FROM THE REVIEWS

"Our country's most eminent jurist, Marshall has, oddly, escaped the attention of serious biographers. Only the third biography of the last eighty years, Smith's copiously researched account is the first to draw upon the full panoply of Marshall papers still being compiled and published. Legal scholars, who focused on Marshall's work as chief justice, have rarely conveyed the richness of his life. And what a life it was . . . Smith tells Marshall's story skillfully."—David C. Frederick, *Civilization*

"Cannot be recommended highly enough."
—Avrum Lank, *Milwaukee Journal/Sentinel*

"A superb biography. It covers all the ground with authority and distinction. It won't have to be done again for a long time—if ever."
—Theodore Draper

"Smith's examination of Marshall's opinions covers the territory in clear, understandable fashion, unburdened by excessive jargon. After reading his portrait of the fourth chief justice, few will doubt Marshall's position as a major definer of the American nation."
—Norman Provizer, *Rocky Mountain News*

"Every so often a book will come on the market that prompts a lawyer to say to his professional colleagues, 'This is a book you *must* read.' Such a book is Jean Edward Smith's fascinating biography of the greatest chief justice this country ever had and one who deserves no less than this splendid story of his life."—Arthur W. Machen, Jr., *Experience*

"A stirring work that captures Marshall's profound impact on our nation and Constitution, not only by exploring and explaining many of the monumental decisions he wrote during his thirty-four years as chief justice, but the broader context of the political struggles over national power that were taking place during his lifetime."—Alexander Wohl, *Legal Times*

"For a well-informed and sensitive treatment of Marshall's long and influential life, this detailed history of the man is well worth reading even for people who think they know him and his times."
—Brent Tarter, *Richmond Times-Dispatch*

"Jean Edward Smith has written the exemplary life of the great man. I hope some modern judges read it."
—Mortimer Sellers, *The Washington Post Book World*

"Some of the best moments of this compendious biography treat Marshall's earlier career as soldier and diplomat—particularly his skillful handling of Talleyrand, the serpentine French foreign minister, and the notorious agents X, Y, and Z."—*The New Yorker*

JOHN MARSHALL

Jean Edward Smith

A Marian Wood / Owl Book

Henry Holt and Company

New York

JOHN MARSHALL

Definer of a Nation

Henry Holt and Company, Inc.
Publishers since 1866
115 West 18th Street
New York, New York 10011

Henry Holt® is a registered trademark
of Henry Holt and Company, Inc.

Published in Canada by Fitzhenry & Whiteside Ltd.,
195 Allstate Parkway, Markham, Ontario L3R 4T8.

Library of Congress Cataloging-in-Publication Data
Smith, Jean Edward.
John Marshall: definer of a nation / Jean Edward Smith.
p.   cm.
ISBN 0-8050-5510-X
Includes bibliographical references and index.
1. Marshall, John, 1755–1835. 2. Judges—United States—
Biography. 3. United States Supreme Court—Biography.
I. Title.
KF8745.M3S63   1996   96-15072
347.73'2634—dc20 [B]   CIP
[347.3073534] [B]

Henry Holt books are available for special promotions and
premiums. For details contact: Director, Special Markets.

First published in hardcover in 1996 by
Henry Holt and Company, Inc.

First Owl Books Edition 1998

A Marian Wood / Owl Book

Designed by Kate Nichols

Printed in the United States of America
All first editions are printed on acid-free paper. ∞

3   5   7   9   10   8   6   4   2

Contents

Preface

Oliver Wendell Holmes said that "if American law were to be represented by a single figure, sceptic and worshipper alike would agree that the figure could be one alone, and that one, John Marshall." Felix Frankfurter declared that "the decisive claim to John Marshall's distinction as a great statesman is as a judge. And he is the only judge who has that distinction." Joseph Story said, "His proudest epitaph may be written in a single line— 'Here lies the expounder of the Constitution.'"

It is my hope that this modest effort may bring home to a new generation of Americans the wisdom and humanity of one of the nation's greatest statesmen. Biographers are prone to cast their subject to fit their own predilections. As Cardinal Newman said, "biographers varnish, they assign motives, they conjecture feelings. But contemporary letters are facts." Accordingly, I have allowed Marshall to speak for himself. I have not put words into his mouth; I have not speculated about his intentions; I have not surmised his feelings unless the evidence was clear.

This book is dedicated to two mentors: Professor William Beaney and Professor Walter Berns. Bill was my thesis advisor at Princeton and has generously read the manuscripts of every book I have written since. If writing can be taught, he has taught me the importance of crisp, declaratory prose in the context of historical accuracy. Walter was a colleague of mine at the University of Toronto for many years. He, too, has inspired me to write as clearly as I can. Bill and Walter disagree on many interpretations of the Constitution, but they are together in their attachment to academic rigor, painstaking research, and scholarly objectivity. I hope this book will warrant their approval.

JOHN MARSHALL

I love his laugh—it is too hearty for an intriguer. . . .

—Joseph Story, 1808

Introduction

&

The Inauguration of 1801

Marshall, Jefferson, and the
Transfer of Power

*Marshall's preeminence was due to the fact that he was
John Marshall.*

—Charles Evans Hughes, 1928

JOHN MARSHALL was the fourth Chief Justice of the United States. Appointed by President Adams during the waning days of his term in 1801, Marshall served as chief justice for thirty-five years. His tenure spanned the terms of five presidents: Jefferson, Madison, Monroe, John Quincy Adams, and Andrew Jackson. Under his leadership, the Supreme Court became a dominant force in American life. The broad powers of the federal government, the authoritative role of the Court, and a legal environment conducive to the growth of the American economy stem from the decisions that flowed from Marshall's pen.

More important, the Marshall Court established the ground rules of American government. The Constitution reflected the will of the people, not the states, said Marshall, and the people made it supreme. That Federalist concept provided the basis for the constitutional decisions of the Marshall era. It was bitterly contested at the time; in many respects it lay at the root of the Civil War. But Marshall's view ultimately prevailed. If George Washington founded the country, John Marshall defined it.

Marshall also established the independence of the judiciary and enhanced its moral authority. Traditionally, justices of high tribunals have written their own opinions, announcing them individually. Under Marshall's leadership, the U.S. Supreme Court initiated the practice of delivering a single opinion of the Court. For the first ten years of his tenure, these were announced by the chief justice himself. That gave the decisions an aura of finality separate opinions could not supply. After 1811, when Joseph Story

1

joined the bench, decisions were parceled out among the justices, but there was always a clearly labeled opinion of the Court, with Marshall delivering the most critical.

A list of Marshall's great decisions reads like the ABCs of American constitutional law. Judicial review—the authority of the Supreme Court to declare acts of Congress and the executive unconstitutional—traces to his landmark opinion in *Marbury v. Madison*.[1] The implied powers of the national government evolved from the decision in *McCulloch v. Maryland*.[2] In the leading cases of *Martin v. Hunter's Lessee*[3] and *Cohens v. Virginia*,[4] the Marshall Court established its jurisdiction over state courts when a federal issue was at stake. The sanctity of contractual arrangements, a concept that underlies the growth of modern business, found expression in *Fletcher v. Peck*[5] and the famous *Dartmouth College* case.[6] Perhaps even more significant, in *Gibbons v. Ogden*,[7] Marshall struck down state efforts to restrain competition and thereby helped to fashion the seamless web of commerce that characterizes the American economy.

Above all, Marshall asserted the authority of the Supreme Court to interpret the Constitution. Today that authority is taken for granted, but it was not universally recognized in 1801. Constitutions are political documents. They define the way a nation is governed. The central issue of whether they were justiciable in courts of law was problematic. The English tradition held that the great constitutional documents of British history were purely political statements that lay in the realm of Parliament to interpret, not the courts. Jefferson subscribed to that view[8]; so did Jackson,[9] and even Abraham Lincoln doubted the authority of the Supreme Court to resolve fundamental constitutional issues in the course of ordinary litigation.[10]

As chief justice, Marshall took the opposite position. Beginning with *Marbury v. Madison*, he consistently held that the Constitution was law. It not only established the political basis of American society, but it was also an important legal document that could be interpreted by the courts. And in matters of law, the decision of the Supreme Court was final.[11] The idea that the Constitution was law, subject to the Court's jurisdiction, was a far-reaching concept. By definition, it established the authority of the Supreme Court as a constitutional body.[12]

Marshall's path was not an easy one, and initially the Court seemed an unlikely competitor for national power. Its early years were marked by rapidly changing personnel. John Jay, the first chief justice, resigned after six years to become governor of New York. John Rutledge of South Carolina, who replaced Jay, served for one term on the Court but failed to win senatorial confirmation. Oliver Ellsworth, the third chief justice, "afflicted with the gravel and the gout,"[13] resigned because of ill health in December 1800. During this period, the nature of the Court's authority was vague and its caseload was light. With a few important exceptions, the early Supreme Court rarely decided a constitutional issue.[14] Its appellate jurisdiction was defined by Congress; it had no regular meeting place; and its term was limited to one month a year.[15]

Marshall overcame these difficulties and asserted the Court's authority. Not surprisingly, his decisions were occasionally unpopular. Some of the most important were taken in the face of hostile chief executives—especially when Jefferson and Jackson were in the White House. Marshall successfully deflected Jefferson's efforts to curtail the judiciary,[16] but he was less successful in dealing with Andrew Jackson, with whom he fought an ongoing battle over the treaty rights of the Cherokee Indians.[17]

Many of the Marshall Court's decisions dealt with recalcitrant state governments. Others protected the vested rights of property against a flood of public and private debt. Those decisions invariably were greeted by adverse public reaction. In the few slave cases to come before the Court,[18] Marshall applied the laws of property. Much to the discomfiture of his fellow Virginians, however, his dicta became increasingly hostile.[19] The holdings went one way, but Marshall restated his aversion to slavery in his commentary.[20]

Despite the criticism that rained down on some of his decisions, Marshall endured. The power of the national government grew, the role of the judiciary expanded, and the opinions of the Marshall Court withstood the test of time. Perhaps it is not surprising that in the wake of his great constitutional holdings, Marshall's personal qualities have been forgotten. His life has been obscured by his achievements. Albert Beveridge, his most distinguished biographer, lamented that less was known of Marshall than of any other great American: "Such exalted encomium has been paid him, that . . . he has become a kind of mythical being, endowed with virtues and wisdom not of this earth. He appears to us as a gigantic figure looming, indistinctly, out of the mists of the past."[21]

That is unfortunate. Marshall's exceptional influence over his prickly and strong-minded colleagues on the Court—there was seldom a dissent while he was chief justice—gives some hint of the warmth of his personality as well as the clarity of his intellect. He was a naturally gifted leader: humorous, low-key, unpretentious, as outgoing as many of his contemporaries were austere. Throughout his life Marshall entertained generously, was a weekend regular at Richmond's famous Quoits Club, and always enjoyed bending an elbow with friends and associates. House Speaker Theodore Sedgwick noted that Marshall was "attached to pleasures, with convivial habits strongly fixed. He is indolent, therefore, [but] when aroused, has strong reasoning powers; they are indeed almost unequalled."[22] Another contemporary, William Wirt, one of America's greatest advocates before the Supreme Court, said of Marshall that "his countenance has a faithful ex-

pression of great good humor and hilarity; while his black eyes—that unerring index—possess an irradiating spirit, which proclaims the imperial powers of the mind that sits enthroned within."[23] And Massachusetts senator
Charles Sumner, who knew Marshall in his later years, spoke of him as "a
model of simplicity . . . ready to laugh; to joke and be joked with."[24]

Joseph Story, Marshall's longtime colleague, said of him:

> The first impression of a stranger, upon introduction to him, was
> generally that of disappointment. It seemed hardly credible that
> such simplicity should be the accompaniment of such acknowledged
> greatness.
>
> Meet him on a stagecoach, as a stranger, and travel with him a
> whole day and you would only be struck by his readiness to admin-
> ister to the accommodations of others and his anxiety to appropriate
> the least to himself. Be with him, the unknown guest at an inn, and
> he seemed adjusted to the very scene, partaking of the warm wel-
> come of its comforts, whenever found; and if not found, resigning
> himself without complaint to the meanest arrangements. You would
> never suspect, in either case, that he was a great man; far less that he
> was the Chief Justice of the United States.[25]

Marshall's political creed was conservative. Like Washington and
Adams, he was skeptical of direct democracy and preferred the checks and
balances imposed by the Constitution. But Marshall was not reactionary. He
believed strongly in representative government, vigorously defended a free
press, and recoiled instinctively from the aristocratic pretensions of some of
his fellow Federalists. Above all, Marshall was an ardent nationalist. He
supported the United States at a time when most people's loyalties ran to
their state. His hero was George Washington. (In his early years as chief justice, Marshall wrote an imposing five-volume biography of Washington,
which remained the definitive account of the first president's life for over
thirty years.)[26] In fact, support for Washington was a litmus test for Marshall.
His long-standing animosity toward his kinsman Thomas Jefferson—Marshall and Jefferson were second cousins—traced in part to Jefferson's partisan criticism of Washington in the late 1790s.

Marshall's nationalism was rooted in his experience during the Revolutionary War. In 1775, at the age of twenty, he joined the army in the fight for
American independence. First with the Culpeper minutemen, and then
with the 11th Virginia regiment, he fought at Great Bridge, Brandywine,
Germantown, and Monmouth. He was with Washington at Valley Forge and
was present at the capture of Stony Point. Toward the end of his life, Mar-

shall acknowledged how important those years had been. "I was confirmed in the habit of considering America as my country and Congress as my government. I had imbibed these sentiments so thoroughly that they constituted a part of my being."[27] The result was that Marshall became an American before he had a chance to become a Virginian.

Nevertheless, Marshall's roots in Virginia ran deep. The eldest of fifteen children, he was born in a simple wooden cabin at the foot of the Blue Ridge Mountains. Like many who were reared in that punishing environment, Marshall's health was robust. Until his late seventies, he regularly walked six miles a day—usually at the quickstep of the Revolutionary War's light infantry. Months before his death, at the age of eighty, the chief justice was still pitching quoits in Richmond on Saturday afternoons, occasionally tipsy from the Quoits Club's powerful rum punch.

Curious as it may seem, Marshall had no significant judicial experience at the time he was appointed chief justice. But he was one of America's most accomplished lawyers.[28] He had been among the first students to complete the legal curriculum prescribed by Chancellor George Wythe at the College of William and Mary,[29] and within ten years of his admission to the bar in 1780, he was recognized as Virginia's leading appellate advocate.[30] A contemporary who watched Marshall in action wrote that he "is superior to every other orator at the Bar . . . in his most surprising talent of placing his case in that point of view suited to the purpose he aims at, throwing a blazing light upon it, and keeping the attention of his hearers fixed upon the object to which he originally directed it."[31] This rare ability to go to the heart of an issue was also noted by Federalist leader Rufus King, who, after hearing Marshall plead a case before the Supreme Court, said, "His head is the best organized of anyone I have known."[32]

Marshall entered politics reluctantly. He had a thriving practice and was speculating heavily in Virginia land titles. Unlike Washington and Jefferson, or Madison and Monroe for that matter, Marshall was not independently wealthy. When he became active in politics following Shays's Rebellion in 1786, it was because he believed that the nation was imperiled. Marshall responded to the threat, speaking out vigorously against the insurrection, and the following spring he was elected to the Virginia assembly. There he supported the subsequent efforts of Washington and Madison at the constitutional convention in Philadelphia, and later he was to map the strategy by which the Virginia legislature submitted the Constitution stripped of crippling amendments to a state ratifying convention.

Once the Constitution had been adopted and the new national government put in place, Marshall returned to private practice. He became the Federalist leader in Virginia but declined Washington's offer to become U.S.

attorney for the state. In 1793, still in private practice, Marshall was elected brigadier general by the Virginia legislature and placed in command of the second brigade of the state militia. Given the unsettled conditions at the time, this was far more than an honorary posting. Two years later Washington invited him into his cabinet as attorney general but Marshall declined. In 1796 he refused appointment as minister to France. The following year he was induced by President Adams to join Charles Cotesworth Pinckney and Elbridge Gerry on a special mission to Paris—a desperate effort to restore cordial ties with revolutionary France. The mission turned out badly from the standpoint of Franco-American relations, but it established Marshall's national reputation. When Talleyrand's representatives (X, Y, and Z) tried to extract a bribe for the French foreign minister, Marshall broke off negotiations and issued a blistering report. He returned to the United States in triumph.[33]

After the XYZ affair, Marshall resumed his law practice in Richmond. In 1798 President Adams offered him a seat on the Supreme Court. Marshall declined. The following year, yielding to the importunings of George Washington,[34] he ran for Congress from Richmond—then a hotbed of Jeffersonian democracy. At a crucial juncture in the campaign, Marshall was endorsed by Patrick Henry, the stormy petrel of Virginia populism. Despite their political differences, Marshall and Henry were warm friends, and Henry's support turned the tide in Marshall's favor. "Tell Marshall that I love him," wrote Henry to an acquaintance in Richmond, "because he acted [in Paris] as a republican, as an American."[35]

During his one year in Congress, Marshall emerged as the leader of the administration's dwindling forces. "We can do nothing without him," Speaker Sedgwick wrote to Rufus King in December 1799.[36] Marshall successfully defended President Adams against charges that he had usurped judicial authority,[37] and at the same time thwarted right-wing Federalist attempts to enact a disputed elections bill that would have given the party the final authority to determine the electoral vote for president.

By this time it was obvious that Marshall was not a doctrinaire Federalist. The key to his politics lay in his nationalism, not his partisanship. He openly criticized the alien and sedition acts of 1798 as useless legislation "calculated to create unnecessary discontents and jealousies at a time when our very existence as a nation may depend on our union."[38] In January 1800, when Jefferson's supporters sought to repeal the Sedition Act, Marshall voted with them. The repeal carried the House 50–48, and Marshall's vote was decisive. For that reason, many Federalists[39] suspected him of being too close to the Republicans, while the Republicans distrusted his ties to Washington and Adams.[40] Those ties were close, but they were bonds of patriotism, not party. Marshall admired Adams's biting intellect, and no one in public life was closer to Washington. When the first president died suddenly in December 1799, the messenger from Mount Vernon sought out Marshall to announce the news, and it was Marshall who delivered the nation's eulogy.

After Washington's death, the Federalists self-destructed. Adams attempted to follow Washington's moderate policies but came under increasing fire from both the left and the right. Jefferson and the Republicans pressed the president for an alliance with France against England, while Hamilton's supporters urged an alliance with England and war against France. Adams was caught in the middle. His neutral course—which ultimately proved correct—had few defenders other than Marshall, who soon became indispensable to the president. It should not be surprising therefore that when Adams purged his cabinet of the Federalist war faction in the spring of 1800, he first nominated Marshall to be secretary of war, which Marshall declined, and then secretary of state, which he accepted.

Marshall served as secretary of state for ten months.[41] When the capital moved from Philadelphia to Washington in June, Adams departed to spend the summer in Massachusetts and left Marshall in charge. From July through October 1800, Marshall was America's de facto chief executive. "He is actually a state conservator," wrote Secretary of the Treasury Oliver Wolcott. "His value ought to be estimated not only by the good he does, but by the mischief he has prevented."[42] Marshall used the opportunity to improve relations with both England and France, and his instructions to the American ministers in London[43] and Paris[44] set United States foreign policy on the course of nonalignment that it would follow for almost a century. That had been George Washington's policy, and Marshall forcefully restated it.

Marshall took no part in the election of 1800 except to offer encouragement to Adams and his running mate, Charles Cotesworth Pinckney of South Carolina, and to lament the decline of national spirit. "There is a tide in the affairs of nations, of parties, and of individuals," he wrote to Congressman Harrison Gray Otis of Massachusetts in August. "I fear that real Americanism is on the ebb."[45]

Three months later, with Jefferson's victory looming, Marshall blamed Federalist miscues for the party's demise. Writing to Judge Richard Peters in Pennsylvania, he said without bitterness that, "however the election may terminate, good men ought still to continue their endeavors for the public happiness. I pray devoutly (which is no very common practice with me) that the future administration may do as little harm as the present and the past."[46] Above all, the outgoing and naturally friendly Marshall deplored the personal vindictiveness that had crept into the campaign. "No one regrets more than I do," he wrote in mid-November, "that intolerant and persecuting spirit which allows no worth out of its own pale, and breaks off all social intercourse as a penalty on an honest avowal of honest opinions."[47]

Marshall sensed that a fundamental political change was at hand. In fact, with the possible exception of 1860, the election of 1800 proved to be the most significant in American history. It marked the introduction of political parties into presidential campaigns and the collapse of the electoral system designed by the Framers of the Constitution. It also ushered in a decisive shift in power. The Federalists were turned out, and the Republicans led by Thomas Jefferson were installed in the White House and Congress.

One cannot understand Marshall without an appreciation of his relationship with Thomas Jefferson, just as one cannot understand his tenure as chief justice except in the context of the exceptional circumstances that brought both men to power in 1801. By then, Marshall had become the nation's most prominent Federalist and the unquestioned leader of the party's moderate wing. Jefferson, at the head of the victorious Republican Party, enjoyed even greater national standing. In the tangled events of late 1800—the sudden resignation of a chief justice, an unexpected deadlock in the electoral college, and an unprecedented transfer of power—Marshall and Jefferson emerged as the central players in a drama that tested the nation's survival.

The Federalists had dominated national politics since 1789. Washington had served two terms as president, and Adams one. But by 1800 the party was badly split between its ultra-conservative faction, led by Hamilton, and the more moderate elements, behind Adams and Marshall. Generally, the Federalists favored a strong central government, were ill-disposed toward states rights, and distrusted direct democracy. They emphasized the vested rights of property, trembled at the thought of popular uprisings, and had taken the lead in framing the Constitution as a bulwark against what many saw as a rising tide of anarchy in various states. The Federalists had successfully arrested the revolutionary thrust of the 1780s and provided the United States with the necessary stability to find its footing. But by 1800 their mandate had worn thin.

The Republicans, by contrast, emphasized majority rule. They deplored the checks and balances built into the federal system and sought to employ their power at the ballot box on behalf of the many—particularly the many who were deeply in debt—against the less numerous class of creditors and the entrenched wealth they represented. Until the election of 1800, Republican strength was concentrated in the various state legislatures. Not surprisingly, the party stressed the authority of the states, favored the yeoman virtues of agrarian society, and tended to be more egalitarian than the Federalists. The extreme wing of the Federalists saw Jefferson's party as a rabble bent on seizing power to foment revolution, while the more radical of Jefferson's supporters viewed the Federalists as dedicated monarchists determined to eradicate representative government.

Those perceptions were sharpened by the ideas of the French Revolution, which figured prominently in the presidential campaign. Jefferson and the Republicans were depicted as agents of the Revolution and the Terror that had accompanied it. For their part, the Federalists were painted as lackeys of the English crown. Neither view was correct. Both parties were deeply committed to the liberal principles of 1776 and to the continued existence of the United States as a free country. Their differences were matters of degree. The Federalists feared national fragmentation, while the Republicans worried about growing centralization. Each party saw the other as a threat to representative government, and as the rhetoric of the campaign escalated, the areas of common understanding receded behind a torrent of invective.

By the late autumn of 1800, it was apparent that Adams had lost and that Jefferson and his running mate, Aaron Burr of New York, would be elected. Under the electoral system designed by the Framers—a system deliberately put in place to thwart the growth of political parties—each member of the electoral college voted for two persons for president, the only stipulation being that one of those persons must be from a different state from that of the elector.[48] There was no distinction between voting for president and voting for vice president. Each elector simply wrote two names on his ballot. When the ballots were tabulated, the person with the largest number of votes became president, while the person with the second largest number was elected vice president. The system was designed to be nonpartisan but had already run into difficulty. In 1796 John Adams had received the largest number of electoral votes and became president, while his principal opponent, Thomas Jefferson, had the second largest number and became vice president.

The formula for mixed government worked poorly, and in 1800 the system simply collapsed. For the first time, each of the parties nominated two candidates. The Federalists backed Adams for president and Pinckney for vice president; the Republicans ran Jefferson and Burr. When the electors met in their respective state capitals, all but one of the Federalist electors voted for Adams and Pinckney,[49] while each of the Republicans cast his votes for Jefferson and Burr. As before, no distinction was made as to who was to be president, who vice president. As a result, Jefferson and Burr each received seventy-three votes; Adams garnered sixty-five; Pinckney, sixty-four; and John Jay one. To the nation's surprise, Thomas Jefferson and Aaron Burr, who had begun the campaign as running mates, found themselves in a dead heat for president.

The Constitution, whose Framers had not anticipated such an event,* provided that in case of a tie in the electoral college, the House of Representatives would choose between the two candidates, each state delegation casting one vote. In hindsight, it may seem curious that Burr, the vice presidential nominee of the Republicans, did not defer to Jefferson. Indeed, Burr had not actively sought the presidency. But when the White House beckoned, he saw his opportunity and stayed in the race. The lame-duck House of Representatives was controlled by the Federalists, and for many of them, Jefferson was anathema. Given the choice between Jefferson and Burr, most preferred Burr, public sentiment to the contrary notwithstanding.

On December 18, 1800, Marshall, in his capacity as secretary of state, wrote the unhappy news of the election to Pinckney in South Carolina:

> According to our present intelligence Mr. Jefferson and Mr. Burr have an equal number of votes and of consequence the House of Representatives must choose between them. It is extremely uncertain on whom the choice will fall. Having myself no voice in the election, and in fact scarcely any wish concerning it, I do not intermeddle with it, but I hear what is said by others, and witness the anxiety of parties.[50]

Marshall added, almost as an afterthought, that Chief Justice Oliver Ellsworth had resigned and that Adams had nominated John Jay to replace him.[51] Should Jay decline, as seemed likely, Marshall thought Adams would choose the senior associate justice, William Cushing of Massachusetts, then sixty-eight. "I shall return to Richmond on the 3d. of March [1801] to recommence practice as a lawyer. If my present wish can succeed so far as respects myself, I shall never again fill any political station whatever."[52]

Ten days later Marshall repeated those sentiments to his wife's brother-in-law, Edward Carrington. He said that while he had hoped to be back in Richmond in February, he would probably have to remain in Washington until March 3, the last day of Adams's term. As for the presidential election, Marshall told Carrington that the outcome "is extremely doubtful," adding "I take no part, and feel no interest in the decision. I consider it as a choice of evils and I really am uncertain which would be the greatest."[53] Marshall went on to say that it appeared that Burr might win. "It is not believed that he would weaken the vital parts of the Constitution, nor is it believed that he has any undue foreign attachments. These opinions incline many who greatly disapprove of him yet to prefer him to the other gentleman who is of-

---

*The Twelfth Amendment, adopted immediately thereafter, required each of the electors to indicate on his ballot which of the two candidates was to be president and which was to be vice president.

fered to their choice. I have only to wish that the best for our common country may be done, but I really do not know what that best is."[54]

The "other gentleman" to whom Marshall referred was Thomas Jefferson, and the reference to "foreign attachments" pertained to Jefferson's sympathy for France. Marshall's long-standing aversion to Jefferson was deeply held and cordially reciprocated. It was a character flaw that Marshall and Jefferson shared equally; a flaw that was captured by the historian Henry Adams who, when speaking of Marshall, wrote that "this great man nourished one weakness. Pure in life; broad in mind, and the despair of bench and bar for the unswerving certainty of his legal method; almost idolized by those who stood nearest him . . . this excellent and amiable man clung to one rooted prejudice: he detested Thomas Jefferson. . . . No argument or entreaty affected his conviction that Jefferson was not an honest man."[55]

Marshall almost invariably retained the friendship of his political opponents, partly as a result of his experience as a trial lawyer, where the cut-and-thrust of the courtroom rarely affected personal relations. More important, Marshall was strenuously convivial and did not make enemies easily. He and James Madison were good friends; Monroe had been close since childhood; and he even enjoyed the company of the abrasive John Randolph. The redoubtable Patrick Henry, the most radical of the great Virginians, remained a friend and admirer. Jefferson was the exception.

Marshall's animosity toward the man he sometimes called "the great lama of the mountain" stemmed from childhood and family heritage and was reinforced by numerous personal encounters over the years. Both Jefferson and Marshall traced their maternal descent to Virginia's illustrious Randolphs. But Marshall's grandmother, Mary Randolph Keith, had been disowned by the family, while Jefferson's ancestors flourished within the fold. Exactly what impact that had on Marshall is unclear, but it certainly set the stage for the subsequent hostility. Albert Beveridge claimed that the animosity sprang from Marshall's bitter experience with Washington at Valley Forge during the bleak winter of 1778. Jefferson was not there. He did not serve in the Continental Army, nor did he share the hardships of war. According to Beveridge, Marshall considered Jefferson a shirker—a fault he never forgave.[56]

Whatever the cause, Marshall's animus was likely reinforced by his in-laws. His mother-in-law, Rebecca Burwell Ambler, had been Jefferson's first fiancée, and she and her family spoke freely of Jefferson's foibles, often in Marshall's presence.[57] But above all, Marshall thought that Jefferson was untrustworthy. If George Washington never told a lie, Marshall believed that Jefferson rarely told the truth. His personal dislike for Jefferson ultimately contributed to his own political skepticism. Looking back many years later,

Marshall said, "I have never believed firmly in [Mr. Jefferson's] infallibility. I have never thought him a particularly wise, sound and practical statesman [and] I have not changed this mode of thinking."[58]

Jefferson, for his part, thought Marshall was a hypocrite. The admittedly partisan Henry Adams suggested that Jefferson's repugnance for Marshall was "tinged with a deeper feeling, bordering at times on fear." Whether the feeling was fear or not, Jefferson certainly acknowledged Marshall's ability, although one would be hard put to say that he respected it. He told Joseph Story that "when conversing with Marshall, I never admit anything. So sure as you admit any position to be good, no matter how remote from the conclusion he seeks to establish, you are gone. So great is his sophistry you must never give him an affirmative answer or you will be forced to grant his conclusion. Why, if he were to ask me if it were daylight or not, I'd reply, 'Sir, I don't know, I can't tell.'"[59]

Jefferson's hostility reflected sharp political differences. Unlike Marshall, Jefferson found it difficult to maintain cordial relations with his opponents, and of those opponents Marshall was often the most formidable.[60] The depth of Jefferson's feeling is best revealed in a letter to Pennsylvania's Albert Gallatin, in which he wrote that Marshall's "inveteracy is profound, and his mind of that gloomy malignity which will never let him forego the opportunity of satiating it on a victim."[61]

The animosity Marshall and Jefferson shared is ironic because in many ways they were very much alike. Both were gifted with exceptional intelligence and both were exceedingly able politicians. They shared the same Virginia heritage, had strong fathers and accomplished mothers (though Jefferson's mother died young), and both were trained as lawyers. They each rejected organized religion (Jefferson more outspokenly), and neither seemed to care a whit about his clothes or personal appearance. Far more significant, both were quintessentially American: Jefferson, the inspired author of the Declaration of Independence; Marshall, the staunch defender of the Constitution. Jefferson, the slaveholder, leaned toward democracy and equality. Marshall, who came to reject slavery, favored republican government, with built-in checks and balances to buffer majority will.

In the final analysis, they had more in common with each other than either cared to admit. Yet it is also true that the contrasts that fueled their rivalry abounded. An exemplary aristocrat who advocated democracy, Jefferson was never comfortable associating with the common man. Marshall, who distrusted democracy, never lost the common touch. Jefferson opposed an energetic central government as a danger to individual liberty; Marshall saw the government in Washington as the keystone of national well-being. Jefferson identified with Virginia; Marshall, with the United States. Jefferson favored agriculture and advocated the virtues of rural life;

Marshall, an avid farmer himself, was more attuned to the needs of commerce and industry. Jefferson was partial to France. Marshall, like Washington, leaned toward Britain. In some respects the differences involved the classic tension between the man of ideas and the man of affairs. Jefferson was at his best when articulating a philosophy of government; Marshall, when applying one. Each exemplified their respective persuasions; each represented an important tendency in American political traditions; yet neither was prepared to accommodate the idiosyncrasies of the other.

Ironically, in the winter of 1800–1801, with the race for president deadlocked, Marshall found himself in a pivotal position. Of all the Federalists, he had been tainted least by the party's defeat. He was recognized as the heir to Washington's mantle of moderation and for the past two years had been the administration's most effective spokesman. Having weathered the fire of the High Federalists, he was, with Adams's defeat, now widely regarded as the party's leader. His support for either Burr or Jefferson would be crucial.

On December 26, 1800, Alexander Hamilton, Jefferson's old nemesis, wrote Marshall to express his opposition to Burr and to suggest that Jefferson be elected.[62] "If there be a man in the world I ought to hate it is Jefferson," wrote Hamilton.[63] "With Burr I have always been personally well. But the public goal must be paramount to every private consideration." Burr was a hopeless bankrupt, Hamilton said, "the *Catiline* of America"[64] who "has no principle public or private. . . . Disgrace abroad [and] ruin at home are the probable fruits of his elevation."[65]

Hamilton was less than honest about his relations with Burr. They were bitter rivals in New York and detested each other. Marshall and Jefferson harbored a mutual dislike, but it paled beside the hatred these two men shared. Nevertheless, Marshall, who did not know Burr, was moved by Hamilton's plea. The day after receiving the letter, Marshall replied candidly to his former comrade-in-arms: "To Mr. Jefferson . . . I have felt almost insuperable objections. His foreign prejudices seem to me totally to unfit him for the chief magistracy of a nation which cannot indulge those prejudices without sustaining deep and permanent injury."[66] Moreover, "in addition to this solid and immovable objection Mr. Jefferson appears to me to be a man who will embody himself with the House of Representatives. By weakening the office of President he will increase his personal power. He will diminish his responsibility, sap the fundamental principles of government and become the leader of that party which is about to constitute the majority of the legislature." Marshall's concern related to Jefferson's well-known preference for legislative rather than presidential government, fearing it would lead to a parliamentary system, which he strongly opposed.

But Marshall's most serious objection pertained to Jefferson's character and what he believed had been his shabby treatment of George Washington. "The Morals of the Author of the letter to Mazzei cannot be pure," he told Hamilton.* Marshall said that "with these impressions concerning Mr. Jefferson I was in some degree disposed to view with less apprehension any other character, and to consider the alternative now offered us as a circumstance not to be entirely neglected."[67]

Nevertheless, Marshall respected Hamilton's judgment. "Your representation of Mr. Burr with whom I am totally unacquainted shows that from him still greater danger than even from Mr. Jefferson may be apprehended. Such a man as you describe is more to be feared and may do more immediate if not greater mischief." As a result, Marshall told Hamilton that he would remain neutral. He would not back Burr, but "I cannot bring myself to aid Mr. Jefferson."[68]

There were rumors that in the event of a deadlock in the House of Representatives (the votes of nine of the sixteen states were required for election), the Federalists would try to retain the presidency temporarily.[69] Some mentioned John Jay as an interim choice;[70] others mentioned Marshall.[71] But Marshall took no part in the matter and did his best to discourage such speculation. The Federalists had lost, and it was now a choice between two evils.[72]

Talk of denying the presidency to the Republicans was idle gossip. A more pressing problem for the Federalists was the replacement of Oliver Ellsworth as chief justice. John Jay, as expected, declined the offer.[73] But Jay's letter did not arrive in Washington until mid-January,[74] and his delay in replying forced Adams's hand. Congress had before it a Federalist measure to revise the judiciary that would reduce the size of the Supreme Court from six justices to five.[75] If Adams delayed naming a replacement until the bill was passed, Ellsworth's resignation in itself would reduce the size of the Court, and the incoming Republican president would name the next chief justice. That left Adams almost no time to find a replacement.

Reflecting on the episode years later, Marshall said, "When I waited on the President with Mr. Jay's letter declining the appointment he said thoughtfully, 'Who shall I nominate now?' I replied that I could not tell. . . . After a moment's hesitation he said, 'I believe I must nominate you.' I had never before heard myself named for the office and had not even thought of it. I was pleased as well as surprised, and bowed in silence. Next day I was nominated."[76]

---

*In April 1796 Jefferson wrote to an old friend, Philip Mazzei, then living in Pisa, mainly about personal matters. But he included in the letter a slightly veiled reference to George Washington as one of the "Samsons in the field and Solomons in the council" who had been "shorn by the harlot England." Mazzei translated the letter into Italian and published it in a Florence newspaper. The Paris *Moniteur* printed a French translation of the Italian version, which eventually made its way into the American press, provoking much criticism of Jefferson.

There is no evidence that Adams had planned to name Marshall, or that he had calculated the move beforehand. Instead, the available information suggests that the pace of events forced the choice.[77] Adams simply could not afford to delay naming a new chief justice if the Federalists were to retain control of the Court. Marshall was at hand, he was prepared to accept the post, and his personal loyalty to the president had been demonstrated time and again over the past year.[78] By choosing Marshall, the petulant Adams was also demonstrating the power he still retained as president. Most Federalists had assumed the nod would go to William Cushing, who had served on the Court since its inception in 1789, or to the next senior justice, William Paterson of New Jersey. Paterson especially had strong support among the Hamiltonian wing of the party. Yet Adams knew that Marshall's standing was unassailable and that the Senate ultimately would have to go along.[79]

Marshall was nonetheless a bitter pill for the High Federalists, and it was they, not the Republicans, who delayed his confirmation. Led by Senator Jonathan Dayton of New Jersey—who wrote that Marshall's nomination was greeted "with grief, astonishment, and almost indignation"[80]—the slim (17–15) Federalist majority in the Senate pressed Adams for a full week to withdraw Marshall's name and submit Paterson's instead. When Adams refused, they reluctantly acquiesced, and on January 27, 1801, John Marshall was confirmed unanimously as Chief Justice of the United States.[81] Two days later the Senate began consideration of the judiciary bill, and passed it the following week.[82]

Senator Dayton continued to fulminate against Adams's "derangement of intellect," explaining that the Federalists "thought it advisable to confirm Mr. Marshall lest another not so well qualified, and most disgusting to the Bench, should be substituted."[83] The Senate's fifteen Republicans, remembering Marshall's past support in Congress and his general moderation, supported the new chief justice enthusiastically.[84] Even Thomas Jefferson, who as vice president presided over the Senate, made no public or private comment, apparently content with Adams's choice.

John Marshall was forty-five years old and in the full vigor of life. "I was unfeignedly gratified at the appointment," he told Justice Story many years later.[85] Marshall, not having anticipated his selection, brought with him no judicial agenda except to preserve the United States. A quarter of a century later, John Adams, then near death, and perhaps forgetting the accidental nature of his original choice, wrote that "the proudest act of my life was the gift of John Marshall to the people of the United States," going on to describe Marshall as a chief justice "equal to Coke or Hale, Holt or Mansfield," the greatest figures of English jurisprudence.[86]

Although the issue of the new chief justice was now settled, Jefferson still faced an uncertain path to the White House. On February 11 the electoral votes were officially counted and the deadlock announced; the House of Representatives then commenced its constitutional task of choosing the next president. While the Federalists commanded a numerical majority in the House, the voting would be by state and Republicans controlled more state delegations. The congressmen balloted nineteen times on February 11 and a total of thirty-five times during the next five days. Republicans voted down the line for Jefferson; Federalists supported Burr. Each ballot showed the same result: eight states for Jefferson, six for Burr, and two state delegations split evenly and therefore abstaining. Jefferson was one state shy of the majority required for election. On the thirty-sixth ballot, the Federalists admitted defeat. Congressman James A. Bayard of Delaware, who was that state's sole representative and thus controlled its vote, told the party's caucus that it was clear Burr could not win and there was no point in continuing to support him. Delaware, he said, would abstain on the next ballot.[87] The Federalists in Vermont and Maryland, the two states that had been equally divided, also abstained, leaving only the Republicans voting. That gave those states to Jefferson. The result was that Jefferson gained a majority of ten states. One state, Delaware, abstained, and the five states that were controlled by the High Federalists held out for Burr to the bitter end.

Jefferson's thirty-sixth ballot victory came on February 17. The inauguration of the president was set by statute for March 4.[88] That left exactly two weeks for an orderly transition, assuming that the charged political climate would permit one. Exuberant Republicans flocked to Washington, Jefferson kept his own counsel as to his future plans, and the outgoing Federalists consolidated their hold on the judiciary. Adams appointed sixteen circuit judges authorized by the new judiciary act and set about filling forty-two relatively minor justice of the peace positions in the District of Columbia—a move further designed to insure stable law enforcement (at least in Federalist eyes) in the nation's capital.[89]

The High Federalists, still unreconciled, feared the worst. By contrast, Marshall, who at Adams's request continued to serve as secretary of state for the remainder of the term,* offered a mixed assessment. Writing to Rufus King, then American minister in London, Marshall urged him to defer any negotiations with the crown until he heard from the new administration. "What the conduct of Mr. Jefferson will be with respect to foreign powers is uncertain. Among those who have supported him are men who on this subject differ widely from each other. The most intelligent among them are in my opinion desirous of preserving peace with Britain but there is a mass of

---

*Marshall was the last, but not the first, to hold the offices of chief justice and secretary of state simultaneously. John Jay, in Washington's first administration, held the positions of secretary of state and chief justice for six months, awaiting Jefferson's return from Paris to take up the cabinet post.

violence and passion in the party which seems to me disposed to press on to war. My private conjecture is that the government will use all its means to excite the resentment and hate of the people against England without designing to proceed to actual hostilities."

Marshall was less optimistic about Jefferson's domestic policies and repeated his fear that the president-elect would seek "to strengthen the state governments at the expense of . . . the Union and to transfer as much as possible the powers remaining with the general government to the House of Representatives."[90]

Despite their personal dislike, Marshall and Jefferson each did their best to facilitate the transition. Jefferson undoubtedly found it easier to deal with the even-tempered Marshall than with the irascible Adams—who would become the first president to boycott his successor's swearing-in*—and Marshall, for his part, had no reason not to cooperate. The preservation of the Union, which was Marshall's primary aim, depended on an orderly transfer of power. In addition, both shared the view that the intemperate rhetoric of the campaign had gotten out of control and that it was time to restore a more civil discourse. When Jefferson informed Marshall that as vice president he had no secretary to help him prepare his messages to Congress,[91] Marshall immediately assigned the chief clerk of the State Department to the president-elect. More significantly, Jefferson asked Marshall to remain as acting secretary of state until James Madison arrived in Washington, which would not be until several days after the inauguration.[92]

Marshall and Jefferson both recognized the enormous significance of the upcoming inauguration and its symbolic importance for the country's future. If handled properly, it would provide a unique testament to the ability of a free people to change their government peacefully. The fear of impending violence was palpable, but the inauguration offered an opportunity for the nation to rally round the new president. With that in mind, Jefferson wrote to Marshall on March 2 to request that he administer the oath of office. From the text of Jefferson's letter, it is not clear whether he was addressing Marshall as secretary of state or chief justice. But that is immaterial. What is more important is that Marshall's presence as the Federalist leader would consummate the changeover. Jefferson said that he intended to take the oath at noon on March 4 in the Senate chamber and promised to be punctual. He asked Marshall to determine the precise wording of the oath that was required.

Marshall replied that afternoon. "I shall with much pleasure attend to administer the oath of Office," he told Jefferson, and "shall make a point of

---

*The two Adamses share this distinction. John Quincy Adams refused to attend Andrew Jackson's inauguration.

being punctual." Marshall said that the State Department's records "furnish no information respecting the oaths which have been heretofore taken. That prescribed in the Constitution seems to me to be the only one which is [appropriate]."[93]

The tension between Marshall and Jefferson yielded to the needs of the nation. On the morning of the inauguration, Marshall began a letter to his old friend in South Carolina, Charles Cotesworth Pinckney. Marshall wanted to thank Pinckney for the congratulations he had written on Marshall's appointment as chief justice and to apprise him of the mood in Washington.

"Today the new political year commences," wrote Marshall. "The new order of things begins. Mr. Adams I believe left the city at 4 o'clock in the morning and Mr. Jefferson will be inaugurated at 12. There are some appearances which surprise me. I wish however more than I hope that the public prosperity and happiness may sustain no diminution under democratic guidance."

Marshall then penned a sentence—one of the most misquoted he ever wrote—summarizing his benign judgment of the new president. In Marshall's words, "The democrats are divided into speculative theorists and absolute terrorists: With the latter I am not disposed to class Mr. Jefferson."[94] In his 1916 biography of Marshall, Beveridge inexplicably omitted the word "not" from this passage, thus giving it the very opposite meaning that Marshall intended.[95] The result was to overstate Marshall's fear of Jefferson and to charge him with a partisanship he did not embrace. Beveridge's false depiction of Marshall's attitude was accepted by a generation of scholars and writers. As a consequence, Marshall was painted far more conservatively than he deserved to be. The High Federalists might have considered Jefferson an "absolute terrorist," but John Marshall certainly did not.*

Marshall also told Pinckney that if Jefferson aligned himself with the terrorists, "it is not difficult to foresee that much calamity is in store for our country—if he does not [so align himself] they will soon become his ene-

---

*Beveridge's misquotation of Marshall was not revealed until 1948 when Professor Richard J. Hooker, writing in the *American Historical Review*, reproduced the original version of Marshall's letter to Pinckney. 53 *AHR* 518–520 (1948). Dumas Malone, Jefferson's exemplary biographer, has suggested most charitably that Beveridge may have seen an incorrect text of the letter. *Jefferson the President: The First Term, 1801–1805* 22, note 7 (Boston: Little, Brown, 1970). Other scholars have been less generous. The fact is that Senator Beveridge loathed Thomas Jefferson and did his utmost to bring Marshall's views into line with his own. For the criticism of Beveridge's treatment of Jefferson made by Max Farrand, W. E. Dodd, Gaillard Hunt, and other scholars, see Claude G. Bowers, *Beveridge and the Progressive Era* 555–557 (Boston: Houghton Mifflin, 1932). For more general criticisms of Beveridge's partisanship concerning Marshall, see Tracy E. Stervey, "Albert J. Beveridge," in *The Marcus W. Jernegan Essays in American Historiography* 390, William T. Hutchinson, ed. (Chicago: University of Chicago Press, 1937); John Braeman, *Albert J. Beveridge* 230–231 (Chicago: University of Chicago Press, 1971).

mies and calumniators."[96] At that point Marshall broke off the letter to attend the inauguration. He arrived at the newly completed Senate chamber well before Jefferson and took his seat alongside Aaron Burr, who had just been sworn in as vice president. Jefferson arrived promptly at noon. His meeting with Marshall on the podium was a dramatic moment in what history has recorded as one of America's most memorable inaugurations.

Perhaps even more than Marshall, Jefferson was determined to establish the precedent of orderly change, and his inaugural address represents one of the greatest statements ever made about the government of a free society.[97] Seeking to restore national harmony, he appealed to the moderate Federalists and attempted to disarm the irreconcilables. He generously praised Washington—"our first and greatest revolutionary character whose preeminent services entitled him to the first place in the country's love"—and modestly asked indulgence for his own errors. It was almost as if he were addressing Marshall directly. Then, in one of the most striking passages, the new president defined the essence of democratic government. While "the will of the majority is in all cases to prevail, that will, to be rightful, must be reasonable. The minority possess their equal rights, which equal laws must protect, and to violate would be oppression." He added, in those often-quoted words, "*We are all republicans; we are all federalists.* If there be any among us who wish to destroy this union, or to change its republican form, let them stand undisturbed, as monuments of the safety with which error of opinion may be tolerated where reason is left free to combat it." Marshall rose to administer the oath, and the ceremony ended.

The years ahead would place these two great statesmen on a collision course. But for the moment, they shared a common purpose. The change of power had been peacefully accomplished. When Marshall returned to his rooms, he finished his letter to Pinckney. "I have administered the oath to the President," he wrote. "You will before this reaches you see his inauguration speech. It is in the general well judged and conciliatory. It is in direct terms giving the lie to the violent party declamation which has elected him; but it is strongly characteristic of the general cast of his political theory."[98]

This book deals with the life of John Marshall. As Chief Justice of the United States for thirty-five years, Marshall transformed the Constitution from a compact among the states into a charter of national life and created a political role for the Supreme Court at the very center of the nation's development. Marshall was a great man in an era that brought forth great men. And the conflicts among them—sometimes petty, often partisan, and occasionally of far-reaching significance—helped the nation to mature and prosper.

Marshall was a man of simple tastes and uncomplicated outlook. Careless of dress, indolent of manner, and a friend to all who approached, he possessed the best-organized mind of his generation. A shrewd politician, a moderate republican, a federalist by principle but a democrat in his daily contacts, Marshall was a patriot and a nationalist. He believed deeply in the United States and carried that faith with him to the grave.

Jefferson and John Adams died on July 4, 1826—the fiftieth anniversary of the Declaration of Independence. Marshall, after a brief illness, died on July 6, 1835. He had gone to Philadelphia that summer for medical treatment, but to no avail. His final words, according to Justice Story, were a prayer for the Union.[99]

On July 8, 1835, as Marshall's funeral cortege made its way through the city, the muffled bells of Philadelphia reverberated their mournful message. As fate would have it, July 8 marked the anniversary of that date in 1776 when Philadelphia's bells had first rung out to celebrate American independence.[100] And then, on that day in 1835, again as if by fate, the greatest of the bells, the Liberty Bell in Independence Hall, went silent. It had cracked while tolling the death of the great chief justice. It was never to ring again.

1

Marshall's Virginia Heritage

The events of my life are too unimportant, and have too
little interest for any person not of my immediate family,
to render them worth communicating or preserving.[1]

W ITH THOSE MODEST WORDS John Marshall commenced a
terse autobiographical sketch for his old friend and colleague
Joseph Story. The year was 1827, and Marshall was seventy-
two. Story had requested the information for a review he was writing of Marshall's *History of the Colonies*, which had recently been republished.[2] Marshall
told Story that he had difficulty recounting the events of his life "since the
mere act of detailing exhibits the appearance of attaching consequence to
them. . . . If I conquer [that difficulty] now, it is because the request is made
by a partial and highly valued friend."[3]

The chief justice thereupon provided Story with a succinct survey of his
early life:

> *I was born on the 24th of September 1755 in the county of Fauquier, at that*
> *time one of the frontier counties of Virginia. My Father possessed scarcely any*
> *fortune, and had received a very limited education;—but was a man to*
> *whom nature had been bountiful, and who had assiduously improved her*
> *gifts. He superintended my education, and gave me an early taste for history*
> *and poetry. At the age of twelve I had transcribed Pope's Essay on Man,*
> *with some of his Moral Essays.*
>
> *There being no grammar school in that part of the country in which my*
> *Father resided I was sent, at fourteen, about one hundred miles from home,*
> *to be placed under the tuition of Mr. Campbell, a clergyman of great re-*
> *spectability. I remained with him one year, after which I was brought home*

*and placed under the care of a Scotch gentleman who was just introduced
into the parish as Pastor, and who resided in my Father's family. He remained in the family one year, at the expiration of which time I had commenced reading Horace and Livy. I continued my studies with no other aid
than my Dictionary. My Father superintended the English part of my education, and to his care I am indebted for anything valuable which I may
have acquired in my youth. He was my only intelligent companion; and was
both a watchful parent and an affectionate friend. The young men within my
reach were entirely uncultivated; and the time I passed with them was devoted to hardy athletic exercises.[4]*

With those sparse words John Marshall sketched the broad outline of his
upbringing. In September 1755 when Marshall was born, Fauquier county,
at the foot of the Blue Ridge Mountains, was perched at the frontier and
lightly settled.[5] Its pioneer inhabitants were nervous and apprehensive that
autumn. Two months before, 5,000 red-coated regulars, the largest force
Britain had ever deployed in the colonies, had been ambushed by the
French and Indians on the banks of the Monongahela. Major General Edward Braddock, the British commander in chief in North America, had been
killed and his command annihilated.[6] The panic flight of the few survivors
shattered the myth of English invincibility. If Wolfe's victory over Mont-
calm on the Plains of Abraham consolidated the British hold on Canada,
Braddock's defeat at the hands of the Indians convinced the American
colonists they must fend for themselves.

George Washington, then twenty-three years old, led the Virginia
rangers who served with Braddock. He saw firsthand the magnitude of Braddock's defeat, as did the other young Virginians who accompanied him. One
Virginian who did not join the campaign was Washington's close friend
Thomas Marshall, the future chief justice's father.[7] Washington and
Thomas Marshall had been raised as neighbors in tidewater's Westmoreland
county and briefly attended school together in Washington parish. Both
were surveyors by profession and had worked together mapping the vast expanse of Virginia's northern neck to chart the way for future settlement.
Like Washington, the elder Marshall was an officer in the Virginia militia,
but with his wife expecting their first child, he remained at home that
summer in the tiny community of Germantown, a settlement of less than
a dozen dwellings, all of which disappeared when the frontier moved
westward.[8]

John Marshall's parents were typical of many young couples in colonial
America. His paternal ancestors were Welsh artisans who came to Virginia
sometime in the late seventeenth or early eighteenth century. His father
was the son of another John Marshall, a small planter who struggled to make

a living on two hundred acres of low, marshy land cut from the wilderness along a minor tributary of the Potomac. That John Marshall was known to his prosperous neighbors as "John of the forest," a pejorative term used by tidewater aristocracy to describe someone less affluent who lived in the woods.[9] In 1722 he married Elizabeth Markham, the younger daughter of a prosperous merchant from Alexandria, Virginia,[10] and together they had six children, Thomas being the eldest. Nothing definite is known about the parents of "John of the forest," and all efforts to chart the chief justice's paternal heritage beyond the second generation have ended in genealogical quicksand. Marshall himself never traced his parentage beyond his grandfather.[11]

By contrast, the chief justice's maternal ancestors came from the remnants of English gentry and Scottish nobility who settled Virginia's great plantations. "My mother was named Mary Keith," wrote Marshall. "She was the daughter of a clergyman, of the name of Keith, who migrated from Scotland and intermarried with a Miss Randolph of James River."[12] Marshall's summary was as delicate as it was precise. His maternal grandmother, the "Miss Randolph of James River," was Mary Isham Randolph, the granddaughter of William Randolph of Turkey Island and Mary Isham of Bermuda Hundred—colonial grandees sometimes referred to as the "Adam and Eve of Virginia." Their descendants include not only Marshall, but Thomas Jefferson, Robert E. Lee, and numerous generations of Randolphs.[13]

The Ishams and the Randolphs were among the first English settlers to arrive in Virginia.[14] The first Randolph, a merchant by the name of Henry, went to Jamestown in 1635. His business flourished, and in 1659 Henry was named clerk of the House of Burgesses. William Randolph, his nephew, arrived a few years later, and trained as a lawyer. He succeeded his uncle as the burgesses's clerk and eventually became attorney general of the colony. In 1680, he married Mary Isham, the much sought after daughter of Henry Isham, one of tidewater Virginia's largest landowners and the social arbiter of the families living on the south bank of the James River.

The Randolph-Isham union proved remarkably fertile. There were nine children and thirty-seven grandchildren. Each of the children married well, and the family holdings multiplied. One son, Richard of *Curles*,* married Jane Bolling, a great-granddaughter of Pocahontas. Another, Sir John Randolph, a distinguished lawyer and scholar, was knighted by George II in 1732, the only Virginian to be given such a rank in the colonial period.[15] A third son, Isham Randolph, who came into possession of the vast Dungeness plantation, was the grandfather of Thomas Jefferson. The descendants of

---

*To distinguish the members of the fast-growing Randolph clan, the various wings of the family were designated by their plantation, e.g. "Richard of *Curles*," "Thomas of *Tuckahoe*," "Isham of *Dungeness*," etc.

William, the eldest son, intermarried with the Blands and the Lees, spawn-
ing additional dynasties. Thomas, the second son of the original William
Randolph and Mary Isham, married the wealthy Judith Fleming of New
Kent county,[16] and established one of the James River's most famous plantations at Tuckahoe. It was from the Tuckahoe Randolphs that Marshall was
descended.

In the early 1730s Mary Isham Randolph, the eldest daughter of
Thomas and Judith of Tuckahoe, then a young girl of sixteen or seventeen,
fell in love and eloped with a slave overseer from her uncle Isham's Dungeness plantation—an Irishman by the name of Enoch Arden.[17] The two were
married secretly and had a child. Eventually they were discovered to be living on remote Elk Island in the James River. According to family chroniclers, the enraged Randolphs descended on the island, killed Arden and the
baby, and took Mary back to Tuckahoe. The tragic loss of her husband and
child shattered Mary's sanity.[18]

Under careful family supervision, Mary recovered gradually, only to fall
in love with yet another man deemed objectionable by the Randolphs. This
time the object of Mary's affection was the Reverend James Keith. Keith
was the minister of Henrico parish, one of the largest and most important
parishes in Virginia.[19] It included not only Tuckahoe and other Randolph
plantations on the James but the rapidly growing town of Richmond as well.
A refugee from the abortive 1719 Jacobite uprising in Scotland, the Reverend Keith was particularly effective in the pulpit. He was a bachelor, but
he was seventeen years older than Mary and, like much of the Anglican
clergy in colonial Virginia, enjoyed a reputation for licentiousness.[20] Mary
and James had an affair and appear to have been discovered *in flagrante
delicto*. The Randolphs, who held two seats on the vestry of Henrico parish,
forced Keith's resignation and did their utmost to prevent the pair from seeing each other. Keith resigned as minister of the parish on October 12,
1733,[21] and departed for Maryland immediately thereafter.[22]

The episode was handled gingerly by church authorities.[23] Commissary
James Blair, the Church of England's representative in Virginia, and a former minister of Henrico parish, wrote to the Bishop of London that "Mr.
Keith has privately left this parish and Country, being guilty of fornication
with a young Gentlewoman, whose friends did so dislike his character that
they would not let her marry him."[24] Blair, however, soon had second
thoughts about the precipitate action against Keith. On March 24, 1734, he
wrote a follow-up letter to the bishop stating that "I gave your Lordship an
account of the misfortune which occasioned [Rev. Keith's resignation] tho' I
did not then know what I have learned since that from some of the circumstances in his case, our Governor recommended him to the Governor of
Maryland."[25] The circumstances are not mentioned by Blair, but presum-

ably pertained to the fact that James Keith and Mary Randolph were deeply in love. The following year Blair rescinded Keith's exile to Maryland and appointed him minister of the frontier parish of Hamilton in what subsequently became Fauquier county.* When Mary came of age, she and James Keith were married, and between them they had eight children, including Marshall's mother.

The Keiths flourished in Fauquier county,[26] but Mary's troubles were not over. Years later she received a letter purporting to come from the Irishman Enoch Arden, triggering a final bout of insanity from which she never recovered. Despite the passage of time, Mary cherished the memory of Arden, and the possibility that he might still be alive filled her with despair— a despair compounded by fears that as a consequence her marriage to the Reverend Keith might be invalid.[27] Were that to be the case, their children would be illegitimate. The question was never resolved conclusively, and for whatever reason Chief Justice Marshall rarely mentioned his tie to the Randolphs.[28]

Marshall was less reluctant to discuss his Keith heritage. James Keith, born in 1697, was the son of a professor at Marischal College in Aberdeen.[29] Most of the Keiths, however, were soldiers: a military family whose lineal descendants bore the title Earl Marischal and who traced their roots to ancient Scottish and Saxon kings. Their soldierly exploits won wide renown and were celebrated in song and legend. Robert Keith, the first Earl Marischal, led the decisive cavalry charge at the battle of Bannockburn in 1314, culminating Scotland's struggle for independence.[30] George Keith (1553–1623), the fifth Earl Marischal, founded Marischal College. His grandson, the seventh Earl Marischal, supported the restoration of Charles II and was keeper of the privy seal of Scotland. Another grandson, John, first Earl of Kintore, held the family castle Dunnottar against Cromwell during the civil wars and preserved the regalia of Scotland, keeping it from falling into the hands of the Puritans.[31]

After the Glorious Revolution of 1688, which brought William and Mary

---

*Commissary James Blair was one of the few persons in Virginia who could have defied the Randolphs openly. The principal founder and first president (for life) of the College of William and Mary, Blair was widely regarded as the *eminence grise* of Virginia politics. As the representative of the Church of England, Blair served on the governor's council for over fifty years and chaired it for much of that period. Circumstances suggest that Keith may have been Blair's protégé or that Blair at least had a special interest in his well-being. Blair, a Scot himself, had been born in that portion of northern Scotland ruled by the Keiths, and was educated at Marischal College in Aberdeen, where he and Keith's father had been classmates. No letters have been found suggesting an ongoing friendship between Blair and the elder Keith, but it was Blair's change of heart that permitted James Keith to return to Virginia. For Blair generally, see Parke Rouse, Jr., *James Blair of Virginia* 5–16, 117–245 (Chapel Hill: University of North Carolina Press, 1971); also see 2 *Fasti Academiae Mariscallanae: Selections from the Records of Marischal College and University, 1593–1860* 196–198, Peter John Anderson, ed. (Aberdeen: New Spalding Club, 1898).

to the throne, the Keiths continued to side with the Scottish James II (the Pretender) and helped to raise the armies that fought on his behalf. The Earl Marischal commanded the Jacobite forces that landed in Scotland in 1719, where they made a desperate but doomed effort to rally the highland clans to the Pretender's cause.[32] When the rebellion failed, the Keiths fled. James Keith, Marshall's grandfather and a first cousin of the Earl Marischal, came to Virginia.[33] His companion, James Francis Edward Keith, the Earl Marischal's younger brother, continued as a soldier, first in the Spanish, then the Russian, and finally in the Prussian army.[34]

Marshall's heritage, the union of working-class fathers and illustrious maternal forebears, was not uncommon in colonial Virginia. The ancestors of his great contemporaries—Washington, Jefferson, Patrick Henry, Madison, and Monroe—reflected similar pairings.[35] Ambitious men of working-class origins frequently became surveyors or lawyers and "married up." Most served as officers in the militia and engaged in local politics—another means of social mobility. All speculated heavily in land, and the fortunate ones prospered. Men such as George Washington, Peter Jefferson, and Thomas Marshall, who worked as surveyors charting the wilderness, were especially well placed to locate desirable tracts and file claims. The daughters of the established gentry, with few eligible suitors to choose from, reached out to select husbands from among these rising young men.

The ancestral parallel between John Marshall and Thomas Jefferson is especially striking. Marshall's father and Peter Jefferson, the president's father, descended from the same stock of Welsh yeomanry. Both inherited modest farms from their own fathers; both became surveyors; both married Randolphs; and neither could trace his distant forebears with any degree of certainty. Peter Jefferson was twenty-two years older than Thomas Marshall and success came correspondingly sooner, but their careers followed remarkably similar paths.

Jefferson, in his own autobiographical sketch, wrote affectionately of his father, using virtually the same words as those chosen by John Marshall to describe his. "My father's education had been quite neglected," said Jefferson, "but being of a strong mind, sound judgment and eager after information, he read much and improved himself." The president noted that his father "was the 3rd or 4th settler of the part of the country in which I live,"[36] and he always took pride in his parents' status as pioneers.[37]

Like Peter Jefferson, Thomas Marshall moved west to exploit the opportunities the frontier provided. In 1752, when "John of the forest" died, he left the bulk of his small estate to his wife Elizabeth for her lifetime, and then to Thomas.[38] The poor land offered little promise, and with the aid of his friend George Washington, Thomas Marshall found employment as a surveyor and land agent for Lord Fairfax. In early 1753 he and his mother abandoned their homestead in Westmoreland county and resettled in the small frontier community of Germantown, in what subsequently became Fauquier county. Captain Thomas Marshall became one of its first and most prominent citizens. He divided the county into districts for tax purposes and several years later was appointed sheriff and tax collector. Since the sheriff, as tax collector, retained a portion of the fees, this was one of the most lucrative positions in colonial America. Later Thomas Marshall became Fauquier county's first magistrate and was elected to the House of Burgesses, where he represented the county virtually without interruption until the revolution.[39] In 1754 he married Mary Randolph Keith, the seventeen-year-old daughter of the Reverend James Keith and Mary Isham Randolph of Tuckahoe. John Marshall, the future chief justice, their first child, was born the following year in circumstances remarkably similar to those in which Thomas Jefferson had been born twelve years earlier.

Lord Fairfax, whose home was at Greenway Court in the Shenandoah Valley, played a pivotal role in the development of the Marshall family. The only peer of the realm to take up permanent residence in North America, "the Proprietor"—as Fairfax was known—was a generous and beloved patron. He not only provided Thomas Marshall (and George Washington as well) with a substantial income, but also offered a model of wisdom and modesty that was exceptionally rare in frontier America. Equally important, by representing his lordship in Fauquier county, Thomas Marshall acquired an immediate social standing that otherwise might have eluded him.

Lord Fairfax's vast holdings, from which he was entitled to collect quitrents,[40] numbered over 5.2 million acres and traced to a royal grant by Charles II in 1649.[41] Known as the northern neck of Virginia, the Fairfax estate included all the land bounded by Chesapeake Bay on the east, the Potomac River on the north, the Rappahannock on the south, and a direct line joining the head springs of the Potomac and the Rappahannock on the west. The area amounted to roughly one quarter of Virginia and included eighteen counties in present-day Virginia and seven in West Virginia.[42] The land was sparsely settled, however, and there were virtually no inhabitants beyond the Blue Ridge Mountains. The task of the Proprietor's agents—men like Washington and Thomas Marshall—was to survey the tract, assist in finding people to settle there, arrange the title transfers, and ultimately collect the modest quitrents, which were often as low as two shillings per hundred acres.

Perhaps even more important than the financial support that Lord Fairfax provided was the access he allowed to his home at Greenway Court, which was an exceptional frontier oasis of learning and culture.[43] Fairfax had been educated at Oxford and as a young man had written the occasional article for Joseph Addison's *Spectator*.[44] He appreciated both the written and the spoken word and had brought with him from England one of the largest libraries in the colonies. Both Washington and Thomas Marshall took full advantage of the resources at Greenway Court, and borrowed freely from the extensive collection of classical and contemporary literature.[45] They relished this access to the world of learning and treasured their association with the man who provided it. The Proprietor's love for the Virginia countryside, his eagerness to aid new settlers, and the confident leadership he exerted on the frontier (Fairfax declined advice that he surrender his exposed position at Greenway Court after Braddock's defeat) contributed significantly to the growth of the American nation.*

During the revolution, Lord Fairfax remained undisturbed at Greenway Court, and George Washington personally undertook to insure his safety.[46] The fact is that Fairfax, the scion of a prominent Whig family in Britain,[47] had little quarrel with American independence. He declined to renounce allegiance to George III, but this was primarily to protect his estates in England, which would have been sequestered had he done so. Nevertheless, the Shenandoah Valley, much of which was still owned by Lord Fairfax, quickly became George Washington's principal source of food for the Continental Army. Similarly, when the paper currency issued by the revolutionary government was deteriorating rapidly in value, Fairfax helped to stabilize the dollar by instructing his numerous collectors to accept it at face value.[48]

Lord Fairfax died in December 1781, at the age of ninety.[49] There is no evidence that the young John Marshall ever met the Proprietor, though he easily could have when he accompanied his father on surveying expeditions for his Lordship. But the example provided by Lord Fairfax, his encouragement of Marshall's father, and the library he shared clearly had an impact on the future chief justice. In later years, Marshall felt emotionally attached to

---

*Andrew Burnaby, a contemporary of Washington and Thomas Marshall, provided a captivating portrait of Fairfax as an English country gentleman thoroughly at home on the American frontier. "He kept many servants, white and black; several hunters; a plentiful but plain table," wrote Burnaby, "and his mansion was the mansion of hospitality. His dress corresponded with his mode of life, and, notwithstanding he had every year new suits of clothes, of the most fashionable and expensive kind, sent out to him from England, which he never put on, was plain in the extreme. His manners were humble, modest, and unaffected; not tinctured in the smallest degree with arrogance, pride, or self-conceit. He was free from the selfish passions, and liberal almost to excess. The produce of his farms, after the deduction of what was necessary for the consumption of his own family, was distributed and given away to the poor planters and settlers in his neighborhood. To these he frequently advanced money, to enable them to go on with their improvements; to clear away the woods, and cultivate the ground; and where the lands proved unfavourable, and not likely to answer the labour and expectation of the planter or husbandman, he usually indemnified him for the expense he had been at in the attempt, and gratuitously granted him fresh lands of a more favourable and promising nature. He was a friend and a father to all who held and lived under him; and as to the country, of which he was the proprietor, he sacrificed every other pursuit, and made every other consideration subordinary, to this great point." Burnaby, *Travels Through the Middle Settlements of North America in the Years 1759 and 1760* 201 (London: Wessels, 1798).

the Fairfax holdings. He often represented the Proprietor's heirs in litigation and subsequently led a syndicate that purchased a remainder interest in the estate.

Thomas Marshall eventually prospered as Lord Fairfax's agent in Fauquier county, but success was hard won. The simple pioneer cabin in Germantown in which the Marshalls initially resided was well constructed,[50] and the family remained there for almost ten years. Thomas Marshall's main source of income was as a surveyor and land agent. Whatever farming the family engaged in was primarily for their own consumption. Clothing was mostly homespun, tools and utensils were fashioned locally, and purchases were restricted to the few staples such as salt and sugar that could not be produced domestically. Reflecting on his childhood many years later, the chief justice recalled how meals frequently consisted of only corn meal mush and how ladies used thorns in the absence of pins to secure their dresses.[51]

The parallels between John Marshall and Thomas Jefferson end abruptly after the early years of childhood. At the age of two, Jefferson's parents returned to Goochland county and, ironically, to Tuckahoe—the ancestral home of Marshall's maternal forebears.[52] Thomas Jefferson's removal to Tuckahoe provided him with a different vantage point from that of Marshall. Jefferson's father had for many years been a close friend of William Randolph's, the older brother of Marshall's grandmother.[53] In 1729, under Virginia's time-honored practice of primogeniture, William had become the sole owner of Tuckahoe and he had taken the unusual step of naming his friend Peter Jefferson, rather than a Randolph, as the executor of his estate and the guardian of his three young children.* When William died in 1745, Jefferson's father moved his family to Tuckahoe and undertook to manage the plantation.[54]

At Tuckahoe, Jefferson was raised in patrician splendor.[55] His early education was assiduously attended to, and although the family returned to Albemarle county in the 1750s, Jefferson's sheltered early years set him apart from Marshall, who grew up on the frontier. Jefferson's close association with the Randolphs widened the gap. While Marshall downplayed his relationship to the family, Jefferson cherished the tie, and his brother and sister subsequently intermarried with other grandchildren of Isham of Dungeness.[56]

Whether their different childhood experiences laid a foundation for the subsequent tension between Marshall and Jefferson is impossible to deter-

---

*In addition to naming Peter Jefferson as his executor, William Randolph specified in his will that if none of his three children should live to maturity, his estate should be divided equally among the children of his youngest sister, Judith Stith. The children of his older sister, Mary Randolph Keith, who ordinarily would have shared in the estate, were not mentioned. In effect, Marshall's grandmother and her children (including Marshall's mother) were disinherited by the Randolphs. William Randolph's will, dated March 2, 1742, with a codicil dated July 20, 1745, was recorded November 19, 1745, and probated May 20, 1746. 5 *Goochland County Will and Deed Book* 73.

mine. Jefferson was certainly aware that his childhood home, Tuckahoe, had been the home of Marshall's grandmother, and he undoubtedly knew of the tragedy that surrounded Mary Randolph Keith and of the enormous gulf that divided her from the Randolphs. Neither Jefferson nor Marshall ever suggested that any of this mattered in the least. But the circumstances are sufficiently bizarre to warrant comment.

Marshall's family moved several times during his childhood, but always farther west and always to take advantage of the opportunities the frontier provided. In the early 1760s, to enable Thomas to superintend the Fairfax lands more easily, the family left Germantown and moved some thirty miles to Leeds Manor, one of the most beautiful regions on the eastern slope of the Blue Ridge. The area had been named personally by Lord Fairfax to commemorate Leeds Castle, the seat of the Fairfax family in England, and the Proprietor had once considered residing there.[57] On the banks of Goose Creek, Thomas Marshall built a simple wooden cabin patterned after the one in Germantown, with two rooms on the first floor and a two-room loft above. Since Marshall's father was not yet well enough established to buy the land, he leased it from Colonel Richard Henry Lee.[58] The Marshalls called their new home "the Hollow," and the ten years they resided there were John Marshall's formative years.

The family grew rapidly. Besides John, there were eight girls and six boys as well as several cousins, such as Humphrey Marshall, a future Kentucky senator, who were raised with the family. Elizabeth, or Eliza, as she was called, the oldest girl, was born in 1756, and her sister Mary in 1757. Eliza later married John's friend, the successful doctor and merchant Rawleigh Colston. Mary wed her cousin Humphrey.

Marshall's brother Thomas was born in 1761, and a second, James Markham, in 1764. Like John, both served as officers in the Continental Army. Thomas became a lawyer and farmer. James married Hester Morris, the daughter of Philadelphia financier Robert Morris, and was a frequent partner with the chief justice in various land acquisitions.

Marshall's sister Lucy, who married the wealthy Virginia planter John Ambler, was born in 1768 and died in 1795. She was the only child not to survive her parents. Alexander Keith Marshall, who became a prominent lawyer in Kentucky, was born in 1770. Louis, a noted physician, educator, and early president of Washington College (now Washington and Lee University), arrived in 1773.

All of the Marshall children were accomplished, literate, and entirely self-educated under their parents' tutelage. Unlike most families of the period, the girls were educated alongside the boys. Senator Humphrey Marshall, who never attended school outside the Marshall household, said his future wife Mary taught him to read.[59] And it was Marshall's sister Susan, married to Judge William McClung of Kentucky, who was considered by the family to be the most gifted intellectually. Jane, another sister, founded a school for young women in Petersburg, one of the first of its kind in Virginia.[60] Nancy, Marshall's youngest sister, married Colonel Joseph Hamilton Daveiss, a prominent Federalist lawyer, who, as United States attorney for Kentucky, sought in vain to indict Aaron Burr for treason. Daveiss was later killed leading a charge at the battle of Tippecanoe.[61]

By any standard, the Marshall household was remarkable. John Marshall, who respected his father enormously, often spoke of his superior intellect and strength of character. It was, said Justice Story, a theme on which he broke out with spontaneous eloquence. Marshall told Story that "My father was a far abler man than any of his sons. To him I owe the solid foundation of all my success in life."[62] Marshall's comment reflected more than an outcropping of filial devotion. Thomas Marshall was ambitious, dedicated, and unflagging in his pursuit of the American dream. From modest beginnings—an abandoned cabin in Germantown and a leased homestead on Goose Creek—he eventually became one of the largest landowners on the Virginia frontier. He was one of George Washington's most trusted advisers, and in his later years he played a prominent role in the settlement of Kentucky.* Upon his death in 1802, he left an estate of more than 200,000 acres in Virginia and Kentucky to be divided among his children.[63]

Thomas Marshall was a large man. Physically powerful and possessed of enormous endurance, he had the ideal characteristics for mapping new country and leading the wave of settlement. He was also a brave man. His courageous leadership of the 3rd Virginia regiment at the battle of Brandywine in 1777 is credited with slowing Cornwallis's advance and saving Washington's army from annihilation. He was also known for his remarkable tolerance at a time when only the Church of England was recognized in the colony. In 1769 he is reported to have constructed a small, nondenomina-

---

*Thomas Marshall was appointed surveyor of the western lands (Kentucky) by the State of Virginia in 1781 and, upon the formation of the Union under the Constitution, was appointed by President Washington to be the Collector of Revenue for Kentucky, a post he held until 1797. His resignation, written to President Adams, undoubtedly expressed the character of the man whom his son loved so dearly. Said Thomas Marshall:

"It may possibly be a subject of enquiry, why, after holding the office during the most critical and troublesome times, I should now resign it, when I am no longer insulted, and abused, for endeavoring to execute the Laws of my Country—when those laws appear to be, more than formerly, respected—and when the probability is, that in future they may be carried into effect with but little difficulty?

"In truth this very change, among other considerations, furnishes a reason for the decision I have made. For having once engaged in the business of revenue, I presently found myself of sufficient importance with the enemies of the Government here to be made an object of their particular malevolence—and while this was the case, I was determined not to be driven from my post." Reprinted in "Thomas Marshall," 1 *Bulletin of the Fauquier Historical Society* 140–141 (July 1922).

tional church on North Cobbler Mountain, and later he intervened with county authorities to prevent the arrest of his brother William, a Baptist preacher of great effectiveness who had riled the anti-Baptist faction of Fauquier's religious establishment.[64] Despite a lack of formal schooling, Thomas Marshall was intellectually accomplished. He invented what became known as Marshall's Meridian Instrument, a surveying device for converting magnetic north to true north that the Virginia Assembly required for all surveys after 1772.[65] George Washington subsequently recommended him to command Virginia's artillery regiment because of his superior mathematical ability. In short, Thomas Marshall's achievements were substantial and his reputation unblemished.

Although Marshall rarely spoke of his mother, he acquired from her a steady temperament and an exceptional respect for the intellectual accomplishments of women.[66] Mary Keith Marshall, as the daughter of a Scottish cleric and teacher, had been educated far beyond the level customary for a Virginia woman of that period.[67] Despite the demands of her large family, she found time to impart to her children a remarkable love of learning. Justice Joseph Bradley wrote that Marshall's mother "was a woman of more than ordinary intellect and character," and noted in his diary that many believed "the Ch[ief] Just[ice] got his brains from his mother's side."[68]

Years later Marshall commented indirectly on the influence of his mother when, as Chief Justice of the United States, he wrote to Richmond publisher Thomas White in support of higher education for women. "I have always believed," wrote Marshall, "that national character . . . depends more on the female part of society than is generally imagined. Precepts from the lips of a beloved mother . . . sink deep in the heart, and make an impression which is seldom entirely effaced. These impressions have an influence on character which may contribute greatly to the happiness or misery, the eminence or insignificancy of the individual."[69] Driving his point home, Marshall told White that "If the agency of the mother in forming the character of her children is, in truth, so considerable as I think it—if she does so much toward making her son what she would wish him to be—how essential is it that she should be fitted for the beneficial performance of these important duties."[70]

Joseph Story captured the chief justice's unusual appreciation of the ability of women when he spoke of the high esteem in which Marshall "held the female sex, as . . . the equals of man. I do not refer to the courtesy and delicate kindness with which he was accustomed to treat the sex; but rather to the unaffected respect with which he spoke of their accomplishments, their talents, their virtues and their excellences."[71]

Marshall's attitude was sufficiently unique to cause Harriet Martineau, an English feminist who knew Marshall in his later years, to note that the chief justice:

maintained through life and carried to his grave a reverence for women, as rare in its kind as in its degree. He brought not only the love and pity . . . which they excite in the minds of the pure, but the steady conviction of their intellectual equality with men, and with this a deep sense of their social injuries. Throughout life he so invariably sustained their cause that no indulgent libertine dared to flatter and humour, no skeptic . . . dared to scoff at the claims of women in the presence of Marshall.[72]

Martineau genuinely admired the chief justice and called him "the most venerated man in the country." In 1835 she undertook a trek across America, and Marshall, who admired her work on behalf of women, insisted on providing her with a letter of introduction in which he pledged himself to be under personal obligation to anyone who might assist her.[73]

It was while the family was living beside Goose Creek that John Marshall's education began in earnest. With no schools in the region, the family hearth became a classroom. In an environment where books were a precious rarity, Thomas Marshall's library stood out as a remarkable exception. His collection of literature, some of which was borrowed from Lord Fairfax, was substantial for the time and included works by Livy, Horace, Pope, Dryden, Milton, and Shakespeare.[74] In his brief autobiographical sketch, Marshall told Story how his father had encouraged his interest in history and poetry and how, at the age of twelve, he had transcribed the works of Alexander Pope. The early exposure to Pope obviously made a lasting impression on Marshall. Sixty years later, at the height of his authority as chief justice, the act of copying out Pope's evocative poetry was one of the few events from his childhood that Marshall still recalled with enthusiasm, and happily wished to record.

That may seem surprising to a contemporary audience. Yet with few books available, and virtually no other form of intellectual stimulation, transcription—and the inevitable memorization that accompanied it—provided an exceptional learning experience. More than the work of any other writer, it was the poetry of Pope that filtered down to a general audience in prerevolutionary America. His name was invoked like a god—or at least a muse—in popular debate, and his verse was quoted and imitated in journals and newspapers to support any issue to which the lines could be made appropriate.[75] Thomas Jefferson annotated his commonplace book with quotations from Pope;[76] George Washington had a six-volume set of Pope's works;[77] and Benjamin Franklin ordered numerous editions from publishers in Philadelphia.[78] Throughout the colonies, ordinary schoolmasters, not unlike Thomas and Mary Marshall, used Pope's verse to teach grammar and moral values simultaneously.[79]

There was good reason for Pope's popularity, and for Marshall's attachment to his works. As a product of the Age of Reason, Pope was the last of the English poets to subscribe to the neoclassical belief that nature was perfect and reason supreme. The neoclassical tradition lacked a sense of original sin and held that morality might be based on common sense. Those ideas are powerfully expressed in Pope's *Essay on Man*, and John Marshall embraced them wholeheartedly. Pope's syllogisms explained the essence of the human condition in a manner that Marshall, a youth of twelve, found easy to comprehend. The effect of such intense exposure to a single author was unavoidable. Pope's optimistic outlook made an indelible impression on Marshall's mind. If any common thread weaves through the life of John Marshall or expresses itself in his political and judicial outlook, it is the belief in the alliance of nature and reason that he took from Pope.

> All Nature is but Art, unknown to thee;
> All Chance, Direction, which thou canst not see;
> All Discord, Harmony not understood;
> All partial Evil, universal Good:
> And, spite of Pride, in erring Reason's spite,
> One truth is clear, WHATEVER IS, IS RIGHT.

In the *Essay on Man*, Pope identified self-interest with the public interest—a powerful talisman for an age of economic expansion and discovery. He also celebrated the virtues of "mixed government," where each element of the population defended its own interest. Man is restrained by "Government and Laws," wrote Pope, and the jarring interests of one element colliding against another created the "music of a well-mixed State." As a formula for constitutional government, the idea of competing interests balancing each other echoed the classical message of Aristotle and Polybius—an idea that came to fruition in the Constitution of the United States, and of which John Marshall was to become the foremost defender.

The future chief justice derived other important advantages from reading Pope. Pope was a master wordsmith—a genius at compressing complex thoughts and expressing them so vividly that his lines continue to enjoy everyday usage. In his introduction to the *Essay on Man*, Pope offered two reasons why he chose to write in verse instead of prose. First, the "principles, maxims, or precepts so written, both strike the reader more strongly at first, and are more easily retained by him afterwards." A second reason for writing in verse, said Pope, was that "I found I could express [these principles] more *shortly* this way than in prose itself; and nothing is more certain, than that much of the *force* as well as *grace* of arguments or instructions, depends on their *conciseness*." Marshall drew an important lesson from that.

Throughout his career, he strived for a similar effect in his writing and, like Pope, was always fond of the pithy phrase. Marshall's decisions bristle with quotable passages converting intricate constitutional doctrines into handy epigrams that, like the iambics of Pope, have become commonplace. Finally, by reading Pope and committing long passages to memory, Marshall was exercising his mind and improving his faculty for retention. The use of pen (or quill) and pencil followed easily.

Marshall's brief attendance at the academy run by the Reverend Archibald Campbell in Washington parish—the same school his father and George Washington had attended briefly—was the only formal schooling he received as a youth. Among his classmates was James Monroe. Legend has it that Marshall and Monroe walked to school together every day, each with books under one arm and a gun slung over his shoulder, "for these were pioneer days and children were taught self-protection from the cradle."[80] Like Scottish parsons through the ages, Campbell ran a tight educational ship. "He was a disciplinarian of the sternest type," said one of Monroe's descendants, and school was "all work and little play. . . . His pupils were regarded as especially well grounded in mathematics and Latin . . . and in their various subsequent careers they were noted for solidity of character."[81]

When Marshall returned to the Hollow, his father, as head of the vestry for Leeds parish, wrote to a friend in Edinburgh requesting that a minister be sent who could double as a teacher for the local children. The man sent over was the Reverend James Thomson, a recently ordained deacon. Thomson initially resided with the Marshall family and tutored the children in Latin in return for his room and board. When Thomson left at the end of the year, Marshall had commenced reading Horace and Livy.

Livy was the most famous of the Roman historians, and the fragments of his history of Rome that Marshall read glorified the republic and extolled the virtues of patriotism. For Livy, however, historical writing had a greater purpose than simply recording the deeds of the past. He saw history as a guide to life (*magistra vitae*); in order to be effective, it must be well written and accessible to the general reader. Marshall's exposure to Livy's tight Latin prose reinforced his determination to use words sparingly. From Livy, as from Pope, Marshall learned how to express himself precisely.[82]

Horace, the Augustan poet, was an even greater stylist than Livy. Like Pope, his memorable phrases have the impact of epigrams, exposing the follies and excesses of the poet's contemporaries. From Horace, Marshall learned to write for effect, to appreciate the ability of the poet to express complex ideas gracefully, and to understand poetry's underlying message about life's vexations and opportunities.[83] That Marshall chose to mention Horace and Livy in his brief sketch for Story suggests that their impact on him was important and that his debt to them was substantial.

Despite the occasional presence of a parson in the house, or the fact that Mary Randolph Keith was the daughter of a minister, piety and religious dogma played little role in the education of the Marshall children. Thomas Marshall and his wife were church members, but they made little attempt to inculcate their beliefs. Instead, the children were encouraged to think for themselves. Senator Humphrey Marshall openly scorned religion; Dr. Louis Marshall confessed agnosticism; and brothers James and Thomas were notably devoid of religious sentiment.[84] John Marshall never rejected the church openly, but his acceptance was environmental rather than doctrinal. Throughout his life the chief justice declined to become a member of any congregation, unable to believe in the divinity of Christ.[85] If Marshall needed reinforcement for that skepticism, it may have come from Pope. The *Essay on Man* is a ringing endorsement of the deist views of the Age of Reason, and although Pope was Catholic, his emphasis on man as a rational being inevitably diminished the role of Christianity.[86]

In 1773 the Marshall family moved once again. Thomas Marshall, by then a man of more substantial means, purchased a 1,700-acre estate adjacent to North Cobbler Mountain, approximately ten miles northwest of the Hollow. He paid almost £1,000 for the property[87]—a substantial sum in colonial Virginia—but the new farm was located adjacent to the main stage road, and the land was much more fertile than the thin soil of Leeds Manor. It was here that Thomas Marshall built Oak Hill, a seven-room frame home with four rooms on the first floor and three above. Although modest in comparison to the estates of Washington, Madison, and Jefferson—to say nothing of those of the Randolphs and the Lees—Oak Hill nevertheless was a substantial home for the period. According to local legend, it had the first glass windows in the region[88] and, with numerous additions and modifications, it remained in the Marshall family for many years.

Marshall's childhood provided a firm underpinning for his career. His family was not wealthy, but neither was it poor. As the oldest child, Marshall learned to accept responsibility early. He acquired the modesty and discretion that a large family frequently instills, and he learned to lead with a light touch. In Marshall's case, the experience of dealing with a clamorous band of younger siblings, earning their affection and respect while holding them to their tasks, proved remarkably useful in later years when dealing with fractious colleagues jealous of their prerogatives.

Marshall also learned the importance of financial independence. He witnessed his family's progression from Germantown, to the Hollow, to Oak Hill. He recognized the work involved as well as the costs entailed. From his father's example, Marshall appreciated the possibilities that America provided. He was probably not yet aware of his own ability, but whatever it was, he was determined to make the most of it.

2

சப

Soldier of the Revolution

1775–1779

About the time I entered my eighteenth year, the controversy
between Great Britain and her colonies had assumed so
serious an aspect as almost to monopolize the attention of
the old and the young. I engaged in it with all the zeal and
enthusiasm which belonged to my age; and devoted more
time to learning the first rudiments of military exercise in
an Independent company of the gentlemen of the county,
to training a militia company in the neighbourhood, and to
the political essays of the day, than to the classics or to
Blackstone.[1]

THAT WAS THE WAY Marshall described for Story the coming of the revolution. He was among the first to concede that the War for Independence could have been avoided. The Peace of Paris of 1763, marking the victorious conclusion of England's seven-year war with France, left the British in firm control of North America east of the Mississippi.* Not only was there no feeling of separatism in the colonies, but in Marshall's words, "the attachment . . . to the mother country was never stronger."[2] Oliver Wolcott of Connecticut said, "The Abilities of a Child might have governed this Country, so strong had been their Attachment to Britain."[3]

The deterioration of this happy relationship had many causes, some deliberate and others accidental, but all centered on the constitutional rela-

---

*Under the provisions of the Peace of Paris, France ceded Canada to Great Britain, retaining only the tiny islands of St. Pierre and Miquelon off Newfoundland. Spain gave East and West Florida to Britain, which became the sixteenth and seventeenth English colonies in North America. In return for the loss of the Floridas, Spain obtained the Louisiana Territory from France, which, in effect, made the Mississippi River the boundary between the British and Spanish empires in North America. For the text of the Treaty of Paris, see George Chalmers, 1 *Collection of Treaties* 467 (London: J. Stockdale, 1790).

tionship between Britain and the colonies. The issue turned on the question of who had the right to levy taxes.[4] Marshall expressed the American attitude as well as anyone in his *Life of George Washington*. Americans, he wrote, "were proud of the land of their ancestors, and gloried in their descent from Englishmen. . . . While the excellence of the English constitution was a rich theme of declamation, every colonist believed himself entitled to its advantages; nor could he admit that, by crossing the Atlantic, his ancestors had relinquished the essential rights of British subjects."[5]

Marshall noted that the nature of the mother country's authority over the colonies had never been accurately defined. "In Britain, it had always been asserted that parliament possessed the power of binding them in all cases whatever. In America, at different times, and in different provinces, different opinion had been entertained on this subject."[6] Marshall went on to say that in New England, "originally settled by republicans, habits of independence had nourished the theory that the colonial assemblies possessed every legislative power not surrendered by compact . . . and were bound by no laws to which their representatives had not assented." By contrast, in the middle and southern colonies, "no question respecting the supremacy of parliament, in matters of general legislation, ever existed." But even these colonies, said Marshall, "denied the right of parliament to tax them internally."[7]

The confusion over the constitutional relationship intensified after the Peace of Paris. Parliament, saddled with enormous debts arising out of the long war with France, sought to shift a substantial portion of its military costs to the colonies. In addition, at a time when land was still the primary source of wealth throughout the world, the crown decreed a halt to English settlement beyond the Appalachians. On October 7, 1763, George III, at the behest of his government, issued a proclamation that forbade the colonies to grant titles to land beyond the sources of the rivers that flowed into the Atlantic.[8] The colonies had not been consulted, nor had the views of the settlers been canvassed. The purpose of the proclamation was to decrease tension with the Indian tribes and thereby reduce Britain's military expenditures.[9] But the colonies saw the move as a ploy to redirect future settlers to Canada, Nova Scotia, and the Floridas, and the crown did little to convince them otherwise.

The king's proclamation was followed in 1764 by parliament's passage of a new revenue act[10] that increased import duties and, in 1765, by the passage of the stamp act—the first direct, internal tax ever laid on the colonies by Britain.[11] Both measures were prompted by the financial burdens of empire, but the colonies regarded them as unwarranted extensions of parliamentary authority. The stamp act, in particular, aroused concern.* "This act excited serious alarm throughout the colonies," said Marshall. "It was sincerely believed to wound vitally the constitution of the country, and to destroy the sacred principles of liberty." Every effort was made "to diffuse among the people a knowledge of the pernicious consequences which must flow from admitting that the colonists could be taxed by a legislature in which they were not represented."[12]

Opposition to taxation without representation provided a common denominator for the colonies. As George Washington wrote to a friend in England, "I think the parliament of Great Britain hath no more right to put their hands into my pocket, without my consent, than I have to put my hands into yours for money."[13] In New York City, an emergency meeting of delegates from nine colonies demanded immediate repeal of the stamp act and demonstrated for the first time the ability of the colonies to work together. In 1766 Britain acknowledged the colonies' concern by repealing the measure,[14] but coupled the repeal with passage of a declaratory act asserting parliament's absolute authority to "bind the colonies . . . in all cases whatsoever."[15] The wording was almost identical to the Irish declaratory act of 1719, which held Ireland in bondage.[16] In the euphoria that greeted the repeal of the stamp act, little notice was taken of the new measure. But the declaratory act augured things to come. The passage of the Townshend acts[17] in 1767, which laid additional duties on imports, the application of the quartering act for housing British soldiers,[18] and the Boston massacre in 1770, in which several colonists were killed when English troops opened fire without orders, rekindled the colonies' discontent.

After several changes of government in London, parliament eventually repealed the Townshend acts, but left a barb that annoyed the colonies even more. Britain revoked all the duties imposed by the acts save for the duty on tea.[19] The decision to retain the tax on tea was arbitrary. In London's view, by keeping the duty on one article, parliament's supremacy over the colonies would be confirmed. Yet as Marshall observed, "seldom has a wise nation adopted a more ill-judged measure."[20]

A confrontation with Britain was averted temporarily because the colonies were able to smuggle undutied tea from Holland. But in 1773 par-

---

*The stamp act was more severe than the title implies. The tax had to be paid in sterling, not colonial currency. That increased the costs considerably since the currency of the colonies was inflated. Every legal paper, plea, demurrer, and so on, would be taxed 3 shillings; other writs, 10 shillings. Every school diploma or degree, £2; licenses, £1 to £4; deeds and property transfers, 5 shillings; newspapers and journals, 1 shilling per page for every paper printed; advertisements, 2 shillings per issue, and so forth. Most galling, perhaps, was that offenses against the stamp act were to be tried in admiralty court, where the defendant did not have the benefit of trial by jury. See especially Edmund Morgan, *The Stamp Act Crisis* 53–70 (Chapel Hill: University of North Carolina Press, 1953).

liament granted the East India Company an effective monopoly of the tea trade.[21] With no competition, the company was able to undersell the smugglers, and the issue of the tax came to a head. As Marshall explained it, "The tea, if landed, would be sold; the duties would consequently be paid; and the precedent for taxing would be established."[22]

Marshall noted that "the same sentiment on this subject appears to have pervaded the whole continent at the same time. This plan of importation was considered by all as a direct attack on the liberties of the people of America, which it was the duty of all to oppose." When several tea-laden ships arrived in Boston in December 1773, a mob disguised as Mohawk Indians descended on the ships and emptied 342 large chests of the precious commodity into the city's harbor. "The dye is now cast," wrote George III to Lord North. "The Colonies must either submit or triumph."[23]

Parliament responded to the Boston Tea Party by passing a series of measures designed to reassert imperial control. The Boston port act closed the harbor of Boston until the tea was paid for;[24] the Massachusetts government act altered the governance of the province by giving the crown the authority to appoint all local officials;[25] an administration of justice act extended that authority to all law enforcement officers;[26] a new quartering act was passed that empowered royal governors to commandeer private houses to shelter British soldiers;[27] and the Quebec act extended the boundary of that province south to the Ohio River, effectively blocking the westward expansion of New York, Pennsylvania, Maryland, and Virginia.[28]

If London thought stern measures would bring the colonies to heel, it was wrong. The laws enacted by parliament, rather than forcing Massachusetts to submit, galvanized American opposition. "All perceived that Boston was to be punished," said Marshall, "and that the object of the punishment was to coerce obedience to a principle they were determined to resist."[29]

Reaction was swiftest in Virginia. The legislature was still in session when news of the Boston port act reached Williamsburg, and the outcry was immediate. On May 24, 1774, the House of Burgesses adopted a resolution drafted by Patrick Henry, Richard Henry Lee, George Mason, and Thomas Jefferson denouncing the British action and designating June 1 as a day of fasting and prayer. Governor Dunmore responded by dissolving the assembly and ordering its members to disperse. The Burgesses adjourned, but before leaving for their homes, the members gathered at the nearby Raleigh Tavern and restated their resolve. "An attack made on one of our sister Colonies to compel submission to arbitrary taxes is an attack made on all British America," said the legislators.[30] Committees of correspondence worked overtime, and a call went out summoning delegates from the various colonies to a special convention.

Of all the colonies, Virginia had come the furthest since 1763. Each colony was divided politically, economically, and socially between the fertile coastal regions, which were settled early, and the vast piedmont areas above the fall line. The contrast was most pronounced in Virginia. Of the fifty-six counties on the roll of the House of Burgesses, thirty-five represented the tidewater area. And in Virginia, tidewater meant tobacco. Extremely labor intensive and ravenous in its demand for nutrients, tobacco had spawned a plantation economy dependent on slavery, hot weather, and British markets.[31] The white population of the tidewater counties was almost exclusively English.[32] Entailed estates, primogeniture, and the large plantations that the cultivation of tobacco required had created a distinct aristocracy that vied with the vice-regal court of the governor at Williamsburg in its manner of living. Historically, the members of this aristocracy—men like Peyton Randolph, Edmund Pendleton, and Robert Carter Nicholas—were staunch supporters of the crown and the established church, and were heavily dependent on the tobacco brokers of Glasgow and Liverpool. Most were deeply in debt to English creditors,[33] and all were at the mercy of a mercantile market that was controlled by the British government's Board of Trade. Tidewater Virginia was bound to Britain by king, religion, and tobacco.[34]

Above the fall line a different situation prevailed.[35] The thin soil, shorter growing season, and distance from deep-water ports made the raising of tobacco far more difficult. Agriculture remained the principal activity, but farming was largely of a subsistence nature. Farmers concentrated on corn, wheat, and livestock, and the surplus was usually consumed within the colonies, making the piedmont substantially less dependent on British markets.[36]

In addition, the population of the Virginia uplands was not exclusively English. As in other colonies, the communities above the fall line were composed of English, Welsh, Scots, French Huguenot, German, and above all, Scots-Irish settlers. The latter were a hardy band of pioneers, Presbyterian rather than Anglican, and skeptical of authority in general but of royal authority in particular.[37] Small farmers for the most part, they were loyal to the crown, but held the king to be bound by parliament's commitment in "the Solemn League and Covenant" to support the Reformation and the "liberties of the kingdom."[38] Thomas Marshall represented this constituency in the House of Burgesses, as did George Washington and George Mason.

For well over a century the tidewater oligarchy had controlled Virginia politics. Piedmont petitions for roads, bridges, and other vital improvements were routinely denied while the colony spent freely to assist the plantation aristocracy. Frontier assertions of democracy, in particular, were greeted with "hearty disfavor and contempt."[39] All of that began to change in the mid-1760s. In the spring of 1765 Patrick Henry, newly elected to the House of Burgesses from upland Louisa County, took on the tidewater establishment over a proposal to create a loan fund primarily for the benefit of spendthrift plantation owners. Henry unleashed his remarkable oratorical talents in the House and won a narrow one-vote victory.[40] It was an unprecedented triumph. The delegates from the piedmont were thrilled with their new champion. George Mason wrote that Henry "is by far the most powerful speaker I have ever heard. Every word he says not only engages, but commands the attention, and your passions are no longer your own when he addresses them."[41]

When news of the stamp act arrived in Williamsburg two weeks later, the Virginia gentry, still smarting over their legislative defeat, were inclined to go along with parliament.[42] Again, however, Henry mounted the rostrum, and on May 24, 1765, his twenty-ninth birthday, he startled all of British North America with his eloquence. To the anguish of the plantation aristocracy, Henry moved a series of resolutions asserting that Virginia's legislature, not parliament, had the "sole exclusive right and power to lay taxes . . . upon the inhabitants of this colony."[43] When Henry reached his famous peroration, "Tarquin and Caesar had each his Brutus, Charles the First his Cromwell, and George the Third—" Speaker John Robinson, a leader of the tidewater forces, shouted "Treason! Treason!" Without faltering an instant, Henry fixed his eye on the Speaker and thundered, "—may profit by their example. *If this be treason, make the most of it.*"[44]

Again, Henry's resolutions carried by one vote, with the members from the upland counties backing them unanimously. Thomas Jefferson, who was then a student at William and Mary, listened to the debate from the doorway of the House. When the members filed out after the vote had been taken, Jefferson reported that he heard Peyton Randolph, who was the king's attorney general at the time, exclaim, "By God, I would have given 500 guineas for a single vote."[45]

From that point on, leadership in the House of Burgesses began to shift to the up-country forces led by Henry.[46] More important, the seeds of revolution had been sown. It was as if Henry's words "sounded an alarm bell" in the minds of Americans and woke them up to the revolutionary day that was dawning.[47] Over the next decade, most of tidewater's plantation owners rallied to the argument of no taxation without representation.[48] In 1774, when the Continental Congress convened, the Virginia aristocrats still hoped for a settlement. Nevertheless, the fact that Peyton Randolph, the former attorney general for George III, was present in Philadelphia indicated how far the pendulum had swung.[49]

The initial Continental Congress was not a radical assembly bent on separation. To the contrary, the delegates adopted a series of resolutions reaffirming their loyalty to the crown and artfully documenting their grievances. Drafted by John Jay, Robert Livingston, and Richard Henry Lee, the message was clear: "Permit us to be as free as yourselves, and we shall ever esteem a union with you to be our greatest glory."[50] The delegates reluctantly voted for an eventual severing of trade with Britain if the coercive acts directed against Massachusetts were not repealed, and agreed to meet again in May 1775.

Congress's plea fell on deaf ears. While the elder Pitt (Lord Chatham), the Earl of Richmond, and Edmund Burke urged compromise, the king's friends and his government demanded firmness. General Thomas Gage, the British commander in chief in North America, told George III that the Americans "will be Lyons, whilst we are Lambs but if we take the resolute part they will undoubtedly prove very meek."[51] After holding that "a rebellion actually exists in Massachusetts Bay," parliament enacted yet another coercive measure, the New England restraining act,[52] which forbade the four colonies of that region to trade with any partner other than Britain and denied their fishermen access to the rich fishing banks off Nova Scotia and Newfoundland.

Three weeks later General Gage took matters into his own hands. Learning of a cache of military supplies in Concord, about twenty miles northwest of Boston, he dispatched a large force of grenadiers and light infantry to destroy them. The battles of Lexington and Concord followed in short order. When the smoke cleared, the British had lost 273 men and the Americans about 90. "This affair," wrote Marshall, "however trivial in itself, was the commencement of a long and obstinate war, and had no inconsiderable influence on that war, by increasing the confidence the Americans felt in themselves."[53]

In Virginia, events moved apace. Meeting in special convention in St. John's Church in Richmond, delegates from the Old Dominion confronted the situation with growing resolve. When Patrick Henry offered his famous motion, "That this colony be immediately put into a state of defence," the outcome was inevitable. The vote was close (65–60),[54] but Henry's tidewater opponents no longer disagreed with him in principle.[55] They were inclined to postpone military preparations, but stirred by Henry's eloquence, they ultimately agreed to take action.

Why stand we here idle? What is it that gentlemen wish? What would they have? Is life so dear, or peace so sweet, as to be purchased at the price of chains and slavery? Forbid it, Almighty God! I know not what course others may take; but as for me, GIVE ME LIBERTY, OR GIVE ME DEATH.[56]

No verbatim transcript of the convention's proceedings was kept, but the testimony of numerous witnesses documents Henry's power. Edward

Carrington, the brother-in-law of John Marshall's wife, was one of many spectators who watched the great orator through an open window of St. John's Church. "Let me be buried at this spot," Carrington said afterward, and upon his death in 1810 his family honored that request.[57] John Marshall told William Wirt many years later that when his father returned to Oak Hill that spring he described the proceedings to the family. Thomas Marshall had represented Fauquier county at the convention, and the chief justice, then an ardent youth eager for action, recalled his father referring to Henry's speech "as one of the most bold, vehement, and animated pieces of eloquence that had ever been delivered."[58]

News of the battles at Lexington and Concord spread quickly throughout the colonies. The law courts were ordered closed, and the various militias began to make ready. In Virginia, hard on the heels of Patrick Henry's address and the resolutions of the Richmond convention, preparations were undertaken in earnest.[59] George Washington wrote to a friend that he wished "the dispute had been left to posterity to determine, but the crisis is arrived when we must assert our rights, or submit to every imposition that can be heaped upon us."[60]

In early May 1775 the militia company of Fauquier county, following a pattern repeated throughout Virginia, mustered for drill in a farmer's field twelve miles west of the courthouse. The fifty or sixty men who assembled with their rifles that day were aware of the crisis but had no inkling of what would be required, or of how they would be asked to serve.[61] Many of the men had considerable experience as Indian fighters on Virginia's frontier, and virtually all were accustomed to the weapons they brought with them. Although they were novice soldiers, they were familiar with the hardships of the outdoors.

When the company's captain did not arrive, responsibility for the drill fell to the company's second in command, nineteen-year-old John Marshall. Under his father's tutelage, Marshall had learned the rudiments of military drill, and, as he modestly explained to the assembled men that morning, he had been appointed their lieutenant "instead of a better."[62]

Marshall drilled the company with what one of those present described as "a perfect temper."[63] When the drill concluded, Marshall spoke for almost an hour about the events in Massachusetts and the likelihood of war. A battalion of minutemen was about to be formed, and Marshall urged the men to join him in signing up. Marshall told Story:

> In the summer of 1775 I was appointed a first lieutenant in a company of minute men designed for actual service, who were assembled in Battalion on the first of September. In a few days we were ordered to march into the lower country for the purpose of defend-

ing it against a small regular and predatory force commanded by Lord Dunmore. I was engaged in the action at the Great Bridge; and was in Norfolk when it was set on fire by a detachment from the British ships lying in the river, and afterwards when the remaining houses were burnt by orders from the Committee of safety.[64]

In July 1775 the Virginia convention met to organize the colony's defense. In addition to providing for two regiments of regular troops (subsequently known as the Virginia Line), the convention authorized the formation of "sixteen battalions of Minute-Men," who would be "more strictly trained to proper discipline than hath hitherto been customary."[65] Patterned after the Massachusetts minutemen at Lexington and Concord, each man who enlisted was given a hunting shirt, a pair of leggings, and 20 shillings a year for the maintenance of his rifle or musket.*

The first and largest battalion formed under the new ordinance was located along the frontier in the Culpeper district, which included Culpeper, Orange, and Fauquier counties.[66] The Culpeper minutemen, as the battalion was styled, numbered upward of 350 men, almost all of whom were expert marksmen. H. J. Eckenrode, Virginia's historian of the revolution, wrote that the minutemen were "by far the most efficient soldiers the colony possessed."[67] Madison wrote to a friend that "the strength of this Colony will lie chiefly in the rifle-men of the Upland Counties, of whom we shall have a great number."[68] John Marshall, one of the earliest to enlist, was commissioned a first lieutenant in the Fauquier Rifles, a company from Fauquier county commanded by Captain William Pickett. Isham Keith, Marshall's cousin, served as an ensign in the same company.[69]

The battalion mustered initially in "Major Clayton's old field," hard by the Culpeper courthouse.[70] Lawrence Taliafero of Orange county was appointed colonel; Edward Stevens of Culpeper county, lieutenant colonel; and John Marshall's father, representing Fauquier county, was selected to be the battalion's major.[71] The yellow flag of the Culpeper minutemen featured a coiled rattlesnake about to strike and the motto "Don't Tread on Me." Patrick Henry's phrase "Liberty or Death" was emblazoned on the

---

*The frontier rifle was a new device in eighteenth-century warfare. Developed originally as a hunting weapon by German gunsmiths in Lancaster, Pennsylvania, it was highly accurate (in experienced hands) at distances up to 200 yards. By contrast, the basic "Brown Bess" infantry musket was reliable only at 50 yards or less. But the musket could be loaded four times more quickly (15 seconds versus 1 minute) and could be fitted with a bayonet, which the frontier rifle could not. Thus, the rifle became a specialized weapon for the sharpshooters of the light infantry. Mark Mayo Boatner, *Encyclopedia of the American Revolution* 934–936 (New York: David McKay, 1966); Ivor Noël Hume, *1775: Another Part of the Field* 297–300, 425 (New York: Knopf, 1966); T. Triplett Russell and John K. Gott, *Fauquier County in the Revolution* 70–81 (Warrenton, Va.: Fauquier County American Bicentennial Commission, 1976).

banner, as well.[72] The battalion wore the uniform of the frontier: fringed trousers, often made of deerskin, and "strong brown linen hunting shirts dyed with leaves."[73] A number of men embroidered "Liberty or Death" on their shirts in large white letters, thus earning the battalion the name of "shirtmen." They carried tomahawks and scalping knives in their belts and were armed with their individual rifles or muskets. To complete the backwoods appearance, each man wore a buck's tail in his hat.

The battalion's frontier garb was designed to intimidate the British redcoats. But the shirtmen's menacing appearance struck terror in the hearts of those living in the more settled regions of Virginia as well. As one of Marshall's fellow soldiers wrote, "The people, hearing that we came from the backwoods, and seeing our savage-looking equipment, seemed as much afraid of us as if we had been Indians."[74] That quickly changed. "We took pride in demeaning ourselves as patriots and gentlemen, and the people soon treated us with respect and kindness."[75]

Another Virginian, reflecting the general state of alarm across the colony, wrote to a friend in Scotland that "All is anarchy and confusion. . . . We are all in arms, exercising and training old and young to the use of the gun. No person goes abroad without his sword, or gun, or pistols. The sound of war echoes from north to south. Every plain is full of armed men, who all wear a hunting shirt, on the left breast of which are sewed, in very legible letters, Liberty or Death."[76]

In mid-September 1775 Patrick Henry, who had assumed command of the Virginia militia, urgently summoned the Culpeper minutemen to Williamsburg to join the Virginia Line facing British forces under Lord Dunmore in the vicinity of Norfolk. The battalion was unprepared when Henry's order arrived,[77] and the minutemen took several weeks to assemble and make the 150-mile trek to Williamsburg, passing by way of Fredericksburg and Richmond.[78] It was an arduous journey, requiring exceptional dedication and enormous stamina. Marshall and his fellow minutemen received no compensation for their service, had no tents, few blankets, no cold-weather clothing or effective rain gear, and no reliable commissary support.

On October 20, 1775, the *Virginia Gazette* of Williamsburg reported that "the Culpeper Battalion of minutemen, all fine fellows, and well-armed (near one half of them with rifles) are now within a few hours march of this city." Once in the capital, the supply situation improved. The battalion bought heavy cloth for winter coats and drew shoes from the colony's public store.

The military situation was critical. Lord Dunmore, supported by a small British fleet standing offshore, had organized a spirited resistance south of the James River along the shore of the Chesapeake. Norfolk, Virginia's largest town and principal seaport, remained in British hands. Like Philadelphia and, to a lesser extent, New York City, Norfolk brimmed with a Scottish merchant class inherently Tory in sentiment.[79] A large percentage of the population had already taken a fresh oath of allegiance to the crown.[80] In addition, Dunmore possessed an effective force of 150 grenadiers from the Fourteenth Regiment of Foot,[81] to which he had added a significant number of militant Loyalists ("the Queen's Own Loyal Virginia Regiment"), and several hundred runaway slaves whom he had armed.[82] The force he assembled had routed the local militia in a minor skirmish near Kempsville,[83] and in Marshall's words, Dunmore "flattered himself that he would soon bring the lower country to submit to royal authority."[84]

If two or three effective British regiments had arrived in Norfolk that autumn, there is no telling what might have happened.[85] "Had I but a few more men here," Lord Dunmore wrote to General Sir William Howe, who had succeeded Gage on September 26, 1775, as the British commander in North America, "I would march immediately to *Williamsburgh* . . . by which I should soon compel the whole Colony to submit."[86] To prevent that possibility, the 2nd Virginia regiment and the Culpeper minutemen were dispatched with great urgency to confront Dunmore's forces.[87] The ensuing battle at Great Bridge, the first and bloodiest battle fought in Virginia during the revolution, effectively terminated royal government in the colony. For John Marshall, it was a baptism by hostile fire.

The city of Norfolk is bounded by the broad expanse of the James River, Chesapeake Bay, and, some miles distant, the Dismal Swamp. Land access is limited, and in 1775 the various overland routes funneled through the flourishing village of Great Bridge, twelve miles to the south. Great Bridge was a shipping point for lumber, tar, potash, and turpentine from the Carolinas. The "great bridge" itself, which formed the centerpiece of a 160-yard causeway, was a long wooden trestle that spanned the south branch of the Elizabeth River where it flowed through the marshes adjacent to the Dismal Swamp. With an eye to controlling the only overland approach to Norfolk, Lord Dunmore had erected a fort on the Norfolk side of the bridge, which was manned by British grenadiers and supported by a dozen pieces of artillery. The position was easily defended since the only way of assaulting the fort was to charge directly across the narrow causeway in the face of Dunmore's cannons. The marshes were impenetrable, and the Americans had too few boats to cross the Elizabeth in strength and attack the British from the rear.

The American and British forces faced each other for several days. It was early December and the weather had turned raw. Lieutenant Colonel Charles Scott of Virginia's 2nd regiment, a veteran of Braddock's ill-fated campaign in 1755, wrote from Great Bridge on December 4, "Last night was the first of my pulling off my clothes for twelve nights successively. Believe me, I never was so fatigued in my whole life."[88] There were occasional skirmishes, and each side brought up reinforcements. The British eventually numbered about 600, including a party of sailors and marines from the frigate HMS *Otter*. The Americans were 700 in number. Four hundred thirty belonged to the 2nd regiment, and the rest were Culpeper minutemen.[89]

On the evening of December 4, Marshall took part in a brief hit-and-run raid across the causeway.[90] The clash lasted fifteen minutes, and the minutemen withdrew in good order with no casualties. Desultory firing continued for several days. The British artillery lobbed the occasional ball at the American breastworks, and the Culpeper sharpshooters tried to pick off any red-coated grenadier who showed himself above the fort's revetments.

Fortunately for the American cause, Lord Dunmore's strategic judgment was not of the same caliber as his troops' tactical deployment. Impatient with the continuing standoff, and perhaps fearing that militia reinforcements were on their way from North Carolina, Dunmore ordered the grenadiers to storm the American breastworks with a frontal assault.[91] The decision reflected Dunmore's contempt for American soldiers, whom he expected would throw down their weapons and run in the face of a sustained bayonet charge by British regulars. That had been his experience at Kempsville the month before, and Dunmore assumed the Virginia Line and Culpeper minutemen would be no different.[92]

Early on the morning of December 9, 1775, the British quietly began to replace the planks in the bridge, which had been removed to prevent the Americans from crossing in force. However, the work took longer than expected, and when the British were finally ready to attack, reveille had just sounded in the American camp.[93] "A lucky time for us," wrote Colonel William Woodford, the American commander, and "rather an improper season for them to make their push, when, of course, all our men must be under arms."[94]

The British assault began with a cannonade against the breastworks. The Americans did not respond immediately. "As the enemy had paid us this compliment several times before," one officer wrote, "we at first concluded [the firing] to be nothing more than a morning salute."[95] No one had considered the possibility that the British would launch an attack straight across the narrow causeway.

After a brief lull, the voices of British noncommissioned officers could be heard ordering their men into ranks. To Marshall and the other Americans, it was a daunting sight, provoking what one patriot called a "superstitious fear of the valor and discipline of the British Army."[96] Led by their commander, Captain Charles Fordyce, the grenadiers of the Fourteenth Foot marched out six abreast in perfect parade order across the narrow causeway. They wore dress uniforms and carried fixed bayonets. After the grenadiers came the marines and sailors, a company of the "Queen's Own" Tory regiment, and the freed slaves. Dunmore had launched his entire command in the attack.[97]

"The alarm was immediately given," Marshall reported, "and, as is the practice with raw troops, the bravest [of the Americans] rushed to the works, where, regardless of order, they kept up a heavy fire on the front of the British column."[98] At the same time, Colonel Stevens led the Culpeper riflemen onto some high ground to the left of the causeway, from which they sent a withering cross fire into the grenadiers' flank. Marshall's father, Major Thomas Marshall, assumed overall command of the troops at the breastworks; Lieutenant John Marshall was with the riflemen on the flank.[99] Colonel Woodford subsequently reported to the Virginia convention that "perhaps a hotter fire never happened, or a greater carnage, for the number of troops" engaged.[100]

Captain Fordyce, at the head of the British column, led his men directly toward the breastworks. When the Americans opened fire, Fordyce went down with a bullet in the knee. He took a handkerchief from his wrist, wrapped it around the wound, stood up, and resumed his place at the head of his troops.[101] Wounded repeatedly, Fordyce continued forward until he fell dead less than a dozen paces from the American position, his body riddled with fourteen bullet wounds. When he went down, the assault collapsed and the remaining troops broke and retreated.

A young British midshipman from H.M.S. *Otter* wrote afterward that

> we marched up to their works with the intrepidity of lions. But alas! we retreated with much fewer brave fellows than we took out. Their fire was so heavy, that, had we not retreated as we did, we should every one have been cut off. Figure to yourself a strong breastwork built across a causeway, on which six men only could advance abreast; a large swamp almost surrounded them; at the back of which were two small breastworks to flank us in our attack on their entrenchments. Under these disadvantages, it was impossible to succeed. . . . We had sixty killed, wounded, and taken prisoners; among whom were the gallant Captain Fordice [*sic*] of the Grenadiers.[102]

A Virginian said, "I then saw the horrors of war in perfection, worse than can be imagined; 10 and 12 bullets thro' many; limbs broken in two or three places; brains turned out. Good God, what a sight."[103] Marshall wrote, "Every grenadier is said to have been killed or wounded in this ill-judged attack, while the Americans did not lose a single man."[104]

That night, under cover of darkness, the British evacuated their fort on the Norfolk side of the causeway. A few hours after the battle, Colonel

Woodford reported to the Virginia convention that Great Bridge "was a second Bunker's Hill, in miniature, with the difference, that we kept our post."[105] The following day, after inspecting the scene more fully, Woodford wrote to Edmund Pendleton, chairman of Virginia's committee of safety, that the British loss was "much greater than I thought yesterday, & the victory [is] complete."[106] Captain Fordyce and the dead grenadiers were buried with full military honors, a deliberate effort, of which Marshall strongly approved, to recognize the dignity of brave men who had died in battle.[107] Small though it was, the battle of Great Bridge proved to be the decisive engagement in the Virginia theater during the early years of the war.

After the victory at Great Bridge, American attention turned to Norfolk. The cosmopolitan residents of the city had little in common with John Marshall and his fellow frontiersmen, and continued to maintain their allegiance to the British crown. Without Norfolk, however, the American hold on Virginia could never be secure. George Washington, commanding the Continental Army outside Boston, wrote to Congress that "the fate of America a great deal depends on [Lord Dunmore] being obliged to evacuate Norfolk this winter."[108] Thomas Jefferson shared Washington's tactical opinion and extravagantly predicted that Norfolk would become a second Carthage. Paraphrasing Cato the Elder, he wrote to his friend John Page, "*Delenda est Norfolk*" [Norfolk must be destroyed].[109]

To the Virginians' surprise, Dunmore chose not to defend the city. Shaken by his defeat at Great Bridge, he took refuge on one of the British ships in the harbor. On the night of December 14, 1775, the American forces, now reinforced by several hundred militiamen from North Carolina, took possession of Norfolk unopposed. With the capture of the city, the war turned nasty. The more rabid Tories fled with their families to Dunmore's ships, and the remaining residents made little secret of their underlying sympathy for the British cause.[110] That poisoned relations between the city and the incoming soldiers. Colonel Scott wrote, "We have got possession of the most horrid place I ever beheld; I mean *Norfolk*. Almost all the inhabitants fled on board the ships. . . . Duty is harder than I ever saw before. Our guards have not been relieved for forty-eight hours."[111] Colonel Robert Howe of North Carolina wrote that the residents of Norfolk "have lost every sense of public virtue or private Honour."[112] Corporal William Wallace of the Culpeper battalion sneered that "all the Damn Torys down this way are glad to get bucks tail to put in their hats now that they may pass for Friends of the Shirtmen."[113]

Although Dunmore had abandoned the city, a substantial British fleet remained offshore, poised to intervene if the opportunity arose. Occasional landing parties attempted to come ashore to secure provisions but were uniformly beaten back. Meanwhile, the sharpshooters from the Culpeper battalion amused themselves by firing at the vessels in the harbor, using the buildings near the water for cover.[114] Lord Dunmore, who seemed intent on pursuing the war from a safe anchorage, demanded that the sniping be stopped. When the Americans refused, he began to bombard the city. At midafternoon on New Year's Day, 1776, the cannonade began. Red-hot shot from the sixty guns of Dunmore's fleet rained on Norfolk for seven hours. The British attack was directed at the buildings on the waterside, which caught fire immediately. The flames spread quickly, and the minutemen, who, as Marshall gently phrased it, "entertained strong prejudices against Norfolk,"[115] not only made no effort to extinguish the fires, but soon joined in the incendiary spree by torching the houses of the Loyalists.

One soldier wrote to his mother that "All night the fire was so great the clouds above the town appeared as red and bright as they do in an evening at sun setting."[116] Norfolk burned for several days. In the end, over 900 houses—more than two-thirds of the city—were destroyed. Food supplies dwindled, the minutemen and soldiers looted on a grand scale, and smallpox broke out, which added to the misery. As one Loyalist wrote to a friend in Scotland, "The Rebels are in the deepest distress, being divested of clothes, ammunition, and lodgings, and, from their not keeping themselves clean, they are overrun with vermin, which, in the Summer season, must breed much sickness. Great numbers of them are already in their hospitals."[117]

In early February Colonel Robert Howe, who had succeeded Colonel Woodford as commander of the American troops, decided to evacuate Norfolk. He received permission from the Virginia convention to burn the remaining 416 houses to deprive the British of their use. When the patriot forces withdrew, nothing was left of the city but "complete desolation, charred timbers, blackened foundations, ashes."[118] The losses were staggering. Norfolk suffered more severely than any city in America during the revolution. Marshall felt great remorse. "Thus was destroyed," he wrote, "the most populous and flourishing town in Virginia. Its destruction was one of those ill-judged measures, of which the consequences are felt long after the motives are forgotten."[119]

The last of the American forces evacuated the ruins of Norfolk on February 6, 1776. The troops were quartered in nearby Kempsville, Great Bridge, and Suffolk—towns that were relatively unscathed and that could be supplied more easily. Marshall's battalion marched to Suffolk, where in early March the minutemen were discharged and sent home.[120] Planting season was at hand, and Dunmore's dwindling force no longer posed a threat to the American consolidation of Virginia.

In the summer of 1776 Virginia's minutemen were demobilized,[121] and in response to the desperate pleas of General Washington for reinforcements, the state convention enacted legislation providing six additional regiments for the Continental Army.[122] Under this statute, Fauquier county was authorized to recruit and select the officers for one company, and it was in the Fauquier company, commanded by Captain William Blackwell, that many former minutemen, including John Marshall, enlisted. Once again Marshall was commissioned a first lieutenant.[123] The authorized strength of the Virginia companies was seventy-five men, but when the Fauquier unit departed to join Washington's forces in January 1777, it numbered less than fifty.[124]

Marshall's company was assigned to Colonel Daniel Morgan's elite rifle regiment, the 11th Virginia, a regiment composed primarily of frontier sharpshooters.[125] Morgan, who began his military career as a teamster with Braddock in 1755, was a favorite among the Virginians and would prove himself to be America's most gifted light infantry commander. At thirty-nine, he was a powerfully built man, well over six feet tall, a superb rider, and a crack shot. He was a first cousin of Daniel Boone as well as a close friend of Washington, Thomas Marshall, and Lord Fairfax. Over the years Morgan had established a well-deserved reputation as a fearless combatant. In 1756 he struck back at a British officer who had slapped him with the flat of his sword and was punished with 500 lashes. (When the officer later apologized, Morgan forgave him.) In 1758 he lost all the teeth on one side of his mouth when an Indian bullet passed through his neck and jaw. Nevertheless, Morgan continued to serve in the militia. In June 1775 he recruited the first company of Virginia riflemen for the Continental Army and marched them 600 miles from northern Virginia to Boston in three weeks without losing a man. Washington used Morgan's rangers as the eyes and ears of his army, and as a reward for his exemplary service, Morgan was promoted to colonel in 1776 and given command of the newly formed 11th Virginia regiment.[126]

Morgan was beloved by his troops and led by example rather than through rigorous discipline. He was as colorful as he was brave, and always carried a turkey-call (a whistle used on the frontier to decoy wild turkey), which he blew to assemble his men. John Marshall and his Fauquier compatriots were delighted at the opportunity to serve with Morgan.[127] They knew that his riflemen were always in the vanguard of the army—the first to be deployed as skirmishers and the last to be called off. Nothing could have suited the twenty-one-year-old Marshall better. Virtually all of Marshall's army service, from 1776 until 1780, was spent as a company officer under Morgan's command, and it was an experience that profoundly influenced the future chief justice.[128]

The first task for the men from Fauquier county was to report to army physicians in Philadelphia to be immunized for smallpox, the scourge of Washington's army. The disease had virtually incapacitated Benedict Arnold's forces during the Quebec offensive, and it was raging virulently among the troops in Washington's winter encampment at Morristown, New Jersey. According to Marshall, it "had proved more fatal . . . than the sword of the enemy."[129] To eliminate the problem, the Continental Congress, at Washington's urging, had authorized vaccination, a procedure that involved exposing patients to a milder form of the smallpox virus. If they could survive this exposure, they would acquire the desired immunity.* Marshall and his fellow Virginians were exposed to the disease safely during the first three months of 1777, and the 11th regiment joined Washington's army at Princeton in early April. In addition to his company duties, Marshall also served as Morgan's regimental adjutant in April and May 1777, and the regimental orderly book for that period is entirely in his handwriting.[130]

In June 1777 Washington sent Morgan with a small detachment of riflemen to reinforce General Horatio Gates, who was facing John Burgoyne's army in upper New York state. Marshall did not take part in the expedition and instead returned full time to his company. Temporary command of the 11th Virginia passed to Lieutenant Colonel Christian Febiger ("Old Denmark"), another experienced fighter cast in the same mold as Morgan. The following month Washington dispatched his light infantry, including the 11th Virginia, on a quick dash from central New Jersey to the Hudson. The purpose was to prevent a link-up between the forces of General Sir William Howe, then quartered in New York City, and the northern army of General Burgoyne. Washington feared that the two British armies were moving to join one another in the Hudson Valley and sought to move his infantry between them.[131] The Americans did not make contact with the British, but the 11th Virginia marched over 300 miles in eighteen days, much of it in the rough terrain of the Watchung Mountains and the Hudson highlands. In later years, Marshall frequently recalled his service as "a regular foot practitioner" in the Continental Army. His long, loping stride—the quickstep of the light infantry—tested the endurance of those who walked with him.[132]

During the march through New Jersey, Marshall's regiment was at the forefront of Washington's army. Its route took it from Morristown to the Hudson River near Nyack, up to Stony Point, west to Chester, New York, and then back to Lambertville, New Jersey. "From the 10th of July we have

*Most countries, and most of the American colonies, rejected the practice of vaccination. Virginia, pursuant to a 1769 statute, prohibited inoculation for smallpox unless specifically approved by the county courts. 8 Hening 371–374. That legislation was not repealed until October 1777. 9 Hening 371–373. For the effect of smallpox on Washington's army, see James E. Gibson, "The Role of Disease in the 70,000 Casualties in the American Revolutionary Army," 17 *College of Physicians of Philadelphia Transactions* 121–127 (1949); William P. Coues, "Washington's Campaign Against Smallpox in the Continental Army," 202 *New England Journal of Medicine* 254–259 (1930); Lyon G. Tyler, "The Old Virginia Line," 12 *Tyler's Quarterly Historical and Genealogical Magazine* 115–116 (1930).

been continually marching," wrote Captain John Chilton, of Virginia. "We have made a complete tour of the Jerseys. . . . This was a forced march . . . and had many impediments. Horses dying on the way, shoeing horses, mending of wagons, &c."[133] On July 30 the 11th Virginia crossed the Delaware into Bucks County, Pennsylvania. The swift current washed away two wagons, and three horses were drowned.[134]

In the summer of 1777, both the Continental Army and the troops under Howe's command numbered about 17,000. But the numerical equality was deceiving. The American troops were inexperienced and ill-disciplined; there was no reliable staff structure to coordinate units in battle; many soldiers lacked proper uniforms and blankets; and the motley assortment of weapons made ammunition resupply difficult. The British, by contrast, had a well-developed staff organization, superior engineers and artillery, standardized weapons, and better-trained troops. And while provisioning the army was a military routine the British had perfected over centuries, Washington had to start from scratch. "No army was ever worse supplied than ours," the commander in chief told Congress on July 19, 1777. "Our Soldiers . . . have scarcely tasted any kind of Vegetables; had but little salt and Vinegar. Soap is another article in great demand. A soldier's pay will not enable him to purchase [soap] by which his . . . consequent dirtiness adds not a little to the diseases of the Army."[135]

General Sir William Howe, the British commander, was also a formidable adversary. A professional soldier (and the son of George I's illegitimate daughter, Maria Sophia[136]), Howe was forty-six—just three years older than Washington—and the physical resemblance between the two men was striking. Washington had served with Braddock, while Howe, as a lieutenant colonel, had commanded the lead battalion of Wolfe's army in its epic victory over the French on the Plains of Abraham. Both men were six feet tall, well proportioned, excellent horsemen, and cut splendid military figures. In addition, the two commanders had proved themselves to be cool and courageous under fire, and were respected and admired by their troops.[137] Of the two, Howe was by far the superior tactician, but he did not have Washington's grasp of the political aspects of the revolution. It is also possible, as some historians have suggested, that Howe was ambivalent about leading a colonial war against Americans.[138]

Nevertheless, Howe's military skills were impressive. In 1776 he had decisively defeated Washington in the first pitched battle of the revolution on Long Island, but Washington had successfully evacuated New York City and kept his defeated army intact.[139] Now, in the summer of 1777, Howe was determined to force Washington's surrender and bring the colonies back into the fold. And he sought to do so with minimal risk and on favorable terrain. Since Washington was deployed in a strong defensive position in central New Jersey, Howe elected to move on Philadelphia from the south, knowing that the American army would have to abandon their redoubt and move southward to meet him.

In early July 1777 Howe began loading his army onto ships in New York harbor. By July 20 he had embarked over 17,000 men, 5,000 horses, hundreds of transport wagons, field pieces, small arms, ammunition, provisions, and a mountain of military impedimenta, onto 284 ships lying offshore. (The Spanish Armada in 1588 numbered only 130 ships.) On July 23 Howe set sail from Sandy Hook, leaving Washington's staff guessing about the fleet's destination. It was an illustration of the sorry state of American intelligence during the revolution. Washington did not learn that the British fleet had been sighted at the mouth of Delaware Bay until July 31, and only then did he surmise that Philadelphia might be Howe's objective. However, the British commander was not finished maneuvering. On August 2 the fleet inexplicably set sail from Delaware Bay, and Washington was unable to determine whether Howe was returning to New York City or heading farther south. As a result, the American army was pinned on the Delaware near Lambertville, awaiting news of Howe's movements.

As it turned out, Howe had decided against navigating the constricted waters of the Delaware River with his enormous fleet, and was headed for Cape Charles and the upper reaches of Chesapeake Bay. The overland distance to Philadelphia would be longer, but the fleet would not be at risk from shore batteries along the Delaware, nor would it have to clear the obstacles the Americans had sunk in the river.

Seasonal offshore winds carried Howe almost to Bermuda before the fleet could tack westward and sail through the entrance of Chesapeake Bay, and it was not until August 22 that Washington finally received word that the ships had been seen "high up in the North East part" of the bay.[140] The British army's destination was now clear, and Washington moved quickly to interpose his forces between the north shore of the Chesapeake, where he assumed Howe would land, and Philadelphia. The American commander in chief now had important advantages. Howe's army was considerably weakened after thirty-two days at sea, many of the horses had died of starvation, and the men were groggy and unfit to go into action immediately. By almost any standard, however, the British amphibious operation was a strategic tour de force. Washington had been flanked out of his defensive position in New Jersey, and Howe, as soon as his army recovered, intended to seek battle in the open fields of eastern Pennsylvania.

As Washington moved the Continental Army south, he elected to march through Philadelphia to buttress that city's waning support for the war. Philadelphia was a hotbed of Tory sentiment, and the commander in chief hoped that a strong show of force might encourage patriotic feeling. Marshall and his fellow officers took pains to ensure that the troops made a good impression. Weapons were cleaned and the men wore sprigs of green in their headgear to give the troops a uniform appearance. Washington, with the Marquis de Lafayette at his side, rode at the head of the column, followed by almost 17,000 armed men who marched twelve abreast down Front Street and up Chestnut. For well over two hours, the column snaked its way through the city to the awe of the disaffected and the delight of the patriots.[141] John Adams, who was present in Philadelphia with the Continental Congress and who witnessed the parade, wrote to his wife Abigail that Washington's troops were "extremely well armed, pretty well clothed, and tolerably disciplined."[142] Another observer noted that "though indifferently dressed, [they] held well-burnished arms and carried them like soldiers, and looked, in short, as if they might have faced an equal number with a reasonable prospect of success."[143]

After the parade, the army marched toward the Chesapeake, and Washington established his base camp near Wilmington. With Morgan away reinforcing Gates, the commander in chief, at Lafayette's urging, created a new light infantry task force to screen the army and harass Howe's advance.[144] This elite unit, hand picked by Lafayette, consisted of 600 men especially selected for their stamina and marksmanship.[145] John Marshall was one of six lieutenants chosen from the Virginia brigade. Command of the new light infantry corps was given to veteran general William Maxwell of New Jersey. Like Morgan's men, or Stonewall Jackson's troops in the Civil War, Maxwell's corps was designed for swift movement and sudden strikes at the enemy's perimeter, and was intended to operate independently well out in front of the army.[146] Washington told Maxwell to be "constantly near the Enemy and to give them every possible annoyance."[147]

General Maxwell immediately moved to intercept Howe and posted his troops astride the principal road from the Chesapeake to Wilmington, some ten miles in front of Washington's main force. With Maxwell exercising direct command, Marshall and his light infantry compatriots bivouacked just south of Cooch's Bridge, a sturdy stone structure spanning Christiana Creek, a minor tributary of the Brandywine. The location was heavily wooded and offered substantial cover for skirmishers. On September 2, 1777, Washington alerted Maxwell to Howe's impending advance. Once again he urged Maxwell "to give them as much trouble as you possibly can."[148] That evening Marshall and his new comrades checked their gear and made ready for the coming battle. They could not defeat the oncoming British, but they could delay them and force Howe to deploy prematurely. Maxwell, electing to ambush the advancing enemy column after it got under way the following morning, strung his men out for a mile or more on both sides of the narrow road below Cooch's Bridge. Marshall's platoon took its position as directed. Maxwell's orders were to shoot and fall back Indian-style until he himself decided upon a stand.[149]

The British vanguard headed straight for the ambush. At about ten o'clock in the morning two German Jäger battalions from Hesse and Ansbach, the lead elements of Lord Cornwallis's infantry corps, came into view and were immediately attacked. As directed, Maxwell's men fell back, skirmishing aggressively. After retreating a half mile or so, Maxwell ordered the troops to hold at a stone fence. The fighting was intense. Lieutenant Colonel Ludwig von Wurmb, who commanded the German battalions, said that after the Americans "had shot themselves out of ammunition the fight was carried on with the sword and bayonet."[150] Once more Maxwell's men retreated up the road, but, in von Wurmb's words, "they immediately made a stand again, and we drove them away a second time."[151] That was at Cooch's Bridge itself. Marshall's platoon was to the immediate left of the structure. Meanwhile, the 2nd battalion of British light infantry moved to flank Maxwell's position, but got mired at the edge of a swamp known locally as Purgatory, a turn of events that, in the words of a British officer, "prevented this spirited affair from becoming so decisive."[152] The British battalion thereupon rejoined the troops engaged at the bridge. Three field pieces were brought up, the 49th Regiment of Foot was deployed, and a final bayonet assault was launched against Maxwell's position. By this time the Americans were greatly outnumbered, and, with their ammunition expended, Marshall and his fellow soldiers broke off contact at 2 P.M. and fell back to rejoin Washington's army.[153]

The battle at Cooch's Bridge, sometimes known as the battle of Iron Hill, was a prelude to the Battle of Brandywine. As was typical for a light infantry assault, all of Maxwell's men were directly engaged, and the casualties were heavy. Maxwell lost 40 of 600 men; Cornwallis's losses, given the nature of the ambush by trained marksmen, were substantially larger. A British deserter reported seeing nine wagons loaded with wounded moving to the rear.[154] With respect to its effect on the war, the battle at Cooch's Bridge was insignificant. It was, however, the first battle ever fought under the American flag. Congress had recently passed the Flag Resolution, and, despite other claims, historians of the revolution consider the battle at Cooch's Bridge the first conducted with the new colors.[155] It seems fitting that John Marshall, the great nationalist chief justice, enjoyed the distinction of participating in the first battle in which the Stars and Stripes were unfurled.

After regrouping, Maxwell's light infantry continued to screen Washington's army, located several miles ahead of the main American position and directly athwart Howe's line of advance.[156] For the next several days Washington and Howe concentrated their forces. "The armies were now within seven miles of each other, with only the Brandywine between them," wrote Marshall.[157] A major battle, which Howe sought and which Washington could not avoid, was imminent. Control of Philadelphia, the nation's capital and largest city, was at stake, and, as Marshall noted, "It was impossible to protect Philadelphia without a victory."[158]

The Brandywine, usually timid, occasionally a torrent, flows southerly from the foothills of Pennsylvania until it meets the Delaware in Wilmington. The stream is easily fordable at a few selected crossings, but deep and treacherous otherwise. Howe's route, if he continued directly toward Philadelphia, would lead him to Chadd's Ford (on the old Baltimore pike), and Washington concentrated his forces on the east side of the river at that point, determined to deny Howe the crossing.

In the early-morning hours of September 11, 1777, Howe began his move against the American position. Marshall reports that "soon after day [break], information was received that the whole British army was in motion, advancing on the direct road leading over Chadd's ford."[159] Once again Maxwell's light infantry was dispatched to delay and harass them. Marshall's unit immediately moved westward and, after marching about three miles, took up a strong defensive position behind a stone wall in the tiny village of Kennett Meetinghouse, halfway between the American and British forces.

Shortly before 9 A.M., the advance elements of Lieutenant General Wilhelm von Knyphausen's corps of British and German infantry came into view. Maxwell's men opened a devastating fire, throwing the enemy into temporary confusion, but Knyphausen's troops rallied quickly and returned the fire.[160] Maxwell's force fell back along the pike, taking cover from time to time and keeping up the fire until they reached Chadd's Ford. There the light infantry were joined by elements of the 11th and 12th Virginia regiments. The Americans counterattacked, retook the high ground on the west bank of the Brandywine, and forced Knyphausen to deploy. With clockwork precision, four British and two Hessian regiments supported by four batteries of artillery immediately came onto line. The artillery raked the American position for thirty minutes, after which the infantry charged with fixed bayonets. Maxwell's troops were forced to withdraw across the river.[161] By 10:30 that morning Knyphausen was in full possession of the hills overlooking the ford. John Marshall, who had been engaged throughout the skirmish, was, with the rest of Maxwell's force, back within the American perimeter.[162]

Throughout the morning of September 11, General Knyphausen marched and countermarched his troops on the heights opposite the American army and, in Marshall's words, "appeared to be making dispositions to force passage of the river."[163] The British preparations convinced Washington that Howe intended to cross the Brandywine with a direct frontal assault at Chadd's Ford, and he deployed his troops accordingly.

But Knyphausen's bluster was a ruse. At 4 A.M., one hour before his corps moved forward, Howe, with Cornwallis's corps in tow, began to move north on a fifteen-mile forced march around the American right. By 1 P.M. Howe had crossed the Brandywine at two little-used fords and, still undiscovered, was closing rapidly on Washington's unprotected right flank with 8,000 men. General Howe had divided his army in two. Knyphausen, with 7,000 men and most of the British artillery, had been sent forward to hold Washington at Chadd's Ford. Cornwallis, with a slightly larger force, was to deliver the major blow at the American position from the flank. Howe accompanied Cornwallis and left Knyphausen on his own to conduct the holding operation. Discovery of the maneuver would have been fatal, but Howe's luck held. Washington initially declined to act on reports of Howe's movement, believing that no responsible commander would divide his forces directly in the face of the enemy.[164]

At 4 P.M., with the British regimental bands playing the "Grenadier March," Cornwallis struck the American right with full fury, and Washington's unprepared forces quickly gave way. Withdrawal turned into retreat, and retreat into rout. Back at Chadd's Ford, Knyphausen now sent his men forward and swept the remaining American defenders from the field. By 6 P.M. the battle was over except for one minor flare-up. Two battalions of British grenadiers, ordered to pursue Washington's retreating army, stumbled on the rear guard composed of Maxwell's light infantry, which again lay in ambush. Marshall and his fellow soldiers held the grenadiers at bay until substantial British reinforcements arrived, whereupon they withdrew under cover of darkness.[165] Altogether, American casualties totaled 300 killed, 600 wounded, and between 300 and 400 taken prisoner. The British lost less than half that number.[166] Marshall had been engaged in the fighting from the first skirmish that morning until the last that night.

In retrospect, Washington was badly outgeneraled at Brandywine. The two armies were more or less equal in size, and Washington held the defensive advantage behind the river, but he was completely unprepared for Howe's envelopment and reacted slowly. As his biographer, Douglas Southall Freeman, observed, the commander in chief "conducted the Brandywine operation as if he was in a daze."[167] Marshall, in his own biography of the first president, apportioned the blame broadly, pointing out that some American units acted admirably under fire, while others "behaved very badly."[168] The American units from Virginia performed especially well. Marshall's father, commanding the 3rd Virginia regiment, was singled out by Washington for special commendation and was widely credited with slowing Cornwallis's advance. The 3rd regiment, "though attacked by much superior numbers, maintained its position without losing an inch of ground, until both its flanks were turned, its ammunition nearly expended, more than half of its officers, and one third of the soldiers killed or wounded. [It] then retired in good order."[169] Lieutenant Colonel William Heth, of a rival American regiment, wrote that "the 3rd Virginia regiment alone had prevented the British grenadiers and light infantry from advancing, long enough to save the army from utter ruin."[170] Thomas Marshall had two horses shot from under him that day, and the Virginia convention, in appreciation for his services, voted him a commemorative sword to mark the event.[171]

Despite defeat on the Brandywine, Washington's army still stood between Howe and Philadelphia. Howe had failed to deliver the knockout blow he sought.[172] At first, Washington attempted to defend the capital, but once again he was outflanked by Howe and withdrew westward to protect his supply base in Reading. Marshall approved Washington's decision, pointing to the sad condition of the army after Brandywine and the need to refit and regroup. Marshall's judgment reflected his personal experience in the field. "An army, maneuvering in an open country, in the face of a very superior enemy, is unavoidably exposed to excessive fatigue, and extreme hardship," he wrote. "The effect of these hardships was much increased by the privations under which the American troops suffered. While in almost continual motion, wading deep rivers, and encountering every vicissitude of the seasons, they were without tents, nearly without shoes, or winter clothes, and often without food."[173]

While Washington's main force hung back, Maxwell's light infantry was reinforced and ordered to harass Howe's advance, but found few opportunities to do so. On September 26, 1777, Howe entered Philadelphia unopposed. Marshall reports that "loud complaints" were made by Maxwell's officers concerning his refusal to offer battle. Whether Marshall was one of the complainants is unclear. A court martial was convened, and Maxwell was quickly acquitted. Marshall's concluding comments are circumspect: "Whether that officer [Maxwell] omitted to seize the proper occasions to annoy the enemy, or the compact and cautious movements of Sir William Howe afforded none, can not easily be ascertained."[174]

During the final week in September, Washington received several thousand needed replacements.[175] In the absence of General Woodford, who had been wounded at Brandywine, Thomas Marshall assumed command of the Virginia brigade, and John Marshall returned to his regiment. Captain Blackwell was ill, and command of the company from Fauquier county fell to the future chief justice. And surprisingly, the military situation, bleak after Brandywine, had taken a turn for the better. Howe had captured Philadelphia, but faced the considerable problem of resupplying his army and maintaining its effectiveness while occupying the American capital. His forces were also being depleted rapidly. Washington had successfully blocked the Delaware River, forcing Howe to detach 3,000 men to protect his supply line back to the Chesapeake. Cornwallis retained four regiments of grenadiers in Philadelphia, and another three regiments had been sent across the Delaware into New Jersey to take possession of the fortifications on that side of the river. That left Howe with about 9,000 effectives at his main camp in Germantown. In the unpredictable ebb and flow of the war, the initiative had shifted to Washington. With his forces rested, and now numerically superior, Washington decided to attack Howe's base camp at first light on October 4, 1777. As Marshall expressed it, the "division of the British force appeared to Washington to furnish a fair opportunity to engage Sir William Howe with advantage."[176]

Washington's attack plan was complex. Like Hannibal at Cannae, the commander in chief proposed to launch a coordinated surprise attack on both flanks and at the center of Howe's camp and crush the unsuspecting British in a giant pincer movement. To mount the attack, Washington divided the army into four separate columns. Each column was required to make a night march of sixteen miles over four different roads that were separated from one another by six or seven miles of rough, broken country and then to arrive simultaneously at four separate points of departure. It was, as one historian has written, "typically the kind of plan easily worked out at headquarters and looking perfect on paper, yet practically impossible for execution in the field."[177] What is most surprising is that despite a series of errors on the American side, the battle of Germantown was close and the British victory a narrow one.

Suffice to say that the American forces did not arrive at their respective departure points on time and the attack was piecemeal. Some units were in the wrong place, some arrived late, and a few never made it to the battlefield at all. The British were taken by surprise, but rallied quickly. As professional soldiers might be expected to do, they fought tenaciously, making a stand at every fence line, and firing and falling back until they formed a compact mass from which to counterattack the scattered American forces. The hardest fighting took place around a massive stone house owned by Pennsylvania's Tory chief justice, Benjamin Chew. From Chew's house, the remnants of six British companies poured a withering fire on the advancing Americans, and in the thick of it was the 11th regiment of the Virginia brigade. John Marshall was wounded in the hand while leading his company in the unsuccessful assault.[178] When the battle ended, the British were still in possession of Germantown, and Washington's army was once again in full retreat. The British lost 70 men, and 450 were wounded. American losses were much heavier: 200 killed, 600 wounded, and 400 taken prisoner. Fifty-three Americans lay dead on the lawn of Chew House alone.[179]

Despite the defeat, the battle at Germantown, combined with Gates's dramatic victory over Burgoyne at Saratoga, had convinced Europe that the

American revolution was genuine and that Washington's army was formidable.[180] The American troops had also gained a great deal of confidence from the encounter. "Our men are in the highest spirits," wrote General Henry Knox, Washington's able chief of artillery. "I know of no ill consequences that can follow the late action; on the contrary, we have gained considerable experience, and our army have a certain proof that the British are vulnerable."[181]

Once again Washington had kept his beaten force intact. The Continental Army remained a force that the victorious Howe could not ignore. Despite two pitched battles—Brandywine and Germantown—Howe had not been able to destroy the American army in the field, and Washington's stature had grown accordingly. Marshall describes with unfeigned admiration how before the battle of Germantown he watched as the commander in chief "rode through every brigade of his army, delivering, in person, his orders, respecting the manner of receiving the enemy, exhorting his troops to rely principally on the bayonet, and encouraging them by the steady firmness of his countenance, as well as by his words, to a vigorous performance of their duty."[182]

Throughout the remainder of October and November 1777, Washington did his utmost to deny Howe easy use of the Delaware. If the British supply line could be interrupted, said Washington, "the acquisition of Philadelphia may, instead of [Howe's] good fortune, prove his ruin."[183] The endeavor proved unsuccessful, and in early December Washington abandoned the effort. On December 19 he took the army into winter quarters at nearby Valley Forge.[184] The decision was a compromise between the alternatives of wintering at Wilmington, which most of his staff favored, and a winter campaign against Howe, which Congress supported but Washington knew was impractical. By keeping the army at nearby Valley Forge, Howe could be threatened without exposing the Continental Army to serious harm.

Like most military compromises, the solution was a poor one. The area around Valley Forge had been stripped so badly by both armies that supplies were virtually impossible to secure.[185] Baron De Kalb, an experienced brigadier general in the French army who had volunteered with Lafayette, wrote that "The idea of wintering in this desert can only have been put in the head of the commanding general by an interested speculator."[186] General James Varnum, who commanded the Rhode Island brigade, complained that "It is unparalleled in the history of mankind to establish winter quarters in a country wasted and without a single magazine."[187]

With the army concentrated at Valley Forge and most roads impassable, provisions of every description were quickly exhausted. For want of blankets, hundreds of men had to sit up all night by fires.[188] Meat ran out, and then flour. Washington wrote Congress in late December that unless supplies were quickly provided, "this army must inevitably . . . starve, dissolve and disperse."[189] The effects of malnutrition were heightened by a shortage of clothing, especially shoes. The morning report of the Virginia brigade on December 23 recorded that only 149 privates were fit for duty, with 257 rendered ineffective for lack of clothing.[190] Eyewitnesses reported that the snow was often red, marked with the blood that flowed from naked, bleeding feet.[191] The lack of shoes and warm clothing created additional sanitary problems, as soldiers were reluctant to brave the elements in search of latrines a healthy distance from their huts. As a result, company streets were polluted with human excrement. The rotting carcasses of hundreds of dead horses, unburied above the hard frozen ground, added to the problem.[192]

Marshall's account of the conditions at Valley Forge marks one of the few occasions in his life when he departed from the understated prose that characterized his writing. In volume two of his *Life of Washington*, he wrote:

> At no period of the war had the situation of the American army been more perilous than at Valley Forge. Even when the troops were not entirely destitute of food, their stock of provisions was so scanty that a quantity sufficient for one week was scarcely in store. . . . The returns of the first of February [1778] exhibit the astonishing number of three thousand nine hundred and eighty-nine men in camp unfit for duty for want of clothes. Scarcely one man of these had a pair of shoes. Even among those capable of doing duty, many were so badly clad, that exposure to the cold of the season must have destroyed them. Although the total of the army included seventeen thousand men, the present effective rank and file amounted to only five thousand and twelve.[193]

Smallpox, camp fever (typhus), dysentery, and scurvy were common at Valley Forge. According to most estimates, over 3,000 American troops died through the cumulative impact of exposure, starvation, and disease.[194] In one Virginia company, only three men came out alive.[195] "Happily," said Marshall, "the real condition of Washington was not well understood by Sir William Howe; and the characteristic attention of that officer to the lives and comfort of his troops saved the American army."[196]

By any measure, conditions at Valley Forge were unspeakable, and there can be no doubt that the men who survived them formed a lasting bond with one another. However, some historians have overestimated the effect that the episode had on individual men. There is no evidence whatever to support Albert Beveridge's assertion that Marshall's animosity toward Jefferson stemmed from Jefferson's absence at Valley Forge.[197] There is no question that Marshall and Jefferson shared a mutual dislike, and in later years, when the hostility between the two men had become acute, Marshall may have remembered that Jefferson was not there. But it strains credulity to believe that as a beleaguered twenty-two-year-old company commander, he would have fretted about Jefferson's absence.

There is no question, however, that the war, and especially the duty at Valley Forge, helped to form Marshall's character. As commander of a small unit, he became familiar with the nature of military leadership and the importance of setting an example for his troops. The time he spent serving under Daniel Morgan reinforced the lessons he had learned earlier from his father. Marshall developed an easy, unaffected style in which command seemed to come naturally. In later years, soldiers who had served with him at Valley Forge described the future chief justice as the most cheerful and optimistic man they knew. He never complained, and when his fellow officers showed their discouragement, Marshall did his utmost to cheer them up. "He was an excellent companion," wrote one, "and idolized by the soldiers and his brother officers, whose gloomy hours were enlivened by his inexhaustible fund of anecdote."[198] The fact that Marshall was athletic may have made the conditions at Valley Forge less grim. He excelled as a runner, and according to numerous accounts he was the only man in the Continental Army who could high jump over six feet—a remarkable achievement in any era.[199]

Conditions at Valley Forge began to improve in the spring of 1778. In desperation, Washington appointed his best field commander, General Nathanael Greene, as quartermaster general, and Greene ruthlessly scoured the middle Atlantic states for food and fodder. "In a few days, the army was rescued from the famine with which it had been threatened, and considerable supplies of provisions were laid up in camp," wrote Marshall.[200] Greene proved that much of the army's suffering had been unnecessary. Aside from the rickety commissary system, Pennsylvania farmers had sold their grain to the British in Philadelphia for hard cash; the farm surplus in the state of New York was sold to civilians in New England; beef supplies from Connecticut failed to materialize; merchants in Boston would not provide government-contracted winter clothing except in exchange for hard cash; and New Jersey's pork spoiled for lack of transport while awaiting shipment to the army.[201] When Greene assumed command, the army simply took what it needed.

Equally propitious, Lieutenant General Friedrich Wilhelm Augustus von Steuben, an unheralded volunteer from the army of Frederick the Great, arrived in camp. Von Steuben, who initially spoke no English, gave the Continental Army the professionalism it was lacking. He rewrote the army's drill manual, composed a training guide for company commanders, and schooled the troops relentlessly in military tactics. Steuben proceeded lesson by lesson, writing in French, which was then translated into English, usually by Alexander Hamilton or John Laurens. Steuben also broke American officers of the English habit of letting sergeants drill the troops and insisted, Prussian-style, that it was the officers' responsibility. Steuben taught by example. Starting in mid-March with a select group of enlisted men, he soon had the whole army watching a Prussian lieutenant general instruct ordinary American soldiers in facings, march steps, and the manual of arms.

Under Steuben's direction, the army was instructed in the proper loading of a musket and the correct use of the bayonet. It learned to march in a column of fours instead of the Indian file of previous campaigns, and to deploy from column to line and line to column. Steuben's Prussian enthusiasm for military service was contagious, and his halting, heavily accented English, punctuated with frequent "goddams," was endearing to officers and soldiers alike. Marshall, as a company commander, benefited immediately from von Steuben's efforts. He wrote afterward that "This gentleman was a real service to the American troops. He established one uniform system of field exercise; and, by his skill and persevering industry, effected important improvements through all ranks of the army during its continuance at Valley Forge."[202] For his efforts, von Steuben was appointed inspector general of the army, and his contribution to the ultimate American victory in the War of Independence ranks second only to Washington's.[203]

Steuben's arrival heralded the change in American fortunes. Shortly thereafter, some 30,000 Charleville muskets were delivered by France. The weather turned prematurely warm, and the shad began their annual migration up the nearby Schuylkill River, affording the army a much-needed change in diet. By April the rancid huts of the soldiers were being cleaned and aired. Long-overdue replacements arrived from Virginia, and Lafayette assumed command of the division to which Marshall's brigade was assigned.[204] The Virginians loved the French nobleman, whom they called "the markwiss," and Marshall wrote with undisguised admiration how Lafayette, "possessing an excellent heart, and all the military enthusiasm of his country . . . demanded no station in the army; would consent to receive no compensation, and offered to serve as a volunteer."[205]

In late April 1778 France recognized the United States as an independent nation, declared war on Great Britain, and joined the battle to secure American independence. By ensuring that the Continental Army survived the desperate winter at Valley Forge, Washington had converted a string of tactical defeats into a strategic victory. General Howe, apparently dissatisfied with the support he had received from Britain, resigned as commander in chief and was succeeded that spring by his second-in-command, Sir Henry Clinton. With France now engaged as America's ally, Britain went on the defensive. Clinton decided that his position in Philadelphia was untenable and evacuated the capital on June 18. He planned to concentrate his forces in the vicinity of New York City, and immediately set out on the long march across New Jersey with Washington in close pursuit.[206] General Morgan's light infantry, including the company from Fauquier county commanded by Marshall, was dispatched by Washington to move out in front of Clinton and impede his progress.[207] Morgan's men felled trees, destroyed bridges, and stopped up the wells. By June 27 Washington, whose army traveled light, had bypassed Clinton and closed off the main overland route to New York at New Brunswick.[208] Rather than risk a contested crossing of the Raritan River with his enormous baggage train, Clinton changed direction and headed toward Sandy Hook.

On the morning of June 28, Washington's advance body fell on the British rear in Monmouth county. A series of American miscues precipitated an untimely retreat by the lead elements, but Washington arrived quickly and rallied the shattered troops. Lafayette referred to the incident in a letter he wrote to Marshall: "Never was General Washington greater in war than in this action. His presence stopped the retreat. His dispositions fired the victory. His fine appearance on horseback, his calm courage, roused by the animation produced by the vexation of the morning [*le dépit de la matinée*] gave him the air best calculated to excite enthusiasm."[209]

Under Washington's direction, the regiments of the main American force wheeled smartly into line of battle to await the British assault. Lafayette recalled how the commander in chief, with von Steuben at his side, rode "all along the lines amid the shouts of the soldiers, cheering them by his voice and example and restoring to our standard the fortunes of the fight."[210] The long months of drill at Valley Forge had paid off. The experienced American army fought a dogged all-day battle with the British at Monmouth. Lord Cornwallis personally led the British assault, first with the Guards' regiments, the Hessians, and the 27th and 44th Foot; then with the dragoons, the grenadiers, and the Black Watch. Through it all, the Americans held. Alexander Hamilton said afterward that never, until he saw the army deploy and fight as it did at Monmouth, had he "known or conceived the value of military discipline."[211]

In one of those lapses that commanders occasionally make in battle, Washington neglected to order Morgan's regiment—which remained well out in front of the British—into action. On the night before the armies collided, Morgan had been instructed to prepare to hit the British flank. But at midday, with the American advance guard in retreat, Washington sent a message to Morgan stating that ". . . as your Corps is out of supporting Distance I would have you confine yourself to observing the motions of the Enemy, unless an opportunity offers of intercepting some small Parties; and by no means to come to an Engagement with the whole Body unless you are tempted by some very evident advantage."[212]

Morgan was at Richmond Mill that day, just three miles away, and eager for battle. Had he been ordered to strike the unprotected British rear (Clinton had reversed directions to meet Washington's oncoming forces), the Battle of Monmouth might have been a decisive American victory. Instead, it ended in a stalemate. Overall, the Americans lost 356 killed and wounded. British losses were similar. Marshall's company, which was not directly engaged, suffered no casualties.

Shortly after the battle of Monmouth, Marshall was promoted to captain, with date of rank July 1, 1777. That made him the fifty-fourth-ranking captain of the Virginia Line.[213] In September, the army underwent a periodic reorganization. The 11th Virginia regiment was redesignated the 7th Virginia regiment, with Morgan retaining command. Marshall commanded the 8th company,[214] which consisted of himself, an ensign, and fifty-two enlisted men, who were primarily friends and neighbors from Fauquier county.[215]

In November Washington and the bulk of the Continental Army went into winter quarters near Middlebrook, New Jersey.[216] Marshall's regiment was camped about a mile north of town, near a rise of land named Chimney Rock. In mid-December Marshall went home on furlough—the first leave he had received since joining the army two years before. He was accompanied by a sergeant, eight privates, and the company drummer, all of whom had reenlisted and who were granted extended furloughs as a reward.[217] They were joined by several French officers who were also on leave and touring America.

When Marshall arrived at Oak Hill with his French guests, he was startled by the deprivation his family had suffered during the war. "When supper time arrived," according to his sister, "mother had the meal prepared for them, and had made into bread a little flour, the last she had, which had been saved for such an occasion. The little ones cried for some." At that point, Marshall realized the desperate need of the family. "He would eat no more of the bread which could not be shared with us," his sister said. "He was greatly distressed at the straits to which 'the fortunes of war' had reduced us, and mother had not intended him to know our condition."[218]

Marshall and the men from his unit returned from furlough in early May 1779,[219] just in time to participate in the capture of Stony Point, New York, an important fortification on the south bank of the Hudson that the British had occupied.[220] Marshall's regiment did not take part in the initial assault, but it joined the covering force supporting the attack and entered the citadel the following morning.[221]

Marshall played a similar role two months later when his friend, Light-

Horse Harry Lee, stormed the British fort at Paulus Hook, New Jersey. Marshall was detached with 200 men to cover Lee's withdrawal,[222] and the episode, in which Lee successfully neutralized the British strongpoint, ended with few casualties.[223] After Paulus Hook, Washington's army remained bivouacked near West Point, keeping a watchful eye on Clinton's somewhat stronger force in New York City. As has always been the case, a soldier at rest is a soldier in search of diversion, and John Marshall, age twenty-four, was no exception. "Never was I a witness to such a scene of lewdness as about Ramapough, particularly at the very venerable Mrs. Sydmon's," Marshall wrote to Major Thomas Posey on September 1, 1779. "I should certainly have thought had I stayed there much longer that all the virtue of the fair sex was centered in our Camp Ladies & should very possibly have begun to think of choosing one of them as a Partner for life."[224] Marshall's 1779 letter to Posey is the earliest of the chief justice's letters that has survived. There is no doubt that he wrote to other friends and family members while he was in the army, but none of those letters have been found.[225]

In December 1779 the army went into winter quarters in Morristown, New Jersey,[226] but the Virginia brigade was spared the ordeal. Fearing that Clinton planned to invade the Carolinas, Washington ordered General Woodford's troops to move south.[227] Many of the volunteers were approaching the end of their three-year commitment, including one-third of the men in Marshall's company.[228] As a result, the Virginia regiments returned to the state. The men whose enlistments had expired were discharged, while the bulk of the officers, including Marshall, were furloughed until additional troops could be recruited.[229] Fifty-one years later, in support of the pension application of an old comrade, Marshall recalled how he and a half-dozen fellow officers of the Virginia Line "walked in together" from Philadelphia that winter.[230]

Marshall retained his commission as a captain in the Continental Army until February 12, 1781, when the Virginia Line was reorganized and all supernumerary officers were discharged. Because of the absence of a written record (the letter to Posey is the singular exception), exactly what he thought at that time is unknown. Junior officers in wartime are usually too busy with daily responsibilities to reflect about the strategy of the conflict, much less the state of the Union. Nevertheless, the mundane concerns of military life in a long, drawn-out struggle provide important insights, and there is no reason to believe that John Marshall was not a keen observer of what went on around him.

Twenty-five years later, when he undertook to write the authorized biography of his commander in chief, those wartime observations, matured by experience, marched across the pages of Marshall's manuscript in quickstep cadences. Above all, there were the lessons about the need for unity of effort, about the dangers of conflicting and sometimes pernicious policies of individual states, about the benefits of limited government and the need for checks and balances. "The many, as often as the few, can abuse power, and trample on the weak, without perceiving that they are tyrants," he wrote.[231]

Marshall did not write about the hunger, or the suffering, or the endless fatigue of those who fought. With the exception of his brief description of conditions at Valley Forge, he said little about the burdens of soldiering. Rarely did he refer to the horror of the battlefield, the fear of being wounded, or the reality of death. All of that touched a part of his soul that Marshall was reluctant to reveal. His readers knew the nature of war and, like him, perhaps preferred to recall only its heroic dimension. What does spring from the pages of Marshall's writing is his deep humanity. His war was not vindictive, and America's enemies were not evil. Generosity, faith in the United States, and an even-handedness toward friend and foe characterized the wartime volumes of Marshall's biography of Washington.

Justice Oliver Wendell Holmes once observed that the two most important events in his life were to have served as a captain in the United States Army during the Civil War and as an associate justice of the Supreme Court. In that order. Holmes treasured his military service, and, as more than one biographer has noted, he was never psychologically mustered out. The same can be said of John Marshall. He relished the title of "general" that he subsequently earned in the Virginia militia, and he peppered his discourse with military metaphors. In his last years, Marshall went far out of his way to assist former soldiers with whom he had fought, and he was never too busy as Chief Justice of the United States to write lengthy letters in longhand to the secretary of war, attesting the pension claims of veterans of the Virginia Line.

The war undoubtedly toughened Marshall. For five years he had exposed himself to concentrated risk as a light infantry officer, and he had survived. Marshall was too modest to talk about his accomplishments, but the strength of his dedication is apparent in a remark he made years later to Joseph Story, when he said that the war confirmed his habit of considering America as his country and Congress as his government. "I had imbibed these sentiments so thoroughly," said the chief justice, "that they constituted a part of my being."[232]

3

⌘

Student and Suitor

*As that part of the Virginia Line which had not marched to
Charleston was dissolving by the expiration of the terms for
which the men had enlisted, the officers were directed to
return home in the winter of 1779–80, in order to take
charge of such men as the legislature should raise for them. I
availed myself of this inactive interval for attending a
course of law lectures given by Mr. Wythe, and of lectures of
natural philosophy given by Mr. Madison, then President of
William and Mary College. The vacation commenced in
July when I left the university, and I obtained a license to
practice law.*[1]

MARSHALL ARRIVED AT OAK HILL shortly after Christmas
1779 and waited in vain for the Virginia assembly to authorize a
new levy for Washington's army. In late February, when there
was still no word from Richmond, he set out on foot to join his father, who
was commanding the state artillery regiment in Yorktown. The unit, known
throughout the state as "Marshall's artillery," had become a family operation. Colonel Thomas Marshall was given command of the regiment shortly
after the battle of Germantown, and he brought with him his son Thomas
and his nephew Humphrey, both of whom served as captains. Another son,
James Markham Marshall, joined them in 1778. Such arrangements were
not unusual in American regiments during the revolution. Family ties provided a bond of loyalty that was difficult to duplicate, and the Marshall clan
was more cohesive than most. In that respect, Yorktown was a forerunner of
things to come. Throughout their adult lives, John Marshall and his siblings
formed joint business ventures, looked for eligible partners for one another,
and offered assistance when difficulties arose.

The Marshall men lived in the commandeered house of a long-departed
Tory Loyalist, which doubled as regimental headquarters. The family of
Jaquelin Ambler resided next door. Ambler, one of the patriarchs of the rev-

olution, was collector of customs in Yorktown and a member of the council of state. He would be elected treasurer of Virginia in 1782 and would hold the post until his death in 1798. The Amblers, like the Randolphs, enjoyed impeccable standing within the tidewater establishment, and the fact that Jaquelin had four young, attractive daughters did not pass unnoticed.

The Ambler pedigree was among Virginia's most illustrious. On the maternal side, Jaquelin Ambler was descended from the immensely wealthy Huguenot family of de la Roche Jaquelin: nobility from the Vendée who had fled to England with their wealth intact shortly before the massacre of French protestants on St. Bartholomew's Day in 1572. Edward Jaquelin, heir to the family fortune, arrived in Virginia in 1697. He settled in Jamestown and proceeded to purchase most of the settlement.[2]

On the paternal side the family was descended from John Ambler, high sheriff of Yorkshire, whose son Richard came to Virginia at the beginning of the eighteenth century and married Elizabeth Jaquelin, one of Edward's several daughters. The Amblers prospered professionally, married advantageously, and, at the time of the revolution, were among the wealthiest families in Virginia. In the early 1760s, in keeping with family tradition, Jaquelin Ambler and his older brother, another Edward, both married extremely well—besting two of America's future statesmen in the process. Edward defeated a despondent George Washington for the hand of the beautiful tidewater heiress Mary Cary, while Jaquelin captured the heart of the equally renowned and attractive Rebecca Burwell, who had been courted by Thomas Jefferson.[3]

The Amblers temporarily fell on hard times in 1780, when virtually no shipping entered the port of Yorktown because of the war.[4] Indeed, like most wars, the War of Independence ushered in a period of significant social mobility. Established families who clung to their Loyalist sentiments lost everything, but even families like the Amblers, who embraced independence, suffered the discomforts of a disrupted economy and a diminution in their standard of living. Some of the Marshalls, particularly those remaining at Oak Hill, experienced similar hardship during the war. For the men of the family, however, the revolution brought adventure and a unique opportunity for advancement. Risking one's life in the cause of liberty did not go unrewarded. Soldiers, and especially officers, who survived the war expected to enjoy the accolades and reap the benefits (including 4,000 acres of free land in the case of Virginia volunteers) that accompanied military service.

By 1780 the standing of the Marshall men had been enhanced significantly. Colonel Thomas Marshall, one of the few heroes of the battle of Brandywine, enjoyed a statewide reputation for bravery under fire. His young sons, Thomas and James Markham, and his nephew, Humphrey, were lifted by the war from the backwoods frontier to become artillery captains in Yorktown. There they mingled with the tidewater gentry and enjoyed the respect bestowed on commissioned officers of the Virginia Line. For twenty-four-year-old John Marshall, a veteran captain of Washington's light infantry, the prospects were even brighter. His impending arrival at Yorktown in the spring of 1780 was eagerly anticipated, not only by his family but by the Amblers next door, as well.[5]

Under ordinary circumstances, a leading tidewater family such as the Amblers would have had little intercourse with the roughhewn Marshalls of Fauquier county. It was the combination of the Amblers' financial difficulties and the Marshalls' military renown that bridged the gap. As commanding officer in Yorktown, Colonel Thomas Marshall was a frequent guest in the Ambler home, and often shared with the family the letters he received from his son John, away at the front with General Washington.[6] "We had been accustomed to hear [of Captain John Marshall] as a very *paragon*," wrote Jaquelin's oldest daughter, Eliza, many years later. "His letters [to his father] were fraught with filial and paternal affection."[7] Marshall's letters made an enormous impression on the Ambler daughters. There were many young officers stationed in Yorktown that winter, including a dozen or so eligible Frenchmen from Admiral Destouches's fleet offshore. But as the Amblers' eldest daughter recalled, "perhaps no officer . . . excited so much interest as Captain Marshall. Our expectations were raised to the highest pitch, and the little circle of York was on tip-toe awaiting his arrival."[8]

In anticipation, the Amblers organized a formal ball in Marshall's honor. According to Eliza, all of the girls "were emulous who should be the first introduced. It is remarkable that my sister Mary, then only fourteen, and diffident beyond all others, declared that we were giving ourselves useless trouble, for that she, for the first time, had made up her mind to go to the ball, though she had not even been to dancing school, and was resolved to set her cap at him, and eclipse us all."[9]

When Marshall eventually arrived in Yorktown, most of the young women were disappointed. Instead of the dashing figure they had expected, they met a gangly, loose-jointed frontiersman whose disheveled appearance may have been appropriate for one of Colonel Daniel Morgan's light infantry officers but was quite unsuited for the garrison world of Yorktown. "When I beheld his awkward figure, unpolished manners, and total negligence of person," Eliza said, "I lost all desire of becoming agreeable in his eyes."[10] Most of the young women shared Eliza's opinion and saw Marshall as another backwoods bumpkin. It was a hasty assessment they soon would regret, for as Eliza noted, "Under the slouched hat there beamed an eye that penetrated at one glance the inmost recesses of the human character; and beneath the slovenly garb there dwelt a heart complete with every virtue."[11]

The only one who did not share in the general disappointment was Eliza's younger sister Mary, affectionately known as Polly. She was utterly charmed by the rustic bearing and simple ways of the inelegant Captain Marshall, who was eleven years her senior and who towered above her on the dance floor.[12]

Polly—Mary Willis Ambler—was born March 18, 1766, the second daughter of Jaquelin and Rebecca Burwell Ambler. When John Marshall met her in the second week of March 1780, she was just shy of her fourteenth birthday. Polly was striking rather than beautiful. She was dark like the French Huguenots, and her strong, aristocratic features were set off by gentle, wide-set brown eyes and a frame of brown curls.

Polly was not tall, probably five foot one or two, and she was slightly built, with a prominent patrician nose, high cheekbones, a thin mouth, and arched eyebrows. The evening of the ball, she wore a light blue gown that had belonged to her mother and that was embarrassingly large for her small frame. Unlike her extroverted sister Eliza, Polly was reticent to the point of shyness. But as her initial expression of interest in Marshall indicated, that reticence concealed an exceptionally strong will.

Marshall was immediately smitten. He had been deprived of female companionship for the last four years, save for the accommodating camp ladies who traveled with the army, and was enchanted by the charms of the delicate Miss Ambler. Reflecting on their first meeting many years later, he said: "I saw her the first week she attained the age of fourteen, and was greatly pleased with her. Girls then came into company much earlier than at present. As my attentions, though without any avowed purpose, nor so open or direct as to alarm, soon became ardent and assiduous, her heart received an impression which could never be effaced."[13] Marshall described Polly as "cheerful, mild, benevolent, serious, humane, intent on self-improvement," and deeply religious. "From native timidity she was opposed to everything adventurous; yet few females possessed more real firmness."[14]

The chief justice's circumspect recollection belies the passion of the young captain of light infantry. A more accurate reflection of Marshall's ardor in 1780 was his oft-quoted remark that "I would have had my wife if I had had to climb Alleghenys of skulls and swim Atlantics of blood."[15] Marshall pursued Polly with incredible determination. Thirty years later he confided to his sister-in-law Eliza that he "looked with astonishment at the present race of lovers" who were so reserved in their pursuit of one another.[16] Beveridge, whose descriptions of Marshall were usually prim and Victorian, wrote that the future chief justice was "a very hurricane of a lover," who "made love as he made war, with all his might."[17]

For the next six weeks, Marshall remained idle in Yorktown, doing whatever odd duties came his way and ingratiating himself with Polly and her family. "During the short stay he made with us," wrote Eliza, "our whole family became attached to him."[18] Every afternoon, and often into the evening, Marshall read to the Ambler girls from the books his father had brought to Yorktown. "Certain it is that whatever taste I may have for reading was entirely gained from him," said Eliza. "He read to us from the best authors, particularly the Poets, with so much taste and feeling, and pathos too, as to give me an idea of their sublimity, which I should never have had an idea of."

An ironic transformation had taken place. John Marshall, the backwoods captain of light infantry, was introducing the sophisticated daughters of tidewater aristocracy to the joys of English literature. According to Eliza, "He lost no opportunity of blending improvement with our amusements, and thereby gave us a taste for books which probably we might never otherwise have had."[19]

Two weeks after Marshall arrived in Yorktown, his father was dispatched by Thomas Jefferson, then Virginia's governor, to undertake a preliminary survey of the Kentucky territory, which at that time was part of the state.[20] Colonel Marshall's vast experience as a surveyor of frontier land for Lord Fairfax made him a logical choice for the assignment. His selection by Jefferson illustrates the high esteem in which the elder Marshall was held by his contemporaries, and it contradicts conventional wisdom that the Marshall family harbored a deep-seated hostility toward Jefferson during the revolution—and vice versa. Thomas Marshall accepted the post with alacrity and immediately took leave of his regiment. With his nephew Humphrey at his side, he made the 500-mile trek to Kentucky in less than three weeks.[21]

In 1780 land was still the primary source of wealth in America, and it provided one of the few reliable hedges against the inflation that was ravaging the country. The virgin wilderness of Kentucky afforded abundant opportunity for those willing to speculate. Thomas Marshall, who had a keen eye for investment, was one of the first to embrace that opportunity. At the age of fifty-three, he led a new wave of settlement in the Kentucky territory and established the foundation for the subsequent wealth of the Marshall family. To raise capital for potential land purchases and to defray the expenses he had incurred as a regimental commander, Thomas Marshall sold 1,000 acres of his Oak Hill estate before leaving Yorktown.[22]

Perhaps because of his father's enthusiasm for the venture, John Marshall lost no time in acquiring land in the new territory. On April 7, 1780, the week after his father's departure, Marshall used £160 of his back pay to purchase the first of many land office warrants from the state of Virginia. That purchase entitled him to lay claim to any 4,000 acres that his father might survey and record for him.[23] This was the beginning of a flurry of land acquisitions in Kentucky.*

It was shortly after his father's departure for Kentucky that Marshall began to study law. Although he had welcomed the opportunity to visit Yorktown, the future chief justice still planned to rejoin Washington's army as soon as the new levy was authorized. But the Virginia legislature had made no progress raising additional men for the Continental Army, and with no troops to command, Marshall was unemployed. At the urging of his family and the Amblers, he enrolled in a series of lectures on the common law offered by Professor George Wythe at the College of William and Mary, ten miles down the road in Williamsburg.

Marshall had already displayed an avid interest in the law. The first American edition of Blackstone's *Commentaries on the Laws of England* was published in 1772, and Thomas Marshall was listed among the charter subscribers. For the next several years, father and son had studied Blackstone together. Family legend asserts that before entering the army, Marshall began to read law in the office of an attorney in Warrenton, walking eighteen miles there and back each day from Oak Hill. "It is said that on that long walk he often carried a large text of legal learning, borrowed from the lawyer to read at night by the light of pine knots when his legal cogitation exhausted his allotment of candles."[24] Marshall himself, years later, wrote to Joseph Delaplaine that "from my infancy I was destined for the bar."[25]

In any event, Marshall was one of eighty-odd students who enrolled at William and Mary when the new term commenced on May 1, 1780,[26] and one of the forty or so who chose to attend the lectures of Chancellor Wythe. His fellow law students included Bushrod Washington, a nephew of the commander in chief, who would be appointed to the Supreme Court in 1798, and Spencer Roane, whose subsequent career as the leading judge on the Virginia court of appeals paralleled Marshall's as chief justice and who ultimately became Marshall's principal judicial antagonist. An ardent antifederalist, a states rights advocate, and a defender of slavery, Roane bitterly opposed national power in general and the authority of the United States Supreme Court in particular. As an ally of Thomas Jefferson, he eventually

---

*On June 15, 1780, Thomas Marshall recorded two further parcels in his son's name, one of 14,717 acres and another of 15,660 acres. An additional 5,000 acres were recorded on behalf of John Marshall on June 24 and yet another 5,000 acres two days later. Before the end of the 1780s, Marshall would claim over 200,000 acres in Kentucky. His father and his brothers would own about twice that amount. Willard Rouse Jillson, *Old Kentucky Entries and Deeds* 124–125, 245, 348, 432, 564 (Louisville, Ky.: Standard Publishing Co., 1926); Jillson, *Kentucky Land Grants* 83–84, 206, 358 (Louisville, Ky.: Standard Publishing Co., 1925); 1 *The Papers of John Marshall* 101–102 (Chapel Hill: University of North Carolina Press, 1974).

would emerge as the political boss of Virginia.[27] But all of that was in the far-distant future. In 1780 Roane, Washington, and Marshall were legal neophytes.

Under college regulations, students were entitled to attend the lectures of two professors. For his second lecture, Marshall elected the course in natural philosophy offered by the Reverend James Madison, a cousin of the future President of the United States. The subject matter dealt primarily with Newtonian physics.[28]

The law lectures that Marshall attended were only the second series offered by Wythe. Previously, lawyers in North America had followed the British method of apprenticing themselves to an established practitioner and "reading law" under his supervision.[29] Usually they read the decisions of King's Bench and the High Court of Chancery and whatever colonial reports might be available. "A dreary ramble," John Adams called it.[30] The problem was that the cases upon which the profession relied were sometimes capricious, occasionally perverse, and often obscure. There were few laws on the statute books to apply, and those that did exist were rarely collected into a single volume, much less codified in usable form. The few treatises and abridgements available—such as the *Institutes* of Sir Edward Coke;[31] Sir Matthew Hale's *Historia Placitorum Coronae*;[32] and the works of Matthew Bacon[33]—focused on individual precedents and provided little guidance in the way of organizing principles or general concepts. Since only the most established and successful lawyers might be fortunate enough to own a copy of one of these works, the novice attorney was consigned to a relentless process of reading cases and memorizing the decisions. The consequence was a legal profession trained to know every precedent in excruciating detail but largely lacking a fundamental understanding of the law. The typical lawyer of the day simply could not see the forest for the trees.

The study of law was transformed radically with the publication of Sir William Blackstone's magisterial *Commentaries on the Laws of England*[34] in 1765. The *Commentaries* reflected Blackstone's attempt to restate the laws of England in a graceful and accessible style. Ignoring the trivial contrarieties that were the focus of earlier treatises, Blackstone presented the common law as a uniform logical system. Conceived as such, it became a robust defense of the existing order of things, something for which Blackstone has often been criticized.[35] However, there is no disputing the contribution the *Commentaries* made as a handbook clarifying the law for lawyers and laymen alike.

Blackstone left Oxford for parliament and the bench before he could create the law school that he had hoped to establish, but his inaugural lecture as Vinerian professor, entitled "On the Study of the Law," provided a formula for legal education and was reprinted as the preface to the first volume of the *Commentaries*.[36] Blackstone believed that the common law was governed by fundamental principles that could be applied to individual cases as they arose. Once the principles were identified, the cases would fall into place. Turning the traditional case method on its head, he advocated a process of deductive reasoning, moving from the broad principles established by experience to the specifics of individual cases. His approach gave the law a coherence that it had lacked and imposed a system of rough order on what previously had been a hodge-podge of individual, unrelated, and often arcane precedents.

Blackstone had a significant influence on the legal profession in Britain,[37] but it was in North America that his work made its greatest impression.[38] When the first American edition of the *Commentaries* appeared in 1772, its original subscribers, in addition to men like Thomas Marshall, included George Wythe, John Jay, James Wilson, Roger Sherman, John Adams, and virtually every leading member of the legal profession.[39] It was also in America, not Britain, where Blackstone's proposal for the study of law came to fruition. Both Jefferson and Wythe, who had been Jefferson's mentor in the 1760s, were powerfully impressed by Blackstone's approach. Both had struggled with the obscure prose of Coke, the absence of modern texts, and the lack of any systematic integration of statutes, case law, and legal concepts. Jefferson deplored Blackstone's innate conservatism,[40] but like Wythe and others, he recognized the value of the English jurist's systematic approach.[41]

In 1779, when Jefferson was elected governor of Virginia and chairman of the board of William and Mary, one of his first acts was to reorganize the college's small faculty.[42] In a sweeping move, he abolished the professorships of divinity and Oriental languages and substituted three new chairs: law and public policy; anatomy, medicine, and chemistry; and modern languages.[43] These were the first professorships of law, medicine, and modern languages in North America.[44] Wythe, who had no serious competition for the post, was appointed professor of law. James McClurg, who held a medical degree from Edinburgh, became the first professor of medicine; and Charles Bellini, a gifted linguist and the college librarian, was appointed the first American professor of modern languages.

McClurg and Bellini were respected scholars, but it was George Wythe who brought the greatest distinction to the college.[45] Like Marshall, Wythe was descended from the Keiths of Scotland,[46] and for years he and his great rival, Edmund Pendleton, had dominated the Virginia bar. Pendleton was the superior advocate; Wythe, the more accomplished craftsman.[47] Self-taught in Greek and Latin—Jefferson considered him the finest classical scholar in Virginia[48]—Wythe had been the colony's attorney general, a member of both the House of Burgesses and the Continental Congress, a signatory to the Declaration of Independence, and the speaker of the Virginia House of Delegates. In 1777 he became one of three judges of the newly established Virginia high court of chancery. He had also been appointed, along with Jefferson and Pendleton, to a three-person commission charged with revising the laws of Virginia to make them consistent with the spirit of the revolution. That famous revision of Virginia's statutes provided for the abolition of primogeniture, the promotion of education, and the guarantee of religious freedom.[49]

Wythe was wedded to Blackstone in his teaching, and his inaugural lecture was cast in Blackstonian terms, stressing the fundamental principles of the law.[50] Reflecting that primary orientation, the curriculum he initiated was wide-ranging. Wythe believed that the young men under his tutelage would not only become lawyers but that some would emerge as the nation's next generation of leaders. He saw William and Mary as "a training ground for republican citizenship."[51] Every morning the students read law under Wythe's supervision: first Blackstone, then the traditional treatises, abridgements, and statutes. Wythe believed that mental vigor was greatest in the mornings, and he assigned the tough work early. Marshall found this schedule congenial. An early riser himself, the future chief justice was most productive just after dawn. Years later in Washington, when he and his judicial colleagues were sharing living quarters at Brown's Indian Queen Hotel, Marshall regularly rose before sunup, took a brisk walk of several miles, and returned to his lodgings for breakfast before any of his fellow justices had awakened.[52]

Wythe lectured at noon on Tuesdays and Thursdays.[53] Afternoons were devoted to reading in related fields, particularly political philosophy. Marshall's mind did not flow easily in theoretical directions,[54] but under Wythe's direction he read and came to appreciate the principal works of Baron Charles Louis de Montesquieu and David Hume.[55] From Montesquieu, whose seminal work, *The Spirit of the Laws*, was translated into English in 1750,[56] Marshall derived a crisp understanding of the doctrine of the separation of powers.[57] Montesquieu was the first modern writer to distinguish the judiciary as an independent branch of government. Departing from prior political theory as well as from English practice, both of which treated the courts as a subordinate arm of the executive, Montesquieu differentiated among the legislative, administrative, and adjudicative functions of government: the threefold separation we are familiar with today. He argued that the preservation of liberty depended on the three functions being kept separate and independent.[58]

Montesquieu's work had an important influence in postcolonial America, and his arguments were cited regularly by the Framers of the Constitution.[59] The doctrine of separation of powers was particularly useful to those who sought to limit legislative authority, since to do so, an independent judiciary was essential. That argument appealed to George Wythe,[60] and Marshall embraced it wholeheartedly.[61]

In David Hume, Marshall found reinforcement for his skepticism of *a priori* principles, and particularly for the theories of natural law. Hume's *Treatise of Human Nature,* published in 1739,[62] effectively destroyed the pretensions of natural law to scientific validity. By carefully distinguishing reason, fact, and value, Hume undermined the old natural law structure that melded the three into a unitary system believed to be derived from God and nature.

When he wrote about law and politics, Hume, like Alexander Pope, stressed the importance of experience. George Wythe drew on Hume to impress upon his students the importance of habit and experience in defining property rights and political authority. Hume called the laws pertaining to property the "rules of justice." He meant that the possession of property should be stable, that property could be transferred by consent, and that agreements must be binding. In Hume's view, stable property ownership was the foundation of a stable society. Consistent with his overall epistemology, Hume's laws were based not on reason or pure theories of justice but on human passions—the aversion to pain and the pursuit of pleasure, reinforced by habit and experience. Wythe found Hume a valuable supplement in teaching the common law, because it too, as Justice Holmes pointed out so eloquently, rests primarily on experience.[63] By legitimizing experience, Hume legitimized the common law.

In addition to traditional lectures and reading courses, Wythe originated the practice of holding moot courts and mock legislatures to give students practical experience. The new laws drafted by Wythe, Jefferson, and Pendleton provided the subjects for the mock legislative sessions. These were held weekly in Williamsburg's old capitol building, the state government having recently moved to Richmond. Wythe presided over the assembly as speaker and chaired the debate among the students. The moot courts, also held in the abandoned building, were similar. John Brown, a classmate of Marshall's who later represented Kentucky in the United States Senate, wrote to his parents that "Mr. Wythe and the other professors sit as Judges. Our Audience consists of the most respectable of the Citizens, before whom we plead Causes given out by Mr. Wythe. Lawyerlike, I assure you."[64] Brown said that he was applying himself "closely to the study of law, and I find it to be a more difficult science than I expected. Those who finish this study in a few months [as Marshall was to do] either have strong natural parts or else they know little about it."[65]

Wythe also assisted in the establishment of the first chapter of Phi Beta Kappa, whose meetings were devoted to debating contemporary issues. Society records indicate that on May 18, 1780, "Capt. John Marshall being recommended as a gentleman who would make a worthy member of this Society was ballotted for & received."[66] Two weeks later he debated the question of "Whether any form of Government is more favourable to public virtue than a Commonwealth," arguing that there were none. The outcome of the debate is not recorded.[67]

Captain Marshall was popular among his classmates, and, being older and more experienced, he was often looked to for leadership. In that capacity, Marshall took advantage of every opportunity to emphasize what he had learned from military service and to stress the importance of a strong national government. Spencer Roane, who was seventeen at the time, later recalled how the chief justice, "a man of the most profound legal attainments," had devoted "his thought, his tongue, and his pen" to the cause of national power for as long as he had known him.[68]

One of the most important tasks that Wythe set for his students was the preparation of a law notebook, or commonplace book,[69] bringing together the statutes and legal precedents they would use when practicing. Wythe recognized the usefulness of a ready reference that placed the law at a young attorney's fingertips. He indicated the material that was most important and urged his students to use his library to record the standard concepts of the common law as interpreted in Virginia.[70] The exercise served two purposes. In bringing together a number of sources on a single subject, a student would invariably absorb something about the relevant concept. Equally important, the summary of sources would provide a valuable reference in their practice.[71]

John Marshall's notebook has survived,[72] and it illustrates the thoroughness with which he applied himself as a student. In fact, to compile a notebook as extensive as Marshall's in the short amount of time he spent at William and Mary also demonstrates, as his classmate John Brown might have phrased it, that Marshall was endowed "with strong natural parts." His written summaries, beginning at A [Abatement] and running through L [Limitation of Action], number 238 manuscript pages and treat more than seventy subjects.[73] They represent an abstract of the corresponding subjects in Blackstone, the first three volumes of Matthew Bacon's *New Abridgment of the Law*,[74] and the *Acts of the Assembly Now in Force in the Colony of Virginia*,[75] a collection compiled in 1769. Occasionally Marshall's thoughts wandered: The names "Ambler," or "Polly Ambler," or "Miss Maria Ambler," or "Miss M. Ambler–J. Marshall," or simply "Polly" are scribbled throughout the manuscript.[76]

During his years in practice, Marshall relied heavily on his commonplace book. The fact that it has survived indicates its importance to him, since the future chief justice was notorious for discarding records that had outlived their usefulness. Unlike George Washington and Thomas Jefferson, Marshall saved none of his letters or memoranda and systematically destroyed his files at regular intervals. He kept his law notes, however, and used them as a guide when new cases arose. Eventually they became embedded in his memory, enabling him to move quickly, almost instinctively, in his arguments from the general principles that were controlling to the specific facts at issue.[77]

Of course, it was not all work in Williamsburg. With the state government having moved to Richmond, Jaquelin Ambler, then a member of the council of state, felt obliged to move as well. In June, when the Ambler family passed through Williamsburg en route to the new capital, Marshall and his friends organized a ball in honor of "the Misses Ambler." Marshall, who by now was deeply in love with Polly, put every effort into making the ball a success. The young men took over the vacant governor's palace and bought what refreshments they could afford. Eliza and Polly were thrilled to be the center of such attention. "The entertainment in itself was like most of the entertainments of the present time, simple and frugal as to its viands, but of the brilliancy of the company too much cannot be said," Eliza wrote several days later.[78] The ball, she said, "consisted of more Beauty and Elegance than I had ever witnessed before, and I was transported with delight at being considered a distinguished personage." Polly's comments were not recorded, but it was apparent that she and Marshall were thinking seriously about each other. Eliza, in the same letter, noted that Marshall "was devoted to my sister."[79]

The Amblers departed for Richmond the next morning, and at the end of July, when lectures ended, Marshall followed them. On July 31, 1780, he called at the state store in Richmond to replenish his military uniforms,[80] and since the Virginia government still had taken no action to raise additional troops for Washington's army, he decided to complete the formalities for admission to the bar. Sometime between July 31 and August 14—the date is not clear—he underwent an examination for his license to practice law. No copy of Marshall's examination survives.[81] According to Virginia statutes in force at the time, a prospective lawyer first had to petition the governor for a license, after which the governor would appoint two lawyers to examine the candidate. If the candidate passed, the governor would grant the license, which entitled the candidate to take the oath of office as an attorney before the appropriate county court.[82] Since Governor Jefferson left Richmond for a lengthy vacation on August 15, Marshall must have filed his petition and undergone examination before that date, because two weeks later, on August 28, 1780, he took his oath before the Fauquier county court in Warrenton.[83]

"It was my design to go immediately to the bar," Marshall told Story,[84] but the courts throughout Virginia were closed to litigants because of the war, and there was simply no business for a fledgling lawyer. Marshall thus idled his time at Oak Hill that autumn, visiting Polly and her family in Richmond once. But he soon grew restless. In late September, with the Virginia legislature still refusing to raise the troops Washington needed, Marshall set out alone to rejoin the army in Philadelphia.[85] As was his habit, he traveled by foot, walking thirty to thirty-five miles a day. When he arrived in the American capital after two weeks on the road, he looked so disreputable that the first hotel he stopped at refused to take him in. Years later, as Chief Justice of the United States, Marshall enjoyed regaling his listeners with the story of how, because of his shabby clothing, long beard, and unkempt hair, he had been turned away by the innkeeper, despite the fact that he was a captain in the Virginia Line and a member of the bar.[86]

By the time Marshall arrived in Philadelphia, the war had turned south. Earlier in the year, Sir Henry Clinton had divided his forces. He kept Knyphausen in New York to menace Washington's dwindling army and dispatched Cornwallis to the Carolinas with the objective of defeating the revolution in the south and returning those colonies to the crown. With 8,500 regulars, Cornwallis captured Charleston, subdued Georgia and South Carolina, and defeated an American army under General Horatio Gates at the Battle of Camden. Had it not been for the failure of his Tory allies at King's Mountain, he would have conquered North Carolina as well.[87] Washington, facing Knyphausen, could spare no reinforcements for the southern theater, but he recognized that the situation was critical. In November, he sent his most able subordinates, General Nathaniel Greene and Baron von Steuben, to take command in the south and raise a new army to confront Cornwallis. Greene assumed overall command in the Carolinas, and von Steuben was delegated the task of revitalizing Virginia's moribund militia and finding reinforcements.[88] Marshall, who was still without a command, accompanied von Steuben to assist in raising troops in Virginia.[89]

The presence of Greene and von Steuben goaded the reluctant Virginia legislature into authorizing a new levy of 3,500 men for the Continental Army. Von Steuben and Marshall did their utmost to recruit them, and by mid-December 1,500 men had volunteered. But the legislature remained unwilling to appropriate money for uniforms and equipment, and many of the recruits deserted. By Christmas 1780 von Steuben was able to send only 700 new troops to Greene, leaving a ragtag remnant of several hundred men in Virginia, many of whom were without weapons. The state was effectively defenseless should Cornwallis move north, but only von Steuben, and perhaps Marshall, appeared to be concerned.[90]

Cornwallis quickly recognized his opportunity. For the previous five years, since the burning of Norfolk on New Year's Day, 1776, Virginia had been spared the war's devastation. The Old Dominion's abundant tobacco crops fortified the credit of Congress abroad; the Shenandoah's agricultural products helped feed the Continental Army; and the state's veteran soldiers—the Virginia Line—provided the backbone of American resistance. If Virginia could be occupied and driven from the war, the revolution would be crushed.[91] Sir Henry Clinton was unwilling to transfer Knyphausen's corps from New York to Virginia as Cornwallis urged, but in late December 1780 he dispatched a raiding party of 1,600 troops under Benedict Arnold* to the state. Arnold's task was to destroy the tobacco crop awaiting shipment abroad as well as any military stores he found and, perhaps more important, to prevent reinforcements from being sent to Greene in North Carolina. If he could rally whatever latent Tory sentiment remained in Virginia, so much the better.

Arnold's raiding party sailed up the James River unopposed and landed at Westover, the Byrd family estate, just below Richmond, on January 3, 1781.[92] The state government fled westward, the militia failed to respond in sufficient numbers, and Arnold entered Richmond two days later. Marshall, who was with von Steuben in nearby Petersburg, marched with the few Continental troops that were available to protect the capital. They were too few in number, and arrived too late.[93] Arnold's men burned a foundry and powder magazine and destroyed a substantial quantity of military stores, 4,000 barrels of tobacco, and large quantities of rum and salt.[94] Two days later the British withdrew, with von Steuben and the small force he had assembled in close pursuit. On January 10 a party of the baron's men under the command of Colonel George Rogers Clark, and including Marshall, set an ambush for Arnold at Hood's Landing, where the James River narrows. In the attack that followed, they killed seventeen of the British before being driven away.[95] Arnold evacuated his troops to Portsmouth, and von Steuben, who by now had gathered a force of 3,000 to 4,000 militia, invested the town to keep Arnold in check.[96]

---

*Benedict Arnold, an early American hero of the Revolution, defected to the British in 1780 and, as part of his reward, was commissioned a brigadier general in the British army. As both Clinton and Cornwallis questioned Arnold's stability, they attached two experienced and effective officers, Colonels David Dundas and John Graves Simcoe, to accompany the expedition into Virginia. Dundas subsequently became commander in chief of the British army (1809–1811) and Simcoe the first lieutenant governor of Upper Canada. The best analysis of Arnold's incursion is Francis Rives Lassiter's "Arnold's Invasion of Virginia," 9 *Swanee Review* 78–93, 185–203 (1901). Also see Willard Sterne Randall, *Benedict Arnold: Patriot and Traitor* 581–584 (New York: William Morrow, 1990).

The failure of the Virginia militia to respond promptly to Arnold's surprise invasion and the government's precipitate flight from Richmond were judged severely. Critics in Virginia and in the Continental Congress sharply chastised Governor Jefferson for not mounting a better defense of the state capital.[97] James Madison remarked sarcastically that he was "glad to hear that Arnold has been at last fired at" after the ambush at Hood's Landing.[98] Jefferson's hasty departure from Richmond in the early-morning hours of January 5 occasioned particularly severe criticism and formed the basis for the charges of cowardice that plagued him throughout his career.[99] Whether Marshall shared this view of Jefferson's behavior is unknown. If he made any comment about the future president's conduct it went unrecorded, and his written treatment of Arnold's raid in the *Life of Washington* makes no mention of Jefferson.[100] Some observers have pointed out that while Jefferson fled from the oncoming British, Marshall, with von Steuben and Clark, moved to intercept them. That comparison ignored the fact that John Marshall was an infantry captain on active service. He was compelled by duty to go forward and meet the British, whereas Jefferson, as governor, had responsibilities that necessitated his evacuation.

In the lull that followed Arnold's raid, Marshall reassessed his situation. Like James Monroe and many other supernumerary officers of the Virginia Line, he decided to resign from the army and pursue a civilian career. Although the war was far from won, the Virginia government remained unwilling to take the measures necessary to raise the additional men required by Washington and Greene. With no troops to command, Marshall grew impatient. And so, after five years of front-line duty, he resigned his commission in February 1781 and proceeded to divide his time between Oak Hill and Richmond, where he resumed his courtship of Polly Ambler. As he told Joseph Story, "I had formed a strong attachment to the young lady whom I afterwards married; and, as we had more officers than soldiers, thought I might without violating the duty I owed my country, pay some attention to my future prospects in life."*[101]

Those prospects were anything but assured. The courts remained closed for the duration of the war (Cornwallis did not surrender at Yorktown

---

*Marshall's explanation is not entirely convincing. His resignation, assuming it was in writing, has been lost. However, it does not ring true that someone with John Marshall's commitment to the United States would resign from military service with the war unwon to pursue his personal career. Arnold still held an important toehold in Virginia, Lafayette and Rochambeau were marching south to reinforce the state, and Cornwallis had begun marching north. Indeed, February 1781 saw the war shift its focus to Virginia, where it finally concluded later in the year.

Two events occurred that month that may shed some light on Marshall's decision. The first has become known as "the affair at Westover." It involved an unauthorized search of Mary Willing Byrd's home by officers of the Virginia Line under the command of Colonel James Innes. This complicated affair is described thoroughly by Julian P. Boyd in 5 *The Papers of Thomas Jeffer-*

until October 1781), and there was little for a young lawyer to do. At that point, Marshall decided to run for a seat in the Virginia legislature. He canvassed his friends and neighbors, and, when elections were held the following spring, he was returned to Richmond as one of the two delegates from Fauquier county.[102] Six months later he was elected to the council of state.

Marshall's courtship of Polly continued. Writing to his wife years later he recalled "our little tiffs & makings up, and all the thousand indescribable but deeply affecting instances of your affection or coldness which constituted for a time the happiness or misery of my life."[103] Persistent family legend holds that when Marshall asked Polly to marry him, she refused.[104] Marshall said good-bye, mounted his horse, and rode off in the direction of Fauquier county. Polly watched him go, and when he disappeared from sight, began weeping hysterically. Nothing could calm her. Her cousin, John Ambler, put his arm around her to console her and surreptitiously snipped a lock of her hair. He then excused himself, raced after Marshall, and gave him the lock. "My father," said Marshall's and Polly's youngest son, "supposing she had sent it, renewed his suit and they were married."[105] Polly afterward placed the snippet of hair in a locket and wore it around her neck for the rest of her life. When she died, Marshall took the locket and wore it until his death.[106]

There is no doubt that Marshall rode away after his proposal was declined, and there is no doubt that John Ambler chased after him with a lock of Polly's hair. However, that portion of the family legend suggesting that John Ambler surreptitiously snipped the lock without Polly's knowledge is

---

son (Appendix I) 671–705 (Princeton: Princeton University Press, 1957). In essence, Mrs. Byrd protested the unwarranted intrusion to von Steuben, who promptly instituted disciplinary action against the officers involved. That pitted Innes and von Steuben in a clash of wills. The investigation into the incident eventually petered out but left a residue of hard feeling between von Steuben and the officers of the Virginia Line. Marshall was in the vicinity of Westover at the time, and whether he was involved in the incident is not known. However, James Innes, then twenty-seven, was a close friend of Marshall's. He had been one of Washington's aides-de-camp, and had fought at Trenton, Brandywine, Germantown, and Monmouth. He had also studied law with Marshall under George Wythe. It is conceivable that Marshall took Innes's side and that this contributed to his decision to resign.

The second incident in February 1781 also involved von Steuben. After calling on all supernumerary officers to assemble at Chesterfield court house on February 10, 1781, von Steuben failed to meet with them until the eighteenth, and then he did so in Petersburg, fifty miles away. That prompted Steuben's aid-de-camp, Major William North, to write to General Greene in North Carolina that "The Baron has unfortunately become universally unpopular, and all ranks of people seem to have taken the greatest disgust at him, and carry it to such a length as to talk of applying to Congress for his recall." Whether this general "disgust" prompted Marshall to resign is also unknown, but again, it seems a more plausible reason that the one he gave Story. For a report of this episode, see 4 *Jefferson Papers* 661–662. Subsequently, Marshall wrote to Greene, perhaps to explain his decision, but that letter has been lost. For reference to the missing correspondence, see 1 *Marshall Papers* 87.

suspect. The entire episode is a curious inversion of the events in Alexander Pope's *The Rape of the Lock*, with which, thanks to Marshall's instruction, Polly was unquestionably familiar. It is much more likely that Polly, recognizing her error, cut her own lock of hair and sent her cousin John with it to retrieve her disappointed suitor. Yet Polly could not admit that she had cut her own hair without seriously compromising her reputation. Alexander Pope had characterized the lock of hair as a woman's virginity and the clipping of the hair as rape, so for Polly to send her own lock to her suitor would have been unseemly. The story thus was altered to protect the young girl's name. For Marshall, however, the meaning of gesture would have been unmistakable.

The wedding took place at eight o'clock on the evening of January 3, 1783, in "The Cottage," the country estate of John Ambler in Hanover county.[107] Polly, who was two months shy of her seventeenth birthday, wore an off-the-shoulder, white brocade dress with shirred sleeves and a short train that flared from the back. After the ceremony, the large wedding party enjoyed an elaborate supper, followed by dancing until "winter dawn shed enough light on the roads for the guests to return to their homes."[108]

John Marshall was twenty-seven years old. He was a lawyer, a war hero, and a member of the council of state. The son of a distinguished frontier family, he was now the son-in-law of Jaquelin Ambler, the treasurer of Virginia and one of the most influential men in the state. Only the financial picture looked bleak. Marshall later confessed that after paying the parson for the ceremony, he had but one guinea to his name.[109] The future may have been uncertain, but John Marshall was choosing his way purposefully.

4

⁂

Husband, Lawyer, Legislator

In April 1787, I was elected into the legislature for the county in which Richmond stands; and although devoted to my profession, entered with a good deal of spirit into the politics of the state. The topics of the day were paper money, the collection of taxes, the preservation of public faith, and the administration of justice. The state of the Confederacy was also a subject of deep solicitude to our statesmen. Mr. Madison was the enlightened advocate of Union and of an efficient federal government; but was not a member of the legislature when the plan of the constitution was proposed to the states by the General Convention. It was at first favorably received; but Mr. P[atrick] Henry and Mr. G[eorge] Mason, and several other gentlemen of great influence were much opposed to it. . . . In addition to state jealousy and pride, which operated powerfully in all large states, there were some unacknowledged motives of no inconsiderable influence in Virginia. In the course of the session, the unceasing efforts of the enemies of the constitution made a deep impression; and before its close, a great majority showed a decided hostility to it. I took an active part in the debates on this question and was uniform in support of the proposed constitution.[1]

T HAT WAS HOW Marshall explained to Story the steps leading to the Virginia convention to ratify the Constitution. The "unacknowledged motives of no inconsiderable influence" to which he alluded pertained to slavery. And it was the question of slavery, although usually unstated during this early period of the nation's history, that contributed to the clamor for states rights in Virginia.

Marshall had been initially elected to the Virginia House of Delegates in the spring of 1782.[2] His fellow delegates included not only Patrick Henry and George Mason but John Tyler, Richard Henry Lee, and James Monroe, who, like Marshall, was serving his first term.[3] The session lasted thirty-eight days but produced little in the way of legislation.[4] Like all delegates,

Marshall was paid 10 shillings a day for his attendance. His pay voucher, submitted July 1, 1782, shows that he drew a total of £24 4s, which included £5 4s for travel from Fauquier county.[5]

During the session in Richmond, Marshall became acquainted with Virginia's leading statesmen. He did not open a law office at the time, devoting himself instead to the politics of the legislature. His primary interest involved the efforts to bring the war to a swift conclusion.* "I partook largely of the sufferings and feelings of the army," Marshall wrote Story, "and brought with me into civil life an ardent devotion to its interests. My immediate entrance into the state legislature opened my view to the causes which had been chiefly instrumental in augmenting those sufferings, and the general tendency of state politics convinced me that no safe and permanent remedy could be found but in a more efficient and better organized general government."[6] Marshall was referring to the continued bickering, much of it personal, that had kept the Virginia House of Delegates deadlocked on most issues. Many of the delegates had known one another for years, and some had formed deep and abiding friendships. For others, familiarity had bred harsh rivalries that could not be put aside without violating Virginia's archaic code of chivalry. Quick action was further inhibited by the general lassitude that prevailed in Richmond. In contrast to the commercialism of the mid-Atlantic and New England states, Virginia's plantation culture placed a premium on leisure and lengthy discussion and set a slow pace, which the legislature emulated.

The state of Virginia had moved its capital to Richmond from Williamsburg in 1780, citing the need to remove the seat of government from easy British attack. In reality, the move westward reflected the changing center of gravity of Virginia politics from tidewater to piedmont. In 1782 the general assembly met in a small frame building, a former warehouse that also served as a site for banquets and dances. (Jefferson's imposing capitol building, designed after the Maison Carrée in Nîmes, was not completed until 1788.) The town of Richmond itself, straddling the falls of the James River, contained fewer than 200 dwellings and had a permanent population of less than 1,200 persons.[7] Unlike the polished coastal settlements at Williamsburg or prewar Norfolk, the town had the raw and unkempt appearance of a frontier boomtown.[8] Streets were unpaved, the capital square was riddled with gullies, and the area around the statehouse was permeated with the pungent aroma of domestic animals.

Given the makeshift nature of the new capital, delegates to the general

---

*The British army did not evacuate Charleston, South Carolina, their last outpost, until December 14, 1782.

assembly found temporary accommodations as best they could, usually in private homes or in one of the half-dozen taverns that clustered around the statehouse. During legislative sessions, the taverns were so crowded that the delegates slept upstairs in beds packed side by side.[9] The dreary conditions were relieved by hard drinking and endless sessions of billards, cards, and backgammon.

Dr. Johann David Schoepf, a German surgeon visiting Richmond while on a tour of North America, captured the flavor of the legislature during Marshall's first term. Reflecting a Teutonic preference for order and discipline, Schoepf wrote: "It is said of the Assembly: It sits; but this is not a true expression, for these members show themselves in every possible position rather than that of sitting still, with dignity and attention."[10]

Schoepf noted that the Virginia assembly was dominated by lawyers. "As in all other public and private societies," he wrote,

> there are certain men who lead the debate, and think and speak for the rest, so it is also in these assemblies. Among the orators here is a certain Mr. Henry who appears to have the greatest influence upon the House. . . . Men of this stamp, either naturally eloquent or become so through their occupation as lawyers, invariably take the most active and influential part in these assemblies. The other members, for the most part farmers without clear and refined ideas, with little education or knowledge of the world, are merely there to give their votes, which are sought, whenever the House is divided. . . .[11]

Marshall made his way quickly in the assembly and was one of the few whom Schoepf observed to be influential. The legislature at that time was loosely divided into two shifting and amorphous factions, one reflecting the views of the Virginia establishment, and the other, led by Patrick Henry, taking a more radical and populist stance. These labels suggest greater specificity than is appropriate, because the factions were never clearly defined, and their membership fluctuated depending on the issue. On one question, however, the division was clear. The establishment forces were concerned with strengthening the Union created by the Articles of Confederation, whereas the radicals were either indifferent or openly hostile to the central government. For the most part, establishment figures such as Madison, Mason, Pendleton, and the various Lees and Randolphs retained control of the assembly, until such time as the always unpredictable Patrick Henry mounted the rostrum. But Henry's attendance was irregular and his intervention infrequent.

Marshall gravitated naturally to the establishment faction. As the son of Thomas Marshall and a veteran officer of the Virginia Line, he was welcomed by his elders, who recognized his ability and responded warmly to his outgoing personality. Marshall was initially appointed to the judiciary committee, a prestigious assignment given the broad terms of reference the committee enjoyed.[12] On May 27, 1782, he was also named to chair a select committee to draft a new militia bill,[13] although no militia legislation was reported out that session. Instead, the House concentrated on passing a long-overdue recruiting bill to supply troops for the Continental Army. As James Madison noted, Virginia "is perhaps under the strongest obligation of any State in the Union to preserve her military contingent on a respectable footing, and unhappily her line is perhaps of all in the most disgraceful condition."[14]

The recruitment bill was strongly supported by the establishment forces, who wanted to include a provision to draft men in those counties whose quota was not filled. Marshall opposed the provision. His experience as a company officer in an army that frequently went hungry made him skeptical of the effectiveness of men forced to serve against their will. Edmund Randolph advised Madison in June that the bill would likely "pass in its present form, but . . . Capt. Marshall, a young man of rising character, will make a furious onset for the abolition of the draft."[15] Randolph's assessment proved correct. Despite Marshall's opposition, the recruitment bill passed in its original form on July 2, 1782—the final day of the session.[16]

When Marshall returned to Richmond the following November for the fall session of the legislature, he was engaged to Polly and the date for the wedding had been set, but his source of livelihood and his ability to support a wife were far from assured. The 10 shillings per diem that he received as a legislator was clearly insufficient, and his law practice was not yet off the ground. It was at this point that Marshall's friends came to his aid. Edmund Randolph, who had become Richmond's leading attorney when George Wythe and Edmund Pendleton were elevated to the bench,[17] offered Marshall the use of his chambers until he was able to establish an office for himself.[18] And on the political front, Polly's father, Jaquelin Ambler, used his influence to win a spot for Marshall on the council of state.[19]

Randolph's offer was particularly generous. The grandson of Sir John Randolph, and thus, Marshall's cousin, Edmund Randolph has served as Virginia's attorney general from 1776 to 1778. Later he would become America's first attorney general and would serve briefly as secretary of state. His own career had benefited significantly in 1774 when Thomas Jefferson decided to enter politics on a full-time basis and turned his law practice over to him.[20] Upon his own election as governor in 1786, he would turn the practice over to Marshall.[21] Bizarre as it may seem, Jefferson's law practice ultimately became John Marshall's.

In the fall of 1782, however, Marshall was just starting out, and Randolph could be credited with considerable perspicacity, because Marshall's slovenly manner of dressing scarcely inspired courtroom confidence. One of the more famous anecdotes about Marshall as a young lawyer relates that an elderly gentleman from the country arrived in Richmond needing a lawyer. Marshall had been recommended highly, but after seeing him, the prospective client decided to go elsewhere. While sitting in the courtroom waiting for his case to be called, the country gentleman observed the proceedings. The first case of the day pitted Marshall against the lawyer he had engaged. Immediately the man from the country knew he had made a mistake. When the first recess came, he approached Marshall, explained that he had given the other lawyer $95 of the $100 which he had brought with him that day, and asked Marshall if he would take the case for the remaining $5. Marshall good-naturedly agreed, adding the story to his repertoire.[22]

With Randolph's help, Marshall eventually established a thriving practice in Richmond. Equally important, his father opened the state's survey office in the Kentucky territory in 1782, and Marshall became an intermediary for investors wishing to convert their land office warrants into surveyed acreage. Nevertheless, the next several years were not easy. Marshall had ongoing financial problems, especially after he married, and initially his clients were few and far between.

A lucky break came in November 1782, when John Banister of Hatcher's Run, near Petersburg, unexpectedly resigned his seat on the council of state. Marshall was elected to fill the vacancy. Virginia's council of state, or privy council, represented an experiment in collective government. Reacting against the prerogative authority that had been concentrated in the royal governor, the framers of Virginia's 1776 constitution established a plural executive that was to be elected by the legislature.[23] Composed of the governor and a council of eight members, the executive was charged with the day-to-day responsibilities of administering the state.[24]

According to the constitution, the governor could act only with the advice and consent of council. The group met every morning in Richmond, usually at 10 A.M., to attend to the day's affairs. The daily meetings were an onerous responsibility, requiring council members to be present in Richmond year-round. They were paid accordingly, each councilor receiving approximately £400 in hard currency, prorated according to attendance—a generous emolument for government service at the time.[25] Indeed, election to the council represented an important step for aspiring politicians in the Old Dominion. Edmund Randolph felt it sufficiently important to write

Madison that "Capt. Marshall, a promising young gentleman of the law is elected into the privy council *vice* Colo. Banister."[26]

Marshall's election to the council at the age of twenty-seven, after serving only one session in the House of Delegates, was unusual but not unprecedented. James Monroe, who was three years younger than Marshall, was also elected in 1782 after serving only one term in the House.[27] Two other members, Samuel Hardy and Beverley Randolph, were twenty-four and twenty-eight years old, respectively. Nevertheless, there is some evidence that Marshall's elbows may have been too sharp and his ambition too close to the surface. One of those who felt jostled was Edmund Pendleton, then serving as president of Virginia's court of appeals. On November 25, 1782, five days after Marshall's election, Pendleton wrote to Madison that "Young Mr. Marshall is elected a Counsellor in the room of Mr. Banister, who resigned. He is clever, but I think too young for that department, which he should rather have earned as a retirement and reward by 10 or 12 years hard service in the Assembly."[28] Curiously, Pendleton had not raised that objection when Monroe had been elevated in July and, indeed, had written to Madison praising Monroe's talents.[29] This suggests that unlike Monroe, who was invariably deferential,[30] Marshall may have appeared too keen to get ahead.

In fact, Marshall and Monroe had powerful patrons who were largely responsible for their quick election to the council of state. Monroe was Jefferson's protégé,* while Marshall benefited from his ties to Randolph and to Jaquelin Ambler, who had been elected treasurer earlier in the year.[31] Then, as now, the person who controlled the state's finances enjoyed considerable influence. Ambler would serve as the Old Dominion's treasurer for sixteen years. Governors came and went with increasing frequency,[32] but Ambler remained in office, his influence growing as each year passed. Like George Wythe, Jaquelin Ambler was a model of probity,[33] and his unsullied reputation made him one of the most powerful men in Richmond.

Marshall's election to the council of state provided a much-needed source of income on the eve of his marriage to Polly—a fact that escaped neither Marshall nor his prospective father-in-law, who was understandably concerned for his daughter's well-being. Family ties provided the glue that held Virginia together, and Jaquelin Ambler intervened on Marshall's behalf

---

*Like Marshall, Monroe had returned to Virginia as a supernumerary officer in December 1779 after serving with Washington since the war's inception. Wounded in the battle of Trenton, he had attained the rank of lieutenant colonel at the time of his resignation. He enrolled in George Wythe's first lecture series at William and Mary in January 1780, but when the Virginia government moved to Richmond that spring, he accompanied Governor Jefferson and continued to study law under Jefferson's tutelage. For a discussion of Monroe as Jefferson's protégé, see Harry Ammon, *James Monroe: The Quest for National Identity* 29–32 (Charlottesville: University Press of Virginia, 1990).

to give his career an important nudge forward. So long as Ambler was treasurer, persons wishing to do business with the state found Marshall a useful go-between, and his law practice grew accordingly.[34]

Marshall's service on the council of state brought him into daily contact with the problems of governing the sprawling commonwealth of Virginia, which at that time extended from the Atlantic to the Mississippi. It included not only the present-day states of West Virginia and Kentucky, but also claims to the vast Northwest Territory stretching from the Ohio River to the Canadian border.

As a member of council, Marshall continued to press the long-overdue problem of revitalizing Virginia's militia.* On February 12, 1783, he wrote to William Leigh Pierce, a former classmate at William and Mary who was on active service in South Carolina, about the difficulties he was encountering. "The grand object of the people is . . . to oppose successfully our British enemies and to establish on the firm base of certainty the independence of America. But [a pettiness] of little interests and passions produces such a distracted contrariety of measures that 'tis sometimes difficult to determine whether some other end is not nearer the hearts of those who guide our Counsels."[35] Marshall went on to explain the difficulties Virginia had encountered in its militia program and described the financial aid the state was providing to the Continental Congress. As an afterthought, he told Pierce "we have vague accounts of peace but they will [reach] you as soon as this letter."[36]

Shortly after Marshall was elected to the council, a question arose that permitted him to assert for the first time the principle for which he will always be remembered: the supremacy of the constitution. In this instance, it was a question of asserting the authority of Virginia's constitution over laws passed by the legislature. The issue involved the authority of the council of state to inquire into the behavior of magistrates and to remove them if they were found to have behaved improperly. This power had been given to the council by an act of the general assembly.[37]

In early February 1783 Governor Benjamin Harrison presented the council with a formal complaint from officials in New Kent county alleging various misdeeds by John Price Posey, a county magistrate.[38] The governor asked for the council's advice as to whether Posey should be removed from office. The council could not respond without first determining whether

---

*Marshall had been elected to the council of state on November 20, 1782. He delayed taking his seat until November 30 so he could shepherd through the House the militia bill that he had drafted. The bill was considered by the committee of the whole house on November 29, but a motion to postpone further consideration until the next session carried 44–35, with Marshall voting against. The following day Marshall resigned from the House and took his oath as a member of council. *Journal of the House of Delegates* 45 (October session, 1782), Virginia State Library.

Posey had committed the offenses alleged, and it was on this point that Marshall balked. In his view, the issue raised important questions about the separation of powers, the independence of the judiciary, and the authority of the legislature to give the executive the power to oversee the courts.

None of these questions had been resolved in Virginia,[39] or in any other state for that matter.[40] Jefferson, who had played a major role in drafting the 1776 Virginia constitution, took the traditional view of parliamentary bodies. He rejected the idea that the constitution was a higher law and argued that it was on a par with other measures passed by the legislature.[41] Madison, by contrast, believed the constitution to be superior to statute law but was not sure how a dispute with the legislature should be resolved.[42] Randolph, Pendleton, and Wythe advocated judicial review to overturn measures that were unconstitutional but were reluctant to see it exercised.

Just three months before the Posey issue came before the council of state, the question of the constitution's supremacy had been raised in the case of *Commonwealth v. Caton*.[43] A complex piece of litigation, the case attracted great notoriety, and John Marshall was one of the many members of the Richmond bar who jammed the tiny courtroom in the makeshift capitol building to hear the arguments of opposing counsel. The issue involved an apparent conflict between the Treason Act[44] passed by the legislature in 1776 and the state constitution.[45] The constitution gave the pardoning power to the governor, while the Treason Act placed it in the hands of the legislature. Edmund Randolph, who, as attorney general, presented Virginia's appeal, argued that the state constitution was "a fundamental law . . . with which every statute of the General Assembly must conform."[46] Anticipating future Federalist arguments in support of the United States Constitution—arguments that sought to reconcile judicial review with representative government—Randolph maintained that the Virginia constitution sprang from the people, "the fountain of power," and established "the first principles of government." Accordingly, said Randolph, the constitution is "a compact, in which the people themselves are the sole parties and which they alone can abrogate." In Randolph's view, it was the responsibility of the court to enforce the will of the people as expressed in the constitution rather than the will of the legislature expressed in the statute.

The judges delivered their opinions on November 2. To the surprise of most who followed the case, the court found that the Treason Act did not violate the "spirit of the constitution," and hence there was no need to rule on its constitutionality. Chief Judge Edmund Pendleton, who as a trial judge during colonial times had deemed the stamp act to be unconstitutional,[47] avoided the issue this time.[48] He stated that the question of judicial review "is indeed a deep, important, and I will add, a tremendous question . . .

[but] I am happy in being of the opinion there is no reason to consider it upon this occasion."[49]

Chancellor Wythe, who concurred in the decision,[50] spoke with some vehemence on the supremacy of the constitution and the nature of judicial review. But Wythe's comments were *obiter dictum*—judicial commentary that went beyond the court's holding and therefore established no precedent. Wythe is reported to have said that as a judge, it was his duty to protect the constitution from legislative encroachment. "Nay more, if the whole legislature . . . should attempt to overleap its bounds, prescribed to them by the people, I, in administering the public justice of the country, will meet the united powers at my seat in this tribunal; and, pointing to the constitution, will say to them, *here is the limit of your authority: and hither, shall you go, but no further.*"[51]

The case of *Commonwealth v. Caton* was still fresh in the minds of Virginians when the Posey matter arose three months later. Marshall, to the dismay of Governor Harrison,[52] seized the opportunity to declare unconstitutional the act of the legislature that had authorized the council to investigate the conduct of the judges. In a well-publicized meeting of the council of state on February 20, 1783, Marshall and his colleagues announced that "The [Council] are of opinion that the Law authorizing the Executive to enquire into the Conduct of a Magistrate . . . is repugnant to the Act of Government, contrary to the fundamental principles of our constitution, and direct[ly] opposite to the tenor of our Laws."[53]

This is the first recorded instance in the United States of an act of a legislature being annulled because it conflicted with the constitution. The council did not question its ultimate authority to remove a judge for cause. However, it asserted that the issue of cause must be ascertained in a court of law. Governor Harrison urged the council to reconsider, but Marshall and his colleagues stood firm. The act of the legislature was unconstitutional in their view, and they refused to execute it.[54]

The assertion of constitutional review by the council of state did not win universal approval. Edmund Randolph, for example, was skeptical of the authority of the executive to refuse to enforce a statute. "The spirit of opposing laws, as being contrary to the constitution, has reached the executive," he wrote Madison on March 15, 1783.[55] "They have lately refused to examine into complaints . . . against a magistrate; alleging that this would be to assume judiciary power, and that the act of the assembly delegating it to the executive, is therefore void." Randolph said that Governor Harrison "conceives himself obliged to report this bold, and, as I think, mistaken step, to the assembly; which means you will probably hear more of it."

As Randolph predicted, when the legislature reconvened in May, Governor Harrison reported the matter to the House of Delegates, indicating that in his view the council had acted improperly.[56] Once again Marshall and his colleagues refused to back down. On May 26 they submitted their own report to the House of Delegates, insisting that the law in question was unconstitutional.[57] Although regrettably, this important constitutional document has been lost,[58] it indicates that Marshall had fully considered the question of constitutional review and had come to the conclusion that the separation of powers gave to each branch of government the authority of judging what was constitutional and what was not.

Whatever Marshall and his colleagues said in their reply to the House must have been convincing, because on June 2 Edmund Pendleton wrote to Madison that the issue was more complex than he originally thought. "The council have replied to the Governor's charge, and so the matter rests. No determination hath yet been made between them, and I am told that there are diversity of opinions which is right. Sure I am something should be *done* [about] it, and if they doubt whether the act in question be constitutional or not, they ought to repeal it and establish a mode of removal . . . which is unexceptionable. . . ."[59] Evidently, the position of Marshall and the council was sustained, because on December 10, 1783, Posey was tried in a judicial proceeding, found guilty of a misdemeanor, and fined £200. As a result of Posey's conviction, the council subsequently advised the governor to vacate his commission.[60]

The reluctance of the general assembly to overturn the council's 1783 decision suggests that the supremacy of the constitution was a concept well understood in Virginia.[61] But whether the executive branch was entitled to exercise constitutional review remained a contentious issue. In December 1785, eight months after Marshall resigned from the council of state, that body reversed itself and agreed to inquire into the conduct of a magistrate from Washington county.[62] Beverley Randolph and Spencer Roane, who had recently been elected to the council, dissented vigorously, and Roane ultimately resigned in protest.[63]

The matter did not end there, however. Both Roane and Marshall were tenacious when it came to the independence of the judiciary, and they refused to let the issue drop. In 1787, when Marshall was reelected to the House of Delegates, he introduced legislation to repeal the original statute that gave the council authority to inquire into the conduct of the judges. The repeal, attached to an act dealing with the appointment of county clerks, was adopted unanimously by the general assembly on January 8, 1788.[64] The proposal, which became chapter XXIII of the acts of the October 1787 session of the legislature, placed the general assembly on record in support of the separation of powers and the supremacy of the constitution.[65]

Marshall's forceful defense of the doctrine of the separation of powers reflected the instruction he received as a student of Chancellor Wythe at William and Mary. It also suggests that Marshall and his council colleagues were uncommonly eager to assert themselves. Jefferson, for example, wrote shortly afterward to Madison that the role of the council of state should be diminished so that it would no longer provide a stepping-stone for "young and ambitious men."[66] Madison agreed that the council should be scrapped, but for different reasons. He saw the executive body as "a grave of useful talents."[67]

Marshall certainly was a young man in a hurry. Albert Beveridge, who apparently was unaware of the council of state's decision in the Posey affair,[68] intuitively perceived that Marshall was too full of himself in those years, basing his inference on Marshall's signature to council minutes, which, he observed, was "totally unlike that of his more mature years."[69] According to Beveridge, Marshall "signed the Council records in large and dashing hand with flourishes—it is the handwriting of a confident, care-free, rollicking young man with a tinge of the dare-devil in him. These signatures are so strangely dissimilar to his later ones that they deserve particular attention. They denote Marshall's sense of his own importance and his certainty of his present situation and prospects."[70]

If Marshall and his colleagues on the council of state were too active, Virginia's general assembly remained moribund. Jefferson railed against it, and Madison perennially complained that the longer the legislature remained in session, the more its meetings degenerated.[71] George Washington, whose efforts to prosecute the War of Independence had frequently been stymied by legislative inaction, noted that "Our Assembly has been . . . employed . . . chiefly in rectifying some of the mistakes of the last, and committing new ones for emendations at the next."[72]

Marshall expressed similar frustration in a letter to Colonel Leven Powell of Loudoun county on December 8, 1783. Powell, the veteran commander of the 16th Virginia regiment who later became one of the few Federalists to represent the state of Congress, was one of Marshall's first clients. In early 1783 he wrote to inquire about the status of his case.[73] Marshall replied that the matter would be tried shortly and then sought to bring Powell up to date on events in Richmond. "This long session [of the general assembly] has not produced a single bill of Public importance, except for the readmission of Commutables."[74] "A bill for the regulation of elections and enforcing the attendance of members is now on the Carpet, and will probably pass. It contains a good deal of necessary matter with some things that appear to me to be impracticable. It is surprising that Gentlemen of character cannot dismiss their private animosities, but will bring them in the Assembly."[75]

Three days later Marshall repeated those sentiments in a letter to James

Monroe, who had recently been elected as one of Virginia's delegates to the Continental Congress, then meeting in Annapolis.[76] No one at this time was closer to Marshall than Monroe. The two men had known each other since the 1760s when they were schoolboys at the Reverend Campbell's academy in Washington parish. They had shared the same cabin at Valley Forge and been elected to the House of Delegates and the council of state the same year. Both were fledgling lawyers and prominent veterans of the Virginia Line, and they shared a fondness for frolic and good times.[77] During lulls in the proceedings in Richmond, especially in the late afternoons and evenings, they whiled away many hours playing cards and billiards at Formicola's, the town's most popular tavern, owned by a recent Italian immigrant, Serrafino Formicola.[78] Whenever a visiting acting troupe came to town, they invariably attended at least one performance together.[79] Thanks to Monroe, who retained most of his incoming letters, a portion of their correspondence survives. It reveals the frankness and, occasionally, the intimacy that existed between the two.

Marshall, who was looking after Monroe's interests in Kentucky, asked him about the status of his land warrant for service in the revolution.[80] He then told Monroe about proceedings in the House. "The Commutable bill has at length passed," and "the attention of the house . . . has been so fixed on the citizen bill that they have scarcely thought on any other subject."[81] Marshall noted that the legislature was ready to cede the Northwest Territory to Congress, but that negotiations were not yet complete.[82]

Monroe replied three weeks later. He asked Marshall to oversee the issuance of his military warrant for western lands[83] and then described the retirement ceremony of General Washington, who had resigned his commission as commander in chief on December 23, 1783. Monroe asked Marshall to look after his "pecuniary interests" while he was away and said how much he regretted recent action by the Virginia legislature to exclude members of the Continental Congress from serving simultaneously in the House of Delegates.[84] He also enclosed a draft resolution that he thought the legislature might use for the cession of the Northwest Territory.

Marshall was deeply moved by Monroe's description of Washington's farewell. "At length then the military career of the greatest man on earth is closed," he replied on January 3, 1784. "May happiness attend him wherever he goes. May he long enjoy those blessings he has secured to his country. When I speak or think of that superior Man my heart overflows with gratitude. May he ever experience from his Countrymen those attentions which such sentiments of themselves produce."[85]

For the next several months Marshall continued to handle Monroe's affairs in Richmond.[86] Monroe urged him to use his influence to hasten the payment of whatever funds might be forthcoming for his service on the council of state. The correspondence reveals the tenuous financial condition of the Old Dominion. The state was broke. Wartime paper money had been withdrawn from circulation, and there was a desperate shortage of hard currency.[87] Marshall told Monroe that he was unable to help. "The exertions of the Treasurer [Jaquelin Ambler] and your other friends here have been ineffectual. There is not one shilling in the Treasury and the keeper of it could not borrow one on the faith of the government. The extreme inclemency of the season has rendered it impossible for the Sheriffs to make [tax] collections and I have my fears that you will not receive [your pay] till some time in April."[88] To make a bad situation worse, Marshall said he had had to fend off some of Monroe's creditors. "I am pressed warmly by [Samuel] Eng [a Richmond merchant] for money, and your old Landlady Mrs. Shera begins now to be a little clamorous."

After the bad news, Marshall turned to lighter subjects. The future chief justice and the fifth President of the United States, then in their late twenties, were like most young men that age. Female virtues were always worth a few words: "This cold weather has operated like magic on our youth," he told Monroe. "They feel the necessity of artificial heat, and quite wearied with lying alone, are all treading the broad road to Matrimony. Little Stewart (could you believe it?) will be married on Thursday to Kitty Hare, and Mr. Dunn will bear your old acquaintance Miss Shera. Tabby Eppes has grown quite fat and buxom, her charms are renovated, and to see her and to love her are now synonymous terms."

In late 1783 Marshall's law practice was still struggling. The fact that he was a member of the council of state, affiliated professionally with Edmund Randolph, and linked personally with the Amblers gave him an advantage. But lawyers, especially young lawyers back from the war, were abundant in Richmond, and the competition for clients was intense. Marshall's account book indicates that during the final quarter of that year he collected only six fees for a total of £5 and a few shillings. That was little more than he won at whist and backgammon,[89] and certainly not enough to support himself and Polly. In fact, establishing their new household cost Marshall considerably more than he was earning.[90] His records show that for the last three months of 1783 his outlay totaled slightly more than £400.[91] Almost all of that was for daily household expenses, furnishings, clothing for Polly and the servants, and Marshall's occasional losses at cards. His income for the same period was £313.

The future chief justice made up the difference temporarily from monies he was holding for Kentucky land purchases. People wishing to invest in Kentucky would often give Marshall the funds to cover his father's surveyor fees. He simply lumped that money with his own income in his account book until such time as he disbursed the funds to the appropriate state agency. In effect, Marshall was giving himself an interest-free loan until his financial situation improved. Today we would question the propriety of such practices, and an attorney would be disciplined severely for commingling a client's money with his own. In 1783, however, there was no expectation that trust funds would be segregated from a lawyer's personal account. Indeed, it was not until well over a century later that regulations to that effect were adopted.* No one appears to have been injured by Marshall's action, and when he received his back pay as a member of council, the purchases were made good.[92]

Marshall's situation was further complicated by the fact that the judges of the general and chancery courts before which he practiced were becoming increasingly uncomfortable with a member of the council of state appearing before them. The Posey affair had undoubtedly colored their judgment, for it underlined the council's ultimate authority to remove a judge. In the eyes of some judges, Marshall's status as a council member gave him unfair leverage.[93]

Marshall decided he had to choose. He could either remain on the council of state and pursue a political career, or he could resign from the council, forfeit the income, and practice law full time. Although his law practice was still struggling, things were beginning to improve. During the first quarter of 1784, his fees totaled £40 and his reputation as an attorney was spreading quickly.[94] Nevertheless, to devote himself entirely to the law would be a gamble. Before choosing, Marshall prudently decided to test the political waters in Fauquier county to ascertain whether he might regain his seat in the House of Delegates. Service in the House, which presented no impediment to practicing before the judges, would enable Marshall to remain active in politics. It would also provide social status and a small additional income. With this in mind, Marshall made a brief trip to Oak Hill in late March, and apparently found the political climate congenial.[95] On April 1, 1784, he submitted his resignation from the council of state to Governor Harrison.[96]

Once Marshall was able to devote himself to the practice of law, his fi-

---

*According to Michael Rigsby, counsel for the Virginia State Bar, "The concept of fiduciary responsibility was unknown in eighteenth-century America. Consequently, practicing lawyers would not have been under any obligation to keep their funds segregated from trust funds of their clients. A regulatory scheme that addressed the issue of distinction was not adopted until 1908 at the national level, when the American Bar Association established a code of ethics, and it was not until 1971 when the State of Virginia prohibited the commingling of funds." Telephone interview, March 19, 1993. Also see *Ethics and the Legal Profession* 26, 34–36, Michael Davis and Frederick A. Elliston, eds. (Buffalo: Prometheus Books, 1986); Mark M. Ortin, *Legal Ethics* 12–18 (Toronto: Cartwright, 1957); and especially, Anton Hermann Chroust, 2 *The Rise of the Legal Profession in America* 261–265 (Norman: University of Oklahoma Press, 1965). For eighteenth-century Virginia legislation regulating the practice of law, but which does not prohibit the commingling of funds, see 9 Hening 404; 12 Hening 36, 339–340, 473.

nancial situation improved dramatically.[97] Albert Gallatin, a recent immigrant from Switzerland who lived in Richmond from 1783 until 1787 and who subsequently became Thomas Jefferson's secretary of the treasury, wrote with nostalgia about his early years in Virginia. Many persons had encouraged him, said Gallatin, but he chose to mention only two: Patrick Henry and John Marshall. Henry encouraged Gallatin to enter politics, and Marshall, "who, though but a young lawyer in 1783, was almost at the head of the bar in 1786, offered to take me in his office without a fee, and assured me that I would become a distinguished lawyer."[98]

Between his old friends from the Virginia Line and his in-laws, Marshall had a ready-made clientele. In May 1784 John Ambler, Polly's cousin, retained him to handle the Ambler family's extensive litigation.[99] At the time, John Ambler was considered to be the richest man in Virginia, having inherited Jamestown Island and numerous other estates. His business affairs were complex, and he could afford the best legal talent in the state. His choice of Marshall was a notable acknowledgment of the future chief justice's ability at the bar. The two men became close friends, and after the death of his own wife in 1787, John Ambler married Marshall's sister Lucy. Later he joined with Marshall, Henry Lee, Rawleigh Colston, and Marshall's brother James to purchase the residue of the Fairfax estate from the Proprietor's heirs.

The fact that John Ambler entrusted his legal affairs to Marshall encouraged other clients to come his way. Marshall's fee income, paltry in 1783, exceeded £1,000 in 1786. That was more than the governor of Virginia was paid,[100] and Marshall's income remained at that level throughout his years of practice in Richmond.[101] He was soon so well established that his name appeared alongside those of Edmund Randolph, Henry Tazewell, John Taylor, and Charles Lee in a paid advertisement in the *Virginia Gazette* announcing that they had agreed among themselves not to undertake any case unless the fee, which was fixed by statute, was paid in advance.[102] The advertisement suggests that the leaders of Richmond's legal fraternity were experiencing difficulty collecting fees from their clients. They may also have been worried about cost-cutting and had agreed not to engage in the practice.

In the spring of 1784, Marshall was back in the legislature.[103] On May 15, shortly after the House of Delegates convened, he wrote to Monroe about the session. As usual, Patrick Henry was a force to be reckoned with. "Mr. Henry arrived yesterday and appears to be charged high with postponement of taxes. If you wish to see a part of the first speech he will make on this subject versified turn to [Charles] Churchill's prophecy of famine and read his description of the highlands of Scotland," a literary allusion in keeping with Marshall's fondness for English poetry.[104]

In the House, Marshall pressed for the adoption of a circuit court system to replace the old Virginia tradition of having county magistrates try most cases.[105] The magistrates were usually lay persons with no judicial experience, whereas the circuit court judges would be lawyers. Opposition to the change was intense. On June 15, 1784, Marshall explained the problem to Charles Simms of Fairfax county, a former officer of the Virginia Line who had become one of his clients. "Those Magistrates who are tenacious of authority will not assent to anything which may diminish their ideal dignity and put into the hands of others a power which they will not exercise themselves."[106] In addition, many county court lawyers "are suspicious that they do not possess abilities or knowledge sufficient to enable them to stand before judges of law." As a result, "every attempt to alter and amend the county court establishment has been ineffectual."

The problem of county court reform was not simply a question of judicial competence. Local magistrates, chosen from the leading citizens of the neighborhood, generally favored local litigants. Reflecting the views of their constituents, they were inclined to assist debtors and were reluctant to order measures such as mortgage foreclosures which would imperil a family's livelihood. Circuit judges, by contrast, were trained in the law, where the rights of creditors were amply protected, and usually they were not from the immediate area, making it less likely that they would be influenced by solicitude for friends and neighbors.

Marshall's sponsorship of the circuit court bill was motivated as much by his commitment to the rights of property as it was by his desire to enhance the quality of local courts in Virginia. Nevertheless, in 1784, court reform was a losing cause. "There are many members of the House of Delegates," he told Simms, "who really appear to be determined against every measure which may expedite and facilitate the business of recovering debts and compelling a strict compliance with contracts. These are sufficient to throw impediments in the way of any improvements on our judiciary system tho they are not so powerful as to shut up our courts altogether."[107]

In June the Continental Congress adjourned for the first time since 1775, and Monroe returned briefly to Richmond before undertaking an expedition to the Northwest Territory. He and Marshall saw each other frequently.[108] They gambled at Formicola's,[109] went to the races, and on at least three occasions that summer went together to the theater.*[110] Polly was

---

*Marshall was an avid theatergoer at a time when the theater was considered beyond the pale by much of America's religious establishment. His surviving letters make no mention of the plays he saw, but his account book indicates that he attended virtually every new performance that came to Richmond. In the summer of 1784, the Dennis Ryan Company, having played in New York, Baltimore, and Annapolis, opened in town. Their repertoire included works by Molière, Sheridan, Alexander Lee, and John O'Keefe. As a reflection of Marshall's interest in the theater, when Richmond opened a new civic theater in 1838, it was named in his honor.

eight months' pregnant and did not accompany them. On July 24, 1784, Polly and John's first child was born, a son named Thomas, after Marshall's father. The baby was delivered by a local midwife, to whom Marshall paid £11 8s.[111] Shortly afterward he engaged a nurse for Polly, who had had a difficult childbirth and who remained in poor health.

When the legislature met for its fall session in late October, Marshall, a seasoned veteran, played an active role. Though he complained to Monroe in early December that "we have as yet done nothing,"[112] the session proved to be one of the general assembly's most productive. The circuit court bill that Marshall favored was again defeated, but the assembly passed two important measures for extending the navigation of the James and Potomac rivers above the fall line.[113] Supported strongly by George Washington, Marshall, and the delegates from the west, the bills authorized construction of the Chesapeake and Ohio Canal linking the Potomac with the Ohio, and the Kanawha Canal joining the James with the Great Kanawha River in West Virginia. The effect would be to open the western lands to waterborne commerce from coastal Virginia and provide an alternative to the route down the Mississippi, the mouth of which was controlled by Spain. In addition, the legislature granted the inventor James Rumsey a ten-year monopoly to build a steamboat using an engine he had recently developed.[114]

In several important areas, however, the legislature failed to take action. The complex question of debts owed to British creditors remained unresolved, and a bill introduced by Patrick Henry to encourage the intermarriage of whites and Indians was defeated.[115] Marshall was disappointed on both counts. He favored paying British debts in full because the failure to do so, he told Monroe, "affords a pretext to the British to retain possession of the forts on the [Great] lakes." In Marshall's view, Virginia's refusal to pay the debts was a violation of the 1783 Treaty of Paris in which Great Britain had recognized American independence,*[116] and represented the unwarranted intrusion of a state into foreign affairs. "I have ever considered [the failure to comply with the treaty] as a measure tending to weaken the federal bands which in my conception are too weak already."[117] As for the intermarriage legislation, Marshall thought it "would be good for this country"

---

*The Treaty of Paris was a *quid pro quo*. In return for independence, the United States promised (Article 4) to reinstate all debts owed by Americans to British creditors. But the treaty was signed on behalf of the United States by the Continental Congress, which had no authority to force the individual states to comply. Virginia, where anti-British sentiment ran strongest, and where the debts were highest, took the lead in erecting impediments to the treaty's execution. In June 1784 the Virginia assembly passed a resolution refusing compliance unless Britain provided compensation for slaves taken from the state. During the October 1784 session, the House of Delegates reversed itself and agreed to provide the required funds to Britain in seven annual payments, but the state Senate refused to agree, killing the legislation.

and deplored its defeat. "Our prejudices oppose themselves to our interests and operate too powerfully for them," he told Monroe.[118] Marshall's sensitivity to the Indians' cause was heartfelt. Fifty years later, in his bitter standoff with President Andrew Jackson over the treaty rights of the Cherokee Nation, he wrote with anguish about "a people once numerous, powerful, and truly independent" who were "gradually sinking beneath our arts and our arms."[119]

When the legislature adjourned in January 1785, Marshall chose not to seek reelection. Later that spring he joined with James Madison, Patrick Henry, Edmund Randolph, James Monroe, Spencer Roane, and two dozen other leading figures in Virginia politics to found the Virginia Constitution Society. The organization sought to provide a forum for the discussion of matters scheduled to come before the legislature.[120] According to a statement in the *Virginia Gazette*, the founders "having associated for the purpose of preserving . . . those pure and sacred principles of liberty . . . and being convinced that the surest mode to secure republican . . . government from lapsing into tyranny is by giving free and frequent information to the people . . . do most solemnly pledge ourselves to . . . keep a watchful eye over the great fundamental rights of the people."[121] Among the dangers the founders promised to guard against were "the innovations of ambition and the designs of faction." The society reflected a rush of enthusiasm in the aftermath of American independence. It met three times in June 1785 but issued no reports and eventually lapsed.

By now Marshall had fixed his future on practicing law in Richmond. As he advised Charles Simms, "My present plan is to pass my summers at Oak Hill and my winters here in Richmond."[122] Marshall's plan advanced considerably in March 1785 with two property transfers, both of which reflected the importance of family in postcolonial Virginia. On March 15 Marshall bought a half-acre lot in the core of Richmond from his father-in-law for a reported price of £10.[123] The transfer was most likely a gift since Marshall's account book indicates that he made no payment.[124] At the same time, he received title to Oak Hill from his father, who had decided to move the family permanently to Kentucky. The deed recorded in Fauquier county indicates that Marshall paid his father a nominal 5s for the estate.[125] Whether additional consideration changed hands is unknown, but also unlikely. Thomas Marshall was well on his way to accumulating a fortune in Kentucky land holdings and no longer needed Oak Hill. Marshall, on the other hand, intended to remain in Virginia. He and his father had always been close, and the transfer arrangement would keep Oak Hill in the family.

In 1785 Marshall set down roots in Richmond. In addition to helping found the first volunteer fire company,[126] he offered himself as a candidate for the city council. There were seventy-six contestants for sixteen posts, and Marshall finished second in the balloting.[127] When the council convened on July 7, he was chosen city recorder, a quasi-judicial post that entailed sitting as a magistrate on the Richmond City hustings court.[128] The hustings court handled minor civil and criminal cases and acted as the city's executive. It appointed and supervised the work of the city officials, granted licenses, and set prices for taverns and other public houses.[129] The trial court itself met monthly, and Marshall served as a magistrate for three years. This was his only judicial experience prior to being appointed Chief Justice of the United States sixteen years later.

Marshall's law practice grew steadily. He spent much of his time on routine matters, such as preparing wills and deeds or advising clients on possible litigation. He represented creditors trying to collect debts and debtors trying to avoid payment. He defended criminals, war veterans, and members of the gentry—anyone who sought his services. The spring and fall terms of the general court, chancery, and the court of appeals were the busiest times for Marshall, some days requiring his constant attendance in the courts.

Marshall's first major case, and his first argument before the court of appeals, occurred in the spring of 1786. He was engaged by the executors of Lord Fairfax to represent their interests in *Hite v. Fairfax*,[130] an important case testing the validity of the Proprietor's original grant to the northern neck. The issue stemmed from competing claims to some 54,000 acres of land located near the southern boundary of the proprietary. The litigation affected not only the claims of Hite's and Fairfax's executors but also brought into question all land titles purchased from Lord Fairfax in the vast area between the Potomac and the Rappahanock. The case was further complicated by the prevailing political winds in Virginia. Independence had brought with it a rising sentiment in favor of sequestering the proprietary lands and overturning the Fairfax title.[131] In fact, it was widely assumed that the court of appeals would administer the coup de grâce to the northern neck proprietary.[132]

The facts of *Hite v. Fairfax* are straightforward. In 1735 Governor William Gooch issued a patent to Jost Hite for 54,000 acres. The patent was in defiance of the earlier royal grant to Lord Fairfax, which the Virginia government at that time disputed. In 1741 Britain's privy council ruled that the lands granted to Hite fell within the proprietorship. To settle the matter, Lord Fairfax agreed to issue a patent for the land to Hite, who would thereupon be obliged to pay quitrents. However, when Hite presented his surveys, Fairfax declined to issue the patent, asserting that Hite's claim included only fertile bottomlands, rendering the adjacent upland areas isolated and inaccessible. Litigation began in 1749 when Hite filed suit to secure title. For a variety of reasons, the case dragged on until 1769, when the general court ruled in favor of Hite and established a commission of seven persons, including Thomas Marshall, to examine the surveys presented by Hite and determine ownership. When the commission report was filed in 1771, the general court issued a final decree, which both parties appealed once again to Britain's privy council. The outbreak of the revolution stayed further proceedings, and in 1780 the case was placed on the docket of the court of appeals. It was carried over from term to term until it finally came before the court on April 29, 1786.[133]

Both sides deployed impressive legal talent. The Hite interests were represented by Edmund Randolph and John Taylor of Caroline, while the Fairfax claim was put forward by Jerman Baker and Marshall. The oral argument lasted six days. Randolph spoke first. Working from elaborate notes, he stressed the equity claim of his clients rather than the strict rules of property, attempting to convert the issue into a dispute between "poor farmers" and "rich lords."[134] Jerman Baker spoke next and argued that the Hites were trespassers since their claim was based on an unauthorized act by the colonial government in 1735. When Taylor's turn came, he questioned the legitimacy of the original royal grant to Lord Fairfax, arguing that it was made and confirmed by Charles II and James II when neither of them was on the throne.

Marshall spoke last, summarizing the case for Fairfax. "From a bare perusal of the papers," he said:

> I should never have apprehended that it would be necessary to defend the title of Lord Fairfax to the northern neck. The long and quiet possession of himself and his predecessors; the acquiescence of the country; the several grants of the crown, together with the various acts of [the] assembly recognizing, and . . . admitting his right, seem to have fixed it on a foundation, not only not to be shaken, but even not to be attempted to be shaken.[135]

Marshall hinged his argument on the fact that Hite had what lawyers call "constructive notice" of Fairfax's prior claim to the land.

> To penetrate into the human mind, and determine with absolute certainty how far particular facts have actually come to the knowledge of a man, is sometimes beyond the reach of the court; but that which a prudent man might and ought to have known, and that which should have excited enquiry, and prompted him to have searched into title, will always be deemed notice to a purchaser.

Unlike his fellow advocates, who relied on their skill at declamation and tended to eschew precedent and authority, Marshall cited Coke and Blackstone extensively to authenticate the validity of the royal grant to Lord Fairfax. The court ultimately held in favor of Hite's claim, but in so doing it reaffirmed the Proprietor's original title. Fairfax's heirs were ordered to convey the lands in question to Hite's descendants.[136] That meant that in the court's view, the Fairfax heirs possessed a valid title to convey. Although they had lost the battle to retain title to the lands in question, the Fairfax heirs had won a far more important victory. In effect, Marshall had taken a major step toward solidifying the property interests of all those in the northern neck who traced their title to Lord Fairfax. Rather than extinguish the proprietary, the decision in *Hite v. Fairfax* spurred further litigation based on the Fairfax title. That litigation would occupy Marshall for the rest of his life. His appearance in this landmark case also solidified his reputation as one of the leaders of the Virginia bar.[137] A fellow lawyer, writing shortly afterward, placed Marshall "at the head of the practice."[138]

That spring Marshall and Polly eagerly anticipated the birth of their second child. On June 15 Rebecca, named after Polly's mother, was born. But tragedy struck quickly. For causes unknown, the infant died five days later. Polly and Marshall were devastated. Polly, at twenty, lacked Marshall's resiliency and continued to grieve over her daughter's death. In September, perhaps as a result of her grief, Polly suffered the miscarriage of another pregnancy and had a mental breakdown.[139] Marshall engaged a neighborhood woman, Betsy Munkus, to help take care of her,[140] and he began to assume responsibility for running the household—doing the shopping, helping with the cleaning, and overseeing the entire array of domestic chores that few men even acknowledged in the late eighteenth century.

In a small town like Richmond, such personal misfortune rarely failed to give rise to gossip that was invariably hurtful. Polly's depression proved to be no exception. Jefferson's daughter Martha, who was living in the capital at the time, wrote to her father that "Mrs. Marshall, once Miss Ambler, is Insane, the loss of two Children is thought to have Occasioned it."[141] Martha's comments about Polly's condition were not confined to her correspondence, and made no friends for her or her father in the Marshall and Ambler households. Polly recovered gradually but never regained her youthful vitality. As it became apparent that she had inherited her mother's frail constitution, Polly gained an ever higher place in her husband's affection. This did not pass unnoticed. Indeed, some speculated that Polly's increasing frailty was not unrelated to the attention Marshall paid to her.[142]

In the autumn of 1786 Marshall made his first and only attempt for statewide office. After one year as governor, Patrick Henry had decided to step down, and Edmund Randolph was elected by the House of Delegates to replace him. That left the attorney general's office vacant, and Marshall decided to seek it. His opponent was his old army friend James Innes.[143] The contest reflected personality and family alliances more than issues, and Innes won a narrow victory.[144] Madison wrote to Jefferson that "Mr. Marshall had a handsome vote."[145] Marshall took the defeat in stride. Randolph had officially turned his law practice over to him,[146] and for the first time Marshall had as many clients as he could handle. One particularly fruitful area of litigation proved to be land titles in the northern neck. Following the decision in *Hite v. Fairfax*, Marshall filed ten bills in chancery on behalf of persons who had bought their land from the Proprietor.[147]

Marshall's political views had crystallized by this time. His pragmatic nature resisted the adoption of a large number of a priori principles, but on four issues his views were firm. He believed in a strong central government, the supremacy of the constitution, the necessity for an independent judiciary, and the unalienable right to possess, enjoy, and augment private property. Marshall's views were consistent with the major currents of eighteenth-century American thought. Locke, Blackstone, Hume, and Montesquieu— the writers most often cited in postcolonial America—stressed that the purpose of government was to protect private rights, especially the right to property, and that the tyranny of the majority was as much to be feared as the tyranny of the crown.

In Marshall's opinion, the power of government derived from the express authority granted by the people. Unlike the British parliament, the American government was not sovereign, and when it acted in the economic sphere, it was bound by the same laws of contract as a private citizen. This view became the law of the land in such leading decisions of the Marshall Court as *Fletcher v. Peck*[148] and the *Dartmouth College* case.[149] The holdings in those cases reaffirmed the vested rights of property against governmental intrusion and helped set the stage for the growth of American capitalism.

Marshall's beliefs had been evolving over the course of his adult life. His commitment to a strong central government was formed during the Revolution. His dedication to the supremacy of the constitution and the independence of the judiciary was reinforced by the Posey affair in 1783. His devotion to the vested rights of property was strengthened by the *Hite v. Fairfax* case and by a second dispute later that year, which thrust Marshall into a quasi-judicial role. The issue involved a long-standing claim of a Philadelphia merchant, Simon Nathan, against the state of Virginia.[150] During the Revolution, Nathan furnished military supplies to General George Rogers Clark and accepted in return several bills of exchange for the value of the goods. Nathan claimed he was entitled to payment in hard currency, but Virginia sought to pay the debt in depreciated paper money, which at the time was worth only 5 percent of its face value. The dispute dragged on for several years until Nathan agreed to submit the matter to arbitration. The Virginia general assembly thereupon appointed Marshall and another prominent lawyer, Cyrus Griffin,* to examine the issue and recommend a settlement.

Because Marshall was the son-in-law of Virginia's treasurer, there may have been some expectation that he would favor the state's position. If that was the case, the assembly was to be gravely disappointed. On December 28, 1786, Marshall and Griffin issued their report and found on all counts in favor of Nathan. "First," they said, "there is no convincing testimony that the bills in question were drawn for depreciated money; secondly, there are considerable proofs that the bills in question were purchased by Mr. Nathan as bills drawn for specie value."[151] Marshall and Griffin said that Virginia could be relieved of its obligation only if fraud on the part of Nathan could be proved, and added that "no such evidence has been adduced."[152]

Disappointed though the general assembly may have been, it acquiesced in the award and ordered the state's executive to pay Nathan what was due.[153] Marshall had served notice that a contract was a contract and that the state of Virginia could not arbitrarily alter its terms. That idea, and its underlying assumptions that property rights were unalienable, became the centerpiece of Marshall's judicial philosophy.

Marshall saw Virginia's effort to revalue its debt to Nathan as a disturbing example of the increasing attacks on private property being made in the name of popular sovereignty. When debt-burdened farmers in western Massachusetts forcibly prevented the courts from proceeding with foreclosure actions, the future chief justice feared the worst. "All is gloom in the eastern states," he wrote to James Wilkinson in early January 1787.[154] "Massachusetts is rent into two equal factions and an appeal I fear has by this time been made to the God of battles." Marshall was referring to the revolt of Daniel Shays, a former captain in the Massachusetts Line, who at that moment was leading a force of 1,100 men toward Springfield to prevent the state supreme court from convening.

"We have contradictory accounts of the motives of the insurgents," said Marshall. "We are sometimes informed that they are a British faction supported secretly from Canada . . . [while] at other times we are told that it is a mere contest for power between [James] Bowdoin [the conservative governor of Massachusetts] and [former governor John] Hancock, and that the

---

*At the time of his appointment, Griffin was a judge of the Confederation's Court of Appeals in Cases of Capture and also a member of the House of Delegates from Lancaster county. Later he served as the last president of the Continental Congress and subsequently became the first judge appointed to the United States District Court in Virginia. 7 *Dictionary of American Biography* 618–619 (New York: Charles Scribner's Sons, 1931).

Hancock faction are aiming at the destruction of all public securities and the subversion of all public faith." To Marshall, that struck at the essential core of government. Nothing was more vital than the preservation of law and order, and nothing was more important than the maintenance of the full faith and credit of the government. "These violent, I fear bloody, dissentions in a state I had thought inferior in wisdom and virtue to none in the union . . . cast a deep shade over that bright prospect which the revolution in America and the establishment of our free governments had opened to the votaires of liberty throughout the globe." Marshall's optimism faded in the face of the threat of anarchy and insurrection. "I fear [this means] that those have truth on their side who say that man is incapable of governing himself. I fear we may live to see another revolution."[155]

Marshall attributed the revolt in Massachusetts to the burden of taxes required to pay the massive public debt incurred during the revolution and to "lax notions" pertaining to the obligation of contract.[156] Hancock's proposed solution of currency devaluation struck Marshall as an unwarranted attack on private property. He also found the attempt of the insurrectionists to disrupt the normal administration of justice particularly reprehensible and deplored "the licentious and turbulent spirit" that claimed to act "in the name of the people."[157]

Shays's Rebellion was forcibly put down by local Massachusetts militia in a brief battle at Springfield on January 25, 1787. In a second encounter, on February 4, Shays's men were routed and the uprising effectively ended. Nevertheless, the rebellion had a profound impact on public opinion, and as Marshall predicted, it delighted the Tories, who viewed it as proof that Americans were incapable of governing themselves. The revolt alarmed virtually every U.S. leader except Jefferson. From his vantage point in Paris as American minister to France, the future president wrote wistfully that "the tree of liberty must be refreshed from time to time with the blood of patriots and tyrants. It is its natural manure."[158]

Jefferson notwithstanding, Shays's Rebellion provided a needed catalyst for those who sought to establish a more effective national government. After the revolt was put down, Marshall wrote to Arthur Lee, who was then in New York as a member of the Confederation's treasury board. Marshall congratulated Lee "on the prospect of reestablishing order and good government in Massachusetts. I think their government will now stand more firmly than before the insurrection provided some examples are made in order to impress on the minds of the people a conviction that punishment will surely follow an attempt to subvert the laws and government of the Commonwealth."[159]

In Virginia, there was little prospect of open revolt, and the House of Delegates had held firm against the reintroduction of paper money.[160] However, elections that spring would provide an important test, and Marshall worried about the outcome. "Our attention is now entirely turned towards the next elections," he told Lee. "The debtors are as usual endeavoring to come into the Assembly and as usual I fear they will succeed."[161] To help head off that danger, Marshall decided to run once again for the House of Delegates, this time offering himself as a candidate from Richmond's Henrico county. Marshall's personal popularity, his work on the hustings court, and his deep involvement in Richmond's civic affairs assured his election.[162]

Under Virginia's revised statutes, the House of Delegates would not convene until October, but the call for a federal convention to meet in Philadelphia had already been issued. Hard on the heels of Shays's Rebellion, the Continental Congress had invited each of the states to send delegates to convene in May "for the sole and express purpose of revising the Articles of Confederation" to "render the federal constitution adequate to the exigencies of government, and the preservation of the union."

The federal convention met in Philadelphia from May 25 to September 17, 1787. Fifty-five delegates from twelve states (Rhode Island boycotted the convention) worked for four months to produce a draft Constitution. It satisfied no one fully. The elaborate system of checks and balances, the separation of legislative, executive, and judicial authority, and the division of power between the national and state governments were novel experiments inspired by a spirit of accommodation rather than any abstract theory of government. Alexander Hamilton, in momentary despair, called the resulting Constitution "a weak and worthless fabric." Delegate Luther Martin of Maryland regarded it as "a stab in the back of the goddess of liberty." Daniel Carroll, also from Maryland, called it "the Continental Congress in two volumes instead of one."

It fell to Benjamin Franklin and James Madison to put the work of the convention into perspective. "The older I grow, the more apt I am to doubt my own judgment," said the octogenarian Franklin. Not only was he astonished that a constitution that was the product of so many compromises could be so good, but "it will astonish our enemies, who are waiting with confidence to hear that our councils are confounded. . . . Thus I consent, Sir, to this Constitution because I expect no better, and because I am not sure that it is not the best." Madison, in transmitting the draft Constitution to the Continental Congress, wrote that "In all our deliberations . . . we kept steadily in our view . . . the consolidation of the Union, in which is involved our prosperity, felicity, safety, perhaps our national existence. . . . The Constitution, which we now present, is the result of a spirit of amity, and of that neutral deference and concession which the peculiarity of our political situation rendered indispensable."[163]

Anticipating that many state legislators might be hostile to the new Constitution, the Framers provided for a special ratification convention to be called in each state. This procedure yielded two important advantages. First, it would permit those who supported the Constitution to elect delegates, including judges and ministers, who were barred from the legislature. Second, it would lend credence to the argument that the Constitution was ratified by the people in special conventions and not by the state governments. Years later, in the hands of the Marshall Court, the argument that the Constitution emerged from the people, not the states, and that the people had made it supreme would become the ultimate rationale for national power. The initial task, however, was to secure ratification, and in Virginia it was too early to predict the outcome.

The House of Delegates that convened in October 1787 was the usual mixed bag of Virginia politics. Traditional leaders such as Patrick Henry, George Mason, and George Nicholas were on hand. So too were Marshall and Monroe, both eager to take part in the constitutional debate. There were also some glaring absences, given the import of the issue before the House. Experienced old hands like Pendleton, Wythe, and Blair were on the bench, Jefferson was representing the United States in Paris, Edmund Randolph was governor, and Madison had gone to New York to direct federalist efforts in the east. Absent too were the titular leaders of the federalist and antifederalist forces, George Washington and Richard Henry Lee. Washington, a staunch supporter of the draft Constitution, quietly added his enormous prestige to secure its adoption, while Lee would prove to be its most perceptive and harshest critic. But both men worked from the sidelines.

The atmosphere in Richmond was charged with anticipation. By October 14 a quorum had assembled and the capital was rife with rumors. A Richmond law student wrote that "Every corner of the city resounds with politicks."[164] A delegate noted that the Constitution "affords matter for conversation to every rank of beings from the Governor to the door keeper," adding that "the opinions appear to be as various as the persons possessing them."[165] James Monroe wrote that it was creating a greater disagreement "among people of character than any issue since the Revolution."[166] Even an old veteran of the legislature like Patrick Henry noticed the eagerness with which the delegates assembled. "Such is the warmth of all the Members of Assembly concerning the new Constitution, that no kind of Business can be done 'til that is considered," he wrote to his brother-in-law in Botetourt county.[167]

Initially those in favor of ratification appeared to have the edge. Madison, who was following events in Virginia closely, wrote to Jefferson that "a very decided majority of the Assembly is said to be zealously in favor of the New Constitution."[168] He warned, however, that it would not be clear sailing. "Individuals of great weight both within and without the Legislature are opposed to it." In particular, Madison mentioned Patrick Henry, the Nelsons, the Cabells, St. George Tucker, John Taylor of Caroline, and "most of the judges." Madison did not mention George Mason or Edmund Randolph, both of whom had been delegates to the Philadelphia convention and both of whom had refused to sign the final draft. How they would react in the coming debate would be crucial.

The opening session of the House provided little in the way of information. Randolph was playing his cards close to his chest, and his address as governor was noncommittal. He noted nineteen items on which he hoped the legislature would take action. The Constitution ranked fourteenth. "The Constitution, proposed by the late Federal Convention has been transmitted to me officially from Congress. I beg leave therefore now to enclose it."[169] That was all. No words of support, and no request to call the ratification convention the Constitution required.

The next day the House of Delegates referred the Constitution to the committee of the whole, but did not begin debate until a week later. Despite the initial groundswell of enthusiasm for ratification, it had become painfully apparent that with Madison absent and Randolph refusing to take sides, the federalist forces in the House were in disarray. Responsibility for introducing the motion calling for a state convention fell to Francis Corbin of Middlesex county. He was an elegant speaker but was woefully ill-suited to carry the banner for a new national government. The son of a prominent Tory who had been the royal receiver-general in Virginia, Corbin had spent the war years in England studying law. While he had not sided openly with the British, neither had he fought for independence. By presenting a man believed to be tainted with crypto-royalist sentiment as the leading spokesman for ratification, the federalists played into the opponents' hands.

The liability of having Corbin serve as spokesman became clear when Patrick Henry rose to reply. Henry's credentials as a patriot were second to none, and he led the attack with his usual gusto. He did not dispute the necessity of calling a convention to debate the Constitution, but he rejected the implication of Corbin's motion that the convention be limited simply to acceptance or rejection. The convention should be allowed to offer amendments, said Henry, and he could not support a motion that did not permit that.[170] Henry's opposition had been taken for granted, although the vehemence of his attack had not been anticipated. None of the federalists, however, were prepared for what happened next. As if on cue, George Mason waded in on Henry's side. Mason had arrived in Richmond only that morning and, as a leading figure in the Virginia establishment, had rarely agreed with Henry in the past. Now he stood with Henry shoulder to shoulder. Mason said he was convinced that "some General government" should be established, but the present proposal was "repugnant to our Highest interests." He told the delegates he would not commit the treasonable act of voting for the Constitution without amendments. In a dramatic gesture that stunned the House, Mason held his right arm aloft and shouted, "I would have lost this Hand, before it should have marked my Name to the new Government."[171]

Henry had turned the tide in the House many times before, and now he and Mason had done it again. It was at this point that Marshall intervened. Fearing a motion from Henry that would explicitly authorize amendments to the draft Constitution, Marshall proposed a compromise. He wanted to avoid an open invitation to alter the text of the document since he realized that if Virginia proposed changes, other states would feel entitled to do likewise. The delicate balance of the Constitution would be destroyed, and it would not be ratified. Marshall decided to blur the issue with a substitute motion. He moved "That the proceedings of the Federal Convention . . . ought to be submitted to a convention of the people, for their full and free investigation and discussion."[172] There was no reference to possible amendments, but neither were they precluded.

Marshall's motion broke the tension. Henry and Mason accepted the wording, and the federalist forces recognized it was the best they could get. When the vote was called, Marshall's substitute motion passed unanimously. Delegates for the convention would be elected in March 1788, and the convention would meet the first Monday in June.

Writing afterward to Madison, Randolph noted Marshall's "happy and politick resolution."[173] If the Constitution "had been propounded by the legislature to the people" on a straight up or down vote, said Randolph, "the constitution could have been rejected and the spirit of the union extinguished." Madison subsequently told Jefferson that if Henry's proposal for amendments had carried, the result would have been either a conditional ratification or a proposal for an entirely new Constitution. "In either event," said Madison, "I think the Constitution and the Union would both be endangered."[174] Marshall was always too modest to discuss the role he played at that critical juncture in the House of Delegates. But without his timely intervention, the fight for ratification in Virginia could have been lost before it began.

5

ᕦᕤ

The Fight for Ratification

When I recollect the wild and enthusiastic democracy with
which my political opinions of that day were tinctured, I
am disposed to describe my devotion to the union, and to a
government competent to its preservation, at least as much
to circumstances as to judgment.[1]

E VER SINCE HIS EXPERIENCE in the War of Independence, Marshall had stood steadfast in the belief that the survival of the United
States depended on national unity, and he now threw himself wholeheartedly into the struggle for ratification of the Constitution. The factors
that fueled his enthusiasm traced back to the political principles he held
dear. At the top of his list of concerns was what he saw as the excessive
power of the various state legislatures and their tendency to serve the interests of a growing class of debtors. He later told Story, "The questions which
were perpetually recurring [in those legislatures] brought annually into
doubt principles which I thought most sound [and] proved that everything
was afloat, and that we had no safe anchorage ground. [This] gave a high
value in my estimation to that article in the constitution which imposes restrictions on the states. I was consequently a determined advocate for its
adoption, and became a candidate for the convention to which it was to be
submitted."[2]

> The county [Henrico] in which I resided was decidedly antifederal,
> but I was at that time popular, and parties had not yet become so bit-
> ter as to extinguish private affections. A great majority of the people
> of Virginia was antifederalist; but in several of the counties most op-
> posed to the adoption of the constitution, individuals of high char-
> acter and great influence came forward as candidates and were
> elected. . . . After an ardent and eloquent discussion to which justice

has never been done . . . the question was carried in the affirmative by a majority of eight voices.[3]

When Marshall referred to questions that "were perpetually recurring" and that "brought . . . into doubt principles which I thought most sound," he meant the financial and political problems associated with a national economy burdened by excessive debt and exhausted credit. Those who owed money sought relief from their debts, usually through their influence in the state legislatures, while the propertied classes to whom money was owed worked just as assiduously to restrict debtor relief and compel strict compliance with the terms of contract. As Marshall's arbitral holding in the Nathan case demonstrated, he was firmly on the side of contract compliance and a stable currency. He deplored the threat posed by the political power of a large debtor class, insisted on the faithful fulfillment of government obligations, and saw an impartial legal system as the bulwark of individual liberty.

For Marshall, liberty centered on the right to be secure in one's property, but it also included those personal liberties that might be threatened by arbitrary power: free speech, a free press, and the right of the accused to a fair trial. He shared the views of Locke, Montesquieu, and Hume that the state was bound by the law and that its primary purpose was to protect the unalienable rights with which free men were endowed. In the battle to protect individual liberties, Marshall saw an independent judiciary as the first line of defense. One of the reasons he supported the adoption of the Constitution so vigorously was that an independent judiciary was a basic tenet of the new system.

The restrictions on the states to which Marshall referred in his letter to Story pertained to the prohibitions contained in Article I, section 10, of the Constitution. The states were enjoined from engaging in foreign affairs, coining money, issuing bills of credit, or depreciating the currency by making anything other than gold or silver legal tender for the payment of debts. In addition, state legislatures were explicitly prohibited from passing *ex post facto* laws and from impairing the obligations of contract. In the minds of the Framers, the *ex post facto* provision would limit state bankruptcy legislation,* while the contract clause would provide essential protection against most

---

*In *Calder v. Bull*, 3 Dallas 386 (1798), one of the first cases of constitutional significance to reach the Supreme Court, the *ex post facto* clause was held to apply only to laws imposing retroactive punishment in criminal cases (by creating criminal sanctions for actions that were legal when carried out or increasing the punishment set for a particular offense and applying that punishment retrospectively) and not to civil disputes. That nullified the Framers' intent. For sharp criticism of that holding, see the opinion of Justice William Johnson in *Satterlee v. Mathewson*, 2 Peters 380 (1829). Also see Suzanna Sherry, "The Founders Unwritten Constitution," 54 *University of Chicago Law Review* 1127–1177 (1987).

other forms of debtor relief. Finally, section 10 took a massive step toward the economic integration of the country by restricting the states' ability to impose import or export duties without the consent of Congress. Marshall saw these various provisions as essential ingredients in the struggle to forge a stronger union: a union that would allow the nation to grow and prosper.

In October 1787, when the House of Delegates passed Marshall's resolution calling for a ratification convention, both sides immediately began jockeying for position. The newspapers filled with articles pro and con; prospective delegates began to issue personal manifestos[4]; and in New York, Madison, Hamilton, and John Jay commenced publication of their remarkable essays defending and explaining the Constitution, *The Federalist* papers.[5] As a counterpoise to the nationalist drumbeat, George Mason issued his *Objections to the Constitution*[6]; Richard Henry Lee published what is generally regarded as the most incisive critique of national power, *Letters from the Federal Farmer*[7]; and Patrick Henry kept up a steady fusillade against the proposed Constitution in public meetings throughout Virginia.[8]

In the House of Delegates the maneuvering was intense. On November 30, 1787, the committee of the whole house reported a series of resolutions to defray the expenses of convention delegates. The resolutions included a motion offered by Patrick Henry to provide funds to send representatives to a second federal convention in the event the Virginia convention "should judge it expedient to propose amendments" to the Constitution.[9] Henry and his supporters carried that motion in the committee of the whole with sixteen votes to spare. As Randolph wrote to Madison, "the current sets violently against the Constitution."[10] Once again, Marshall went to work to fashion a compromise with Henry, and the final bill, passed on December 13, 1787, made no reference to a second federal convention.[11] Instead, it provided funds for communicating with Virginia's "sister states or the conventions thereof" and "collecting the sentiments of the union respecting the proposed federal constitution."[12] As with Marshall's earlier compromise resolution, the measure was passed by the House of Delegates unanimously.[13] It left open the possibility of amendments but deferred that decision until the convention.

With public opinion throughout the country so volatile, the federalist forces concentrated on the Virginia convention, believing that how the Old Dominion voted would determine the fate of the Union. The Framers of the Constitution had provided that the document would go into effect as soon as it was ratified by nine states. Conventions in Delaware, Pennsylvania, and New Jersey approved the document in December 1787. The vote was unanimous in Delaware and New Jersey, but in Pennsylvania, the nation's second most populous state, ratification had come only after a bitter struggle. Unwilling legislators had been taken forcibly to the statehouse to get the quorum needed to call the ratifying convention, and at the convention itself, federalist delegates stifled all opposition, not even permitting the Constitution's opponents to have their speeches printed in the record.[14]

Georgia ratified unanimously on January 2, 1788. George Washington wrote, "If a weak State with Indians on its back and the Spaniards on its flank does not see the necessity of a General Government there must I think be wickedness or insanity in the way."[15] Connecticut followed Georgia a few days later, and Massachusetts came next. An early straw vote in the Bay State convention had indicated 192 delegates against the Constitution and only 144 in favor. Unlike Virginia, where the Constitution's opponents insisted slavery would be in jeopardy under a federal system, opponents in Massachusetts asserted that the new national government would become the pawn of slaveowners in the South. But the federalists outmaneuvered their opponents in Massachusetts and ultimately won a narrow eighteen-vote victory. Maryland ratified in April 1788 and South Carolina in May. That brought the total to eight. Of the remaining states, New York and Virginia were crucial. The Virginia convention would assemble June 2 and New York, two weeks later. New Hampshire would also convene in June, but federalist forces were outnumbered in the Granite State and had adjourned an earlier convention in February to avoid defeat.[16] North Carolina and Rhode Island, both in the grip of strong antifederalist coalitions, sulked on the sidelines, their legislatures declining even to call a ratification convention.

And so it was in Virginia, the next state to meet, where the issue was joined. With one-fifth of the population of the Union (twice that of Pennsylvania, three times that of New York),[17] and over one-third of the nation's commerce, Virginia became the focus of the constitutional debate. Ironically, it was one of the few states that had prospered under the Articles of Confederation. Its ports were accessible year-round; a series of long, navigable rivers provided inexpensive avenues for commerce up to the fall line; the upland road system had become increasingly well developed; and continued immigration contributed to a rapidly growing population. Virginia's farm products, especially grain, timber, and tobacco, provided valuable cargoes for the trade ships returning to Europe, and the state's revenue from customs duties, a primary source of government income, had risen substantially during the 1780s.[18]

The Old Dominion's prosperity was not shared equally by its inhabitants, however, and a continued shortage of hard currency created serious problems for those whose credit had been exhausted—primarily the small farmers and artisans of the piedmont, the Shenandoah Valley, and the Kentucky territory. The result was an erratic distribution of sentiment favoring and opposing the Constitution. Virginians who had profited from the state's autonomy were reluctant to ratify, and those deeply in debt were afraid of the Constitution's bias toward tight money and contract compliance. Both groups opposed the diminution of state sovereignty that would result from the new federal system. Enthusiasm for the Constitution was further dampened by the prospect of having to pay the massive prewar debt owed to British creditors,[19] while the lack of a Bill of Rights, and especially a guarantee of religious freedom, turned many nonestablished faiths, particularly the Baptists, against the document. The matter of free navigation of the Mississippi also became an issue, since many in the West feared that a northern-dominated central government might conclude a treaty with Spain closing the Mississippi to navigation.[20] Finally, there was the question of slavery, which cast its shadow over every political debate in Virginia. Patrick Henry was concerned about what a strong federal government would do about slavery in the South and alternately filled his listeners with fear and laughter with his homey exclamation, "They'll free your niggers."[21]

In short, the Constitution was in trouble in Virginia and the outcome of the convention was in doubt. "So small . . . was the majority in favour," Marshall wrote, "that had the influence of character been removed, the intrinsic merits of the instrument would not have secured its adoption."[22] Patrick Henry put it more directly. "I am satisfied 4/5 of our Inhabitants are opposed to the new Scheme of Government," he wrote to General John Lamb in New York. "Indeed, in the part of this country lying north of the James River I am confident 9/10 are opposed to it. And yet strange as it may seem, the Members in Convention appear equal on both Sides; so that the Majority which way soever it goes will be small. The Friends and Seekers of Power have with their usual Subtlety wriggled themselves into the Choice of the People by assuming Shapes as various as the Faces of [the] Men address[ed] on such Occasions."[23]

In accordance with Marshall's October resolution, the election for delegates was held in each county on the first court day in March. That day varied from county to county, with tidewater counties meeting earlier than those in the West. Each county, regardless of population, was authorized two delegates. This was a sleeper clause in Marshall's motion that benefited the federalists since the plantation country where the Constitution was favored generally had a much smaller voting population than the piedmont. A contemporary assessment of the election results, compiled by a New York merchant and published in the *Massachusettts Sentinel*, reported that of the 168 delegates, the federalists had elected 85, the antifederalists 66, 3 were neutral, and 14 from the West unaccounted for.[24] Since the fourteen to be elected from the West would probably be antifederalist, the result was too close to call.[25]

The roster of convention delegates reads like a "Who's Who" of Virginia politics: the Cabells, the Lees, George and Wilson Nicholas, Marshall's friends Archibald Stuart, Bushrod Washington, and James Webb, and some forty-seven veterans of the Virginia Line, almost all of whom belonged to the strongly nationalist Society of the Cincinnati, and who formed a solid bloc of support for the Constitution. Patrick Henry and James Madison were there of course, as were Edmund Pendleton and George Mason. Chancellor Wythe and Judge John Blair were elected from York county, Attorney General James Innes from Williamsburg, and Governor Edmund Randolph and Marshall from Richmond's Henrico county. Randolph had been elected easily, but Marshall's victory over Dr. William Foushee was close, 198 votes to 187.[26] As he later told Story, the victory reflected his personal popularity, not his federalist views, since Henrico county was strongly antifederalist. In fact, one month before the election, Randolph had written to Madison that "Marshall is in danger; but F[oushee] is not popular enough on other scores to be elected, although he is perfectly a Henryite."[27] This was one of many instances in Marshall's long career when his engaging personality gave him an advantage. The voters might disagree with his politics, but they liked him and voted for him. In retrospect, it seems curious that the state's voters chose men of stature whom they liked rather than men with whom they agreed. Marshall is an obvious example, but so is Pendleton, who was elected without opposition in antifederalist Caroline county, and for that matter, Madison himself, who had to surmount substantial Baptist opposition in Orange county. This unusual circumstance was in large part responsible for Virginia's ratification of the Constitution since Madison, Pendleton, and Marshall each played an important role in the debate that ultimately gave the "yes" forces their narrow margin of victory.

The convention debate proved to be crucial, because the battle lines were not as sharply drawn as either Marshall or Henry suggested. While it is true that Madison, Marshall, and Innes favored ratifying the Constitution without amendments, and that Patrick Henry headed the faction irreconcilably opposed, most members of the convention stood somewhere in between. Some, such as Pendleton and Randolph, favored ratification first and amendments afterward.[28] Pendleton, the unquestioned leader of the tidewater conservatives, took a pragmatic tack. "In all political cases," he told Madison, "if we can't get the very best, we must take the best we can get, provided it is preferable to the thing to be changed."[29] Randolph was more cautious. He had refused to sign the final draft of the Constitution in Philadelphia because he felt it contained too many ambiguities, but after Maryland and South Carolina ratified the document, he recognized that the equation had changed. "The accession of eight states reduced our deliberations to the single question of union or no union," he told Madison.[30] As a result, he urged that amendments be added after ratification.

An even larger group of delegates, nominally headed by Mason and Monroe, favored a stronger central government but believed the Constitution should be amended before ratification. Jefferson, who followed events closely from Paris, fell into that category as well. "As to the new Constitution," he wrote to Edward Carrington, "I find myself nearly a Neutral."[31] Jefferson's lengthy critique of the document pointed out with remarkable evenhandedness its pluses and minuses.[32] The essence of Jefferson's concern was summarized best by biographer Merrill Peterson, who noted that Jefferson not only was eager for a bill of rights, but, unlike Madison and Marshall, was decidedly ambivalent about "a system rigged to substitute the countervailing forces of self-interest for the defect of public virtue and the supposed danger of majority rule."[33]

James Monroe, who, with Marshall, was one of the most prominent of Virginia's younger leaders elected to the convention, did not believe that "a conditional ratification would, in the remotest degree, endanger the Union." In his view, prior amendments were harmless. "They secure our rights without altering a single feature."[34] George Mason's opposition to ratification without amendments stemmed from his belief that, once ratified, the Constitution would never be changed. Mason was the author of the Virginia Declaration of Rights of 1776, and he genuinely feared that without a bill of rights individual liberty would be imperiled. "The laws of the general government being paramount to the laws and constitution of the several states," said Mason, "the Declaration of Rights in the separate states are no security."[35] Unlike Patrick Henry, with whom he found himself uncomfortably allied, the northern Virginia planter was not unalterably opposed to the Constitution and made it clear that he "would adopt it sooner than jeopardize the union."[36] At bottom, what Mason sought was "to give the [national] government sufficient energy, on real republican principles; but . . . to withhold such powers as are not absolutely necessary."[37] In effect, the bulk of the delegates, ranging from Pendleton and Randolph to Mason and Monroe, worked to balance the federalists' commitment to union with the antifederalists' devotion to individual liberty. "Men of intelligence, patriotism, property, and independent circumstances are thus divided," Madison wrote Jefferson.[38]

The unquestioned leader of the irreconcilables was Patrick Henry. "The first thing I have at heart is American liberty," he told his constituents, "the second thing is American union." Henry's powerful critique of a strong central government issued from an honest fear of despotic power, and many of the objections he was to raise in the convention have been raised time and again in the years that followed, although seldom with the same eloquence.

Opposite Henry, James Madison anchored the nationalist end of the spectrum. His tough-minded, interest-based view of politics defined the central thrust of the Constitution. "Let ambition counter ambition," he wrote in *Federalist 51*, and his advocacy of ratification without amendments was uncompromising. "The question on which the proposed Constitution must turn," he wrote to Edmund Pendleton, "is the simple one whether the Union shall or shall not be continued. There is in my opinion no middle ground to be taken."[39] Marshall, who admired both Henry and Madison, captured the essence of their historic confrontation. Patrick Henry was much more than an orator, said Marshall. He was "a learned lawyer, a most accurate thinker, and a profound reasoner. If I were called upon to say who of all the men I have known had the greatest power to convince, I should perhaps say Mr. Madison, while Mr. Henry had without doubt the greatest power to persuade."[40]

And so the lines were drawn. The power to convince versus the power to persuade. The Constitution would be debated and analyzed in Virginia as it would be in no other state. The arguments would be eloquent, powerful, and prophetic, and would bear comparison with those of any other assembly, in any place, at any time. In April, after his election as a delegate, Marshall bought a copy of the first volume of *The Federalist*, several hundred of which had been shipped by Madison to Richmond.[41] He also undertook an uncharacteristic effort to spruce up his appearance. His account book shows that between the end of March and the beginning of June 1788, he bought two pair of shoes, silk stockings, linen for shirts, nankin for breeches, a new coat, a waistcoat, and a hat.[42] Clothes were not the only items that Marshall bought in preparation for the convention. His account book shows that he laid in a large supply of bottles, corks, and glasses and on May 20 bought several barrels of wine for £20. His market expenditures for meat, cheese, and vegetables rose accordingly. Since Marshall's house was in easy walking distance of where the convention was to meet, it seems obvious that he anticipated playing host, providing refreshments for many of the delegates, and engaging in the informal arm-twisting that he so enjoyed. Polly, whose health continued to deteriorate, did not participate in that spring's entertaining, and Marshall looked after the arrangements alone.

On Sunday, June 1, 1788, the mass of the delegates began to arrive in Richmond. For their convenience, the stage schedules had been changed and extra vehicles laid on at Fredricksburg and Williamsburg.[43] The weather was hot and unseasonably dry, the result of an unusual spring drought that had killed nearly all the young tobacco plants.[44] The dust along the unpaved streets of Richmond was ankle-deep, billowing with every breeze, and coloring the vegetation a sooty gray. That afternoon, the taverns and rooming houses filled with delegates exchanging greetings and catching up with the latest news. An air of expectation hung over the city. The old hands from the legislative assembly were present, but many of the convention delegates had never been to Richmond and had never seen the principal actors of the coming drama. Monroe and Marshall were relative unknowns, and Madison and Randolph, although they were familiar names, had been little seen outside the legislature. On the other hand, Patrick Henry and Edmund Pendleton were mythic figures, heroes from a vanishing past about whom the delegates' fathers and even grandfathers had spoken.[45] One of the memorable descriptions of the scene that Sunday afternoon was drawn by Hugh Blair Grigsby, the primary historian of the convention. According to Grigsby's account, late in the day, from the heights of Shockoe Hill, the approach of two men could be observed.

> Though not personal enemies, they rarely thought alike on the greatest questions of the age, and they came aptly enough by different roads. One was seen advancing from the south side of the James, driving a plain and topless gig. . . . The other approached from the north side of the river in an elegant vehicle then known as a phaeton, which was driven so slowly that its occupant was seen at a glance to be pressed by age or infirmity. . . . His imposing stature, the elegance of his dress, the dignity of his mien, his venerable age, bespoke no ordinary man. . . . They met on the steps of the Swan and exchanged salutations. Public expectation was at its height when it was known that Patrick Henry and Edmund Pendleton, who, for a quarter of a century, had been at the head of the two great parties of that day, were about to engage in another fierce conflict in the councils of their country.[46]

The next morning, Monday, June 2, 1788, the delegates crowded into the capitol building. Poorly ventilated, the House chamber was already hot and stuffy. The room was ill-suited for so large an assembly in such scorching weather. Thanks to the presence of Madison, the federalists were ready and their strategy was laid out. By prior arrangement, when the convention was called to order, Paul Carrington, the respected chief judge of the general court, representing Charlotte county, nominated Edmund Pendleton to be the convention's president. Pendleton had presided over the Virginia conventions of 1775 and 1776, and with him in the chair, the prospects for ratification would be greatly enhanced. Henry and the antifederalists were painfully aware of that but had no candidate ready to oppose him. In fact, so great was Pendleton's stature that rather than risk a defeat so early, the Constitution's opponents seconded the inevitable, and Pendleton was elected unanimously.

Henry and his cohorts did object, however, when the federalists moved to have a stenographer take shorthand notes of the debates—the first time that had ever been attempted in a parliamentary setting. They eventually gave way, and the Virginia convention thus became the first body to have its debates recorded verbatim, although the antifederalists remained suspicious of the project and in the end declined to correct their speeches in the convention transcript.[47] After the organizational details were complete, the sweltering delegates voted to adjourn and meet the next day in the more spacious quarters of Richmond's New Academy, a commodious wooden structure built two years earlier in the cooler reaches of Shockoe Hill.

When the convention resumed the next morning, it became apparent that despite age and infirmity, Pendleton's political skills were as sharp as ever. He crisply instructed the clerk to read the resolution of the Continental Congress calling the federal convention in Philadelphia. He then inserted into the record the report of the convention to Congress and the text of Marshall's motion passed by the general assembly that provided for the Virginia convention. By so doing, the federalists immediately established the statutory authority of the convention to ratify the Constitution, thus preempting any objections Henry might raise on that point.[48]

But the momentum shifted quickly to the antifederalists. Startled by the abruptness of Pendleton's maneuver, George Mason was quickly on his feet seeking recognition, thus depriving Madison's men of the next move. In an instant, the incessant hum of the convention stilled, and the delegates leaned forward to catch Mason's words. They were aware that the anticipated confrontation was at hand. Erect and vigorous at sixty-two, and dressed in deep mourning in memory of his daughter, the snowy-haired Mason spoke in a full, clear voice.[49] "I hope and trust that this Convention . . . will 'freely and fully' investigate this important subject. The fullest and clearest investigation of the proposed Constitution [is] indispensably necessary. The subject therefore, ought to obtain the freest discussion, *clause by clause*, before any general previous question be put to a vote."[50] Mason's proposal for a clause-by-clause analysis took the federalists by surprise. Madison and his supporters were at their best analyzing the specific parts of the Constitution, while Patrick Henry's strength lay in attacking the proposed federal system as a whole. Thus, Mason's proposal seemed to play into the hands of his opponents.

When Mason finished, John Tyler of Charles City county, another antifederalist, moved that consideration be done in committee of the whole—the customary legislative procedure for amending or "marking up" documents under consideration. Passage of Tyler's motion without agreement on the clause-by-clause analysis proposed by Mason would open the door for amendments at any stage. Mindful of this, Mason rose again. He acknowledged the advantage of going into committee of the whole but insisted on a clause-by-clause discussion before any votes were taken.

Madison now sought Pendleton's eye and blandly agreed with Mason. The Constitution would first be debated in detail before any motions were put. Pendleton recognized the advantage that was being offered, terminated the debate, and put Mason's suggestion to a vote. The convention thereupon resolved that no motions would be entertained until the entire Constitution had been "discussed, clause-by-clause, through all its parts."[51]

Madison wrote afterward to Washington that he was "a good deal elated" by the procedure adopted,[52] and traditional interpretations of the Virginia convention describe Mason's action as a blunder.[53] In reality, Mason knew perfectly well what he was doing.[54] Unlike Henry, he was not irreconcilably opposed to the Constitution, and he believed the best way of remedying its defects was to call attention to them in a clause-by-clause debate. Such a procedure would expose the weaknesses of the document while avoiding premature action that might destroy it.[55]

When the convention met on Wednesday, it immediately went into committee of the whole. Pendleton turned the chair over to George Wythe. This was standard parliamentary practice for consideration by committee of the whole, but it was also illustrative of the federalists' careful tactics. Pendleton was masterful in debate, and by vacating the chair, he was free to take part. Wythe, who was not as good on the floor, was flawless in the chair and could be relied on to retain control of the convention's agenda.

As soon as Wythe took the gavel, Patrick Henry demanded recognition. Chafing under Mason's clause-by-clause restriction, he was determined to make one final assault on the Constitution as a whole. Refusing to be bound by the procedures Pendleton had put in place, Henry moved for a rereading of the acts that had authorized the federal convention. He proposed to show that the convention had exceeded its powers. With one bold stroke he hoped to defeat ratification of the document.

But it was too late. The federalists were ready. On the opposite side of the chamber, Pendleton slowly pulled himself up out of his chair, helped by those around him, and was immediately recognized by Wythe. "We are not to consider," said Pendleton coldly, "whether the federal Convention exceeded their powers. This Constitution was transmitted to Congress by that convention; by the Congress transmitted to our legislature; by them recommended to the people; the people have sent us hither to determine whether this government be a proper one or not."[56] Pendleton said that the delegates who assembled in Philadelphia had found the old system "so thoroughly defective as not to admit revising" and accordingly "had submitted a new system for our consideration."

Pendleton's intervention was decisive. Henry withdrew his motion, and the clause-by-clause battle over the Constitution began. The clerk read the Preamble and the first two sections of Article I, and then the debate commenced. First on his feet was George Nicholas of Albemarle county, the federalists' most formidable orator.[57] An experienced parliamentarian, a former colonel in the Virginia Line, and the brother-in-law of Edmund Randolph, the portly Nicholas had an instinct for the jugular. As Marshall had phrased it earlier to Monroe, Nicholas was "a politician not famed for hitting a happy medium."[58] If Madison was the federalists' tactician and Pendleton their eminent authority, Nicholas was their battering ram. For two hours he held the convention in rapt attention with a set speech that focused on the Articles just read. As Nicholas took his seat, Patrick Henry rose to answer. The speech that followed was vintage Henry. Taking aim at the Preamble, Henry fashioned his address into a powerful attack on the Constitution as a whole. "What right had [the Philadelphia convention] to say *We, the people?*"[59] he asked.

> Who authorized them to speak the language, *We, the people*, instead of *We, the states?* . . . That they exceeded their power is perfectly clear. . . . The Federal Convention ought to have amended the old system; for this purpose they were solely delegated; the object of their mission extended to no other consideration.[60]

The federalists knew that Henry's persuasive power was so great it would be dangerous to let his arguments go unanswered. As soon as Henry concluded his remarks, Edmund Randolph, in accordance with Madison's well-calculated strategy,[61] began the federalist rebuttal. As governor, Randolph was in a unique position at the convention. His views on the Constitution were still tightly guarded from all but a few, and many considered him an unknown quantity. The antifederalists anticipated that he would ask for amendments prior to ratification, and Governor George Clinton of New York, an unremitting opponent of the Constitution, had written to Randolph to arrange for a second federal convention.[62] The hall quieted as Randolph began to speak, each delegate eager to hear the governor's explanation of why he had not signed the Constitution in Philadelphia. Randolph began slowly, his resonant, lilting voice carrying his listeners effortlessly. "I am a child of the revolution," he told the assembly as he proceeded to detail the need for a strong central government. These introductory remarks surprised no one. But what followed was a thunderbolt. "As with me," said Randolph, "the only question has ever been between previous or subsequent amendments." The Virginia convention, he said, had been scheduled so late, and so many states had already take action, that there was no longer any possibility of amending the Constitution beforehand "without inevitable ruin to the Union, and the Union is the anchor of our political salvation."[63]

The antifederalists were stunned. Not only had Henry's oratorical spell been broken, but Randolph had gone over to the enemy. "Young Arnold," gasped Mason, "Young Arnold," which in 1788 was about the most heinous epithet in a Virginian's lexicon.[64] Mason himself now sought recognition, and again the chamber stilled. The hour was late, but what a day it had been: Henry and Pendleton crossing swords, then Nicholas, followed by Henry again, Governor Randolph, and now George Mason. It was a spectacle that few who witnessed would ever forget. When Mason spoke, he sought to allay the damage Randolph had done with a careful analysis of Article I and the vast powers that it granted to the national government. Would not these powers soon destroy the governments of the states? asked Mason. "Should this power be restrained, I shall withdraw my objections to this part of the Constitution; but as it stands, it is an objection so strong in my mind, that its amendment is with me a *sine qua non* of its adoption."[65]

Madison had kept himself in reserve to answer Mason, and now took the floor.[66] Short in stature, diffident in manner, Madison always spoke casually, as if expressing some thought that had just occurred to him. He often carried a hat in his hand, with his notes in his hat, and eschewed the rhetorical flourishes of speakers like Henry and Randolph. Madison was not a spellbinder, but as Marshall observed, no one possessed greater power to move men's minds. And as the principal advocate of the Constitution, his words carried a special weight.

Madison focused directly on Mason's criticism of national power and spoke gently of the countervailing authority of the states, almost as if he were correcting a friend in personal conversation. Having made his point, Madison noted the late hour and suggested adjournment. He said he would hold the remainder of his remarks "until a more convenient time."[67] That evening, from his room at the Swan, Madison recounted the day's proceedings in a letter to George Washington. Randolph had committed himself fully to the federalist cause, said Madison, while Henry and Mason had "made a lame figure and appeared to take different and awkward ground."[68] He told Washington that the federalists "are a good deal elated by the existing prospect," but that it was too early to claim victory because the election results from Kentucky were "extremely tainted" and the status of the fourteen western delegates was still in doubt.

The following morning, June 5, the delegates assembled early on Shockoe Hill, eagerly anticipating Madison's reply to Henry and Mason. After the routine business of the convention had been dealt with, Pendleton turned the gavel over to Wythe and was helped to his seat on the floor. According to the rules of the House of Delegates, which the convention had adopted, Madison, as the last speaker of the previous day, was entitled to the floor, but he was nowhere to be seen. The word spread that he had been taken ill suddenly and confined to his room.[69] That may or may not have been true. Madison's diminutive stature and weak, reedy voice made him unsuited to initiate the federalist offensive. The Constitution's proponents needed a vibrant speaker who could dispel the lingering effects of Henry's oration, and Madison simply was not the man for the job. Had he been present, he could not have avoided speaking, and the federalist momentum would have been lost.

For a moment there was a stillness in the hall as the delegates turned anxiously to Henry and Mason.[70] Suddenly it was the aged Pendleton who was struggling to get to his feet. It was another federalist masterstroke. Because of his advanced age and failing health, no one had expected Pendleton to carry a major share of the debate. Hugh Blair Grigsby reports that the very effort made by the enfeebled Pendleton to rise to his feet brought tears to the eyes of many older delegates, and the packed hall grew silent to catch his every word.[71] Frail though he was, Pendleton soon demonstrated why he had dominated the Virginia bar for the past half century, as he coolly and methodically dismantled Henry's case. Pendleton avoided theatrics. With crisp logic and well-chosen words, he attacked Henry point by point. It was the address of a great lawyer pleading his last case. His closing lines were magnificent. "I belong to no party and seek no influence for myself. My age and situation, I trust, will sufficiently demonstrate the truth of this assertion." And then, with traditional understatement, he concluded that "I am perfectly satisfied with this part of the system."[72]

Henry sought recognition to reply. All his life he had been opposed by Pendleton, and now, once again, in the greatest battle of their careers, his ancient rival had won another round. But before Henry could catch George Wythe's eye, another federalist, a tall, young officer clearly accustomed to command, was on his feet addressing the convention. Light-Horse Harry Lee, the commander of Washington's cavalry and a close friend and Princeton classmate of James Madison, was taking direct aim at Henry in a tone that few would have dared assume. First Pendleton, then Lee. So great were the federalists' fears of Henry that they were launching a two-pronged attack.

Finally it was the great orator's turn to reply. Henry spoke for three hours, delivering the longest and what many believe to be the ablest address he ever made before a political body. Although Pendleton and Lee had captured the morning's momentum, the day ultimately belonged to Henry. Marshall liked and respected Henry, and although they were often on different sides politically, they got along well. In fact, Marshall was personally much closer to Henry than he was to Madison or Pendleton. In subsequent years, the two would occasionally act as co-counsel in major cases: Henry the spellbinding advocate, Marshall the supreme logician. At the convention, however, Marshall was still too young to rank as a major player, and so, like his colleagues and collaborators on the federalist benches, he nervously awaited Henry's renewed attack.

Henry began to speak in his customary mild and hesitant manner.[73] "I wish I was possessed of talents, or possessed of anything that might enable me to elucidate this great subject," he said. "I am not free from suspicion; I am apt to entertain doubts." His voice grew stronger as the balanced cadences marched across the convention floor. Again and again he hit his central point that the proposed new government would be a consolidated national undertaking and not a confederation of the states. That issue would be fought out repeatedly during the next seventy-five years, eventually by force of arms, and it would be concluded by the victory of the Union just a few miles from the spot where Henry now stood. Henry accurately perceived the diminished role of the states under the Constitution, and he made that the central issue in his fight against ratification:

> The Confederation—this same despised government—merits in my opinion the highest encomium. It carried us through a long and dangerous war. It rendered us victorious in that bloody conflict with a powerful nation. It has secured us a territory greater than any European monarch possesses. And shall a government which has been this strong and vigorous be accused of imbecility and abandoned for want of energy? Consider what you are about to do before you part with this government.

Henry then turned to Pendleton. He acknowledged the federalist argument that public licentiousness was dangerous and must be guarded against, but he put that fear into a different perspective. "We are cautioned by the honorable gentleman, who presides, against faction and turbulence. . . . I am not well versed in history," said Henry, "but I will submit to your recollection, whether liberty has been destroyed most often by the licentiousness of the people, or by the tyranny of the rulers."

At that point, Henry shifted his argument to examine the Constitution itself. "[It] is said to have beautiful features; but when I come to examine these features, sir, they appear to me horribly frightful. Among other deformities it has an awful squinting—*it squints toward monarchy.* . . . Your President may easily become a king."[74]

The effect of Henry's attack was devastating. Indeed, his impact was so great that Grigsby reports that if Henry had concluded his remarks with a motion to postpone indefinitely further consideration of the Constitution, "it would have succeeded by a considerable majority."[75] Fortunately for the federalist forces, such a motion was out of order under the procedure the convention had adopted. And so Henry concluded on the same note of modesty with which he had begun. "May you be fully apprised of the dangers of the new plan of government, not by fatal experience, but by some abler advocate than I."*[76]

The federalists were stunned. Their worst fears had come true. Henry had the convention in the palm of his hand. The following day, Friday, June 6, the federalists used their control of convention procedure to monopolize the debate. Randolph and Nicholas spoke, and then Madison entered the debate with the first of a series of tightly argued discourses that put the Constitution into perspective. On Saturday, it was Henry's turn once more, and when the convention adjourned for the weekend, it was clear that the Constitution hung by a thread.

On Monday, Henry and Mason made a dramatic entrance into the convention hall. Walking arm in arm from their quarters in the Swan, they stopped on the steps of the New Academy and conferred earnestly for some minutes. Grigsby reports that the throng of delegates around the two chieftains was so great that they made their way to their seats with great difficulty.[77] The titans still held the floor: Henry, Mason, and now William Grayson for the antifederalists; Randolph, Nicholas, Madison, and Lee for the Constitution. The debate turned ugly. The federalists realized they had to neutralize Henry, and the task was assigned to Randolph and Lee. Randolph asserted that Henry had been deceitful. "If our friendship must fall, *let it fall, like Lucifer, never to rise again!*" shouted Randolph. Lee taunted Henry for not having served in the army during the war and, indeed, for his eloquence itself, which Lee insinuated could not be trusted. "He calls his assertions *facts*," Lee exclaimed. "I hold his unsupported authority in contempt."[78] Henry chose not to reply to Lee's caustic attack, and the convention adjourned on Monday shaken by the change of tone in the debate.†

Whether for that reason or not, both sides revised their strategy. On the next day, Tuesday, June 10, two fresh faces were sent into the debate. The old hands had become testy, and a change of pace seemed in order. James Monroe spoke for the antifederalists and Marshall for the Constitution.

---

*The human dimension of Henry's appeal can be judged by the fact that as he approached the height of his argument, his eye ranged over the convention and caught the face of his son, whom Henry had left at home to take care of the family during his absence. Henry hesitated for a moment, stooped down, and whispered to a friend who was sitting before him: "Dawson [John Dawson of Spotsylvannia county], I see my son in the hall. Take him out." Dawson did as he was asked and promptly returned with the news that Mrs. Henry had given birth to a son and that both she and the child were doing well. Hugh Blair Grigsby, 1 *History of the Virginia Federal Convention of 1788* 119 (Richmond, Virginia Historical Society, 1890).

†While Henry did not respond to Lee's attack, he was stung by the accusations that Randolph leveled against him. That evening Colonel William Cabell of Amherst county, whom Henry had named as his second, called on Randolph to set time and place for a duel. But in the discussion that followed, cooler heads prevailed and the challenge was not offered. Grigsby, 1 *Virginia Federal Convention* 162–165.

Monroe versus Marshall. The schoolboy chums, wartime friends, and political and personal companions were now squaring off in debate. Monroe, like Madison, was poor at public speaking and was selected by the antifederalists because of his military background. Thus far, no officer from Washington's army had spoken against the Constitution, and the antifederalists needed to demonstrate their patriotism, especially after Light-Horse Harry Lee's slashing attack on Henry. The fact that Monroe was known to be a protégé of Jefferson may also have recommended him, since each side sought to invoke Jefferson's support.[79]

Monroe delivered a lengthy speech strewn with metaphors that traced the history of federalism from ancient Greece to the New England confederacy. Like Monroe himself, the speech was sincere but lacked the fire of previous addresses. Patrick Henry, who always thought well of Monroe, said, "He is slow, but give him time and he is sure."[80] Indeed, it was precisely that sureness that eventually brought Monroe great success. However, the delegates were little interested in detailed quotations from Polybius celebrating the Achaean league, and Monroe's effort fell flat.

Next up was Marshall, who delivered another set piece. Unlike Monroe, Marshall avoided historical analogies and, like the accomplished appellate lawyer he had become, dealt crisply with the Constitution in the understated style he had perfected. Grigsby draws a winsome portrait of the "tall young man, slovenly dressed in loose summer apparel, with piercing black eyes," who spoke that afternoon:

> His manners, like those of Monroe, were in strange contrast with those of Edmund Randolph . . . and had been formed in the tutelage of the camp. . . ; his habits were convivial almost to excess; and he regarded as matters beneath his notice those appliances of dress and demeanor which are commonly considered not unimportant to advancement in a public profession. . . . [81]

Marshall's speech was not remarkable, but it provides the first statement of his views on the document of which he was to become the nation's foremost interpreter. It is clear from his address that those views were shaped to an extraordinary degree by his military service. Marshall delivered the carefully crafted speech of a lawyer, not a statesman, and its appeal lay in the rigor of the arguments, not its political persuasiveness. The speech lacked both Henry's moving rhetoric and Randolph's elegant turn of phrase. Marshall could not match Madison's encyclopedic knowledge of the issues, and at thirty-three he lacked the physical presence of Mason and Pendleton. However, the crispness of his arguments appealed to the lawyers among the delegates.

Much of Marshall's speech was cast as a reply to Henry. Among other things, Henry had claimed that the unwritten British constitution was superior to that proposed by the federal Convention, a contention that Marshall rejected. "It matters not . . . whether [the British constitution] be a wise one," said Marshall. "I think, that for America at least, the Government on your table is very much superior to it."[82]

> I ask you, if your House of Representatives would be better than it is, if a hundredth part of the people were to elect a majority of them? If your Senators were for life, would they be more agreeable to you? If your President were not accountable to you for his conduct; if it were a constitutional maxim that he could do no wrong, would you be safer than you are now? If you can answer *yes* to these questions, then adopt the British constitution. If not, then good as that government may be, this is better.[83]

Marshall stressed the need for experience with the proposed Constitution before embarking on attempts to change it. If that "experience shall show us any inconveniences, we can then correct it. But until we have experience on the subject, amendments, as well as the Constitution itself, are to try. Let us try it, and keep our hands free to change it when necessary."

"What are objects of the national government?" asked Marshall. "To protect the United States and to promote the general welfare." He focused on the twin objectives of defending the country from foreign attack and ensuring domestic stability. Thirty-one years later, he returned to the theme of national power in the great case of *McCulloch v. Maryland*. "Let the end be legitimate, let it be within the scope of the Constitution, and all means which are appropriate, which are plainly adapted to that end, which are not prohibited, but consistent with the letter and the spirit of the Constitution, are constitutional."[84]

Marshall concluded with an analysis of the Constitution's safeguards against arbitrary power. The absence of such safeguards had been the central thrust of Henry's attack, and Marshall, as he might have done in argument before the court of appeals, replied with a tightly structured exposition on the virtues of the separation of powers. "The object of our inquiry is, *Is the power necessary—and is it guarded?*"

Marshall's defense of the Constitution was not confined to the convention floor. Practicing the lobbying skills he had learned in Virginia's House of Delegates, he was much in evidence in Richmond's taverns and public houses, pleading the federalist cause with thirsty delegates over a glass or two. The Swan was the inn of choice for Virginia's more affluent delegates.

An unpretentious wooden building on the north side of Broad Street, just at the crest of Shockoe Hill, it was home to Madison, Henry, Pendleton, and Mason. The furnishings were plain and the rooms small, but the food was good, the wine was better, and when the weather was warm, one could sit on the large verandah and hear the roar of the river in the background.[85]

Below the hill were a number of other taverns and public houses, the most popular of which was Formicola's. It was also Marshall's favorite. Far less elegant than the Swan, it had two public rooms downstairs and two rooms above that served as common bedrooms for the delegates. The atmosphere was raucous, the food and drink were plentiful, and the delegates could unwind quickly from a long day's tensions.[86]

In the evenings, Marshall regularly invited the committed and the uncommitted to his home for dinner. Gouverneur Morris, in Richmond to support the federalist cause, dined with Marshall on Thursday, June 12, and provided his host with a doggerel of his observations at the convention:

> The State's determined Resolution
> Was to discuss the Constitution
> For this the members come together
> Melting with Zeal and sultry Weather,
> And here to their eternal Praise
> To find its Hist'ry spend three Days
> The next three days they nobly roam
> Thru ev'ry Region far from Home . . .
> Fellows who freedom never knew
> To tell us what we ought do
> The next three days they kindly dip ye
> Deep in the River Mississippi
> Nine days thus spent e'er they begin
> Let us suppose them fairly in
> And then resolve me gentle friend
> How many Months before they End.[87]

Marshall obviously appreciated Morris's humor, because the verse was one of the few writings he ever saved. And in looking back at the Virginia convention, it is easy to overlook the importance of entertainment and fellowship in cementing both the federalist and antifederalist coalitions. Madison and Mason may have been all business, but Marshall and Henry could not be described in those terms, and nor could Monroe or Light-Horse Harry Lee. The ratification process entailed more than the speeches delivered to the convention. Marshall's greatest contribution may well have been to balance Henry's affability in Richmond's public houses[88] and to gain the confidence of the delegates from Kentucky, where the Marshall name carried great weight.

Nevertheless, it was an uphill struggle. By the end of the second week, the momentum had shifted to the antifederalists. Gouverneur Morris reported to Hamilton that "matters are not going so well in this State as the Friends of America could wish."[89] Madison, in despair at his inability to counter Henry in debate, told Washington that "the business is in the most ticklish state that can be imagined. The majority will certainly be very small on whatever side it may finally lie; and I dare not encourage much expectation that it will be on the favorable side."[90]

On Monday, June 16, the convention began to consider the grant of powers to the national government contained in Article I, section 8. In the general debate that followed, Henry, Madison, Randolph, and Mason all spoke, with the antifederalists concentrating their fire on the militia clause. William Grayson of Prince William county, who was perhaps the most accomplished scholar on the antifederalist side,[91] asserted that the Constitution left the states no control of their militias. Following Grayson's speech, Marshall rose to deliver the federalist reply. His brief answer, framed in the rhetoric of an ongoing floor debate, is noteworthy for its concise restatement of federalist dogma: Both the national government and the various state governments are creations of the people, said Marshall, and the people, who are sovereign, can take power from one government and transfer it to the other. "The State Governments did not derive their powers from the General Government. But each government derived its powers from the people; and each was to act according to the powers given it." Years later the Marshall Court invoked that rationale in the consolidation of national power. It was not a novel viewpoint, but it is illustrative of Marshall's consistency that he espoused it as early as 1788.

Far more important for the future of constitutional development was the discussion that took place on the judiciary. In many respects, the establishment of a federal court system was the most controversial aspect of the Constitution, and the battle over Article III, the judiciary article, proved to be the last great battle of the convention. Today, with more than 200 years of hindsight, it is difficult to understand why the creation of a national judiciary was so contentious in 1788. Part of the opposition stemmed from a fear that the power of the states would be diminished. But an even greater fear was that a federal judiciary would be unresponsive to local needs, that it would impose the rules made by a distant Congress, and perhaps above all, that it would favor the legal rights of creditors over the equity claims of respondents. The federal judges would be appointed, not elected; their jurisdiction would include a substantial number of issues presently tried in state courts (for example, all suits between citizens of different states, regardless of the subject matter, could be tried in federal court); and they would become the final interpreters of federal laws, treaties, and the Constitution.

With the Constitution teetering in the balance, both sides prepared for the final confrontation. The antifederalists scented victory. "Tomorrow the Judiciary comes on and we shall exert our whole force," William Grayson wrote to a friend in New York. He predicted that if the debate were "conducted in an able & masterly manner," the opponents could pick up the votes they needed.[92] Mason, it was agreed, would head the attack, with Henry and Grayson to follow. The federalists, with their backs to the wall, picked Pendleton to lead the fight, supported by Marshall, while Madison and Randolph would patrol the flanks and answer any questions that the two principal speakers overlooked.

The choice of the venerable Pendleton was a foregone conclusion. No delegate, not even Henry, could match the skill of Virginia's chief judge in the cut and thrust of debate, and no one enjoyed greater respect. Pendleton's frailty added to his aura of wisdom and experience, and the obvious effort that it required for him to rise and speak gave additional gravity to his remarks. The selection of Marshall for the supporting role was something of a surprise. He was junior in age and experience to both Madison and Randolph. He lacked the former's understanding of the debate in Philadelphia that lay behind Article III, and he could not match Randolph's eloquence. But the leaders of the federalist cause turned to Marshall because no one else, not even Pendleton, could provide the tight logical analysis of the federal court structure that was required. The judiciary article had to be explained point by point to the delegates, and no one was better at synthesizing a mass of detail and making it comprehensible than Marshall.

On Thursday, June 19, the clerk read the first two sections of Article III. Pendleton began the defense. A national judiciary was necessary, he said, "to arrest the executive arm, prevent arbitrary punishments, and give a fair trial, that the innocent may be guarded, and the guilty brought to just punishment, and that honesty and industry be protected, and injustice and fraud be prevented."[93]

Pendleton pointed out that the "power of the judiciary must be coextensive with the legislative power, and reach all parts of society intended to be governed." He continued for thirty minutes, detailing the nature of federal jurisdiction, but his voice weakened and his comments soon became inaudible.[94] The ancient warrior was helped to his seat, unable to complete his remarks.

Mason spoke next and held the floor for several hours, detailing the antifederalist objections to a national judiciary. He concentrated on the broad sweep of federal jurisdiction and particularly on the authority given to federal courts to try suits between citizens of different states, known today as diversity jurisdiction. "Can we not trust our state courts with the decision of these?" asked Mason. "If I have a controversy with a man in Maryland—if a man in Maryland has my bond for a hundred pounds—are not the state courts competent to try it? Is it suspected that they would enforce the payment if unjust, or refuse to enforce it if just? The very idea is ridiculous."[95]

It is important to remember that when Mason spoke, there were no courts other than the state courts. Article III did not make the federal courts superior to the state courts. The two were to exist side by side. Nevertheless, the addition of an entirely new judicial system appeared to many as an unwelcome intrusion.

Mason's extended remarks struck at the core of federal power, for without a national judiciary the laws of Congress would be subject to varying judicial interpretations in every state of the Union. Madison replied briefly, but the hour was late and the convention adjourned with Henry and Marshall slated to speak the next day.[96]

When the convention resumed, Henry took up the issues Mason had omitted. Paying ironic tribute to Pendleton, he deplored the fact that Virginia's judges might become federal judges.

> If we are to be deprived of that class of men, and if they are to combine against us with the Federal Government, *we are gone!* I regard the Virginia judiciary as one of the best barriers against the strides of power. So few are the barriers against the encroachments and usurpations of Congress, that when I see this last barrier, the independency of the judges impaired, I am persuaded that I see the prostration of all our rights.[97]

Henry's eye for the blemishes in the Constitution was unerring, and he seized on the words that would later lead to the Eleventh Amendment: the fact that the federal courts were given jurisdiction in suits "between a State and Citizens of another State."* Madison had incorrectly asserted that a state could not be a made a defendant in such proceedings, and Henry took him to task. "His construction [of the text] is to me perfectly incomprehensible. . . . If gentlemen pervert the most clear expressions, and the usual meaning of the language of the people, there is an end to all argument."

---

*In *Chisholm v. Georgia*, 2 Dallas 419 (1793), the Supreme Court (Iredell dissenting) held that federal jurisdiction extended to suits initiated against a state by citizens of another state and entered a default judgment against Georgia on Chisholm's behalf. The State of Georgia refused to comply, and immediately thereafter the Eleventh Amendment was added to the Constitution providing that "The Judicial power of the United States shall not be construed to extend to any suit . . . commenced or prosecuted against one of the United States by Citizens of another State, or by Citizens or Subjects of any Foreign State."

Henry's conclusion was a damning indictment of the federalists. "If gentlemen take this liberty" of loose construction now in debate, "what will they not do when our rights and liberties are in their power?"[98]

> A Constitution, sir, ought to be, like a beacon, held up to the public eye, so as to be understood by every man.[99]

Pendleton replied briefly, but age and infirmity quickly got the better of him. Mason responded, again stressing his objections to federal diversity jurisdiction, and then from across the chamber, Marshall caught Wythe's eye. Neither Pendleton nor Madison had been able to blunt the antifederalist attack, and the burden fell to the junior delegate from Henrico county.[100]

Marshall took direct issue with Mason and Henry, and his detailed analysis made the complicated provisions of Article III appear rational and acceptable. From his remarks, there seems little doubt that he had carefully studied Mason's speech the night before. But Marshall's argument was most noteworthy for its constant reference to the judiciary as the defender of the Constitution and of individual liberty. The views Marshall had first expressed as a member of the council of state in the Posey case obviously were deeply held, and he rebuked the antifederalists for presuming that a national judiciary would become the pliant tool of an oppressive government. Congress's powers were delegated by the Constitution, said Marshall. "If they were to make a law not warranted by any of the powers enumerated, it would be considered by the Judges as an infringement of the Constitution which they are to guard. They would not consider such a law as coming under their jurisdiction. *They would declare it void.*"[101]

"What is the purpose of a judiciary?" Marshall asked Mason. It is, he said, "to execute the laws in a peaceable orderly manner, without shedding blood . . . or availing yourselves of force. If this be the case, where can its jurisdiction be more necessary than here? To what quarter will you look for protection from an infringement on the Constitution, if you will not give the power of the Judiciary? There is no other body that can afford such protection."

Marshall returned repeatedly to the theme that any oppressive laws passed by Congress "would be void." "The Honorable Member says laws may be executed tyrannically. Where is the independency of your Judges? If a law be executed tyrannically in Virginia, to what can you trust? To your Judiciary. What security do you have for justice? Their independence. Will it not be so in the Federal Court?"

Marshall pointed out that the members of Congress "can be changed at our pleasure. Where power may be trusted, and there is no motive to abuse it, it seems to me to be as well to leave it undetermined, as to fix it in the

Constitution."[102] That pragmatic attachment to muddling through characterized Marshall's long career, and his speech to the Virginia convention revealed his deepest feelings. He told his listeners, "We ought well to weigh the good and evil before we determine. We ought be well convinced, that the evil will be really produced before we decide against [the Constitution]. If we be convinced that the good greatly preponderates, though there be small defects in it, shall we give up that which is really good, when we can remove the little mischief it may contain, in the plain easy method pointed out in the system itself?"

Marshall's presentation recaptured the ground that Mason and Henry had taken. The future chief justice's precise knowledge of legal procedure struck the antifederalists where they were weakest. His familiarity with the postrevolutionary development of Virginia's legal system far surpassed that of Mason and Henry, and his point-by-point refutation of Mason's charges reassured those wavering supporters of the Constitution who may have been shaken the day before.

Marshall's speech concluded the federalist defense of Article III. That night Madison wrote to Hamilton that "a great effort is making" against the federal judiciary. "At present . . . we still retain a majority of 3 or 4, and if we can weather the storm . . . I shall hold the danger to be pretty well over."[103] On Sunday, when the dust from the week's debate had settled, he wrote somewhat more confidently that "The Judiciary Department has been on the anvil for several days," but the antifederalist attacks "have apparently made less impression than was feared." Madison suggested that time was now running on the side of ratification, but he said the majority was likely to be so small, that "ordinary casualties . . . may vary the result."[104]

On Monday, June 23, the discussion of the Constitution concluded with Henry attempting a final counterattack. He complimented Marshall but said he thought he was wrong. "I have the highest veneration and respect for the honorable gentleman and I have experienced his candor on all occasions, but, Mr. Chairman, in this instance, he is so materially mistaken that I cannot but observe, he is much in error."[105] Coming from Henry, the comment was a tribute, and Marshall made a gracious reply.[106]

The following morning, Tuesday, June 24, the delegates assembled early, ready for the final motions to be put. Henry came prepared to submit a number of amendments, the acceptance of which would postpone ratification indefinitely. To forestall him, the federalists played another trump card. They selected the universally respected George Wythe, who had chaired the debate, to introduce the motion for adoption. When Pendleton called the session to order, he called on Thomas Mathews of Norfolk to take the chair, and Mathews immediately recognized Wythe. Wythe's support for the Constitution was well known, and his handling of the bruising debate in committee of the whole had been masterly. His introduction of the motion for ratification gave it additional prestige. As soon as Wythe introduced the motion to ratify, Henry was on his feet, claiming it was premature. He urged that the Constitution be amended before ratification. "If you will . . . stipulate that there are rights which no man under heaven can take from you, you shall have me going along with you; not otherwise."[107] Henry then introduced his own motion, which proposed a number of amendments to the Constitution as well as a bill of rights and which mandated that the revised text be submitted to the other states for their consideration before ratification.

Next to take the floor was Governor Randolph, who bitterly charged Henry with being a secessionist and who spoke at length on the dangers of attempting to amend the Constitution before ratification. Mason, Dawson, and Grayson spoke for the antifederalists, followed by Madison, who made a forceful yet conciliatory plea for ratification. "It is worthy of our consideration," said Madison, "that those who prepared [the Constitution] found difficulties not to be described in its formation: mutual deference and concession were absolutely necessary. Had they been inflexibly tenacious of their individual opinions, they would never have concurred."[108]

Then it was Henry's turn once again, and he unleashed the full force of his oratory. "He [Madison] tells you of the important blessings which he imagines will result to us . . . from the adoption of this system. I see the awful immensity of the dangers with which it is pregnant."[109] At that point, Richmond was suddenly enveloped in darkness. A tremendous thunderstorm erupted that broke the long spring drought and shook the New Academy building to its foundation, adding an extraordinary counterpoint to Henry's forebodings. Henry tried to continue, but the wind and rain proved too much and he was forced to conclude.[100] The convention then adjourned, ready to vote the following day.

On the day of the voting, the delegates were once again in their places early. The federalists anticipated a narrow victory, but no one could be sure. Even if they won, there was considerable concern as to what Henry and his supporters might attempt. Two months before, Madison had been convinced that "desperate measures" would "be his game."[111] On their side, the antifederalists worried that if the Constitution were ratified, the convention would adjourn without taking any action on proposed amendments or a bill of rights.

As soon as Pendleton called Mathews to the chair, Nicholas sought recognition and moved that Wythe's motion to ratify be read. With uncharacteristic generosity he assured Henry and his followers that after ratification the federalists would gladly agree to amendments that would promote liberty without destroying the spirit of the Constitution. The antagonism of the past three weeks began to fade, and as the vote neared, both sides inexplicably seemed to draw together. John Tyler of Charles City county moved that Henry's motion calling for amendments and a bill of rights be read. A brief flurry of debate followed, with a number of delegates who had not spoken seeking to be heard. Then Henry rose to address the convention for the last time. He offered an elegant valedictory, but the fire was gone. Henry urged prior amendments to the Constitution, but he assured his listeners that he would acquiesce to the convention's decision.

> If I shall be in the minority, I shall have those painful sensations which arise from a conviction of being overpowered in a good cause. Yet I will be a peaceable citizen. . . . I wish not to go to violence, but will wait with hopes that the spirit which predominated in the Revolution is not yet gone, nor the cause of those who are attached to the Revolution yet lost.[112]

After Randolph had made one final plea for the Union, the committee rose and Pendleton returned to the chair. Wythe's motion to ratify was read, and then Henry moved a substitute resolution:

> *Resolved*, That, previous to the ratification of the new Constitution . . . , a declaration of rights . . . together with amendments to the most exceptionable parts of the said Constitution . . . ought to be referred by this Convention to the other states . . . for their consideration.[113]

The final test was at hand. Pendleton ordered the clerk to call the roll on Henry's motion to amend. One after the other, the delegates were called by county, alphabetically. The vote seesawed. The delegates from Albemarle, Augusta, Berkeley, and Botetourt voted no, while those from Amelia, Amherst, Bedford, and Bourbon voted aye. The next ten counties were from southside Virginia, where the opponents of ratification were strongest. When the last of these counties voted, Henry led, 25–12. Then the votes began to shift. Slowly the federalists gained ground. Marshall's lobbying efforts with the Kentucky delegates bore fruit when Fayette county was called and Humphrey Marshall, defying the instructions from his constituents, voted no. So did John Breckinridge and Rice Bullock of Jefferson county. These were Kentucky votes that the antifederalists could not afford to lose. When Henrico county was called, Marshall and Randolph voted no, making the count 38 to 35. Several more counties were called, and the vote knotted at 40–40. Back and forth it went. Lancaster county voted no, Loudoun and Louisa split, and Lunenburg voted aye. The vote was 47–47. The next four counties, all from Kentucky, voted aye and Henry led 55–47.

Several counties from tidewater were called and voted no, and when Norfolk, Northampton, and Northumberland were called, all voted no. The score was deadlocked once again, 60–60. The lead shifted to Henry, then to the federalists.

When Samuel Edmiston and James Montgomery of Washington county voted Aye, it was 80–82 against Henry with six votes remaining. At last, the federalists could breathe easily. Light-Horse Harry Lee and Bushrod Washington of Westmoreland county voted no. Next were Judge Blair and Chancellor Wythe of York county, who also voted no. Then came James Innes from Williamsburg, and Thomas Mathews from Norfolk borough. Two more nos. The final vote on Henry's substitute motion was 80–88. The amendment failed; the Constitution was safe. Pendleton instructed the clerk to call the roll on Wythe's original motion to ratify. The vote was repeated, this time with the federalists voting aye and the opponents, no. One delegate, David Patteson of Chesterfield county, switched to the federalists, and the final tally on the Constitution was 89 to 79.[114]

When Pendleton announced the vote, there was no rejoicing on the federalist benches. The margin was too thin, and Henry's forces remained formidable. The general assembly was known to be hostile to the Constitution, and it was unclear whether the fight would be continued. That night a group of diehard antifederalists met to plan strategy to prevent the establishment of a new government. Henry was sent for and asked to preside. He accepted, but once in the chair told his supporters that although he had opposed the Constitution, he had done so "in the proper place." The question was now settled, said Henry, and he advised those present that "as true and faithful republicans," they had all better go home.[115]

The following day Spencer Roane, Henry's son-in-law, wrote to a friend that

> The decision has been distressing and awful ... and it is generally believed will be so received by the people. The minority is a very respectable one indeed, and made a most noble stand in defense of the liberties of the people. ... There is no rejoicing on account of the vote of ratification—it would not be prudent to do so; and the federalists behave with moderation and do not exalt their success.[116]

After the vote was announced, Pendleton appointed two committees. The first committee, consisting of Randolph, Nicholas, Madison, Marshall, and Corbin, all federalists, was instructed to prepare the formal document of ratification for transmission to the Continental Congress. The second committee, composed of twenty members equally divided between federalists and opponents, was charged with preparing the amendments that Virginia would propose to the Constitution after it went into effect. Chaired by George Wythe, the committee included Henry, Mason, and Grayson, as well as Madison, Marshall, and Randolph.[117]

The first committee, whose work was a formality, reported back the next day. The amendment-drafting committee reported on Friday. It recommended a bill of rights patterned after the Virginia Declaration of Rights that Mason had framed, with added guarantees of free speech, peaceable assembly, and due process as well as protection against unreasonable searches and seizures, cruel and unusual punishments, and the quartering of soldiers in private homes.[118] These became the bases for the First, Third, Fourth, Fifth, and Eighth Amendments to the Constitution. There is no record of the committee's proceedings, and Marshall's exact role in preparing the draft bill of rights is unclear. But his subsequent statements on free speech and due process suggest that he was in complete agreement.

In addition to a bill of rights, the committee recommended some twenty changes to the text of the Constitution. These were based on Henry's proposals to the convention and included substantial restrictions on the power of the national government to tax and to wage war. There was also a proposal to rewrite Article III and strip federal courts of diversity jurisdiction as well as the authority to try suits between a state and citizens of another state. Marshall opposed these revisions,[119] and ultimately they were put forward by the convention largely as a gesture of respect for Patrick Henry and the principled fight against ratification that he had led. It was an important conciliatory move by the federalists, yet with two exceptions,[120] none of Henry's proposals ever became a part of the Constitution.

Marshall's participation in the Virginia convention was the climactic point of his early life. The struggle for ratification was narrowly won, and the future chief justice had done his share, on and off the convention floor, to secure the votes that were needed. His relentless, point-by-point defense of the judiciary article marked him as Virginia's leading authority on the federal court system and further enhanced his reputation as an advocate. To have bested Henry and Mason at that critical juncture was no small accomplishment, and to have done so while retaining the friendship of his opponents speaks volumes about Marshall's character and personality. Powerful in argument, insistent in logic, confident in debate, Marshall had learned to conceal his talent behind a smokescreen of folksiness and bonhomie.*

---

*Both Henry and Mason were impressed with Marshall's ability as an advocate. Henry was soon collaborating with Marshall in several of the most important cases to come before the courts during the next decade (see Chapter 6), and Mason began using Marshall to handle his legal matters in Richmond. 3 *The Papers of George Mason* 1168–1169, Robert A. Rutland, ed. (Chapel Hill: University of North Carolina Press, 1970). Madison must also have formed a favorable impression of Marshall's technical skills because he utilized him to prepare a property deed midway through the convention. 1 *Marshall Papers* 412.

The battle over national power was just beginning. With the ratification of the Constitution, the venue shifted. But the struggle would continue on and off for the next seventy-five years. As a front-line officer in the Continental Army, Marshall had contributed his share during the struggle for independence. As a delegate to the Virginia ratification convention, he had assisted materially in the birth of the federal government. During the next decade, he would devote himself to his professional obligations in Richmond—always keeping an eye on the state of the nation, but content to allow others to bear the responsibility and reap the benefits of government service. Marshall's dedication to the law, and the success that he achieved, prepared him as well as anything could have for the role he was ultimately called upon to play. Having fought for the nation and having helped to create it, he would eventually become the Constitution's primary interpreter and defender.

6

ベ

At the Richmond Bar

FTER VIRGINIA RATIFIED THE CONSTITUTION, Marshall
retired from the legislature. As he told Story, "I felt that those great
principles of public policy which I considered essential to the general happiness were secure . . . and I willingly relinquished public life to devote myself to my profession."[1] Marshall said that Henrico county was "so
thoroughly antifederal" that his reelection to the House of Delegates would
have been doubtful in any event. "This however was not my motive for withdrawing from the legislature. My practice had become very considerable, and
I could not spare from its claims on me so much time as would be necessary
to maintain such a standing in the legislature as I was desirous of preserving."[2]

Given Marshall's role at the ratifying convention, it was not surprising
that the federalists soon pressed him to become Richmond's candidate for
the U.S. House of Representatives. Marshall indicated to Story that he believed he could have been elected because the powerful antifederalist vote
"was almost equally divided between two candidates who were equally obstinate and much embittered against each other."

> The struggle between the ambition of being engaged in the organi-
> zation of government, and the conviction of the injury which would
> be sustained by my private affairs was at length terminated in the
> victory of prudence, after which the federalists set up and elected
> Colonel [Samuel] Griffin, who obtained rather more than one third
> of the votes in the district which constituted a plurality.[3]

Griffin was the first to recognize the debt he owed Marshall for having declined the federalist nomination. Eager to repay the favor, one of his first acts upon arriving in New York for the initial session of Congress was to recommend that Marshall be appointed United States attorney for Virginia.[4] President Washington, who had already retained Marshall to handle his own legal matters, readily agreed and submitted his name to the Senate for approval when the Congress convened. Marshall was confirmed unanimously, and on September 30, 1789, Washington wrote to him enclosing his commission.[5] "The high importance of the Judicial System in our national Government made it an indispensable duty to select such characters to fill the several offices in it as would discharge their respective trusts with honor to themselves and advantage to their Country."[6]

The appointment took Marshall by surprise. No one had spoken to him about it, and his name had been put forward without his consent. Griffin simply assumed that Marshall would accept the post. However, as Marshall later told Story, much as he would have liked to have been United States attorney, the demands imposed by that job would have forced him to cut back his lucrative practice at the state courts in Richmond. The federal court met in Charlottesville and Williamsburg, and Marshall realized that the situation would be unworkable.[7] Accordingly, on October 14, 1789, he wrote to Washington, declining the post.

> I thank you sir very sincerely for the honor which I feel is done me by an appointment flowing from your choice, and I beg leave to declare that it is with real regret I decline accepting an office which has to me been rendered highly valuable by the hand which bestowed it. Could a due attention to the duties of the office have consisted with my practice in the superior courts of this State I should with great satisfaction have endeavored to discharge them, but the sessions of the federal and state courts being at the same time in different places an attendance on the one becomes incompatible with the duties of an Attorney in the other.[8]

By 1789 Marshall's professional life had hit full stride. His income approached £1,500 annually, and his practice, like that of most successful lawyers of the time, depended on volume rather than retainers from one or two major clients. Most of Marshall's fees derived from litigation. These were set by statute and ranged from slightly more than £1 for routine case work to £5 for chancery suits and suits involving land titles.[9] Marshall's account book for 1789 indicates that he served over 300 clients that year, and out of those 300, only half a dozen paid fees exceeding £10.[10] It was the need to service this large clientele that lay behind his refusal to accept the post of United States attorney. Always candid about the necessity to earn a living, Marshall wrote hastily to Archibald Stuart in December 1789 that "A client is just come in—pray heaven he may have money."[11]

Marshall found the remuneration he was looking for in the work he did before the Virginia court of appeals. Appellate cases commanded substantially higher fees than cases in the general court, and, fortunately for Marshall, they were the type best suited to his talents. His ability to digest a complicated factual record, deploy the relevant legal principles, and fashion a tight logical argument made him one of the most successful practitioners before the state's highest court. Beginning with *Hite v. Fairfax* in 1786, he appeared in 125 cases before that tribunal over the course of the next ten years and was the counsel of record in almost every major case to come before it.[12] Marshall had a special knack for rebuttal. If there was the slightest flaw in a tightly woven case, he would detect it and proceed to unravel the fabric. Of the 125 cases he argued before the court, he won 67, lost 56, and 2 decisions were divided.[13]

During the years that Marshall practiced in Richmond, the court of appeals was headed by Edmund Pendleton, whose judicial influence on Marshall was profound. Pendleton exercised tremendous control over his colleagues on the Virginia court. "If he went wrong, they all went wrong, for without him they could not go at all," wrote one observer,[14] and it was from Pendleton that Marshall learned the importance of having the court speak primarily through its chief, a practice he instituted on the United States Supreme Court when he became chief justice in 1801.

One of the most important cases Marshall argued before Pendleton was *Bracken v. College of William and Mary*,[15] a 1790 case involving the independence of private educational institutions from government control. *Bracken* provides additional insight into Marshall's early views on constitutional interpretation, and his argument before the court of appeals presages his famous *Dartmouth College* decision of thirty years later.[16] Like the *Dartmouth* case, *Bracken* raised important issues concerning the interpretation of corporate charters. Marshall, not surprisingly, argued that charters, like constitutions, should be interpreted broadly. "In all institutions which are to be durable, only great leading and general principles ought to be immutable."[17]

The issue involved the dismissal of the Reverend John Bracken by William and Mary's board of visitors in 1779. When the board, under Jefferson's leadership, abolished the professorships of classics and Oriental languages, Bracken was one of those who lost his post.[18] He brought suit, asking the court to issue a writ of *mandamus* ordering the college to restore him to his position. Bracken contended that the board lacked the authority under its charter to dismiss professors and that his employment had been wrongfully terminated. The case raised the question of the relative authority of the board of visitors versus that of the faculty, as well as a more general dispute as to the appropriate direction the curriculum should take. The faculty favored the traditional approach emphasizing the classics, while the board sought to introduce the study of law, medicine, and modern languages.

The record of the proceedings in general court was destroyed in the Richmond fire of 1865, but it would appear that the question of whether the court should issue the writ of *mandamus* was adjourned to the court of appeals sometime in the late 1780s.[19] Marshall was retained by the college in 1787, and the case finally made it to the head of the docket in December 1790.

Marshall argued that the court lacked jurisdiction because William and Mary was not a public entity but "a private eleemosynary institution" governed entirely by its own board of visitors. Accordingly, said Marshall, a writ of *mandamus*, which was a common law device to compel a government official to take action, was not an appropriate remedy.[20]

As to the merits of the Reverend Bracken's claim, Marshall argued that the board acted within its implicit powers to change the college's curriculum. The college charter was broadly written, he said, and gave to the board the "power to make such laws for the government of the college, from time to time, *according to their various occasion and circumstance*, as to them should seem most fit and expedient."[21] Marshall said this necessarily included the power to modify the curriculum "because a particular branch of science, which, at one period of time would be deemed all important, might at another be thought not worth acquiring."

Marshall recognized that the interpretation of constitutional provisions required considerable discretion, but he seldom stated his views as crisply as he did before the court of appeals in 1790. He was opposed by John Taylor of Caroline, who represented Bracken, and who made an equally powerful argument for the strict interpretation of the college's charter. This early encounter between Marshall and Taylor foreshadowed the confrontation the two men would have later in their careers over the nature of the United States Constitution. Marshall, as chief justice, would hold that the Constitution established broad, general principles, while Taylor would become one of the most articulate defenders of states rights and what today might be called original intent. "The constitution of the college, like all other constitutions, ought to be preserved inviolate," said Taylor.[22]

The judges of the court of appeals who heard the case, in addition to chief judge Pendleton, included Paul Carrington, William Fleming, Peter Lyons, and Spencer Roane. They ignored Marshall's contention that the court lacked jurisdiction over "private eleemosynary institutions," but accepted his argument that the college's charter should be interpreted broadly. On December 8, 1790, the court ruled "on the merits of the case" that the

Reverend Bracken was not entitled to a writ of *mandamus* to restore his position.[23]

Several other cases that Marshall argued during his years in Richmond were of more than routine interest. In two of them, the Bizarre murder inquest and *Ware v. Hylton*,[24] the British debt case, he joined forces with Patrick Henry to provide his clients with what was, arguably, the most formidable combination of legal talent ever assembled. Marshall and Henry got along well. They enjoyed each other's company, shared a mutual respect, and eventually became warm friends.* They also worked well together, and their talents complemented each other perfectly. Marshall fashioned the strategy and developed the points at issue with his crisp, logical style; Henry, ever engaging and always eloquent, provided the spark that gave electricity to the cause.

The Bizarre inquest saw Marshall teamed with Henry in one of the most lurid criminal dramas in Virginia's history. In the winter of 1792–93, the state was rocked by rumors of adultery and infanticide among the Randolphs. Richard Randolph, the grandson of Richard of Curles and the master of the aptly named Bizarre plantation in Cumberland county, was said to have fathered a child by his sister-in-law, Nancy, and then to have killed the infant at birth. The dreadful incident allegedly occurred at Glenlyvar, the plantation of Richard's cousin Randolph Harrison. On the night of October 1, 1792, Richard, his wife Judith, and Nancy were Harrison's overnight guests. In the early-morning hours, after Nancy supposedly had given birth, Richard was reported to have suffocated the child and then deposited it on a pile of wood shingles some distance behind the mansion, where it was discovered by the plantation's slaves. The story quickly began to circulate, at first among the slaves, but soon traveling to the white community where it spread like wildfire, gaining embellishments and growing more horrible with each retelling.

The tale appeared plausible enough. Ann Cary Randolph, known as Nancy, was a vivacious and strong-willed daughter of Jefferson's boyhood friend Thomas Mann Randolph of Tuckahoe. In 1791 the sixteen-year-old Nancy quarreled with her father over the choosing of a husband and decided to move in with her sister Judith and Judith's husband, Richard Ran-

---

*When President Washington's second term was about to expire, New York federalists asked Marshall to explore with Henry whether he would be interested in seeking the presidency as Washington's successor. Marshall met with Henry on May 22, 1796, and afterward informed the New Yorkers that Henry was "unwilling to embark in the business. His unwillingness I think proceeds from an apprehension of the difficulties to be encountered by those who shall fill high executive offices." Marshall to Rufus King, May 24, 1796. 3 *The Papers of John Marshall* 28 (Chapel Hill: University of North Carolina Press, 1979).

dolph, at Bizarre. Nancy had a host of suitors, including Richard's two younger brothers, Theodoric and John, who was subsequently known as John of Roanoke. Nancy and Theodoric soon fell in love and planned to marry. But in February 1792, before they could do so, Theodoric took ill and died suddenly, leaving Nancy alone and despondent. Following Theodoric's death, Richard was often observed to be extremely solicitous of Nancy. Many believed that they had seen them embrace as lovers might. Others recalled seeing a change in Nancy's youthful figure, while some, Jefferson's daughter Martha included, remembered that Nancy was often ill, perhaps with morning sickness, and had once requested some gum guaiacum, which was popularly believed to induce abortion.[25]

On the night of October 1, Richard, Judith, Nancy, and Archibald Randolph, Nancy's escort, arrived by carriage at Randolph Harrison's home shortly before dinner. Nancy was so unwell that she immediately went upstairs to bed. However, she emerged a short while later for dinner and seemed to be quite recovered. Soon after the meal Nancy again went upstairs to her room. Judith and Richard, who had the adjacent room, went to bed shortly afterward.

In the middle of the night, a woman's screams, coming from the second floor of the house, were loud enough to wake the Harrisons in their main-floor bedroom. Mrs. Harrison ran upstairs only to find Nancy's door locked. She knocked and Richard opened the door. Mrs. Harrison stayed with Nancy for some time, but when she found her resting easier she left and returned downstairs.[26] The next morning Mrs. Harrison found Nancy in bed, closely wrapped in blankets. She saw some blood on the pillow case and the stairs, but could not see either the sheets or the quilt. Nancy remained in bed that day and did not return to Bizarre until the following weekend. Mrs. Harrison thought nothing more about the mysterious evening until she was told several weeks later by one of the servants that Nancy had miscarried. Mrs. Harrison then reexamined the bed and found that an attempt had been made to wash it, but that it was still badly stained. Mr. Harrison likewise believed nothing was amiss until five or six weeks later when a slave took him to the woodpile and showed him a stain on the shingles where the fetus allegedly had been placed.[27]

By December, the story of what was presumed to have happened at Glenlyvar had become common gossip. Richard was said to have fathered the child, adding adultery to the accusation of infanticide. Seeking desperately to quell the rumors, Nancy, Judith, and Richard spent several days in January 1793 in Williamsburg with Richard's stepfather, St. George Tucker. Tucker had succeeded George Wythe as professor of law at William and Mary and was also a judge on the general court. On Tucker's recommendation, Richard sought out Marshall, who devised the strategy that ultimately brought the matter to a head.

Marshall did not know whether Richard was culpable, and there is no evidence that he ever inquired. Insofar as he was concerned, his client was innocent until proven guilty in a court of law. Consequently, he advised Richard to get the matter before a court as quickly as possible. There was no body of a dead child—no *corpus deliciti*—to establish that a crime had been committed and no witnesses who could testify to the existence of one. The evidence that did exist consisted merely of hearsay and innuendo. Believing that no charges would be laid and that Richard would be set free, Marshall advised him to appear before the court and ask to be either tried or released. This would not end the gossip, but it would mean that as a matter of law Richard and, by implication, Nancy were innocent.[28] Accordingly, on March 29, 1793, Richard notified several newspapers that he intended to appear before the Cumberland county court when it met for its April term.[29] As Marshall had urged, Richard was daring the slanderers to come forward. If they were unwilling to come to court, Randolph asked them to publish their charges together with the evidence so that the public might judge for themselves.

As the term of court approached, Marshall went over tactics with Richard. Since the testimony would be taken in open session, he recommended that Richard retain Patrick Henry to examine the witnesses. In Marshall's view, Henry was the finest trial lawyer in Virginia, and when it came to handling witnesses, he had no peer. Richard followed Marshall's suggestion and, according to legend, offered Henry £250 to represent him—an exorbitant fee for the period.[30] Henry initially declined. He was not well, and had been living in semiretirement on his plantation at Red Hill for the past two years. Richard nevertheless persisted, doubled the fee, and promised that the inquest would be held shortly.[31] Henry's biographer indicates that the great statesman discussed the matter with his wife. "Dolly," he said, "Mr. Randolph seems very anxious that I should appear for him, and 500 Guineas is a large sum. Don't you think I could make a trip [to Cumberland courthouse] in the carriage?"[32] Mrs. Henry knew her husband well enough to know that he longed for the drama of another courtroom confrontation, and she consented to his appearance. Marshall would prepare the case, organize the defense, and handle the details, while Henry, as he had so often done, would administer the coup de grâce.

On April 22, 1793, Richard appeared before one or more of the justices of the peace who had assembled to conduct the Cumberland county court. It is not known how the charges were formally made, but a magistrate ordered that Richard be held by the sheriff for an official inquest to be conducted by the entire county court, which was composed of sixteen magistrates.*[33] There was no provision for bail at that point in the proceedings, and Richard was held in custody until the magistrates, together with whatever witnesses were called, assembled on April 29.

No official transcript of the proceedings was made. The only information available about the testimony derives from the notes taken by Marshall.[34] According to his records, seventeen witnesses were called. Several said they had observed Richard and Nancy embrace, and a few commented on Nancy's alteration in size, but none could provide direct evidence that a child had been born or subsequently killed. Richard testified in his own defense but, pursuant to common law procedure, was not sworn under oath.[35] Virginia statutes precluded the slaves from testifying, and although she had been examined by one of the magistrates before the inquest, Nancy did not take the stand.[36] Martha Jefferson, who was one of the witnesses to appear, testified that she believed Nancy to have been pregnant, but the Harrisons testified that they had found nothing suspect. The other witnesses were either friendly or were extremely careful, under Henry's watchful eye, to say nothing that could not be substantiated. The one exception was Nancy's gossiping aunt, Mary Cary Page. Mrs. Page's father was Archibald Cary of Warwick county. A former member of the Virginia House of Delegates, Cary had once threatened to plant a dagger in Patrick Henry's heart, an incident that Henry had not forgotten.

On the witness stand, Mrs. Page told the court at great length how Nancy had refused to allow her to examine her body. In Mrs. Page's eyes, this was highly suspicious behavior. Lowering her voice, Mrs. Page confided that she had surreptitiously observed a suggestively plump-looking Nancy through a crack in Nancy's bedroom door while the young woman was undressing.

Henry, savoring Mrs. Page's testimony, waited just long enough for the comment about seeing Nancy through the crack of the bedroom door to sink in. "Which eye did you peep with?" he asked in a tone heavy with sarcasm. The courtroom, which Henry had slowly won over by his deft handling of the earlier witnesses, erupted with laughter as Mrs. Page flushed with embarrassment. When the laughter subsided, Henry's voice boomed out to the magistrates, "Great God, deliver us from eavesdroppers!"[37]

---

*Virginia law provided that a free person charged with a crime would be brought before a magistrate who could determine whether an examination by the whole county court was necessary. If the magistrate so decided, he would order the accused held in jail, direct material witnesses to appear, and instruct the sheriff to summon the entire court to assemble for the examination. If the offense was a capital crime, the examining court would decide whether the prisoner should be released or be held for trial in the district court having jurisdiction. 1 Shepherd 20–21 (1792).

Marshall delivered the closing argument and summarized the evidence for the court. He noted that Richard's apparent attachment to Nancy was the normal affection that a brother might bestow on a sister who had lost her betrothed under tragic circumstances. He observed that the witnesses differed as to whether Nancy had appeared pregnant or not and that those who knew her best doubted it. In any case, an increase in a woman's girth could be caused by many things. As for the gum guaiacum, it had various uses, and if Nancy had wanted to induce an abortion she would surely have been more circumspect about taking it. The events at Glenlyvar excited no suspicion at the time they occurred, he said, and Nancy had resumed a regular, active life when she returned to Bizarre. Marshall dwelt last on Nancy's refusal to be examined by the officious Mrs. Page and noted that "the pride of conscious innocence was sufficient to produce the refusal." He concluded with customary understatement: "The friends of Mrs. Randolph cannot deny that there is some foundation on which suspicion may build. Nor can it be denied by her enemies but that every circumstance may be accounted for, without imparting guilt to her. In this situation, candor will not condemn or exclude from society, a person who may only be unfortunate."[38]

The affection of the judges for the young woman was more evident than their sympathy for her brother-in-law.[39] Accordingly, Marshall rested his case on Nancy's innocence. Cumberland county's sixteen magistrates did not retire to reach a verdict. When Marshall concluded, they signaled one another by eye and gesture and then announced their decision. No charges would be forwarded and the matter of *Commonwealth v. Randolph* was dismissed.[40] The packed courtroom erupted in cheers and applause. Henry and Marshall had prevailed, and Richard was set free.

The dismissal of the charges did not halt the gossip or repair the animosity that had developed among the various Randolphs over the incident. The Tuckahoe clan never forgave Patrick Henry for his demolition of Mrs. Page,[41] and Richard, Judith, and Nancy were ostracized by many in society. Thomas Jefferson, who followed the affair from Philadelphia, essentially agreed with Marshall and Henry, and cautioned his daughter against bitterness. Jefferson said that Nancy had suffered enough, and he urged Martha to "provide commiseration and comfort regardless of what the trifling or malignant may think."[42] Richard Randolph never recovered from the scandal. He died three years later, despondent to the end. Nancy continued to live with her sister Judith at Bizarre for several years and later moved to New York, where she struggled to support herself by teaching school.[43]

Not until 1815 was the truth of what happened at Glenlyvar revealed, when Nancy was finally provoked into telling her side of the story. First in a letter to John Randolph that was widely distributed among friends and family, and then in a series of private letters to St. George Tucker, she explained that in 1792, she and Theodoric had been very much in love and had become engaged to be married. They had conceived a child, but Theodoric had died almost immediately afterward. "We should have been married, if Death had not snatched him away a few days after the scene which began the history of my sorrows."[44] Nancy said that on September 30, the night before the dinner at Glenlyvar, she had given birth to Theodoric's child at Bizarre, but the child was stillborn. Richard Randolph knew what had happened, she said, but he never told anyone, not when he became the object of the community's scorn, and not even when he was threatened with a murder trial. "He was a man of honor," said Nancy.[45]

Marshall's next great legal challenge, and his next great partnership with Patrick Henry, arose only one month after the conclusion of the Bizarre inquest when the bellweather British debt case, *Ware v. Hylton*, came before the United States circuit court in Richmond.[46] The status of British debts—the money owed by individual Americans to English creditors—had been a controversial issue since the revolution, and it continued to embitter relations between the two countries until well into the nineteenth century. The extent of American indebtedness was enormous, approaching £5 million sterling, with almost half of that (£2.3 million) owed by Virginians.[47] That debt was divided almost equally between the piedmont region and tidewater. In the piedmont, stores operated by Scottish merchants had extended credit generously to the small farmers and artisans of the area. In tidewater, the large planters and merchants had dealt with English consignment houses, which also extended credit liberally.[48]

Like colonial nations throughout history, Americans bridled at their increasing debt load. Their enthusiasm for independence was fueled in no small measure by the prospect of freeing themselves from their financial bondage to British creditors. In 1777 the Virginia legislature took an important step in that direction when it passed an act for sequestering British property.[49] Under the act, citizens could rid themselves of their debts to British subjects by paying an equivalent amount into the state treasury. Payment could be made in Virginia's paper currency even though the debt was in sterling. The legislature saw the proposal as a useful way of raising money to bolster the state's depleted finances. They had no intention of passing the funds on to the British.[50]

Initially, few Virginians took advantage of the scheme. But as the state's currency depreciated in value, it soon became possible to pay off the original debt at a fraction of its value, and canny Virginians responded in droves.[51] Jefferson, for example, made two payments totaling £2,666 to discharge the indebtedness of an estate of which he was executor; George Washington paid £5,008; Edmund Pendleton, £103; Judge John Blair, £1,005; and there were abundant entires in the state's ledger for the Randolphs, Byrds, Blands, Burwells, and other prominent families.[52]

A second act, passed by the Virginia legislature in May 1782, declared "that no debt or demand whatsoever, originally due to a subject to Great Britain, shall be recoverable in any court in this commonwealth."[53] This constituted a total bar to recovery, and the state courts simply refused to hear any suits on the subject. Having effectively insulated themselves from their British debts, Virginians began to believe that for all practical purposes the debts had been dissolved.

The British creditors saw the issue differently. Despite the war, they continued to insist on full payment, plus accrued interest. The problem was formally addressed by the 1783 Treaty of Paris, which granted American independence. Article 4 of the treaty explicitly stipulated that creditors were to "meet with no lawful impediment to the recovery of the full value in sterling money, of all *bona fide* debts heretofore contracted."[54]

Under the Articles of Confederation, Article 4 of the Treaty of Paris remained a dead letter. The states, Virginia in particular, refused to comply, and the Continental Congress lacked the means to enforce the treaty.[55] By 1786 the British government had become sufficiently exasperated by the states' refusal to honor Article 4 that renewed hostilities with the United States were a distinct possibility.[56] This threat, as much as the fear of anarchy triggered by Shays's Rebellion in Massachusetts, led to the calling of the Philadelphia convention and the drafting of the Constitution.

The Framers addressed the problem of noncompliance with the Treaty of Paris directly. Article VI of the United States Constitution stated in no uncertain terms: ". . . all treaties made . . . under the Authority of the United States shall be the supreme Law of the Land; and the Judges of every State shall be bound thereby, any Thing in the Constitution or Laws of any State to the Contrary notwithstanding." The carefully chosen phraseology of the article had the effect of making the Treaty of Paris apply retroactively as the supreme law of the land. Virginia and the other states would be forced by federal authority to comply with its terms. Of equal import, the judiciary article of the Constitution, the one so vigorously contested at the Virginia ratifying convention, provided that the federal courts, not the state courts, would have jurisdiction over suits brought by foreigners against American citizens.[57] That effectively ended Virginia's judicial blockade and paved the way for British creditors to bring suit.

With the establishment of the federal circuit courts in 1790, British creditors were able to commence litigation to recover the money owed to them. In fact, the vast majority of the cases filed in the federal courts in Virginia following the adoption of the Constitution were for the recovery of British debts. More than 100 such suits were brought at the first term of court, and within a year the number of actions filed exceeded 200. Many more potential plaintiffs waited on the sidelines until the first test cases were decided.[58]

The Virginians, especially those who owed money, followed the development with enormous anxiety. "I observe that the British Merchants have begun to prosecute the Recovery of their old debts before the people are in a situation to pay," Thomas Pleasants, a prominent James River merchant, wrote to Madison in July 1790.[59] Some Virginians blamed the new national government for reviving the issue, and almost all believed that it was unrealistic to expect the matter to be settled in private lawsuits. The antagonisms generated by the War of Independence made it impossible to separate the question of prewar British debts from the larger issue of diplomatic relations between the United States and Great Britain. The parties to the suits became symbols of the dignity of their respective nations, and the public looked increasingly to the governments of the countries to settle the matter in international negotiations.

For a time, Virginians managed to keep the issue of prewar British debts in legal limbo. Not unlike southern segregationists of the 1950s and 1960s, they devised a series of stratagems to frustrate collection in the courts. The elaborate arguments were primarily political, and the master strategist was, ironically, John Marshall. Devout federalist, champion of the new Constitution, and an advocate of compliance with the Treaty of Paris during his tenure in the House of Delegates, Marshall served as the primary counsel for virtually all of the defendants.[60] The Randolphs, Harrisons, Byrds, and even Thomas Jefferson turned to Marshall. In fact, so numerous were his British debt cases, and so elaborate was the defense he fashioned, that Marshall had his pleadings printed rather than writing each one in longhand. These printed forms, with the names of the litigants and the particular facts at issue inserted in Marshall's hand, survive in great numbers among the papers of the federal circuit court in Richmond.

Marshall established four lines of defense. First, he argued that if the debtor had paid the funds into the Virginia sequestration office, the debt was legally discharged. Second, he maintained that the Virginia statute of 1782, which barred recovery, had not been repealed and was therefore still in force. Third, he contended that because Britain had failed to honor those provisions of the Treaty of Paris requiring compensation to be paid for slaves carried off during the war and for the evacuation of the forts in the Northwest Territory, the treaty was void. Finally, he argued that whatever right the British plaintiffs may have had was "totally annulled" by the dissolution of the "then subsisting government" on July 4, 1776. Whether Marshall seriously believed he could prevail in court is not known. But if his purpose was merely to delay a decision until the matter was settled at the governmental level, the obstacle course he constructed was remarkably effective.

The initial test case, *Jones v. Walker*, did not make it to the circuit court's docket until November 1791, eighteen months after the first suits were filed.[61] One reason for the delay, aside from the complex nature of eighteenth-century litigation, was that the new federal judges were reluctant to confront the array of constitutional issues raised in Marshall's pleadings. Thanks to the intricate defense he had stitched together, the British debt cases posed uncomfortable issues that went far beyond the common law of contract. Were the laws of Virginia compelled to yield to the Treaty of Paris as the "supreme law of the land"? If the treaty automatically superseded conflicting state laws, did it also nullify prior state actions taken under those laws, such as Virginia's sequestration scheme? Was the treaty of 1783 void because of British noncompliance? And equally vexing, did the judiciary have the authority to declare a treaty void? All of these questions had to be dealt with, and the judges procrastinated as long as they could.[62]

When *Jones v. Walker* finally came before the court for oral argument, the atmosphere in Richmond was electric.[63] The House of Delegates adjourned so that members could attend the trial, and the commodious courtroom, more than ample for most cases, was jammed to capacity. A contemporary observer reported that an even larger audience stood on the patio outside, listening to the arguments through the open windows.[64]

The facts of the case were straightforward. William Jones was the surviving partner of the Bristol commission firm of Farell and Jones, perhaps the largest and most important British company trading with tidewater planters before the war. The defendant, Dr. Thomas Walker, was a noted surgeon, a veteran of the Virginia Line, and a successful land speculator. In 1779 Walker had paid £2,150 into the Virginia treasury to discharge his debt to the Bristol firm. Now, in 1791, under the terms of the treaty, the Bristol firm was trying to recover its money.* Marshall was the attorney of record for Dr. Walker, and he was joined by Patrick Henry, Alexander Campbell, and Virginia's attorney general, James Innes. The plaintiff's case was put by Jerman Baker, assisted by Andrew Ronald, John Wickham, and Burwell Starke, thus bringing together eight of the most able lawyers in Virginia.[65]

Marshall's defense strategy relied on the pyrotechnics of Patrick Henry, who spoke for three days and converted the trial into a contest between American independence and British tyranny. "The conduct of that nation becomes once more the subject of investigation," said Henry, as he pro-

---

*In 1779, the £2,150 paid in Virginia paper currency by Dr. Walker to liquidate his debt had a specie value of £107.

ceeded to detail a catalogue of injustices flowing from the crown.[66] The effect was all that Marshall and his client could have hoped for. By the time Henry had finished, the debtors in attendance must have been persuaded that they did not owe a shilling to their British creditors.[67] All eight counsel spoke extensively, but it was Henry's effort that dominated the proceedings.

The trial came to naught, however, when Justice Blair left the bench before the arguments concluded. His son had died suddenly, and he departed to attend the funeral. In Blair's absence, Justice Johnson and Judge Griffin declined to render judgment. The case was continued through two court terms in 1792. In the meantime, William Jones died and John Tyndale Ware, his administrator, was substituted as plaintiff. Because of the delays related to the substitution, a similar suit, *Ware v. Hylton*, which was already pending, was substituted as the test case,[68] and a second hearing on the question of British debts was scheduled for May 24, 1793.[69] Once again Marshall, with the help of Patrick Henry, made ready to confound British claims.

This time the case was heard by Chief Justice John Jay, Justice James Iredell, and district judge Cyrus Griffin. The arguments presented were a repeat of those submitted in 1791. Henry held forth with another epic performance, and Marshall, as usual, argued the law.[70] "The discussion," one observer reported, "was one of the most brilliant exhibitions ever witnessed at the Bar of Virginia."[71] The Countess of Huntingdon, who was visiting Richmond and heard the arguments, said that "If every one had spoken in Westminster Hall, they would have been honored with a peerage."[72] Another observer, John Nicholas of Albemarle county, wrote to John Breckinridge in Kentucky that "I have just returned from Richmond where I have been listening to a very lengthy and able argument on the subject of British debts. The bar all acquitted themselves well, but most of all our friend Marshall, it was acknowledged on all hands, excelled himself in *sound sense* and *argument*, which you know is saying an immensity."[73]

The most reliable evidence of the quality of the arguments is found in the decisions of the judges. Chief Justice Jay said the cause "has been ingeniously and industriously managed."[74] Justice Iredell said:

> The cause has been spoken to at the bar, with a degree of ability equal to any occasion. I shall as long as I live remember with pleasure and respect the arguments which I have heard on this case. They have discovered an ingenuity, a depth of investigation, and a power of reasoning fully equal to anything I have ever witnessed, and some of them have been adorned with a splendor of eloquence surpassing what I have ever felt before. Fatigue has given way under its influence, and the heart has been warmed; while the understanding has been instructed.[75]

Iredell's latter remarks were addressed to Henry.[76] "Gracious God! He is an orator indeed," the Supreme Court justice said to Jay as they left the courtroom.[77] The court had little difficulty dismissing defense arguments that the rights of the creditors had lapsed with the Declaration of Independence in 1776, and they unanimously rejected the contention that the judiciary had the authority to declare a treaty void. Likewise, they held that the Virginia act of 1782 was overturned by Article VI of the Constitution, which made the Treaty of Paris the supreme law of the land. On the question of sequestration, however, Iredell and Judge Griffin ruled that those Virginians who had made payment into the state treasury had legitimately discharged their personal debt and that, in effect, the state of Virginia had assumed the burden. British creditors still had a right to payment, but they should seek redress from the state, not the debtor.[78] Over Jay's vigorous dissent, Iredell and Griffin held that Article 4 of the Treaty of Paris did not overturn the Virginia sequestration statute of 1777.

The circuit court decision in *Ware v. Hylton* eliminated three of the four defenses Marshall had fashioned to protect Virginia's debtors. However, for those who had paid into the state treasury, the holding provided reassurance that they were no longer liable. Based on the strength of Jay's dissent, Ware appealed that portion of the decision to the Supreme Court, setting the stage for one of the most important decisions ever rendered by the Court. Because of a series of procedural delays, the case was not heard until February 1796. Marshall argued the appeal for Virginia's debtors with Alexander Campbell. Patrick Henry, who had retired from practice, chose not to make the trip to Philadelphia. This was the only case in which Marshall appeared before the Supreme Court, and he was hampered in his presentation by his unwillingness to diminish the scope of the supremacy clause of the Constitution.[79] Instead, he sought to reconcile the Constitution and the Virginia sequestration statute by construing the Treaty of Paris in such a way as to permit Virginia's earlier action. The result was a brilliant piece of advocacy that demonstrated Marshall's effectiveness in bending words to suit his purpose. But he failed to convince the four sitting justices[80] that the Virginia sequestration statute fell outside the scope of the peace treaty, and they unanimously overturned the circuit court holding, thus depriving Virginia debtors of their last defense.[81]

Despite his defeat in *Ware v. Hylton*, Marshall's reputation as a leading member of the Virginia bar was now secure. On an extended tour of North America in the 1790s, the Duke de la Rochefoucault-Liancourt spent considerable time in Richmond and kept an extensive record of his impressions. He noted that "Mr. Edmund Randolph, heretofore Secretary of State of the Union, ... follows here the profession of lawyer. ... He has a great practice, and stands in that respect nearly on a par with Mr. J. Marshall, the most esteemed and celebrated counsellor in this town."[82] Marshall, he said, "is beyond all doubt one of those who rank highest in the public opinion at Richmond."

> He is what is termed a federalist, and perhaps at times somewhat warm in support of his opinions, but never exceeding the bounds of propriety. . . . He may be considered as a distinguished character in the United States. His political enemies allow him to possess great talents, but accuse him of ambition. I know not whether the charge be well or ill grounded, or whether that ambition might ever be able to impel him to a dereliction of his principles—a conduct of which I am inclined to disbelieve the possibility on his part. He has already refused several employments under the general government, preferring the income derived from his professional labours (which is more than sufficient for his moderate system of economy), together with a life of tranquil ease in the midst of his family and in his native town. Even by his friends he is taxed with some little propensity to indolence; but even if this reproach were well founded, he nevertheless displays great superiority in his profession when he applies his mind to business.[83]

Marshall's "moderate system of economy," as the duke phrased it, may have been modest by the standards of European nobility, and certainly was less opulent than that of Washington, Jefferson, and Madison, but it was scarcely threadbare. In the autumn of 1788, just after the Virginian ratification convention adjourned, Marshall purchased a half-acre lot in what was known as the court end of Richmond and commenced construction of a suitable home for his growing family.[84] Ultimately the Marshalls would have ten children, although only six lived to adulthood. The court end had become the most fashionable area of Virginia's rapidly growing capital, deriving its name from its proximity of the statehouse and the law courts. Marshall's lot stood at the corner of the Ninth and I Streets.[85] It was a short walk from the capitol building, and his neighbors included many of his fellow attorneys as well as most of his in-laws. Jaquelin Ambler lived nearby, as did three of Polly's brothers-in-law: Edward Carrington, Daniel Call, and the merchant George Fisher. Spencer Roane and John Wickham lived in the neighborhood, as did John Brockenbrough, president of the Bank of Virginia, Thomas Ritchie, publisher of the Richmond *Enquirer*, William Wirt, Judge Philip Nicholas, and Marshall's sometime political rival, Dr. William Foushee.

Marshall's house was substantial but not elaborate. Built of brick in the symmetrical Federal style of the period, the house took two years to complete and cost Marshall a little more than £1,200, which was roughly equivalent to one year's income.[86] The building was forty-five feet square, two and a half stories high, and contained nine rooms, including an especially large dining room that soon became the setting for Marshall's famous "lawyers' dinners"—the sumptuous stag affairs that he hosted monthly for his colleagues in Richmond. The rooms downstairs were paneled, with classical wainscoting. A porcelain bowl given to Marshall by Patrick Henry was prominently displayed on a sideboard in the dining room. Years later Marshall acquired a set of state china that had originally been ordered in France by President Monroe. A parsimonious Congress had refused to pay the bill, and Marshall purchased the set for himself to save Monroe embarrassment.[87]

Insurance records indicate that there were several outbuildings, including the kitchen, laundry, stable, a small cabin for Marshall's servant couple, and his law office, a typical arrangement at the time in affluent circles.[88] Marshall's house, along with John Wickham's, was one of the few to survive the great fire of 1865, and it is now open to the public.[89] None of the outbuildings has survived.

Perhaps reflecting the mood of conviviality induced by the ratification convention, Marshall took the lead in the summer of 1788 in organizing Richmond's first men's social club, the celebrated Quoits Club or, as it was sometimes called, the Barbecue Club. Every Saturday afternoon from May through September, members assembled at Reverend John Buchanan's farm located on the outskirts of Richmond, about a mile west of Marshall's house. Membership was restricted to thirty, plus the governor and the city's two parsons, the Presbyterian minister John D. Blair, and the Episcopalian bishop, the Reverend Buchanan.[90] Most of Marshall's neighbors belonged to the Quoits Club, as did the city's principal merchants and politicians. The all-male coterie would devour a sumptuous lunch set on a long trestle table under a rough frame structure built to shield the men from the sun. Marshall and John Wickham were the club's first caterers, "and as they were *bon vivants* . . . they obtained for dinner the best the market afforded."[91] The meal was served promptly at 12:30 P.M., and the principal dish was always a barbecued pig.[92] According to a contemporary report:

> Mr. Marshall sat at the head and Mr. Wickham at the foot of the table. A better dinner of the substantials of life was rarely seen. The only dessert they indulged in was a steaming, juicy mutton chop, cooked to a turn, and a "devilled ham," highly seasoned with mustard, cayenne pepper, and a slight flavouring of Worcester sauce, and these were passed along the board.[93]

The rules of the club prohibited wine except on special occasions. Instead, the members imbibed a potent punch concocted by Marshall and

Wickham containing brandy, rum, and Madeira "poured into a bowl one-third filled with ice (no water), and sweetened." Lemons were added for garnish.[94] The rules prohibited the discussion of business, politics, or religion, and those who transgressed were fined a case of champagne, which the members would drink at the next meeting.

After the meal was consumed, the quoits players adjourned to the pits. Each player had his own set of quoits, usually made of brass, and kept highly polished by John Wickham's servant, Jasper Crouch, who served as one of the club's stewards. Marshall, however, had

> a set of the largest, most uncouth, rough iron quoits, which very few in the club could throw with any accuracy from hub to hub; but he threw them with great ease, and frequently rung the peg. . . . We have seen Mr. Marshall, in later times, when he was Chief Justice of the United States, on his hands and knees, with a straw and a pen-knife, the blade of the knife stuck through the straw, holding it between the edge of the quoit and the hub, and when it was a very doubtful question [as to which quoit was closest], pinching or biting off the ends of the straw until it would fit a hair.[95]

Marshall remained a club regular until he died, and relished the Saturday respite with his friends and neighbors, many of whom were his political adversaries.[96] He also participated enthusiastically in Richmond's St. Taminy festival, an annual celebration honoring America's mythical patron saint, facetiously canonized around 1770.* On May 1 of each year, members of the Sons of St. Taminy dressed as Indians and paraded through the city. This was followed by an elaborate banquet and occasionally a ball. Marshall's account book indicates that each year's celebration cost him £2, which suggests that the food and drink were copiously laid on.[97]

Marshall's style was not without its critics. Jefferson, who was always ill at ease in the tavern, criticized his "lax lounging manners."[98] George Mason, who used Marshall for his own legal work, thought he was often indolent,[99] and at least one writer has suggested that Polly's nervous affliction was partially attributable to her sitting up at night waiting for Marshall to return home from a late evening of cards and billiards.[100]

For all his natural sociability, however, Marshall took his work seriously and insisted that justice be administered equitably. This was never more ev-

---

*The name originated from Indian Chief Tamenende, or Tammany, a respected leader of the Delaware tribe. The Sons of St. Taminy [Tammany] was an offshoot of several patriotic societies formed during the Revolution. Members performed charitable works such as poor relief. These societies were forerunners of New York's Democratic organization, Tammany Hall. See *Dictionary of Americanisms*, Mitford M. Mathews, ed. (Chicago: University of Chicago Press, 1951).

ident than in his efforts to seek mercy in the 1793 murder conviction of Angelica Barnett. Angelica Barnett was a young black woman, free, not a slave,
whose home had been broken into late one night by a white man named Peter Franklin. Franklin was allegedly on an unofficial search for runaway
slaves. When no runaways were found, Franklin became abusive, assaulted
Barnett in front of her family, and threatened to kill her with the bludgeon
he carried. As Franklin advanced toward her, Barnett struck him in the head
with an ax. Franklin died from the wound four days later. Barnett was tried
for murder, convicted, and sentenced to hang.[101] The conviction and sentence raised an outcry throughout Richmond, and Polly, apparently for the
first and only time in her life, signed a public petition with three dozen of
the city's most prominent women asking Governor Henry Lee for mercy.[102]

To aggravate matters, Barnett was raped by a cellmate while in prison
and became pregnant.[103] Lee granted a temporary stay of execution,[104] and
while it was pending, Marshall joined with the leaders of the Richmond bar
to request clemency. Angelica Barnett "was possessed of many of the rights
of a free Citizen," said the petitioners, including "the great right of personal
immunity in her own house. This, unquestionably was invaded, . . . and it is
at least reasonable to presume that many of the Circumstances alleged by
the prisoner in her justification, might have been proved if her associates
were not incompetent by law to give Testimony against a White person."[105]
Marshall said he was not familiar with the evidence, but from what he had
heard of Barnett's character, he joined the petition for mercy. Governor Lee
received the lawyers' petition on September 12, 1793, and pardoned Barnett
that evening—one day before her scheduled execution.[106]

Marshall's view of slavery matured during this period. He owned several
slaves who performed routine household duties, but as he was never involved in large-scale agriculture, he had no significant holdings. In the 1790s
Marshall tried four slave cases before the court of appeals, and in three of
them he represented the slaves. His account book indicates that he received
no payment for the cases, and so one must assume that he volunteered his
services. Marshall's principal servant, Robin Spurlock, who, although a slave,
was a leading figure among Richmond's blacks, and it is likely that he
brought the cases to Marshall's attention.*[107]

The issue in each case involved intermarriage between blacks and Indians. Indians were free and enjoyed various rights granted in treaties they
had signed with the state of Virginia and the federal government. Under

---

*Spurlock remained with Marshall until the chief justice's death in 1835. In his will, Marshall
provided for Spurlock's freedom should he desire it; otherwise he might choose which of Marshall's children he would live with.

tribal law, Indian status was matrilineal, and Virginia statutes pertaining to Indians had adopted this rule.[108] Thus, all children of Indian women were considered to be Indian and therefore free persons, and that included the children of an Indian mother married to a slave. Slaveowners frequently ignored the law and treated the children of such couples as slaves. The only recourse for the child was to seek legal redress, but few had the means to do so. As a member of the legislature, Marshall had helped draft a bill to punish "persons guilty of selling free persons as slaves,"[109] and it is likely that Spurlock had little difficulty persuading him to take such cases free of charge.

In *Hannah v. Davis*,[110] Marshall teamed with James Monroe to establish the rule of maternal descent that subsequently served as the controlling precedent.[111] Six years later, in *Coleman v. Dick & Pat*, an action for assault and battery and false imprisonment brought by two slaves seeking their freedom on the basis of maternal descent, Marshall told the court that it was "useless to cite cases to establish such plain principles of law" and won a unanimous decision.[112] His concern for mistreated slaves and Indians was deeply held and earned him the respect of his fellow attorneys, many of whom were reluctant to accept such cases.

Marshall's dominant position at the Richmond bar was reinforced in the summer of 1794 when he was appointed Virginia's acting attorney general during James Innes's temporary absence from the state. In August 1794 President Washington had asked Innes to go to Kentucky and explain to the residents of the territory the current state of negotiations with Spain concerning navigation of the Mississippi River—a hot topic on the frontier, and one that Washington wanted handled promptly.[113] Innes accepted the mission and, with the approval of Governor Lee and the council of state, asked Marshall to stand in for him during the six months or so that he would be absent.[114] Marshall's duties as acting attorney general consisted primarily in rendering legal opinions to Governor Lee and the council of state. These were routine and broke no new ground.[115] Marshall acted as Virginia's attorney general until Innes returned in April 1795, and his account book indicates that he received no pay for his services.

Later that summer President Washington tried to persuade Marshall to move to Philadelphia and join his cabinet as Attorney General of the United States. William Bradford, who had replaced Edmund Randolph a year earlier, had died on August 23, 1795, and Washington instinctively turned to Marshall with the offer. "The salary annexed thereto and the prospect of a lucrative practice in this city . . . must be as well known to you . . . better perhaps . . . than they are to me, and therefore I shall say nothing concerning them." Washington added, "If your answer is in the affirmative, it will readily occur to you that no unnecessary time should be lost in repairing to this place. If on the contrary it should be in the negative (which I should be very sorry for) it might be as well to say nothing of this offer. But in either case I pray you to give me an answer as promptly as you can."[116]

Marshall replied by return post. Much as he would have liked to join Washington's administration, he said that the pressure of his personal business affairs simply would not permit it. "While the business I have undertaken to complete in Richmond forbids me to change my situation tho for one indefinitely more eligible, permit me Sir to express my sincere acknowledgements for the offer your letter contains, and the real pride and gratification I feel at the favorable opinion it indicates."[117]

The business in Richmond to which Marshall alluded involved his efforts to purchase a substantial portion of the Fairfax estate from Lord Fairfax's heirs and to obtain a clear title to the property. Neither task was proving easy. Because of his birth and upbringing, Marshall was committed emotionally to the northern neck lands. He was endeavoring to negotiate a settlement with the Virginia government that would recognize the state's claim to the bulk of the proprietary, while protecting the Fairfax claim to what were known as the "manor lands," the lands Lord Fairfax had set aside for his personal use. And it was these manor lands that Marshall sought to buy.

Marshall's interest in purchasing the manor lands, totaling about 215,000 acres, traced to the 1786 decision in *Hite v. Fairfax*, which implicitly recognized the Fairfax claim to the proprietary.[118] Lord Fairfax's heir, the Reverend Denny Martin Fairfax, lived in England, had no interest in moving to North America, and was eager to sell his holdings.[119] The state of Virginia, however, saw the proprietary as a potential source of revenue and had begun to confiscate and sell off those portions that had not already been appropriated.[120] Denny Fairfax retained Marshall to defend his interests against the confiscations, and Marshall soon became convinced that he could defend the Fairfax title against all comers, including the state of Virginia. If he was correct, the manor lands would provide an exceptional investment opportunity. Few Virginians believed that the proprietary could withstand the state's challenge, and this lowered the price of the property substantially. Still, it was a high-stakes gamble, and Marshall was betting his financial future that his legal judgment would prevail.

The issue was joined initially in the case of *Hunter v. Fairfax*, which was tried before a Virginia district court in Winchester in 1794. The state of Virginia, asserting title under the common law doctrine of *escheat*,* had sold a

---

*The doctrine of *escheat* holds that nonresident aliens cannot inherit property and that upon the death of the original owner, the land *escheats*, or reverts, to the commonwealth. Virginia contended that Fairfax's heir, Denny Martin, was a British subject who had never established residence in Virginia. Since he was therefore ineligible to inherit the Fairfax estate, the estate accordingly *escheated* to the state.

788-acre tract of the proprietary to David Hunter.[121] Denny Martin Fairfax filed a legal objection, and Hunter brought suit to gain a clear title. St. George Tucker, sitting as the trial judge, ruled against Hunter and rejected Virginia's attempt to confiscate the land. To invoke the doctrine of *escheat*, said Tucker, the state had to initiate proceedings in a court of law and give Martin an opportunity to respond. Until Virginia did so, the courts would protect Martin's claim.[122]

Tucker's holding represented a limited victory, but Marshall believed that the case for Denny Martin was much stronger since it rested on the Treaty of Paris, which prohibited any additional confiscations of the property of British subjects after 1783. In Marshall's view, the treaty provision, now the supreme law of the land, protected Denny Martin's title.[124] Marshall was now working both sides of the street with the Treaty of Paris. In the British debt cases, he argued that it did not apply, while in the Fairfax litigation he insisted that it was controlling.

So great was Marshall's confidence in his ability to prevail against Virginia's claim to the proprietary that in late 1792 he dispatched his brother James to London to negotiate with Denny Martin for the purchase of the manor lands. In February 1793 Martin and James reached an agreement under which the Marshalls contracted to buy the two most important manors, Leeds and South Branch, totalling 215,000 acres, for £20,000 sterling. The transfer date was set for February 1, 1794, provided Martin could convey a clear title at that time.[125]

At less than 2 shillings an acre for some of the best land in northern Virginia, the price was a bargain. In its *escheat* sales, Virginia was selling much less desirable land for 5 shillings an acre. But the bargain would be realized only if Marshall was able to defend the Fairfax title successfully, and the prospects of doing that were growing dim. As if on cue, as soon as the purchase agreement was signed in London, the state of Virginia accelerated its attack on the proprietary by proceeding with *escheat* actions in the various county courts in the northern neck. Anti-British sentiment was running high in Virginia, and the legislature, responding to that sentiment, adopted resolutions calling for suspension of the Treaty of Paris and for a more rigorous effort to confiscate remaining British property by *escheat*.[126] Although couched in general terms, the latter resolution was aimed specifically at the Fairfax holdings.

By the autumn of 1794, the various county courts had uniformly ruled in favor of the state of Virginia's claim. Denny Martin, working through Marshall, appealed these decisions to the court of appeals in Richmond, setting the stage for the state's highest court to rule explicitly on the Fairfax title. As fate would have it, Marshall now found himself representing both parties to the case. He was retained by Martin, but with James Innes in Kentucky, he was also Virginia's acting attorney general. Because of the obvious conflict, Marshall stepped aside as the state's chief legal officer. At that point, the council of state, recognizing the importance of the litigation, went to Patrick Henry, who was told that he could set his own fee if he took the case.[127] The great orator, now in the twilight of his career, declined.[128] The state then retained John Wickham and Alexander Campbell, but Campbell committed suicide before the appeal could be argued.[129]

Marshall was troubled by the delay. It was apparent to all involved that if he lost, he would appeal to the federal courts. However, confounding his plans and strengthening the hand of Virginia considerably, Congress had just approved the Eleventh Amendment to the Constitution. The amendment was designed to prevent states from being sued in federal court by citizens of other states and by foreigners.[130] If ratified by the states, which seemed certain, Denny Martin Fairfax could lose the right to carry an appeal against Virginia into federal court.[131]

Increasingly worried that his plan to purchase the Fairfax estate might miscarry, Marshall advised Denny Martin to make contact in London with the British officials then negotiating the Jay Treaty to obtain explicit recognition of the Fairfax title in the treaty.[132] Martin did not receive Marshall's letter until two weeks after the Jay Treaty had been initialed, but fortuitously, Article 9 of that treaty provided that British subjects would be treated "as if they were natives" of the United States insofar as land ownership was concerned.[133] This clause meant that the doctrine of *escheat* could not be invoked and that Martin would be fully entitled to inherit the Fairfax estate—but only if the courts held the Jay Treaty to apply. This was a big proviso. Marshall was certain the federal courts would uphold the treaty, but whether the Virginia court of appeals would do so was not clear.

The problem, then, was to get the question of the Fairfax title out of the state courts and into federal court. With the Eleventh Amendment pending, Marshall turned to the earlier litigation between Martin and Hunter. Since the State of Virginia was not a party to that case, the Eleventh Amendment would not bar an appeal to federal authority. The question of the Fairfax title was equally at stake in both cases, and by returning to the private lawsuit, Marshall believed that a satisfactory judgment might be obtained.

Accordingly, in April 1795 Marshall filed suit against Hunter on Martin's behalf in the United States circuit court.[134] In effect, he was making a detour around the Virginia court of appeals and going directly to federal court with the issue, anticipating that a federal ruling on behalf of Fairfax would be controlling.[135] Virginia officials immediately recognized the significance of the case and engaged counsel on Hunter's behalf.[136] On June 6, 1795, the United States circuit court (Justice James Wilson and Judge Cyrus Griffin) ruled in favor of Fairfax in a brief *per curiam* decision.[137] Hunter appealed the judgment to the Supreme Court. This was a precursor of the great case, *Martin v. Hunter's Lessee*, ultimately decided by the Marshall Court in 1816.[138] The Virginia legislature, painfully aware that the state had been outmaneuvered, responded to the circuit court decision with a resolution denying "the authority of the federal courts to decide cases affecting titles to lands under the grants of this commonwealth to the citizens thereof."[139] That threw down the gauntlet to federal authority, but calmer heads eventually prevailed and, after the third reading, the motion was tabled.[140] Nevertheless, it was clear that the stakes were rising substantially.

The fact is, both Marshall and the Virginia authorities were becoming increasingly worried about the litigation. The state executive feared that the Supreme Court might rule that the Treaty of Paris applied and uphold the Fairfax title. That would undercut the state's efforts to confiscate and resell the unappropriated lands in the northern neck, which thus far had been uncontested. On his part, Marshall feared that the Virginia court of appeals might reject the Fairfax claim before the Supreme Court could act. Marshall and his partners were interested only in the 215,000 acres of manor lands that Fairfax owned personally. The state's primary interest was in the vast two million or so unappropriated acres of the proprietary that Lord Fairfax had held under the original royal grant but had not disposed of. A court decision, whether it was the United States Supreme Court upholding the Fairfax title or the Virginia court of appeals rejecting it, would produce a winner-take-all situation, and neither party was prepared to risk that. Accordingly, a compromise seemed in order.

In November 1796 Marshall was once again a member of the House of Delegates, and in that capacity he helped to fashion a proposal that accommodated the interests of everyone concerned. Introduced by Robert Andrews of Williamsburg, the resolution noted that the United States circuit court had found for Fairfax and that the issue was presently pending "in the court of appeals in this state."[141] A decision either way, said the resolution, "is likely to produce a great disquietude among a considerable body of the people." The committee then went on to note "a spirit of accommodation among those interested may prevail."[142] The compromise proposal called on Denny Martin to convey the entire proprietary to James Marshall, who was still in London. James Marshall would then convey the unappropriated land to the state, and in return, Virginia would recognize the residual Fairfax title to the manor lands.

It was a clear-cut way to ensure that each side obtained what it wanted most. On November 24, 1796, Marshall accepted the terms on behalf of Denny Martin,[143] and on December 10 the assembly enacted the settlement.[144] After the various transfers went through, the state gained title to all of the unappropriated lands in the proprietary, and Denny Martin retained the manor lands in his own name. He had contracted to sell these to the Marshalls as soon as they could raise the money, and Marshall's next task was to raise the £20,000 agreed upon. That would prove to be almost as difficult as the battle to acquire a clear title had been, and the deal was not consummated until October 16, 1806. In the interim, Marshall had to pay interest on the purchase price, and the burden of doing so cast a pall over his financial situation for the next half-dozen years. The money was raised eventually, and Marshall, after various sales and exchanges with his brother James and his brother-in-law Rawleigh Colston, ended up with 50,000 acres of prime Virginia real estate.[145]

7

Virginia Federalist

T HE CONSTITUTION'S NARROW VICTORY at the Virginia convention was just the beginning of the debate over the distribution of political power between the national government and the states. Madison warned Hamilton[1] and Washington[2] that the antifederalists would concentrate their efforts in the various state legislatures. Marshall wrote afterward that "conflict between the powers of the general and state governments was coeval with those governments. The old line of division was still as strongly marked as ever."[3] The Constitution's opponents thought that "liberty could be endangered only by encroachments upon the states, and that it was the great duty of patriotism to restrain the powers of the general government within the narrowest possible limits." On the other hand, the federalists "sincerely believed that the real danger which threatened the republic was to be looked for in the undue ascendency of the states."[4]

Washington tried to bridge the gap by including in his cabinet federalist Alexander Hamilton as secretary of the treasury and republican Thomas Jefferson as secretary of state, and initially the effort appeared successful. In June 1790 the two men actually struck a deal resolving the two most controversial issues then confronting the government: the funding of the public debt and the location of the nation's capital. Hamilton, always attuned to the nation's business interests, had sought to put the country's finances in order by having the federal government assume the various state debts and pay them off at face value. In his view, that would establish the basis for a sound currency and restore investor confidence in the public treasury. The antifederalists, fearing a nationalist grab for power and believing fervently that such a move would unduly reward speculators in government bonds, vigorously opposed the measure. The fiercest opposition was in the state of Virginia, which had already discharged its debts and had nothing to gain from the proposal. On the other hand, the Virginians were uneasy over the prospect that the future capital might be located in the North, and that provided the basis for a compromise. Jefferson agreed to find the necessary Virginia votes in Congress to pass the debt assumption bill, and in return Hamilton agreed to deliver enough northern votes to establish the capital on the Potomac.[5]

But the harmony was short-lived. When the federalists came forward in 1791 with a proposal to incorporate a national bank, the republicans charged that the measure was unconstitutional. At that time, banking was entirely under state control, and the powerful states rights faction insisted that there was no basis in the Constitution for the national government to intervene. In a tightly argued memorandum submitted at Washington's request, Jefferson asserted that the enumerated powers given to Congress did not include any authority over banking. In Jefferson's eyes, the list of enumerated powers in Article I of the Constitution was exhaustive, and he rejected the claim that the government enjoyed any implicit or inherent powers that extended beyond the literal text of the document. "To take a single step beyond the boundaries thus specially drawn around the powers of Congress is to take possession of a boundless field of power, no longer susceptible of any definition."[6]

Hamilton responded with an equally well reasoned memorandum that set forth the doctrine of implied powers. "The powers contained in a constitution," he told Washington, "ought to be construed liberally in advancement of the public good. . . . The means by which natural exigencies are to be provided for, national inconveniences obviated, and national prosperity promoted are of such infinite variety, extent, and complexity, that there must of necessity be great latitude of discretion in the selection and application of those means."[7] Hamilton said, "This *general principle* is *inherent* in the very *definition* of government." Every power vested in a government includes "a right to employ the *means* requisite . . . to the attainment of the ends of such power."

The battle lines were drawn. Jefferson and Hamilton became the protagonists in the struggle over the national bank, and the arguments they brought forth as to how the Constitution should be interpreted provided the rallying points around which the nation's two great political parties coalesced. Marshall later wrote that it was the debate over the bank that led "to the complete organization of those distinct and visible parties, which, in their long and dubious conflict for power, have . . . shaken the United States to their centre."[8]

The Federalists, designated now with a capital F, were led by Washington and Hamilton. They embraced the idea of a strong national government and saw the broad words of the Constitution as a means to that end. Their opponents, increasingly known as Republicans, were led by Jefferson, Madison, and Monroe. The Republicans favored states rights and sought to restrict the growth of national power by insisting on a narrow reading of the constitutional text.

At the national level, the parties were almost equally balanced, and each engaged in feverish recruiting efforts. Marshall was courted assiduously by the Federalists. As Jefferson wrote to Madison in the summer of 1792, "I learn that [Hamilton] has expressed the strongest desire that Marshall should come into Congress from Richmond, declaring that there is no man in Virginia whom he wishes so much to see there; and I am told that Marshall has expressed half a mind to come. Hence I conclude that Hamilton has plied him well with flattery and solicitation and I think nothing better could be done than to make him a judge."[9] Jefferson, of course, had the state court in mind, but the idea that Marshall could be parked on the bench was one that he would come to regret.

The division of American opinion into organized political parties coincided with the increasing radicalization of the French Revolution and the subsequent war between Britain and France. These events inevitably reinforced the battle lines that had been drawn. The Republicans backed the revolution and supported France; the Federalists recoiled from the reign of terror and favored Britain. Washington was caught in the middle as he tried to steer the United States on a neutral course between the belligerents. "I trust that we shall have too just a sense of our own interest to originate any cause that may involve us," he wrote to a friend in the spring of 1793.[10]

The president's task was complicated by the arrival of the new minister of the French republic, Citizen Edmond Charles Genet, who landed in Charleston, South Carolina, on April 8, 1793. Genet was greeted by an immense crowd of supporters, and his overland journey to Philadelphia became a triumphal procession as he appealed directly to the American people to support the French cause.[11] As Marshall told Story:

> The arrival and conduct of Mr. Genet excited great sensation throughout the southern states. We were all strongly attached to France— scarcely any man more strongly than myself. I sincerely believed human liberty to depend in a great measure on the success of the French revolution. My partiality to France, however, did not so entirely pervert my understanding as to render me insensible to the danger of permitting a foreign minister to mingle himself in the management of our affairs, and to intrude himself between our government and people.[12]

The Washington administration was even more concerned than Marshall about Genet's activities. On April 22, in an effort to prevent the United States from becoming embroiled in hostilities, the president issued his famous neutrality proclamation forbidding American citizens from aiding either Britain or France.[13] Initially the proclamation was welcomed by both countries.[14] Not surprisingly, however, each nation sought to interpret the document to its own advantage. That led Washington to ask the Supreme Court for guidance as to the meaning of neutrality. The episode became a seminal event in the evolution of American foreign policy. Chief Justice John Jay, speaking for the Supreme Court, declined to give Washington the advice he sought. The Court's refusal to respond established the fundamental principle that the United States Supreme Court will not render advisory opinions. Jay said that the Constitution made each of the three branches of government independent and that "as judges of a court of last resort" it would be inappropriate for the justices to consider the question Washington had asked.[15] Court decisions were binding, whereas an advisory opinion could be accepted or rejected as the president desired. Jay's response allowed him to emphasize the finality of the Supreme Court's decisions and to dodge the political hot potato Washington had thrown to the justices.

Equally important, by issuing the proclamation on his own authority, Washington set a controversial precedent for presidential prerogative in foreign affairs. His unilateral action gave rise to a profound debate about the relative authority of Congress and the president in shaping American foreign policy. It began with Hamilton and Madison squaring off in a series of articles published in Philadelphia's *Gazette of the United States*. Hamilton, writing under the pseudonym "Pacificus,"[16] argued that the Constitution entrusted the conduct of foreign relations to the executive branch, "subject only to the *exceptions* and *qualifications* which are expressed in the instrument."[17] Madison replied as "Helvidius,"[18] asserting that Congress was the policymaking arm of the national government and that it possessed full authority over foreign affairs, except for that *specifically* granted to the president.*

---

*The controversy over who controls American foreign policy has been a recurring one, but the arguments brought forth in subsequent debate have rarely introduced elements not considered in the original Pacificus-Helvidius exchange. Indeed, so fundamental was this exchange between Hamilton and Madison that until the Civil War the essays were included in the various editions of *The Federalist*. In 1863 Henry B. Dawson established the modern practice of omitting them, and later editors have followed that practice. See *The Federalist* (Washington, D.C.: J. & G.S. Gideon, 1818–1857). Also see Edward S. Corwin, *The President's Control of Foreign Relations* (Princeton, N.J.: Princeton University Press, 1917), which contains most of the essays with Corwin's commentary. For the full text, see *The Letters of Pacificus and Helvidius*, Richard Loss, ed. (Delmar, N.Y.: Scholars' Facsimiles & Reprints, 1976).

The debate quickly spread across the country. At Hamilton's urging, Federalists in the North and South held public meetings to support the president. The largest and most celebrated meeting was organized by Marshall in Richmond on August 17, 1793.[19] Marshall convinced George Wythe, a staunch Republican and a close friend of Jefferson's, to chair the gathering. He also drafted the resolutions that were approved and wrote the meeting's extravagant letter of praise to President Washington commending his sagacious conduct of the country's foreign policy.[20] The resolutions, which were adopted unanimously, supported American neutrality, endorsed the president's proclamation, and, without mentioning Genet by name, criticized foreign intervention in the domestic affairs of the United States.[21]

The Federalist campaign to elicit public backing took Jefferson's supporters by surprise.[22] The shock was especially great in Virginia, which until then had been considered a Republican stronghold. Madison and Monroe responded with a series of pro-French resolutions that were introduced at public meetings across the state, and on September 4, Monroe published the first of four essays in the *Virginia Gazette and Advertiser*, warning all Republicans to be on guard. Writing under the pseudonym "Agricola,"[23] Monroe claimed that the Richmond meeting had been organized by the "enemies of the French revolution, who are likewise the partisans for monarchy," whose sole object was a closer union with Britain. Their ultimate goal, he said, was to transform the United States into a monarchy.[24] In view of that danger, Monroe urged the citizens of Virginia to make it known that the sentiments expressed by "the faction in Richmond" were not those of the people as a whole.[25]

The tone of Monroe's essay suggests that Marshall's activities were causing considerable anxiety in the Republican camp. On September 2, 1793, Madison incorrectly told Jefferson that Marshall, having acquired the Fairfax estate, "has lately obtained pecuniary aid from the [National] Bank or persons connected with it. I think it certain that he must have felt in the moment of the purchase an absolute dependence on the monied interest, which will explain him to every one that reflects, in the active character he is assuming."[26] The truth is that in 1793 Marshall had just begun the lengthy process of acquiring the Fairfax property. He and his brother James had signed an initial purchase agreement, but title was not cleared until 1796, and the first payment was not made until 1797. Moreover, the money borrowed for the purchase came from the Netherlands, not the United States. Monroe wrote to Jefferson as well, ascribing the events in Richmond to Marshall whom, he said, could only be classed with John Jay and Rufus King in the pantheon of Republican demons.[27] Jay and King had organized similar public meetings in New York to support the president, and both were being castigated by the Republican press.[28]

As was so often the case in Virginia, politics had taken a personal turn. On the Federalist side were Washington, Governor Henry Lee, and Marshall, who had quietly become the president's most effective lieutenant in the state. For the Republicans, it was Jefferson supported by the ever-reliable Monroe and most members of the legislature. Two of the key players, however, had changed sides. Madison, previously the principal advocate of a strong central government, was firmly in the Republican camp, while Patrick Henry was moving closer to the Federalists. Madison's shift reflected the change in public opinion in Virginia, whereas Henry's move was made largely for personal reasons—he detested Thomas Jefferson.[29] Marshall explained the growing animosity of the period to Story:

> The resentments of the great political party which led Virginia had been directed toward me for some time, but [the Richmond rally] brought it into active operation. I was attacked with great virulence in the papers and was so far honoured in Virginia as to be associated with Alexander Hamilton, at least so far as to be termed his instrument. With equal vivacity I defended myself and the measures of the government. My constant effort was to show that the conduct of our government respecting its foreign relations were such as a just self-respect and a regard for our rights as a sovereign nation rendered indispensable, and that our independence was brought into real danger by the overgrown and inordinate influence of France.[30]

On September 8 Marshall responded to Monroe in the first of the four essays that also appeared in the *Gazette and Advertiser*.[31] The Monroe-Marshall exchange does not approach the stature of the Pacificus-Helvidius letters in either the elegance of the arguments employed or the comprehensiveness of the issues addressed. Monroe and Marshall were speaking to the Virginia electorate, not the nation at large, and their writing had a parochial slant.

Marshall wrote under two pen names, "Aristides" and "Gracchus," not to conceal his authorship but because he was addressing two separate aspects of the controversy.[32] As Aristides he dealt with the conduct of Citizen Genet, and as Gracchus he attempted to refute Monroe's charge that the Washington administration favored monarchy.[33] Marshall's task was made somewhat easier by the alarmist tone Monroe had adopted. With careful irony he ridiculed Agricola for pretending to support neutrality yet being unwilling to join the citizens of Richmond in praising the president's neutrality proclamation. He scoffed at the suggestion that there was an anti-French party in America. "If there be among us men who are enemies to the French revolution, or who are friends to monarchy, I know them not."[34]

The harshness of the exchange illustrates how political passions had risen since the ratification of the Constitution. Marshall and Monroe, once the best of friends, now were bitter opponents. The enmity was a malignant outgrowth of the good-natured rivalry that had commenced at the Virginia ratification convention. Far from bringing the opposing factions together, the establishment of the federal government actually widened the political rift by providing a larger and more visible arena in which existing antagonisms could play themselves out. Marshall proved that he was able to hold his own in the rough-and-tumble of this renewed partisan strife, and as Monroe's most recent biographer has concluded, his performance in the exchange of letters "was far livelier than Monroe's. Both modeled their publications on the popular *Spectator* style, but Marshall had a lighter and more ironical touch than his opponent."[35]

In retrospect, the Marshall-Monroe exchange marked the beginning of national party warfare in Virginia. Marshall became the surrogate for Hamilton and Washington, while Monroe effectively promoted Jefferson's cause. Marshall's essays may have been the more tightly reasoned and his style more incisive, but Monroe's polemical ability probably tipped the debate to the Republicans. Agricola's boldness in criticizing Washington struck a new note in the nation's politics,[36] and the use of foreign policy as a litmus test of partisan allegiance would define the difference between the two parties for the next decade. Marshall was unhappy about that. As he wrote to Archibald Stuart shortly after his exchange with Monroe, "Our foreign affairs are becoming somewhat perplexed and I fancy the American Government will have occasion for all its wisdom to conduct it steadily through the threatened storm. I now begin to hope that we shall not increase its embarrassments by our indiscreet intemperance."[37]

As Washington's effort to maintain American neutrality became an increasingly divisive issue, England and France each sought to test the administration's resolve. France asserted its right under the Revolutionary War's treaty of alliance to use American ports for raids on British shipping in the West Indies,[38] and Britain, whose navy controlled the seas, commenced seizing American vessels bound for France and pressing American seamen into British service. Beginning in mid-1793, Great Britain seized over 300 American ships, bringing the two countries to the verge of war. Marshall, who remained firm in his support of American neutrality, fretted over the British action. "We fear, and not without reason, a war," he wrote to a friend in the spring of 1794.[39] "The man does not live who wishes for peace more than I do, but the outrages upon us are beyond human bearing. . . . Pray Heaven we may weather the storm."

The possibility of war with Britain prompted Congress to reexamine the neglected condition of the nation's armed forces. The examination focused on the various state militias, which, because there was no standing army, were the country's first line of defense.[40] Under Governor Lee, Virginia took the lead in attempting to put its militia in fighting trim. In December 1793 Marshall, because of his prior military experience, was elected a brigadier general by the general assembly and given command of the state's second brigade.[41] Initially Marshall's duties were routine, consisting largely of supervising the brigade's organization and securing sufficient equipment. But with the passage of the Neutrality Act in June 1794,[42] he was soon on active service.

Under the act, American citizens were prohibited from aiding either of the belligerents. Section 3 specifically forbade the outfitting of privateers to prey on commercial shipping. Shortly after the measure was passed, the British consul in Norfolk warned Governor Lee that a group of French sympathizers led by a Captain John Sinclair were fitting out a vessel as a privateer near Smithfield, on the James River. Lee dispatched a United States marshal and a few militia to investigate. They found that Sinclair was indeed outfitting a ship, the *Unicorn*, and they seized it. Having done so, however, they found themselves outnumbered and in a precarious position, as Sinclair and his collaborators prepared to retake the vessel. County authorities were pro-French and unwilling to intervene. Consequently, Governor Lee ordered Marshall to the scene with the nineteenth regiment of the state militia. Lee told Marshall to ride immediately to Smithfield at the head of the cavalry. "The Artillery and Light Infantry will follow by water."[43]

Lee wanted Marshall to seize the *Unicorn*, but he wanted him to do it peacefully, and Marshall complied with his instructions. On July 23 he reported to the government that his troops were on the scene and that "Every idea of resisting with violence the execution of the laws seems to have been abandoned."[44] Marshall said that a search of Captain Sinclair's house revealed thirteen cannons and a variety of small arms. These had been seized and the *Unicorn* was being made ready to sail upriver under guard. Marshall told Lee that the local militia had not been supportive, but that the difficulty rested with the officers and not with the men.

The following week Marshall ordered his troops back to Richmond. He advised the governor that it was apparent that Sinclair had planned to take action. The weapons seized had been loaded and were ready to fire. "The situation of the [Sinclair] house is such as completely to command the Deck of the Vessel. I do not think that 100 men placed in the Vessel could have protected her ten minutes from fifteen [men] placed in the House."[45] Marshall said that the arrival of the state militia made a profound impact on the people of Isle of Wight county, especially the commanding officers of the local forces. "They seem not to have been sufficiently impressed with the importance of maintaining the sovereignty of the laws, they seem not to have thought it a duty of strong and universal obligation to effect this object, but I do believe that a more proper mode of thinking is beginning to prevail."[46]

Almost as soon as the expedition to Smithfield ended, Marshall's brigade was ordered to assist in quelling the Whiskey Rebellion in Pennsylvania.[47] Governor Lee assumed command of the operation, but this time Marshall did not accompany his unit. The state courts were in session, and Marshall had just been appointed Virginia's acting attorney general.[48] There was an abundance of qualified officers in the Virginia militia, and so with Lee's approval, Marshall remained in Richmond to handle the state's business before the court.

Confronted with dissent at home and the possibility of war abroad, Washington did his utmost to steer a steady course. To ease tensions with Britain, the president dispatched Chief Justice John Jay as a special envoy to London with instructions to settle as many of the outstanding problems as possible. If the British were receptive, Washington told Jay to negotiate a commercial treaty that would ensure continuing economic ties between the two countries. In so doing, however, Jay was explicitly cautioned not "to derogate from our treaties and engagements with France."[49]

To balance Jay's appointment and to restore a modicum of bipartisanship to the country's foreign policy, Monroe was named as American minister to France. Both appointments were well intentioned. Jay was more than eager to put commercial ties with Britain on a firm footing, while Monroe, perhaps the most Francophile of the Republicans, went to Paris determined to restore amity between the two countries.

Neither appointment worked out as anticipated. Jay succeeded in negotiating the treaty that unofficially bears his name,[50] but its pro-British tenor seriously infringed upon the spirit, if not the text, of the 1778 alliance with France. Although the treaty averted war between America and Great Britain, its terms were perceived to be so unfavorable to the United States that it precipitated a firestorm of opposition that destroyed the political consensus Washington had worked so hard to achieve. The French denounced the Jay Treaty, and the Republicans undertook a campaign of vilification so intense that its ratification was seriously threatened. Monroe, for his part, soon found himself dangerously out of step with the administration, and his continued tenure in Paris became another bone of contention between the Republicans and the Federalists.

As the battle between the parties intensified in Virginia, Marshall found himself back in the thick of it. In 1795 he yielded to popular pressure in Richmond and was again elected to the House of Delegates.[51] Marshall's return to the legislature caused concern among the Republicans, but Jefferson saw a silver lining. "Though Marshall will be able to embarrass the Republican party in the assembly a good deal," he wrote to Madison, yet upon the whole his having gone into it will be of service. He has been, hitherto, able to do more mischief acting under the mask of Republicanism than he will be able to do after throwing it plainly off. His lax lounging manners have made him popular with the bulk of the people of Richmond; and a profound hypocrisy, with many thinking men of our country. But having come forth in the plentitude of his English principles the latter will see that it is high time to make him known.[52]

Shortly after Marshall's election, Washington's administration suffered a serious setback when Edmund Randolph was forced to resign as secretary of state. Randolph, who was sympathetic to France, had been indiscreet in his conversations with Genet's successor, Joseph Fauchet, and apparently had advised the French to step up their efforts to influence American public opinion. Fauchet transmitted Randolph's advice to Paris, but his letter was intercepted by the British and turned over to the president, who promptly asked for Randolph's resignation.[53] Washington was then confronted with the need to find a successor who could manage the country's strained relations with Britain and France with an even hand. Supreme Court justices William Paterson of New Jersey and Thomas Johnson of Maryland declined, as did Charles Cotesworth Pinckney of South Carolina.[54] Washington evidently considered offering the post to Marshall, but as he wrote to Hamilton, "Mr. Marshall, of Virginia, has declined the office of Attorney General, and I am pretty certain would accept of no other." Almost pleadingly, the president asked, "What am I to do for a Secretary of State?"[55]

Without waiting for Hamilton's reply, Washington decided to consult Marshall about the possibility of Patrick Henry assuming the post. "I would have [approached] Mr. Henry first," the president said, "but for ignorance of his political sentiments, for I should consider it an act of governmental suicide to bring a man into so high an office, who was unfriendly to the constitution."[56] Washington asked for Marshall's advice. His confidence in Marshall's judgment can be gauged by the fact that the president enclosed a personal letter to Henry that was to be forwarded to him if Marshall agreed. "My letter to Mr. Henry is left open for your perusal. . . . If it goes forward, seal it; if not, return it to [me]."[57]

Marshall favored the offer to Henry. It was unlikely that Henry would accept, he told Washington, but "a more deadly death-blow could not be given to the [Republican] faction in Virginia, and perhaps elsewhere. . . . In the present crisis, Mr. Henry may reasonably be calculated on as taking the side of the government, even though he may retain his old prejudices against the Constitution." Marshall thought that as Henry's wealth increased, he was becoming increasingly interested in the protection of private property "which must additionally attract him to the existing government. Add to this that he has no affection for the present leaders of the opposition in Virginia."[58]

As Marshall had anticipated, Henry declined Washington's offer and the president thereupon promoted his secretary of war, Timothy Pickering, to succeed Randolph. Pickering was a leader of the High Federalist faction of the party and was vociferously anti-French. Shortly after appointing Pickering, Washington signed the Jay Treaty. Together, the two actions tilted American foreign policy toward Britain. Marshall, who was now back in the legislature, knew that another struggle was at hand, and he prepared once again to do battle on Washington's behalf. As he told Story:

> Throughout that part of the year which followed the advice of the senate to ratify Mr. Jay's treaty, the whole country was agitated with that question. The commotion began at Boston and seemed to rush through the Union with a rapidity and violence which set human reason and common sense at defiance. The first effort was to deter the President from ratifying the instrument—the next to induce Congress to refuse the necessary appropriations. On this occasion too a meeting of the citizens of Richmond was convened and I carried a series of resolutions approving the conduct of the President.[59]

As he had done three years before, Marshall organized another public meeting at the Richmond statehouse. On April 25, 1796, almost 400 people jammed the assembly chamber for an all-day session to rally support for the president. The gathering was initially ill-disposed toward the treaty, but Marshall apparently won the audience over with what was described as a "masterly" presentation.[60]

As soon as the meeting adjourned, Marshall reported the happy outcome to Rufus King and Alexander Hamilton in New York. "The ruling party in Virginia are extremely irritated at the vote today," he wrote to King, "and will spare no exertion to obtain a majority in other counties." Marshall said he was trying to counter their efforts, but "*exitus in dubio est* [the outcome is uncertain]."[61]

Marshall wrote a more extensive report to Hamilton, stating that the meeting "was more numerous than I have ever seen at this place and after a very ardent and zealous discussion . . . a decided majority declared in favor of a resolution [supporting the treaty.]"[62] Marshall warned that "a majority of counties will avow sentiments opposed to ours, but the division of the state will appear to be much more considerable than has been stated. In some of the districts there will certainly be a majority who will concur with us, and that perhaps may have some effect."

Edmund Randolph, who was understandably bitter at having been summarily dismissed by Washington, also attended the Richmond meeting and
filed a somewhat more jaundiced report with Madison. He said that Marshall had packed the meeting with British merchants, federal office holders,
people seeking government jobs, "and many without a shadow of a freehold." It was Randolph's opinion that "Marshall's argument was inconsistent and shifting, concluding every third sentence with the horrors of war."
However, he acknowledged that the Federalists had carried the day.[63]

The debate over the Jay Treaty did not end with the rally in Richmond.
"This was a subject," said Marshall, "in which every man who mingled in
public affairs was compelled to take part, and I determined to make myself
master of it."[64] Marshall told Story that he

> perused carefully all the resolutions which were passed throughout
> the United States condemning the treaty and compared them with
> the instrument itself. Accustomed as I was to political misrepresen-
> tation, I could not view without some surprise the numerous gross
> misrepresentations which were made on this occasion; and the viru-
> lent asperity, with which the common terms of decency in which na-
> tions express their compacts with each other, was assailed."[65]

Marshall said that "the constitutionality of the treaty was attacked with peculiar vehemence, and, strange as it may appear, there was scarcely a man in
Virginia who did not believe that a commercial treaty was an infringement of
the power given to Congress to regulate commerce."[66]

When the House of Delegates took up the matter, Marshall was ready.

> One or two of my cautious friends advised me not to engage in the
> debate. They said it . . . would destroy me totally. . . . I answered
> that the subject would not be introduced by me; but, if it should be
> brought before the house by others, I should undoubtedly take the
> part which became an independent member. The subject was intro-
> duced; and the constitutional objections were brought forward most
> triumphantly. There was perhaps never a political question . . . which
> was susceptible of more complete demonstration, and I was fully
> prepared not only on the words of the constitution and the universal
> practice of nations, but to show . . . that Mr. Jefferson and the whole
> delegation from Virginia in Congress . . . had manifested unequivo-
> cally the opinion that a commercial treaty was constitutional.
>
> I had reason to know that a politician even in times of violent
> party strife maintains his respectability by showing his strength; and

is most safe when he encounters prejudice most fearlessly. There was scarcely an intelligent man in the house who did not yield his opinion on the constitutional question.[67]

Justice James Iredell, who was in Richmond to preside at circuit court and who witnessed the debate, wrote afterward that "there were few members [of the House] who were not convinced by Mr. Marshall's arguments as to [the treaty's] being constitutional, which few members thought it was before the debate began, and some of the speakers on the other side had the candor to acknowledge their convictions though not in the House."[68]

Marshall did not know if the published accounts of the debate were written by impartial observers or by some of his friends, but he told Story that his contribution was "spoken of in such extravagant terms" that the next winter, when he went to Philadelphia to argue *Ware v. Hylton* before the Supreme Court, he was greeted with an outpouring of enthusiasm by Federalists in Congress. "The particular subject which introduced me to their notice was at that time so interesting, and a Virginian who supported . . . the measures of the government was such a *rara avis*, that I was received by them all with a degree of kindness which I had not anticipated."[69]

Shortly after the debate in the House of Delegates, Washington yielded to Secretary of State Pickering's importunings to recall Monroe from Paris on the grounds that he was too sympathetic to the French. Washington hoped to replace Monroe with someone who was friendly toward France but who was also a Federalist and, if possible, a southerner. As the president expressed it, someone "who will promote not thwart the neutrality policy of the government, and at the same time will not be obnoxious to the People among whom he is sent."[70] His first choice was Marshall, and his second, Charles Cotesworth Pinckney of South Carolina.

On July 8, 1796, Washington dispatched an urgent letter to Marshall in Richmond. "In confidence I inform you," wrote the president, "that it has become indispensably necessary to recall our Minister at Paris; and to send one in his place who will explain faithfully, the views of this government, and ascertain those of France. Nothing would be more pleasing to me, than that you should be this Organ; if it were only for a temporary absence of a few months."[71] Washington said he realized that the chances were slight that Marshall would accept, and so he enclosed a second letter addressed to Pinckney. If Marshall did not want to go to Paris, the president asked him to forward the letter to Pinckney, "in order that as little delay as possible be incurred."

Marshall was flattered by the offer, but as Washington had expected, he declined. The Fairfax litigation was coming to a head, and Marshall simply could not put it aside. As he told Washington:

[If] it [were] possible for me in the present crisis in my affairs to leave the United States, such is my conviction of the importance of that duty which you would confide in me . . . that I would certainly forego any consideration not decisive with respect to my future fortunes, and would surmount that just diffidence I have ever entertained of myself, to make one effort to convey truly and faithfully to the government of France those sentiments which I have ever believed to be entertained by that of the United States.[72]

In the autumn of 1796, as Washington's term drew to a close, Marshall took up the cudgels for the president one last time. As a parting gesture, the Federalists in the Virginia House of Delegates moved a resolution expressing the confidence of the assembly in "the virtue, patriotism, and wisdom of the President of the United States." In a calculated affront, the Republicans moved to strike the word *wisdom* from the resolution. Marshall led the Federalist efforts on the floor and, as he later told Story, "in the debate, the whole course of the administration was reviewed, and the whole talent of each party brought into action. Will it be believed that the word was retained by a very small majority? A very small majority in the legislature of Virginia acknowledged the wisdom of General Washington."[73]

In the final months of his term, reflecting the daily influence of Pickering, Washington moved ever closer to the anti-French stand of the High Federalists. The behavior of France toward the United States, he told Hamilton, is "outrageous beyond conception; not to be warranted by her treaties with us; by the Law of Nations; by any principle of justice; or even by a regard to decent appearances."[74] In that context, Washington's Farewell Address is often cited as a model of national self-interest and impartiality.[75] In fact, it was a partisan defense of Federalist foreign policy and a bitter critique of French intervention in American affairs.[76]

In the subsequent presidential campaign between Adams and Jefferson, Pierre Adet, who had succeeded Fauchet as the French minister to the United States, openly intervened on Jefferson's behalf,[77] although he candidly informed Paris that either candidate would be better for France than Washington had been.[78] Indeed, once Adams was elected, it appeared as though a breakthrough in Franco-American relations might be at hand. In his brief inaugural address, the new president reaffirmed his "personal esteem for the French nation" and his intention, "by amicable negotiation" to "investigate every just cause of complaint."[79] He consulted several times with Jefferson, who was now vice president, about improving relations with France, and even contemplated sending his former rival to Paris to settle the differences between the two countries.[80] Jefferson quickly had second thoughts about such a mission, but he acknowledged that the outstanding problems, unless dealt with promptly, would likely propel the nations toward war. Marshall shared those concerns. Little did he realize that he would soon be called upon to fill the spot Jefferson had declined.

In many respects, the tension with France reflected the tension with Great Britain three years earlier. Jay's mission to London had pulled Britain and the United States back from the brink of war, but the Jay Treaty itself had become one of the most serious problems for Franco-American relations. Paris considered it not only a violation of the alliance of 1778 but part of a larger conspiracy to thwart the aims of the French Revolution.[81] After failing to prevent the treaty's ratification, France retaliated by attacking American shipping in the West Indies and confiscating the cargoes of U.S.-flag vessels in French ports. Debts for grain purchases in America went unpaid, and the Directory, which now ruled France,* sought to punish the United States by severing diplomatic relations. Adet notified the American government that he had been recalled to Paris and that the Directory would appoint no successor. When Pinckney arrived in Paris to succeed Monroe, Charles Delacroix, the French foreign minister, refused to accept his credentials and ordered him to leave the country immediately.[82]

French attacks on American commerce, combined with Pinckney's expulsion from Paris, led Adams to convene a special session of Congress to deal with the crisis. The president told the lawmakers that he wanted to avoid war with France but at the same time intended to preserve American dignity. He asked that U.S. military and naval forces be augmented and stressed the urgency of negotiating an end to the crisis. Although firm in tone, Adams emphasized the need for a peaceful settlement. But like Washington, he could not resist a gibe at France for meddling in American politics, and he condemned French efforts "to foster and establish a division between the government and people of the United States." The Federalists welcomed the president's remarks, but the Republicans were enraged at the reference to French influence. They focused on the military measures Adams had requested and denounced what they saw as a continued drift toward war. Adams's speech had been intended to achieve national unity. Instead, it led to increased polarization.[83]

Adams nevertheless persisted in his efforts to resolve the French crisis. The president looked on it as an opportunity to assert his own leadership and to escape from Washington's shadow. "My entrance into office is marked by a misunderstanding with France, which I shall endeavor to reconcile," he wrote to his son shortly after the inauguration.[84] Having once served as the American minister to France, Adams understood the French government far

---

*The Directory was a five-person executive established by the Thermidorian Constitution of 1795, following the Reign of Terror. It ruled France until supplanted by Napoleon in 1799.

better than Washington, and he recognized that an extraordinary initiative would be required to get negotiations moving. Since Jefferson remained reluctant to go to Paris, the president contemplated sending Madison to break the deadlock. His appointment would rally Republican support, and, given Madison's unstinting support for the French Revolution, would be well received by the Directory as well. But when the High Federalists in his cabinet opposed the nomination, Adams backed off to maintain party unity.[85]

The president then focused on Pinckney. A strong argument could be made in favor of sending Pinckney back to Paris to assuage national honor. But Adams feared that Pinckney, if sent alone, might be rebuffed again. He therefore decided to choose two additional envoys and send a diplomatic triumvirate to France. Such a gesture would attract French attention, and if the two additional envoys were chosen judiciously, domestic support could be rallied for the diplomatic mission.

For one of the new appointees, Adams wanted his old friend and colleague from Massachusetts, Elbridge Gerry. Gerry was a Republican and sympathetic to France, but because of their long personal friendship the president felt he could trust him.[86] Once again the cabinet balked. Adams then turned to another Massachusetts man, Francis Dana, the state's chief justice, who had once been the president's secretary.[87] Dana's name was submitted to the Senate and he was duly confirmed, but he declined the appointment for reasons of ill health. Adams submitted Gerry's name a second time, and this time the cabinet concurred.[88]

For the final envoy, Adams wanted a representative from Virginia. Madison, who was at the top of his list, had already been rejected by the cabinet, so the president went directly to Marshall. Should Marshall decline, Adams planned to approach Ludwell Lee, Thomas Lee, and Bushrod Washington.[89] There is no indication that the cabinet disagreed with the choice of Marshall, and he was confirmed by the Senate (22–6) on July 5, 1797. The three envoys, officially designated as "envoys extraordinary and ministers plenipotentiary to the French Republic," were charged to "dissipate umbrages, remove prejudices, and rectify error and adjust all differences by a treaty between the two powers."

On June 6, 1797, the day after the Senate voted confirmation, Secretary of State Pickering wrote to inform Marshall of his appointment. "Your knowledge of the state of the political affairs of the United States, especially in relation to France, renders any explanation of the cause and object of the Extraordinary Commission unnecessary," said Pickering.[90]

Marshall accepted immediately. He advised Pickering by return post that he would undertake the assignment and made ready to leave Richmond within a fortnight.[91] As he told Story, his attachment to the legal profession had not changed.

On the other hand I felt a very deep interest in the state of our controversy with France. I was most anxious and believed the government to be most anxious for the adjustment of our differences with that republic. I felt some confidence in the good dispositions which I should carry with me into the negotiation, and in the temperate firmness with which I should aid in the investigations which would be made. The subject was familiar to me, and had occupied a large portion of my thoughts. I will confess that the éclat which would attend a successful termination of the differences between the two countries had no small influence over a mind in which ambition, though subjected to control, was not absolutely extinguished.

But the consideration which decided me was this. The mission was temporary, and could not be of long duration. I should return after a short absence, to my profession, with no diminution of character, and, I trusted, with no diminution of practice. My clients would know immediately that I should soon return and I could make arrangements with the gentlemen of the bar which would prevent my business from suffering in the meantime.[92]

Marshall's explanation is not convincing. It is true that the Fairfax title had been cleared and that Marshall's presence in Richmond was no longer essential. It is also probable that ambition was a factor in his decision. Nevertheless, in light of Marshall's repeated refusals to join Washington's administration, it is surprising that he was willing to drop everything and depart for Paris at the request of a president whom he had never met, for a mission that was uncertain, and the duration of which was unknown. It is even more surprising when one considers that except for the occasional visit to a distant county seat to attend a session of court, and three quick trips to Philadelphia in 1796, Marshall had rarely been away from home overnight since his marriage in 1783.

Polly, who had become increasingly frail, was again three months' pregnant, and had already lost four children through miscarriage or during infancy.* It was unlikely that Marshall would be back from Paris for the birth of the child, should Polly carry the pregnancy to term. In addition, there was a large house to be cared for and three children to raise. Thomas, the eldest, was thirteen and needed close supervision. Jaquelin was ten, and daughter Mary, a three-year-old toddler, would have been a handful for a healthy mother, much less one in Polly's condition. Marshall may have felt that since

---

*The Marshall's first daughter, Rebecca, died when five days old, June 21, 1786, and Polly miscarried another pregnancy that autumn. A second daughter, Mary Ann, was born November 24, 1789, and died August 1, 1792. A son, John James, was born February 13, 1792, and died on June 10 of that year.

Polly's parents and her three sisters lived nearby she would be looked after, and he undoubtedly counted on his principal servant, Robin Spurlock, to run the household. Still, to leave for Paris so suddenly and with such scant preparation was an abrupt departure from Marshall's normally relaxed style.

In retrospect, it appears that Marshall's decision to accept the post was motivated largely by his inability to finance the Fairfax purchase. By the spring of 1797 this had become a pressing concern. The legislative compromise under which Denny Martin would convey the Fairfax interest to James Marshall and then to the State of Virginia had been enacted,[93] but the Marshalls had been unable to raise the money to pay Martin, and until Martin received payment, the deal could not go through. Originally the Marshalls had planned to finance their purchase with a loan from James's father-in-law, Philadelphia financier Robert Morris. However, by the time the title had been cleared and the legislative compromise agreed to, Morris's financial empire was in shambles and he was unable to provide the necessary funds. James had been in Europe for two years trying to raise funds to cover Morris's various ventures but had met with little success.[94] Although he had negotiated a small loan for the purchase of South Branch Manor, the smaller of the two Fairfax manors,[95] he had not been able to raise the funds to pay Martin for transferring the entire proprietary.

Marshall undoubtedly considered it necessary to go to Europe to assist James in finding the money. Whatever correspondence there was between the two has been lost,[96] but Marshall spent his first several days in Europe meeting with bankers in Amsterdam. Immediately thereafter, James paid Denny Martin £2,625 for the unappropriated lands in the proprietary. Martin then conveyed the domain to James, who in turn conveyed it to the State of Virginia, consummating the legislative compromise by which the Marshalls gained clear title to the manors. Martin's deed to James was not recorded until Marshall returned to Richmond in June 1798, suggesting that Marshall brought it back with him from Europe.*[97]

News of Marshall's appointment as diplomatic envoy was greeted enthusiastically by the Federalists, but the Republicans were skeptical. One exception was Marshall's old friend St. George Tucker. Tucker attended a farewell dinner for Marshall at the Eagle Tavern in Richmond and had a private conversation with him afterward. Immediately following that discus-

---

*Jefferson, who was critical of Marshall's Fairfax purchase, wrote in his *Anas* that "Mr. John Marshall has said here [in Philadelphia] that had he not been appointed minister to France, he was desperate in his affairs and must have sold his estate and that immediately. That that appointment was the greatest God-send that could have ever befallen a man. I have this from [Senator] J[ohn] Brown and [Senator] S[tevens] T[homson] Mason." *The Complete Anas of Thomas Jefferson* 355 (New York: Da Capo Press, 1950). Albert J. Beveridge, who was always skeptical of Jefferson, wrote that "his information in this matter was indisputably correct." Beveridge, 2 *Life of Marshall* 211, note 4.

sion, Tucker wrote to a friend "that of all the to'ther side men that I know he [Marshall] appears to me to preserve the best disposition to conciliate and to preserve our pacific relations with France."[98]

Tucker's views to the contrary, French representatives in the United States, like most Republicans, were skeptical of Adams's appointees. Alexandre Hauterive, the French consul in New York, who, after Adet's recall had become France's senior official in the United States,[99] informed Paris that if Adams had chosen Madison, Aaron Burr, or Chancellor Robert R. Livingston of New York, it would have suggested that he wanted to reach a settlement.[100] Instead, "he has named a group of men who are most unfavorably disposed toward France." Hauterive wrote that Pinckney, though of good character, was bitter at not having been received by Delacroix, and that Dana was an inveterate Tory whose "personality is as fiery as his mind is narrow."[101]

> Mr. Marshall is a man of a very pronounced character who hides neither his support for the English cause nor his distance from anything that favors French interests. This quality of frankness, which sometimes shows his quick temper, is supported by a high standard of conduct, by a certain knowledge of human nature and of business, and by many talents. All of this has gained for him the complete confidence of the Federalist Party.[102]

Hauterive said that the choice of Marshall "is an expression of intent on the part of the president which is as astonishing as [the anti-French] views contained in his address to Congress." Pierre Adet was even more critical of Adams's choices. Back in Paris, he warned Delacroix about the envoys with unique Gallic imagery: "their protestations are false and their caresses faithless."[103]

Marshall's attitude toward the assignment appears to have been typically nonchalant. He was concerned about improving relations with France, but his personal affairs dominated his thinking. It may also be true that at the age of forty-two, he embarked on the mission with a sense of adventure. The future chief justice had never been abroad. Now, at Adams's behest, he was going to Paris to negotiate with revolutionary France, the most powerful country on the continent. He casually rode out from Richmond on horseback early on the morning of June 21, 1797, accompanied by his servant Dick, a young black man whom he had purchased in 1790[104] and whose job it would be to return home with the horses. Marshall's plans were to stop at Mount Vernon to consult with George Washington and then to board a ship in Alexandria bound for Philadelphia—a far easier passage than the overland route he had taken on foot so often during the revolution.

Polly was distraught at Marshall's departure and could not be convinced that the mission was necessary. Up until the last moment she pleaded with him not to go.[105] Their parting was bitter, and Marshall, seeking to make amends, wrote seven anguished letters within the next two weeks to console her.[106] The letters seem to have had little effect on Polly, since she wrote to Marshall only once during the entire year that he was away.[107] Their marriage survived, but the strains induced by Marshall's abrupt departure for Paris were considerable.[108]

After two days of hard riding, Marshall arrived at Mount Vernon on the evening of June 22. Washington insisted that he spend the next day with him, and the two men had a wide-ranging discussion covering a variety of issues, particularly the worsening situation with France. Marshall revered Washington, and it is safe to assume that the former president's growing hostility to the French regime influenced his attitude toward the Directory.

On July 1, 1797, Marshall arrived in Philadelphia and dined with President Adams that evening. They developed an immediate liking for each other. Marshall said that Adams was "a sensible, plain, candid, good tempered man and consequently I was much pleased with him."[109] Adams described Marshall in identical terms. "He is a plain man, very sensible, cautious, guarded, and learned in the law of nations. I think you will be pleased with him," the president wrote to Elbridge Gerry.[110]

That same evening Monroe, who had just returned to Philadelphia after being removed from his post in France, was fêted at a grand public dinner at Oeller's Hotel hosted by Vice President Jefferson and attended by more than fifty Republican dignitaries. The gala for Monroe, conspicuously honoring his service in Paris, was designed to embarrass the administration and was duly reported to the Directory, further encouraging their belief that a powerful pro-French party stood ready to assume power in the United States.[111]

Marshall made no effort to meet Monroe while in Philadelphia and appears to have been more worried about the situation in Richmond than in Paris. A letter of July 3 to Polly shows him clearly concerned about her health. In it he also described the dinner with the president and told her that the following evening he had visited with Robert Morris and his family. Morris was experiencing hard times, said Marshall, but the family was not showing it. He told Polly that he was doing his best to keep busy so that he would not brood too much "over my much loved and absent wife. . . . Our separation will not I trust be long and letters do everything to draw its sting."[112]

The next day was the Fourth of July, and Philadelphia celebrated independence lavishly.[113] Marshall again wrote to Polly on the fifth. "I have been extremely chagrined as not having yet received a letter from you." He put on the best face that he could, telling Polly he assumed she was well "as I hear nothing indicating the contrary. But you know not how solicitous, how anxiously solicitous, I am to hear it from yourself. Write me that you are well and in good spirits and I shall set out on my voyage with a lightened heart."[114]

Polly responded to Marshall's entreaties, and four days later he acknowledged receiving a long-awaited letter from her. Polly's letter has been lost, but judging from Marshall's reply, she told him that although her health had improved, she was depressed and unhappy. Marshall said he hoped her mind would soon become tranquil. "Good health will produce good spirits and I would not on any consideration relinquish the hope that you will possess both. Remember, that if your situation should be as suspected [an allusion to Polly's pregnancy], melancholy may inflict punishment on an innocent for whose sake you ought to preserve a serene and composed mind."*[115]

On July 14 Marshall wrote that he was about to sail and that he hoped to reach Amsterdam by the end of August. If all went well, he planned to be home by Christmas. He told Polly he had received a letter from their son Tom. "I am happy to perceive from it that you retain your better health. I flatter myself you do because he does not mention your health. Thus I will continue to please myself concerning you and to believe that you are well and happy."[116]

Marshall's extended stay in Philadelphia permitted him to explore the full range of American policy with Adams and Pickering, as well as with Alexander Hamilton, who was in the capital at the time. Hamilton and Adams were estranged, but the former secretary of the treasury, now governor of New York, had lobbied long and hard during the previous six months to improve relations with France.[117] He and Marshall were close, and except perhaps for Washington, there was no one whose opinions Marshall respected more. If Washington had counseled Marshall to be on guard, Hamilton undoubtedly impressed on him the necessity to come to an agreement.

It is not known whether Marshall saw Jefferson in Philadelphia, but the chances are that he did not. Jefferson kept a meticulous record of his appointments, and there is no indication of the two having met that summer. Although Jefferson was vice president, he was also the leader of the opposition party, and he made no secret of the fact that he thought Adams was leading the country to war. Jefferson's views were colored not only by his sympathy for France but by his abiding hatred of Great Britain. One biographer has suggested that the great Virginian's fears of British influence were largely groundless,[118] but in 1797 Jefferson genuinely believed that the Federalists were intent on serving the interests of Britain and that more than a

---

*On January 13, 1798, Polly gave birth to a son, named John Marshall.

few of them had monarchical aspirations. His solution was a military victory by revolutionary France and the establishment of a republican government in Britain. "Nothing can establish firmly the republican principles of our [own] government but an establishment of them in England. France will be the apostle of this," he wrote to Edmund Randolph.[119]

Jefferson apparently had no doubts about an eventual French victory,[120] and he thought the best course for the United States was to delay negotiations until then. As Marshall prepared to depart, Jefferson told Joseph Létombe, the French consul in Philadelphia, that the Directory should receive the envoys, "listen to them, and then drag out the negotiations at length and mollify them by the urbanity of the proceedings."[121]

Létombe passed Jefferson's advice on to Paris. "May the French, then, know how to temporize," he wrote to Delacroix. "It is up to the Directory, Citizen Minister, whether it is suitable to imitate the wisdom of Fabius. . . . "[122] Létombe wrote twice more to Paris about the mission. On July 18 he reported Marshall's departure,[123] and on July 25 he added his final observations about the envoys. Pinckney and Marshall were lawyers, Létombe said. "The first has a reputation for being a mad patriot; the other for being a true Federalist, especially since he acquired Lord Fairfax's Virginia lands."[124] Létombe ridiculed Pinckney's negotiating talents but said that "Mr. Marshall, a sly one, is planning to try his hand at diplomacy in Paris."[125]

Létombe's views were confirmed by Hauterive in New York. He told Delacroix that "the three Commissioners will be very much at sea in Paris. . . . I believe them to be expecting an unpleasant reception. The likelihood of such a welcome has undoubtedly played a key role in the planning of their strategy. However, I am certain that nothing will throw them off balance as much as a polite but cold reception, infrequent, vague and private meetings and no foreseeable end to the talks."[126] Hauterive's assessment of what the envoys anticipated was correct, and his suggestion of how to deal with Marshall, Pinckney, and Gerry set the tone of French policy.

The envoys' detailed instructions, which were transmitted to them by Pickering on July 15,[127] were surprisingly flexible and emphasized the need to preserve American neutrality. France, if possible, should accept the Jay Treaty. In return, the United States would interpose no objections should the French acquire the Louisiana Territory from Spain, negotiations for which were then under way. At the same time, the Revolutionary War's treaty of alliance should be renegotiated to relieve the United States of the obligation of guaranteeing French possessions in the West Indies. The envoys were instructed to try to recover damages for shipping losses inflicted by French privateers, but they were told not to press that issue if France would accept the Jay Treaty. Marshall and his colleagues were given wide latitude to resolve the outstanding differences between the two countries, without encroaching on American treaty obligations with Great Britain. The *sine qua non* was to avoid war, and the opening of negotiations was seen as an important step in that direction. The only limitations placed on the envoys were that they should not agree to any restrictions on American commerce and that they should avoid authorizing any loans to France so long as hostilities with Britain continued.

On July 18 Marshall's vessel, the brigantine *Grace*, was ready to sail. The lack of a favorable wind slowed the ship's passage out of Delaware Bay, and two days later Marshall wrote a final letter from America to Polly, which was carried ashore by the pilot when he departed. Marshall said his cabin "is neat and clean . . . and I find that I sleep very soundly. We have for the voyage [a sufficient amount] of salt provisions, livestock and poultry, and as we lay in our own liquors I have taken care to provide myself with plenty of excellent porter wine and brandy."[128] Because of the summer calms, Marshall feared a lengthy passage. "We have met in the bay several vessels. One from Liverpool had been at sea nine weeks . . . I hope we shall do better but fears mingle with my hopes." Once again he urged Polly to write. "Some of your letters may miscarry but some will reach me and my heart can feel till my return no pleasure comparable to what will be given it by a line from you telling me that all remains well."

Marshall wrote once again while at sea, hoping to give the letter to a passing ship bound for the United States. "We have not made quite a third of our way to Amsterdam," he told Polly on August 3. "My only solicitudes are for the success of my mission and for the much loved persons I leave behind. Sometimes I am melancholy, and sink into fears concerning you but I shake them off as fast as possible and please myself with the delightful picture of our meeting on my return."[129]

8

✑

Mission to Paris

(The XYZ Affair)

T HE *GRACE* MADE LANDFALL at the mouth of Texel River in the
Netherlands on the morning of August 29, 1797, six weeks after sailing from Philadelphia.[1] The river's entrance, the only deep-water
egress from the port of Amsterdam, was blockaded by the British navy with
the Dutch fleet bottled up inside. Marshall was enormously impressed by
this display of naval power. He wrote immediately to inform George Washington. "Until our arrival in Holland we saw only British and neutral vessels.
This, added to the blockade of the Dutch fleet in Texel, of the French fleet
in Brest, and of the Spanish fleet in Cadiz manifests the entire dominion
which one nation at present possesses over the seas."[2] Marshall's ship was
stopped three times by blockading frigates, but he said that "the conduct of
those who came on board was such as would proceed from general orders . . .
calculated to conciliate America. Whether this be occasioned by a sense of
justice and good faith, or solely by the hope that the contrast which it exhibits to the conduct of France, its effects on our commerce are the same."[3]

That evening, after an uneventful passage up the Texel, the *Grace* docked
in Amsterdam[4] where Marshall received what he believed to be encouraging news. "Tayleran [Talleyrand] Perigord," had just become foreign minister, he wrote to a friend in Virginia,[5] and at his direction, French border
officials had been instructed to issue passports to the American envoys and
facilitate their journey to Paris. "This is civil and ensures the commencement of negotiation," said Marshall a trifle optimistically.[6]

Charles Maurice de Talleyrand-Périgord, whose career as French foreign minister spanned four decades, would prove to be one of the most able diplomats in European history. Seemingly impervious to political strife, coups d'état, and military defeat, he remained in office through the Directory, the Consulate, the empire of Napoleon, the restoration of Louis XVIII, the reign of Charles X, and the July Monarchy of Louis Philippe. Political loyalty was not among the virtues of this superb tactician, who habitually trimmed his sails to fit the prevailing wind, but his durability gave French foreign policy a continuity that few nations have enjoyed. Talleyrand cut his diplomatic teeth on the American envoys sent by Adams in 1797, and the mistakes he made in his negotiations with them were mistakes he never repeated. The wily master of political intrigue met his match in the appellate advocate from Virginia, who soon assumed the quiet but steady direction of the envoys' strategy. A Franco-American war was narrowly averted, and both nations emerged from the encounter with a vastly greater understanding of the intricacies of dealing with each other.

Talleyrand, the same age as Marshall, was descended from one of the oldest families in France. (In the tenth century, one of his ancestors had reportedly demanded of Hugh Capet, "Who made you king?"[7]) As an infant, he had been dropped by a careless nurse. The resulting injury to his foot never healed properly and left him with a permanent limp. Thus incapacitated for military service, he was forced by his parents to renounce his rights as the eldest son in favor of a younger brother and to enter the church. He studied at Saint-Sulpice, was ordained, and in 1780 became the clergy's agent-general, charged with managing the church's sprawling financial affairs—a task admirably suited to his exceptional administrative ability and worldly inclination. As a reward for his diligence, Louis XVI named him Bishop of Autun, although even then Talleyrand's devotion to his faith remained less than complete. The evening of his installation, after vowing to obey the apostolic succession of Saint Peter, he had dinner as usual with his longtime consort, Adelaide de Flahaut, at their apartment in the Louvre.[8]

Talleyrand's friends sardonically called him "l'Abbé de Périgord," and his secular demeanor fitted the times. Like Marshall, he thrived on social companionship and cultivated a relaxed style that the uninitiated often mistook for lassitude. Indeed, the two men had much in common. Both could be breathtakingly charming. Talleyrand was the epitome of Parisian grace, while Marshall personified the open friendliness of the American frontier. Talleyrand valued civility and reflection, understood the importance of diplomacy and negotiation, and when presented with the choice of a circuitous or a direct route to his objective, invariably chose the former. Marshall appeared more direct, but that directness often concealed a subtlety that Talleyrand reluctantly came to admire. Both men valued political stability, but both were also gamblers by nature, willing to risk success or failure on the tenacious defense of a carefully calculated position.

When the winds of political change began to blow in 1789, Talleyrand quickly distanced himself from the doomed monarchy. He represented the clergy (the first estate) in the initial Estates-General, where he advocated the nationalization of church property. Although he was promptly excommunicated by Pius VI for this, Talleyrand's position was not anticlerical. He envisaged the church in a secular role, its clergy the spiritual functionaries of the state, vested with educational and social responsibilities, and supplying a moral stewardship that would satisfy the popular yearning for belief.*

With the advent of the Reign of Terror, Talleyrand went into exile, first in Great Britain and then in the United States, where he concentrated on amassing a personal fortune. From 1794 to 1796 he was a consultant for the Holland Land Company, selling frontier land to Europeans, and became involved in various speculative ventures with Henry Knox and Robert Morris.[9] During the years he spent in the United States, Talleyrand struck up a lasting friendship with Alexander Hamilton.[10] Reflecting his own attachment to *realpolitik*, Hamilton considered Talleyrand "the greatest modern statesman, because he had so well known when it was necessary both to suffer wrong to be done and to do it."[11] Talleyrand returned the compliment and was reported to have said: "I consider Napoleon, Pitt, and Hamilton as the three greatest men of our age, and if I had to choose, I would unhesitatingly give the first place to Hamilton."[12] Talleyrand found much of American life incomprehensible, especially the reluctance of its leading officials to profit from public service. Seeing Hamilton working late at night in his law office, he told friends that he could not understand how the man who had "made the fortune of his country" had to "work all night in order to support his family."[13]

In 1796, after the Terror subsided, Talleyrand returned to France and was elected to the academic Institut National, where, in two papers on North America,[14] he argued that the United States and Britain were linked by language, culture, and trade patterns rather than formal alliances, and that economic self-interest had dissipated the hostility caused by the War of Independence.[15] Unlike the Directory, which looked on American neutrality as a hostile act, Talleyrand maintained that if the United States abandoned neutrality it would ally itself with England. That did not seem

---

*To illustrate the important role of the church in consolidating the revolutionary faith by combining piety and patriotism, Talleyrand conceived and presided over the mammoth Fête de la Fédération on the Champ de Mars in Paris, July 14, 1790—the first anniversary of the taking of the Bastille. For a description of Talleyrand's role in that event, see Simon Schama, *Citizens: A Chronicle of the French Revolution* 509–514 (New York: Knopf, 1989).

imminent, but he argued that it was important to avoid that eventuality if possible.[16]

Through the influence of his friend and former lover Germaine de Staël,[17] Talleyrand was named to succeed Charles Delacroix as foreign minister on July 18, 1797.[18] After months of intrigue to obtain the post, Talleyrand was overjoyed. "I'll hold the job," he exulted. "I have to make an immense fortune out of it, a really immense fortune."[19] Notwithstanding Talleyrand's venality, his replacement of Delacroix was a positive step for Franco-American relations. It paralleled the transition in Philadelphia from Washington to Adams. Neither shift produced a sharp reversal in policy, but each side softened its tone. "If the commissioners [appointed by Adams] come with powers . . . to negotiate on a basis compatible with the dignity of the Republic and her interests, the differences will soon be terminated," Talleyrand wrote to Létombe shortly after assuming office.[20] Joseph Pitcairn, an American merchant living in Paris and a neighbor of Talleyrand's, wrote to Rufus King in August 1797 that the new foreign minister "has for us many advantages over his predecessor—he is superior in natural talents and in acquired—but above all he knows America and particularly her leading men very well."[21]

Initially, Talleyrand's control over French foreign policy was limited. He complained privately that the Directory treated him like an office boy, confining his duties "to signing passports and other administrative documents."[22] However, his position was so insecure that he dared not reveal his dissatisfaction. To be foreign minister during the First Republic was a risky undertaking. Of Talleyrand's fourteen predecessors, five had been killed, four were in exile, and at least two others had been imprisoned.[23] Wilhelm Sandoz-Rollin, the Prussian minister in Paris, told Berlin shortly after Talleyrand's appointment that it would be "a phenomenon of wit and management" if he were able to hang on since, except for Paul Barras, "the other Directors scarcely speak to him."[24]

Ironically, Talleyrand's ambiguous status with the Directory not only served him well when Napoleon supplanted it but soon left American affairs almost exclusively in his hands. With the armies of revolutionary France sweeping across Europe, the Directors had far more important concerns in 1797. In fact, the proceedings of the Directory, which met daily, contain scarcely a reference to the United States.[25] Because of the Directory's inattention, Talleyrand enjoyed more freedom of action concerning the United States than he enjoyed in other areas, but even so, he was not disposed to spend much time on a country that he said was "not of greater consequence . . . nor ought to be treated with greater respect, than Geneva or Genoa."[26]

The American envoys would soon run head on into this contempt, but in the fall of 1797 the main players in the unfolding diplomatic drama remained widely scattered. When Marshall arrived in Amsterdam, he was surprised to learn that his fellow envoy, Charles Cotesworth Pinckney, was waiting for him not there but in The Hague, and that Elbridge Gerry's ship was still at sea. William Vans Murray, the American minister to the Netherlands, wrote Marshall from The Hague on September 2 to say that he and Pinckney were anxiously awaiting his arrival. "You will find [Pinckney] a clear-sighted and honorable man, and of pleasing friendly manners. He knows you well, though he never saw you, and is prepared to appreciate everything good about you with cordiality and partiality. If the third commissioner [Elbridge Gerry] is as congenial as I believe you two will be, there is every reason for us all to expect glory from the battle [even] if we do not triumph in success."[27] Murray ended the letter on a suggestive note, jokingly asking Marshall whether he came "as a *single* man. Madame T[allie]n will like you the more if you have."[28] The reference was to the beautiful Jeanne Marie Thérésa Cabarrus, the wife of Jean Tallien, leader of the Thermidorian reaction against Robespierre and the Reign of Terror. Madame Tallien, one of the most fascinating women of her time, was the leader of French revolutionary fashion and had been dubbed by the Paris press "*notre dame de Thermidor.*"[29]

Rather than joining Pinckney immediately, Marshall remained in Amsterdam until September 3. Amsterdam was the banking and commercial capital of the Netherlands, and Marshall wanted to consult Dutch bankers about raising additional money for the Fairfax purchase. He arrived in The Hague on September 4. As Murray had predicted, he and Pinckney hit it off immediately, and they remained close friends until the latter's death in 1825. Pinckney, a large, heavyset man, was nine years older than Marshall and, like the future chief justice, was blessed with robust health and a warm, avuncular personality.[30] He was descended from a wealthy family of South Carolina merchants, planters, and lawyers, and had prospered practicing law in Charleston. What he lacked in blistering intellect, he more than made up for in solid dependability. It has been said of Pinckney that he was honor and duty personified.[31] Writing to Justice Story many years afterward, Marshall said approvingly that he was a man "of high and even romantic honor," whom he found to be very sensible.[32]

Pinckney benefited from having received an outstanding education abroad, which included schooling at Westminster School and Christ Church College at Oxford and legal training in London's Middle Temple. Of the three envoys, he was the only one who spoke French, a skill he had acquired while studying at the Royal Military College in Caen. Like Marshall, Pinckney was addressed as "General," but in his case the title traced to the Revolutionary War in which he had served as a brigadier general in the South

Carolina Line. Pinckney had fought at Brandywine and Germantown, although his path and Marshall's had not crossed. Subsequently, he had represented South Carolina at the constitutional convention in Philadelphia and led the fight for ratification in his state.

In politics, Pinckney and Marshall were much alike. Neither was rabidly partisan, but each identified strongly with the national government and feared the narrow self-interest of the states. Pinckney said the doctrine of state sovereignty was a heresy "which can never benefit us, but may bring on us the most serious distresses."[33] Like Marshall, he had declined several appointments proffered by Washington but had willingly undertaken the arduous journey to France as Monroe's successor, believing peace with that country to be of vital importance. In that respect, and despite his rebuff by Delacroix, Pinckney was more positive about France than Marshall. While both men supported the French Revolution, Pinckney had been among those who welcomed Citizen Genet at Charleston, and he vigorously supported the principles of the Republic, although he was often taken aback by the lack of public virtue he observed among members of the French government. Later he would run for vice president on the Federalist ticket with Adams in 1800, and was himself the Federalist nominee for president in 1804 and 1808.

In The Hague, the two envoys waited impatiently for Gerry to join them. On September 9 Marshall wrote Polly that "we shall wait a week or ten days longer and shall then proceed on our journey. You cannot conceive (yes you can conceive) how these delays perplex and mortify me."[34] Somewhat belatedly, Marshall realized he was in for more than he had anticipated. "I fear I cannot return until spring, and that fear excites very much uneasiness and even regret at my having ever consented to cross the Atlantic." He went on to describe the beauty of The Hague, but lamented the insular nature of Dutch society. "In fact, we seem to have no communication but with Americans or those who are employed by America or who have property in our country."[35]

On the same day that Marshall wrote to Polly, he dispatched a longer letter to Pickering. A marginal note entered by the State Department indicates the letter arrived in Philadelphia three months later (December 15, 1797)[36]— an illustration of the slowness of communications in the 1790s and, correspondingly, of the wide discretion exercised by American diplomats who could not refer pressing issues to Philadelphia for settlement. When an envoy was sent overseas, he was put on a long leash, and the fate of the nation's foreign relations was in his hands. Pickering had given Marshall, Pinckney, and Gerry broad policy instructions. How they carried out those instructions was left to them.

Marshall wrote to inform Pickering that there had been a coup d'état in

Paris on September 4, in which the more radical members of the Directory, aided by soldiers provided by Napoleon, had moved against their moderate and conservative opponents. The results of the most recent election, in which the moderates had triumphed, were nullified. Almost 200 deputies were arrested, forty-two newspapers closed, and the Directory's two dissident members, Lazare Carnot and François Barthélemy, were removed.[37] "The majority of the Directory by one bold stroke has probably prostrated the opposition," said Marshall.[38] "If this step has really been taken it is impossible to foresee its results. I am however persuaded that foreign nations will derive no benefit from it."

Marshall was startled that the overthrow of elected officials was taken so lightly in Europe, and he actually anticipated the rise of a figure like Napoleon. "The course of this wonderful people sets at defiance all human calculation," he told Pickering. "Any other nation which could practice and quietly submit to such a total subversion of principles would be considered . . . on the eve of military despotism. For the sake of human happiness I hope this will not be the lot of France."[39]

The following week Marshall wrote to Pickering with more details about the coup.

> The constitution of France may survive this wound, but the constitution of no other nation on earth could survive it . . . the [opposition] members of the legislature have been seized by order of the Directory, without observing any of the forms [the constitution] wisely prescribes. . . . These excesses cannot have been necessary. A wanton contempt of rules so essential to the very being of a republic could not have been exhibited by men who wished to preserve it.[40]

Having vented his displeasure at the overthrow of constitutional government, Marshall reassured Pickering that he was not going to meddle in French affairs.

> I am sensible, sir, that we have nothing to do with the internal revolutions of a sovereign nation which decides on its own fate. No remark on it will be made by me, nor will any sentiment be uttered which can have the appearance of intermeddling, even in thought, with their proper concerns. Our business is to labor the accommodation of differences, and to that sole object will all our efforts tend. France may assume what form of government she pleases, and may administer it as she pleases—our object and our duty remain the same.

Nevertheless, he cautioned Pickering that the chances for settlement had decreased. "All power is now in the undivided possession of those who have directed against us those hostile measures of which we so justly complain."[41]

When Elbridge Gerry still had not arrived in The Hague by September 18, Marshall and Pinckney set out for Paris without him. They traveled in separate coaches, Pinckney with his family and Marshall with his secretary, John Brown, a former clerk of the Virginia court of appeals,[42] and John Gamble, the eighteen-year-old son of a close friend in Richmond who was touring Europe before entering Princeton. None of the men in Marshall's party spoke French, a fact that caused some difficulty when their coach broke down and they had to deal with local tradesmen. After this incident, they were joined by Major Henry Rutledge, Pinckney's secretary and nephew, who had greater familiarity with the language. He wrote to his father in South Carolina that he had accompanied Pinckney as far as Chambray, "but some accident having happened to Genl. Marshall's wheels, it was thought best to transfer me to his party, as being better able to squabble in French with the blacksmiths." Three of the four wheels on Marshall's coach eventually had to be replaced, and as Rutledge reported, "after a great deal of imposition and noise, in which there was nothing very remarkable except the good temper of Genl. Marshall, we got through our difficulties and arrived [in Paris] a few hours after my Uncle."[43]

Altogether the trip took nine days. Gerry, who landed near Rotterdam on September 18, went first to The Hague and did not arrive in Paris until October 4. Vans Murray, with whom Gerry stayed in the Dutch capital, wrote to Marshall with remarkable perspicacity that "You will find him stored with much congressional and general knowledge—not well acquainted with mankind—and with the very best intentions and a tender and friendly heart. He is too, though he appears from a certain hesitation of manners at first, a man of cordiality, and will cooperate with you with sincerity and kindness."[44] Murray warned Marshall that Gerry believed a powerful pro-British party existed in the United States that was working against France. "I have attempted to disabuse him, but I consider this view as a radical error, productive of great consequences."

An elfin man with an exceptionally large head, Elbridge Gerry, at fifty-three, was the oldest of the envoys. A Yankee merchant from Marblehead who had taken up the cudgels early in the fight for independence, Gerry detested everything associated with Great Britain, especially the class system and the monarchy. He was one of the few statesmen who had signed both the Declaration of Independence and the Articles of Confederation, and he had served repeatedly in the Continental Congress on behalf of his native

Massachusetts. Like Pinckney, Gerry was a delegate at the constitutional convention in Philadelphia, where he had joined George Mason and Edmund Randolph in opposing the final document. Elected as an antifederalist to the first and second congresses, he formed close ties to Jefferson and Madison while retaining the friendship of John Adams, for whom he voted in 1796 as a Massachusetts elector. Like Adams, Gerry was governed by a strong streak of Puritan independence and was most comfortable when stubbornly advocating dissenting viewpoints.[45] His greatest vice was his unpredictability. He was a loose cannon on the floor of whatever assembly he adorned.[46] "Poor Gerry always had a wrong kink in his head," said his good friend Abigail Adams.[47]

According to his most recent biographer, Gerry's contrariness grew out of his ferocious attachment to the republican ideal. It was a classical abstraction that he took literally, and his devotion to it often rendered him incapable of distinguishing between small points and major issues.[48] Educated at Harvard and steeped in the literature of Greece and Rome, he viewed politics as an unceasing struggle between liberty and power. The inevitable disharmony between his ideal of republican virtue and the world he confronted left Gerry eternally suspicious. It was, according to his otherwise respectful son-in-law, "the weakest trait of his mind."[49] Nevertheless, there was no gainsaying his intellect, and of the three envoys, Gerry was by far the most sympathetic to France. After his tenure in Paris, he served as governor of Massachusetts, where his partisan efforts to redistrict the state for the Republicans' advantage added the term *gerrymander* to the nation's political vocabulary. Elected vice president on the ticket with Madison in 1812, he died in office two years later.

On their arrival in Paris, the envoys took up residence in a massive townhouse at 1131 rue de Grenelle, three blocks from the foreign ministry. The owner of the house retained an apartment on the top floor; the third floor accommodated the envoys' three secretaries; the Pinckneys occupied the main floor; and Gerry and Marshall each had a small apartment on the ground floor. Gerry complained that his quarters were so dangerous that he had to keep two loaded pistols under his pillow. Mrs. Pinckney described the furnishings as "not very fresh." The supply of sheets, she said, was adequate but there were no towels, few carpets, the mirrors were cracked, and many of the chimneys did not work.[50] The accommodations had been arranged by James Mountflorence, the American vice consul in Paris,[51] but neither Marshall nor Gerry felt they were satisfactory.

Talleyrand was informed immediately of Marshall's and Pinckney's arrival. On September 28 he wrote to Létombe in Philadelphia that the envoys were in Paris and that "negotiations should soon be underway." He was guardedly optimistic. "It is impossible to speculate on the possible outcome. I can only reiterate what I have said in previous dispatches: namely, we will do everything in our power to reestablish harmonious relations between the two Republics—something which is particularly in the best interest of the United States."[52] Talleyrand's condescension reflected the growing military might of France and the hubris of a government that had shown little but contempt for the neutral nations of Europe. He now planned to dictate terms to the United States in the same way that his predecessors had dictated to the Netherlands, Spain, and the various German principalities.

On October 8, four days after Gerry's arrival, the envoys paid a formal call on the foreign minister, whose official residence at 471 rue du Bac was just a short distance from their apartments. They waited briefly while Talleyrand was closeted with the minister from Portugal. When that interview concluded, he received them cordially and, at Pinckney's request, provided them with diplomatic identification ("cards of hospitality") to ease their stay in Paris. Talleyrand said he was preparing a memorandum for the Directory on the subject of Franco-American relations[53] and asked that negotiations be deferred until it was finished. He indicated that the memorandum would be completed in two or three days, at which time the Directory would decide how to proceed. The envoys spoke English, in which Talleyrand was fluent. The foreign minister, as befitted his position, spoke French.[54] The meeting lasted fifteen minutes. Marshall reported that Talleyrand's manner "was polite and easy." The envoys were disappointed at the delay in opening negotiations but nevertheless believed they were off to a good start.[55]

In his memorandum, Talleyrand urged the Directory to normalize relations with the United States. He argued that France bore at least some responsibility for the despised Jay Treaty, insofar as French officials had failed to communicate their objections to Philadelphia before it was signed. Talleyrand blamed the failure on Delacroix's policy of not talking to the Americans. He noted that President Washington, during his last two years in office, had turned against France, but Adams, if not sympathetic, was at least neutral. Talleyrand cited the president's narrow margin of victory over Jefferson as a factor that would dictate caution and pointed to Adams's prompt appointment of the three special envoys as an indication that the president sought peace. He went on to suggest that France's long-term interests, particularly the welfare of its colonies in the West Indies, lay in a peaceful settlement of the outstanding issues. "War leads to no useful result," he told the Directory.[56]

As a preliminary to opening negotiations, Talleyrand said he intended to ask the envoys to explain several passages of President Adams's May 16 speech to Congress, which he thought were hostile to France. "If dignity requires that we not remain insensitive to such remarks, it can just as well sanction the preventing of a recurrence by [demanding an] explanation—not too humiliating to our adversary, however, so that without hurting anyone's self-esteem, we can proceed rapidly towards what is useful, without obstacles on either side, without ulterior motives, without mistrust."[57] Whether Talleyrand's reference to Adams's speech represented a genuine concern, or whether it was a negotiating ploy to lever the envoys into complying with his demands, will never be known for certain. But it was a curiously self-righteous insertion that revealed Talleyrand's faulty assessment of the United States and that soon became a major stumbling block in the negotiations.[58]

After their initial reception, the envoys heard nothing further from Talleyrand for almost a week. Marshall wrote to Charles Lee, Adams's attorney general, that the delay "will appear as strange to you as it does to us. Our appointment was known in the beginning of August. . . . Yet our reception and the commencement of our negotiations are delayed in order to receive a report. In the meantime our vessels are everyday condemned [by French courts]."[59]

On October 14 Talleyrand cautiously played his first card. The envoys were informed that the Directory was "excessively exasperated" with the United States and had decided to demand an explanation of several passages in President Adams's speech to Congress that they considered offensive. The Americans received this information indirectly, via the foreign minister's private secretary, Baron d'Osmond,[60] who met with the United States vice consul, James Mountflorence, who then had tea with General Pinckney. Pinckney was told that unless a satisfactory explanation was given, the Directory would not receive the envoys officially, which would mean that negotiations could not begin. Talleyrand, so his secretary said, "was extremely sorry and had endeavored in vain to soften the Directory."[61] In effect, Talleyrand was ascribing to the Directory the policy he himself had recommended, and he sought to ingratiate himself with the envoys by intimating that he opposed it.

Pinckney informed Marshall and Gerry of the overture, and the three men decided not to respond. Marshall observed that the manner of transmitting the request was so irregular that there was no reason to reply.[62] Afterward they reread Adams's speech and found nothing that required an explanation.[63] It was apparent, however, that they were becoming impatient. Marshall wrote in the journal he was keeping that "we have had several conversations on the extraordinary silence of the Government concerning our reception. The plunder of our commerce sustains no abatement . . . [yet] our reception is postponed in a manner most unusual and contemptuous."[64]

In retrospect, Talleyrand's tactics appear obvious. He wanted to settle the outstanding issues but was in no hurry to do so. From his perspective, the matter was not urgent. By not receiving Marshall, Pinckney, and Gerry, he sought to exert pressure indirectly and to prepare the envoys for a demand for money—a *douceur*, or sweetener—that he would soon make. After he received the money, he would remove the obstacles he had erected. Negotiations would begin, and Talleyrand would have reaped a sizable reward.

It was not an unusual strategy. The tradition of French statesmen receiving considerations from foreign governments had been rendered more or less acceptable by long usage. During the War of Independence, Silas Deane, the American purchasing agent in Paris, had found it necessary to pay a *douceur* when doing business in France,[65] and the practice had become even more widespread in the First Republic. As Sandoz-Rollin told Berlin, "it has become the custom under the Directory that every large transaction should be preceded by a *douceur*."[66] The American mission was to be no exception, and Talleyrand expected the envoys to obey this unwritten rule of French diplomacy. What was unusual, perhaps, was the relentlessness with which Talleyrand pursued the bribe. "The Minister of Foreign Relations," wrote Sandoz-Rollin, "has declared loftily that he loves money and that he is determined, when he retires from public office, not to be forced on the public dole."[67] In an age when venality was common, Talleyrand was remarkable only for the extent of his greed.*

In the meantime, the envoys waited. Not surprisingly, Marshall's patience began to wear thin. He recognized that Talleyrand was delaying negotiations deliberately, and he urged his colleagues to send a letter requesting that discussions begin. "I am willing to wait two or three days longer, but not more. The existing state of things is to France the most beneficial and the most desirable, but to America it is ruinous."[68]

At this point Gerry objected, playing the role his critics had predicted. In his view, a letter demanding that negotiations begin would only irritate the Directory, and it might give them an excuse to break off discussions completely. Marshall reported that Pinckney agreed with his own view, "but we are both anxious to proceed with the full assent of Mr. Gerry. We are restrained by a high respect for his opinions and by a wish to preserve unanimity in everything." As a result, the envoys continued to wait, assuming Talleyrand would contact them.

True to form, on October 18 Talleyrand initiated a second indirect ap-

---

*Talleyrand's personal profit during his first two years as foreign minister for expediting treaties, guaranteeing immunity for neutral territory, and other such favors has been estimated at between 13 and 14 million francs, and between 1797 and 1804 at 30 million francs. George LaCour-Gayet, 1 *Talleyrand 1754–1838* 237–238 (Paris: Payot, 1928); Louis Bastide, *Vie politique et religieuse de Talleyrand-Périgord* 227 (Paris: Faure, 1838); J. F. Bernard, *Talleyrand: Biography* 207 note (New York: G. P. Putnam's Sons, 1973).

proach, although he still refused to meet the Americans officially. Shortly after breakfast that morning, Nicholas Hubbard, an Englishman by birth and
a partner in the Amsterdam bank that had financed the national debt of the
United States, called on the envoys to assure them that their personal
checks would be honored by the bank while they were in Paris.[69] Gerry was
not present, but Hubbard asked Pinckney if he would receive a visit that
evening from a colleague of his, Jean Conrad Hottinguer, whom he said had
an important message from Talleyrand. Hottinguer, a Swiss banker, was an
associate of Hubbard's in a European syndicate that speculated in American
investments. He had lived in the United States and, during the early 1790s,
had been involved with Talleyrand and Robert Morris in various land purchases in Pennsylvania.[70] He was acquainted with Pinckney, and he also
knew James Marshall, having helped negotiate the loan that enabled the
Marshalls to purchase South Branch Manor in the summer of 1797.[71]
Whether Talleyrand knew of the link between Hottinguer and James Marshall is not known. However, given the notoriety of the Fairfax purchase, it
is not unlikely. In any case, Marshall never alluded to the connection. In referring to Hottinguer in his journal, he said merely that Hubbard had described him as "a man of truth and reputation, and that any communications
he should make might be relied on."[72] Ultimately, Hottinguer would become "X," the first of three Talleyrand intermediaries subsequently described in American diplomatic dispatches as X, Y, and Z.

Pinckney agreed to receive Hottinguer, who arrived that evening while
the three envoys were having dinner. Pinckney excused himself from the
table and retired with Hottinguer to an adjoining room. There Hottinguer
informed the South Carolinian that he had a message from Talleyrand. He
repeated that some members of the Directory were exasperated with
Adams's speech and that Talleyrand was attempting to calm them.[73] Hottinguer then outlined the conditions for negotiations to begin. The envoys
would have to "give satisfaction to the honor of France" concerning Adams's
speech; the United States would have to pay all claims that Americans had
lodged against the French government; the American government would
have to assume responsibility for paying for the damage done by French privateers; and it would also have to make a substantial loan to the French government. Finally, the envoys would have to provide an additional *pot de vin*
of £50,000 to Talleyrand—a bribe to soothe the thirsty throat of government.[74]

When Pinckney reported the conversation to Marshall and Gerry, the
latter was noncommittal, but Marshall was furious. "I was decidedly of the
opinion and so expressed myself that such a proposition could not be made
by a nation from whom any treaty short of the absolute surrender of the independence of the United States was to be expected." Marshall told his col

leagues the terms were ridiculous and that they should ignore them. He again suggested that they write directly to Talleyrand and express their concern about the present state of affairs between the two countries.[75] Marshall insisted that negotiations be conducted face to face with the foreign minister and that the terms presented through Hottinguer were unacceptable.[76] Gerry, however, advocated a more conciliatory approach. To maintain unanimity, it was eventually agreed that Pinckney should meet with Hottinguer to obtain further details. Despite Marshall's warning, the envoys were already being drawn into Talleyrand's net.

The following evening, October 19, Hottinguer returned to Pinckney's apartment with a written statement setting out the French demands.[77] It commenced with the notation that "a person who possesses the confidence of the Directory" would provide his services to smooth the way for an accord by giving Adams's speech "a softening turn." That person, said Hottinguer, was Talleyrand.[78] The document then set out the explicit requirements for a settlement. These had been refined somewhat since Hottinguer's oral presentation to Pinckney. American claims against France were to be adjudicated by a bilateral commission, but whatever payments were awarded "are to be advanced by the American government itself." France still wanted a loan, but the American government could protect its neutrality by disguising the money as an advance payment to French citizens for debts owed to them by various Americans. "There shall also be first taken from this loan certain sums for the purpose of making the customary distributions in diplomatic affairs," a euphemism for Talleyrand's bribe.[79]

When the envoys discussed their response the next morning, Marshall again urged that they terminate "this indirect mode of procedure."[80] Pinckney agreed, but Gerry, who feared that a hard line might lead to war, continued to advocate caution. Marshall and Pinckney argued with Gerry for several hours, but as Marshall reported, "no impression was made."[81]

That evening, while the envoys were still debating their response, Hottinguer returned for a third time, bringing with him Pierre Bellamy, whom he introduced as a close friend of Talleyrand's. Like Hubbard and Hottinguer, Bellamy was a banker (a partner in the Hamburg firm of Ricci and Bellamy) and an import merchant. More important, he was Talleyrand's personal banker. He would become "Y" in the envoys' dispatches. As if to amplify Hottinguer's earlier remarks, Bellamy repeated that Talleyrand was favorably disposed toward the United States and that he still cherished memories of the kindness with which he had been treated there. Indeed, he was "extremely solicitous of repaying these kindnesses" by using "his good offices with the Directory" to aid in the negotiations.[82] However, since the Directory had not officially received the envoys, and since it also had not deputized Talleyrand to communicate with them, the foreign minister had authorized Bellamy to present certain proposals that, if acceptable, could form the basis of a treaty between France and the United States. Bellamy said that if the envoys agreed, he would tell Talleyrand, who would then intercede with the Directory to open negotiations.[83]

At that point, Bellamy pulled from his pocket a French translation of Adams's speech with the offending portions indicated.*[84] These would have to be repudiated, said Bellamy. After that, negotiations could begin, but "I will not disguise from you that this satisfaction, being made, the essential part of the treaty remains to be adjusted: *il faut de l'argent—il faut beaucoup de l'argent.*" [It will require money—it will require a great deal of money.][85] When Marshall asked whether they were to understand that unless the demands were agreed to, the American envoys would not be officially received by the Directory, Bellamy hedged. He had no instructions on that point, he said.[86]

After Hottinguer and Bellamy left, the envoys discussed their predicament. Marshall said the propositions were preposterous, and Pinckney agreed. Moreover, even if the conditions had been acceptable, Hottinguer and Bellamy "had no authority to bind the government of France."[87] Marshall told his colleagues it was contrary to the interests of the United States "to carry on this clandestine negotiation" and that the longer it continued, the more they would entangle themselves. Once again Gerry disagreed,[88] and the discussion became heated. After several hours, however, he yielded and it was agreed that the envoys would break off the informal discussions. Hottinguer and Bellamy were coming for breakfast the next morning, and they would be told at that time.

But the next morning, October 21, 1797, the envoys found themselves being manipulated once again. Hottinguer arrived for breakfast at nine, but Bellamy did not appear until ten, explaining that he had been closeted with Talleyrand.[89] Bellamy reiterated that the Directory was so incensed by Adams's speech that they had decided not to receive the envoys until the president's remarks were disavowed. Bellamy said that he and Talleyrand were aware of the pain the envoys "must feel in complying with this demand, but that the Directory would not dispense with it: that we must consider it as the indispensable preliminary to obtain a reception, *unless we could find the means to change their determination in this particular.*"[90]

When the envoys pressed Bellamy as to what he meant, he said he was

---

*The offending passage in Adams's speech stated: "While we are endeavoring to adjust all our differences with France by amicable negotiations, the progress of the war in Europe, *the depredations on our commerce,* the personal injuries to our citizens, and general complexion of our affairs, render it my indispensable duty to recommend to your consideration effectual measures of defence." Talleyrand's emphasis. See 3 *The Papers of John Marshall* 288, note 7 (Chapel Hill: University of North Carolina Press, 1979).

not authorized to suggest the means. However, if they wanted his personal opinion, it was a question of money. Bellamy proceeded to explain how the United States should advance to France 32 million Dutch florins. After France concluded a peace treaty with Holland, the Dutch government would repay the loan and no one would lose anything. In effect, the United States would merely be advancing to France the 32 million on the credit of the Netherlands. When Marshall asked whether the *douceur* of £50,000 was in addition to this sum, Bellamy said yes.[91] What Bellamy did not say was that he and Hottinguer expected to make a sizable profit handling the Dutch loan through their banks.

Once again the envoys withdrew to an adjoining room to formulate their response. Gerry urged that they delay a formal answer and tell Talleyrand's emissaries that they wanted time to consider the proposals. "I improperly interrupted him," said Marshall, "and declared that I would not consent to any proposition of the sort; that the subject [had] already [been] considered and that so far as my voice would go I would not permit it to be supposed longer that we could deliberate on such propositions."[92]

The discussion became acrimonious. Finally Marshall proposed a compromise. "Out of respect to the opinions of Mr. Gerry," Marshall said he would return to Philadelphia for instructions provided that the French would suspend further attacks on American shipping in the interim. Gerry agreed, and Marshall wrote a memorandum for them to present to Bellamy and Hottinguer summarizing the arrangement. Gerry thought Marshall's draft was too harshly worded and wrote out a substitute, which the envoys then read to Talleyrand's agents.[93] Bellamy was told he could make a copy if he wished, but he refused.

Bellamy was frustrated that the envoys had not accepted his proposal, and he lost his temper. He threatened them with expulsion from France unless they either repudiated Adams's speech or paid the money demanded. The banker said they would never be received by the Directory and he shuddered at the consequences.[94] Bellamy and Hottinguer departed, the former repeating his warning that the Americans would immediately receive a letter from Talleyrand ordering them to leave Paris.[95]

The next day Marshall prepared the first of two lengthy dispatches for Pickering describing what had happened. All three envoys signed the message. It did not arrive in Philadelphia until the following spring,[96] and until then the American government knew nothing of what was taking place. The envoys were on their own. Their only sources of guidance were Pickering's broad directive of the previous summer and their own sense of what was appropriate. First and foremost in the minds of all three men was a determination to do nothing that would discredit the United States.

Marshall made that sentiment clear in a letter to Vans Murray, written the same day as the dispatch to Pickering. "We are not, and I believe we shall not be received [by the Directory]. I cannot be explicit with you; but I am persuaded that, however unsuccessful our mission may be, our conduct can never be disapproved by our country. I am preparing for orders, which I daily expect, to leave France."[97]

Three days later Marshall expressed similar thoughts to George Washington. The French government, he wrote, "seems to be radically hostile to our country. I could wish to form a contrary opinion, but to do so I must shut my eyes on every subject which presents itself to them." He told Washington that "the Atlantic only can save us," and added that the envoys were making arrangements to leave Paris.[98]

Pinckney and Gerry shared Marshall's pessimism. Mrs. Pinckney packed the family's belongings, anticipating a hurried departure,[99] while Pinckney wrote angrily to Murray that "we experience a haughtiness which is unexampled in the history and practice of nations. . . . I would give a handsome fee for one half hour with you. '*I could a tale unfold.*'"[100] Gerry was no less frustrated. "The ministers of the U[nited] States here are in a very unpleasant situation," he wrote. "They are not to be received by the Directory, and having no power to negotiate upon certain propositions informally made, which the most extravagant imagination of any citizen of the United States could never have suggested, they expect every moment a formal hint to depart. The fact is a small cargo of Mexican dollars would be more efficient in a negotiation at present than two cargoes of Ambassadors."[101]

Talleyrand was nonplussed by the American response, which contrasted sharply with the eagerness of the neutral states of Europe to placate France. Confronted with the triumvirate's refusal to deal with Bellamy and Hottinguer, he dispatched a third intermediary to revive the negotiations. This was Lucien Hauteval, "Z" in subsequent dispatches, a wealthy sugar planter from Santo Domingo who had lived in Boston, where he had been acquainted with Gerry.[102] Hauteval had moved to Paris in 1796 and was known to be especially friendly toward the United States. He was a close friend of Talleyrand's and often submitted memoranda to him dealing with Franco-American relations and the future of Santo Domingo. Hauteval was not a business associate of the foreign minister, and he appeared to be a man of integrity, so much so that even Marshall came to respect his affection for the United States.[103]

On the morning of October 22, Hauteval called on the envoys but found only Gerry at home, Marshall and the Pinckneys having decided to visit St. Cloud.[104] Hauteval assured Gerry that Talleyrand was well disposed toward the United States, that he was disappointed he had not seen more of the envoys in their private capacities, and that he would welcome further contact. The foreign minister, he said, had explicitly asked him to call on Gerry to deliver the message.[105] Hauteval also explained to Gerry that the loan to France and the *douceur* for Talleyrand were prerequisites for doing business with the Directory, but he wanted it understood that unlike Bellamy and Hottinguer, he did not represent Talleyrand in business matters and came simply as his friend.[106] Gerry suggested that the message should be delivered to all three envoys, whereupon Hauteval paid a return visit the following day to see Marshall and Pinckney. However, when Hauteval suggested that they call on Talleyrand privately, the two demurred. They told Hauteval that it would be inappropriate for them to call on Talleyrand unless they were officially invited. Gerry, on the other hand, who had known Talleyrand slightly from Boston,[107] thought that a personal visit might be in order and agreed to accompany Hauteval to the foreign ministry the following day.[108] Talleyrand was with the Directory when they arrived, and an appointment for Gerry was set for the evening of October 28.

For several days the envoys heard nothing further. Then, on October 27, the day before Gerry's scheduled meeting with Talleyrand, Hottinguer visited them at noon. Austria had just made peace with France,[109] and the mood in Paris was euphoric. Hottinguer warned the envoys that the Directory's hand had been strengthened by the victory and that they were becoming impatient with the United States. Unless that attitude could be softened, war might ensue.[110]

The envoys stood their ground. Pinckney and Gerry replied that the Austrian collapse had been anticipated and that it would not affect their conduct in any way.[111] When Hottinguer reminded them of France's military power and said that the Directory would now move against those nations that had been neutral, including the United States, Pinckney, who was finding it difficult to control his indignation, replied that they were fully aware of the situation and still refused to pay tribute.[112] Gerry added they had no authority to negotiate a loan in any event.

Marshall's journal captures the remarkable scene that followed:

> Mr. Hottinguer again expatiated on the power and violence of France. He urged the danger of our situation, and pressed the policy of softening [the Directory] and thereby obtaining time. . . . Mr. Gerry told him that if war should be made on us by France it would be obviously forced on us. . . . General Pinckney told him that all America deprecated a war with France, but that our present situation was more ruinous to us than a declared war could be. That at present our commerce was plundered unprotected but that if war was declared we should seek the means of protection.
>
> Mr. Hottinguer said he hoped we would never form a connection with Britain. General Pinckney answered that he hoped so too . . .

but that if France should attack us we must seek the best means of self defense. Mr. Hottinguer again returned to the subject of money. Said he, "Gentlemen, you do not speak to the point. It is money. It is expected that you will offer money." General Pinckney said we had spoken to that point very explicitly and had given an answer. "No," he said, "you have not. What is your answer?" General Pinckney replied, "*No, no, not a sixpence.*"

He asked if our government did not know that nothing was to be obtained here without money? General Pinckney replied that our government had not even suspected such a state of things. He appeared surprised at that and said there was not an American in Paris who could not have given this information. General Pinckney told him that the letters of our minister [James Monroe] had indicated a very contrary temper in the government of France and had represented it as acting entirely upon principle. . . .

The conversation continued for nearly two hours, and the public and private advance of money was pressed and pressed again in a variety of forms. At length Mr. H. said that he did not blame us, that our determination was certainly proper if we could keep it, but he showed decidedly his opinion to be that we could not keep it. He said he would communicate our conversation to the minister.[113]

Gerry and Hauteval met with Talleyrand the following day. The foreign minister was cordial but did not modify his demand for money. When he told Gerry that France required a loan from the United States, the New Englander replied that they had no authority to make such a commitment, but if formal negotiations commenced, one of the envoys would return to Philadelphia for instructions. Talleyrand responded abruptly that the Directory was accustomed to dispatch business promptly and could not wait so long—an astonishing statement in view of the fact France had kept the American envoys waiting for the last six weeks. Talleyrand suggested the envoys themselves assume the authority to make the loan; they were ministers plenipotentiary and a loan "was an absolute *sine qua non.*"[114] Talleyrand then told Gerry that the Directory had just passed a decree [*arrêté*] demanding that Adams's speech be disavowed.[115] He said he would delay the decree for a week in order to give the envoys time to "find other means" that might dissuade the Directory from issuing it—a clear invitation to provide the *douceur* his agents had demanded.[116]

Gerry and Hauteval returned to the envoys' lodgings and informed Marshall and Pinckney of what had happened. The three agreed they would not meet Talleyrand's demand and that a week would make no difference. Accordingly, they told Hauteval to inform Talleyrand there was no reason for delay. If the Directory wanted to issue the decree and order them out of France, it might as well do so immediately. "We did not wish to suspend it for an instant," wrote Marshall. "We were as ready to receive it now as we should be eight days hence."[117]

The following day Hottinguer called on the envoys with yet another message from Talleyrand. He said the foreign minister was "extremely anxious to be of service" to the envoys and wanted to make one last effort to secure their cooperation.[118] As reported by Marshall, "A great deal of the same conversation which had passed at our former interviews was repeated. The power and the haughtiness of France was again displayed to us. We were told that the destruction of England was inevitable, and that the wealth and arts of that nation would naturally pass over to America if that event should find us at peace."[119]

Talleyrand was attempting to whet the Americans' appetite for plunder. The message also marked a shift in the foreign minister's negotiating stance. The envoys were told that if they paid the *douceur*, two of them could remain in Paris while the third returned to America for instructions about the loan. The Directory would not receive them, but Talleyrand would meet with them and commence informal discussions on the issues outstanding. The envoys asked Hottinguer if France would return the cargoes of American ships still in its custody if they accepted the proposal. He said no. They asked if France would suspend further attacks on American commerce. Again Hottinguer said no.

Marshall responded sharply that they could see no benefit in paying the bribe. "We told him that France had taken violently from America more than $15 million, and [had] treated us as enemies in every respect. That we had come to restore harmony between the two nations . . . and that in lieu of this we were told that if we would pay [a bribe of £50,000] we might be permitted to remain in Paris which could only give us the benefit of seeing the plays and operas of Paris for the winter. . . ."[120]

Unless the envoys paid Talleyrand's fee, Hottinguer replied, they would be ordered to leave. They should carefully consider the consequences, he added menacingly, implying immediate physical danger and possible imprisonment. Pinckney, Marshall, and Gerry were unmoved. When Hottinguer asked if Bellamy could call on them again, Marshall replied they would be happy to see him personally, "but if he came only with the expectation that we should [agree] to advance money without previously establishing a solid and permanent reconciliation, he might save himself the trouble because it was a subject we had considered maturely and on which we were immovable."

Confronted with the envoys' refusal, Talleyrand made a desperate effort to extract his *douceur*. The next morning, October 30, 1797, Bellamy and

Hottinguer wangled another breakfast invitation with the envoys. Bellamy harangued them for an hour about the power and glory of France. He said that because of the victory of Bonaparte's armies in Austria, Talleyrand was in a much stronger position. Accordingly, he could now offer more generous terms. Bellamy thereupon gave the envoys a sheet of paper containing Talleyrand's new terms of settlement.[121] Bellamy stressed that although the proposals were Talleyrand's, the foreign minister would not take responsibility for them and could not guarantee that the Directory would approve them. He would only "undertake to use his influence with the Directory in support of them."[122]

Talleyrand's revised terms reflected his eagerness for money. Two of the envoys could remain in Paris while the third returned to America to obtain instructions concerning a loan to France. A mutually agreed five-member commission would adjudicate American shipping claims against French privateers. The judgments awarded would be paid initially by the United States as "an advance to the French Republic, who will repay it in a time and manner to be agreed upon." Negotiations for a new treaty would proceed forthwith, so as to be ready for signature when the envoy returned to France with instructions about the loan, the implication being that without the loan there would be no treaty. Finally, Talleyrand indicated that further confiscations of American property would be suspended while the envoy was away, as would further attacks on American shipping by French privateers. What was not in the proposed terms was also important. Talleyrand had dropped all references to Adams's speech and no longer demanded that it be explained or repudiated. Hottinguer informed the envoys, however, that Talleyrand would not submit the proposed terms to the Directory until he received £50,000, "or the greater part of it," which suggests the price was now negotiable as well.[123]

Bellamy's manner was officious, and he patronized the envoys with boasts of French power and American weakness. Even worse, he threatened that the envoys would be blamed if an agreement was not reached, and touted the strength of "the French party in America," which, he said, French diplomacy would exploit.[124] Marshall, Pinckney, and Gerry took a jaundiced view of Talleyrand's offer. Their written response, which was delivered the next day, summarily rejected the proposal that the United States advance the money to satisfy American shipping claims but left the door open for the settlement of other issues. On one point, however, the envoys were firm. "No diplomatic gratification can precede the ratification of the treaty."[125] There would be no bribe.

Talleyrand did not respond to the American counterproposal. Instead, on November 3 Hottinguer called on the envoys and showed them a draft of a letter that he said the foreign minister had written requesting an explanation of Adams's speech.[126] Hottinguer said it would be sent to them unless they agreed to the terms he and Bellamy had presented earlier. When Marshall, Pinckney, and Gerry repeated their unwillingness to consider the matter, Hottinguer told them with some exasperation that the French government had received fresh intelligence from the United States that if Aaron Burr and James Madison had been sent to Paris instead of the three of them, an agreement between the two countries would already have been reached,[127] adding that Talleyrand was preparing a memorandum to France's supporters in America complaining about the unfriendly behavior of the envoys; if the talks collapsed, it would be blamed on the Federalists.[128]

That evening Marshall wrote to Attorney General Charles Lee in Philadelphia that "our situation is more intricate and difficult than you can believe."[129] After detailing Hottinguer's latest threats, Marshall said he and his colleagues had agreed "to refuse to hold any further indirect discourse" with Talleyrand's agents but had not yet agreed on a plan of action. Whatever they decided to do would cost money. "No person here seems to think that peace ought to be demanded, but by ministers with a full hand."

Talleyrand was not prepared to give up, and he believed that time was on his side. The United States was not going to declare war on France; Jefferson and the Republicans would prevent an alliance with Great Britain; and perhaps most important, delay would likely benefit the Republicans and work against the Federalists. In the long run, that would be to France's advantage. Meanwhile, the French army, now placed under the sole command of Napoleon, was gaining strength each day.

Accordingly, in early November Talleyrand switched his intermediaries but not his tactics. On November 8 Caron de Beaumarchais, a wealthy Parisian merchant who had assisted the colonies during the War of Independence and who had substantial business interests in the United States (Marshall represented him in Virginia[130]), called on the envoys to gauge their mood.[131] He reported to Talleyrand that he could detect no change in the Americans' attitude.[132] Simultaneously, James Mountflorence, the American vice counsel, approached Pinckney on the foreign minister's behalf. The South Carolinian rebuffed the overture.[133] Pinckney told Mountflorence to inform Talleyrand that the envoys were "extremely disgusted" with their reception in Paris; "that we were the ministers of a republic wishing very earnestly to be on friendly terms with France; that we expected at least to have been heard and felt very sensibly the contempt manifested for our country through us. That we neither came to buy or beg a peace but to treat as an independent nation on the subjects of differences subsisting between us."[134] When Mountflorence informed Talleyrand of Pinckney's reply, the foreign minister said the Americans "were more haughty in their conduct than any other ministers" in France. If they had come forward as requested, "their treaty might have been finished by this time."[135]

On November 8 Marshall wrote a second lengthy dispatch to Pickering, describing in detail the overtures made on Talleyrand's behalf.[136] This, too, was signed by Pinckney and Gerry. The material in this dispatch, along with Marshall's earlier letter of October 22, would be made public in the spring of 1798 and would create an outpouring of patriotism in America. France would be roundly condemned, Talleyrand castigated, the envoys hailed for their steadfastness, and the fortunes of the Federalists revitalized. But that was six months away. In November 1797 Marshall and his colleagues were simply doing their duty as best they could under extremely trying circumstances.

On November 27, 1797, when there was still no response from the Directory and no indication from Talleyrand as to when negotiations might begin, the envoys reconfirmed the grim situation to Pickering.

> Frequent and urgent attempts have been made to inveigle us again into negotiation with persons not officially authorized, of which the obtaining money is the basis. But we have persisted in declining to have any further communication relative to diplomatic business with persons of that description, and we mean to adhere to this determination. We are sorry to inform you, that the present disposition of the government of this country appears to be as unfriendly toward ours as ever, and that we have very little prospect of succeeding in our mission.[137]

Marshall expressed his own views to Pickering in a separate letter. He noted that preparations were under way for an invasion of England but doubted that France could mount it effectively. "An army passing the channel unprotected by a sufficient fleet would risk a great deal in its passage, and should it even effect a landing it must succeed or perish."[138] Instead, he thought the preparations cloaked French designs on Spain and Portugal, and that even Switzerland was threatened with partition. More to the point, he was annoyed rather than alarmed by Talleyrand's failure to meet with the envoys. "My own private opinion is that this haughty, ambitious government is not willing to come to an absolute rupture with America during the present state of war with England but [at the same time] will not condescend to act with justice or to treat us as a free and independent nation."[139]

Throughout the fall and winter, Marshall was sustained by his opinion that France did not want war with the United States and that Talleyrand was simply extending negotiations as long as he could. That view allowed the envoys to retain more equanimity than might otherwise have been possible.

In important ways, each of the envoys contributed substantially. Marshall provided balance and direction, Pinckney supplied unshakable dedication and firmness, and Gerry, ever prepared to see the French point of view, restrained his colleagues from precipitously breaking off discussions—which in the last analysis placed the responsibility on Talleyrand.

Bleak as the situation appeared, the envoys were determined to wait Talleyrand out. Accordingly, Marshall and Gerry took steps to improve their accommodations. Jefferson had anticipated that the ambiance of the city would "mollify" the envoys and make them more amenable.[140] Marshall had no intention of being mollified, but neither did he plan to live the life of an ascetic. Together with Gerry, he began to savor the delights of Paris.* In mid-November, with the assistance of Joel Barlow, a wealthy merchant who was the unofficial head of the American community,[141] they found more congenial quarters in the elegant mansion (*hôtel particular*) of the Marquise Reine-Philiberte de Villette at 54 rue de Vaugirard, facing the Luxembourg Gardens. Gerry was given a commodious suite of four rooms on the second floor, while the future chief justice made do with three superbly appointed rooms on the ground floor. The rent was £12$^1/_2$ per month, £5 less than each man had paid for the less desirable lodgings near the foreign ministry.[142]

The beautiful and charming Marquise de Villette, an accomplished young widow with two small children, provided her guests with an immediate entrée to Parisian society. The daughter of impoverished nobility from the vicinity of Ferney, near Lake Geneva (her father was an officer in the king's guard), she had been destined for a convent until the elderly Voltaire, who lived nearby and who had seen her grow up, intervened and adopted her. Voltaire could not accept the idea that she be cloistered. He called her *belle et bonne* (beautiful and good),[143] and she became a cherished daughter to him, comforting him during his last years with her pleasing ways. "The sickly old man found some of the lost fire of his youth in the company of this young girl," a contemporary observed, and she was always able to soothe his irritability and impatience.[144] It was Voltaire who, at the age of eighty-three, taught Reine-Philiberte how to dance[145] and who arranged for her marriage in 1777 to the Marquis de Villette, an extremely wealthy but dissolute figure who died of his excesses in 1793. Because of her irrepressible cheerfulness, her beauty, her intelligence, and her social position, the marquise was a fa-

---

*For anyone not involved in politics, the intellectual and social life in Paris under the Directory was vibrant. Wilhelm von Humboldt, who arrived with his family in November 1797, wrote to Johann Christof Friedrich von Schiller that "Any one like me who pursues such harmless things as ancient literature . . . is everywhere left in peace, but particularly here now, where the police are exceptionally good and yet not burdensome with formalities and spying, where foreigners are treated with the greatest affability, and where a live and genuine interest in science and scholarship obtains." December 7, 1797, *Neue Briefe an Schiller, 1796–1803* 175, F. C. Ebrard, ed. (Berlin: Paetel, 1911).

vorite with the expatriate American community. Her salon was frequented by men of letters eager to bask in Voltaire's reflected glory as well as by those members of the old nobility who had made peace with the revolution. She had been imprisoned for nine months during the Terror, but even the most extreme of Robespierre's supporters could not bring themselves to execute her.[146] Among her friends were the Maréchale de Luxembourg, the Duchesse de Lauzun, the Comtesse de Boufflers, and Madame Jeanne Cabarrus Tallien, *notre dame de Thermidor*,[147] about whom Vans Murray had joked to Marshall.[148]

The marquise's house on the rue de Vaugirard was a shrine to Voltaire. The central feature of her Paris drawing room was a magnificent Houdon bust of Voltaire under which she burned incense. Voltaire's robe was prominently displayed, as were some of his writings, and, most unusual, even macabre, his heart was preserved in a silver case for all to see.[149]

Madame de Villette took an immediate liking to her American guests, as did they to her. She sat with them each afternoon for hours, taught them to speak French, and soon began to play the role of hostess, organizing dinners and parties for them. When resident American artist John Vanderlyn painted her portrait with her nine-year-old son (Voltaire Charles de Villette), she insisted that Gerry and Marshall also sit for Vanderlyn. The Gerry portrait, one of Vanderlyn's most famous, hangs in the Fogg Art Museum at Harvard.[150] Marshall, more modest, or perhaps more self-conscious at forty-two, settled for a miniature, which is the earliest rendition of his likeness.[51] The marquise occasionally took her guests to her country estate for the weekend, and whenever she did so, she arranged for a fourth person, a lady friend, to accompany them.

Gerry and Marshall were enchanted. Gerry sent his wife a glowing description of Madame de Villette, in which he called her "one of the finest women in Paris; on account of the goodness of her heart, her excellent morals, and the richness of her mind." After retelling her background and relation to Voltaire, Gerry added, almost as an afterthought, "She is not handsome, but such a woman as you would like. I have given you a particular history of this lady . . . knowing it will gratify you to hear how minutely I am situated."[152] Gerry's defensive comment that the marquise was not a handsome woman was doubtless intended to reassure the absent Ann Gerry, who was spending the winter of 1797–1798 in Marblehead.

Marshall was more circumspect. On November 27 he wrote to Polly about his stay in Paris. After complaining that he had not heard from her since his arrival in Europe, Marshall told his wife that the city "presents one incessant round of amusement and dissipation. . . . Every day you may see something new, magnificent, and beautiful; every night you may see a spectacle which astonishes and enchants the imagination. The most lively fancy aided by the strongest description cannot equal the reality of the opera. All that you can conceive and a great deal more than you can conceive . . . is to be found in this gay metropolis, but I suspect it would not be easy to find a friend." He then referred to his new accommodations:

> I have changed my lodgings much for the better. I lived till within a few days in a house where I kept my own apartments perfectly in the style of a miserable old bachelor without any mixture of female society. I now have rooms in the house of a very accomplished, a very sensible, and I believe a very amiable lady whose temper, very contrary to the general character of her country women, is domestic and who generally sits with us two or three hours in the afternoon. This renders my situation less unpleasant than it has been but nothing can make it eligible.[153]

Curiously, the letter was unsigned. It is the only letter of Marshall's extant that is unsigned and, as such, is sufficiently unusual to raise the question of whether Marshall and the Marquise de Villette were more than friends. Polly may have assumed so, and family chroniclers imply as much.[154] Marshall's letter did not arrive in Richmond until January 1798, when Polly was still recuperating from the birth of their son, John. She immediately went into a deep depression, lost interest in everything, including the new baby, and eventually had to be taken by her sister Eliza to the Carrington estate in Cumberland county.[155]

Such evidence as there is of a romance between Marshall and the marquise is circumstantial at best. Mrs. Pinckney wrote titillatingly to a friend in South Carolina that the Marquise de Villette "is an agreable pleasing woman, about 32 years of age. She always dines with the two *bachelors*, and renders their situation very agreeable."[156] Marshall was sufficiently captivated by the marquise to forgo an appointment he had with Pinckney in order to accompany her to the theater for the opening of Voltaire's *Mahomet.*[157] "What could I do [when she] invited me?" he wrote apologetically to the South Carolinian the next day. "You will excuse my going but will think I ought to have sent [a message] to stop you [from coming over]. I'm sure I ought, but it did not occur to me."[158] After leaving Paris in the spring, Marshall wrote to Fulwar Skipwith[159] from Bordeaux, asking him to say goodbye once more to Madame de Villette. "Say to her, in my name and in the handsomest manner, everything which respectful friendship can dictate. When you have done that, you will have rendered not quite half justice to my sentiments."[160] And to Pinckney he wrote, "I . . . shall bid an eternal adieu to Europe . . . and to its crimes. Mark, I mean only political crimes, for those of a private nature are really some of them so lovely that it requires men of as much virtue and less good temper than you and myself to hate them."[161]

It would be surprising if Marshall had not been attracted to Madame de Villette. She was a mature, warmhearted woman of exceptional beauty and unrivaled charm, as outgoing and vivacious as Polly was shy. It would be equally surprising if she had not been attracted to Marshall, who, at forty-two, was strikingly handsome, his jet-black hair and penetrating black eyes setting off a six-foot frame that contrasted noticeably with that of most Frenchmen of the era. Marshall was not polished in the continental manner, but women were drawn to him by the combination of his natural Virginia courtliness, his robust good humor, and his vigorous intellect. If he and the Marquise de Villette were intimate, it would not have been an unusual occurrence in the Paris of the 1790s. But whatever the extent of their relationship, it remained private, and the attachment, if there was one, ended when Marshall returned to America.

Some historians have suggested that Madame de Villette was a *femme fatale*, an agent of Talleyrand who seduced the Americans with her charm.[162] There is no evidence to support this claim. The French police had an informer who watched Madame de Villette's house and who tried to keep an eye on Marshall and Gerry, albeit without much success. The police dossier on Madame de Villette contains a report from this informer indicating that the envoys met nightly at her house.[163] When the police commissioner passed that information on to Talleyrand, the foreign minister immediately expressed his gratitude.[164] "The surveillance you have ordered, citizen colleague, can only produce welcome results at a time when the machinations of the foreign coalition, be it in the Republic or elsewhere, can only be dubious."[165] If Madame de Villette had been working for Talleyrand, it would not have been necessary to dispatch police informers to spy on the envoys. Moreover, the French archives, which are known for the completeness of their holdings, have no record of any communication between Talleyrand and the marquise.

After two months in Paris, the envoys had yet to be received officially, and the demands for tribute continued. In early December[166] Gerry dined with Talleyrand, Hottinguer, Bellamy, and Hauteval. It was an early effort by the French to pry Gerry away from Marshall and Pinckney. However, when Hottinguer asked point-blank whether the *douceur* they had requested would be paid, Gerry said firmly that it would not.[167] Two weeks later Hottinguer visited Pinckney to renew the plea and was again turned down.[168] On December 17 Bellamy called on Gerry with another invitation to visit

Talleyrand and then approached Marshall about his relations with Caron de Beaumarchais. Marshall wrote about the conversation in his journal:

> He observed that he had not known until lately that I was advocate for that gentleman in his cause against the State of Virginia, and that Mr. de Beaumarchais . . . had expressed sentiments of high regard for me. I replied that Mr. de Beaumarchais' cause was of great magnitude and very uncertain and consequently that a portion of the interest he felt in it would very naturally be transferred to his Advocate.
>
> He immediately said (low and apart) that Mr. de Beaumarchais had consented, provided his claim could be established, to sacrifice £50,000 sterling of it, as the private gratification, which had been required of us, so that the gratification might be made without any loss to the American Government.* I answered that a gratification on any terms or in any form was a subject which we approached with much fear and difficulty, as we were not authorized by our Government to make one, nor had it been expected that one would be necessary; that I could not undertake to say whether my colleagues would consent to it in any state of things, but I could undertake to say that no one of us would consent to it unless it was preceded or accompanied by a full and entire recognition of the claims of our Citizens and a satisfactory arrangement on the objects of our mission.[169]

Marshall immediately informed Pinckney of the overture, and he, too, rejected Hottinguer's suggestion.[170] The envoys gathered in Marshall's suite the following day to assess the situation and reaffirmed their decision to have no further dealings with Talleyrand's intermediaries. Marshall and Pinckney, who were becoming increasingly apprehensive about Gerry's resolve, asked him to pass that message along to anyone who should approach him and make clear that "we could not enter into any engagements for

---

*Beaumarchais had won a judgment against the state of Virginia for £145,000 sterling as compensation for goods provided to the state during the Revolution, a decision that the state had appealed. As explained by Bellamy, Beaumarchais proposed to sign an agreement "to relinquish £45,000 if the whole should be finally recovered, leaving only £100,000 for himself: that the £45,000 might accrue to the United States who would in this case lose but a small part of the £50,000." In other words, the *douceur* of £50,000 was still to be paid, and recovery of most of it contingent on Beaumarchais's prevailing in the appeal. See Envoys to Pickering, December 24, 1797, Exhibit C: Gerry's Memorandum, 3 *Marshall Papers* 332. Litigation of Beaumarchais's claim remained before the courts for decades. Congress considered the matter on five separate occasions, and the matter was finally settled in 1835, for 800,000 francs. Albert Beveridge, 2 *The Life of John Marshall* 292, note 2 (Boston: Houghton Mifflin, 1916).

money."[171] At Marshall's suggestion, they also agreed to send a letter to Talleyrand "stating the objects of our mission and discussing the subjects of difference between the two nations in like manner as if we had been actually received and to close the letter with requesting the Government to open negotiations with us or grant us our passports."[172] If Talleyrand would not see them officially, the future chief justice believed that it was important to place the American position on the record.

Marshall immediately began drafting the statement, and Gerry, accompanied by Bellamy, visited Talleyrand at his office in the foreign ministry. Talleyrand confirmed that the proposals made by Bellamy "might always be relied on" and then for Gerry's benefit wrote the proposals on a sheet of paper, showed it to him, and then burned it.[173] Gerry expressed no opinion on the offer but invited Talleyrand for dinner at Madame de Villette's on December 30.[174]

The day before Christmas, Marshall wrote a synopsis of the situation to Rufus King in London. The envoys had remained in Paris, he said, because they were prepared to "submit to any situation however irksome" if a settlement appeared possible. "But submission has its limits and if we have not actually passed, we are certainly approaching them. Repeated efforts for a bribe and for a loan continue to be made. We are assured that if we remain here six months longer we shall not be received but on condition of complying with these demands."[175] Marshall then asked King for his advice. "What ought we to do? We regret the impossibility of consulting our government. . . . We must act upon our own judgments and our opinion is that we ought not to remain much longer." Marshall said that unless negotiations commenced soon, they intended to leave Paris in mid-January.[176]

Whatever doubts Marshall may have had were put to rest by King's response.[177] After exhorting the envoys to act in concert,[178] King said the Directory, through Talleyrand, had just offered to make peace with Great Britain for a bribe of £1 million sterling, which was to be split among the Directors, "Talleyrand's department to have shared one hundred thousand pounds." He said Britain might have agreed if "she could have put confidence in the corrupt agents" with whom she had to deal.* Insofar as King was concerned, the British action "confirms the propriety of your resolution not to treat with any unauthorized persons, and on the subject of bribes and loans I do not perceive that under any circumstances you consent to them. *To ransom our country from injustice and power would be to invite dishonor and injury because there can be no guarantee against them.*"[179]

---

*King's reference is to Jean Hottinguer and Pierre Bellamy, who went to London in December to represent Talleyrand in confidential discussions with the British. See King to Pickering, December 23, 1797, 2 *Life and Correspondence of Rufus King* 261, Charles R. King, ed. (New York: G. P. Putnam's Sons, 1896).

King's warning about the importance of unanimity was well timed. Until now Gerry had stayed in step with Marshall and Pinckney, largely because they had been willing to accommodate his idiosyncrasies. But as time wore on, Gerry became increasingly apprehensive about Talleyrand's threats concerning the danger of war. Marshall, for his part, was convinced France did not want war with the United States, certainly not while the conflict with England was unresolved, and he was certain that Talleyrand was bluffing.[180] Pinckney felt that Talleyrand's motives were immaterial. A man of principle, the South Carolinian was convinced that the envoys were right and that America would ultimately prevail.[181] Gerry shared Pinckney's confidence that America could defend itself, but he worried about the ideological consequences of a war with France. It was this issue that ultimately caused a rift between Gerry and his colleagues. For Gerry, the American Revolution had marked the dawn of a new age in which the United States was charged with the mission of assisting the spread of republicanism throughout the world. In a letter to Vans Murray, he wrote of his belief that a war between the two great republics, the United States and France, "would disgrace republicanism and make it the scoff of despots."[182] Like Jefferson, Gerry was obsessed with the fear that a war with France would drive the United States into Britain's embrace, with dire consequences for both American independence and the republican ideal. "God grant that none of these events take place."[183]

The American memorial to Talleyrand, signed by all three envoys but written by Marshall, was a lengthy defense of United States neutrality and a restatement of the American claims against France.[184] Albert Beveridge may have exaggerated when he wrote that "the statement by Marshall remains to this day one of the ablest state papers ever produced by American diplomacy,"[185] but Marshall admirably delineated American grievances. Vans Murray, after reading the document, wrote to John Quincy Adams that the argument was "unanswerable." Marshall, he said, was "one of the most powerful reasoners I have ever met."[186] The memorial to Talleyrand was one of Marshall's finest efforts, although, as Murray noted, its impact would be greater in America than in Paris. Overall, Marshall's tone was conciliatory and respectful. He closed with a wish that negotiations commence. If that was not possible, the envoys "would leave France with the most deep felt regret." They did not give Talleyrand an ultimatum or demand their passports, but their intent was clear.[187]

Talleyrand did not reply immediately and continued to approach the envoys indirectly, seeking to deal with each one individually. Pierre du Pont de Nemours,[188] an old friend of the Pinckneys from an earlier visit to Charleston, visited the general; Beaumarchais dealt with Marshall; and Talleyrand turned his attention to Gerry. On February 1, at Talleyrand's behest,

du Pont called on Pinckney to ask if the envoys had received any new instructions from the United States.[189] The following day Beaumarchais visited Marshall to say that the French government expected the envoys to
make the next move: "that it still supposed we would perceive our interests
so clearly in a connection with France that we would propose to make the
pecuniary advances required of us."[190]

Two days later Talleyrand met with Gerry and turned his considerable
charm on the New Englander, whose "attachment to France and conciliatory disposition was well known." Talleyrand suggested that in the future
the French government should perhaps deal exclusively with Gerry.[191]
When Gerry returned to Madame de Villette's he told Marshall of his wide-
ranging discussion with Talleyrand. He said he had raised some matters on
his own initiative and that Talleyrand had made some propositions to him
that he could not discuss with either Marshall or Pinckney. Gerry told Marshall that he had to give Talleyrand an answer "tomorrow or the day after,"
adding portentously that it would probably determine whether there would
be "peace or war."[192]

Marshall correctly surmised that Talleyrand intended to blame him and
Pinckney for the failure of the negotiations and to credit Gerry if they were
successful. "I am led irresistibly by this train of thought to the opinion that
the communication made to Mr. Gerry in secret is a proposition to furnish
passports to General Pinckney and myself and to retain him for the purpose
of negotiating the differences between the two Republics." Marshall was
sure that Talleyrand did not want to break off negotiations completely, but
he was equally certain that Talleyrand would be pleased "to retain only one
Minister and to chuse that one."[193] So long as one of the envoys remained in
Paris, the danger of an Anglo-American alliance would be minimized. If
Gerry remained and Talleyrand concluded a new treaty with him, the Republican cause in the United States would be strengthened considerably.

The following day Marshall told Pinckney of his suspicions.[194] They
agreed to let Gerry decide for himself how he should answer Talleyrand.
They could probably not keep him from meeting with the foreign minister
in any event, and by not making an issue of it, they left the responsibility
entirely on the New Englander's shoulders.

Gerry returned to see Talleyrand on February 6 and again on February
7. He cryptically informed his colleagues that he had rejected one of Talleyrand's proposals but was considering a second, reiterating that the issue
of war or peace probably depended on his decision.[195] Marshall wrote that
he and Pinckney did not know what the propositions contained, "except
that Mr. Gerry says they are perfectly new." Marshall warned Gerry that Talleyrand was unlikely to offer anything the United States could accept but
simply wanted to prolong the discussions until the war with England was

concluded.[196] Gerry was unconvinced, and the private meetings with Talleyrand continued.

Two days later Gerry and Marshall attended the theater with Madame de Villette. When they returned to their lodgings, Gerry said that he had had "a very extraordinary conversation" that day with Talleyrand's secretary, Louis Paul d'Autremont,[197] but that he was not at liberty to reveal its substance. Marshall, who had grown weary of Gerry's posturing, said he did not want to hear of it and headed off to his apartment. At this point, Gerry once again raised the subject of Talleyrand's *douceur*. Marshall repeated that as far as he and Pinckney were concerned, the matter was closed. Gerry then disclosed that Autremont had told him that the Directory had decided to order all three envoys out within twenty-four hours but that Talleyrand was holding it up to give the envoys time to reconsider. Marshall was unimpressed. He went over the previous ground with Gerry and insisted that the French were simply up to their usual tricks. "Mr. Gerry was a little warm and the conversation was rather unpleasant."[198]

As Marshall had predicted, the French did not order the envoys to leave, and Talleyrand continued his efforts to extract his sweetener. On February 14, following another round of conversations with the foreign minister, Gerry told Marshall that unless they paid the money there would be no treaty.[199] Talleyrand repeated that sentiment to Major Rutledge, Pinckney's secretary, several days later.[200] On February 20 Caron de Beaumarchais called once more on Marshall for the same purpose.[201] Autremont paid Gerry a return visit on February 25 and suggested that the envoys agree to a loan to France that would be payable not at present, but when the war with Britain was over. The timing of the payment would allow the Americans to preserve the facade of neutrality. Gerry jumped at the idea and presented it to Marshall and Pinckney the following evening at Madame de Villette's.[202]

Pinckney declared that Autremont's suggestion was no different from the previous proposals because there was nothing to prevent the French from using the loan commitment as collateral to raise money immediately.[203] Marshall added that Autremont had no authority to bind the French government and that this had been one of the major problems all along. Gerry argued that a settlement of this sort was the only means of avoiding war, and he disagreed that the envoys were prevented by their instructions from approving such a loan. Marshall retraced the old arguments for Gerry's benefit. It was a question of American independence, he said, and if they granted the loan under duress, "we no longer acted for ourselves but according to the will of France." As he had maintained throughout, Marshall said that he did not think peace or war depended on the loan. The French threat to order the envoys out of France "had been repeated three times but had never been executed." Marshall told Gerry that the French were reluctant "to part with us during the uncertain state of war with England" and were only "amusing us" in the meantime. If anything "could preserve us from the calamity of war," he told Gerry, "it was a firm and moderate conduct on our part." Marshall suggested that they leave France and await the outcome of the conflict with Great Britain. That would compel France to be more conciliatory, and they would have "impressed her with the conviction that the accommodation could only be made on terms compatible with the liberty of our country."[204]

On February 26 Beaumarchais informed Marshall of another long conversation he had had with Talleyrand in which the point was made repeatedly that "peace or war depended on a loan."[205] Gerry also continued to press for the loan, while Marshall just as firmly rejected the idea. Pinckney told Gerry that he had learned from a friend of Talleyrand, presumably Pierre du Pont, that the French foreign minister planned to send Pinckney and Marshall away and retain only Gerry in Paris, with whom he then would negotiate a treaty. Pinckney was convinced that Talleyrand had made this statement to du Pont knowing that the latter would pass the information along, hoping thereby to sow dissent among the envoys.[206] Gerry, when pressed by Pinckney, acknowledged that this indeed was Talleyrand's plan. Marshall wrote in his journal that he was now convinced the proposal for a loan to France payable at the end of the war had been Gerry's idea in the first place. "It would be a contribution for the purpose of conquering Britain," and fit neatly with Gerry's anglophobia.[207]

At length the envoys decided to seek another meeting with Talleyrand. Their unity was fraying fast, but Marshall drew on his skills as a mediator to fashion an agreement among them, albeit one that satisfied neither Gerry nor Pinckney. If Talleyrand asked for a loan payable after peace with England had been concluded, the envoys would agree to consult Philadelphia. Otherwise, they would inform him that no money would be forthcoming.[208]

The meeting was scheduled for 3 P.M. on March 2, and the envoys were ushered in promptly. It was their first face-to-face meeting with Talleyrand in five months. After the customary expressions of goodwill, Talleyrand reiterated the Directory's displeasure with Adams's speech (he added Washington's Farewell Address for good measure) and again urged the envoys to find some means to dispel that dissatisfaction. He alluded directly to a loan and indicated that it was an absolute precondition of doing business with the Directory. When Gerry mentioned making the loan payable after the war, Talleyrand said that was a possibility providing there was some immediate aid. Marshall asked whether the loan was an ultimatum. "Mr. Talleyrand did not give a direct answer to the question. He said that the government insisted on some act which would demonstrate our friendly disposition towards . . . the republic. Once this was done, he said the adjustment of complaints would be easy."[209]

That evening at Madame de Villette's, as the envoys reviewed their meeting with Talleyrand, the division among them remained as sharp as ever. Marshall and Pinckney continued to oppose a loan under any circumstances, while Gerry insisted that it was the only way to prevent war with France. "We parted, neither having made any sort of impression on the other," wrote Marshall.[210]

The following morning Gerry sought to continue the discussion. According to Marshall, "I told him, that my judgment was not more perfectly convinced that the floor was wood, or that I stood on my feet and not my head, than that our instructions would not permit us to make the loan required."[211] Marshall then said that since neither he nor Pinckney was going to change his mind, Gerry's only alternatives were to negotiate the loan himself or to return to Philadelphia for fresh instructions. Marshall added that he and Gerry could make the trip together, leaving Pinckney in Paris to maintain relations between the two countries. Recognizing perhaps that this was as far as Marshall would go, Gerry agreed to the suggestion, and on that basis it was decided to request one more interview with Talleyrand.[212]

Talleyrand agreed to see the envoys on March 6. Just before they left Madame de Villette's that day, Gerry asked Marshall if he would consider inserting a statement in a treaty that the complaints of Presidents Washington and Adams against France "were founded in mistake." Marshall exploded at the suggestion. "I should tell an absolute lye, if I should say that our complaints were founded in mistake," said Marshall. "He replied hastily and with warmth, that he wished to God I would propose something which was accommodating: that I would propose nothing myself and objected to everything which he proposed. . . . I felt a momentary irritation, which I afterwards regretted, and told Mr. Gerry that I was not accustomed to such language, and did not permit myself to use it with respect to him or his opinions."[213]

When the envoys met with Talleyrand, the foreign minister made it clear that although the loan might be payable after the war, France intended to make use of it immediately. However, in an effort to persuade the envoys, he spoke at length about how the transaction could be concealed from public view. Britain need never know what the United States was doing. Marshall objected. He told Talleyrand that any act by the United States permitting one of the belligerents to raise money for immediate use "would be furnishing aid to that power and would be taking a part in the war." On that point, Marshall said their instructions were clear. In an effort to find a compromise, Gerry said that he and Marshall were prepared to return to the

United States for new instructions, but Talleyrand made no reply. The meeting ended inconclusively, with Marshall and Pinckney assuming that they would be ordered to leave Paris shortly.[214]

Events, however, overtook them. At the very moment when the envoys were meeting with Talleyrand, Marshall's two long dispatches describing French chicanery were being devoured by Adams and Pickering in Philadelphia. Written on October 22 and November 8, the letters were posted in Amsterdam on November 28 and arrived in the United States on March 4. The messages were encoded, and they were not deciphered and ready for the president's perusal until the morning of March 6. Until then the American government had absolutely no idea what had happened in Paris.

"Are our commissioners guillotined," Washington asked, "or what else is the occasion of their silence?"[215] Jefferson, who continued to believe that delay worked to the Republicans' advantage,* was far less concerned. "We have still not a word from our Envoys," he wrote to Madison in mid-February. "This long silence (if they have been silent) proves things are not going on very roughly. If they have not been silent, it proves their information, if made public, would check the disposition to arm."[216]

When Marshall's dispatches finally arrived in Philadelphia, Jefferson could not have been more wrong. Adams initially declined to make the letters public, believing the lives of the envoys would be endangered. But as word of their contents leaked out, the Republicans in Congress demanded that the messages be published, and Adams happily complied. The furor that ensued destroyed the Republicans' chance for victory in the upcoming congressional elections. The cause of France was discredited; a burst of patriotism swelled the ranks of the Federalists; and Marshall emerged as the man of the hour. Talleyrand's hopes of benefiting from domestic discord in the United States were dashed, and his venality, once exposed, tarnished the image of the pro-French faction for years to come.

The Republicans were thunderstruck. Madison was amazed that Talleyrand, who had lived in America and knew American attitudes, could have blundered so badly. "I do not allude to [his] depravity," he wrote Jefferson. "It's his unparalleled stupidity [that] fills me with astonishment."[217] Jefferson said the disclosures "produced such a shock on the republican mind, as has never been seen since our independence."[218] George Washington wrote that the dispatches should "open the eyes of the blindest" to French du-

---

*On January 17, 1798, Létombe wrote to Talleyrand that "The Vice-President still argues that the Directory has everything to gain here by temporizing, and he repeats to me incessantly that Machiavelli's maxim, '*Nil repentè*' [never repent] is the soul of great affairs." Archives du Ministère des Affaires Étrangères, 49 *Correspondance Politique: États-Unis* 145.

plicity,[219] while Abigail Adams told her sister that "the Jacobins in the Senate and House were struck dumb and opened not their mouths."[220]

Before publishing the dispatches, Pickering deleted the names of Hottinguer, Bellamy, and Hauteval and substituted the letters X, Y, and Z, thus giving the affair the pithy nomenclature it has enjoyed through history. Jefferson subsequently took the position that nothing so farfetched could possibly have happened, and he called it "a dish cooked up by Marshall, where the swindlers are made to appear as the French government."[221] However, Marshall faithfully reported events as they unfolded, and even Gerry, who had signed the letters along with Marshall and Pinckney, never questioned their accuracy.

There was a beguiling quality to the envoy's dispatches, a plainspoken depiction of American integrity that stood in sharp contrast to French corruption and cynicism. Marshall did not make his case artlessly, and he knew as well as anyone how to put together a brief that would convince his audience. Talleyrand's behavior spoke for itself. The callous insensitivity of the Directory's demand that the three ministers apologize for their presidents' remarks, the blatant insistence on a *douceur*, and, above all, the refusal of France even to recognize the envoys' official status—a slap in the face of all Americans—gave Pinckney's retort, "No. No. Not a sixpence," an eloquence rarely matched in the annals of diplomacy.

In Paris, meanwhile, the negotiations turned increasingly into a game of cat and mouse. Marshall and Pinckney were now convinced that no agreement could be made with France except on the most humiliating terms, and they were determined to place responsibility for the rupture on Talleyrand. Rather than request their passports, they wanted Talleyrand to order them to leave Paris. That would reveal the duplicity of French policy and, they hoped, would deter Gerry from negotiating alone. Marshall and Pinckney were as yet unaware of the impact of their dispatches in Philadelphia,* but both were experienced politicians and understood the advantage that would accrue to the Federalists from exposing the Directory's demand for tribute.

On March 8 Marshall wrote once more to bring George Washington up

---

*On March 23, 1798, Secretary of State Pickering sent revised instructions to the envoys. After expressing outrage at the failure of French authorities to receive the envoys officially, Pickering said that President Adams had directed that, if the envoys were in official negotiations with their duly authorized French counterparts, they were to remain and conclude the treaty. However, if they still had not been officially received by the Directory, "you are to demand your passports and return. . . . [I]n no event is a treaty to be purchased with money by loan or otherwise. A loan . . . would violate our neutrality and a *douceur* to the men now in power might by their successors be urged as a reason for annulling the treaty. . . ." Although the letter did not arrive in Paris until after Marshall's and Pinckney's departure, it indicates clearly that their interpretation of their instructions pertaining to a postdated loan was correct. For the text of Pickering's instructions, see 3 *Marshall Papers* 422–424.

to date. He reiterated that the prospects for a treaty looked dim and that when the Directory realized that a loan would not be forthcoming, he and Pinckney would be ordered to leave.[222] In a letter to Charles Lee written two days later, Marshall's frustration with the situation in Paris fairly bubbled over: "I have cursed a thousand times the moment when a sense of duty induced me to undertake this painful embassy, but I must now make the best of it."[223]

The next move was Talleyrand's, and it was another bluff. On March 14 Caron de Beaumarchais called on Marshall to say that the Directory had decided to sequester the property of all Americans in France unless the loan was forthcoming. He also said it had been decided to order Pinckney and Marshall to leave, but Talleyrand was delaying the order for several days to allow them to reconsider.[224] Marshall replied that there was no point in delay; he would not change his mind about the loan. Beaumarchais then said that the government preferred to deal with Gerry.

> He would not conceal from me, that our positive refusal to comply with the demands of France was attributed principally to me, who was considered as entirely English. I felt some little resentment and answered that the French government thought no such thing; that neither government nor any man in France thought me English, but they knew I was not French; they knew that I would not sacrifice my duty and the interests of my own country to any nation on earth.[225]

Over the months in Paris, Beaumarchais and Marshall had become friends, and the Frenchman explained how the government planned to use its supporters in the United States to discredit him. "I told him I was much obliged to him [for the information], but that I relied entirely on my conduct itself for its justification." Marshall said that he recorded the conversation carefully because he was convinced that Talleyrand had initiated it and that Beaumarchais would give him a full report.[226]

When Marshall told Gerry about his discussion with Beaumarchais, the New Englander said he would not agree to stay in Paris alone. Marshall wrote that he doubted Gerry's resolve—a judgment that ultimately proved to be correct.[227] Talleyrand accurately perceived the potential crack in the envoy's unanimity, and he stepped up his efforts to court Gerry, who continued to meet with him privately.[228] On March 20, just before dinner, Gerry returned to Madame de Villette's with a lengthy letter from Talleyrand responding to the envoy's January memorial and concluding with the announcement that "Notwithstanding the kind of prejudice which has been entertained against them, the Executive Directory is disposed to treat with one of the three [envoys], whose opinions, presumed to be more impartial, promise, in the course of the explanations, more of that reciprocal confidence which is indispensable."[229]

Without mentioning names, Talleyrand sought to make it clear that he would henceforth deal only with Gerry. He knew that Marshall and Pinckney were determined to leave unless they were accredited,[230] and his letter was calculated to maneuver the two men into asking for their passports. In so doing, the Americans would imply an acceptance of France's decision to negotiate only with Gerry.

The bulk of Talleyrand's lengthy reply dealt with French grievances against the United States, the most prominent of which were the Jay Treaty, President Adams's speech of May 16, 1797, and the refusal of the envoys to be "sincerely conciliatory," presumably a reference to the troublesome *douceur*. The tone was harsh and scarcely designed to provide the basis for an accord. Pinckney called it "weak in argument, but irritating and insulting in style."[231] Most surprisingly, Talleyrand dealt at length with the attacks on France in American newspapers, which he attributed to the American government.[232] He appealed to the people of the United States to reject "the prejudices with which it has been designed to inspire them," apparently believing he was making things difficult for the Federalists.

On March 21 and again on March 22, the envoys met in the drawing room of Madame de Villette's to consider their response. Whether they remained in Paris or not, they agreed it was important to answer Talleyrand in writing, and Marshall once again was assigned to prepare the reply. It was also agreed that Marshall should state clearly that "no one of the Ministers could consent to remain on a business committed to all three, and that none of us felt ourselves at liberty to withdraw, but by the direction of our own government, from a service which had been entrusted to us."[233] In other words, the envoys wanted to make clear they were still prepared to negotiate, but they would do so only as a team and that it would not be up to France to choose the negotiator.

Marshall worked on the reply for a week. It was not as tightly argued as the memorandum he had written in January, but the points made by Talleyrand were refuted and the tone was conciliatory.[234] The passage in which Marshall rejected Talleyrand's assertion that the American government had manipulated the press was especially eloquent.

The Genius of the Constitution and the opinions of the people of the United States cannot be overruled by those who administer the government. Among those principles deemed sacred in America, among those precious rights considered as forming the bulwark of their liberties, which the Government contemplates with awful reverence; . . . there is not one . . . more deeply impressed on the public mind, than liberty of the press. That this liberty is often carried to excess, that it has sometimes degenerated into licentiousness, is seen and lamented; but the remedy has not yet been discovered. Perhaps it is an evil inseparable from the good to which it is allied, perhaps it is a shoot which cannot be stripped from the stalk, without wounding vitally the plant from which it is torn. However desirable those measures may be, which might correct without enslaving the press, they have never yet been devised in America. No regulations exist which enable the government to suppress whatever calumnies or invectives any individual may choose to offer to the public eye, or to punish such calumnies and invectives otherwise, than by a legal prosecution in the courts, which are alike open to all who consider themselves as injured.[235]

Marshall went on to say that "nothing can be more notorious than the calumnies and invectives with which the wisest measures and the most virtuous characters of the United States have been pursued and traduced." But that was "a calamity incident to the nature of liberty" and went hand in hand with a free government.[236]

The question of whether Gerry should remain in Paris was more troublesome. Gerry told his colleagues that "he would sooner be thrown into the Seine than consent to stay," and Pinckney somewhat menacingly asserted that he had better not. "I was perfectly silent," Marshall recorded.[237] But the united front soon crumbled. On March 23 Talleyrand's secretary called at Madame de Villette's to see Gerry but, finding him absent, spoke to Marshall instead. The Directory was exceedingly irritated at the envoys, he said, but their wrath might be softened if Marshall would apply "to the French government to permit General Pinckney and myself to return . . . while Mr. Gerry should remain until such powers should be received, as would enable him to take those measures, which would preserve peace with France." Autremont told Marshall that if such a request was not submitted within three days, "we should be all three ordered off," a threat that left Marshall unmoved. "I told him that personally nothing could be more desirable to me than to return immediately to the United States: that I regretted the order, but only regretted it as it manifested an increasing hostility on the part of France towards the United States."[238]

When Gerry returned that afternoon, Marshall told him of the conversation. At that point Gerry recanted his previous resolve and insisted that Marshall send Talleyrand the letter requesting his and Pinckney's passports. Marshall flatly refused. Gerry then said that to prevent a war he would stay. The New Englander had broken ranks.

Marshall stood his ground because he was certain that this latest threat was a bluff like all the others. Talleyrand was not willing to order all three envoys to leave, or even two of them if he could avoid it. He was merely trying to entice them to take the initiative and leave of their own volition. Unlike Gerry, Marshall was still confident that while the conflict with England remained unsettled, the French government would not risk bringing the United States into the fray. He told Gerry that if Talleyrand wanted him and Pinckney to leave, he would have to say so.

Talleyrand was furious, and for two weeks he and Marshall tried to stare each other down. On March 30 Autremont returned to repeat the threat that all three envoys would be ordered out unless Marshall and Pinckney requested their passports. Again Marshall demurred.[239] Then it was Caron de Beaumarchais's turn to shuttle back and forth between Marshall and Talleyrand. Marshall demanded a letter of safe conduct from Talleyrand.[240] The foreign minister hedged.[241] Talleyrand insisted that Marshall not stop in England on his return journey.[242] Marshall said it depended on the guarantee of safe conduct.[243] On April 10 Marshall told Beaumarchais that the last vessel bound for the United States would leave France shortly. There would not be another for at least a month. If Talleyrand did not want Marshall to return to the United States via England, he would have to act quickly.[244] Talleyrand responded that if Marshall wanted a passport, he would have to go to the consulate and give his "name, stature, age, complexion etc." just as an ordinary citizen would.[245] Marshall replied, again through Beaumarchais, that he was a minister, not a private citizen, and that France could not deprive him of that status: "it was conferred upon me not by Mr. Talleyrand, but by the government of the United States."[246] Talleyrand told Beaumarchais that Marshall had been the problem all along and that "so soon as I was gone the negotiation would be carried on; . . . that all I sought for was to produce a rupture in such a manner as to throw the whole blame on France; and that this would be brought about, if the French government should order us out of the country."[247] Beaumarchais, who must have felt like a tennis ball, told Talleyrand that Marshall had no desire to cast blame on France but was unwilling to take the blame himself. He had been sent to Paris by the United States, and it was his duty to be there. If the French wanted him to leave, it was only appropriate that they should say so.[248]

Beaumarchais's assessment proved correct. Marshall told his friend that unless he received a written statement from Talleyrand "signifying the positive objection of the government to me," he intended to remain at his post.[249] In the final exchange, Talleyrand, now thoroughly exasperated, indicated to Beaumarchais that whether Marshall went or stayed made no difference. He would "send for Mr. Gerry and open negotiations with him regardless."[250] Marshall replied that Gerry might do what he wished after he and Pinckney left, but so long as the two remained, Gerry had no power to act alone.[251] Marshall added that on this point all three envoys were quite clear. Recognizing that he had been backed into a corner, Talleyrand capitulated. On April 13, without further réclame, the foreign minister wrote to request that Marshall and Pinckney depart, and enclosed their passports plus a letter of safe conduct.[252]

There was a final, bitter scene with Gerry before Marshall and Pinckney left. Pinckney did most of the talking, which left Gerry much shaken.[253] "I never met a man of less candor and so much duplicity as Mr. Gerry," he told Rufus King shortly afterward.[254] Mrs. Pinckney was more outspoken, charging that Gerry "had been false to his colleagues and wanting to his country."[255] Once again Marshall remained silent. He had gained his point already. Talleyrand had been compelled to take responsibility for the failure of the mission, and Marshall was confident that Gerry, who was now deeply impressed with the difficulty of his position, would do nothing alone.* On April 23 the future chief justice set sail for New York on the American brig *Alexander Hamilton*. Marshall thought it was "a very excellent vessel but for the sin of her name which makes my return in her almost as criminal as if I had taken England in my way."[256] Pinckney, whose daughter was ill, spent several additional months in southern France, and sailed from Bordeaux on August 5 on the Prussian ship *The Hope of Emden*.[257]

Gerry remained in Paris another four months. Talleyrand pressed him relentlessly to assume the authority to negotiate on behalf of the United States, and Gerry steadfastly refused.[258] He proved to be as much of a hairsplitter with the foreign minister as he had been with Marshall and Pinckney and eventually wore him down by not budging an inch. In the fallout from the XYZ affair, Gerry was reviled unmercifully in the United States for his servility to a corrupt regime, and many attributed his conduct to partisan politics, accusing him of deliberately dividing the mission in order that he might negotiate a peace treaty with France and bring glory to the Republicans. That charge is wide of the mark. Gerry remained in Paris because he took Talleyrand at his word that war would ensue if he left.[259] He was miserable about remaining, viewed himself as a hostage in the cause of peace,[260] and urged Adams to extricate him from his predicament by appointing a new set of commissioners as soon as possible.[261]

---

*Vans Murray wrote with dismay to John Quincy Adams that Gerry was too much of an innocent to remain in Paris unchaperoned. "I know him so well as to say that of all men I know in America, he is perhaps the least qualified to play a part in Paris, either among the men or the women— he is too virtuous for the last—too little acquainted with the world and himself for the first—and could do no possible good but in a relative character as one of three envoys." April 13, 1798, "Letters of William Vans Murray to John Quincy Adams, 1797–1803," Worthington C. Ford, ed., in *Annual Report of the American Historical Association for the Year 1912* 394 (Washington, D.C.: Government Printing Office, 1914).

In the end, Gerry's decision to stay in Paris proved fruitful. When news of the XYZ affair drifted back to Paris, Talleyrand was hard put to explain his behavior. The United States began to prepare for war with France and, in short order, renounced the treaty of alliance of 1778, suspended trade, and authorized the seizure of all French privateers as legitimate prizes.[262] The Federalist party was rejuvenated by the affair, while the Republicans and the pro-French faction in the United States found themselves on the ropes.[263] Moving quickly, Talleyrand and the Directory reversed themselves. They dropped their demands for a loan, made no further mention of a *douceur*, gave up requesting an apology for President Adams's speech, put an end to French privateers' raids on American commerce, and ceased making an issue of the Jay Treaty. Gerry did not directly contribute to any of these developments, but he provided a continuing American presence in Paris that facilitated the resumption of negotiations. When he returned to the United States, he brought Adams the official assurances of the French government that it genuinely sought peace.[264]

Talleyrand had learned his lesson about meddling in American politics. He resumed negotiations with the Federalists who held power, not with the out-of-office Republicans. In the summer of 1798, he dispatched Louis André Pichon to The Hague to consult with Vans Murray, and it was the Pichon-Murray discussions that led Adams to appoint a new negotiating team.[265] That team was received with full honors in Paris, and the dispute was soon settled. Murray told Pichon that, in dealing with Gerry, Talleyrand had mistaken his man, and that he should have pursued negotiations with Marshall.[266] Ironically, it was Marshall, as secretary of state, who presided over the final stages of the Franco-American discussions that produced the Convention of Môrtefontaine in 1800 that finally established peace between the two nations.

9

ᐁᑭ

To Congress from
Richmond

*On my arrival in New York I found the whole country in
a state of agitation on the subject of our mission. Our dispatches had been published and their effect on public opinion had fully equalled my anticipation.*

*I returned to Richmond with a full determination to
devote myself entirely to my professional duties, and was
not a little delighted to find that my prospect at the bar had
sustained no material injury from my absence. My friends
welcomed my return with the most flattering reception, and
pressed me to become a candidate for Congress. My refusal
was peremptory, and I did not believe it possible that my
determination could be shaken. I was however mistaken.[1]*

THE *ALEXANDER HAMILTON* DOCKED in New York on Sunday,
June 17, 1798, fifty-three days en route from Bordeaux.[2] The frenzy
for war with France, triggered by the publication of the XYZ dispatches, was at its height, and as the first of the envoys to return, Marshall
became an instant celebrity. The *New York Commercial Advertiser* printed an
extra edition announcing his arrival, and plans were laid for a gala reception.
Politicians of all persuasions immediately sought Marshall's support. The
High Federalists, the ultra-conservative wing of the party, pushed for an immediate declaration of war against France and anticipated that Marshall
would support them. The less numerous moderate Federalists, headed by
Adams, vacillated between war and peace. They sought to preserve American integrity abroad, but in the last analysis were unwilling to declare war
unless the United States were attacked. They were unsure of Marshall's position. The Republican party, reeling from the revelations of French chicanery, sought to avoid war at all costs and feared the impact of the envoys'
return.[3]

Marshall immediately made it clear that he backed President Adams and the moderates. He cut short plans for a reception in New York and booked the first coach for Philadelphia so that he might report immediately to the president.[4] Marshall's companion on the coach was Edward Livingston, a leading Republican congressman from New York and one of Jefferson's principal allies. Marshall spoke candidly to Livingston and repeated his view that France did not want a war with the United States while the conflict with England continued. He thought Talleyrand had been stalling because it was in France's interest to do so. Marshall said the envoys had been treated shabbily, but he did not think that was sufficient reason to go to war. In fact, he told Livingston that he would not support a declaration of war unless the United States were attacked.[5] Later that day Marshall repeated to both Adams and Secretary of State Pickering his view that the Directory did not want a war with the United States and that it believed protracted negotiations gave France an advantage.[6]

Jefferson was also interested in Marshall's views and canceled plans to leave Philadelphia to await his arrival.[7] When Livingston reported his conversation on the coach, the Republican chieftain was much relieved. "M[arshall] is not hot enough for his friends," he informed Madison,[8] and for the first but not the last time, the two great Randolph descendants, political rivals though they were, tacitly cooperated to prevent what each viewed as a national catastrophe. Neither wanted war with France. Both worked to avoid it. Without Marshall's support, the High Federalists could not get their war wagon harnessed. On the other hand, Adams knew that he could hold to a middle course with Marshall on his side. Jefferson, for his part, understood that if France recanted, war could be averted. Accordingly, whenever the opportunity presented itself, Marshall spoke out against war, and Jefferson advised the Directory to mend its ways.

As for the hero's welcome, Philadelphia more than made up for what Marshall had bypassed in New York. The Federalist leadership, determined to capitalize on the returning envoy's popularity, staged a reception the likes of which the nation had not seen since Washington's first inauguration. At Frankfort, six miles from the city, Marshall's coach was met by Secretary of State Pickering, a large party of dignitaries, and three troops of cavalry resplendent in dress uniforms. As the cavalcade lumbered toward the capital, the Pennsylvania regiment of artillery thundered a salute. Philadelphia's church bells pealed a continuous welcome that lasted late into the night. One newspaper reported that "the streets, the windows, and even the tops of houses in many instances, were crowded with people" who gave Marshall "a sincere and hearty welcome."[9] A leading Federalist journal noted that this "was not the shout of a giddy populace, responsive to the flattering cant of a hypocritical demagogue [but] the voice of respect, affection and gratitude, towards a man who, at the hazard of his life, had displayed the most eminent talents and fortitude in the support of the interest and honour of his country."[10]

Elias Boudinot, director of the mint and one of the party who met Marshall at Frankfort, wrote to his wife that Marshall was "rather disconcerted at the unexpected honor of his reception."[11] A European who witnessed the welcome described the future chief justice as "a man of more than forty years, quite handsome and one could recognize in his bearing that he had breathed the air of Paris."[12]

The following day the speaker of the house, Jonathan Dayton of New Jersey, led a congressional delegation to invite Marshall to a dinner planned in his honor.[13] Numerous testimonials were addressed to him from various civic organizations throughout the nation commending his conduct in Paris. Marshall responded in each instance with a statement supporting the moderate policy of President Adams.[14] When a committee of New Jersey militia officers assured him they were resolved "to enforce by the sword, those injured rights which the milder means of negotiation have failed to secure," he replied that "all honorable means of avoiding war should be essayed before the sword be appealed to."[15]

Jefferson twice called on Marshall at his hotel, wanting a firsthand report, but found him out on both occasions. He subsequently sent a note explaining that a prior commitment prevented him from attending the gala celebration in Marshall's honor. Jefferson wrote that he had stopped by the hotel twice, but an unfortunate slip of the pen led him to say that he "was so lucky as to find that he [Marshall] was out on both occasions." Jefferson reread the note before dispatching it and, rather than write a new one, simply interlined *un* before the word *lucky*.[16] Marshall took no offense and sent a conciliatory reply thanking Jefferson for calling. He said he was leaving for Virginia the next day and offered to carry any letters to the state that the vice president might care to send.*[17]

The banquet for Marshall at Oeller's Hotel was a Federalist extravaganza. Some 120 distinguished guests, including Speaker Dayton, members of the cabinet, and justices of the Supreme Court, paid tribute to the envoy's "patriotic firmness" in Paris. The meal was lavish, and a total of sixteen toasts were delivered.[18] Of these, the thirteenth, "Millions for defense, but not a cent for tribute," proposed by Congressman Robert Goodloe Harper of

---

*Years later, when the animosity between the two was at its height, Marshall, at least according to family legend, is reported to have said that Jefferson's initial omission of the prefix *un* to the word *lucky* was one occasion where "Jefferson had come near to telling the truth." There is no indication that Marshall felt that way at the time, and the story may be apocryphal. See Sallie E. Marshall Hardy, "John Marshall, third chief justice of the United States, as son, brother, husband, and friend," 8 *The Green Bag* 482–483 (1896).

South Carolina, received the loudest applause. The phrase quickly became a Federalist battle cry, and the words have reverberated through the pages of American history.

Early on the morning of June 25, 1798, Marshall left Philadelphia for Winchester and a reunion with Polly, who had been with her relatives in northern Virginia since the birth of their son John. He planned to travel by public coach. When the future chief justice arrived at the depot and found that all the seats on the vehicle were taken, he nimbly climbed up and sat outside next to the driver. A visiting Polish nobleman, Julian Niemcewicz, who had witnessed Marshall's triumphant arrival in Philadelphia, was equally impressed with his departure. "No incident . . . better paints a picture of the government, the attitudes and habits of this country," he wrote. "The height of office, the applause of the populace, great favor with all, never erases from the American mind the idea of equality and simplicity."[19]

Marshall's journey to Winchester was punctuated by demonstrations similar to his reception in Philadelphia. In Lancaster and in York, Pennsylvania, and in Frederick, Maryland, he was met by local cavalry units and the cheers of townspeople.[20] Invariably he was treated to additional banquets, toasts, and various expressions of gratitude. In Frederick, he purchased a horse for the last leg of his journey, and rode into Winchester quietly on the evening of June 28, to find Polly bedridden and still under the care of a physician. In many respects, Polly's affliction was as much emotional as physical. She suffered from a profound melancholy, which her husband's extended absence had made worse. Although not an invalid, Polly remained a recluse for the remainder of her life. In the years ahead, she did not entertain, rarely left her bedroom, and remained extremely sensitive to the slightest noise or commotion.

Marshall remained in Winchester for five weeks. Polly's health improved, but she was still not well enough to accompany him when he headed out for Richmond on August 3, 1798. On Wednesday, August 8, as Marshall approached the city, he was met on the outskirts by the Richmond Troop of Horse, the Light Infantry Blues, Governor James Wood, and a host of state officials and former officers who had served in the revolution. As the extended column approached the city, the Richmond artillery company fired an eleven-gun salute in Marshall's honor, the appropriate greeting for a brigadier general. Saturday evening 200 citizens gathered for another banquet. After a flowery tribute by Bushrod Washington,[21] Marshall delivered his first set speech since returning from Paris. Moderate in tone, he implored the nation to be on guard but at the same time downplayed the possibility of war.[22]

Shortly after arriving in Richmond, Marshall wrote to Pickering urgently requesting payment for his mission to France. "The derangements produced by my absence and the dispersion of my family oblige me to make either sales which I do not wish, or to delay payments of money which, I ought not to delay, unless I can receive payment from the treasury."[23] Marshall's reference to payments "I ought not to delay" pertained to the interest due Denny Martin Fairfax for the purchase of Leeds Manor. Marshall's original acceptance of the mission to Paris had hinged on the salary attached to it, and he now urgently needed the funds to make good the Fairfax acquisition.[24] Overall, Marshall received $19,963.97 for the twelve months he spent in Paris. From that amount, $1,372.19 went for the salary of his secretary, John Brown, leaving Marshall something in excess of $18,000.[25] Marshall's travel costs and his expenses in Paris amounted to roughly $5,000,[26] which meant that he realized over $13,000 from the mission. That amount was more than twice his normal annual income. It was also an extremely generous emolument for public service. President Adams's salary was $25,000; Vice President Jefferson, the secretary of state, and the secretary of the treasury each received $5,000; and other cabinet officers were paid $4,000.[27] The extra income enabled Marshall to meet the interest payments on the Fairfax estate for the next two years, but his financial situation remained precarious.

By the summer of 1798, the nation's political parties found themselves once again equally balanced. The Federalists were still reaping the benefits of the publication of the XYZ dispatches, but the zealousness of the party's conservative wing to lead the country into war had triggered a reaction that redounded to the Republicans' advantage. As Fisher Ames of Massachusetts lamented, "Truth had indeed mowed down the Republicans, but in six weeks they will sprout again, as unconquerable as the weeds."[28]

Wilson Cary Nicholas of Albemarle county, a close friend of both Jefferson's and Marshall's, expressed the prevailing sentiment in a long and thoughtful letter to Marshall in mid-August. Nicholas said he had been "long convinced that we have sufficient cause for War with France according to the usage of nations, but I believe the best interests of this country would be sacrificed by going to War." He told Marshall that "the only pretence for it is the protection of commerce, and I have no doubt that our commerce would be more impaired by war than it would be without it, and that we shall have . . . an immense accumulation of debt, and a dangerous increase of executive power and influence."[29]

Marshall did not disagree; nor, for that matter, did Adams. The difficulty was that the High Federalists had taken advantage of the outcry against France to ram through Congress a military bill authorizing a vastly expanded standing army[30] and a revenue measure to support it.[31] George Washington was recalled to active duty to head the army—symbolically, his commission as lieutenant general was reactivated on July 4, 1798—and had it not been for the reluctance of Adams and Marshall, the party very likely would have carried a declaration of war against France on July 5.[32]

The party also capitalized on the situation to pass the infamous alien and sedition acts of 1798—an ill-considered attempt to stifle domestic criticism. These laws involved four measures passed by Congress in June and July. The first, the Naturalization Act of June 18, 1798, extended the period of residence required for naturalization from five years to fourteen. The Federalists believed that most immigrants voted Republican, and they sought to keep them off the voters rolls as long as possible. The Alien Act of June 25, 1798, authorized the president to expel any nonnaturalized person of foreign birth whom he judged "dangerous to the peace and safety of the United States." The Alien Enemies Act of July 6, 1798, authorized the president, in the event of war, to designate as alien enemies any citizen or subject of a hostile nation residing in the United States and to make regulations to their apprehension, restraint, or removal. The Sedition Act of July 14, 1798, perhaps the most notorious of the acts, made it a crime to utter or publish "any false, scandalous, and malicious writing or writings against the Government of the United States, or either House of the Congress of the United States, with intent to defame . . . or to bring them . . . into contempt or disrepute. . . ."[33]

Marshall watched these developments with growing concern. He said nothing to Adams, but in mid-August wrote to Pickering about the drift of Federalist policy. He was particularly concerned with the passage of the alien and sedition acts. In fact, Marshall was the only party leader to question the legislation and the only one to recognize that the acts gave the Republicans an issue with which to win back popular support.[34] The High Federalists, in their eagerness to put the country on a war footing, had overreached. Marshall was especially critical of the party's effort to restrict debate. The Sedition Act, he told Pickering, was "viewed by a great many well meaning men as unwarranted by the Constitution," an unmistakable reference to the First Amendment, which had been deliberately framed to prohibit prosecution for seditious libel.[35] Marshall had been on the drafting committee at the Virginia convention that had initially framed the amendment, and he did not want his silence on the new Federalist legislation to be viewed as consent. He told Pickering that many persons in Virginia hated the government and would criticize the sedition law automatically. "But there are also many who are guided by very different motives and who tho less noisy in their complaints are seriously uneasy on the subject."[36]

George Washington also watched the unfolding events with growing alarm, but more with an eye to partisanship and to what he saw as Jefferson's embrace of the French cause. The former president feared that the Republicans were selling America short. Washington, now in nominal command of an army that had yet to be raised,[37] focused on the upcoming congressional elections in an effort to ensure a Federalist victory. In that sense, the elections of April 1799 marked the general's emergence as an authentic party man.[38] At the time, the Federalists held only four of Virginia's nineteen seats in the House of Representatives.* In the late summer of 1798, eight months before the election, Washington began to scour the state for suitable candidates. As Marshall later expressed it, Washington worked "to induce men whose talents he respected, but who had declined political life, to enter the national and state legislatures."[39]

In mid-August Marshall wrote to his old commander in chief to tell him that he planned to attend court in Frederick county in early September. If Washington was going to be at home, Marshall said, he would like to pay a courtesy call at Mount Vernon en route. The former president replied immediately. He told Marshall that he would be delighted to see him and said he was most anxious to discuss politics with him.[40] At the same time, Washington dispatched a note to his nephew Bushrod, who, like Marshall, was practicing law in Richmond, asking him to come as well. "I learnt with much pleasure . . . of General Marshall's intention to make me a visit," the former president wrote. "I wish it of all things; and it is from the ardent desire that I have to see him that I have not delayed a moment to express it." Washington told his nephew that "the crisis is most important. The temper of the people in this State is so violent and outrageous, that I wish to converse with General Marshall and yourself on the elections which must come soon."[41]

Marshall and Bushrod arrived at Mount Vernon shortly before breakfast on September 3 and stayed until the morning of September 6.[42] In long walks across the meadows, in discussions on the broad piazza, and in conversations at the dinner table, the ex-president pressed his guests to run for Congress: Bushrod from Westmoreland county where the Washington family had its roots, and Marshall from the district of Richmond and Henrico county. Both seats were held by Republicans, and the old chief recognized that men of considerable stature would be required to dislodge them. "General Washington urged the importance of the crisis," wrote Marshall, and insisted that "every man who could contribute to the success of sound opinion was required by the most sacred duty to offer his services to the public."[43]

Bushrod Washington, confronted by his uncle's preemptory command of "Bushrod, it must be done," soon acquiesced.[44] Marshall, however, remained firm in his determination to return to his practice. He told the for-

---

*As the most populous state, Virginia had 19 of the 106 seats in the House, and 15 of those were filled by Republicans. Massachusetts and Pennsylvania, the next most populous states, had 13 seats each, which were divided 11–2 in favor of the Federalists in the former and 8–5 in favor of the Republicans in the latter. Overall, the Federalists controlled the House during the Fifth Congress, 56–50.

mer president that he doubted his ability to do any good, that he had already promised his support to another candidate, and that he needed his income as a lawyer to pay for the remainder of the Fairfax estate. "I told him that I had made large pecuniary engagements which required close attention to my profession and which would distress me should the emoluments derived from it be abandoned."[45] On the afternoon of September 5, Marshall rode into Alexandria to attend a banquet in his honor that Washington had hastily arranged. Again he was celebrated for his steadfast conduct in Paris, but even that heady experience did not shake his resolve to avoid being drawn into political life.[46]

Washington was unrelenting. That evening, after the banquet, he gave Marshall a stern directive to run for office. Marshall hesitated to take offense at Washington's manner, and his respect for the aged general prevented him from replying sharply, but his resolve was unshaken. For three days the two men had engaged in a fierce battle of wills. It was a rare experience for Washington to have his wishes rejected so openly, but Marshall felt strongly that his first responsibility was to solidify his family's financial situation. Neither man, it seemed, was prepared to yield.

In deference to Washington, Marshall decided to rise before dawn and ride out from Mount Vernon before the argument could be renewed. It may have been an intervention of fate, but the former president anticipated Marshall's intent. At first light, when Marshall opened the front door and stepped out onto the piazza to make his way to the stable, Washington was waiting for him. Some reports hold that he was dressed once again in his uniform as lieutenant general and commander in chief. Whether this was the case or not, Washington was determined to make a final plea. Many years later Marshall wrote that the conversation that morning "was one of the most interesting I was ever engaged in," as the former president made a personal appeal based on his own example. "He had withdrawn from office with a declaration of his determination never again, under any circumstances, to enter public life. No man could be more sincere in that declaration, nor could any man feel stronger motives for adhering to it. No man could make a stronger sacrifice than he did in breaking that resolution, thus publicly made, and which he had believed to be unalterable. Yet I saw him, in opposition to his public declaration, in opposition to his private feelings, consenting under a sense of duty, to surrender the sweets of retirement, and again to enter the most arduous and perilous station which an individual could fill. My resolution yielded to this representation, and I became a candidate for Congress."[47]

As Marshall rode back to Richmond, he reflected on what he had done. Against his better judgment he had yielded to Washington's insistence and soon would be a candidate for public office once more. The race would not be easy. By passing the alien and sedition acts, the Federalist Congress had frittered away the advantage over the Republicans that they had gained with the XYZ affair.[48] The fear of war was also diminishing. On August 1, 1798, Sir Horatio Nelson, Rear-Admiral of the Blue, had caught the French fleet at anchor off the shoals of Aboukir Bay near Alexandria, Egypt, and destroyed it. Nelson's dramatic victory in the Battle of the Nile cut off Napoleon's army and effectively ended any prospect of a French invasion of the United States, regardless of how remote that possibility may have been. Meanwhile, it was becoming increasingly clear that Talleyrand and the Directory had changed their tune. Reports filtering back from Vans Murray in The Hague, as well as from Pinckney in Bordeaux and Gerry in Paris, indicated that French belligerence had subsided.

A more immediate concern for Marshall was his opponent in the congressional campaign, John Clopton. The Republican incumbent, Clopton was a member of a locally prominent family and had represented the district in Congress for four years. In Virginia, incumbents were returned regularly, and Clopton was as well known to most voters as Marshall. Both men had been officers in the Virginia Line; both were lawyers (Marshall the more successful—not always an asset in the eyes of a cranky electorate); both had served in the legislature; and both were outgoing campaigners who were generally as well liked by their opponents as by their supporters.[49] The thirteenth district, like most of Virginia, tilted Republican, but the town of Richmond was a pro-Marshall bastion, and in each of the five counties composing the constituency there was a strong Federalist minority.* Marshall recognized that if he were to win he would need to take the uncommitted and the moderate Republican vote away from Clopton. The campaign, consequently, would have to be waged in the middle ground.

Marshall may not have realized it, but it was inevitable that he would become the central figure in the Virginia congressional elections that year.[50] Because of his prominence, he rallied the Federalist forces throughout the state simply by becoming a candidate. Yet that very prominence made him the primary target of the Republicans, who stoutly resisted his effort to unseat one of their own in an important district.

To minimize Republican attacks, Marshall moved immediately to distance himself from the alien and sedition acts. A newspaper exchange with

---

*The district was composed of Charles City, Hanover, Henrico, James City, and New Kent counties, which, geographically, constituted that part of Virginia between the James and York Rivers below the fall line. In general, Federalist strength in Virginia was greatest among the state's merchants and middle-class farmers. The Republican party, led by large planters, relied for its support upon an agrarian coalition of planters and small farmers. Norman K. Risjord, "The Virginia Federalists," 33 *Journal of Southern History* 498–502 (1967). Also see Myron F. Wehtje, "The Congressional Elections of 1799 in Virginia," 29 *West Virginia History* 257–259 (1968).

"a Freeholder" provided the opportunity. On September 19, just after announcing his candidacy, the Richmond *Virginia Gazette* published what purported to be a letter from a local freeholder requesting Marshall's views on five issues central to the campaign. The questions were an invitation to the candidate to put his position on the record, and they were phrased in a manner so sympathetic that it is likely that Marshall either wrote them himself or was closely involved in their preparation.[51] The "freeholder" asked Marshall to state his views on the Constitution, on alliances with foreign nations, on closer ties with Great Britain, on the administration's policy toward France, and on the alien and sedition acts.[52]

Marshall replied the next day, noting that "every citizen has a right to know the political sentiments of the man who is proposed as his representative; and mine have never been of a nature to shun examination." He replied to the questions in order, the answers providing a crisp restatement of the moderate Federalism that he embraced. Marshall said the Constitution, *sanctioned by the will of the people*, was the rock of our political salvation.[53] That seemingly innocuous response was in fact a powerful affirmation of Federalist doctrine that the Constitution emerged from the people, not the states.

On the subject of foreign alliances, Marshall registered his opposition. "America has no motive for forming such connections, and very powerful motives for avoiding them." He said he also opposed closer links with Great Britain, and he explained his position with a paraphrase of Washington's Farewell Address:

> We ought to have commercial intercourse with all, but political ties with none. Let us buy as cheap and sell as dear as possible. Let commerce go where individual . . . interest will carry it; but let us never connect ourselves with any people whatever.

By raising the question of ties with Britain early in the campaign, Marshall hoped to deny the Republicans an issue. He had been tarred as pro-British during the debate on the Jay Treaty, and he wanted to shed that label quickly.

With respect to France, Marshall said the administration's policy was designed to preserve American neutrality and independence. The alternative would be to "have relinquished the rights of self-government, and have become one of the colonies of France." He treated the matter briefly because his role in Paris was so well known that additional discussion was unnecessary.

The final and most serious question involved Marshall's position on the alien and sedition acts, and it presented the future chief justice with an opportunity to back away from Federalist dogma and assert his independence. Throughout his life, Marshall consistently championed the virtues of free speech, a free press, and the liberty of the individual. He wanted to be sure that the voters of the thirteenth district understood that he opposed the alien and sedition acts because they threatened these fundamental freedoms.

"I am not an advocate for the alien and sedition bills," Marshall stated. "Had I been in Congress when they passed, I should . . . certainly have opposed them." He was against them, he said, "because I think them useless; and because they are calculated to create, unnecessarily, discontents and jealousies at a time when our very existence, as a nation, may depend on our union." Marshall suggested that if the bills had been opposed in Congress by a man of moderate Federalist principles such as himself, good sense would have prevailed, and they would never have been enacted. As for their repeal, he would, if elected, "obey the wishes of my constituents." Marshall said he thought the most effective course was simply to allow the acts to expire, as they were scheduled to do in 1801. "I shall, indisputably, oppose their revival."

By placing himself on the record at the beginning of the campaign, Marshall denied Clopton the opportunity to brand him with the excesses of High Federalism. He had rejected closer ties with Great Britain, minimized the danger from France, and placed himself in the Virginia mainstream that opposed the alien and sedition acts. It was an effective electoral gambit that did no violence to Marshall's convictions. Political moderation came naturally to him, and on this occasion it coincided with the thirteenth district's center of gravity.

Marshall's moderate views were not only well received by his constituents but set the tone for the Federalist campaign in Virginia. Circulated widely, his comments drew support from many Republicans and helped narrow partisan differences.[54] For the Federalist elite in New England, however, Marshall suddenly became persona non grata. Fisher Ames of Massachusetts said that Marshall had given aid and succor to the enemy. "No correct man, no incorrect man, even, whose affections are wedded to the government, would give his name to the opposers of the [sedition] law. . . . This he has done. Excuses may palliate, future zeal in the cause may partially atone, but his character is done for."[55] Theodore Sedgwick, equally wedded to the principles of High Federalism, declared that Marshall's "mysterious and unpardonable conduct" had aided "French villainy." Archfool Gerry, he said, had never behaved more mischievously. In Sedgwick's opinion, Marshall had "degraded himself by a mean and paltry electioneering trick."[56] Even the more circumspect Harrison Gray Otis condemned

Marshall *"ore rotundo"* [with round full voice], as did Rufus King and William Vans Murray.[57] Pickering likewise deplored Marshall's statement. Better than most, however, he knew Marshall's views and discounted the possibility that he was compromising them. "I have not met one good federalist who does not regret his answers to the Freeholder," he wrote to Sedgwick, "but I am sorry that it should be imagined to be an 'electioneering trick' [because] General Marshall is incapable of doing a dishonourable act."[58] Only George Cabot among the Massachusetts junta defended Marshall. He urged his colleagues not to be so critical and reminded them of political reality in Virginia. Marshall was the only Richmond Federalist who could be elected, he said, and once in office he would be a valuable asset.[59]

President Adams was not worried by Marshall's statements. On September 13, 1798, after learning of the death of United States Supreme Court Justice James Wilson, he immediately instructed Pickering to prepare nomination papers for Marshall to succeed him.[60] Pickering doubted that Marshall would accept the post, but he complied with the president's wishes. On September 20 he dispatched two letters to Marshall in Richmond. The first was the official notification of Adams's decision. The second was a personal letter indicating that he understood Marshall might decline the post and asking his opinion as to whether Bushrod Washington might accept the nomination.[61] Marshall received both of Pickering's letters on September 27, and replied the next day. As expected, he declined Wilson's seat, but told Pickering that Bushrod Washington would accept the appointment, "and I am equally confident that a more proper person could not be named."[62]

Adams accepted Marshall's decision with regret. "I still think that General Marshall ought to be preferred," he wrote to Pickering. "Of the three envoys, the conduct of Marshall alone has been entirely satisfactory, and ought to be marked by the most decided approbation of the public. He has raised the American people in their own esteem, and if the influence of truth and justice, reason and argument is not lost in Europe, has raised the consideration of the United States in that quarter of the world."[63]

In Virginia, meanwhile, the campaign accelerated. Since Marshall and Clopton were not far apart on the major issues, the fight descended to a personal level. The two candidates tried to remain above the battle (Marshall made no further public statements), but their supporters engaged in repeated efforts to vilify their party's rival, and both candidates suffered equally. Marshall was usually thick-skinned in such matters, but when Pickering wrote to ask him to prepare a public report on the XYZ affair,[64] he respectfully declined. Half in jest, Marshall said that "as a punishment for some unknown sins" he had agreed to run for Congress.

In consequence of this the whole malignancy of Antifederalism . . .
has become uncommonly active. The jacobin presses which abound
with us . . . teem with publications of which the object is to poison
still further the public opinion and which are leveled particularly at
me. Anything written by me on French affairs would whet and
sharpen up the sting of every abusive scribbler. To protect myself
from the vexations of these newspaper altercations . . . I wish if possible to avoid appearing in print myself.[65]

The two most vicious campaign attacks involved a Federalist assault on
Clopton written by someone calling himself "Buckskin" that appeared in
Richmond's *Virginia Gazette*,[66] and a Republican broadside against Marshall
consisting of five essays published in the *Aurora* entitled *The Letters of Curtius*.[67] Buckskin charged that Clopton had libeled Adams by calling the president a traitor who grasped at absolute power by bribing the majority of the
House of Representatives. Clopton immediately denied the charge, and the
proof that Buckskin claimed he possessed failed to materialize.[68] *The Letters
of Curtius*, written by John Thompson, a young lawyer from Petersburg and
a gifted polemicist, chastised Marshall for his slippery replies to the "freeholder" and resurrected the accusations about his pro-British sentiments.
"Notwithstanding the magnitude of your talents, you are ridiculously awkward in the arts of dissimulation and hypocrisy," said Curtius. "It is painful
to attack . . . a man whose talents are splendid and whose private character
is amiable, but sacred duties . . . to the cause of truth and liberty require it.
You have lost forever the affection of a nation and the applause of a world. In
vain will you pursue the thorny and rugged path that leads to fame."[69]
Thompson's attack drew fire from a number of Marshall's supporters, including one who wrote in a colloquial, backwoods dialect and who signed
himself simply as "Hodge." "You is rite again," Hodge told Curtius, "when
you says this Marshall's principals is proved by none but tories and refugees,
for Washington luvs the same principals, and you nose what a tory he was
but 20 years ago."[70]

The campaign became even more heated in December 1798 when the
Republican-dominated Virginia assembly passed its version of what historians call the Kentucky and Virginia Resolutions of 1798. The Kentucky resolution was drafted by Jefferson; the Virginia resolution by Madison. Both
were defiant protests against the alien and sedition acts. They asserted the
right of a state to refuse to comply with any federal legislation it considered
unconstitutional.[71] The resolutions were based on the idea that the Constitution was a compact among the states and that the authority of the national
government was strictly limited to the enumerated powers that the states
had delegated to it. When the federal government exceeded those powers,

as the resolutions maintained it had done in passing the alien and sedition acts, "the states . . . are in duty bound to interpose" themselves. The argument harked back to a memorandum Jefferson had written on the subject of the national bank seven years before[72] and stood in direct opposition to the Federalist theory of Union, which held that the Constitution reflected the will of the people, not the states, and was therefore superior to the states.*

The "compact theory" underlying the Kentucky and Virginia Resolutions became the constitutional basis for the arguments of states rights advocates. During the nullification crisis of 1832,[73] "the principles of '98" became a rallying cry for South Carolina secessionists. In 1859 a new edition of the resolutions gave southern spokesmen renewed justification for arguments they put forward in favor of state sovereignty and secession. As one of Jefferson's leading biographers has written, "the secessionist movement was a remarkable testament to the compact theory of government, which Jefferson, more than anyone, had fixed upon the American mind."[74]

After adopting the resolutions, the Kentucky and Virginia legislatures appealed to the other states to join them, but none did so. Ten states explicitly rejected the resolutions, while the other four took no action at all.[75] Even in Virginia, reaction to Jefferson's strategy of nullification was swift, negative, and vociferous,[76] forcing Clopton on the defensive. Just as Marshall had to distance himself from the High Federalists, Clopton soon found that the thirteenth district was more attached to the Union than Jefferson had assumed. In a series of letters to his constituents, Clopton backed away from the extreme view of state sovereignty reflected in the resolutions and assured voters of his support for the Constitution, "from which I have never knowingly deviated."[77]

Marshall held his fire. The Federalist response to the resolutions was delivered by Henry Lee, who had taken Bushrod Washington's place as the Federalist candidate in Westmoreland county. In a series of essays entitled "Plain Truth," published in Richmond's *Virginia Gazette*, Lee effectively restated the view that it was the people, not the states, who had created the Union, and that the individual states could not nullify the wishes of the people of the Union expressed in national legislation.[78] "Plain Truth" was a strongly reasoned, nationalist interpretation of the Constitution, and it

---

*The Federalist argument was cast in its most direct form by Justice James Wilson in the leading case of *Chisholm v. Georgia*, 2 Dallas 419 (1793). The people, said Wilson, were sovereign. They had originally created the states, and, when they afterward created the Union, they could take from the states some of the powers they had originally given to them and vest those powers in the Union. Specifically, the people could make the states (and Georgia in particular) subject to the jurisdiction of the federal courts, as they had done in Article III, section 2 of the Constitution. Accordingly, "as to the purpose of the Union, the States are not sovereign." Wilson's reasoning survived, although the Eleventh Amendment, adopted immediately thereafter, nullified the holding.

forced the citizens of Virginia to consider whether the state legislature, in passing the resolutions, had usurped their sovereignty.[79]

Thanks to Lee's efforts Marshall was able to devote himself to the informal campaigning at which he excelled. He attended barbecues, shared drinks with voters, and displayed the "lax, lounging manners" that so infuriated Jefferson. The journalist James Callender, a bitter enemy of all Federalists, wrote that Marshall sought votes by telling Republicans that he and Clopton saw eye to eye on most issues, by "dancing around bonfires," and by spending "five or six thousand dollars upon barbecues." In Callender's words, Marshall was "the paymaster of strong liquors, the barbecue representative of Richmond."[80] Though Callender's estimate of Marshall's campaign costs was undoubtedly high, his description of Marshall's tactics was reasonably accurate.

As the campaign progressed, the lead seesawed back and forth between Marshall and Clopton. In January 1799 Marshall told George Washington that he was "by no means certain who will be elected for this district" and that the Republicans throughout the country were concentrating their fire on him.[81] Madison expressed a similar opinion in a letter to Jefferson two weeks later. "The opinion still prevails that Marshall will be disappointed," he said, "but it is agreed that the maximum effort will be used in his favor, and we know that in that case, the issue must be attended with some uncertainty."[82]

Marshall's hopes suffered a setback when rumors began to circulate that Patrick Henry favored Clopton. The great Virginian had been retired for six years, and the animosities that had swirled about him had yielded to an acclaim bordering on reverence among his fellow citizens. Marshall's candidacy would be fatally damaged if Henry opposed him publicly. Aware of the danger, Archibald Blair, the longtime clerk of the state's executive council and a friend of both men, wrote the old warrior to tell him that the Republicans were claiming that Henry opposed Marshall because "he belonged to the aristocratic party in the state."[83] Henry's response was all that Marshall could have hoped for. His reply to Blair was full of affection for Marshall, and Henry sent it knowing full well that it would be circulated widely and would dismay the Republicans.

Henry prefaced his remarks to Blair with a sharp attack on the Virginia resolutions and for good measure added a swipe at the government of France. The resolutions threatened the "dissolution of the Nation," the French Republic aimed to destroy "virtue, morality, and religion."[84]

> Can it be thought that with these sentiments I should utter anything tending to prejudice General Marshall's election? Very far from it indeed. Independently of the high gratification I felt from his public

ministry [to France], he ever stood high in my esteem as a private citizen. His temper and disposition were always pleasant, his talents and integrity unquestioned. These things are sufficient to place that gentleman far above any competitor in the district for Congress. But, when you add the particular information and insight which he has gained, and is able to communicate to our public councils, it is really astonishing that even blindness should hesitate in the choice.[85]

Henry said that he would vote for Marshall for Congress in preference "to any citizen in the state at this juncture," with the single exception of George Washington.[86]

Henry's letter worked as expected. Clopton's temporary advantage was nullified and by spring the election was once again too close to call. Jefferson, who followed the race intently, remained optimistic. "The tide is evidently turning . . . from Marshall's romance," he wrote to Edmund Pendleton.[87] Marshall remained cautious. "The fate of my election is extremely uncertain," he told his brother James on April 3. "The means used to defeat it are despicable in the extreme and yet they succeed. Nothing I believe more debases or pollutes the human mind than faction."[88]

Election day, April 24, 1799, had a festive air about it. There were no written or printed ballots at that time in Virginia, and the voter merely announced his choice to the election judges seated behind a long table placed on the courthouse green.[89] Suffrage was limited to male freeholders twenty-one years or older, and it was customary for the candidates to sit alongside the judges, where they acted as scrutineers. When a voter announced his choice, the candidate for whom he voted rose, shook the voter's hand, and thanked him for his support. All of this took place before a partisan crowd that grew in size as the day wore on. Each party provided a barrel of whiskey, and voters often tested both barrels before making their choice. The liquor warmed the spirits of the crowd, who greeted each vote with the appropriate cheers and catcalls. The contest between Clopton and Marshall was tight, and throughout the day the lead shifted back and forth between the two men. Each party worked hard to get absent voters to the courthouse, and late in the afternoon the Federalists brought in Parsons Blair and Buchanan. The two spiritual leaders of Richmond's flock were friends of both Marshall and Clopton, and although they inclined toward Federalism, they had tried to avoid committing themselves to either candidate. Eventually, however, they were coaxed to the poll. A contemporary account describes the arrival of the two parsons:

> There were shoutings and hurrahs perfectly deafening. Men were shaking fists at each other, rolling up their sleeves, cursing and

swearing with angry and furious denunciations. Some became wild with agitation. Then came Mr. Thomas Rutherford and voted for Marshall, and there was again a tie . . . Parson Blair came forward. A swaggering fellow, just above him said, "Here comes two preachers, dead shot for Marshall." Both candidates knew them intimately and rose from their seats, and the shout was terrific.

"Mr. Blair," said the sheriff, "who do you vote for?" "John Marshall," said he. Mr. Marshall replied, "Your vote is appreciated, Mr. Blair." . . . [And then] Parson Buchanan was at the sheriff's elbow.

The whole Federal party, and the Democrats too, thought this vote was certain, beyond the possibility of a doubt, for Marshall. "Who do you vote for, Mr. Buchanan?" "For John Clopton," said the good man. Mr. Clopton said, "Mr. Buchanan, I shall treasure that vote in my memory. It will be regarded as a feather in my cap forever." The astonishment expressed in Mr. Marshall's face, in Parson Blair's countenance, by the friends of Mr. Buchanan generally, can only be imagined. . . .

When our friends entered the carriage on their return home, Parson Buchanan said, "Brother Blair, we might as well have staid [*sic*] at home. When I was forced against my will to go, I simply determined to balance your vote, and now we shall hear no complaints of the clergy interfering in elections."[90]

When the votes from all of the counties in the thirteenth district were tallied, Marshall won by a total of 114.* "For the honor of the District, I wish the Majority had been greater," George Washington told him, "but let us be content."[91] In Philadelphia, Marshall's victory was greeted with enthusiasm. Pickering wrote to inform Rufus King of Federalist triumphs in New York, adding that "still more important, is, that General Marshall is elected a member of Congress for his district."[92] But many High Federalists remained apprehensive. Theodore Sedgwick told King that if Marshall should shape his political conduct according to "his public declaration relative to the alien and sedition acts, it would have been better that his insignificant predecessor should have been re-elected." Sedgwick said that because of Marshall's stature he would probably set the tone for federal politics south of the Susquehanna. He thereupon urged King to write to Marshall about the importance of party discipline since "there never has been an instance where

---

*No official returns have survived, but newspaper reports indicate that Clopton defeated Marshall in Hanover county by 7 votes, 317–310. Marshall carried Henrico county (which included Richmond) 299–250 and New Kent county 162–137. His margin of victory in Charles City county was reported to be 35 votes and in James City county, 12. *Virginia Gazette and General Advertiser*, April 26, 30, 1799; *Gazette of the United States* (Philadelphia), May 2, 1799.

the commencement of a political career was so important as that of General Marshall."[93]

Jefferson was disheartened by the Federalist victories in Virginia—the party won eight of the state's nineteen congressional seats, double the number in the previous Congress—and especially by Marshall's triumph in Richmond. "It marks a taint in that part of the State which I had not expected," he wrote to Archibald Stuart in May.[94] Jefferson blamed Patrick Henry. "His apostasy must be unaccountable to those who do not know all the recesses of his heart."[95]

Shortly after the election, Marshall undertook a long-delayed journey to visit his father in Kentucky. Thomas Marshall, now sixty-nine, had retired as the federal tax collector in Kentucky two years previous, and his health was failing.[96] Marshall and his father had always been close, and although they had not seen each other in fifteen years, they had corresponded regularly. Now, as the end approached, Marshall wished to see his father for a last time. The trip was entirely personal, although Jefferson, still smarting from Marshall's election victory, feared other motives were involved. "The visit of the apostle Marshall to Kentucky excites anxiety," he wrote to Wilson Cary Nicholas, "however, we doubt not that his poisons will be effectively counterworked."[97] In fact, Marshall made no public statements while in Kentucky and did not even bother to sound out public opinion.

In the fall of 1799 Marshall argued a number of cases before the United States circuit court and the Virginia court of appeals. The most important was the great Virginia manumission case of *Pleasants v. Pleasants*.[98] The litigation arose over the will of John Pleasants who died in 1771, and who had wanted to free his slaves upon his death. Virginia law prohibited private manumission, so the elder Pleasants bequeathed the slaves to his children on condition that if a law were subsequently enacted allowing manumission, the legatees would free the slaves at that time. In 1782 the Virginia general assembly passed legislation permitting manumission,[99] and Robert Pleasants, John Pleasants's son and executor, brought suit to compel the other heirs to comply with their father's wishes. The heirs resisted, and the suit dragged on for almost six years. Popular passions were aroused, mostly against manumission.[100] Finally, in September 1798, Chancellor Wythe, before whom the case was tried, not only ruled in favor of the slaves' immediate freedom but held that they were entitled to the profit from their labor since 1782.[101]

The case came before the Virginia court of appeals a year later. The stakes were enormous, involving the freedom of as many as 400 slaves and economic losses that could total hundreds of thousands of dollars.[102] Marshall and John Warden represented Robert Pleasants on behalf of the slaves. They were opposed by John Wickham and Edmund Randolph. The issues on appeal were complex and involved, among other things, the "rule against perpetuities," a revered canon of property law that holds that the vesting of an estate cannot be postponed beyond a reasonable period.[103] In his closing arguments, Marshall maintained that the rule did not apply because the slaves were not simply property. They were also the beneficiaries of the will, and the "right to freedom . . . clearly passed by the will."[104] Moving into uncharted legal terrain, Marshall argued forcefully that the rule against perpetuities was inapplicable when human liberty was involved. The appellate court agreed, but in a 2–1 decision it restricted Wythe's broad holding and set aside the award of damages.

The Sixth Congress assembled in Philadelphia in early December 1799. Marshall arrived several days early, this time accompanied by Polly, who, although six months' pregnant,* did not want to relive the anguish she had felt during the long months Marshall was away in Paris. On the surface, the Federalists appeared to be in good shape in 1799. They held the presidency and both houses of Congress, and their majority in the House of Representatives had increased from six to twenty.[105] They had also done particularly well in the South, winning twenty-two of the thirty-seven congressional seats from Virginia, the Carolinas, and Georgia. In reality, however, the party was badly split between the High Federalists, mainly from north of the Delaware, and the moderates from the South. The High Federalists despised Adams, while the moderates were steadfast in their support of the president. In addition, mounting opposition to the alien and sedition acts, a large standing army, and the high taxes necessary to support it continued to work to the party's disadvantage. The Republicans had already rebounded in Pennsylvania and in several of the southern legislatures. In addition, Adams's decision to resume negotiations with France† had antagonized the High Federalists. Unlike the pragmatic Southerners who had learned the

---

*The Marshalls' eighth child, and the fifth to survive, named James Keith Marshall, was born in Philadelphia, February 13, 1800.

†In February 1799, in response to the conciliatory messages he had received from Vans Murray in The Hague, Adams chose to renew the negotiations with France that had been broken off when Marshall, Pinckney, and Gerry departed. He nominated Murray to be U.S. minister to Paris to conduct the talks. Marshall approved the move and wrote immediately to Charles Lee indicating his support. That letter has been lost, although Lee sent it on to Adams, who derived great satisfaction from it. A fractious Senate held up Murray's confirmation, at which point Adams nominated a new triumvirate composed of Chief Justice Oliver Ellsworth, Patrick Henry, and Murray. These men were confirmed over High Federalist objections on February 27, 1799. Henry stepped back because of ill health and was replaced by Governor William R. Davie of North Carolina, but because of continuing difficulties within his own administration, Adams did not dispatch the envoys until early November. At approximately the same time (November 9, 1799), Napoleon ousted the Directory, taking power as First Consul. The effect was to make France even more conciliatory toward the United States. See Charles Lee to Adams, March 14, 1799; Adams to Lee, March 20, 1799, 8 *Works of John Adams* 628–629, Charles Frances Adams, ed. (Boston: Little, Brown, 1850).

political skills of compromise and accommodation, the New England Federalists saw themselves, like English parliamentarians, as men of "enlightened views and virtuous sentiments" whose duty it was to lead and correct public opinion, not follow it. Above all, that meant stamping out what they perceived as the Jacobin menace at home and abroad. While moderates such as Marshall sought to build electoral coalitions within a diverse constituency, the High Federalists believed that adjusting to popular passions was to pander to the unenlightened and to promote cowardice, hypocrisy, and opportunism.

As Sedgwick had predicted, Marshall found himself cast as the natural leader of the moderates,[106] and he was quite unprepared for the belligerency of the High Federalists. Shortly after arriving in Philadelphia, he wrote to his brother James that the situation was "much more critical than I had conjectured. The eastern people are very much dissatisfied with the President on account of the [Ellsworth] mission to France. They are strongly disposed to desert him and to push some other candidate. . . . Perhaps this ill humor may evaporate before the election comes on—but at present it wears a very serious aspect."[107] Marshall was especially concerned over the fact that government revenues were inadequate to cover the military expenditures so dear to the hearts of the High Federalists. He told James that "this difficulty ought to have been foreseen when it was determined to execute the law for raising the army."

Ordinarily, Marshall favored strong defense measures, but he expressed surprise that "many influential characters" wanted to retain a large standing army when the nation was no longer threatened. "I am apprehensive that our people would receive with very ill temper a system which should keep up an army of observation at the expense of the annual addition of five million [dollars] to our debt. The effect of it would most probably be that the hands which hold the reins [of power] would be entirely changed."[108] From the perspective of the High Federalists, Marshall's sensitivity to public opinion made him suspect. It was precisely this sensitivity, however, that made him Adams's most valuable supporter in the House.

Marshall's first test came with the election of Speaker. The last three Speakers had come from the middle states or New England, and Marshall thought it would improve party harmony to choose a Southerner for the post.[109] The leading prospect was John Rutledge of South Carolina, who had chaired the committee of detail at the Constitutional Convention and whose distinguished career stretched back over twenty-five years. Marshall nominated Rutledge, only to confront virulent opposition from the congressional phalanx of High Federalists. The New Englanders had never forgiven Rutledge for his criticism of the Jay Treaty. In December 1795 they had defeated his nomination for Chief Justice of the United States and now, four years later, they were determined to prevent him from becoming Speaker. Instead, they insisted on one of their own, former senator Theodore Sedgwick of Massachusetts, as rigid an ideologue and as bitter a critic of Adams's policy as any High Federalist around.[110]

The contest between Rutledge and Sedgwick raged for three meetings of the Federalist caucus with neither side giving ground. With the House set to convene for its first session, Rutledge instructed Marshall to withdraw his name in favor of Sedgwick, lest the Republicans take advantage of the split in Federalist ranks to elect one of their own.[111] The rift in the party was mended, thanks in no small measure to the graciousness of Rutledge and the accommodating style of Marshall.

Within a few days, Federalists of all complexions recognized that the key to party reconciliation lay with Marshall, whose good humor could bridge even the widest gaps. Marshall refused to take political differences personally, and, Jefferson aside, there were few people with whom he could not work easily. Many years later, in describing his congressional experience for Story, he emphasized the personal aspect far more than the political. "There was a good deal of talent in [the Sixth] Congress both for and against the administration, and I contracted friendships with several gentlemen whom I shall never cease to value."[112]

One of Marshall's most rewarding friendships was with Albert Gallatin, the Republican leader in the House. Gallatin had lived in Richmond for five years in the early 1780s, and it was Marshall who had initially urged him to practice law. They were warm friends but sharp rivals. Marshall also formed an abiding friendship with Theodore Sedgwick, the leader of the High Federalists. "I have been much in company with General Marshall since we arrived in this City," Sedgwick wrote to Rufus King shortly after his election as Speaker. "He possesses great powers and has much dexterity in the application of them. He is highly and deservedly respected by the friends of Government from the South."[113] Sedgwick was still troubled by Marshall's concern for public opinion but was now inclined to give him some leeway. "He is disposed . . . to express great respect for the sovereign people and to quote their opinions as evidence of truth. I believe his intentions are perfectly honorable, and yet I do believe he would have been a more decided man had his education been on the other side of the Delaware."[114]

Following Sedgwick's election as Speaker and the organization of the House, the first order of business was to receive the president's State of the Union address. Adams spoke on December 3. He defended the record of his administration and indicated his hope that negotiations with France would be successful.[115] It was customary in those days for Congress to submit a written response to the president's message, and Marshall, by common consent, was asked to draft the reply. The task was delicate because of the controversy surrounding the Ellsworth mission. Adams was convinced that his decision to dispatch the envoys was correct. He had the support of the southern moderates, but the High Federalists were certain he was wrong. Meanwhile, the Republicans hoped the mission would succeed so that the quasi-war with France could end, but they were loath to see Adams get the credit. Marshall handled the problem adroitly. He drafted a message that politely echoed the president's sentiments on all of the topics he had raised but that was worded sufficiently vaguely to avoid a floor fight on any specific issue. Marshall praised the character of the envoys selected by Adams, twice noted the president's sincerity, and pointedly hoped, not without a touch of irony, "that similar dispositions may be displayed on the part of France." The success of the mission, he wrote, "depends not on America alone," an expression that seemed to satisfy the distemper of the High Federalists.[116] As with most compromises, no one was completely satisfied, but the contentious issues had been dealt with artfully and Marshall's draft passed unanimously.[117] Adams, whose relations with Congress were strained at the best of times, was delighted. He could scarcely believe the "full and unqualified" praise of the message.[118]

Almost as soon as Congress's reply had been transmitted to President Adams, unconfirmed reports of the sudden death of George Washington began to trickle in to Philadelphia.* It was a Wednesday afternoon, December 18, 1799, and the House was in session handling routine business. Marshall was immediately sought out by his colleagues and asked to move an adjournment.[119] Like all who had heard the news, he was overcome with grief as he took the floor. The normally dry-as-dust official report in the *Annals of Congress* noted that Mr. Marshall began "in a voice that bespoke the anguish of his mind, and a countenance expressive of the deepest regret."[120] He briefly informed the House of what had happened, noted that the news was unverified, lamented that it was probably true, and immediately moved an adjournment until the next day. "The House of Representatives can be but ill-fitted for public business after receiving information of this national calamity."[121]

When the House reconvened on Thursday, Marshall, by tradition, still had the floor, and it was he who delivered the congressional eulogy. With an economy of words he paid tribute to Washington's service to the nation, concluding with the famous refrain:

> *First in war,*
> *First in peace,*
> *First in the hearts of his countrymen.*[122]

*Washington died of acute tonsillitis at Mount Vernon during the evening of December 14, 1799.

For generations those words have been associated with George Washington, and they have usually been attributed to Marshall, who delivered them. The phrase, however, was actually written by Henry Lee, who had given it to Marshall the night before. Lee had anticipated speaking, but recognized that this would be inappropriate because of the rules of the House, so he deferred to Marshall who had the floor. Marshall, for his part, always did his best to see that Lee was credited for the words.[123]

Following the eulogy, Marshall was appointed co-chairman of the joint congressional committee handling the arrangements for Washington's funeral. The former president was buried quietly at Mount Vernon, but in Philadelphia his death was marked with solemn grandeur. Marshall and Speaker Sedgwick led a black-clad funeral procession on foot from Congress Hall to the German Lutheran Church six blocks away, and this time Lee gave the eulogy. Vice President Jefferson, in a curious display of petulance, refused to attend the services, a partisan move that scarcely elevated him in Marshall's estimation.[124] After the funeral, Marshall introduced legislation on behalf of the joint committee calling for a monument to Washington to be constructed in the new capital, the District of Columbia.[125] Marshall also became the former president's official biographer and the custodian of his political legacy.[126]

By Christmas of 1799 Marshall had superseded Harrison Gray Otis and Robert Goodloe Harper as leader of the Federalist forces in the House and he was working actively to reorient the party in a more moderate direction. Samuel Eliot Morison, Otis's biographer, noted the "judicial moderation and statesmanlike qualities of the very highest order" that Marshall brought to the task.[127] In a similar vein, Oliver Wolcott, the administratively competent but politically lackluster successor to Alexander Hamilton at the Treasury, conceded the party's debt to Marshall but feared that "he is too much disposed to govern the world according to the rules of logic."[128] Marshall expressed his own preference for compromise and consensus in a letter to his brother-in-law John Ambler.[129] "I hope a mutual spirit of toleration and forbearance will succeed to the violence which seemed in too great a degree to govern last year. As far as I can judge from present appearances this will be a temperate session and I wish most devoutly that the prevalence of moderation here may diffuse the same spirit among our fellow citizens at large."[130]

In January Marshall displayed his talent for bringing diverse interests together when he intervened to save two of the most important measures to come before the House. First with the army bill and then with legislation to establish a uniform system of bankruptcy throughout the United States, Marshall introduced crucial amendments that garnered enough votes to allow each measure to pass.

The army bill emerged by accident. On New Year's Day, 1800, the Republicans suddenly put forward a resolution to disband the standing army that had been created in the aftermath of the XYZ affair. The army had proved both expensive and unpopular, and Washington, its nominal commander, was dead. With the Ellsworth mission en route to Paris and the crisis with France winding down, it made eminent sense to do away with the new army and save the country an impending $5 million deficit. Marshall did not disagree with the Republicans, but after a year's experience fencing with Talleyrand, he believed it would undermine Ellsworth's efforts in Paris if the United States disarmed before an agreement had been reached. In addition, the concept of a standing army was an article of faith among the High Federalists. To disband it suddenly would be a crippling blow to party morale, particularly if the move were made at the instigation of the Republicans. Marshall struggled to find a compromise, but it proved difficult because of the intensity of feeling that had developed over the issue during the previous two years.

First in Marshall's view, it was important to defeat the Republican motion in order to protect Ellsworth and rally the High Federalists. He took the lead in the House debate and brought with him the southern moderates who held the balance of power. He reminded the members that because of the spoliation of American shipping, "we are at war with France, although it is not in declared form," and attributed the recent improvement in relations to the fact that the United States had armed itself. When America was weak, "even discussion was denied"; when America armed, "immediately a different language was used, and the rights of an independent nation were allowed her."[131]

Marshall said the bill offered by the Republicans was too drastic. It offered no middle ground, and if enacted, it would cripple negotiations with France. He proposed a compromise. The army would suspend enlistments but would not dismiss the troops already in active service until the envoys in Paris indicated that an agreement was likely. Debate on the Republican motion continued until January 10, 1800, when it was put to a vote and defeated, the House moderates following Marshall's lead. The next week a committee headed by Marshall introduced his compromise bill. It passed the House on January 24.[132] In the spring, when the news flowing back from Paris indicated that the envoys would be received with full honors by the Bonaparte regime, even the High Federalists recognized that the new army had to be demobilized. Robert Goodloe Harper of South Carolina put forward the motion for demobilization on May 7, with a provision, proposed by Marshall, that the demobilization be carried out at the discretion of the president as soon as he thought the diplomatic situation warranted it.[133]

The bankruptcy bill also came before the House in January. The month before, Marshall had been appointed to a select committee along with

James A. Bayard of Delaware to draft a uniform bankruptcy statute for the United States.[134] At the time, the concept of bankruptcy was still very much in its infancy. There was no federal legislation, and most states simply adhered to the common law practice of imprisonment for debt. Marshall had no personal stake in the legislation, but he was touched by the plight of his close friend Robert Morris, who had been forced to declare insolvency in 1798, and who had been languishing in Philadelphia's Prune Street Jail ever since.[135]

The committee worked on the bill for a month and reported it on January 6, 1800.[136] Previous Congresses had considered similar measures, but they had invariably been defeated by an unlikely alliance of states rights Republicans and tight-money Federalists. The Republicans opposed expanding federal authority, while the tight-money Federalists objected to bankruptcy legislation in principle. Under the bill reported, the common law practice of imprisonment for debt would be terminated, and bankruptcy actions would be transferred to the federal district courts where uniform procedures, specified in the statute, would be followed. As in the past, the measure was exceedingly controversial, with supporters and opponents about equally balanced. In an effort to tilt the Republican vote in favor of the bill, Marshall added a provision specifying that the issue of bankruptcy and the extent of debts outstanding would be decided by a jury. Lobbying for and against the measure was intense, and one opponent complained to Madison of "the out of doors efforts" employed by the bill's supporters— undoubtedly a wry tribute to Marshall's convivial style.[137]

On February 11 Bayard and Marshall beat back (24–63) an amendment that would have eliminated the bill's retroactive provision. Ten days later the House approved the measure by the narrowest of margins, 48–48, with Speaker Sedgwick delivering the casting vote in favor.[138] Sedgwick and the High Federalists were none too pleased with Marshall's jury provision, but bowed to the inevitable. "The law is far from being such as I wished," the Speaker wrote to Rufus King. "The trial of the question of bankrupt or not, by jury, will be found inconvenient, embarrassing and dilatory. The mischief was occasioned by Virginia Theory. It was the whim of General Marshall; with him a *sine qua non* of assent to the measure, and without him the bill must have been lost. . . ."[139]

Marshall's efforts to find a middle ground between the High Federalists and the more doctrinaire Republicans of the Sixth Congress were largely effective. Partisanship was never far from the surface, however, particularly with presidential elections due later in the year.[140] A looming issue in the campaign related to President Adams's decision to extradite to Great Britain a seaman charged with mutiny and murder abroad the Royal Navy's frigate HMS *Hermione*. Thomas Nash, alias Jonathan Robbins,[141] had been a member of the crew of the *Hermione*. In 1797 the crew had mutinied, murdered the ship's officers, and taken the vessel to a Spanish port, where they sold it.[142] The crew then scattered, many quietly making their way into the American merchant marine.

In early 1799 Nash turned up in Charleston, South Carolina, a crew member on the American schooner *Tanner's Delight*. At the request of the British consul, he was arrested pending extradition to Great Britain under the Jay Treaty.[143] Nash, a boastful, hard-drinking sailor, admitted having served on the *Hermione* but swore he was an American citizen. He said his name was Jonathan Robbins, of Danbury, Connecticut, and he claimed that he had been pressed into service in the British navy against his will and had not taken part in the mutiny. As was often the case in such incidents, Nash had papers attesting to his American citizenship, although they were of dubious authenticity. When the British petitioned the United States district court in Charleston for Nash's extradition, the presiding judge, believing that a decision to extradite rested with the executive branch, declined to turn Nash over without instructions from the State Department. At the request of the British minister, Adams looked into the case and, on May 21, 1799, approved the extradition. Following a court hearing to determine probable cause,[144] Nash was turned over to the Royal Navy, taken to Jamaica, tried by court-martial, found guilty, and hanged.

News of Nash's execution spread quickly. The Republican press seized on the issue, asserting that Adams had sacrificed an innocent American to British vengeance.[145] The hue and cry was taken up in Congress, and on February 20, 1800, Edward Livingston of New York, on behalf of the Republicans, moved to censure Adams for his handling of the case. Initially the Republicans attempted to prove that Nash was the American Jonathan Robbins.[146] When they were unable to do this, they claimed that Adams had "dangerously interfered" with the independence of the judiciary by ordering that the seaman be extradited. The issue immediately became one involving the separation of powers and the respective authority of the president and the courts. The Republicans maintained that the Constitution gave to the judiciary the authority to decide "all questions arising under the Constitution, laws, and treaties of the United States";* that extradition, since it was a matter regulated by treaty, should properly be decided by the courts; and that Adams's action constituted an egregious infringement of judicial authority.[147]

The Republicans had the administration on the defensive, and for the next three weeks they hammered away at Adams's alleged misuse of executive power. "I think no circumstance since the establishment of our govern-

*Article III, section 2, of the Constitution states that "The judicial Power shall extend to all Cases, in Law and Equity, arising under this Constitution, the Laws of the United States, and Treaties made, or which shall be made, under their authority. . . ."

ment has affected the popular mind more," Jefferson wrote to a supporter in South Carolina.[148] By the end of February, Marshall had become visibly irritated by the refusal of the Republicans to move on to other business. They would not bring Livingston's censure motion to a vote, but neither would they abandon the debate. "Every stratagem seems to be used to give this business an undue impression in the public mind," he complained to his brother James.[149]

The debate dragged on for another week as the Republican press trumpeted charges of Adams's malfeasance. On Wednesday, March 5, 1800, the House transacted no other business except the Robbins case, and on Thursday, Wilson Cary Nicholas of Virginia spoke for three hours on the issue, and Gallatin spoke for two.[150] On Friday, March 7, when the House convened, it was Marshall, rumpled and untidy as usual, who caught Sedgwick's eye and took the floor. As the administration's strongest voice in the House, he was determined to bring the issue to a head. It was time to end the debate and evaluate the evidence at hand, he said. The House grew still and members of both parties flocked in from the cloakroom and corridors as Marshall began to analyze and demolish the case against Adams. Gallatin took a seat nearby and began taking notes, preparing for the rebuttal he would certainly be called upon to give as the Republican leader. Marshall spoke for three hours.[151] Point by point he raised each charge the Republicans had mounted, and point by point he demonstrated why each did not apply. Marshall examined the Jay Treaty, jurisdiction over crimes at sea, the law of nations, and the rules of extradition. He buttressed his case with extensive citations from Coke, Grotius, Hawkins's *Pleas of the Crown*, Roman civil law, and the relevant American statutes. It was a forensic tour de force that combined relentless logic with a sparse eloquence rarely attained in the halls of Congress. After Marshall had spoken for thirty minutes, Gallatin put down his pencil and paper and became absorbed in Marshall's reasoning. A few minutes later he got up, went to the space in back of the seats, and paced up and down while Marshall proceeded.

The principal charge against Adams was that he had usurped judicial authority. Marshall disputed the Republican contention that the Constitution expressly gave the courts the power to decide *all questions* arising under the Constitution, treaties, and laws of the United States. What the Constitution actually said was that the judicial power of the United States extended "to all *cases in law and equity* arising under the Constitution, laws and treaties of the United States."[152] The distinction, said Marshall, was crucial.

A case in law or equity was a term well understood, and of limited signification. It was a controversy between parties that had taken shape for judicial decision. If the judicial power extended to every *question* under the Constitution it would involve almost every subject proper for legislative discussion and decision. If [it extended] to every *question* under the laws and treaties of the United States, it would involve almost every subject on which the executive could act. The division of power [among the branches of government] could exist no longer, and the other departments would be swallowed up by the judiciary.[153]

Marshall said that "by extending the judicial power to all *cases in law and equity*, the Constitution had never been understood" to confer any political power on the courts. The meaning of *"cases in law and equity"* was clear. "A question must assume a legal form, for forensic litigation, and judicial decision. There must be parties to come to court, who can be reached by its process, and bound by its power, whose rights admit of ultimate decision by a tribunal to which they are bound to submit."

Marshall was drawing a distinction between legal issues and political questions. Not everything that arises under the Constitution involves a legal issue. Some matters are political. And the courts are empowered to render decisions on legal issues only. They have no authority to decide political questions. These are the province of the executive and the legislature. Three years later in the great case of *Marbury v. Madison*, Marshall employed that distinction to establish the authority of the Supreme Court to interpret the Constitution in matters of law. While explicitly recognizing that political questions might raise constitutional issues, Marshall stated that these questions were ultimately the responsibility of the president and Congress.[154] The distinction that Marshall drew between legal issues and political questions has become one of the cornerstones of American constitutional law. In the case of the Vietnam war, for example, important constitutional questions were raised about the war powers, but these were political questions, not legal ones. Federal courts consistently declined to entertain suits testing the war's constitutionality, citing the distinction first articulated by Marshall in his speech on the *Robbins* case.[155]

Marshall maintained that extradition was a political decision affecting the nation's treaty obligations with a foreign power.[156] As such, it fell under the jurisdiction of the president, not the judiciary. Marshall then moved on to discuss the president's general responsibility in the field of foreign affairs. His remarks, taken out of context, have frequently been miscited in the continuing battle concerning executive power. In defending Adams's decision to extradite Nash, Marshall said: "The President is the sole organ of the nation in its external relations, and its sole representative with foreign nations. Of consequence the demand of a foreign nation can only be made on him."

Marshall meant that foreign nations deal with the United States exclusively through the president. "He possesses the whole executive power. He holds and directs the force of the nation." As a result, "any act to be performed by the force of the nation," such as extradition, "is to be performed through him."

When Marshall referred to the president as the nation's "sole organ . . . in its external relations," he was not suggesting that the president was primarily responsible for formulating American foreign policy or exclusively charged with determining its content.[157] Marshall was explicit that it was Congress, not the president, which bore the final responsibility for making the nation's policy. Even the president's choice of means could be regulated by Congress. After referring to the president as "sole organ," Marshall said that "Congress unquestionably may prescribe the mode; and Congress may devolve on others the whole execution of the [treaty]; but till this is done, it seems the duty of the executive department to execute the [treaty] by any means it possesses." Said differently, the president enjoys broad discretion in foreign relations until Congress acts. Once Congress has acted, the president is bound by its decision. Under the Constitution, an act of Congress is the supreme law of the land, and it is the president's constitutional responsibility "to take care that the laws be faithfully executed."[158]

Because of the length of his speech, Marshall did not summarize or recapitulate his remarks, and simply thanked the House for its indulgence. The fact is, no summary was necessary. The case Marshall laid out was compelling. Gallatin, who stood at the rear of the chamber, made no effort to gain the floor. Nicholas, Livingston, and other Republican members immediately crowded round him, urging that he reply. "Gentlemen," said Gallatin, "answer it yourself. For my part, I think it is unanswerable."[159]

That was certainly Joseph Story's impression. He pronounced Marshall's speech on the *Robbins* case "one of the most consummate juridical arguments which was ever pronounced in the halls of legislation. . . . a *Réponse san réplique*, an answer so powerful that it admitted no reply."[160] Story later wrote that Marshall's speech "settled then and forever the points of international law on which the controversy hinged. . . . Whoever reads that speech, even at this distance of time, when the topics have lost much of their interest, will be struck with the prodigious power of analysis and reasoning which it displays, and which are enhanced by the consideration that the whole subject was then confessedly new in many of its aspects."[161]

The next day, Saturday, March 8, Livingston's motion to censure Adams was defeated 61–35. six Republicans voting with Marshall. On March 10 the Federalists pressed their advantage and introduced a resolution approving the conduct of the president. That passed by a similarly lopsided vote, 62–35. Adams was exonerated and the *Robbins* case lost its resonance as a campaign issue.[162]

Throughout the Sixth Congress, Marshall repeatedly defended Adams from partisan attack, whether by the Republicans or the High Federalists. The future chief justice had become the president's spokesman, not by design so much as because he and Adams simply agreed on most issues. The president was often out of step with his own party, and Marshall was too. As a Southerner and as a Virginian, he had strong views about the Constitution, and as Sedgwick noted, those views occasionally set him apart from party orthodoxy. On two crucial party-line measures to come before the House, repeal of the Sedition Act and a proposed Disputed Elections Bill, Marshall rejected the party discipline and voted with the Republicans.

Repeal of the Sedition Act was a litmus test for the Republicans, just as its retention was an article of faith for the High Federalists. At the end of January, the Republican minority brought the act to the floor and moved its repeal. Marshall did not speak in the debate, but as he had promised his constituents, he voted for the motion to repeal the measure and took enough southern Federalists with him that the motion passed 50–48.[163] (If Marshall had voted with his party, the result would have been a 49–49 tie, and Speaker Sedgwick would have cast a deciding vote against repeal.)

After the preliminary motion passed, a complicated series of parliamentary maneuvers ensued. Republican floor leadership appears to have been lax, because James Bayard of Delaware was able to introduce a Federalist amendment that would have replaced the repealed act with the even more obnoxious common law of seditious libel. The Republicans did not have the votes on the floor to defeat it. Marshall voted with the Republicans against the proposal, but Bayard's amendment carried by a majority of four. The amended motion to repeal was then put to a vote, and for the third time Marshall joined with the Republicans. This time the votes were there, and the amended motion failed.[164] As a result, the Sedition Act remained on the books and expired on schedule, March 3, 1801. Marshall's three votes on the issue made it clear, however, that he would not support his party's position to restrict free speech or curtail freedom of the press.

Marshall's opposition to the Disputed Elections Bill placed him even more at odds with the High Federalist core of the party. With all eyes focused on the upcoming presidential election, Federalist senator James Ross of Pennsylvania introduced a bill calling for the establishment of a Grand Committee of the House and Senate that would rule on the validity of the electoral votes cast in the various states. If the bill were passed, the Federalist-dominated Congress would become the final arbiter of the election, and Jefferson's electoral chances would be dealt a crippling blow. Despite his personal antipathy to the vice president, Marshall thought that the measure was not only wrong-headed but a clear violation of Article II of the Constitution, which specified the procedure for choosing the president. If the electoral college could not reach a decision, the Constitution stated clearly that the responsibility devolved upon the House of Representatives.

When the bill reached the House at the end of March, Marshall worked the cloakrooms and corridors assiduously, voicing his objections and lining up the opposition vote.[165] When the measure came to the floor, he not only spoke against it but offered a series of amendments of such wide application that a select committee was appointed to redraft the bill. Marshall was named chairman, and the resulting committee draft, known as "John Marshall's amendment," withheld from the Grand Committee any power of decision, assigning it simply the responsibility of reporting the electoral votes cast in each state.[166] Marshall's modifications to the Ross bill gutted the measure. It no longer provided the Federalists with a vehicle to alter the electoral vote for president, and it was killed in the Senate, with all the Federalist senators voting against.[167]

As the sixth congressional session drew to a close in the spring of 1800, Marshall had established himself as the leader of "popular Federalism." He had prevented the party from enacting the more egregious items on its legislative agenda and had offered timely compromises to secure the enactment of national legislation on bankruptcy and the demobilization of the standing army. He had emerged as President Adams's most reliable supporter in the House and the most articulate defender of the principles of moderation for which both he and Adams stood.

Reflecting on the session as a whole, Marshall welcomed the diminution of partisan rancor. Speaker Sedgwick took a more pessimistic view, calling the session "long, tedious, and unproductive." He lamented the "feebleness of character" in the House, which he ascribed in no small measure to Marshall's lack of commitment to Federalist principles. "Marshall was looked up to as the man whose great and commanding genius was to enlighten and direct national councils," Sedgwick wrote to Rufus King. "This was the greatest sentiment, although some . . . thought him temporizing while others deemed him feeble. None had in my opinion justly appreciated his character. As his character has stamped itself on the measures of the present session, I am desirous of letting you know how I view it." Sedgwick proceeded to give King one of the most famous thumbnail sketches of Marshall ever written:

> He is a man of a very affectionate disposition, of great simplicity of manners and honest and honorable in all his conduct.
>
> He is attached to pleasure, with convivial habits strongly fixed. He is indolent, therefore; and indisposed to take part in the common business of the House.
>
> He has a strong attachment to popularity but [is] indisposed to

sacrifice to it his integrity; hence it is that he is disposed on all popular subjects to feel the public pulse and hence results indecision
and *an expression* of doubt. Doubts suggested by him create in more
feeble minds those which are immovable. He is disposed . . . to express great respect from the sovereign people, and to quote their
opinions as evidence of truth. The latter is of all things the most destructive of personal independence and of that weight of character
which a great man ought to possess.[168]

If Sedgwick and the High Federalists were critical of Marshall, John
Adams was overjoyed to have found an effective ally in the House.[169] The
presidential election was looming, and Adams desperately needed to reassert
his control over the party and tamp down the revolt of the party's conservative wing. The High Federalists had been unhappy with the president's
moderate leadership for years, and they were now actively plotting to replace
him.[170] Alexander Hamilton was leading the effort, and there were many in
the party, including some in Adams's own cabinet, who looked at Hamilton
rather than the president for direction. With Congress winding down and
some members already leaving town, Adams decided to take advantage of
the situation to reorganize his cabinet and replace people of dubious loyalty
with his own men. Adams's first target was his affable secretary of war, James
McHenry of Maryland, whose friendship with Hamilton traced back to the
Revolutionary War when both had served on Washington's staff.

On the evening of May 5, 1800, Adams summoned an unsuspecting
McHenry away from a dinner party, ostensibly to settle a minor item of department business. The matter in question was settled quickly, whereupon
the president flew into a rage against Hamilton and accused McHenry of being his accomplice.[171] When McHenry tried to defend himself, Adams let
loose another tirade about the inefficiency of the War Department. At this
point, the secretary submitted his resignation, which Adams promptly accepted. The president brooded about the choice of a successor for a day and
then, on the morning of May 7, in typical fashion, sent Marshall's name to
the Senate without bothering to consult him.[172] That afternoon Marshall
stopped by the War Department to make some routine inquiries for several
of his constituents, and only then did he learn of what had happened. He
later described the scene to Justice Story:

In May 1800, as I was about to leave Philadelphia . . . for the purpose
of attending the courts in Richmond, I stepped into the war office in
order to make some enquiries respecting patents for some of my military friends, and was a good deal struck with a strange sort of mysterious coldness which I soon observed in the countenance of Mr.

McHenry, the secretary of war, with whom I had long been on terms of friendly intimacy. I however prosecuted my enquiries until they brought me into conversation with Mr. Fitzsimmons the chief clerk, who congratulated me on being placed at the head of that department, and expressed the pleasure it gave all those who were engaged in it. I did not understand him, and was really surprised at hearing that I had been nominated to the senate as secretary of war. I did not believe myself to be well qualified for this department, and was not yet willing to abandon my hopes of reinstating myself at the bar. I therefore addressed a letter to Mr. Adams making my acknowledgements for his notice of me, and requesting that he withdraw my name from the senate, as I was not willing openly to decline a place in an administration which I was disposed cordially to support.[173]

Marshall told Adams that he appreciated the confidence the president had shown in him, but "I must pray you sir to withdraw the nomination."[174] For whatever reason, Adams declined to do so, and the Senate duly confirmed Marshall as secretary of war on May 9, 1800. By that time, Marshall was already on his way to Richmond to pick up the pieces of his fast-disintegrating law practice. The United States circuit court convened on May 22, and he had several cases to prepare.[175] Moreover, his salary as a congressman had scarcely covered his and Polly's living expenses in Philadelphia.[176] With another interest payment due on Leeds Manor, Marshall desperately needed to win back his former clients and restore the profitability of his practice.

Adams was not prepared to give up so easily. Marshall was the one person in Congress he felt close to, and one of the few in Philadelphia who had repeatedly demonstrated a personal loyalty to the president. If Adams was going to assert his control over the party, he needed Marshall close at hand. Accordingly, on May 10, while Marshall was still en route to Richmond, Adams asked Secretary of State Timothy Pickering to resign. Pickering, an obstinate, self-righteous man, refused, and Adams, unwilling to back down, announced Pickering's dismissal at noon, May 12.[177] That afternoon the president sent Marshall's name to the Senate as Pickering's successor.* Once again Marshall had not been consulted. The Senate acted promptly and Marshall was confirmed unanimously as secretary of state on May 13. Charles Lee, who stayed on as attorney general, wrote to Marshall in Richmond that afternoon enclosing his commission of office.[178]

Marshall now had a serious decision to make. He was committed to the president, but his family obligations were compelling. Perhaps the most se-

---

*Samuel Dexter of Massachusetts was nominated at the same time to be secretary of war. Records of the U.S. Senate, RG 46, National Archives.

rious problem was Polly's reluctance to leave home. Six months in Philadelphia had convinced her she did not want to leave Richmond again.[179] On the other hand, the salary of the secretary of state would be sufficient to support Marshall's comfortable lifestyle and cover the interest payments due on the Fairfax estate. This was an important consideration, as Marshall's law practice had suffered during his absence from Richmond. The city bristled with attorneys, and the success of a practice hinged on continuity. Many of Marshall's former clients had become reluctant to retain his services, because, as a member of Congress, he was not always on hand to shepherd their litigation through the courts.

Adams's offer was attractive to Marshall for more than financial reasons, however. Marshall's sojourn in Paris had whetted his appetite for diplomacy, and he was eager to renew his involvement in the conduct of the nation's foreign policy. The president's detached administrative style would give Marshall ample room to shape policy as he saw fit. Marshall was also genuinely fond of Adams, and he welcomed the opportunity to continue working with the president. He shared Adams's goal of ending the bitter ideological struggle between the radical Republicans and the High Federalists by building a strong centrist coalition.[180] Finally there was the question of pride. Marshall was in a political battle that had become personal. He explained his decision to Story:

> My decided preference was still for the bar. But on becoming a candidate for Congress I was given up as a lawyer, and considered generally as entirely a political man. I lost my business altogether, and perceived very clearly that I could not recover any portion of it without retiring from Congress. Even then I could not hope to regain the ground I had lost. This experiment however I was willing to make, and would have made had my political enemies been quiet.
>
> But the press teemed with so much falsehood, with such continued and irritating abuse of me that I could not bring myself to yield to it. I could not conquer a stubbornness of temper which determines a man to make head against and struggle with injustice. I felt that I must continue a candidate for Congress and consequently could not replace myself at the bar.
>
> On the other hand the office was precisely that which I wished, and for which I had vanity enough to think myself fitted. I should remain in it while the party remained in power; should a revolution take place it would at all events relieve me from the competition for Congress without yielding to my adversaries, and enable me to return once more to the bar in the character of a lawyer having no possible view to politics. I determined to accept the office.[181]

10

Secretary of State

MARSHALL'S APPOINTMENT as secretary of state was widely applauded. The Federalists recognized his ability, while the Republicans, who had worked easily with him in Congress, rejoiced that Adams had not named someone more objectionable. The Philadelphia *Aurora*, which was usually unrelenting in its attacks on the government, actually managed a few words of praise. "In genuine federal principles, General Marshall is as inflexible as Mr. Pickering," it told its readers. "But in the negotiation with France, the General may not have imbibed so strong prejudices—and, having been one of the Envoys to that Republic, he may be supposed to be more conversant with some of the points in dispute than Col. Pickering, and consequently to be preferred."[1] Even in France, Marshall's appointment was hailed. The semiofficial *Gazettes de France*, reflecting the views of the Bonaparte regime, noted approvingly: "This is the gentleman who some time since came as Envoy from the United States; and who so virtuously and so spiritedly refused to fill the pockets of some of *our gentry* with Dutch inscriptions, and millions of livres."[2]

Among the Federalists, it was Pickering himself who urged a closing of ranks behind Marshall. The office of secretary of state "was never better filled," he told supporters.[3] A further note of support was sounded by Charles Cotesworth Pinckney, recently back from Paris and widely rumored to be the High Federalist alternative to Adams. Pinckney wrote former Secretary of War McHenry that "you may rely on [Marshall's] federalism, and be certain that he will not unite with Jefferson and the Jacobins."[4] Abigail Adams, who was as pleased as her husband with the appointment, wrote to her son that the nation needed "cool dispassionate Heads, as well as honest Hearts."[5] Marshall, whose loyalty to the president was unquestioned, qualified on both counts.

The future chief justice assumed his duties in mid-June. The infant government had already begun the task of moving from Philadelphia to Washington—which at the time was little more than a malarial swamp on the banks of the Potomac, midway between the villages of Alexandria and Georgetown. President Adams arrived in the new capital June 2, and Marshall, who remained in Richmond until the court session ended on June 4, came several days later. For the journey to the capital, Marshall shared a stagecoach with Justice Samuel Chase, who had just presided over the sedition trial of James Callender in Richmond.[6] Once in Washington, Marshall, Adams, and Samuel Dexter, the incoming secretary of war, lodged together in the Washington City Hotel, a three-story brick building that had recently opened. The hotel was located on the present site of the Supreme Court building, immediately across from the capitol, which was still several months from completion.[7] The three men worked out of their hotel rooms for a week, at which point Adams departed to spend the summer in Quincy, Massachusetts, leaving Marshall in charge of the government. He told Story many years later: "I was very well received by the President, and was on very cordial terms with all the cabinet except Mr. Oliver Wolcott. He at first suspected that I was hostile to the two ex-secretaries [Pickering and McHenry], and to himself, because they were all three supposed to be unfriendly to the President to whom I was truly attached. My conduct soon convinced him however that I had no feeling of that sort, after which I had the satisfaction of finding myself on the same cordial footing with him as with the rest of the cabinet."[8]

With Adams out of town, Marshall had his hands full. His most pressing task, which went well beyond the traditional duties of the secretary of state, was to hold together the badly splintered Federalist party. Despite his defection on the alien and sedition acts and the Ross bill, Marshall was liked and respected by the High Federalists. Throughout the summer he worked diligently on Adams's behalf to tamp down the revolt that was brewing. He constantly reminded the president's opponents of the importance of the upcoming presidential election. Jefferson and Burr were running against Adams and Pinckney, and Marshall feared the consequences of a Republican victory in the fall. "By union we can securely maintain our ground," he wrote to Sedgwick. "Without it we must sink and with us all sound, correct American principles."[9]

Like Adams, Marshall believed that peace with France and Britain was the most important issue in the campaign. Together with Henry Lee and Polly's brother-in-law, Edward Carrington, he crafted the election statement of the Federalist state committee in Virginia. The document asserted the committee's vigorous support for Adams's policy and reads like a catechism of Marshall's views on American neutrality. "We forget," said the committee, "that our government has preserved us from two impending wars . . . with the two most powerful nations of the world . . . without any sacrifice to the national interest, or of the national honor. We forget that we have been preserved from a close alliance with either of those two nations . . . and the inevitable consequence of war with the other; and that we remain completely free and independent."[10]

Marshall's campaign efforts were only partially successful. He may have prevented Adams from being dumped in several states, but he was unable to contain the public attacks on the president from members of his own party. Written by Hamilton and others,[11] these broadsides lambasted Adams for his political moderation, his willingness to compromise with the Republicans, and, above all, his decision to send the Ellsworth mission to Paris and resume negotiations with France. Despite Marshall's unstinting support for the president,[12] the party's internal strife would contribute directly to its eventual defeat.

As secretary of state and president's principal cabinet officer, Marshall was confronted with a vast array of governmental responsibilities. In 1800 the Department of State was the focal point of domestic as well as foreign policy, and the department's duties included granting patents and copyrights; taking the census (1800 was a census year); recording land grants throughout the vast federal domain; supervising the mint (which remained in Philadelphia and which, as a matter of administrative curiosity, fell under the jurisdiction of the State Department rather than the Treasury); printing and distributing government documents; and governing the territories of the United States. The administration of justice also came under the department's purview, since the position of attorney general was purely advisory to the president. In short, the secretary of state, in addition to his diplomatic and political duties, was responsible for all the activities of the federal government except those involving the Treasury, the military, and the post office—functions that today are handled by the Patent Office, the Bureau of the Census, the Government Printing Office, the Department of the Interior, and the Department of Justice. Marshall was assisted in these myriad tasks by a chief clerk and seven other people, bringing to a total of nine the entire staff of the department.

In addition to the statutory responsibilities of the department, Marshall confronted the immediate problems associated with constructing the new federal city in Washington and moving the government from Philadelphia. He was charged by Adams with supervising the work of the district commissioners laying out the city as well as overseeing construction of the capitol and the president's mansion. This task became more pressing in the autumn of 1800 as Congress prepared to convene and the Adamses sought to move in.[13] As winter neared and the president's mansion was still not complete, Marshall barraged the commissioners with requests to speed up their work. With the president and his wife expected shortly, he told them that it was "really important that you should put as many workers as you can . . . on that House for one week," so that it "may be finished time enough to be cleaned and aired before the arrival of Mrs. Adams. . . . Pray suffer no more painting to be done in any part of the house."[14] Later, when the Adamses had moved in, Marshall complained to the commissioners that so many curiosity seekers were "constantly passing thro' all the rooms of the President's House, that it is impossible for him to have the furniture set out, or the rooms put in order." He said that "some decent person" should be stationed at the entrance to prevent unauthorized persons from roaming around inside.[15]

In foreign affairs, which was Marshall's principal concern, it was a period of quiet peril. The Barbary pirates were stepping up their attacks on American shipping in the Mediterranean, as were freebooting privateers fitted out in Spain. These problems were not new, but they required constant attention lest one erupt into a full-scale crisis.[16] Far more important, however, was the ongoing quasi-war with France and the fate of the Ellsworth mission. Deteriorating relations with Britain ranked a close second. The principal difficulty involved the festering claims of British creditors against individual Americans, which, despite the Jay Treaty, still had not been paid. As the primary lawyer for Virginia's debtors in the early 1790s, Marshall had developed the strategy that initially frustrated British claimants. Now, as secretary of state, he was on the other side of the fence and faced an unraveling diplomatic accord that threatened to destroy the amity between the two nations.

Under the Jay Treaty, the claims of British creditors were to be settled by a special bilateral arbitration commission, but the commission had fallen apart in the summer of 1799, when the American arbiters walked out following a bitter disagreement over procedure. Neither government had found a way to resolve the impasse. Three months before he was removed from office, Pickering had proposed creating a new commission,[17] but the British were not satisfied with its composition. In April 1800 Lord Grenville, foreign secretary in the Pitt government, suggested an alternate version, which the Americans rejected.[18] Later that month Grenville hinted to Rufus

King, who was still the American minister to the Court of St. James, that a lump-sum payment from the United States might be the easiest way to resolve the dispute and that Britain would then assume responsibility for paying the individual creditors. King reported the conversation to Marshall,[19] who, on July 21, 1800, passed the suggestion along to the president in Quincy.

Marshall made no recommendation, although he asked Adams whether a lump-sum payment to Britain could "afford just cause of discontent to France."[20] The idea of concealing a lump-sum payment under the guise of reimbursing individual creditors had been one of Talleyrand's gambits during the XYZ affair. Marshall had refused to consider it because of the deleterious effect it would have had on American neutrality, and he was equally dubious about sending money directly to Great Britain. Adams, however, did not think it was a problem. The debts, he told Marshall, had been contracted by private American citizens and were owed to British subjects. Unlike Talleyrand, the British were seeking payment of legitimate debts. By making payment to the crown, the United States was simply acknowledging these debts. "No foreign country has anything to do with it," said Adams. The greatest problem would be "agreeing upon a sum," but the president liked the idea and told Marshall that they should give it a try.[21]

Despite his initial doubts, Marshall soon came to the same conclusion. On July 26, and well before receiving the president's reply, he wrote to Adams that "I am greatly inclined to believe that we shall never be able to extricate ourselves from this affair on better terms." Marshall said that a sum of $5 million, "or perhaps a million sterling" might be appropriate.[22] Adams officially embraced the idea on August 11. He told Marshall that £1 million sterling might be high, but "I agree with you . . . that it is better to pay more than we conjecture is due than go through all the trouble and run all the risk of an arbitration."[23]

Armed with the president's approval, Marshall wrote to King in mid-August instructing him to negotiate a lump-sum settlement with Britain and end the dispute. He told King to seek the lowest possible amount. Adams, he said, "will be satisfied with four million dollars. He will not consent to exceed one million sterling."[24] Marshall had learned from his experience in Paris that the diplomatic representative on the spot is best able to judge the situation, and so except for setting limits on the amount of the settlement, he left the negotiations completely in King's hands. After reading Marshall's concise instructions to King, Adams wrote, "I do not know how the subject could have been better digested."[25]

As a result of the administration's prompt action in dealing with Lord Grenville's proposal, tensions with Great Britain were reduced, and the complex process of arriving at an acceptable figure began. In 1802 King concluded an agreement by which the United States would pay Britain

£600,000 sterling, divided into three annual installments. By then Jefferson had succeeded Adams as president, and the Pitt government had been replaced by the ministry of Henry Addington. Marshall was no longer secretary of state, nor was Grenville foreign secretary.[26]

A second source of conflict with Great Britain stemmed from the Royal Navy's continued impressment of American seamen, its seizure of American goods on the high seas, and the condemnation of American vessels by British prize courts. These were simmering grievances related to Britain's infringement of American neutrality. As one of the Paris envoys, Marshall had strenuously protested similar incursions by France in his negotiations with Talleyrand. Now, as secretary of state, he took up the same problem with Britain. On September 20, 1800, Marshall wrote once more to King restating American policy and instructing him to raise the outstanding issues immediately with Lord Grenville.

Marshall's September letter to King is one of his most memorable compositions. Its balanced tone foreshadowed his great Supreme Court decisions, and the precision of his language left little room for conjecture. The message captured the essence of American neutrality and emphasized the necessity for evenhandedness. American complaints against Britain were crisply stated, and Marshall again deferred to King's tactical judgment. The historian Andrew J. Montague extravagantly termed Marshall's communiqué "a document ranking among the very greatest of American state papers, and perhaps unequalled in the diplomatic contributions of the English-speaking world."[27] Beveridge called it "a state paper which, in ability, dignity, and eloquence, suggests [Marshall's] famous Jonathan Robbins speech and equals his memorial to Talleyrand."[28] The letter is not as lengthy as the message to Talleyrand and its focus is sharper. The object of the American government, Marshall told King, was to preserve an exact neutrality between England and France. "Separated far from Europe, we mean not to mingle in their quarrels. This determination was early declared, and has never been changed. In pursuance of it we have avoided, and we shall continue to avoid, any political connections which might engage us further than is compatible with the neutrality we profess. . . ."[29]

Marshall said that the aggressive actions first of Britain, and then of France, had "forced us to . . . prepare for war. We have repelled, and we will continue to repel, whatever injuries are inflicted upon us. But this is a situation of necessity, not of choice. It is one in which we are placed—not by our own acts—but by the acts of others." He then sketched America's unhappy experience with both countries. "We still pursue peace. We will embrace it if it can be obtained without violating our national honor or our national faith, but we will reject, without hesitation, all propositions which may compromise the one or the other."

Marshall instructed King to reassure Britain that the Ellsworth mission to Paris was consistent with America's past policy of strict neutrality. If the Pitt government had apprehensions, "you will, by a plain and candid representation of the truth, endeavor to remove them." Once that was done, Marshall told King to raise "the irritating and injurious vexations we sustain." He thereupon provided the minister with what amounted to a legal brief dealing with three broad areas: the seizure of American goods as contraband, the unjust decisions of British prize courts, and the impressment of American seamen. His restatement of the law of nations gave King more than ample justification to assert that Britain was at fault.

Marshall reserved his toughest language for the one-sided decisions of British courts of vice admiralty, which, he said, invariably held in favor of the privateers. "The most effectual restraint [against unjust seizures] is an upright judiciary which will decide impartially between the parties, and uniformly condemn the captor in costs and damages where the seizure has been made without probable cause. If this practice be not honestly and rigidly observed, there will exist no restraint on the captors." Marshall implied that the admiralty courts were corrupt, and he placed the responsibility for the problem with the British government. "Only by infusing a spirit of justice and respect for law into the courts of vice admiralty" can these "irritating vexations be restrained. . . . This spirit can only be infused by uniformly discountenancing and punishing those who tarnish the seat of justice . . . by converting themselves from Judges into mere instruments of plunder."[30]

As for the impressment of American seamen, "they are dragged on board British ships of war . . . and forced by violence there to serve until conclusive testimonials of their birth can be obtained. . . . It is an act of violence for which there is no palliative." Marshall told King that if the Royal Navy did not desist, "an open rupture is inevitable."[31]

Marshall's letter to King was a masterful display of statesmanship. With Adams on an extended sojourn in Quincy, Marshall was attempting to reinvigorate American foreign policy by asserting an active neutrality. The Royal Navy and the courts of vice admiralty had displayed a blatant disregard for American rights. Marshall not only asked King to make the appropriate protest, but provided him with a working memorandum that effectively set forth the position of the United States. Marshall's letter to King marked the beginning of a shift in American foreign policy away form the pro-British orientation of Washington's second term. Henceforth, Britain would enjoy no special relationship with the United States. Marshall understood full well the implication of his letter. Although he had always advocated a policy of neutrality toward the great powers of Europe, he had come to believe that "the hardest thing for the Federalists to bear was the charge of British influence."[32]

In his dealings with France, Marshall took the opposite tack. Peaceful overtures from Paris would be warmly reciprocated, and the Bonaparte regime appeared much more conciliatory toward the United States than the Directory had been. Messages from the French capital traveled at a snail's pace, and there still was no word from Ellsworth as to his mission's reception, but Marshall was confident that things were going well. Knowing Talleyrand as he did, he assumed that negotiations would be protracted, but that this was not necessarily cause for alarm.[33] In late August he alerted Adams to the possibility that a treaty might not be forthcoming. With or without a treaty, however, Marshall was temperate in his judgment and asked the president whether the quasi-war against France "ought to be continued, if on their part a change of conduct shall be manifest."[34] Adams replied on September 4 that he was undecided. He asked Marshall's opinion as to whether he should "recommend to Congress an immediate and general Declaration of War against the French Republic." That, said Adams, would clarify the situation and would give the public a clear-cut choice.[35]

Marshall was apparently for just such an invitation from the president, and he again took the opportunity to urge patience and restraint. "I am greatly inclined to think that the present government [of France] is much inclined to correct . . . the follies of the past," he told Adams. "Considerable steps in this direction have already been taken, and I expect the same course will be continued. Should this expectation not be disappointed there will . . . exist no cause for war, except to obtain compensation for past injuries," and that, said Marshall, was not sufficient justification.[36]

Marshall's instinct proved correct. At the very time he and Adams were exchanging views, the Ellsworth envoys and their French counterparts, led by Joseph Bonaparte, had already reached a settlement more comprehensive than either side had initially thought possible. Officially labeled the Convention of Môrtefontaine, the agreement provided for "a firm, inviolable, and universal peace."[37] Rules were specified to prevent future maritime abuses, arrangements were made for the payment of debts due each country, port privileges were placed on a most-favored-nation basis, and the French, eager to undermine Britain's continuing blockade, accepted the American wording that "free ships [make] free goods." The accord was signed amid great festivities at the Château de Môrtefontaine, Joseph's country residence about eighteen miles north of Paris, on October 3, 1800. The American envoys were the guests of honor. Napoleon, his family, and practically every important official in the French government were present.[38]

Although two of the most contentious issues, indemnities for past damages and the status of the treaty of alliance of 1778, were deferred for future consideration, the French and American envoys were pleased with the settlement. The United States did not obtain everything it sought, but as Vans

Murray wrote to Marshall, "We were all profoundly convinced . . . that we should agree to that treaty rather than make none."[39] Oliver Ellsworth wrote that at least the conflict with France had ended. "Be assured, more could not be done without too great a sacrifice, and as the reign of Jacobinism is over in France, and appearances are strong in favor of a general peace, I hope you will think it was better to sign a convention than to do nothing."[40]

News of the agreement filtered back to the United States slowly. In early November the Baltimore *Telegraph and Daily Advertiser* carried the "Glorious News" of an agreement but printed no details of the treaty, and the official text did not reach Washington for another five weeks.[41] With the outcome of the 1800 presidential election still in doubt, the delay added to the already tense atmosphere in the capital. The High Federalists, who were unrelenting in their opposition to France, were chastened by word of a possible agreement; the Republicans were equally apprehensive; and both factions, for diametrically opposite reasons, fretted about the possible contents of the document.

Marshall, by contrast, remained optimistic. On November 18, 1800, he wrote to his old friend St. George Tucker that "I believe confidently that an accommodation has taken place with France, tho we have as yet no official account of it." Like Adams, Marshall hoped fervently for peace and he rejoiced to Tucker that the quasi-war was over. "I think it is time for peace to be universal."*[42]

The members of the House and Senate were now trickling into Washington for the second session of the Sixth Congress, scheduled to convene on November 17. Bad weather and poor roads had delayed many legislators, and a quorum was not achieved until four days later. In some ways, the nation's capital was like Richmond in the 1780s. The representatives and senators lived huddled together in rooming houses clustered around Capitol

---

*Marshall was writing to Tucker in response to Tucker's plea for leniency for Richmond journalist James Callender, who had been convicted under the Sedition Act for his pamphlet *The Prospect Before Us*. Tucker asked Marshall to intercede with Adams, suggesting that what Callender had written was no more libelous of the president than what Hamilton had written. "I have no hesitation in declaring to My friend John Marshall, that I should feel myself obliged to HIM for his humane interposition on behalf of a man, whom I cannot but consider as suffering an unconstitutional punishment."

Marshall's reply made it abundantly clear that he agreed with Tucker that the Sedition Act was unconstitutional. "Whatever doubts some of us may entertain," wrote Marshall, the president was convinced the act was constitutional and could not be persuaded by arguments to the contrary. Marshall said "my own private judgment would have been against [Callender's] being prosecuted, but I am not quite sure that is a sufficient reason for interposing. . . ." As for Hamilton's attack, "I wish for his sake [it] had never been seen by any person. I have no doubt that it wounds and irritates the person at whom it is directed infinitely more than *The Prospect Before Us*, because its author is worthy of attention and his shaft may stick." Tucker to Marshall, March 6, 1800, 6 *The Papers of John Marshall* 4–5 (Chapel Hill: University of North Carolina Press, 1990); Marshall to Tucker, November 18, 1800, *ibid*. 14–15.

Hill, the streets were unpaved, and the town had a rough, frontier quality about it. Albert Gallatin, in Washington for the first time, wrote his wife that "the whole of the Federal city [consists of] seven or eight boarding houses, one tailor, one shoemaker, one printer, a washing woman, a grocery shop, a pamphlets and stationery shop, a small dry-goods shop, and an oyster house."[43] Representative Roger Griswold of Connecticut, obviously accustomed to more congenial surroundings, called it "both melancholy and ludicrous . . . a city in ruins."[44] Oliver Wolcott was even less charitable. "The people are poor," he wrote. "As far as I can judge they live like fishes, by eating each other."[45]

On November 22 President Adams, not yet a lame duck, delivered his fourth State of Union address. Written by Marshall at Adams's request,[46] the message was moderate in tone, a valedictory befitting a successful administration. Revenues were up, commerce was flourishing, negotiations with Britain were under way, and a friendship treaty with Prussia had just been concluded. There was still no official word from Paris, but the outlook was positive. Napoleon had received the American envoys "with the respect due to their character," and the president told Congress that he hoped that an agreement would be forthcoming.

Two weeks later, William R. Davie arrived in Washington with the official text of the Convention of Môrtefontaine. Simultaneous with Davie's arrival, Marshall was informed by Pinckney that the Republican electors had prevailed in South Carolina, the last state in the Union to report its results.[47] The outcome in South Carolina put Jefferson and Burr over the top. Twelve years of Federalist rule had come to an end. Adams took the defeat stoically,[48] and Marshall began making plans to return to Richmond and pick up the tattered remnants of his law practice.[49]

Since the new administration would not take office until March 4, Adams and Marshall had three more months in office. Adams especially was determined to remain at the helm until his term expired, and on December 16 he submitted the French treaty to the Senate for approval. Marshall had written a message for the president urging acceptance, but Adams chose not to use it and sent the convention forward without embellishment.[50] Both he and Marshall were pleased with what the Ellsworth mission had accomplished and, like the envoys, agreed that it was best to restore peaceful relations with France even though several important issues remained unresolved. The Federalist-controlled Senate was not so sure, and debate dragged on for several weeks.[51] The Republicans and the moderates favored ratification, but the High Federalists remained unconvinced. Harrison Gray Otis called the agreement "another chapter in the book of humiliation."[52] Fisher Ames wrote, "We are, by treaty, to embrace France, and Frenchmen will swarm in our porridge-pots."[53] Another legislator was so disgusted with the prospect of peace with France that he assumed Ellsworth must have been "rendered feeble by disease."[54]

Having lost his bid for reelection, Adams had even less influence than usual with the High Federalists, and Marshall was unable to win the opponents over. Rejection of the convention would "utterly ruin the Federal party and endanger our internal tranquillity," he told Sedgwick.[55] Nevertheless, when the vote was taken on January 23, 1801, the Senate rejected the convention 16–14, well short of the two-thirds majority required for approval. All of the negative votes were cast by Federalists.[56] Adams was appalled, and Marshall was dumbfounded.

The fact is, the party had thrown a temper tantrum—a splenetic outburst of resentment against Adams, against France, and against the impending loss of power that the election had made inevitable. Reality dawned quickly. To the discomfiture of Federalist senators, the Convention of Môrtefontaine was extremely popular throughout the country, not only among Jefferson's supporters but also with the business community, which wanted the quasi-war to end so that trade could be restored with France.[57] Marshall and others pointed out that if the party did not back Adams and adopt the treaty, the incoming Jefferson administration would negotiate a new one that they would find even more objectionable.[58] The scales were tipped when Marshall released a letter he had just received from Rufus King in London stating that the British government found nothing objectionable in the treaty.[59] That took the wind out of the High Federalists' sails. Adams resubmitted the treaty, and on February 3, 1801, the Senate reversed itself and approved the Convention of Môrtefontaine, 22–9, five of the president's opponents switching sides. Peace with France was restored, although Jefferson did not promulgate the treaty officially until almost a year later.[60]

The Senate fight over the Convention of Môrtefontaine coincided with the resignation of Oliver Ellsworth as chief justice.[61] As a replacement, Adams instinctively went first to his old friend John Jay, who was stepping down as governor of New York. When Jay declined,[62] the president turned to Marshall. For the past two years, first in Congress, then as secretary of state, no one had been more loyal to Adams than Marshall, and no one shared the president's views of moderate Federalism more completely.

Adams's decision came as a surprise, especially to Marshall.* In retrospect, however, the choice appears inevitable. Apart from his devotion to the president, Marshall was one of the few Federalists to command the respect of both parties and one of the few who would bring to the Court both

---

*The details surrounding Marshall's appointment and confirmation as chief justice are set forth in the introduction.

legislative and executive experience. He had represented the United States abroad with distinction, and, with the possible exception of Adams himself, no Federalist stood higher in public esteem. In addition, Marshall's legal skills were superb. His analytical mind and his pragmatic bent had made him one of Adams's most trusted colleagues, and his personal integrity was unchallenged.

There was also no one, save perhaps Madison, who could equal Marshall's understanding of the Constitution, and even Madison fell short when grappling with the provisions of Article III, which defined the powers and jurisdiction of the federal courts. Marshall's masterly restatement of the nature of judicial authority and the power of the president in the *Robbins* case had not only defused an explosive political issue but had authoritatively defined the separation of powers. His September 20 instruction to King, which Adams had endorsed, displayed an exceptional knowledge of the law of nations, admiralty law, and the nature of citizenship. Its evenhandedness was a Marshall hallmark. As Senator Richard Stockton of New Jersey told Adams, Marshall's appointment as chief justice "merits the certain approbation of all impartial men here."[63]

Although Marshall lacked judicial experience, he did not lack a judicial temperament. His moderate political views reflected a fundamental tolerance for opposing opinions, and he saw the courts as the ultimate defenders of individual liberty. Marshall was no friend of omnipotent government, and as his votes on the Sedition Act confirmed, he valued freedom of speech and freedom of the press as the essential prerequisites of representative government. Above all, Marshall was devoted to the Union. With Jefferson and the states rights supporters taking power, Adams may well have believed that it was important to add an articulate defender of national supremacy to the Court, particularly one who came from Virginia.

On January 31, 1801, Adams signed Marshall's commission as Chief Justice of the United States.[64] Four days later, following Senate approval of the Convention of Môrtefontaine, Marshall formally advised the president of his acceptance.

I pray you to accept my grateful acknowledgements for the honor conferred on me in appointing me Chief Justice of the United States.

This additional and flattering mark of your good opinion has made an impression on my mind which time will not efface.

I shall enter immediately on the duties of the office and hope never to give you occasion to regret having made this appointment. With the most respectful attachment, I am Sir your Obedt. Servt.

J. Marshall[65]

Adams replied in the same generous vein and requested that Marshall continue to discharge the duties of secretary of state until Jefferson took office.[66] Since the treaty with France had been approved, Marshall's tasks were mostly pro forma, but at the end of February, just before leaving office, he wrote a brief memorandum for James Madison, the incoming secretary of state, summarizing the diplomatic problems confronting the United States. The problems with the Barbary powers needed to be addressed; "our affairs with Spain will command very serious attention"; Great Britain was stepping up its attacks on American shipping; and the negotiations between Rufus King and Lord Grenville concerning payment of the debts owed British creditors required immediate attention.

Marshall said he feared an agreement had already been concluded. "I say I fear so because it is very much my wish that [the issue] should be found in a situation to be abandoned or pursued as shall in the opinion of the [incoming] administration be most conducive to the public interest, and it is for this reason that I recommend the most immediate attention to the subject."[67] From the tenor of Marshall's memorandum, it is clear that he harbored no resentment against the new administration and was doing his utmost to facilitate the transition.

Thus ended Marshall's tenure as secretary of state. The Supreme Court had already convened for its February term; Marshall had presented his commission as chief justice and had taken the oath of office. He was forty-five years old. For the next thirty-five years he would preside as Chief Justice of the United States. "He hit the Constitution much as the Lord hit the chaos, at a time when everything needed creating," wrote one observer.[68] President James A. Garfield said, "Marshall found the Constitution paper and made it power. He found a skeleton and clothed it with flesh and blood."[69] The prickly John Randolph of Roanoke noted that Marshall's "real worth was never known until he was appointed Chief Justice."[70]

To Marshall, more than to any other person, belongs the credit for establishing the foundations of constitutional interpretation. The magisterial character of his great opinions has never been equaled. Clear, concise, and eloquent, they are in many ways a rarity: legal documents that can be read and understood by the ordinary citizen as well as by the most learned practitioner. Lord Bryce, in his masterful analysis of the American system of government, perhaps best described Marshall's contribution:

> His work of building up and working out the Constitution was accomplished not so much by the decisions he gave as by the judgments which for their philosophical breadth, the luminous exactness of the reasoning, and the fine political sense which pervades them,

have never been surpassed and rarely equaled by the most famous jurists of modern Europe or of ancient Rome. . . . He grasped with extraordinary force and clearness the cardinal idea that the creation of a national government implies the grant of all such subsidiary powers as are requisite to the effectuation of its main powers and purposes, but he developed and applied this idea with so much prudence and sobriety, never treading on purely political ground, never indulging in the temptation to theorize, but content to follow out as a lawyer the consequences of legal principles, that the Constitution seemed not so much to rise under his hands to its full stature, as to be gradually unveiled by him till it stood revealed in the harmonious perfection of the form which its framers had designed.[71]

Bryce said that the "admirable flexibility and capacity for growth" that distinguish the American Constitution from all other written constitutions is largely attributable to Marshall, "yet not more to his courage as to his caution."

11

⁂

Opinion of the Court

The course of every tribunal must necessarily be, that the opinion which is delivered as the opinion of the court, is previously submitted to the judges; and, if any of the reasoning be disapproved, it must be so modified as to receive the approbation of all, before it can be delivered as the opinion of all.

John Marshall, "A Friend of the Union"

MARSHALL'S APPOINTMENT as chief justice coincided with the beginning of a new political era. Adams had yielded the presidency to Jefferson, the Republicans had gained control of both Houses of Congress, and the seat of government had moved from Philadelphia to Washington. The Jeffersonian revolution had begun. The doctrine of states rights was ascendant. The judiciary remained dominated by Federalist appointees, but in Marshall's view the courts should be if not above politics, at least above partisanship. That distinction was ambiguous. "Of the importance of the judiciary at all times, but more especially the present I am very fully impressed," he wrote to Charles Cotesworth Pinckney on the morning of Jefferson's inauguration. "I shall endeavor in the new office to which I am called not to disappoint my friends."[1]

Marshall was the first chief justice to preside over the Supreme Court in Washington. When he took the post, he assumed leadership of a court that enjoyed little prestige and even less authority. In 1788 Alexander Hamilton had written that "the judiciary is beyond comparison the weakest of the three branches,"[2] and little had happened in the interim to prove him wrong. For the first year and a half of its existence, the Supreme Court did not decide a single case.[3] In the sixteen active terms between 1790 and 1800, only sixty-three cases were reported, less than a dozen of which were significant.[4] Above all, the authority of the Court to interpret the Constitution was not yet clear. Certainly it did not possess the power of an ultimate arbiter whose decisions would be binding on the other two branches of government.[5]

The Supreme Court of the United States was a court of law, not a constitutional court. It was established to hear law cases, not expound the Constitution. Its jurisdiction was expressly limited, and its appellate role was determined by statute. Congress and the president enjoyed far more extensive constitutional authority. Tradition and usage recognized the Constitution as a political document specifying how the nation was to be governed. The two "political" branches of government, the legislative and the executive, maintained primary responsibility for its interpretation. The authority of the legislature derived from the concept of legislative supremacy, which the Continental Congress had inherited from the British Parliament.[6] The executive's authority to interpret the Constitution resembled the royal prerogative. Washington had placed a distinctive stamp on the office and with his neutrality proclamation had already established the president's authority to interpret the Constitution. As a result, both Congress and the executive could lay greater claim to constitutional finality than the Court.

The Supreme Court's jurisdiction over the states was also in question. When the Court had asserted its authority to try a sovereign state as a defendant in a private lawsuit, as it did in the 1793 case of *Chisholm v. Georgia*,[7] the decision was quickly reversed by the Eleventh Amendment. In addition, the Court was plagued by problems of rapid turnover and poor attendance. Of the six original appointees to the Court in 1789, only William Cushing remained on the bench. Court sessions were brief, and the lack of a quorum often caused cases to be carried over—and sometimes required sessions to be canceled entirely.[8]

The problem of leadership on the Court was particularly acute. John Jay, the first chief justice, resigned in 1795 to become governor of New York.[9] Alexander Hamilton declined Washington's entreaties to succeed Jay,[10] and the Senate, on partisan grounds, rejected the nomination of John Rutledge of South Carolina.[11] Washington then offered the position to Patrick Henry. When Henry stepped aside because of his age,[12] the president appointed William Cushing of Massachusetts, the senior associate justice. Cushing was immediately confirmed by the Senate but, like Henry, declined to accept the post because of age and infirmities.[13] Following Cushing's refusal, Washington turned to Oliver Ellsworth of Connecticut who, as a United States senator, had been the principal drafter of the Judiciary Act of 1789 that had created the federal court system. Ellsworth was confirmed on March 3, 1796, and presided over the Court for six terms, but resigned because of ill health in October 1800.[14] The chief justiceship began to resemble a revolving door.[15] Jay was offered the position once again but declined, citing the failure of the Supreme Court to "acquire the public confidence and respect which, as the last resort of the justice of the nation, it should possess."[16]

Jay and Ellsworth, the only two men who had actually served as chief justice, had unintentionally contributed to the lack of public esteem for the Court. Both men had relinquished their duties as chief justice to assume diplomatic missions abroad: Jay to negotiate the treaty with Great Britain that bears his name, Ellsworth to conclude the Convention of Môrtefontaine. Each undertaking, while important for American foreign relations, caused the two chief justices to miss several terms of Court and to neglect completely their duties on circuit. More significantly, they had been involved in the negotiations as agents of the president. Aside from the damage this did to the doctrine of the separation of powers, Jay and Ellsworth were perceived as Federalist partisans, which further diminished the stature of the Court.[17]

Other justices were even more directly involved in Federalist causes. As trial judges on circuit, all had enthusiastically enforced the Sedition Act, and none had questioned its constitutionality. Justices Chase and Paterson, in particular, had made a habit of haranguing juries in the name of Federalist virtue.[18] In a still more egregious entry into partisan politics, Chase and Bushrod Washington had campaigned actively for Adams in 1800.[19]

Perhaps even more contentious, all the justices except Chase had sustained criminal convictions under English common law even when no federal statute had been violated.[20] This tendency to create crimes by judicial fiat* was particularly infuriating to the vast majority of citizens who believed the Constitution had established a government of limited powers.[21] Inevitably, the Supreme Court came to be perceived as an organ of Federalist policy, and its judicial standing eroded accordingly.

So lightly was the Court regarded, and so slight was its prestige, that when the government moved to Washington, no provision was made for it to be housed. In 1796 a planning committee of the House of Representatives had recommended "a building for the Judiciary," but no money had been provided and no plans had been drawn up.[22] Two years later the project was

---

*The argument in favor of convicting under the common law was that "crime" must be punished, and if Congress failed to act, it was the duty of the courts to act without the authority of statute. Marshall did not accept that argument. In a lengthy letter to St. George Tucker in November 1800, Marshall said he agreed with Tucker that the Constitution did not confer *"any grant of general jurisdiction in cases at common law."* (Tucker had sent Marshall a copy of his recently published pamphlet, *Examination of the Question, "How Far the Common Law of England Is the Law of the Federal Government of the United States".*) See 6 *The Papers of John Marshall* 23–25 (Chapel Hill: University of North Carolina Press, 1990). Tucker's emphasis.

Subsequently, as chief justice, Marshall insisted that the jurisdiction of federal courts was not "regulated by the common law" but rather "by written law" (*Ex Parte Bollman*, 4 Cranch 75, 93 [1807]), and in the leading case of *United States v. Hudson and Goodwin* (7 Cranch 32 [1812]), the Marshall Court definitively rejected common law jurisdiction. Also see Marshall's holdings on circuit in *United States v. Smith* (C.C.D. Va. 1809), and *Livingston vs. Jefferson*, 15 F. Cas. 660 (C.C.D. Va. 1811) (No. 8411), in which he stated that "the jurisdiction of the courts of the United States depends, exclusively, on the constitution and laws of the United States" (at p. 667).

officially shelved with a notation that "the immediate erection of that edifice is not considered so essential as houses for the accommodation of Congress, of the President and the Executive offices."[23]

As secretary of state, Marshall apparently shared that view. Charged by Adams with overseeing construction of the federal city, he neither noted the need nor made arrangements for space to house the Court. In early December 1800 the district commissioners wrote to him suggesting that a committee room in the capitol be set aside temporarily for the Court. Alternatively, they recommended that the Court be provided "one or two rooms in the new Executive or War Office, and the Judges . . . with private lodgings in Georgetown."[24] If Marshall replied, that letter has been lost. The probability is that he did not, because six weeks later the commissioners wrote to him again asking for instructions as to where the Court was to be housed.[25] Once again no reply from Marshall has been found, but it is likely that he instructed the commissioners to seek a room on Capitol Hill, because on January 20, 1801, the Speaker of the House laid before that body a request that the Supreme Court be accommodated in the capitol.[26] Three days later, with the Senate concurring, the House resolved "That leave be given to the Commissioners of the City of Washington to use one of the rooms on the first floor of the Capitol for holding the present session of the Supreme Court of the United States."[27]

The room assigned to the Court, and in which it met until 1808, was Committee Room 2, located on the ground floor of the north wing, adjacent to the main staircase. Benjamin Latrobe, the capitol architect, described it as noisy, "a half-finished committee room meanly furnished, and very inconvenient."[28] The Court had no library, no office space, no clerks or secretaries, and the official reporter, Alexander J. Dallas, a distinguished member of the Pennsylvania bar,[29] had resigned rather than make the trip to Washington. Initially there was no bench for the justices, and they sat at individual desks placed on a raised platform. Even these meager quarters were not reserved for the Supreme Court exclusively, but had to be shared with the district and circuit courts of the District of Columbia.[30]

It was in this makeshift courtroom on a cold and rainy February morning that John Marshall took the oath as Chief Justice of the United States.[31] As befitted the Court's low profile, the event was little noted and sparsely attended.[32] Marshall, however, was already asserting leadership subtly. Breaking with tradition, he wore a plain black robe in the republican fashion of the judges of the Virginia court of appeals. The other justices, Cushing, Chase, and Washington,* were attired either in the traditional scarlet and ermine of

---

*Justices Moore and Paterson did not attend the February term.

the King's Bench[33] or their individual academic gowns—the "party-colored robes" of an oppressive judiciary, in the words of Senator Stevens Thomson Mason.[34] By wearing black, Marshall was making a quiet statement. He had seen the Federalists self-destruct electorally through an excess of hubris, and he recognized that the Court was on shaky ground. Why flaunt the colors of the English judiciary when the black robes worn by Pendleton and Wythe would do just as well? The decision had symbolic importance, but the chief justice had another motive. Marshall was a small-r republican and he was uncomfortable with trappings of power. Like Ulysses S. Grant, who wore his general's stars on the uniform of an army private, Marshall preferred simplicity to pomp, understatement to extravagance. Authority followed from ability as much as from rank, and the new chief justice, not unlike the young man of twenty who good-naturedly drilled his Fauquier county neighbors in the manual of arms, was preparing to lead his judicial colleagues onto new ground.

Marshall's first task was to remove the Court from partisan politics and reassert its judicial authority. Black robes might help, but otherwise the February term in 1801 offered little opportunity. One case was routinely disposed of *per curiam*, and a number of lawyers were admitted to practice, but with only four justices in attendance, the bulk of litigation was carried over to the August term.[35] The Court adjourned February 10 without having made a ripple in the national press.

Marshall's last judicial duty that spring was to swear Jefferson in as president. At the new president's request,[36] he continued as acting secretary of state until March 5, when Levi Lincoln replaced him, pending Madison's arrival in Washington.[37] The following day Marshall departed for Richmond and did not return to the capital until the first week of August, when the Court reconvened. This time, setting a pattern that would continue for most of his tenure, Marshall had arranged rooms for his colleagues at Conrad and McMunn's boardinghouse, the same Capitol Hill hostelry where Jefferson had stayed prior to his inauguration. None of the justices brought his wife, and Marshall, perhaps mindful of his happy existence as the eldest of fifteen children, or the military camaraderie at Valley Forge, elected to bring his colleagues together under one roof. It was another subtle move to enhance the identity of the Court, and its importance in explaining the cohesion of the Marshall years can scarcely be overstated.[38] From 1801 on, whenever the Court convened, the justices lived together in the same hotel or boardinghouse, the chief justice benignly presiding over his extended judicial family. Years later, Justice Story described what it meant to eat, sleep, and drink with his colleagues. "My brethren are very interesting men with whom I live in the most frank and unaffected intimacy," he wrote to a friend in Massachusetts.[39] "We are all united as one, with a mutual esteem which makes even the labors of Jurisprudence light. . . . We moot every question as we proceed, and familiar conferences at our lodgings often come to a very quick and, I trust, a very accurate opinion, in a few hours.*[40]

Whether Marshall's decision to reserve rooms for his colleagues in the overcrowded village of Washington was part of a carefully planned strategy or simply a friendly gesture, there is no question that the results were fortuitous for the nation's highest court. The justices' communal existence provided an environment in which Marshall's conviviality could flourish. The qualities of clear thinking and political insight that had made him the natural leader of the delegation to Paris and that had propelled him to the leadership of the Adams Federalists in Congress now were free to work their effect on five potentially fractious associates who had had little experience working together and who were profoundly jealous of their individual prerogatives.[41]

The personal chemistry among the justices was especially important. At sixty-nine, William Cushing was roughly the same age as Marshall's father and had been admitted to the bar in the year of Marshall's birth. Devoted to his wife, who always accompanied him on circuit, he was childless and might well have seen in Marshall the son he never had. A man of stern New England determination, Cushing had faced down armed mobs during Shays's Rebellion to conduct court on schedule. He became chief justice of the Supreme Judicial Court of Massachusetts, was Washington's first appointee to the bench, and was reputedly the last American jurist to wear a wig.[42] His strength lay in the field of constitutional law (he had helped to frame the Massachusetts constitution), and his opinion in *Chisholm v. Georgia* was a strong restatement of nationalist principles.[43] By 1801 Cushing's sharpness had dulled, yet he carried himself with quiet dignity and listened to arguments attentively.[44] His literary tastes were wide-ranging (his wife often read to him), and he was a close friend of John and Abigail Adams, a fact that may also have drawn him to Marshall.

Justice William Paterson of New Jersey, the next senior justice, was ten years older than Marshall and had been the choice of the High Federalists to succeed Ellsworth. Irish by birth, Paterson graduated from Princeton in 1763, studied law under Richard Stockton, and became New Jersey's first attorney general in 1776. As a delegate to the Constitutional Convention in Philadelphia, he authored the famous "New Jersey plan" that called for a unicameral legislature in which each state would enjoy equal representa-

---

*Story wrote to his wife that "the Judges live with perfect harmony. . . . Our intercourse is perfectly familiar and unrestrained, and our social hours when undisturbed with labors of law, are passed in gay and frank conversation, which at once enlivens and instructs." Story to Sarah W. Story, March 5, 1812, in William W. Story, 1 *Life and Letters of Joseph Story* 217–218 (Boston: Little, Brown, 1851).

tion. Paterson's proposal was favored by the small states, but he eventually endorsed the Great Compromise and enthusiastically led the fight for ratification in New Jersey. He was elected to the United States Senate in 1788 and, along with Ellsworth, was one of the principal drafters of the Judiciary Act of 1789.[45] In 1790 he became governor of New Jersey and held that post until 1793 when Washington tapped him for the Court.

Paterson's legal credentials were impressive.[46] As governor, he had initiated a compilation of the statutes in force in New Jersey,[47] and his private practice had been one of the state's most lucrative. Like Cushing, his opinions on the Court tilted strongly in favor of national power,[48] and on circuit he had been one of the most vigorous enforcers of the Sedition Act.* Nevertheless, Paterson had been embarrassed by the efforts of hard-core Federalists to make him chief justice[49] and had written Marshall immediately upon his confirmation to congratulate him. Marshall replied by return post,[50] and although the two men had not been well acquainted, they quickly became close friends. They both possessed superb legal minds and shared a Celtic penchant for strong drink and good talk. "'Laugh where we can' is one of the best maxims to pass through life with ease and comfort," Paterson had once counseled his High Federalist friends,[51] and it was on his recommendation that Marshall was awarded an honorary LL.D. by Princeton in 1802.[52]

Samuel Chase of Maryland was the most outspoken of Marshall's colleagues and would soon become the storm center in the Republican assault on the judiciary. Fourteen years older than the chief justice, he was appointed to the Court by Washington in 1796. His temperament was mercurial, and he was instinctively opposed to doing anything under the slightest duress. He was generally acknowledged to be the most intellectually gifted of the justices, but, like Elbridge Gerry, he was something of a loose cannon. Princeton professor Edward Corwin has characterized him as "a born leader of insurrection."[53] Chase had spearheaded the drive for independence in Maryland and was the only member of the Marshall Court to have signed the Declaration of Independence.[54] As a member of the Continental Congress, he had backed Washington steadfastly against the various intrigues

---

*Paterson presided over the trial of Congressman Matthew Lyon of Vermont, the first person to be convicted under the Sedition Act. Because of his sharp criticism of President Adams, Lyon was accused of attempting "to stir up sedition and bring the President and Government of the United States into contempt." He was found guilty and sentenced by Paterson to four months' imprisonment and a fine of $1,000, an exceedingly high figure at the time. The conviction of a sitting member of Congress was regarded by Jefferson and the Republicans as a serious attack on the Constitution itself, and Paterson's role did not pass unnoticed. Francis Wharton, *State Trials of the United States during the Administrations of Washington and Adams* 333–341 (Philadelphia: Casey and Hart, 1849); Jefferson to John Taylor, November 26, 1798, 4 *The Writings of Thomas Jefferson* 259–261, H.A. Washington, ed. (New York: H. W. Derby, 1861).

mounted against him, a fact that the president undoubtedly recalled when he appointed Chase. On the Court his opinions ranked with those of James Wilson in their grasp of constitutional issues. In *Ware v. Hylton*, the famous British debt case argued by Marshall, Chase, in firm, clear language, established the supremacy of treaties over state laws to the contrary.[55] In *Hylton v. United States*, another 1796 case, he laid down a definition of a "direct" tax that was accepted for the next 100 years.[56] But as a trial judge on circuit, Chase was a holy terror, and when it came to enforcing the Sedition Act, he had no peer. His intemperate, overbearing charges to the jury earned him the reputation of an American Jeffreys,[57] and the sentences he handed out to the government's opponents tended to justify that label.[58] Chase was by no means a reactionary, however. Of all the justices of the Supreme Court in the eighteenth century, he was the only one who had refused to convict under the common law, and his holding to that effect in *United States v. Worrall*[59] was later adopted by the Marshall Court.[60]

Physically, Chase was enormous, well over six feet, with a massive head, broad face, and thick white hair. Massachusetts congressman Manasseh Cutler described him as one of the largest men he had ever seen.[61] And despite his turbulent disposition, he was not without a rough and ready charm that his intimates found appealing. Indeed, it was in the close quarters at Conrad and McMunn's that Chase's human qualities came to be appreciated. Story wrote that Chase

> abounds with good humor [and] amuses you extremely by his anecdotes and pleasantry. His first approach is formidable, but all difficulty vanishes when you once understand him. In person, in manners, in unwieldy strength, in severity of reproof, in real tenderness of heart; and above all in intellect, he is the living, I had almost said the exact, image of Samuel Johnson. . . . I like him hugely.[62]

Bushrod Washington, who, at thirty-eight, was the youngest member of the Court, had been on the bench for two years. He was the son of George Washington's brother Augustine and reputedly the general's favorite nephew.[63] In appearance and temperament, he was the polar opposite of Chase. Short in stature, frail, and boyish in appearance, he had lost the sight of one eye because of excessive reading in poor light. Where Chase was bluff and blustery, Washington was mild and conciliatory. Where Chase was offputting because of his thunder, Washington was difficult to know because of his reticence. As with Chase, however, Washington found respect and camaraderie in the intimacy of Conrad and McMunn's.[64] That, at least, was Story's conclusion, who said of Washington that "his mind was solid, rather than brilliant; sagacious and searching, rather than quick and eager."[65]

No one in public life was closer to Marshall than Bushrod Washington, and in the twenty-nine years they served together on the Court, they differed in opinion on only three occasions.[66] That was not because Washington was under Marshall's tutelage. It was simply that the two men saw matters the same way.[67] Both had studied under Wythe at William and Mary in 1780; both revered the memory of George Washington (after Martha Washington's death in 1802, Bushrod lived at Mt. Vernon); both were delegates to the Virginia ratification convention; and both had served together in the House of Delegates, where they had worked hard for the principles of moderate Federalism. As lawyers in Richmond during the 1780s and 1790s, each had had ample opportunity to appreciate the other's talents and virtues, and their personal lives frequently intertwined. The two men were already collaborating on a proposed biography of Washington and were each coping with the demands of an invalid wife. Both were also concerned about the fate of slaves who had been set free. Bushrod became the first president of the American Colonization Society, which sought to relocate freed blacks in Liberia, and Marshall later became president of its Virginia branch.[68]

The most recently appointed associate justice, Alfred Moore of North Carolina, was, at forty-five, the same age as Marshall. Witty, animated, and caustic in debate, he was one of the founders of the University of North Carolina and was widely regarded as the most able lawyer in North Carolina at the time of his appointment.[69] Like Marshall, Moore had served as a junior officer in the Revolutionary War and shared an attachment to moderate Federalism. In physical appearance, he was even smaller than Bushrod, standing only four feet five inches tall and weighing between eighty and ninety pounds. Like the elfin Gerry, his head was large for his body, and he was fine featured and dark-eyed.[70] Of the five original associate justices of the Marshall Court, he was the most even-tempered and the easiest to get along with.

These were Marshall's compatriots, the members of his judicial family: the elderly Cushing, the canny Paterson, the headstrong Chase, the reticent Bushrod, and the tiny Alfred Moore. They gathered slowly that August. Moore was the first to arrive, the beneficiary of seasonal winds that had facilitated his waterborne journey from Buchoi, his tobacco and rice plantation in Brunswick, the southernmost county in North Carolina. By Tuesday, August 4, a quorum was present, and the Court convened in its makeshift quarters, the oppressive heat of a Washington summer moderated only slightly by the thick masonry walls of the new capitol. Following Marshall's lead, the justices were clad in black, a symbolic peace offering to the Republican ascendancy.[71]

Marshall's courtroom appearance was not imposing. William Wirt, who had known Marshall for years, wrote shortly after his appointment that "the

Chief Justice of the United States is tall, meager, emaciated; his muscles relaxed, and his joints so loosely connected, as not only to disqualify him for any vigorous exertion of the body, but to destroy everything like elegance and harmony in his air and movements."[72] Joseph Story, as a young lawyer pleading his first case before the Court,[73] described Marshall in similar terms:

> Marshall is of a tall, slender figure, not graceful or imposing, but erect and steady. His hair is black, his eyes small and twinkling, his forehead rather low. . . . His manners are plain yet dignified; and an unaffected modesty diffuses itself through all his actions. His dress is very simple, yet neat; his language chaste but hardly elegant. . . . In conversation he is quite familiar. . . . His thoughts are always clear and ingenious, sometimes striking . . . he possesses great subtilty [*sic*] of mind, but it is only occasionally exhibited. I love his laugh— it is too hearty for an intriguer—and his good temper and unwearied patience are equally agreeable on the bench and in the study. His genius is, in my opinion, vigorous and powerful, less rapid than discriminating, and less vivid than uniform in its light. He examines the intricacies of a subject with calm and persevering circumspection, and unravels the mysteries with irresistible acuteness.[74]

The August term commenced with the case of *Talbot v. Seeman*, a major prize case arising out of the quasi-war with France.[75] In *Talbot*, the constitutional status of the quasi-war was once again called into question. The *American Daily Advertiser* called it "A cause of very great importance both on account of the legal principles applicable to neutral shipping and the magnitude of the pecuniary interest involved in the event, being no less than $180,000."[76] It was also a case that divided sharply along partisan lines, the Federalists supporting the rights of the American captor, the Republicans against. Two prominent Federalist lawyers, Congressman James A. Bayard of Delaware and Jared Ingersoll of Philadelphia, represented the appellant, Captain Silas Talbot, commander of the famous American frigate *Constitution* ("Old Ironsides").[77] Two equally prominent Republicans, John T. Mason of Maryland[78] and Alexander Dallas, appeared for the respondent.

The case involved the *Constitution*'s capture of the *Amelia*, an armed merchant vessel owned by a Hamburg businessman, Hans Seeman.* In 1799 the *Amelia*, bound from Calcutta to Hamburg with a load of valuable

---

*The *Amelia* mounted eight carriage guns, which, given the threat of pirates, was standard for merchantmen at that time. Because the Hanseatic city of Hamburg was neutral in the war between Britain and France, the *Amelia* was considered a neutral ship.

cargo, had been seized on the high seas by the French corvette *La Diligente*. Refitted with a prize crew, it was under sail to the French West Indies for condemnation when it was intercepted by the *Constitution* and redirected to New York for adjudication. Captain Talbot, on behalf of himself and his crew, claimed half the value of the vessel for rescuing it from the French. Seeman insisted that the ship should be returned to him without paying salvage since it was a neutral vessel and hence in no danger from French condemnation proceedings. The U.S. district court ruled in favor of Talbot, but when the matter was appealed, Justice Washington, sitting on circuit, reversed the ruling. Washington held that under international law the *Amelia* was not a lawful prize. Accordingly, Captain Talbot had rendered no service to its owners in recovering it.[79] As befitted the high drama attached to the case, the appeal before Washington had been argued by Alexander Hamilton on behalf of Captain Talbot, while his nemesis, Aaron Burr, appeared for Seeman.

The argument before the Supreme Court lasted four days. Bayard and Ingersoll maintained that because the *Amelia* was armed and flying French colors, Captain Talbot was justified in seizing her; that in so doing he had saved the ship from inevitable condemnation by a French admiralty court; and that he was entitled to compensation for his efforts. But when Bayard sought to read into the record President Adams's interpretation of the relevant congressional legislation that would have supported Talbot's action, the justices objected. Paterson said that statutory interpretation was a task for the Court and that the president's views were not binding.[80] Chase and Moore agreed. Marshall said, "I have no objection to hearing them, but they will have no influence on my opinion."[81] Ultimately, the Court refused to hear what Adams had said.[82]

When it came time for Dallas and Mason to respond, they emphasized that the *Amelia* was a neutral ship and that it was unlikely that she would have been condemned by French courts. The United States and France were not at war, they argued, and in seizing the ship, Captain Talbot had gone far beyond what Congress had authorized. They said that Justice Washington's holding on circuit was correct and that it should be affirmed.[83]

Marshall and his colleagues wrestled with the case for almost a week. In the evenings at Conrad and McMunn's, at mealtimes, and over the weekend, the justices discussed the arguments that had been presented. Congress was not in session, Jefferson and Madison were on holiday, and what little social life there was in the scraggly village of Washington revolved around the boardinghouse.[84] By Sunday evening the justices had reached a consensus. It was now a matter of announcing it. *Talbot v. Seeman* is inordinately important in the history of American jurisprudence because it is the first case in which the justices of the Supreme Court labeled their decision the "Opinion of the Court." Marshall, amiable, and considerate as always, not only brought his boardinghous into a unanimous agreement concerning the law but also conv that the Court should speak with one voice. That style had been by Edmund Pendleton on the Virginia court of appeals,[85] and Ma phasized its effectiveness to his colleagues. If a complex, politically charged case like *Talbot* could be resolved with a single opinion, not only would the holding enjoy greater legitimacy, but the identity of the Supreme Court as a nation's highest tribunal would become manifest and its prestige would be enhanced enormously.

Like Pendleton, Marshall believed that the Court should speak through its chief justice. That would add to the Court's aura of authority. Once again his colleagues concurred. During the next four years, the Marshall Court rendered forty-six written decisions, all of which were unanimous. Marshall participated in forty-two, and in each of those he announced the opinion of the Court.* Whether he circulated his drafts among his colleagues is unknown since no annotated manuscripts from that period have survived.[86] But whether he did or not, it is certain, given the independence of strong-willed colleagues like Chase and Paterson, that his opinions reflected the Court's consensus.[87]

In *Talbot*, it seems obvious that Marshall was as much concerned about the cohesion of the Court as he was about the holding. The process of achieving unanimity and speaking with one voice was as important to him as the outcome, and his opinion judiciously balanced the claims of all the parties concerned. As chief justice, Marshall had a rare knack for expressing compromise with clarity, and *Talbot v. Seeman* is an example of that dexterity. The issue hinged on whether *Constitution*'s taking of the *Amelia* was lawful, which in turn depended on the nature of relations between France and the United States in 1799. Marshall began the Court's opinion with a bow to Congress. In a passage often quoted, he stated that the nation's war powers belonged exclusively to the legislature: "The whole powers of war being, by the Constitution of the United States, vested in Congress, the Acts of that body can alone be resorted to as our guides in this enquiry."[88] Since the Constitution specifies that the president is the commander in chief, Marshall's observation was a slight overstatement. Nevertheless, from a political

---

*In four cases, *Stuart v. Laird*, 1 Cranch 299 (1803), *Ogden v. Blackledge*, 2 Cranch 272 (1804), *Lambert's Lessee v. Paine*, 3 Cranch 95 (1805), and *Marine Insurance Co. v. Wilson*, 3 Cranch 187 (1805), Marshall recused himself. He had tried *Stuart v. Laird* and *Ogden v. Blackledge* on circuit; in *Lambert's Lessee* he had represented one of the parties; and in *Marine Insurance* he had a remote financial interest. In both *Laird* and *Blackledge*, the Court's decision was announced by the senior justice present: Paterson in *Laird*, Cushing in *Blackledge*. In *Lambert* and *Marine Insurance*, the justices announced their opinions *seriatim*.

standpoint, it did not hurt for a Federalist Court to acknowledge Congress's preeminence.

After a lengthy survey of the relevant legislation, Marshall held that Congress had authorized the taking of any French ship that might threaten American commerce. "The *Amelia* was an armed vessel commanded and manned by Frenchmen. . . . It is not then to be questioned, but that there was probable cause to bring her in for adjudication."[89] In arriving at that conclusion, Marshall had to extrapolate considerably. There were no statutes on point, and he relied on what he called "the real intent of Congress."[90] This aspect of the decision represented an important breakthrough for the Court insofar as it was asserting its right to determine what Congress meant when the laws were silent.

Having held the seizure to be lawful, Marshall turned to the question of whether Captain Talbot was entitled to salvage. That depended on whether he had rendered a service to Seeman. Marshall said that a neutral vessel normally is in no danger of condemnation. However, the laws of France authorized the seizure of vessels laden with products from English colonies.[91] Since the *Amelia* was bringing goods from India, then part of the British empire, her condemnation by a French court of admiralty was "extremely probable."[92] By recapturing her, Captain Talbot had rendered "an essential service, and the Court is therefore of the opinion that the re-captor is entitled to salvage."[93]

Marshall did not restore the district court judgment, however, which had awarded half the value of the vessel. That would have amounted to a clear-cut victory for Captain Talbot. The Federalists would have rejoiced, and the Republicans would have taken it as another illustration of the bias of the federal judiciary. Instead, he once again went beyond the record to apply a standard of reasonableness. The *Amelia* was, after all, a neutral vessel, and "according to the law of nations, a neutral is generally to be restored without salvage."[94] Marshall said that "considering the circumstances . . . one-sixth appears to be a reasonable allowance."[95] The Court thus allowed Talbot to collect salvage for rescuing the *Amelia*, but cut his award by two-thirds. There was no statutory basis for such a judgment; the Court simply adopted a figure that seemed appropriate.

Marshall was not finished. To ease the impact of the holding for Seeman, the Court allowed him to deduct his costs from the money that was due Talbot.[96] That too was not customary, since a losing litigant is rarely awarded costs. Finally, as a gesture to Bushrod, Marshall said that his holding on circuit reversing the district court had been correct and that it was incorrect only in not allowing salvage. Washington had been reversed, but it had been done as gently as possible.[97]

The decision in *Talbot v. Seeman* is a textbook example of navigating through a minefield. Determined to remove the Court from partisan politics, Marshall steered adroitly between the Federalists' belief in the quasi-war and the Republicans' doubts about its legitimacy. Congress received a big bouquet concerning its war powers, and the military action undertaken by the *Constitution* was vindicated. Captain Talbot and his crew were awarded salvage, but the amount of that award, after deducting costs, was not appreciable.* In principle, the Federalist view of the quasi-war was sustained, but in practice, the Republicans could not complain about the judgment. The *Aurora* commended Marshall for examining "at length the arguments urged on each side." The *National Intelligencer,* the organ of Jefferson's party in Washington, reprinted the entire text of the decision, explaining to readers its importance.[98]

Talbot v. Seeman illustrated Marshall's ability to find a middle ground. Under his low-key leadership, his colleagues, previously accustomed to expressing their individual views in *seriatim* opinions, worked through the complex issues together to reach a unanimous decision, a decision that they allowed Marshall to report. This seminal holding set a pattern that was followed not only by the Marshall Court but in virtually every Supreme Court decision since. The "Opinion of the Court" is a unique American innovation, and it can be traced to Marshall in *Talbot.*

When the Court adjourned, Marshall could reflect on a useful beginning. The Court had avoided taking sides in the quasi-war, it had explicitly recognized that the war powers belonged to Congress, and it had established its broad authority to interpret what Congress intended. Marshall had pulled the Court together. It had risen above partisanship to speak with one voice, and its collective identity had been established. The road ahead would be perilous, but Marshall and his colleagues had proved that they could work together. Judicial authority was intact.

---

*This was not the first time that Marshall and Talbot had crossed paths. As secretary of state, Marshall had been confronted with Talbot's seizure of a French privateer, the *Sandwich*, in the Spanish port of Puerto Plata, on the island of Santo Domingo. The Spanish minister to the United States protested the violation of Spain's territorial waters by the *Constitution* and demanded that the *Sandwich* be released. Marshall agreed that the capture was unauthorized and, in Adams's name, ordered Captain Talbot to return the vessel "to the minister of his Catholic Majesty." Marshall to Adams, July 26, 1800, 4 *Marshall Papers* 190. Also see Carlos Martinez de Yrujo to Marshall, July 7, 1800, *ibid.* 178–180.

Talbot, or his crew, apparently balked at returning the *Sandwich*, at which point Marshall dug in his heels. "If the executive of the United States cannot restore a vessel captured by a national ship, in violation of the law of nations, it is easy to perceive how much inconvenience may result," he wrote to Adams. Marshall recommended that they obtain a judgment in U.S. district court, Adams agreed, and in October 1800 the court ruled that Captain Talbot had acted improperly and ordered him to surrender the vessel. Marshall to Adams, September 6, 1800, *ibid.* 260–261; Carlos Martinez de Yrujo to Marshall, October 15, 1800, *ibid.* 327.

12

The Gathering Storm

IN 1801 the December term of the Court coincided with the initial session of the Seventh Congress. For the first time in the nation's history, the Republicans controlled both the House and the Senate.[1] It had been almost a year since the watershed elections of 1800, and Jefferson's followers had waited impatiently to correct what they saw as the country's wrong turnings. On Monday, December 7, with Congress convening on the upper floors of the capitol, the Supreme Court, still in drab Committee Room 2, met one floor below. Only Justices Cushing and Paterson were on hand, and the Court immediately adjourned for the day.

The next day the Court got down to business. All of the justices except Alfred Moore were present, and there were half a dozen cases on the docket. Marshall called the Court to order, announced its intention to hear argument in another prize case arising from the quasi-war, *United States v. Schooner Peggy*,[2] and adjourned the proceedings shortly after eleven so that the justices could listen to Jefferson's state of the union message.[3] This was the president's first opportunity since his inauguration to announce his agenda. Breaking with tradition, Jefferson did not appear before Congress as Washington and Adams had done, but sent a written message through his secretary, Meriwether Lewis.[4] Marshall, as chief justice, had donned a black robe to denote his republicanism; Jefferson, not to be outdone, was understating the president's authority by departing from the speech-from-the-throne style of delivery of his Federalist predecessors.[5]

Jefferson avoided stridency, but his message lacked the eloquence of his inaugural address. He spoke of the need to cut taxes, to reduce the size of the national government, and to scale back the military. As Marshall had anticipated, the states rights message was front and center.[6] Jefferson made reference to the judiciary, a continuing sore spot for the Republicans, but only in passing: "The judiciary system of the United States, *and especially that portion of it recently erected*, will of course present itself to the contemplation of Congress. . . ."[7] Jefferson's allusion was to the Judiciary Act of 1801, passed during the closing days of Adams's term. His comment was so mild, however, that it triggered little alarm.[8] Irreconcilables like Fisher Ames smelled a rat,[9] and Hamilton wrote that Jefferson's comment was "the symptom of a pigmy mind,"[10] but moderate Federalists were reassured. John Quincy Adams wrote shortly afterward that a great tranquility prevailed throughout the country and that "the violence of party spirit has very much subsided."[11]

Marshall and his colleagues evidenced little concern about Jefferson's remarks and, for the remainder of the week, listened to argument in *Schooner Peggy*. Like *Talbot v. Seeman*, the case pitted Federalists against Republicans, and it involved President Jefferson directly. The *Peggy* was an armed French merchant vessel captured during the quasi-war. It was condemned as a prize by the United States circuit court in Connecticut on September 23, 1800, and ordered sold. Seven days later, however, the Convention of Môrtefontaine was signed in Paris by Oliver Ellsworth.[12] Article 4 of the convention provided that vessels that had been captured but "not yet definitively condemned" should be restored to their original owners. Since the circuit court judgment had not been executed when the convention was signed, Jefferson believed the *Peggy* fell under the terms of Article 4. Shortly after assuming office, he directed the United States attorney for Connecticut, Pierrepont Edwards, to have the proceeds from the ship's sale paid over to its French owners. The court clerk holding the money refused to comply, and Justice Cushing sustained him, ruling that the president's order was invalid. Jefferson saw the decision as another example of political interference by Federalist judges.[13]

The case involved the application of the Convention of Môrtefontaine. It was complicated by the fact that the convention had not been officially promulgated by the president and, therefore, in a technical sense was not part of the supreme law of the land.* Marshall, whose sympathies lay com-

---

*On February 18, 1801, the Convention of Môrtefontaine was ratified by President Adams, with the advice and consent of the Senate, with the exception of Article 2, pertaining to the postponement of American shipping claims against France, to which the Senate had objected. On July 31, 1801, Napoleon accepted the Senate's reservation, noting that France interpreted it to mean that the United States was waiving future claims to indemnity. Jefferson considered that Napoleon's modification required renewed Senate approval but had not resubmitted the convention when *United States v. Schooner Peggy* came before the Court.

pletely with Jefferson in this matter, may have been the first to recognize the problem. He allowed the argument to proceed through the week of December 7–12, continued it on Monday, December 14, and again on Thursday, December 17.[14] In the meantime, Jefferson transmitted the convention to the Senate for approval.[15] The Senate gave its advice and consent by the required two-thirds majority on December 19,[16] and Jefferson promulgated the convention the morning of December 21.[17] Immediately thereafter, Marshall delivered the opinion of the Court.[18]

Just as in the aftermath of the XYZ affair, when Marshall and Jefferson had tacitly worked together to avert a war with France,[19] so too did they cooperate in the case of *United States v. Schooner Peggy*. If Marshall had wanted to embarrass Jefferson, or if he had shared the partisan Federalist view of the issue, he would not have withheld the Court's decision until the president was able to put the Convention of Môrtefontaine into effect. Once the convention was ratified, a unanimous Court, speaking through the chief justice, upheld Jefferson's interpretation of the convention with a ringing restatement of the treaty power. Marshall said that "Where a treaty is the law of the land, and as such affects the rights of parties litigating in court, that treaty as much binds those rights . . . as an act of congress." He noted that in private cases between individual litigants, a court "ought to struggle hard" to avoid an interpretation that would affect the rights of the parties.

> But in great national concerns where individual rights, acquired by war, are sacrificed for national purposes, the contract, making the sacrifice, ought always to receive a construction conforming to its manifest import; *and if the nation has given up the vested rights of its citizens, it is not for the court, but for the government, to consider whether it be a case proper for compensation.*[20]

For Marshall, the case of the *Schooner Peggy* gave the Court an opportunity to assert the authority of the president and Congress to conduct the country's foreign affairs. It also provided an opportunity to distinguish between legal issues, which were properly justiciable before the Court, and overriding international obligations, which were not. The decision reflected a studied restraint and manifested Marshall's continuing determination to distance the Court from partisan politics. For Jefferson, the Court's decision was a vindication of his desire to repair relations with France. It was also a potential olive branch from the judiciary.

The next case on the docket was *Wilson v. Mason*, an important case involving diversity jurisdiction that allowed Marshall to assert the Supreme Court's appellate authority despite state laws to the contrary.[21] The issue involved contested land titles in Kentucky between George Wilson, a citizen of that state, and the Virginia heirs of George Mason.[22] According to a compact the two states had signed in 1794, there could be no appeal from a trial court's decision in land title cases.[23] The original suit was brought in the United States district court in Kentucky, which in 1800 ruled in favor of the Mason claim. Wilson appealed that judgment to the Supreme Court, as he was permitted to do under federal legislation.[24] The question for the Court was whether the appeal could be maintained, given the compact between Virginia and Kentucky prohibiting such an action.

Wilson v. Mason was Marshall's first constitutional case. It is important because it illustrates his determination to uphold national authority. Speaking once again for a unanimous Court, Marshall said:

> The Constitution of the United States, to which the parties to this compact had assented, gave jurisdiction to the federal courts in controversies between citizens of different states. The same Constitution vested in this court an appellate jurisdiction in all cases where original jurisdiction was given to the inferior courts, with only "such exceptions" and "under such regulations as the Congress shall make."[25]

Marshall noted that Congress, "in pursuance of the Constitution," had passed legislation that gave the Supreme Court appellate jurisdiction in cases such as this, and that legislation was controlling. By contrast, he said that if the compact between Virginia and Kentucky were permitted to govern the case, it would mean that "the legislatures of any two states might, by agreement between themselves, annul the Constitution of the United States."[26] The jurisdictional issue disposed of, the Court went on to reverse the holding of the lower court and to find in favor of Wilson.[27]

Despite the best efforts of Marshall and Jefferson to reduce partisan tension, a new storm was brewing on the horizon. On Wednesday, December 16, 1801, the day after the decision in *Wilson v. Mason* was announced, Charles Lee, who had been attorney general under Washington and Adams, appeared before the Court to request an order directing Secretary of State Madison to show cause why a writ of *mandamus** should not be issued com-

---

*A writ of *mandamus* is a judicial command instructing an officer of the government to perform a particular act. It is an ancient common law writ described by Blackstone as "a command issuing in the king's name, from the court of King's Bench, and directed to any person, corporation, or inferior court . . . within the king's dominions, requiring them to do some particular thing therein specified, which appertains to their office and duty, and which the court of King's Bench had previously determined, or at least supposes to be consonant to right and justice." William Blackstone, 3 *Commentaries on the Laws of England* 110 (Oxford: Clarendon Press, 1765).

Section 13 of the Judiciary Act of 1789 authorized the Supreme Court "to issue . . . writs of *mandamus* in cases warranted by the principles and usages of law, to any courts appointed, or persons holding office, under the authority of the United States." 1 *United States Statutes at Large* 81.

manding Madison to deliver certain justice of the peace commissions for the District of Columbia.[28] Lee was one of the half-dozen lawyers who argued regularly before the Court, and his appearance, in itself, was not out of the ordinary. But his seemingly routine request launched litigation in what has been called the mother of constitutional landmarks, *Marbury v. Madison.*[29]

The facts of this famous case are well known. A week before Jefferson took office, the lame-duck Federalist Congress enacted legislation authorizing the president to appoint a number of justices of the peace in the nation's capital.[30] On March 2, 1801, two days before his term expired, President Adams nominated forty-two persons for that office. The nominees were duly confirmed by the Senate on March 3, shortly before adjournment.[31] Adams immediately signed the commissions, and Marshall, as secretary of state, affixed the Great Seal of the United States.[32] In the last-minute rush of the transition, however, the commissions were not delivered.[33] When Jefferson assumed office, he found them lying on a table in the State Department and instructed that they not be sent out.[34] Jefferson was greatly vexed by Adams's so-called midnight appointments,[35] but these particular ones were minor, and his response was measured. The act authorizing the justices of the peace permitted the president to determine the number of appointments, and Jefferson, intent on economy, decided merely to reduce the number by twelve.[36] The following day he gave recess appointments to thirty persons, including twenty-five of those originally named by Adams, plus five of his own choosing.[37] Among those not reappointed was William Marbury, a prominent Federalist businessman in Georgetown.[38] The episode attracted little attention at the time,[39] although the *National Intelligencer* praised Jefferson's generosity in reappointing so many of Adams's choices.[40]

It was now nine months later when Lee appeared before the court to request a writ of *mandamus* compelling Madison to give Marbury his undelivered commission.[41] When Lee explained the purpose of the order, Marshall asked Attorney General Levi Lincoln, who was present in Court, whether he had anything to offer. Lincoln replied that he had no instructions on the subject. He said Mr. Madison had just received notice of Lee's request and had not had time to consider it. Lincoln told Marshall he would "leave the proceedings under the discretion of the Court."[42] There is no indication, either in the Court minutes or in newspaper reports, that Lincoln expressed any concern over the request. Marshall consulted his colleagues on the bench and found that only Chase was prepared to rule at that time. He then said that the Court would take the question under advisement. Two days later, after an opportunity to review the matter, Marshall announced the Court's decision to entertain the motion and issued a preliminary order to Secretary of State Madison requesting him to show cause why a writ of *man-*

damus should not be granted. The chief justice set the fourth day of the next term of Court, scheduled for June 1802, to hear argument.[43]

Thus far, the case had all the earmarks of a routine judicial proceeding. A writ, authorized by statute, had been requested, and the Court, conforming to normal practice, had requested the person against whom the order was directed to respond with an explanation as to why it should not be granted. This was the standard adversarial process by which courts conducted their business. The only unusual feature of the case was that the order was directed to the secretary of state. Marshall had occupied that position, and if there had been anything irregular, he would certainly have been aware of it. There is absolutely no evidence that the chief justice sought to provoke a confrontation with Jefferson or the administration.[44] There is also no indication that either Jefferson or Madison initially took umbrage at the request. Both men were avid letter writers, and their correspondence from the period contains no reference to the matter. James Monroe, who was governor of Virginia at the time and who regularly wrote to Jefferson warning of impending Federalist plots, also made no mention of the case in his correspondence.[45] Extremists in both parties would eventually escalate the issue, but in December 1801 Marshall and Jefferson were still trying to moderate the partisanship that had engulfed the nation.[46] In fact, three days after granting Lee's request, the Court handed down its decision in *United States v. Schooner Peggy*, a decision that could scarcely be described as hostile to the administration.[47]

Regardless of Marshall's intentions, a collision between the Court and the administration may have been unavoidable. The problem was not Marbury's writ, but the Judiciary Act of 1801,[48] which continued to rankle Jefferson's supporters. In his message to Congress, the president had obliquely recommended its review. But there was no call for immediate action. The storm broke on January 6, 1802, when Senator John Breckinridge of Kentucky moved the act's repeal. The motion was seconded by Stevens Thomson Mason of Virginia, the Senate majority leader. Both men had Jefferson's confidence,* and it has often been assumed that they were acting at the president's behest.[49] This may or may not have been the case. Jefferson was certainly committed to repealing the judiciary law,[50] but whether he was prepared to move against it at the beginning of the session is open to doubt. Such an action would rekindle partisan passions and jeopardize the widespread popularity the Republican party had acquired since assuming office.[51] Indeed, Jefferson's most distinguished biographer has suggested that

---

*Breckinridge had been Jefferson's intermediary in the introduction of the Kentucky Resolutions in 1798, and Mason, a close personal friend, was one of the president's most reliable supporters in his home state. Dumas Malone, *Jefferson and the Ordeal of Liberty* 401–402, 405 (Boston: Little, Brown, 1962).

Breckinridge and Thomson may have been self-starters in moving repeal: partisan zealots who left the president no alternative.[52]

The issue of timing is more important than it may seem. By acting precipitously, Breckinridge and Mason unleashed a storm of opposition. A calibrated revision of the offending legislation became impossible, and the desirable features of the act were jettisoned along with its overtly partisan provisions. In addition, ordinary judicial processes, like the Court's order to Madison, came to be perceived in a different light, and the political atmosphere in the United States was poisoned for almost a decade.

Republican objections to the Judiciary Act of 1801 were well founded. Designed to correct long-recognized deficiencies in the judicial system created by the Founding Fathers, the act was rammed through Congress at the last moment by the outgoing Federalists. That gave the act an unmistakably partisan flavor, and the manner in which it was initially administered by President Adams tainted it further. But the act itself was not without merit,[53] and in a cooler political climate—arguably, the one that Jefferson and Marshall were striving to create—the political overgrowth might have been pruned without damaging the measure's root structure.

The act enlarged the jurisdiction of the federal courts to the full extent provided by the Constitution[54] and made the courts more accessible to individual litigants.[55] The old appellate system, in which justices of the Supreme Court rode circuit, was replaced with a new tier of sixteen circuit judges, and provisions were made for a reorganization of the district courts. Because of the lessened workload, the number of Supreme Court justices would be reduced from six to five when the next vacancy occurred.[56]

These provisions did not spring forth suddenly in the aftermath of the Republican victory in 1800 but had been the subject of debate virtually since the creation of the federal judiciary in 1789.[57] The two most controversial items were the expansion of federal court jurisdiction and the addition of sixteen circuit judges. These struck at the core of the continuing conflict between Republicans and Federalists. As in 1789, the conflict reflected fundamental economic differences: Creditors, absentee landowners, and the commercial establishment believed their interests would be better protected by federal authority, while most farmers, artisans, and the settlers of new lands preferred the state courts where judges were elected and the political power of local residents had a correspondingly greater impact.

Few issues were more politically charged than the question of land titles, which were in great confusion and the subject of constant litigation. The situation was particularly acute in Georgia and Kentucky, where there was widespread fear that the federal courts would support the prior claims of nonresident land companies over the title deeds of recent settlers.[58] Marshall had grappled with that issue in *Wilson v. Mason*[59] and had upheld the rights of local Kentuckians against out-of-state claimants. In so doing, however, he had established the appellate authority of the Supreme Court as the ultimate arbiter of land title cases involving nonresident litigants. That was a red flag to legislators from Georgia and Kentucky, whose constituents clamored for repeal of the 1801 Act. As Thomas Todd, then a judge on the Kentucky court of appeals, wrote to John Breckinridge,

> I apprehend great danger and mischief from the [Federal] Court in this State; a great part of the lands here are claimed by non-residents, numberless disputes will arise between them and our own citizens, they will bring their suits in the Federal Court even when they have but little prospect of success here, *with a determination to appeal to the Supreme Court;* the distance is so great, the scarcity of money and [the] indigent circumstances of many of our citizens such that they will not be able to follow the appeal, they must either give up their lands or be forced into an ungenerous and unjust compromise.[60]

As a result of the expansion of federal court jurisdiction, Republicans perceived the 1801 Judiciary Act as a partisan measure. This impression was only deepened by Adams's midnight appointment of sixteen leading Federalists to the judgeships on the newly created circuit courts. Although Adams did not appoint any extremists to the bench,[61] there was not one Republican judge in the entire federal judiciary when Jefferson took office.* "The Federalists have retired into the judiciary as a stronghold, and from that battery all the works of republicanism are to be beaten down and erased," the new president told John Dickinson.[62] Congressman William Branch Giles of Virginia, far more radical than Jefferson, wrote that "the revolution is incomplete so long as the judiciary is in possession of the enemy."[63] For Giles the answer was clear: "an absolute repeal of the whole judicial system, terminating the present offices . . . and restraining to the proper constitutional extent the jurisdiction of the courts."[64]

As chief justice, Marshall had done his utmost to deflect Republican

---

*Marshall's influence in the appointment of the midnight judges is unclear. At Adams's request he had continued as secretary of state, but there is no correspondence between the two concerning the judgeships. Professor Kathryn Turner, whose law journal article "The Midnight Judges" has stood the test of time, writes that "The degree of [Marshall's] influence . . . cannot be established. It may have been more substantial than the evidence indicates or it may have been relatively small. In the close association which the two men shared during these weeks, discussion of those under consideration for the circuit court positions *may* have taken place; together they *may* have arrived at some decisions. Adams, in a state of mind wherein hurt, anger, and humiliation appear to have been mixed in equal portions at the trying end of his administration, and bereft of the comforting presence and counsel of his wife, may well have relied on the advice of the highly esteemed and trusted Marshall. There is, however, no way of knowing." 109 *University of Pennsylvania Law Review* 494, 496 (1961). Turner's emphasis.

criticism, and with the December term complete, he was well on his way to establishing the Supreme Court as a coherent voice in national affairs. The justices spoke with newfound unanimity; the edge of partisanship had been dulled; and the collective identity of the Court as the nation's highest tribunal had become increasingly manifest. But the Republican onslaught could no longer be diverted. Years of resentment against what many perceived as an oppressive Federalist judiciary had surged forward and now expressed itself in a clamor to repeal the 1801 Judiciary Act. Marshall was back in Richmond when Breckinridge introduced his motion in the Senate, and there is no evidence that he played any role in the debate that followed. Indeed, because of his judicial position, any intervention by Marshall would have been singularly inappropriate. He undoubtedly followed the discussion in the press, but if he wrote or received any letters on the subject, that correspondence has been lost.[65]

Few debates in congressional history have been as heated as the debate over the repeal of the judiciary law. The Senate devoted the entire month of January to the issue, considering no other legislation during this period. The Republicans, ably led by Breckinridge and Mason, concentrated their attack on the expansion of federal jurisdiction and the partisan nature of Adams's appointments. Litigation over land titles figured prominently in the debate,[66] as did the added cost of the new circuit judges. All the Republican speakers defended Congress's right to repeal the measure, but contrary to popular belief, the Supreme Court's order to Madison to show cause in the *Marbury* case was mentioned only in passing and was in no way central to the debate.[67] The Federalists, who were led with equal effectiveness by Gouverneur Morris, maintained that the newly appointed circuit judges were protected by the Constitution, that their continued tenure was essential for an independent judiciary, and that the only way they could be removed was by impeachment.

The nation's press immediately took sides in the debate, and the political temperature rose accordingly. In the Senate, the battle was closely fought. The bill to repeal the Act of 1801 passed its second reading with the tie-breaking vote of Vice President Aaron Burr. On the third reading, however, Burr defected and voted with the Federalists to refer the bill to committee.* That decision was reversed two days later with the arrival of a Republican absentee who had not voted previously. Finally, on February 3, 1802, the bill received final reading and passed by one vote, 16–15.[68]

In the House, where the Republican majority was larger, the debate was

---

*The Republicans never forgave Burr for his betrayal, and to this day the vice president's motives for changing his vote have never been adequately explained. See Dumas Malone, *Jefferson the President: The First Term* 124–125 (Boston: Little, Brown, 1970).

sharper as both sides became increasingly intemperate. Virginia's hot-tempered radical, William Branch Giles, led the Republican forces and cast the struggle as one between despotism and democracy. Giles built an extravagant case against judicial tyranny, but when he attacked the Marshall Court for its show-cause order to Madison,[69] Representative James A. Bayard of Delaware, the House minority leader, quickly called him to task. A request to show cause was merely a preliminary proceeding, Bayard reminded Giles, and involved no implication that a writ of *mandamus* would be issued, or that the Court would assume jurisdiction.[70]

The debate in the House continued through the month of February, and on March 3 the Republican leaders put the measure to a vote. By 59–32, the House of Representatives supported the bill, and the Judiciary Act of 1801 was repealed.[71] In striking the act from the books, Congress asserted its constitutional authority to determine the organization of the federal courts.[72] Nevertheless, the Federalists continued to argue with great vehemence that in so doing, Congress had infringed upon two equally pertinent provisions of the Constitution: the guarantee that "Judges . . . shall hold their Offices during good Behavior," and the stipulation that their salaries "shall not be diminished" while in office.[73] As a result, Alexander Hamilton suggested to Bayard that the repeal be tested before the Supreme Court "as soon as possible."[74] Indeed, a fear that the issue would come before the Court propelled the Republican majority in Congress to quickly pass substitute legislation reorganizing the judiciary, requiring the justices to ride circuit once more, abolishing the June and December terms of the Court (created by the Act of 1801), and restoring the old February term but not the August term. That meant that the Supreme Court would not meet again until February 1803, a gap of fourteen months.*[75] This last action, in particular, struck a raw nerve among the Federalists. "Are the gentlemen afraid of the judges?" asked Bayard. "Are they afraid that they will pronounce the repealing law void?"[76]

Marshall took the repeal calmly, and he appears to have considered Congress's action inevitable. When Oliver Wolcott sent him a copy of the new judiciary act that the Republicans had proposed, he expressed no concern. In fact, he told Wolcott that there were "some defects in the system which I presume will be remedied as they involve no party or political questions, but

---

*The provision that the Supreme Court convene every February for a term of four weeks, rather than hold two separate two-week terms, was designed to minimize the justices' travel requirements. The journey to Washington from New England (in the case of Cushing) or from lower North Carolina (in the case of Moore) was an arduous one. The downside of the provision was the fourteen-month gap from December 1801 until February 1803. Except for that, there is no evidence that the justices were unhappy with the change. For the text of the bill then pending, see 11 *Annals of Congress* 1332–1342.

relate only to the mode of carrying causes from the circuit to the supreme court."* Marshall told Wolcott that he regretted the cancelation of the June term of the Court, "but I have no doubt that the immediate operation of the bill will be insisted on."[77]

The following day, April 6, 1802, he wrote to Justice Paterson about the bill then pending. "You have I doubt not seen that arrangement of our future duties as marked out in the bill lately reported to the Senate. They are less burdensome than heretofore, or than I expected."[78] Marshall was unconcerned about Congress's repeal of the Act of 1801, but he told Paterson that he was troubled by the provision that the justices be required to sit on circuit. He considered that a conflict of duty since the justices would be trying cases that they might later hear on appeal. Marshall said that if the provision had been a new one, he would have been unwilling to take up circuit duties without consulting his colleagues. In light of the former practice of the justices to ride circuit, however, "I consider it as decided and that whatever my own scruples may be I am bound by the decision."[79]

The week afterward, Marshall wrote a lengthy letter to James Bayard about some unsettled accounts from his tenure as secretary of state. He made no mention of the bill before Congress but told Bayard he would be in Washington the following week to wrap up his business at the State Department.[80] Marshall stayed in Alexandria during his visit and met with Bayard on several occasions. The two were devoted friends. They shared the tenets of moderate Federalism and had always worked together easily. Like Marshall, Bayard was strenuously convivial and got along famously with his political opponents—except for "the Monticello crowd," whom he despised.[81] His closest friend was his Republican rival from Delaware, Caesar Rodney. In an Alexandria tavern that April, Bayard and Marshall informally reviewed the political situation in Washington.

Bayard said that the Federalists wanted to test the constitutionality of the Judiciary Act's repeal. Marshall, who could offer no official advice, gave Bayard his personal view that the repeal was constitutional and that the new statute should be obeyed. He said that the circuit judges appointed by Adams were now without authority and that they should adjourn any proceedings then pending.[82] Marshall's advice was consistent with his general view of the Constitution, and he was warning his friend against tilting at

---

*Marshall was referring to the reorganization of the circuit courts, which was the major provision of the Act. Instead of three circuits there would now be six, with a justice of the Supreme Court permanently assigned to each. That justice would serve with the various district judges on the circuit court twice a year. Years later, speaking for the Court in *United States v. Daniel*, Marshall said explicitly that the Act of 1802 was a "great improvement of the pre-existing system." 6 Wheaton 542, 547 (1821). This case is sometimes miscited as *United States v. Duvall*. See Charles Warren, 1 *The Supreme Court in United States History* 209, note 2 (Boston: Little, Brown, 1926).

windmills. He reminded Bayard that the text of Article III gave Congress explicit authority to establish such inferior courts as it thought proper and placed no limits on that power.[83] Marshall did indicate, however, that he had doubts about the renewed provision that the justices of the Supreme Court ride circuit, and, at Bayard's urging, he agreed to consult his colleagues on the matter.[84]

Bayard immediately reported Marshall's views to a conclave of Federalist congressional leaders, including Gouverneur Morris, Roger Griswold of Connecticut, and David Ogden of New York.[85] Morris noted: "I am neither surprised nor disappointed for it accords with my idea of the Judge [Marshall]."[86] Bayard apparently shared Marshall's opinion, or so Morris reported.[87] Nevertheless, the party's leadership decided to press on. "The business must not stop here," wrote Morris.[88] Just as Jefferson may have been propelled into premature action by his congressional allies Breckinridge and Mason, Marshall and the Court were about to be drawn into the fray by the Federalist irreconcilables in Congress. Extremists in both parties had taken control of the agenda, and the political temperature continued to rise.

As Marshall had promised, he wrote to his fellow justices from Alexandria asking for their views on the renewed requirement that they ride circuit. Marshall's letter to Paterson is all that survives,[89] but the various replies he received makes it clear that each of the justices was polled.[90] Marshall told his colleagues:

> This is not a subject to be lightly resolved on. The consequences of refusing to carry the law into effect may be very serious. For myself personally I disregard them, and so I am persuaded does every other Gentleman on the bench when put in competition with what he thinks his duty. But the conviction of duty ought to be very strong before the measure is resolved on.[91]

Marshall pointed out that because the justices had served on circuit in the past, it "will detract very much in the public estimation" if they should refuse to do so now.

Marshall was determined to keep the Court out of partisan politics. His informal advice to Bayard that the repeal of the Act of 1801 was constitutional was a clear signal to the Federalists to pull in their horns, and his letters to his colleagues were so cautiously phrased that it is clear the chief justice was making every effort to contain the crisis. By placing his colleagues on record early, he was attempting to minimize the possibility of future recriminations. Bushrod Washington, the first to reply, told Marshall that the question of whether the justices should ride circuit should be "considered as settled and should not again be moved."[92] Cushing said that "to be consistent . . . we must abide by the old practice."[93] Paterson told Marshall that he agreed with Bushrod. "Practice has fixed construction, which it is too late to disturb."[94] Only the combative Chase thought the justices ought not resume their duties on circuit, but even he observed that the position would be difficult to sustain. "The burthen of deciding so momentous a question, under the present circumstances of our country, would be very great on all the Judges assembled, but an individual Judge, declining to take a Circuit, must sink under it."[95] Marshall was pleased with the result. It was apparent that his colleagues did not want to pursue the matter. He told Paterson that he was "privately gratified" and that he would acquiesce "with much pleasure."[96]

That summer, when it came time for the justices to join their district court colleagues on circuit, each dutifully complied. The radical Republicans, who had feared that Marshall would head a judicial revolt and might even overturn their legislation, now openly commended him for his course of action.[97] A break in the storm clouds appeared to be in the offing, but it vanished quickly. Whether they realized it or not, Marshall and Jefferson were on a collision course. Neither had sought it. Marshall had worked assiduously to remove the Court from partisan politics, and Jefferson, just as assiduously, had pursued a policy of cautious moderation, intent on weaning the moderate Federalists from their hard-core allies.[98] But the repeal of the Judiciary Act of 1801 had rekindled old animosities. The Federalist leadership perceived the subsequent passage of the Judiciary Act of 1802 to be an act of vengeance. Marshall, who deplored the increased bitterness, wrote to Rufus King, somewhat in despair, that the disposition of the parties to come together, "which was strongly displayed by the minority twelve months past, exists no longer." He told King that, contrary to what he had hoped, "our political tempests will long, very long, exist, after those who are now tossed about by them shall be at rest."[99]

That melancholy mood persisted for several months—a rare interlude for the usually ebullient Marshall. In November 1802 he wrote to his old friend Charles Cotesworth Pinckney, "There is so much in the political world to wound honest men who have honorable feelings that I am disgusted with it and begin to see things through a much more gloomy medium than I once thought possible."[100]

13

⁂

Marbury v. Madison

*It is emphatically the province and duty of the judicial
department to say what the law is.*

John Marshall
Marbury v. Madison

I N THE AUTUMN of 1802, Marshall and his fellow justices resumed their
duties on circuit. Rather than precipitate a crisis with the Republican
majority in Congress over the new Judiciary Act, the chief justice chose to
respect its provisions, hoping thereby to steer the Court away from conflict.
It was a decision that reflected Marshall's basic political moderation and
conformed to his strongly held view that the judiciary should remain nonpartisan—a view that, in 1802, was shared neither by the irreconcilables
in his own party nor by the radical wing of the Republicans. Above all, it
was consistent with his understanding of the Constitution. Each branch of
government was entrusted with specific responsibilities, and Congress
was given explicit authority to organize the lower courts. Marshall might
disagree with the manner in which congressional discretion had been exercised, but he was not about to challenge the plenary nature of that discretion.

As chief justice, Marshall was assigned by the Judiciary Act of 1802 to
the fifth circuit, comprising the districts of Virginia and North Carolina.[1]
This assignment was fortunate given that Bushrod Washington was also
from Virginia and Alfred Moore from North Carolina. Had there been any
legislative hostility toward Marshall when the act was passed, he could easily have been given a more distant posting. As it was, the fifth circuit was the
most convenient he could possibly have had, for it meant he could discharge
the bulk of his duties without leaving home. The Virginia circuit met in
Richmond and was the nation's busiest. The North Carolina circuit, which

convened in Raleigh, was far less active, and required Marshall's presence for less than a week at a time.[2]

Despite Marshall's determination to shield the Court from partisan politics, the High Federalists were unwilling to let matters rest. Convinced that the repeal of the Judiciary Act of 1801 was the opening salvo of a Republican campaign to dismantle the entire federal judiciary and perhaps even the Constitution itself, the party's hard core went on the offensive.[3] Their initial gambit was to have the repeal measure quickly declared unconstitutional, but this was frustrated by the new Judiciary Act, which delayed the next session of the Supreme Court until February 1803. Their next maneuver was an attempt to persuade the justices to refuse to ride circuit. Such a refusal would have vitiated the Republican substitute legislation and would have created a constitutional crisis from which the High Federalists hoped to benefit. That strategy came to naught as well when Marshall and his colleagues refused to cooperate. The irreconcilables were left with four options, all of which they began to pursue vigorously.

The first element of the High Federalist assault involved a public campaign calling upon Marshall and his associates to declare the repeal act unconstitutional when the Court reconvened.[4] Next, the High Federalists planned to have the displaced circuit judges, led by Oliver Wolcott, petition Congress to be reinstated.[5] Third, they made preparations to introduce a number of test cases into the circuit courts, hoping eventually to carry them forward to the Supreme Court. Finally, the pending litigation of William Marbury and his associates was seen as another opportunity to whip up public support. The inevitable result of this four-pronged attack was to exacerbate an already delicate political situation and to widen the division between the two parties—exactly what Marshall and Jefferson had hoped to avoid.[6]

The issue between the High Federalists and the justices of the Marshall Court was joined first on September 18, 1802, when Bushrod Washington opened circuit court in Hartford, Connecticut. Roger Griswold, a charter member of the High Federalist braintrust, used the occasion to challenge the authority of the circuit court to hear two cases then pending, insisting that the judges appointed by Adams still held office and that their courts were the appropriate venue. Washington immediately dismissed Griswold's motion and ordered that the docket be called.[7]

A similar incident occurred shortly afterward in Boston when Justice Cushing called the first circuit to order. Theophilus Parsons, another High Federalist chieftain (and subsequently chief judge of the supreme judicial court of Massachusetts), questioned the constitutionality of the court, at which point Cushing adjourned proceedings until the next day. During the intervening twenty-four hours the judges evidently made it plain how they intended to rule, because when the court reconvened, Parsons, "very much mortified," dropped his plea and the court resumed its business.[8] In New Jersey, another test case was mounted when one of the deposed midnight judges brought suit before Justice Paterson contesting the constitutionality of the repealing act of 1802. That, too, was summarily dismissed.[9]

The principal High Federalist assault was reserved for the fifth circuit in Richmond, where Marshall was presiding. Once again, it was the chief justice's old friend Charles Lee who led the attack. The issue involved an earlier judgment won by a Maryland resident, John Laird, against Hugh Stuart, a citizen of Virginia, in one of the circuit courts that had been abolished by the Republican Congress. The judgment of that court was now before Marshall for execution. Lee immediately challenged Marshall's authority to hear the matter. He repeated the arguments made by Griswold and Parsons that the Repeal Act of 1802 was unconstitutional, and he questioned Congress's authority to compel the justices of the Supreme Court to ride circuit. "If it be said that the practice from the year 1789 to 1801 is against us, we answer that the practice was wrong, that it crept in unawares, without consideration and without opposition."[10] Marshall dismissed both of Lee's arguments and ordered the judgment in favor of Laird to be executed.[11] Lee thereupon appealed Marshall's decision to the Supreme Court (*Stuart v. Laird*), thus setting the stage for the final High Federalist challenge to Congress's actions in 1802.

In going forward with their appeal, the High Federalists once again betrayed their sense of unreality. Bushrod Washington, Cushing, Paterson, and Marshall had all ruled against them on circuit, and there was little likelihood that the justices would reverse themselves come February. But the party's irreconcilables were determined to press on, confident that their position was correct. That moral certitude unsettled the radical Republicans—who should have known better—and the political rhetoric escalated. The Supreme Court unwillingly now became the focus of the struggle over the judiciary that had commenced two years earlier on the floor of Congress.

Marshall was not affected by the High Federalist offensive. His dark mood of autumn had passed, and he had emerged from it more resolved than ever to extricate the Court from the morass of partisan politics. Before he could confront that challenge, however, there were circuit court duties to complete. Shortly after Christmas, Marshall set out for Raleigh and his first session of court in North Carolina. The distance from Richmond to Raleigh over the post road was 165 miles, and the weather being fair, Marshall made the trip in three days. Like Richmond, which had inherited the mantle of government from Williamsburg, Raleigh had recently become the capital of North Carolina. The state government had moved to Raleigh from coastal New Bern in 1792, and the new capital had all the trappings of a piedmont frontier town as it struggled to accommodate the various legislators and state officials who descended upon it. Jonathan Mason, a former United States senator from Massachusetts, described the town as "a miserable place, nothing but a few wooden buildings and a brick Court House."[12]

In 1803 Raleigh's population numbered fewer than 1,000. Marshall found lodging in the boardinghouse of Henry H. Cooke—a rickety frame structure about a quarter of a mile from the courthouse. The rooms were spartan, and Marshall had to gather his own wood and make his own fires. But for the next thirty-two years he stayed with Cooke whenever he held court in Raleigh.[13] "Everything here [is] as pleasant as I could expect," he wrote to Polly on January 2, and it is obvious from his letter that his buoyancy had returned.

> You will laugh at my vexation when you hear the various calamities that have befallen me. In the first place when I came to review my funds, I had the mortification to discover that I had lost 15 silver dollars out of my waist coat pocket. They had worn through the various mendings the pocket had sustained and sought their liberty in the sands of Carolina. I determined not to vex myself with what could not be remedied and ordered Peter to take out my clothes that I might dress for court when to my astonishment and grief after fumbling several minutes in the portmanteau, staring at vacancy, and sweating most profusely he turned to me with the doleful tidings that I had no pair of breeches.
>
> You may be sure this piece of intelligence was not very graciously received. However, after a little scolding I determined to make the best of my situation and immediately set out to get a pair made. I thought I should be a *sans culotte* only one day and that for the residue of the term [December 30, 1802–January 5, 1803] I might be well enough dressed for the appearance of the first day to be forgotten. But, "the greatest of evils, I found, was followed by still greater!" Not a tailor in town could be prevailed on to work for me. They were all so busy that it was impossible to attend to my wants however pressing they might be, and I have the extreme mortification to pass the whole term without that important article of dress I have mentioned.[14]

Because of the repeal of the Judiciary Act of 1801, the circuit court had not met for almost a year, and Marshall found a full docket awaiting him.[15] One case, *Ogden v. Blackledge*, which eventually came before the Supreme Court,[16] permitted him to restate his views concerning the separation of powers and the necessity of preventing legislative encroachment upon the courts. Marshall's comment was gratuitous,* but his decision upholding the claims of British creditors against citizens of North Carolina was subsequently sustained by the high court.[17]

On the bench in Raleigh, just as in Richmond, Marshall was careful not to betray any sign of political partisanship—a determination that, with the continuing exception of Chase, his colleagues now shared. The *Raleigh Register* reported that his charge to the grand jury in *Ogden v. Blackedge* was "concise and appropriate, fully explaining their duty, without the least political intermixture."[18] The *Minerva*, another North Carolina paper, called it "elegant and learned."[19] Consistent with the cautious judicial posture Marshall had adopted, he declined to give copies of his jury charge to the press. According to the *Minerva*, "the Chief Justice [said] that he had laid it down as a rule from which he did not intend to depart, not to allow his charges to be published."[20]

Marshall's efforts to avoid partisanship would soon be tested. When Congress reconvened in January 1803, the High Federalists launched their offensive. The Supreme Court was scheduled to meet on February 7, with both *Marbury v. Madison* and *Stuart v. Laird* on the docket. On January 27, in accordance with the strategy previously agreed upon, eleven of the deposed circuit judges presented personal memorials to the House and Senate requesting Congress to define their status and urging that the issue of their compensation be referred to the Court.[21] The Federalist press devoted considerable space to the appeal, although the *Aurora* perhaps more accurately noted that "The judges . . . this day brought forth the mouse from the mountain."[22]

The ensuing debate was viciously partisan. In the House, the Federalists urged that the constitutionality of the Repeal Act be referred to the Supreme Court.[23] The Republicans responded that the people, not the courts, were the judges of the constitutionality of acts of Congress.[24] "If the petitioners can bring their case before the Supreme Court, let them do so," said John Nicholas of Virginia. "If the Supreme Court shall arrogate this power to themselves, and declare our law to be unconstitutional, it will then behoove us to act. Our duty is clear."[25] With the threat of legislative reprisal in the air, the House rejected the judges' petition, thirty-seven voting in favor, sixty-one against.[26]

---

*Although it was not essential to his decision, Marshall noted that the Bill of Rights of North Carolina provided for the separation of powers and that if the legislature, by statute, usurped the judicial function, the statute "is therefore in my judgment, void." When the case came before the Supreme Court in 1804, Justice Cushing, who was presiding (Marshall recused himself), declined to hear argument on that point holding it was not relevant. *Ogden v. Blackledge*, 2 Cranch 272, 276 (1804). For Marshall's circuit court opinion, see 6 *The Papers of John Marshall* 147–149 (Chapel Hill: University of North Carolina Press, 1990).

The debate in the Senate was even more heated, and the Supreme Court again became the focal point of the controversy. The Federalist onslaught was led by Gouverneur Morris of New York, Jonathan Dayton of New Jersey, and James Ross of Pennsylvania. The Judiciary, said Ross, was "the only body to which we could look" for protection from laws that were unconstitutional. "The Constitution is the supreme law: it is the duty of a judge to compare acts of the Legislature with this great charter, and pronounce whether the special delegated power [of Congress] has been exceeded or not."[27]

The Republicans answered that the judges' petition "was nothing more than an attempt to inflame the public mind"[28] and deplored the divisive tactics of their opponents. "Would not peace and union have been better promoted by keeping the subject out of sight, and not by attempting . . . to irritate party animosities?" asked Wilson Cary Nicholas of Virginia.[29] None of the Republican senators questioned the Supreme Court's authority to declare an act of Congress unconstitutional. But as John Breckinridge of Kentucky noted, since "the courts can decide that question without our interference," why should the Senate become involved?[30] Like the House, the Senate voted down the judges' petition, although the vote was much closer, 13–15.[31]

The High Federalists continued to press forward. On January 28, the day after the House rejected the memorial of the former judges, Senator John Howard of Maryland introduced a request from William Marbury, Robert Hooe, and Dennis Ramsay for a certified copy of the Senate's executive journal from March 1801, attesting their confirmation as justices of the peace.[32] Howard ingenuously observed that "the request was so reasonable that he concluded it would pass without objection."[33]

In raising Marbury's request before the Senate, the High Federalists' purpose was twofold. Secretary of State Madison had not responded to the Supreme Court's show cause order, nor had he provided the claimants with the documentation they sought pertaining to their original appointments. As a result, the trio of litigants could offer no tangible proof that their commissions had been withheld. A copy of the Senate's journal would at least establish that they had been duly appointed.[34] A more important consideration, however, was that by raising the issue on the eve of the Supreme Court's February term, the High Federalists were putting pressure on the justices. The party press reported the debate extensively, and, for the first time since December 1801, public awareness rekindled. If Marshall and his colleagues had hoped to dispose of Marbury's request quietly, the party's militants were serving notice that this would not be possible.

The Senate Republicans recognized immediately that Marbury and his colleagues were pawns in a game of constitutional confrontation initiated by the High Federalists. John Breckinridge attacked the request for the Senate journal as an unwarranted attempt to assail the president. His action converted the issue into a showdown between Jefferson and the Court—raising the stakes even higher. "The suit is now pending on a *mandamus* to the secretary of state. The Senate ought not to aid the Judiciary in their invasion of the rights of the Executive."[35]

Other Republicans picked up the theme. General James Jackson of Georgia, who, with Breckinridge, was one of the Senate's most radical Republicans, said he would "never lend his aid to set the Judiciary above the Executive."[36] Robert Wright of Maryland called Marbury's request "an audacious attempt to pry into Executive secrets, by a tribunal which had no authority to do any such thing; and to enable the Supreme Court to assume an unheard of and unfounded power, if not despotism."[37] DeWitt Clinton of New York noted that "a great Constitutional question is now agitated in [the Supreme] Court, involving the right to control the Executive."[38] The Republicans eventually defeated Marbury's request, again in a 13–15 vote,[39] but the High Federalists had succeeded in making the authority of the Supreme Court the central issue in their campaign. *Marbury v. Madison*, which had begun as a routine exercise in judicial procedure fourteen months earlier, was now center stage. Marshall's effort to remove the judiciary from partisanship had been thwarted by the irreconcilables in his own party. The *Aurora* was right on target when it referred to William Marbury as "the person *used* by the *tories* to blow up this bubble."[40]

The Supreme Court was now the focus of the nation's partisanship. Despite the long cooling off period since the Court last met in December 1801, and notwithstanding the justices' evident reluctance to become involved, Committee Room 2 had become the venue where the animosity between the High Federalists and their radical opponents would be played out. In *Marbury*, the Court was being asked to issue a writ of command to Jefferson's secretary of state; in *Stuart v. Laird*, it was being challenged to overturn the Republican-passed Judiciary Act of 1802. Both cases threatened to produce a constitutional crisis, which Marshall recognized the Court could not win. Even more seriously, each threatened to upend the nonpartisan stance the justices had adopted and, with it, the Supreme Court's legitimacy as the nation's highest tribunal.

First to be argued was *Marbury v. Madison*,[41] which, unlike virtually all cases to come before the Supreme Court, was one in which the justices sat as a trial court. Marbury's request for a writ of *mandamus* was not an appeal from a lower court holding but an original action brought before the Supreme Court under section 13 of the old Judiciary Act of 1789.[42] Marbury and his associates had to demonstrate why the writ should be issued, and on February 10, Charles Lee opened his argument on their behalf.[43] Madison, who still had not responded to the Court's order to show cause, continued to ignore the matter, which gave the proceedings an especially eerie quality. Not only were the justices sitting in judgment in an original action, but one of the parties to the case was not even represented—a bold challenge to the Court's authority.

Because the Senate had refused to provide an extract of its executive journal, Lee was confronted at the outset with the necessity of proving that his clients had been nominated and confirmed as justices of the peace. The one person who could provide direct evidence on that point was Marshall himself who, as secretary of state, had affixed the seals to their commissions. In fact, it was actually Marshall who had been remiss in seeing that the documents were sent out.[44] Lee chose not to call the chief justice and initially attempted to build his case on the testimony of the State Department's chief clerk, Jacob Wagner, and his assistant, Daniel Brent. Both proved to be unwilling witnesses and claimed executive privilege. Despite their reluctance, Marshall ordered them to be sworn. They could object to any specific question they might be asked, he said, but the Court would decide whether they were required to answer.[45] The collision of the Court and the executive branch, which both Marshall and Jefferson had attempted to avoid, appeared to be at hand.

Wagner and Brent chose not to press the issue of executive privilege. Under oath, Wagner testified that he was working as Jefferson's personal secretary at the time of the transition and had no direct knowledge of the justice of the peace commissions. He said he had heard that the commissions for Marbury and Robert Hooe had been signed by President Adams, but that by some accident the one for Dennis Ramsay had not been.[46] When Lee asked, "who gave you that information?" Wagner declined to answer and Marshall upheld his refusal, saying that the question was not pertinent. Brent, also under oath, said he had seen the commissions but did not think they had been sent out. He did not know what had happened to them.[47]

Lee called as his next witness Attorney General Levi Lincoln, who had replaced Marshall as interim secretary of state the day after Jefferson's inauguration. Lincoln presumably had been aware of Jefferson's order not to deliver the commissions, but as acting secretary of state, and therefore the president's principal deputy, his claim to executive privilege was compelling. Lincoln was also the nation's attorney general, however, and an officer of the Court. His position was delicate, and he asked Marshall whether he was required to testify. On the one hand, said Lincoln, he respected the jurisdiction of the Court; on the other, he felt himself bound to maintain the rights and privileges of the executive. If the Court decided that his testimony was essential, he asked that Lee's questions be put in writing so that he might have time to consider them.[48]

Marshall was sympathetic to Lincoln's plight. He granted the attorney general's request and instructed Lee to put his queries in writing. Lee wrote out the four questions he wished to ask, and the chief justice, after consulting his colleagues, told Lincoln that the Court felt he should answer the questions, but that he could take whatever time he needed to consider them. Marshall said that Lincoln need not disclose anything that was confidential and that he certainly need not incriminate himself.[49] It was apparent from the interchange between Marshall and Lincoln that each was doing his utmost to prevent the issue from escalating into a full-blown confrontation between the executive branch and the Court. Lincoln deferred to the Court's authority; Marshall made it plain that the Court would respect executive privilege.

At that point Lincoln requested that he be given until the following morning to reply, noting that he was due shortly at a committee hearing dealing with claims against the United States submitted by the state of Georgia.[50] Marshall agreed, and the Court adjourned. The first day's testimony was complete. It had been a trying experience. The Supreme Court was ill-suited to the role of a trial court, and taking direct testimony was time-consuming. It was evident to those in attendance that the justices were uncomfortable, and Madison's failure to respond continued to cast a shadow over the proceedings.

When the Court reconvened on Friday, February 11, Lincoln took the improvised witness stand. He noted his objection to Lee's first question, stating that he could not say what had happened to the commissions because he did not know whether Secretary Madison had ever had possession of them. Marshall upheld Lincoln's objection and ruled that the question was immaterial.[51] Lincoln thereupon responded to Lee's three remaining interrogatories. He said that he had seen the commissions and that they had been signed by President Adams and sealed with the Great Seal of the United States. But he told the Court that he did not recollect whether any of them had been made out to Marbury, Hooe, or Ramsay. He said that he also did not know whether any of the commissions had been sent out, but did not believe that any had been.[52] At that point Lincoln was excused. With considerable tact and a great deal of understanding, the chief justice and the attorney general had avoided the collision the High Federalists were trying to engineer. In requiring that Lee put his questions in writing, the Court had preempted the possibility of a dramatic interrogation of Lincoln that would undoubtedly have fanned the flames of partisanship.

The fact is, the Federalists had had little success thus far in making their case. As his final piece of evidence, Lee submitted an affidavit made out by James Marshall, the chief justice's brother, attesting to the fact that he had seen the commissions in the office of the secretary of state, that he had attempted without success to deliver a number of them in Alexandria, and that he had returned them to the State Department. Lee asserted that the existence of the commissions was thus proved, and moved on to his closing argument.[53]

When Lee concluded, Marshall asked Lincoln whether he wished to respond. Lincoln said he had received no instructions from Secretary Madison and therefore would remain silent. According to press reports, Marshall was uncomfortable that the traditional adversarial process had not been followed. Eager to hear argument from the opposing side, he said that the Court "would attend to the observations of any person who was disposed to offer his sentiments."[54] When no one responded, Marshall said that the Court would postpone judgment and moved on to other business.

The Supreme Court was now in a no-win situation. It had avoided a clash between the Jefferson administration and its High Federalists opponents in the courtroom, but an even greater collision was in the offing. If the Court issued a writ of *mandamus*, it was abundantly clear that Madison would ignore it. Since the Court lacked the means to enforce the writ, the judiciary would be exposed as powerless. Executive authority would have prevailed simply by standing aside and doing nothing. Public opinion would back Madison; the Republicans would wax triumphant; and another check on majority power would have been dissipated.

On the other hand, if the Court did not issue the writ to which Marbury was entitled, and which was unmistakably provided for by statute, the judiciary would be deemed a paper tiger. It would be seen as unwilling to confront the Republican behemoth, and an unworthy guardian of constitutional principle. For two weeks, Marshall and his colleagues wrestled with the dilemma. In the interim, Chase was taken ill and the Court removed its sessions to the living room of nearby Stelle's Hotel to accommodate him— Stelle's Hotel, a three-story brick structure on the present site of the Library of Congress, had become the justices' common lodging after Conrad and McMunn's was destroyed in a fire.[55]

Some of the pressure that had been building was lifted when the High Federalists turned their fire on Jefferson over his reluctance to take action against Spain for its closure of the port of New Orleans.* The crisis on the lower Mississippi had been festering for several months, and on Monday, February 14, three days after the conclusion of Lee's argument in *Marbury*

---

*In 1800 Spain ceded the Louisiana Territory to France by the Treaty of St. Ildefonso. But the terms of the treaty were complex, and, pending their fulfillment, the Spanish retained control of the area. In October 1802 the Spanish Intendant, acting under orders from Madrid, withdrew the right of American citizens to deposit goods in New Orleans prior to their being shipped abroad. That decision effectively closed the Mississippi to American shipping, with potentially disastrous results for the economies of Kentucky and Tennessee. Popular response in the West clamored for

v. Madison, Senator James Ross of Pennsylvania introduced legislation instructing the president to use military force to take possession of New Orleans and calling 50,000 state militia into national service to assist.[56] The
resolution was a serious challenge to the president's authority to conduct the
nation's foreign relations. It was also a deliberate effort to scuttle a peaceful
settlement. Debate on the measure consumed the Senate and the administration for the next two weeks, diverting attention from the Court and the
pending decision on Marbury's request.

On Thursday, February 24, while the Senate debate still raged, the justices assembled in the living room of Stelle's Hotel to announce their decision. Once again their holding was unanimous, and once again it was the
chief justice who spoke for the Court. Marshall began slowly, reading the
opinion in the same low but persuasive voice that characterized his years at
the bar. He noted that Madison had not shown cause why the writ of *mandamus* should not be issued. A less astute, or a more partisan, judge might
have ruled for Marbury by default. Such a decision would have been defen-
sible under the normal rules of the adversarial process and would have precipitated the constitutional crisis the High Federalists longed for. But a
constitutional crisis was precisely what Marshall sought to avoid. Thus, having acknowledged Madison's noncompliance, the chief justice let the matter rest. "The peculiar delicacy of this case," said Marshall, "the novelty of
some of its circumstances, and the real difficulty attending the points which
occur in it, require a complete exposition of the principles on which the
opinion to be given by the Court is founded."[57]

Marshall turned to the question of whether Marbury was entitled to his
commission as a justice of the peace. By tackling this question first, the chief
justice was throwing a sop to the High Federalists. He traced the legislation
by which the office was created, examined the appointment process specified by the Constitution, and noted that the process was complete when the
president signed the commissions and the secretary of state affixed the seal.
Delivery of the documents was not required. Marshall said that since Marbury's commission had been signed and sealed, he was duly appointed as a
justice of the peace for a term of five years. That appointment was not revo-
cable but was vested in Marbury's legal rights, "which are protected by the
laws of this country. To withhold his commission, therefore, is an act deemed
by the Court not warranted by law, but violative of a vested legal right."

---

the seizure of New Orleans, and to head off war, Jefferson dispatched Monroe to Paris with instructions to purchase sufficient territory from France to secure American navigation of the Mississippi. These negotiations were pending when *Marbury v. Madison* came before the Court. See
E. W. Lyon, "The Closing of the Port of New Orleans," 37 *American Historical Review* 280–286
(1932).

Having established Marbury's right to the office, Marshall then asked whether the laws afforded a remedy. "The very essence of civil liberty," he said, "consists in the right of every individual to claim the protection of the laws whenever he receives an injury." Marshall's voice quickened as he moved along. As an advocate, he had been renowned for commencing his summations in a halting and disjointed manner, picking up momentum as he proceeded, and soaring to a tightly crafted conclusion. To those listening in the living room at Stelle's, it seemed inevitable that the Court was building its case to issue the writ Marbury had requested.

Marshall briefly recited several instances in which executive departments had been held accountable by the judiciary.[58] He then turned to the nature of presidential authority. Marshall was now on the familiar ground he had laid out in his speech to the House of Representatives on the Robbins case. The distinction he had drawn between political questions and legal issues was about to become the constitutional law of the United States. The Republicans in the audience pricked up their ears when Marshall said that the Constitution invested the president "with certain important political powers, in the exercise of which he is to use his own discretion, and is accountable only to his country in his political character, and to his own conscience."

To assist him in his political role, Marshall said, the president was entitled to appoint certain subordinates who were responsible exclusively to him. "In such cases, their acts are his acts; and whatever opinion may be entertained of the manner in which executive discretion may be used, still there exists, and can exist, no power to control that discretion. The subjects are political. They respect the nation, not individual rights, and being entrusted to the executive, the decision of the executive is conclusive."

Marshall noted that the secretary of state, in particular, is required to conform to the president's will. "He is the mere organ by whom that will is communicated. The acts of such an officer, as an officer, can never be examinable by the courts."

For those in attendance, the direction of the Court appeared to have changed. As a former secretary of state, Marshall's words carried special meaning, and he was now presenting a powerful defense of executive prerogative. If the partisans of 1803 had reflected for a moment, they would have realized that that position was perfectly consistent with the moderate federalism Marshall had always espoused and undoubtedly provided a common denominator for his colleagues on the Court.

Marshall was not finished. The High Federalists had initially thought the Court was about to issue the writ of *mandamus*. The Republicans now anticipated that it would not. The chief justice again shifted ground. He said that the secretary of state, in addition to his political responsibilities, also had certain purely administrative duties. These were prescribed by law and involved no discretion. When those duties pertained to the rights of individuals, a person "who considers himself injured has a right to resort to the laws of his country for a remedy." Marshall said that Marbury had a legal title to the office to which he had been appointed and a consequent right to his commission. Madison's refusal to deliver it was "a plain violation of that right," and Marbury was fully entitled to seek redress in the courts.

The advantage shifted back to the High Federalists. Marshall had been speaking for over an hour (when complete, the decision would exceed 11,000 words) and was weaving an intricate pattern that riveted the attention of those who now crowded into the makeshift courtroom at Stelle's. Word had spread quickly that the chief justice was delivering a momentous decision, and numerous members of the House and Senate had joined the regular practitioners in attendance. A constitutional crisis of epic proportions appeared to be in the making, and the audience hung on every word.

It was nearly noon when Marshall warmed to his conclusion. The only question remaining, he said, was whether Marbury "is entitled to the remedy for which he applies." That depended on two factors: "the nature of the writ applied for, and the powers of this Court." For the next twenty minutes, Marshall examined the nature of a writ of *mandamus*. Once again he balanced Marbury's right to the writ with the delicacy of issuing a command to the secretary of state. For the first time, the chief justice took aim at the Republican critics of the Court. Is it not amazing, he asked, that "the assertion by an individual, of his legal claims, in a court of justice . . . should at first be considered by some, as an attempt to intrude into the cabinet, and to intermeddle with the prerogatives of the executive? It is scarcely necessary for the Court to disclaim all pretensions to such a jurisdiction. An extravagance, so absurd and excessive, could not have been entertained for one moment."

To reassure the nation at large, Marshall provided a powerful restatement of the judicial function. "The province of the Court," he said, "is, solely, to decide the rights of individuals, not to inquire how the executive, or executive officers, perform duties in which they have a discretion. Questions, in their nature political, or which are, by the Constitution and laws, submitted to the executive, can never be made in this Court."

Marshall said that Marbury's petition, "so far from being an intrusion into the secrets of the cabinet," merely involved obtaining the copy of a paper to which "the law gives a right on the payment of ten cents."[59] He then held that since no political discretion was involved, a writ of *mandamus* compelling Madison to do what the statute required was the appropriate remedy. "It only remains to be inquired whether it can issue from this Court."

Lee and Lincoln were now on the edge of their seats. Marshall had structured his decision to heighten the suspense. It was one o'clock and the tension palpable as the chief justice recited section 13 of the Judiciary Act of 1789, giving the Supreme Court the power to issue writs of *mandamus*. The statutory authority of the Court was clear, said Marshall, *unless the law was unconstitutional*.

With the outcome still in doubt, Marshall commenced the constitutional exposition for which *Marbury v. Madison* is famous. The Constitution, he said, vested the judicial power of the United States "in one Supreme Court, and in such inferior courts as Congress shall, from time to time, ordain and establish." The Supreme Court's appellate jurisdiction was determined by Congress, but its original jurisdiction—those cases in which it sits as a trial court—was fixed by the Constitution. Marshall noted that the text of the Constitution was precise. The Supreme Court's original jurisdiction was expressly limited to cases "affecting ambassadors, other public ministers and consuls, and those in which a state shall be a party." That enumeration was complete and could not be increased by Congress. As a result, the authority Congress gave to the Supreme Court to issue writs of *mandamus* "appears not to be warranted by the Constitution." Congress had acted to expand the original jurisdiction of the Court as stipulated by the Constitution, and that, said Marshall, it could not do.

Could a law that was unconstitutional be enforced by the courts? According to Marshall, the question was deeply interesting, "but happily not of an intricacy proportioned to its interest." The people of the United States had established the Constitution as the supreme law of the land. It "organizes the government, and assigns, to different departments, their respective powers." The powers of Congress were limited. "To what purpose are powers limited, and to what purpose is that limitation committed to writing, if these limits may, at any time, be [exceeded] by those intended to be restrained?" Like a stern schoolmaster lecturing errant pupils, Marshall observed that "It is a proposition too plain to be contested, that the Constitution controls any legislative act repugnant to it." Otherwise, the legislature may alter the Constitution at will. "Between these alternatives there is no middle ground. The Constitution is either a superior, paramount law, unchangeable by ordinary means, or it is on a level with ordinary legislative acts, and like other acts, is alterable when the legislature shall please to alter it."

Marshall said it was absolutely clear that all of those who had framed written constitutions—an implicit reference to the various state constitutions—intended those documents to be supreme. As a result, "an act of the legislature, repugnant to the Constitution, is void. This theory is essentially attached to a written constitution, and is consequently to be considered, by this Court, as one of the fundamental principles of our society."

Marshall was now defending the perimeter of judicial authority. In a sentence that has echoed through the years, the chief justice announced that "It is emphatically the province and duty of the judicial department to say what the law is." And then, the critical link in his argument: The Constitution was law. It could be interpreted by the courts in ordinary litigation. "If two laws conflict with each other, the courts must decide on the operation of each." If a law and the Constitution are in conflict, and if both apply to a particular case, "the Court must determine which of these conflicting rules governs the case. This is the essence of judicial duty."

At that point, Marshall's conclusion was inescapable. If the courts are obliged to interpret the Constitution, and if the Constitution "is superior to any ordinary act of the legislature—the Constitution, and not such ordinary act, must govern the case to which they both apply."

Earlier in the Court's decision, Marshall had recognized vast areas of political discretion that were not subject to judicial scrutiny. Now, in conclusion, he was driving home the point that the Constitution was a legal document and that, in matters of law, the decision of the Court was final. It was a principle, he said, "essential to all written constitutions, that a law repugnant to the Constitution is void, and that *courts*, as well as other departments, are bound by that instrument."

Since Congress had no authority to expand the original jurisdiction of the Supreme Court by granting it the power to issue writs of *mandamus*, the rule to Secretary of State Madison to show cause "must be discharged." At fifteen minutes before two o'clock on February 24, 1803, after a decision that had required almost four hours for Marshall to read, the case of *Marbury v. Madison* was dismissed.

It was a judicial tour de force. Marshall had converted a no-win situation into a massive victory. The authority of the Supreme Court to declare an act of Congress unconstitutional was now the law of the land. Typically, Marshall's decision paid heed to the claims raised on both sides of the case. The High Federalists were awarded the nominal prize of hearing that Marbury was entitled to his commission, and the Republicans gained a victory with the dismissal of the rule to show cause. But the real winner was the Supreme Court and, some might say, the Constitution itself.

The legal precedent for judicial review, that unique American doctrine that permits the Supreme Court to declare acts of Congress and the executive unconstitutional, traces to the holding in *Marbury v. Madison*. Marshall did not say that the Supreme Court was the ultimate arbiter of the Constitution. He did not say that the authority to interpret the Constitution rested exclusively with the Court, and he certainly did not endorse grandiose schemes that envisaged the Supreme Court as a board of review sitting in judgment on each act of Congress to determine its constitutionality.[60] He simply stated that the Constitution was law, and that as a judicial matter, it could be interpreted by the Court in cases that came before it.

The following week, in a cursory opinion of four paragraphs, Justice Paterson, speaking for another unanimous Court, dismissed the High Federalist appeal against the judiciary act of 1802 in the case of *Stuart v. Laird*.[61] "The question is at rest," said Paterson, "and ought not now to be disturbed."*[62] The judicial challenge mounted by the High Federalists had been defeated. The Marshall Court had twice demonstrated that it would not be made an instrument of partisan politics. The rule to show cause directed to Madison had been dismissed, and Congress's authority to determine the organization of the lower courts had been sustained. The Republicans, many of whom had anticipated that the Court would rule against them, were overjoyed at the holdings.[63] The Federalists, who were the big losers, were somewhat mollified by the careful phrasing of Marshall's decision in *Marbury*. Above all, the Supreme Court had avoided the trap that the irreconcilables had prepared for it.

Sir Lewis Namier, the distinguished British historian, once observed that scholars are inclined to remember the present and to forget the past. In few instances is that more evident than in the treatment of *Marbury v. Madison*. Biographers, historians, and legal scholars have read back into the case the bitter hostility between Jefferson and Marshall that developed during the treason trial of Aaron Burr in 1807. The two men were never fond of each other, but in 1803, when the decision in *Marbury* came down, they shared a continuing concern to moderate the partisanship that divided the nation. The president did not comment publicly or privately on the decision at the time, and Marshall's assertion of the Court's authority to declare an act of Congress unconstitutional was not controversial.[64] In fact, it was consistent with the views that Jefferson himself had expressed in the draft of his first message to Congress in December 1801.† In later years Jefferson became a bitter critic of *Marbury v. Madison*. But his ire was directed solely at

---

*Charles Warren, one of the most eminent historians of the Supreme Court, notes that "No more striking example of the non-partisanship of the American Judiciary can be found than this decision by a Court composed wholly of Federalists, upholding, contrary to its personal and political views, a detested Republican measure." 1 *The Supreme Court in United States History* 272 (Boston: Little, Brown, 1926).

†In a lengthy discourse on the Sedition Act, Jefferson made it clear that he believed each branch of government had a right to decide for itself on the constitutionality of matters before it. In words with which Marshall would not have disagreed, Jefferson said, "Our country has thought it proper to distribute the powers of its government among three equal and independent authorities, constituting each a check on one or both of the others, in all attempts to impair its constitution. To make each an effectual check, it must have a right in cases which arise within the line of its proper functions, where, equally with the others, it acts in the last resort and without appeal, to decide on the validity of an act according to its own judgment, and uncontrolled by the opin-

Marshall's *obiter dictum* concerning Marbury's right to his commission, not at the Court's exercise of judicial review.[65]

The Republican press, which often took its cue from the president in such matters, not only refrained from criticizing the decision but reported the Court's holding extensively and advised readers of its importance.[66] Several newspapers printed Marshall's opinion verbatim—all 11,000 words. The *National Intelligencer* devoted three issues to the holding,[67] the *New York Spectator* two,[68] and the *Aurora* two,[69] each paper preempting much of its coverage of the crisis on the lower Mississippi to do so. By contrast, the Federalist press devoted little attention to the decision. Praise for it was markedly restrained, and what little there was focused on Marshall's comments about Marbury's right to his commission, not the Court's holding that section 13 of the Judiciary Act was unconstitutional. An exception was the *Washington Federalist*, the organ of the moderate wing of the party, which printed the complete text of the decision.[70] Like the Republican press, it commented on the conciliatory nature of the holding, which it said "will remain as a monument of the wisdom, impartiality and independence of the Supreme Court."[71]

In Congress, which remained in session until March 3, not one word of criticism was offered, in either the House or the Senate. The authority of the Supreme Court to overturn an act of Congress went unchallenged, and Marshall's reasoning was not questioned. The chief justice's contemporaries recognized that the decision fit squarely with his preference for moderation, and even the most radical Republicans hailed his efforts to extricate the Court from the partisanship that had engulfed it. The *Aurora*, in a rare tribute to someone outside the Republican fold, saluted Marshall as the hero of the hour. "The weight of your authority . . . calmed the tumult of faction, and you stood, as you must continue to stand, a star of the first magnitude."[72]

The decision itself is one of the great constitutional documents of American history. Marshall's unadorned prose evoked the spirit of constitutional balance: a government of laws, not of men. The ideas he expressed were not new, nor were they tailored for political expediency. The distinction between political questions within the purview of the executive, discretion and legal issues within the jurisdiction of the Court, was a constitutional

---

ions of any other department. We have accordingly, in more than once instance, seen the opinions of different departments in opposition to each other, and no ill ensue."

At the last minute, Jefferson deleted the passage for fear that it would be "chicaned" by his political opponents. It was first discovered and made public by Charles A. Beard in his *Economic Origins of Jeffersonian Democracy* 454–455 (New York: Macmillan, 1915). For a discussion of Jefferson's views on the "tripartite" theory of constitutional interpretation, which suggests that the theoretical differences between him and Marshall have been greatly exaggerated, see Dumas Malone, *Jefferson the President: The First Term* 151–156 (Boston: Little, Brown, 1970).

principle he had articulated convincingly during the debate on the *Robbins* case in 1800. The supremacy of the Constitution, the separation of powers, and the corresponding authority of the Court to declare an act of the legislature void when judicial independence was threatened were principles he had held dear since his days as a student of George Wythe at William and Mary. In 1783, as a member of Virginia's council of state, Marshall had refused to enforce an act of the legislature authorizing the executive to review the conduct of judges.[73] In 1788, as a member of the House of Delegates, he had joined in introducing legislation reaffirming the separation of powers and withdrawing from Virginia's executive any authority over the judiciary, a measure that passed the House unanimously.[74] At the Virginia ratification convention later that year, he had defended the authority of the judiciary to declare an act of Congress unconstitutional.[75] Even more to the point, on circuit in Raleigh in January 1803, just one month before handing down the decision in *Marbury*, he had indicated that an act of the North Carolina legislature infringing judicial authority was void.[76]

With the decision in *Marbury v. Madison*, Marshall was neither embarking on a crusade for judicial supremacy, nor was he charting new territory. In restrained language, he interposed the Court as a check against legislative omnipotence and affirmed the principles that lie at the root of constitutional government. The people, not the government, are sovereign, and the Constitution reflects their will. By exercising judicial review, the Court was merely enforcing the will of the people as expressed in the Constitution, over the desire of the government as expressed in the statute. Marshall's reverence for the Constitution set the tone of the decision. The care and patience with which he elucidated the issues elevated the Court above partisanship. Marshall articulated the virtues of limited government. Read in its entirety, *Marbury v. Madison* is an essay on the necessity for moderation. It is a primer on representative government, a rationale for the rule of law. It is the first of Marshall's great constitutional decisions, and perhaps his most eloquent.

14

14

✦✦

The Center Holds

THE SUPREME COURT handed down its decision in *Stuart v. Laird*
on Thursday, March 2, 1803, and adjourned immediately thereafter.[1] Congress followed suit the next day. It would be another year
before either body met again, and the future was unclear. On the one hand,
a *modus vivendi* between the judiciary and the Jefferson administration appeared possible. The Court's decisions in *Marbury v. Madison* and *Stuart v.
Laird* reflected Marshall's determination to rise above partisanship, and had
been hailed by most Republicans as such. For its part, the administration
seemed content with the repeal of the "midnight judges act" and the new
moderation the judiciary was displaying. Jefferson faced reelection in 1804
and was eager to bring as many Federalists under the Republican tent as
possible. That effort would be undermined by a renewed assault on the
courts. Indeed, if the Court and the administration had been the only players in 1803, it is possible that an accommodation would have been reached.[2]

But the hand of fate was not so easily satisfied. The radical Republicans,
led by William Branch Giles and John Randolph, two of Jefferson's staunch
Virginia allies, continued to see the judiciary in partisan terms, as did their
High Federalist opponents. Neither could accept the idea of an independent, free-standing judicial system as a third branch of government. The
American experiment in the separation of powers was still in its trial stages.
When Giles referred to the judiciary as "a fortress in possession of the enemy" and called for the wholesale removal of judges so that the courts could
be synchronized with Congress and the president,[3] he was merely express-

ing traditional ideas that died hard.[4] Ironically, those ideas were as congenial to Federalist irreconcilables such as Gouverneur Morris and Timothy Pickering as they were to Giles and Randolph, all of whom saw the courts as major players in the game of partisan politics. That rendered accommodation problematic. Until the independence of the judiciary was more firmly established, or until the extremists in both parties were brought under control, a rapprochement between the administration and the judiciary was unlikely.

On March 2, just before leaving Washington for Richmond, Marshall expressed his concern to Oliver Wolcott. "We have fallen upon evil times, and I do not clearly perceive a prospect of better."[5] Samuel Chase, who was slowly recovering from the gout that had crippled him and whose combative instincts had been restrained by Marshall, apparently shared the chief justice's concern. "Things must take their natural Course, from *bad* to *worse*," he wrote to a friend several days later.[6]

Back in Richmond, Marshall immediately turned his attention to the quasi-official biography of Washington he had agreed to write. In 1799, when the first president died, he had bequeathed his public and private papers to his nephew Bushrod,[7] and Bushrod had conceived the idea of using the papers as the basis of a biography. Initially he had planned to write the biography together with Washington's longtime secretary, Tobias Lear. But by the spring of 1800 he had had second thoughts, due in part to his own failing eyesight, and he approached Marshall. "I cannot help thinking that General Marshall may be induced to undertake the writing of the history," he wrote Lear.[8] Bushrod said he was "extremely anxious to see this work commenced" and that Marshall, who was then a member of Congress, was the one person who could do "full Justice to the Subject."[9] Marshall had announced the news of Washington's death, had given the nation's memorial address in Congress, had chaired the committee that made the funeral arrangements for the former president's burial, and was head of the commission planning a monument in the capital. No one in public life had been closer to Washington in his final years.

Exactly when Marshall agreed is not certain, but by the autumn of 1800 he was committed.[10] As befitted old friends, there was no formal contract. The understanding was that Bushrod would provide Washington's papers and handle the publishing arrangements, while Marshall would do the writing. The income would be divided equally. Marshall was unable to begin the project immediately, having just been appointed secretary of state. Nevertheless, Bushrod let it be known what they were planning and began to solicit bids from various publishers.

In December 1800 Lear delivered the first trunk of Washington's papers to Marshall, but it was not until the summer of 1801, after his first term of Court, that he began to write.[11] Over the next five years, while performing his duties as chief justice and presiding over the biennial sessions of the circuit courts in Richmond and Raleigh, Marshall wrote a five-volume biography of George Washington, totaling over 3,200 pages. The first volume was a history of the British colonies; volumes two, three, and four dealt with the revolution; volume five, published in 1807, covered Washington's presidency and the first decade of the United States under the Constitution.[12] The work was not so much a biography as a history of the American people. Marshall began with the first settlements in Jamestown and Plymouth, and traced the growth of the nation, concluding with Washington's death in 1799. In a sense, Marshall became America's first nationalist historian.[13] He wrote about Washington and the United States as if they were inseparable. In his youth, Marshall had been nurtured on the histories of Livy, which celebrated the Roman republic. His outlook and much of his phraseology were shaped by his reading of Alexander Pope and of Voltaire, under whose influence he had fallen during his year in Paris. Marshall appreciated the contribution literature could make to civic culture, and his *Life of Washington* became an object lesson in public virtue.[14]

Book writing was a new challenge for Marshall, and it is fair to say that he had no idea how much work would be involved or how long it would take. Throughout his life, the chief justice cultivated a relaxed image of idleness and lassitude, but the fact is that he was superbly disciplined. He rose well before dawn every day; by noon he had done a full day's work and was free for more informal activities. That was his normal routine. The problem was that the *Life of Washington* imposed far greater demands. Marshall had always been able to write quickly and was accustomed to writing under deadlines, but for the most part, his previous efforts had been singular exertions—the XYZ dispatches from Paris, the *Robbins* speech, the decision in *Marbury*—after which he could put the matter aside. Book writing, especially a five-volume project, was a long-term commitment with onerous daily requirements. Marshall soon recognized the toll it was taking. "I had to learn that under the pressure of constant application the spring of the mind loses its elasticity," he acknowledged to his publisher after the first volume was completed.[15]

From the beginning, Bushrod and Marshall assumed that the book would be a commercial success. They believed the public would buy at least 30,000 copies of the five-volume set, and Bushrod had based his negotiations on that figure. According to his calculations, the volumes would sell for $3 apiece. He and Marshall would get $1, and the publisher would retain $2. By simple arithmetic (30,000 x 5 x $1.00), royalties should total $150,000, which meant that he and Marshall could expect to receive $75,000 each.

Those calculations proved hopelessly optimistic. After negotiating with a number of publishers, none of whom was prepared to offer a cash advance,

Bushrod eventually came to terms with Caleb P. Wayne, editor of the *Gazette of the United States*, the nation's leading Federalist newspaper. Under their agreement, Marshall and Bushrod would receive $1 for each volume sold, but there would be no payment until the third volume had been published. This arrangement would allow Wayne to recoup his costs and ensure that Marshall produced the manuscripts on schedule. Marshall did not want to sign the contract[16] and initially did not want to be identified as the author of the biography. He eventually relented on both points when Wayne and Bushrod insisted, but even then he refused to be identified as chief justice.[17] His name was printed in extremely small type near the bottom of the title page, well below that of "The Honourable Bushrod Washington," under whose inspection it was said the books were written.

Wayne played the traditional role of publisher-printer-bookseller, and, as was standard in the early 1800s, the books were sold by subscription. Originally, Wayne meant to tour the major cities and collect subscriptions himself, but he soon realized that was unfeasible. Instead, he authorized local postmasters to take subscribers' names and collect the money. There were 1,250 postmasters in the United States, he told Marshall, and "All letters to and from these men go free of postage."[18] As the publication date of the first volume neared, Wayne also engaged two commission salesmen, Mason Locke Weems, who would later write his own biography of Washington, and John Ormrod, a Philadelphia printer, to scour the country.[19] Weems covered the southern states; Ormrod, the north.

Marshall took an avid interest in the sale of subscriptions and wrote numerous letters to friends throughout the South introducing Weems. "You will much oblige me by naming to him such persons as he may probably apply to with success, and by giving him your countenance," the chief justice wrote to Judge Henry Potter, his colleague on the North Carolina circuit, early in 1804.[20]

After a year of advertising, Wayne had sold 4,000 subscriptions. It was a record for a work that had not been published, although the number fell far below Marshall's and Bushrod's expectations. Bushrod was particularly disappointed, and asked Wayne whether the postmasters, who, under Jefferson, were largely "democrats," had put their heart into the work. "I would not give one honest *soliciting* agent for 1250 quiescent postmasters."[21] Wayne assured Washington that the problem was not the postmasters but the cost of the volumes and the delay in publication. Three dollars was a high price for a work of unknown quality that had not yet appeared.[22]

Eventually, the project did become a commercial success, though not the bonanza that Marshall and Bushrod had anticipated.[23] Over 7,000 copies of the set were sold, which, together with foreign rights, produced $39,000 in royalties.[24] Bushrod and Marshall netted $19,500 each. Marshall's share enabled him to make the final payment on Leeds Manor to the heirs of Denny Martin, and the title to the last Fairfax property in Virginia was transferred to him and his brother James on October 18, 1806.[25]

The *Life of Washington* was quickly translated into French, German, and Dutch, and American demand remained strong for a number of years. Throughout his life, Marshall tinkered with the manuscript, constantly revising and rephrasing it.[26] From the time the work was first published in 1805, there have been over three dozen editions, the most recent in 1983, and the set is still in print.[27] Shortly before he died, Marshall prepared a two-volume abridgement for schoolchildren.[28] That went through twenty editions before it was replaced as the basic text of Washington's life.

Critical reaction to the biography was mixed. Marshall's judicial prose did not make for scintillating reading, and those who expected a literary masterpiece were disappointed. British commentators, accustomed to the works of Boswell and Gibbon, were particularly harsh. The *Edinburgh Review* called the *Life of Washington* "unpardonably deficient in all that constitutes the soul and charm of biography. . . . We look in vain . . . for any sketch or anecdote that might fix a distinguishing feature of private character in the memory."[29] John Adams, whose views of Washington were ambivalent, called the work "a mausoleum, 100 feet square at the base and 200 feet high."[30] On the other hand, James Madison found it "highly respectable, as a specimen of historical composition."[31] In general, Federalist reviewers praised Marshall for his candor, and the Republican press found nothing objectionable in the first four volumes, which concluded Washington's military career. Only in volume five, where he dealt with the bitter party strife of the 1790s, did Marshall venture onto perilous ground. "I have reason to fear that the imprudent task I have just executed will draw upon me a degree of odium and calumny which I might perhaps otherwise have escaped," he confessed afterward. "But having undertaken it I have endeavored to detail the events of a most turbulent and factious period without unnecessarily wounding the dominant [Republican] party, but without a cowardly abandonment of the truth."[32] As Marshall anticipated, Republican criticism was severe.[33]

Overall, the judgment of history has been favorable.[34] Marshall's rendition of the War of Independence, particularly the events in which he participated, at times achieves the grace and urgency of Grant's military *Memoirs*.[35] His portrayal of conditions at Valley Forge is the best that has been written, and his description of the formation of the Union under the Constitution is a model of trenchant political analysis. As a documentary source book, the volumes are invaluable.[36] Jared Sparks, who undertook a more conventional biography of Washington several decades later, noted that "after the able, accurate, and comprehensive work of Chief Justice Marshall, it would be presumptuous to attempt a historical biography of Washington."[37] Washington Irving, another biographer of the first president, relied heavily on Marshall's work.[38] Joseph Story, reviewing a separate edition of the first volume (published in 1824), called the *Life of Washington* "the most authentic history of the colonies, which is extant."[39]

Writing 100 years later, Professor Charles Beard found the *Life of Washington* to be "masterly." He hailed Marshall as "a historian of great acumen [who] sketched with an unerring hand the economic conflict which led to the adoption of the Constitution,"[40] and thereupon proceeded to quote from him for three solid pages in his own seminal work on the Constitution. Subsequently, in his work on Jeffersonian democracy, Beard paid homage to Marshall, "who, in his *Life of Washington*, expounded in a few passages of that remarkable clarity and precision which characterized his opinions from the bench, the economic nature of the grievances on which the Republicans thrived."[41] More recently, historians Stanley Elkins and Eric McKitrick, winners of the 1994 National Book Award for *The Age of Federalism*, relied implicitly on Marshall's reconstruction of the differences between Hamilton and Jefferson for the framework of their discussion of the origin of the Federalist and Republican parties.[42]

The *Life of Washington* may be even more important for what it reveals about Marshall's views concerning the Constitution.[43] The theoretical underpinnings of the great decisions of the Marshall Court are laid out in the pages describing the origins of the Constitution. The centrifugal force of the individual states is a threat to the Union. National well-being requires national unity, and the power of the central government must be commensurate with its responsibilities. In foreign relations, the United States must speak with one voice. Public obligations are a public trust and must be rigorously adhered to. Commercial activity requires uniform regulation. The obligations of contract must be strictly enforced. In *McCulloch v. Maryland*,[44] *Fletcher v. Peck*,[45] *Gibbons v. Ogden*,[46] and the *Dartmouth College* case,[47] those views became the law of the land.

As the *Life of Washington* makes clear, Marshall believed that the Constitution established the organic unity of the United States and that the powers granted to the national government were meant to be interpreted broadly. Marshall does not explicitly address the role of the Court, but he refers time and again to the need for balance and moderation. Washington exemplified those traits, and Marshall's description of him provides what may well be the best brief statement of the chief justice's own principles[48]:

> In speculation, he was a real republican, devoted to the constitution of his country, and to that system of equal political rights on which it is founded. But between a balanced republic and a democracy, the

real difference is like that between order and chaos. Real liberty, he thought, was to be preserved only by preserving the authority of the laws, and maintaining the energy of government. Scarcely did society present two characters which, in his opinion, less resembled each other, than a patriot and a demagogue.[49]

Jefferson took particular offense at that passage, inferring that the reference to a demagogue was an implicit reference to him. In fact, Jefferson had been deeply suspicious of Marshall's motives from the outset. When he first learned that Marshall was writing the biography of Washington, the president assumed it was a partisan gambit to influence the 1804 election. So great was his concern that he immediately wrote to his friend Joel Barlow, who was still in Paris, and asked him to write a Republican rejoinder. "John Marshall is writing the life of General Washington from his papers. It is intended to come out just in time to influence the next presidential election. It is written therefore principally with a view to election purposes, but it will consequently be out in time to aid you with information as well as to point out the perversions of truth necessary to be rectified."[50] Jefferson told Barlow that he and Madison would make their papers available to him and that he should return to the United States as soon as possible.

Insofar as the 1804 election was concerned, Jefferson had little to fear. By November Marshall had published only the first two volumes, concluding with the distress of the army at Valley Forge. Nevertheless, Jefferson's reaction reflects the distrust he and Marshall had of each other. Although both men were moderate politically, each instinctively misread the other's motives. Marshall, for example, refused to credit Jefferson's effort to diminish the partisanship that beset the nation and invariably linked him with the rhetoric of the radical Republicans. Jefferson, as his response to the *Life of Washington* suggests, saw Marshall in High Federalist colors and declined to accept at face value his attempt to remove the Court from partisan politics. Each thought the other devious. Marshall could not understand the internal problems that bedeviled the Republicans and could not appreciate how difficult it was for Jefferson to rein in the radicals. Jefferson could not understand Marshall's attachment to an independent judiciary and could not appreciate that his reverence for the Constitution transcended his earlier incarnation as Federalist leader in Virginia.

These deep-seated differences were exacerbated by the personal antipathy each man had for the other. As president and chief justice, they maintained an uneasy equilibrium that personified the separation of powers. Each jealously guarded the prerogatives of his office and, at the personal level, begrudged the success of the other. Yet for all their differences, each represented a vital current in the American mainstream. Jefferson believed passionately in majority rule. Marshall, just as earnestly, feared majority tyranny. Jefferson was attached to liberty and equality. Marshall stood for the rule of law and a government of checks and balances. Jefferson tilted to the left and Marshall to the right, but between them they encompassed the vast center of the political spectrum. Regardless of their mutual distrust, the author of the Declaration of Independence and the man destined to become the guardian of the Constitution were each essential to the emerging American consensus. Neither wanted a constitutional confrontation, and it was ultimately that common concern that kept the country on an even keel.

Shortly after the Court adjourned in the spring of 1803, Jefferson, in an extraordinary display of presidential prerogative, resolved the crisis on the lower Mississippi with an agreement to purchase the entire Louisiana territory from Napoleon for $15 million. The agreement involved substantial risk. The boundaries of the province were unresolved; Napoleon's title to the territory was cloudy*; Spain remained in possession of the area; France had promised the Spanish crown never to dispose of Louisiana to a third party; and in any event, the French constitution prohibited the alienation of national territory without a vote of the legislative assembly. Nevertheless, when presented with the opportunity to double the size of the United States and ensure unimpeded navigation of the Mississippi, Jefferson acted with alacrity.[51]

Under the terms of the treaty of cession, the inhabitants of the Louisiana territory were granted the rights of American citizens and eventual admission to the Union. That raised additional constitutional problems. In his conflict with Hamilton over the establishment of the national bank, Jefferson had argued that the government possessed no power not expressly granted by the Constitution, and initially he had qualms about his authority to consummate the purchase.[52] But the issue quickly resolved itself along partisan lines. When the treaty came before the Senate for approval, the normally strict-constructionist Republicans voted unanimously in favor of it, while the Federalists, who under Washington and Adams had championed presidential prerogative, voted nay.[53] The radical Republicans from the

---

*Under the Treaty of St. Ildefonso, October 1, 1800, by which Spain agreed to retrocede Louisiana to France, Napoleon undertook, as a prior condition, to establish in Italy a minor kingdom for the Prince of Parma, the son-in-law of the Spanish monarchs. It was agreed that six months thereafter, the king of Spain would retrocede Louisiana to France. By the summer of 1802, Napoleon had been unable to obtain recognition of the new "kingdom" by the major European powers, but he reassured the Spanish crown of his intent. Accordingly, on October 15, Spain agreed to transfer Louisiana despite the fact that the prior condition specified in the Treaty of St. Ildefonso had not been fulfilled. In the spring of 1803, however, when Jefferson agreed to purchase Louisiana from France, that transfer had not yet taken place. See A. P. Whitaker, "The Retrocession of Louisiana in Spanish Policy," 39 *American Historical Review* 454–476 (1934).

West waxed eloquent about the access to new lands. The Federalists cited constitutional objections to expanding the size of the Union without the consent of the states. In effect, the parties had changed sides.

Marshall had no doubt that the acquisition of Louisiana was constitutional. When the issue finally came before the Court in 1828, his decision was unequivocal.[54] Speaking for his colleagues, Marshall said that "the Constitution confers absolutely on the government of the Union, the powers of making war, and of making treaties; consequently, that government possesses the power of acquiring territory, either by conquest or by treaty." Since the Constitution said nothing explicitly about the authority to acquire territory, Marshall held that it was implicit in the war power and the treaty power. The states did not have to be consulted, and the "ceded territory becomes a part of the nation to which it is annexed."[55]

As for the boundaries of the purchase, the most contentious issue was whether the territory known as West Florida* was included. Jefferson, studying old maps of French Louisiana, was convinced that it was[56]; Talleyrand, when asked, was evasive[57]; and the Spanish rejected the claim. The United States eventually took possession of the area under color of the treaty of cession, and when the issue came before the Court, Marshall once again upheld Jefferson's interpretation. Reiterating the distinction between legal issues and political questions he had drawn in *Marbury v. Madison*, the chief justice deferred to the president and Congress:

> If those departments which are intrusted with the foreign intercourse of the nation, which assert and maintain its interests against foreign powers, have unequivocally asserted the rights of dominion over a country of which it is in possession, and which it claims under a treaty; if the legislature has acted on the construction thus asserted, it is not in its own courts that this construction is to be denied. *A question like this respecting the boundaries of nations, is . . . more a political*

---

*West Florida was the area along the Gulf coast between the Iberville and Perdido Rivers that today comprises the littoral of Alabama and Mississippi, including the ports of Mobile, Gulfport, and Biloxi. It was part of the area ceded by France to Great Britain after the Seven Years War in 1763, and during the period of French rule, it was unmistakably part of the Louisiana Territory. After the war, the British immediately transferred the area to the Spanish, who annexed it to their existing Florida holdings, designating the areas Louisiana, West Florida, and East Florida respectively. Consequently, under Spanish rule, West Florida was not part of Louisiana. The Treaty of St. Ildefonso stated ambiguously that Spain was retroceding to France "the colony or province of Louisiana, with the same extent that it now has in the hands of Spain, and that it had when France possessed it." The words were chosen by Talleyrand and deliberately conveyed two different meanings. France could claim that West Florida was included; Spain could assert that it was not. Talleyrand was undoubtedly convinced that if the issue should be tested, France's interpretation would prevail. See I. J. Cox, *West Florida Controversy* 80–81 (Baltimore: Johns Hopkins Press, 1918).

than a legal question, and in its discussion, the courts of every country must respect the will of the legislature. . . .[58]

In the autumn of 1803, with the Louisiana purchase finalized and navigation of the Mississippi assured, Marshall presided over the circuit court in Richmond.[59] After Christmas, he made another trip to Raleigh where he sat with Judge Potter on the North Carolina circuit.[60] After completing his duties on circuit, he returned home and wrote to Potter that "with a little breaking down, walking, and traveling in a wagon I reached Virginia agreeably enough without any accident to procrastinate the journey."[61] Traveling on circuit was the most arduous task the justices faced, and Marshall, who had only to journey to Raleigh twice a year, was far more fortunate than his colleagues. Justice Cushing, on the first circuit in New England, had been badly injured on several occasions when his coach overturned; Chase was almost drowned when his ferry was swept away on the rain-swollen Susquehanna; and Alfred Moore confronted danger constantly in the backwoods of South Carolina and Georgia.

This year it was Justice Paterson, on circuit in New Jersey, who suffered serious injury. "The coachee in which I was returning home overset down a precipice of ten feet," he wrote to Marshall. The fifty-eight-year-old Paterson said he was "so much injured, particularly in my right side and left shoulder, that I am not yet able to dress, undress, *etc.*, without assistance." He told Marshall that his physicians had instructed him not to travel to Washington, and that as a result he would miss the 1804 term of the Court. "Permit me to suggest the propriety of your writing to Judge Moore, and urging the necessity of his attendance at the next term. It would be an unpleasant circumstance, if a number of judges, sufficient to constitute a quorum, should not attend." Marshall regretted Paterson's misfortune, but chose not to write to Moore, assuming that the North Carolina jurist would have left for Washington before a letter could reach him. However, Moore was also in poor health, did not attend the 1804 term, and resigned from the Court at the end of February.

As the 1804 term drew near, Marshall's efforts to remove the Court from partisan politics suffered a major setback. In early January the mercurial John Randolph introduced a resolution in the House of Representatives calling for an investigation into the conduct of Justice Chase.[62] Randolph had been openly critical for some time of the moderate course being pursued by Jefferson,[63] and he would soon break completely with the administration. The evidence suggests that by attacking Chase—a large, slow-moving target—Randolph hoped to rally the party's radicals and force Jefferson to adopt a more aggressive attitude toward the judiciary.[64] There is certainly nothing in the record to indicate that Randolph made his motion either at the request of the president or with his consent.[65]

After four days of heated debate, the House adopted Randolph's motion, a number of moderate Republicans joining the Federalists in opposition.[66] Chase, who lived nearby in Baltimore, followed the proceedings in the House closely and immediately wrote to Marshall asking for his support. Several of the accusations against Chase involved his alleged misconduct when he had presided over the sedition trial of James Callender in Richmond in 1800. Chase asked Marshall to obtain statements from the members of the bar who had been present and made clear his determination to fight the charges.[67]

As soon as Marshall received Chase's letter, he sought out a number of lawyers who had witnessed the trial. He told Chase that he would bring their statements to Washington when the Court convened in February. Marshall had little sympathy for Chase's free-wheeling partisanship on the bench and, indeed, had devoted considerable energy as chief justice to moderating the Marylander's outspokenness. But he was appalled that the Republican majority would go after his colleague for actions that had occurred so many years earlier. Besides, Marshall knew that in the heat of trials, judges sometimes ruled incorrectly. That was what the appellate process was designed to remedy. Marshall told Chase that even if errors had been made, "it certainly constitutes a very extraordinary ground for an impeachment."[68]

Marshall was not an advocate of judicial supremacy, but he was determined to defend the independence of the Court. He reminded Chase that in ancient times, juries were subject to an attaint* for deciding incorrectly. "The present doctrine seems to be that a Judge giving a legal opinion contrary to the will of the legislature is liable to impeachment." Marshall then told Chase that if the legislature did not agree with a judge's holding, they should reverse it by statute. Just as "the old doctrine of attaint has yielded to the silent, moderate but not less operative influence of new trials, I think the modern doctrine of impeachment should yield to an appellate jurisdiction in the legislature. A reversal of those legal opinions deemed unsound by the legislature would certainly better comport with the mildness of our character than a removal of the Judge who had rendered them unknowing of his fault."[69]

---

*Attaint was an old English practice designed to determine whether a jury had given a false verdict. The inquiry was made by a grand assize of twenty-four persons, usually knights, and if they found the verdict to be a false one, the judgment was that the jurors should become infamous, forfeit their property, be imprisoned, and have their wives and children thrust out of doors, their houses razed, their trees extirpated, and their meadows plowed up. Sir William Blackstone, 3 *Commentaries on the Laws of England* 404 (Oxford: Clarendon Press, 1765).

The House of Representatives investigated Chase's activities for the next several months. Meanwhile, when the Court convened on February 6, a record twenty-two cases were pending. With Paterson and Moore absent, the workload fell to Marshall, Chase, Cushing, and Washington. As a result of Randolph's motion, the atmosphere was charged once again. Marshall's and Jefferson's separate efforts to lower the political temperature seemed to have gone for naught. The radical Republicans were seeking to make the Court an issue, just as in 1803 the High Federalists had sought to engage the Court in their partisan struggle. Also reminiscent of 1803, the Court's docket included two well-publicized cases that divided along party lines.

In *Murray v. Schooner Charming Betsy*,[70] the politically explosive issue of expatriation was front and center. Jefferson and the Republicans believed that expatriation—the ability to renounce one's citizenship and accept a different allegiance—was the natural right of all Americans. Most Federalists disagreed, holding that citizenship was permanent and that one could change allegiance only with the approval of the government.[71]

The case involved the capture of the *Charming Betsy*, a schooner out of St. Thomas flying Danish colors, by the U.S.S. *Constellation* during the quasi-war with France. *Constellation*, a sister ship of the *Constitution*, was commanded by Captain Alexander Murray and had already acquired legendary status as a result of its dramatic capture of the thirty-eight-gun French frigate *Insurgente* off the island of Nevis in 1799—the first victory for the United States Navy since John Paul Jones had forced H.M.S. *Serapis* to strike its colors twenty years earlier.[72] The *Charming Betsy* was owned by Jared Shattuck, an American by birth who in 1789 had moved to St. Thomas, a Danish colony in the Virgin Islands. He had sworn allegiance to the Danish crown and conducted business as a Danish subject. In the summer of 1800, the *Charming Betsy* set out from St. Thomas to Guadaloupe with a cargo of American produce. She was intercepted and captured by a French privateer and then retaken by the *Constellation*. Captain Murray presumed Shattuck to be an American citizen who was trading with the enemy in violation of the nonintercourse act, thereby making the schooner a lawful prize. The vessel was taken to Philadelphia for condemnation, but the trial court ruled that the seizure was illegal, holding that Shattuck was a Danish subject. It ordered the *Charming Betsy* restored and awarded heavy damages against Captain Murray. The issue before the Supreme Court turned on whether the nonintercourse act, which barred American citizens from trading with France, applied to Shattuck.

Speaking once again for a unanimous Court, Marshall restricted the applicability of the nonintercourse act to the narrowest possible limits. "An act of Congress," he said, "ought never to be construed to violate the law of nations if any other possible construction remains, and consequently can never be construed to violate neutral rights, or to affect neutral commerce, further than is warranted by the law of nations as understood in this country."[73] He then stepped gingerly around the expatriation controversy. Marshall personally believed in permanent allegiance,* but he saw no reason for the judiciary to become embroiled in so partisan an issue. "Whether a person born within the *United States* . . . can divest himself absolutely of that character otherwise than in such manner prescribed by law, is a question which it is not necessary at present to decide."[74] Instead, Marshall devised the concept of foreign commercial domicile to apply to businessmen residing abroad. Shattuck, because of his residence in St. Thomas and his oath of allegiance to Denmark, had removed himself from the protection of the United States and was temporarily clothed with Danish nationality. It was another of Marshall's judicious compromises. The Federalist idea of perpetual allegiance was not rejected, but for all practical purposes Shattuck was to be treated as a Dane. "It is therefore the opinion of the court, that the *Charming Betsy* . . . being at the time of her recapture the *bona fide* property of a *Danish* burgher, is not forfeitable."[75]

Marshall was troubled by one aspect of the holding. As a former soldier, he sympathized with Captain Murray who, he said, had "acted upon correct motives, from a sense of duty." As a result, "this hard case ought not to be rendered still more so by a decision in any respect oppressive." The Court restored the vessel to Shattuck, but substantially reduced the damages assessed against the *Constellation*'s captain.[76]

The questions of obeying the orders of a superior officer and of the respective war powers of the president and Congress were central to the other major case before the Court that term, *Little v. Barreme*.[77] Captain George Little, commanding the frigate U.S.S. *Boston* on station off Santo Domingo, had intercepted and captured the Danish brig *Flying Fish* en route from Jérémie to St. Thomas, suspecting it of being an American vessel trading with the enemy. Little was acting in accordance with the orders of President Adams to intercept any suspected American ship sailing *to* or *from* a French port. The difficulty was that Congress had authorized the president to seize only those vessels sailing *to* French ports. The *Flying Fish* was sailing *from* a French port, not *to* one. The trial court ordered the brig and its cargo restored to its owners, and the circuit court added an award of damages against Captain Little for acting contrary to the law. The question before the Supreme Court was whether the orders of President Adams mitigated Captain Little's liability.

---

*Marshall never took an explicit judicial position on expatriation, although he expressed his personal views in a 1814 letter to Timothy Pickering. "In truth," he wrote, "it is a question upon which I never entertained a *scintilla* of doubt." Marshall to Pickering, April 11, 1814, Pickering Papers, Massachusetts Historical Society. Marshall's emphasis.

Speaking once more for his colleagues, Marshall said that in the absence of congressional legislation, the president might well have issued the orders to the navy that he did. However, once Congress had specified the manner by which the nonintercourse act was to be enforced, the president no longer enjoyed that discretion. The orders of the president, since they were contrary to the act, could not shield Captain Little from responsibility. Again, however, Marshall was troubled by the effect the holding might have on the military.

> I was much inclined to think that a distinction ought to be taken between acts of civil and those of military officers; and between proceedings within the body of the country and those on the high seas. That implicit obedience which military men usually pay to the orders of their superiors, which indeed is indispensably necessary to every military system, appeared to me strongly to imply the principle that those orders, if not to perform a prohibited act, ought to justify the person whose general duty it is to obey them, and who is placed by the laws of his country in a situation which in general requires that he should obey them. . . .[78]

Marshall said he had been convinced by his fellow justices that he was mistaken. "I acquiesce in [the opinion] of my brethren . . . that the instructions [of the president] cannot change the nature of the transaction, or legalize an act which without those instructions would have been plain trespass."

The Court's decision in *Little v. Barreme* established an important precedent concerning the president's authority as commander in chief. Marshall held that the president enjoys an inherent discretion to deal with military emergencies as they arise, provided that Congress has not acted. Once Congress takes action, presidential discretion is limited. In 1952, when President Truman disregarded the Taft-Hartley Act and seized the nation's steel mills, the decision in *Little v. Barreme* was cited repeatedly by the justices as the controlling precedent explaining why President Truman had exceeded his authority.[79]

Little v. Barreme also stands for the principle that the orders of a superior, even if they are from the commander in chief, do not exempt a military officer from personal responsibility. To say that one was "just following orders" is not an acceptable excuse. That premise became a central feature of the American military system after the decision.[80]

Finally, *Little v. Barreme* provides a rare insight into the workings of the Marshall Court and should put to rest any assumption that the chief justice's colleagues were pliant tools in the hands of a master manipulator. Marshall spoke for the Court, and the decision was unanimous, but the text of the opinion makes it obvious that he had disagreed with his colleagues initially and then had yielded to their judgment. The opinion reveals the extent to which the justices discussed decisions collectively and the premium they placed on consensus. Dissents were discouraged, and in this instance Marshall preferred to yield than to break ranks.

The day after the decision in *Little v. Barreme* was handed down, Alfred Moore's resignation from the Court arrived in Washington. Although Moore was the same age as Marshall, he had been ailing for several years and was no longer able to make the annual journey to the nation's capital to attend the sessions of the Supreme Court, much less carry out his duties on circuit. As Senator William Plumer quaintly put it to a friend in New Hampshire, "Judge Moore, from a full conviction of a speedy removal by writ of *habeas corpus* returnable in Heaven's Chancery, has resigned his office."[81]

Moore's resignation gave Jefferson his first opportunity to alter the complexion of the Court. The president had just been renominated by his party's congressional caucus for a second term[82] and was determined to find a Republican jurist who would break the Federalist monopoly on the Court. At the same time, he wanted someone who would not be objectionable to the nation's legal community. "The importance of filling this vacancy with a Republican and a man of sufficient talents to be useful is obvious," wrote treasury secretary Albert Gallatin.[83] Because of Moore's circuit responsibilities in Georgia and South Carolina, Gallatin recommended that a South Carolinian be named ("the practice in Georgia is as loose as it is in New England"), and after an extensive search, Jefferson settled on William Johnson, who at thirty-two would become the youngest person appointed to the Court.[84] Johnson was then a judge on the South Carolina supreme court and, like the mainstays of Jefferson's cabinet, was a political moderate acceptable to most Federalists. "He is a zealous Democrat," wrote Senator Plumer, "but is said to be honest and capable."[85] The son of a blacksmith, Johnson had worked his way through Princeton and graduated at the head of his class in 1790. He returned to Charleston to read law in the office of Marshall's old friend, Charles Cotesworth Pinckney, for whom he acquired enormous personal and professional respect. Elected to the South Carolina legislature in 1794, he had shunned any attachment with the Charleston Republican Society and had sided with the Federalists on local issues involving tax reform, bank charters, and the revision of the state's judiciary. Plumer said admiringly, "He has, without the aid of family, friends, or connections, by his talents and persevering industry raised himself to office."[86] Story wrote that Johnson had "a strong mathematical head, and considerable soundness of erudition . . . less of metaphysics, and more of logic."[87] Once on the Court, Johnson occasionally dissented from his colleagues on economic issues, and he disliked Marshall's habit of always speaking for the Court. But as Jefferson would soon learn, his support for national authority surpassed that of the chief justice himself.

Shortly after Johnson's appointment, and before the Court adjourned in March, Marshall provided a deposition to the House committee of inquiry concerning Chase. The subject was the Callender trial in Richmond. One of the witnesses against Chase swore that he had heard Chase and Bushrod Washington (in the presence of Marshall) discussing the Callender case in the lobby of Stelle's Hotel. Chase had allegedly told Bushrod that if he had known that Callender was an enemy of Jefferson, he "would scarcely have fined him so high."[88] Marshall deposed that he vaguely recalled the incident but said that the conversation was not to be taken seriously. The justices often joked among themselves, said Marshall, and he would not respect his colleagues as he did if he thought "such motives for judicial conduct" had been acknowledged by Chase, or if they had not been condemned by Washington.[89]

The 1804 term of the Court ended on March 6. Of the twenty-two cases that had been pending, decisions were rendered in fourteen: Marshall delivered eight, Cushing one, and five were *per curiam*.[90] The Chase controversy notwithstanding, the term was another benchmark in the establishment of the Court's stature. John Quincy Adams, recently elected to the United States Senate from Massachusetts, wrote to a friend after arguing his first two cases before the justices[91] that "I have never witnessed a collection of such powerful legal oratory as at this session of the Supreme Court."[92]

The House investigation into Chase's conduct concluded March 12. Two weeks later the formal articles of impeachment, drafted by John Randolph, were laid before the House.[93] The charges pertained to incidents ranging from oppressive conduct and mistaken rulings during the trials of John Fries and James Callender in 1800, to a highly partisan charge to a grand jury in Baltimore in the spring of 1803.[94] All charges related to Chase's conduct on circuit; none pertained to his role as an associate justice of the Supreme Court. Back in Richmond working on the *Life of Washington*, Marshall was plainly disturbed by what he considered a political vendetta. "I have just received the articles of impeachment against Judge Chase," he wrote to his brother James on April 1. "They are sufficient to alarm the friends of a pure and, of course, an independent judiciary, if among those who rule our land there are any of that description."[95] It being late in the session, the House deferred action on Randolph's recommendations until the next term, scheduled to convene in November.[96]

During the spring and summer of 1804, Marshall was preoccupied with the *Life of Washington*. The first volume was published in June, the second in September, and volume three, which covered the period from the battle of

Monmouth to Cornwallis's surrender at Yorktown, appeared in November. On circuit in Richmond, Marshall heard a dozen cases, including his first major criminal case, *United States v. Logwood.*[97] Thomas Logwood, a prominent Buckingham county planter, was part of a counterfeiting ring manufacturing bogus U.S. banknotes. A federal grand jury, which included John Randolph among its members, indicted Logwood on five counts. He was convicted on four, Marshall dismissing one charge on a technicality.[98] Each count was punishable by ten years in prison and a $5,000 fine.

In passing sentence, Marshall tempered justice with mercy. He said he did not believe that "a separate punishment could be inflicted for every separate charge, because according to this principle, the punishment might be so multiplied . . . as to exceed the very greatest limit which the *letter* of the law had assigned."[99] Accordingly, he sentenced Logwood to a combined total of ten years' imprisonment on all four counts. John Randolph, who had remained in Richmond to witness the trial and who was on the verge of breaking completely with Jefferson, was profoundly impressed by Marshall's demeanor on the bench and even more by the Solomon-like sentence he handed down. Contrary as it may seem, the man who led the Republicans in the House and who had initiated Chase's impeachment had become a fervent admirer of the nation's chief justice. "If a clearer head and sounder heart than Mr. Justice M. possessed be on earth, I have never found them," wrote Randolph.[100]

Chase, in the meantime, was organizing his defense. A formidable opponent on any occasion, the elderly giant girded for the last great battle of his career. That summer he assembled a defense team of the nation's most distinguished lawyers, headed by his old Maryland friend Luther Martin, who, after the death of Patrick Henry, was generally regarded as the greatest trial lawyer in the country.[101] Martin had represented Maryland at the constitutional convention in 1787 and would serve as the state's attorney general for the next twenty-eight years. Beloved by his fellow lawyers, he was a reprobate genius: a notorious alcoholic whose fondness for liquor rarely impaired his performance in the courtroom.*[102]

The Eighth Congress reconvened for its second session in early November 1804. On December 3 Randolph formally submitted the articles of

---

*Martin subsequently led the defense of Aaron Burr when Burr was tried for treason. Years later, he appeared before Chase in circuit court in Baltimore and was visibly intoxicated. "I am surprised that you can so prostitute your talents," Chase said. Martin is supposed to have replied, "Sir, I never prostituted my talents except when I defended you and Colonel Burr." Chase angrily instructed the clerk to cite Martin for contempt, but when presented with the paper for his signature, the elderly judge, recollecting their forty-year friendship and all he owed to Martin, put his quill down, saying "this hand could never sign a citation against Luther Martin." Paul S. Clarkson and R. Samuel Jett, *Luther Martin of Maryland* 280 (Baltimore: Johns Hopkins Press, 1970).

impeachment to the House, which approved them more or less along party lines.[103] Randolph was named to manage the trial in the Senate; in retrospect, that was a serious error.[104] Aside from his brittle personality and his estrangement from the administration, Randolph was not a lawyer, and the bulk of the charges against Chase involved technical legal issues. Although he was a gifted orator, Randolph lacked an understanding of the rules of evidence and had no experience in building a case before a jury. Chase, on the other hand, was a superb lawyer, and his defense team included the best legal talent in the country.

The Senate trial began on February 4, 1805, with Vice President Aaron Burr presiding. There were thirty-four senators present, twenty-five Republicans, and nine Federalists. Twenty-three votes, or two-thirds of the Senate, were required for conviction, which meant that if the decision went along party lines, the Republicans had the necessary votes to remove Chase.

The first day was devoted to Chase's reply to the charges against him, and he delivered a masterful performance. Racked by gout and barely able to stand, the elderly justice spoke for three and a half hours. One by one he examined the articles of impeachment and raised a number of detailed, complex, and often very subtle legal objections. Chase concluded by acknowledging that he could have made procedural mistakes while presiding, but these had been "honest errors," not impeachable offenses. As for his partisan charges to grand juries, Chase defended his right as a citizen to speak out on political topics. He noted that "it has been the practice in this country . . . for the judges to express [themselves] from the bench," and, although Marshall deplored the practice, Chase was quite correct.[105]

Randolph's rebuttal fell flat. In congressional debate, he could be moving and persuasive. But against the remorseless logic of Chase's defense, his rhetorical response was unconvincing and his lack of legal training all too apparent. "This speech is the most feeble . . . that I ever heard him make," said Senator Plumer of New Hampshire.[106]

From that point on, the prosecution's case deteriorated. The House managers defined "high Crimes and Misdemeanors" in political terms, holding that the Senate's power of impeachment was unlimited and that it did not require proof of criminality or corruption.[107] Chase's defense team responded with tight legal arguments insisting that to be impeachable, a judge's conduct must constitute an indictable offense. The text of the Constitution permits both interpretations, but Randolph's histrionics scuttled the prosecution's effort almost from the beginning.[108]

On February 16 Marshall was called as a witness for the defense.[109] He was questioned concerning Chase's conduct at Callender's trial in Richmond and, under cross-examination, acknowledged that Chase and Callender's attorneys had often clashed. However, he declined to place the blame exclusively on Chase.

MR. RANDOLPH.   Then I will make the question more particular by asking whether the interruptions of counsel were much more frequent than usual?

MR. MARSHALL.   The counsel appeared to me to wish to bring before the jury arguments to prove that the sedition law was unconstitutional and Mr. Chase said that that was not a proper question to go to the jury; and whenever any attempt was made to bring that point before the jury, the counsel for [Callender] were stopped. . . .

MR. RANDOLPH.   Is it the practice in courts when counsel objects to the legality of an opinion given by the court to hear arguments of counsel against such an opinion?

MR. MARSHALL.   If the counsel have not been already heard, it is usual to hear them, in order that they may change or confirm the opinion of the court, when there is any doubt entertained. There is however no positive rule on the subject, and the course pursued by the court will depend upon the circumstances. Where a judge believes that the point is perfectly clear and settled, he will scarcely permit the question to be agitated. However, it is considered as decorous on the part of the Judge to listen, while the counsel abstain from urging unimportant arguments.[110]

Throughout his testimony, Marshall was understated and judicious. He discussed Chase's rulings in the context of a bitter trial in which the defense attorneys were angling for every advantage. More important, he adhered closely to the strategy of Chase's lawyers and dealt exclusively with the legal issues. The High Federalists were disappointed that he did not meet the radical Republicans head on and dispute the political nature of the accusations against Chase.[111] Marshall took the position that the burden of proof rested with the prosecution and that the most effective defense strategy was to cast an element of doubt on each of the charges that had been brought. He was also aware that his effort to remove the judiciary from partisanship would suffer a severe setback if, in Chase's defense, he were to take a partisan stance.

Marshall's judgment was vindicated when the Senate voted on the articles of impeachment. On March 1, 1805, as the clerk called the roll, Chase was acquitted on all counts. Not a single vote was cast against him on any of the articles alleging procedural mistakes at Callender's trial.[112] Only on the charge that Chase had badgered the Baltimore grand jury was there a majority for conviction, but even that fell far short of the required two-thirds. As expected, the nine Federalist senators voted across the board for acquittal. A minimum of six Republicans joined them on each count. Even Senator Giles voted not guilty four times. Senator William Cocke of Tennessee, who cast his vote against Chase seven times, admitted afterward that he was glad the justice had been acquitted because it "would have a tendency to mitigate the irritation of party spirit."[113] Republicans as well as Federalists were responsible for Chase's acquittal.[114] "The venerable judge whose head bears the frost of seventy winters, is honorably acquitted," wrote Senator Plumer to his son. "I never witnessed, in any place, such a display of learning as the counsel for the accused exhibited."[115]

There is no simple explanation of why so many Republicans voted for Chase's acquittal. Some genuinely believed he was being treated unfairly. Many believed the charges were not proved. Others were unwilling to weaken the independence of the judiciary. As one historian noted, "their grievances against the courts before 1800 were real enough, but Marshall had initiated a period of judicial self-restraint, and there existed in 1805 little evidence to substantiate the radicals' claim of judicial tyranny."[116] The most important factor, however, may have been the struggle under way within the Republican party. Randolph and the radicals, having split with the administration, were now beyond the pale.[117] Jefferson, Madison, Gallatin, and Lincoln were determined to pursue a policy of conciliation with the moderate Federalists, and the Chase impeachment had no place in their plans.

It has been suggested that the move against Chase was merely a prelude to an assault on the Supreme Court itself. Marshall and Paterson were said to be the next targets.[118] There is no evidence to support such a charge, other than the hyperbole of the High Federalists. Indeed, there is considerable evidence to the contrary. Throughout Chase's prosecution, John Randolph repeatedly contrasted Chase's conduct during the Callender trial with the manner in which Marshall presided on circuit. "Look at the case of Logwood," said Randolph. "The able and excellent judge, whose worth was never fully known until he was raised to the bench, who presided at that trial, uttered not one syllable that could prejudice the defense of the prisoner. . . . The Chief Justice knew that, sooner or later, the law was an overmatch for the dishonest, and leaving the cause of the commonwealth to its attorney, he disdained to descend from his great elevation to the low level of a public prosecutor. He let the law take its course."[119]

On March 1, the same day that the Senate acquitted Chase, Jefferson wrote to Marshall to request that he attend the inauguration and administer the oath of office. Three days later, standing on the same spot where Burr had announced Chase's acquittal, Marshall swore Jefferson in as president for a second term. They would soon be at loggerheads, and they would remain bitter antagonists for the remainder of their lives, but in March 1805, just as at Jefferson's first inaugural in 1801, their presence on the podium symbolized the triumph of conciliation and compromise. The earlier efforts of the High Federalists to politicize the judiciary had been frustrated, and, with the acquittal of Chase, the assault of the radical Republicans on the Court had been repulsed. Confronted first from the right and then from the left, the center had held.

Chase changed his ways and never again allowed his Federalist predilections to intrude into the trials over which he presided.[120] "Judge Chase delivered a short and pertinent charge to the grand jury," the *National Intelligencer* reported on May 5. "His remarks were pointed, modest, and well applied."[121] Other Federalist judges followed suit. Among the Republicans, the effects of Chase's acquittal were equally far-reaching. The trial did not represent a defeat for the party, as it has often been represented to be, but a victory for the administration's policy of conciliation. By the end of the 1805 term, the independence of the Federal judiciary had been established, setting the stage for an extended period of constitutional stability. Marshall's efforts to extricate the Court from partisanship and the ability of the moderates to consolidate their control of the Republican party had proved effective. There would be further efforts to circumscribe the power of the judiciary, but these would be relatively easily disposed of through an alliance between the moderates of both parties.[122]

15

Treason Defined

CHASE'S IMPEACHMENT TRIAL cast a shadow over the 1805 term of the Court. Despite the distraction, the justices heard twenty-three cases,[1] one of which, *United States v. Fisher*,[2] was of constitutional importance. The issue involved the portion of the Bankruptcy Act of 1800 that gave the federal government first claim to an insolvent person's assets.[3] Marshall, along with Robert Goodloe Harper of South Carolina, had been the principal author of the measure in the House of Representatives.[4] Now Marshall was sitting in judgment, while Harper, representing Fisher, urged that the act was unconstitutional. The government's case was argued by Alexander J. Dallas, the United States attorney for Pennsylvania and one of the most outspoken Republican lawyers of the period. The Republicans had opposed passage of the legislation in 1800 for many of the reasons that Harper now asserted on Fisher's behalf, while Dallas's argument before the Court resembled the position originally put forth by the Federalists.[5]

The decision in *Fisher* turned on the implied powers of the national government. Did the *necessary and proper* clause of the Constitution* authorize passage of the act? Should the clause be interpreted broadly or narrowly? That was the question on which Hamilton and Jefferson had divided during

---

*Article 1, section 8, after enumerating the specific powers granted to Congress and the national government, states that Congress shall have the authority "To make all Laws which shall be necessary and proper for carrying into Execution the foregoing Powers, and all other Powers vested by this Constitution in the government of the United States, or in any Department or Office thereof."

Washington's first term. It was also the issue that underlay the formation of the Federalist and Republican parties. Marshall was addressing the question for the first time as chief justice, and, in upholding the bankruptcy statute, he sketched out the doctrine of implied powers that he would develop more fully in *McCulloch v. Maryland*[6] fourteen years later.

"It would be incorrect, and would produce endless difficulties," said Marshall, "if the opinion should be maintained that no law was authorized which was not indispensably necessary to give effect to a specified power. . . . Congress must possess the choice of means, and must be empowered to use any means which are in fact conducive to the exercise of a power granted by the Constitution."[7] Marshall's words are a paraphrase of the language used by Hamilton in his 1791 memorandum to Washington defending the constitutionality of the national bank,[8] and it appears that he was consciously using the same phraseology.

The decision in *Fisher* was handed down February 21, 1805. At the time, Marshall was working on the fifth and final volume of the *Life of Washington*. The sixth chapter dealt with the conflict between Hamilton and Jefferson over the national bank, and, in a tightly written appendix, Marshall restated, often verbatim, the arguments each laid before Washington concerning the *necessary and proper clause*.[9] Hamilton had written that the word *necessary* often means no more than "needful, requisite, incidental, useful, or conducive to." Marshall heightened the impact by adding authoritatively, "This is the true sense in which the word is used in the constitution."[10] It seems clear that in Marshall's mind Hamilton had been correct, and *United States v. Fisher* gave him the opportunity to say so.

Back in Richmond by the middle of March, Marshall devoted himself to the manuscript for the final volume of the *Life of Washington*. In June he presided over the circuit courts in Richmond and Raleigh, and that summer he and Polly, as had become their habit, went to Oak Hill in the foothills of the Blue Ridge Mountains to escape the heat. In the fall he again held court in Richmond and Raleigh,[11] and returned to Washington in February for the 1806 term of the Court. The Republicans were still lobbing an occasional cannon shot in the direction of the judiciary,[12] but Chase's acquittal had dampened their ardor. Indeed, the extremists on both sides had been chastened. Judges throughout the federal system hewed carefully to the nonpartisan line Marshall had established, and the radical Republicans ceased to consider impeachment an option.[13]

The 1806 term of the Supreme Court was uneventful. The justices decided a record twenty-six cases, but none had constitutional significance. Marshall wrote the opinion in nineteen. The remainder were decided *per curiam*, except for three in which Marshall recused himself and his colleagues delivered their opinions *seriatim*.[14] Marshall's leadership of the Court was now an established fact. Except for Justice Paterson's dissent in one case that term,[15] every decision was unanimous. Even Jefferson's appointee, Justice William Johnson, found no reason to disagree with his Federalist brethren.[16]

Marshall finished the *Life of Washington* in June 1806. He had been ill that spring and as he told his publisher, "The delay, which is greater than I expected, has been occasioned in part by my personal indisposition and in part by the necessity of going over the work and expunging about one third of it."[17] The book would not appear until the following year, and its publication would provoke a firestorm of Republican reaction.

In the autumn of 1806, Marshall received an honorary LL.D. from Harvard, which at that time was a bastion of High Federalism. The party's ultras had come to terms with Marshall's moderate stance, and the award was recommended by Dr. John Eliot, the president of the Massachusetts Historical Society.[18] Autumn also brought the unhappy news that Justice Paterson had passed away. Paterson had never recovered from the accident in which his coach overturned, and he died September 9, 1806, en route to Ballston Springs, New York, to receive treatment for his injuries. To fill the vacancy, Jefferson turned to Brockholst Livingston. Livingston was a Princeton classmate of James Madison's and had been recommended for the Court by both Madison and Levi Lincoln at the time of William Johnson's appointment. A judge on the New York Supreme Court and a moderate Republican, he was widely regarded as one of the nation's leading authorities on commercial law, a field that was rapidly expanding with the nation's economic growth.

Livingston was forty-nine when he was appointed—two years younger than Marshall—and the scion of one of America's most distinguished families. He had served as a junior officer during the Revolutionary War, fighting at Saratoga and Bennington. After the war he read law in Albany. He entered New York politics as a Federalist, but broke with the party over the Jay Treaty (he and Jay were brothers-in-law) and gradually, under Madison's tutelage, gravitated to the Republicans. As a young man, Livingston was headstrong and rambunctious. In 1798 he had killed a man in a duel,[19] but as he matured, his youthful exuberance yielded to a genial affability. He was confirmed unanimously by the Senate, took his seat during the February 1807 term, and quickly became a fixture of the Marshall Court. During his sixteen years on the bench, he wrote thirty-eight opinions, mainly in the fields of prize law and negotiable instruments,[20] and dissented only eight times in over 400 cases. Story alluded to his quickness of mind, calling him "a very able and independent judge. . . . He is luminous, decisive, earnest and impressive on the bench. In private society he is accessible and easy, and enjoys with great good humor the vivacities . . . of the wit and moralist."[21] More than anyone, except for Marshall himself, it was Livingston with his infectious high spirits who helped to make the justices of those years "a band of brothers."[22]

Jefferson's third and final opportunity to add to the Court arose in the spring of 1807, when Congress created an additional judgeship to handle the cases arising in the new states of Ohio, Tennessee, and Kentucky. This brought the number of justices to seven, and Jefferson nominated Thomas Todd, the chief justice of the Kentucky Supreme Court. A staunch Republican well versed in the land laws of the western states, Todd was forty-two years old. Like Marshall, he had been raised on the Virginia frontier, and the two hit it off immediately. Todd remained on the Court until his death in 1826, and during those nineteen years he gave the chief justice his unwavering support, much to Jefferson's disappointment. Of the 644 decisions handed down during that period, Todd delivered the Court's opinion eleven times (all but one involving land law) and dissented only once—a five-line disclaimer concerning an indemnity bond in the very first case in which he participated.[23] Contemporary accounts describe him as "a dark complexioned, good-looking, substantial man . . . patient and candid in investigation, clear and sagacious in judgment."[24] Todd's principal contribution was on circuit, where he struggled mightily to unsnarl the tangled web of frontier land titles. "The law should be construed so as to advance the remedy and suppress the mischief," he said while holding court in Nashville.[25] Justice Story wrote that it was to Todd's honor "that though bred in a different political school from that of the Chief Justice, he never failed to sustain those great principles of constitutional law on which the security of the Union depends. He never gave up to party what he thought belonged to the country."[26]

Jefferson's three appointees to the Court, Johnson, Livingston, and Todd, were distinguished state jurists and respected lawyers. Although certified Republicans, they were all judicial moderates. Each was confirmed unanimously by the Senate, and each became a valued contributor to the jurisprudence of the Marshall Court, bringing his particular expertise to the deliberations of the justices. Johnson, as his biographer has written, "stood with Marshall in supporting national power to meet the unforseeable needs of the future" and shared the chief justice's attachment to judicial independence[27]; Livingston added depth and understanding in the increasing number of commercial cases that came before the court; Todd was the justices' expert on real property. Like Marshall, they valued the Supreme Court as an institution and were willing to have their contributions reflected silently in the unanimous decisions the chief justice announced. In that sense, the Marshall Court was a team. Their common lodgings fostered camaraderie, and whatever tensions existed arose out of the specifics of a particular case and quickly dissipated once a decision was reached. Cushing and Chase, the senior justices, blended as easily with Jefferson's Republican appointees as did Washington and Marshall, the chief justice's conviviality and gentle charm creating an atmosphere in which judicial accord came easily. Disputes typically were resolved over the dinner table. The meals were as sumptuous as time permitted, and the wine flowed copiously. As Story noted, Marshall was "brought up on Federalism and Madeira, and he was not a man to outgrow his early prejudices."[28]

In late 1806 the interlude of calm that had followed Chase's acquittal was interrupted by disturbing news from the West concerning the activities of Aaron Burr. When Burr left office as vice president after Jefferson's first term, he was a ruined man. After fourteen years in politics, his once-flourishing law practice was gone, and he was deeply in debt. He was distrusted by Republicans and Federalists alike, and his personal reputation lay in tatters for having challenged and killed Alexander Hamilton in their famous duel in 1804. Unlike Livingston, who was deemed to have acted honorably, Burr was under indictment for willful murder in both New York and New Jersey.[29]

To revive his fortunes, the former vice president set out for the area beyond the Appalachians, where he began making plans to liberate Mexico from Spanish rule and, failing that, to settle the vast land grant of Baron Bastrop on the Washita River, west of the Mississippi.[30] Whether Burr also intended to detach the western states and establish a new nation remains unclear. As one reflective historian has noted, the evidence is sufficiently ambiguous to persuade his supporters of his innocence and his detractors of his guilt.[31] Burr's defenders insist that his aims were military: to provoke a war with Spain, to liberate Mexico, and ultimately to free South America from Spanish rule. From this perspective, Burr was a patriot and his enterprise reflected the expansionist impulses of nineteenth-century America—the same impulses that had led Jefferson to consummate the Louisiana Purchase. Burr's enemies assert that his expedition against Spain masked a traitorous design to detach the trans-Allegheny region from the United States and establish himself as the ruler of a vast empire extending from the Mississippi valley to Mexico City. Both hypotheses are credible, but it is equally likely that Burr, the supreme opportunist, had no fixed plans and was content merely to follow events as they unfolded.[32]

Rumors of Burr's activities circulated freely, and in March 1806 Joseph Hamilton Daveiss, the United States attorney for Kentucky, alerted Jefferson to what was afoot. During the next six months Daveiss wrote eight letters to Jefferson describing Burr's activities. It is not clear why, but Jefferson declined to act. Daveiss was a Federalist holdover who had recently married Marshall's youngest sister, and it is possible that his warnings were dismissed as a partisan effort to discredit western Republicans, many of whom were friendly with Burr.[33] In reality, Daveiss was a fiercely independent man who despised Burr for having killed his idol and namesake, Alexander Hamilton. In the summer of 1806, he had sought an indictment on his own authority against the former vice president for planning to invade Mexico and plotting western secession, but a Kentucky grand jury declined to return a true bill. Burr was defended by Henry Clay, and many frontiersmen, sympathetic to liberating Mexican lands, believed that Burr had the tacit support of the administration in Washington.[34]

Jefferson did not become alarmed by Burr's activities until November 1806, when additional reports filtered in from the West. On November 27, the president issued a proclamation declaring that a conspiracy to engage in a military expedition against Spain had been discovered and commanding all persons engaged therein to cease and desist. Jefferson directed all civil and military authorities "to be vigilant . . . in searching out and bringing to condign punishment all persons engaged . . . in such enterprise."[35] Burr was not mentioned by name, and there was no allegation of treason. The proclamation alluded only to the plot against Spain. Nevertheless, Jefferson had become convinced that Burr's activities were treasonable. Writing to Governor John Langdon of New Hampshire, the president said that "Our Catiline is at the head of an armed body, and his object is to seize New Orleans, from there attack Mexico, place himself on the throne of Montezuma, add Louisiana to his empire, and the Western States from the Allegheny, if he can. I do not believe he will attain the crown but neither am I certain the halter will get its due."[36]

Jefferson's proclamation cut the ground out from under Burr. Throughout the West, men who had supported the Mexican endeavor rushed to dissociate themselves from him. The Lexington *Gazette*, a longtime backer of the former vice president, reflected the shift in an editorial. "Some weeks ago it was our opinion that Burr's designs were not unfavorable to the interests of the Union. . . . We now declare that opinion changed by the President's proclamation."[37] By Christmas 1806 it was apparent that Burr's efforts had been contained. Jefferson told Senator William Plumer, his holiday dinner guest, that he was confident that the conspiracy would be put down without much trouble or expense.[38]

Thus far, very few facts had been made public. On January 16, 1806, with rumors of the failed adventure swirling, John Randolph, now thoroughly estranged from the administration, rose in the House to demand an explanation of the president's November proclamation, claiming that Jefferson had presented no evidence to support his charges. After a heated debate, the House approved Randolph's resolutions requesting the executive to come forward with any information in its possession "touching any illegal combination of private individuals against the peace and safety of the Union."[39]

Stung by Randolph's attack, Jefferson lost his customary composure. On January 22 he sent a special message to Congress providing a summary of events and castigating Burr as the "archconspirator" in a treasonous enterprise to divide the nation.[40] The president acknowledged that because of sketchy information it was "difficult to sort out the real facts," but he said that Burr's "guilt is placed beyond question." This was the first time that Burr's name had been officially linked with the plot. It was also the first allegation of treason, and Jefferson overplayed his hand. Randolph's queries were disposed of, but the president had convicted Burr before a trial could be held. Jefferson's precipitous action tainted subsequent proceedings and made it appear as if he had been embarked from the outset on a personal vendetta against the man who had almost snatched the presidency from him in 1800.

John Adams, whose personal breach with Jefferson had healed, recognized the president's mistake. Writing immediately afterward to Dr. Benjamin Rush, Adams said that even if Burr's "guilt is as clear as the noonday sun, the first magistrate ought not to have pronounced it so before a jury had tried him."[41] The former president noted that although he had never thought as highly of Burr's talents as others had, "I never believed him to be a fool. Politicians have no more regard for the Truth than the Devil [and] I suspect that this Lying Spirit has been at Work concerning Burr."

In his message to Congress, Jefferson said that two of Burr's accomplices, Dr. Erich Bollman and Samuel Swartwout, had been apprehended in New Orleans by General James Wilkinson, the acting governor of the territory, and were being sent to Washington for trial. He did not tell Congress that the two men had been denied access to counsel or that Wilkinson had defied a writ of *habeas corpus* issued by the supreme court of the Orleans territory commanding their release. He also offered no convincing explanation why the pair were being sent to Washington rather than being tried in the district where the alleged offense was committed—a patent violation of the Sixth Amendment to the Constitution.[42] Jefferson, it seems, was determined to press charges of treason against anyone connected with the plot and was willing to cast a blind eye at General Wilkinson's disregard for the rights of the accused.[43] When the prisoners landed in Charleston, military authorities transshipped them to Baltimore, disregarding another writ of *habeas corpus* for their release, this one issued by the presiding judge of the United States district court in South Carolina.[44]

Bollman and Swartwout arrived in Washington under heavy military guard on January 23, the day after Jefferson's message to Congress. The two were placed in confinement at the Marine Barracks, and Jefferson personally called on the United States attorney, Walter Jones, to deliver a letter he had received from Wilkinson describing their activities. He instructed Jones to go to court immediately and seek a bench warrant charging the two with treason.[45]

That afternoon, to ensure that the prisoners would not be freed with another writ of *habeas corpus*, Senator William Branch Giles introduced legislation to suspend the writ for three months in all cases involving persons charged with "treason, misprison of treason, or other high crime or misdemeanor endangering the peace, safety, or neutrality of the United States."[46] The bill was worded in such a way as to legalize Wilkinson's arrest of Bollman and Swartwout and to keep the pair in confinement. The Senate, which appears to have been swept away by the day's events, met in closed session and immediately passed the resolution with only James Bayard of Delaware rising in opposition.[47] "How the Senate could have passed such an act which would have permitted such deeds of tyranny is strange and incomprehensible," wrote Rufus King of New York.[48] Indeed, the Senate's action that day remains inexplicable, except as a reflection of the momentary panic gripping Washington. Over the weekend calmer heads prevailed, and when Giles's measure was introduced in the House on Monday, it was soundly defeated 113–19, with both parties uniting to condemn what one member called "the most extraordinary proposition" ever made to them for consideration.[49]

On Tuesday, January 27, the day after the House defeated the bill to suspend *habeas corpus*, Bollman and Swartwout were arraigned in the circuit court of the District of Columbia and committed without bail to stand trial for treason.[50] When the Supreme Court convened for its 1807 term the following week, the capital was rife with anticipation. It was clear that the fate of Bollman and Swartwout would soon be brought before it. Indeed, on Thursday, February 5, the fourth day of the new term, Charles Lee, who had been retained as counsel by Samuel Swartwout, appeared before the justices requesting a new writ of *habeas corpus* to free the prisoners.[51]

There were two issues before the Court. The first was strictly procedural: Did the Court have the authority to issue a writ of *habeas corpus*? The second raised the constitutional issue of the Sixth Amendment. Could Bollman and Swartwout be tried for treason in Washington? On February 13, 1807, Marshall delivered the opinion of the Court on the procedural issue.[52] He began cautiously. To ensure that the Court would not be condemned for overstepping its authority, the chief justice disavowed any jurisdiction based on common law—that old bugaboo of the Republicans. The term *habeas corpus* could be defined at common law, "but the power to award the writ by any of the courts of the U[nited] States must be given by written law."[53] Marshall thereupon held that section 14 of the Judiciary Act[54] gave the justices of the Supreme Court explicit authority to issue writs of *habeas corpus*. He distinguished the writ of *habeas corpus* for which Bollman and Swartwout had applied from the writ of *mandamus* in *Marbury v. Madison*.[55] Marshall noted that Bollman and Swartwout had not presented their applications to the Supreme Court in the first instance. Had they done so, said Marshall, the case would have fallen under the Court's original jurisdiction. The holding in *Marbury* would have applied. But the case of Bollman and Swartwout was clearly appellate, since "it is a revision of a decision of an inferior court, by which a citizen has been committed to jail."[56] Accordingly, Congress had not overstepped its authority when it granted the Court the power to issue the writ of *habeas corpus*.

On Monday, February 16, with the Court's jurisdiction established, Lee moved that Bollman and Swartwout be released. For the next four days Marshall, Johnson, Chase, and Washington* heard arguments on whether the circuit court in Washington had jurisdiction over Bollman and Swartwout and whether the evidence submitted to the court was sufficient to hold the prisoners on a charge of treason. At the close of argument on Thursday, Marshall said the Court had not yet been able to reach a decision but that the prisoners could be released on bail. Two days later Marshall ordered Bollman and Swartwout discharged. All four justices were agreed that the pair could not be tried in the District of Columbia. The four were also agreed that there was no evidence to support a charge of treason against Bollman. Marshall, Chase, and Washington believed the same to be true of Swartwout. Johnson apparently did not agree, but he remained silent, content with Marshall's phrasing of the decision.

Quoting the constitutional definition of treason, Marshall said that "Treason against the United States shall consist only in levying War against them, or in adhering to their Enemies, giving them Aid and Comfort."[57] For Bollman and Swartwout to be guilty, "war must be actually levied against the United States. However flagitious may be the crime of conspiring to subvert by force the government of our country, such conspiracy is not treason."

Marshall then added a paragraph that was more loosely worded than the situation required:

> It is not the intention of the Court to say that no individual can be guilty of this crime who has not appeared in arms against his country. On the contrary, if war be actually levied . . . all of those who perform any part, however minute or however remote from the scene of action, and who are actually leagued in the general conspiracy, are to be considered as traitors. But there must be an actual assembling of men for the treasonable purpose, to constitute a levying of war.

---

*Brockholst Livingston left Washington over the weekend of February 14–15 to attend his critically ill daughter in New York. Justice Cushing was ailing and also did not sit.

Marshall's intent was to permit charges of treason to be brought against all parties involved once an overt act of rebellion had taken place. But there had to be an overt act. That becomes clear as the opinion continues. Stripped from context, however, the paragraph gives the impression that the net may be cast more broadly. It is one of the few times during Marshall's tenure as chief justice that his prose lacked the necessary clarity.

After examining the evidence against Bollman and Swartwout, Marshall said that the information indicated that Burr's plans were directed against Spain, and that this constituted a high misdemeanor but not treason.[58] "There is not one syllable which has a necessary or a natural reference to an enterprise against any territory of the United States." Marshall pointed out that the Framers of the Constitution not only had defined the crime of treason narrowly but had been careful to specify the nature of the proof required: the testimony of two witnesses to the same overt act, or a confession in open court. "It is therefore more safe as well as more consonant to the principles of our Constitution that the crime of treason should not be extended to doubtful cases."

The Court's decision to release Bollman and Swartwout infuriated Jefferson's more outspoken supporters. Senator Giles threatened to introduce an amendment to the Constitution that would deprive the Supreme Court of all jurisdiction in criminal cases, and according to John Quincy Adams, there was renewed talk of impeachment.[59] Overall, however, public reaction was muted. On the issue of treason, the Court had spoken with one voice and, if anything, it was Jefferson, not Marshall, who was seen as having overstepped his authority.[60] The Court adjourned the following week, having decided, in addition to *Bollman and Swartwout*, seventeen of the eighteen cases on its docket. Marshall delivered the opinion in nine, Johnson spoke for the Court in a Kentucky case involving Senator Humphrey Marshall,[61] and seven decisions were *per curiam*. Except for *Bollman and Swartwout*, none of the cases involved constitutional issues.

While Bollman and Swartwout were fighting treason charges in Washington, Burr was engaged in a battle of his own in Mississippi. When Jefferson issued his conspiracy proclamation in November 1806, Burr was slowly floating down the Ohio and Mississippi Rivers with nine longboats and sixty young adventurers, quite unaware of the hue and cry being raised against him. On December 31, 1806, his party passed Fort Massoc, Kentucky. The commanding officer informed Andrew Jackson that there was "nothing the least alarming, [Burr] having nothing on board that would even suffer a conjecture, more than a man bound to market."[62] Not until Burr reached the Mississippi Territory several weeks later was he confronted by civil authorities and charged with treason.[63] He immediately offered to surrender himself and allow his boats to be searched. The search turned up only a few rifles and hunting pieces, and convinced local authorities in Natchez that Burr was unequipped for anything other than the settlement of Baron Bastrop's Washita lands, and poorly supplied even for that. "His object is agriculture, and his boats are the vehicles of emigration," Governor Cowles Mead wrote the War Department.[64] Burr voluntarily went before the United States district court for the territory, and a special grand jury refused to return an indictment. "We are of the opinion that Aaron Burr has not been guilty of any crime or misdemeanor against the laws of the United States or of this Territory, or given any just alarm or inquietude to the good people of the Territory."[65]

When the grand jury was dismissed, Burr asked to be discharged. The judge, Thomas Rodney, the father of attorney general Caesar Rodney, denied the request and summarily ordered Burr to renew his bond or be jailed. Burr met bond but, at the advice of friends in the Mississippi Territory who feared for his life, went into hiding. He was apprehended by military authorities on February 19 in Washington county, held in the stockade at Fort Stoddart on the Tombigbee River for two weeks, and then sent north to the nation's capital to stand trial. "Colonel Burr . . . passed by my door the day before yesterday under a strong guard," wrote John Randolph from southside Virginia. "To guard against enquiring as much as possible he was accoutered in a shabby suit of homespun with an old white hat flopped over his face."[66]

When Burr's party reached Fredricksburg, Jefferson redirected it to Richmond.[67] The Supreme Court's decision in *Bollman* had made it clear that Burr could not be tried in Washington, but the president believed a case could be made for trying Burr in Richmond. The initial staging point for Burr's expedition had been Blennerhasset's Island on the Ohio River. The island lay inside the boundaries of Wood county, Virginia (now West Virginia), and thus was within the jurisdiction of the fifth circuit court in Richmond—the very court over which Marshall presided. Burr had not been physically present on the island and, in fact, did not join the party until it reached the confluence of the Cumberland and Ohio Rivers. However, in the *Bollman* decision, Marshall had said that if a treasonable act had occurred, "all those who perform any part, however minute, or however remote from the scene of action . . . are to be considered as traitors."[68] Jefferson was convinced that the activity at Blennerhasset's Island was treasonable and ordered Burr taken to Richmond to stand trial.[69]

The former vice president arrived in Richmond under heavy military guard on the evening of March 26. Four days later he was arraigned before Marshall, both for commencing a military expedition against Spain and for treason. The treason charge stemmed from the allegation that Burr had assembled an armed force to attack New Orleans. The prosecution was led by

George Hay, the United States attorney for Virginia, and attorney general Caesar Rodney. Burr was defended by John Wickham and Edmund Randolph, the doyens of the Richmond bar. This pretrial hearing was Rodney's only appearance in the case. He had been a friend of Burr's for years and had little enthusiasm for prosecuting him. "I rejoice that men of talents . . . have come forward to defend the prisoner, notwithstanding the general opinion of his guilt," said Rodney. "For my part, I wish for nothing but that justice may be done."[70] After concluding the argument for the government, he departed from Richmond, leaving the case in Hay's hands.[71]

On April 1 Marshall delivered his decision. He said that to hold Burr for trial, the prosecution did not have to prove the accusations against him, but it did have to show probable cause.[72] He said the evidence introduced would support holding Burr on the charge of initiating an expedition against Spain but was insufficient to substantiate the charge of treason. As in the *Bollman* case, Marshall distinguished between a conspiracy to commit treason and the overt act itself. There was reason to believe that Burr had treasonable designs, but those designs had not ripened into a levying of war against the United States, and that was what the Constitution required.

"Treason," said Marshall, "may be machinated in secret, but it can be perpetrated only in open day and in the eye of the world. . . . The assembling of forces to levy war is a visible transaction, and numbers must witness it. . . . Several months have elapsed, since this fact did occur, if it ever occurred. More than five weeks have elapsed since the Supreme Court declared the necessity of proving the fact, if it exists. Why is it not proved?"[73] Marshall said he could not assume that the government was remiss in seeking the proof; the only conclusion remaining was that the evidence did not exist. He ordered the prisoner held for the grand jury on the charge of initiating an expedition against Spanish territory but dismissed the treason charge. Bail was set at $10,000.[74]

Marshall was disturbed by the Burr drama. Since the government could prosecute and probably convict Burr of mounting a military expedition against Spain, he could not understand why Jefferson persisted with the treason charge. Aside from the lack of clear and convincing proof, the chief justice was troubled by the implications of an action for treason. It was a dangerous precedent for the new nation. As a member of Congress, Marshall had fought his fellow Federalists over the alien and sedition acts. Now the equation was reversed, and it was the Republican administration that was taking advantage of its office to bring the coercive power of the state against its opponents.

Marshall was forthright in announcing his concern. "As treason is the most atrocious offence which can be committed against the political body, so it is the charge which is most capable of being employed as the instrument of those malignant and vindictive passions which may rage in the bosoms of contending parties struggling for power."[75] The fact that the charge was leveled against a former vice president also made Marshall uneasy. His year in Paris under the Directory had convinced him of the danger of political justice, and he was concerned by the parallels he saw. Moreover, Marshall recognized that by applying the constitutional test for treason scrupulously, he would likely reopen the quarrel between the judiciary and the administration. His efforts to remove the Court from partisanship would be set back, and the judiciary would again become the object of Republican attack.

Those fears were soon realized. Jefferson saw Marshall's preliminary decision in Richmond as partisan obstruction. "The Federalists make Burr's cause their own, and exert their whole influence to shield him from punishment," he wrote to a friend the day after the holding came down.[76] "It is unfortunate that Federalism is still predominant in our judiciary department, which is consequently in opposition to the legislative and executive branches, and is able to baffle their measures often." Three weeks later, writing from Monticello to Senator Giles, the president criticized the judiciary at length, asserting that it was only "the tricks of the judges" that stood between Burr and the gallows. "The nation will judge both the offender and the judges for themselves. If a member of the executive or legislature does wrong, the day is never far distant when the people will remove him." Jefferson told Giles that the only recourse was to amend the Constitution to make the judiciary responsible to the people. "If their protection of Burr produces this amendment, it will do more good than his condemnation would have done." Jefferson's letter to Giles is one of the most damning pieces of correspondence insofar as the president's disregard for civil liberties is concerned. He repeatedly refers to the judgment of the people concerning Burr's guilt and denigrates the procedural guarantees of the law. The evidence, he told Giles, "will satisfy the world, if not the judges, of Burr's guilt."[77]

After Rodney withdrew from the case, Jefferson assumed control of the prosecution. He devoted several Cabinet meetings to the matter and instructed Madison to find additional funds to bring witnesses from great distances.[78] On the eve of the trial he forwarded to Hay a sheaf of blank pardons he had signed. Hay was instructed to fill them out "at discretion, if [he] should find a defect of evidence, and believe that this would supply it."[79] This was a carte blanche for the prosecuting attorney to grant presidential pardons in order to secure testimony against Burr. Jefferson told Hay to avoid giving them "to the gross offenders, unless it be visible that the principal [Burr] will otherwise escape."[80]

The proceedings against Burr resumed on May 22. Marshall was joined on the bench by district judge Cyrus Griffin, and a grand jury of distinguished Virginia freeholders was impaneled. Several days of legal skirmishing followed. On May 25 Hay gave notice that he intended to resubmit his earlier motion that Burr be held for treason. After six hours of bitter argument, with both sides playing to public opinion, Marshall ruled in favor of the prosecution. The court, he said, regretted the publicity that would accompany the motion, "but the remedy is not to be obtained by suppressing motions, which either party has a right to make."[81]

Argument on Hay's motion continued for several days. When the prosecution attempted to introduce affidavits pertaining to Burr's plans, the defense objected that the documents had not been properly authenticated. Marshall upheld the objection, emphasizing that the rules of evidence would be strictly enforced. "The interest, which the people have in this prosecution, has been stated, but the best and true interest of the people is to be found in a rigid adherence to those rules which preserve the fairness of criminal prosecutions in every stage."[82] On May 28 Marshall decided to call a halt to the proceedings. Rather than rule once again on Hay's motion to try Burr for treason, the chief justice said he would leave the decision to the grand jury.[83] Burr voluntarily increased his bond by an additional $10,000, and the court recessed, waiting for the government's witnesses to arrive.[84]

Both sides now worked assiduously to buttress their cases. Burr had arrayed a formidable defense team, including not only Wickham and Randolph, but two younger lawyers, Benjamin Botts and John Baker. They were joined on May 28 by the greatest of all defense counsel, Luther Martin. Martin had been a close friend of Burr's for many years and was infatuated with Burr's daughter Theodosia, the wife of South Carolina governor Joseph Alston. As he had done during the Chase impeachment trial, he donated his formidable talents free of charge.[85] Hay meanwhile secured the services of Virginia's lieutenant governor, Alexander MacRae, a sarcastic, hard-bitten Republican, always effective before a jury, and the young William Wirt, a rising star of the Richmond bar, destined in the years ahead to equal, if not surpass, Luther Martin as the nation's leading advocate as well as the profession's most prominent inebriate.

Jefferson, who was plainly dissatisfied with the course the trial was taking, peppered Hay with instructions.[86] "Stop . . . citing *Marbury v. Madison* as authority," said the president. "I have long wished for a proper occasion to have the gratuitous opinion in that case brought before the public, and denounced as not law."* Jefferson was still more outspoken in a personal let-

---

*Jefferson's objections pertained to Marshall's *dictum* concerning Marbury's right to his commission, not to the holding that section 13 of the Judiciary Act of 1789 was unconstitutional. Jefferson to Hay, June 2, 1807, 11 *Writings of Thomas Jefferson* 213–216, Andrew A. Lipscomb, ed. (Washington, D.C.: Thomas Jefferson Memorial Association, 1903).

ter to his son-in-law. The procedural guarantees afforded Burr, he said, showed "the original error of establishing a judiciary independent of the nation, and which, from the citadel of the law can turn its guns on those they were meant to defend, and control and fashion their proceedings to its own will."[87]

On Tuesday, June 9, Burr and his attorneys came into court seeking certain documents in the administration's possession that the defense asserted were important to their case.[88] Burr said that if Hay would provide the documents, a court order would not be necessary; otherwise they would move for a subpoena *duces tecum** requiring the president to produce the papers. Hay, who was caught off guard by Burr's request, volunteered to obtain the documents "if the court thinks them material." Marshall said he could not determine whether the papers were relevant without seeing them and would much prefer that opposing counsel work the matter out themselves. After several acrimonious exchanges before the bench, it became apparent that an agreement could not be reached. At that point, Marshall said he would issue the subpoena if Hay was satisfied that the court had the authority to do so. Hay had no instructions in the matter and evidently decided it was best not to concede the point without Jefferson's approval. Accordingly, he told Marshall that he was not satisfied that the court had the authority to subpoena the president, whereupon the chief justice asked for oral argument on the matter.[89]

Hay wrote to Jefferson immediately and urged him to provide the papers as soon as possible, lest Burr and his attorneys use the issue to inflame public opinion. "Luther Martin has been here a long time, perfectly inactive," said Hay. The combative barrister was looking for an opportunity to attack the administration, and this would "furnish a topic."[90] As Hay anticipated, several days of rancorous debate followed, and the defense took advantage of the opportunity to put the prosecution on the defensive. First Wickham, then Martin, and then Randolph lambasted the administration for depriving Burr of the evidence he needed for his defense, but it was Martin who drove the issue home. "The president has undertaken to prejudge my client by declaring, that 'Of his guilt there can be no doubt.' He has assumed to himself the knowledge of the Supreme Being. . . . He has let slip the dogs of war, the hell-hounds of persecution, to hunt down my friend." Warming to his task, Martin asked whether Jefferson, "who has

---

*A subpoena *duces tecum* [Latin, meaning "to bring with you"] requires the party to whom the subpoena is issued to appear in court and bring with him whatever document or piece of evidence is specified. In argument before the court, Wickham made it clear that the defense did not seek Jefferson's attendance, but only the production of the documents. 1 *Reports of the Trials of Colonel Aaron Burr* 115, David Robertson, ed. (Philadelphia: Hopkins and Earle, 1808).

raised all this absurd clamor, would pretend to keep back the papers which are wanted for this trial, where life itself is at stake?"[91]

Not since Patrick Henry's "Liberty or Death" oration in 1776 had Richmond heard such eloquent defiance of government authority. MacRae responded gamely that "a subpoena may issue against [the president] as well as against any other man" but that executive confidentiality had to be respected. He cited Marshall's holding in *Marbury v. Madison* as authority.[92] It remained for William Wirt to deflect the attack on Jefferson. What do Burr's attorneys expect "from these perpetual philippics against the government?" he asked. "Do they flatter themselves that this court feel political prejudices which will supply the place of argument and innocence on the part of the prisoner? . . . Do they use the court merely as a canal, through which they may pour upon the world their undeserved invectives against the government?"[93]

Jefferson did not suffer criticism easily, and he was enraged by Martin's attack. In a letter to Hay, the president wrote that he thought Martin had been privy to Burr's plans and asked whether he should be indicted, "*particeps criminis* [as an accomplice] with Burr." Such action, he said, "will put down this unprincipled and impudent federal bull-dog, and add another proof that the most clamorous of Burr's defenders are all his accomplices."[94]

The argument on Burr's motion to subpoena Jefferson continued for two days. On Saturday, June 13, Marshall rendered his historic decision. The president was not above the law. Burr would be granted his subpoena. "The propriety of introducing any paper into a case as testimony, must depend on the character of the paper, not the character of the person who holds it."[95]

The chief justice said that "the genius and character of our laws and usages are friendly, not to condemnation at all events, but to a fair and impartial trial; and they consequently allow to the accused the right of preparing the means to secure such a trial."[96] He noted that two issues were involved: whether a subpoena could be served on the president, and the question of executive privilege. Marshall disposed of the first issue quickly. The president, unlike the king of England, was subject to the law and bound by the Constitution. The only exemption "would be because his duties as chief magistrate demand his whole time for national objects." Marshall said it was apparent that the demands of office were "not unremitting," and he implied that a convenient time could always be found. The president would be protected "from being harassed by vexatious and unnecessary subpoenas" by the conduct of the court when the subpoena was returned. Whatever objections the chief executive might have could be considered at that time. Accordingly, "the court can perceive no legal objection to issuing a subpoena *duces tecum* to any person whatever, provided, the case be such as to justify the process."[97]

On the question of executive privilege, Marshall was circumspect. He acknowledged that there might be documents in the possession of the executive that should not be made public. "What ought to be done under such circumstances presents a delicate question, the discussion of which, it is hoped, will never be rendered necessary in this country." At the present time, however, the question did not arise. There was no indication that the material Burr sought contained any matter "the disclosure of which, would endanger public safety." Marshall explicitly recognized the right of the executive to object to the disclosure of such information. If the documents Burr wanted "contain any matter which it would be imprudent to disclose, which it is not the wish of the executive to disclose, such matter, if it be not immediately and essentially applicable to the point, will, of course, be suppressed." But having given the executive the right to object, Marshall made it clear that the final decision rested with the court, not the president. "Everything of this kind," he said, "will have its due consideration on the return of the subpoena."

In conclusion, Marshall noted that the prosecution had said a great deal about the disrespect to the president implied by issuing a subpoena. The chief justice commented dryly that he felt as much respect for the president "as is compatible with his official duties. To go beyond these would exhibit a conduct which would deserve some appellation other than the term respect." Moreover, said Marshall, showing undue deference to the president could taint the outcome of the case.

> Should it terminate as is expected[98] on the part of the United States, all of those who are concerned in it should certainly regret that a paper which the accused believed essential to his defense . . . had been withheld from him. I will not say that this circumstance would in any degree tarnish the reputation of the government, but I will say that it would justly tarnish the reputation of the court which had given its sanction to its being withheld.*[99]

---

*Paul Freund, writing in the *Harvard Law Review*, concludes that Marshall's holding established four principles of American jurisprudence:

1. There is no absolute privilege in a criminal case for communications to which the President is a party.
2. Upon a particularized claim of privilege by the President, the court, giving due respect to the President's judgment, will weigh the claim against the materiality of the evidence and the need of the accused for its production.
3. For the purposes of determining whether disclosure is required, the material sought may be ordered produced for *in camera* inspection by the court, with the participation of counsel and, it seems, the accused.

Marshall's decision momentarily reversed the thrust of public opinion and placed the administration on the defensive. Republican prejudice against executive authority was gratified, and the party press temporarily stilled its criticism of the chief justice.[100] Perhaps reflecting the public mood, Jefferson's initial response was conciliatory. Writing to Hay on June 12, he asserted the president's prerogative to determine what papers to make available but immediately forwarded copies of the documents Burr requested. "Reserving the necessary right of the President of the U.S. to decide, independently of all other authority, what papers, coming to him as President, the public interests permit to be communicated, and to whom, I assure you of my readiness under that restriction, voluntarily to furnish on all occasions, whatever the purposes of justice may require."[101]

Five days later Jefferson wrote an official follow-up to Hay indicating that the terms of the subpoena had been "substantially fulfilled" and explaining at greater length the necessity for executive confidentiality.[102] Jefferson also included a personal note.[103] He told Hay that his official letter was written "in a spirit of conciliation and with the desire to avoid conflicts of authority between the high branches of government which would discredit it equally at home and abroad." He said it was understandable that Burr wanted to "divert the public attention from him to this battle of giants"—a reference to himself and Marshall. Jefferson then thought better of his wording and struck out the phrase, writing instead that Burr sought to "convert his Trial into a contest between the judiciary and Exec[utive] authorities." Jefferson told Hay he was surprised "that the Chief Justice should lend himself to it, and take the first step to bring it on," and said he doubted if Marshall's "prudence or good sense will permit him to press it." Nevertheless, Jefferson was apprehensive that the court might attempt to compel his appearance, and instructed Hay to warn him immediately. He also asked whether Judge Griffin, who was sitting with Marshall, might not be prevailed upon "to divide his [Marshall's] court and procure a truce at least in so critical a conjuncture." In conclusion, Jefferson said the powers given to the executive by the Constitution were sufficient to guard against "judiciary vengeance," and he hoped "the discretion of the Chief Justice will suffer this question to lie over for the present."[104]

By mid-June the government's witnesses had arrived in Richmond, and the proceedings before the grand jury commenced. On June 24, after hear-

---

4. In lieu of such production, the court may direct that inferences shall be drawn in favor of the accused, or that the prosecution be dismissed.

Freund goes on to note that in the case of President Nixon and the Watergate tapes, "these principles were largely confirmed, and the mechanics of an *in camera* inspection were refined." "Forward: On Presidential Privilege," 88 *Harvard Law Review* 13, 30–31 (1974).

ing the testimony of forty-eight persons, foreman John Randolph came into court and announced that the grand jury had voted to indict Burr for treason as well as on the charge of instigating war against Spain. Marshall immediately ordered Burr taken into custody, and two days later the former vice president entered a plea of not guilty. Marshall thereupon dismissed the grand jury with what the court reporter termed a short and elegant speech "in which he complimented them upon the great patience and cheerful attention with which they had performed the arduous and laborious duties in which they had been so long engaged."[105] The date for Burr's trial was set for the first Monday in August.

The indictment against Burr focused on the activities at Blennerhasset's Island on December 10, 1806. It charged that on that day, the former vice president,

> not having the fear of God before his eyes . . . but being moved and seduced by the instigation of the devil, wickedly devising and intending the peace and tranquility of the United States to disturb; and to stir, move and excite insurrection, rebellion and war . . . with a great multitude of persons . . . did falsely and traitorously assemble and join themselves together . . . and then and there with force and arms did falsely and traitorously and in a warlike and hostile manner, array and dispose themselves against the said United States. . . .[106]

As soon as the indictment came down, Marshall recognized that his discussion of treason in the *Bollman* decision had been too loosely worded.[107] The grand jury had imputed Burr's presence on Blennerhasset's Island, even though the prosecution conceded he had not been there. If the former vice president was to be tried for treason, the definition of that crime must be clear. Accordingly, on June 29, Marshall wrote to his fellow justices soliciting their advice. "Many points of difficulty will arise before the petit jury which cannot be foreseen and on which I must decide according to the best lights I possess. But there are some which will certainly occur, respecting which considerable doubts may be entertained, and on which I most anxiously desire the aid of all the Judges."[108]

Marshall said the most important problem pertained to the issue of *constructive treason*.* "How far is this doctrine to be carried in the United States? If a body of men assemble for a treasonable purpose, does this implicate all

---

*The premise of the common law doctrine of constructive treason, as stated by Sir Edward Coke, is that "in treason all of the *participes criminis* are principals; there being . . . no accessories to that crime; and that every act, which in the case of a felony, would render a man an accessory, will, in case of treason, make him a principal." The origins of the rule are traced authoritatively in St. George Tucker's edition of Blackstone's *Commentaries*, a work cited repeatedly during the proceedings

of those who are concerned in the conspiracy whether acquainted with the assemblage or not?" The chief justice acknowledged that the opinion of the Court in *Bollman* "certainly adopts the doctrine of constructive treason. How far does that case carry this doctrine? Ought the expressions in that opinion be revised?"

Marshall told his colleagues that he recognized that judges were reluctant to state their opinions on cases not before them and that he would not be asking their advice if Burr's case could be carried to the Supreme Court. But if the government pursued the issue, the question of constructive treason would come forward in the various circuits, "and I am sure there would be a strong and general repugnance to giving contradictory decisions on the same points. Such a circumstance would be disreputable to the Judges themselves as well as to our judicial system."[109]

Burr's trial convened on August 3. To accommodate the throng of spectators who had flocked to Richmond, the court met in the commodious chamber of the Virginia House of Delegates, but even that room was insufficient to seat the curious crowds eager to see the "archtraitor" brought to justice. Because of the publicity the case had received, jury selection was a long and tedious process. From the initial forty-eight-man venire, only four jurors were chosen. After the defense had rejected forty-four prospective jurors for cause, the prosecution claimed that Burr's lawyers were stalling. Marshall's response was characteristically moderate. The issue, he said, was not whether potential jurymen had ever expressed an opinion concerning Burr, but whether they "will fairly hear the testimony which may be offered to them."[110]

After Marshall's ruling, Hay moved for another venire of forty-eight to be called and said he was willing to ask for an additional five hundred names if necessary. When the new venire was assembled, Burr suggested that to save time he be allowed to select the remaining eight jurors from their ranks. Hay agreed, on the condition that the court ask those selected whether they thought they should be disqualified. "If they themselves are satisfied, the government should also be satisfied."[111] The eight prospective jurors were then brought before the bench and Marshall said, "Gentlemen, if you have made up, and expressed any opinion, either for, or against the accused, you ought to express it."

---

against Burr. 4 *Blackstone's Commentaries with Notes of Reference to the Constitution and Laws of the United States* . . . Appendix, Note B, "Concerning Treason," 41–47 (Philadelphia: Birch and Smith, 1803).

Tucker, a stout-hearted Republican, maintained that the Framers intentionally defined treason in the Constitution to preclude adoption of constructive treason, and that they emphasized their determination by stating that "Treason . . . shall consist ONLY in levying war against [the United States], or in adhering to their enemies." Tucker said the word *ONLY* was explicit, and he capitalized it to help make his point. The entire note is devoted to rejecting the idea of constructive treason.

MR. BURR. The law presumes every man to be innocent, until he have been proven to be guilty. According to the rules of law, it is therefore the duty of every citizen, who serves on this jury, to hold himself completely unbiased; it is no disqualification then, for a man to come forward, and declare, that he believes me to be innocent.

CHIEF JUSTICE. The law certainly presumes every man to be innocent, till the contrary be proved; but if a juryman give an opinion in favor of the prisoner, he must be rejected.[112]

Two of the persons said they thought Burr was guilty, two more names were added from the venire list, and the jury was finally impaneled the morning of August 17.[113] Marshall arranged for them to be sequestered on the upper floors of the capitol when court was not in session and, at the urging of both sides, announced that the trial would convene daily at 9 A.M. and continue until 4 P.M.

With the jury in place, Hay opened the case for the prosecution. After reviewing the Constitution's definition of treason, he acknowledged that Burr was not actually present at Blennerhasset's Island on December 10, when the alleged act of levying war against the United States took place. However, he cited Marshall's words in *Bollman* that "If war be actually levied, all of those who perform any part . . . *however remote from the scene of action*, and who are actually leagued in the general conspiracy, are to be considered as traitors." Burr was guilty because he was the mastermind behind the plot and had procured the assemblage.[114]

Hay then called the government's first witness, General William Eaton, a former diplomat and soldier-of-fortune who was down on his luck and to whom Burr had allegedly explained his enterprise while still vice president. Burr objected immediately, claiming that testimony about his intent was irrelevant until the act of treason had been established. Botts, Wickham, and Martin chimed in, and Charles Lee, who had been added to the defense, said that to hear collateral evidence about Burr's intentions before an overt act of levying war had been proved "put the cart before the horse."[115] William Wirt, who had become the mainstay of the government team, responded that it was up to the prosecution to determine how its case should be presented and that to proceed chronologically made eminent good sense. "If you were to write a history of the late revolution, would you begin with the siege of Yorktown?"[116] The argument raged for an additional three hours. At 4 P.M. Marshall adjourned, indicating that he would rule on Burr's motion the next day.

When court reconvened, Marshall delivered a handwritten decision of some 2,000 words that attempted to strike a balance between the two positions. "As is not infrequent, the argument on both sides appears to be . . .

Thomas Marshall

Mary Randolph Keith Marshall

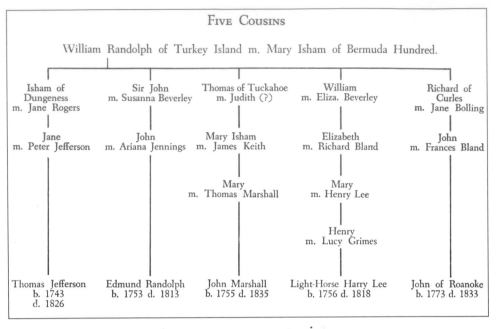

FIVE COUSINS

William Randolph of Turkey Island m. Mary Isham of Bermuda Hundred.

Isham of Dungeness m. Jane Rogers	Sir John m. Susanna Beverley	Thomas of Tuckahoe m. Judith (?)	William m. Eliza. Beverley	Richard of Curles m. Jane Bolling
Jane m. Peter Jefferson	John m. Ariana Jennings	Mary Isham m. James Keith	Elizabeth m. Richard Bland	John m. Frances Bland
		Mary m. Thomas Marshall	Mary m. Henry Lee	
			Henry m. Lucy Grimes	
Thomas Jefferson b. 1743 d. 1826	Edmund Randolph b. 1753 d. 1813	John Marshall b. 1755 d. 1835	Light-Horse Harry Lee b. 1756 d. 1818	John of Roanoke b. 1773 d. 1833

The Randolph Heritage

Lord Fairfax

Patrick Henry

George Wythe

Assumpsit.   Polly Ambler

The Pl't must set forth every thing essential to the
gist of the action with such certainty that it may
appear there was cause of action. but the law
requires no greater certainty than the nature of the
thing requires

The Def't must shew there was no contract, or that the
contract was void & without consideration or that
he has performed it

March &c   An entire promise cannot be apportioned.
in Ba. 483 The Def't cannot plead that he has revoked the promise

Polly Ambler

Polly.

Marshall's Law Notebook

Polly Ambler, 1783

James Madison

James Monroe

Marshall House, Richmond

Marshall in Paris, 1797

Talleyrand

Charles Cotesworth Pinckney

Elbridge Gerry

Marquise de Villette and Voltaire Robert de Villette

Albert Gallatin

Washington's Funeral, 1799

Gentlemen of the Senate.

I nominate John Marshall Secretary of State to be a Chief Justice of the United States in the place of John Jay who has declined his appointment

John Adams

United States
Jan 20ᵗʰ 1801.

Nomination

John Adams

Justice William Cushing

Justice Samuel Chase

Justice William Paterson

Justice Alfred Moore

Marshall in Richmond, 1808

Centerfold: The Marshall Court

1812–1823

(in order of seniority)

John Marshall

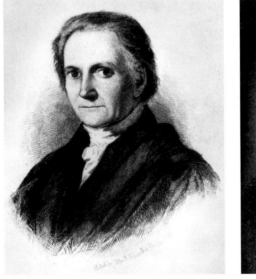

Bushrod Washington

William Johnson

Brockholst Livingston

Thomas Todd

Gabriel Duvall

Joseph Story

Polly, 1799

THE
LIFE
OF

GEORGE WASHINGTON,

COMMANDER IN CHIEF

OF THE

AMERICAN FORCES,

DURING THE WAR WHICH ESTABLISHED THE INDEPENDENCE
OF HIS COUNTRY,

AND

FIRST PRESIDENT

OF THE

UNITED STATES.

COMPILED
UNDER THE INSPECTION OF
THE HONOURABLE BUSHROD WASHINGTON,

FROM

ORIGINAL PAPERS

BEQUEATHED TO HIM BY HIS DECEASED RELATIVE, AND NOW IN POSSESSION
OF THE AUTHOR.

TO WHICH IS PREFIXED,

AN INTRODUCTION,

CONTAINING

A COMPENDIOUS VIEW OF THE COLONIES PLANTED BY THE ENGLISH

ON THE

CONTINENT OF NORTH AMERICA,

FROM THEIR SETTLEMENT
TO THE COMMENCEMENT OF THAT WAR WHICH TERMINATED IN THEIR

INDEPENDENCE.

BY JOHN MARSHALL.

VOL. I.

PHILADELPHIA:
PRINTED AND PUBLISHED BY C. P. WAYNE.

1804.

Title Page

William Marbury

Aaron Burr

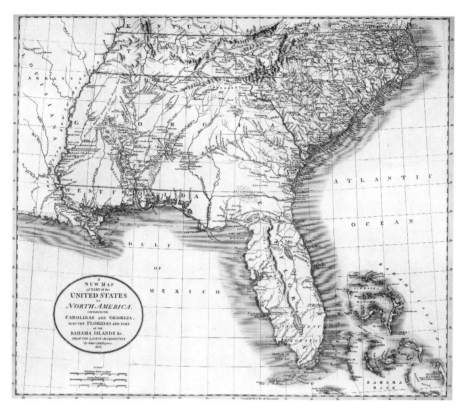

Yazoo and the Floridas

Capture of the *Venus*, 1812

John Randolph

Luther Martin

Henry Clay

Spencer Roane

Marshall's Survey Map, 1812

Daniel Webster

Lottery Ticket, *Cohens v. Virginia*

(*left to right*) Congressman Hugh Nelson (Va.), Washington, Livingston, Marshall, and Story. This is the only group portrait of the justices and is part of Samuel Finley Breese Morse's large painting, *The Old House of Representatives* (1821).

Fauquier White Sulphur Springs. (The cottages of Marshall and
Monroe are side-by-side between the fountain and the inn.)

"I am completely floored."

Virginia Constitutional Convention, 1829–1830
Monroe presiding, Madison speaking, Marshall seated directly behind
Madison.

Jackson's Inauguration

Justice Story

U.S. Capitol, 1830

Marshall in Philadelphia, 1831

Oak Hill

Tombstone

JOHN MARSHALL.
Son of Thomas and Mary Marshall
was born the 24ᵈ of September 1755.
Intermarried with Mary Willis Ambler
the 3ʳᵈ of January 1783.
Departed this life
the 6ᵗʰ day of July 1835.

correct." Marshall said it was normal to begin by establishing the alleged act, but there was no hard and fast rule to that effect. The prosecution could proceed in whichever order it wished, provided that the evidence about Burr's intentions focused on the overt act alleged in the indictment. Information about the defendant's "general evil disposition" was merely corroborative and could not be introduced until an act of treason had been established.[117]

Eaton was recalled to the stand. He related his conversations with Burr in 1805 but was of little help to the government's side. "Concerning certain transactions which are said to have happened at Blennerhasset's Island, or any agency which Aaron Burr may be supposed to have had in them, I know nothing."[118] Next on the stand was Commodore Thomas Truxtun, legendary commander of the U.S.S. *Constellation* and an old friend of the former vice president's, who had often spoken with him about his projects against Mexico. "I know nothing of overt acts, treasonable designs or conversations on the part of Colonel Burr," said Truxtun.[119]

During the next several days, ten more witnesses were called, most of whom had been present on Blennerhasset's Island. None was able to establish that an act of levying war against the United States had taken place. Finally, on Thursday, August 20, Burr and his attorneys objected to the continued introduction of collateral testimony before the prosecution established that an overt act of treason had occurred.[120] The prosecution responded that the question of whether war had been levied was a matter of fact for the jury to decide and that the court should allow the government to place its entire case before them.[121] Once again Marshall sought to strike a balance. The defense had a *right* to object to the admissibility of evidence, and might insist on it, but he suggested that the motion be postponed.[122] Hay then volunteered that he had only two more witnesses concerning the events on Blennerhasset's Island. After they testified, the defense could make its motion if it wished.[123]

When the government's final witnesses added nothing of substance, Burr's attorneys launched their counterattack. Wickham led off and delivered what Richmond lawyer Littleton Tazewell called "the greatest forensic effort of the American bar."[124] For two days Wickham, in the lean, elegant style that was his hallmark, examined the law of treason. He concentrated his attack on the concept of constructive treason. Emphasizing traditional Republican objections to federal common law jurisdiction in criminal matters, Wickham said that "no person can be punished for treason unless they come within the precise description provided by the Constitution."[125] The elderly Randolph followed with the last great speech of his career. He, too, focused on "the pernicious doctrine of constructive treason."[126] Citing Jefferson's declaration that Burr was guilty, he noted that "if the doctrine of treason be not kept within precise limits, but left vague and undefined, it gives the triumphant party the means of subjecting and destroying the other."[127] Wickham and Randolph placed the prosecution in the unhappy position of having to defend the idea of constructive treason—which was anathema to most Republicans, Jefferson's position on the matter notwithstanding. Only Wirt rose to the occasion, and his speech, "Who is Blennerhasset?" describing Burr's seduction of Harman Blennerhasset, became an instant classic of legal declamation.[128] Wirt was followed by Botts on behalf of Burr, and then Hay summarized for the prosecution.

On August 27 Luther Martin, the "rear-guard of Burr's forensic army,"[129] rose to conclude for the defense. Martin spoke for fourteen hours over a period of three days and, despite heavy drinking, was in perfect command of his faculties. Friends and foes alike conceded that Martin gave a magnificent performance, summoning the precedents, laying out the facts, and finishing with a masterful disquisition on constitutional law. His final words were directed at Marshall and Judge Griffin. It is easy to do our duty in fair weather, intoned Martin, but "when the tempest rages, when the thunders roar, and the lightnings blaze around us—it is then that the truly brave man stands firm at his post. . . . May that God who now looks down upon us, so illuminate your understandings that you may know what is right; and may he nerve your souls with firmness and fortitude to act according to that knowledge."[130]

It was shortly before 4 P.M. on Saturday, August 29, when the arguments concluded. Marshall announced that the court would adjourn until Monday, at which time he would render a decision on the defense's motion to suspend further testimony. After ensuring that Judge Griffin was agreed, Marshall began writing his opinion Saturday evening. He continued all day Sunday, worked late into the night, and was up well before dawn Monday morning to add the final touches. As always, he wrote in longhand with a quill pen, and, as in *Marbury v. Madison*, he had time for only one draft. When he finished, Marshall had written 25,000 words—the longest decision of his career. Unlike his great constitutional opinions for the Supreme Court, it is studded with citations to precedent, learned treatises, and legal authority.[131] With virtually no opportunity to revise or tighten what he had written, it is often repetitive. But as with all of his decisions, it marches inexorably across the legal landscape, disposing of the issues in sequence and in the end providing a solid judicial restatement of the law of treason designed to ensure that it would never again be used as an instrument of political persecution.

When court convened at 9 A.M., Marshall was ready. All weekend the fate of Burr had hung in the balance, and on Monday morning the chamber of the House of Delegates was jammed with spectators awaiting the chief justice's decision. Marshall immediately began to read in the soft Virginia tones that characterized his comments from the bench. He praised the prosecution and the defense for "a degree of eloquence" seldom seen and "a depth of research" that was invaluable.[132] The issue, he said, was clear. Both sides agreed that Burr was not present when the overt act alleged in the indictment took place. The Constitution required the testimony of two witnesses to that act. If the act itself could not be proved, was the testimony linking Burr to those on Blennerhasset's Island relevant?

Marshall reviewed the constitutional definition of treason at great length. The crime consisted of levying war against the United States. He sidestepped the issue of constructive treason ("a question of vast importance which it would be proper for the Supreme Court to take a fit occasion to decide") and dealt with the facts of the case. The indictment

> charges the prisoner with levying war against the United States, and alleges an overt act of levying war. That overt act must be proved . . . by two witnesses. It is not proved by a single witness.
>
> If it be said that the advising or procurement of treason is a secret transaction which can scarcely ever be proved in the manner required by this opinion, the answer which will readily suggest itself is, that the difficulty of proving a fact will not justify conviction without proof.

Marshall proceeded to hold that the indictment itself was faulty. The government had fictionally placed Burr on Blennerhasset's Island, when it should have stated "the true facts of the case." Setting an important precedent for civil liberties, Marshall noted that the Sixth Amendment to the Constitution required that in "all criminal prosecutions the accused should . . . be informed of the nature and cause of the accusations" against him.[133] Burr could not defend himself unless he was given accurate notice "which may reasonably suggest to him the point on which the accusation turns." Fictitious indictments, a handy weapon for government prosecutors, could not be accepted.

As for the decision in *Bollman*, Marshall said that that opinion "does not touch the case of a person who advises or procures an assemblage and does nothing further." Such activity would be a conspiracy to levy war, but not an actual levying of war. "It is not enough to be leagued in the conspiracy, and that war be levied, but it is also necessary to perform a part. . . . This part . . . may be minute, it may not be the actual appearance in arms, and it may be remote from the scene of action . . . but it must be a part. *This part, however minute or remote constitutes the overt act on which alone the person who performs it can be convicted.*"

It was almost 2 P.M., and the court's decision on the defense motion to suspend further testimony still had not been rendered. Marshall paused, and before proceeding he addressed the public pressure (including the threat of impeachment) that had been leveled against himself and Judge Griffin.

> That this court dares not usurp power is most true. That this court dares not shrink from its duty is not less true.
>
> No man is desirous of placing himself in a disagreeable situation. No man is desirous of becoming the peculiar subject of calumny. No man, might he let the bitter cup pass from him without self-reproach, would drain it to the bottom. But if he has no choice in the case; if there is no alternative presented to him but a dereliction of duty or the opprobrium of those who are denominated the world, he merits the contempt as well as the indignation of his country who can hesitate which to embrace.

The audience that had crowded into the House chamber was hushed. The Chief Justice of the United States was speaking, and in words reminiscent of *Marbury v. Madison*, he reaffirmed judicial authority. "It is of necessity the peculiar province of the court to judge the admissibility of testimony." Marshall said that after a complete review of the arguments on both sides, the court had come to the conclusion that the defense motion must prevail. "No testimony relative to the conduct or declarations of the prisoner elsewhere and subsequent to the transactions on Blennerhasset's Island can be admitted, because such testimony, being in its nature merely corroborative, and incompetent to prove the overt act itself, is irrelevant, until there be proof of the overt act by two witnesses."

He then sent the case to the jury. "The jury have now heard the opinion of the court on the law of the case. They will apply that law to the facts, and will find a verdict of guilty or not guilty as their own consciences may direct." The jury retired briefly and, with no testimony to incriminate Burr, returned a verdict of not guilty.[134] The following day Hay moved that the former vice president be committed to the United States district court in Kentucky, Tennessee, or the Mississippi Territory to be retried for treason "in the district where the overt act was committed."[135] Marshall gently dismissed Hay's plea, pointing out that charges were still pending against Burr for inciting war against Spain and that he was still in the custody of the fifth circuit. After Burr had been tried on that charge, Hay could renew his motion if he wished.[136]

Jefferson was incensed by the acquittal. Rather than acknowledge that the prosecution's case was shaky, the president blamed Marshall for interfering.[137] He told Hay that the chief justice's motives had been "not only to clear Burr, but to prevent the evidence from ever going before the world." It is not clear what evidence Jefferson had in mind, since if Hay was in possession of any, he surely would have introduced it. Hoping to salvage something from the case, the president attempted to use the outcome as an opportunity to curtail the judiciary. The confrontation between Jefferson and Marshall was now direct. The former president told Hay that the trial record would be "laid before Congress, that they may . . . provide the proper remedy."[138] As for the misdemeanor charge against Burr, he urged Hay to proceed immediately. "If defeated, it will heap coals of fire on the head of the Judge."[139]

Burr's trial for inciting war against Spain commenced September 9.[140] Six days later, after calling more than fifty witnesses, Hay moved that the indictment be dismissed *nolle prosequi* [without further intention to prosecute] and that the jury be excused.[141] The evidence, taken as a whole, showed unmistakably that Burr's objective was the settlement of the Washita lands and that he would not have initiated a war to liberate Mexico unless the United States and Spain had been at war.[142] Marshall ruled that the jury could not be excused without the defendant's consent. Burr insisted on having a verdict, and, after a short consultation *in camera*, the jurors once again found him to be not guilty.[143]

Marshall did not emerge from the Burr trial unscathed. He was excoriated briefly in the Republican press,[144] and a mob in Baltimore burned his likeness in effigy. That autumn Jefferson sent the trial record to Congress. In his message, the president said pointedly, "You will be enabled to judge whether the defect was in the testimony, in the law, or in the administration of the law, and wherever it shall be found, the Legislature alone can apply or originate the remedy."[145] If that was an invitation for the House to commence impeachment proceedings or for a constitutional amendment to limit judicial authority, Congress ignored it, preoccupied with other problems.[146] The international situation required immediate attention, and the possibility of war with Great Britain loomed ominously on the horizon. British naval vessels were impressing American citizens on the high seas, and the nation clamored for action.* The Burr trial began to recede into history, but the break between Jefferson and Marshall, so long in the making, was now complete.

---

*In the summer of 1807, while the Burr trial was at its height, the British man-of-war *Leopard* intercepted and fired on the U.S. frigate *Chesapeake* just outside American territorial waters. The *Chesapeake* was fresh out of Norfolk and was not fitted out for battle. *Leopard* drew alongside and, without warning, poured several broadsides into the American vessel, shooting away her masts, destroying her rigging, killing three, and injuring eighteen. *Chesapeake*, totally disabled, struck her colors. The British boarded and removed four sailors alleged to be British subjects—three of whom were American citizens. Immediately public attention shifted from events in Richmond to the incident at sea.

A month after the trial ended, Marshall expressed his own views in a letter to Judge Richard Peters. Peters had sent the chief justice a printed copy of his own admiralty decisions, and Marshall wrote an acknowledgment. "I received it while fatigued and occupied with the most unpleasant case which has ever been brought before a Judge in this or perhaps in any other country which affected to be governed by laws." Marshall said that he had galloped to Oak Hill as soon as the trial was over and then had held circuit in North Carolina and Richmond.

> Thus you perceive that I have sufficient bodily employment to prevent my mind from perplexing itself about attentions paid me in Baltimore and elsewhere. I wish I could have had an opportunity to let [the trial] go off as a jest . . . but it was most deplorably serious and I could not give the subject a different aspect by treating it in any manner which was in my power. I might perhaps have made it less serious to myself by obeying the public will instead of the public law, and throwing a little more of the sombre upon others.[147]

Marshall had done his duty as he saw it. The proceedings against Burr lapsed and Jefferson's term ended the following year. Under Madison, a rapprochement between the executive and the judiciary was quickly achieved. Marshall always considered the Burr trial to be the most disagreeable experience in his thirty-five years on the bench. He had no affection for Burr, especially after the death of Hamilton, yet he was determined that the text of the Constitution be adhered to.*[148]

---

*Consonant with Marshall's holding in the Burr trial, Justice Livingston, on circuit in Vermont in the autumn of 1808, further restricted the application of the treason clause by holding that it could not be employed as a weapon to enforce federal laws. The Jefferson administration, acting through Attorney General Caesar Rodney, had attempted to enforce the Embargo Act prohibiting trade with Great Britain by bringing indictments for treason against those smuggling goods between Canada and the United States. Livingston ruled that the indictment could not be sustained. "No single act in opposition to or in evasion of a law, however violent or flagrant, when the object is private gain, can be construed into levying war against the United States." *United States v. Hoxie*, 26 F. Cas. 397 (C.C.D. Vt. 1808), Federal Cases No. 15407.

16

Yazoo

MARSHALL ENDURED the Burr trial with stoic determination. Except for his letter to Judge Peters, he showed little emotion concerning the events of 1807. His experience in politics, and especially his year in Paris, had prepared him to be the center of controversy, and although he did not relish the notoriety, he accepted it as one of the inevitable consequences of public life. Polly was less able to weather the storm. Unaccustomed to the tension of a long and bitter trial and unable to comprehend the continuous criticism to which her husband had been subjected, she collapsed under the pressure. When news arrived that a crowd in Baltimore had hanged Marshall in effigy, Polly suffered a nervous collapse.[1] She took to her bed and became a virtual invalid. So severe was her depression, and so extreme her sensitivity to any noise or disturbance, that the Richmond Common Council temporarily halted the ringing of the town bell and muffled the striking of the town clock.[2]

Marshall responded to Polly's affliction with increasing affection and did everything he could to shield his wife from any intrusion. It was not uncommon for the chief justice to get up at any hour of the night and steal downstairs to drive away some wandering horse or cow whose sounds had disturbed her.[3] The barking of neighborhood dogs posed a special problem. Aside from being family pets, the dogs were essential for the protection of life and property, but the alarm they sounded broke the stillness Polly needed so desperately. Marshall intervened only when the problem became persistent, and he did so as delicately as possible. When a dog of his neighbor, John Rawlings, barked incessantly one summer, Marshall wrote Rawlings a kindly note, calling his attention to Polly's distressed condition. "During this spell of hot weather she had been kept almost perpetually awake [by the dog's barking]. Last night she could not sleep two hours. Her situation is deplorable, and if this state of things continues she cannot live."[4]

As the years passed, Polly showed little improvement. Her extreme nervousness was compounded by anemia, and she suffered from spells of severe weakness. In 1816 Marshall wrote to his brother Louis that "My wife continues in wretched health. Her nervous system is so affected that she cannot sit in a room while a person walks across the floor. I am now preparing to convey her out of town in order to escape the noisy rejoicing of the [Christmas] season which is now approaching."[5] Grandchildren reported that when Marshall entered the house, he would always take off his shoes at the door and put on his slippers to avoid making any noise that would disturb Polly.[6] When the chief justice hosted his famous lawyers' dinners each fall and winter, his wife was carried across the street to the home of her sister, Eliza Carrington. She withdrew from society and lived out the remainder of her years in isolation, lovingly cared for by her husband.

Richmond residents grew accustomed to seeing the tall, ungainly, negligently dressed Chief Justice of the United States shopping in the farmers' market.[7] As had long been his custom, Marshall rose well before dawn to go for a brisk walk of four to five miles through the meandering Shockoe Valley. He returned through the rows of farm carts that lined the creek bank, where he made his daily purchases of meat, vegetables, butter, and eggs. He never hurried, and habitually lingered at the market, chatting with everyone, learning the gossip, and listening to the ceaseless political talk. One day, as he loitered with his produce, a young gentleman new to Richmond, who had never seen Marshall before, offered the poorly dressed chief justice a small coin to carry a plump turkey he had just purchased. Marshall obligingly added the turkey to his own provisions and trudged respectfully behind his new employer to a house not far from his own, whereupon he handed the bird to its owner and pocketed the coin flipped in his direction. The incident, witnessed by many at the market, sent the city into gales of laughter, although Marshall kindly noted that "we were going the same way" and it seemed only neighborly.[8]

Richmond residents were not as well prepared for the sight of the chief justice, mop in hand, leading his servants in the weekly housecleaning. Numerous callers at the Marshall house reported him with his sleeves rolled up and a handkerchief tied about his head, helping to scrub the floors and set the house to order.[9]

Polly's dependence on Marshall brought the couple closer together as the years went by. Shortly after the chief justice's death, descendants found tucked among some papers a poem Marshall had composed for his wife. He had originally written it for a friend's book of autographs, but had withheld it "in the apprehension that it might be thought light and unbecoming the gravity of [someone] seventy-three."[10]

Lines Written for a Lady's Album

In early youth, when life was young
　　And spirits light and gay,
When music breathed from every tongue
　　And every month was May;

When buoyant hope in colours bright
　　Her vivid pictures drew,
When every object gave delight
　　And every scene was new;

My heart with ready homage bowed
　　At lovely woman's shrine,
And every wish that she avowed
　　Became a wish of mine;

Now age with hoary frost congeals
　　Gay fancy's flowing stream,
And the unwelcome truth reveals
　　That life is but a dream;

Yet still with homage true I bow
　　At woman's sacred shrine,
And if she will a wish avow
　　That wish must still be mine.

My old wife! My youth grown rich and tender with years!

In late January, Marshall left Polly under the watchful eyes of her sisters and hurried to Washington for the 1808 term of the court. There were thirty cases on the docket, several of which threatened a renewed confrontation with the administration and all of which were slated to be argued during the six weeks commencing February 1. The justices continued their practice of keeping common lodgings, and they had settled into a routine. They convened Court at eleven, and listened to arguments until four. Then they returned to their hotel for dinner at five and commenced their evening conference at six.[11] Marshall set the pace. As he wrote Polly, "I rise early, pour [*sic*] over law cases, go to court and return at the same hour and pass the evening in consultation with the Judges."[12] The judges' conference usually lasted until eight and was conducted every evening except Sunday, unless the justices were invited out.*[13]

It was during these nightly conferences that pending cases were discussed and the position of the Court determined.[14] Issues were mooted as they arose, partly because written briefs were not always submitted and the justices had to rely on the oral arguments they had just heard.[15] These sessions, which Marshall instituted, were the origin of what today is known as "the Conference," the twice-weekly meeting in which the justices transact the business of the Court. Then, as now, no one was present but the justices, no notes were taken, and what took place can only be surmised from the opinions of the Court. These informal after-dinner meetings, undoubtedly lubricated with well-chosen Madeira, allowed the justices to exchange views frankly and to arrive at a common understanding on the points at issue. Story wrote that the discussions were freewheeling, a "pleasant and animated interchange of legal acumen."[16] They were invaluable not only in establishing the collective identity of the Court but also in providing firm, clear guidance as to the law in a given case. And for a legal profession accustomed to the *seriatim* opinions of individual judges, nothing was more helpful than to know with certainty what the law was.

Peisch v. Ware,[17] decided March, 9, 1808, illustrates the importance of the conference in permitting the Court to speak authoritatively. The case involved a conflict between federal and state laws concerning salvage activities in coastal waters. The ship *Favourite,* bound from Bordeaux to Philadelphia with a cargo of wine and brandy, was discovered abandoned and adrift in Delaware Bay, her masts gone, her rudder and anchor cables missing, and in danger of being carried out to sea by the tide. A salvage party rescued the derelict and was rewarded half the value of the cargo by a Delaware arbitration tribunal.[18] At that point, federal authorities intervened and attempted to seize the cargo, asserting that it had been imported in violation of the revenue laws and consequently should be forfeited to the United States.

The case was argued from March 1 to March 4.[19] Five days later Mar-

---

*When it came time for the justices to pay their customary formal call on the president, Justice Johnson, the South Carolina Republican, questioned whether they should go, given Jefferson's intemperate criticism of Marshall's handling of the Burr trial. Attorney General Caesar Rodney told Jefferson that the justices divided three to three, with Bushrod Washington casting the deciding vote in favor of calling. How Marshall voted is not known, but he and Washington rarely differed. Rodney to Jefferson, October 31, 1808, quoted in Charles Warren, 1 *The Supreme Court in United States History* 336–337 (Boston: Little, Brown, 1926).

shall announced that the justices were agreed that no forfeiture was required. Reflecting the sentiment of his new Republican colleagues, Marshall interpreted the nation's revenue laws narrowly, deferred to state judicial authority, and produced a unanimous decision.[20] As for the original salvage award, the holding was more complicated:

> [T]he opinion of the majority is that the sentence of the [Delaware arbitration tribunal] ought to be affirmed. This opinion however is made up on different grounds. Two of the Judges are of the opinion that the award was fairly entered into. . . . Two other Judges who do not think the award obligatory view it as the opinion of fair and intelligent men on the spot. . . . Three Judges are of opinion that the award is of no validity and ought to have no influence. They think . . . that the salvage allowed is too great.
>
> They acquiesce however cheerfully in the opinion of the majority of the Court, and express their dissent from that opinion solely for the purpose of preventing this sentence from having more than its due influence on future salvage cases.

In effect, Marshall had hammered together an opinion of the Court that was acceptable to all of his colleagues. The views of the dissenters were acknowledged, but no separate dissenting opinions were filed. The Court spoke with one voice, and that was the voice of the chief justice.

Marshall's efforts to remove the Court from partisanship had suffered a severe setback during the Burr trial. Now it was the deteriorating international situation that thrust the justices into the crucible of political conflict. As a result of the *Leopard*'s unprovoked attack on the *Chesapeake* the previous summer, the divisive issue of expatriation was again front and center. Great Britain maintained that under the common law, no British subject could voluntarily expatriate himself. As a result, the Royal Navy was justified in impressing those persons who had become naturalized American citizens. Old-guard Federalists generally agreed with the British doctrine, but the mass of the country was up in arms, demanding satisfaction for *Leopard*'s action. Two important cases, *McIlvaine v. Coxe's Lessee*[21] and *Dawson's Lessee v. Godfrey*,[22] raised the issue of expatriation. In both the Court, acting unanimously, sidestepped ruling on the common law doctrine. Marshall did not participate in either case, but given the dexterity with which the justices avoided entanglement in one of the raging political issues of the day, scholars have suggested that the chief justice unquestionably steered the decisions in conference.[23]

An equally contentious case, and one that brought the Court into direct conflict with the administration, involved the decisions of British prize courts against American shipping. The Royal Navy routinely intercepted and took possession of American merchant vessels bound for Europe, and British prize courts routinely condemned the vessels for blockade running. In *Croudson v. Leonard*,[24] the Court was asked to decide whether American insurance companies were liable for such seizures. The insurers maintained that blockade running was an offense at international law and that British condemnation proceedings absolved the companies of responsibility. The shipowners and the Jefferson administration contended that the decisions of the admiralty courts were biased and that the United States should not comply with British rules against neutral shipping.[25] The Court divided on the issue, with Marshall, Cushing, Washington, and Johnson upholding the British rule, and Chase and Livingston dissenting.[26] *Croudson* was the last case decided during the 1808 term. Whether it was because of the press of time, because the Court was divided, or because the decision was sure to create conflict with the administration, Marshall assigned the majority opinion to Justice Johnson. If the Court was going to affirm British doctrine, it was doubtless wise to have the holding announced by one of Jefferson's appointees.[27]

The 1808 term of the Court ended March 16. Of the thirty cases that had been pending, Marshall wrote the opinion in twenty-two. In three cases he recused himself,[28] two cases were decided *per curiam*, and two were dismissed for lack of jurisdiction. The only case in which Marshall participated and did not write the opinion was *Croudson v. Leonard*. Overall, the Court continued in remarkable agreement. Marshall occasionally noted a division on specific points, but in total, only two individual dissents were filed.[29]

It was not until the Court adjourned that the justices were confronted with the most serious consequences of unraveling relations with Great Britain. Jefferson's response to the capture of American ships and the impressment of American seamen was to forbid all foreign trade by the United States. Under prodding from the administration, Congress, in the spring of 1808, passed a series of embargo acts prohibiting American vessels from sailing abroad.[30] Customs officials were instructed to detain such ships in port, and, under the Act of April 25, 1808, even vessels bound for American destinations were to be held if, in the opinion of the customs officer, their cargo was to be sold abroad.[31] In interpreting the statute, Jefferson went far beyond the text of what Congress provided and told Secretary of the Treasury Gallatin that *every* shipment of food, lumber, tobacco, and cotton, regardless of its destination, was sufficiently suspicious to justify holding a vessel.[32] The effect was to close American ports to all commerce, paralyzing the shipping industry and causing great hardship, particularly in the New England states, New York, and the seaports to the south.

Jefferson's rationale for the embargo rested on his belief that England was so dependent on American trade that its economy would collapse if trade were stopped. In reality, Britain found trading partners elsewhere, and its shipping industry profited enormously from the absence of American competition. Republicans defended the embargo as a measure that protected American shipowners from having their vessels seized, but the shipowners, who had thrived on trade with England, wanted no part of it.[33]

As the embargo took effect, enforcement became an increasing problem, and it was inevitable that the federal courts would be drawn in. The president's order to interdict even those vessels bound for American ports were especially contentious, and on May 24, 1808, Adam Gilchrist, a shipowner in Charleston, South Carolina, sought to test its legality. The vessel involved was loaded with rice destined for Baltimore. Acting pursuant to Jefferson's instructions, Simeon Theus, the collector of customs in Charleston, had refused to give the ship permission to sail, although he personally did not think the rice was bound for Europe.[34] Gilchrist appeared before Justice Johnson in circuit court and petitioned for a writ of *mandamus* ordering Theus to grant clearance.[35] The United States attorney for South Carolina did not oppose the petition, and four days later Johnson issued the writ, holding that Jefferson's instructions to the collector were unauthorized by the statute and that without the sanction of law, "the collector is not justified . . . in increasing restraints on commerce." Johnson added a stinging rebuff to the president. "The officers of our government, from the highest to the lowest, are equally subject to legal restraint; and it is confidently believed that all of them feel themselves equally incapable . . . to attempt an unsanctioned encroachment on individual liberty."[36]

Johnson's decision hit the country like a bombshell. Except for Marshall's holding in the Burr case, no decision by a federal court was reported more widely or received greater editorial attention.[37] Federalists hailed Johnson's integrity and independence, while Republican assailed the decision as another example of judicial high-handedness. Jefferson was indignant that his embargo policy should be frustrated by his own appointee and viewed Johnson's holding as a personal insult.[38] At the president's behest, Attorney General Rodney issued his own opinion rejecting the power of federal judges to issue writs of *mandamus* to executive officers. Ironically, he cited Marshall's decision in *Marbury v. Madison* as the definitive authority.[39] Jefferson distributed Rodney's opinion to the press, thereby ratcheting the controversy a notch higher.

Justice Johnson, who was still smarting over Jefferson's conduct during the Burr trial, interpreted the president's move as another threat to judicial autonomy. Addressing the issue in open court, he called Jefferson's action "an act unprecedented in the history of executive conduct" and said that it "could be intended for no other purpose than to secure the public opinion on the side of the executive and in opposition to the judiciary."[40] The fact that Johnson was a Republican and was speaking in South Carolina, a hotbed of Republicanism, gave his remarks extraordinary impact. After repeatedly invoking Marshall's holding in *Marbury,* Johnson said that "The courts do not pretend to impose any restraint upon any officer of government, but what results from a just construction of the laws of the United States. Of these laws the courts are the constitutional expositors, and every department of government must submit to their exposition."[41] No federal judge, Marshall included, ever spoke more concisely in defense of judicial authority.

Johnson's spirited response struck a raw nerve among Republicans. "You can scarcely elevate a man to a seat in a Court of Justice before he catches the leprosy of the bench," Rodney told Jefferson.[42] First Marshall, now Johnson, had defied the president. "It is high time for the people to apply a remedy," said the attorney general. "The judicial power, if permitted, will swallow the rest. They will become omnipotent."[43]

Johnson had not addressed the constitutionality of the embargo in the *Gilchrist* case, having confined himself to dealing with the issue of the president's executive order. Marshall expressed no comment on Johnson's ruling, and the issue never came before the Supreme Court. Later in the year a United States district court in Massachusetts upheld Congress's authority to impose the embargo, and no appeal was taken.[44] Given Marshall's earlier decisions about the implied powers of Congress in *United States v. Fisher,*[45] it was clear that the Supreme Court would not overturn the embargo.[46] In fact, sixteen years later in *Gibbons v. Ogden,* the great case dealing with Congress's authority to regulate commerce, Marshall referred explicitly to "the *universally acknowledged power* of the Government to impose embargoes."*[47]

Although the embargo was constitutional, it proved to be a political disaster for Jefferson. New England seethed with resentment, town meetings

---

*There is no evidence that Marshall ever questioned the constitutionality of the embargo, although there is ample evidence that he strongly opposed it as a private citizen. In December 1808, upon receipt of two speeches from Senator Timothy Pickering advocating repeal, Marshall acknowledged Pickering's effort, replying that "If sound argument and correct reasoning could save our country it would be saved. Nothing can be more completely demonstrated than the inefficacy of the embargo, yet that demonstration seems to be of no avail. I fear most seriously that the same spirit which so tenaciously maintains this measure will impel us to a war with the only power which protects any part of the civilized world from the despotism of that tyrant [Napoleon] with whom we shall then be arranged." Marshall congratulated Pickering on his analysis of the motives behind the embargo, and then, recognizing perhaps that he may have been too candid, closed with the admonition that "I abstain from remarks on this question." Marshall to Pickering, December 19, 1808, 7 *The Papers of John Marshall* 188 (Chapel Hill: University of North Carolina Press, 1993). For the text of Pickering's speeches, November 30 and December 1, 1808, see Ralph R. Shaw and Richard H. Shoemaker, eds., *American Bibliography . . . 1801–1819,* #15938, #15941 (New York: Scarecrow Press, 1958).

passed resolutions advocating secession, and juries simply refused to convict those charged with violating the law.[48] Jefferson's mistake was the Federalists' opportunity. Just as the ill-conceived alien and sedition acts in 1798 had revived the flagging Republican cause, the embargo gave the Federalists a renewed lease on life. In the 1804 presidential election, Jefferson had carried every state except Connecticut and Delaware, and by 1807 every state government except Connecticut was in Republican hands. But the tide now turned. Federalist spokesmen rallied opposition to the embargo, and the Republicans found themselves divided. Madison was nominated by the party's congressional caucus to succeed Jefferson, but the New York legislature broke ranks and supported Vice President George Clinton as an anti-embargo Republican, while in Virginia James Monroe, who had split with Jefferson over foreign policy, was nominated by a dissident faction as an "Old Republican."[49]

The Federalists once again chose Charles Cotesworth Pinckney as their candidate, and on September 21 Marshall wrote from Richmond to apprise his former companion of the dim chances of carrying the Old Dominion. "Virginia remains devoted to the present system of measures," said Marshall. "In some parts of the state an impression has been made, but it is very partial. We may have three federal members in the next Congress, possibly four.[50] But at the Presidential ticket, nothing can be done. In our general ticket the voice of the minority is lost."[51] In referring to "our general ticket," Marshall was alluding to the fact that Virginia apportioned its electoral vote on a statewide, winner-take-all basis; it was one of the first states to do so.[52] That meant that the Federalists had no chance of choosing any of the state's twenty-four electors.

Marshall told Pinckney that since becoming chief justice, he had "absolutely withdrawn from the busy circles in which politics are discussed." He said he had devoted himself to his small farm outside Richmond, "and scarcely ever read a newspaper. My attempts to produce an indifference to what was passing around me would I believe have been nearly successful had they not been totally defeated by events so serious . . . that they . . . appear . . . to place . . . the independence of our country in the most serious danger. I however can only look on with silent and anxious concern. I can render no service."[53]

Except for expressing his views to Pinckney, Marshall took no part in the 1808 election. As the voting approached, he wrote once more to explain that the Federalists in Richmond, despairing of carrying the state for the party, had decided to support Monroe. Marshall said he was not present when the decision was taken, but had been informed about it and had decided to alert Pinckney so that the action would not be misunderstood.[54]

The federalists of Virginia constitute a small and oppressed minority in our state. Between rival democratic candidates for the Presidency they were divided. . . . The superior talents of Mr. Madison would probably have placed us in his scale and had not recent events [related to the embargo] induced the opinion that this prejudices with respect to our foreign relations were still more inveterate and incurable than those of either of his competitors.

Marshall told Pinckney that "this circumstance, and this circumstance singly," caused those at the meeting "to support the Monroe ticket as the only mode in which they could aid the federalist cause."[55]

While the Federalists gained ground in the 1808 election, once more they went down to defeat. Pinckney carried four New England states and Delaware, and picked up additional electors in Maryland and North Carolina, but Madison outdistanced him easily.[56] In Virginia, the Monroe slate failed miserably. The final results gave Madison's electors 14,665 votes as opposed to 3,408 for Monroe. Pinckney received only 760 votes, most Federalists having cast their ballots for Monroe.*[57]

When the Court convened on February 6 for its 1809 term, the embargo was on its last legs. New England Republicans had joined the clamor for its repeal, and Jefferson was forced to concede that the measure had been a failure. Three days before leaving office, he signed a bill that had been rushed through Congress, ending the embargo.[58] Madison was freed of an unpopular legacy, and on March 4, amid a festive air of celebration, Marshall administered the oath of office to the fourth President of the United States. During his service as chief justice, Marshall would administer the oath on nine separate occasions to five different chief executives, but the changeover in 1809, marking the end of Jefferson's term, was undoubtedly one of his most pleasurable.

With the change of administration, the conflict over the separation of powers ended. Madison did not share the Jeffersonian view that the courts were subordinate to the popular will. Rather, he fully subscribed to a division of governmental authority among three coordinate and coequal branches.[59] In effect, the battle for an independent judiciary had been won by default. Despite sharp differences over foreign policy, Marshall and Madison saw eye to eye on the organization and role of the federal government, but the 1809 term of the Court quickly put each man to the test.

---

*As a result of his defection, Monroe remained in the political wilderness for the next two years. Gradually his personal breach with Jefferson healed, and in January 1810, when Governor John Tyler resigned to accept a seat on the federal bench (replacing Judge Cyrus Griffin), Monroe was elected governor. Three months later Madison appointed him secretary of state. Harry Ammon, *James Monroe: The Quest for National Identity* 270–288 (Charlottesville: University Press of Virginia, 1991).

The embargo had triggered a wave of resentment against the national government. In a very real sense, the Union was in peril. Massachusetts and Connecticut, reeling under the impact of the trade cutoff, were threatening the nullification of federal statutes,[60] while Pennsylvania and Georgia, traditional breeding grounds of radicalism, were again challenging the jurisdiction of the federal courts.[61] The threat from Pennsylvania was the most immediate. The issue involved a dispute dating from the Revolutionary War and pertained to a salvage award rendered by a federal prize court holding the state of Pennsylvania liable.[62] The state refused to recognize the authority of the court and declined to pay the judgment. In 1803 the case was revived, and Judge Richard Peters, of the United States district court in Pennsylvania, decreed that the funds be paid.[63] Once again Pennsylvania refused, the legislature instructing the governor "to protect the just rights of the State . . . by any means necessary from any process issued out of any federal court."[64] Reluctant to precipitate a showdown between federal and state authority,[65] Peters declined to order that his judgment be executed. The matter remained in abeyance until 1809, when Attorney General Caesar Rodney, acting in his private capacity as a lawyer, appeared before the Supreme Court on behalf of the frustrated claimant and requested a preemptory writ of *mandamus* directing Judge Peters to enforce his decree. The case has been styled *United States v. Peters*,[66] although Judge Peters was merely a nominal defendant, and it involved an immediate clash between the judicial authority of the federal government and the sovereign power of one of the states.

In response to the attorney general's request, the Supreme Court unhesitatingly reasserted the supremacy of the national government. In a decision remarkable for its directness, Marshall, speaking once more for a unanimous Court, said that "if the legislatures of the several states may at will annul the judgments of the courts of the United States and destroy the rights acquired under those judgments, the Constitution itself becomes a solemn mockery."[67] The chief justice chose his words with exactitude, aiming at separatist sentiment in New England as much as in the refractory Pennsylvania legislature. Forcible resistance by a state to national authority, he said, "must be deprecated by all; and the people of Pennsylvania, not less than the citizens of every other state, must feel a deep interest in resisting principles so destructive of the Union." After briefly examining the merits of the case, Marshall held that there was no legal basis for Pennsylvania's resistance. He said the Court regretted that it was forced to take action, "but it is a solemn duty, and therefore must be performed. A preemptory *mandamus* must be awarded."[68]

Pennsylvania did not yield easily. When the Supreme Court's decision was announced, Governor Simon Snyder called out the state militia to prevent the judgment from being executed, and the legislature adopted another series of resolutions rejecting the jurisdiction of the federal courts. This time Judge Peters stood his ground. He responded with an order directing the state to comply, and a federal grand jury indicted the commanding general of the militia for resisting the laws of the United States. At that point, Governor Snyder appealed to President Madison for support. Snyder said he hoped the president would "justly discriminate between opposition to the Constitution . . . and that of resisting the decree of a Judge founded on a usurpation of power."[69] Had Jefferson still been president, there is no telling what might have happened.[70] Madison, however, did not flinch. Confronted with a near rebellion in Pennsylvania, he brushed aside the governor's request, noting that "it would be unnecessary, if not improper" for him to reexamine the case. "The Executive of the United States is not only unauthorized to prevent the execution of a decree sanctioned by the Supreme Court of the United States, but is expressly enjoined, by statute, to carry into effect any such decree where opposition may be made to it."[71]

Madison's firm but polite reply ended the matter. Snyder beat a hasty retreat, state troops were withdrawn, and the legislature appropriated the money to comply with the judgment. Brigadier General Michael Bright, the militia commander, was brought to trial in federal court before Justice Washington, where he was convicted and sentenced to be fined and imprisoned.[72]

Coming in the first months of Madison's term, *United States v. Peters* was a pivotal case. It not only helped terminate the long-standing hostility between the executive and judicial branches, but in fact ushered in an era of mutual support. The Republican press, which since the Burr trial had nothing good to say about the judiciary, now rallied around it. "We have heard much talk about the independence of the Judiciary," wrote the *Aurora*, "but here is a point at which the independence of the Judiciary, in its strict and constitutional sense, exists and demands to be supported, and in which it must be supported, or there is an end to government. . . . The decree of the court must be obeyed."[73] The Supreme Court's authority was on the upswing, and the 1809 term saw the justices working at the height of their efficiency. A record forty-five cases had been on the docket, and the Court rendered decisions in forty-one. Of those, Marshall wrote the opinion in thirty, Cushing in two, Livingston in one, Washington in one, and seven decisions were *per curiam*. Johnson dissented twice, but otherwise the decisions were unanimous.

That spring, and again in the fall, Marshall presided over the circuit court in Raleigh and Richmond. On December 10, during the term in Richmond, he received a long, intimate, and totally unexpected letter from his old friend Gouverneur Morris in New York.[74] Morris, who was two years older than Marshall, was extremely successful financially and had kept his hand in politics as Federalist leader in the Empire State. The two men had not met or corresponded since Morris's term in the Senate expired in 1803, and now the New York leader was writing to Marshall about an affair of the heart. It was an old memory revived. Morris had developed a relationship with Nancy Randolph of Tuckahoe, the much-maligned young lady whose reputation Marshall and Patrick Henry had defended at the Bizarre murder inquest in 1793. Morris was twenty-four years older than Nancy, and, as delicately as possible, he sought Marshall's opinion.

Morris had originally met Nancy while visiting her father, Thomas Mann Randolph, at Tuckahoe in 1786. She was then a child of eleven. They did not renew their acquaintance until late in 1808, when he discovered her destitute in New York. Morris, a bachelor, felt sorry for the daughter of his old friend and took her into his spacious residence as his housekeeper. Over the next year the two fell in love. Morris told Marshall there was considerable gossip in New York about her involvement in the events that had taken place years earlier at Glenlyvar, and he asked if there were any basis for it. Morris said he didn't care personally, but he was afraid the charges would be used to discredit the Federalist cause. "The Object of this Letter is to ask you frankly the Reputation Miss Randolph left in Virginia, and the Standing she held in Society."[75]

Marshall replied instantly. He told Morris that if any indiscretion was ascribed to Nancy, "the suspicion has never reached my ears."[76] He recalled that the infanticide charge "was very public and excited much attention. Some circumstances addressed in support of it were ambiguous, and rumor, with her usual industry, spread a thousand others which were probably invented by malignant, or magnified by those who love to supply any defects in the story they relate." Marshall said that Nancy's plight in Virginia had been made more difficult because a part of her family "avowed their belief of her guilt. Yet that sister [Judith] who had the fairest means of judging the transaction, and who was most injured by the fact if true, continued to treat her with an affection apparently unabated."

Marshall did not reveal any details of his lawyer-client relationship in the case, but he told Morris that in a matter that had been so publicized, "public opinion would necessarily be divided. Many believed the accusations brought against Miss Randolph to be true, while others attached no criminality to her conduct and believed her to be the victim of a concurrence of unfortunate circumstances. *Among the latter class of persons were the ladies with whom I am connected.*"[77]

Marshall's letter reached Morris on December 23. The next morning he proposed to Nancy, and the following day, Christmas, 1809, they were married. Three days later Morris wrote to Marshall explaining his decision. He thanked the chief justice for his candor and said that as a result he had dismissed the gossip as unimportant. Nancy fulfilled all of his expectations as a wife, said Morris, and he had absolutely no regrets.[78]

Marshall returned to Washington in early February for the 1810 term of the Court, a term that, with the possible exception of 1803, would prove to be the most important during his tenure as chief justice. In 1803, in *Marbury v. Madison*,[79] the Court had established its authority to declare an act of Congress unconstitutional. In 1810, in another landmark case, *Fletcher v. Peck*,[80] it would assert its authority to strike down state laws repugnant to the Constitution. After *Marbury*, the Marshall Court never again pronounced a federal law unconstitutional. By contrast, *Fletcher v. Peck* was the first of a series of decisions nullifying state legislation. These decisions include some of the most important holdings in American constitutional law: *McCulloch v. Maryland*[81]; the *Dartmouth College* case[82]; *Gibbons v. Ogden*[83]; and the great Cherokee case, *Worcester v. Georgia*.[84] As Justice Holmes noted, "I do not think the United States would come to an end if we lost our power to declare an Act of Congress void. I do think the Union would be imperilled if we could not make that declaration as to the laws of the several states."[85]

Aside from its contribution to the consolidation of the union, the Marshall Court's ruling in *Fletcher v. Peck* was perhaps even more significant for its invocation of the contract clause of the Constitution* as a general restraint against state interference with the right to acquire private property. From 1810 onward, commercial transactions enjoyed substantial constitutional protection—a vital restatement of the Constitution's underlying Lockean premise that government was limited and that property, along with life and liberty, was one of the unalienable rights the law was designed to protect. For Marshall's generation, property was a dynamic concept. It referred not merely to existing possessions but also to the industrious acquisition of wealth.[86] Madison expressed it best in *Federalist 10* when he said that "the first object of Government" is the protection of the "different and unequal facilities of acquiring property." That is also the sense in which John Adams used it: "Property must be secured, or liberty cannot exist."[87]

Fletcher v. Peck was one of the legacies of the Yazoo land scandal of 1795, in which a corrupt Georgia legislature had sold some 35 million acres—comprising most of the present states of Alabama and Mississippi—to four New England land companies for 1½¢ an acre. In retrospect, the transaction appears to have been an incredible betrayal of public trust. All but one mem-

---

*Article I, section 10, provides that "No State shall enter into any Treaty, Alliance, or Confederation; grant Letters of Marque and Reprisal; coin Money; emit Bills of Credit; make any Thing but gold and silver Coin a Tender in Payment of Debts; pass any Bill of Attainder, ex post facto Law, *or Law impairing the Obligation of Contracts*, or grant any Title of Nobility." (Emphasis added.) For the debate in the Federal Convention pertaining to the contract clause, see Max Farrand, 2 *Records of the Federal Convention* 440ff (New Haven, Conn.: Yale University Press, 1911).

ber of the Georgia legislature profited personally from the deal, and several made substantial fortunes. Nevertheless, the transaction was not without merit.[88] Georgia's treasury was empty; the Indian-fighting militia was clamoring for its pay; the state's meager population was poor; the public reputation of the new investors was unblemished; and they were offering $500,000 in hard currency for unsettled land in the wilderness.[89] That was a sizable sum in 1795.* In addition, Georgia's title to the territory was cloudy. The land was occupied by the great Indian tribes of the Southeast Confederacy (Creeks, Cherokees, Choctaws, and Chickasaws), whose title had not been extinguished. It was also claimed by Spain as well as by the federal government. As one historian has written, "No one could say what was the value of Georgia's title, but however good the title might be, the State would have been fortunate to make it a free gift to any authority strong enough to deal with the Creeks and Cherokees alone."[90]

The taint attached to the sale ignited a firestorm across Georgia. Rival politicians fanned the flames, and in the election that took place later in 1795, the old legislature was swept out of office. The incoming assembly, as its first order of business, passed an act rescinding the grant.[91] The lands that had been sold were declared to be "the sole property of the State," and all documents relating to the original transaction were ordered expunged from the records. These and the official copy of the 1795 act were burned in an elaborate public ceremony on the statehouse square, the fire supplied from heaven by means of a magnifying glass that concentrated the sun's rays into a flame.[92]

Yazoo might have remained a local affair had not the four companies that purchased the land resold so much of it, and so quickly, to so many good-faith purchasers throughout the United States. The announcement of Georgia's rescinding act aroused widespread consternation and gave rise to a vociferous national controversy over the propriety of the original grant and the authority of the state to revoke it. Claiming ignorance of the fraud that had attended passage of the 1795 act, investors sought to recoup their money by petitioning Congress. Their determined efforts made the Yazoo controversy a staple issue in the halls of Congress for nearly twenty years.[93]

Judicial remedies appeared limited. The Eleventh Amendment barred suits against the states in federal courts, and the 1796 rescinding act forbade Georgia's courts from exercising jurisdiction. Thus it came about that in 1803, Robert Fletcher, of Amherst, New Hampshire, brought a private lawsuit against John Peck of Boston, one of the original Yazoo purchasers, to test

---

*In 1789 and again in 1790, the Georgia legislature had attempted to sell the land for $200,000, but both sales had fallen through when the would-be investors failed to raise the money. C. Peter Magrath, *Yazoo: Law and Politics in the New Republic* 4–6 (Providence, R.I.: Brown University Press, 1966).

Peck's title to the land. The case was based on Peck's subsequent sale of 15,000 acres of land to Fletcher. Fletcher contended that because of Georgia's rescinding act, Peck no longer owned the land, and sought his money back. The evidence suggests that the suit was deliberately arranged between friendly parties to obtain a judgment from the Supreme Court as to the validity of the Yazoo titles.[94] If the state of Georgia had the authority to rescind the original grant, Fletcher was entitled to the return of his money. If Georgia lacked that authority, then the rescinding act was without force and Peck's original title to the land was good.

Justice Cushing heard the case on circuit in 1807 and ruled for Peck.[95] The appeal was argued before the Supreme Court in March 1809, set aside on a technicality,[96] and reargued in 1810. Luther Martin appeared on behalf of Fletcher and once was so intoxicated that Marshall took the unprecedented action of adjourning temporarily so that the old Federal bulldog could recover.[97] Robert Goodloe Harper and Joseph Story represented Peck and argued the case for the land companies.[98]

The justices mulled over their decision for almost a month. Finally, on March 16, the second to last day of the 1810 term, Marshall announced the opinion of the Court.[99] As was his habit in difficult cases, he began elliptically. The first issue was whether Georgia had the authority to sell the land in 1795, or whether the state's constitution prohibited such a sale. Marshall deferred to the legislature. In a famous passage, reiterated countless times by the Supreme Court in the years since, the chief justice emphasized the necessity for judicial restraint.

> The question, whether a law be void for its repugnancy to the constitution, is at all times a question of much delicacy, which ought seldom, if ever, to be decided in the affirmative, in a doubtful case. The Court, when compelled by duty to render such a judgment, would be unworthy of its station, if it were unmindful of the solemn obligations which that situation imposes. But it is not on slight implication and vague conjecture that the legislature is to be pronounced to have transcended its powers, and its acts to be considered as void. The opposition between the constitution and the law should be such that the judge feels a clear and strong conviction of their incompatibility with each other.[100]

Having established the limits of judicial review, Marshall held that Georgia's constitution imposed no bar to the original sale. As for the motives of the legislature, these too were beyond judicial cognizance. "That corruption should find its way into the governments of our infant republics and contaminate the very source of legislation . . . are circumstances most deeply to be deplored." But the validity of a law does not depend on the motives of its framers. Even if the Court could investigate the question of legislative corruption, what standard would it use? "Must it be direct corruption, or would interest or undue influence of any kind be sufficient?" Does the majority of the legislature have to be corrupt, or would any taint suffice? "If the majority . . . be corrupted, it may well be doubted whether it be within the province of the judiciary to control their conduct; and, if less than a majority act from impure motives, the principle by which judicial interference would be regulated is not clearly discerned."

Marshall was drawing an important line. The spheres of the government departments were distinct. To have inquired into the bribery charges leveled against the Georgia legislature would have prompted a vast number of suits attacking state legislation throughout the Union. Ever since he had become chief justice, Marshall had attempted to distinguish between law and politics. To entertain the issue of legislative corruption would thrust the Court once more into the political arena.[101] Marshall said it would be "indecent, in the extreme . . . to enter into an inquiry respecting the corruption of the sovereign power of a state." If the act in question does not violate the constitution, if it conforms to all procedural requirements, then "a court of law cannot sustain a suit [based] on the allegation that the act is a nullity [because] of the impure motives which influenced certain members of the legislature." Thus far Marshall had trod lightly. His deference to Georgia's sovereignty and his reluctance to examine the motives of the state's legislators shielded the Court from charges that it was overstepping its authority. There was sound reason for not probing the inner motives of legislatures, and for the most part, this is a principle to which the Supreme Court has adhered.[102]*

Marshall turned to the rescinding act of 1796. Did it square with well-understood legal concepts? Could the state of Georgia extinguish the titles of innocent purchasers? Was the legislature the judge in its own cause? "There are certain great principles of justice," he said, "that ought not to be entirely disregarded." A transfer of property obtained by fraud would be set aside. "But the rights of third persons, who purchase the property unaware of the previous fraud, cannot be ignored." If that principle were not respected, "all titles would be insecure, and the intercourse between man and man would be very seriously obstructed."

---

*Marshall's holding as to the irrelevance of legislative motives, abandoned temporarily by activist Courts in the late-nineteenth and early-twentieth centuries, was vigorously reaffirmed in 1936. In words that Marshall himself might have used, Justice Harlan Fiske Stone, speaking for the Court in *Sozinsky v. United States*, held that "Inquiry into the hidden motives which may move Congress to exercise a power constitutionally conferred upon it is beyond the competency of the courts." 300 U.S. 506, 513–514 (1936).

This was the nub of the issue. Marshall and his colleagues on the Court were determined to maintain a legal environment in which title deeds were secure. It was true, said Marshall, that as a general rule, one legislature is competent to repeal the acts of its predecessors. But if someone has taken action under a law that has been passed, a succeeding legislature cannot undo that action. "The past cannot be recalled. Conveyances have been made, and those conveyances have vested legal estates."

Marshall's attack on the rescinding act was grounded in traditional ideas of limited government. The rules of society imposed restraints on legislative power. "Where are those limits to be found, if the property of an individual, fairly and honestly acquired, may be seized without compensation?"

The heart of the decision was yet to come. Marshall noted that the validity of the rescinding act "might well be doubted," even if Georgia were a completely sovereign power. But Georgia was not sovereign. "She is a part of a large empire, she is a member of the American union. That union has a Constitution, the supremacy of which all acknowledge, and which imposes limits to the legislatures of the several states." In particular, said Marshall, "The Constitution of the United States declares that no state shall pass any . . . law impairing the obligation of contracts. Does the case now under consideration come within this prohibitory section of the Constitution?"

According to Marshall, a contract was a compact between two or more parties. It bound a party to perform a particular act, or it related to something that had already been performed. Contracts that had been performed were like grants. They extinguished the interest of the grantor and implied an agreement not to reassert that interest. "A party is therefore always estopped by his own grant."[103]

Marshall said it was clear that the Constitution protected such grants.[104] The question before the Court was whether a grant given by a state was excluded from that protection. "Is the [contract] clause to be considered as inhibiting the state from impairing the obligation of contracts between two individuals, but as excluding from that inhibition contracts made with itself?" Marshall framed the question to permit only one response. "The words" of the Constitution, he said, "contain no such distinction. They are general, and are applicable to contracts of every description."[105] Whatever might be thought about state sovereignty, said the chief justice:

[I]t is not to be disguised that the Framers of the Constitution viewed, with some apprehension, the violent acts which might grow out of the feelings of the moment; and that the people of the United States, in adopting that instrument, have manifested a desire to shield themselves and their property from the effects of those sudden and strong passions to which men are exposed. The restrictions on the legislative power of the states are obviously founded in this sentiment; and the Constitution of the United States contains what may be deemed a Bill of Rights for the people of each State. . . . The power of the legislature over the lives and fortunes of individuals is expressly restrained.[106]

Marshall was retracing the ground he had covered in his biography of Washington.[107] The decision in *Fletcher v. Peck* was clear. "It is the unanimous opinion of the Court that . . . the state of Georgia was restrained, either by general principles which are common to our free institutions, or by the particular provisions of the Constitution of the United States, from passing a law whereby the estate [of an innocent purchaser] could be impaired and rendered null and void."

The reference to "general principles" was a nod to Justice Johnson, who filed a concurring opinion in which he agreed that the motives of the Georgia legislature were beyond judicial scrutiny and that the state was prohibited from reasserting its original title to the land. However, Johnson based his holding on "general principle," not the contract clause.[108] As always, Marshall was concerned to reach a unanimous decision. Linking the notions of general principle and the contract clause in the ruling allowed him to achieve that.*

In strictly legal terms, Marshall's opinion in *Fletcher v. Peck* broke no new ground. The Court adhered to the long-settled rule of Anglo-American equity jurisprudence that the title of an innocent purchaser cannot be set aside.[109] In that respect, the decision was not unexpected.[110] The Madison administration, besieged by New England separatists, welcomed the holding as a means of defusing northern resentment over the issue. The president had always been one of the leading advocates of compromise with the Yazoo claimants. In 1803, as one of three commissioners appointed by Jefferson to investigate the problem, he had recommended that the claimants be compensated, but the plan had miscarried.[111] Now, armed with the Court's decision, the administration renewed its efforts, and on March 31, 1814, Congress finally passed a bill providing $5 million to settle the Yazoo claims.[112]

Fletcher v. Peck was one of those rare cases in which everyone profited. The original purchasers, including the members of the 1795 legislature, were generously compensated; their opponents in Georgia acquired political office; and the state resold the land to the United States for $1,250,000— which was more than double the original sale price. The federal government

---

*Johnson's language in favor of overturning the 1796 rescinding act was actually more vigorous than Marshall's. "When the legislature have once conveyed their interest or property in any subject to the individual, they have lost all control over it; have nothing to act upon; it has passed from them; is vested in the individual; becomes intimately blended with his existence, as essentially so as the blood that circulates through his system." 6 Cranch 87, 143 (1810).

received territory it had long wanted, and because the land continued to rise in value (due principally to Eli Whitney's invention of the cotton gin), the government was able to resell it at a substantial profit. The Court benefited from the case since the decision helped to bring the judiciary and the Madison administration into closer alignment. In *United States v. Peters* the year before, Madison had given the Court the full backing of the executive branch. In *Fletcher*, the justices, a majority of whom were Republicans,* gave the cause of the Yazoo claimants the blessing of legitimacy, which in turn helped the administration garner the votes in Congress to secure a settlement.[113]

The true significance of the decision, however, lies in what scholars refer to as the doctrine of vested rights.[114] Property acquired a position of primacy among American constitutional values. The contract clause, read broadly, became a weapon with which to strike down state legislation impairing the acquisition of private property. A stable legal environment in which commercial transactions could be relied on—an environment essential to the growth of the American economy—henceforth enjoyed constitutional protection. When Marshall referred to the contract clause as "a Bill of Rights for the people of each state," he was tapping a wellspring of public sentiment. In 1810 only three state constitutions contained contract clauses similar to the one in the federal Constitution.[115] By the time of the Civil War, twenty-three additional states had adopted contract clauses.[116] These new clauses were invariably inserted into the Bill of Rights sections of the state constitutions. As one historian has noted, *Fletcher v. Peck* "was a decision in nearly perfect harmony with the attitudes and values of most politically conscious Americans."[117]

When the Court adjourned in 1810, it had considered thirty-nine cases. Marshall delivered the decisions in twenty-three, six were *per curiam*, and three were dismissed or withdrawn. Of the remainder, Livingston announced the opinion of the Court in three, Johnson in two, and Washington in two. The Supreme Court of the United States had become a coherent force. Unanimity had become the norm. Marshall was largely responsible for that, not simply because of the range of his intellect, but because of the camaraderie and fellowship he fostered. Indeed, the only dissent of the term was filed by Marshall himself, who broke with his colleagues over the jurisdiction of French admiralty courts in a minor prize case.[118] By the end of the 1810 term, the Court had emerged as a definitive interpreter of the Constitution. In landmark cases like *Marbury v. Madison* and *Fletcher v. Peck*, it was not only announcing the law authoritatively but was shaping the nature of the Union for future generations.

---

*Justices Cushing and Chase were ailing and did not take part in *Fletcher v. Peck*. That left Marshall and Bushrod Washington of the old Federalists, plus Jefferson's three Republican appointees: William Johnson, Brockholst Livingston, and Thomas Todd.

17

"A Band of Brothers"

WITH POLLY AN INVALID, the task of raising the six Marshall children fell primarily to the chief justice. Thomas, the eldest child, born in 1784, had graduated from Princeton at nineteen. He practiced law in Richmond briefly, but because of ill health was unable to work regularly. In 1809 he married the daughter of a James River plantation family; as a wedding present, Marshall gave them Oak Hill. The couple retired to Fauquier county and devoted themselves to farming. Tom was diligent and gifted, and, on occasion, represented the county in the legislature. Of all the Marshall children, he was the closest to his father and shared most of the chief justice's views. In 1832 he emerged as a leader in the struggle to end slavery in Virginia. Unfortunately, whatever public career he might have enjoyed ended abruptly with his accidental death in 1835.

Jaquelin Ambler Marshall, three years younger than Thomas, studied medicine briefly and dabbled in theology. Like Thomas, he moved to Fauquier county to live at Prospect Hill, a large tract given to him by his father as a wedding present. The Marshall family history says of Jaquelin that "With very little ambition, he was satisfied to superintend his farm and to entertain his select friends."[1]

The Marshall's only daughter, Mary, was fifteen in 1810, and that autumn the chief justice, recognizing his limitations, took her to live with his sister Elizabeth (Mrs. Rawleigh Colston), at the Colston's Honeywood estate in Berkeley county. Mary remained there for over a year, received instruction from a private tutor, and returned to Richmond in late 1811. Two years later, at the age of eighteen, she married her cousin and next-door neighbor, Jaquelin Harvie.[2]

The three youngest children—John, who was twelve in 1810, James Keith, who was ten, and Edward, five—were a source of continuing concern for Marshall. Although he would later send all three to Harvard, he worried about their ultimate employment. That spring, shortly after the Court adjourned, he asked Bushrod Washington to make inquiries for him concerning future apprenticeships for the boys with the Philadelphia investment house of Willing & Francis. Washington was traveling to Philadelphia on circuit, and the justices frequently undertook errands for each other. Never one to let pass an opportunity to restock his wine cellar, Marshall also asked Washington to purchase some Madeira for him from a commission merchant.[3]

In April Washington wrote to Marshall that "Messrs. Willing & Francis consent to receive the eldest of the boys. Mr. Willing, to whom I spoke, expressed the pleasure it would afford him to oblige you. He thinks that the age of 16 is [best] for a young man to enter upon this branch of education, considering that his preceding years ought to be employed in acquiring a thorough knowledge of Arithmetic, Geography, and Mathematics."[4] Washington had also looked after the Madeira. "The half pipe of wine* is secured for you. Be so good as to direct me how to contrive it to you." Bushrod told Marshall that the wine had been shipped from London packed in a bulk cargo of flour, and he suggested that it be crated "to protect it from plunder on its passage" to Norfolk.[5]

During the summer of 1810, Marshall was repeatedly consulted by Benjamin Latrobe, the Surveyor of Public Buildings in Washington, concerning new quarters for the Court. During his second term, Jefferson had redesigned the interior of the capitol. The Senate chamber was moved from the first floor to the second, and the Supreme Court and the Library of Congress were moved into the vacated space on the first floor. Congress appropriated the bulk of the funds required for the renovation, but in 1808 the Senate struck from the bill the money for the courtroom and library. Latrobe told Marshall that the difficulty was created by the two senators from the Old Line state. "None of the senators would have cared much about it had not those of Maryland been active in exciting hostility. . . . Mr. [Samuel] Smith has been an active enemy to the city, as the probable rival of Baltimore, [while] Mr. [Philip] Reid hates the city. I cannot tell why, and being gouty, the idea of sitting upstairs displeased him exceedingly."[6]

---

*A "pipe" is an old English measure of fluids, equivalent to two hogsheads, or 126 gallons. Because of Marshall's well-known affinity for fine Madeira, Washington wine merchants soon began labeling their best brand *The Supreme Court*. Frances Norton Mason, *My Dearest Polly* 220 (Richmond, Va.: Garrett & Massie, 1961).

Latrobe told Marshall that he had nevertheless continued work on the courtroom, since the new Senate chamber could not be finished until the room underneath it was done.[7] The problem was that he had run out of money and could not fit out and furnish the room without tapping the contingency fund of the judiciary. Latrobe enclosed an itemized catalog of expenditures totalling $2,411.24. The list included $413 for mahogany tables, $213 for seven chairs for the justices, and $120 for six cast-iron stoves.[8] Marshall was delighted that Latrobe had gone ahead with the work and promptly returned to him a certificate of approval.[9] Charles Ingersoll, a noted Philadelphia attorney, described the new courtroom as follows:

> Under the Senate Chamber is the Hall of Justice, the ceiling of which is not unfancifully formed by the arches that support the former. The Judges in their robes of solemn black are raised on seats of grave mahogany; and below them is the bar; and behind that an arcade, still higher, so contrived as to afford auditors double rows of terrace seats thrown in segments around the transverse arch under which the Judges sit.[10]

The Court was a major social attraction in Washington. Ingersoll reported that when he attended, "one side of the fine forensic colonnade was occupied by a party of ladies, who were . . . sacrificing some impatient moments to the inscrutable mysteries of pleading. On the opposite side was a group of Indians, who are here on a visit to the President, in their native costume, their straight black hair hanging in plaits down their tawny shoulders, with moccasins on their feet, rings in their ears and noses, and large plates of silver on their arms and breasts."[11]

In the autumn of 1810 Justice Cushing, the last of President Washington's original appointees, died at the age of seventy-eight. Madison now had an opportunity to reshape the Court. Jefferson, watching events from Monticello, was ecstatic. "Old Cushing is dead," he wrote treasury secretary Albert Gallatin.[12] "The event is a fortunate one, and so timed as to be a Godsend for me." Jefferson told Gallatin that the Court had defied the will of the nation for the last ten years. That could be changed "by the appointment of a decided Republican, with nothing equivocal about it. But who will it be?" In Jefferson's view, the most deserving candidate, considering that the appointee should come from New England, was former attorney general Levi Lincoln of Massachusetts.

No one was more concerned about the fate of the judiciary in 1810 than Jefferson. Aside from his long-standing view that the courts, like the president and Congress, should be responsible to the people,[13] the former chief executive was now the defendant in a massive civil suit filed by former congressman Edward Livingston in the circuit court in Richmond—the very court over which Marshall presided. Livingston had been Republican leader in the House, then mayor of New York City, and had broken with Jefferson over Burr.* The pending case involved Jefferson's executive order to federal officials in New Orleans to seize extensive alluvial lands (the *Batture*) that Livingston claimed. Livingston offered to submit the ownership of the property to arbitration, but the president declined. When Congress also refused to provide relief, Livingston sued Jefferson personally for $100,000.

"Were this case before an impartial Court, it would never give me a moment's concern," Jefferson wrote to William Branch Giles. "But Livingston would never have brought it in such a Court. The deep-seated enmity of one Judge [Marshall] and the utter nullity of the other [Cyrus Griffin], with the precedents of the Burr case, lessen the confidence which the justice of any cause should give me. Should the Federalists, from Livingston's example, undertake to harass and run me down with prosecutions before Federal Judges, I see neither rest nor safety before me."[14]

When Judge Griffin became terminally ill that summer, Jefferson wrote immediately to Madison seeking a friendly replacement. "The state has suffered long enough by having such a cypher in so important an office, infinitely the more from the want of any counterpoint to the rancorous hatred which Marshall bears to the government of his country, and from the cunning and sophistry within which he is able to enshroud himself."[15] Jefferson told Madison that when it should become necessary to replace Griffin, "It will be difficult to find a character of firmness enough to preserve his independence on the same bench with Marshall." One possibility, said the former president, was Governor John Tyler, a staunch Republican who was actively seeking the position.[16] Madison and Marshall were on good terms, and the president harbored no animosity toward the chief justice, but he agreed that Tyler, who had supported the ticket vigorously in 1808 (and who had been a state judge for twenty years), deserved the appointment. When Griffin died late in 1810, the president duly nominated him.

Jefferson may have been grasping at straws and, as he sometimes did, may have been reading too much into the motives of others. Marshall and his new associate were not close friends, but they had known each other for almost thirty years.[17] They were political opponents, but there was no bitterness between them. Tyler was a regular at the famous lawyers' dinners Marshall hosted, and he respected the chief justice's legal acumen. He served on the federal bench in Richmond from 1811 until his death two

---

*Livingston subsequently served as Andrew Jackson's civilian aide during the battle of New Orleans, was elected to Congress from Louisiana, and in 1829 was appointed by Jackson to be secretary of state. In that capacity, he wrote Jackson's Nullification Proclamation in 1832, and he later served as United States minister to France.

years later, and there is no record of his ever having dissented from Marshall's judgment.[18]

Livingston's lawsuit brought Jefferson's fear of Marshall to the surface. That autumn he told Albert Gallatin that the outcome of the litigation ought to be clear, but "what it will be, no one can tell. . . . [Marshall's] decisions, his instructions to a jury, his allowances and disallowances and garblings of evidence, must all be subjects of appeal. I consider that as my only chance of saving my fortune from entire wreck. And to whom is my appeal? From the judge in Burr's case to himself and his associate judges in the case of *Marbury v. Madison*."[19]

Thus, in October 1810, with Tyler's appointment secured, Jefferson turned his attention to the Supreme Court. Once again he focused on political control. "Another circumstance of congratulation is the death of Cushing," he wrote to Madison.[20] The people, said Jefferson, have made the president and Congress responsible to them, "and have steadily maintained the reformation in those branches. . . . The death of Cushing gives an opportunity of closing the reformation by [appointing] a successor of unquestionable republican principles." The former president urged Madison to nominate Levi Lincoln. His "firm republicanism and known integrity will give complete confidence to the public in the long desired reformation of the judiciary." Jefferson said his second choice would be postmaster general Gideon Granger of Connecticut. There were also some "pseudo-republicans" from New England whom he urged Madison to avoid. George Blake, the United States attorney in Boston, "calls himself a republican, but never was one at heart." Even more obnoxious were Joseph Story and Massachusetts congressman Ezekiel Bacon. They "are exactly the men who deserted us on [the embargo] and carried off the majority. The former is unquestionably a tory, and both are too young."[21]

Madison was uncertain about Lincoln's legal skills,[22] but he had no doubt about the former attorney general's Republican attachment. He told Jefferson that Lincoln would most likely decline (his eyesight was failing),[23] but nevertheless, on October 20, offered the nomination to him. "I am not unaware of the infirmity which is said to afflict your eyes," the president wrote, "but these are not the organs most employed in the functions of a Judge."[24] Lincoln pondered the possibility until late November and then turned down the offer.[25] Madison, however, had become determined to have the former attorney general on the Court and, despite the rejection, forwarded Lincoln's name to the Senate on January 2, 1811. Lincoln wasimmediately confirmed, Madison signed his commission as an associate justice of the Supreme Court, and Republican leaders throughout the country urged him to accept.[26] Once again Lincoln declined, this time more firmly.[27] Madison now was left in a quandry. The Court was due to convene for the 1811 term in February, and Cushing's seat remained un-filled.

On February 4, with the Court scheduled to meet that day, Madison as-tounded virtually everyone by passing over Jefferson's suggestion of Gideon Granger and nominating his old friend from Connecticut, Alexander Wol-cott.[28] Other than being the Republican leader in the state, Wolcott had lit-tle to recommend him, and he was decisively rejected by the Senate, 9–24. Wolcott's rejection created an immediate crisis for Marshall and the Court.[29] Under the Judiciary Act of 1801, four justices were required to constitute a quorum. The act specified that if a quorum could not be mustered within ten days, the Court was to adjourn and its business carried over to the next term. Although Marshall, Bushrod Washington, and Livingston were pres-ent on February 4, Chase was critically ill and Johnson and Todd were un-able to attend. With Cushing's seat vacant, the Court lacked a quorum. On February 14, for the first and only time during Marshall's tenure, the justices adjourned without doing business. The 1811 term was canceled.

On his third attempt to fill Cushing's seat, Madison selected John Quincy Adams, then in St. Petersburg as American minister to Russia. On February 22, one week after the Court adjourned, Madison submitted Adams's name to the Senate, and he was confirmed unanimously the next day. Both parties applauded the appointment.[30] Marshall, who was con-cerned about Adams's presidential ambitions, was less enthusiastic. When informed of the nomination by Massachusetts senator Timothy Pickering, he replied that "it is certainly devoutly to be wished that the politician may completely merge in the Judge. Nothing is more to be deprecated than the transfer of party politics to the seat of Justice."[31]

Marshall's skepticism was well founded. Adams's goal was the presi-dency, not the Supreme Court, and when eventually notified of the ap-pointment, he declined. But the process was a lengthy one, and by late autumn 1811 Cushing's seat was still not filled. The delay was due to the lack of reliable communications between Washington and St. Petersburg. With the British fleet blockading the continent and Napoleon interdicting overland traffic, the sending of messages between Washington and the Russian capital was difficult and time-consuming. Adams did not receive notification of his appointment until the end of May,[32] and his decision was not delivered to Madison until the second week of November.[33] Without al-luding directly to his political ambitions, Adams told Madison that the law was "never among those [disciplines] most congenial to my temper," and "I have long entertained a deep and serious distrust of my qualifications for a seat on the bench."[34]

Adams's refusal caught Madison by surprise. The situation was compli-cated further during the summer when Justice Chase died. Chase was seventy and had served on the Court for sixteen years. His death afforded Madison an even greater opportunity to reshape the highest rung of the judiciary since it would bring to five the number of Republican appointees, but time was of the essence. The Court would convene for its 1812 term in February, and the president now needed two nominees: a New Englander for Cushing's seat and someone from Maryland or Delaware to replace Chase.[35] Among the prominent Republican candidates for the latter post were two members of Madison's own cabinet: Secretary of State Robert Smith of Maryland, and Attorney General Caesar Rodney from Delaware.[36]

On November 15, immediately after receiving Adams's reply, the president again astounded observers by sending to the Senate the names of two men, neither of whom had been political front-runners. Having tried and failed three times to make a high-profile Republican appointment, Madison turned to experience and expertise. He was shaping the Court, but in a professional manner that Marshall applauded. For Chase's seat, the president passed over his cabinet and chose the urbane Gabriel Duvall, a former chief justice of Maryland, who had been comptroller of the treasury since 1802 and was then fifty-nine.[37] To succeed Cushing, Madison disregarded Jefferson's persistent advice and named Joseph Story of Massachusetts, who, at thirty-two, would replace Johnson as the youngest person ever appointed to the Supreme Court.

Madison had known Duvall since the two had served together in the Third and Fourth Congresses. He liked him personally,[38] as did everyone in Washington, and thought he would add solidity to the Court.[39] Why the president chose Story has never been fully explained,[40] although, in retrospect, it may not be that difficult to understand. The two were undoubtedly acquainted. Story served briefly in Congress from 1808 to 1809 and at the time of his appointment was speaker of the Massachusetts House of Representatives. He was already an outstanding figure at the bar in Massachusetts and Washington, and had successfully argued the landmark case of *Fletcher v. Peck*[41] in support of the position Madison embraced. He was recognized as one of the nation's leading legal scholars* and had written a well-received treatise on civil litigation that Madison may have read.[42] He had also compiled annotated American editions of several standard works on pleading.[43] As Story's principal biographer has suggested, the president, a serious scholar himself, may simply have felt that Story was the most qualified candidate for the Court and may have recognized "a congeniality between his own and Story's nationalism."[44]

---

*Theophilus Parsons, chief justice of the Supreme Judicial Court of Massachusetts, and St. George Tucker, who held George Wythe's old chair at William and Mary, enjoyed primacy as scholars, but Parsons was a prominent Federalist, and with Marshall and Washington already on the Court, the appointment of another Virginian was out of the question.

Three days after Madison submitted the nominations to the Senate, Duvall and Story were confirmed unanimously. The composition of the legendary Marshall Court was now fixed. For the next eleven years, until the death of Brockholst Livingston in 1823, its membership would not change. Each February the same men, now truly "a band of brothers," would convene in Washington, share their meals and accommodations, and, under Marshall's genial leadership, provide a definitive interpretation of the nation's laws. The great constitutional decisions establishing national supremacy stem from this period. Equally important, and too often overlooked, are the authoritative holdings of the Court in commercial law, real property, and admiralty—decisions that provided the legal foundation for the expansion of American economy throughout the nineteenth century.

There are numerous reasons for the cohesion of this remarkable Marshall Court. Conventional wisdom holds that Marshall dominated his colleagues and that the justices obediently followed his lead.[45] That explanation demeans both Marshall and the six men who comprised the Supreme Court of the United States from 1812 to 1823. As Justice Frankfurter observed, "Marshall himself, hard headed as he was and free from obvious self-deception, would doubtless be greatly amused by the claim that he was the whole of his Court."[46]

Marshall led the Court, but his leadership was collegial. The justices reasoned collectively, even when Marshall assembled the final product. In that sense he was the moderator, not the master, of the Court and he wore his authority with gentle deference.[47] His credentials as the definitive interpreter of the judiciary article of the Constitution at the Virginia convention, his diplomatic success in Paris, his leadership of the Adams Federalists in Congress, his service as secretary of state, his judicial temperament, and the quality of his mind made him the Court's natural leader.[48] Marshall also had a genius for soothing ruffled egos. Through his tact and patience, he brought forth the best of what each justice had to give.

Marshall's colleagues were men of substantial accomplishment. Five had legislative experience, and two, Johnson and Story, had been speakers of their state legislatures. Four had served as justices on state supreme courts, and two, Duvall and Todd, had been chief justice. Story brought an unparalleled knowledge of ancient and comparative law to the Court, while Bushrod Washington and William Johnson were, like Marshall, authors of repute. All had had flourishing practices before they were appointed to the bench, and their collective experience covered a wide spectrum of the law.

In origin and social background, the justices were a diverse group. Five were southerners, the exceptions being Livingston from New York and Story from Massachusetts. Washington, Duvall, and Todd belonged to the plantation class by birth, while Marshall and Johnson were of humbler origins and tended to be closer to the commercial community than to the landed gentry. Livingston was the only native-born aristocrat among the justices, and Story personified the virtues and foibles of Puritan New England. Only two of the justices, Marshall and Washington, had studied law academically, but Johnson had profited from the lectures on jurisprudence of John Witherspoon at Princeton,[49] and Story had been inspired by similar lessons in civic virtue at Harvard.[50]

The justices were also distinct from one another in personality, character, and style, but each presided over his circuit with remarkable effectiveness. Story and Johnson were naturally outspoken and argumentative, and frequently disagreed with each other. Washington and Todd were reflective and reticent. Gabriel Duvall exuded patrician charm, while Livingston continuously exhibited the boisterous good humor of a man half his age. Marshall lubricated the wheels of justice with fine Madeira, and even Story, who initially abstained from alcohol, was soon convinced that a glass of wine fell within the jurisdiction of the Court.*[51]

Partisan politics mattered little among the justices. Marshall and Washington were moderate Federalists, while the remaining five were moderate Republicans. They shared common values and a common legal frame of reference. As one historian has noted, despite differences in age, talent, and experience, they all belonged to America's revolutionary generation. Duvall, Livingston, Marshall, Todd, and Washington had served as junior officers or enlisted men during the war. They had witnessed at first hand the state particularism, economic disorganization, and sectional rivalry that almost destroyed the revolutionary effort. Story and Johnson, who were too young to have participated, had learned from their fathers' experiences: William Johnson, Sr., was a member of the Liberty Tree Society in Charleston, and Elisha Story had been an "Indian" at the Boston Tea Party. Doctrinal differences were not resolved simply by a shared revolutionary experience, but it mattered considerably that these disagreements took place

---

*President Josiah Quincy of Harvard, a friend of Story's, once accompanied the justice to Washington. When Quincy inquired about the city, Story warned him that "I can do very little for you there, as we judges take no part in the society of the place. We dine once a year with the President, and that is all. On other days we take our dinner together, and discuss at table the questions which are argued before us. We are great ascetics, and even deny ourselves wine, except in wet weather."

Quincy reports that Story paused at that point, as if thinking that the act of mortification he had mentioned placed too severe a tax upon human credulity, and presently added: "What I say about wine, sir, gives you our rule; but it does sometimes happen that the Chief Justice will say to me, when the cloth is removed, 'Brother Story, step to the window and see if it looks like rain.' And if I tell him that the sun is brightly shining, Judge Marshall will sometimes reply, 'All the better, for our jurisdiction extends over so large a territory that the doctrine of chances makes it certain that it must be raining somewhere.'" Joseph Quincy, *Figures of the Past* 89–90 (Boston: Roberts Brothers, 1883).

in such a context.[52] In that sense, each of the justices shared with Marshall a reverence for the Constitution, a respect for the Court, and a love for the Union.

Madison certainly did not nominate Duvall and Story to appease Marshall, but there is no question that their appointments accelerated the growing rapport between the Court and the executive branch. This rapport was becoming increasingly important as the international situation deteriorated. War clouds with Great Britain were on the horizon, and the country was bitterly divided. New England and the middle Atlantic states favored conciliation; the West and the South stood solidly for war. Aside from the litigation that would inevitably be produced in the event of hostilities, Madison recognized the importance of judicial support in preserving national unity. Thus, in November 1811, the president went out of his way to see that Marshall was informed of administration policy. On November 6 James Monroe, who had succeeded Robert Smith as secretary of state and who had restored his own warm relationship with Marshall, forwarded to the chief justice the text of Madison's state of the union address for his perusal.[53] Such solicitude was a new experience for Marshall, and he responded graciously. "Permit me to thank you for this polite mark of recollection," he wrote Monroe, and then acknowledged the special consideration.[54] Marshall strongly disapproved of the drift toward war, but he felt reassured by Monroe's overture that the fight for an independent judiciary had been won.

In November Marshall journeyed to Raleigh to hold court, returning to Richmond for the fall term of the Virginia circuit immediately afterward. Prominent on the docket was the emotion-packed case of *Livingston v. Jefferson*,[55] which was argued during the first three days of December 1811. Livingston was represented by John Wickham; Jefferson by George Hay and William Wirt—the same counsel who had opposed one another in the Burr trial. Livingston charged that Jefferson, by instructing federal officials to take possession of the *Batture*,* was guilty of trespass. Jefferson countered

---

*Batture is the French word for a sandbank deposited by the currents of a meandering stream. In New Orleans, a large *batture* had accumulated along the bank of the Mississippi where it curved through the "Crescent City," altering the course of the river and creating an extensive alluvial plain suitable for development. Such river meanderings have always created legal problems, and the Mississippi has been especially apt to change course.

In 1805 the New Orleans *batture* was claimed both by the city and by the adjacent riparian landowners. Livingston, who had acquired part of the *batture* from one of the landowners, brought suit in the Superior Court of the New Orleans Territory to establish his ownership against the claims asserted by the city. He won the case and thus acquired a valid legal title to the land.

The judgment was protested by city officials, but since Louisiana was not yet a state, there was no appellate route from the Superior Court. Its decision was final. Accordingly, Governor Claiborne, on behalf of the city of New Orleans, requested President Jefferson to assert prior United States ownership of the *batture*. This Jefferson did, not by commencing legal action, but by challenging the jurisdiction of the court. He asserted that an action for trespass could be tried only in the district where the land was located.[56] This was known as the local action rule. It was based on the common law distinction between injury to a person (trespass *vie et armis*), which was actionable anywhere, and injury to land (trespass *quare clausum fregit*). Land violations, so the argument went, required a detailed knowledge of the context in which the property was situated, and only a local jury could provide that.*[57]

On December 5 Judge Tyler and Marshall announced their opinions individually. Both upheld Jefferson's objection and ordered the case dismissed. Tyler, who spoke first, treated the arguments briefly, stating that he was too ill to expand further.[58] Marshall spoke at length, setting out the rationale, and came to the same conclusion. He noted there were no precedents to the contrary. Lord Mansfield, he said, had struggled against the local action rule but had been expressly overruled.[59] True, it was an English decision, and the decisions of British courts since the War of Independence were not binding. "But they are entitled to that respect which is due

---

by directing the United States marshal simply to take possession of the land, using whatever force was necessary. Simultaneously, the secretary of war authorized the local military commander to use military force to regain the *batture* should the governor request it. When Livingston volunteered to litigate the matter, Jefferson turned a deaf ear.

Jefferson's peremptory behavior toward Livingston, especially his refusal to instruct the attorney general to go into federal court to assert the United States' claim to the *batture*, has never been adequately explained. Most writers on the subject have attributed Jefferson's motivation to his personal hostility toward Livingston, arising in part from the latter's support for Aaron Burr in 1800. Dumas Malone, Jefferson's most sympathetic biographer, concludes that the president "resorted to an uncharacteristic exercise of authority. Furthermore, his subsequent defense of his actions bordered at times on desperation. He does not appear at his best in this affair."

Professor Ronan E. Degnan, after an extensive review of the legal issues involved, states, "This piece does not dispute that Thomas Jefferson was a great national hero whose memory is properly revered to this day. Still, if all one knew about Jefferson was his conduct in the matter of the New Orleans *batture* and his treatment of Edward Livingston, a different conclusion would emerge, a portrait of a petty politician and a contriver extraordinaire who was not at all above manipulating the federal judiciary to serve his own selfish purposes. I end still admiring Jefferson, but less ardently than before this inquiry commenced." Malone, *The Sage of Monticello* 73 (Boston: Little, Brown, 1977); Degnan, "Livingston v. Jefferson—*A Freestanding Footnote*," 75 *California Law Review* 115, 127–128 (1987). Also see George Dargo, *Jefferson's Louisiana: Politics and the Clash of Legal Traditions* 74–99 (Cambridge, Mass.: Harvard University Press, 1975); William B. Hatcher, *Edward Livingston: Jeffersonian Republican and Jacksonian Democrat* 180–189 (University City: Louisiana State University Press, 1940).

*Jefferson did not maintain, except in passing, that the suit should be dismissed because he was acting in his official capacity as president and thus enjoyed sovereign immunity. Today that would most likely be a president's first response, and, given the holding of the Supreme Court in *Nixon v. Fitzgerald*, 457 U.S. 731 (1982), it would probably prevail. In 1811 that defense was narrowly conceived. It was available to the government itself, but not to the individual officer. Indeed, since the state was immune from liability for the unlawful acts of its agents, the agents themselves remained liable on standard agency principles. See David E. Engdahl, "Immunity and Accountability for Positive Government Wrongs," 44 *University of Colorado Law Review* 1, 14–21 (1972).

to the opinions of wise men who have maturely studied the subject they decide."

Marshall then came to the nub of the problem. The local action rule meant that Jefferson could be sued only in New Orleans. But the federal law then in force specified that a defendant could be brought to trial only where he resided, or where he was found and served with process. Unlike today, no other federal court would do.[60] That meant that Livingston would be unable to bring suit. The incident was, in effect, a wrong without a remedy. Marshall said that the resulting "total failure of justice . . . appeared to me to be entitled to particular weight." But he acknowledged there was nothing he could do. The local action rule must prevail. "I must submit to it. The law . . . is in favor of the defendant."[61] The case must be dismissed.[62]

It is apparent from Marshall's final paragraph that he regretted holding as he did. Judge Tyler later told Jefferson that Marshall "gave a sensible opinion" but had wanted to refer the case to the Supreme Court. "I pressed the propriety of [its] being decided, and letting the parties act as they pleased . . . to which he consented."[63] Neither Marshall nor Jefferson commented about the case at the time. Years later Marshall told Story that he believed his *Livingston* opinion rankled Jefferson more than that in *Marbury v. Madison*. "The case of the *mandamus* may be the cloak, but the *batture* is recollected with still more resentment."[64]

Later that December, tragedy struck Richmond when the city playhouse, jammed with a holiday audience, went up in flames, killing seventy people and injuring over a hundred. Marshall had not attended the theater that evening, but he rushed to the scene to help fight the fire and rescue those who could be saved. The following day he was named to head a committee to raise funds for a memorial to the victims, a project that culminated in the building of Richmond's Monumental Church on the site of the former theater. Marshall, though he did not belong to the church, and though he had difficulty accepting the divinity of Christ, nevertheless purchased a pew near the chancel and attended regularly.[65] For the chief justice, it was a matter of "setting a good example" for his friends and neighbors, rather than a reflection of devout faith.[66]

In January Marshall began making plans for his annual trip to Washington and the 1812 session of the Court. The justices had not met for two years, and the docket was crowded with forty cases, many of which had been carried over from the 1811 term. In addition, Duvall and Story would be joining the Court for the first time, and Marshall wanted to be there when they arrived to ensure they were settled in properly.

Unfortunately, events intervened to frustrate Marshall's plans. Seasonal rains had turned Virginia's roads into a quagmire, and as Marshall's coach descended a steep incline leading to the Rappahannock, it overturned, injuring all the passengers. Marshall broke his collarbone and was unable to travel for a week. The Court convened as scheduled on Monday, February 3, with Bushrod Washington presiding. The chief justice arrived ten days later. Four cases had already been argued, but the bulk of the docket was still ahead. Marshall's arm was in a sling, and he was in considerable pain, but he was determined to be present. A number of important admiralty cases arising out of the Napoleonic wars were set to be argued, and one, *Schooner Exchange v. McFaddon*,[67] tested the ability of the citizens of the United States to file a claim against a foreign warship in American territorial waters. The case had serious foreign policy implications and threatened to involve the nation in a naval confrontation with France.

The case was argued before a full Court from February 24 to 26. Five days later Marshall delivered the decision of his colleagues, carefully distinguishing between legal issues, which were justiciable, and overriding international obligations, which were not. Marshall's opinion in *The Exchange* represents the basic constitutional holding elaborating that distinction. Professor John Bassett Moore of Columbia University said that it was Marshall's greatest decision in the realm of international law.[68] The historian Charles Warren called it "an opinion which has ever since constituted one of the great fundamental decisions in international law."[69] Joseph Story, in his *Commentaries on the Constitution*, quoted Marshall at length, noting that it was the Court's definitive holding on sovereign immunity.[70]

The schooner *Exchange* was a merchant vessel originally owned by two Maryland businessmen, John McFaddon and William Greetham. On a voyage from Baltimore to Spain in 1810, the ship had been captured by a French privateer, condemned as a prize, and armed and refitted as a Napoleonic man-of-war. Renamed the *Balaou* and sailing under the tricolor, the vessel was forced by bad weather to put into the port of Philadelphia for repairs. The former owners immediately filed suit in United States district court to repossess the ship. The case was argued in the context of the war at sea between Britain and France and the continued depredations made by the belligerents on neutral shipping. The claimants maintained that their only chance of recovering their property was through the federal courts. The Madison administration, which was determined to maintain good relations with Napoleon, appeared on behalf of France. It argued that under international law, a naval vessel belonging to a nation at peace with the United States was not subject to the jurisdiction of American courts. Judge Richard Peters, who heard the case in Philadelphia, agreed with the government's contention and dismissed the suit. The circuit court reversed the decision, and an appeal was immediately taken to the Supreme Court. Because of the enormous importance of the case for Franco-American relations, *Exchange v. McFaddon* was given priority over other cases on the docket. The Supreme

Court had reluctantly become a major player in American foreign policy. An adverse decision, said the administration, would "amount to a judicial declaration of war" against France.[71]

Marshall despised Napoleon and was privately critical of what he considered the pusillanimous attitude of the Madison administration toward France.[72] However, the issue in *The Exchange* involved the comity of nations, and for Marshall, that took precedence. It was his long-standing view, expressed first in the House of Representatives during the debate on the Robbins case in 1800, that American foreign relations were entrusted by the Constitution to the president and Congress. Such matters involved the sovereignty of the nation rather than individual rights. Speaking for a unanimous Court, the chief justice said that the wrongs complained of by the ship's claimants were "rather questions of policy than of law" and "are for diplomatic rather than legal discussion."

Much to the relief of the Madison administration, Marshall held that regardless of its previous ownership, *The Exchange* was now a national vessel "in the service of the Emperor of France." As such, it had "come into American territory under an implied promise that . . . it should be exempt from the jurisdiction of the country." Marshall said that was a well-understood principle of international law. "A nation would justly be considered as violating its faith, although that faith might not be expressly plighted, which should suddenly and without previous notice, exercise its territorial powers in a manner not consonant to the usages and received obligations of the civilized world."

Reflecting the collegial process by which he and his colleagues arrived at their decisions, Marshall said that "I am directed to deliver it, as the opinion of the Court, that the sentence of the circuit court reversing the sentence of the district court in the case of *The Exchange* be reversed, and that of the district court, dismissing the [claim] be affirmed." In so holding, Marshall was bringing the United States in line with other countries where, without the separation of powers, law courts would invariably adhere to their government's foreign policy. A separate judicial branch, coordinate and coequal with the president and Congress, could create mischief in international affairs if it acted independently. Foreign nations had to know who represented the United States, and Marshall was making it clear that it was the executive branch and not the Court.* The consequence is that individual

---

*Marshall made that point explicit on circuit in North Carolina later in May. In *United States v. Brig Diana* he held that although it was Congress that formulated policy, "the President was the only constitutional channel of diplomatic intercourse with foreign nations; and the only organ of communication to the people of the United States upon this subject." *Raleigh Register and North Carolina Gazette*, May 22, 1812.

property rights must occasionally yield to the imperatives of foreign policy, a position that the Supreme Court has consistently affirmed.[73]

The 1812 term saw the Court working at its collegial best. Perhaps to free Marshall (who was still in pain as a result of his injury) of the labor of writing every opinion, each of the justices pitched in and delivered at least one decision. Marshall still did the lion's share, announcing the opinion of the Court in twenty cases. Washington delivered the opinion in five, Johnson in three, Story in two, and Duvall, Livingston, and Todd each in one.[74] Johnson dissented on a minor technical point in one case,[75] and Todd delivered one concurring opinion.[76] Otherwise, all of the decisions were unanimous. Justice Todd was preoccupied during the term courting Dolley Madison's vivacious younger sister, Lucy Payne Washington. Todd was a widower; Lucy, the widow of George Steptoe Washington, Bushrod's brother. To the astonishment of Washington society, the stolid, bulky Todd bested Lucy's numerous suitors, and the pair were married in an elaborate White House ceremony shortly after the Court adjourned.[77]

Although he was delighted with Todd's good fortune, Marshall returned to Richmond that spring with a heavy heart. The nation, he was convinced, was drifting inexorably toward war. President Madison shared Jefferson's antipathy toward England, and the war hawks in Congress, led by Henry Clay and John C. Calhoun, looked acquisitively at Canada and the West Indies. Marshall believed France to be more culpable than Great Britain as far as the violation of American rights was concerned, and he doubted whether the United States could prevail in an all-out war against Britain, but for the most part, he kept these opinions to himself. "I know little of what is passing—much less what is in reserve for us," he wrote John Randolph in mid-June.[78] After complimenting Randolph for his vigorous opposition to the war, the chief justice suggested that the combined efforts of the administration and the leading figures in Congress to inflame public opinion made hostilities inevitable. "I cannot help fearing that real genuine liberty has as much to apprehend from its clamorous votaries as from quarters that are more suspected. In popular governments it is, I fear, possible for a majority to exercise power tyrannically."

When Congress declared war against Great Britain on June 18, Monroe immediately sent Marshall the relevant documents supporting that decision. The gesture reflected a combination of friendship and political calculation. By keeping Marshall apprised of the situation, the administration not only was exhibiting a special courtesy toward the judiciary but obviously was hoping that it could garner the chief justice's support. Marshall responded graciously to the overture, but his anxiety at the prospect of war was obvious. "Permit me to subjoin to my thanks for this mark of your attention my fervent wish that this momentous measure may, in its operation on the interest and honor of our country, disappoint only its enemies." Marshall told Monroe their friendship was not in jeopardy. Nevertheless, he avoided any endorsement of the administration's policy.[79]

The next day the chief justice received a personal letter from John Randolph complaining about Speaker Henry Clay's efforts to curtail debate in the House. In particular, Clay, in his rulings from the chair, had attempted to silence Randolph, who had been one of Madison's most outspoken critics.[80] Marshall had never been a political ally of the acerbic Randolph, but over the years the two had become close friends. His lengthy reply, written for Randolph's eyes only, illustrates his anguish concerning the war. Marshall's mood had turned black, and he worried about the nation's future.

> To what are we to impute this disregard of [free speech] which time has rendered venerable, which early impressions had surrounded with a sort of religious reverence, and whose utility has the sanction of the experience and consent of the ages? Does the execrable doctrine that the end will justify the means derive its prevalence from temporary causes or from such as are permanent and deeply rooted in our system and habits?

Such moralizing was uncharacteristic of Marshall. He apologized to Randolph and said that he was going immediately to his farm "where I shall forget as far as I can forget the occurrences of the political world."[81]

For a brief period that summer, there was a boomlet among Maryland Federalists to nominate the chief justice as a peace candidate for president.[82] Marshall gave the effort no support. Instead, he urged the party to make common cause with antiwar Republicans. Writing in reply to a letter he had received from Robert Smith of Baltimore, Marshall said that

> the declaration of war has appeared to me, as it has to you, to be one of those portentous acts which ought to concentrate on itself the efforts of all those who can take an active part in rescuing their country from the ruin it threatens. All minor considerations should be waived; the lines of subdivisions between parties, if not absolutely effaced, should at least be covered for a time; and the great division between the friends of peace and the advocates of war ought alone to remain.

In Marshall's view, "all who wish peace ought to unite in the means which may facilitate its attainment, whatever may have been their differences of opinion on other points."[83]

Charles Cotesworth Pinckney, who had been the Federalist nominee for president in 1804 and 1808, and who often took his cue from Marshall, repeated that theme the following month. Writing to the party's nominating caucus, Pinckney said that it would be prudent to support any Republican who would promise a "speedy and honorable peace."[84] Marshall and Pinckney both recognized that the South was so thoroughly Republican that the only hope of defeating Madison lay in supporting a rival from his own party. Even that, however, was a slender hope. The Federalist caucus duly endorsed DeWitt Clinton of New York, who was running against the president as an antiwar Republican, but the effort was to little avail. That fall Madison was reelected handily, 128 electoral votes to Clinton's 89.

After writing to Smith in July, Marshall said nothing further concerning the 1812 campaign. He was occupied that summer with preparations to lead a survey party that would map a route linking the James River with the tributaries of the Ohio across the Appalachians. Curious as it may seem, John Marshall, the Chief Justice of the United States, had been asked by the Virginia legislature to chair a commission to determine the feasibility of opening the James to trans-Appalachian commerce. The project involved making a detailed investigation of the streambeds on both sides of the mountains to assess their navigability, recommending the construction of canals where necessary, and laying out a turnpike route across the mountains that would join the head waters of the two river systems. Perhaps still stranger is that Marshall, at the age of fifty-seven, decided to lead the survey himself through this largely uncharted territory.

Marshall was thrilled at the prospect. All his life he had advocated linking the James and the Potomac to the country beyond the Appalachians. In his biography of George Washington, he had written approvingly of Washington's plans to improve the nation's inland waterways. The first president had been convinced, said Marshall, "that the rivers of Virginia afforded a more convenient, and a more direct course . . . for bringing the trade of the West to the Atlantic."[85] In 1784 Washington had suggested "the appointment of commissioners of integrity and ability, exempt from the suspicion of prejudice, whose duty it would be, after an examination of the James and the Potomac, to search out the nearest and best portages between those waters and the streams capable of improvement which run into the Ohio."[86] Marshall now had the good fortune to conduct the very survey that Washington had recommended.

The time was propitious. Thousands of settlers were taking up new lands over the mountains, and the chief justice believed it was important, both economically and politically, that they be tied to the East rather than to the South via the Mississippi, or to Canada by way of the St. Lawrence.[87] Robert Fulton's invention of the steamboat had also excited the country's imagination. It was now possible to navigate upstream against strong river currents. On a personal level, Marshall was inspired by the example of his father who, in 1780, had been appointed by Jefferson to survey the Kentucky territory. The chief justice had not handled a surveyor's chain or a spirit level since his youth, but the prospect of a new adventure, an adventure tinged perhaps with danger, excited his boyish enthusiasm.

On September 1, 1812, Marshall set out with a party of twenty-two men on a flatboat from Lynchburg. They ascended the James to the mouth of Dunlop's Creek, portaged over the mountains to the Greenbrier River, made their way down that stream to New River, and then proceeded to the Kanawha, a major tributary of the Ohio. The trip totaled 250 miles and took six weeks. The route Marshall mapped is the one that subsequently was followed by the Chesapeake and Ohio Railroad and by Interstate 64.

Once the survey was complete, Marshall consolidated the data and wrote the final report. It was a task not dissimilar from the one that he regularly performed in preparing the opinions of the Court. Just as Marshall's judicial associates trusted him to state their views with clarity, the Virginia legislature counted on his majestic prose to help make their vision a reality. As one historian has written, the report of the Marshall commission was a seminal event in the history of Virginia. "Combining concrete proposals with a statesmanlike vision of potential benefits, this report was the first step towards the realization of the long-standing aspiration of Virginia statesmen to establish a commercial route linking the eastern and western sections of the commonwealth."[88]

Marshall's river commission report unfolds like his great constitutional decisions in *Marbury v. Madison* and *Fletcher v. Peck*. He began by describing the conditions his party encountered, moved on to explain how the difficulties could be surmounted, and concluded with an analysis of the advantages that would accrue from linking the James with the Ohio. According to Marshall, the navigation of the James from Crow's Ferry to the Cow Pasture River ("a distance of 36 miles and 59 poles"*) presented little difficulty. "The falls are no where formidable; there are long stretches of smooth water, and the shallows may be so deepened as to afford water for boats bringing down from six to eight tons." From the Cow Pasture River to Dunlop's Creek, the difficulties were more substantial. "The masses of water diminishes, and the elevation increases. The shoals became longer and shallower,

---

*A pole (the same as a rod) equals 16.5 feet. One mile contains 320 poles. Marshall's written report summarized the distances and elevations, emphasizing the rate of vertical change between key points. The survey map itself, and the accompanying text, provided the information in much greater detail. *A Survey of the Head Waters of the James River and the Greenbrier, Jacksons River, and the Great Kanawha or New River, and the High Road between Them.* Virginia Board of Public Works, Richmond, Va., 1813.

and the intervals of smooth water shorter." Marshall believed that portion of the river could also be made navigable, but at somewhat greater expense.[89]

Marshall noted that because it had been a dry autumn, the overland portage was not difficult. The river system west of the mountains presented more formidable obstacles, however. The Greenbrier was so shallow and rock-strewn that at one point Marshall's party had been able to advance only three miles in two days. New River had been still more difficult. "Having to search its intricate way, and force a passage through a long chain of lofty and ragged mountains, whose feet it washes, [New River] exhibits an almost continuous succession of shoals and falls, from which the navigator is sometimes, though rarely, relieved by a fine sheet of deep placid water."

Having described the impediments and indicated how they might be overcome, Marshall turned to the advantages the project offered. If the legislature chose merely to improve the navigation of the James and to build a turnpike over the mountains, agriculture in the western part of the state would be enhanced, industry would flourish, and the population would increase quickly. Marshall said that if the legislature should decide to make New River safe for navigation, as well, even greater advantages would accrue. "Not only will that part of our own State which lies on the Kanawha and the Ohio receive their supplies and send much of their produce to market through James River, but an immense tract of fertile country, a great part of the States of Kentucky and Ohio, will probably give their commerce in the same direction."

Invoking the larger issues at stake, Marshall noted that positive action by Virginia would advance the cohesion of the Union. Reflecting his long-held view as to the importance of economic growth in building the nation, Marshall said that the

> intimate connection which generally attends free commercial intercourse, the strong ties which are formed by material interest, and the interchange of good offices, bring together individuals of different counties, and are well calculated to cherish those friendly sentiments, those amicable dispositions which at present unite Virginia to a considerable portion of the Western peoples. At all times, the cultivation of these dispositions must be desirable; but in the vicissitudes of human affairs, in that mysterious future, which is in reserve, and is yet hidden from us, events may occur to render their preservation too valuable to be estimated in dollars and cents.

Because of the War of 1812, Marshall's report was not acted upon for several years. In 1816, however, with peace restored, the Virginia legislature established a fund for public works and instituted an extensive program of river improvements and road construction.[90] The report of the Marshall commission served as the basis for the state's principal project, the James River waterway. Marshall remained an active supporter of the enterprise for the remainder of his life, serving as a delegate to Virginia's internal improvements convention held in Charlottesville in 1828 and helping to raise private capital for the newly chartered James River and Kanawha Company.[91]

On January 6, 1813, Judge John Tyler died, after a long illness. Tyler had served with Marshall on the Virginia circuit for two years. His death meant another vacancy for Madison to fill, and Marshall, who was now communicating regularly with Monroe, wrote to the secretary of state on January 18, urging that the seat be filled quickly. "In making this communication I trust I shall not be considered as impertinently endeavoring to hurry the nomination of the President, but simply as wishing to apprise him of the fact."[92] Marshall suggested no candidate for the post, but he could not have been more pleased when, the following week, President Madison sent the name of St. George Tucker to the Senate. Tucker was a certified Republican in good standing and the nation's leading legal scholar. His edition of Blackstone's *Commentaries* was already an American classic.[93] He was also one of Marshall's dearest friends. It had been at Tucker's request that Marshall had undertaken Richard Randolph's defense in the Bizarre murder inquest in 1793, and it had been Tucker's advice that Marshall had sought before leaving Richmond for Paris in 1797. It was also Tucker's vigorous rejection of the doctrine of constructive treason that Marshall had relied on during the Burr trial.[94] The two had remained in close contact over the years, and their professional respect for each other permitted them to disagree forcefully on points of law without becoming personal or partisan.[95] By naming Tucker, Madison was strengthening the federal judiciary in Virginia, just as he had buttressed the Court in Washington and New England with Story's appointment.[96]

When the Supreme Court convened on February 1 for its 1813 term, there were forty-six cases on the docket. Except for Thomas Todd, who remained in Kentucky with his new wife, all of the justices were present. Once again the Court was virtually unanimous in its holdings, and, as in 1812, the decisions were distributed among the justices, with each delivering at least two opinions.[97] None of the cases dealt with constitutional issues, although matters of international law again figured prominently.*

---

*In *Williams v. Armroyd*, 7 Cranch 423, Marshall extended the Court's holding in *The Exchange* to exclude the decisions of French prize courts from judicial review, even if a vessel's seizure had been patently illegal. Emphasizing that the responsibility for the nation's foreign policy rested with Congress, Marshall said that until Congress declared the French rules of seizure to be void, the judicial branch was bound, under accepted principles of international comity, to

The 1813 session of the Court coincided with Madison's second inauguration. On March 4, in the chamber of the House of Representatives, Marshall administered the oath of office for the fourth time. The chief justice still opposed the president's decision to go to war with Britain, but he derived great satisfaction from Madison's obvious appreciation of the need for an independent judiciary. Marshall did not let his views on the war interfere with his ongoing effort to keep the Court free from political entanglement. Throughout the conflict, he and his colleagues enforced the strictures of international law impartially, even against the commercial interests of American citizens. In a long series of cases, chiefly involving marine insurance companies, the Court held American traders to the strictest performance of their duties under the law of nations.[98]

Madison's inauguration provided the last festive occasion for the country in 1813. The problem was that the war with Britain was gong badly. General Sir Isaac Brock, commanding the small British garrison in Upper Canada, decisively defeated successive American invasion attempts mounted from Detroit, Fort Dearborn (Chicago), and across the Niagara River at Queenston Heights. The disasters on the Canadian border were followed by the loss of the initiative at sea when Admiral Sir John Warren arrived off the Atlantic coast with a powerful naval force from Bermuda and orders to "bring the war home to the Americans." Warren's ships successfully blockaded the ports from New York southward, entered Chesapeake Bay, and in June took possession of the town of Hampton, opposite Norfolk at the mouth of the James River. On June 24 a British squadron sailed upriver and dropped anchor at Sandy Point, forty miles below Richmond. As in 1781, when Benedict Arnold sacked the city, Virginia's capital was threatened. Once again Marshall responded to the city's defense.

With a British attack deemed imminent, the Richmond city fathers, meeting in emergency session, appointed a committee of vigilance "to organize and carry into immediate operation such defensive measures as they may think best for the defense of the City."[99] Marshall was named to head the fortifications subcommittee and was instructed to coordinate his efforts with the governor and the officers of the Nineteenth Regiment of the Virginia militia. He immediately undertook a survey of the city's resources. Two days later, on June 28, he presented a written report to the town coun-

---

apply the decisions of the French courts. Those decisions, he said, "retain the obligation common to all sentences whether erroneous or otherwise, and bind property which is their object; whatever opinion other co-ordinate tribunals may entertain of their propriety, or of the laws under which they were rendered." If Congress should provide different instructions, Marshall indicated that the Court would have no difficulty restoring the property to its original owner. Without a congressional declaration of national policy, however, the judiciary was powerless to provide a remedy, even though the property was subsequently found in American territory.

cil dismissing the idea that Richmond could be fortified to protect it against the British.[100] The chief justice carefully detailed the possibilities of a fortified defense and one by one ruled them out.

> There is in this city or its immediate vicinity no particular height or eminence which overlooks and commands the whole town. There is no spot on which a battery could be erected, that would annoy an enemy in whatever direction he might approach. . . . Nor is it necessary for an invading army to enter the city by any particular route. Any one or more of five or six roads might be used. . . . The fortification of any particular spot therefore, would afford no protection to the city, nor would the defense of any particular road impede the advance of [an] enemy into the center of town. A very small circuit would enable him to avoid our works, and to enter the town where the way would be open to him. . . . No works would afford any essential advantage unless the whole town . . . should be enclosed and regularly fortified. Such works would require sums unattainable by us; and, if erected, would require a garrison for their defense more than sufficient to beat the enemy in the open field.

Marshall was still a light infantryman at heart. He said that Richmond had to be saved by operations in the field: "by facing the enemy with a force which may deter him from any attempt to penetrate the interior of our country, and which may impress him with the danger of separating himself from his ships." Unless that could be done, Richmond was doomed. Victory lay in maneuver. "Throughout the world," said the chief justice, "open towns belong to the army which is master of the country."

The initial invasion scare passed quickly. The Nineteenth Regiment was in the field blocking the British advance from Sandy Point, and at the end of June the British attack squadron sailed downriver and rejoined the main battle fleet in the Chesapeake. The committee of vigilance continued to meet sporadically, and Richmond suffered several more invasion scares, but the city was never attacked. Marshall went about his usual routine, helped out from time to time drilling new recruits for the militia,[101] and in November deferred holding circuit in North Carolina, lest he be needed at home.

18

National Supremacy

THE 1814 TERM saw the Supreme Court dealing with a host of issues arising from the war. Questions of prize law, the rules of belligerency, and trading with the enemy dominated the agenda. For the first time, the fabled unanimity of the justices crumbled. Marshall and Livingston were inclined to interpret the powers of the government narrowly, while Story and Washington tended to take a more nationalist stance. Johnson, Duvall, and Todd oscillated between the two camps, but usually sided with Marshall. The Court did not question the wisdom of the war. On the contrary, it did its utmost to enforce the measures adopted by Congress.[1] But in the conflict between global commerce and the rights of a belligerent to interdict trade, the justices were hard pressed to maintain the unity of the Marshall Court.[2]

In *Brown v. United States*,[3] the first case to be decided in the 1814 term, the justices divided over the president's war powers. The issue involved property in the United States owned by British subjects. Did the war give the president the power to seize this property without specific congressional authorization? Speaking for the majority, Marshall held that the disposition of enemy property was a matter of public policy that should be determined by Congress, not the president or the courts. The right to confiscate such property, he said, was well settled. But the law of nations, "introduced by commerce in favor of moderation and humanity" and received "throughout the civilized world," required that "the exercise of such an extreme power must be specifically asserted." Until Congress acted, the property could not be seized. The president enjoyed no inherent authority to do so.[4] Story, joined by Washington, dissented.[5] Story took a broader view of presidential prerogative than Marshall did, and the chief justice was unable to reconcile their differences in conference.*

In *The Venus*,[6] a leading prize case, the Court again divided. Washington and Story spoke for the majority while Marshall tabled one of his rare dissents.[7] The case raised important questions concerning citizenship, the implications of living abroad, and the distinction between native-born Americans and those who acquired citizenship through naturalization. The merchant ship *Venus* had sailed from Liverpool for New York in the summer of 1812, before news of the United States declaration of war reached Britain. It was captured on the high seas by the American privateer *Dolphin* and condemned as an enemy prize. The problem was that the *Venus* was owned by American citizens. Although they had been born in Great Britain, they had lived in the United States for many years and had become naturalized. One of them had returned to England for business purposes and was living there when the war began.

The Court upheld the seizure of the vessel on the grounds that one of its owners was an English resident. Implicit in the decision was the view that a naturalized American citizen reverted to his original status when he returned to the country of his birth. Marshall's stinging twenty-nine-page dissent challenged the distinction between naturalized Americans and those who were native born. For him, the two classes of citizenship were identical. "[I]f I may be excused for borrowing from the common law a term particularly appropriate, I think the United States are *estopped* from saying that they have not placed this adopted son on a level with those born in the United States." Marshall argued that it was immaterial that one of the owners had returned to England. A businessman's commercial domicile had nothing to do with his allegiance as a citizen. "The stranger merely residing in a country during peace, however long his stay, . . . cannot . . . be considered as in-

---

*Justice Story's dissent in *Brown* marks the first exposition of the view that the president enjoys sweeping discretionary powers in time of war. "I think," said Story, that the president "must, as an incident of the office, have a right to employ all the usual and customary means acknowledged in war." It was Story's opinion that the duty to preserve the sovereignty of the nation rested with the president. "The best manner of annoying, injuring and pressing the enemy, must . . . vary under different circumstances; and the executive is responsible to the nation for the faithful discharge of his duty, under the changes of hostilities."

Story's dissent is the direct antecedent of the broad view of presidential power expressed by Justice Sutherland, speaking for the Court in the noted case of *United States v. Curtiss-Wright*, 299 U.S. 304 (1936). Marshall's majority opinion in *Brown*, circumscribing presidential authority, is reflected in the decision of the Supreme Court in the famous steel-seizure case during the Korean War, *Youngstown Sheet and Tube v. Sawyer*, 343 U.S. 579 (1952).

corporated into that society, so as, immediately on a declaration of war, to become the enemy of his own."*

Altogether, the Court decided more than twenty cases related to the war, and the occasional dissents merely reinforced the Court's reputation as the nonpartisan arbiter of the nation's laws.[8] The *National Intelligencer*, the Republican organ of the Madison administration, described the Supreme Court in 1814 as "a branch of the Government which it is important to hold in due veneration, and whose decisions are entitled to the highest respect."[9] Oral arguments before the Court now drew national attention, and the daily sessions were crowded with spectators. Story wrote to friends in Massachusetts that "the arguments of this Term have been conducted with unusual ability." The lawyers appearing before the Court have drawn "crowded houses; all of the belles of the city have attended and have been entranced for hours."[10]

Dolley Madison was a frequent visitor to the Court, and her effect on the proceedings was electric. As one senator's wife wrote in the midst of the 1814 term:

> Curiosity led me to join the female crowd who throng the court room. . . . One day Mr. [William] Pinkney [the attorney general] had finished his argument and was just about seating himself when Mrs. Madison and a train of ladies entered. He recommenced, went over the same ground, using fewer arguments, but scattering more flowers. I am certain he thought more of the female part of his audience than of the court, and on concluding, he recognized their presence, when he said, "He would not weary the court, by going thro a long list of cases to prove his argument, as it would not only be fatiguing to them, but inimical to the laws of good taste, which *on the present occasion* (bowing low) he wished to obey."[11]

Shortly after the Court adjourned in 1814, the war took another turn for the worse when Napoleon abdicated to the island of Elba. That freed the British army on the continent for duty in North America. Two months later

---

*One hundred fifty years later the Supreme Court endorsed Marshall's position. Said Justice Douglas, speaking for the Court in *Schneider v. Rusk*, 377 U.S. 163 (1964), "Living abroad, whether the citizen be naturalized or native born, is no badge of lack of allegiance." At issue was a provision of the Nationality Act of 1952 that stripped naturalized Americans of their U.S. citizenship after three years' residence in their country of birth. According to the Court, "This statute proceeds on the impermissible assumption that naturalized citizens as a class are less reliable and bear less allegiance to this country than do the native born. This is an assumption that it is impossible for us to make." Also see, *Afroyim v. Rusk*, 387 U.S. 253 (1986).

an expeditionary force under General Sir Robert Ross sailed from Bordeaux for Chesapeake Bay with instructions "to destroy and lay waste such towns and districts" as he might find assailable. The British government wanted to bring the war home to the United States, especially in its Atlantic midsection. On August 16 Ross's army landed on the banks of the Patuxent River, less than sixty miles from Washington. Since there was no American intelligence service, the only information available in the capital was the rumor that the British had landed. Nothing was known of the size of Ross's force or its movements. So desperate was the government for information that Secretary of State James Monroe led a detachment of cavalry to scout out the British position.

Monroe came upon the enemy at Benedict, Maryland. He accurately estimated that the force consisted of 5,000 infantry, with supporting artillery but no cavalry, and concluded that it was bound for Washington. Despite Monroe's timely warning, the city remained defenseless. Of the 95,000 militiamen who were called to active duty, only 7,000 poorly armed men reported. On August 24, after a brief skirmish at the village of Bladensburg in which the undisciplined American units were routed, the British entered the capital unscathed. All of the public buildings in Washington, including the capitol and the President's House, were burned, and the American government was turned out of doors. The British then moved on to Baltimore, where the Maryland militia, unlike the troops defending Washington, put up a stout-hearted resistance. General Ross was killed leading a landing party against Fort McHenry on September 12, and with his death, the British campaign on the Chesapeake ended.

The Supreme Court shared the fate of other government departments. Its first-floor room in the capitol was torched, the furniture was destroyed, and whatever books and records remained were vandalized. But the structure survived. As Benjamin Latrobe reported afterward, "Great efforts were made to destroy the Court-room, which was built with uncommon solidity, by collecting into it and setting fire to the furniture of the adjacent rooms. By this means the columns were cracked exceedingly, but it still stood and the vault[ed ceiling] was uninjured. It was, however, very slenderly supported and its condition dangerous."[12]

Congress met in special session that fall in a Washington hotel and quickly arranged for the construction of a temporary meeting place while the capitol was being repaired. But it neglected to make any provision for the Supreme Court.[13] On December 29 Marshall wrote Bushrod Washington at Mount Vernon to inquire about the situation. "Can you inform me what provision is made for us? Where and in what kind of room are we to sit?"[14]

Marshall was especially concerned to find common lodgings for the justices. He told Washington:

We must rely upon you to make enquiries, and, if it be in your power, to make arrangements for our accommodation. If it be practicable to keep us together, you know how desirable this will be. If that be impracticable we must be as near each other as possible. Perhaps we may dine together should we be compelled to lodge in different houses. Do me the favor to give me all the information in your power on this interesting subject.

Washington's reply has been lost, but the justices discovered that their old lodgings in Stelle's Hotel were still available, the British having spared most private buildings in Washington. Temporary quarters for the Court were established in the Pennsylvania Avenue home of Elias Caldwell, the court clerk. Marshall and his colleagues met there for both the 1815 and 1816 terms and returned to the refurbished capitol in 1817.

When the justices assembled in February 1815, peace had been restored. American commissioners meeting with their British counterparts in Ghent, the ancient capital of Flanders, concluded a treaty of peace on Christmas Eve, 1814. Both sides agreed to disagree on everything except for a restoration of the status quo ante. Hostilities were to cease immediately, and prewar boundaries be restored.[15] Andrew Jackson's decisive victory at the Battle of New Orleans on January 8, 1815, permitted the United States to end the "Second War of Independence" in a blaze of glory, but the victory had no effect on the outcome of the struggle.

The mood in Washington was jubilant. Despite the inconvenience of temporary quarters, the justices, and Marshall in particular, rejoiced that the war was over. Harvard educator George Ticknor, who like many others chose to attend Court for the drama it provided, wrote to his father one of the few contemporary descriptions of the chief justice and his colleagues that has survived. "I passed the whole of this morning in the Supreme Court," wrote Ticknor. "The room in which the Judges are compelled temporarily to sit is, like everything else that is official, uncomfortable, and unfit for the purposes for which it is used. They sat—I thought inconveniently—at the upper end; but as they were all dressed in flowing black robes, and were fully powdered, they looked dignified."[16] As for Marshall, Ticknor told his father that

> The Chief Justice of the United States is the first lawyer—if not, indeed, the first *man* in the country. You must then imagine before you a man who is tall to awkwardness, with a large head of hair, which looked as if it had been lately tied or combed, and with dirty boots. You must imagine him, too, with a strangeness in his manners, which arises neither from awkwardness nor from formality, but seems to be

a curious compound of both. . . . His style and tones in conversation are uncommonly mild, gentle, and conciliatory; and before I had been with him half an hour, I had forgotten the carelessness of his dress and person, and observed only the quick intelligence of his eyes, and the open interest he discovered in the subjects on which he spoke, by the perpetual variations of his countenance.[17]

With hostilities at an end, harmony returned to the Court. Forty-three cases were on the docket in 1815, and with two exceptions, each decision was unanimous.[18] Todd remained in Kentucky, and Duvall did not deliver an opinion, but otherwise the justices continued their pattern of parceling out the decisions. Marshall spoke for the Court twenty times, Story nine, Washington four, Livingston three, Johnson twice, and five decisions were *per curiam*.

The most prominent case pertained to the seizure by an American privateer of neutral cargo on board an armed British vessel, the *Nereide*.[19] The issue involved the property of Manuel Pinto, a Spanish subject who, in 1813, had chartered the *Nereide* to carry his goods (valued at £10,000 sterling) from England to South America. Sailing from Portsmouth under convoy, the *Nereide* was separated from her escort in a storm, captured near Madeira by the American privateer *Governor Tompkins*, and condemned as an enemy prize by the U.S. district court in New York. Although international law held that neutral goods were exempt from condemnation even if found on belligerent vessels, it was not clear whether the exemption applied to cases in which the belligerent vessel was armed and resisted capture, as the *Nereide* had done.

The case was argued before the Court for four days and pitted the leaders of the American bar against each other.[20] "Few cases have excited more interest," wrote the *New York Evening Post*, "not only on account of the value of the property in controversy, but the important questions of national law which were involved in it."[21] Speaking for the Court, Marshall held that neutral goods were always exempt from seizure on the high seas. It is "universally recognized as the original rule of the law of nations that a neutral merchant may ship his goods on a vessel belonging to a nation at war," said the chief justice. That right is "founded on the plain and simple principle that the property of a friend remains his property wherever it may be found." Accordingly, such merchandise "does not cease to be neutral because it is placed on an armed belligerent ship, nor when that vessel exercises the undoubted belligerent right to resist capture by the enemy."

One of the collateral issues involved the application of Spanish law, which permitted neutral property found on belligerent vessels to be confiscated. Since the property in question was Spanish, lawyers for the American privateer argued that the Spanish rule should be applied to retaliate against Spain for its earlier seizure of American goods. Marshall rejected that contention out of hand. "The Court is decidedly of the opinion that reciprocating to the subjects of a nation, or retaliating on them, its unjust proceedings toward our citizens, is a political, not a legal measure. It is for the consideration of the Government, not of its courts. . . . It is not for us to depart from the beaten track prescribed for us, and to tread the devious and intricate path of politics."[22]

The principle announced by Marshall that neutral property must be respected and that enemy bottoms do not make enemy goods represented an important statement on behalf of free trade. That principle remains a fundamental doctrine of the United States. It was formally adopted by the international community in the 1856 Declaration of Paris and continues to be a basic rule of the law of nations.[23]

As soon as the Court adjourned in 1815, the realities of parenting came home to Marshall. The two oldest boys, Thomas and Jaquelin, were well settled. Thomas was farming in Fauquier county, and Jaquelin, still living at home, was applying himself seriously to the study of medicine. However, the chief justice's headstrong and flirtatious daughter Mary had married her cousin and childhood sweetheart the day after she turned eighteen, which she was free to do under Virginia law. Whether Marshall disapproved of the marriage is open to question, but the timing of the event suggests that he had not granted his permission while Mary was subject to his legal control. Marshall was even more concerned about his two younger sons, John and James. Both were at Harvard, and both were in serious trouble. After a year of dissipation and rebellion, John Marshall, Jr., then seventeen, was expelled from the college on March 20. According to faculty records, "Representation being made . . . that Marshall of the Sophomore Class had been engaged in a course of immoral and dissolute conduct, which has been long continued and under circumstances that left little hope of his reform, it was voted that he be dismissed from College and not be permitted to return before the expiration of a year, and then only to a degraded standing."[24] James, a freshman, was disciplined at the same time for breaking a window, and was fined for exhibiting "an improper attitude at worship."[25]

Marshall took the matter in hand as best he could. Not wishing James to suffer the same fate as his older brother, the chief justice wrote to Bushrod Washington, who was on circuit in Philadelphia, about the possibility of placing the young man with the investment house of Willing & Francis immediately. "He is now at Cambridge," said Marshall, "but I should remove him without hesitation the instant it becomes proper to place him in a counting house."[26] After reminding Bushrod of his earlier inquiry to Mr. Willing on the boys' behalf,[27] the chief justice asked him to approach the firm once more. "If they are willing to take [James], let me know what are their terms and when they wish him to come." Washington's reply has not survived, but Harvard records indicate that James Keith Marshall withdrew from college on May 2, 1815, to join the firm of Willing & Francis in Philadelphia.

Marshall's concern that his son might stray from the straight and narrow is evident from the letter he sent the firm prior to James's arrival. The chief justice asked for all the assistance they could provide. "I am extremely anxious respecting the conduct and morals of my son [and] I cannot help feeling some solicitude about the place where he boards and the society to which he may be introduced. . . . Without presuming to ask what may be burdensome, the more you exercise the authority of a father, a Guardian, and a master the more I shall be indebted to you, and the more grateful I shall be for your goodness." Marshall said that James's "first sliding into bad company" should be "firmly and sternly corrected. He considers himself as bound to you, and I am ready to execute any paper to that effect you may wish."[28] James Keith Marshall remained with the firm of Willing & Francis until 1818. He learned the trade of a banker, but chose not to follow that profession. He returned to Virginia,[29] lived at home for several years, married, and, like Thomas, took up farming in Fauquier county on a country estate, Leeds Manor, that Marshall gave him as a wedding present.

John's future was more problematic. Marshall was remorseful over his son's dismissal from Harvard and recognized his own limitations as a parent. "I have been excessively pained at his misconduct and cannot entirely excuse myself for the unlimited confidence I placed in him," the chief justice wrote to Harvard professor Joseph Cogswell.[30] "I think myself in some measure accessory to his disgrace." Marshall was aware that John, whom he called "my culpable son," had a drinking problem and that he was unlikely to mend his ways. He wanted to help his son retrieve his reputation, but

> I fear he will not avail himself of any opportunity which may be afforded him. I grieve to perceive in him no mark of sincere penitence, no deep conviction of his faults, no resolute determination to correct them. . . . In the wounded feelings of a father anxious for the welfare of a son of whose unworthiness he is unwilling to be convinced, your goodness will I trust find an apology for the trouble given you by this letter.

John, Jr., did not return to Richmond after his expulsion, but remained in Cambridge living on his father's credit. In late April Marshall wrote again to Cogswell and asked him to send John home immediately.[31] One month later he sent Cogswell a bank draft to cover the debts his son had accumulated. "Be so obliging as to present my respectful compliments to the President [John Thornton Kirkland]," said Marshall. "I am much obliged by the measures he took for the correction of John, and am truly chagrined that a son of mine should have proved so unworthy of his attentions, and should have thrown away the advantages he might have derived from the instruction he might have received."[32]

John Marshall, Jr., never returned to Harvard. Like his brothers, he moved to Fauquier county, married well, and received an estate as a wedding present from his father, which he subsequently called Mount Blanc. John was popular with his neighbors and well liked throughout the county, yet he continued to drink too much. He died in 1833, at the age of thirty-five, deeply in debt and unable to provide for his wife and three young children, whom Marshall took it upon himself to support.[33]

During the summer of 1815, Marshall and Bushrod conceived the idea of publishing the voluminous papers of George Washington. Marshall thought that with careful editing, he and Bushrod could reduce the mass of documents to ten or twelve large volumes. As with the biography that Marshall had written, the royalties would be divided equally. One of the problems, however, was that Bushrod had Washington's personal letters, while Marshall had the official correspondence. "This will produce some difficulty," the chief justice said, since the documents "ought to be published in the order in which they were written blending letters to different characters together."[34] Marshall worked sporadically at the project for the next ten years. Ultimately he gave up the idea, and he and Washington turned the papers over to Professor Jared Sparks of Harvard, who subsequently published twelve volumes of the first president's papers. Bushrod and Marshall received half of the royalties from Sparks, which eventually amounted to $30,000.[35]

Marshall's personal correspondence was extensive during this period of his life, but since he retained none of the letters he received and made no copies of those he wrote, the record can be traced only through the persons who preserved his letters. One of those who did was federal judge Richard Peters in Philadelphia, and it was to Peters that Marshall made some of his most candid comments concerning judicial procedure. Peters wrote in early October 1815 to ask Marshall's views on judges setting aside jury verdicts because of irregularities during a trial. When was a judge authorized to do so?[36] Marshall replied that "the setting aside of verdicts is very much within the discretion of the judge who tried the cause," although "it must be a very strong case" to do so.[37] He said there were "considerable objections to setting aside a verdict where it conforms to the right of the cause. To say nothing of *precious* time consumed in a second trial (time that might be so pleasantly employed on the farm), the justice of the case is committed to some hazard by being carried before another jury; and, in any event, a party who has committed no fault, is subjected to costs and delay." Marshall told Peters that he would "terminate those *wise* reflections by observing that if I approved the verdict I would let it stand; if I did not, although my disapprobation might not be sufficient to set it aside had all been perfectly *en règle* [according to the rules], I would avail myself on the irregularity to award a new trial."[38]

When the Court reconvened for the 1816 term, it was facing a judicial insurrection. The war with Britain was over and the brief stirrings of New England separatism had been contained,* but now the appellate jurisdiction of the Supreme Court—its authority to hear appeals from the various states—was under direct attack by the highest court in Virginia. The Judiciary Act of 1789 had given state and federal courts concurrent jurisdiction in many areas. For the First Congress, it was partially a matter of compromise with the antifederalists and partially a matter of convenience. The state courts were already in place, and by allowing them to try some federal issues, the size of the national judiciary could be kept small. To ensure uniform interpretation among the numerous state courts, section 25 of the act allowed appeals from the highest court in each state to the Supreme Court whenever the Constitution, treaties, or a federal law was involved. During the years 1789 to 1813, the Court had heard sixteen such appeals without serious opposition.[39] When the federal judiciary had clashed with the state of Pennsylvania on 1809 over the decision of Judge Peters,[40] Virginia had been the first to rally to the Supreme Court's side.[41] In 1812, in a major case involving state taxes and land tenure, New Jersey accepted without a murmur the Court's decision invalidating a state law that had been appealed from the state judiciary.[42] But in 1816, the Virginia court of appeals and the Supreme Court were on a collision course. The issue involved Marshall's brother James directly and the chief justice himself at the margins. The case was *Martin v. Hunter's Lessee*.[43] It would become a landmark in the struggle for national supremacy, and the decision, a judicial tour de force written by Justice Story, would become the keystone in the arch of the Supreme Court's appellate authority.

The litigation involved conflicting claims to a 739-acre segment of the former estate of Lord Fairfax.[44] David Hunter, a large-scale investor in west-

---

*In 1814 the five New England states, protesting the war with Great Britain, flirted briefly with the idea of leaving the Union. Meeting in secret session in Hartford, Connecticut, on December 14, 1814, delegates from Massachusetts, Rhode Island, Connecticut, New Hampshire, and Vermont considered adopting an ordinance of secession. Moderate forces eventually gained control, and the convention adjourned the following month, issuing a final report affirming national unity. The Hartford Convention, as the gathering is called, is considered the high-water mark of New England separatism.

ern land, purchased the parcel from the state of Virginia under the various confiscation statutes the legislature enacted during the Revolution. Denny Martin, who was Lord Fairfax's heir, asserted ownership by inheritance, reinforced by the treaty of peace with Great Britain in 1783 and the Jay Treaty. Marshall and his brothers agreed to purchase Martin's interest in 1793. Under the compromise worked out with the Virginia legislature four years later, the Marshalls acquired uncontested title to the lands Lord Fairfax had set aside for his personal use, while the state gained the remainder of the proprietary.[45] The issue in the dispute was whether the land Hunter had purchased fell within that appropriated by Lord Fairfax for himself and thus belonged to the Marshalls, or whether it was part of that which the state had acquired.

The case languished in the state courts until 1810, when the Virginia court of appeals, interpreting the legislative compromise narrowly, upheld Hunter's claim. At that point Marshall urged his brother James, to whom the property actually belonged,[46] to appeal the state court's finding to the Supreme Court on a writ of error. "If the decision of the Supreme Court is against us," wrote Marshall, it "will save the expense of further litigation."[47] Marshall was not concerned about the impact of an adverse ruling because the disputed parcel was small, and the possible precedent would affect no more than 5,000 acres, the title to which was being similarly contested. It was preferable, he thought, to get the matter resolved rather than continue the legal uncertainty.[48]

When the case came before the court in 1812 (*Fairfax's Devisee v. Hunter's Lessee*[49]), Marshall recused himself, and Justice Story, speaking for the majority,[50] reversed the Virginia court of appeals, ruling that the treaties with Britain nullified the state's confiscation statutes. Accordingly, since Virginia had never acquired title to the property, it could not have sold it to Hunter. Story used the occasion to strike a blow for the supremacy of the Union. His powerfully written decision emasculating Virginia's confiscation statutes threw down the gauntlet to the defenders of states rights in the Old Dominion. Story's tone seemed deliberately provocative, suggesting that the Court was itching for a fight.[51] A writ of *mandamus* was dispatched to the Virginia court of appeals ordering it to reverse itself and to execute the judgment of the Supreme Court in favor of Martin.[52]

If Story and his colleagues were eager to do battle, they soon got their wish. The Virginia court of appeals not only refused to comply with the Supreme Court's ruling, but explicitly challenged the constitutionality of the Court's appellate authority. After rehearing the matter, the Richmond judges were unanimous that "the appellate power of the Supreme Court of the United States does not extend to this Court"; that section 25 of the Judiciary Act of 1789 was unconstitutional; and that "the proceedings in the

Supreme Court in *Fairfax's Devisee v. Hunter's Lessee* were *coram non judice** in relation to this Court."[53]

Judge Spencer Roane, the dominant voice on the court,[54] sounded the tocsin for resistance to federal authority. "No calamity would be more to be deplored by the American people, than a vortex in the general government, which would engulf and sweep away every vestige of the state constitutions." Just as Story's decision had been an invocation of national authority, Roane's response was a states rights treatise on the nature of the Union, which he maintained was merely a confederacy of sovereign states whose governments "remain in full force." The federal government, by contrast, was limited to exercising those powers that were *expressly* authorized by the compact to which the states had consented. For Roane and other states rights Virginians, the jurisdiction of the Supreme Court of the United States and that of the court of appeals in Richmond were parallel. Each was sovereign in its own sphere, and neither had jurisdiction over the other.[55]

The Virginia court of appeals' defiance of the Supreme Court's mandate in *Fairfax's Devisee v. Hunter's Lessee* converted what was a routine title dispute into a constitutional confrontation of the first order. To deny the constitutionality of section 25 of the Judiciary Act would strip the Court of a significant portion of its jurisdiction. Decisions of state courts on constitutional issues, treaties, and federal laws would become final and, inevitably, contradictory. The unifying role that the Supreme Court had played would be terminated, and the meaning of the Constitution would soon vary from state to state. As one historian has written, the refusal by the court of appeals to enforce the Supreme Court's ruling had become "Virginia's equivalent of the Hartford Convention. The issue equalled, if it did not surpass, that in *Marbury*: It looked back to the Virginia and Kentucky Resolutions [of 1798], from which Roane drew his arguments, and forward to the great struggle of the 1820s and beyond that to the Civil War."[56]

At this point Marshall intervened. On December 16, 1815, the day the court of appeals decision was handed down, he wrote out a petition for a second writ of error asserting that the Virginia judges had erred in holding section 25 of the Judiciary Act unconstitutional.[57] The appellate authority of the Supreme Court was at stake, and time was of the essence. If Virginia's challenge was not answered promptly, the court of appeals would appear to have prevailed and the erosion of the Supreme Court's authority would have begun. For that reason it was essential that the case be placed on the docket of the 1816 term, and to do so, the papers had to be filed immediately.[58]

Coram non judice, literally "in the presence of a person not a judge," is a common law expression applied to a case decided by a court not having jurisdiction in the matter, thus rendering the judgment void.

Marshall's decision to intervene was prompted by the constitutional significance of the case rather than a personal stake in the litigation. His involvement was consistent with prevailing standards of judicial conduct, and it was never made an issue by his opponents on the court of appeals in Richmond.[59] As a judge, Marshall was sensitive to the conflict of interest posed by the Fairfax cases, and he routinely withdrew when they came before him on circuit and in the Supreme Court. He refused to sit not only in cases in which he or his relatives had a personal interest, but in all cases where the Fairfax title might be involved.[60] As he told St. George Tucker after recusing himself from three cases on circuit in Richmond, "though neither myself nor any of my connexions [*sic*] are interested, I cannot sit because the Fairfax title is implicated."[61]

The case, now designated *Martin v. Hunter's Lessee*,[62] was argued before the Supreme Court for three days. On March 20, 1816, Justice Story, speaking now for all of his colleagues save Marshall, who had recused himself, reversed the Virginia court of appeals with a masterly restatement of the nature and extent of the Supreme Court's appellate authority. Story's opinion in *Martin* ranks among the greatest constitutional pronouncements ever rendered by the Court. The issue was straightforward. Was section 25 of the Judiciary Act of 1789 constitutional? Could Congress give the Supreme Court appellate jurisdiction over state courts when a federal issue was involved?

As Marshall might have done, Story began with a conciliatory nod to the judges in Richmond. "The questions involved are of great importance and delicacy," he said, and the "unwelcome task" that the Court confronted was compounded by the deference it felt toward the Virginia court of appeals. Story then examined the Constitution and the intent of the Framers with exhaustive precision. The conclusion, he said, was inescapable. Contrary to the assertion of Judge Roane, "the Constitution of the United States was established not by the states . . . but, as the preamble declared, by 'the people of the United States.'" The people were sovereign, not the states. And the people, in order to erect and preserve an effective national government, could grant that government certain powers over the states. The appellate jurisdiction given to the Supreme Court in all cases involving federal laws, treaties, and the Constitution of the United States was but one example in which the people, by adopting the Constitution, intentionally deprived the states of a portion of their sovereignty.

Justice Johnson, who had dissented in the earlier case of *Fairfax's Devisee v. Hunter's Lessee*,[63] added a powerful concurring opinion. He noted that the issue involved a "collision between the judicial powers of the Union and one of the greatest States in the Union," but argued that "the General Government must cease to exist, wherever it loses the power of protecting itself in the exercise of its constitutional powers."[64] The Court held the Judiciary Act of 1789 to be constitutional and, for the second time, reversed the decision of the Virginia court of appeals. To avoid further friction, the Court did not issue another mandate to the judges in Richmond, but simply turned its judgment over to James Marshall. No further legal steps were required because the effect of the decision was to confirm the possession of those who had purchased the tract from him years earlier.[65]

The decision in *Martin v. Hunter's Lessee* did not end the quarrel over the extent of the Supreme Court's appellate authority. States rights advocates in Virginia and elsewhere continued to maintain that the Constitution reflected a compact among sovereign states, while the advocates of national supremacy, with the Marshall Court in the vanguard, asserted that the Union reflected the will of the people. It was the people who had created the states originally. It was also the people who had created the Constitution. It followed logically that the people could take from the states some of the powers they had previously given them and bestow those powers on the national government. Article I of the Constitution took certain legislative powers from the states and gave them to Congress. Article II gave certain executive powers to the president. Article III took certain powers that previously resided in the states and gave them to the Court.

Martin v. Hunter's Lessee provided the rationale for the supremacy of the Union. It was the first in a series of powerful nationalist decisions—*McCulloch v. Maryland*, *Cohens v. Virginia*, and *Gibbons v. Ogden*—in which Marshall and his colleagues, relying on the doctrine of popular sovereignty, stitched together the common fabric of the country. This was the golden age of the Marshall Court. It was also the "Era of Good Feeling,"[66] that brief period in American history when partisan strife receded and nation-building accelerated. Relations with Great Britain became friendly; Congress adopted America's first protective tariff and rechartered the national bank; and the Court emerged as the primary vehicle for translating the new spirit of nationalism into constitutional doctrine.

In the autumn of 1816, James Monroe was elected president over token Federalist opposition.[67] Monroe personified the new era. Having experienced the vengeance of radical Republicanism in Virginia, he had become committed to reconciling party differences and reducing sectional rivalry.[68] His inauguration in March 1817 was a celebration of national unity. Eight thousand people—the largest crowd thus far to witness a new president take the oath of office—gathered in front of the east portico of the capitol.[69] Promptly at noon, the new president made his way to the rostrum, accompanied by Madison, Marshall, and the associate justices of the Supreme Court.[70] The justices, attired in their black robes, were especially prominent. Their presence symbolized the emerging national consensus. The rapprochement between the executive branch and the Court, which had commenced under Madison, came to fruition during the Monroe administration, as the great nationalist decisions of the Marshall Court moved in harmony with the spirit of the new age.*

In 1817 the Court left its quarters in the home of Elias Caldwell and moved to a temporary office in the basement of the capitol—a gloomy, windowless room described by Daniel Webster as "little better than a dungeon."[71] It would meet there for two years. In keeping with the drab setting, the 1817 and 1818 terms were uneventful. The dockets were crowded with admiralty cases, but the Court rendered no judgment of lasting significance.[72] The justices continued their practice of parceling out the decisions, but now, more than ever, the Supreme Court spoke with one voice.[73] In 1817, of the forty-two cases reported, forty-one decisions were unanimous. The sole dissent was filed by Marshall in a routine land title case arising in Kentucky.[74] In 1818 the Court decided thirty-eight cases, again with only one dissent, this time by Justice Johnson, who spoke for himself, Marshall, and Washington in a minor prize case.[75]

Despite their dingy official quarters, Marshall and his colleagues had become the center of attention in Washington. The capital's social season began in earnest with the opening of the Court's term. "The city begins to be gay, but the season of greatest festivity is after the Supreme Court commences its session," wrote a correspondent for the *New York Commercial Advertiser.*[76] "The arrival of the Judges, counsellors, parties, etc., connected

---

*In 1817, as a reflection of the esteem the Court now enjoyed, Congress passed an act providing for an official Supreme Court reporter at an annual salary of $1,000 (3 *United States Statutes at Large* 376). This gave the *Reports* of the Supreme Court official status. While the bill was pending, Marshall was consulted by Senator Dudley Chase of Vermont, chairman of the Senate Judiciary Committee. Rather than submit his own views, Marshall consulted his colleagues and then spoke for the Court as a whole. "From experience, the Judges think there is much reason to apprehend that the publication of the decisions of the Supreme Court will remain on a very precarious footing, if the Reporter is to depend solely on the sales of his work for . . . his compensation."

Recognizing that his reply would be widely circulated in Congress, Marshall staked out the Court's role. "That the cases determined in the Supreme Court should be reported with accuracy and promptness is essential to correctness and uniformity of decision in all the courts of the United States. It is also to be recollected that from the same tribunal the public receives that exposition of the Constitution, laws, and treaties of the United States as applicable to the cases of individuals, which must ultimately prevail."

For the benefit of states rights senators, Marshall made the case for judicial comity as delicately as possible. "It is a minor consideration," he told Chase, "that even in cases where the decisions of the Supreme Court are not to be considered an authority except in the courts of the United States, some advantage may be derived from their being known. It is certainly to be wished that independent tribunals having concurrent jurisdiction over the same subject, should concur in the principles on which they determine the cases coming before them. . . . On great commercial questions especially it is desirable that the judicial opinions of all parts of the Union should be the same." Marshall to Chase, February 7, 1817, 8 *The Papers of John Marshall* 148–149 (Chapel Hill: University of North Carolina Press, 1995).

with the High Court creates a stir in the metropolis. There are now tea and dining parties daily. The President gives two superb dinners a week, and . . . every other Wednesday evening Mrs. Monroe holds a drawing room."

Marshall's affability contributed to the celebratory atmosphere. "Since my being in this place I have been more in company than I wish and more than is consistent with the mass of business we have to go through," he wrote to Polly in February 1817.[77] "I have been invited to dine with the President, with our own [cabinet] secretaries, and with the minister of France [Baron de Neuville]. Tomorrow I dine with the British minister [Sir Charles Bagot]." Marshall responded warmly to such invitations, and, at sixty-two, he still appreciated the charms of a beautiful hostess. "I have been very much pleased with the French minister and with his lady," he told Polly. "She is among the most simple and domestic women I ever saw." Marshall likely was unaware of it, but the words he chose to describe the attractive Baroness de Neuville were virtually identical to those he had used twenty years earlier in his letter to Polly about Madame de Villette. Perhaps he did recognize the similarity, however, because he promptly added that "in the midst of these gay circles my mind is carried to my own fireside and to my beloved wife."

Another witness to the Court's newfound popularity was Secretary of State John Quincy Adams, who wrote to a friend in Massachusetts that

> We had the Judiciary company to dine with us this day. Chief Justice Marshall, the Judges Johnson, Story, and Todd, Attorney General Wirt, also Messrs. Harper, Hopkinson, Ogden, Webster, Wheaton, and Winder, all counsellors of the Court. . . . We had a very pleasant and convivial party. There is more social ease and enjoyment in these companies, when all of the guests are familiarly acquainted with one another, than at our usual dinner parties during the session of Congress, when we have from fifteen to twenty members assembled from various parts of the Union, and scarcely acquainted together.[78]

It fell to Charles Ingersoll of Philadelphia, more starchy than many of his colleagues, to question the justices' social proclivities. "Fie on them for dining out so continuously," he wrote in his diary.

> It seems to me that the dinner-giving system has increased very much since I first knew this great watering place . . . where amusement is a business, a need, to which almost everyone is given up from 5 o'clock until bedtime. . . . In my opinion, a Judge should never dine out in term time except Saturday and Sunday, if then. In

England, I am told, they hardly ever do, and I fancy the pillars of Westminster Hall would marvel much if they could see the Supreme Court of the United States begin a day's session, aye, after robing and taking their places, by receiving from the marshal their cards of invitation and taking up their pens to answer them before the first of cases is called for hearing.[79]

The friendship between Marshall and Monroe was particularly close. Schoolboy chums, bunkmates at Valley Forge, and youthful comrades in postwar Richmond, they were no longer separated by a political divide. Marshall was especially fond of Monroe's daughter Eliza, who often served as the president's hostess when Mrs. Monroe was too ill to appear, and he had even developed a grudging affection for Eliza's elderly husband, George Hay, the United States attorney for Virginia.[80] Marshall was now summering at Fauquier White Sulphur Springs, a resort near Warrenton whose virtues had been touted years earlier by Thomas Jefferson.[81] At Marshall's suggestion, the Monroes began spending their summers there as well, the president's cottage side by side that of the chief justice. Polly sometimes accompanied Marshall in the summer, but she was often too frail to undertake the journey.[82]

In 1819 the Court returned to its remarkable vaulted chamber on the first floor of the capitol. This splendid room, the last in the Senate wing to be restored, would be home to the justices for the next forty years. The move to more commodious quarters also heralded the end of the drought of constitutional cases. The 1819 term began with three major cases on the docket, and the nation awaited the Court's decisions with anticipation. Story was caught up in the mood. "The next Term of the Supreme Court will probably be the most interesting ever known," he wrote in December 1818.[83] "Several great constitutional questions, the constitutionality of the insolvent laws [*Sturgis v. Crowninshield*], of taxing the Bank of the United States [*McCulloch v. Maryland*], and of the Dartmouth College new charter [*Dartmouth College v. Woodward*], will probably be splendidly argued."

The *Dartmouth College* case had been argued the previous term, but Marshall had postponed the Court's decision. Although the justices had conferred on the case, some had not made up their minds, and those who had did not agree.[84] Rather than sound an uncertain trumpet, Marshall decided to carry the case over. Most observers assumed that it would be reargued, but on the second day of the 1819 term, the chief justice confounded the throng in attendance by announcing that the Court had come to a conclusion. Without further comment, he began to read the momentous decision.[85]

What had happened was that over the lengthy recess, each of the justices had reconsidered the case. Marshall had drafted an opinion for the

Court, as had Story and Washington. When the justices reassembled in their quarters at Davis's Hotel on February 1, Marshall read his opinion to his colleagues and found that all but Gabriel Duvall agreed with it. The justices decided that it was unnecessary to have the case reargued. Marshall would simply announce the decision of the Court, Story and Washington would add their concurrences, and Duvall's dissent would be noted.[86]

Dartmouth College is a pivotal case in America's economic development. It presented a classic example of taking private property for public use and raised fundamental questions about the nature of corporate structures. Was a corporation a private entity protected by the Constitution, or was it a public institution subject to legislative control? The issue hinged on the contract clause of the Constitution. Was a corporate charter a contract? Specifically, was the charter of Dartmouth College a contract protected by the contract clause against impairment by the New Hampshire legislature? The case had ramifications far beyond the realm of higher education. If the property of a corporation were entitled to the same protection as that of an individual, the corporate device would become a valuable vehicle for private investment. On the other hand, if a corporation were subject to legislative control, its commercial utility would be restricted and investors would be reluctant to buy stock.

The case came to the Court encrusted with the politics of the Granite State.[87] Dartmouth College (named for the Earl of Dartmouth) had been chartered in 1769 as a private educational institution, and like Harvard, Princeton, and Yale, it was governed by a self-perpetuating board of trustees. Dartmouth's board had become largely Federalist and it was supported by Federalist interests in New Hampshire.[88] When William Plumer, a Jeffersonian-Republican, was elected governor in 1816, he immediately declared that Dartmouth's charter, with its provision for perpetual governance by trustees, was "hostile to the spirit and genius of free government."[89] That summer, the Republican legislature passed an act that revised the college's charter by establishing a board of overseers to be appointed by the governor, and that changed the name of the school from Dartmouth College to Dartmouth University. The effect of the legislation was to transform the college into a state university under state control.[90]

Daniel Webster, who was a Dartmouth alumnus, argued the case for the college, and his masterful presentation established forever his reputation at the bar.[91] Blending citations from the Constitution, statutes, and the common law, he fashioned a telling attack on the legislature's attempt to take private property "away from one . . . and give it to another."[92] His peroration, forever enshrined in the college halls of Hanover, New Hampshire, reduced Marshall and his colleagues to tears:

This Sir, is my case. It is the case, not merely of that humble institution; it is the case of every college in our Land. . . . It is more. It is, in some sense, the case of every man who has property of which he may be stripped. For the question is simply this: shall our State legislatures be allowed to take *that which is not their own*, to turn it from its original use, and apply it to such ends or purposes as they, in their discretion, shall see fit? Sir, you may destroy this little institution. . . . You may put it out; but if you do, you must carry through your work! You must extinguish, one after another, all these great lights of science, which, for more than a century, have thrown their radiance over our Land! It is, Sir, as I have said, a small college. And yet *there are those who love it.* . . . Sir, I know not how others may feel, but, for myself, when I see my alma mater surrounded, like Caesar in the senate house, by those who are reiterating stab upon stab, I will not, for this right hand, have her say to me, *et tu quoque, mi fili!* [and you also, my son!]*[93]

Marshall's decision began in typically roundabout style. "This Court can be insensible neither to the magnitude nor delicacy of the question," he said, but "on the judges of this Court is imposed the high and solemn duty of protecting even from legislative violation, those contracts which the Constitution of our country has placed beyond legislative control; and, however irksome the task may be, this is a duty from which we dare not shrink."[94]

After briefly stating the facts of the case, the chief justice addressed the issue of the charter's status directly. "It can require no argument to prove," he said, that the charter incorporating Dartmouth College was a contract.[95] The question before the Court was whether it was the type of contract protected by the Constitution. Specifically, was a corporate charter a grant of political authority, or did it confer private property rights? Using arguments

---

*Whether Webster delivered those precise words is a source of controversy among scholars. There is no controversy, however, about the effect of his presentation. Justice Story wrote that "When [Webster] came to his peroration, there was in his whole air and manner, in the fiery flashings of his eye, the darkness of his contracted brow, the sudden and flying flushes of his cheeks, the quivering and scarcely manageable movements of his lips in the deep guttural tones of his voice, in the struggle to suppress his emotions, in the almost convulsive clenchings of his hands without a seeming consciousness of the act, there was in these things what gave to his oratory an almost superhuman influence. . . . The whole audience had been wrought up to the highest excitement, many were dissolved in tears; many betrayed the most agitating mental struggles; many were sinking under exhausting efforts to conceal their own emotions. When Mr. Webster ceased to speak, it was some minutes before anyone seemed inclined to break the silence." Joseph Story, unpublished manuscript, Library of Congress, quoted in G. Edward White, *The Marshall Court and Cultural Change: 1815–35* 617, in The Oliver Wendell Holmes Devise, 3–4 *History of the Supreme Court of the United States* (New York: Macmillan, 1988).

analogous to those he had employed on behalf of the College of William and Mary thirty years earlier (*Bracken v. College of William and Mary*[96]), Marshall held that Dartmouth was "a private eleemosynary institution, endowed with a capacity to take property for objects unconnected with government"; that its trustees "are not public officers, nor is it a civil institution, participating in the administration of government." He went on to strike a powerful blow for the freedom of education.

> That education is an object of national concern, and a proper subject of legislation, all admit. That there may be an institution founded by government, and placed entirely under its immediate control, the officers of which would be public officers, amenable exclusively to government, none will deny. But is Dartmouth College such an institution? Is education altogether in the hands of government? Does every teacher of youth become a public officer, and do donations for the purpose of education necessarily become public property?

Marshall answered each question in the negative.[97]

The chief justice then turned to the nature of a corporation. In a definition destined for constitutional immortality, he said:

> A corporation is an artificial being, invisible, intangible; and existing only in the contemplation of the law. . . . It possesses only those properties which the charter of its creation confers upon it. . . . Among the most important are immortality, and . . . individuality. . . . By these means, a perpetual succession of individuals are capable of acting for the promotion of a particular object, like one immortal being. But . . . it is no more a State instrument, than a natural person exercising the same powers would be.

Marshall said that a charter of incorporation did not transform a private body into a public institution, nor did it "transfer to the government any new power over it. The character of civil institutions does not grow out of their incorporation, but out of the manner in which they are formed, and the objects for which they are created." Choosing his words with precision, he announced that "The opinion of the Court, after mature deliberation, is that this is a contract, the obligation of which cannot be impaired without violating the Constitution of the United States."[98]

Marshall noted that although Dartmouth's charter had been granted by the crown, it was nonetheless binding on the state of New Hampshire.[99] "A repeal of [Dartmouth College's] charter at any time prior to the adoption of the present Constitution of the United States, would have been an extraordinary and unprecedented act of power," he said, but one within the scope of the legislature's authority. The Constitution of the United States, however, restricted the legislature's freedom of action. Specifically, according to Article I, section 10, it could pass no act "impairing the obligation of contracts."

Marshall said the New Hampshire law failed this test. "The whole power of governing the college is transferred from the trustees . . . to the executive of New Hampshire. The management and application of the funds of this eleemosynary institution, which are placed by donors in the hands of trustees . . . are placed by this act under the control of the government of the State. The will of the State is substituted for the will of the donors, in every essential operation of the college." Speaking for all of his colleagues except Duvall, Marshall then struck down the New Hampshire legislation as "repugnant to the Constitution of the United States."[100]

Like all of Marshall's great constitutional decisions, the *Dartmouth College* opinion is uncluttered with citations to cases and precedent. That reflected a deliberate choice rather than ignorance or carelessness. Marshall's argument to the Virginia court of appeals on behalf of the College of William and Mary in 1790 was replete with references to common law decisions pertaining to eleemosynary institutions, and there can be no doubt that he was minutely familiar with the precedent.[101] But as he usually did when wrestling with fundamental constitutional questions, Marshall preferred to reason from general principles. Daniel Webster said afterward that "The Chief Justice's opinion was in his own peculiar way. He reasoned along from step to step; and, not referring to the cases, adopted the principles of them, and worked the whole into a close, connected, and very able argument."[102] Joseph Hopkinson, who was Webster's co-counsel, told the president of Dartmouth that "Our triumph . . . has been complete. Five judges, only six attending, concur not only in a decision in our favor, but in placing it upon principles broad and deep, and which secure corporations of this description from legislative despotism and party violence for the future."[103] The Washington correspondent of the *Boston Daily Advertiser* reported that "It is one of the most elaborate and able opinions I have ever heard. It was drawn up by the Chief Justice, and bears the marks of a great and vigorous mind, exercising all its powers in search of truth, and in support of a great constitutional principle."[104] The *Columbia Centinel* said it was "the most able and elaborate opinion which, perhaps, has ever been pronounced in a Court of Judicature."[105] Sixty years later Chief Justice Morrison Remick Waite, in what may be the ultimate tribute, noted that the principles enunciated by Marshall in the *Dartmouth College* case were so "imbedded in the jurisprudence of the United States as to make them to all intents and purposes a part of the Constitution itself."[106]

Aside from its economic impact,* few cases better illustrate Marshall's ability to bring his colleagues together. When the case was initially argued, only Bushrod Washington sided with the chief justice. Todd and Duvall supported the New Hampshire legislature, while Johnson, Livingston, and Story were undecided.[107] Rather than reveal a divided Court, Marshall held off announcing a decision. During the recess, the three undecided justices gravitated to his position. The chief justice exerted no pressure on them directly or indirectly. But the idea that the Court should speak with one voice had become so ingrained among the brethren that the desire to reach a consensus was irresistible. Story, Livingston, and Johnson arrived at their conclusions independently, but the atmosphere of collegiality that Marshall had fostered over the years undoubtedly facilitated their move.[108]

Justice Johnson's shift was particularly noteworthy. Occasionally described as the great dissenter on the Marshall Court,[109] Johnson, like Story, was frequently more nationalist than the chief justice himself, and the *Dartmouth College* case involved a question of national power. It pitted the collective will of the people of the United States, expressed in the contract clause of the Constitution, against the legislative authority of a single state. Over the years, Johnson had also become very close to Marshall. In 1819 the South Carolinian was at work on a biography of General Nathanael Greene. Not only did Marshall's biography of Washington provide a model, but the chief justice, who had served briefly under Greene, offered constant encouragement to his colleague.[110] Thus Johnson, who nine years earlier had objected to the Court's invocation of the contract clause against the Georgia legislature in *Fletcher v. Peck*,[111] now embraced Marshall's much more far-reaching application of the clause to protect corporate rights against the state of New Hampshire.[112]

Two weeks after the decision in the *Dartmouth College* case, the Court extended the contract clause to overturn state bankruptcy legislation that had a retroactive effect. The case was *Sturgis v. Crowninshield*,[113] and once more it was Marshall who spoke for his colleagues. At issue was a New York law passed in 1811 that permitted debtors to be relieved of their debts by assigning their property to their creditors. A month before the statute was passed, Richard Crowninshield, a textile merchant in New York City, borrowed $1,543.78 from Josiah Sturgis. The following autumn Crowninshield's business venture failed. He declared bankruptcy under the New

---

*Until the *Dartmouth College* case, the corporate device was used almost exclusively in the United States for religious, educational, or political purposes. By the end of the eighteenth century, American states had chartered 310 corporations, but only eight of these were employed to produce goods. By 1830 there were 1,900 corporations in New England alone, well over half of which were involved in commerce and production. See E. Merrick Dodd, *American Business Corporations until 1860* 11 (Cambridge, Mass.: Harvard University Press, 1954).

York statute, and, over Sturgis's objection, his debts were discharged. Crowninshield moved to Massachusetts, founded a new textile business, and began to prosper. In 1816 Sturgis brought suit in federal court to recover his debt, arguing that the New York law impaired the obligation of contracts.[114]

The case came to the Court in the midst of the financial panic of 1818–1819. The postwar credit bubble had burst, commodity prices had collapsed, and land values had plummeted. As a result, many were unable to repay the money they had borrowed. Economic distress was rampant, with creditors and debtors alike caught in the collapse. The ability of the states to respond to the crisis hinged on the Court's decision.

Two issues were involved. First, the Constitution gave Congress the power to establish "uniform laws on the subject of Bankruptcies."[115] However, there was no federal statute then on the books,* and the question for the Court was whether the Constitution's grant of authority to the federal government precluded action by the states. The second issue involved the contract clause. If Congress's power over bankruptcies was not exclusive, and if the states could legislate in the field, did the New York statute nevertheless constitute an impairment of the obligation of contract?

For Marshall, forging a consensus in *Sturgis* was more complicated than it had been in the *Dartmouth College* case. In *Dartmouth*, his colleagues had been divided when the case first came before the Court, but the division had been *in camera*. In *Sturgis v. Crowninshield*, four of the justices had already ruled on circuit, and they were divided equally. Story and Washington had held that the states were prevented from enacting bankruptcy legislation by the power given to Congress. They had also suggested that the contract clause would be infringed by such legislation.[116] Justice Livingston, however, had upheld the New York statute that was before the Court,[117] and Justice Johnson had ruled in South Carolina that the states and the federal government enjoyed concurrent jurisdiction over bankruptcy legislation.[118] Marshall succeeded in bringing the Court to a unanimous decision, although Justice Johnson said later that the judgment was "as much of a compromise as a legal adjudication."[119]

---

*In 1800 Marshall, as the leader of the Adams Federalists in the House of Representatives, had pushed the nation's first bankruptcy law through Congress (2 *United States Statutes at Large* 85–86; 10 *Annals of Congress* 691–692, 713–716; see Chapter 9). The measure was strongly opposed by Jefferson's supporters, and in 1803 the Republican Congress repealed it (13 *Annals of Congress* 215, 613, 1246). Congress did not enact another bankruptcy statute until 1841. Charles Warren, *Bankruptcy in United States History* 19–79 (Cambridge, Mass.: Harvard University Press, 1935).

In light of the Court's decision in *Sturgis v. Crowninshield*, it should be noted that in 1800 Marshall led the debate against a Republican amendment that would have eliminated the bill's retroactive effect. Marshall was not against retroactive debt relief. However, he thought the national government should enact it, not the states (10 *Annals of Congress* 519–520, 533–534).

On the issue of whether the Constitution's grant of authority to Congress precluded state action, the chief justice said that until Congress acted, the states were free to do so. "It is not the mere existence of the power, but its exercise, which is incompatible with the exercise of the same power by the States. It is not the right to establish these uniform laws, but their actual establishment, which is inconsistent with the partial acts of the States."[120] Marshall recognized that unless the states were permitted to act, no relief would be forthcoming. His decision was a pragmatic response to the economic emergency the country confronted.* It also reflected his long-standing views on the issue. Writing years earlier to Bushrod Washington about the authority given to Congress to establish uniform bankruptcy laws, Marshall said that "unless Congress shall act on the subject, I should feel much difficulty in saying that the legislative power of the states respecting it is suspended by this part of the Constitution."[121]

Having held that the national government and the states enjoyed concurrent jurisdiction over bankruptcy legislation, at least until Congress acted, Marshall turned to the contract clause. "The words of the Constitution," he said, "are incapable of being misunderstood. They admit of no variety of construction, and are acknowledged to apply to that species of contract, an engagement between man and man for the payment of money, which has been entered into." Marshall said that the intent of the Framers had been "to establish a great principle, that contracts should be inviolable." As a result, the words of the contract clause "prohibit the passage of any law discharging a contract without performance." Marshall said the decision was "confined to the case actually under consideration." Accordingly, the Court did not strike down the New York law, but only its retroactive effect.[122] Justice Johnson noted afterward that "denying [the state] the power to act on anterior contracts could do no harm, but, in fact, imposed a restriction conceived in the true spirit of the Constitution."[123]

Marshall's decision in *Sturgis v. Crowninshield* was an artful compromise. With the chief justice's encouragement, the Court endorsed the position that Livingston and Johnson had taken on circuit. Until Congress acted, the states were free to do so. In return, the justices agreed that the contract clause of the Constitution invalidated any law that affected contracts made prior to the law's passage. The decision left open the question of whether a state law discharging a debtor from a subsequent contract was constitutional.[124]

The final case in the 1819 trilogy, *McCulloch v. Maryland*,[125] came before

---

*In 1934 Chief Justice Charles Evans Hughes responded in a similar fashion to the economic crisis spawned by the Great Depression when, despite overwhelming precedent to the contrary, he led a majority of the Court to uphold the Minnesota Mortgage Moratorium Law. *Home Building and Loan Association v. Blaisdell,* 290 U.S. 398 (1934).

the Court on February 22. Like *Sturgis*, it grew out of the financial panic gripping the country. The case involved the authority of the state of Maryland to tax the transactions of the Bank of the United States* and went to the root of the relationship between the national government and the states. Because of its abiding significance, *McCulloch v. Maryland* may be the most important case in the history of the Supreme Court. The questions Marshall addressed—the extent of federal power, the limits of state sovereignty, the nature of the Union, and the principles by which the Constitution should be interpreted—are of continuing relevance, and the answers he provided have shaped the nation's growth for almost two centuries. Albert Beveridge wrote that if Marshall's "fame rested solely on this one effort, it would be secure."[126]

The Bank of the United States had been a source of controversy since its inception. The question of its constitutionality had split Washington's cabinet, and Marshall, in his *Life of Washington*, had ascribed the formation of political parties in the United States to the division that occurred.[127] Federalists favored the bank; Republicans opposed it. The Federalist view prevailed and, in 1791, Congress chartered the First Bank of the United States for a period of twenty years. When the bank's charter expired in 1811, the Republicans blocked its renewal. But the nation's growing financial difficulties, exacerbated by the War of 1812, strengthened the case for a federal banking system. The Republicans eventually came around on the issue, and in 1816 Congress voted to charter the Second Bank of the United States. President Madison, who as a congressman in 1791 had been one of the bank's leading opponents, unhesitatingly signed the measure into law.[128]

Initially the bank flourished. Its liberal credit policies fueled a postwar economic boom. Branches were established in each of the states, and the institution was hailed as the engine of prosperity. But the bank's expansionary policies proved its undoing. When overheated commodity prices fell sharply in 1818, the bank, short of cash reserves, shifted to a policy of contraction. It abruptly called in its loans, forcing many businesses and state banks into insolvency. Financial panic ensued, and the "monster" bank was blamed for the collapse. Outraged state legislatures responded with a variety of measures designed to curtail the bank's activities. Maryland's method was to levy a heavy stamp tax on all banks "not chartered by the legislature."[129]

---

*The Bank of the United States was not an official government institution but a commercial banking system operating under a charter granted by Congress. It was intended to provide an alternative to the state-chartered banks then in operation. While it provided certain banking services to the federal government, its management was in private hands and the bulk of its capital was raised from private investors. See Bray Hammond, *Banks and Politics in America from the Revolution to the Civil War* 251–262 (Princeton, N.J.: Princeton University Press, 1957); Plous and Baker, "*McCulloch v. Maryland*: Right Principle, Wrong Case," 9 *Stanford Law Review* 710 (1957).

When the tax went into effect, James McCulloch, the manager of the Baltimore branch of the bank, refused to pay. He was convicted in county court. The judgment was affirmed by the Maryland court of appeals, and the conviction was carried to the Supreme Court on a writ of error. The case was complicated by allegations of corruption surrounding McCulloch. The Baltimore branch of the bank had been the most active in the nation, and as its manager, McCulloch had approved numerous loans and overdrafts for himself and his associates. Rumors of misconduct were swirling in Washington, but the full extent of McCulloch's culpability did not come to light until well after the Supreme Court had rendered its decision.[130]

Because the case involved an explicit confrontation between national and state authority, its importance was immediately evident. The Court relaxed its rule restricting the number of lawyers to two for each party, and as a consequence six of the country's most distinguished lawyers appeared in the cause. Maryland was represented by Luther Martin, then seventy-five years old and making his last appearance at the bar. He was assisted by two seasoned appellate advocates, Joseph Hopkinson and Walter Jones. The bank was represented by Daniel Webster, flush from his victory in the *Dartmouth College* case, William Wirt, the attorney general of the United States, and the legendary William Pinkney, who was widely regarded as the greatest lawyer of his era. The argument before the Court consumed nine days—three times that normally allowed for major cases—and was an example of the adversarial process honed to its sharpest edge. Marshall said afterward that both sides had displayed "a splendor of eloquence, and a strength of argument seldom, if ever, surpassed."[131]

Counsel for Maryland argued for a strict construction of the Constitution and for the sovereignty of the individual states. "The Constitution was formed and adopted, not by the people of the United States at large, but by the people of the respective states. . . . It is therefore a compact between the states, and all the powers which are not expressly relinquished by it, are reserved to the states."[132] Webster and Wirt made the case for the implied powers of Congress. On March 1, 1819, Pinkney concluded for the bank. He spoke for three days. "Never, in my whole life, have I heard a greater speech," said Story. "All the cobwebs of sophistry and metaphysics about States rights and State sovereignty he brushed away with a mighty besom."[133]

On March 6, only three days after the arguments concluded, Marshall delivered the opinion of a unanimous Court.[134] The first question, he said, was whether Congress had the power to charter a bank. After noting that the bill to incorporate the bank "did not steal upon an unsuspecting legislature, and pass unobserved," but had been endorsed repeatedly by both the executive and legislative branches, the chief justice turned to the Constitution. "Counsel for the State of Maryland have deemed it of some importance to consider it as not emanating from the people, but as the act of sovereign and independent states. The powers of the general government, it has been said, are delegated by the states, who alone are truly sovereign."

Marshall said it would be difficult to sustain this proposition. The Convention that framed the Constitution "was indeed elected by the state legislatures. But the instrument, when it came from their hands, was a mere proposal" without obligation attached to it. It was submitted by Congress to the people, who assembled by convention in the various states.

> It is true, they assembled in their several states—and where else should they have assembled? No political dreamer was ever wild enough to think of breaking down the lines which separate the states, and of compounding the American people into one common mass. When they act, they act in their states. But the measures they adopt do not, on that account, cease to be measures of the people themselves, or become measures of the state governments.

Then, in words that have often been paraphrased, Marshall held that "The government of the Union . . . is, emphatically and truly, a government of the people. In form and substance it emanates from them. Its powers are granted by them, and are to be exercised directly on them, and for their benefit."

The chief justice said that the Constitution was drawn in general terms. If it attempted to detail all of the powers of government, it "would partake of the prolixity of a legal code, and could scarcely be embraced by the human mind. It would probably never be understood by the public. Its nature, therefore, requires that only its great outlines should be marked, its important objects designated, and the minor ingredients which compose those objects be deduced from the nature of the objects themselves." Using another phrase that has reverberated through the years, Marshall said, "we must never forget that it is *a constitution* we are expounding."

> We admit, as all must admit, that the powers of the government are limited, and that its limits are not to be transcended. But we think the sound construction of the Constitution must allow to the national legislature that discretion, with respect to the means by which the powers it confers are to be carried into execution, which will enable that body to perform the high duties assigned to it, in the manner most beneficial to the people. . . .
>
> Let the end be legitimate, let it be within the scope of the Constitution, and all means which are appropriate, which are plainly adapted to that end, which are not prohibited, but consist with the letter and spirit of the Constitution, are constitutional.

Marshall rejected the idea that the Supreme Court should exercise detailed oversight of congressional discretion.

> Should Congress, in the execution of its powers, adopt measures which are prohibited by the Constitution . . . it would become the painful duty of this tribunal . . . to say that such an act was not the law of the land. But where the law is not prohibited, and is really calculated to effect any of the objects entrusted to the government, to undertake here to inquire into the degree of its necessity, would be to pass the line which circumscribes the judicial department, and to tread on legislative ground. This Court disclaims all pretensions to such a power.

Concluding more forcefully than usual, Marshall said that "after the most deliberate consideration, it is the unanimous and decided opinion of this Court, that the act to incorporate the Bank of the United States is a law made in pursuance of the Constitution, and is part of the supreme law of the land."

Could Maryland tax the bank? The chief justice invoked first principles. The Constitution and the laws made in pursuance thereof were supreme, he said. They controlled the constitutions and laws of the respective states.

> From this, which may almost be termed an axiom, other propositions are deduced as corollaries. These are,

> 1st.—That a power to create implies a power to preserve.

> 2nd.—That a power to destroy, if wielded by a different hand, is hostile to, and incompatible with these powers to create and preserve.

> 3rd.—That where this repugnancy exists, the authority which is supreme must control. . . .

Then, in one of the most famous lines he ever wrote, Marshall held that "the power to tax involves the power to destroy." If the states could tax the bank, "they may tax the mail; they may tax the mint; they may tax patent rights; they may tax the judicial process; they may tax all the means employed by the government. . . .This was not intended by the American people. They did not design to make their government dependent on the states."

Marshall's prose came forth in epic periods reminiscent of Alexander Pope. After briefly tracing the arguments made by Hamilton and Madison in the *Federalist,* he said that "the Court has bestowed on this subject its most deliberate consideration. The result is a conviction that the states have no power, by taxation or otherwise, to retard, impede, burden, or in any manner control, the operations of the constitutional laws enacted by Congress to carry into execution the powers vested in the general government." Marshall finished by saying that "We are unanimously of opinion, that the law passed by the legislature of Maryland, imposing a tax on the Bank of the United States, is unconstitutional and void."

The Court's decision in *McCulloch v. Maryland* is a ringing restatement of national supremacy. Marshall's eloquent phrases have been invoked repeatedly by later generations of jurists and legislators to justify the expansion of national authority at the expense of the states. At the time, however, Marshall could not have envisaged the modern federal government with its greatly augmented powers to regulate the economy and promote social welfare. His decision was a defensive one. In 1819 the Court was concerned with preserving the Union against the powerful centrifugal forces that constantly threatened its dissolution. *McCulloch* did not so much expand federal sovereignty as restrict state sovereignty.[135] As one scholar has written, the Court's intention was to enable the federal government to exercise its powers effectively and to prevent state encroachments upon its legitimate operations.[136]

Marshall's decision emphasized judicial restraint. In upholding Congress's power to charter the bank, he reaffirmed the limited conception of judicial review that he had announced sixteen years earlier in *Marbury v. Madison*. Discretion in policy matters rested with Congress; the Supreme Court would not presume to judge "the degree of necessity" that had motivated the legislative branch. When Marshall spoke of the Constitution as "intended for ages to come" and of the need to adapt it "to the various *crises* of human affairs," he was alluding to the responsibility of Congress, not the Court,[137] and the limits on Congress were defined by the political process, not the judiciary.

When the Court adjourned on March 12, it had decided thirty-three cases. With the exception of the dissent by Duvall in the *Dartmouth College* case, each decision was unanimous. Marshall delivered fourteen, Story nine, Johnson five, Washington two, Livingston and Duvall one each, and one decision was *per curiam*, but regardless of who wrote the decision, the Supreme Court of the United States spoke with one voice.

19

Steamboats

ARSHALL'S OPINION in *McCulloch* immediately drew national attention. Newspapers throughout the country published the text in full.[1] In the North and East, where the bank was still popular and the recession less severe, the decision drew substantial support. Webster wrote Story that the opinion was "universally praised. Indeed, I think it admirable. Great things have been done at this session."[2] The *Boston Daily Advertiser* called the decision "one of the most able judgments ever delivered."[3] The *National Intelligencer*, reflecting the views of the Monroe administration, said "The Supreme Judicial authority of the Nation has rarely, if ever, pronounced an opinion more interesting in its views or more important as to its operation."[4]

Reaction in the South and West was mixed. A leading Georgia paper hailed the decision as "a very interesting adjudication" and said that the struggle between the national and state banks should continue until one or the other was rooted out. "In such a struggle, we should hope, as the least of two evils, that the Bank of the United States should prevail, for in banking, as in government, one tyrant may be better endured than two or three hundred."[5] The *Kentucky Gazette* wrote, "This interesting decision cannot be too highly appreciated, and it will furnish a happy lesson to local politicians against their right to infringe upon the National Constitution or upon the laws of Congress. We hope to see no more interference by State Legislatures."[6] On the other hand, a Mississippi newspaper said, "The last vestige of the sovereignty and independence of the individual States composing the

National Confederacy is obliterated at one fell sweep."[7] *Niles Weekly Register* in Baltimore, partially reflecting wounded state pride, delivered a series of attacks on the decision, calling it "a total prostration of State-Rights and the loss of the liberties of the Nation. . . . A deadly blow has been struck at the Sovereignty of the States, and from a quarter so far removed from the people as to be hardly accessible to public opinion. . . . Nothing but the tongue of an angel can convince us of [the decision's] compatibility with the Constitution."[8]

Opposition was fiercest in Virginia. The Richmond Junto,* the powerful Republican clique that dominated politics in the Old Dominion, were still smarting over the rebuke given the Virginia court of appeals in *Martin v. Hunter's Lessee* three years earlier.[9] The decision in *McCulloch v. Maryland* rubbed salt in the wound. These men were Marshall's neighbors: Thomas Ritchie, editor of the Richmond *Enquirer*, the state's most influential newspaper; Judge Spencer Roane, the most outspoken defender of state rights on the court of appeals; and William Brockenbrough, a judge of the Virginia general court who was Roane's first cousin. Ritchie lived one block away, Brockenbrough two, and Roane's substantial property abutted Marshall's on the east, separated symbolically by a deep gulley. They moved in the same social circles as the chief justice, their children had been playmates, and they had known one another for at least thirty years.[10] They were also political rivals of long standing. The Junto saw the Court's decision in *McCulloch* as a mortal threat to Virginia's sovereignty and a potential threat to slavery, that most peculiar and jealously guarded institution.[11] They were determined to resist the decision or, more precisely, to undermine the rationale upon which it rested.

The issue was joined on March 23, 1819, when the Richmond *Enquirer* published an appeal from Ritchie urging that the holding in *McCulloch v. Maryland* "be controverted and exposed." He called on "those firm Republicans of the Old School [a swipe at Monroe] to rally round the banners of the constitution, defending the rights of the states against federal usurpation."[12]

Marshall, having returned to Richmond after the Court adjourned, had already been apprised of the impending attack. The day after Ritchie's

---

*"Junto" is an English corruption of the Spanish *junta*, meaning council, group, or congress. In political usage it describes a small coterie or cabal, and was applied disparagingly to the advisors of Charles I, to the Rump under Cromwell, and to the leading members of the great Whig houses who controlled the English government in the reigns of William III and Queen Anne. In Virginia, the term was applied to the small group of men who controlled the state Republican party. Based in Richmond and led by Spencer Roane until his death in 1822, the Junto set the agenda for Virginia politics during the first half of the nineteenth century. See Harry Ammon, "The Richmond Junto, 1800–1824," 60 *Virginia Magazine of History and Biography* 395–418 (1953); Joseph H. Harrison, Jr., "Oligarchs and Democrats: The Richmond Junto," 78 *ibid*. 184–198 (1970).

statement appeared, he wrote to Story that "our opinion in the bank case has roused the sleeping spirit of Virginia—if indeed it ever sleeps. It will, I understand, be attacked in the papers with some asperity; and as those who favor it never write for the public it will remain undefended and of course be considered as *damnably heretical*."[13]

Ritchie's announcement created a stir among Marshall's friends in the court end section of Richmond, and it is one of the few times in his life that the chief justice felt needled. Ordinarily, he let criticism pass without comment. And he almost never discussed previous decisions of the Court. But on March 27, three days after writing to Story, he wrote to Bushrod Washington expressing his dismay. "Great dissatisfaction has been given to the politicians of Virginia by our opinion on the bank question. They have no objection to a decision in favor of the bank, since the good patriots who administer the government wished it and would probably have been seriously offended with us had we dared to have decided otherwise. *But they required an obsequious, silent opinion without reasons*."[14]

Marshall told Washington that "we shall be denounced bitterly in the papers and, as not a word will be said on the other side, we shall undoubtedly be condemned as a pack of consolidating aristocrats. The legislature and executive who have enacted the [Bank] law . . . will escape with impunity, while the poor court . . . of whom nobody is afraid, bears all the obloquy of the measure."

On March 30 the Junto fired its opening salvo when the *Enquirer* published the first of two lengthy essays by Judge Brockenbrough, written under the pseudonym "Amphictyon,"[15] attacking the Court's decision.[16] As a good neighbor, Brockenbrough treated Marshall with elaborate courtesy.[17] Yet his attack was harsh. Scarcely mentioning the bank, he focused on the finding that the Constitution derived from the people, not the states, and sharply criticized the idea that the powers of the federal government should be construed liberally. Perhaps seeking to bait Marshall, he zeroed in on the Court's tradition of speaking with one voice. Diehard Republicans, Jefferson especially,[18] had always resented the unanimity of the Supreme Court's decisions under Marshall, since it gave the holdings an unchallengeable aura of authority. Brockenbrough suggested that the justices had undoubtedly disagreed on various aspects of the case but that those disagreements had been masked by Marshall's opinion. "On this great constitutional question, affecting the rights of the several states composing our confederacy . . . the people had surely a right to expect that each judge should assign his own reasons for the vote which he gave." After rehearsing the compact theory at great length, Brockenbrough concluded ominously that Virginia would "never employ force to support her doctrines, till other measures have entirely failed."[19]

Brockenbrough's attack goaded Marshall into a public response. In the 1790s he had engaged in a vitriolic newspaper exchange with Monroe concerning Washington's foreign policy,[20] but as chief justice he had left the defense of the Court to others. In the spring and early summer of 1819, however, he took up his pen once again. This was the only time during Marshall's thirty-five years as chief justice that he entered a public dispute. The fact that he did so is an indication of how seriously he took the Junto's assault. If the attacks on the Court went unanswered, Marshall feared that the states rights virus would spread throughout the country. There was also an important personal dimension. The fact that the charges came from his neighbors in Richmond made a difference. For better or worse, Marshall's pride was involved. His standing in the community was affected by the Junto's attack. The criticism of the Court was no longer impersonal. Had "Amphictyon" been writing from Baltimore or Charleston, the chief justice might not have felt the same obligation to respond.

Believing that his prestige was on the line, Marshall replied to Brockenbrough in two essays published in the Philadelphia *Union* in late April.[21] He signed himself "A Friend to the Union," throwing down the gauntlet to his states rights opponents. To Marshall's great discomfiture, his effort misfired. The *Union's* editor had radically altered what he had written, and the articles appeared garbled and confused. The chief justice told Bushrod that it was "a curious piece of work." The editor has "cut out the middle of the first number to be inserted into the middle of the second; and to show his perfect impartially he has cut out the middle of the second number to be inserted in the first. He has thrown these disrupted parts together without the least regard to their fitness and made a curious mixture—a sort of *Olla podrida* [a traditional Spanish stew], which, however good the ingredients may be . . . is rather nauseous to the intellectual palate."[22]

Marshall, now totally engaged in the fight, wanted the essays printed in their "true shape." He asked Washington to have them republished as soon as possible in the Alexandria *Gazette*.[23] The chief justice said that unless the record was corrected, "the democracy in Virginia" would continue to exploit the issue. "An effort is certainly making to induce the legislature which will meet in December to take up the subject and to pass resolutions not very unlike those which were called forth by the alien and sedition laws in 1799." Marshall felt that if the Richmond Junto were successful, "the Constitution would be converted into the old confederation."[24]

The republished essays dealt effectively with the arguments advanced by Brockenbrough. Nevertheless, Amphictyon clearly had gotten under Marshall's skin, especially with his attack on the Court's unanimity. In his reply, Marshall said that an opinion of the Court was exactly that: It reflected the thinking of all the justices both as to the reasoning involved and the positions adopted. "The chief justice never speaks in . . . his own person, but as the mere organ of the Court." Marshall said it was incredible to believe that "the judges of the Supreme Court, men of high and respectable character, would sit by in silence while great constitutional principles of which they disapproved were advanced in their name."[25]

Whether the chief justice should have replied to Amphictyon is doubtful. From the standpoint of political efficacy, he might have been better advised to allow the attack to go unanswered. Brockenbrough's outcry found little resonance elsewhere, and it appears that Marshall was overreacting to what, in some respects, was a Richmond neighborhood squabble. Supreme Court Reporter Henry Wheaton, for example, thought the chief justice was exhibiting an "unusual degree of solicitude" over the issue. Wheaton wrote there was little likelihood that the Virginians would find any other state "to join in their crusade against federal authority."[26]

The fact is, Marshall's response spurred the Junto into further action. As soon as the chief justice's reply to Amphictyon was published, Judge Spencer Roane let it be known that he, too, would enter the lists.[27] Marshall wrote Bushrod, "It is said that some other essays written by a very great man are now preparing and will soon appear."[28] Although Marshall and Roane were next-door neighbors, they did not like each other, and the chief justice made no effort to conceal that fact in his letter to Bushrod.

The reason for the animosity between Marshall and Roane is unclear. Roane was Patrick Henry's son-in-law, and in the 1780s he and Marshall served together harmoniously in the Virginia legislature. Roane was appointed to the court of appeals in 1794, and on many issues, such as judicial review, his view and Marshall's coincided.[29] The fact that Roane led the state Republican organization does not adequately explain the tension between the two, since Marshall remained good friends with virtually all of his political opponents. Some scholars have suggested that Roane was Jefferson's candidate to be chief justice in 1801, but there is no evidence to support that.[30] At the time, Jefferson knew Roane primarily as Patrick Henry's son-in-law, and Henry and Jefferson had been at loggerheads for years. In addition, Jefferson had not opposed Marshall's appointment.[31] The inescapable conclusion is that Marshall's dislike of Roane, which was warmly reciprocated, was essentially personal, and that these personal feelings poisoned their relationship.

Like his father-in-law, Roane was an enormously gifted politician. But unlike Henry, he preferred to lead from behind the scenes. He possessed a vigorous intellect, and his knowledge of the law was profound, but in fairness to Marshall, Roane was not an easy man to like. His sometime political ally Alexander MacRae, himself an outspoken Republican, former lieutenant governor, and a member of the prosecution in the Burr trial, described

Roane as a man of "strong passions and morose manners . . . and eminently qualified to become the founder of a new political sect. He was ambitious of distinction, impatient of equality, and could not endure a superior." In MacRae's opinion, Roane acted like a despot, but in his political views he was "a democratic republican."[32] His rabid advocacy of states rights set the course for the Republican party in Virginia and contributed in no small measure to the attitudes and mindset that led ultimately to the Civil War.*

On June 11, 1819, the *Enquirer* published the first of four essays by Roane attacking Marshall's reasoning in *McCulloch v. Maryland*.[33] Roane was a far more accomplished polemicist than Brockenbrough, and he indicted the Court with bitter invective. Writing under the pseudonym "Hampden," for John Hampden, a leader in the constitutional struggle against the despotism of Charles I, Roane said that the Supreme Court, "by a judicial *coup de main*," had assumed the power to amend the Constitution and had given Congress an unlimited power of attorney "which portends destruction of the liberties of the American people."[34] In essence, Roane charged that *McCulloch* manifested a sinister design to overthrow the Constitution, trample the rights of the states, and establish a consolidated central government of unlimited powers.[35] He stressed that the Constitution "was not adopted by the people of the United States, as one people," but by the people in each of the states.[36] Finally, like Brockenbrough, he attacked the Marshall Court's unanimity and castigated those justices who "had before been accounted Republicans." Roane said that "few men come out from high stations as pure as they went in."[37]

Two days after Roane's second article appeared, Marshall told Bushrod that "the storm which has been for some time threatening the Judges has at length burst on their heads, and a most serious hurricane it is."[38] This was a storm that had developed its own momentum. Later Marshall acknowledged that the efforts of Amphictyon and Hampden were having little ef-

---

*John Quincy Adams, who was then secretary of state, took a more cynical view. "Roane glorifies himself as a very virtuous patriot, and holds himself out as a sort of Jefferson or Madison. All of this is 'close ambition varnished over with zeal.' Jefferson and Madison did attain power . . . under the banner of State rights and State sovereignty. They . . . pretended the Government of the Union had no powers but such as were expressly delegated by the Constitution. Mr. Jefferson was elected President . . . and the first thing he did was to purchase Louisiana—an assumption of implied power greater . . . than all the assumptions of implied powers in the twelve years of the Washington and Adams administrations put together. The Virginia opposition to implied powers is a convenient weapon, to be taken up or laid aside as it suits the purposes of State turbulence and ambition." J. Q. Adams thought that Roane harbored presidential ambitions and was employing the same tactics as those used by Jefferson. "[The Virginians] still possess in a superior degree the art of political management. They will be favored by circumstances [and] by the success of the former example. The tactics of the former war are again resorted to and Roane comes forward as the champion of Virginia." October 28, 1821, 5 *The Memoirs of John Quincy Adams* 264–265, Charles Francis Adams, ed. (Philadelphia: J. B. Lippincott, 1875).

fect,[39] but in mid-June 1819 he was caught up in the exchange. "I find myself more stimulated on this subject than on any other," he told Washington. "I believe the design to be to injure the Judges and impair the Constitution."[40] Marshall said he intended to answer Roane and, once again, requested Washington to arrange for the publication of his articles in the Alexandria *Gazette*. "I shall send them on in successive numbers, but do not wish the first to be published till I shall have seen the last of Hampden." The chief justice, who this time signed himself "A Friend of the Constitution," was concerned that his identity not be revealed. He told Washington to burn the manuscripts after the printer had finished with them and to send two copies of the articles to his son at Oak Hill. "I do not wish them to come to me lest some suspicion of the author should be created."[41]

Marshall wrote a total of nine essays in reply to Roane. They appeared in the *Gazette* from June 30 to July 15, and they reveal what one scholar has called Marshall's "passionate personal commitment to the principles of *McCulloch*."[42] The linchpin of the chief justice's argument was the sovereignty of the people. "The question discussed by the Court was not whether the Constitution was the act of the people in mass, or in the states, but whether the Constitution was the act of the people or the state governments."[43] Marshall said "our Constitution is not a league of independent states. It is a government; and has all the constituent parts of a government. It has established legislative, executive, and judicial departments, all of which act directly on the people, not through the medium of the state governments." Marshall's essays are studded with detail. His citations to scholarly authority and precedent effectively addressed the charges raised by Roane. "Let 'Hampden' succeed," wrote the chief justice, "and the Constitution will be radically changed. The government of the whole will be prostrate at the foot of its members; and that grand effort of wisdom, virtue, and patriotism which produced it will be totally defeated."[44]

The intemperate exchange between Marshall and Roane had little immediate effect. Madison, from retirement at his estate in Orange county, wrote to Roane that the chief justice had erred in addressing general principles in *McCulloch*. The former president favored the bank and agreed with Marshall that the state of Maryland had no power to tax it, but he deplored the broad discretion that the Court's decision had accorded to Congress.[45] Jefferson's position was more complex. On the one hand, he wanted the Supreme Court to declare the bank unconstitutional, but on the other he resented Marshall's authority. He told Roane that despite the appointment of five Republican justices "the leaven of the old mass seems to assimilate to itself the new, and after twenty years . . . we find the Judiciary on every occasion still driving us into consolidation."[46]

In December 1819 the Virginia House of Delegates began consideration of a series of resolutions protesting the Supreme Court's decision in *McCulloch* and urging the adoption of a constitutional amendment that would create a new court to decide questions involving the distribution of power between the federal government and the states. The resolutions were adopted by the House in February 1820, along with a motion condemning Congress for its attempt to make Missouri's admission to the Union dependent upon the prohibition of slavery within its borders.[47] Although the measures failed passage in the state senate, what had been implicit in the Richmond Junto's opposition to *McCulloch v. Maryland* had now been made explicit. As one writer has noted, "Compact theory and the issue of slavery had become intertwined."[48]

The question of Missouri's admission to the Union now took center stage. When the justices reassembled in Washington for the 1820 term of the Court, the nation's attention was riveted on the debate then under way. The issue involved the question of slavery in the Louisiana Territory and whether Congress had the authority to prohibit it.* Since there was no explicit provision in the Constitution, did Congress have the implicit power to do so? Marshall's broad view of the "necessary and proper clause" in *McCulloch v. Maryland* suggested that it did. But the constitutional battleground had shifted from the Supreme Court to the floor of Congress.

The "Missouri question" divided the nation between North and South. Southern states, with Virginia in the lead, were indignant that Congress would attempt to legislate on slavery. They viewed the issue as a matter of private property and disputed the federal government's authority to impose restrictions on the admission of new states. States rightists in the Old Dominion believed that such legislation would make the new states less equal than the other states in the Union. A number of Virginians believed that Marshall's decision in *McCulloch v. Maryland* was at the root of the problem. Spencer Roane told Senator James Barbour in December 1819 that "the Bank case has established the principle"; the Missouri question was simply "a particular measure" that flowed from it.[49] Congressman James Johnson from southside Virginia, paraphrasing Patrick Henry's famous attack on executive power, said that Marshall's sweeping interpretation of the necessary and proper clause "has a strong squinting not only at monarchy but at despotism."[50]

In the North the reaction was the reverse. Not only was there widespread support for a broad reading of Congress's powers, but a new common

---

*Slavery existed under French law throughout the vast territory of the Louisiana Purchase, and Congress had done nothing to disturb it. Louisiana entered the Union as a slave state in 1812, and the institution was widespread among the cotton and corn plantations that had been established in the rich bottomlands on the west bank of the Mississippi to the north and along the lower Missouri River. Opponents argued that the admission of Missouri as a slave state would imply federal sanction of slavery and portend the spread of the institution westward.

denominator had emerged. Surviving Federalist politicians and most Republicans saw the issue of slavery as one that transcended party differences. Finally, there was the question of political balance. To admit Missouri as a slave state would upset the delicate equilibrium that had existed since 1787. Rufus King wrote that it would "settle forever the dominion of the Union. Not only the President but a majority of the Supreme Judiciary will forever hereafter come from the slave region."[51] Southerners, of course, feared exactly the opposite.

Battle lines hardened during the winter of 1819–1820. Scarcely an issue of Thomas Ritchie's Richmond *Enquirer* went to press without an essay on the Missouri question. In the North, town meetings poured forth a torrent of moral outrage.[52] Each side talked openly of dividing the Union unless its demands were met, and civil war was not ruled out. "Who would have thought," said one southern senator, "that the little *speck* we . . . saw [last session] was to be swelled into the importance that it has now assumed, and that upon its decision depends the duration of the Union."[53]

Congress was deadlocked on the issue. In the House those who wished to impose restrictions on Missouri held a ten-vote advantage, whereas in the Senate the pro-slavery forces were in firm command. Resolution of the impasse required nearly three months, but eventually calmer heads—led by House Speaker Henry Clay—fashioned a compromise. Missouri would be admitted to the Union as a slave state, but henceforth slavery would be prohibited in the territory north of Missouri's southern boundary, latitude 36°30'. To provide balance, Maine, which had just detached itself from Massachusetts, would be admitted to the Union as a free state. That would make twelve of each. This was the Missouri Compromise of 1820, and its acceptance was a near-run thing. Virginia held out to the bitter end. Justice Story, who, like all of the justices, was following the debate intently, wrote that "Virginia is the most outrageous against compromise; she insists that the Territories [west of the Mississippi] shall be free to have slaves, and uses all sorts of threats against all who dare propose a surrender of this privilege. . . . You would not have supposed that there was a State in the Union, entitled to any confidence or character, except Virginia."[54] The Richmond Junto were especially determined to defend a principle. With the compromise nearing a vote, Spencer Roane wrote to Monroe that he would rather take the South out of the Union than be "damned [*sic*] up in a land of slaves by the Eastern people."[55] On March 2, 1820, after a series of narrow votes on the individual components of the package, the House went on record in favor of the Missouri Compromise 134–42. All nineteen members from Virginia voted against.[56]

The Missouri question overshadowed the 1820 term of the Court. The justices considered twenty-seven cases, but none were of constitutional significance. Marshall delivered ten decisions, and the others were divided among his colleagues. Livingston dissented from Story's opinion in a case involving piracy,[57] and Johnson dissented in a Tennessee land case.[58] Otherwise, all of the Court's decisions were unanimous.

In the spring of 1820 the sleeping spirit of Virginia awoke with a vengeance. Reaction to the Missouri Compromise dominated public discourse. "We scarcely ever recollect to have tasted a bitterer cup," wrote Thomas Ritchie in the *Enquirer*. "A constitution warped from its legitimate bearings, an immense region closed forever against Southern and Western people—such is the 'sorry sight' which rises to our view."[59] Later that year the *Enquirer* published what would become a textbook for southern secessionists, John Taylor's *Construction Construed and Constitutions Vindicated*.[60] "If any book is capable of arousing the people," wrote Ritchie, "it is this one."[61]

John Taylor of Caroline had devoted a lifetime to states rights. The argument for strict construction of the Constitution that he put forth in 1820 was similar to the powerful case he had made when opposing Marshall over the college charter of William and Mary in 1790.[62] This time, however, Taylor's plea was a call to action. "The Missouri question is not yet closed. . . . The usurpation of federal power . . . is again to be attempted. . . . The charter [of the Bank of the United States] has been justified on principles so bold and alarming, that no man who loves the Constitution can fold his arms in apathy."[63] Taylor devoted five of sixteen chapters to attacking Marshall's decision in *McCulloch v. Maryland*. The essence of the Court's doctrine, said Taylor, was that the powers of the national government were limited, but the means by which it could pursue them were unlimited. "As ends may be made to beget means, so means may be made to beget ends, until the cohabitation shall rear a progeny of unconstitutional bastards which were not begotten by the people."[64] In Taylor's presentation, slavery, states rights, and compact theory marched in unison. He concluded with a threat of secession and civil war.[65]

Taylor was not a member of the Richmond Junto. In fact, he had been in bad odor with Virginia's leadership since the election of 1808 when he had supported Monroe. Almost overnight he was elevated to the role of elder statesman. Elected to the United States Senate in 1822, he continued to wage an unremitting campaign against national power until his death two years later.[66]

Another elder statesman also was heard from. Jefferson, who for the past decade had avoided public exposure, began to issue a stream of warnings about the consolidating tendencies of the national government. "I had for a long time ceased to read newspapers, or pay any attention to public affairs," he wrote to Maine senator John Holmes in April 1820. But the Missouri question, "like a fire bell in the night, awakened and filled me with terror. I consider it at once the knell of the Union."[67] Jefferson singled out the Supreme Court for special attack. "The judiciary," he told Thomas Ritchie, "is a subtle corps of sappers and miners constantly working underground to undermine the foundations of our confederated fabric."[68] To Albert Gallatin he confided his fear that Congress would soon outlaw slavery throughout the United States, and complained bitterly that "the steady tenor" of the Court has been "to break down the constitutional barriers between the co-ordinated powers of the States and of the Union."[69] To his friend Archibald Thweat, Jefferson noted "the inroads daily making by the federal [government] into the jurisdiction of its co-ordinate associates, the State governments. The legislative and executive branches may sometimes err, but elections and dependence will bring them to rights. The judiciary branch is the instrument which, working like gravity, without intermission, is to press us at last into one consolidated mass."[70]

If Spencer Roane needed any encouragement, Jefferson provided it. After acknowledging that the passage of time inevitably brought change, he warned the leader of the Junto that it also brought corruption. "The great object of my fear is the federal judiciary. That body, like gravity, ever acting, with noiseless foot, and unalarming advance, gaining ground step by step, and holding what it gains, is engulfing insidiously the [state] governments into the jaws of that which feeds them. . . . Let the eye of vigilance never be closed."[71]

Jefferson was especially critical of the Supreme Court's habit of speaking with one voice. He told Thomas Ritchie that the justices "consider themselves secure for life" and "sculk from responsibility. . . . An opinion is huddled up in conclave, perhaps by a majority of one, delivered as if unanimous, and with silent acquiescence of lazy or timid associates, by a crafty chief judge, who sophisticates the law to his mind, by the turn of his own reasoning." The former president said that the justices should be required by law to announce their opinions *seriatim*. "A judiciary independent of a king . . . is a good thing; but independence of the will of the nation is a solecism, at least in a republican government."[72]

Marshall soon got a chance to reply. On June 1, 1820, Philip and Mendes Cohen, managers of the Norfolk branch of Cohens Lottery and Exchange Office of Baltimore, were charged by authorities in Norfolk with selling tickets for the National Lottery in violation of Virginia law. The National Lottery was an ongoing activity authorized by an Act of Congress[73] and conducted by the city government of the District of Columbia, to raise money for municipal purposes. In January 1820 the Virginia legislature, in an effort to promote the state's own lotteries, had enacted a statute prohibiting the sale of out-of-state lottery tickets. The Cohens were convicted in local court and fined $100. They appealed to the Supreme Court, asserting that the National Lottery, like the national bank, was a federal institution immune from state regulation.

This was scarcely a trivial issue or a minor infraction involving two unsavory figures at the margin of society. Lotteries were one of the chief means by which governments raised capital in the early nineteenth century.[74] For Virginia to close its borders to the National Lottery would have a significant impact and, arguably, violated not only the sovereign immunity of the federal government, but the free flow of commerce guaranteed by the Constitution.

Philip and Mendes Cohen had a vital stake in the outcome. Cohens' Lottery and Exchange Office was a leading vendor of lottery tickets in the United States with branch offices in New York, Philadelphia, and Charleston, in addition to the Virginia operation centered in Norfolk, and a mail order service that sold tickets nationwide.* For Virginia to curtail the firm's activities would be a serious blow, with possible ramifications in other states. Accordingly, the Cohens engaged two of the nation's leading lawyers to handle their appeal: David Ogden of New York and William Pinkney from Baltimore. Pinkney was on the case from the moment Philip and Mendes were arrested. Then serving as a United States senator from Maryland, he was well acquainted with the Cohen family. He was also committed to a broad interpretation of the necessary and proper clause and to the doctrine of sovereign immunity. The day after the Cohens were indicted, he drafted a letter to *Niles Weekly Register*, which he persuaded four prominent lawyers to cosign, arguing that state governments were prohibited by the Constitution from interfering with Congress's attempt to improve conditions in the nation's capital and that a lottery was an appropriate means for Congress to select.[75] The Cohens' case was not about a $100 fine for a petty gaming violation. Like *McCulloch v. Maryland*, it was about the future of the Union.

For Virginia, the issue was states rights. The procedural question was

---

*The Cohen firm was founded in 1812 by Jacob I. Cohen, the eldest of six sons of Judith and Israel Cohen, who had emigrated from Bavaria to the United States in 1803. As the business grew, Jacob brought each of his brothers into the firm. In Baltimore, where the home office was located, the Cohen family had already become part of the city's financial establishment. A reputable firm in a not so reputable business—the Cohens were known for paying prize winners immediately—lotteries led to banking, and banking to insurance and stock brokerage. The Cohen family sponsored the Hebrew congregation in Baltimore, and in 1826, when Maryland's law prohibiting Jews from holding office was repealed, Jacob was elected to the city council. He later became president of the Baltimore Fire Insurance Company and a director of the Baltimore and Ohio Railroad. Philip Cohen subsequently became postmaster of Norfolk, and Mendes was elected to the Maryland legislature and also became a director of the Baltimore and Ohio Railroad. Two other brothers, Benjamin and David, helped to found the Baltimore Stock Exchange. Both served as president of that organization, and Benjamin was president at the time of his death in 1845. W. Ray Luce, "The Cohen Brothers of Baltimore: From Lotteries to Banking," 68 *Maryland Historical Magazine* 288–308 (1973); Aaron Baroway, "The Cohens of Maryland," 18 *ibid.* 363–373 (1923).

preeminent. Did the Supreme Court of the United States have appellate jurisdiction over the decisions of state courts, applying state law, in state criminal trials? Could the Cohen brothers appeal their Norfolk conviction to federal authority? When the Supreme Court issued the writ of error to allow the case to come forward, it triggered a wave of indignation throughout the Old Dominion. The Junto leaders insisted that the Eleventh Amendment to the Constitution* precluded individual appeals against the state of Virginia and that section 25 of the Judiciary Act—the source of the Court's jurisdiction in *Martin v. Hunter's Lessee*—did not apply.[76] In December 1820 the state legislature adopted a series of resolutions denying the Supreme Court's authority and instructing Virginia's lawyers to confine their argument exclusively to the question of jurisdiction.[77]

Marshall took a detached view of the case. Unlike his overreaction to the Junto's criticism of *McCulloch*, he was comfortable that the anguished cries from Richmond had found little support. When he arrived in Washington on February 7 for the 1821 term, there were forty-one cases on the docket, with *Cohens v. Virginia*[78] well down the list. All of the justices except Bushrod Washington, who was confined to his bed at Mount Vernon, were on hand. Marshall wrote to Washington that he should not fret about being absent. "We all think that it would be madness to encounter the hazard of joining us, unless your health should be entirely restored."[79] After mentioning several cases that were pending, the chief justice suggested that Washington might join the brethren later in the term.

> It is probable that the case from Virginia, which has excited so much commotion in our legislature, will be set to some late day and it certainly is desirable that the Court should be as full as possible when it is decided. I mention these things as eventually to be wished, but as depending altogether on your being able to pass a few days in Washington with perfect safety to yourself; for we all concur in advising you not to encounter the slightest hazard to your health from any consideration whatever.

Washington's health did not improve in time for him to join his colleagues, and when *Cohens* was argued on February 18, only six justices were present. The case for Virginia was presented by Alexander Smythe and Philip Barbour. Barbour was a member of Congress and a fierce defender of

---

*The Eleventh Amendment, adopted in protest against the jurisdiction asserted by the Supreme Court in *Chisholm v. Georgia*, 2 Dallas 419 (1793) (see Chapter 7), states that "The Judicial power of the United States shall not be construed to extend to any suit in law or equity, commenced or prosecuted against one of the United States by Citizens of another State, or by Citizens or Subjects of any Foreign State."

states rights who later would be appointed to the Court by Andrew Jackson.[80] He immediately moved that the case be dismissed for lack of jurisdiction. Argument centered on that issue for two days, as counsel for Virginia truculently disputed the Supreme Court's authority to hear the Cohens' appeal. Smythe concluded with a thinly veiled threat of rebellion. "Nothing can so much endanger [the federal government] as exciting the hostility of the State governments. With them is to determine how long this government shall endure."[81] When Smythe finished, Ogden and Pinkney argued the case for federal jurisdiction with great precision, citing precedent and text extensively.[82]

Marshall held the decision for two weeks. There were two issues to be dealt with. The first was procedural and involved the jurisdiction of the Court: Could it hear an appeal from a criminal conviction in the Virginia courts? The second question went to the merits of the case: Could Virginia prohibit the sale of lottery tickets authorized by Congress? Was the National Lottery analogous to the national bank? If so, the decision in *McCulloch* would be controlling.

For Marshall and his colleagues the procedural issue was paramount. An act of Congress was involved, and if the Supreme Court did not enjoy ultimate appellate authority, each state would be free to interpret federal legislation as it wished. There would soon be as many interpretations as there were states, and the unity of the nation would not survive. That was not what the Framers had intended, and it was not what the Constitution said. Accordingly, the Court's jurisdiction appeared to be on firm ground.

The merits of the case were more complicated. Lottery tickets were not like banking, and a strong argument could be made that each state possessed inherent authority to provide for the health and morals of its citizens. There was also a practical question. The Court could easily enforce its decision as to jurisdiction, but it could not compel Virginia to admit federal lottery tickets against its will. If Virginia defied the Court and persisted in arresting those selling out-of-state ducats, there would be little the justices could do. Marshall was too astute to press an issue the Court could not win. By the end of February, the judgment seemed clear. The Supreme Court would uphold its authority to hear appeals from state courts when a federal issue was involved, but it would defer to Virginia's residual right to prohibit out-of-state lottery tickets. The Cohens appeal would be heard but denied.

This required some maneuvering. Thus far only the procedural question had been argued. Virginia's lawyers had refused to discuss the merits of the case, and counsel for the Cohens had not addressed the issue, either. For the Court to uphold Virginia without the state's having made its case would be a rank departure from precedent and would appear suspect. Accordingly, Marshall, presumably working through Story, obtained Daniel Webster to make the case for Virginia. Ostensibly, the Court's decision would affect every state, and Webster, so it was reported, was the counsel for New York in a similar case that was making its way forward.[83] On Friday, March 2, Webster duly appeared before the Court and argued the case for the states. David Ogden and Attorney General William Wirt appeared on behalf of the Cohens. The arguments were brief, almost *pro forma*, and revolved around the question of whether congressional legislation pertaining to the District of Columbia was national in scope or merely municipal.[84] If national, Virginia could not interdict the lottery tickets; if merely municipal, the tickets enjoyed no special protection.

The following day, Saturday, March 3, 1821, Marshall delivered the opinion of the Court on the jurisdictional issue. The decision was unanimous. Marshall's opinion is a state paper of the first magnitude, and in the years ahead it would become a powerful bulwark of national unity. The decision settled forever the authority of the Supreme Court to hear appeals from the various state judicial systems when a federal issue was involved and provided an essential restatement of the supremacy of the Union. In *Marbury v. Madison* the Marshall Court established the principle of judicial review; in *McCulloch v. Maryland* it authenticated the implied powers of Congress; in *Cohens v. Virginia* it met the compact theory of states rights head on and vanquished it from judicial discourse.[85]

The lawyers for Virginia, said Marshall,

> maintain that the nation does not possess a department capable of restraining peaceably, and by authority of law, any attempts which may be made, by a part, against the legitimate powers of the whole; and that the government is reduced to the alternative of submitting to such attempts, or of resisting them by force. They maintain that the Constitution of the United States has provided no tribunal for the final construction of itself, or of the laws or treaties of the nation; but that this power may be exercised in the last resort by the courts of every State in the Union.

Marshall said that "the mischievous consequences of the construction contended for on the part of Virginia . . . would prostrate . . . the government and its laws at the feet of every State in the Union. . . . Each member will possess a *veto* on the will of the whole."

In words analogous to those he had used in *McCulloch*, Marshall observed that

> a Constitution is framed for ages to come, and is designed to approach immortality as nearly as human institutions can approach it.

Its course is not always tranquil. It is exposed to storms and tempests, and its framers must be unwise statesmen indeed, if they have not provided it, as far as nature will permit, with the means of self-preservation from the perils it may be destined to encounter. No government ought to be so defective in its organization, as not to contain the means of securing the execution of its laws against other dangers than those which occur every day.

Addressing the precise issue at bar, the chief justice held that the judicial power of the Union extends "to all cases arising under the Constitution or a law of the United States, whoever may be the parties to the case." The Eleventh Amendment did not shield Virginia. It was the nature of the cause, not the identity of the parties, that determined the Court's jurisdiction. In a holding vital to the Supreme Court's appellate authority, Marshall said that "the defendant who removes a judgment rendered against him by a State Court into this Court for the purpose of re-examining the question [of] whether that judgment violates the Constitution or the laws of the United States, does not commence or prosecute a suit against a State." Accordingly, he said, the case of *Cohens v. Virginia* was governed by the text of the original Constitution, not the Eleventh Amendment. And Article III of the Constitution gave the Court appellate authority whenever a federal issue was involved.

The most powerful passage in Marshall's opinion dealt with the nature of the Union. With both Congress and the Court under attack in Richmond, the chief justice pulled out all the stops. His words reflect his abiding love for the United States and provide the most eloquent evocation of the nation ever delivered in a judicial setting.

In war we are one people. In making peace, we are one people. In all commercial regulations, we are one and the same people. In many other respects, the American people are one, and the government which is alone capable of controlling and managing their interests in all these respects, is the government of the Union. It is their government, and in that character they have no other. America has chosen to be, in many respects, and for many purposes, a nation; and for all these purposes, her government is complete; to all these objects, it is competent. The people have declared, that in the exercise of all powers given for these objects, it is supreme. It can, then, in effecting these objects, legitimately control all individuals or governments within the American territory. The constitution and laws of a State, so far as they are repugnant to the Constitution and laws of the United States, are absolutely void. These States are constituent

parts of the United States. They are members of one great empire—
for some purposes sovereign, for some purposes subordinate.

Marshall said that "after having bestowed upon this question the most
deliberate consideration of which we are capable, the Court is unanimously
of the opinion that [Virginia's] objections to its jurisdiction are not sustained" and that Philip Barbour's motion to dismiss the case was overruled.
The Court then adjourned for the weekend.

On Monday, March 5, its jurisdiction sustained, Marshall addressed the
merits of the Cohens' appeal. Speaking once more for all of his colleagues
save the absent Washington, the chief justice held that Congress had not intended to authorize the sale of lottery tickets in Virginia and that the object
of the National Lottery was "entirely local." It was confined to the District
of Columbia. As a result, Virginia could legitimately restrict the sale of national lottery tickets within its borders. Marshall implied that Congress
could establish an interstate lottery if it wished, but that it had not done so
in this instance. The Virginia statute under which the Cohens were convicted was upheld. In effect, Virginia had won the battle but lost the war.

As soon as the Court's brief decision on the merits of the case was announced, the justices adjourned to attend Monroe's second inauguration. By
law the new president's term began on March 4, but in 1821 that date fell
on a Sunday. When Monroe asked Marshall how the oath-taking should be
handled, the chief justice, after consulting his colleagues, suggested that it
be postponed until Monday, March 5, "unless some official duty should require its being taken on Sunday."[86] Monday dawned rainy and cold, and a
crowd of 3,000 was forced to squeeze inside the newly restored House
chamber, to which the ceremony was moved at the last minute. After Marshall administered the oath—the sixth time he had done so—Monroe spoke
briefly and optimistically about the nation's future. There was "every reason
to believe," said the president, that because of "the good sense of the people," the American system of government "will soon attain the highest degree of perfection of which human institutions are capable." Monroe
departed to the accompaniment of "Yankee Doodle" played by the Marine
Band.[87] That evening Marshall and his colleagues attended the inaugural
ball at Brown's Indian Queen Hotel.

When the Court adjourned at the end of March, it had decided forty-one
cases. Marshall delivered the opinion in twelve, and the others were
parceled out.[88] Whether it was in response to Jefferson and the Richmond
Junto or not, all forty-one decisions that the Court announced were unanimous. As Marshall told Story, "we have external and political enemies
enough to preserve internal peace. The harmony of the bench will, I hope
and pray, never be disturbed."[89]

Cohens v. Virginia immediately drew national attention. Marshall's opinion was warmly approved by moderate Republicans outside the Old Dominion and by the remaining Federalists. The Monroe administration appeared well pleased. Gales and Seaton, publishers of the *National Intelligencer*, the Republican establishment's newspaper, wrote immediately to the chief justice to request a copy of the decision.[90] The *New York American*, another Republican journal, said that "the whole argument against the jurisdiction of the Supreme Court has been completely demolished in the opinion delivered by Chief Justice Marshall."[91] In much of the South, reaction was similar. The *Southern Patriot* in Charleston said, "Such illustrations of the true theory and intention of the Constitution are of the highest public utility. . . . That branch of the opinion of the Court which regards the question of jurisdiction presents one of the best connected and most vigorous constitutional arguments that we have seen."[92]

The Richmond Junto responded predictably. Thomas Ritchie, writing in the *Enquirer*, complained that "the very title of the case [*Cohens v. Virginia*] is enough to stir one's blood." Echoing the sentiment of his mentor at Monticello, Ritchie said that "the Judiciary power, with a foot as noiseless as time and a spirit as greedy as the grave, is sweeping to their destruction the rights of the States."[93] Spencer Roane did not take the field initially. Instead, he sought help from Virginia's greatest authority on the intent of the Framers. In mid-April he wrote to enlist Madison's support in the Junto's crusade. Would the former president write an article attacking the decision in *Cohens v. Virginia?*[94] Madison responded tepidly. He told Roane that although the Court's tendency to mingle dicta with its judgments was regrettable, he did not share the Junto's apprehension. He discounted Roane's fears of Marshall's "ingenious and fatal sophistries" and the Supreme Court's "usurpations," suggesting that Congress was a far greater problem than the Court. "Whatever may be the latitude of jurisdiction assumed by the judicial power of the United States, it is less formidable to the reserved sovereignty of the States than the latitude of power it has assigned to the national legislature."[95] The following month he told Roane that "on the abstract question whether the federal or the State decisions ought to prevail, the sounder policy would be to yield to the claims of the former."*[96]

---

*Madison remained true to his convictions. In 1823, in a powerful letter setting out his position, he told Jefferson of his correspondence with Roane and said, "A paramount, or even a definitive, authority in the individual States would soon make the Constitution and laws different in different States and thus destroy that equality and uniformity of rights and duties which form the essence of the compact. . . . Believing, as I do, that the [Federal] Convention regarded a provision within the Constitution for deciding in a peaceable and regular mode all cases arising in the course of its operation as essential to an adequate system of Government; that it intended the authority vested in the Judicial Department as a final resort, in relation to the States, for cases resulting to it in the exercise of its functions, and that this intention is expressed by the articles

Unable to mobilize Madison in the cause, Roane again entered the fray. In a series of articles published in the Richmond *Enquirer* under the pseudonym "Algernon Sidney,"[97] he lambasted the decision in *Cohens* with broadside after broadside.[98] Calling the Court's holding "a most monstrous and unexampled decision," Roane said that "it can only be accounted for from that love of power which all history informs us infects and corrupts those who possess it." The Supreme Court of the United States, he said, was at the "zenith of despotic power. . . . Appointed in one generation, it claims to make laws and constitutions for another." The Republican justices who had concurred with Marshall were denounced with particular venom. "How else is it that they also go to all lengths with the ultra-federal leader who is at the head of their court? That leader is honorably distinguished from you messieurs judges. He is true to his former politics. He has even pushed them to an extreme never until now anticipated. He must be equally delighted and *surprised* to find his *Republican* brothers going with him." How is it that they go with him, not only as to the holding, "but as to all the points and positions contained in the most lengthy, artful and alarming opinions?" Roane said it was because they were "on the side of the government that feeds them."[99]

Roane was always able to raise Marshall's hackles, and his attack on *Cohens* proved no exception. On June 2, shortly after the initial Algernon Sidney articles appeared, the chief justice wrote Story that "the old *friend* of the court seems inflamed with more than a double portion of ire. . . . The opinion of the Supreme Court in the case of *Cohens v. The Commonwealth of Virginia* is attacked with a degree of virulence superior even to that which was employed in the Bank question."[100] Two weeks later, as Roane's fusillade continued, Marshall said that

---

declaring that the federal Constitution and laws shall be the supreme law of the land, and that the Judicial power of the United States shall extend to all cases arising under them: Believing, moreover, that this was the prevailing view of the subject when the Constitution was adopted and put into execution; that it has so continued through the long period which has elapsed; and that even at this time an appeal to a national decision would prove that no general change has taken place: Thus believing, I have never yielded my original opinion, indicated in the *Federalist*, No. 39, to the ingenious reasonings of Col. [John] Taylor [of Caroline] against this construction of the Constitution."

In *Federalist* 39, Madison wrote that "in controversies relating to the boundaries between the [national and state] jurisdictions, the tribunal which is ultimately to decide, is to be established under the general Government. . . . Some such tribunal is clearly essential to prevent an appeal to the sword, and a dissolution of the compact; and it ought to be established under the general, rather than under the local Governments." Marshall was unaware of Madison's letter to Jefferson, but he could scarcely have asked for more vigorous support.

Madison to Jefferson, June 27, 1823; see also Madison to Joseph G. Cabell, September 7, 1829, expressing the same view. 3 *Letters and Other Writings of James Madison* 323–328, William C. Rives and Philip R. Ferdall, eds. (Philadelphia: J. B. Lippincott, 1865).

for coarseness and malignity Algernon Sidney surpasses all party writers who have ever made pretensions to any decency of character. There is on this subject no such thing as a free press in Virginia; and the calumnies and misrepresentations of this gentleman will remain uncontradicted and will by many be believed to be true. He will be supposed to be the champion of state rights instead of being what he really is, the champion of dismemberment.[101]

Several weeks later, with the animosity between Marshall and Roane at its peak, the chief justice wrote Bushrod Washington that there was only "one man in the United States who could or would write such pieces. If you have not seen them I recommend them to you as being an excitement to stagnating spirits as powerful as the essence of chian [Cayenne pepper] to a palate that has lost its discriminating power."[102]

Story, who was avidly following the contretemps from his home in Salem, wrote Marshall in late June that Virginia was once again out of step with the nation. "The people here are disposed to place confidence in Courts, and when they decide after full argument, they are generally satisfied." Story said that "Massachusetts is attached to the Union and has no jealousy of its powers. . . . We should dread to see the government reduced as Virginia wishes it, to a confederacy. We are disposed to construe the Constitution of the U.S. as a *frame of government* and not as a petty charter granted to a paltry corporation for the purpose of regulating a fishery or collecting a toll."[103] Story told Marshall that "the opinion of our best lawyers is unequivocally with the Supreme Court. . . . They consider your opinion in *Cohens v. Virginia* . . . as the greatest of your judgments. Allow me to say that nowhere is your reputation more sincerely cherished than here; and however strange it may sound in Virginia, if you were known here only by this last opinion, you could not wish for more unequivocal fame."

Story was especially riled by Jefferson's role in the states rights movement. Although the former president had as yet made no public statement concerning the Court, he had written the year before to William Jarvis of Pittsfield, Massachusetts, criticizing the independence of the judiciary and suggesting that it be made accountable to public opinion. Jefferson wrote in response to a book Jarvis had written,[104] and now the book was on display, along with Jefferson's letter, in a Boston bookstore. Story told Marshall that Jefferson's "obvious design is . . . to prostrate the judicial authority and annihilate all public reverence for its dignity. There never was a period in my life when the opinions would not have shocked me; but *at his age* and in these critical times they fill me alternately with indignation and melancholy. Can he wish yet to have influence enough to destroy the Government of his Country?" On a more congenial note, Story said he was sending to Richmond "a quintal of our best dumb fish" for Marshall's enjoyment.* "I shall send you in the true spirit of cookery a written direction how to cook the fish, which is as essential as the fish itself."[105]

When Marshall received Story's letter, he replied immediately. "What you say of Mr. Jefferson . . . rather grieves than surprises me. It grieves me because his influence is still so great that many will adopt his opinions however unsound they may be."[106] The chief justice said that Jefferson's hostility was not difficult to fathom. "He is among the most ambitious, and I suspect among the most unforgiving of men. His great power is over the mass of the people and this power is chiefly acquired by professions of democracy. Every check on the wild impulse of the moment is a check on his own power, and he is unfriendly to the source from which it flows. He looks, of course, with ill will at an independent judiciary."[107]

Marshall expressed a similar sentiment to the son of Henry Lee. "Those Virginians who opposed the opinions and political views of Mr. Jefferson seem to have been considered rather as rebellious subjects than legitimate enemies entitled to the rights of political war."[108]

It was at this point that Jefferson sidled into the assault on the Court. Like Madison, he was reluctant to enter the debate directly. But unlike the father of the Constitution, he strongly supported the Richmond Junto's states rights stance. Accordingly, he concocted a plan with Roane and Ritchie to have the *Enquirer* publish a "cooked up extract" of a letter he had written, leaving the recipient's name blank. He sent this to Roane, who passed it on to Ritchie, who published it July 17, 1821.[109] Ritchie prefaced the letter with a brief editorial, in which he wrote that the former president was pursuing "the even tenor of his brilliant course, unswayed by the fashionable heresies of the time."[110] In his letter, Jefferson heaped extravagant praise on the states rights views expressed by John Taylor in *Construction Construed and Constitutions Vindicated*. He did not mention the decision in *Cohens* specifically, but said that the federal government and the states had distinct spheres of responsibility. In Jefferson's view, the national government was designed to manage foreign affairs, while domestic matters rested with the states. Both levels of government were "equally supreme" and "as independent as different nations."[111] In cases of dispute between the two, the appeal should be to a special convention of the people, not to the functionaries of either government—an implicit criticism not only of the Court's decisions in *McCulloch* and *Cohens* but of the action of Congress in the Missouri Compromise, as well.

---

*"Dumb fish" was a Massachusetts colloquialism for salted cod, the expression derived from "dun fish," pertaining to the dunnish color of the cured fish. A quintal is 100 pounds.

Jefferson's letter was reprinted widely. The former president still had many supporters, and public sentiment threatened to shift. As the rhetoric escalated, the Monroe administration, led by Secretary of War John C. Calhoun, commenced an urgent effort to control the damage.[112] The *National Intelligencer* published a series of articles attempting to rebut Jefferson's remarks. Could any principle "be more dangerous or more irreconcilable to the principles of our government than that which makes . . . decisions [of the state courts] final on questions arising under the Constitution?" asked the editors.[113] Throughout the summer the *Enquirer* and the *National Intelligencer* traded accusations. Other papers joined in, most of the comments supporting the Court.[114]

In September Marshall wrote to Story that Roane's essays had obviously been inspired by Jefferson. "Although the coarseness of the language belongs exclusively to the author, its acerbity has been increased by his communication with the great Lama of the mountains."[115] Marshall said that

> a deep design to convert our government into a mere league of States has taken strong hold . . . in Virginia. The attack upon the judiciary is in fact an attack upon the Union. The judicial department is well understood to be that through which the government may be attacked most successfully, because it is without patronage, and of course without power, and it is equally well understood that every subtraction from its jurisdiction is a vital wound to the government itself. . . . The whole attack, if not originating with Mr. Jefferson, is obviously approved and guided by him. It is therefore formidable in other states as well, and it behooves the friends of the Union to be more on the alert than they have been.

Turning to lighter things, Marshall told Story that the quintal of cod had arrived and that he would try "to observe your instructions in the cooking department. I hope to succeed; but be this as it may, I promise to feed on the fish with an appetite which would not disgrace a genuine descendant of one of the Pilgrims."

By the end of 1821 the debate had subsided and the Court emerged from it largely unscathed. A year-end attempt by Senator Richard M. Johnson of Kentucky to amend the Constitution to make the Senate rather than the Supreme Court the forum for review of state court decisions failed miserably. The proposal was so preposterous that it was rejected even by the state of Virginia, and no further effort was made that session to repeal section 25 of the Judiciary Act of 1789, the immediate source of the Court's appellate authority.[116] Webster wrote to Story that there was "less reality in all this smoke" than he had originally thought.[117] Jefferson continued to fulminate against the Court in his private correspondence but said nothing more in public. "Tranquility at my age is the supreme good of life," he told Ohio lawyer Charles Hammond.[118] The Virginia legislature also moved on to other matters. In the spring of 1822, Thomas Ritchie said editorially in the *Enquirer* that Virginia "forbears at present presenting her opinions."[119] Spencer Roane became ill that spring, and with his death in September, the Junto's assault on the Court collapsed. The storm had passed. Marshall's holdings concerning national supremacy remained intact. As for the importance of the decision in *Cohens v. Virginia*, one historian has written that with one fell swoop, "Marshall was able to define the jurisdiction of the Supreme Court, give the major interpretation of the Eleventh Amendment, amplify an earlier decision that cases could be appealed from state courts to federal courts, and keep open the possibility that Congress could enact laws for the District of Columbia which would overrule state legislation."[120]

In contrast to 1819 and 1821, the next two terms of the Court were uneventful. In 1822 the justices considered thirty-one cases; in 1823 they handled thirty.[121] With two exceptions—one each year—all of the decisions were unanimous.[122] Only one case was of constitutional importance, and Marshall recused himself because of potential family involvement.*[123]

Shortly after the Court adjourned in 1822, President Monroe informally asked the justices for their opinion on the extent to which the national government could fund public works projects throughout the country. Monroe had just vetoed the Cumberland Road bill on the constitutional grounds that Congress lacked textual authority to undertake internal improvements. He sent a copy of his lengthy veto message to each of the justices for their comments.[124] Marshall responded with a personal note and was noncommittal.[125] Story explicitly declined to comment on the constitutional issue.[126] Justice Johnson, however, in what one scholar has termed "one of the most interesting and unusual [incidents] in our political history,"[127] undertook to poll his colleagues on the president's behalf. Afterward, Johnson wrote Monroe that "the Judges are deeply sensible of the mark of confidence bestowed on them in this instance and should be unworthy of that confidence did they attempt to conceal their true opinion." He said they all agreed

that the decision on the Bank question [*McCulloch v. Maryland*] completely commits them on the subject of internal improvement, as ap-

---

*In a leading nonconstitutional case, *Johnson v. McIntosh*, 8 Wheaton 543 (1823), the Marshall Court dealt definitively with the nature of the Indian title to land in North America. The case will be treated in the context of the Cherokee cases of the 1830s, which are discussed in the next chapter.

plied to Post Roads and Military Roads. On other points it is impossible to resist the lucid and conclusive reasoning contained in [that decision]. The principle assumed in the case of the Bank is that the granting of the principal power carries with it the grant of all adequate and appropriate means of executing it. That selection of these means must rest with the General Government, and as to that power and those means the Constitution makes the Government of the U.S. supreme.[128]

Johnson's extraordinary letter makes clear the degree to which the justices subscribed to Marshall's reasoning in *McCulloch*. It also represents the single departure in American constitutional history from the principle that the Supreme Court will not render advisory opinions.[129] Although Johnson's letter to Monroe was a personal one, and although the chief justice and his colleagues remained in the background, it seems obvious that the first Republican appointee to the Bench sought to dispel any apprehension Monroe might have felt concerning the attitude of the Court.

The following year the curtain came down on the most celebrated era of the Marshall Court. On March 18, 1823, as the term drew to a close, Justice Brockholst Livingston died of pneumonia. He was sixty-six years old and had served on the Court for sixteen years. Livingston's health had been frail for some time, but his sudden death came as a shock to Marshall. For the last twelve years, since the appointment of Story and Duvall in 1811, the composition of the Court had not changed. These twelve years remain by far the longest period of continuous membership in the Court's history.[130] The same seven men gathered each February in Washington, shared their meals and lodgings, and hammered together an exceptional record of judicial accomplishment. During this period the Court decided 457 cases, 437 of which were unanimous. That remarkable consensus established the reputation of the Supreme Court not only as the ultimate legal authority in the nation but as a body that was reliable, predictable, and definitive when it spoke. Marshall wrote the lion's share of the decisions, but regardless of the author, it was clear that whoever delivered the opinion of the Court was speaking for all of his colleagues.* Livingston wrote his share of decisions, and he ranked with Story and Johnson in

---

*It was during this period that the Court's mode of delivering its opinions became fixed. As Justice Johnson expressed it, they would agree "to appoint someone to deliver the opinion of the majority, but leave it to the discretion of the rest of the judges to record the opinions or not ad libitum" [at liberty]. A clearly labeled opinion of the Court made the decision authoritative, but the independence of the individual justices was not infringed. Donald G. Morgan, Justice William Johnson: The First Dissenter 181–182 (Columbia: University of South Carolina Press, 1954).

the number of dissents he filed.[131] More important, however, was Livingston's personal contribution to the Court's harmony. He was easily the most amiable and even-tempered of the brethren. His unfailing good humor was always on tap to relieve a tense interchange or to turn a black cloud bright. Marshall called him "one of the kindest hearted men in the world."[132]

The question was who would replace him. On March 24, 1823, Monroe offered the position to his longtime secretary of the navy, Smith Thompson. Like Livingston, Thompson was from New York, and had served as the state's chief justice from 1814 to 1818. Those whom Monroe consulted— John Quincy Adams, John C. Calhoun, and William Wirt—strongly endorsed the choice. Thompson, however, had pronounced presidential ambitions and believed he could win the Republican nomination in 1824. As a result, he deferred accepting Monroe's offer for several months while he attempted to lever his fellow New Yorker, Senator Martin Van Buren, onto the Court in exchange for Van Buren's support for president.* Van Buren anchored the party's radical wing in the Senate and was among the most partisan of Republicans. Rumors that he might be appointed to the Court caused immediate concern among the justices.[133] Story wrote Marshall that he felt "deep anxiety as to the successor of our lamented friend, Judge Livingston. I have heard strange rumours on the subject."[134] Marshall, who had heard the same rumors, shared Story's alarm. "Our Presidents I fear will never again seek to make our department respectable."[135]

In fact, Monroe was unaware of Thompson's maneuvering and had no intention of appointing Van Buren.[136] "The President would sooner appoint an alligator," the New York senator quipped.[137] When that became apparent to Thompson, he mustered whatever grace he could and accepted the nomination.[138] Monroe sent his name to the Senate in December, and Thompson took his seat February 10, 1824.

Thompson brought a new dimension to the Court. More accurately, he represented a throwback to the pre-Marshall era when justices of the Supreme Court saw no contradiction between their judicial duties and open participation in elective politics. Unlike the early justices who had been Federalists, Thompson was a Republican. But like them, he did not shed his political aspirations when he joined the Court. He ran for governor of New York in 1828 (losing to Van Buren 106,444 to 136,794), and only gradu-

---

*This bizarre episode is documented in the extensive correspondence among Thompson, Van Buren, Rufus King, and President Monroe in the spring of 1823. The letters are cogently quoted and summarized by G. Edward White, *The Marshall Court and Cultural Change, 1815–1835* 310–315, in The Oliver Wendell Holmes Devise, 3–4 *History of the Supreme Court of the United States* (New York: Macmillan, 1988).

ally, as his political fortunes waned, did he reconcile himself to remaining on the Bench.[139] However, in one respect Thompson fit in. He was sociable and enjoyed good company. As soon as he was appointed, he sold his house in Washington, resumed permanent residence in Albany (where circuit duties required his presence), and joined the justices each February in their communal quarters at Brown's Hotel.[140]

Aside from his concern over Livingston's replacement, Marshall was preoccupied during the spring and summer of 1823 with preparing his youngest son, Edward Carrington, for the rigors of Harvard. Insofar as higher education was concerned, the Marshall family had not fared well. John, Jr., had been expelled from Harvard; James Keith left voluntarily to pursue a commercial career in Philadelphia; Jaquelin was practicing as a doctor but had no formal medical education; and Mary, as was the custom of the period, had married early and had not attended college. Only Thomas, the oldest child, had completed college (he graduated from Princeton in 1807), and the chief justice hoped that Edward could duplicate that achievement.

Marshall decided that it would be best to send his son to Cambridge early so that he could prepare for classes with a private tutor. The chief justice had discussed the matter at some length with Story when they were in Washington, and on June 1 he wrote to confirm arrangements. Marshall asked Story if he would advise Edward "respecting the person with whom he should study, and respecting his place of boarding, should you be able to do so without, in any manner, distracting your attention from official duties."[141] Marshall said he would prefer for Edward to live in the college, "but presume this cannot be allowed until he is admitted as a scholar." He also told Story that he was unfamiliar with Harvard's current billing practices and asked for information. "It will be my choice to pay in advance where I can do so with convenience." In the interim, Marshall (who was evidently strapped for cash) sent Story a postdated check for $100. "I have given some money to my son . . . but probably not enough. I will therefore thank you, after receiving the amount of my draft, to furnish him as he may require. . . . I will not encourage expensive habits in my son, but I do not wish to treat him over parsimoniously."[142]

Three weeks later Edward arrived in Boston. Story told Marshall that he had written to President Kirkland on his son's behalf and that they had found a place for him in a private boardinghouse in Cambridge "under the instruction of two of the Tutors of the College." Story said that after Harvard's commencement in August, rooms in the college should be available. "I shall personally attend to this. . . . In the meantime I wish you to understand that I do not feel it any burden or trouble to attend to his concerns and that I shall take great pleasure in aiding him in all the ways within my powers."*[143]

The correspondence between Marshall and Story provides a rare glimpse of the inner workings of the Court.[144] They wrote to each other several times a year during the 1820s, frequently discussing cases on circuit and sometimes alluding to issues that might come forward on appeal. In a contentious bank case that he had tried in Richmond,[145] Marshall acknowledged he would probably be reversed. "The Judge however who draws the opinion must have more ingenuity than I have if he draws a good one."[146] On a sticky procedural point that had arisen in another case, he told Story that he had reluctantly followed a ruling by Justice Thompson in New York but would raise the matter when the brethren reassembled. "It is a point on which the practice ought certainly to be uniform."[147] Sometimes the correspondence was purely personal. Marshall reciprocated Story's shipment of salted cod with two barrels of family flour. "Your name is marked on the heads of the barrels, and I hope you receive them safely. They are part of the stock laid up for my own use, and, though not quite so white as we usually make flour of that description, in consequence of the dryness of the wheat when ground, will, I trust, be found very good."[148]

There was a jocular tone to the letters, even when dealing with matters of utmost seriousness. "Our brother Johnson has hung himself on a democratic snag in a hedge composed entirely of thorny states rights in South Carolina," Marshall wrote in September 1823.[149] He was referring to Justice Johnson's decision on circuit overturning South Carolina's Negro Seamen Act† as repugnant to the Constitution.[150] Marshall told Story that "the decision has been considered as another act of judicial usurpation," and that the

---

*Edward Carrington Marshall remained at Harvard for three years, graduating with the class of 1826. Story watched over him and sent Marshall regular reports on his son's progress. Like his brothers, Edward settled in Fauquier county, devoted himself to farming, and served four terms in the Virginia legislature, where he was one of four senators to vote against the ordinance of secession in 1861. Impoverished by the Civil War, he was given a clerkship in the federal pension office by President Grant. The family history notes that Edward was fond of the classics. "His profound scholarship, his literary acquirements and cordial manners made him a welcome companion in the most learned circles of society." W. M. Paxton, *The Marshall Family* 103–104 (Cincinnati: Robert Clarke & Co., 1885).

†In December 1822, the South Carolina legislature, fearing the spread of subversive ideas among the slaves, enacted a measure that required free Negroes employed on incoming vessels to be seized and held in jail until the vessel departed. The ships' captains were made responsible, and Negro seamen who did not comply were to be sold into slavery. 7 *Statutes at Large of South Carolina* 461. The measure was passed during a wave of hysteria following a threatened slave revolt planned by a free Negro, Denmark Vesey. Justice Johnson was critical from the outset of what he considered South Carolina's overreaction, and when the act came before him in *Elkison v. Deliesseline*, 8 Fed. Cas. 493 (C.C.D. S.C.) (No. 4,366) (1823), he declared it unconstitutional. If a seaman could be banned because of "the color of his skin," why not "the color of his eye or his hair?" Johnson said the authority of the federal government to regulate commerce "is paramount and

attitude of many South Carolinians was, "if this be the Constitution, it is better to break that instrument than to submit."[151]

Marshall sympathized with Johnson. He told Story that Virginia had "the twin brother" to the law their South Carolina colleague had overturned. "A case was brought before me in which I might have considered its constitutionality, but it was not absolutely necessary and, as I am not fond of butting against a wall in sport, I escaped on the construction of the act."[152] Johnson, who was less cautious than Marshall, met the issue head on. As a result, he was subjected to a chorus of denunciation throughout the South. The *Charleston Mercury* said he had betrayed his native state.[153] *Niles Weekly Register* called the decision "more dangerous to the existence of the Union" than the Missouri question had been.[154] When Johnson sent a copy of the decision to Jefferson, the former president did not respond.[155] The fact is that Johnson found few defenders apart from his brothers on the Court.[156]

Such was the situation when the justices convened in 1824. South Carolina seethed with disunion; slavery and the compact theory had become inseparable; and Jefferson resumed his attack on the judiciary. Despite twenty-three years of Republican presidents—and five Republican appointees to the bench—the sage of Monticello continued to fume against the Supreme Court, which he claimed was still Federalist "almost to a man."[157]

Efforts to curtail the Court were again put forward. Representatives from Kentucky proposed the repeal of section 25 of the Judiciary Act, while others advocated altering the size of the Court or the number of justices required to decide a constitutional issue. Marshall told Story they should entrust their salvation to Providence.[158] To assist Providence, the chief justice wrote to Henry Clay.[159] One of "the most dangerous things in legislation," Marshall told the House Speaker, "is to enact a general law of great and extensive influence to effect a particular object; or to legislate for a nation under a strong excitement which must be suspected to influence the judgment. If the mental eye be directed to a single object, it is not easy for the legislator, intent only on that object, to look all around him, and to perceive and guard against the serious mischief with which his measure may burn [*sic*]."[160] Clay was receptive to Marshall's admonition, and Congress once again deferred action.

The first case on the Court's 1824 docket was the great steamboat controversy, *Gibbons v. Ogden*,[161] a case destined to achieve fame as "the emancipation proclamation of American commerce."[162] The issue involved a

exclusive." The words of the Constitution imply a "total, unlimited grant" to Congress which "sweeps away the whole subject, and leaves nothing for the states to act upon." *Ibid.* 495. Also see Philip M. Hamer, "Great Britain, the United States, and the Negro Seamen Acts, 1822–1848," 1 *Journal of Southern History* 4 (1935); Morgan, *Justice William Johnson* 126–146, 190–202.

monopoly granted by the New York legislature to Robert Fulton and Robert Livingston to operate steamboats in the state's waters. Fulton and Livingston had pioneered the development of steam navigation, and in 1808 they received an exclusive license to exploit their invention.* Three years later they were granted a similar monopoly by Louisiana for navigation on the lower Mississippi. As the success of the steamboat became apparent, numerous competitors attempted to enter the field. Other states charted rival companies; Connecticut and New Jersey passed retaliatory legislation authorizing the seizure of vessels licensed in New York; and commercial relations among the states turned ugly. Attorney General William Wirt said that the three states of the mid-Atlantic region were "on the eve of civil war."[163]

Protracted litigation ensued. The monopoly was challenged in the courts, but the initial suits were either dismissed or the exclusive grant to Livingston and Fulton was sustained.[164] Finally, in 1819, a test case emerged that eventually made its way to the Supreme Court. For several years Colonel Aaron Ogden had been operating a ferry service between New York City and New Jersey under a licence granted by the Livingston monopoly. In 1818 Thomas Gibbons opened a rival service with two steamboats—the *Bellona* and the *Stoudinger*—licensed under the federal coasting act.[165] The *Bellona* was piloted by Cornelius Vanderbilt, then on the threshold of his business career. With Vanderbilt's acumen, the line quickly cut into Ogden's profits. He responded by securing a restraining order in state court against Gibbons's vessels. Gibbons then appealed to the Supreme Court, asserting that the federal coasting act gave his steamboats the right to "navigate the waters of any state," New York legislation to the contrary notwithstanding. Procedural difficulties caused the case to be put off until the 1824 term, and by then the issue had acquired national significance. Could a state restrict commercial traffic through the grant of transportation monopolies? Could New York limit the operation of steamboats on the Hudson River and Long Island Sound? By analogy, could Louisiana restrict navigation on the lower Mississippi to a single firm? If the monopolies were upheld, the economic

---

*In 1798 Livingston secured from the New York legislature an act giving him the exclusive right to operate steamboats in the rivers and other waters of the state if he could build a boat capable of making four miles an hour moving upstream against the current of the Hudson. (Act of March 27, 1798, *Laws of New York, 1798* 382–383.) The act was extended several times, and on August 17, 1807, the steam-powered *Clermont*, developed by Fulton and Livingston, successfully navigated the Hudson between New York and Albany, achieving the required speed. On April 11, 1808, the legislature confirmed the agreement, giving Livingston and Fulton a monopoly for thirty years. All other persons were forbidden to navigate New York waters by steam without a license from Livingston and Fulton. An unlicensed vessel, "together with the engine, tackle, and apparel thereof," was to be seized and forfeited to them. Act of April 11, 1808, *Laws of New York, 1807–1809* 407–408. See Maurice Glen Baxter, *The Steamboat Monopoly* (New York: Knopf, 1972); Thomas Knox, *Life of Robert Fulton and a History of Steam Navigation* 72–93 (New York: G. P. Putnam's Sons, 1896).

expansion of the nation would be severely restricted. The issue turned on the commerce clause of the Constitution.[166]

Argument commenced on February 4, 1824, and continued for five days. Gibbons was represented by Daniel Webster and Attorney General William Wirt—the same team that had successfully argued *McCulloch v. Maryland*. Webster was forty-two years old and at the height of his forensic powers. "We in the South have not his superior and you in the North have not his equal," said Congressman William Lowndes of South Carolina.[167] Webster was the first to address the Court and he framed the issue as broadly as possible*: Congress's power to regulate commerce was exclusive, and whether it had acted or not, the states were powerless to intervene.[168] The reporter covering the Supreme Court for the *Washington Republican* called it "one of the most powerful arguments we ever have heard."[169] Story wrote that the clarity and simplicity of Webster's argument was compelling. "Whoever, with a view of the real difficulties of the case and the known ability of his opponents, shall sit down to the task of perusing this argument, will find that it is equally remarkable for profoundness and sagacity, for the choice and comprehensiveness of the topics, and for the delicacy and tact with which they were handled."[170] Webster described the scene in Court as follows:

> I can see the Chief Justice as he looked at that moment. Chief Justice Marshall always wrote with a quill. He never adopted the barbarous invention of steel pens. And always, before counsel began to argue, the Chief Justice would nib his pen; and then, when everything was ready, pulling up the sleeves of his gown, he would nod to the counsel who was to address him, as much as to say, "I am ready; now you may go on." I think I never experienced more intellectual pleasure than in arguing that novel question to a great man who could appreciate it, and take it in. . . . [171]

Thomas Oakley responded for Ogden, followed by Thomas Addis Emmet. Oakley, said the *New York Statesman*, "was not at all intimidated by the able argument of his antagonist, but set about attacking the ramparts of the

---

*Webster told his biographer that he had stayed up all night the evening before preparing his argument, and that "he thought he never on any occasion had so completely the free use of his faculties. . . . At nine A.M., after eleven hours of continuous intellectual effort, his brief was completed. He sent for the barber and was shaved; he took a very slight breakfast of tea and crackers; he looked over his papers to see if they were all in order; he read the morning journals to amuse and change his thoughts, and then he went into Court and made that grand argument which, as Judge [James Moore] Wayne said about twenty years afterward 'released every creek and river, every lake and harbor in our country from the interference of monopolies.'" George Ticknor Curtis, 1 *Life of Daniel Webster* 216–217 (New York: D. Appleton, 1870). (Justice Wayne's comment was in *The Passenger Cases*, 7 Howard 283, 437 [1849].)

law which had been erected, with his usual coolness and deliberation."[172] Emmet, a renowned orator in the Irish tradition who had been trained at Trinity College in Dublin, spoke for two days. His argument filled eighty pages in *Wheaton's Reports* and was studded with citations that sought to establish the concurrent power of the states to regulate commerce in the absence of congressional legislation. William Wirt, who made the final argument, surpassed both Webster and Emmet in eloquence. Chancellor George Bibb of Kentucky, who was in Court when Wirt spoke, called his summation "the greatest display that I have ever heard at the Bar since the days of Patrick Henry."[173]

The Court's decision did not come with the usual swiftness. On February 19, the week after the arguments concluded, Marshall fell on the ice and dislocated his shoulder. He was returning from dinner at the White House and slipped as he was stepping from his carriage, hitting his head and shoulder. He was unconscious for several minutes. A doctor was called, the shoulder reset, his head wrapped in bandages, and he was confined to his lodgings for the next two weeks.[174] "Old men do not get over sprains and hurts as quickly as young ones," he wrote Polly four days after the accident. "Although I feel no pain when perfectly still, yet I cannot get up and move about without difficulty, and cannot put on my coat. Of course I cannot go to Court." Marshall said he was making good progress. "The doctors say I mend a great deal faster than they expected. . . . The swelling has gone entirely down, and I have not the slightest appearance of fever."[175]

The chief justice, now in his sixty-ninth year, immediately became the object of the capital's sympathy. "All my friends have called to see me," he told Polly. "The President himself has visited me and expressed his wish to serve me in any manner that may be in his power." Even more surprising, said Marshall, all of the Cabinet wives had called on him, "some more than once, and have brought me more jelly than I can eat."

In a moment of tenderness, Marshall told Polly that he spent his time in bed thinking about their courtship.

> You must know then that I begin with the ball at Yorktown, and with the dinner of fish at your house the next day: I then retrace my visit to Yorktown, our splendid assembly at the Palace in Williamsburg, my visit to Richmond . . . my return the ensuing fall and the very welcome reception you gave me . . . our little tiffs and makings up, my feelings when Major Dick* was courting you, my trip to the cottage, the lock of hair, my visit again to Richmond the ensuing fall,

---

*Alexander Dick, an officer in the Virginia Line, was two years older than Marshall and had been a rival suitor of Polly's. Major Dick succeeded his father, Charles Dick, as superintendent of the gun factory in Fredericksburg in 1783 and died two years later. 5 *The Papers of John Marshall* 207, note 4 (Chapel Hill: University of North Carolina Press, 1985).

and all the thousand indescribable but deeply affecting instances of your affection or coldness which constituted for a time the happiness or misery of my life and will always be recollected with a degree of interest which can never be lost while recollection remains. Thus it is that I find amusement for those hours which I spend without company or books.

By the following week Marshall was able to sit at his desk, and, with his colleagues in agreement, he began to compose the decision in *Gibbons v. Ogden*. The tension in Washington mounted sharply. "Inquiries are hourly made respecting the anxiously-looked-for decision of the Supreme Court in this important case," wrote the *New York Statesman*.[176] On Monday, March 2, with the opinion completed, Marshall returned to Court, although still very much in pain. According to one correspondent,

> This morning, his Honor, Chief Justice Marshall appeared for the first time since his confinement . . . and took his seat on the bench. His return to his elevated and important station is welcomed by every member of the Bench and the Bar, and the whole community. The Court-room was thronged at an early hour in anticipation of what has taken place—the reading of the opinion of the Court in the great *Steamboat Case*.[177]

As soon as he was seated, Marshall began to read from his notes. His voice was feeble and barely audible in the crowded courtroom, and many persons collected near the bench to hear him.[178] His arm was still in a sling, and it was apparent that the accident had sapped his energy. As always in difficult states rights cases, he began by paying deference to the state involved. The state of New York believed its laws were constitutional, and that view was entitled to great respect. But respect did not mean that the Court was compelled to accept the state's opinion. The Constitution was at issue, and in interpreting it the justices must exercise "that independence which people of the United States expect from this department."[179] Marshall thereupon restated his view that the words of the founding document should be interpreted according to their normal meaning. "The enlightened patriots who framed our Constitution, and the people who adopted it, must be understood to have employed words in their natural sense, and to have intended what they said."

He turned to the commerce clause. "The words are, 'Congress shall have power to regulate commerce with foreign nations, and among the several states, and with the Indian tribes.'" What did "commerce" mean? What did *regulate* entail? And what was the significance of the word *among*? Marshall proceeded to define the words with such clarity that their meaning has been etched in the nation's law for almost two centuries. The seamless web of economic activity that characterizes the United States—the inability of the states to impose burdens on commerce or to favor their own products—traces directly to the holding of the Court in *Gibbons v. Ogden*. It is no exaggeration to say, as did Albert Beveridge, that few events in history have done more to knit the American people into a single nation than that decision.[180]

"Commerce," said Marshall, "is undoubtedly traffic, but it is something more: it is intercourse. It describes the commercial intercourse between nations, and parts of nations, in all its branches, and is regulated by prescribing rules for carrying on that intercourse. . . . Commerce among the States cannot stop at the boundary line of each State, but may be introduced into the interior." He went on to say that Congress's power to regulate commerce was complete and "may be exercised to its utmost extent, and acknowledges no limitations," other than those prescribed in the Constitution itself. The chief justice said it was obvious that the power to regulate commerce included the power to regulate navigation and that this power extended to the waters of every state in the Union. "The sole question is, can a State regulate commerce with foreign nations and among the several States, while Congress is regulating it?" Was there concurrent jurisdiction?

Before answering that question, Marshall laid out the limits of federal authority. It is evident from his phrasing that he was attempting to strike a balance. He distinguished between Congress's power to regulate interstate commerce and the residual authority of each state to enact "inspection laws, quarantine laws, health laws of every description, as well as laws for regulating the internal commerce of a State." Such laws, he said, "form a portion of that immense mass of legislation, which embraces every thing within the territory of a State not surrendered to the general government." Those laws might have an impact on commerce, but they should not be considered attempts to regulate commerce. "All experience shows, that the same measures, or measures scarcely distinguishable from each other, may flow from distinct powers; but this does not prove that the powers themselves are identical."

Clearly, then, the states had important residual powers which they were free to exercise.* If in so doing, however, they should clash with federal leg-

---

*Five years later, in *Willson v. Blackbird Creek Marsh Co.*, 2 Peters 245 (1829), Marshall explicitly recognized that state laws might affect interstate matters when issues of health were involved. In that case the Court held that a dam constructed under state authority could validly close a stream to interstate commerce because the dam had been erected as a health measure to drain the surrounding marshes. Such action, said Marshall, did not involve an attempt by the state to regulate

islation, Marshall said that it was "unequivocally manifest that Congress may control the State laws, so far as it may be necessary to control them, for the regulation of commerce." If New York's steamboat laws conflicted with an act of Congress, "it will be immaterial whether those laws were passed in virtue of a concurrent power to regulate commerce . . . or in virtue of their power to regulate their domestic trade and police." In both instances, said Marshall, the New York legislation must yield.

After examining the federal coasting act under which Gibbons's vessels were licensed and comparing it to the New York legislation that had granted the monopoly to Livingston and Fulton, Marshall held that the Empire State's statutes came "in direct collision" with the act of Congress and could not stand.† The stranglehold of the steamboat monopoly was overturned. The waterways of the United States—one of the prime means of transportation in the 1820s—were opened to competition. But Marshall was not finished. He concluded the opinion with a sharp denunciation of states rights extremists, who, he said, threatened the Union's survival.

> Powerful and ingenious minds, taking, as postulates, that the powers expressly granted to the government of the Union are to be contracted by construction into the narrowest possible compass, and that the original powers of the States are retained, if any possible construction will retain them . . . explain away the Constitution of our country, and leave it, a magnificent structure to look at, but totally unfit for use. They may so entangle and perplex the understanding, as to obscure principles which were before thought quite

---

commerce but reflected the exercise of the state's police powers and hence was not an invasion of the field granted to Congress. The state law, he said, was not "repugnant to the power to regulate commerce in its dormant state." 2 Peters 252. Presumably, if Congress had acted explicitly to forbid the dam, the federal law would have prevailed.

†Because of the conflict between the federal coasting act and the New York monopoly laws, Marshall did not directly address the question of whether the state enjoyed concurrent authority to regulate interstate commerce in the absence of congressional legislation. But he implied that it did not. Referring to the argument made by Webster, Marshall said, "It has been contended by counsel for the appellant, that, as the word, 'to regulate', implies . . . full power over the thing to be regulated, it excludes, necessarily, the action of all others that would perform the same operation on the same thing. . . . It produces a uniform whole, which is as much disturbed and deranged by changing what the regulating power designs to leave unregulated, as that on which it has operated. There is great force to this argument, and the Court is not satisfied that it has been refuted." 9 Wheaton 209.

In *Cooley v. Board of Wardens of the Port of Philadelphia*, 12 Howard 299 (1852), the Taney Court held that matters primarily local in scope could be regulated by the states in the absence of federal legislation but that once Congress acted, the federal law prevailed. This was an important element in what is known as "the Cooley Doctrine"—a pragmatic attempt by the Court to clarify the relationship between the national government and the states concerning the regulation of commerce.

plain, and induce doubts where, if the mind were to pursue its own course, none would be perceived.

Marshall did not refer to John Taylor of Caroline or to the Richmond Junto by name, but there is no doubt that these were his targets. Justice Johnson, who was still under fire in South Carolina for overturning the Negro Seamen Act, was equally concerned about the states rights clamor and added an uncompromising concurrence to Marshall's opinion. Taking a bolder stance than the chief justice, Johnson explicitly rejected the idea that the states enjoyed any power whatsoever to regulate commerce. With words similar to those he had used on circuit in *Elkison v. Deliesseline*, he said that Congress's power was exclusive and "carries with it the whole subject, leaving nothing for the states to act upon."[181]

Reaction to the Court's decision was overwhelmingly favorable. Throughout the country, Marshall's opinion was hailed as a breakthrough for free enterprise. With virtually no exceptions, the nation's press rejoiced at the destruction of the obnoxious steamboat monopoly. Many New York papers published the opinion in full. The *New York Evening Post* said that it would "command the assent of every impartial mind competent to embrace such a subject" and was "written with great clearness, perspicuity and, considering the importance of the subject, with great conciseness." Another said that it was "probably the strongest document in support of the Federal Government that has ever been issued." A third said the opinion "presents one of the most powerful efforts of the human mind that has ever been displayed from the bench of any Court." In New Jersey, the press hailed the breakup of "the unprincipled steamboat monopoly. The waters are now free." Newspapers in Kentucky, Georgia, and Missouri joined the chorus.[182] Even in South Carolina the holding was greeted with approval. "This decision will have an important bearing upon the navigation companies of New York, which have been brought into existence and pampered by the unnatural and unconstitutional measures adopted by the Legislature of the State," wrote the *Charleston Courier*.[183]

Negative reaction centered in Virginia, and even there it was moderate. John Randolph wrote that he did not object to the holding but that the chief justice had written too much.

No one admires more than I do the extraordinary powers of Marshall's mind; no one respects more his amiable deportment in private life. He is the most unpretending and unassuming of men. His abilities and his virtues render him an ornament not only to Virginia, but to our Nation. I cannot, however, help thinking that he was too long at the Bar before he ascended the Bench; and that, like our friend

T[azewell?], he had injured, by the indiscriminate defense of right or wrong, the tone of his perception . . . of truth or falsehood.[184]

The Richmond *Enquirer* called the opinion "too elaborate, too long, and travelling beyond the record." It warned that the decision, like *McCulloch* and *Cohens*, would eventually sweep aside the state governments.[185]

The effects of the decision were immediate. Steamboat navigation of American waters increased at an incredible rate.[186] *Niles Weekly Register* reported in November 1824 that the number of steamers plying New York waters had already jumped from six to forty-three. Of more long-term consequence, the opening of the Hudson River and Long Island Sound to the free passage of steamboats propelled the growth of New York as a commercial center. The Hudson was the gateway to the Erie Canal, and with it access to the Great Lakes and the territory beyond. New England manufacturing benefited as well, because it became cheap and easy to transport anthracite coal from Pennsylvania. But the political impact of the decision in *Gibbons v. Ogden* may have been even more important. Marshall's broad view of the commerce power represented a radical departure from the restricted notion of federal authority exemplified in President Monroe's veto of the Cumberland Road bill in 1822. It marked another step in the growth of national power and almost at once became a mighty weapon in the hands of such statesmen as Henry Clay and Daniel Webster, who favored projects requiring an extension of federal authority. In the words of Chief Justice Harlan Fiske Stone, writing more than 100 years after Marshall's decision, "it will be the judgment of history that the Commerce clause and the wise interpretation of it, perhaps more than any other contributing element, have united to bind the several states into a nation."[187]

On March 27, 1824, the Court adjourned, and Marshall returned to Richmond the next day.[188] He decided to travel by steamboat. He was no longer in pain, but he still could not use his arm and wanted to avoid the jostling of a two-day trip on the overland stage. The chief justice had never made the journey by steamer, and *Gibbons* had whetted his interest. Having broken the steamboat monopoly and having touted the advantages of steam navigation in his 1812 report on linking the James and Ohio Rivers, Marshall wanted to experience the marvel of moving upstream against a strong current. "I shall reach Richmond in the steam boat which comes up on Friday night," he wrote Polly. "I imagine the boat will not be up before nine o'clock at night, in which case I shall remain on it all night."[189] At the age of sixty-nine, and not fully recovered from a serious injury, the chief justice was as excited as a child at the opportunity to return home by steamboat.

20

The Chief Justice and Old Hickory

MARSHALL SPENT THE SPRING of 1824 at circuit court and in the summer worked sporadically at preparing George Washington's voluminous correspondence for publication.[1] That fall his attention turned to the upcoming visit of General Lafayette to Virginia. Earlier in the year, Congress had tendered an invitation to the marquis to visit the United States in conjunction with the fiftieth anniversary of American independence. Lafayette, who was in financial distress, accepted with alacrity and arrived in New York on August 15, 1824. His triumphal tour of the nation, which lasted more than a year, is without parallel in American history. He was universally greeted as the "Guest of the Nation," and local dignitaries and town corporations cheerfully picked up the bill for the lavish receptions that were held in his honor. At the conclusion of his visit, Congress voted him a much-needed grant of $200,000 and gave him a township of land in the West as a token of the nation's affection.[2]

After landing in New York, Lafayette turned northward and spent the remainder of August and early September touring New England. He arrived in Washington on September 12 and immediately went to Warrenton, in Fauquier county, where both Monroe and Marshall were summering. The first reception was a sumptuous dinner served outdoors under an arbor at the town tavern. Lafayette sat in the place of honor flanked by the president and the chief justice—both of whom had served under him at Valley Forge. Lafayette was sixty-seven, Monroe sixty-six, and Marshall sixty-nine. The president was honored by a toast for his "exalted merit and spotless integrity." Lafayette toasted "the old Virginia Line and their descendants in

Fauquier county." Then a toast was offered to Marshall, "the soldier, the statesman, the jurist."

Marshall rose to respond. "It would not be easy," he said, "to express my thanks for the kindness which I have experienced today. To be associated with the men at this table cannot fail to be highly gratifying." He nodded respectfully toward Lafayette: "one who relinquished all the pleasures and enjoyments which Europe could furnish to encounter the dangers and share the toils and privations which were the lot of all those who engaged in our struggle for independence." He then turned to Monroe, now finishing his eighth and final year as president. The warmth between the two was apparent. "I am proud to recognize one of my earliest associates; one with whom I have frequently acted in the most trying scenes; for whom I have felt, and still retain, the most affectionate and respected esteem, without a taint of that bitter spirit which has been too long the scourge of our country."

Marshall then addressed his friends and neighbors from Fauquier county who were at the banquet.

> I can never forget that this county was the residence of the revered author of my being, who continued to be your representative until his military character first, and his removal afterwards, made him ineligible; that in this county I first breathed the vital air; that in it my infancy was cradled and my youth reared up and encouraged; that in the first dawn of manhood I marched from it with the gallant young men of the day to that glorious conflict which gave independence to these states, and birth to this mighty nation. Here my affections as well as my interest still remain, and all my sons are planted among you.

Marshall closed with another toast: "To the people of Fauquier—Brave soldiers in time of war, good citizens in time of peace, and intelligent patriots at all times."[3]

In mid-October Lafayette attended the anniversary celebration of Cornwallis's surrender in Yorktown and then traveled to Norfolk, Williamsburg, and Richmond. Marshall and Secretary of War John C. Calhoun accompanied him.[4] In Richmond, Marshall was fêted along with Lafayette. The bands repeatedly broke into "Hail, Columbia," the old Federalist anthem, and Marshall presided over the various dinners given in Lafayette's honor. When the Frenchman toasted the state of Virginia, Marshall graciously responded with a toast dear to his heart: "To rational liberty—the cause of mankind. Its friends cannot despair when they behold its champions."[5] The highpoint of the celebrations took place on the steps of the state capitol, where a bust of the marquis was dedicated. Flanking the bust was an honor guard composed of the remaining veterans of the Virginia Line, headed by the chief justice. Marshall addressed Lafayette on their behalf.

He told Lafayette that his role was indelibly impressed in the memory of all Virginians. "In the bosoms of none is it more deeply engraved than in those of the men who stand before you. Some of us served under you in that memorable campaign; many in the course of the war. While duty required obedience, your conduct inspired confidence and love. Time, which has thinned our ranks, and enfeebled our bodies, has not impaired these feelings."[6] That evening Marshall hosted a private dinner for Lafayette at his house, and the following day the general departed with his entourage for Albemarle county and a reunion with Jefferson and Madison.[7]

For Marshall, Lafayette's visit evoked the spirit of the Revolution and the nation's founding. The chief justice was always awkward at social events, but he nevertheless retained his youthful enthusiasm for gala balls and formal banquets, and he delighted in the attention that was shown to the state's distinguished visitor. During the celebrations, he was especially taken with the beauty and charm of Eliza Lambert, a younger sister of Richmond's mayor, who had sung for Lafayette at a dinner hosted by the city at the Eagle Tavern. Marshall was so captivated by Eliza's singing that he immediately wrote her a poem to commemorate the evening[8]:

From the Chameleon
To the Mocking Bird

Where learnt you the notes of that soul melting measure?
Sweet mimic who taught you to carol that song?
From Eliza 'twas caught, whom e'en birds hear with pleasure,
As lightly she tripped the green meadow along.

O breathe them again while with rapture I listen,
Every beat of my heart is responsive to thee;
And my eyes to behold thee with ecstacy glisten,
With thy grey breast reclined on that high poplar tree.

It was not the sweet liquid note of the black bird,
Nor was it the partridges whistle so clear,
Nor was it the soft sounding lay of the blue bird.
With these sly deceiver you've cheated my ear.

Nor was it the call that deceived the young red breast,
Nor sweetest of all the shy woodlark in air,
But the song little minstrel of her that can sing best,
The sounds that so oft have delighted my ear.

Then come airy warbler, live near to my dwelling
And in circles around wave thy bright glossy wing,
Keep my heart thus forever with ecstacy swelling,
Oh, cheat me thus sweetly whenever you sing.

Did Marshall think of himself as a chameleon? He was always able to poke fun at his own caution and once wrote a letter to John Randolph in which he spoke of himself as a centipede who always had one foot "in contact with the subject on which he moves," compared with Randolph, who, like a gallant horseman, could clear at one leap both fence and ditch.[9] Was Marshall's poem to Eliza a love poem? If Marshall was attracted to Eliza, it is likely that his feelings were manifested vicariously and that nothing more passed between the two. Miss Lambert later had a relationship with Edgar Allan Poe, who is reported to have been enthralled by her beauty and her intellect.[10]

In November 1824 the country was caught up in another presidential election. This time there were four candidates, divided more or less along regional lines. John Quincy Adams, the secretary of state, was running as a moderate to succeed the moderate Monroe. He drew support primarily from the North. Andrew Jackson emerged as the candidate of popular democracy. His strength was concentrated in Pennsylvania, the uplands of the Carolinas, and the states bordering the Mississippi. Treasury secretary William Crawford, who had stepped aside for Monroe in 1816, was in the race as the candidate of the Old South; and Henry Clay vied with Jackson for support on the frontier. When the 261 electoral votes were counted, none of the candidates received a majority. Adams carried New York and New England with 84, Jackson stood first with 99, Crawford had 41, and Clay 37. That meant that for the second time in twenty-five years, the election would be thrown into the House of Representatives. As was his habit, Marshall took no part in the election and did not cast a ballot. He respected Adams, and he knew both Jackson and Crawford, but he had hoped against the odds that Clay would prevail.[11]

When the Court convened in February 1825, there were twenty-seven cases on the docket. Marshall reached Washington on the weekend of February 7–8, called immediately upon President Monroe,[12] and then wrote Polly of his arrival. "I am now sitting by a good fire in an excellent room, the same I occupied last year, scribbling to my beloved wife. Neither Judge Johnson nor Story has arrived, and our brother Todd I am told is so very unwell that we have reason to fear we shall never see him again. Story too has been sick, but is on the way and we look for him today." Marshall told Polly that the roads from Richmond had never been in better condition. "I reached Alexandria on Saturday evening before five, and have never before got in by daylight, seldom earlier than nine, and once or twice as late as eleven." As any caring husband might do, he thanked his wife for reminding him to wear his warm cloak. "I could not help congratulating myself on the comfort I enjoyed compared to the suffering I should have felt had I come without it."

Congress had been in session for almost a month when Marshall arrived, but it had not yet voted to elect a president. Under the Twelfth Amendment, which had been added to the Constitution after the confusion over Jefferson's election in 1801, the House of Representatives was to choose from among the top three candidates in the electoral college, each state again having one vote. With twenty-four states in the Union, the votes of thirteen were needed to win. Crawford, who had finished third, suffered a paralytic stroke before Congress met and was out of the running. That left Adams and Jackson. The hero of New Orleans had the solid support of eleven states but needed two more. Adams had seven states and needed six. Clay, who had been eliminated, controlled the votes of three states and was eagerly courted by both camps. James Buchanan was believed to have promised Clay the post of secretary of state on Jackson's behalf, and it was widely assumed that Adams had made the same offer. Clay, whose rivalry with Jackson was of long standing, threw his support to Adams. This left the New Englander three states short, and three states were still in doubt. Missouri and Illinois were each represented by one congressman, and were wavering. Both states had gone for Jackson in the election, but their representatives were believed to prefer Adams. Maryland, with a congressional delegation of nine, was divided four for Jackson, four for Adams, and one undecided. No one was quite sure how the state would vote. On Monday, February 9, when the issue finally came before the House, Maryland, by a majority of one congressman, voted for Adams. To the nation's amazement, John Quincy Adams was elected, thirteen states to eleven. Adams had picked up all six states that had not been initially committed and became the first minority president in the nation's history.

"You were probably as much surprised as I was to find that the President was elected on the first ballot," Marshall wrote to his brother James.[13] The chief justice attributed Adams's victory to Clay's supporters. Marshall told his brother that Adams needed support in the West and that he would likely bring Clay into his cabinet. When Adams did appoint Clay to the state department, Jackson's supporters were predictably furious. John Randolph called it a corrupt bargain: "the combination of the puritan with the black-leg." Clay challenged Randolph to a duel. Both fired at each other, and fortunately both missed. Such was the presidential transition in 1825.

Three days after Adams took office, Marshall sent Monroe a new edition of the first volume of the *Life of Washington*. He had revised the text and published it separately under the title A *History of the English Colonies in North America*.[14] In a rare sentimental mood, Marshall said the book was offered "as a mark of the affectionate recollections excited in the bosom of the author when he looks back to times long since gone by." Once again he praised Monroe's conduct as president.[15]

The 1825 term brought the issue of the African slave trade before the Marshall Court for the first time.[16] The case involved the *Antelope*, a slave ship intercepted off the southern coast of the United States by the revenue cutter *Dallas*. At the time of her capture, *Antelope* was flying the colors of Venezuela and was carrying a cargo of 281 Africans claimed by Portuguese and Spanish slavers. Congress had prohibited the importation of slaves into the United States in 1808,[17] and subsequent legislation had defined the slave trade as piracy and made participation by Americans punishable by death.[18] But the slave trade was not illegal in Spain, Portugal, or Venezuela, and the *Antelope* was taken in international waters. The question before the Court pertained to the disposition of the Africans found onboard. The United States, represented by Attorney General Wirt and Francis Scott Key, argued that the seizure of the *Antelope* was authorized by congressional statutes for the suppression of piracy, that the Africans had been lawfully brought into the country by the *Dallas*, and that they should be freed and returned to Africa.[19] Wirt called it a conflict between "a claim to freedom and a claim to property."[20] Counsel for the Spanish and Portuguese governments demanded restitution of the Africans, whom they said had been "acquired as property . . . in the regular course of legitimate commerce."[21] The case was argued for five days—one-sixth of the 1825 term—and attracted overflow audiences each day.

On March 16, two weeks after the arguments concluded, Marshall delivered the opinion of a unanimous Court. The chief justice castigated the slave trade; held that because it was contrary to natural law, it could be maintained only by positive law; recognized that it was permissible under existing usage of the law of nations; and, after weighing the respective claims of the United States, Spain, and Portugal, devised a formula that set 80 percent of the Africans free.[22] "That every man has a natural right to the fruits of his own labor, is generally admitted; and that no other person can rightfully deprive him of those fruits, and appropriate them against his will, seems to be the necessary result of this admission."[23]

Marshall said that although Congress had defined the slave trade as piracy, it could not prescribe the rules for other nations. Under international law, "the legality of the seizure of a vessel engaged in the slave trade depends on the law of the country to which the vessel belongs." Since the *Antelope* flew the flag of a country that permitted the slave trade, the vessel must be restored. That, said Marshall, was the principle involved.

Having established the general rule, Marshall turned to the specifics of the case. He said that the Portuguese claim to the Africans had not been proved, and the Spanish claim could be substantiated for only a small number. As a result, "all of the Africans now in possession of the marshal . . . which were brought in with the *Antelope*, except those which may be designated as the property of Spanish claimants, ought to be delivered up to the United States, to be disposed of according to law." Under Marshall's ruling, only thirty-nine Africans were subsequently identified as "Spanish" and sold into slavery; the remainder were set free and transported to Liberia.[24]

Marshall's decision in the *Antelope* reflects the approach he often took in highly contentious cases. The principle enunciated went in one direction, but the pragmatic application of that principle allowed the Court to arrive at a decision more in conformity with the natural justice of the case. In the *Antelope*, Marshall balanced his personal abhorrence of the slave trade with what he called "the mandate of the law." The strictures of international law were observed, but the results were not displeasing to those who opposed slavery. Equally important, the decision allowed the Court to speak with one voice on an issue that threatened to tear the nation apart. The formula Marshall adopted satisfied his slave-owning colleagues William Johnson and Bushrod Washington and did no violence to the strong antislavery views of Story and Smith Thompson.

Four years later, in the major case of *Boyce v. Anderson*,[25] Marshall addressed one of the most heated issues of the day: Was a slave a person or an article of merchandise? The question came before the Court after the drowning of several slaves in a steamboat accident.* If the slaves were considered freight, the carrier would have an absolute liability for their loss. If they were persons, the steamboat would be liable only if negligence could be proved. Much to the dismay of many southern slaveowners,[26] Marshall held that a slave was a person. Choosing his words with great deliberateness, the chief justice hit the issue head on: "A slave has volition, and has feelings which cannot be entirely disregarded. He cannot be stowed away as a common package. In the nature of things, and in his character, he resembles a passenger, not a package of goods."[27]

The issue of slavery itself never came before the Marshall Court. However, the chief justice's personal views were not complicated. He abhorred the practice, and as the years passed, he became increasingly concerned about its pernicious effects. Temperamentally, he rejected the radicalism of

---

*The slaves belonged to Robert Boyce and were traveling down the Mississippi on the steamboat *Teche* when the vessel caught fire and sank. The passengers, including the slaves, escaped to shore and were picked up by a small boat from the steamer *Washington*. As the boat neared the *Washington* it capsized and the slaves drowned.

the abolitionists. He thought the "malignant effects" of "insane fanaticism" would "defeat all practicable good by the pursuit of an unattainable object."[28] Yet he was equally repelled by the unrelenting antipathy of so many of his fellow Southerners to gradual change. Marshall expressed that antipathy in an 1826 letter to his old Massachusetts friend Timothy Pickering:

> I concur with your thinking that nothing portends more calamity and mischief to the southern states than their slave population; yet they seem to cherish the evil and to view with immovable prejudice and dislike every thing which may tend to diminish it. I do not wonder that they should resist any attempt . . . to interfere with the rights of property, but they have a feverish jealousy of measures which may do good without the hazard of harm that is, I think, very unwise.[29]

In a similar vein, Marshall wrote to Lafayette deploring the South's "jealousy" on the subject of slavery, which, he said, was a great impediment to any experiment that might lead to emancipation. "The disposition to expel slavery from our bosoms, or even to diminish the evil, does not, I think, gain strength in the South."[30] In another letter, Marshall lamented Virginia's lack of progress on the two principal problems confronting the state: internal improvements and slavery. "On the first, I despair. On the second we might do much if our unfortunate political prejudices did not restrain us from asking the aid of the federal government. As far as I can judge, that aid, if asked, would be freely and liberally given."[31]

Marshall was referring to proposals sponsored by Rufus King and others to use part of the proceeds from the sale of government land in the West to emancipate slaves and promote their immigration to Africa.[32] In his darker moments, he recognized the scheme was unlikely to be acted upon, and at times he despaired that slavery was "incurable but by convulsion."[33] Nevertheless, he believed that colonization provided the most effective solution.

Marshall's attachment to the idea of colonization was tenaciously held. In December 1816 he is reported to have made the hazardous winter journey from Richmond to Washington to attend the initial organizational meeting of the American Society for Colonizing the Free People of Color.[34] The society was the brainchild of the Reverend Robert Finley of New Jersey, Francis Scott Key, and Elias Caldwell, the veteran clerk of the Supreme Court. Speaker of the House Henry Clay presided at the meeting, and the attendees included John Randolph, Daniel Webster, and most of the lawyers from the Washington area who practiced before the Court. Bushrod Washington was elected the first president of the society, and the sixteen vice presidents included Clay, Secretary of the Treasury William Crawford, and Andrew Jackson.[35] In 1823 Marshall helped establish the Richmond-

Manchester Auxiliary to the society, and in 1825 he organized the first contingent of 105 Africans to sail from Norfolk to Liberia.[36]

But the society soon found itself at cross-purposes. Many believed its purpose was limited to the removal of free Africans—whom most slaveowners feared as a destabilizing influence. Others saw the society as a vehicle for emancipation. That dispute led Marshall in 1827 to found the independent Virginia Society for Colonization, and he served as its president and principal fund-raiser until his death.*[37] "I cannot entertain a doubt that Liberia is the best retreat that can be found for our people of color. The soil is good, and the colonist will receive a sufficient quantity for cultivation. Instruction in all religious and moral duties is carefully attended to, and the education of children is an object of primary solicitude with the Society."[38]

In 1833, when the British parliament abolished slavery in the remaining colonies, Marshall rejoiced that it might provide an example to the South. As one family member wrote, "He now saw hope for his beloved Virginia, which he had seen sinking lower and lower among the States. The cause was that work had become disreputable in a country where a degraded class is held to enforced labor. . . . Now there was hope, for he considered that in this act of the British the decree had gone forth against American slavery, and its doom was sealed."[39]

Aside from the *Antelope*, the 1825 term of the Supreme Court was routine. All twenty-seven cases on the docket were decided unanimously. Marshall spoke for the Court ten times, Story seven, Johnson five, Washington three, and Thompson two. There was occasional sniping in the halls of Congress and sporadic efforts to curtail the Court's authority, but its prestige had become so great that these efforts were doomed to failure.[40] Former critics of the Court now rallied to its defense. Congressman Philip Barbour of Virginia, who had argued vigorously against federal jurisdiction in *Cohens v. Virginia*, called the Court the repository of "the peace and tranquility of the Union." He dismissed charges that it was a danger to states rights. If, after forty years, the power of the Court had not been abused, the people "might reasonably expect that it would not be, hereafter."[41] Martin Van Buren, a perennial foe of judicial power, acknowledged that the justices possessed

---

*Marshall's views were effectively expressed in a letter of appreciation to an unknown donor: "Will you pardon me," he writes, "if I deem this a fit occasion to express my profound sense of your strenuous and continual exertions in the great cause of humanity—the restoration of the descendants of Africans in these United States to the land of their ancestors. No object unites more entirely in its favor those motives which actuate the Christian, the Philanthropist, and the Patriot; and you have promoted it not only by large pecuniary contributions, but by those laudable researches which may furnish inducements to the intelligent statesman to embark in an enterprize which promises great future advantages to his country. Go on sir,—assured of the approbation of your own heart, and of a great portion of the wise and the good." Addressee unknown, no date, Manuscript Collection, Princeton University Library.

"talents of the highest order and spotless integrity" and that "the uncommon man who now presides over the Court . . . is in all human probability the ablest Judge now sitting upon any Bench in the world."[42] A states rights South Carolina senator said that "the independence of the Judiciary is at the very basis of our institutions. . . . However high the tempest may blow, individuals may hear the calm and steady voice of the Judiciary warning them of their danger."[43] Attorney General William Wirt captured the mood of the country:

> The importance of the Court in the administration of the Federal Government begins to be generally understood and acknowledged. The local irritations at some of their decisions (as in Virginia and Kentucky for instance) are greatly overbalanced by the general approbation with which those same decisions have been received throughout the Union. If there are a few exasperated portions of our people who would be for narrowing the sphere of action of the Court and subduing its energies . . . , there is a far greater number of our countrymen who would wish to see it in the free and independent exercise of its constitutional powers, as the best means of preserving the Constitution itself.[44]

As for the chief justice, Wirt said, "I verily believe there is not a spark of vanity in his composition—unless it be that venial and hospitable nature which induces him to pride himself on giving his friends the best glass of Madeira in Virginia."[45]

Marshall spent the summer of 1825 revising the remainder of the *Life of Washington* for a new edition. He told Bushrod that it would be ready by winter, "should any printer be disposed to engage in publication. This however is a business which we cannot press."[46] Later he apologized to his colleague for being tardy in answering his mail. "I received your letter a few days past and ought immediately to have answered it, but when you reach my age you will find that when a man is engaged as I am at present, a thing postponed is very apt to slip the memory and to be longer neglected than it ought to be."[47] On circuit in Richmond that fall, Marshall was joined on the bench by his old friend George Hay, the longtime United States attorney for Virginia, whom Adams appointed to succeed the ailing St. George Tucker. Hay was the fourth district judge to serve with Marshall, and he held the post until his death in 1830.

The 1826 term of the Court commenced on Monday, February 6. Marshall left Richmond by stage early on the Friday before and arrived in Alexandria Saturday evening. On Sunday he wrote to Polly. "I am now in an excellent room with a good fire and am a day sooner than usual in Washington. My usual practice has been to remain a day in Alexandria, but I came on this morning from a desire to end my journey while the weather is good. Mr. Washington and Mr. Duvall are here, and we expect our brothers Story and Thompson today. Judge Johnson unfortunately took the course by way of Norfolk and cannot, in consequence of it, be here till Wednesday or Thursday. Mr. Todd is unable to perform the journey."[48]

As Marshall feared, Justice Todd, who had missed the 1824 and 1825 terms of the Court, was critically ill. He died a this home in Frankfort, Kentucky, on February 7, at the age of sixty-one. During his nineteen years on the Court, Todd wrote only fourteen opinions (eleven for the Court, two concurrences, and one dissent). But as a Jeffersonian appointee from Kentucky and linked by marriage to Madison, he provided important political balance, and he undoubtedly contributed in conference to the collective judgments that Marshall announced. Todd was an impressive man with a commanding physical presence who comported himself with quiet, amiable dignity. He was at his best on circuit in Kentucky.[49] His silent acquiescence in Marshall's opinions helped legitimize the decisions of the Court and added immeasurably to the prestige that the tribunal now enjoyed. To replace Todd, Adams sought another Kentuckian, and turned to the forty-nine-year-old Robert Trimble, who for the last nine years had been the United States district judge for the state. Trimble had repeatedly come under fire in Kentucky for his holdings in support of national authority. He was the first federal court judge named to the Bench and was also John Quincy Adams's only appointee to the Court. He was confirmed by the Senate 27–5 on May 9, 1826 (Senator John Rowan of Kentucky voted against), and took his seat the following year.[50] Trimble served on the Court for only two years and died of "malignant bilious fever" in 1828.[51]

Todd's death cast a pall over the 1826 term of the Court.[52] One week into the term, Marshall wrote Polly that "I am settled down in my old habits as regularly as if I was still on the right side of seventy. I get up as early as ever, take my walk of three miles by seven, think of you, and then set down to business." Marshall said he had a bad case of influenza, but was recovering. "If you had no other reason to know how old I am, you would be reminded of it by my dwelling on this trifling indisposition."

Despite Todd's death, the social scene in Washington remained buoyant. Marshall said he had received "three invitations for evening parties this week. If you were here and would go with me, I am not sure that my influenza or court business would keep me so constantly within doors, but as it is I do not feast my eyes with gazing at the numerous belles who flock to this place during the winters."[53] In March Marshall told Polly that he had attended a White House reception given by Mrs. Adams. The crowd, he said, was enormous, "but I saw very few there whom I know and fewer still in whom I take any interest. A person as old as I am feels that his home is his place of most comfort, and his old wife the companion in the world in whose society he is most happy."[54]

Like all of his colleagues, Marshall was feeling his age. Livingston and Todd were gone. Bushrod Washington, the senior justice, had been on the Court twenty-eight years; Marshall, twenty-five; William Johnson, twenty-two; Story and Duvall, fifteen. Duvall's hearing had failed and, at seventy-three, the oldest of the justices, he walked with difficulty. Justice Washington's health was poor, and Johnson and Story suffered periodically from influenza. But the camaraderie and affection among the justices was as strong as ever. Marshall was the shepherd of the flock. He was closest to Washington and Story, but he had great affection for Johnson, as well.[55]

The harmony of the Court was reflected in its decisions. In 1826, for the third time during Marshall's tenure as chief justice—and for the second year in succession—all of the judgments were unanimous. Marshall wrote eleven, two were *per curiam*, and the remainder were parceled out. *Niles Weekly Register*, which had criticized the Court mercilessly after the decision in *McCulloch v. Maryland*, noted benignly that "we have often thought that no person could behold this venerable body without profound respect for the virtue and talents concentrated on its bench, and with a degree of confidence that, as there must be some power in every government having final effect, it could hardly be vested anywhere more safely than in the Supreme Court, as at present filled."[56]

Later that spring Marshall accepted Harvard professor Jared Sparks's offer to edit the papers of George Washington. Marshall was caught up in preparing a new edition of his own biography of the first president, and he recognized the monumental task that editing the papers entailed. Story acted as a go-between in the negotiations, and the ultimate arrangement, according to which Marshall and Bushrod would share half the royalties, delighted the chief justice. Marshall wrote Sparks that he was "gratified at the expectation of seeing General Washington's works ushered to the world by a gentleman whose literary reputation ensures full justice to his memory."[57]

In April Sparks visited Marshall in Richmond. His account captures the essence of the chief justice in his seventy-first year:

Called on Chief Justice Marshall; entered his yard through a broken wooden gate, fastened by a leather strap and opened with some difficulty, rang, and an old lady came to the door. I asked if Judge Marshall was at home. "No," said she, "he is not in the house; he may be in the office," and pointed to a small brick building in one corner of the yard.

I knocked at the door, and it was opened by a tall, venerable-looking man, dressed with extreme plainness, and having an air of affability in his manners. I introduced myself as the person who had just received a letter from him concerning General Washington's letters, and he immediately entered into conversation on that subject. He appeared to think favorably of my project, but intimated that all the papers were entirely at the disposal of Judge Washington. He said that he had read with care all General Washington's letters in the copies left by him, and intimated that a selection only could with propriety be printed, as there was in many of them a repetition, not only of ideas, but of language. This was a necessary consequence of his writing to so many persons on the same subjects, and nearly at the same time. . . .

Such and other things were the topics of conversation, till the short hour of a ceremonious visit had run out. I retired much pleased with the urbanity and kindly manners of the Chief Justice. There is consistency in all things about him,—his house, grounds, office, himself, bear marks of a primitive simplicity and plainness rarely to be seen combined.[58]

Marshall continued his good-natured correspondence with Story. "I sent you by the *General Jackson* (because the name must render every part of its cargo valuable in your estimation) a small cask of hams which I hope you will find tolerably good in themselves. They are packed in hickory ashes; and our Ladies, who are skilful in the management of their Hams, say that they must be taken out on their arrival and put in a cool dry place as the hickory ashes may probably become lye on the voyage."[59]

One issue that particularly vexed Marshall was the refusal of Congress to reimburse James Monroe for the expenses he had incurred while representing the United States in London and Paris before the War of 1812. As secretary of state and then as president, Monroe was not able to pursue his claims, and when he filed for repayment after he left office, Congress turned a deaf ear.[60] The former president, who was deeply in debt and who was seeking all the support he could muster, sent Marshall an itemized accounting of his claim. Forty years earlier, when they were both serving in the House of Delegates, Marshall had assisted Monroe with his finances, and he now commiserated with his old friend. "I am greatly flattered by your letter and the accompanying documents," Marshall replied. "There was undoutedly great reason for your requesting such a final settlement . . . and in making that settlement I think you have a right to expect that the justice of your country will not be stinted."[61] In May of 1826, when Congress still had not acted, Marshall chaired a testimonial dinner for Monroe's benefit at the Eagle Tavern.[62]

Another elder statesman was in even more serious financial straits. By 1826 Thomas Jefferson was effectively bankrupt. His estates were heavily mortgaged, and his debts exceeded $100,000.[63] Jefferson appealed to the legislature for permission to dispose of Monticello in a public lottery. Monroe, despite his own financial embarrassment, offered support, and so did Marshall. Dumas Malone, Jefferson's distinguished biographer, reports that "expressions of sympathy and appreciation by friends and former foes were a balm to Jefferson's spirit."[64] In addition to the lottery, numerous cities formed committees to raise subscriptions, "not over $5 each," for the former president's benefit. Marshall chaired the Richmond committee, and after Mr. Jefferson's death on July 4, he served on the committee of arrangements for a day of public mourning.[65] Marshall's opinion of Jefferson's politics had not changed. But he did not begrudge the dignity to which he felt the former president was entitled.

That fall Marshall proved that the Chief Justice of the United States is as prone to social faux pas as the father of any son anticipating marriage. Edward Marshall, now in his last year at Harvard, had met a young woman named Harriet Fay through Justice Story. Miss Fay was the daughter of Story's brother-in-law, Judge Samuel Fay, a probate judge in Middlesex county and a long-serving member of Harvard's Board of Overseers. The Fays were Boston aristocracy, their lineage as distinguished as the Amblers or the Randolphs.*[66] Edward wrote Marshall that he and Harriet were in love, that he had proposed marriage, and that his proposal had been accepted. Edward indicated they would soon be married, and implied that he had received Judge Fay's permission.

Marshall did not know Judge Fay, but he decided to write him nonetheless to assure him that his daughter would be well received. "I had feared that the almost entire separation of Miss Fay from her natural friends and all the companions of her youth would be too great a sacrifice to be made, and, if made, would produce permanent unhappiness. That she has been induced to make it cheerfully is the best proof of that sincere affection which

---

*Dr. Oliver Wendell Holmes, who was four years younger than Edward Marshall, was one of many young men captivated by Harriet Fay. He described her in an article in the *Atlantic Monthly*:

> Among my schoolmates at the Port School was a young girl of singular loveliness. I once before referred to her as "the golden blond," but did not trust myself to describe her charms. The day of her appearance in the school was almost as much of a revelation to us boys as the appearance of Miranda was to Caliban. Her abounding natural curls were so full of sunshine, her skin was so delicately white, her smile and her voice were so all-subduing, that half our heads were turned. Her fascinations were everywhere confessed a few years afterwards; and when I last met her, though she said she was a grandmother, I questioned her statement, for her winning looks and ways would still have made her admired in any company.

Oliver Wendell Holmes, "Cinders from the Ashes," 23 *Atlantic Monthly* 115–123 (January 1869).

is, I am persuaded, when mutual, the never failing source of felicity to those who are united under its influence." Marshall said that Harriet "will be received by [Edward's] mother and myself as our own daughter, and with that parental affection which is the best though an inadequate substitute for the deep loss she will sustain in parting from Mrs. Fay and yourself."[67]

Judge Fay's reply has not survived, but it arrived in Richmond on October 14, 1826. From Marshall's response, it is obvious that he had made a serious error. Not only had Edward not spoken with Fay, but the judge clearly disapproved of the marriage and quite possibly of Edward himself. The fact that Judge Fay had eloped with Harriet's mother in 1801 did not moderate his New England scorn.[68] Marshall was chagrined at his own presumptuousness, yet he was not entirely sympathetic with the judge. The following day he dispatched a formal apology. It is written with the care and precision (there are numerous strike-overs and rephrasings) that Marshall ordinarily reserved for constitutional decisions of the first magnitude. His poignant concern for the feelings of the young couple is written between the lines. "It must have appeared very strange," he told Fay, "that while your objections to a connection between our families remained immovable, I should treat it as an affair already arranged." The chief justice said he had written "under a total misunderstanding of the actual state of things. I have not seen Edward since May; but his letters to his mother and myself . . . state his reception with delight, and dwell on his expected union with the lady of his choice, in the language of a young man who sees nothing but felicity before him." Marshall acknowledged that Edward had not written explicitly that Fay had given his approval,

> but everything he said implied that all obstacles were removed, and that the event was certain, though the time was not fixed. Not doubting that you had viewed the attachment, which I then supposed to be mutual, between our children, with as much indulgence as myself, my heart told me that . . . it could not be displeasing to a Father totally unacquainted with the connections of the gentleman who was to marry his daughter, and to remove her a great distance from her friends, to be assured that she would be received with cordial and tender affection by the family into which she was about to enter.

Marshall pointedly told Fay that he hoped Edward had been informed of the judge's decision and that it had been made "with the approbation of Mrs. and Miss Fay." Harriet apparently was seriously ill, and the chief justice closed with a wish for her recovery. "It is not an empty compliment when I say that I am grieved to hear of the feeble state of health in which

Miss Fay finds herself. I have accustomed myself to take an interest in what concerns her which I cannot instantly dismiss, and shall enquire respecting her health with the sincere wish to hear that the threatening and obstinate symptoms of which you speak have yielded to medicine and exercise."[69]

Marshall did not correspond with Story about the episode, but that fall he did write to chastise his friend for a speech he had given at Harvard. Story had presented to the Phi Beta Kappa society a speech entitled "Literary Condition of the Age," and he had sent the chief justice a copy. "I have read it with real pleasure," wrote Marshall,

> and am particularly gratified with your eulogy on the ladies. It is a matter of great satisfaction to me to find another Judge, who, though not as old as myself, thinks justly of the fair sex, and commits his sentiments to print. I was a little mortified, however, to find that you had not admitted the name of Miss [Jane] Austen into your list of favorites. I had just finished reading her novels when I received your discourse, and was so much pleased with them that I looked in it for her name, and was rather disappointed at not finding it. . . . I count on your making some apology for this omission.[70]

Marshall, who had been reared on the works of Homer and Alexander Pope, found genuine pleasure in literature and spent many hours, particularly in the evenings, reading aloud to Polly.[71] He was especially fond of the works of Sir Walter Scott and the English poets.[72] Several years later he told Story that after his retirement he planned "to read nothing but novels and poetry."[73] Indeed, the fact that Marshall was reading the novels of Jane Austen at the time he wrote to Judge Fay seems strikingly appropriate, for the episode has a distinctly Austenian quality about it.[74]

The 1827 term of the Supreme Court clarified two important constitutional issues, one relating to the commerce clause, the other to state bankruptcy legislation. In *Brown v. Maryland*,[75] dealing once again with the commerce clause, the Court struck down a Maryland statute that imposed a $50 license tax on importers of foreign goods. Such measures, said Marshall, interfered with the authority of the federal government to regulate commerce and violated the Constitution's prohibition against state import duties.

> The oppressed and degraded [condition] of commerce previous to the adoption of the Constitution can scarcely be forgotten. . . . It may be doubted whether any of the evils proceeding from the feebleness of the federal government contributed more to that great revolution which introduced the present system, than the deep and general conviction that commerce ought to be regulated by Con-

gress. It is not, therefore, [a] matter of surprise that the grant should be as extensive as the mischief, and should comprehend all foreign commerce and commerce among the states.[76]

The second case, *Ogden v. Saunders*,[77] concerned state bankruptcy legislation. Eight years earlier, in *Sturgis v. Crowninshield*, the Court had rejected the application of New York's insolvency law to contracts entered into before the act was passed. But the effect of the law on debts contracted after its passage remained unclear. This latter issue had first come before the Court in 1824 when George Ogden sought to discharge his debt to John Saunders. Ogden was a citizen of New York; Saunders, a citizen of Kentucky. Their contract had been made after the New York law was adopted. The case was argued March 3–4, 1824. Justice Todd was absent, and in conference the remaining justices divided three to three. Marshall, Story, and Duvall believed that federal bankruptcy jurisdiction was exclusive and that all such state legislation violated the contract clause of the Constitution. That interpretation would have closed the loophole left open in *Sturgis v. Crowninshield*. Justices Washington, Johnson, and Thompson, on the other hand, thought the New York legislation was valid. Congress had not yet acted in the matter, and the parties to the contract had notice of the state's insolvency law when their agreement was entered into. With the Court divided evenly, the justices elected to carry the case over and await Todd's return. Todd missed the next two terms, however, and it was not until 1827 that Trimble took his seat.

With the Court once more at full strength, the case (along with several similar ones from other states) was reargued. Daniel Webster and Henry Wheaton appeared on behalf of those who claimed the state laws were unconstitutional. They were opposed by William Wirt, Edward Livingston, and David Ogden. On February 18, 1827, the Court announced its decision, and for the first and only time during his tenure as chief justice, Marshall found himself in dissent on a constitutional issue.* Trimble agreed with Washington, Johnson, and Thompson that the state laws did not impair the

---

*Marshall's lengthy dissent in *Ogden* was most likely written shortly after the case was argued in 1824 and, anticipating Todd's return, was intended to be the opinion of the Court. In it, Marshall made clear that the federal issue was controlling. "When we consider the nature of our Union; that it is intended to make us, in a great measure, one people, as to commercial objects; that, so far as respects the intercommunication of individuals, the lines of separation between the States are, in many respects, obliterated; it would not be a matter of surprise, if on the delicate subjects of contracts once formed, the interference of State legislation should be greatly abridged, or entirely forbidden." He also spoke at length about the sanctity of contract, which, he said, "results from the right which every man retains to acquire property, to dispose of that property according to his own judgment, and to pledge himself for a future act. *These rights are not given by society, but are brought into it.*" 12 Wheaton 346. Emphasis added.

obligation of contract. That disposed of the companion cases to *Ogden v. Saunders* and, in effect, gave the states authority to enact bankruptcy legislation until Congress entered the field. The issue in *Ogden* was more complicated since it involved a contract with an out-of-state citizen. That question was reargued, and Justice Johnson shifted sides. On the larger federal issue that was now posed, the South Carolinian agreed with Marshall, Story, and Duvall that the New York law was invalid. Speaking for the new majority, Johnson said that "When the states pass beyond their own limits and act upon the rights of citizens of other states, there arises a conflict of sovereign power, and a collision with the judicial powers granted to the United States which render the exercise of such a power incompatible with the rights of other states and with the Constitution of the United States."[78] In effect, Marshall lost the principle that all state bankruptcy legislation was unconstitutional, but with Johnson's concurrence the impact of the decision was restricted. Overall, the 1827 term was one of the Court's most productive. The justices considered seventy-six cases and rendered decisions in forty-seven, of which forty-four were unanimous.[79]

Marshall was reminded that term of the ephemeral nature of political alliances. Shortly after the Court met he received a letter from his cousin and lifelong friend, Humphrey Marshall, the former United States Senator from Kentucky. Humphrey sought the chief justice's assistance in his son's efforts to become the United States attorney for the state. "I know he is backward," said Humphrey, but "having myself suffered by the ill-will of this state towards the former President Adams, I should feel some compensation were his son, to place mine, in a situation where he could serve both his country and himself." What was surprising was that the former senator who had once fought a celebrated duel with Henry Clay was now closely aligned with the great commoner. "In truth," he wrote, "was now Mr. Clay in the cabinet . . . I should have no expectation of [my son] getting the appointment."[80]

Marshall forwarded Humphrey's letter to Clay with a lukewarm recommendation. "I have much repugnance to solicit for my friends, especially where the office is in a different state from that in which I reside, and shall not venture to make an application to the President; but if you think the communication of the enclosed letter can be of any service to my Nephew [Thomas A. Marshall] and are yourself inclined to favour his pretensions, you will oblige me by laying it before him."[81]

If Marshall was uneasy about helping his friends and relatives secure government positions, he was more than eager to assist former comrades of the Virginia Line. That summer in Richmond he happened to meet his old friend from Culpeper county, Captain Philip Slaughter. Slaughter had served with Marshall in the Culpeper minutemen and then in the Eleventh Virginia regiment under Colonel Daniel Morgan. They had fought beside each other at Great Bridge, Brandywine, and Germantown, and had shared a cabin at Valley Forge. Slaughter was down on his luck. Marshall took him home and, after several days, learned that he was in town to borrow money from a moneylender to save his farm from foreclosure.[82] Marshall asked how much he needed, and Slaughter said $3,000. The chief justice walked across the yard to his office, wrote out a check for that amount, and gave it to his old friend. Slaughter refused to take it, but Marshall insisted. "Secure it to my grandchildren and I will be satisfied."[83] Later in the summer when Slaughter sent Marshall a check for $100 to apply to the loan, the chief justice returned it. "I know you too well to feel the slightest apprehension concerning the debt. . . . I have only to request that you will not precipitate a sale [of your farm] on disadvantageous terms."[84] Marshall said nothing of the loan to Polly or his children. In his will, he devised the deed-in-trust that Slaughter had given him to his son James, and from James it passed to Marshall's grandson John, who collected the money after Philip Slaughter's death.[85]

The 1828 term of the Court was uneventful. The justices rendered decisions in fifty-five cases, all but two of which were unanimous.[86] The nature of the cases coming before the Court was changing—the number of prize and admiralty cases decreased while those relating to the nation's economic development increased substantially. But there were no cases of constitutional significance.[87] Despite his age, or perhaps because of it, Marshall was at the height of his intellectual powers. Shortly after the 1828 term, Attorney General William Wirt wrote a friend that Marshall's mind was on "a scale of an Atlantic Ocean" while the minds around him "were mere ponds in comparison. To hear that man in full stretch is to feel annihilated."[88]

Inevitably, the chief justice's attention drifted to the upcoming presidential election. Just before Christmas he had written pessimistically to Story about the uncontrollable forces pulling the nation apart.

> I begin to doubt whether it will long be practicable peaceably to elect a chief magistrate possessing the powers which the Constitution confers on the President of the United States, or such powers as are necessary for the government of this great country with due regard for its essential interests. I begin to fear that our Constitution is not doomed to be so long lived as its real friends have hoped. What may follow sets conjecture at defiance. I shall not live to witness and bewail the consequences of those furious passions which seem to belong to man.[89]

Marshall was especially concerned about the rabid partisanship of Jackson's supporters, the vituperative attacks they leveled at Adams and Clay, and the extent to which presidential politics had engulfed the work of Congress. "It is infinitely to be deplored that the contests concerning the election of the President, and the factions they generate, should mingle themselves with the legislation of the country," he wrote to Lafayette. "I fear, however, it is a disease for which no remedy is attainable."[90]

In private, Marshall made no secret of his opposition to Jackson. Nevertheless, he was embarrassed when the *Marylander*, a Democratic paper in Baltimore, published an item quoting him as saying that although he had not voted in twenty years, he intended to this time. "Should Jackson be elected, I should look upon the government as virtually dissolved."[91] The comment was republished widely, and Marshall felt it necessary to respond. Writing to John Pleasants, publisher of the Richmond *Whig and Advertizer*, the chief justice said

> you are authorized to declare that the *Marylander* has been misinformed. I admit having said in private that, though I had not voted since the establishment of the general ticket system [in Virginia], and had believed that I never should vote during its continuance, I might probably depart from my resolution in this instance from the strong sense I felt of the injustice of the charges of corruption against the president and secretary of state. I never did use the other expression ascribed to me.[92]

Henry Clay was touched by Marshall's rejoinder and wrote immediately to express his appreciation. "I know that you were moved by your well known love of truth and justice, but that does not abate the force of my personal obligation to you. Indeed, I regret that it became necessary that you should have to say publicly one word on the agitating topic of the day, because it will subject you to a part of that abuse which is indiscriminately applied to . . . everything standing in the way of the elevation of a certain individual."[93]

Story also wrote to express his concern.[94] Marshall replied that he was "a good deal provoked at the publication in the *Marylander*, not because I have any objection to its being known that my private judgment is in favor of the reelection of Mr. Adams, but because I have great objections to being represented in the character of a furious partisan. Intemperate language does not become my age or office and is foreign to my disposition and habits."[95]

Late that summer Justice Trimble died at his home in Paris, Kentucky. He had been on the Court only two years yet had written sixteen opinions. Almost immediately a bitter political contest developed over his replacement. That contest was compounded by Jackson's decisive victory over Adams in November.[96] Democrats felt the vacancy should be left to Jackson to fill; Whigs urged Adams to send his own appointee to the Senate while there was still time. Clay, who was concerned that Adams nominate someone, and who was particularly interested that another Kentuckian be named, wrote to Marshall urging the appointment of ex-senator John J. Crittenden.[97] Crittenden was a distinguished lawyer, a prominent Whig, and had been appointed by Adams to be the United States attorney for Kentucky (over Humphrey Marshall's son). Clay asked the chief justice if he would recommend Crittenden to the president.

Marshall replied on November 20. "I need not say how deeply I regret the loss of Judge Trimble. He was distinguished for sound sense, uprightness of intention, and legal knowledge. His superior cannot be found. I wish we may find his equal." Marshall said he was deeply interested in who would replace Trimble and that he assumed Adams would make the appointment. But he told Clay that he did not know Crittenden and did not believe he should suggest anyone to the president unless he was asked. "It has the appearance of assuming more than I am willing to assume."[98] Nevertheless, Marshall acknowledged that Crittenden was highly regarded. "Were I myself to designate the successor of Mr. Trimble, I do not know the man I could prefer to him." Clay had what he wanted. He showed Marshall's letter to John Quincy Adams, who promptly sent Crittenden's name forward.[99]

Did Clay take advantage of the chief justice's frankness? That is one possible interpretation. But Marshall was not a political novice, and he would have known that his comments were unlikely to remain confidential. Perhaps he was taking advantage of Clay's inquiry to reinforce the chances of someone he thought desirable. In any event, the matter came to naught, as the Senate voted 23–17 to defer the nomination until Jackson was inaugurated.

In 1829, because of the increasing volume of litigation, the beginning of the Court term was moved forward to the second Monday in January. There was some difficulty, however, assembling a quorum. On February 1, Marshall wrote Polly that "our sick Judges have at length arrived and we are as busy as men can be.* I do not walk as far as I formerly did, but I still keep up the practice of walking in the morning." As was always the case after a presidential election, the capital was focused on the victor's arrival, and Marshall was no exception. "General Jackson is expected in the city within a fortnight, and is to put up in this house," he told Polly. "I shall of course wait on him. It is said that he feels the loss of Mrs. Jackson very seriously. It

---

*Justices Duvall and Thompson missed the first three weeks of the 1829 term because of illness, and Justice Johnson was delayed because of the injuries he sustained when his stagecoach overturned on a bad stretch of a road.

would be strange if he did not. A man who at his age [Jackson was sixty-one] loses a good wife loses a friend whose place cannot be supplanted."[100] The chief justice felt Jackson's loss keenly. Polly's health had continued to deteriorate, and Marshall had just learned that his daughter-in-law Margaret, the wife of his son James, had died. She was thirty-seven and left seven children, the youngest three years old. It was in the context of a shared sadness that Marshall administered the oath of office to Jackson on March 4. A vast throng, estimated at over 15,000, witnessed the ceremony. Marshall wrote to Polly afterward that "people have flocked to Washington from every quarter of the United States. . . . A great ball was given at night to celebrate the election. I of course did not attend it."[101]

Two days after the inauguration, Jackson startled his more clamorous supporters by nominating John McLean of Ohio to fill Trimble's seat on the Court. McLean was a moderate Whig who had served effectively as postmaster general under both Monroe and Adams. Before that he had been a judge on the Ohio supreme court. A political rival of Henry Clay, he had remained on good terms with Jackson throughout the 1828 campaign, and it was widely believed that he harbored presidential ambitions four years hence. He was also known to be opposed to the political spoils system. So long as he remained in the cabinet, it would be impossible to restaff the post office with reliable Democrats. By elevating McLean, Jackson demonstrated the adroitness that made him so formidable. With one stroke, he was shelving a potential presidential opponent,[102] opening the post office to his supporters, rewarding a foe of his old enemy Henry Clay, and disarming the Whigs with a judicial appointment they could only applaud.[103] Marshall, who had feared that Jackson might name one of his more radical followers (Senator John Rowan of Kentucky had been mentioned), was delighted. He was even more pleased when Jackson did not withdraw the nomination of Joseph Hopkinson, an old Federalist and old friend of Marshall's, to be United States district judge in Pennsylvania. "The President it is said, is not himself inclined to proscription," Marshall wrote Hopkinson. "This I am inclined to believe, because I think a President of the United States will always be more disposed to conciliate than exasperate; and must always feel some reluctance at inflicting injury."[104]

McLean was confirmed unanimously March 7, 1829, but did not take his seat until the following year. Ultimately, he would serve on the Court for thirty-two years and would hew closely to the nationalist position Marshall had staked out.[105] Apart from Jackson's inauguration and the appointment of McLean, the 1829 term of the Court was routine. The six justices present rendered decisions in forty-five cases, forty-four of which were unanimous. Marshall wrote seventeen opinions for the Court, and the others were distributed more or less equally.[106]

That spring Marshall was approached by the citizens of Richmond to represent the city in Virginia's upcoming constitutional convention. The spirit of Jacksonian democracy had swept the country, and in many states the pressure for reform was irresistible. Virginia's constitution, written in 1776, proved particularly vulnerable. It restricted suffrage to the male owners of real property, counted slaves in apportioning representation in the legislature, and ensured that the property-owning elite of the eastern counties would enjoy perpetual political control. The western counties had for years agitated for reform, and in 1829 the legislature reluctantly acquiesced, issuing the call for a constitutional convention to meet in Richmond in October.

Marshall initially rejected entreaties that he serve as a delegate.[107] It was not because he was Chief Justice of the United States. That was no impediment. But at seventy-four, he was afraid he was too old—*"non sum qualis eram* [I am not what I once was]."[108] Eventually he yielded. "I am almost ashamed of my weakness and irresolution," he wrote Story. "I have acted like a girl addressed by a gentleman she does not positively dislike, but is unwilling to marry. She is sure to yield to the advice and persuasion of her friends."[109] Virginia's two ex-presidents, Madison and Monroe, surrendered to similar pressures. Madison was a spry seventy-eight; Monroe was much less so at seventy-one. The three elder statesmen not only added dignity to the proceedings but provided a powerful force for compromise, adding their wisdom and prestige to bring the eastern and western counties together.

The convention assembled in the chamber of the House of Delegates, Monday, October 5, 1829. The evening before, Marshall entertained the two ex-presidents at a quiet dinner in his home. Madison was accompanied by his wife Dolley, who was still as charming and radiant as when she presided over Washington society as first lady.[110] Monroe, a widower, was accompanied by his daughter, Eliza Hay—who had always been one of Marshall's favorites. Polly, now dreadfully weak, came downstairs to receive her guests but asked to be excused shortly afterward.[111] The next morning the three elder statesmen led the procession of delegates into the House chamber. As the oldest delegate present, Madison assumed the chair and, by prearrangement, moved that Monroe be elected the convention's president.* Marshall seconded the nomination, and Monroe was installed by acclamation.

---

*Because the work of the convention was to be conducted in committee of the whole, the post of president was largely honorific. Madison and Marshall, being older than Monroe, were offered the position first, and both declined. Monroe, whose health was failing, was persuaded to take the post, but he was forced to resign in early December when he became ill. The committee of the whole was chaired by Philip Barbour, who thereupon assumed the president's post, as well. Harry Ammon, *James Monroe: The Quest for National Identity* 564 (Charlottesville: University Press of Virginia, 1990).

The convention lasted fourteen weeks. Madison chaired the committee on legislation; Marshall, the committee on the judiciary. Both men attended the convention every day, sitting next to each other on the front bench. After each session the two could be seen walking down the hill to Marshall's house, which became a focal point for entertaining delegates of all persuasions. Madison, Monroe, Governor William Giles, John Randolph, Littleton Tazewell, and Philip Barbour, regardless of their political disagreements, met often at the chief justice's table and partook liberally of his food and Madeira.[112] One convention delegate reported seeing Marshall at the market before sunrise, wearing a plain black suit, "stalking along between rows of meat and vegetables, catering for his household."[113]

The most divisive issues at the convention involved suffrage and legislative apportionment. Suffrage fell under Marshall's committee; apportionment under Madison's. The western delegates pressed for universal manhood suffrage, while conservatives from the East sought to retain Virginia's freehold property qualification—ownership of fifty acres of unimproved land or twenty-five acres with a house on it. After weeks of debate, the convention was deadlocked. Marshall, who favored the freehold requirement, and Madison, who stopped short of advocating universal suffrage, then proposed a compromise, which the convention accepted. At their recommendation, the right to vote was extended to all householders and heads of households who paid taxes. The freehold requirement was abolished, but a moderate property qualification remained.[114]

The issue of apportionment proved more intractable. Delegates from the West insisted that only whites be enumerated; those from the East demanded that slaves continue to be counted. Again the convention deadlocked, and this time it was Madison, supported by Marshall, who proposed the compromise: apportion the lower house of the legislature based on the state's white population, but use the federal formula of counting slaves as three-fifths of a person in apportioning the Senate. Because of the unyielding opposition of the state's slaveowners, the compromise was rejected, and the convention bypassed the issue. It was subsequently set by statute in a manner that favored the slaveholding counties of the East.

In early January the convention began its consideration of the judiciary article of the constitution. Marshall had written the preliminary draft, and his proposal provided for the tenure of state judges—a proposal that flew in the face of Jeffersonian orthodoxy. Governor Giles led the opposition, and the traditional arguments were brought forth with renewed vehemence. Marshall told the convention that "the Judicial Department comes home in its effects to every man's fireside: it passes on his property, his reputation, his life, his all. Is it not to the last degree important, that [a judge] should be rendered perfectly and completely independent, with nothing to influence or control him but God and his conscience?" Giles countered, "I am as much in favor of the complete independence of the judiciary as the warmest advocate of that principle, but I am in favor of its responsibility also. . . . I would make all the Judges responsible, not to God and their own consciences only, but to a human tribunal."[115]

Debate on the judiciary article continued for almost two weeks. In the beginning, as various amendments were offered, Marshall commanded only a bare majority. But as the debate wore on, the combination of his prestige, his cordial demeanor, and his relentless logic proved overwhelming. John Randolph, who had once led the fight to make the justices of the Supreme Court responsible to public opinion, rallied to Marshall's side. "The argument of the Chief Justice is unshaken and unanswerable," he told the convention. "It is as strong as the fortress of Gibraltar."[116] Another delegate spoke of "the reverence manifested for Chief Justice Marshall. The gentleness of his temper, the purity of his motives, the sincerity of his conviction, and his wisdom, were confessed by all."[117] A third commented on his "revolutionary and patriarchal" appearance. "Tall, in a long surtout of blue, with a face of genius and an eye of fire, his mind possessed a rare faculty of condensation; he distilled an argument down to its essence."[118]

Marshall's summation was magnificent. "The independence of all those who try causes between man and man, and between man and his government, can be maintained only by the tenure of their office," he told the convention. His voice trembled with emotion as he said, "I have always thought, from my earliest youth till now, that the greatest scourge an angry Heaven ever inflicted upon an ungrateful and sinning people, was an ignorant, a corrupt, or a dependent Judiciary. Will you draw down this curse upon Virginia?" Marshall said that the ancestors of those in the convention hall had always believed in the importance of an independent judiciary. "We all thought so till very lately; and I trust the vote of this day will show that we still think so."[119]

When the clerk called the roll of delegates, judicial tenure was sustained, 56–29. The judiciary article in Virginia's new constitution was then approved essentially as Marshall had written it.[120] Afterward he told Story that the final document was "not precisely what any of us wished, but it is better than we feared."[121] Madison expressed it more eloquently when he wrote Lafayette, "The peculiar difficulties which will have been overcome ought to render the experiment a new evidence of the capacity of men for self-government."[122]

Marshall succeeded in salvaging judicial independence in Virginia. But as a result he missed the first three weeks of the 1830 term of the Court and, perhaps, the opportunity to keep the brethren in collegial accord. It was a difficult decision. Marshall realized that if he left the convention before the judiciary article was approved, the tenure of Virginia's judges would be lost.* But McLean would be joining the Court for the first time, and perhaps even more important, Bushrod Washington, after thirty-one years on the Bench, died on circuit in Philadelphia on November 26. With Bushrod's death, Marshall had lost a great friend and a valuable ally.[123] Jackson, again to the consternation of his party's radical wing, passed over Pennsylvania's chief justice, John Bannister Gibson, who was an outspoken critic of the Marshall Court,[124] and nominated Henry Baldwin of Pittsburgh, another judicial moderate. Story called the appointment "quite satisfactory to those who wish well to the country and the Court."[125] Webster, happy that Gibson had been sidetracked, wrote that Baldwin "is supposed to be, substantively, a *sound* man, and he is undoubtedly a man of some talents."[126] Even John Quincy Adams, who saw little to praise in anything Jackson did, applauded the appointment.[127] Perhaps because McLean and Baldwin were considered reliable, Marshall did not worry about their settling into the justices' routine, or if he did, he considered his presence in Richmond more important.

That contrasts sharply with Marshall's previous behavior. And with the shepherd away in Richmond, the flock scattered. For the first time in twenty-nine years, the justices were not housed under one roof and did not take their meals together. On January 20, when the chief justice arrived, he found that McLean, who had brought his family to Washington several years earlier, was continuing to live with them, and that Johnson, now the senior justice, was also living separately. "In consequence," Marshall wrote Polly, "we cannot carry on our business as fast as usual."[128] Perhaps it was an omen; perhaps it was a contributing factor; perhaps it was simply that the composition of the Court had changed. Whatever the reason, the remarkable unity of the Marshall Court would soon splinter.

Initially, the change was not noticeable. "Everything goes on as usual," the chief justice told his wife. "I take my walk in the morning, work hard all day, eat a hearty dinner, sleep sound at night and sometimes comb my hair before I go to bed. While this operation is performing, I always think with tenderness of my sweet barber in Richmond. It is the most delightful sentiment I have."[129] When the term ended on March 22, the Court had considered fifty-eight cases. Although he had arrived three weeks late, Marshall delivered the decision in twenty-four. Story wrote eight; Johnson seven;

---

*On January 8, 1830, he wrote to Story, "The crisis of our constitution is now upon us. A strong disposition to prostrate the judiciary has shown itself and has succeeded to a considerable extent. I do not know what is in reserve. The most important principles will be determined this week or early in the next. I had determined to abandon everything and had taken my seat in the stage [to Washington] on Saturday. Those who concur with me in opinion have pressed me so earnestly to remain with them a few days that I have consented to postpone my journey, and shall not be present at the meeting of the Court." Story Papers, Massachusetts Historical Society.

McLean and Baldwin each wrote six; Thompson five; and two decisions were *per curiam*. But the dissents were up sharply. Except for Marshall and Duvall, each justice dissented at least once, and Johnson departed from his colleagues on three occasions.[130]

In the leading constitutional case of *Craig v. Missouri*,[131] in which the Court struck down Missouri's attempt to issue bills of credit, the justices divided four to three. However, in *Providence Bank v. Billings*,[132] another great case involving the contract clause, the justices continued to speak with one voice as Marshall upheld Rhode Island's authority to tax private corporations it had previously chartered. Modifying the absolute protection given to corporate charters in the *Dartmouth College* case, the chief justice stressed that the power to tax was an essential aspect of government, that it was shared by every citizen, and that it could not be relinquished by implication. Unless a legislative charter explicity exempted a corporation from taxation, no exemption could be assumed to have been made. The Constitution, said Marshall, "was not intended to furnish the corrective to every abuse of power which may be committed by state governments. The interest, wisdom, and justice of the representative body and its relation with its constituents, furnish the only security, where there is no express contract, against unjust and excessive taxation, as well as against unwise legislation generally."[133] The Court's decision was hailed by Whigs and Democrats alike.[134] Efforts to curtail the judiciary, which were always lurking in states rights circles, were undermined, and the term ended on a political high note.

In the spring of 1830, the doctrine of nullification burst forth upon the country. Previously expounded by John C. Calhoun in a little-known pamphlet,[135] it was Senator Robert Y. Hayne of South Carolina who introduced the term to national discourse. The occasion arose in debate over an innocuous Senate resolution concerning public lands. Citing the Kentucky and Virginia Resolutions of 1798, Hayne argued that the Union was a creature of the states; that its powers were expressly limited; and that if a sovereign state believed the federal government had exceeded its authority, the state could nullify the offending measure.[136] Daniel Webster's famous reply to Hayne evoked the nation's case with powerful effect: "Liberty *and* Union, now and forever, one and inseparable."[137] Ironically, the intensity of Webster's lengthy and devastating Senate response elevated the issue to national debate.* South Carolinians rushed to the verbal barricades, as did

---

*Marshall had difficulty believing that anyone could have taken Hayne seriously. As he wrote to Congressman Edward Everett of Massachusetts, "The idea that a state may constitutionally nullify an act of Congress is so extravagant in itself, and so repugnant to the existence of Union between the states, that I could with difficulty bring myself to believe it was seriously entertained by any person." Marshall went on to say that "the division of opinion already exhibited in South Carolina is . . . a security against her attempting this mad project alone. . . . However frantic we

states rightists in Missouri and Georgia. Andrew Jackson met the assault without flinching. The president considered himself a states rights devotee, yet he never questioned the supremacy of the Union. After enduring a torrent of nullification oratory at the Democrats' annual dinner celebrating Jefferson's birthday, Old Hickory closed the evening with a dramatic toast of his own. Glowering at Vice President Calhoun, the author of the heresy, Jackson said: "Our Federal Union—it *must* be preserved," upon which he drained his glass.[138]

Madison also answered the challenge. Dismayed that his statements in 1798 against the alien and sedition acts were being turned against the Union, the former president responded with his final, most carefully considered interpretation of the nature and powers of the federal government. In a detailed letter published in the October 1830 issue of the *North American Review*, Madison restated the views of the Framers concerning federal supremacy. He emphasized that the Constitution reflected the work of the people, not the states, and insisted that the Supreme Court, despite occasional lapses, was the final arbiter of disputes between the national government and the states.[139] As for nullification, Madison said that "there is not a shadow of countenance in the Constitution . . . for this preposterous and anarchical pretension."[140]

Marshall was delighted. "Mr. Madison . . . is himself again," the chief justice wrote Story. "He avows the opinions of his best days and must be pardoned for his oblique insinuations that some of the opinions of our court are not approved. Contrast this delicate hint with the language Mr. Jefferson has applied to us."[141] Indeed, the friends of the Union could scarcely have wished for more powerful support. The president stood in the vanguard of the nation's defenders, the father of the Constitution had entered the fray, and as the Court's decisions in *Willson v. Blackbird Creek Marsh Co.*[142] and *Providence Bank* indicated, the chief justice and his colleagues were not insensitive to the legitimate demands of the states. The Supreme Court was the bulwark of national power, but the justices were equally aware of the important prerogatives that the Constitution left with the states.

The 1831 term opened like all the others. The chief justice wrote Polly that "I rise early, pore over law cases, go to Court and return at the same hour and pass the evening in consultation with the judges. Visitors sometimes drop in upon us, but their visits are short and we always return them by card."[143] Marshall's health remained robust. In addition to his brisk early-morning walk, he habitually paced himself an additional mile coming and

---

may be on many subjects, let the naked question of dismemberment be presented to us, and I am persuaded that there is not a southern state which would not recoil from it with disgust." November 3, 1830, Everett Papers, Massachusetts Historical Society.

going from Brown's Indian Queen Hotel to the capitol each day. "I was ashamed of myself . . . to see the Chief Justice, who is seventy-five years old, tracking up to Court on foot," wrote Congressman Everett of Massachusetts. "In his youth, he was dissipated: attended horse races and cock fights, gamed, bet, and drank. In my youth I was a demure lad, indulged in no dissipation, ran the gauntlet of Europe without being betrayed into vice, then I am, at the age of thirty-seven, obliged to drive up to the Capitol, while the Old Chief Justice walks."[144]

Trouble arose early in the term. The cases pending before the Court were not especially difficult or contentious. The problem was Justice Baldwin. Although neither he nor his colleagues was aware of it at the time, Baldwin was in the early stages of a mental breakdown.* He became disruptive in conference and was personally disagreeable, querulous, and erratic. One observer reported that he would sit for hours in his darkened room, staring at the walls.[145] The following year Baldwin suffered a total collapse while presiding on circuit,[146] and he missed the entire 1833 term of the Court because of mental illness. In 1831, however, the illness was just beginning to manifest itself. Baldwin took exception to all of the Court's practices—including living at Brown's Indian Queen Hotel, which he thought was too expensive. He found Story's learned views particularly offensive,[147] complained repeatedly about Reporter Richard Peters, and issued a record nine dissents in the forty-two cases the Court decided.[148] The unity of the Marshall Court dissolved, not over an issue of principle, but over a personality disorder.

Marshall's response was charitable. The chief justice was more perplexed than angry, and he was especially concerned about where the justices would be quartered the following year in light of Baldwin's objections. "I am apprehensive that the revolutionary spirit which displayed itself in our circle will, like most other revolutions, work inconvenience and mischief in its progress," he wrote Story in May. "I believe Mr. Brown does not count on boarding the Judges next winter; and if any other arrangement is made, tis entirely unknown to me. We have, like most other unquiet men, discontented with things as they are, discarded accommodations which are reasonably convenient, without providing a substitute."[149] Marshall said he was concerned as to what would happen. "If the Judges scatter *ad libitum* [at lib-

---

*Baldwin's disorder was apparently brought on by financial difficulties, which eventually forced him into bankruptcy. His obituary notes that his "former free and warm-hearted commonality was with a few rare exceptions, abandoned, and . . . he would dwell, with diseased interest, on incidents which, in his sounder mind, could never have attracted his notice, and could too often regard his truest friends with suspicion and distrust. . . . [Eventually a] malady manifested itself which . . . made him temporarily incapable of his public duties." "The Late Mr. Justice Baldwin," 6 *Pennsylvania Law Journal* 1, 6 (1846).

erty], the docket I fear will remain quite compact, losing very few causes; and the few it may lose, will probably be carried off by *seriatim* opinions. Old men however are timid, and I hope my fears may be unfounded."

Two months later the chief justice wrote Story that he was still concerned about where the justices would board during the 1832 term. Marshall said he had not joined in the discussion the last day of Court because he felt he was "a bird of passage whose continuance with you cannot be long."[150] Then the bombshell. In absolute confidence, Marshall told his old friend that he planned to step down, but wanted Jackson's successor to name his replacement. "You know how much importance I attach to the character of the person who is to succeed me." However, Marshall had miscalculated when the election would occur. He told Story that he had mistakenly assumed the election would be in the fall, and had realized only belatedly that the president had another year in office. "This obliges me to look forward to our quarters for the next winter." Marshall said that Justice Baldwin had undertaken to handle the arrangements, but that so far nothing had been done. As a result, they might have to provide for themselves. "You, Judge Thompson, Judge Duvall and myself may, I hope, contrive to mess together. Brother Duvall must be with us or he will be unable to attend consultations."[151]

Story shared Marshall's concern, but he was overwhelmed that summer by the sudden death of his ten-year-old daughter. "She was as beautiful and perfect as any human being could be."[152] Story asked whether the chief justice and his wife had ever met with similar calamities.

Marshall replied with deep emotion:

You ask me if Mrs. Marshall and myself have ever lost a child. We have lost four—three of them bidding fairer for health and life than any that have survived them. One, a daughter about six or seven was brought fresh to our minds by what you say of yours. She was one of the most fascinating children I ever saw. She was followed within a fortnight by a brother whose death was attended by a circumstance we can never forget. When the child was supposed to be dying I tore the distracted mother from the bedside. We soon afterwards heard a noise in the room which we considered as indicating the death of the infant. We believed him to be dead. I went into the room and found him still breathing. I returned and as the pang of his death had been felt by his mother, and I was confident he must die, I concealed his being alive and prevailed on her to take refuge with her mother who lived the next door across an open square from her. The child lived two days during which I was agonized with its condition and with the occasional hope, though the case was desperate, that I might enrapture his mother with the intelligence of his restoration to us. After the event had taken place, his mother could not bear to return to the house she had left and remained with her mother a fortnight. I then addressed to her a letter in verse in which our mutual loss was deplored, our lost children spoken of with the parental feeling which belonged to the occasion, her affection for those which survived was appealed to, and her religious confidence in the wisdom and goodness of providence excited. The letter closed with a pressing invitation to return to me and her children.

Marshall told Story that he had looked for a copy of the verse, "but tis lost."[153]

In the spring of 1831, Marshall's health began to fail. Walking became difficult, and at times it was painful for him to urinate. When he set out in his gig for circuit court in Raleigh, Polly had the servants prepare a special cushion for him to ease the trip.[154] But travel made the condition worse, and by summer the pain had become unbearable. The Marshall family physician accurately diagnosed the problem as stones in the bladder, but the chief justice refused to believe him. Instead, he began to treat himself, taking a variety of medicines and painkillers that sapped his strength and interfered with his concentration. "My nerves, my digestion, and my head were seriously affected," he later wrote Story. "I found myself unequal to the effective consideration of any subject, and had determined to resign at the close of the year."[155] Marshall caught himself, discontinued the drugs, and when the pain did not subside, decided to seek the aid of America's foremost surgeon, Dr. Philip Syng Physick, in Philadelphia.[156]

Dr. Physick was then sixty-three and in semiretirement. He nevertheless agreed to examine Marshall, and confirmed that the problem was bladder stones. The chief justice was impressed by the doctor's thoroughness. "He deliberates very much, is determined to do nothing rashly, and seems to be perfectly the master of my case," he wrote Polly.[157] Marshall did not tell his wife of Dr. Physick's diagnosis, nor did he mention that an operation would be necessary. He simply said that the treatment would begin shortly. "I flatter myself that his efforts will be successful."

It was another week before Dr. Physick was ready to operate. Initially, there was difficulty procuring a satisfactory room, then torrential rains set in, confining Dr. Physick to his house.[158] The doctor was also apprehensive about doing the surgery himself since he had not performed a major operation in several years. His assistants intervened, insisting that the chief justice was seventy-six and that only the doctor had the skill and experience necessary to pull him through.[159] That argument was apparently sufficient to convince Dr. Physick, who scheduled the operation for the morning of October 13. The day before, the chief justice wrote to Polly, to his son James

Keith Marshall, and to Story. He told Polly that the treatment Dr. Physick prescribed was about to begin, but still did not mention that it entailed an operation. "My room is now preparing, and he has just left me with directions to take a table spoonful of castor oil two hours after dinner."[160] To James Keith he confided what was to happen and was optimistic about the outcome.[161] Marshall told Story about the operation at greater length and made it clear that he planned to attend the next term of Court. "Our brother Baldwin is here. He seems to have resumed the dispositions which impressed us both so favorably the first term. This is as it should be." Marshall said he still worried about their accommodations and would see to them after he recovered. If he should survive the operation and not be cured, the chief justice planned to resign. "I cannot be insensible to the gloom which lours over us. I have a repugnance to abandoning you under such circumstances . . . but the solemn convictions of my judgment sustained by some pride of character admonish me not to hazard the disgrace of continuing in office, a mere inefficient pageant."[162]

The morning of the operation, Dr. Physick's assistant, Dr. Jacob Randolph, arrived to prepare Marshall for the ordeal. He found the chief justice in good spirits and eating his breakfast. "Well, Doctor, you find me taking breakfast, and I assure you that I have had a good one. I thought very probably this might be my last chance, and therefore I was determined to enjoy it and eat heartily."[163] Marshall told Dr. Randolph that he did not feel the least anxiety about the operation. He knew that the odds were against him, but he preferred to die rather than live with the pain and misery he suffered.[164] He asked when the operation would be performed. Randolph said eleven, and Marshall asked whether he could go to sleep.

"I was a good deal surprised at this question," Randolph recalled, "but told him that if he could sleep it would be very desirable. He immediately placed himself upon the bed and fell into a profound sleep, and continued so until I was obliged to rouse him in order to undergo the operation. He exhibited the same fortitude, scarcely uttering a murmur throughout the whole procedure, which, from the peculiar nature of the complaint, was necessarily tedious."[165]

The grim operation, known as a lithotomy, was performed without anesthetic.[166] Dr. Physick made an incision into Marshall's body from below, entered the bladder at its neck, and with forceps began to remove the stone. To the doctor's surprise, he found not one stone but numerous smaller ones ranging in size from a large pea to a pinhead. Working quickly lest the chief justice expire, Dr. Physick removed over a thousand small particles and then washed the bladder with barley water to catch any fragment that might have eluded his forceps.

The operation was an astonishing success. Dr. Randolph said afterward that although it had been performed with great skill, Marshall's recovery "was in a great degree owing to his extraordinary self-possession, and to the calm and philosophical views which he took of his case."[167]

Marshall's quick convalescence was equally astonishing. On November 8 he wrote to Polly, "I have at length risen from my bed and am able to hold a pen. The most delightful use I can make of it is to tell you that I am getting well and have well founded hopes that I shall be entirely free from the painful disease with which I have been so long afflicted."[168] Two days later he wrote Story that he was able to walk across the room. "This I do with a tottering and feeble step." Marshall said he planned to return to Richmond by boat and that he intended to convene circuit court later in the month. The chief justice also told Story that he had attended to their accommodations in Washington. Arrangements had been made for five of them (Marshall, Story, Duvall, Thompson, and Baldwin) to board with Tench Ringold, the marshal of the District of Columbia, in his large home at 18th and F Streets—about two miles from the capitol. Justice Johnson would board separately,* and McLean would continue to live with his family. "Our brother Baldwin has called on me frequently. He is in good health and spirits, and I, always sanguine, hope that the next term will exhibit dispositions more resembling those displayed in the first [rather] than the last."[169]

Marshall left Philadelphia on Saturday, November 19, on the steamboat *William Penn* bound for Baltimore. After "a very tempestuous passage down the [Chesapeake] bay," he arrived in Richmond on Wednesday.[170] Marshall's health was now restored, but a greater sadness awaited him. While he was away, Polly's condition had become critical. Marshall realized that the end was near. On December 19 he wrote to his brother James, "My poor wife lies dangerously ill and has been for more than a fortnight. She is confined to her bed and my fears are stronger than my hopes, though the doctor thinks her rather better today."[171] For the next week Marshall remained at Polly's bedside. On the day before Christmas, she removed from her neck the locket containing the strand of hair from her courtship and placed it around his. Marshall wore it for the remainder of his life.[172] The next day, Christmas 1831, Polly died.

Marshall was grief stricken. A few weeks later when the Court convened, Story entered the chief justice's room at Mr. Ringold's and found him in tears. Marshall told his old associate that he rarely passed a night without crying for Polly. "She must have been a very extraordinary woman," Story wrote his wife, "and I think he is the most extraordinary man I ever saw, for the depth and tenderness of his feeling."[173]

On Christmas Day a year later, Marshall wrote a moving tribute to

---

*As it turned out, Justice Johnson missed the entire 1832 term because of illness.

Polly.[174] He closed with the lines General Burgoyne had written for his own departed wife:

> Encompassed in an angel's frame,
>   An angel's virtues lay;
> Too soon did heaven assert its claim
>   And take its own away.
> My Mary's worth, my Mary's charms
>   Can never more return.
> What now shall fill these widowed arms?
>   Ah, me! My Mary's urn!
> Ah, me! My Mary's urn!!!

In 1832 the Marshall Court found itself on a collision course with the state of Georgia concerning the rights of the Cherokee Indians. A decade earlier, in *Johnson v. McIntosh*,[175] a case involving the Piankeshaw Indians in Illinois, Marshall had explicitly recognized the Indian title to the lands in their possession. Speaking for a unanimous Court, the chief justice said that Great Britain had acquired sovereignty over North America through discovery and conquest; that the United States had succeeded to the British claim; and that the Indians, although they did not own their tribal land outright, nevertheless enjoyed the right of continued occupancy. They could transfer the land to the federal government or to other members of the tribe, but they could not sell it to outside purchasers. Marshall expressed skepticism concerning "the original justice" of the nation's sovereign claim to the Indian land. Nevertheless, he termed it a political decision that the Court could not reverse.

> However extravagant the pretension of converting the discovery of an inhabited country into conquest may appear; if the principle has been converted in the first instance, and afterwards sustained; if a country has been acquired and held under it; if the property of the great mass of the community originates in it, it becomes the law of the land, and cannot be questioned. So too with the concomitant principle, that the Indian inhabitants are to be considered merely as occupants, to be protected, indeed, while in peace, in the possession of their lands, but to be deemed incapable of transferring the absolute title to others.*

---

*Marshall's holding concerning native title to tribal lands established the basic rule of North American jurisprudence, not only in the United States but in Canada as well. In 1973, for example, the Supreme Court of Canada characterized the decision in *Johnson v. McIntosh* as "the *locus*

The decision of the Court in *McIntosh*, combined with numerous American treaties with the Indian tribes, appeared to safeguard native lands from encroachment by white settlers. But the protection was more apparent than real. In the late 1820s, when gold was discovered on the Cherokee lands in Georgia, the state enacted a series of laws that abolished the Indian nation, distributed its territory (some nine million acres) to the several adjacent counties, and declared that after June 1, 1830, all Cherokee laws and customs would be null and void. The Cherokees appealed first to President Jackson, then to Congress, and finally to the Court. Jackson said that Georgia had jurisdiction over all persons within its limits and turned a deaf ear; Congress proposed to relocate the Indians west of the Mississippi; only the Court offered the Cherokees an opportunity to preserve their land and their way of life.

Before a test case could be heard,[176] Georgia demonstrated its contempt for the federal judiciary by hanging a Cherokee named George Tassels for a murder committed in Indian territory. Despite treaties to the contrary, Tassels was tried in state court and convicted. Marshall himself issued a writ of error granting an appeal to the Supreme Court, but the state authorities defiantly proceeded with the execution.[177] The Georgia legislature resolved that "the interference by the chief justice of the supreme court of the United States, in the administration of the criminal laws of this state, is a flagrant violation of her rights." The governor was directed to "disregard any and every mandate and process . . . purporting to proceed from the chief justice or any associate justice of the Supreme Court of the United States."[178]

It was in that context that the case of *Cherokee Nation v. The State of Georgia* came before the Court on March 5, 1831. Speaking on behalf of the Cherokees, former attorney general William Wirt moved for an injunction to prevent Georgia from enforcing its Indian laws. Four days later, the last day of the 1831 term, Marshall announced the decision of the Court.[179] "If courts were permitted to indulge their sympathies," said the chief justice,

> a case better calculated to excite them can scarcely be imagined. A people, once numerous, powerful, and truly independent, found by our ancestors in the quiet and uncontrolled possession of an am-

---

classicus of the principles governing aboriginal title." *Calder v. Attorney-General of British Columbia*, [1973] S.C.R. 313, 380. By contrast, the jurisprudence in British East Africa, Australia, and the Portuguese and Spanish colonies denied any aboriginal title whatever, holding the land to be *terra nullus*. Not until 1992, in the leading case of *Mabo v. Queensland*, 107 ALR 1, did the High Court of Australia reverse previous decisions and acknowledge native title along the lines Marshall laid out in 1823. For a general review of the importance of *Johnson v. McIntosh*, see John Hurley, "Aboriginal Rights, the Constitution and the Marshall Court," 17 *Revue Juridique Themis* 403–443 (1983).

ple domain, gradually sinking beneath our superior policy . . . have
yielded their lands, by successive treaties, each of which contains a
solemn guarantee of the residue, until they retain no more of their
formerly extensive territory than is deemed necessary to the comfortable subsistence.

Unfortunately, said Marshall, the justices lacked the authority to hear
the case. The jurisdiction of the Supreme Court was fixed by the Constitution. In order for the Cherokees to bring suit against Georgia, they would
have to be a foreign nation, and clearly they were not. "They may, more correctly, perhaps, be denominated domestic dependent nations. . . . they are
in a state of pupilage; their relation to the United States resembles that of a
ward to his guardian. They look to our government for protection; rely upon
its kindness and its power; appeal to it for relief of their wants." Accordingly,
"the framers of our Constitution had not the Indian tribes in view, when
they opened the courts of the Union to controversies between a state or the
citizens thereof and foreign states." The Cherokees lacked standing to sue.

Marshall, whose sympathies were with the Indians, declined to override
the textual mandate of the Constitution. "If it be true, that the Cherokee
nation have rights, this is not the tribunal in which those rights are to be asserted. If it be true, that wrongs have been inflicted, and that still greater are
to be apprehended, this is not the tribunal which can redress the past or prevent the future." Throughout his opinion, Marshall implied that if a proper
test case could be brought before the Court, an appropriate decision could
be rendered. The laws of Georgia might even be overturned. But *Cherokee
Nation* was not such a case.

The following year exactly such a case arose. Samuel Worcester, a Con-
gregationalist minister from Vermont, and Elihu Butler, an associate, were
arrested and convicted for violating one of Georgia's recently enacted
statutes that prohibited nonnatives from living on Cherokee land without a
license from the state. The Georgia law contravened various United States
treaties with the Cherokee. In addition, Worcester and Butler held permits
issued by the president pursuant to an act of Congress to conduct missionary work among the Indians. Nevertheless, the pair were sentenced by a
state court to four years at hard labor. They immediately appealed to the
Supreme Court, and this time the Court's jurisdiction was clear. Just as in
Cohens v. Virginia, a federal issue was involved. The Cherokees had lacked
standing to sue because they were not a foreign nation. But there was no
question that Worcester and Butler could come forward as individual litigants.

Marshall seized the opportunity. Over Baldwin's dissent, he declared
Georgia's Indian laws unconstitutional and ordered the missionaries re-

leased. Marshall was seventy-six years old. He had just recovered from a severe operation and had recently experienced the death of his wife. Yet his twenty-eight-page decision in *Worcester v. Georgia*[180] is one of the most powerful he ever delivered. He said that Georgia had arrested Worcester while he was "under the guardianship of treaties guaranteeing the country in which he resided"; that Worcester was performing missionary duties which Congress had recommended; and that he had been convicted under a statute "repugnant to the Constitution, laws, and treaties of the United States." Not only was that statute unconstitutional, but the whole "system of legislation lately adopted by the Legislature of Georgia in relation to the Cherokee Nation" was "repugnant to the Constitution, laws, and treaties of the United States." It, too, was struck down.

Harriet Martineau, the famous English feminist, described the scene:

> I watched the assemblage when the Chief Justice was delivering the judgment . . . judges on either hand, gazing at him more like learners than associates. . . . These men absorbed in what they are listening to, thinking neither of themselves nor each other, while they are watched by the group of idlers and listeners. Among them the newspaper corps. The dark Cherokee chiefs, the stragglers from far West, the gay ladies in their waving plumes, and the members of either [H]ouse that have stepped in to listen; all these I have seen constitute the silent assemblage, while the mild voice of the aged Chief Justice sounded through the Court.[181]

The Supreme Court was on record. The Indian laws passed by the state of Georgia were unconstitutional. "The Court has done its duty," Story wrote, "let the nation now do theirs."[182] But the nation was unwilling. Georgia again ignored the Court; Worcester and Butler remained in prison; and President Jackson is reported to have said, "Well, John Marshall has made his decision, now let him enforce it."[183] Jackson probably did not say that, and at that point the president had no responsibility for enforcing the judgment. The decree issued by the Supreme Court merely instructed Georgia to reverse its decision and release the missionaries. The Court adjourned shortly thereafter, which meant that the decree could not be enforced until the 1833 term and that the state would not be in defiance until then.[184]

When the Supreme Court adjourned in 1832, it had considered fifty-five cases. Justice Baldwin disagreed with his colleagues seven times but did not file a written opinion in any case. Marshall dissented once,[185] Thompson once,[186] and the other decisions were unanimous. At the age of seventy-six, Marshall continued to write the lion's share, speaking for the Court twenty-one times.

By mid-1832 the nation's attention was focused on Jackson's reelection and the renewed furor over states rights in the South. Georgia, in the aftermath of the *Cherokee* cases, looked as if it might join the incorrigibles in South Carolina threatening nullification, and the mood had turned rancorous in Virginia, as well. In August Marshall wrote Story that "things to the South wear a very serious aspect. If we can trust appearances, the leaders are determined to risk all the consequences of dismemberment."[187] As the states rights rhetoric escalated that autumn, Marshall's spirits sagged. In late September he wrote to Story in an even more despondent mood. "I yield slowly and reluctantly to the conviction that the Constitution cannot last. The Union has been prolonged thus far by miracles. I fear they cannot continue."[188]

But a miracle of sorts was in the offing. Jackson was swept back into office in November[189] and immediately moved to suppress the impending states rights revolt. When South Carolina passed an ordinance of nullification declaring the federal tariff act unconstitutional and refusing compliance, Old Hickory reinforced the garrisons at Forts Moultrie and Sumter, ordered the treasury department's revenue cutters to enforce the tariff, and on December 10, 1832, issued his famous proclamation to the people of South Carolina calling the hand of the nullification forces. A state could not decide which laws to obey and which to refuse, said Jackson. Using phraseology similar to Marshall's in *McCulloch v. Maryland* and *Cohens v. Virginia*, the president said that the Constitution had established "a government in which all the people are represented, which operates directly on the people individually, not upon the states." Jackson said the Supreme Court was the ultimate arbiter of the constitutionality of the nation's laws and that if the Court held a statute to be constitutional, it must be obeyed.

> The laws of the United States must be executed. I have no discretionary power on the subject; my duty is emphatically pronounced in the Constitution. Those who told you that you might peaceably prevent the execution have deceived you.... They know that a forcible opposition could alone prevent the execution of the laws, and they know that such opposition must be repelled. Their object is disunion. But be not deceived by names. Disunion by armed force is *treason*. Are you really ready to incur its guilt?[190]

Marshall was delighted. He compared Jackson's action with Washington's quelling of the Whiskey Rebellion in 1794.[191] After a dinner at the White House, Story wrote to his wife that since Jackson's proclamation and message to Congress, "the Chief Justice and myself have become his warmest supporters, and shall continue so just as long as he maintains the principles contained in them. Who would have dreamed of such an occurrence?"[192]

The Court, which had done so much to establish national supremacy, found itself riding a crest of approval. Peace had been made with the Jackson administration; congressional criticism had ceased; and the inauguration on March 4—Marshall's ninth and last—proved to be one of his most enjoyable. Story told his wife that "the Chief Justice looked more vigorous than usual. He seemed to revive and enjoy anew his green, old age." Seeking a respite from the Court's labors, Story and Marshall attended the theater to see Miss Fanny Kemble, a noted actress of the period. "On the Chief Justice's entrance into the box, he was cheered in a marked manner," said Story. "He behaved as he always does, with extreme modesty, and seemed not to know that the compliment was intended for him."[193]

The 1833 term of the Court was equally congenial. The justices decided forty-one cases, all but one of which was unanimous.[194] In the leading constitutional case of *Barron v. Baltimore*,[195] Marshall, speaking for all of his colleagues, held that the guarantees of the Bill of Rights applied only to the national government, not to the states. "These Amendments demanded security against the apprehended encroachments of the General Government, not against those of the local governments." As a member of the Virginia committee that had drafted the original proposals in 1788, Marshall said that "serious fears were extensively entertained" that the powers of the new federal government "might be exercised in a manner dangerous to liberty." The Bill of Rights was designed to prevent that. The states were not its object of concern.

In the spring of 1833, Story published his famous *Commentaries on the Constitution of the United States*,[196] which he dedicated to Marshall. "I shall read them eagerly," said the chief justice. "I greatly fear that, south of the Potomac, where it is most wanted, it will be least used. It is a Mohammedan rule, I understand, 'never to dispute with the ignorant,' and we of the true faith in the South abjure the contamination of infidel political works. It would give our orthodox Nullifyer a fever to read the heresies of your commentaries."[197]

The 1834 term of the Court was uneventful. Justice Johnson was critically ill and remained in South Carolina. Duvall was often absent, and the justices deferred three important constitutional cases.[198] Marshall said:

> The practice of this Court is not (except in cases of absolute necessity) to deliver any judgment in cases where constitutional questions are involved unless four Judges concur in opinion, thus making the decision that of a majority of the whole Court. In the present cases four Judges do not concur. . . . The Court therefore direct these

cases to be reargued at the next term, under the expectation that a larger number of Judges may then be present.[199]

The 1834 docket was crowded with nonconstitutional issues, however, and the justices decided sixty-one cases, all but one unanimously.[200] Marshall spoke for the Court twenty-nine times. The other decisions were rendered by Story, McLean, and Thompson.

Charles Sumner, who had recently graduated from Harvard Law School, was visiting Washington for the first time in 1834. "Every day's attendance in the political part of the capitol shows me clearly that all speeches there are delivered to the people beyond, and not to Senators and Representatives present. In the Supreme Court, the object of speaking is to convince. The more I see of politics, the more I learn to love the law." Reveling in the intimacy of Washington society, Sumner told his parents that he had dined with the justices in their boardinghouse the past Sunday. "Judges Marshall, Story, Thompson, and Duvall were present, who, with myself, made up the company, with two waiters in attendance. Sunday here is a much gayer day than with us. No conversation is forbidden, and nothing which goes to cause cheerfulness, if not hilarity. The world and all things are talked of as much as on any other day. Judge Marshall is a model of simplicity—'in wit a man, simplicity a child.'"[201]

On August 4, 1834, Justice Johnson died after a long and debilitating illness. Once again Jackson disappointed his party's radicals and named Congressman James M. Wayne of Georgia to fill the vacancy. Wayne, though a Democrat, was a judicial moderate. He had served five years on the Georgia supreme court, and as a member of Congress he had vigorously supported Jackson's stand against nullification. He was confirmed instantly by the Senate and joined the Court at the beginning of the 1835 term. "Mr. Wayne has taken his seat on the Bench," said the *Niles Register*, "of which lofty place all parties agree on considering him worthy, believing that he will not be a partisan Judge."[202] Thus far, Jackson had filled three vacancies on the Court, and each time he had surprised supporters and opponents alike by choosing appointees (McLean, Baldwin, and Wayne) of unquestioned judicial stature. Marshall said nothing either publicly or privately about Wayne's appointment, but there was no question that it enhanced the reputation of the Court.[203]

The president was less fortunate with his next selection. Before the Court met in 1835, Justice Duvall, who was eighty-one and now totally deaf, resigned, creating another vacancy. Jackson turned to his former attorney general and secretary of the treasury, Roger Brooke Taney of Maryland. Because of Taney's role in terminating the Bank of the United States (as treasury secretary he had withdrawn the government's deposits from the bank), the Whigs, aided by Calhoun's states rights supporters, bitterly opposed his nomination. Marshall, who knew Taney as attorney general and who respected his legal acumen, favored confirmation,[204] as did Duvall.[205] But on the last day of the 1835 session, the Senate voted 24–21 to postpone further consideration of Taney, effectively killing the appointment.

Aside from the fight over Taney's nomination, the 1835 term of the Court proceeded in routine fashion. The justices considered forty-one cases and rendered unanimous decisions in thirty-seven.[206] Marshall, now in his eightieth year, delivered seventeen opinions of the Court. The others were divided more or less equally. In the final case decided that year, *Mitchel v. United States*,[207] Marshall spoke for the last time as chief justice. The case involved land titles in Florida, and after tracing the history of the litigation, Marshall rendered a tribute to the Court:

> Though the hope of deciding causes to the mutual satisfaction of the parties would be chimerical, that of convincing them that the case has been fully and fairly considered, that due attention has been given to the arguments of counsel, and that the best judgment of the Court has been exercised on the case, may be sometimes indulged. Even this is not always attainable. In the excitement produced by ardent controversy, gentlemen view the same object through such different media, that minds not unfrequently receive therefrom precisely opposite impressions. The Court, however, must see with its own eyes, and exercise its own judgment, guided by its own reason.

Throughout the 1830s Marshall kept in close contact with his sons in Fauquier county. He assisted them financially, provided legal advice, and encouraged their efforts at farming. He was especially concerned about the progress of his grandchildren. "Every man ought to be intimately acquainted with the history of his own country," he advised one grandson, John Marshall, Jr. The chief justice thought that proficiency in English composition was even more important. No doubt reflecting on his own childhood experience reading Alexander Pope, Marshall encouraged him to transcribe the work of established writers. "The early habit of arranging our thoughts with regularity, so as to point them to the object to be proved, will be of great advantage. In both, clearness and precision are the most essential qualities. The man who by seeking embellishment hazards confusion, is greatly mistaken in what constitutes good writing. The meaning ought never to be mistaken. Indeed, the reader should never be obliged to search for it."[208]

Marshall was now making plans to retire and move to Oak Hill.[209] In preparation, he was beginning to move some of his personal possessions. "I was informed by Mr. [Antoine Charles] Cazanove [the Alexandria merchant] of the arrival of a pipe and two quarter casks of wine from Madeira," the chief justice wrote to his son James. "The pipe is of high colored Madeira for myself. The two quarter casks are of the strawcolored for your brother Jaquelin." He had also purchased some mahogany chairs and a sofa. Marshall asked James if he would see to their delivery. "Let the wine be brought by a wagoner who is entirely trustworthy," he cautioned.[210]

Marshall's health was failing quickly. He realized the extent of his decline, but bore it with good humor. "Could I find a mill that would grind old men, and restore youth, I might indulge the hope of recovering my former vigor and tastes for the enjoyments of life," he wrote court reporter Richard Peters. "But as that is impossible, I must be content with patching myself up and dragging on as well as I can."[211]

Several times a week Marshall walked the two miles from his house to Shockoe Hill cemetery to visit Polly's grave. In early June 1835 he collapsed on the journey and was carried home by two men who were passing by. Marshall immediately went to Philadelphia to consult Dr. Physick. This time his ailment was diagnosed as a diseased liver, which had become greatly enlarged. The pressure of the enlarged liver upon his stomach had compressed it to such an extent that Marshall could not retain the smallest amount of nutriment. He was wasting away.

Edward Carrington Marshall, the chief justice's youngest son, had gone with him to Philadelphia, and when the stay there became longer than anticipated, Marshall's eldest son, Thomas Marshall, set out to replace Edward. On June 29, when Thomas was passing through Baltimore, a summer thunderstorm erupted and he took shelter in a nearby building. A clap of lightning hit the building's chimney, which collapsed, striking Thomas and killing him instantly. Marshall was not informed of his son's death. During the next several days he grew weaker but remained alert. At six o'clock on the evening of July 6, 1835, John Marshall died. According to Dr. Nathaniel Chapman, who was present, the chief justice was "perfectly in his senses to the last and as death approached nearer to him his pain ceased and he went off without a struggle."[212] Polly's locket was around his neck to the end.

The nation's grief was profound. Flags flew at half staff throughout the country, and many towns and cities declared extended periods of mourning. Eulogies from Marshall's friends and admirers were legion. His intimates in Richmond's Quoits Club voted that his place should not be filled and that "the number of the club should remain one less than it was before his death."[213] The tributes from his adversaries were even more impressive. Thomas Ritchie, publisher of the Richmond *Enquirer*, said that Marshall "was as much loved as he was respected. There was about him so little of 'the insolence of office,' and so much of the benignity of the man, that his presence always produced the most delightful impressions. There was something irresistibly winning about him."[214]

Andrew Jackson wrote that

Having set a high value upon the learning, talents, and patriotism of Judge Marshall, and upon the good he has done his country in one of its most exalted and responsible offices, I have been gratified at seeing that sentiments equally favorable have been cherished by his fellow citizens, and that there has been no disposition, even with those who dissent from some of his expositions of our constitutional law (of whom it is perhaps proper that I should say I am one), to withhold from his memory the highest tribute of respect. In the revolutionary struggles for our National independence, and particularly in the subsequent discussions which established the forms and settled the practice of our system of Government, the opinions of John Marshall were expressed with the energy and clearness which were peculiar to his strong mind, and gave him a rank amongst the greatest men of his age which he fully sustained on the bench of the Supreme Court.[215]

Marshall was buried next to Polly in Shockoe Hill cemetery. The words on his tomb were written by him two days before he died, leaving nothing but the final date to be supplied.

John Marshall
son of Thomas and Mary Marshall
was born the 24th of September 1755
Intermarried with Mary Willis Ambler
the 3rd of January 1783
Departed this life
the sixth day of July 1835

Notes

Joseph Story's comment about Marshall was made in a letter to Samuel Fay, February 25, 1808, after meeting the chief justice for the first time. Story, a leading Boston lawyer, had just appeared before the Supreme Court as the attorney for the appellant in the famous Yazoo lands case, *Fletcher v. Peck*, ultimately reported at 6 Cranch 87 (1810). See 1 *Life and Letters of Joseph Story* 167, William W. Story, ed. (Boston: Charles C. Little and James Brown, 1851).

Introduction

The Charles Evans Hughes quotation is from Hughes's *The Supreme Court of the United States* 58 (New York: Columbia University Press, 1928).

1. 1 Cranch 137 (1803).
2. 4 Wheaton 316 (1819).
3. 1 Wheaton 304 (1816). Because he was personally involved in the case (see Chapter 18), Marshall recused himself in *Martin*, and the decision was written by Story.
4. 6 Wheaton 264 (1821).
5. 6 Cranch 87 (1810).
6. *Dartmouth College v. Woodward*, 4 Wheaton 518 (1819).
7. 9 Wheaton 1 (1824).
8. Thomas Jefferson to Abigail Adams, September 11, 1804, 8 *The Works of Thomas Jefferson* 310, Paul Leicester Ford, ed. (New York: G. P. Putnam's Sons, 1905). Also see Jefferson to William C. Jarvis, September 28, 1820, 12 *ibid.* 161–164.
9. Andrew Jackson, Veto Message on the Bill to Recharter the Bank of the United States, 2 *Messages and Papers of the Presidents* 581–583, James D. Richardson, ed. (Washington, D.C.: Government Printing Office, 1896–1899).
10. Abraham Lincoln, First Inaugural Address, March 4, 1861, 6 *Messages and Papers* 9–10.
11. *Marbury v. Madison*, 1 Cranch 137, 177.
12. Marshall did not suggest, nor did he ever maintain, that the Supreme Court was the "ultimate" interpreter of the Constitution or that its jurisdiction over constitutional matters was

exclusive. His definition of judicial review was restricted and pertained only to the Court's authority to invalidate acts of Congress and the executive when those measures infringed upon the Court's judicial authority. In this context, see especially Robert Lowry Clinton, *Marbury v. Madison and Judicial Review* 1–18 *et seq.* (Lawrence: University of Kansas Press, 1989); Jesse H. Choper, *Judicial Review and the National Political Process: A Functional Reconsideration of the Role of the Supreme Court* 62, 212–213, 382–386 (Chicago: University of Chicago Press, 1980); Hadley Arkes, "On the Moral Standing of the President as an Interpreter of the Constitution," 20 *PS* 637–642 (Summer 1987); Christopher Wolfe, *The Rise of Modern Judicial Review: From Constitutional Interpretation to Judge-made Law* 3–11 (New York: Basic Books, 1986); Wallace Mendelson, "Was Chief Justice Marshall an Activist?" in Stephen C. Halpern and Charles M. Lamb, eds. *Supreme Court Activism and Restraint* 57 (Lexington; Mass.: Lexington Books, 1982). For expansive interpretations of Marshall's holding by the modern Supreme Court, interpretations that go far beyond what Marshall said, see *Cooper v. Aaron* 358 U.S. 1, 18 (1958); *Baker v. Carr*, 369 U.S. 186, 211 (1962); and *United States v. Nixon* 418 U.S. 683, 703–704 (1974).

13. John Adams to John Jay, December 19, 1800. 9 *The Works of John Adams* 91–92, Charles Francis Adams, ed. (Boston: Little, Brown, 1854).

14. Three notable exceptions were *Chisholm v. Georgia*, 2 Dallas 419 (1793), holding the state of Georgia subject to the jurisdiction of federal courts in civil suits, which triggered the Eleventh Amendment to the Constitution; *Ware v. Hylton*, 3 Dallas 199 (1796), holding treaties to be the supreme law of the land; and *Calder v. Bull*, 3 Dallas 386 (1798), restricting the *ex post facto* provision of the Constitution to criminal laws only.

15. For a review of the early difficulties of the Court, see Julius Goebel, Jr., *History of the Supreme Court of the United States: Antecedents and Beginnings to 1801* (New York: Macmillan, 1971), as well as the classic account by Charles Warren, 1 *The Supreme Court in United States History* 31–168, rev. ed. (Boston: Little, Brown, 1926).

16. See especially Leonard Baker, *John Marshall: A Life in Law* 363ff. (New York: Macmillan, 1974).

17. *Cherokee Nation v. Georgia*, 5 Peters 1 (1831); *Worcester v. Georgia*, 6 Peters 515 (1832).

18. *Scott v. Negro London*, 3 Cranch 324 (1806); *Spires v. Willson* 4 Cranch 400 (1808); *Scott v. Negro Ben*, 6 Cranch 3 (1810); *Wood v. Davis* 7 Cranch 271 (1812); *Mimi Queen v. Hepburn*, 7 Cranch 290 (1813); *The Antelope*, 10 Wheaton 66 (1825); *Boyce v. Anderson*, 2 Peters 151 (1829); *McCutchen v. Marshall*, 8 Peters 220 (1834). None of these cases dealt with constitutional issues, none with fugitives or slavery in the territories, and none provided the Court with an opportunity to consider slavery per se. See Kent Newmyer, "On Assessing the Court in History," 21 *Stanford Law Review* 540, 542 (1969).

19. The Marshall name became generally associated with the fight against slavery in Virginia. Marshall himself was the first president of the Richmond chapter of the American Colonization Society, a movement to resettle freed slaves in Liberia. Taking a more radical position was his eldest son, Thomas, who, representing Fauquier county, led the 1832 fight in the Virginia assembly for black emancipation. Cf. D. M. Roper, "In Quest of Judicial Objectivity: The Marshall Court and the Legitimation of Slavery," 21 *Stanford Law Review* 532–539 (1969). The title of the article is misleading. Roper (at p. 537) notes that the title is "ill-advised," and that "the Marshall Court's carefully objective and sometimes explicitly reluctant participation in the legal system's accommodation of the institution of slavery was far from an expression of approval."

20. Speaking for the Court in *The Antelope*, Marshall called the slave trade "this criminal and inhuman traffic . . . [which] is contrary to the law of nature." 10 Wheaton 120. Marshall's views on slavery are discussed perceptively in Robert K. Faulkner, *The Jurisprudence of John Marshall* 49–51 (Princeton, N.J.: Princeton University Press, 1968).

21. Albert J. Beveridge, 1 *The Life of John Marshall* v (Boston: Houghton Mifflin, 1916).

22. Sedgwick to Rufus King, May 11, 1800, 3 *Life and Correspondence of Rufus King* 236–238, Charles R. King, ed. (New York: G. P. Putnam's Sons, 1896).

23. William Wirt, *The Letters of a British Spy* 114–124, 2nd ed. (Baltimore: Lucas, 1803).

24. 1 *Memoirs and Letters of Charles Sumner* 137, Edward L. Pierce, ed. (London: Low, Marston, Searle, & Rivington, 1878).

25. The quotation is from the eulogy delivered by Justice Story at the request of the Suffolk [Massachusetts] Bar, October 15, 1835. Reprinted in 3 *John Marshall: Life, Character, and Judicial Services* 327, 363–364, John F. Dillon, ed. (Chicago: Callaghan, 1903).

26. John Marshall, *The Life of George Washington*, 5 vols. (Philadelphia: C. P. Wayne, 1805–1807).

27. John Marshall, *An Autobiographical Sketch* 9–10, John Stokes Adams, ed. (Ann Arbor: University of Michigan Press, 1937).

28. I am indebted to Graeme Barry, B.A., LL.B., M.A., for his legal research and suggestions concerning Marshall's career as a lawyer.

29. George Wythe held the first chair of legal studies established in America and, following the example of Sir William Blackstone at Oxford, sought to promote the systematic study of the common law. Marshall was an early product of this structured approach to legal education, and his law notebook is a 238-page restatement of legal principles derived from Matthew Bacon's *New Abridgement of the Law*, Blackstone's *Commentaries on the Laws of England*, and the Acts of the Virginia assembly. See especially William F. Swindler, "John Marshall's Preparation for the Bar," 11 *American Journal of Legal History* 207–213 (1967).

30. It has become fashionable to assert that John Marshall had a shoddy legal education and was unfamiliar with the precedents of common law. Both assertions are seriously in error. Marshall had what was considered a superb legal education for the time, and as a brief perusal of his appellate arguments will demonstrate, he was abundantly familiar with precedent and cited it with telling effect.

　　The argument that Marshall was unfamiliar with common law precedent was first made by Albert Beveridge, who, for whatever reason, sought to emphasize Marshall's political sagacity and downplay his legal talent. Beveridge developed the argument at some length in volume 2 of his *Life of Marshall* (pp. 178–180) but cited no evidence other than an 1841 law review article by Gustavus Schmidt. See "Reminiscences of the Late Chief Justice Marshall," 1 *Louisiana Law Journal* 80–99 (May 1841). In fact, Beveridge miscited Schmidt. What Schmidt said was:

> The extent of Mr. Marshalls [*sic*] legal attainments is sufficiently attested by his decisions . . . which on account of the familiar acquaintance they display with the principles of international, public, and common law, and the perspicuity and elegance of their style, as well as the convincing force of their reasoning must be viewed as models of judicial eloquence. And yet, Mr. Marshall can hardly be regarded as a learned lawyer, in the sense in which this word is often employed; as his acquaintance with the roman jurisprudence, as well as with the laws of foreign counties, was not very extensive. He was what is called a *common law lawyer*, in the best and noblest acceptation of the term. He was educated for the bar at a period, when Digests, abridgments and all the numerous facilities, which now smooth the path of the law student were unknown. . . . It was thus no easy task to become an able lawyer, and it required no common share of industry and perseverance to amass sufficient knowledge of the law, to make even a decent appearance in the forum . . . Mr. Marshall succeeded, in a comparatively short time, to muster the elements of the common law, and to place himself at the head of the profession in Virginia, on a level with a Randolph, a Pendleton and a Wythe, names which will forever remain illustrious in the legal profession. That this was not achieved without great labor will readily be believed; and it affords convincing proof both of the energy of character, which Mr. M. possessed, and of his aptitude for study and reflection. . . . (Pp. 81–83, emphasis in original.)

31. Letter of Benjamin H. Latrobe, May 31, 1796, in John E. Semmes, *John H.B. Latrobe and His Times* 7–9 (Baltimore: Norman, Remington, 1917).

32. King to Charles Cotesworth Pinckney, October 17, 1797, 2 *Life of King* 234–235. King's comments were made after listening to Marshall present Virginia's unsuccessful appeal to the Supreme Court in *Ware v. Hylton*, 3 Dallas 199—the only case Marshall ever argued before the Court.

33. A banquet in Philadelphia celebrating Marshall's return was the occasion for the famous toast, "Millions for defense, but not one cent for tribute." Samuel Eliot Morison, *The Oxford*

History of the American People 350 (New York: Oxford University Press, 1965). See also Burton Alva Konkle, *Joseph Hopkinson, 1770–1842, Jurist: Scholar: Inspirer of the Arts, Author of Hail Columbia* 69–84 (Philadelphia: University of Pennsylvania Press, 1931).

34. For an account of Washington's 1798 conference with Marshall (and Bushrod Washington), see Martin Van Buren, *The Autobiography of Martin Van Buren*, John C. Fitzpatrick, ed., in 2 *Annual Report of the American Historical Association for the Year 1918* (Washington, D.C.: Government Printing Office, 1920).

35. Henry wrote to a friend in Richmond (who immediately published the letter) that "General Marshall . . . ever stood high in my esteem as a private citizen. His temper and disposition were always pleasant, his talents and integrity unquestioned. These things are sufficient to place that gentleman far above any competitor in the District for Congress." Henry to Archibald Blair, January 8, 1799, in William Wirt Henry, 2 *Patrick Henry: Life, Correspondence, and Speeches* 591–594 (New York: Charles Scribner's Sons, 1891).

36. Sedgwick to King, December 29, 1799, 3 *Life of King* 163.

37. The charges stemmed from Adams's decision to extradite a fugitive, Jonathan Robbins, to Great Britain. Justice Story said that Marshall's speech in the House of Representatives was "one of the most consummate judicial arguments which was ever pronounced in the halls of legislation. . . . It silenced opposition and settled then and forever the points of international law on which the controversy hinged." Quoted in John F. Dillon, 3 *John Marshall: Life, Character, and Judicial Services* 357–358. It was in his famous speech on the Robbins case that Marshall referred to the president as "the sole organ of the nation in its external relations and its sole representative with foreign nations." 4 *The Papers of John Marshall* 104 (Chapel Hill: University of North Carolina Press, 1984).

38. John Marshall, "Letter to a Freeholder," September 20, 1798, printed in the *Virginia Herald* (Fredericksburg), October 2, 1798. 3 *Marshall Papers* 503–506. Marshall said he would not have voted for the measures, probably could have prevented their enactment had he been in Congress, and certainly would not vote for their renewal.

39. Fisher Ames of Massachusetts, a leader of the High Federalists, wrote of Marshall, "No correct man—no incorrect man even—whose affections and feelings are wedded to the government, would give his name to the base opposers of the law, as a means for its annoyance. Excuses may palliate; future zeal in the cause may partially atone; but his character is done for. . . . False Federalists . . . should be dealt hardly by. . . . The moderates are the meanest of cowards, the falsest of hypocrites." Ames to Christopher Gore, December 18, 1798, 1 *Works of Fisher Ames* 246, Seth Ames, ed. (Boston: Little, Brown, 1854).

40. John Thompson, *The Letters of Curtius* (Richmond: S. Pleasants, 1804); Henry Adams, *The Life of Albert Gallatin* 212, 227 (Philadelphia: J. B. Lippincott, 1879).

41. Marshall later observed that "I was very well received by the President, and was on very cordial terms with all the cabinet except Mr. Wolcott [Oliver Wolcott, Jr., secretary of the treasury]. He at first suspected that I was hostile to the two ex-secretaries [Timothy Pickering and James McHenry], and to himself, because they were all three supposed to be unfriendly to the President to whom I was truly attached. My conduct soon convinced him however that I had no feeling of that sort, after which I had the satisfaction of finding myself on the same cordial footing with him as with the rest of the cabinet." *Autobiographical Sketch* 29.

42. Wolcott to Fisher Ames, August 10, 1800, in Oliver Wolcott, 2 *Memoirs of the Administrations of Washington and John Adams* 401–402, George Gibbs, ed. (New York: Van Norden, 1846).

43. Marshall to Rufus King, September 20, 1800, 2 *American State Papers: Foreign Relations* 489, Walter Lowrie and Matthew St. Clair Clarke, eds. (Washington, D.C.: Gales and Seaton, 1832) Reprinted in 4 *Marshall Papers* 283–297. The diplomatic historian Andrew J. Montague called Marshall's letter to King "a document ranking among the very greatest of American papers, and perhaps unequaled in the diplomatic contributions of the English-speaking world." "John Marshall," in *American Secretaries of State and their Diplomacy* 247, 265, Samuel Flagg Bemis, ed. (New York: Knopf, 1927).

44. Marshall to David Humphreys, September 8, 1800, *Naval Documents Related to the Quasi-War Between the United States and France* 326–331 (Washington, D.C.: Government Printing Office, 1938). Reprinted in 4 *Marshall Papers* 266–273.

45. Marshall to Harrison Gray Otis, August 5, 1800, *ibid*. 204–205.
46. Marshall to Richard Peters, October 30, 1800, *ibid*. 336.
47. Marshall to St. George Tucker, November 18, 1800, 6 *ibid*. 14–15.
48. According to Article II, section 1, of the Constitution: "The electors shall meet in their respective States, and vote by Ballot for two Persons, of whom one at least shall not be an Inhabitant of the same State with themselves."
49. A Federalist elector in Rhode Island voted for John Jay instead of Pinckney. See David Hackett Fischer, *The Revolution of American Conservatism: The Federalist Party in the Era of Jeffersonian Democracy* 281 (New York: Harper & Row, 1965).
50. Marshall to Charles Cotesworth Pinckney, December 18, 1800, 6 *Marshall Papers* 41.
51. "I have nominated you to your old station," Adams wrote to Jay on December 19, 1800. "This is as independent of the inconstancy of the people, as it is of the will of a President. In the future administration of our country, the firmest security we can have against the effects of visionary schemes or fluctuating theories, will be in a solid judiciary; and nothing will cheer the hopes of the best men so much as your acceptance of this appointment." 9 *Works of John Adams* 91–92.
52. Marshall to Pinckney, 6 *Marshall Papers* 41.
53. Marshall to Edward Carrington, December 28, 1800, *ibid*. 44–45.
54. *Ibid*.
55. Henry Adams, 1 *History of the United States During the Administration of Thomas Jefferson* 132 (New York: Literary Classics of the United States, 1986). Adams's original edition was published in 1882 by Charles Scribner.
56. Beveridge, 1 *Life of Marshall* 125–130; Baker, *Marshall* 68–69, 345.
57. Dumas Malone, *Jefferson the Virginian* 81–85, 358–359 (Boston: Little, Brown, 1948). A 1781 letter from Eliza Ambler (Marshall's future sister-in-law) detailing Jefferson's flight as governor when the British invaded Virginia was later published in "An Old Virginia Correspondence," 84 *Atlantic Monthly* 538–539 (1899).
58. Marshall to Henry Lee, October 25, 1830, Marshall Papers, Williamsburg, Va.
59. The quotation is from Justice Story, who told the anecdote in one of his lectures at the Harvard Law School. It was recorded by Rutherford B. Hayes, one of Story's students, in his diary entry of September 20, 1843. Charles R. Williams, 1 *Life of Rutherford Birchard Hayes* 33 (Columbus, Ohio: F. J. Hear, 1928). Story referred to the quotation in his eulogy to Marshall, without mentioning Jefferson's name. Dillon, 3 *Marshall: Life, Character and Judicial Services* 370.
60. Jefferson to Madison, November 26, 1795, 8 *Works of Jefferson* 197–199.
61. Jefferson to Albert Gallatin, September 27, 1810, 1 *The Writings of Albert Gallatin* 492, Henry Adams, ed. (Philadelphia: J. B. Lippincott, 1879). Senator Henry Cabot Lodge, who was not an admirer of Jefferson, called the third president's dislike of Marshall "the hatred of a timid man, of acute, subtle, brilliant intellect and creeping methods, for the man of powerful mind, who was as simple and direct as he was absolutely fearless and who marched straight to his object with his head up and his eyes on his foe." "John Marshall, Statesman," 172 *North American Review* 198 (February 1901).
62. Hamilton's letter to Marshall has been lost. Given the nature of Marshall's reply, which was preserved among Hamilton's papers, it has long been assumed that Hamilton's message to him was similar to that sent at the same time to other Federalist leaders expressing Hamilton's virulent opposition to Burr. See Hamilton to Oliver Wolcott, December 16, 1800; to Gouverneur Morris, December 19; to Theodore Sedgwick, December 22; to Harrison Gray Otis, December 23; and to James A. Bayard, December 27, 1800. 25 *The Papers of Alexander Hamilton* 257–277, Harold C. Syrett, ed. (New York: Columbia University Press, 1977).
63. Hamilton to Gouverneur Morris, December 26, 1800, *ibid*. 275.
64. Hamilton to Wolcott, December 16, 1800, *ibid*. 257. The reference is to Lucius Sergius Catilina (108–62 B.C.), a Roman politician who conspired to assassinate the consuls and plunder Rome, and who was foiled by Cicero.
65. Hamilton to Bayard, December 27, 1800, *ibid*. 275–277.
66. Marshall to Hamilton, January 1, 1801, 6 *Marshall Papers* 46–47.

67. The Mazzei letter, and Marshall's sharp commentary, are published in 2 *Life of George Washington* appendix, 23–32, rev. ed. (Philadelphia: Crissy, 1832). James Madison's balanced judgment of the incident, written many years later, was that allowances "ought to be made for a habit in Mr. Jefferson as in others of great genius of expressing in strong and round terms, impressions of the moment." Madison to N. P. Trist, May 1832, 9 *Writings of James Madison* 479, Gaillard Hunt, ed. (New York: G. P. Putnam's Sons, 1909–10).

68. Marshall to Hamilton, January 1, 1801, 6 *Marshall Papers* 46–47.

69. On December 26, 1800, Jefferson wrote to Madison that the Federalists were seeking a deadlock "to pass a bill giving the government to Mr. Jay, appointed Chief Justice, or to Marshall as Sec'y of State." 9 *Works of Jefferson* 161. Also see Jefferson to Tench Coxe, *ibid*. 162. Jefferson offered no substantiation. Under the unusual circumstances of the election, Jefferson's apprehension is understandable, but it proved to be unfounded.

70. *Salem Gazette*, January 16, 1801; *The Aurora* (Philadelphia), January 10, 15, 1801, cited in Warren, 1 *Supreme Court* 182, note 2.

71. Monroe to Jefferson, January 6, January 18, January 27, 1801; 3 *The Writings of James Monroe* 253–257, Stanislaus Murray Hamilton, ed. (New York: G. P. Putnam's Sons, 1898–1903).

72. Beveridge, 2 *Life of Marshall* 539–540.

73. Jay to Marshall, January 2, 1801, 6 *Marshall Papers* 49; Jay to Adams, January 2, 1801, 4 *The Correspondence and Public Papers of John Jay* 285–286, Henry P. Johnston, ed. (New York: G. P. Putnam's Sons, 1890–93). Jay's letter to Adams declining the appointment illustrates the problems Marshall initially faced as chief justice. Said Jay, "I left the bench perfectly convinced that under a system so defective it would not obtain the energy, weight, and dignity which was essential . . . ; nor acquire the public confidence and respect which, as the last resort of the justice of the nation, it should possess. Hence I am induced to doubt both the propriety and the expediency of my returning to the bench under the present system."

74. Kathryn Turner, "The Appointment of Chief Justice John Marshall," 17 *William and Mary Quarterly* 143, 152, note 40, 3rd series (1960).

75. The ostensible reason for the reduction was to prevent a tie vote on the Court. But if Ellsworth's vacancy were to have been filled, the effect would have been to deny a new Republican president an opportunity to fill the first vacancy. See William W. Crosskey, 2 *Politics and the Constitution in the History of the United States* 759 (Chicago: University of Chicago Press, 1953).

76. Marshall, *Autobiographical Sketch* 30.

77. Turner, "Appointment of Marshall," 155ff.

78. Some Federalists, such as Oliver Wolcott, suggested that it was actually Adams who had followed Marshall's policies over the previous year. "With regard to Gen. Marshall," wrote Wolcott, "every one who knew that great man, knew that he possessed to an extraordinary degree the faculty of putting his own ideas into the minds of others, unconsciously to them." Wolcott, 2 *Memoirs* 350.

79. On January 26, 1801, Adams, with evident satisfaction, wrote to Elias Boudinot that he had nominated "a gentleman in the full vigor of middle age, in the full habits of business, and whose reading in the science [of the law] is fresh in his head." 9 *Works of John Adams* 94.

80. When Marshall's name was announced, Senator Dayton wrote to Justice Paterson that it was "contrary to the hopes and expectation of us all." January 20, 1801, William Paterson Papers, New Jersey Historical Society.

81. 1 *Senate Executive Journal* 371, 374 (1801). By contrast, Marshall's confirmation as secretary of state was whisked through in one day, May 13, 1800.

82. February 7, 1801, 11 *Annals of Congress* 915. The bill was signed into law by Adams on February 13, 1801. 2 *United States Statutes at Large* 89.

83. Dayton to Paterson, January 28, 1801, William Paterson Papers, New Jersey Historical Society.

84. Beveridge, 2 *Life of Marshall* 555.

85. Marshall, *Autobiographical Sketch* 30.

86. Adams to Marshall, August 17, 1825, Marshall Papers, Williamsburg, Va.

87. Bayard's correspondence provides the best insight into the voting in the House of Repre-

sentatives. See *Papers of James A. Bayard, 1796–1815*, Elizabeth Donnan, ed., in 2 *Annual Report of the American Historical Association for the Year 1913* 116–132 (Washington, D.C.: Government Printing Office, 1915). Also see the letter of Rep. Robert Goodloe Harper to his South Carolina constituents, February 24, 1801, *ibid*. 132–137.

88. Act of March 1, 1792, 1 *United States Statutes at Large* 239.
89. Act of February 27, 1801, 11 *Annals of Congress* 1554.
90. Marshall to King, February 26, 1801, 6 *Marshall Papers* 82–83.
91. Jefferson to Marshall, March 2, 1801, *ibid*. 86.
92. Jefferson to Marshall, March 4, 1801, *ibid*. 88. Madison was in ill health and did not arrive in Washington until May. Marshall served as secretary of state until March 5, at which time he was temporarily replaced by Levi Lincoln, Jefferson's attorney general. As Dumas Malone has pointed out, there is no foundation for the canard that Lincoln forcibly took possession of the office on the night preceding the inauguration. Dumas Malone, *Jefferson the President: The First Term, 1801–1805* 34 (Boston: Little, Brown, 1970).
93. Marshall to Jefferson, March 2, 1801, 6 *Marshall Papers* 86–87.
94. Marshall to Pinckney, March 4, 1801, *ibid*. 89–90.
95. Beveridge, 3 *Life of Marshall* 11.
96. Marshall to Pinckney, March 4, 1801, 6 *Marshall Papers* 89–90.
97. For the text of Jefferson's first inaugural, see 9 *Works of Jefferson* 193–200. Emphasis added.
98. 6 *Marshall Papers* 89–90.
99. As reported by Justice Story in Dillon, 3 *John Marshall: Life, Character, and Judicial Services* 344.
100. David Kimball, *Venerable Relic: The Story of the Liberty Bell* (Philadelphia: Eastern National Park and Monument Association, 1989).

1: Marshall's Virginia Heritage

1. John Marshall, *An Autobiographical Sketch*, John Stokes Adams, ed. (Ann Arbor: University of Michigan Press, 1937). The quotation appears on p. 3.
2. Marshall had prefixed a history of the colonies to his five volume *The Life of George Washington* (Philadelphia: C. P. Wayne, 1805–07). In 1824 it was published as a separate work by Abraham Small of Philadelphia: John Marshall, *A History of the Colonies planted by the English on the Continent of North America, from their Settlement, to the Commencement of that War, which terminated in their Independence*. Story's review appeared in 26 *North American Review* 1–40 (January 1828).
3. Marshall, *Autobiographical Sketch* 3.
4. *Ibid*. 3–4.
5. "The Genesis of Fauquier," 1 *Bulletin of the Fauquier County Historical Society* 109–113 (July 1922); H. C. Groome, *Fauquier During the Proprietorship* 82–112 (Richmond, Va.: Old Dominion Press, 1927).
6. Braddock, an officer in the Coldstream Guards, was commander in chief of all British forces in North America. His task force included two regiments of infantry (the 44th and 48th), plus supporting artillery, engineers, a large supply train, and eleven companies of colonial militia. The defeat is thoroughly treated in Winthrop Sargent's magnificent classic *History of An Expedition against Fort Du Quesne in 1755; under Major-General Edward Braddock* (Philadelphia: Lippincott, Grambo & Co., 1855). Marshall's treatment of the campaign, a work of remarkable literary merit, appears in volume 1 of his *Life of George Washington* at pp. 294–306. Marshall describes Washington's role in volume 2, pp. 13–21. For more recent works, see Charles Hamilton, *Braddock's Defeat* (Norman: University of Oklahoma Press, 1959), and Lee McCardell, *Ill-starred General: Braddock of the Coldstream Guards* (Pittsburgh: University of Pittsburgh Press, 1958).
7. W. M. Paxton, in his history of the Marshall family, asserts that Lieutenant Thomas Marshall originally joined Braddock's expedition but was left behind to aid the construction of Fort Necessity. Paxton, *The Marshall Family* 20 (Cincinnati: Robert Clarke & Co., 1885). This ap-

pears to be incorrect. Beveridge dismisses the claim, citing a letter to Thomas Marshall from his sister Elizabeth Marshall Martin, dated June 15, 1755, referring to Braddock's progress. If Thomas had been with Braddock, his sister would not have so written. Albert J. Beveridge, 1 *The Life of John Marshall* 8, note 2 (Boston: Houghton Mifflin, 1916). More significantly, Thomas Marshall's name was not on the meticulous roster kept by George Washington of those Virginians who joined the expedition. Washington Papers, Library of Congress.

8. The community of Germantown is believed to be the oldest settlement in Fauquier county. It was established in 1721 by twelve German families—miners and metalworkers—who went to Virginia in 1714 under the auspices of Governor Alexander Spottswood and Baron Christopher de Graffenried to exploit the mineral deposits of Virginia's piedmont. Each family was assigned a lot of 150 acres, with a leasehold for ninety-nine years. The community was described in 1748 by the Reverend Mathew G. Gottschalk as being similar to "a village in Germany where the houses are far apart. It is situated along a little creek, Lucken [Licking] Run. They are from the Siegen District [in Westphalia] and are all Reformed people. . . . There is a church and a school house." But the settlement at Germantown did not last. With land to the west readily available, all but one of the German families soon moved on. And it was in the abandoned homestead of the Fishback family, one of the original settler families, that the Marshalls resided in 1755. H. C. Groome, *Fauquier During the Proprietorship* 113–130; Charles E. Kemper, "The History of Germantown," 2 *Bulletin of the Fauquier County Historical Society* 125–133 (July 1922). Also see Charles E. Kemper, "The Early Westward Movement in Virginia," 13 *Virginia Magazine of History and Biography* 362–370 (1906); "Germantown, Fauquier's First Settlement," 3 *News and Notes from The Fauquier Historical Society* 1–2 (Summer 1981).

9. Douglas Southall Freeman, 1 *George Washington: A Biography* 51 (New York: Charles Scribner's Sons, 1948). Also see Beveridge, 1 *Life of Marshall* 13, note 1, citing the oral testimony of W. G. Stanard, secretary of the Virginia Historical Society, and Professor H. J. Eckenrode of Richmond College.

10. Marshall family legend, related by the chief justice's oldest sister, Eliza Colston, holds that Elizabeth Markham was the stepdaughter of the famous pirate Blackbeard. According to the tale, when John Markham, the Alexandria merchant, died in the early 1700s, his young widow took up with and then married a dashing naval personage whom she subsequently learned was Blackbeard. The Markham children were purposely sent away from the Alexandria homestead, and Elizabeth, still a young girl, found a home with her uncles, William and Lewis Markham, in Westmoreland County. There she met and married the original John Marshall, "John of the forest." For Eliza Colston's recounting of the matter, see Paxton, *Marshall Family* 15–17.

11. Beveridge, 1 *Life of Marshall* 14–15. Cf. Paxton, *Marshall Family* 5–13.

12. Marshall's comments were contained in an autobiographical letter he wrote to Joseph Delaplaine of Philadelphia, March 22, 1818. The letter was read in full in a memorial address by Justice Horace Gray in Richmond, Virginia, February 4, 1901, and reprinted in 1 *John Marshall: Life, Character, and Judicial Services* 54–55, John F. Dillon, ed. (Chicago: Callaghan, 1903).

13. For details of the early Randolphs, see especially Gerald Steffens Cowden, "The Randolphs of Turkey Island: A Prosopography of the First Three Generations, 1650–1806," unpublished Ph.D. dissertation, College of William and Mary, 1977. Also see Jonathan Daniels, *The Randolphs of Virginia* (Garden City, N.Y.: Doubleday, 1972); H. J. Eckenrode, *The Randolphs: The Story of a Virginia Family* (Indianapolis: Bobbs-Merrill, 1946); Robert Isham Randolph, *The Randolphs of Virginia* (Chicago: private printing, 1936); W. C. Bruce, 1 *John Randolph of Roanoke* 9–17 (New York: Putnam, 1922); Roberta Lee Randolph, *The First Randolphs of Virginia* (Washington, D.C.: Public Affairs Press, 1961); Wassell Randolph, *William Randolph I. of Turkey Island* (Memphis, Tenn.: Seebode Mimeo Service, 1949); *Collected Letters of John Randolph of Roanoke to Dr. John Brockenbrough, 1812–1833*, Keith Shorey, ed. (New Brunswick, N.J.: Transaction, Inc., 1988).

14. For a genealogical chart of the ancestors of William Randolph, tracing the heritage to the fif-

teenth century, see W. G. Stanard, "Major Robert Beverley and His Descendants," 3 *Virginia Magazine of History and Biography* 261–271 (1896). The Isham family heritage is described in "Narrative of Bacon's Rebellion," 4 *ibid.* 117–153 (1897); "Virginia Gleanings in England," 18 *ibid.* 80–92 (1910). Also see Roberta Lee Randolph, *The First Randolphs* 28–34.

15. Sir John Randolph, 1693–1737, was widely regarded as the ablest lawyer in the colonies during the early eighteenth century. He served successively as clerk of the House of Burgesses, King's Attorney, Speaker of the House of Burgesses, and treasurer of the colony of Virginia. Daniels, *Randolphs of Virginia* 43–48; Richard Lee Morton, 2 *Colonial Virginia* 520–522 (Chapel Hill: University of North Carolina Press, 1960); Eckenrode, *Randolphs* 44–51. For Sir John, see W. A. Shaw, 2 *The Knights of England* 284 (London: Sherratt & Hughes, 1906).

16. *The Secret Diary of William Byrd of Westover 1709–1712* 321, note 1, Louis B. Wright and Marion Tinling, eds. (Richmond, Va.: Dietz, 1941); "Genealogy of the Fleming Family," 23 *Virginia Magazine of History and Biography* 325–326 (1915).

17. The story of Mary Isham Randolph was related by Colonel William Byrd of Westover, following his visit to Tuckahoe in September 1732. Colonel Byrd reported that the overseer [Enoch Arden] was without

> one visible Qualification, except Impudence, to recommend him to a Female's Inclinations. But there is sometimes such a Charm in that Hibernian Endowment, that frail Woman can't withstand it, tho' it stand alone without any other Recommendation. Had she run away with a Gentleman or a pretty Fellow, there might have been some excuse for her, tho' he were of inferior Fortune: but to stoop to a dirty Plebian, without any kind of merit, is the lowest Prostitution. I found the family justly enraged at it; and tho' I had more good Nature than to join in her Condemnation, yet I could devise no Excuse for so senseless a Prank as this young Gentlewoman had play'd.

The Writings of Colonel William Byrd of Westover in Virginia 338, John Spencer Bassett, ed. (New York: Doubleday, Page & Co., 1901).

18. Daniels, *Randolphs of Virginia* 50–51.

19. Henrico parish, among the oldest in Virginia, was the site of Pocahontas's baptism and wedding. The original church, Curles Church, was situated on Richard Randolph's Curles plantation, near the town of Varina. In the late 1740s the bulk of the congregation began to meet in Richmond, and the vestry seat was officially moved to the newly constructed St. John's Church in 1749. See the Reverend Lewis D. Burton, "Annals of Henrico Parish," in *History of Henrico Parish, 1611–1904* 5–20, J. Staunton Moore, ed. (Richmond, Va.: Bossieux, 1904).

20. Paxton, *Marshall Family* 24–25, 31–32; Keith family papers, Virginia Historical Society, Richmond, Virginia. A recent history of the city of Aberdeen described James Keith as "a shadowy seventeenth-century alumnus of Marischal College." Alexander Keith, *A Thousand Years of Aberdeen* 213 note (Aberdeen, Va.: Aberdeen University Press, 1972).

21. Mary's brother William was the senior vestryman and church warden of Henrico parish, and Richard Randolph of Curles plantation was also a vestryman. Virginia's statutes explicitly charged the church warden with presenting offenders to the vestry for punishment. Offences included, *inter alia*, "those foule and abominable sins of drunkennesse, fornication, and adultery. . . ." William Waller Hening, 2 *The Statutes at Large: Being a Collection of All of the Laws of Virginia* 51–52 (Richmond, Va.: Samuel Pleasants, 1809–1823). For the vestry minutes accepting James Keith's resignation, see Dr. R. A. Brock, "Vestry Book of Henrico parish, Virginia, 1730–1773," in Moore, *History of Henrico Parish* 13–16.

22. The Randolphs did not object to their daughter marrying clergy. Rather, their objection was directed at Keith personally. Mary's younger sister Judith subsequently married the Reverend William Stith, who succeeded Keith as the minister of Henrico parish and who later became president of William and Mary.

23. Bishop Meade, in what is considered the standard church history of the period, simply states that "Of the Rev. Mr. Keith . . . I have not been able to obtain all the information I desire and hope for. From all that I can learn, he was a worthy man." 2 *Old Churches, Ministers, and Families of Virginia* 216 (Philadelphia: J. B. Lippincott, 1861). Similar references are contained in Edward Lewis Goodwin, *The Colonial Church in Virginia* 284 (Milwaukee: More-

house Publishing Co., 1927); and Frederick Lewis Weis, *The Colonial Clergy in Virginia, North Carolina, and South Carolina* 29 (Baltimore: Genealogical Publishing Co., 1976). The scant documentation of the episode concludes on September 20, 1735, when Governor Gooch wrote to the Bishop of London to announce a replacement for Keith in Henrico parish. The new minister, wrote Gooch, will "by his Conduct, make amends to the People for the failings of that unhappy Gentleman [Rev. Keith]." No further explanation was provided. See Reverend G. McLaren Brydon, "The Virginia Clergy," 32 *Virginia Magazine of History and Biography* 333–334 (1924).

24. James Blair to Bishop of London, January 15, 1734. Correspondence of the Bishop of London with some miscellaneous papers, 1695–1776, Fulham Palace Papers, 15, 122. Cited in Cowden, "The Randolphs of Turkey Island," 411.

25. Blair's follow-up letter is reproduced in William Stevens Perry, 1 *Historical Collections Relating to the American Colonial Church* 358 (Hartford, Conn.: The Church Press, 1870).

26. See especially Stella Pickett Hardy, "Fauquier County Keiths," in *Colonial Families of the Southern States of America* 311–313 (Baltimore: Genealogical Publishing Co., 1968). Also see Larry King, *Keith Kinfolks: Descendants of James Keith, Sr.* (Henderson, Tenn.: private printing, 1979).

27. During her later years, Mary Randolph Keith lived with her granddaughter, Eliza Marshall (Mrs. Rawleigh Colston), the chief justice's eldest sister, and it was she who corroborated the story for family chronicler James Paxton. See *Marshall Family* 25–26.

28. Most of Marshall's biographers have been equally chary of tracing the Randolph tie. Beveridge, for example, treats the Elk Island episode in a footnote. 1 *Life of Marshall* 17, note 7. For additional commentary on Marshall's early biographers, see Edward S. Corwin, "John Marshall," in 6 *Dictionary of American Biography* 315 (New York: Charles Scribner's Sons, 1935). Leonard Baker makes no reference whatever to the episode in his biography, *John Marshall: A Life in Law* (New York: Macmillan, 1974).

29. Paxton asserts not only that James was the son of a professor in Marischal College at Aberdeen but that the professor was also a bishop. That is incorrect. James's father was George Keith, an uncle and tutor of the Earl Marischal, who lost his chair at the college in 1717 for siding with the Pretender. See John Malcolm Bulloch, *A History of the University of Aberdeen, 1495–1895* 140–141 (London: Hodder & Stoughton, 1895). Robert Keith, a cousin, was Bishop of Fife from 1733 to 1743, but he was too young to have been the father of James Keith. For the bishops of Scotland, see *Crockford's Clerical Directory* 1748–1749 (London: Oxford University Press, 1960). Cf. Paxton, *Marshall Family* 25.

30. Robert Keith's exploits were described by Sir Walter Scott in his epic poem "Lord of the Isles." For the battle of Bannockburn, see John E. Morris, *Bannockburn* (Cambridge: Cambridge University Press, 1914); General Sir Philip Christison, *Bannockburn: The Story of the Battle* (Edinburgh: Scottish National Trust, 1962).

31. For a concise discussion of the role of the Keiths in England's civil war, see 10 *Dictionary of National Biography* 1204–1224, Sir Leslie Stephen and Sir Sidney Lee, eds. (London: Oxford University Press, 1917). A more extensive history of the Keiths is provided by Peter Buchan in his *An Historical and Authentic Account of the Ancient and Noble Family of Keith* (Peterhead: P. Buchan, 1820). Dunnottar, one of the most extensive and important castles in Scotland, is described in Frank Roy Fraprie, *The Castles and Keeps of Scotland* 110–115 (Boston: L.C. Page & Co., 1907). Because it was the strongest fortress in Scotland, Dunnottar was selected as the place of deposit for the national regalia. The preservation of the treasure is described by Fraprie at pp. 113–115.

32. For details of the 1719 rising and the role of the Keiths, see Sir Charles Petrie, *The Jacobite Movement: The Last Phase, 1716–1807* 15–29 (London: Eyre & Spottiswoode, 1932); Bruce Lenman, *The Jacobite Cause* 59–72 (Glasgow: Richard Drew Publishing, 1986); Frank McLynn, *The Jacobites* 102–104 (London: Routledge & Kegan Paul, 1985); William Kirk Dickson, *The Jacobite Attempt of 1719* xxx-lix (Edinburgh: Edinburgh University Press, 1895).

33. Paxton, *Marshall Family* 24; Allan B. Magruder, *John Marshall* 5 (Boston: Houghton, Mifflin, 1890); Beveridge, 1 *Life of Marshall* 17. Magruder refers to James Keith as the "cousin-

german to the last Earl Marischal and to Field Marshal James Keith," a seldom-employed usage to denote a first-cousin relationship.

34. John Hill Burton, *The Scot Abroad* 331–47 (Edinburgh: Blackwood, 1864); Buchan, *Ancient and Noble Family of Keith* 68–84. James Francis Edward Keith was created a field marshal by Frederick the Great in 1747. During the Seven Years' War, he conducted the masterly Prussian retreat from Olmütz and was mortally wounded while rallying his troops at the battle of Hochkirchen. Keith's role at Olmütz and Hochkirchen are described in F. W. Longman, *Frederick the Great and the Seven Years' War* 147–153 (New York: Charles Scribner's Sons, 1900).

35. George Washington's great-grandfather was a merchant seaman who settled in Virginia and married well. Washington's father twice married landed heiresses, and Washington himself repeated the practice when he married the widow Martha Dandridge Custis, one of the wealthiest women in the colonies. See Freeman, 1 *George Washington* 16–17; 2 *ibid.* 300–301, 404; Charles Cecil Wall, *George Washington: Citizen-Soldier* 24 (Charlottesville: University Press of Virginia, 1980); John E. Ferling, *The First of Men: A Life of George Washington* 2 (Knoxville: University of Tennessee Press, 1988).

James Madison's ancestors were carpenters, but they achieved success rapidly through similarly advantageous marriages, particularly the marriage of Madison's grandfather to Frances Taylor, eldest daughter of James Taylor, a large Virginia landowner. Irving Brant, 1 *James Madison: The Virginia Revolutionary* 24–27 (Indianapolis: Bobbs-Merrill, 1941). James Monroe's ancestors, like Washington's, were seventeenth-century mariners who landed in the colonies and married well. See Daniel Gilman, *American Statesman: James Monroe* 4 (Boston: Houghton Mifflin, 1890); George Morgan, *Life of James Monroe* 11–14 (Boston: Small, Maynard, 1921).

Patrick Henry's father arrived from Scotland in 1727 and married into one of Virginia's oldest and richest families when he wed the young, attractive widow of the prosperous John Syme, herself a Dabney. William Wirt Henry, 1 *Patrick Henry: Life, Correspondence and Speeches* 1–7 (New York: Scribner, 1891); Clifford Dowdey, *The Virginia Dynasties* 338–339 (Boston: Little, Brown, 1969).

36. 1 *The Works of Thomas Jefferson* 4–5, Paul Leicester Ford, ed. (New York: G. P. Putnam's Sons, 1904).

37. Dumas Malone, *Jefferson the Virginian* 3–5 (Boston: Little, Brown, 1948).

38. Will of "John of the forest," made April 1, 1752, probated May 26, 1752, and recorded June 22, 1752. 9 *Records of Westmoreland County, Deeds and Wills* 419. It is reproduced as Appendix II in Beveridge, 1 *Life of Marshall* 485–486.

39. Thomas Marshall briefly stepped down from the House of Burgesses in 1767 when he became sheriff of Fauquier county and again briefly in 1773 when he was appointed clerk of Dunmore county (now Shenandoah county).

40. Quitrents were an outgrowth of feudalism, the period during which small landholders owed service to their liege lord. By paying a small annual fee, known as a quitrent, the landholder acknowledged the lord's tenure, and freed himself of any other service that might be required. See especially B. W. Bond, "The Quit-Rent System in the American Colonies," 17 *American Historical Review* 496–516 (1912).

41. On September 18, 1649, Charles II, then living in exile at St. Germain-en-Laye near Paris, granted to his "right trusty and beloved" companions, the two Culpeper brothers, "in consideration of many services done," that portion of the Old Dominion of Virginia "bounded by and within the heads of the Rivers of Tappahonocke als Rappahanock and Quiriough or Patawomecke Rivers." The bedraggled exile court of Charles II had little concept of the vast extent of the area designated, and with Cromwell in firm control in England, the gift was virtually worthless. After the Restoration, however, the grant was duly recorded (over the loud protests of colonial officials in Jamestown), and on April 6, 1671 the General Court of Virginia accepted the patent. A revised patent was issued by James II to Thomas Lord Culpeper on September 27, 1688, and the grant was made perpetual. Shortly thereafter, James II was driven from the throne, Lord Culpeper died, and the estate passed to his daughter, Catherine, Lady Fairfax. As luck would have it, her husband, the fifth Lord Fair-

fax, was a staunch supporter of William and Mary, and commanded the Yorkshire cavalry that had secured the north of England on their behalf. Subsequently an officer in the Life Guards, Lord Fairfax had little difficulty gaining renewed royal affirmation of the grant, once again to the consternation of colonial officials in Virginia. His son Thomas, the sixth Lord Fairfax, inherited the estate in 1710 while still a child. After visiting the proprietary in 1735, Lord Fairfax moved to Virginia in 1747. See especially Stuart E. Brown, Jr., *Virginia Baron: The Story of Thomas 6th Lord Fairfax* 49–100 (Berryville, Va.: Chesapeake Book Co., 1965), and Freeman, 1 *George Washington* 447–524, wherein the tangled affairs of the proprietary are carefully rendered.

42. Lord Fairfax's northern neck proprietary included the following counties in Virginia: Lancaster, Northumberland, Richmond, Westmoreland, King George, Stafford, Prince William, Fairfax, Culpeper, Fauquier, Loudon, Madison, Rappahannock, Shenandoah, Warren, Clarke, Frederick, and three-quarters of Page county. In West Virginia: Jefferson, Berkeley, Morgan, Hampshire, Mineral, Hardy (nine-sixteenths), and Grant (two-thirds).

43. Freeman, 1 *George Washington* 202; Washington Irving, 1 *The Life of Washington* 26–27, 3rd ed. (New York: G. P. Putnam, 1856); Silas Weir Mitchell, *The Youth of Washington Told in the Form of An Autobiography* 76–77 (New York: Century, 1904); Beveridge, 1 *Life of Marshall* 49–50.

44. Andrew Burnaby, *Travels Through the Middle Settlements of North America in the Years 1759 and 1760* 197–198, 3rd ed. (London: Wessels, 1798); Irving, 1 *Life of Washington* 33; Jared Sparks, 1 *The Life of George Washington* 12 (London: Henry Colburn, 1839); Lorenzo Sabine, 1 *Biographical Sketches of Loyalists of the American Revolution* 409 (Boston: Little, Brown, 1864); Meade, 2 *Old Churches of Virginia* 282–283.

45. The inventory of the contents of Lord Fairfax's library, made upon his death, is reprinted in Stuart Brown, *Virginia Baron* 192–193. In addition to a twenty-volume set of *Universal History*, thirteen volumes of Swift's *Works*, and twenty-four volumes of bound magazines, the library included the works of most contemporary English writers as well as the standard classics and legal texts of the period.

46. Brown, *Virginia Baron* 178.

47. In Britain, Fairfax's distinguished ancestors had consistently opposed tyrannical government. Ferdinando (1584–1648), the second Lord Fairfax, commanded the right wing of the parliamentary forces at Marston Moor. Thomas, "Black Tom" (1612–1671), the third Lord Fairfax, was the head of Cromwell's army and the hero of the battle of Naseby, in which Charles I was driven from power. When the Commonwealth turned oppressive after Cromwell's death, the Fairfaxes supported the restoration of Charles II to reestablish order.

48. General Charles Lee, Washington's second in command, provided the details of Lord Fairfax's assistance to the cause of independence in Lee's petition to the Virginia Legislature on Fairfax's behalf. See Brown, *Virginia Baron* 183–184.

49. Parson Weems wrote apocryphally that Lord Fairfax, upon hearing the news of Cornwallis's defeat in 1781, called out to his servant, "Come, Joe! Carry me to my bed! for I'm sure 'tis high time for me to die!" Mason Locke Weems, *The Life of George Washington* 26, republished by Harvard University Press in 1962. Weems's account does not ring true. As Lord Fairfax's biographer notes, his more likely comment would have been that it "serves the Tories right." Brown, *Virginia Baron* 187.

50. The cabins of the original German settlers were built with Teutonic thoroughness. More or less alike and constructed cooperatively, the cabins consisted of a ground floor 16 feet by 26 feet, divided into two rooms, with a loft overhead. According to an eyewitness account,

> the sills [of the cabins] were of hewn oak 10 ½ in. by 9 in., mortised at the ends and secured by 1 in. oak pins. The studding consisted of 4 in. by 7 in. oak, mortised and pinned to the sills. . . . The house was weatherboarded outside with boards of heart of yellow poplar 10 in. by 1 in., rabbited and laid on flat with ⅜ in. bead. The walls inside were made by plastering a composition of small stones in a red clay and straw mortar between the studding [the famous wattle and daub used by the Germans in their construction since the Middle Ages], the surface being levelled smooth and white washed. The rafters were 4 in. by 4 in. oak and the roof covering consisted of boards 4

ft. long, 7 in. wide and ⅜ in. thick, overlapping like shingles. The joists were 4 in. by 7 in. oak and the floor was laid with 10 in. dressed boards nailed down with handmade 20d. nails. . . . All hardware, nails, hinges and latches were of hand wrought iron.

And like many settlers' homes of the period, there was a spring in the cellar. H. C. Groome, *Fauquier During the Proprietorship* 130, note 17.

51. Cited in John Esten Cooke, "Early Days of John Marshall," 3 *Historical Magazine and Notes and Queries Concerning the Antiquities, History and Biography of America* 165–169 (June 1859).

52. In April 1690 William Randolph of Turkey Island purchased 3,256 acres on Tuckahoe Creek from Edmond Jennings of York County for 1,500 pounds of tobacco. The name "Tuckahoe" was derived from a root eaten by the Indians and called "tockahoe" by them. An early description of the root is provided by William Strachey, the first secretary of the colony of Virginia, in his *The Historie of Travell into Virginia Britannia* (1612), reprint ed., Louis B. Wright and Virginia Freund, eds. (London: Hakluyt Society, 1953). Also see Roberta Lee Randolph, *The First Randolphs* 43, as well as Jefferson Randolph Anderson, "Tuckahoe and the Tuckahoe Randolphs," 45 *Virginia Magazine of History and Biography* 55–86 (1937).

53. It was William who had played the leading role in the tragedy of Elk Island, and it was also he who, as warden of Henrico parish, had forced the resignation of James Keith. As a result, the estrangement between him and his oldest sister, Marshall's mother, was complete.

54. Thomas Jefferson's earliest recorded recollection was of being carried on a pillow by a mounted slave on the journey from Shadwell to Tuckahoe. See Henry S. Randall, 1 *The Life of Thomas Jefferson* 11 (New York: Derby & Jackson, 1858). For further discussion of the Tuckahoe plantation, see Thomas Tileston Waterman, *Mansions of Virginia* 85–92 (Chapel Hill: University of North Carolina Press, 1946); R. A. Lancaster, Jr., *Historic Virginia Homes and Churches* 168–173 (Philadelphia: J. B. Lippincott, 1915); Thomas Anburey, 2 *Travels through the Interior Parts of America* 318–319 (London: W. Lane, 1789); "Virginia Council Journals," 32 *Virginia Magazine of History and Biography* 390–395 (1924); J. R. Anderson, "Tuckahoe and the Tuckahoe Randolphs," 45 *ibid.* 55–56 (1937); *Annual Report of the Monticello Association* 9–13 (1936); as well as Edith Tunis Sale, *Interiors of Virginia Houses of Colonial Times* 387–1406 (Richmond, Va.: W. Byrd Press, 1927).

55. By 1746 Tuckahoe had become one of the most productive plantations on the James River. Dumas Malone reports that Peter Jefferson "directed the activities of at least seven slave overseers." Between 1745 and 1751, Tuckahoe produced 667,336 pounds of tobacco, Virginia's principal cash crop. Malone, *Jefferson the Virginian* 20.

56. In 1769 Jefferson's sister Lucy married her first cousin, Charles Lilburne Lewis. In 1780 Jefferson's brother Randolph married Anne Jefferson Lewis, a sister of Charles Lilburne Lewis, also a first cousin. All four were grandchildren of Isham of Dungeness. For a genealogical chart, see *ibid.* 429.

57. Brown, *Virginia Baron* 88, 109–110.

58. In 1765 Thomas Marshall leased 330 acres "whereon the said Thomas Marshall now lives" from Ludwell Lee and Colonel Richard Henry Lee for an annual rent of £5, plus quitrents and land tax. The lease was "for and during the natural lives of . . . Thomas Marshall, Mary Marshall his wife, and John Marshall his son and . . . the longest liver of them." Records of Fauquier County, 2 *Deed Book* 424. Frances B. Foster of The Plains, Virginia, wrote in 1937 that "This old cabin gives little evidence of having been the home of such distinguished persons as those who . . . occupied it. There are two rooms on the first floor and two attic rooms. A huge stone chimney is its best feature. . . . The windows are the same small cabin windows, and the floor seems to be the original, being wide boards well worn. Two enormous trees and the old stone meat house in the yard add to its quaintness." *Old Homes and Families of Fauquier County, Virginia* 217 (Berryville, Va.: Virginia Book Company, no date.)

59. Anderson Chenault Quisenberry, *The Life and Times of Hon. Humphrey Marshall* 10 (Winchester, Ky.: Sun Publishing Co., 1892).

60. Jane Marshall Taylor was regarded in Petersburg as a formidable "lady of genius and information," and her school was academically rigorous. "Mrs. Taylor," the local rector reported

in 1824, "makes her pupils read the Grecian, Roman, and English historians at large, not in abridged form." Andrew Syme to Duncan Cameron, December 29, 1824, reported in Suzanne Lebsock, *The Free Woman of Petersburg: Status and Culture in a Southern Town, 1784–1860* 173–174, 206 (New York: W. W. Norton, 1984). For Jane's husband, see Edward A. Wyatt, IV, "George Keith Taylor, 1769–1815: Virginia Federalist and Humanitarian," 16 *William and Mary Quarterly* 16–17, second series (1936).

61. Joseph Hamilton Daveiss, 1774–1811, was a self-taught lawyer of exceptional ability who was appointed United States Attorney for Kentucky by President Adams in 1800. His middle name, self-selected, was chosen to reflect his admiration for Alexander Hamilton. In 1801 he argued the case of *Wilson v. Mason*, 1 Cranch 45, before the Supreme Court, and two years later married Chief Justice Marshall's sister, Nancy. An ally in Kentucky of Senator Humphrey Marshall, he was eventually relieved as U.S. Attorney by President Jefferson. For Daveiss's subsequent attack on Jefferson, see his pamphlet, *View of the President's Conduct Concerning the Conspiracy of 1806* (Frankfort, Ky.: J. M. Street, 1807). The sword Daveiss wore at Tippecanoe is preserved in the vault of the Masonic Widows and Orphans Home in Louisville.

62. Joseph Story, "Eulogy to John Marshall," October 15, 1835, in Dillon, 3 *John Marshall: Life, Character, and Judicial Services* 330.

63. Extracts of Thomas Marshall's will, executed June 26, 1798, in Woodford county, Ky., recorded in Mason county, Ky., Book B, p. 212, and probated February 15, 1803, are reproduced in Paxton, *Marshall Family* 23–24.

64. Maria Newton Marshall, *Recollections and Reflections of Fielding Lewis Marshall* 65 (Orange, Va.: private printing, 1911); Louis Payton Little, *Imprisoned Preachers and Religious Liberty in Virginia* 197–198 (Lynchburg, Va.: J. P. Bell, 1938).

65. No example of "Marshall's Meridian Instrument" survives, although it was widely advertised in Virginia before the Revolution. A 1784 inventory of Thomas Jefferson's scientific instruments includes the notation: *Marshall's meridian instrument, mahog/cin/20*, indicating that it was made in part of mahogany (or housed in a mahogany case) and that Jefferson paid $20 for it. The May 7, 1772, issue of the *Virginia Gazette* (Williamsburg) carried the following advertisement:

> GENTLEMEN, Surveyors, and others, may be supplied with MR THOMAS MAR-SHALL'S new invented instrument for finding the VARIATION of the NEEDLE by the Subscriber. This Instrument is extremely simple and cheap, and will be singularly Serviceable to Surveyors if the Act takes Place which obliges them to return Plot and protract their Surveys by the true Meridian.

The act referred to in the ad was passed by the Virginia Assembly in the spring of 1772. Silvio A. Bedini, "Marshall's Meridian Instrument," 7 *Professional Surveyor* 26ff. (July/August 1987); *ibid.* 60 (September/October 1987).

66. Marshall's mother survived her husband by seven years and died in Washington, Mason County, Kentucky, in 1809. Her son Thomas, with whom she had been living, inscribed her tombstone as follows:

Marshall
Mary Randolph Keith
1737–1809

She was good, not brilliant; useful, not
ornamental, and the mother of 15 children.

Cited in T. Triplett Russell and John K. Gott, "An Historical Vignette of Oak Hill," 20 (unpublished paper of the Fauquier County Commission on the Bicentennial of the United States Constitution, 27 September 1987).

67. Andrew Burnaby, in his *Travels Through North America*, reports that Virginia women at the time had very little education (p. 57). Sometimes the daughters of prominent and wealthy

families could not read or write. Philip Alexander Bruce, 1 *Institutional History of Virginia in the Seventeenth Century* 454–455 (New York: G. P. Putnam's Sons, 1910). Even when private tutors were employed, the girls in the family were usually taught only rudimentary reading and writing, primary emphasis being placed upon "their future sphere as homemakers." Thomas Woody, 1 *A History of Women's Education in the United States* 273 (New York: Octagon Books, 1929). Edmund Morgan notes that "it was a generally accepted belief that the capacities of a girl could never equal those of her brothers. A girl was not expected to go beyond the study of reading, writing, and arithmetic. There was no sense in bothering her head with Greek and Latin, for she would never be able to undertake the advanced liberal education for which these were the foundation." *Virginians at Home: Family Life in the Eighteenth Century* 17 (Charlottesville: University of Virginia Press, 1952). The Marshall household was obviously an exception to this rule. Cf. Julia Cherry Spruill, *Women's Life & Work in the Southern Colonies* 193 (New York: Russell & Russell, 1938).

68. Diary of Justice Joseph P. Bradley, June 17, 1886, Bradley Papers, New Jersey Historical Society.

69. Marshall to White, November 29, 1824, in James M. Garnett, *Lectures on Female Education* 8, 4th ed. (Richmond: Thomas W. White, 1825).

70. *Ibid.*

71. Story went on to say that as chief justice, Marshall "paid a voluntary homage to the genius of women and to the beautiful productions of it which now adorn almost every branch of literature and learning. He read those productions with a glowing gratitude. He proudly proclaimed their merits and vindicated on all occasions their claims to the highest distinction. And he did not hesitate to assign to the great female authors of our day a rank not inferior to that of the most gifted and polished of the other sex." Story's remarks are reprinted in Dillon, 3 *John Marshall: Life, Character and Judicial Services* 365–366.

72. Harriet Martineau, 1 *Retrospect of Western Travel* 150 (London: Saunders and Otley, 1838). Martineau's autobiography is peppered with references to the great chief justice. See 2 *Harriet Martineau's Autobiography* Maria Weston Chapman, ed. (London: Smith, Elder & Co., 1877). Also see Harriet Martineau, *Society in America*, Seymour Martin Lipset, ed. (Garden City, N.Y.: Doubleday, 1962).

73. The text of Marshall's letter is reprinted in Chapman, 1 *Autobiography* 395–396.

74. François Alexandre Frédéric La Rochefoucauld-Liancourt, 3 *Travels Through the United States of North America* 232 (London: R. Phillips, 1800). Justice Story believed that in addition to Pope, Livy, and Horace, the Marshall family possessed works by Dryden, Milton, and Shakespeare. Dillon, 3 *John Marshall: Life Character and Judicial Services* 331.

75. James D. Hart, *The Popular Book: A History of American Literary Taste* 27 (New York: Oxford University Press, 1950).

76. *The Literary Bible of Thomas Jefferson: His Commonplace Book* 130–132, Gilbert Chinard, ed. (Baltimore: The Johns Hopkins Press, 1928).

77. Agnes Marie Sibley, *Alexander Pope's Prestige in America, 1725–1835* 11 (New York: Columbia University Press, 1949).

78. Hart, *Popular Book* 27.

79. *Ibid.*

80. Rose Gouverneur Hoes, "James Monroe's Childhood and Youth," MS Collection, James Monroe Law Office, Fredricksburg, Va. (no date).

81. *Ibid.*

82. See especially A. H. McDonald, "The Style of Livy," 47 *Journal of Roman Studies* 155 (1957).

83. L. P. Wilkinson, *Horace and His Lyric Poetry* (Cambridge: Cambridge University Press, 1951).

84. 6 *Dictionary of American Biography* 310–313; 325–326; Paxton, *Marshall Family* 69, 80–83. Dr. Louis Marshall later recanted and became a prominent lay member of the Presbyterian church.

85. Dillon, 3 *John Marshall: Life, Character, Judicial Services* 14–17.

86. See especially Douglas H. White, *Pope and the Context of Controversy* 11–12 (Chicago: University of Chicago Press, 1970); Geoffrey Tillotson, *Pope and Human Nature* 41 (Oxford: Oxford University Press, 1958); Maynard Mack, *Alexander Pope: A Life* 523–525 (New York:

W. W. Norton, 1985); M. H. Abrams et al., 1 *The Norton Anthology of English Literature* 2242–2243, 4th ed. (New York: W. W. Norton, 1979); Hoxie Neale Fairchild, 1 *Religious Trends in English Poetry* 499–500 (New York: Columbia University Press, 1939).

87. Thomas Marshall paid Thomas Turner "nine hundred and twenty pounds ten shillings current money of Virginia." Records of Fauquier County, 5 *Deed Book* 282.

88. The original seven-room frame home at Oak Hill is described at length in T. Triplett Russell and John K. Gott, "An Historical Vignette of Oak Hill," 11–14. The authors attribute the building to colonial architect John Ariss and note its similarity to "Kenmore" in Fredricksburg, which Ariss built. They note the nine-over-nine windows with slender muntins and that "the north chimney, laid in Flemish bond with glazed headers in an elaborate pattern, is one of the finest in northern Virginia." Also see Frances B. Foster, "OAK HILL," *Old Homes and Families of Fauquier County* 147–150; Mayme Ober Peak, "Oak Hill: The Fauquier Home of Chief Justice Marshall," 49 *House Beautiful* 288 (April 1921).

2: Soldier of the Revolution

1. John Marshall, *An Autobiographical Sketch* 5, John Stokes Adams, ed. (Ann Arbor: University of Michigan Press, 1937).

2. John Marshall, 1 *The Life of George Washington* 360, reprint ed. (Fredricksburg, Va.: The Citizens' Guild, 1926). A useful confirmation of Marshall's thesis is provided by Theodore Draper, *The American Revolution* (New York: Times Books/Random House, 1996).

3. Cited in Samuel Eliot Morison, *The Oxford History of the American People* 182 (New York: Oxford University Press, 1965).

4. For a reasoned assessment of British policy, see Jack M. Sosin, *Whitehall and the Wilderness* (Lincoln: University of Nebraska Press, 1961).

5. Marshall, 1 *Life of Washington* 361–362.

6. *Ibid.* 362.

7. *Ibid.* 362–364.

8. *British Royal Proclamations Relating to America: 1603–1783* 212, 215–216, Clarence Saunders Brigham, ed. (Worcester, Mass.: American Antiquarian Society, 1911).

9. See especially Sosin, *Whitehall and the Wilderness* 27–78.

10. "An act for granting certain duties in the British colonies and plantations in America." 4 George III, c. 15, 26 *The Statutes at Large* 33–52, Danby Pickering, ed. (Cambridge: Joseph Bentham, 1764).

11. "An act for applying certain stamp duties." 5 George III, c. 12, 26 *Statutes at Large* 179–204.

12. Marshall, 1 *Life of Washington* 369–370.

13. Washington to Bryan Fairfax, July 20, 1774, 3 *The Writings of George Washington* 233, John C. Fitzpatrick, ed. (Washington, D.C.: Government Printing Office, 1931).

14. "An act to repeal an act made in the last session of Parliament . . ." 6 George III, c. 11, 27 *Statutes at Large* 19.

15. "An act for the better securing the dependency of his Majesty's dominions in America . . ." 6 George III, c. 12, *ibid.* 19–20.

16. "An act for the better securing of the dependency of the kingdom of Ireland . . ." 6 George I, c. 6, *ibid.* 205.

17. "An act for granting to his Majesty additional duties . . ." 7 George III, c. 58; also see 7 George III, c. 55, c. 56, c. 57, and c. 59, 27 *ibid.* 599–610.

18. "An act for punishing mutiny and desertion . . ." 5 George III, c. 33, 26 *ibid.* 305–318.

19. "An act to repeal . . ." 10 George III, c. 17, 28 *ibid.* 294–295.

20. Marshall, 1 *Life of Washington* 401. In his writings, Marshall was seldom overtly critical of the actions of others, and "ill judged" was the strongest term of condemnation that he employed. When Marshall said something was "ill judged," it meant that in his view a horrible mistake had been made.

21. "An act . . . to empower the commissioners of the treasury to grant licences to the East India Company . . ." 13 George III, c. 44, 30 *Statutes at Large* 74–77.

22. Marshall, 1 *Life of Washington* 413.

23. 3 *The Correspondence of King George the Third* 131, Sir John Fortescue, ed. (London: Macmillan, 1927).

24. "An act to discontinue . . . the landing and discharging . . . of goods . . . at the town of Boston." 14 George III, c. 19, 30 *Statutes at Large* 336–341.

25. "An act for the better regulating of the government . . . of Massachusett's [*sic*] Bay." 14 George III, c. 45, *ibid.* 381–390.

26. "An act for the impartial administration of justice . . ." 14 George III, c. 39, *ibid.* 410.

27. "An act for the better providing suitable quarters . . ." 14 George III, c. 54, *ibid.* 410.

28. "An act . . . for the government of the province of Quebec . . ." 14 George III, c. 83, *ibid.* 549–554. For the policy implications of the Quebec Act, see Sosin, *Whitehall and the Wilderness* 239–255. An equally important aspect of the Quebec Act was the acceptance of Catholicism and the French civil law, both of which were anathema to the American colonies. The issue of Catholicism as a contributor to the American Revolution is treated carefully in Charles H. Metzger, *The Quebec Act* (New York: United States Catholic Historical Society, 1936).

29. Marshall, 1 *Life of Washington* 419.

30. Cited in Morison, *History of the American People* 206.

31. Lewis Cecil Gray, 1 *History of Agriculture in the Southern United States to 1860* 223 (Glouster, Mass.: Peter Smith, 1958); Arthur Pierce Middleton, *Tobacco Coast: A Maritime History of Chesapeake Bay in the Colonial Era* 157–158 (Newport News, Va.: Mariners' Museum, 1953).

32. Evarts B. Greene and Virginia Harrington, *American Population Before the Federal Census of 1790* 141 (New York: Columbia University Press, 1932); Stella H. Sutherland, *Population Distribution in Colonial America* 174–176 (New York: Columbia University Press, 1936); U.S. Bureau of the Census, *Statistical History of the United States: From Colonial Times to the Present* 1168 (New York: Basic Books, 1976).

33. As Jefferson noted, the debts of Virginia planters to English creditors "had become hereditary from father to son, for many generations, so that the planters were a species of property, annexed to certain mercantile houses in London." Quoted in Merrill D. Peterson, *Thomas Jefferson and the New Nation* 41 (New York: Oxford University Press, 1970).

34. See in particular, T. H. Breen, *Tobacco Culture: The Mentality of the Great Tidewater Planters on the Eve of the Revolution* (Princeton: Princeton University Press, 1985).

35. For the contrast between tidewater and piedmont, see the useful empirical study by Robert E. and B. Katherine Brown, *Virginia, 1705–1786: Democracy or Aristocracy?* 7–62, 271–283 (East Lansing: Michigan State University Press, 1964).

36. Gray, *Agriculture in the Southern United States* 214–215, 255; J. Potter, "The Growth of Population in America, 1700–1860," *Population in History*, D. V. Glass and D.E.C. Eversley, eds. (London: Edward Arnold, 1965).

37. During the Revolution Major General Charles Lee, Washington's eccentric second in command, referred to the government of the piedmont counties in Virginia as "a Mac-ocracy, by which I mean that a banditti of low Scotch-Irish whose names generally begin with Mac— and who are either the sons of imported servants, or themselves imported servants—are the Lords Paramount, and in such wild, beastly hands as these the *Respublica Diutius Stare Non Potest* [the Republic can stand no longer]—God knows what is to become of us." Charles Lee, 4 *The Lee Papers* 42 (New York: N.Y. Historical Society, 1872–1875). For a less jaundiced assessment, see Virginius Dabney, *Virginia: The New Dominion* 91–98 (Garden City, N.Y.: Doubleday, 1971).

38. The Solemn League and Covenant was negotiated with the parliamentary forces during England's civil war. Under this accord, the Scots agreed to provide military assistance, and in return, the English Parliament agreed to establish Scottish Presbyterianism throughout England, Scotland, and Wales. See David Stevenson, *The Covenanters: The National Covenant and Scotland* 52–54 (Edinburgh: The Saltire Society, 1988); Allan I. Macinnes, *Charles I and the Making of the Covenanting Movement* 175–176 (Edinburgh: John Donald, 1991).

   The role of religion, and the fear that the crown had latent Catholic tendencies, had a major impact in Virginia. As historian Rhys Isaac notes, "The spectre of the popish menace, long part of Anglo-American folk culture, was raised afresh by Parliament's recent steps in the 1770s to establish the Roman Catholic church in the conquered French province of Quebec." Isaac quotes a popular Virginia tune categorizing George III's advisors as "Papish knaves" and questioning whether "free born men" should be "ruled by Popish law." Rhys Isaac, *The Transformation of Virginia: 1740–1790* 258 (Chapel Hill: University of North Carolina Press, 1982).

39. Charles Henry Ambler, *Sectionalism in Virginia from 1776 to 1861* 3–5 (Chicago: University of Chicago Press, 1910). Republished in 1964 by Russell & Russell (New York).

40. Henry's remarkable speaking ability had already been demonstrated in the *Parsons' Case* in Hanover County, in which he defeated the clergy's efforts to overturn the so-called two-penny law that restricted their compensation. See especially, William Wirt Henry, 1 *Patrick Henry: Life, Correspondence and Speeches* 30–48 (New York: Charles Scribner's Sons, 1891). The best account of the loan-fund affair is Thomas Jefferson's report to William Wirt, written by Jefferson for Wirt's biography of Patrick Henry. Jefferson noted that Henry "carried with him all of the members of the upper counties, and left a minority composed merely of the aristocracy of the country." William Wirt, *Sketches of the Life and Character of Patrick Henry* 69–71 (Ithaca, N.Y.: Mack, Andrus, Co., 1848).

41. Cited in Charles Campbell, *History of the Colony and Ancient Dominion of Virginia* 574 (Philadelphia: J. B. Lippincott, 1860).

42. For Virginia reaction to the Stamp Act, see Warren M. Billings, John E. Selby, and Thad W. Tate, *Colonial Virginia: A History* 285–308 (White Plains, N.Y.: KTO Press, 1986).

43. The text of Henry's resolutions, originally written out by him on a blank page in an old copy of *Coke On Littleton*, have been lost. Henry wrote out a second copy and left it in a sealed envelope, along with his will, to be opened by his executors. It is reprinted in Henry, 1 *Patrick Henry* 80–81.

44. "Letter from Virginia," June 14, 1765, *Gazetteer* (London), August 13, 1765, cited in Henry, 1 *Patrick Henry* 86. Emphasis added.

45. Jefferson to Wirt, in Wirt, *Sketches of Patrick Henry* 51–52.

46. Jefferson to Daniel Webster, cited in Henry, 1 *Patrick Henry* 86.

47. Cited in Morison, *History of the American People* 187.

48. John E. Selby, *The Revolution in Virginia, 1775–1783* 38–40 (Williamsburg, Va.: The Colonial Williamsburg Foundation, 1988); Isaac, *Transformation of Virginia* 183–246.

49. Peyton Randolph was the eldest son of Sir John Randolph of Tazewell Hall. As Professor William H. Nelson has noted, the First Continental Congress was essentially conservative in its origins, seeking to negotiate a solution with Britain without war. But "the decisions of [the Congress], and the establishment of the Congress itself as a nucleus of an American national government, were mortal blows to the Tories." *The American Tory* 64 (Oxford: Clarendon Press, 1961).

50. First Continental Congress, Declaration of Rights, cited in Marshall, 1 *Life of Washington* 430.

51. 3 *Correspondence of George the Third* 59.

52. "An act to restrain trade and commerce [in New England]," 15 George III, c.10, 31 *Statutes at Large* 4–11.

53. Cited in Marshall, 1 *Life of Washington* 449.

54. H. J. Eckenrode, *The Revolution in Virginia* 47–49 (Boston: Houghton Mifflin, 1916).

55. Thomas Jefferson, in describing the Virginia Convention, said of Henry's opponents that "These were honest, able men, who had begun the opposition [to the crown] . . . but with a moderation more adapted to their age and experience. Subsequent events favored the bolder spirits of Henry . . . with whom I went on all points. Sensible, however, to the unanimity among our constituents, although we often wished to have gone faster, we slacked our pace, that our less ardent colleagues might keep up with us; and they, on their part, differing nothing from us in principle, quickened their gait somewhat beyond that which prudence might . . . have advised." Jefferson's remarks were made to William Wirt and are quoted in Wirt, *Sketches of Patrick Henry* 96.

56. The text of Henry's speech, together with the comments of those who heard it, is in Henry, 1 *Patrick Henry* 260–272.

57. *Ibid.* 270. The author has visited Carrington's grave.

58. Wirt, *Sketches of Patrick Henry* 95.

59. The Richmond convention ordered the Virginia militia law of 1738 put into immediate execution. That statute provided for an annual muster to be held in each county during the month of September and for musters of individual companies every three months, or at more frequent intervals if the commanding captain so desired. In addition to reviving the old statute, the convention established that militia companies were to consist of sixty-eight men, commanded by a captain, two lieutenants, one ensign, four sergeants, and two corporals. They were to be armed with rifles, if possible, but otherwise with muskets. The militiamen drilled in the military exercises prescribed for British forces in 1764. The full text of the British drill manual was printed as an appendix to the convention's *Journal*. See *Journal of the Proceedings of the Convention, held at Richmond on the 20th Day of March 1775* 14–19, 29 et seq. (Williamsburg, Va.: Alexander Purdie, 1775); William Walter Hening, 5 *The Statutes at Large: Being a Collection of all of the Laws of Virginia* 18 (Richmond, Va.: Samuel Pleasants, 1823).

60. Fitzpatrick, 3 *Writings of Washington* 24–25.

61. As Rhys Isaac has noted, "It was imperative for the patriot gentry to communicate to the populace not only their fearful view of what awaited Virginians should they remain supine, but also the vision of the good life that inspired the struggle." *Transformation of Virginia* 244.

62. Thomas Marshall, as a captain in the Virginia militia, had at one time commanded the Fauquier county unit. The details of the May 1775 drill were provided by an eyewitness to Horace Binney, who included the account in his eulogy to Marshall in Philadelphia, September 24, 1835. Horace Binney, *An Eulogy on the Life and Character of John Marshall* 23 (Philadelphia: J. Crissy and G. Goodman, 1835). Cf. T. Triplett Russell and John K. Gott, *Fauquier County in the Revolution* 66–67 (Warrenton, Va.: Fauquier County American Bicentennial Commission, 1976).

63. Binney, *Eulogy of John Marshall* 22.

64. Marshall, *Autobiographical Sketch* 5.

65. The Virginia Convention proceedings are reported in 3 *American Archives* 366–430, Peter Force, ed. (Washington, D.C.: Matthew St. Clair Clarke and Peter Force, 1840). The ordinance passed by the convention provided for twenty days of intensive battalion training and a monthly training period of four days at company level. Once again, the British military manual of 1764 was prescribed as the basic field regulation. *Ibid.* 400–404.

66. E. M. Sanchez-Saavedra, "All Fine Fellows and Well-Armed," 14 *Virginia Cavalcade* 4–11 (1974).

67. Eckenrode, *Revolution in Virginia* 60.

68. Madison to William Bradford, June 19, 1775, 1 *The Papers of James Madison* 153, William T. Hutchinson et al., eds. (Chicago: University of Chicago Press, 1962).

69. Sanchez-Saavedra, 14 *Virginia Cavalcade* 5; Russell and Gott, *Fauquier County in the Revolution* 66–67.

70. John Marshall, letter, February 6, 1832, Revolutionary War Pension Files, David Jamieson file, S-5607, Record Group 15, National Archives; Philip Slaughter, *History of St. Mark's Parish* 107–108 (Baltimore: Innes & Co., 1877), reprinted in Raleigh Travers Green, *Genealogical and Historical Notes on Culpeper County, Virginia* (Culpeper, Va.: R. T. Green, 1900).

71. E. M. Sanchez-Saavedra, *Guide to Virginia Military Organizations in the American Revolution* 16–17 (Richmond, Va.: Virginia State Library, 1978).

72. Edward W. Richardson, *Standards and Colors of the American Revolution* 136–137 (Philadelphia: University of Pennsylvania Press, 1982).

73. Slaughter, *History of St. Mark's Parish* 107–108. The shirts were made at public expense and cost one shilling eight pence per shirt. Entry dated November 23, 1775, *Day Book Oct. 12, 1775–Oct. 17, 1776*, Records of the Public Store in Williamsburg, Virginia State Library.

74. Slaughter, *History of St. Mark's Parish* 107.

75. *Ibid.*

76. Letter, A Gentleman in Virginia to his friend in Edinburgh, September 1, 1775, in Force, 3 *American Archives* 620–621.

77. The Virginia Committee on Safety, which had been established by the convention to over-

see military operations, did not make provision for the issuance of tents, kettles, and canteens to the minutemen units until September 21, 1775. *Ibid.* 757.

78. The battalion's route of march is detailed in an affidavit of William Burton, reprinted in 9 *William and Mary Quarterly* 213–214, 1st series (1903). Also see Russell and Gott, *Fauquier County in the Revolution* 73–75.

79. Thomas J. Wertenbaker, *Norfolk: Historic Southern Port*, Marvin W. Schlegel, ed. (Durham, N.C.: Duke University Press, 1931).

80. Eckenrode, *Revolution in Virginia* 70–71; Selby, *Revolution in Virginia* 68–69.

81. The Fourteenth Regiment of Foot was scattered in separate units all along the coast from St. Augustine to New York. On December 1, 1775, there were 133 enlisted men and 13 officers present for duty in Norfolk. Force, 4 *American Archives* 349–350.

82. *Ibid.* 58–73; Campbell, *History of Virginia* 623–635; Dabney, *Virginia: The New Dominion* 130–131. On November 7, 1775, Lord Dunmore issued a proclamation offering freedom to each slave who would run away from his master and "resort to his Majesty's STANDARD." Ironically, that brought the waverers among the plantation aristocracy quickly on to the patriotic side. The former slaves were formed into the "Royal Ethiopian Regiment," issued cast-off items from Dunmore's ships, and wore simple frocks with the words "Liberty or Slaves" painted on them, mocking the minutemen's "Liberty or Death."

83. For the November 26, 1775, report of Captain Samuel Leslie of the 14th Infantry to General Howe on the encounter at Kempsville, see Force, 3 *American Archives* 1717. Also see Edmund Pendleton to Richard Henry Lee, November 27, 1775, 4 *ibid.* 201–202.

84. Marshall 2 *Life of Washington* 342.

85. Eckenrode *Revolution in Virginia* 72.

86. Dunmore to Howe, November 30, 1775, in Force, 3 *American Archives* 1713–1714. Emphasis in original.

87. For details of the march of the Culpeper minutemen from Williamsburg to Great Bridge, see Ivor Noël Hume, *1775: Another Part of the Field* 381 ff. (New York: Knopf, 1966); John Daly Burk, 3 *The History of Virginia from Its First Settlement to the Present Day* 440 (Petersburg, Va.: Dickson and Pescud, 1804–1816); as well as Lord Dunmore's account in his letter to General Howe, November 30, 1775. Force, 3 *American Archives* 1713–1714.

88. Force, 4 *American Archives* 171–172.

89. Woodford to Virginia Convention, December 10, 1775, *ibid.* 228.

90. Russell and Gott, *Fauquier County in the Revolution* 84.

91. Legend has it that a reliable servant of Thomas Marshall was sent into the British camp claiming to be a deserter. As instructed by the elder Marshall, he informed the British that the American forces did not number more than 300 "shirtmen," that they were hungry and their morale was low, but that reinforcements were expected shortly from North Carolina. The ruse was designed to precipitate a British attack. The legend cannot be verified. For Colonel Woodford's account of the incident, see Woodford to the Virginia Convention, December 10, 1775, in Force, 4 *American Archives* 228. Also see Woodford to Pendleton, December 10, 1775, *ibid.* 233; Allan B. Magruder, *John Marshall* 17 (Boston: Houghton, 1890); Theodorick Bland, *The Bland Papers* 39–41 (Petersburg, Va.: E. and J. C. Ruffin, 1840); Burk, 3 *History of Virginia* 85; Benson J. Lossing, 2 *The Pictorial Field-Book of the Revolution* 535–536 (New York: Harper and Bros., 1852). Cf. Percy B. Caley, "Dunmore: Colonial Governor of New York and Virginia," 699–704, unpublished Ph.D. dissertation, University of Pittsburgh, 1939. Dunmore explained the decision to Lord Dartmouth, Secretary of State for Colonial Affairs, as a preventive strike. "Being informed that the Rebels had procured some Cannon from North Carolina, and that they were also to be reinforced from Williamsburgh and knowing that our little Fort was not in a condition to withstand any thing heavier than a Musquet shot, I thought it advisable to risque something to save the Fort." December 13, 1775. Cited in Hume, *1775* 432.

92. Lord Dunmore was not alone in that assessment. Captain Matthew Squire of H.M.S. *Otter* wrote to his commander, Admiral Graves, "I have great reason to suppose, and hope from their being such cowards, and cold weather coming on that they [the Americans at Great

Bridge] will return to their respective homes, and we shall be quiet for the remainder of the winter." December 2, 1775, in Force, 4 *American Archives* 351–352.

93. Woodford to Pendleton, December 10, 1775, *ibid.* 233.

94. Woodford to Virginia Convention, December 10, 1775, *ibid.* 228.

95. Letter of Major Spotswood, December 9, 1775, *ibid.* 224. Also see Woodford to Pendleton, *ibid.* 233.

96. Benjamin Rush, *The Autobiography of Benjamin Rush* 156, George W. Corner, ed. (Princeton, N.J.: Princeton University Press, 1948).

97. Hume, *1775* 431.

98. Marshall, 2 *Life of Washington* 132. Various secondary accounts suggest that the Americans held their fire until the British were within fifty yards of the breastworks. Marshall and Woodford, both of whom were present, state otherwise, and I have followed their account. The American troops were untrained and completely without battle experience. To assume that they would have held their fire like disciplined veterans does not ring true.

99. Russell and Gott, *Fauquier County in the Revolution* 87–88

100. Woodford to Virginia Convention, December 10, 1775, in Force, 4 *American Archives* 228–229, note.

101. Hume, *1775* 434–435; *ibid.* 228–229, note.

102. Letter, January 9, 1776, *ibid.* 540.

103. Richard Kidder Meade to Richard Bland, December 18, 1775, 1 *Bland Papers* 39.

104. Marshall, 2 *Life of Washington* 132.

105. Woodford to Virginia Convention, December 10, 1775, in Force, 4 *American Archives* 228.

106. Woodford to Pendleton, December 10, 1775, *ibid.* 233.

107. Leonard Baker, *John Marshall: A Life in Law* 56–57 (New York: Macmillan, 1974). Helen Calvert Maxwell, a Norfolk acquaintance of Captain Fordyce's, reported that before the battle, Fordyce had given "his watch to his friend [Capt. James Maxwell] with a message for his wife, for he knew, as he said, that he was going to his death." Helen Maxwell, "My Mother," 2 *Lower Norfolk County Virginia Antiquary* 137.

108. Washington to Congress, December 18, 1775, in Fitzpatrick, 4 *Writings of Washington* 172. Washington was more explicit to Richard Henry Lee. "If that man [Dunmore] is not crushed before spring, he will become the most formidable enemy America has. . . . I do not think forcing his Lordship on shipboard is sufficient; nothing less than depriving him of life or liberty will secure the peace to Virginia." *Ibid.* 186.

109. Cited in 14 *Virginia Magazine of History and Biography* 251 (1906).

110. Eckenrode, *Revolution in Virginia* 83–86.

111. Force, 4 *American Archives* 292.

112. Howe to Pendleton, December 13, 1775. 1 *Richmond College Historical Papers* 125, D.R. Anderson, ed. (Richmond, Va.: Richmond College, 1915).

113. Cited in Sanchez-Saavedra, "All Fine Fellows," 11.

114. Marshall, 2 *Life of Washington* 133. Also see Force, 4 *American Archives* 539.

115. Marshall, 2 *Life of Washington* 133.

116. William Campbell to Margaret Campbell, January 15, 1776, cited in Selby, *Revolution in Virginia* 8.3

117. Force, 4 *American Archives* 1166.

118. *Ibid.* 539.

119. Marshall, 2 *Life of Washington* 133.

120. Affidavit of John Marshall in support of pension claim of William Payne, April 26, 1832, Pension file 8938, Record Group 15, National Archives.

121. Lyon G. Tyler, "The Old Virginia Line in the Middle States During the American Revolution," 12 *Tyler's Quarterly Historical and Genealogical Magazine* 1 (1930); 9 Hening 134.

122. 9 Hening 180–184; "Virginia's Soldiers in the Revolution," 19 *Virginia Magazine of History and Biography* 406 (1911).

123. 1 *The Papers of John Marshall* 4, note 6 (Chapel Hill: University of North Carolina Press, 1974); Russell and Gott, *Fauquier County in the Revolution* 168–171.

124. 1 *Marshall Papers* 4–6; Force, 3 *American Archives* 616, 694–695; John R. Sellers, "The Virginia Continental Line 1775–1780," unpublished Ph.D. dissertation, Tulane University, 1968; Tyler, "Old Virginia Line," 19.

125. The 11th regiment of the Virginia Line was assigned to Brigadier General William Woodford's First Virginia Brigade, which was part of the division commanded by Major General Adam Stephen. Woodford's brigade was composed of the 3rd, 7th, 11th, and 15th Virginia regiments.

126. After the war Morgan became a prosperous farmer and, like Marshall, a staunch Federalist. He commanded the troops that put down the Whiskey Rebellion in Pennsylvania in 1795, was elected to Congress in 1797, and, by the time of his death in 1802, owned more than 250,000 acres in Virginia, Maryland, and Pennsylvania. James Graham, *The Life of General Daniel Morgan* (New York: Derby and Jackson, 1856); Don Higginbotham, *Daniel Morgan: Revolutionary Riflemen* (Chapel Hill: University of North Carolina Press, 1961); North Callahan, *Daniel Morgan: Ranger of the Revolution* (New York: Holt, Rinehart, and Winston, 1961).

127. Russell and Gott, *Fauquier County in the Revolution* 69, 168. John Marshall's intense admiration for Morgan can be appreciated by perusing Marshall's description of Morgan's attack on Quebec, in 2 *Life of Washington* 107–109.

128. When Morgan retired from Congress because of ill health in 1799, Marshall wrote to his brother, James Markham Marshall, "I regret very sincerely the situation of Genl. Morgan and wish you should see him to present me respectfully and affectionately to him." April 3, 1799, 4 *Marshall Papers* 10–11.

129. Marshall, 2 *Life of Washington* 263.

130. Orderly Book, 1777, Febiger Papers, Historical Society of Pennsylvania. For the duties of an adjutant, see John M. Wright, "Some Notes on the Continental Army," 11 *William and Mary Quarterly* 99–100, 2nd series (1931).

131. "Howe's designs are most unquestionably against the [Hudson] highlands," Washington wrote on July 12, 1777. Fitzpatrick, 8 *Writings of Washington* 355, 386, 414, 454; Christopher Ward, 1 *The War of the Revolution* 328–329 (New York: Macmillan, 1952).

132. Marshall's comment was quoted by Justice Horace Gray in his *An Address on the Life, Character and Influence of Chief Justice Marshall* 34 (Washington, D.C.: Pearson, 1901).

133. John Chilton to Charles Chilton, August 17, 1777, in Tyler, "Old Virginia Line," 130. Chilton was a captain in the 3rd Virginia regiment and was killed at the Battle of Brandywine, September 11, 1777. During the march through New Jersey, he shared a tent with Captain William Blackwell, John Marshall's company commander. *Ibid.* 131.

134. Diary of Philip Slaughter, College of William and Mary Library; Tyler, "Old Virginia Line," 284; Sellers, "Virginia Continental Line," 241.

135. Fitzpatrick, 8 *Writings of Washington* 441.

136. General Howe's father was Emmanuel, Second Viscount Howe, who married Maria Sophia, the daughter of the Baroness Kilmansegge (afterward Countess Darlington), who was the mistress of George I.

137. John F. Watson, 2 *Annals of Philadelphia and Pennsylvania* 287 (Philadelphia: J. F. Watson, 1844); George Trevelyan, 4 *The American Revolution* (New York: Longmans, Green, 1905–1922). Also see Troyer S. Anderson, *The Command of the Howe Brothers During the American Revolution* (New York: Oxford University Press, 1936).

138. Willard M. Wallace, *Appeal to Arms: A Military History of the American Revolution* 180–181 (New York: Harper & Brothers, 1951); Howe to Lord George Germain, October 22, 1777, in 2 *Stopford-Sackville MSS* 80, Historical Manuscripts Commission (London: His Majesty's Stationery Office, 1904).

139. The classic work on the battle of Long Island is Henry P. Johnston, *The Campaign of 1776 Around New York and Brooklyn. Including a New and Circumstantial Account of the Battle of Long Island and the Loss of New York* 115–116 (Brooklyn, N.Y.: Long Island Historical Society, 1878). Also see Ward, 1 *War of the Revolution* 202–274.

140. Fitzpatrick, 9 *Writings of Washington* 115–116.

141. Tyler, "Old Virginia Line," 287; Wright, "Continental Army," 85.

142. *Familiar Letters of John Adams and His Wife Abigail Adams During the Revolution* 198, Charles

Francis Adams, ed. (New York: Houghton Mifflin, 1875). Adams qualified his exuberance. "They don't step exactly in time. They don't hold up their heads quite erect, nor turn out their toes so exactly as they ought. They don't all of them cock their hats; and such as do, don't all wear them the same way." *Ibid.*

143. Alexander Graydon, *Memoirs of His Own Time* 291 (Philadelphia: Lindsay & Blakiston, 1846).

144. Ward, *War of the Revolution* 338; Marshall, *2 Life of Washington* 296; John F. Reed, *Campaign to Valley Forge: July 1, 1777–December 19, 1777* 88–89 (Philadelphia: University of Pennsylvania Press, 1965). For Howe's strategy see Evan W.H. Fyers, "General Sir William Howe's Operations in Pennsylvania, 1777," 9 *Society of Army Historical Research Journal* 173, 187 (1930); Robert F. Seybolt, "A Contemporary British Account of General Sir William Howe's Military Operations in 1777," 40 *American Antiquarian Society Proceedings* 1, 76 (new series, part 1) (1930).

145. Reed, *Campaign to Valley Forge* 88. According to Washington's orders of August 28, 1777, the light infantry corps would consist of 1 field-grade officer, 2 captains, 6 lieutenants, 8 sergeants, and 100 rank and file from each of the six brigades. Fitzpatrick, 9 *Writings of Washington* 71.

146. For the role of light infantry in the Revolutionary War, see John W. Wright, "The Rifle in the American Revolution," 29 *American Historical Review* 294–295 (1924); Eric Robson, "British Light Infantry in the Eighteenth Century: The Effect of American Conditions," 62 *Army Quarterly* 209–222 (1891).

147. Fitzpatrick, 9 *Writings of Washington* 146–147.

148. *Ibid.* 148.

149. Reed, *Campaign to Valley Forge* 100.

150. Lieutenant Colonel von Wurmb to Colonel von Jungkenn, *Letters from Major Baurmeister to Colonel von Jungkenn* 9, Bernhard A. Uhlendorf and Edna Vosper, eds. (Philadelphia: Historical Society of Pennsylvania, 1936) Also see "Letters of Major Baurmeister during the Philadelphia Campaign," Bernard A. Uhlendorf and Edna Vosper, eds., 59 *Pennsylvania Magazine of History and Biography* 399–401 (1935).

151. 59 *Pennsylvania Magazine of History and Biography* 399–401.

152. "Journals of Captain John Montresor," *New York Historical Society Collections, 1881* 445–446 (New York: New York Historical Society, 1882).

153. Marshall, *2 Life of Washington* 297. Also see Ward, *1 War of the Revolution* 338–339; Reed, *Campaign to Valley Forge* 101–103; Edward W. Cooch, *The Battle of Cooch's Bridge* (Wilmington, Del.: W. N. Cann, 1940).

154. Fitzpatrick, 9 *Writings of Washington* 173, 187; Reed, *Campaign to Valley Forge* 102–103; Ward, 1 *War of the Revolution* 466, note 20.

155. On June 14, 1777, Congress passed the Flag Resolution providing for a flag of thirteen stripes red and white alternately and thirteen white stars in a field of blue. For its use at Cooch's Bridge, see Mark Mayo Boatner III, *Encyclopedia of the American Revolution* 283 (New York: David McKay, 1966); Milo M. Quaife, Melvin J. Weig, and Roy E. Appleman, *The History of the United States Flag from the Revolution to the Present* 50 (New York: Harper & Row, 1961).

156. Ward, 1 *War of the Revolution* 340.

157. Marshall, 2 *Life of Washington* 299.

158. *Ibid.*

159. *Ibid.*

160. Ward, 1 *War of the Revolution* 343.

161. Lieutenant General Wilhelm Knyphausen to Lord George Germain, Oct. 21, 1777, in Fyers, "Howe's Operations in Pennsylvania," 33–34.

162. Marshall, 2 *Life of Washington* 299–300.

163. *Ibid.* 299.

164. Henry A. Muhlenberg, *The Life of Major-General Peter Muhlenberg* 492 (Philadelphia: Carey and Hart, 1849).

165. George Bancroft, 5 *History of the United States of America From the Discovery of the Continent* 179 (New York: D. Appleton, 1885).

166. Marshall, 2 *Life of Washington* 303–305.
167. Douglas Southall Freeman, 4 *George Washington: A Biography* 488 (New York: Charles Scribner's Sons, 1951).
168. Marshall, 2 *Life of Washington* 303–305.
169. *Ibid.* 304, note. In a letter published by the *Virginia Gazette*, October 3, 1777, one soldier at Brandywine wrote that "Col. Marshall, of the 3rd regiment, attacked the enemy's left column with his single regiment, and at first repulsed them; but, overpowered by numbers, was obliged to retire, which he did in good order."
170. Cited in Russell and Gott, *Fauquier County in the Revolution* 208.
171. Fitzpatrick, 9 *Writings of Washington* 301–302; *Virginia Gazette*, November 21, 1777.
172. Washington to Congress, September 11, 1777, in Fitzpatrick, 6 *Writings of Washington* 44–46; Marshall, 2 *Life of Washington* 306; Russell and Gott, *Fauquier County in the Revolution* 212; Reed, *Campaign to Valley Forge* 140. Cf. 1 *Marshall Papers* 11, note 5; Albert J. Beveridge, 1 *The Life of John Marshall* 103 (Boston: Houghton Mifflin, 1916).
173. Marshall, 2 *Life of Washington* 312.
174. *Ibid.* 317. Also see Paul David Nelson, *Anthony Wayne* 68 (Bloomington: Indiana University Press, 1985). The General Order convening the court of inquiry to investigate Maxwell's behavior is in Fitzpatrick, 9 *Writings of Washington* at p. 379; the order convening the court martial at 9 *ibid.* 438; and the judgment of the court martial at 10 *ibid.* 3–4. According to the text, "The Court, having considered the charges [of intoxication], and evidences, are unanimously of opinion, that Brigadier General Maxwell, while he commanded the light troops, was not at any time disguised with liquor, so as to disqualify him in any measure from doing his duty."
175. Ward, 1 *War of the Revolution* 362.
176. Marshall, 2 *Life of Washington* 321.
177. Ward, 1 *War of the Revolution* 365. For a crisp discussion of the flaws of Washington's plan, see Freeman, 4 *George Washington* 510–519.
178. Marshall's wound was not serious, and he never spoke of it in later years. It was revealed in the pension application of William Kearns, a soldier in Marshall's company, and certified correct by Marshall in 1828. Pension File W7965, Record Group 15, National Archives. Also see 1 *Marshall Papers* 9, note 4.
179. Ward, 1 *War of the Revolution* 371. Also see Alfred B. Lambdin, "Battle of Germantown," 1 *Pennsylvania Magazine of History and Biography* 377 (1877); Tyler, "Old Virginia Line," 28; Reed, *Campaign to Valley Forge* 214–239.
180. Sir George Trevelyan, the leading British historian of the Revolution, wrote of Germantown that "Eminent generals and statesmen of sagacity, in every European court, were profoundly impressed by learning that a new army, raised within the year, and undaunted by a series of recent disasters, had assailed a victorious enemy in its own quarters and had only been repulsed after a sharp and dubious conflict." 4 *American Revolution* 249.
181. Knox to Congress, cited in Reed, *Campaign to Valley Forge* 244.
182. Marshall, 2 *Life of Washington* 352. Marshall notes explicitly that he personally observed Washington's efforts that day.
183. Fitzpatrick, 9 *Writings of Washington* 259.
184. The Valley Forge experience has drawn its due measure of scholarly study. Book-length treatments are contained in Alfred H. Bill, *Valley Forge: The Making of an Army* (New York: Harper, 1952); W. Herbert Burk, *Historical and Topographical Guide to Valley Forge* (Philadelphia: Winston, 1910); Donald B. Chidsey, *Valley Forge* (New York: Crown, 1959); Ronald E. Heaton, *Valley Forge, Yesterday and Today* (Norristown, Pa.: Heaton, 1956); John J. Stoudt, *Ordeal at Valley Forge* (Philadelphia: University of Pennsylvania Press, 1963); Frank H. Taylor, *Valley Forge: A Chronicle of American Heroism* (Philadelphia: Nagle, 1905); Harry E. Wildes, *Valley Forge* (New York: Macmillan, 1938). Articles include Edward M. Chase, "Valley Forge," 32 *Quartermaster Review* 44–46 (1952); Douglas Macfarlan, "Revolutionary War Hospitals in the Pennsylvania Campaign 1777–78," 59 *Picket Post* 23–30 (1958); Fred J. Wilkins, "Steuben Screamed But Things Happened and an Army Was Born at Valley Forge," 20

Picket Post 7–13 (1948); H. F. Wilkinson, "Here Was Born a Nation," 10 *Quartermaster Review* 9–25 (1930). Printed primary sources include Henry Woodman, *The History of Valley Forge* (Oaks, Pa.: Francis, 1922); "Diary of Lieutenant James McMichael of the Pennsylvania Line 1776–1778," 16 *Pennsylvania Magazine of History and Biography* 129–159 (1892); "Diary Kept at Valley Forge by Albigence Waldo, Surgeon in the Continental Army, 1777–1778," 5 *Historical Magazine* 129–134, 1st Series (1861); "The Journal of Ebenezer Wild," 6 *Massachusetts Historical Society Proceedings* 78–160, 2nd Series (1890).

185. Rupert Hughes, 3 *George Washington: The Savior of the States, 1777–1781* 231 (New York: W. Morrow, 1926–1930).
186. Friedrich Kapp, *The Life of John Kalb* 137 (New York: Henry Holt, 1884).
187. Jared Sparks, 5 *The Writings of George Washington* 241 note (Boston: Little, Brown, 1855).
188. Washington to Congress, December 23, 1777, in Fitzpatrick, 10 *Writings of Washington* 195.
189. *Ibid.*
190. Heaton, *Valley Forge* 30.
191. Woodman, *History of Valley Forge* 62; Freeman, 4 *Washington* 570.
192. Taylor, *Valley Forge* 46; Stoudt, *Ordeal at Valley Forge* 119; Chidsey, *Valley Forge* 25, 71; 10 *Writings of Washington* 195.
193. Marshall, 2 *Life of Washington* 433.
194. "Diary Kept by Albigence Waldo, Surgeon in the Continental Army," 130.
195. Trevelyan, 4 *American Revolution* 299.
196. Marshall, 2 *Life of Washington* 434.
197. Beveridge, 1 *Life of Marshall* 126–130. Beveridge cites a December 18, 1777, letter from Washington to Benjamin Harrison in Virginia, urging that Virginia send its best men to Congress. "Where is Mason—Wythe—Jefferson?" asks Washington (Fitzpatrick, 7 *Writings of Washington* 301–302). From Washington's query to Harrison, Beveridge extrapolates Marshall's hatred of Jefferson. "Is it not a reasonable inference that the Virginia officers in the familiar talk of comrades, spoke of Jefferson in terms less mild?" asked Beveridge (at p. 127). Well, maybe. But what about Mason and Wythe? And what about the fact that Washington's query was written before the army encamped at Valley Forge? And the fact that Washington was talking about Congress, not the army? Furthermore, is it conceivable that junior officers from Virginia would have been privy to the thoughts of the commander in chief, even assuming that Washington might have wanted Jefferson to render greater support?
198. Cited in Joseph Story, "Chief Justice John Marshall's Public Life and Services," 27 *North American Review* 8 (1828).
199. James Bradley Thayer, *John Marshall* 12 (Boston: Houghton Mifflin, 1904); Beveridge, 1 *Life of Marshall* 132.
200. Marshall, 2 *Life of Washington* 432.
201. John C. Miller, *Triumph of Freedom* 222–223 (Boston: Little, Brown, 1948); Wallace, *Appeal to Arms* 169.
202. Marshall, 2 *Life of Washington* 439.
203. For Steuben's contribution generally, see Freeman, 4 *Washington* 616; Wilkins, "Steuben Screamed"; John McAuley Palmer, *General von Steuben* (New Haven, Conn.: Yale University Press, 1937).
204. For the arrival of muskets, see Chase, "Valley Forge," 45; for the Virginians, see Stoudt, *Ordeal at Valley Forge* 231.
205. Marshall, 2 *Life of Washington* 436.
206. Taylor, *Valley Forge* 65; Wildes, *Valley Forge* 259; Bill, *Valley Forge* 204; Woodman, *History of Valley Forge* 204.
207. The best account of the Battle of Monmouth remains William S. Stryker, *The Battle of Monmouth* (Princeton, N.J.: Princeton University Press, 1927). Also see Samuel Steele Smith, *The Battle of Monmouth* (Monmouth Beach, N.J.: Philip Freneau, 1964); Ward, 2 *War of the Revolution* 576–586. For Morgan's movements, see Stryker *Battle of Monmouth* 55–56 as well as Theodore Thayer, *The Making of a Scapegoat: Washington and Lee at Monmouth* 65–66 (Port Washington, N.Y.: Kennikat Press, 1976).

208. The route of the army is in *The George Washington Atlas*, plate 38, Lawrence Martin, ed. (Washington, D.C.: George Washington Bicentennial Commission, 1932).

209. Lafayette to Marshall, cited in Marshall, 3 *Life of Washington* 22, note.

210. Cited in Ward, 2 *War of the Revolution* 581.

211. Cited in Stryker, *Battle of Monmouth* 209.

212. Fitzpatrick, 9 *Writings of Washington* 126–127.

213. 1 *Marshall Papers* 27, note 1. Marshall was promoted on the list of September 8, 1778, recommended by the promotion board under the presidency of Colonel James Wood.

214. J. Potter, "Rank Roll of Virginia Line Officers," September 8, 1778, National Archives, Orderly Book No. 28, Record Group 93; Peter Angelokos, "Arrangements of the several regiments of the First Virginia Brigade," September 14, 1778, *ibid.*; *Journals of the Continental Congress, 1774–1789*, Worthington C. Ford, ed. (Washington, D.C.: Government Printing Office, 1904–1937).

215. Payroll, White Plains, N.Y., August 30, 1778. 1 *Marshall Papers* 22–26; Sanchez-Saavedra, *Guide to Virginia Military Organizations* 53.

216. Marshall's brigade reached Middlebrook on December 10, 1778. See Peter Angelokos, "The Army at Middlebrook, 1778–1779," 70 *New Jersey Historical Society Proceedings* 98, 105–106 (1952); Sellers, "Virginia Continental Line," 325; Fitzpatrick, 13 *Writings of Washington* 328, 376–377.

217. John Marshall refers to his furlough in his affidavit in the pension file of Humphrey Marshall, S-31234, Record Group 15, National Archives. Also see 1 *Marshall Papers* 27, note 1, as well as the muster rolls of January 14, February 3, March 6, April 5, and May 7, 1779, Record Group 93, National Archives.

218. Sallie E. Marshall Hardy, "John Marshall as Son, Brother, Husband, Friend," 8 *The Green Bag* 480 (1896).

219. 1 *Marshall Papers* 27, note 1.

220. For details of the operation at Stony Point, see Henry P. Johnston, *The Storming of Stony Point* (New York: James T. White & Co., 1900); I. W. Sklarsky, *The Revolution's Boldest Venture* (Port Washington, N.Y.: Kennikat Press, 1965); Edmund P. Bessell, "The Storming of Stony Point," 72 *National Historical Magazine* 47 (1938).

221. See Marshall's affidavit in the pension file of Churchill Gibbs, S46002, Record Group 15, National Archives; also see 3 *Life of Washington* 129, where he states "The author was in the covering party, visited the fort the next day, and conversed with the officers who had been engaged in storming the works." For the role of the covering party, see Johnston, *Storming of Stony Point* 164; Sklarsky, *Boldest Venture* 68, 78–80. Cf. Beveridge. 1 *Life of Marshall* 138–141.

222. Marshall, 3 *Life of Washington* 139 note., Cf. Thomas A. Boyd, *Light-Horse Harry Lee* 46 (New York: Charles Scribner's Sons, 1931); Beveridge, 1 *Life of Marshall* 142.

223. For Lee's operation against Paulus Hook, see William H. Richardson, *Washington and the "Enterprise Against Paulus Hook"* (Jersey City, N.J.: New Jersey Trust Co., 1938); Boyd, *Light Horse Harry Lee*; and Henry Lee, *Memoirs of the War in the Southern Department of the United States*, General Robert E. Lee, ed. (New York: University Publishing Co., 1869). Also see Freeman, 5 *Washington* 125–129.

224. Marshall to "Major Thomas Posey, Light Infantry," September 1, 1779, 1 *Marshall Papers* 32–34. Camp ladies were an essential adjunct of eighteenth-century warfare. They did all of the army's laundry, most of the cooking, and frequently provided important companionship. Washington recognized the necessity of such accompaniment and, in 1777, suggested the figure of 6 women per 100 men as the army's norm. Because of the better pay and better rations, the figure in the British army was somewhat higher. See George and Anne Forty, *They Also Served* 214 (Speldhurst, Kent: Midas Books, 1979); Walter Hart Blumenthal, *Women Camp Followers of the American Revolution* 59–83 (New York: Arno Press, 1974); Fitzpatrick, 9 *Writings of Washington* 17, 126; 22 *ibid.* 203; 26 *ibid.* 199. On March 16, 1802, Congress fixed by statute the number of women eligible to draw rations at four per company. Raphael P. Thian, *Legislative History of the General Staff of the Army* 332 (Washington, D.C.: Government Printing Office, 1901).

225. In *My Dearest Polly*, Marshall's great-granddaughter, Frances Norton Mason, writes of the fre-

quent wartime letters Marshall sent to his father, who was stationed at Yorktown. *My Dearest Polly* 5 (Richmond: Garrett & Massie, 1961). None of these letters has survived.

226. For the muster roll of Marshall's company in the 7th Virginia regiment, dated December 9, 1779, in Morristown, see 1 *Marshall Papers* 35–37.
227. Fitzpatrick, 7 *Writings of Washington* 220, 237, 253.
228. Muster roll, December 9, 1779, 1 *Marshall Papers* 35–37.
229. Russell and Gott, *Fauquier County in the Revolution* 322–326.
230. Marshall to Chittenden Lyon, December 24, 1830, pension file of William Baylis, S12953, Record Group 15, National Archives.
231. Marshall, 2 *Life of Washington* 148.
232. Marshall, *Autobiographical Sketch* 14.

3: Student and Suitor

1. John Marshall, *An Autobiographical Sketch* 6, John Stokes Adams, ed. (Ann Arbor: University of Michigan Press, 1937).
2. "The Ambler Family," *Richmond Critic*, January 20, 1889. For the family de la Roche Jaquelin, see Bishop Meade, 1 *Old Churches, Ministers and Families of Virginia* 103–105, 463–465 (Philadelphia: J. B. Lippincott, 1861); Louise Pecquet du Bellet, 1 *Some Prominent Virginia Families* 9, reprint ed. (Baltimore: Genealogical Publishing Co., 1976).
3. Rebecca Burwell, the "Belinda" of Jefferson's college days, was born May 29, 1746, the daughter of Lewis Burwell, president of the governor's council and acting governor of Virginia in 1750. For an account of Jefferson's courtship and Rebecca's subsequent marriage to Jaquelin Ambler, see Dumas Malone, *Jefferson the Virginian* 81–85 (Boston: Little, Brown, 1948) For Jefferson's own comments, see his letter to William Fleming, 20 March 1764, in 1 *The Papers of Thomas Jefferson* 15–16, Julian P. Boyd, ed. (Princeton, N.J.: Princeton University Press, 1950).
4. The families of Jaquelin and Edward Ambler are described by Bishop Meade in 1 *Old Churches, Ministers and Families of Virginia* 106–108. Also see 33 *Virginia Magazine of History and Biography* 187–188 (1925), and W. M. Paxton, *The Marshall Family* 42–45 (Cincinnati: Robert Clarke & Co., 1885). For Jaquelin's straitened circumstances in 1780, see Elizabeth Ambler Carrington, "An Old Virginia Correspondence," 84 *Atlantic Monthly* 535 536 (1899).
5. Carrington, "An Old Virginia Correspondence," 547.
6. None of Marshall's letters to his father has survived.
7. Elizabeth Ambler Carrington to her sister Nancy, written in 1810. "An Old Virginia Correspondence," 545–548. Italics in original.
8. *Ibid*. 547.
9. *Ibid*.
10. *Ibid*.
11. *Ibid*.
12. Frances Norton Mason, *My Dearest Polly* 6 (Richmond: Garrett & Massie, 1961).
13. John Marshall, Anniversary Eulogy to Mary W. Marshall, December 25, 1832, Virginia State Library, Richmond, Virginia.
14. *Ibid*.
15. Senator Joseph E. McDonald to Senator Beveridge, reported in Albert J. Beveridge, 1 *The Life of John Marshall* 163, note 3 (Boston: Houghton Mifflin, 1916).
16. Carrington, " An Old Virginia Correspondence," 548.
17. Beveridge, 1 *Life of Marshall* 163.
18. Elizabeth Ambler Carrington to Nancy, "An Old Virginia Correspondence."
19. *Ibid*.
20. In 1780 the Kentucky territory was divided into three counties: Fayette, Lincoln, and Jefferson, with Fayette in the east and Jefferson in the west. Thomas Marshall was sent to Fayette County, and to cover his expenses he was entitled to claim half of the land he surveyed—an arrangement that was scarcely extravagant with Kentucky land selling for 25¢ an

acre. See Martin Marshall McKnight, "The Marshalls of Kentucky," *Kentucky Progress Magazine* 29–30. Also see Irwin S. Rhodes, "John Marshall and the Western Country, Early Days," 18 *Bulletin of the Historical and Philosophical Society of Ohio* 117–136 (April 1960).

21. Humphrey Marshall, 1 *History of Kentucky* 4, 104 (Frankfort, Ky.: Henry Gore, 1812).

22. On March 28, 1780, Thomas Marshall executed a deed for 1,000 acres to Major Thomas Massey, for which Marshall received £30,000. Marshall had purchased the land for only £500 seven years before, and the price increase reflected the rampant inflation sweeping Virginia at the time. Records of Fauquier County, 7 Deed Book 533.

23. Land Office Warrant, No. 4583, Richmond, April 7, 1780, 1 *The Papers of John Marshall* 104 (Chapel Hill: University of North Carolina Press, 1974).

24. Mason, *My Dearest Polly* 7.

25. Marshall to Delaplaine, March 22, 1818, in John Edward Oster, *Political and Economic Doctrines of John Marshall* 197–198 (New York: Neale, 1914).

26. At the time Marshall enrolled, William and Mary had no specific entrance requirements. As President Madison wrote to the president of Yale, "The Doors of ye University are open to all, nor is even a knowledge in ye an[cien]t Languages a previous Requisite for Entrance." Reprinted in 16 *William and Mary Quarterly* 215, 1st series (1908).

27. For a brief summary of Roane (including his antagonism to Marshall), see "Judge Spencer Roane of Virginia: Champion of States Rights—Foe of John Marshall," 66 *Harvard Law Review* 1242–1259 (1953), as well as the specialized study of Rex Beach, "Spencer Roane and the Richmond Junto," 22 *William and Mary Quarterly* 1–17, 2nd series (1942). William E. Dodd's "Chief Justice Marshall and Virginia," 12 *American Historical Review* 776–787 (July 1907) provides additional insight into the Marshall-Roane rivalry. The most complete treatment of Roane's career is in Margaret E. Horsnell, *Spencer Roane: Judicial Advocate of Jeffersonian Principles* (New York: Garland Publishing, 1986). Also see the earlier "Spencer Roane of Virginia: 1762–1822," by Clyde Christian Gelback, unpublished Ph.D. dissertation, University of Pittsburgh, 1955.

28. William and Mary College Papers, Bound Volumes, Notes on Professors' Lectures A–M, Swem Library. Also see John Brown to William Preston, January 26, 1780, in "Glimpses of Old College Life," 9 *William and Mary Quarterly* 75, 1st series (1900).

29. See, in particular, E. Lee Shepard, "Breaking into the Profession: Establishing a Law Practice in Antebellum Virginia," 48 *Journal of Southern History* 393–410 (1982).

30. 3 *The Works of John Adams* 50 note, Charles Francis Adams, ed. (Boston: Little, Brown, 1854). Also see Charles Warren, *History of the American Bar* 35–38 (Boston: Little, Brown, 1911).

31. Sir Edward Coke, *The first part of the Institutes of the laws of England: or A commentary upon Littleton*, 12th ed. (London: Nutt, Gosling, 1738). This work is known as *Coke on Littleton*.

32. Sir Matthew Hale, *Historia Placitorum Coronae*, 2 vols. (London: E. & R. Nutt and R. Gosling, 1736), commonly cited as Hale, *Pleas of the Crown*.

33. Matthew Bacon, *A New Abridgement of the Law*, 6 vols. (London: E. & R. Nutt, and R. Gosling, 1736). In the Library of Congress's record set of this first edition, George Wythe's book plate appears in volume 2 and his autograph in volume 4.

34. Sir William Blackstone, *Commentaries on the Laws of England*, 4 vols. (Oxford: Clarendon Press, 1765–1769).

35. Jeremy Bentham, in particular, railed against Blackstone's "complacent conservatism" and "sugar-coated optimism." For contemporary criticism, see Professor Duncan Kennedy, "The Structure of Blackstone's Commentaries," 28 *Buffalo Law Review* 205–382 (1978–79). Kennedy calls Blackstone "a pivotal figure in the development of . . . the liberal mode of American legal thought. His work set out together, for the first time in English, all the themes that right to the present day characterize attempts to legitimate the status quo through doctrinal exegesis." At p. 211.

36. Blackstone's inaugural lecture was read at Oxford, 25 October 1758. A facsimile of the first edition of the *Commentaries* (with an introduction by Stanley M. Katz) was published by the University of Chicago Press in 1979. "On the Study of the Law" appears at pp. 2–37.

37. David Lockmiller, *Sir William Blackstone* (Chapel Hill: University of North Carolina Press, 1938); L. C. Warden, *Life of Blackstone* (Charlottesville, Va.: Michie, 1938).

38. See, in particular, J. R. Pole, *Paths to the American Past* (New York: Oxford University Press, 1979); Kennedy, "Structure of Blackstone's Commentaries," 284–312, 354–382; and the early work of Daniel Boorstin, *The Mysterious Science of the Law: An Essay on Blackstone's Commentaries* (Cambridge, Mass.: Harvard University Press, 1941). Also see Beverly Zweiben, *How Blackstone Lost the Colonies: English Law, Colonial Lawyers, and the American Revolution* (New York: Garland, 1991).

39. *Commentaries on the Laws of England. In four books. By Sir William Blackstone, Knt. one of his Majesty's judges of the Court of Common Pleas.* "Re-printed from the British copy, page for page with the last edition. America: Printed for the subscriber, by Robert Bell, at the late Union library, in Third-street, Philadelphia, 1771–1772."

40. For a useful analysis of Jefferson's legal career, see Frank L. Dewey, *Thomas Jefferson: Lawyer* (Charlottesville: University Press of Virginia, 1986). Also see Edward Dumbauld, *Thomas Jefferson and the Law* (Norman: University of Oklahoma Press, 1978). For Jefferson on Blackstone, see Dumbauld, pp. 8–11

41. Malone, *Jefferson the Virginian* 71.

42. Richard Beale Davis, *Intellectual Life in Jefferson's Virginia* 50–51 (Chapel Hill: University of North Carolina Press, 1964). Also see, Robert P. Thomson, "The Reform of the College of William and Mary, 1763–1780," 115 *Proceedings of the American Philosophical Society* 187–213 (1971).

43. Thomas Jefferson, 1 *The Writings of Thomas Jefferson* 74, Andrew A. Lipscomb, ed. (Washington, D.C.: The Thomas Jefferson Memorial Association, 1903).

44. Malone, *Jefferson the Virginian* 285; Robert M. Hughes, "William and Mary, The First American Law School," 2 *William and Mary Quarterly* 4–41, 2nd series (1922).

45. Jefferson to Ralph Izard, 13 *Jefferson Papers* 372. Beverley Tucker, whose father, St. George Tucker, succeeded Wythe at William and Mary, described the importance of Wythe's intellect for the college: "The difficulty was to find men to fill these important posts. *Integrity* and *talent* were abundant, but a *learned* lawyer was a *rara avis*. . . . There was but one man in the state who had any claims to the character. I speak of the venerable Chancellor Wythe. . . ." Beverley Tucker, *Principles of Pleading* (1846), quoted in Dice Robbins Anderson, "The Teacher of Jefferson and Marshall," 15 *South Atlantic Quarterly* 334 (1916). Emphasis in original.

46. Wythe's mother (Elizabeth Walker) was the granddaughter of George Keith, a brother of the ninth Earl Marischal, who studied at Marischal College and graduated with a master's degree from the University of Aberdeen in 1658. Destined for the Church of England, George Keith defected to Quakerism, served prominently in Pennsylvania, later recanted, and was ordained an Anglican minister by the Bishop of London in 1700. In 1702 he returned to America and became an active proselytizer for the Church of England. He is described by Quaker historian James Bowden as "Quick in perception and acute in argument," traits that characterized Wythe and Marshall. See James Bowden, 2 *The History of the Society of Friends in North America* 76 (London: C. Gilpin, Cash, 1854).

47. Anderson, "Teacher of Jefferson and Marshall," 327, 332.

48. Malone, *Jefferson the Virginian* 68.

49. For Wythe's role on the revising commission, see Imogene Brown, *American Aristides: A Biography of George Wythe* 174–198 (Rutherford, N.J.: Fairleigh Dickinson Press, 1981). For the general nature of the law revision, see Charles T. Cullen, "Completing the Revisal of the Laws in Post-Revolutionary Virginia," 82 *Virginia Magazine of History and Biography* 84–99 (1974); as well as C. Ray Keim, "Primogeniture and Entail in Colonial Virginia," 25 *William and Mary Quarterly* 545–586, 3rd series (1968).

50. Joyce Blackburn, *George Wythe of Williamsburg* 103–105 (New York: Harper & Row, 1975); Brown, *American Aristides* 203. Compare Charles T. Cullen, "New Light on John Marshall's Legal Education and Admission to the Bar," 16 *American Journal of Legal History* 345 (1972).

51. Cited in W. Edwin Hemphill, "George Wythe: America's First Law Professor and Teacher of Jefferson, Marshall, and Clay," 44, unpublished M. A. thesis, Emory University, 1933.

52. Marshall to Polly, January 21, 1830, Marshall Papers, Williamsburg, Va.

53. The actual texts of Wythe's lectures have not been located, although they existed in manuscript form as late as 1810. Brown, *American Aristides* 229–230, note 25.

54. Justice Felix Frankfurter, then a professor of law at Harvard, caught the essence of Marshall when he described the chief justice as having "a temperament to which abstract theorizing was never congenial." Frankfurter, *The Commerce Clause Under Marshall, Taney, and White* 14–15 (Chapel Hill: University of North Carolina Press, 1937).

55. In a carefully researched 1984 article in the *American Political Science Review (APSR)*, Donald S. Lutz provided compelling statistical evidence of the impact of Montesquieu, Blackstone, and Hume on American political thought from 1760 to 1805. Of all the political writers cited in debate during that period, Montesquieu ranked first (8.3 percent), Blackstone second (7.9 percent), and Hume fourth (2.7 percent). The authors of both the *Federalist* and *Antifederalist* papers also relied primarily on Montesquieu and Blackstone in mounting their appeals. Lutz, "The Relative Influence of European Writers on Late Eighteenth-Century America Political Thought," 78 *APSR* 189–197 (March 1984).

56. Baron Charles Louis de Montesquieu, *The Spirit of the Laws*, Thomas Nugent, trans. (London: J. Nourse and P. Vaillant, 1750). The most readily available modern edition is that edited by David Wallace Carrithers and published by the University of California Press in 1977.

57. See especially William E. Nelson, "The Eighteenth-Century Background of John Marshall's Constitutional Jurisprudence," 76 *Michigan Law Review* 893, 903–904 (1977-78).

58. Montesquieu, *Spirit of the Laws* 152, Book XI, sec. 6.

59. Paul M. Spurlin, *Montesquieu in America* (Baton Rouge: Louisiana State University Press, 1940). Also see Merle Curti, *The Growth of American Thought* 123 (New York: Harper & Row, 1943); Fernand Cattelain, *Étude sur l'influence de Montesquieu dans les constitutions américaines* (Besançon: Millot Frères, 1927); H. Kunst, *Montesquieu und die Verfassungen der Vereinigten Statten von Amerika* (Munich and Berlin: Liebmann, 1922).

60. Blackburn, *Wythe of Williamsburg* 105.

61. Thomas Jefferson rejected Montesquieu for the same reason that Wythe and Marshall embraced him. While Wythe and Marshall cherished an independent judiciary as a counterpoise to the popular will, Jefferson favored unlimited popular sovereignty. Jefferson, for example, did not even note Montesquieu's famous Book XI advocating judicial independence in his commonplace book and later disparaged the separation of powers in his conversations with Lafayette. See Gilbert Chinard, *Pensées choisies tirées du Commonplace Book de Thomas Jefferson* 259, (Paris: Société d'Édition "Les Belles Lettres," 1925); Chinard, *Thomas Jefferson: Apostle of Americans* 232–233 (Boston: Little, Brown, 1929). Also see Dumas Malone, *Jefferson the Virginian* 176–177 (Boston: Little, Brown, 1948).

62. David Hume, *A Treatise of Human Nature* (London: J. Noon, 1739).

63. "The life of law has not been logic: it has been experience," wrote Holmes. "The felt necessities of time, the prevalent moral and political theories, intuitions of public policy, even the prejudices which judges share with their fellow-men, have had a good deal more to do than the syllogism in determining the rules by which men should be governed." Oliver Wendell Holmes, Jr., *The Common Law* 1 (Boston: Little, Brown, 1881).

64. Brown's letters describing his student days in Williamsburg are reprinted in "Glimpses of Old College Life," 9 *William and Mary Quarterly* 19–23, 75–83, 1st series (1900).

65. John Brown to his uncle, Colonel William Preston, Smithfield, Va., February 15, 1780, *ibid.* 76.

66. "Original Records of the Phi Beta Kappa Society," 4 *William and Mary Quarterly* 213–261, at 236, 1st series (1896). Marshall was the fortieth member of Phi Beta Kappa, Bushrod Washington the forty-first, and Spencer Roane the twenty-ninth.

67. *Ibid.* 236. William Short, later Jefferson's private secretary, recalled almost forty years afterward that his argument on the issue that day had been "far superior" to Marshall's. William Short to Greenbury William Ridgeley, Nov. 10, 1817, 64 *Maryland Historical Magazine* 367 (Winter 1969). In fact, the Phi Beta Kappa minutes indicate that it was Peyton Short, William's brother, who opposed Marshall and that "Mr. Peyton Short, being unprepared, was silent on ye occasion." 4 *William and Mary Quarterly* 236.

68. Roane's comment appears in an article he published in the Richmond *Enquirer*, March 30, 1819, attacking Marshall's decision in *McCulloch v. Maryland*. See Chapter 18. The comment has usually been attributed to Roane, although recent evidence suggests it was made by John Brockenbrough.

69. The term "common place" is a literal translation of *locus communis*, referring to "a general theme or argument applicable to many particular cases" and subsequently (by the sixteenth century) referring to a book of such arguments. 2 *Oxford English Dictionary* 693 (London: Oxford University Press, 1961). Commonplacing was the standard procedure followed by persons preparing for the bar from the early sixteenth century well into the nineteenth. See, for example, Sir Matthew Hale's recommendations in his introduction to Sir Henry Rolle's *Un Abridgment des Plusiers Cases et Resolutions del Commun Ley* (London: Crooke, 1668).

70. For an analysis of the law books available in Williamsburg in 1780, including George Wythe's collection, see Appendix C in William Swindler's unpublished manuscript, "Marshall's Law Notes," volume 3 of a projected series of studies on the bicentennial of American legal education. Swindler Papers, Swem Library, College of William and Mary.

71. Albert Beveridge asserted that Marshall's notebook was based on Wythe's lectures rather than commonplacing. 1 *Life of Marshall* 174. Recent research by Professor William Swindler and Charles T. Cullen, associate editor of the *Marshall Papers*, contradicts Beveridge's hypothesis. Swindler and Cullen argue that the precision of the numerous citations simply could not have been obtained through oral lectures. Furthermore, it is inconceivable that an experienced advocate like Wythe would have lectured alphabetically, as if reading from a dictionary. William F. Swindler, "John Marshall's Preparation for the Bar—Some Observations on His Law Notes," 11 *American Journal of Legal History* 208–209 (1967); Cullen, "New Light on John Marshall's Legal Education," 347–348; 1 *Marshall Papers* 38.

72. Marshall's original manuscript, carefully laminated and rebound, is in the library of the College of William and Mary. A lengthy extract, with an important editorial introduction, is reprinted in 1 *Marshall Papers* 37–87. A useful summary is provided by Swindler, "Marshall's Preparation for the Bar," 201–213. Also see Cullen, "New Light on Marshall's Legal Education," 345–351.

73. Marshall's manuscript terminates with several blank pages headed "Mayhem," "Maintenance," "Mandamus," and "Master & Servant," which indicates that he intended to continue his commonplacing but was prevented from doing so. In 1783 Marshall began a record of his accounts in the back of the notebook—a project in which he soon lost interest.

74. Bacon, *A New Abridgment of the Law.*

75. This compilation of Virginia statutes was the primary compilation during the colonial period and was not superseded until William Waller Hening's collection was published in 1823. Hening, *The Statutes at Large: Being a Collection of All of the Laws of Virginia* (Richmond, Va.: Samuel Pleasants, 1809–1823).

76. While Marshall's notebook reveals little original thought, it indicates his exceptional ability to synthesize a wide range of precedent and bring it to bear on a single issue. The entries in the book also illustrate the subjects Marshall considered most important in preparing for practice. Land law, which was the primary basis of a lucrative practice in Virginia, occupies thirty-four pages (e.g., ejectment, estates, leases), with another thirty-four pages devoted to related matters (covenant, devises, inheritance). Material on the various forms of action also received a good deal of attention.

77. The case of *Crump's Executors v. Dudley* (3 Call 506 [1790]) is a good example. The dispute involved a sale of assets by a prospective bride the day before her marriage. Marshall, representing the Dudleys, sought to have the sale set aside and in his argument relied on common law precedents pertaining to husband and wife. The sale, he contended, fell within the category of agreements by a wife before marriage that were voided by the marriage. "Equity," Marshall had written in his notebook, "will set aside the intended wife's contracts entered into before marriage when they appear to have been made with an intent to deceive & cheat the hsbd." 1 *Marshall Papers* 74.

    In his argument before the court, Marshall emphasized implicit property considerations as a motive for matrimony. "That could not be mentioned," he said, "since it is not to be expected that declarations to that effect could be made by a gentleman who is endeavouring to obtain a lady's affection." Marshall won the case in Virginia's high court of chancery, but lost on appeal. 3 Call 514.

78. Elizabeth Jaquelin Ambler to Mildred Smith, from Richmond, 1780, "An Old Virginia Correspondence," 536–537.

79. *Ibid.*

80. Military records indicate that Captain John Marshall, 7th regiment, was issued three summer vests and breeches, a hat, and a pair of shoes. Accounts of Military Stores, July 31, 1780, Box 37, War Office Papers, Virginia State Library.

81. 1 *Marshall Papers* 41.

82. For a description of Virginia regulations in 1780, see Cullen, "New Light on Marshall's Admission to the Bar," 349–351.

83. Marshall's appearance to take the oath as an attorney is recorded in the minutes of the Fauquier county court for August 28, 1780. Minute Book, Office of the Clerk, Fauquier County Circuit Court, Warrenton, Va.

84. Marshall, *Autobiographical Sketch* 6–7.

85. U.S. Congress, *Biographical Directory of the American Congress* 1503–1504 (Washington, D.C.: Government Printing Office, 1972).

86. 2 *Southern Literary Messenger* 183 (February 1836).

87. Christopher Ward, 2 *The War of the Revolution* 655–747 (New York: Macmillan, 1952).

88. George Washington Greene, 3 *The Life of Nathanael Greene* 48–59 (New York: Hurd and Houghton, 1871); Francis Vinton Greene, *General Greene* 158–171 (New York: D. Appleton, 1913); John McAuley Palmer, *General von Steuben*, 237–244 (New Haven, Conn.: Yale University Press, 1937).

89. It is not clear from the records that have survived whether Marshall traveled south with the immediate party of Greene and von Steuben, or whether he led the support train of ten wagons dispatched from Philadelphia by his former commander, Colonel Christian Febiger ("Old Denmark"), on November 8, 1780.

90. Two letters from Marshall to Greene, the earliest dated December 22,1780, and describing military conditions in Virginia, have been lost. Originally located among the papers of General Nathanael Greene, they are catalogued in 1 *Marshall Papers* 87.

91. Sir Henry Clinton and Earl Charles Cornwallis, 2 *Narrative of the Campaign of 1781 in North America* 12 (Philadelphia: J. Campbell, 1865–1866).

92. Mary Willing Byrd, the widow of William Byrd III, and the owner of Westover, was the cousin of Arnold's wife and was a prominent Tory sympathizer. John E. Selby, *The Revolution in Virginia: 1775–1783* 268 (Williamsburg, Va.: Colonial Williamsburg Foundation, 1988).

93. For Marshall's description of Arnold's raid, see Marshall, 3 *The Life of George Washington* 334–336, reprint ed. (Fredricksburg, Va.: The Citizens' Guild, 1928).

94. *Ibid.* 335. Arnold's report of the raid's success is in Williard Sterne Randall, *Benedict Arnold: Patriot and Traitor* 583 (New York: William Morrow, 1990).

95. Palmer, *von Steuben* 250.

96. *Ibid.*

97. In addition to warnings of impending danger from Greene and von Steuben, Jefferson had received several letters from General Washington warning of a probable invasion and urging the governor to be prepared. 20 *The Writings of George Washington* 31, 147, 190, John C. Fitzpatrick ed. (Washington, D.C.: Government Printing Office, 1931–1944); and 21 *ibid.* 21. Also see Francis Rives Lassiter, "Arnold's Invasion of Virginia," 9 *Swanee Review* 78, 82 (1901).

Light-Horse Harry Lee, no friend of Jefferson, was particularly scathing, suggesting that the governor had clumsily left "the archives of the State, its reputation and all the military stores deposited in the magazines of the metropolis at the mercy of a small corps conducted by a traitor." Henry Lee, *Memoirs of the War in the Southern Department* 298–300, General Robert E. Lee, ed. (New York: University Publishing Co., 1869). Also see, 4 *Jefferson Papers* 256–278.

Baron von Steuben's biographer, the highly regarded military scholar John A. Palmer, was more charitable, calling Jefferson a man of letters, not a man of action. Palmer, *von Steuben* 249, 257. An equally balanced view, which is not uncritical of Jefferson, is provided by Malone in *Jefferson the Virginian* 336–350. Also see Jane Carson, *James Innes and His Brothers of the F.H. C.* 123–134 (Williamsburg, Va.: The Colonial Williamsburg Foundation, 1965).

98. Madison to Edmund Pendleton, January 23, 1781, 2 *The Papers of James Madison* 287, William E. Hutchinson et al., eds. (Chicago: University of Chicago Press, 1962). Also see Madison to Pendleton, January 16, 1781, *ibid.* 286–287.

99. Selby, *Revolution in Virginia* 223. Eliza Ambler, Marshall's future sister-in-law, was in Richmond at the time, and her subsequent letter to her friend Mildred Smith detailing Jefferson's flight has often been quoted by Jefferson's foes. The text, well known in Jefferson's lifetime, scarcely improved relations between him and Marshall. See "An Old Virginia Correspondence," 538–539.

100. Marshall, 3 *Life of Washington* 334–337.

101. Marshall, *Autobiographical Sketch* 6.

102. The election certificate, filed by Fauquier county sheriff E. Moher on April 22, 1782, states that "I have Caused the free holders of the said County, to meet at the Courthouse . . . who have Elected John Marshall and William Pickett Esqrs. to serve as Delegates in the General Assembly." Election Records, Virginia State Library, Richmond. There is no record of the number of votes cast or how they were distributed.

103. Marshall to Polly, February 23, 1826, Marshall Papers, Williamsburg, Va.

104. Mason, *My Dearest Polly* 19.

105. As told by Edward Carrington Marshall in 9 *The Green Bag* 481 (December 1896).

106. The locket is on permanent display at the Marshall House in Richmond.

107. According to Virginia statutes that dated to 1631, a marriage license issued by the governor or his agent was required before a wedding could take place. 1 Hening 156. In 1660 a law was passed requiring a marriage bond. Persons who wished to be married were required to appear before the county clerk and give bond with sufficient security that there was no lawful cause to prevent the marriage. The clerk then prepared the license, which was presented to the minister who performed the ceremony. 2 Hening 18, 55. John Marshall's marriage bond, in the sum of £50, was filed with the clerk of Henrico county, January 1, 1783. Jaquelin Ambler's approval was sworn to by him that same day. 1 *Marshall Papers* 92–93.

108. Mason, *My Dearest Polly* 20.

109. Eliza Ambler Carrington to her sister Nancy, "An Old Virginia Correspondence," 548.

4: Husband, Lawyer, Legislator

1. John Marshall, *An Autobiographical Sketch* 7–9, John Stokes Adams, ed. (Ann Arbor: University of Michigan Press, 1937).

2. For the text of the oath that Marshall took, see 1 *The Papers of John Marshall* 87–88 (Chapel Hill: University of North Carolina Press, 1974).

3. Thomas Jefferson, although elected to the House of Delegates without opposition from Albemarle county in 1782, eventually declined to serve, citing the need to attend to his private affairs as well as to be with his fatally ill wife. See the correspondence between Jefferson and Monroe, April 15, and May 12, 1782, in 1 *The Writings of James Monroe* 15–17, Stanislaus Murray Hamilton, ed. (New York: Putnam, 1898–1903) and 6 *The Papers of Thomas Jefferson* 184–187, Julian P. Boyd, ed. (Princeton, N.J.: Princeton University Press, 1952). Also see Dumas Malone, *Jefferson the Virginian* 394–395 (Boston: Little, Brown, 1948).

4. So inconclusive was the May session of the House of Delegates that its journal was one of the few that was not printed. See *Journal of the House of Delegates of the Commonwealth of Virginia* (Richmond, Va.: Thomas W. White, 1828). Hereinafter cited as *JHDV*. The manuscript version of the journal is preserved in the Virginia State Library.

5. Travel costs at the time were compensated at the rate of 2 pounds of tobacco per mile, the price of tobacco being reckoned at 20 shillings per hundredweight—and the distance Marshall traveled totaled 250 miles. Marshall's pay voucher is reprinted in 1 *Marshall Papers* 88.

6. Marshall, *Autobiographical Sketch* 10.

7. Richmond's population in 1782 was surprisingly young. According to the tax list, 34 percent were children fifteen or younger, 44 percent fell in the range from sixteen to thirty, and only about one in five had passed his or her thirty-first birthday. Of the black population, 10 per-

cent were listed as free. With 138 households reported, 87 owned slaves, 45 owned cattle, and 73 owned horses. By occupation, the 1782 tax census reported 36 merchants, 22 craftsmen, 19 carpenters, 5 barbers, 4 doctors, 4 printers, 1 chemist, 1 schoolmaster, and 6 seamstresses and washwomen. Harry M. Ward and Harold E. Greer, Jr., *Richmond During the Revolution: 1775–1783* 8–9, 16 (Charlottesville: University Press of Virginia, 1977).

8. *Ibid.*
9. W. Asbury Christian, *Richmond: Her Past and Present* 29 (Richmond: L. H. Jenkins, 1912); Virginius Dabney, *Richmond: The Story of a City* 36 (Garden City, N.Y.: Doubleday, 1976).
10. Johann David Schoepf, 2 *Travels in the Confederation* 55, Alfred J. Morrison, trans. (Philadelphia: W. J. Campbell, 1911).
11. *Ibid.* 56–57.
12. Marshall was assigned to the judiciary committee, styled the Committee for Courts of Justice, May 25, 1782. Its work included the final drafting of legislation, general oversight of the courts and judicial system, and matters normally handled by a finance committee, such as taxes and currency. Minute Book, House of Delegates, May 25, 1782.
13. May 27, 1782, *ibid.*
14. Madison to Pendleton, April 2, 1782, 4 *The Papers of James Madison* 130–131, William E. Hutchinson et al., eds. (Chicago: University of Chicago Press, 1967).
15. Randolph to Madison, June 20, 1782, *ibid.* 358.
16. Minute Book, House of Delegates, July 2, 1782; William Waller Hening, 11 *The Statutes at Large: Being a Collection of All of the Laws of Virginia* 14–20 (Richmond, Va.: Samuel Pleasants, 1809–1823). For a concise summary of the act, see 4 *Madison Papers* 362, note 48.
17. In 1782 Pendleton and Wythe both sat on the high court of chancery as well as the court of appeals, of which Pendleton was chief judge. John J. Reardon, *Edmund Randolph: A Biography* 61–63 (New York: Macmillan, 1974); David John Mays, 2 *Edmund Pendleton, 1721–1803: A Biography* 156 (Cambridge, Mass.: Harvard University Press, 1952). For the extent and importance of Randolph's practice, see "Sketches of his own family written by Littleton Waller Tazewell for the use of his children" (Norfolk, Va.: 1823) in Tazewell Family Papers, Virginia State Library. Also see Moncure Daniel Conway, *Omitted Chapters of History Disclosed in the Life and Papers of Edmund Randolph* 36–43 (New York: G. P. Putnam's Sons, 1888).
18. 5 *Marshall Papers* liii.
19. The Journal of the Council of State for November 20, 1782, states that "John Marshall esquire having been elected a Member of the Privy Council or Council of State . . . , *and producing a Certificate from under the hand of Jaq. Ambler esqr. of his having qualified according to law;* he took his seat on the board." Emphasis added.
20. On August 24, 1774, Randolph, then twenty-one years old, printed a circular informing Jefferson's clients that the practice was now his. An original of the circular is in the Parker Family Papers; Brown, Picton and Hornley Library, Liverpool, England. A photocopy is in the possession of the Colonial Williamsburg Foundation. Jefferson's reasons for abandoning his practice are unclear. Dumas Malone suggests that Jefferson had lost both his zest and his respect for the law. Frank Dewey suggests that he wanted to devote his time to his family and the construction of Monticello. Reardon, *Edmund Randolph* 15; Frank L. Dewey, *Thomas Jefferson: Lawyer* 107–113 (Charlottesville: University Press of Virginia, 1986); and Edward Dumbauld, *Thomas Jefferson and the Law* 88–89 (Norman: University of Oklahoma Press, 1978).
21. On November 22, 1786, following his election as governor, Randolph ran an ad in the *Virginia Independent Chronicle* of Richmond saying, "I beg leave to inform my clients that John Marshall, Esq., will succeed to my business in general." See 4 *Virginia Calendar of State Papers* 184; Reardon, *Edmund Randolph* 88; Christian, *Richmond—Her Past and Present* 30.
22. Henry Howe, *Historical Collections of Virginia* 266, reprint ed. (Baltimore: Regional Publishing Company, 1969); *Century Magazine* 1 (June 4, 1859). Also see Sallie E. Marshall Hardy, "Some Virginia Lawyers of the Past and Present," 10 *The Green Bag* 23–24 (1898).
23. *Virginia Constitution: 1776* 9–10 (Williamsburg, Va.: Alexander Purdie, 1776).
24. The governor, who presided over the council (but had no vote), was elected for a term of one year and could be reelected twice. Councilors were elected for an indefinite period, but the

constitution authorized the legislature to remove two members of the council every three years. In practice, the removal power proved unnecessary because there were enough resignations and deaths to effect a sufficient turnover in membership. 9 Hening 115–116. For resignations, see 3 *Journal of the Council of State of Virginia, passim*, Wilmer L. Hall, ed. (Richmond, Va.: Virginia State Library, 1952). Hereinafter cited as *JCSV*.

25. When Marshall took his seat in 1782, the eight members of the council of state shared an appropriation of £3,200. 10 Hening 483.

26. 5 *Madison Papers* 339. Emphasis added.

27. Monroe was elected to the council at the close of the June session of the legislature. Minute Book, House of Delegates, July 2, 1782. Also see Harry Ammon, *James Monroe: The Quest for National Identity* 37–40 (Charlottesville: University Press of Virginia, 1990).

28. 5 *Madison Papers* 318–319.

29. Pendleton to Madison, April 15, 1782, 19 *Proceedings of the Massachusetts Historical Society* 150, series 2 (1965).

30. When Monroe left military service, General Charles Lee, who took an avuncular interest in Monroe's career, urged him to overcome his "*mauvaise honte* [false modesty]," which Lee felt was inhibiting Monroe's advancement. Lee to Monroe, July 18, 1780. Charles Lee, 3 *The Lee Papers* 429 (New York: New York Historical Society, 1872).

31. "Empty as the strong box is," wrote Pendleton to Madison, "I am told there is a warm contest for this office." Pendleton supported Ambler, believing his opponent, Foster Webb, "too young for the dignity and importance of that office." David John Mays, 2 *The Letters and Papers of Edmund Pendleton* 392 (Charlottesville: University Press of Virginia, 1967).

32. As treasurer, Jaquelin Ambler served under five governors: Benjamin Harrison (1781–1784), Patrick Henry (1784–1786), Edmund Randolph (1786–1788), Beverley Randolph (1788–1791), and Henry Lee (1791–1792).

33. Bishop Meade reports that as treasurer, Jaquelin Ambler was famous for "his scrupulous integrity." According to Meade: "Whilst Treasurer, one of his clerks robbed the Treasury of £5,000. The officers whose duty it was to examine the Treasurer's books for that year failed to detect the defalcation, and reported to the Legislature that the Treasurer's books balanced as they should do. Mr. Ambler was the first to find out the villainy and immediately reported it to the Legislature, [which] caused a re-examination of the books to take place, re-elected him to the office, and passed an act in which they declared their confidence in his character, so far from being impaired by the event, had been greatly increased; whereupon he immediately paid the £5,000 into the treasury, out of his own funds, and determined to continue in office." 1 *Old Churches, Ministers and Families of Virginia* 106 (Philadelphia: J. B. Lippincott, 1861).

34. See, for example, the letter from Marshall to William Heth, March 1, 1783, in which Marshall tells Heth that he has presented a request of Heth "to the Treasurer," i.e., Jaquelin Ambler. That undoubtedly assured Heth greater responsiveness than if Heth had approached Ambler directly. 1 *Marshall Papers* 98–99.

35. Marshall to William Leigh Pierce, February 12, 1783, *ibid.* 94–96.

36. *Ibid.*

37. The Virginia legislation of 2 December 1778 delegated to the executive the power, after a conclusive hearing, to remove a magistrate for "misconduct, neglect of duty, or malpractices." 9 Hening 478. For reference to debate on the bill before passage, see *JHDV* 14, 20, 31–32, 94 (October term, 1778).

38. 3 *JCSV* 221–222. The complaint was filed by Bartholomew Dandridge, a brother of Mrs. George Washington, and accused Posey, a justice of the peace who had represented New Kent County in the general assembly in 1780–1781, of "grossly mismanaging" the estate of the late John Parke Custis, a son of Martha Dandridge Custis Washington by her first husband. Posey was the administrator of the estate but allegedly had converted it to his own use. Executive Communications, Virginia State Library. Also see 6 *Madison Papers* 347, note 5.

39. St. George Tucker, in his 1803 annotated edition of Blackstone's *Commentaries*, cited the 1778 execution of a Virginia brigand, Josiah Phillips, as an early example of judicial review. 1 *Blackstone's Commentaries with Notes of Reference to the Constitution and Laws of the United States*

and to the Commonwealth of Virginia 293 (Philadelphia: Birch and Small, 1803). The Phillips case involved an inoperative bill of attainder passed by the general assembly and provides an early example of legislative excess, but does not offer a precedent for judicial review. It is discussed definitively in William Winslow Crosskey, 2 *Politics and the Constitution in the History of the United States* 944–948 (Chicago: University of Chicago Press, 1953).

40. Constitutional scholars are divided as to whether the unreported case of *Holmes v. Walton*, decided by the New Jersey supreme court in 1780, constituted a precedent for judicial review. The decision, rendered by Chief Justice David Brearley, declined to accept the verdict brought in by a jury of six persons rather than the twelve persons customary at common law. (A New Jersey statute of October 8, 1778, allowed a six-man jury.) See Austin Scott, "Holmes v. Walton: The New Jersey Precedent," 4 *American Historical Review* 456–460 (1899). Compare Crosskey, 2 *Politics and the Constitution* 948–952, which disputes the possible precedent. A balanced assessment is provided by Raoul Berger, *Congress v. the Supreme Court* 40–41 (Cambridge, Mass.: Harvard University Press, 1969).

41. Jefferson's views, expressed originally in a memorandum for Barbé-Marois and more extensively in his *Notes on the State of Virginia*, held that the Virginia constitution of 1776 was not the supreme expression of the will of the people but mere statute law that the legislature was free to change. In addition to noting that the 1776 constitution contained no amending formula, Jefferson argued that when the Virginia delegates met in May 1776 (the constitution was promulgated May 6), "Independence, and the establishment of a new form of government, were not even yet the objects of the people at large."

   In Jefferson's opinion, since neither independence nor a new form of government had "been opened to the mass of the people," the voters were "not thinking of independence and a permanent republic" when they elected delegates to the convention. Accordingly, the voters could not have vested the delegates with the power to make a constitution, could not have regarded the convention as possessing a higher status than the legislature, and, consequently, must have viewed the constitution as equivalent only to a statute. See *Notes on the State of Virginia by Thomas Jefferson* 110–129, William Peden, ed. (Chapel Hill: University of North Carolina Press, 1955); 6 *Jefferson Papers* 246–249, 270–280; 6 *Madison Papers* 318–321.

42. Madison's views on judicial review were complex. He conceded the supremacy of the constitution and the need to prevent the enactment of unconstitutional legislation, but he did not believe that the judiciary had the ultimate authority to decide the issue. In Madison's words,

   A revisionary power is meant as a check to precipitate, to unjust, and to unconstitutional laws. These important ends would . . . be more effectually secured, without disarming the Legislature of its requisite authority, by requiring bills to be separately communicated to the Executive and Judiciary departments. . . . In State Constitutions and indeed in the Federal one also, no provision is made for the case of a disagreement in expounding them; and as the Courts are generally the last in making their decisions, it results to them . . . to stamp [a law] with its final character. *This makes the Judiciary Department paramount in fact to the Legislature, which was never intended and can never be proper.*

   6 *Madison Papers* 309. Emphasis added.

43. *Commonwealth of Virginia v. Caton, et al.*, 4 Call 5 (1782).

44. 9 Hening 115–116.

45. *Commonwealth v. Caton*, or "the Case of the Prisoners," involved the conviction for treason of John Caton, Joshua Hopkins, and James Lamb, three prominent Tories from southeastern Virginia. They were sentenced to hang, but before judgment could be executed, the House of Delegates voted to pardon them. The Senate refused to concur. A complex mix of constitutional issues was at stake.

   First was the Treason Act, which gave the power to pardon to the general assembly, in conflict with the Constitution, which gave the pardoning power to the governor. Second, if there was a conflict, could the court of appeals hold a statute passed by the assembly to be invalid? Third, if there was no conflict and the statute was valid, could a pardon be granted by only one house of the general assembly? The release of the prisoners was stayed pending an appeal by the state, and the court of appeals, sitting *en banc* [in the bench], heard the matter on October 31, 1782.

The court did not resolve the question of its authority to declare an act of the legislature unconstitutional because the judges found that the Treason Act was not in conflict with the Constitution. Chief Judge Pendleton, speaking for his colleagues, reconciled the act with "the spirit, and not the words of the constitution," which he acknowledged were "inaccurate" and permitted various interpretations. 4 Call at 19. Accordingly, the case turned on whether a one-house pardon satisfied the act's requirement that it be granted by the "General Assembly." The court divided 6–2, the majority holding that the pardon by the House of Delegates alone was invalid and ordered that the prisoners not be released. Edmund Randolph wrote immediately afterward to Madison that "There surely was prudence in the path, which they took. But I doubt not, that to any but lawyers the construction, by which the [constitution and Treason Act] were reconciled, would appear unintelligible." 5 *Madison Papers* 262–263.

Pendleton told Madison that

> The great constitutional question, as it was called in our papers . . . was determined in the Court of Appeals by 6 Judges against two, that the Treason Act was not at Variance with the Constitu[tio]n but a proper exercise of the Power reserved to the Legislature by the latter, of direct[in]g in what other cases . . . the Executive should be restrain'd from Pardoning, including in it the power of direct[in]g the mode of Pardon in all such Cases, provided such mode should necessarily involve the Consent of the House of Delegates which it was thought preserved the Spirit of the Constitution & was the best Interpretation w[hi]ch the Inaccurate words of the Constitution would admit of; consequently it stands as the opinion of the Judiciary here that a Traitor can't be pardon'd but by the Consent of both Houses of the Assembly.
> *Ibid.* 261.

46. Edmund Randolph's argument is reported in 6 *ibid.* 321, note 8. The most cogent analysis of Randolph's view is provided by Charles F. Hobson in "The Early Career of John Randolph," 154–156, unpublished Ph.D. dissertation, Emory University, 1971.

47. The stamp act crisis in 1766 had brought the courts in Virginia to a virtual standstill. The judges were unsure whether to apply the required stamps to their documents or refuse to comply with the act pending its possible repeal. Pendleton, then a judge in Caroline county, took the lead, urging his fellow judges to take up any matter within their jurisdiction regardless of stamps "on the ground that the Stamp Act was unconstitutional and should be disregarded." Mays, 1 *Edmund Pendleton*, 156–173. Also see Pendleton's letter to Colonel James Madison, February 15, 1766, 19 *Proceedings of the Massachusetts Historical Society* 109–112, 2nd series (1965).

48. Pendleton was in the unenviable position of having presided over both the convention that had drafted the constitution and the legislature that had passed the treason act. As Pendleton's biographer, David John Mays, noted, "So far as we know, [Pendleton] had not criticized the clumsy constitutional provision during the Convention that drafted it, and, as Speaker of the House, he had let the Act pass unchallenged, although its constitutionality was even then a matter of grave doubt." Mays, 2 *Edmund Pendleton* 195. Since both actions took place on his watch, it would have been awkward for Pendleton to hold that there was a conflict.

49. 4 Call 5, 17–18.

50. *Ibid.* 13.

51. 4 Call 5 at 8. Professor Crosskey has suggested that the passage quoted was "singularly shrill" for George Wythe and has speculated that Daniel Call, the reporter, may have embellished Wythe's remarks. Volume 4 of Call's Virginia Reports was not published until 1827, some forty-five years after *Caton*, and Call may deliberately have sought to strengthen the argument for judicial review. However, Wythe's biographers are unanimous that the quotation is genuine. Compare Crosskey, 2 *Politics and the Constitution* 952, and Imogene Brown, *American Aristides: A Biography of George Wythe* 249–251 (Rutherford, N.J.: Fairleigh Dickinson University Press, 1981). Also see: William Clarkin, *Serene Patriot: The Life of George Wythe*

160–161 (Albany, N.Y.: Alan Publications, 1970); Joyce Blackburn, *George Wythe of Williamsburg* 69–71 (New York: Harper & Row, 1975); Raoul Berger, *Congress v. the Supreme Court* 103, note 263.

52. Randolph to Madison, March 15, 1783, 6 *Madison Papers* 347.

53. Decision of the Council of State, 3 *JCSV* 221–222. 1 *Marshall Papers* 96–97.

54. In *Dr. Bonham's Case* in 1610, Sir Edward Coke, then judge of the Court of Common Pleas, stated that "when an act of parliament is against common right and reason or repugnant, or impossible to be performed, the common law will control it, and adjudge such act to be void." 1 *Coke's Reports* 116, 118a (1610). Coke believed that the common law attorney possessed a special learning in the law that placed him on an almost equal footing with the crown and parliament. Coke's statement in *Dr. Bonham's Case* never became constitutional doctrine in Britain. Nevertheless, it was freely cited in North America, especially in the years leading up to the Revolution. In February 1761 James Otis, in the famous Writs of Assistance case in Boston, mounted a powerful argument that acts "against the Constitution" and "against natural equity" are void, and in 1772, in the Virginia case of *Robin v. Hardaway*, Thomson Mason argued that "all acts of the legislature apparently contrary to natural right and justice are, in our laws, and must be, in the nature of things, considered as void." As a point of interest, John Adams was the court reporter who recorded Otis's remarks, and it was Thomas Jefferson who captured Mason's comments. See 2 *The Works of John Adams* 521–525, Charles Francis Adams, ed. (Boston: Little, Brown, 1851); *Jefferson's Reports* 109, 114 (1772), collected and published posthumously by Jefferson's grandson, Thomas J. Randolph (London: Colburn and Beatty, 1829).

55. Randolph to Madison, March 15, 1783, 6 *Madison Papers* 335.

56. Harrison to House of Delegates, May 20, 1783, Executive Communications, Virginia State Library; *JHDV* 14 (May 21, 1783).

57. *JHDV* 22 (May 26, 1783).

58. Receipt of the communication from Marshall and the members of the executive is noted in the handwritten Minute Book of the House of Delegates, "Monday, the 26th of May, 1783," with the notation that it was referred to the committee of the "Whole [House] on [the state of the] Comm[onwealth]." The communication cannot be located in the archives of the State of Virginia, and according to Conley Edwards, the state archivist, must be presumed lost. Interview, April 9, 1993.

59. Pendleton to Madison, June 2, 1783, 7 *Madison Papers* 106. Pendleton's emphasis.

60. 3 *JCSV* 386. 25 *The Writings of George Washington* 443–446, John C. Fitzpatrick, ed. (Washington, D.C.: Government Printing Office, 1931–1944). In March 1786, in a separate proceeding, Posey was convicted of defrauding Dandridge, the administrator of John Parke Custis's estate. In July of the next year, Posey was imprisoned in New Kent county for assaulting the sheriff. Escaping from his cell, Posey set fire to the jail on the night of July 15, 1787, and totally destroyed both the jail and the clerk's office with all of its records. Found guilty of arson, he was hanged in Richmond, January 25, 1788. 4 *Calendar of Virginia State Papers* 95, 225, 329–330, 367, 376, 459; "A Strange Story of the Firing of the Courthouse," 4 *William and Mary Quarterly* 115–116, 1st series (1895–1896).

61. See Thad W. Tate, "The Social Contract in America, 1774–1787: Revolutionary Theory as a Conservative Instrument," 22 *William and Mary Quarterly* 384, 3rd series (1965).

62. On December 13, 1785, charges of malfeasance were brought in the council of state against Arthur Campbell, a magistrate in Washington county. Over the written dissent of Beverley Randolph, who cited the constitutional precedent that had been established in the Posey affair, the majority of the council (Sampson Mathews, James McClurg, Joseph Jones, and Miles Selden) agreed to investigate the charges against Campbell and set a date on which to do so. In so deciding, the council referred explicitly to the power given to it by legislative enactment ("An act to extend the Powers of the Governor and Council," 9 Hening 478), thereby affirming its constitutionality. 3 *JCSV* 497–498.

63. Roane did not attend the December 13, 1785, meeting when the Campbell matter arose. But at two subsequent meetings (April 4 and August 31, 1786) in which the findings against Campbell were adduced, Roane dissented, explicitly challenging the authority of the coun-

cil to proceed. *Ibid.* 540–541, 576–577. Following the August 31 meeting, Roane resigned from the council, and although no copy of his resignation has been found, Roane's biographers tie his decision to the Campbell matter. See especially Jon Kukla, "A Spectrum of Sentiments: Virginia's Federalists, Antifederalists, and 'Federalists Who Are For Amendments,' 1787–1788," 96 *Virginia Magazine of History and Biography* 286–287 (1988). Also see Clyde Christian Gelback, "Spencer Roane of Virginia: 1762–1822: A Judicial Advocate of States Rights," 18–23, unpublished Ph.D. dissertation, University of Pittsburgh, 1955; Margaret Eileen Horsnell, *Spencer Roane: Judicial Advocate of Jeffersonian Principles* 16–20 (New York: Garland Publishing, 1986).

In 1787, following repeal of the offending statute by the general assembly, Campbell, who had been removed from office earlier, attempted to resume his duties as magistrate. He was sued in a civil action, *Edmiston v. Campbell*, for wrongly exercising the authority of a magistrate, and fined £300. Campbell appealed his conviction to the general court, where it was heard in 1792 by a four-judge panel, including Spencer Roane. On November 19, 1792, the general court reversed Campbell's conviction, holding that "the executive council cannot constitutionally remove a justice from office." *Edmiston v. Campbell*, 3 Virginia Reports 16, 18 (1792). Also see 1 *Blackstone's Commentaries* 125. Roane's views on judicial review, which paralleled Marshall's, are laid out more extensively in *Kamper v. Hawkins*, 3 Virginia Reports 20 (1792), in which he stated that "the judiciary may and ought not only to refuse to execute a law expressly repugnant to the Constitution, but also one which is, by a plain and natural construction, in opposition to the fundamental principles thereof." At pp. 35–36.

64. *JHDV* 141 (October term, 1787). For the handwritten bill (no date), see House of Delegates Rough Bill, October 1787–December 1788, Box 11, Virginia State Library.

65. 12 Hening 507.

66. 6 *Jefferson Papers* 549.

67. 7 *ibid.* 35.

68. Presumably, Beveridge would have treated the matter had he been aware of it. But as Julian Boyd has noted, Beveridge dealt with Marshall's "very active, though brief career" on the council of state in a surprisingly cursory manner. 6 *ibid.* 279, note.

69. Albert J. Beveridge, 1 *The Life of John Marshall* 210–211 (Boston: Houghton Mifflin, 1916).

70. *Ibid.*

71. Madison told Washington that "the present Assembly may perhaps be regarded as pleading most powerfully the cause of the new Government, for it is impossible for stronger proofs to be found than in their conduct, of the necessity of some such anchor against the fluctuations which threaten shipwreck to our liberty." Madison to Washington, December 14, 1787. 10 *Madison Papers* 327.

72. Washington to Madison, January 10, 1787, in Fitzpatrick 11 *Writings of Washington* 208.

73. *Powell v. Burwell's Estate* (1786), 1 *Marshall Papers* 352.

74. "An act to amend the several acts of the assembly for ascertaining certain taxes and duties, and for establishing a permanent revenue." 11 Hening 299–306. In effect, the Commutables Act permitted the payment of taxes in tangible goods and was a reflection of the shortage of currency in the state.

75. 1 *Marshall Papers* 108–109.

76. Marshall to Monroe, December 12, 1783, *ibid.* 109.

77. Ammon, *James Monroe* 38.

78. Dabney, *Richmond* 36; 1 *Marshall Papers* 313, note 8.

79. *Ibid.* 343, 347.

80. Marshall to Monroe, December 12, 1783, *ibid.* 109–111.

81. The question of citizenship, one of the most divisive in postcolonial America, involved the status of Loyalists who had fled the state and sought to return. If they were deemed citizens, they could bring suits and have judgments executed against real property, and that aroused considerable opposition. Patrick Henry and Richard Henry Lee favored the readmission of all persons without distinction as to what they had done. In December 1783 the General Assembly reached a compromise that forbade the return of all persons who had been residents of the United States on April 19, 1775, and had subsequently borne arms against the United

States. All other former residents were allowed to return and were granted all rights of citizenship save those of voting or holding office. See Isaac Samuel Harrell, *Loyalism in Virginia* 133–140 (Durham, N.C.: Duke University Press, 1926); 9 Hening 322–325. Also see 1 *Jefferson Papers* 476–479; 7 *Madison Papers* 100–101, 120–121, 182–183, 198–199.

82. Congress's reply to Virginia's offer had arrived in Richmond when Marshall wrote. It was sent by Governor Harrison to the House of Delegates on December 11, 1783, and approved four days later. *JHDV* 53, 62, 71, 82 (October term, 1783).

83. Monroe's military warrant was no. 2368, for 5,333 acres and was issued by the Virginia government February 2, 1784.

84. For the 1783 Act of the Virginia legislature, see 11 Hening 249–250. It was repealed in May 1784. *Ibid.* 365.

85. Marshall to Monroe, January 3, 1784, 1 *Marshall Papers* 113.

86. Marshall to Monroe, February 7, 1784, *ibid.* 115. Also see Marshall to Monroe, February 19, 1784, *ibid.* 115–116.

87. See especially Merrill Jensen, *The New Nation: A History of the United States During Confederation, 1781–1789* 314 (New York: Knopf, 1950). For the consequences of the return to hard currency and what became a temporary barter economy, see Andrew C. McLaughlin, *The Confederation and the Constitution* 48–49 (New York: Collier, 1962); Chester Whitney Wright, *Economic History of the United States* 180–188, 2nd ed. (New York: McGraw-Hill, 1949); Henry Phillips, *Historical Sketches of the Paper Currency of the American Colonies* 200–206 (Roxbury, Mass.: W. Elliot Woodward, 1865).

88. Marshall to Monroe, February 24, 1784, 1 *Marshall Papers* 116–118.

89. *Ibid.* 295–298. During the last quarter of 1783, Marshall's winnings at whist and backgammon totaled £5 2s. But during the same period he also reported losing £3 14s at whist.

90. *Ibid.* 296

91. The precise figure is £406 5s 7d. *Ibid.* 293–303.

92. Marshall's record of accounts indicates that from October 1783 through March 1784, he received a total of £98 18s 9d earmarked for his father and that the appropriate disbursement was not made until April 1784, just after he received a government warrant of £100, reflecting his back pay as a member of the council of state. As Marshall's income from his law practice increased, the time interval between receiving survey fees for his father and making the corresponding disbursement diminished until August 1785, when the account became current. *Ibid.* 295–337.

93. For the judges' objections, see Marshall to Monroe, April 17, 1784, *ibid.* 120–121.

94. *Ibid.* 300–301.

95. Marshall's record of expenses indicates that the trip to Fauquier county cost £4 15s. *Ibid.* 300.

96. Marshall to Harrison, April 1, 1874, *ibid.* 118.

97. The index of Marshall's success in the courtroom is his account book. Other documentation pertaining to his early law practice is spotty. Records and correspondence have been lost or destroyed, and a considerable portion of the official proceedings was burned in the Richmond fire of 1865. The editors of the *Marshall Papers* have retrieved what is available, and a summary of Marshall's cases in Richmond's general court, the high court of chancery, and the court of appeals from 1784 to 1788 is contained *ibid.* 123–252.

98. Gallatin to William Maxwell, February 15, 1848, 2 *The Writings of Albert Gallatin* 659–660, Henry Adams, ed. (Philadelphia: J. B. Lippincott, 1879).

99. Marshall to John Ambler, May 7, 1784, 1 *Marshall Papers* 122.

100. The salary of the governor of Virginia was fixed by statute at £1,000 annually. 10 Hening 278–279. Also see William Wirt Henry, 1 *Patrick Henry: Life, Correspondence, and Speeches* 457 (New York: Charles Scribner's Sons, 1891).

101. Marshall's account book is sometimes vague about specific income entries. That is because Marshall was keeping the record for himself, not posterity, and a shorthand entry told him what he wanted to remember. The records suggest that Marshall's approximate income from his legal practice between 1786 and 1795 was as follows:

1786	£1,075
1787	1,090
1788	1,085
1789	1,029
1790	1,415
1791	1,233
1792	941
1793	957
1794	1,093
1795	1,046

1 *Marshall Papers* 347–413; 2 *ibid.* 341–498.

102. *Virginia Gazette and General Advertizer*, November 6, 1784. 1 *Marshall Papers* 126–127.

103. Marshall was reelected as the delegate from Fauquier county, apparently without opposition, April 26, 1784. Election certificate, April 26, 1784, Election Records, Virginia State Library.

104. Marshall was referring to Charles Churchill's *The Prophecy of Famine* (London: private printing, 1763), which describes Scotland's impoverished highlands as follows:

> No living thing, whate'er its food, feasts there,
> But the Cameleon, who can feast on air.
> No birds, except as birds of passage, flew,
> No bee was known to hum, no dove to coo.
> No streams as amber smooth, as amber clear,
> Were seen to glide, or heard to warble here.
> Rebellion's spring, which thro' the country ran.
> Furnished, with bitter draughts, the steady clan.

Henry's famous 1784 speech against the tax law ranks with his "liberty or death" address in 1775 as one of his greatest orations, and, once again, it turned the tide in the House. A contemporary reported that Henry's "delineations of the wants and wretchedness [of the people in the upper counties] was so minute, so full of feeling, and withal so true, that he could scarcely fail to enlist on his side every sympathetic mind." Cited in Robert Douthat Meade, *Patrick Henry: Practical Revolutionary* 267–268 (Philadelphia: J. B. Lippincott, 1969). Also see George Morgan, *The True Patrick Henry* 314–315 (Philadelphia: J. B. Lippincott, 1907).

105. Marshall and Spencer Roane were added to the committee to draft county court legislation on June 2, 1784. *JHDV* 32 (May term, 1784).

106. Marshall to Simms, June 16, 1784. 1 *Marshall Papers* 124–125.

107. *Ibid.*

108. Ammon, *James Monroe* 45.

109. Marshall's account book indicates that on June 22, 1784, he lost £19 at whist—not an inconsiderable sum. It also notes theater ticket purchases for himself and "Colo. Monroe" on June 26, July 3, and July 13. 1 *Marshall Papers* 305–306.

110. Martin Staples Shockley, "John Marshall and the Richmond Theatre," 1–4, unpublished paper, Marshall Papers Project, Williamsburg, Virginia. Also see Shockley's "The Richmond Theatre, 1780–1790," 60 *Virginia Magazine of History and Biography* 421–436 (1952), as well as George O. Seilhamer, 1 *History of the American Theatre* 85–91 (Philadelphia: Globe Printing House, 1889); George C.D. Odell, 1 *Annals of the New York Stage* 226–227 (New York: Columbia University Press, 1927); and Arthur Hornblow, 1 *A History of the Theater in America from its Beginnings to the Present Time* 169 (Philadelphia: B. Blom, 1919).

111. 1 *Marshall Papers* 308.

112. Marshall to Monroe, December 2, 1784, *ibid.* 129–132.

113. "An act for clearing and improving the navigation of James River," 11 Hening 450–462; and "An act for opening and extending the navigation of Potowmack river," *ibid.* 510–525.

114. *Ibid.* 502. Rumsey's boat was unveiled at Shepherdstown on the Potomac, December 3,

1787. For a preliminary description of the boat, see *JHDV* 84 (May term, 1784). Also see Madison to Jefferson, January 9, 1785, 7 *Jefferson Papers* 592–593. When the session ended in January, Marshall wrote to George Muter, a fellow veteran of the Virginia Line from Fauquier county who had moved to Kentucky, that the two canal measures were "of the utmost consequence, both to you and us. They are, to open the communication between the James and Potomac Rivers with the western waters. Should this succeed, and should Mr. Rumsey's scheme for making boats to work against the stream answer the expectation of our sanguine gentlemen, the communication between us will be easy, and we shall have but little occasion to contest the navigation of the Mississippi." Marshall to Muter, January 7, 1785, 1 *Marshall Papers* 133–135.

115. Both Henry and Marshall believed that the intermarriage of whites and Indians would not only improve relations between the two but would lead to "a better race of human beings." Henry's bill provided that every white man who married an Indian woman should be paid £10 in hard currency plus an additional £5 for each child—a substantial sum in 1784. If a white woman should marry an Indian man, the bill provided that £10 would be deposited with the county court, which would be used to buy livestock for them, that the couple should receive an additional £3 annually for clothes, and that every child born to the couple should be educated at state expense between the ages of ten and twenty-one. The bill survived first and second readings, but failed final passage because Henry had been elected governor in the interim and thus was unable to lead the debate in the House. For the text of Henry's proposal, see William Wirt, *Sketches of the Life and Character of Patrick Henry* 170–174, rev. ed. (Ithaca, N.Y.: Mack, 1848). Also see Henry, 2 *Patrick Henry* 218–219; Meade, *Patrick Henry: Practical Revolutionary* 264–265.

116. *JVHD* 41, 54, 72–75, 81 (May 1784); Emory Evans, "Private Indebtedness and the Revolution in Virginia, 1776 to 1796," 28 *William and Mary Quarterly* 349–374, 3rd series (1971). Also see Madison to Jefferson, January 9, 1785, 7 *Jefferson Papers* 595–596. The text of the Treaty of Paris is reprinted in Richard B. Morris, *The Peacemakers* 461–465 (New York: Harper & Row, 1965).

117. 1 *Marshall Papers* 129–132.

118. Marshall to Monroe, December 2, 1784, *ibid.* 131.

119. *Cherokee Nation v. Georgia*, 5 Peters 1 (1831).

120. In addition to Madison, Henry, Randolph, Monroe, Roane, and Marshall, the founders included John Blair, Robert Andrews (professor of mathematics at William and Mary), James McClurg, John Page (future governor of Virginia), Mann Page, the other James Madison, Thomas Lomax, William Short, William Fleming, John Breckinridge, Archibald Stuart, Joseph Jones, William Nelson, R. H. Lee, Philip Mazzei, Wilson Cary Nicholas, John Taylor, John Brown, Alexander White, and Arthur Lee.

   For the text of the Constitution Society announcement, see 1 *Marshall Papers* 140–142. For a discussion of the society, see J. G. de Roulhac Hamilton, "A Society for the Preservation of Liberty," 32 *American Historical Review* 550–552, 702–793 (1927); Bess Furman, "Signed, Sealed—and Forgotten! The Story of a Premier Promoter of the Constitution," 71 *Daughters of the American Revolution Magazine* 1004–1009 (1937).

121. *Virginia Gazette*, April 23, 1785.

122. Marshall to Simms, June 16, 1784, 1 *Marshall Papers* 124–125.

123. Lot No. 480, Record Book, Office of the Clerk of the Law and Equity Court, Richmond, March 15, 1785. The lot is located on the city block now occupied by the Federal Building, 400 N. 8th Street.

124. 1 *Marshall Papers* 322–323. Marshall did, however, pay £4 9s in taxes on the lot on March 25, 1785. If the taxes were that steep, even the reported selling price of £10, assuming Marshall paid it, would have been nominal.

125. Deed Book, Office of the Clerk of Fauquier County Circuit Court, Warrenton, Va., March 16, 1785.

126. Known as "The Fellowship Fire Company of Richmond," Marshall was one of the original forty-four members. 1 *Marshall Papers* 248–249.

127. Leonard Baker, *John Marshall: A Life in Law* 98 (New York: Macmillan, 1974).

128. 1 Minutes of the Richmond City Common Hall 104–107, Virginia State Library.

129. For a general discussion of the responsibilities of the Richmond hustings court, see 1 *Marshall Papers* 169–172 and the notes cited therein.

130. *Hite v. Fairfax*, 4 Call 42 (1786).

131. Lord's Fairfax's proprietary interests had been protected while he was alive. The Virginia legislation of October 1777 abolishing quitrents explicitly excepted the northern neck (9 Hening 359–361), and the sequestration act of that year designed for the protection of British estates from "waste, destruction and loss" did not touch the Fairfax holdings (*ibid.* 377–380). But following the Proprietor's death in 1781, the legislature began to assert a claim to the estate. In 1782 the general assembly passed two acts designed to establish the Commonwealth's control. The first, stipulating that "there is reason to suppose that the said proprietorship hath descended upon alien enemies," provided that future quitrents be paid to the state (*ibid.* 128), and the second validated all existing surveys filed with Lord Fairfax "until some mode shall be taken up and adopted by the general assembly concerning the Northern Neck" (*ibid.* 159). Then, in October 1785, the assembly voted to take possession of all land office papers in the northern neck and authorized the governor henceforth to grant title to the remaining unappropriated land in the proprietary, amounting to approximately 2.5 million acres (12 *ibid.* 111). Governor Henry began granting title to these lands in 1786, and during the next ten years, the state derived more than £100,000 from such land sales. In this connection, see John A. Treon, "Martin v. Hunter's Lessee: A Case History," 44, unpublished Ph.D. dissertation, University of Virginia, 1970.

132. *Ibid.* 51.

133. For a discussion of the earlier litigation, see Stuart E. Brown, Jr., *Virginia Baron: The Story of Thomas 6th Lord Fairfax* 74–100 (Berryville, Va.: Chesapeake Book Co., 1965); Josiah L. Dickinson, *The Fairfax Proprietary* 9–21 (Front Royal, Va.: Warren Press, 1959); and H. C. Groome, *Fauquier During the Proprietorship* 30–81 (Richmond, Va.: Old Dominion Press, 1927).

134. "Edmund Randolph Court Notes," Clark-Hite Manuscript, The Filson Club, Louisville, Ky.; 4 Call 58–62.

135. For the text of Marshall's argument, see *ibid.* 69–81; 4 *Marshall Papers* 153–164.

136. 4 Call 43, 81.

137. See especially Reardon, *Edmund Randolph* 71–73.

138. William Nelson to William Short, January 11, 1787, William Short Papers, Library of Congress.

139. Marshall's account book indicates that on September 22, 1786, he paid three doctors (Drs. Foushee, McClurg, and Mackie) a total of £42 in fees for Polly's treatment. 1 *Marshall Papers* 360.

140. Betsy Munkus, for whom no biographical information survives, was paid 16 shillings monthly for taking care of Polly from 1786 until April 2, 1790. *Ibid.* 371, note 64.

141. Martha Jefferson Carr to Thomas Jefferson, February 26, 1787. 15 *Jefferson Papers* 634–635.

142. Francis Norton Mason, *My Dearest Polly* 41, 60, 113 (Richmond: Garrett & Massie, 1961).

143. Madison to Washington, November 1, 1786, 9 *Madison Papers* 155.

144. The House of Delegates first considered filling the attorney general post on November 10, 1786, but adjourned the matter from day to day until November 23, when the election was held. *JHDV* 35–55 (October term, 1786).

145. Madison to Jefferson, December 4, 1786, 9 *Madison Papers* 191.

146. Randolph's advertisement advising clients that Marshall would take over the practice appeared in the *Virginia Independent Chronicle* (Richmond), November 22, 1786.

147. Copies of the bills in chancery are among the Clark-Hite Papers at The Filson Club, Louisville, Kentucky, the original court records having been destroyed in the 1865 Richmond fire. For the actions listed, see 1 *Marshall Papers* 188–192.

148. *Fletcher v. Peck*, 6 Cranch 87 (1810).

149. *Dartmouth College v. Woodward*, 4 Wheaton 58 (1819).

150. For the history of Nathan's claim, see 3 *Madison Papers* 21, note 1; 6 *Jefferson Papers* 321–324.

151. Arbitrar's Award, December 28, 1786, Executive Communications, Virginia State Library; 1 *Marshall Papers* 198.

152. *Ibid.*

153. Resolutions of January 10 and January 11, 1787, *JHDV* 152, 155 (October term, 1786); 4 *JCSV* 30.

154. Marshall to Wilkinson, January 5, 1787, 1 *Marshall Papers* 199–201. Also see 12 *American Historical Review* 346–348 (1906–1907).

155. 1 *Marshall Papers* 199–201. For Shays's Rebellion generally, see the classic *History of the Insurrection in Massachusetts in 1786 and of the Rebellion Consequent Thereon* by George Richards Minot, originally published in 1788, reprint ed. (New York: Da Capo Press, 1971). Also see David P. Szatmary, *Shays's Rebellion: The Making of an Agrarian Insurrection* (Amherst: University of Massachusetts Press, 1980); Robert J. Taylor, *Western Massachusetts in the Revolution* 128–167 (Providence, R.I.: Brown University Press, 1954).

156. John Marshall, 4 *The Life of George Washington* 221, reprint ed. (Fredricksburg, Va.: The Citizens' Guild, 1926).

157. *Ibid.*

158. Jefferson to William Stephens Smith, November 13, 1787, 12 *Jefferson Papers* 355–357.

159. Marshall to Arthur Lee, March 5, 1787, 1 *Marshall Papers* 205–206.

160. In late 1786, the House had voted against paper money 84–17. Madison to his father (James Madison Senior), November 1, 1786, 9 *Madison Papers* 153.

161. 1 *Marshall Papers* 206.

162. Marshall was elected as one of two delegates from Henrico county, April 2, 1787. The election certificate provides no indication of the votes cast. Election Records, Virginia State Library.

163. George Washington to Congress, September 17, 1787, 2 *Records of the Federal Convention of 1787* 666–667, Max Farrand, ed. (New Haven: Yale University Press, 1911).

164. James Breckinridge to John Breckinridge, October 31, 1787, Breckinridge Family Papers, Library of Congress.

165. George Lee Turbeville to Arthur Lee, October 28, 1787, 13 *Documentary History of the Ratification of the Constitution* 505, John P. Kaminski and Gaspare J. Saladino, eds. (Madison: State Historical Society of Wisconsin, 1976).

166. Monroe to Madison, October 13, 1787, 1 *Writings of Monroe* 176.

167. Patrick Henry to Thomas Madison, October 21, 1787.

168. Madison to Jefferson, October 24, 1787, 12 *Jefferson Papers* 283–284.

169. Randolph to the Speaker of the House of Delegates, October 15, 1787, Executive Letterbook, Virginia State Library.

170. *JHDV* 12 (October 25, 1787).

171. *Ibid.* 15 (October 25, 1787). Madison subsequently told Jefferson that Mason had "left Philadelphia in an exceeding bad humour indeed. A number of little circumstances arising in part from the impatience which prevailed towards the close of business, conspired to whet his acrimony. He returned to Virginia with a fixed disposition to prevent the adoption of the plan if possible. . . . Being now under the necessity of justifying his refusal to sign, he will of course, muster every possible [objection]." October 24, 1787, 12 *Jefferson Papers* 280.

172. *JHDV* 15 (October 25, 1787).

173. Randolph to Madison, October 23, 1787, in Reardon, *Edmund Randolph* 127.

174. Madison to Jefferson 5 *The Writings of James Madison* 121–122, Gaillard Hunt, ed. (New York: G. P. Putnam's Sons, 1900–1910).

5: The Fight for Ratification

1. John Marshall, *An Autobiographical Sketch* 9, John Stokes Adams, ed. (Ann Arbor: University of Michigan Press, 1937).

2. *Ibid.*

3. *Ibid.* 10–11. Marshall's reference to eight votes pertains to the margin by which Patrick Henry's preliminary motion to amend the Constitution was defeated.

4. In Richmond, the *Virginia Independent Chronicle* published a series of antifederalist essays un-

der various pseudonyms between October 1787 and June 1788. These are reprinted in volume 4 of *The Complete Anti-Federalist*, Herbert J. Storing, ed. (Chicago: University of Chicago Press, 1981). Most of the favorable articles are reprinted in John P. Kaminski and Gaspare J. Saladino, *Documentary History of the Ratification of the Constitution* (Madison: University of Wisconsin Press, 1983). Two favorable articles of unknown authorship, signed *Americanus*, and published by the Richmond *Independent Chronicle* on December 5 and December 19, 1787, could have been written by Marshall but cannot be positively attributed to him.

5. *The Federalist* essays appeared in various New York City newspapers from October 27, 1787, to May 28, 1788. They were collected and published in two volumes, the first on March 22, 1788, and the second on May 28, 1788. *The Federalist; A Collection of Essays, Written in Favour of the New Constitution, As Agreed Upon by the Federal Convention, September 17, 1787* (Philadelphia: John and Archibald McLean, 1788).

The authoritative modern text of *The Federalist* is that edited by Jacob E. Cooke and published by Wesleyan University Press in 1961. The best reference work is *The Federalist Concordance*, Thomas S. Engeman, Edward J. Erler, and Thomas B. Hofeller, eds. (Middletown, Conn.: Wesleyan University Press, 1980). For analysis, see especially Martin Diamond, "The Federalist," in *History of Political Philosophy* 573–593, Leo Strauss and Joseph Cropsey, eds. (Chicago: University of Chicago Press, 1963).

6. George Mason, "Objections to the Constitution," November 1787, republished in *The Origins of the American Constitution: A Documentary History* 255–258, Michael Kammen, ed. (New York: Penguin Books, 1986).

7. Richard Henry Lee, "Letters from the Federal Farmer," initially published in the *Poughkeepsie Country Journal*, November 1787–January 1788. The first five letters were republished in a pamphlet entitled *Observations Leading to a Fair Examination of the System of Government Proposed by the Late Convention; And to Several Essential and Necessary Alterations to It. In a Number of Letters from the Federal Farmer to the Republican* (New York: Thomas Greenleaf, 1787). It is available in Kaminski, *Documentary History* 261–301. Lee's authorship of the letters is disputed by modern scholars, but he was a delegate to the Continental Congress in New York when the letters were published, and in 1787 and 1788 he was deemed to be the author.

8. David A. McCants, *Patrick Henry, the Orator* 74 (Westport, Conn.: Greenwood Press, 1990).

9. *Journal of the House of Delegates of the Commonwealth of Virginia* 77 (October term, 1787). Hereinafter cited as *JHDV*.

10. Randolph to Madison, December 27, 1787. 10 *The Papers of James Madison* 262, William T. Hutchinson et al., eds. (Chicago: University of Chicago Press, 1972). Also see John J. Reardon, *Edmund Randolph: A Biography* 129 (New York: Macmillan, 1975).

11. *JHDV* 81, 86, 88, 95 (October term, 1787); William Waller Hening, 12 *The Statutes at Large: Being a Collection of all of the Laws of Virginia* 462–463 (Richmond, Va.: Samuel Pleasants, 1809–1823).

12. *Ibid.* 463.

13. *JHDV* 95 (October term, 1787).

14. John Bach McMaster and Frederick D. Stone, *Pennsylvania and the Federal Constitution, 1787–1788* 4, 14–15 (Lancaster, Pa.: Inquirer Publishing, 1888).

15. 29 *The Writings of George Washington* 386, John C. Fitzpatrick, ed. (Washington, D.C.: Government Printing Office, 1931).

16. Madison to Pendleton, March 3, 1788; to Randolph, March 3, 1788; and to Washington, March 3, 1788, 5 *The Writings of James Madison* 110, 113, 110, Gaillard Hunt, ed. (New York: G. P. Putnam's Sons, 1904).

17. Hugh Blair Grigsby, 1 *History of the Virginia Federal Convention of 1788* 8–16, reprint ed. (New York: Da Capo Press, 1969). Three-eighths of Virginia's population were slaves.

18. *Ibid.* 16–20.

19. The "supremacy clause" in Article VI of the Constitution was added specifically to make the 1783 Treaty of Paris with Great Britain and all other treaties "made, or which shall be made, under the authority of the United States . . . the supreme Law of the Land . . . any Thing in the Constitution or Laws of any State to the Contrary notwithstanding,"

20. "No pain is spared to inculcate a belief that the Government proposed will without scruple or delay, barter away the right of navigation to the river Mississippi," wrote George Washington. Fitzpatrick, 29 *Writings of Washington* 450.

21. Quoted in George Morgan, *The True Patrick Henry* 353, note (Philadelphia: J. B. Lippincott, 1907).

22. John Marshall, 4 *The Life of George Washington* 242, reprint ed. (Fredricksburg, Va.: The Citizens' Guild, 1926).

23. Henry to General John Lamb, June 9, 1788. Original in New York Historical Society. Reprinted (and slightly edited) in Issac Q. Leake, *Memoirs of the Life and Times of General John Lamb* 307 (Albany, N.Y.: J. Muncell, 1850).

24. On April 28, 1788, David Henley, a New York tobacco buyer, wrote a lengthy letter to his father, Samuel Henley, in Boston describing the elections in Virginia and tabulating the results by county. Henley, because of his business connections, was apparently in close touch with prominent Virginia federalists, and his list proved to be surprisingly accurate. Of the 151 delegates listed as federalist or antifederalist, 146 voted as predicted—an illustration of the efficacy of the federalist intelligence network prior to the convention. For Henley's tabulation and a useful analysis, see F. Claiborne Johnston, Jr., "Federalist, Doubtful, and Antifederalist: A Note on the Virginia Convention of 1788," 96 *Virginia Magazine of History and Biography* 333–344 (1988).

25. 1 Grigsby, *Federal Convention* 36, note 1; Albert J. Beveridge, 1 *The Life of John Marshall* 360 (Boston: Houghton Mifflin, 1916).

26. *Virginia Independent Chronicle* (Richmond), March 5, 1788.

27. Randolph to Madison, February 29, 1788, 10 *Madison Papers* 542.

28. As Pendleton wrote to Richard Henry Lee, "You have been truly informed of my Sentiments being in favor of Amendments, but against insisting on their Incorporation previous to and as a *sine qua non* of Adoption, or of a Convention being previously called to consider them." June 14, 1788, 2 *The Letters and Papers of Edmund Pendleton 1734–1803* 530, David John Mays, ed. (Charlottesville: University Press of Virginia, 1967).

29. Pendleton to Madison, December 19, 1786, *ibid.* 491.

30. Randolph to Madison, April 17, 1788, 9 *Madison Papers* 26–27.

31. Jefferson to Edward Carrington, December 21, 1787, 12 *The Papers of Thomas Jefferson* 446, Julian P. Boyd, ed. (Princeton, N.J.: Princeton University Press, 1955).

32. Jefferson to Madison, December 20, 1787, *ibid.* 438–443.

33. Merrill D. Peterson, *Jefferson and Madison and the Making of Constitutions* 9–10 (Charlottesville: University Press of Virginia, 1987).

34. 3 *Debates in the Several State Conventions on the Adoption of the Federal Constitution* 207–222, Jonathan Elliot, ed. (Philadelphia: J. B. Lippincott, 1907).

35. 3 *The Papers of George Mason* 991, Robert A. Rutland, ed. (Chapel Hill: University of North Carolina Press, 1970).

36. Randolph to Madison, October 29, 1787, 10 *Madison Papers* 230.

37. Elliot, 3 *Debates* 271.

38. Madison to Jefferson, December 9, 1787, 12 *Jefferson Papers* 410.

39. Madison to Pendleton, February 21, 1788, 10 *Madison Papers* 108.

40. Quoted in William Wirt Henry, 2 *Patrick Henry: Life, Correspondence, and Speeches* 376 (New York: Charles Scribner's Sons, 1891).

41. 1 *The Papers of John Marshall* 409 (Chapel Hill: University of North Carolina Press, 1974). The first volume of *The Federalist*, containing essays 1–36, was published in Philadelphia on March 22, 1788, by John and Archibald McLean. Volume 2 did not appear until May 28, 1788, and Marshall's account book does not indicate that he purchased it. Marshall paid 12s for volume 1 and the English edition of Jefferson's *Notes on the State of Virginia*, which had been published in 1787.

42. 1 *Marshall Papers* 403–413.

43. *Virginia Gazette* (Richmond), May 22, 1788.

44. Grigsby, 1 *Federal Convention* 25.

45. *Ibid.* 33.

46. *Ibid.* 27–28.

47. Kate Mason Rowland, 2 *The Life of George Mason* 222 (New York: Russell & Russell, 1964).

48. Elliot, 3 *Debates* 3.

49. Grigsby, 1 *Federal Convention* 69–70.

50. Elliot, 3 *Debates* 3. Emphasis added.

51. *Ibid.*

52. Madison to Washington, June 4, 1788, 10 *Madison Papers* 124. Also see Washington to John Jay, June 8, 1788, 11 *Writings of George Washington* 271, Worthington C. Ford, ed. (New York: G. P. Putnam's Sons, 1889).

53. See, for example, Grigsby, 1 *Federal Convention* 72–73; Beveridge, 1 *Life of Marshall* 369–370; Helen Hill Miller, *George Mason: Gentleman Revolutionary* 287–289 (Chapel Hill: University of North Carolina Press, 1975).

54. Mason's strategy reflected a prior discussion and agreement with Richard Henry Lee. Lee to Mason, May 7, 1788, 2 *The Letters of Richard Henry Lee* 466–469, James Curtis Ballagh, ed. (New York: Macmillan, 1914).

55. Rowland 2 *Life of Mason* 224; David John Mays, 2 *Edmund Pendleton, 1721–1803: A Biography* 230 (Cambridge, Mass.: Harvard University Press, 1952); Jon Kukla, "A Spectrum of Sentiments: Virginia's Federalists, Antifederalists, and Federalists Who Are For Amendments," 96 *Virginia Magazine of History and Biography* 286–287 (1988).

56. Elliot, 3 *Debates* 6; Grigsby, 1 *Federal Convention* 217–218.

57. Elliot, 3 *Debates* 7.

58. Marshall to Monroe, December 12, 1873, 1 *Marshall Papers* 110.

59. Elliot, 3 *Debates* 7–21.

60. *Ibid.*

61. *Ibid.* 21–23.

62. Randolph received Clinton's letter in late May and laid it before the council of state, which advised him to transmit it to the general assembly, scheduled to meet in late June after the convention. Accordingly, Randolph did not advise the convention of the letter from Clinton, for which he was later severely criticized. See Randolph to the Speaker [Thomas Mathews], June 23, 1788, Executive Letterbook, Virginia State Library. For Clinton's letter, dated May 8, 1788, see Executive Communications, Virginia State Library.

63. Elliot, 3 *Debates* 25.

64. Grigsby, 1 *Federal Convention* 91.

65. Elliot, 3 *Debates* 29–34.

66. Grigsby, 1 *Federal Convention* 93.

67. Elliot, 3 *Debates* 34–35; Grigsby, 1 *Federal Convention* 95–99.

68. Madison to Washington, June 4, 1788, 1 *Letters and Other Writings of James Madison* 398, William C. Rives and Philip R. Ferdall, eds. (Philadelphia: J. B. Lippincott, 1865).

69. Grigsby, 1 *Federal Convention* 101. Madison wrote to Tench Coxe on June 11 that he was suffering from a bilious attack when he reached the convention and was "extremely feeble." Madison Papers, Library of Congress.

70. Grigsby, 1 *Federal Convention* 101.

71. *Ibid.* 101–102.

72. Elliot, 3 *Debates* 35–41.

73. Marshall to Monroe, December 12, 1783, 1 *Marshall Papers* 110–111.

74. Elliot, 3 *Debates* 41–43. Emphasis added.

75. Grigsby, 1 *Federal Convention* 118, note.

76. Elliot, *Debates* 64.

77. Grigsby, *Federal Convention* 151.

78. Elliot, 3 *Debates* 176–187. Emphasis added.

79. The slowness of communication between Paris and Richmond undoubtedly contributed, but Jefferson's views on the Constitution remained ambiguous. In February 1788 Jefferson had written to W. S. Smith that "Were I still in America, I would advocate [the Constitution]

warmly till nine [states] adopted, and then warmly take the other side to convince the remaining four [states] that they ought not to come into it till the declaration of rights is annexed to it."

Dumas Malone notes that, "The problem with Jefferson's stance is that his remarks were
always behind events in the New World" and that his early criticisms "were used by opponents of the Constitution to obstruct its passage." *Jefferson and the Rights of Man* 172 (Boston:
Little, Brown, 1951).

80. Quoted in Grigsby, 1 *Federal Convention* 168, note.

81. *Ibid.* 176–177.

82. 1 *Marshall Papers* 256–270.

83. *Ibid.*

84. 4 Wheaton 316, 384 (1819).

85. George Wythe Munford, *The Two Parsons; Cupid's Sports; The Dream; and The Jewels of Virginia*
349 (Richmond, Va.: J.D.K. Sleight, 1884); John Ferdinand Dalziel Smyth, *A Tour in the
United States of America* 50 (London: Robinson, 1784).

86. Johann David Schoepf, 2 *Travels in the Confederation* 64 (Philadelphia: W. J. Campbell, 1911).

87. 1 *Marshall Papers* 271–272. Morris's handwritten verse (on the reverse side of Marshall's dinner invitation) is among the Marshall Papers in Williamsburg, Va.

88. Henry did not drink, but he had once worked as a bartender, had manufactured liquor, and
was comfortably at home in a tavern atmosphere. Jefferson said of Henry that he displayed
"a passion for music, dancing, and pleasantry" and that "he so excelled at sociability that it
attached everyone to him." Richard R. Beeman, *Patrick Henry: A Biography* 50 (New York:
McGraw-Hill, 1974).

89. On June 13, 1788, Morris advised Hamilton that Henry's rhetoric notwithstanding, "there
are as you well know certain dark Modes of operating on the Minds of Members which like
contagious Diseases are only known for their effects," an allusion to the lobbying efforts by
the antifederalists. Morris added that "My Religion steps in where my Understanding falters
and I feel Faith as I lose Confidence. Things will yet go right but when and how I dare not
predict." 5 *The Papers of Alexander Hamilton* 7, Harold C. Syrett, ed. (New York: Columbia
University Press, 1961).

90. Madison to Washington, 1 *Madison Letters* 399.

91. Grayson had been educated at Oxford and studied law in the Inner Temple. His knowledge
of the classics rivaled that of Wythe, and he later served as Virginia's first senator under the
Constitution.

92. Grayson to Nathan Dane, June 18, 1788, Dane Papers, Library of Congress.

93. Elliot, 3 *Debates* 517–521.

94. *Ibid.* 521.

95. *Ibid.* 526.

96. Grigsby, 1 *Federal Convention* 290.

97. *Ibid.* 292.

98. Elliot, 3 *Debates* 543.

99. *Ibid.* 579.

100. Mays, 2 *Edmund Pendleton* 262–263.

101. Marshall's three speeches to the Virginia convention are collected in volume 1 of the *Marshall Papers* at pp. 252–285. The quotation appears on p. 277. Emphasis added.

102. *Ibid.* 279.

103. Madison to Hamilton, June 20, 1788, 5 *Hamilton Papers* 13–14. Also see Madison's letter to
his father on the same date, 1 *Letters of Madison* 400.

104. Madison to Hamilton, June 22, 1788, 5 *Hamilton Papers* 61.

105. Elliot, 3 *Debates* 578.

106. *Ibid.*

107. *Ibid.* 593.

108. *Ibid.* 618.

109. *Ibid.* 625.

110. *Ibid.*

111. Madison to Randolph, April 10, 1788, 1 *Letters of Madison* 385–387.
112. Elliot, 3 *Debates* 652.
113. *Ibid.* 653.
114. *Ibid.* 653–655.
115. 1 *Southern Literary Messenger* 332, cited in Rowland, 2 *Life of Mason* 274.
116. Roane to Philip Aylett, June 26, 1788, Manuscript Collection, New York Public Library.
117. Elliot, 3 *Debates* 655–656.
118. *Ibid.* 657–659.
119. The Virginia convention accepted all of the committee's recommendations except Henry's proposal to restrict the federal government's taxing power. When the convention voted to strike that, Marshall voted in favor. *Ibid.* 662.
120. The two proposals made by Henry that eventually became part of the Constitution were his suggestion that "each state . . . shall respectively retain every power . . . which is not . . . delegated to Congress," which became the basis for the Tenth Amendment, and his suggestion that the authority of the federal courts to try suits between a state and citizens of another state be removed, which became the basis for the Eleventh Amendment.

6: At the Richmond Bar

1. John Marshall, An *Autobiographical Sketch* 11, John Stokes Adams, ed. (Ann Arbor: University of Michigan Press, 1937).
2. *Ibid.*
3. *Ibid.* 11–12.
4. See Washington to Marshall, November 23, 1789, 2 *The Papers of John Marshall* 44 (Chapel Hill: University of North Carolina Press, 1977).
5. Marshall's commission as United States attorney for Virginia is reprinted, *ibid.* 41.
6. Washington to Marshall, September 30, 1789, *ibid.* 41–42.
7. Marshall, *Autobiographical Sketch* 12.
8. Marshall to Washington, October 14, 1789, 2 *Marshall Papers* 42–43.
9. William Waller Hening, 7 *The Statutes at Large: Being a Collection of All of the Laws of Virginia* 400–401 (Richmond, Va.: Samuel Pleasants, 1809–1823).
10. 2 *Marshall Papers* 354–381.
11. Marshall to Archibald Stuart, December 1789, *ibid.* 47–48.
12. "JM's Court of Appeals Cases," 5 *ibid.* 451–467.
13. *Ibid.* Marshall's arguments in the Court of Appeals from 1786 to 1800 are recorded in the two volumes of Virginia Reports edited by Bushrod Washington and the four volumes of Daniel Call. Marshall's presentations before the court contain references to more than two dozen collections of cases in the English courts of King's Bench, Common Pleas, Exchequer, and the High Court of Chancery, dating from the reign of Elizabeth I to his own time. For cases in the common law, he used the reports of Coke (1572–1616), Yelverton, Ventris, Levinz, and Salkeld covering the seventeenth century, and Lord Raymond, Strange, Hardwicke, Wilson, Burrow, Cowper, and Douglas extending over the eighteenth century. On the chancery side, Marshall had recourse to *Cases in Chancery, Precedents in Chancery, Equity Cases Abridged*, Vernon, Peere Williams, Talbot, Atkyns, and Brown.
14. Nathaniel Beverley Tucker, *The Principles of Pleading* 57–59 (Boston: Little, Brown, 1846). Also see John David Mays, 2 *Edmund Pendleton, 1721–1803: A Biography* 297–299 (Cambridge, Mass.: Harvard University Press, 1952).
15. *Bracken v. College of William and Mary*, 3 Call 577 (1790). For extensive commentary pertaining to the facts and issues involved, see 2 *Marshall Papers* 67–72.
16. *Dartmouth College v. Woodward*, 4 Wheaton 518 (1819). The similarity to *Bracken* is discussed in Florian Bartosic, "With John Marshall from William and Mary to Dartmouth College," 7 *William and Mary Law Review* 259–266 (1966).
17. Marshall's argument is most readily available in 2 *Marshall Papers* 72–81. The quotation cited appears on p. 74.

18. Bracken, the rector of Williamburg's Bruton Parish Church, had been appointed master of the college's grammar school sometime between 1775 and 1777. The grammar school prepared students for admission through training in Greek and Latin grammar, and as master of the school, Bracken also served as a professor of classics. See Rutherford Goodwin, "The Reverend John Bracken (1745–1818), Rector of Bruton Parish and President of the College of William and Mary in Virginia," 10 *Historical Magazine of the Protestant Episcopal Church* 354–389 (1941).

19. 2 *Marshall Papers* 71, notes 2 and 3.

20. Marshall anchored his argument on Lord Holt's definition of eleemosynary institutions in *Philips v. Bury*, 90 English Reports 469–471 (King's Bench, 1694), and related English precedent.

21. Clause 9, *The Charter of Transfer and Statutes of the College of William and Mary in Virginia* 30, 31, cited in 2 *Marshall Papers* 73, note 4. Marshall's emphasis.

22. For Taylor generally, see Henry H. Simms, *Life of John Taylor* (Richmond, Va.: William Byrd Press, 1932). The quotation appears at p. 42.

23. 3 Call 597.

24. 3 Dallas 199 (1796).

25. Gum guaiacum was a drug used in the eighteenth and nineteenth centuries for the treatment of chronic rheumatism, skin disorders, gout, and colic. The standard medical treatise of the period notes that "several physicians have apprehended mischief from the use of the guaiacum," but the nature of the mischief is not identified. William Cullen, 2 *A Treatise of the Materia Medica* 139–142, Benjamin Barton Smith, ed. (Philadelphia: Edward Parker, 1812).

26. For Mrs. Harrison's statement, see 2 *Marshall Papers* 171–172.

27. For Randolph Harrison's testimony, *ibid.* 170–171.

28. Marshall's notes of the inquest are pointed toward establishing Nancy's innocence. *Ibid.* 168–178.

29. Richard Randolph to the public, March 29, 1793, in the *Virginia Gazette and General Advertiser* (Richmond), April 3, 1793.

30. William Wirt Henry, 2 *Patrick Henry: Life, Correspondence and Speeches* 490 (New York: Charles Scribner's Sons, 1891); Robert Douthat Meade, 2 *Patrick Henry: Practical Revolutionary* 419 (Philadelphia: J. B. Lippincott, 1969).

31. There is no documentary evidence to support the assertion that Henry received £500 for representing Randolph. To the contrary, Cumberland county court records show that Richard paid Henry £140—itself an incredible fee—with a note due May 30, 1793. Cumberland County Court Order Book, 1792–1797, 217, Virginia State Library. Marshall received no fee for his services, or at least he did not record one in his account book.

32. Meade, *Patrick Henry* 419.

33. *Virginia Gazette*, May 15, 1793; Cumberland County Court Order Book: 1792–1797, 161, Virginia State Library.

34. 2 *Marshall Papers* 161–178. The editors of the *Marshall Papers*, puzzled by the purpose of the notes, suggest that they may have been written afterward by Marshall from the rough notes that he took at the hearing and given to St. George Tucker for Tucker's subsequent use.

35. Under the common law, the accused was not sworn at this stage in the proceedings. Theodore F.T. Plucknett. *A Concise History of the Common Law* 437, 5th ed. (Boston: Little, Brown, 1956).

36. Ann [Nancy] Randolph Morris to John Randolph, January 16, 1815. Quoted in William Cabell Bruce, 2 *John Randolph of Roanoke* 284 (New York: G. P. Putnam's Sons, 1922).

37. Meade, *Patrick Henry* 420.

38. 2 *Marshall Papers* 177–178.

39. Meade, *Patrick Henry* 419–420.

40. The Cumberland County Court Order Book contains the following handwritten entry for April 29, 1793:

> At a court held for Cumberland county the twenty ninth day of April one thousand seven hundred and ninety-three for the examination of Richard Randolph who stands

committed and charged with feloniously murdering a child said to be born of Nancy Randolph, present [here follows a list of the sixteen magistrates]. The court being thus constituted the prisoner was led to the bar in custody of the sheriff to whose custody he was before committed for the felony aforesaid and being charged with the same denied the fact, whereupon, sundry witnesses were sworn and examined touching the premises and the prisoner heard in his defence. On consideration whereof and of the circumstances reflecting the fact, it is the opinion of the Court that the said Richard is not guilty of the felony wherewith he stands charged and that he be discharged out of custody and go hence thereof without day. (At p. 88.)

41. Meade, *Patrick Henry* 420.
42. Thomas Jefferson to Martha Jefferson. April 28, 1793. *The Family Letters of Thomas Jefferson* 115, Edwin Morris Betts and James Adam Bear, Jr., eds. (Columbia: University of Missouri Press, 1966). Also see Dumas Malone, *Jefferson and the Ordeal of Liberty* 172–174 (Boston: Little, Brown 1962).
43. 2 *The Diary and Letters of Gouverneur Morris* 515–516, Anne Cary Morris, ed. (London: Kagan, Paul, Trench, 1899).
44. Nancy's letter to Randolph (January 16, 1815) is published in Bruce, *2 Randolph of Roanoke* 274–295. Her letters to St. George Tucker, dated December 13, 1814, and February 9, March 2, and March 20, 1815, were discovered in the 1970s among the Tucker-Coleman Papers, Swem Library, College of William and Mary.
45. Ann C[ary] Morris to John Randolph, January 16, 1815, in Bruce, *2 Randolph of Roanoke* 283.
46. The circuit court decision was not reported, but see *Ware v. Hylton*, Appellate Case File No. 4, RG 267, National Archives. The most complete documentation of the circuit court arguments is in 5 *Marshall Papers* 293–313. Also see Charles F. Hobson, "The Recovery of British Debts in the Federal Circuit Courts of Virginia, 1790 to 1793," 92 *Virginia Magazine of History and Biography* 189, note 36 (1984).
47. The following table, extracted from that prepared by the British Foreign Office, February 5, 1791, lists the debts outstanding by state (Delaware for some reason is omitted). The original, in the British Records Office, is available most readily in Samuel Flagg Bemis, *Jay's Treaty: A Study in Commerce and Diplomacy* 103, note 19 (New York: Macmillan, 1923). The figures include fourteen years' accumulated interest.

	British Debts (in £ sterling)
Virginia	2,305,408
Maryland	517,455
S. Carolina	687,953
N. Carolina	379,344
Georgia	247,782
Pennsylvania	229,452
New York	175,095
Rhode Island	49,208
Massachusetts	287,982
Connecticut	28,653
New Hampshire	21,795
New Jersey	524
Total	4,930,656

48. Emory G. Evans, "Private Indebtedness and the Revolution in Virginia, 1776 to 1796," 28 *William and Mary Quarterly* 373, 3rd series (1971); Richard B. Sheridan, "The British Debt Crisis of 1772 and the American Colonies," 20 *Journal of Economic History* 168 (1960).
49. 9 Hening 379–380.
50. Hobson, "Recovery of British Debts," 178.
51. The rate of depreciation was set by statute in 1781. 10 Hening 472–473.

52. 9 *The Papers of Thomas Jefferson* 16, Julian P. Boyd, ed. (Princeton, N.J.: Princeton University Press, 1950). For a complete list of payees, see the Records of the Treasurer's Office, Journal of Receipts, Virginia State Library.

53. 9 Hening 75–76.

54. 2 *Treaties and Other International Acts of the United States of America* 154, David Hunter Miller, ed. (Washington, D.C.: Government Printing Office, 1931–1948).

55. Beginning in 1784, the Virginia legislature defeated several attempts to remove the legal impediments to the recovery of British debts until such time as the state received compensation for the slaves the British had removed during the war. Virginia's courts also effectively barred suits by British litigants by placing the claims on what was called the "British docket" where they languished unheard. In effect, until the legislature moved to rescind the earlier acts barring British recovery, the state courts remained closed to creditors. As Edmund Pendleton wrote to Madison, it was "the province of the legislature to determine how the treaty [of Paris] is to be performed." March 31, 1783. 6 *The Papers of James Madison* 422–423, William T. Hutchinson et al., eds. (Chicago: University of Chicago Press, 1962). Also see Evans, "Private Indebtedness and the Revolution in Virginia," 356–367.

56. See, for example, A. L. Burt, *The United States, Great Britain, and British North America from the Revolution to the Establishment of Peace after the War of 1812* 98 (New Haven, Conn.: Yale University Press, 1940). Compare Charles R. Ritcheson, *Aftermath of Revolution: British Policy Toward the United States, 1783-1795* 49-90 (Dallas: Southern Methodist University Press, 1969).

57. According to Article III, section 2, "The judicial Power [of the United States] shall extend . . . to Controversies . . . between a State, or the Citizens thereof, and foreign States, Citizens or Subjects."

58. Hobson, "Recovery of British Debts," 182.

59. Pleasants to Madison, July 10, 1790, 13 *Madison Papers* 273.

60. Hobson, "Recovery of British Debts," 185.

61. For the pleadings in *Jones v. Walker*, see 5 *Marshall Papers* 264–294.

62. This paragraph relies heavily on the analysis of Charles Hobson, "Recovery of British Debts," 186–187.

63. Under the Judiciary Act of 1789, Supreme Court justices were required to ride circuit and sit as trial judges with members of the district court on an ad hoc basis. For that term of the circuit court, the panel of judges was composed of Supreme Court justices John Blair of Virginia, Thomas Johnson of Maryland, and district judge Cyrus Griffin. 1 *United States Statutes at Large* 75 (1789).

64. William Wirt, *Sketches of the Life and Character of Patrick Henry* 225, revised ed. (Ithaca, N.Y.: Mack, 1848).

65. Hobson, "Recovery of British Debts," 187.

66. A stenographic report of arguments in *Jones v. Walker* was taken by David Robertson, the reporter who recorded the debates at the Virginia ratifying convention in 1788. That report is no longer extant, but William Wirt, in his *Sketches of Patrick Henry*, used Robertson's report to recapture the essence of Henry's speech. The presentations of the other seven counsel have been lost. See Wirt, pp. 226–258.

67. The best description of Henry's effort is *ibid.* 222–260. Also see Meade, *Patrick Henry* 407–412.

68. 5 *Marshall Papers* 268.

69. The facts of *Ware v. Hylton* did not differ substantially from those of *Jones v. Walker*. Daniel L. Hylton was a prosperous James River merchant who in 1774 executed a bond to Farell and Jones to settle an account balance of nearly £1,500 sterling. In 1780, under Virginia's sequestration law, Hylton paid £953 in depreciated currency (equivalent to £15 specie) into the Virginia treasury in partial fulfillment of his debt to the Bristol firm. Jones had filed suit to recover the original sum plus accrued interest in 1790, and Ware succeeded to the cause.

70. Marshall addressed the court on May 29 and 30. The notes of his argument, taken in longhand by Justice Iredell, are published together with explanatory footnotes in 5 *Marshall Papers* 300–313. In addition to Blackstone, the decisions of King's Bench and contemporary

American holdings, Marshall cited extensive textual references to Hugo Grotius, *The Rights of War and Peace* (London: Irvy and Marby, 1738); Emmerich Vattel, *The Law of Nations* (Dublin: White, 1792); Jean Jacques Burlamaqui, *The Principles of Natural and Politic Law*, Thomas Nugent, trans. (London: J. Nourse, 1763); Cornelius van Bynkershoek, *A Treatise on the Law of War* (Philadelphia: Farrand and Nicholas, 1790); and Samuel Freiherr von Pufendorf, *On the Law of Nature and Nations* (London: Varnan and Osborne, 1716).

71. Cited in Leonard Baker, *John Marshall: A Life In Law* 161 (New York: Macmillan, 1974).

72. Henry Howe, *Historical Collections of Virginia* 221–222, reprint ed. (Baltimore: Regional Publishing Co., 1969).

73. John Nicholas to John Breckinridge, June 9, 1793, 9 Breckinridge Family Papers 1974, Library of Congress. Emphasis in original.

74. Jay's opinion was mislabeled as *Jones v. Walker* instead of *Ware v. Hylton*. The quotation is at 13 Fed. Cas. 1060, 1061, Case 7,507 (n.d.).

75. Justice Iredell's circuit court opinion is reported in *Ware v. Hylton*, 3 Dallas 199, 256–280 (1796). Judge Griffin's opinion, if written, has been lost.

76. John Randolph, who was one of those present in the courtroom, believed Henry's presentation to have been the best the great Virginian ever delivered. Bruce, 1 *Randolph of Roanoke* 146. Also see 2 *Patrick Henry* 474–475.

77. John Randolph is the source of Iredell's quotation, having overheard the remark as Iredell, Jay, and Griffin filed out of the courtroom. Bruce, 1 *Randolph of Roanoke* 146.

78. The implications of this holding for the creditors were severe, because in 1788 Virginia had enacted legislation reducing the state's liability under the sequestration scheme to the actual specie value of the amount that had been paid. 12 Hening 529–539.

79. For Marshall's Supreme Court argument, see 3 Dallas 199, 210–215 (1796). Also see 3 *Marshall Papers* 4–14; 5 *ibid.* 317–327.

80. Chief Justice Jay and Justice Iredell, who had heard *Ware v. Hylton* on circuit, did not sit for the appeal. That left Justices Samuel Chase, William Paterson, James Wilson, and William Cushing to try the issue.

81. After *Ware v. Hylton*, British creditors began to obtain judgments with increasing frequency. Nevertheless, at jury trials Virginia juries routinely deducted interest for the eight years of the war, and those creditors who obtained judgments were often unable to collect because the debtors had died, moved away, become insolvent, or so distributed their property as to prevent execution of the judgment.

Ultimately, the question of British debts was resolved at the negotiating table. In that sense, Marshall's delaying tactics saved most Virginia debtors from having to pay the money owed. The Jay Treaty of 1794 established an arbitration commission for hearing the claims of British creditors. The commission met in Philadelphia beginning in May 1797, and British plaintiffs immediately shifted their interest from the courts to the commission. But after two years of hearings, the commission lapsed. Further negotiations between the United States and Britain (briefly involving Marshall as secretary of state) led to the Convention of 1802, by which the United States paid Britain an indemnity of £600,000 sterling. The money was distributed to British creditors by an all-British commission meeting in London. Most Virginia debtors ultimately paid nothing.

82. Duke de la Rochefoucault-Liancourt, 2 *Travels Through the United States of North America* 38 (London: R. Phillips, 1799).

83. *Ibid.* 61–62.

84. Marshall's account book indicates that he began paying construction costs on his house in October 1788, although the deed for the property was not recorded until July 7, 1789. The deed states that Marshall paid £150 for the lot, although his account book shows only one payment of £50 to the vendor, which was made on January 14, 1790. See 2 *Marshall Papers* 8–12, 28, 382. The deed is recorded in 1 *Richmond City Hustings Book* 29, Virginia State Library.

On January 4, 1791, Marshall purchased an adjacent half-acre lot for £50, giving him a full acre in the heart of Richmond. 2 *Marshall Papers* 85.

85. In 1845, I Street was renamed Marshall Street in honor of the chief justice.

86. For Marshall's construction account, see 2 *Marshall Papers* 8–12.

87. Baker, *John Marshall* 183.

88. 3 *Marshall Papers* 34–37.

89. Marshall's house remained in the Marshall family until the early 1900s, when it was acquired by the City of Richmond. In 1911 The Association for the Preservation of Virginia Antiquities was entrusted with its care and preservation. Some of Marshall's original furnishings are in the house, and over the years a number of similar period items have been added.

90. For the Barbecue Club generally, see George Wythe Munford, *The Two Parsons; Cupid's Sports; The Dream; and The Jewel of Virginia* 326–341 (Richmond, Va.: J.D.K. Sleight, 1884); Edmund Berkeley, Jr., "Quoits, the Sport of Gentlemen," 15 *Virginia Cavalcade* 11–21 (1965).

91. From *The Two Parsons*, as cited in *A Richmond Reader, 1733–1783* 269, Maurice Dulce and David P. Jordan, eds. (Chapel Hill: University of North Carolina Press, 1983).

92. Sallie E. Marshall Hardy, "John Marshall," 8 *The Green Bag* 482 (December 1896).

93. Dulce and Jordan, *Richmond Reader* 269.

94. Hardy, "John Marshall," 482.

95. Dulce and Jordan, *Richmond Reader* 270; also see Samuel Mordecai, *Richmond in By-Gone Days* 183–190 (Richmond, Va.: G. M. West, 1856).

96. For the record of Marshall's dues to the Quoits Club between 1793 and 1795, see 2 *Marshall Papers* 461, 465, 475, 494.

97. 1 *ibid.* 303, 329, 357; 2 *ibid.* 458, 459.

98. Jefferson to Madison, November 26, 1795, 8 *The Works of Thomas Jefferson* 197–198, Paul Leicester Ford, ed. (New York: G. P. Putnam's Sons, 1904).

99. 3 *The Papers of George Mason* 1268, Robert A. Rutland, ed. (Chapel Hill: University of North Carolina Press, 1970).

100. C.M.C., "The Home Life of Chief Justice Marshall," 12 *William and Mary Quarterly* 67–69, 2nd series (1932).

101. 6 *Calendar of Virginia State Papers* 337–338, Sherwin McRae, ed. (Richmond, Va.: Superintendent of Public Printing, 1886). Under Virginia law, which prevented blacks (free or slave) from testifying against whites, Barnett's family was not permitted to give evidence at the trial. 12 Hening 182 (1785).

102. 6 *Calendar of Virginia State Papers* 344–345. Also see 342–343.

103. *Ibid.* 363–364.

104. *Ibid.* 393.

105. *Ibid.* 530–531.

106. September 12, 1793, *Journal of the Council of State of Virginia, passim*, Wilmer Hall, ed. (Richmond, Va.: Virginia State Library, 1952). Also see 2 *Marshall Papers* 207–209.

107. C.M.C. "Home Life of Marshall," 265.

108. 3 Hening 464–467.

109. *Journal of the House of Delegates of the Commonwealth* 126–128 (October term, 1787) (Richmond, Va.: Thomas W. White, 1828). Hereinafter cited as *JHDV*. Marshall also voted against a measure during the 1787 session that would have required free slaves to leave Virginia. *Ibid.*

110. 1 *Marshall Papers* 218–220. The case was originally reported by St. George Tucker in his casebook and is among the Tucker-Coleman Papers at Swem Library, College of William and Mary.

111. The precedent of *Hannah v. Davis* is cited by St. George Tucker in his 1803 edition of Blackstone's *Commentaries*, vol. 2, note H, "On the Law of Slavery in Virginia." Also see Helen Tunnicliff Catterall, 1 *Judicial Papers Concerning American Slavery and the Negro* 94–95 (Washington, D.C.: Carnegie Institution, 1926).

112. 1 Washington 233 (1793).

113. Edmund Randolph, Secretary of State, to James Innes, August 8, 1794, 1 *American State Papers: Miscellaneous* 926, Walter Lowrie and Walter S. Franklin, eds. (Washington, D.C.: Gales and Seaton, 1834). If Innes declined, Randolph asked him to inquire whether Marshall would accept the mission to Kentucky.

114. Henry Lee to Innes, August 14, 1794, Executive Letterbooks, Virginia State Library; August 14, 1794, Journal of the Virginia Council of State, Virginia State Library.

115. The eight extant opinions rendered by Marshall are contained in 2 *Marshall Papers* 291 ff.

116. Washington to Marshall, August 26, 1795, *ibid.* 319–320.

117. Marshall to Washington, August 31, 1795, 2 *ibid.* 320.

118. 4 Call 69–81 (1786). See Chapter 4 and the sources cited therein.

119. Marshall to Richard Henry Lee, January 18, 1793, 2 *Marshall Papers* 138–139.

120. By the end of 1785, the state had assumed responsibility for all of the unappropriated lands of the proprietary—approximately 2.5 million acres. In late 1786 Governor Patrick Henry began granting title to portions of these lands, and during the next ten years the state derived more than £100,000 from such land sales. John Alfred Treon, "Martin v. Hunter's Lessee: A Case History," 102, unpublished Ph.D. dissertation, University of Virginia, 1970.

121. David Hunter was one of numerous purchasers of the Fairfax lands from the Virginia government. Overall, Hunter purchased 9,000 acres in Berkeley, Shenandoah, and Hampshire counties in 1788, paying £25 per hundred acres. 5 *Marshall Papers* 229–230.

122. St. George Tucker, "Notes on Cases in the General Court, District Courts, and Court of Appeals in Virginia, 1786–1811," *Hunter v. Fairfax*, April 22, 1794. Tucker-Colman Papers, Swem Library, College of William and Mary.

123. 8 *United States Statutes at Large* 80. 12 *Treaties and other International Agreements of the United States of America, 1776–1949* 11, Charles I. Bevans, ed. (Washington, D.C.: Government Printing Office, 1974).

124. 2 *Marshall Papers* 142–143. Lord Fairfax died in 1781, and pursuant to his will, Denny Martin inherited the estate at that time. It was Marshall's opinion that the state of Virginia could have moved to invoke the doctrine of *escheat* between 1781 and 1783, but that after that date, it was precluded from doing so by the Treaty of Paris.

125. For the purchase contract, see 2 *Marshall Papers* 150–156.

126. Samuel Shepherd, 1 *The Statutes at Large of Virginia, From October Session 1792, to December Session 1806* 285 (Richmond, Va.: S. Shepherd, 1835); Isaac Samuel Harrell, *Loyalism in Virginia: Chapters in the Economic History of the Revolution* 103–111 (Durham, N.C.: Duke University Press, 1926).

127. Henry, 2 *Patrick Henry* 504.

128. On December 24, 1794, Governor Robert Brooke wrote to Henry that "The course is . . . now depending in the court of appeals, and as it is not only important in itself, but its discussion will govern in all similar cases, the Executive . . . are extremely anxious to commit its management to the most competent counsel. Under the hope that your undertaking for the State on this occasion will not be incompatible with your other avocations . . . I take the liberty of requesting you to advocate it in this instance at the ensuing term." Executive Letterbooks, Virginia State Library.

129. "Our unfortunate friend is no more," Marshall wrote to Henry Lee on July 18, 1796. "A dose of laudanum taken for the purpose has rid him of the world and its cares. For him they had so accumulated as to become too heavy to be borne longer. The burden was laid down on Monday night and yesterday I saw him interred." 3 *Marshall Papers* 35.

130. The Eleventh Amendment was prompted by the decision of the Supreme Court in *Chisholm v. Georgia*, 2 Dallas 419 (1793), which had sustained federal jurisdiction in a suit initiated against the state of Georgia by a citizen from South Carolina based on Article III of the Constitution. Believing this to be an unwarranted diminution of state sovereignty, Congress introduced the Eleventh Amendment as a corrective. It was approved March 4, 1794, and ratified by the necessary number of states on February 7, 1795. Official announcement of the ratification was made by President Adams January 8, 1798. According to the text of the Amendment:

> The Judicial power of the United States shall not be construed to extend to any suit in law or equity, commenced or prosecuted against one of the United States by Citizens of another State, *or by Citizens or Subjects of any Foreign State.* (Emphasis added).

131. Twenty-five years later, in the landmark case of *Cohens v. Virginia*, 6 Wheaton 264 (1821), Chief Justice Marshall effectively nullified the Eleventh Amendment when a federal issue was at stake. See Chapter 19. But in 1794 the prevailing view was that the amendment constituted an absolute bar. As Rawleigh Colston wrote to Thomas Gregory on December 4, 1794, "It is suggested by Mr. Fairfax's counsel [John Marshall] that the trial has been delayed, as he conceives, until a certain amendment of the Federal Constitution shall be adopted by our State legislature now in session, in consequence of which Mr. Fairfax will be deprived of his right of appeal from the state to the federal jurisdiction."

132. 2 *Marshall Papers* 144.

133. Article 9 of the Jay Treaty of 1794 states:

> It is agreed, that British Subjects who now hold Lands in the Territories of the United States, and American Citizens who now hold Lands in the Dominions of His Majesty, shall continue to hold them according to the nature and Tenure of their respective Estates and Titles therein, and may grant, Sell or Devise the same to whom they please, in like manner as if they were Natives; and that neither they nor their Heirs or assigns shall, so far as may respect the said Lands, and the legal remedies incident thereto, be regarded as Aliens.

> 8 *United States Statutes at Large* 116; Bevans, 12 *Treaties and other International Agreements* 21.

134. Marshall's pleadings for this action in ejectment took the form of an elaborate fiction that had been devised under the common law to test title to real estate. On behalf of Denny Martin Fairfax, the real plaintiff, Marshall fabricated an imaginary lease to "George Goodtitle," who was subsequently "ejected" by the imaginary "Peter Plunderer," taken to be the tenant of the real defendant, David Hunter. In addition to "Goodtitle" and "Plunderer," who were descendants of John Doe and Richard Roe, Marshall also utilized the names of Plaintiffs Aminidif Seekright, Simon Seekright, and Timothy Trititle, and defendant Ferdinand Dreadnought, Timothy Thrustout, and Nicholas Notitle in ejectment actions. Ejectment fictions were abolished by statute in Virginia in 1849. J. H. Baker, *An Introduction to English Legal History* 164–168 (London: Butterworths, 1971); Frederick W. Maitland, *Equity also the Forms of Action at Common Law* 351–353 (Cambridge: Cambridge University Press, 1926); 5 *Marshall Papers* 236–239.

135. For the complete pleadings in *Fairfax v. Hunter* (1795), see *ibid*. 228–263.

136. 2 *ibid*. 145.

137. 5 *ibid*. 249.

138. 1 Wheaton 304 (1816).

139. *JHDV* 179 (October term, 1795).

140. *Ibid*.

141. *Ibid*. 3, 4, 9, 10 (November term, 1796).

142. *Ibid*.

143. Marshall to John Wise, Speaker of the House of Delegates, November 24, 1796, 3 *Marshall Papers*.

144. 2 Shepherd 22–23 (1796). On August 30, 1797, Denny Martin Fairfax transferred title to the unappropriated land to James Marshall. The deed was recorded in Richmond in June 1798, whereupon the general assembly directed the governor to honor the Fairfax title to the manor lands "as if he the said Denny [Martin] had been a native citizen of this commonwealth, and as if no escheat or forfeiture thereof had ever taken place." *Ibid*. 140. On October 10, 1798, James Marshall completed the transaction by deeding "all Northern Neck lands recited in the Act of 1796" to the state. 2 *Marshall Papers* 147–148.

145. *Ibid*. 148–149.

7: Virginia Federalist

1. Madison to Hamilton, June 27, 1788, 5 *The Papers of Alexander Hamilton* 109–110, Harold C. Syrett, ed. (New York: Columbia University Press, 1977).

2. Madison to Washington, June 27, 1788, 1 *Letters and Other Writings of James Madison* 402, William C. Rives and Philip R. Ferdall, eds. (Philadelphia: J. B. Lippincott & Co., 1865).

3. John Marshall, 4 *The Life of George Washington* 394–395, reprint ed. (Fredericksburg, Va.: The Citizens' Guild, 1926).

4. *Ibid.*

5. Jefferson to Monroe, June 20, 1790, 6 *The Works of Thomas Jefferson* 78–80, Paul Leicester Ford, ed. (New York: G. P. Putnam's Sons, 1904).

6. "Opinion on the Constitutionality of a National Bank of the United States," 6 *Works of Jefferson* 198.

7. "Opinion as to the Constitutionality of the Bank of the United States," 3 *Works of Alexander Hamilton* 445–493, Henry Cabot Lodge, ed. (New York: G. P. Putnam's Sons, 1904). Hamilton's emphasis.

8. Marshall, 4 *Life of Washington* 397.

9. Jefferson to Madison, June 29, 1792, 7 *Works of Jefferson* 129–130. No correspondence between Hamilton and Marshall during this period has been found. However, on March 27, 1794, Marshall wrote to Archibald Stuart in Staunton, Virginia, about a proposed trip to Philadelphia the two had agreed to take that winter to "superintend for a while the proceedings of Congress." Why they should have wanted to do that is not explained. 2 *The Papers of John Marshall* 261 (Chapel Hill: University of North Carolina Press, 1977).

10. Washington to David Humphreys, March 23, 1793, 12 *The Writings of George Washington* 276, Worthington C. Ford, ed. (New York: G. P. Putnam's Sons, 1889).

11. For the Genet episode in general, see Harry Ammon, *The Genet Mission* (New York: Norton, 1973). Also see Albert Hall Bowman, *The Struggle for Neutrality* 56–75 (Knoxville: University of Tennessee Press, 1974); Alexander DeConde, *Entangling Alliance: Politics and Diplomacy under George Washington* 182–220 (Durham, N.C.: Duke University Press, 1958).

12. John Marshall, *An Autobiographical Sketch* 13–14. John Stokes Adams ed. (Ann Arbor: University of Michigan Press, 1937).

13. 1 *American State Papers: Foreign Relations* 140, Walter Lowrie and Matthew St. Clair Clarke, eds. (Washington, D.C.: Gates & Seaton, 1833).

14. 3 *Marshall Papers* 73 and the sources cited therein.

15. Letter from John Jay and the Associate Justices to President Washington, August 8, 1793, 3 *The Correspondence and Public Papers of John Jay* 486–489, H. Johnston, ed. (New York: G. P. Putnam's Sons, 1893). Also see *Hayburn's Case*, 2 Dallas 409, 441 (1792).

16. Hamilton chose the disarming pseudonym "Pacificus" to emphasize the need for peace through preparedness and to champion executive power. Jacob Ernest Cooke, *Alexander Hamilton* 128–129 (New York: Charles Scribner's Sons, 1982); John C. Miller, *Alexander Hamilton: Portrait in Paradox* 370–371 (New York: Harper & Row, 1959).

17. The Pacificus articles are most easily located in *The Letters of Pacificus and Helvidius*, Richard Loss, ed. (Delmar, N.Y.: Scholars' Facsimilies & Reprints, 1976). Hamilton's emphasis.

18. Madison wrote under the name "Helvidius" to invoke the spirit of Helvidius Priscus, a Roman Stoic in the first century A.D., who forcefully upheld the principle that the emperor should act only with the consent of the Senate. His uncompromising stance caused him to be put to death by the emperor Vespasian. For the portrait of Helvidius drawn by Tacitus, see Jakub Pigón, "Helvidius Priscus, Eprius Marcellus, and *Iudicium Senatus*: Observations on Tacitus, *Histories* 4.7–8" 42 *Classical Quarterly* 235–246 (1992). Also see William C. Rives, 3 *History of the Life and Times of James Madison* 353–354 (Boston: Little, Brown, 1868).

19. Harry Ammon, *James Monroe: The Quest for National Identity* 102 (Charlottesville: University Press of Virginia, 1990).

20. Marshall, *Autobiographical Sketch* 14.

21. For the text of the resolutions, as well as the letter to President Washington, see 2 *Marshall Papers* 196–200.

22. Harry Ammon, "Agricola *Versus* Aristides: James Monroe, John Marshall, and the Genet Affair in Virginia," 74 *Virginia Magazine of History and Biography* 315 (1966).

23. Gnaeus Julius Agricola (A.D. 37–93) completed the Roman conquest of Britain in a series of military victories and is credited with inducing the Britons to adopt the customs and civi-

lization of Rome. The primary reference is by Tacitus, who was Agricola's son-in-law. An English edition of *The Life of Agricola* was published in Glasgow in 1763 (R. Urie), with which Monroe was probably familiar.

24. Ammon, *James Monroe* 106.

25. Ammon, "Agricola," 316.

26. Madison to Jefferson, September 2, 1793, *The Papers of James Madison*, William T. Hutchinson et al., eds. (Chicago: University of Chicago Press, 1972).

27. Monroe to Jefferson, September 3, 1793, 1 *The Writings of James Monroe* 274–276, Stanislaus Murray Hamilton, ed. (New York: G. P. Putnam's Sons, 1898).

28. For the role of Jay and King, see Robert Ernst, *Rufus King: American Federalist* 189–193 (Chapel Hill: University of North Carolina Press, 1968).

29. Henry's negative opinion of Jefferson during this period is carefully laid out in Henry Mayer, *A Son of Thunder: Patrick Henry and the American Republic* 468–471 (New York: Franklin Watts, 1986). Also see Richard R. Beeman, *Patrick Henry: A Biography* 132–133, 186–187 (New York: McGraw-Hill, 1974).

30. Marshall, *Autobiographical Sketch* 14.

31. *Virginia Gazette and General Advertiser* (Richmond), September 11, 1793, reprinted in 2 *Marshall Papers* 201–207.

32. Aristides (530–468 B.C.) was a conservative Athenian statesman who levied tax assessments that were considered so equitable that he won the title of "the Just." Plutarch seized upon that title to weave a fanciful portrait of Aristides, and it is undoubtedly from Plutarch that Marshall's knowledge of Aristides derived. The Gracchi were a plebeian family prominent in Rome in the third and second centuries B.C. "Gracchus," used by Marshall, refers to Gaius Sempronius Gracchus (153–121 B.C.), who, as tribune, took the part of the plebeians (Latins outside Rome who were not yet Roman citizens) and freed slaves, incurring the hatred and opposition of the aristocratic party, by whom he was killed in 121 B.C. Marshall's familiarity with Gracchus probably derived from Plutarch's *Gaius Gracchus*.

33. Marshall's Aristides letters appeared in the *Virginia Gazette and General Advertiser*, September 11 and November 20, 1793. The Gracchus letters appeared on October 16 and November 13. For text, see 2 *Marshall Papers* 201–207, 221–228, 231–247.

34. *Ibid.* 203.

35. Ammon, "Agricola," 317.

36. Ammon, "Agricola," 320. Also see Philip Marsh, *Monroe's Defense of Jefferson and Freneau against Hamilton* (Oxford, Ohio: privately published, 1948).

37. Marshall to Stuart, ca. December 1793, 2 *Marshall Papers* 251.

38. For the text of the 1778 Treaty of Alliance with France, see 2 *Treaties and Other International Acts of the United States* 35–44, David Hunter Miller, ed. (Washington, D.C.: Government Printing Office, 1931).

39. Marshall to Stuart, March 27, 1793, 2 *Marshall Papers* 262.

40. Richard H. Kohn, *Eagle and Sword: The Federalists and the Creation of the Military Establishment in America, 1783–1802* 85–95 (New York: Free Press, 1975).

41. *Journal of the House of Delegates of the Commonwealth of Virginia* 102, 104 (October term, 1793) (Richmond: Thomas W. White, 1828). Hereinafter cited as *JHDV*.

42. 1 *United States Statutes at Large* 381–384.

43. Lee to Marshall, July 21, 1794, 2 *Marshall Papers* 273–274.

44. Marshall to Lee, July 23, 1794, *ibid.* 275–276.

45. Marshall to Lee, July 28, 1794, *ibid.* 276–278.

46. *Ibid.* Also see Lee to Marshall, July 30, 1794, *ibid.* 278–279.

47. *Ibid.* 280. For the Whiskey Rebellion generally, see Leland D. Baldwin, *Whiskey Rebels: The Story of a Frontier Uprising* (Pittsburgh: University of Pittsburgh Press, 1939; Kohn, *Eagle and Sword* 158–173.

48. 2 *Marshall Papers* 183.

49. For Jay's instructions, see *The Record of American Diplomacy* 77–80, Ruhl J. Bartlett, ed. (New York: Alfred A. Knopf, 1964).

50. 12 *Treaties and other International Agreements of the United States* 21, Charles I. Bevans, ed. (Washington, D.C.: Government Printing Office, 1974).
51. As Marshall explained his election to Story:

> The public and frequent altercations in which I was unavoidably engaged gradually weakened my decision never again to go into the legislature, and I was beginning to think of changing my determination on that subject, when the election of 1795 came on.
>
> From the time of my withdrawing from the legislature two opposing candidates had divided the city, the one was my intimate friend [John Harvie] whose sentiments were very much those which I entertained, and the other [Alexander McRobert] was an infuriated politician who thought every resistance to the will of France subserviency to Britain, and an adhesion of despots against liberty. Each election between these gentlemen, who were both popular, had been decided by a small majority; and that which was approaching was entirely doubtful.
>
> I attended at the polls to give my vote early and return to the court which was then in session at the other end of town. As soon as the election commenced a gentleman came forward and demanded that a poll should be taken for me. I was a good deal surprised at this entirely unexpected proposition and declared my decided dissent. I said that if any fellow citizens wished it I would become a candidate at the next succeeding election, but that I could not consent to serve this year because my wishes and my honour were engaged for one of the candidates. I then voted for my friend and left the polls for the court which was open and waiting for me. The gentleman said he had a right to demand a poll for whom he pleased, and persisted in his demand that one should be opened for me—I might if elected refuse to obey the voice of my constituents if I chose to do so. He then gave his vote for me.
>
> As this was entirely unexpected—not even known to my brother who though of the same political opinions with myself was the active and leading partisan of the candidate against whom I had voted, the election was almost suspended for ten or twelve minutes, and a consultation took place among the principal freeholders. They then came in and in the evening information was brought to me that I was elected. I regretted this for the sake of my friend. In other respects I was well satisfied at being again in the assembly.

Marshall, *Autobiographical Sketch* 14–15.
52. Jefferson to Madison, November 26, 1795, 8 *Works of Jefferson* 197–198.
53. The episode is described in John J. Reardon, *Edmund Randolph: A Biography* 307–334 (New York: Macmillan, 1975). Also see Irving Brant, "Edmund Randolph, Not Guilty," 7 *William and Mary Quarterly* 179–198, 3rd series (1950). For Marshall's commentary, see 5 *Life of Washington* 394–396.
54. Washington to Edward Carrington, October 9, 1795, 11 *The Writings of George Washington* 78, Jared Sparks, ed. (Boston: Little, Brown, 1855).
55. Washington to Hamilton, October 29, 1795, 13 *ibid*. 131.
56. Washington to Carrington, October 9, 1795, 11 *ibid*. 78. For the text of Washington's letter to Henry, see *ibid*. 81–82.
57. *Ibid*.
58. Carrington to Washington, October 13, 1795, *ibid*. 80–82, note. For Marshall's subsequent comments, see 5 *Life of Washington* 396–397.
59. Marshall, *Autobiographical Sketch* 16–17.
60. Joseph Story, "Eulogy on the Life of John Marshall," in 3 *John Marshall: Life, Character and Judicial Services* 352, John F. Dillon, ed. (Chicago: Callaghan, 1903).
61. Marshall to King, April 25, 1796, 3 *Marshall Papers* 23–24.
62. Marshall to Hamilton, April 25, 1796, *ibid*.
63. Randolph to Madison, April 25, 1796, in Reardon, *Edmund Randolph* 343.
64. Marshall, *Autobiographical Sketch* 17.
65. *Ibid*.

66. *Ibid.*
67. *Ibid.*
68. Griffith J. McRee, 2 *Life and Correspondence of James Iredell* 456 (New York: Appleton, 1857).
69. Marshall, *Autobiographical Sketch* 19–20. At the age of seventy, Marshall's memory occasionally was faulty. There is no doubt that he was well received by the Federalists in Philadelphia when he went to argue *Ware v. Hylton*, but that was in February 1796, several months prior to the debate in the House of Delegates.
70. Washington to Timothy Pickering, July 8, 1796, in Ford, 13 *Writings of Washington* 236.
71. Washington to Marshall, July 8, 1796, 3 *Marshall Papers* 31–32.
72. Marshall to Washington, July 11, 1796, *ibid.* 32–33. For Washington's reply, *ibid.* 33–34. General Pinckney accepted Washington's offer and was named United States minister to France at the end of July.
73. Marshall, *Autobiographical Sketch* 20–21; *JHDV* (December 10,1796). Compare Albert J. Beveridge, 2 *The Life of John Marshall* 158–163 (Boston: Houghton Mifflin, 1916); Richard R. Beeman, *The Old Dominion and the New Nation* 150–151 (Lexington: University of Kentucky Press, 1972).
74. Washington to Hamilton, January 22, 1797, 20 *Hamilton Papers* 476.
75. Felix Gilbert, *To the Farewell Address* 115–136 (Princeton, N.J.: Princeton University Press, 1961). Also see Samuel Flagg Bemis, "Washington's Farewell Address, A Foreign Policy of Independence," 39 *American Historical Review* 254–255 (1934).
76. The Farewell Address is reproduced in full in volume 5 of Marshall's *Life of Washington*, at pp. 279–306.
77. Manning J. Dauer, *The Adams Federalists* 96–97 (Baltimore: The Johns Hopkins Press, 1968); Bowman, *Struggle for Neutrality* 262–278; Page Smith, 2 *John Adams* 112–113 (Garden City, N.Y.: Doubleday, 1962).
78. Adet to Delacroix, December 18, 1796, *Correspondence of the French Ministers to the United States, 1791–1797*, Frederick Jackson Turner, ed., in 2 *Annual Report of the American Historical Association for the Year 1903* 978–980 (Washington, D.C.: Government Printing Office, 1904).
79. 9 *The Works of John Adams* 105–111, Charles Francis Adams, ed. (Boston: Little, Brown, 1850).
80. Dumas Malone, *Jefferson and the Ordeal of Liberty* 295–301 (Boston: Little, Brown, 1962); Smith, 2 *Adams* 917–925; Dauer, *Adams Federalists* 120–128.
81. French objections were not groundless. The Jay treaty ignored the principle of "free ships, free goods" and greatly expanded the list of contraband articles. As Samuel Flagg Bemis noted, these measures "were in some sense incompatible with the Franco-American treaty of 1778 but not a violation of it." Samuel Flagg Bemis, *A Diplomatic History of the United States* 103 (New York: Holt, 1950).
82. Pinckney to Pickering, December 20, 1796, 2 *American State Papers: Foreign Relations* 5–10, 18. Also see E. Wilson Lyon, "The Directory and the United States," 43 *American Historical Review* 514–516 (1938); William Stinchcombe, *The XYZ Affair* 14 (Westport, Conn.: Greenwood Press, 1980).
83. 7 *Annals of Congress* 54–59. Adams's speech was postponed for one day because of the lack of a quorum on May 15. For a useful synopsis of Republican criticism, see Stanley Elkins and Eric McKitrick, *The Age of Federalism* 552 (New York: Oxford University Press, 1993).
84. Adams to J. Q. Adams, March 31, 1797, 8 *Works of John Adams* 537.
85. Oliver Wolcott to Hamilton, March 31, 1797, 20 *Hamilton Papers* 569–574; Dauer, *Adams Federalists* 125–126; also see Stinchcombe *XYZ* 29, note 12 and the sources cited therein. Madison was unwilling to accept the assignment, as well. The idea that he would go to Paris was "pure fiction," he told Jefferson. Madison to Jefferson, January 22, 1797, 16 *Madison Papers* 471.
86. James T. Austin, 2 *The Life of Elbridge Gerry* 134–135 (Boston: Wells, 1829).
87. See James McHenry to Timothy Pickering, February 23, 1811 in Henry Cabot Lodge, *Life and Letters of George Cabot* 204 (Boston: Little, Brown, 1878); 1 *Memoirs of the Administrations of Washington and John Adams: edited from the papers of Oliver Wolcott, Secretary of the Treasury*

462–471, George Gibbs, ed. (New York: William Van Norden, 1846); Adams to Gerry, June 20, 1797, Adams Papers, Massachusetts Historical Society.

88. Pickering to Charles Cotesworth Pinckney, June 1, 1797, Timothy Pickering Papers, Massachusetts Historical Society. Nevertheless, there was little enthusiasm for Gerry. "No appointment could have been more injudicious," House Speaker Thomas Sedgwick wrote to Rufus King, June 24, 1797. 2 *The Life and Correspondence of Rufus King* 193, Charles R. King, ed. (New York: G. P. Putnam's Sons, 1896).

89. Memorandum, "Questions to be proposed," May 26, 1797, Adams Papers, Massachusetts Historical Society.

90. Pickering to Marshall, June 6, 1797, 3 *Marshall Papers* 86.

91. Marshall's letter to Pickering has been lost, but on June 12, 1797, less than a week after the offer was made, Pickering informed Pinckney that Marshall had accepted. RG 59, National Archives. Cited in 3 *Marshall Papers* 80, note 2.

92. Marshall, *Autobiographical Sketch* 21–22.

93. 2 Shepherd 22–23 (1796). See Chapter 6.

94. Morris to John Marshall, December 30, 1796; January 23, 1796, 3 *Marshall Papers* 60–61, 63.

95. *Ibid.* 80, note 4. For details of the purchase of South Branch Manor, see 6 *ibid.* 543–544.

96. 3 *ibid.* 80, and note 6.

97. 2 *ibid.* 148.

98. Tucker to John Page, June 23, 1797, cited in Leonard Baker, *John Marshall: A Life In Law* 221 (New York: Macmillan, 1974). Tucker's reference to "side men" indicates that it was assumed that Pinckney, as the senior of the envoys, would be the principal spokesman.

99. Alexandre Maurice Blanc de Lanaute, comte d'Hauterive (1754–1830). See Francis B. Childs, "A Secret Agent's Advice on America: 1797," in *Nationalism and Internationalism* 18–26, Edward Mead Earle, ed. (New York: Columbia University Press, 1950).

100. Hauterive to Citizen Adet, May 22–27, 1797, Archives du Ministère des Affaires Étrangères, 2 *Correspondance Politique: États-Unis, Supplément* 162. Hereinafter cited as *CPE-U.*

101. Hauterive to Citizen Adet, June 3, 1797, *ibid.* 165–166. Hauterive wrote before Dana declined the posting.

102. *Ibid.* Emphasis added.

103. Adet to Delacroix, October 3. 1796. *Correspondence of the French Ministers to the United States* 950–952.

104. 2 *Marshall Papers* 396.

105. Frances Norton Mason, *My Dearest Polly* 89–90 (Richmond, Va.: Garrett and Massie, 1961).

106. Marshall to Polly, June 24, 1797, 3 *Marshall Papers* 92.

107. Polly's letter was dated June 30 and has been lost. See Marshall to Polly, July 10, 1797, *ibid.* 97.

108. Marshall wrote to Polly upon his arrival in The Hague, September 9, 1797, and again from Paris, November 27, 1797. If he wrote additional letters, they have been lost.

109. Marshall to Polly, July 3, 1797, *ibid.* 94–95.

110. Adams to Gerry, July 17, 1797, 8 *Works of John Adams* 549. At the time of Marshall's appointment, Abigail wrote to John Quincy Adams that Marshall was "said to be a very fair and Honorable man, and truly American, a lawyer by profession, against whom no objection is offered, but that he is not Frenchman enough for those who would have sent Jefferson or Madison." Stewart Mitchell, *New Letters of Abigail Adams* 94 (Boston: Houghton Mifflin, 1947).

111. Dumas Malone, 1 *Jefferson and the Ordeal of Liberty* 324–325; Ammon, *James Monroe* 158.

112. 3 *Marshall Papers* 94–95.

113. *Ibid.* 94, note.

114. Marshall to Polly, July 5, 1797, *ibid.* 95–96.

115. Marshall to Polly, July 10, 1797, *ibid.* 97–98.

116. Marshall to Polly, July 14, 1797, *ibid.* 101–102.

117. "We seem to be where we were with G. Britain when Mr. Jay was sent there—and I cannot discern but that the Spirit of the Policy then pursued with regard to England will be the

proper one now in respect to France," Hamilton wrote to Washington in January 1797. Also see Hamilton to Theodore Sedgwick, January 20, February 26, 1797; to Pickering, March 22, 29, May 11, 1797; to Oliver Wolcott, March 30, April 5, 1797. 20 *Hamilton Papers* 470, 474, 521–522, 545, 556–557, 567–568, 575.

118. Dumas Malone, *Jefferson and the Rights of Man* 315–317, 322 (Boston: Little, Brown, 1951).

119. Jefferson to Randolph, June 27, 1797, 7 *Works of Jefferson* 142–156.

120. Jefferson to Madison, May 18, 1797; to Thomas Pinckney, May 29, 1797; to Peregrine Fitzhugh, June 4, 1797; to French Strother, June 8, 1797; to Madison, June 8, 15, 1797; to Aaron Burr, June 17, 1797; to Elbridge Gerry, June 21, 1797; to Edward Rutledge, June 24, 1797; to Edmund Randolph, June 27, 1797. *Ibid.* 124–130, 134–140, 142–156.

121. Létombe to Citizen Delacroix, July 7, 1797, 47 *CPE-U* 347. During this period, Létombe refers in four separate dispatches to having met with Jefferson: May 16, 30, June 5, 6. In a later dispatch, Létombe told Paris that the vice president said that he should "not hesitate to drop in on him any time I liked." January 17, 1798, *ibid.* 49, 145.

122. July 7, 1797, *ibid.*

123. July 18, 1797, *ibid.*

124. July 25, 1797, *ibid.*

125. *Ibid.*

126. *Ibid.*

127. Pickering to Envoys, July 15, 1797, 3 *Marshall Papers* 102–119.

128. Marshall to Polly, July 20, 1797, *ibid.* 120–122.

129. Marshall to Polly, August 3, 1797, *ibid.* 122–123. Marshall was unable to place the letter aboard a passing vessel and mailed it from Amsterdam on August 29.

8: Mission to Paris (The XYZ Affair)

1. Marshall to Pickering, September 2, 1797, 3 *The Papers of John Marshall* 128–130 (Chapel Hill: University of North Carolina Press, 1979).

2. Marshall to Washington, September 15, 1797, *ibid.* 138–147. Also see Marshall to Edward Carrington, September 2, 1797, *ibid.* 123–127.

3. Marshall to Washington, *ibid.* 138–147.

4. Marshall to Carrington, *ibid.* 123–127.

5. *Ibid.*

6. *Ibid.* Also see Marshall to Pickering, September 2, 1797, *ibid.* 132–138.

7. The question was put by Adalbert, Count of Périgord. See Georges LaCour-Gayet, 1 *Talleyrand: 1754–1838*, 72 (Paris: Payot, 1928).

8. The Comtesse de Flahaut, the illegitimate daughter of a farmer-general of France, was the sister-in-law of the Comte d'Angivilliers, who, as superintendent of the king's buildings, had provided her with a private apartment in the Louvre. In the early 1780s she and Talleyrand established a happy ménage, and in 1785 a son was born to them. See Simon Schama, *Citizens: A Chronicle of the French Revolution* 227 (New York: Knopf, 1989). Louis Madelin, *Talleyrand: A Vivid Biography of the Amoral, Unscrupulous, and Fascinating French Statesman* 16, Rosalie Feltenstein, trans. (New York: Roy, 1948).

9. See William Stinchcombe, "The Diplomacy of the WXYZ Affair," 34 *William and Mary Quarterly* 602–606, 3rd series (1977). Also see Edwin R. Baldridge, "Talleyrand's Visit to Pennsylvania, 1794–1796," 36 *Pennsylvania History* 159 (1969). Morris's petition in bankruptcy indicates that Talleyrand contracted conditionally in 1796 to buy a large tract of New York land from Morris for $142,500.42 but stepped back, leaving Morris owing Talleyrand an unspecified sum that Talleyrand had put down as a deposit. Entry 325, Morris petition, Papers of Robert Morris, Queen's College, New York. There is no indication that Talleyrand met Marshall in the United States. John Quincy Adams wrote to William Vans Murray that Talleyrand was a naturalized American citizen "and took the oath." July 10, 1798, *The Writings of John Quincy Adams* 341 note (Washington, D.C.: American Historical Association, 1914).

10. Nathan Schachner, *Alexander Hamilton* 345 (New York: Appleton-Century, 1946).

11. *2 Life, Letters. and Journals of George Ticknor* 113 (Boston: Sampson Low, Marston, Searle, and Rivington, 1876).

12. Charles Maurice Camille de Talleyrand-Périgord Dino, *Étude sur la République des États-Unis d'Amérique* 192 (New York: Hurd & Houghton, 1876). Also see 1 *The Memoirs of the Prince de Talleyrand* 181–182, duc de Broglie, ed., R. Ledos de Beaufort, trans. (New York: G. P. Putnam's Sons, 1891).

13. Talleyrand-Périgord Dino, *Étude sur la République* 192. Also see J.F. Bernard, *Talleyrand: A Biography* 160–161 (New York: G. P. Putnam's Sons, 1973).

14. Charles Maurice de Talleyrand-Périgord, "Commercial Relations of the United States with England," April 4, 1797, and "An Essay upon the Advantages to be Derived from New Colonies," July 3, 1797 (Boston: Thomas B. Wait, 1809). Also see Georges LaCour-Gayet, 1 *Talleyrand* 214–218.

15. Talleyrand-Périgord, "Commercial Relations of the United States with England," 12.

16. *Ibid.* Also see William Stinchcombe, *The XYZ Affair* 35–46 (Westport, Conn.: Greenwood Press, 1980).

17. Madame Anne Louise Germaine de Staël (1766–1817), daughter of the great Protestant banker and controller-general of France, Jacques Necker, was a leading figure in Parisian intellectual circles. Best known for her remarkable literary achievements (*Sophie*, 1786; *Lettres sur J. J. Rousseau*, 1788; *Réflexions sur le procès de la reine*, 1793), she was the wife of the Swedish minister, Baron Eric Magnus de Staël-Holstein.

18. Talleyrand's appointment as foreign minister involved considerable accident and caprice, and has never been more than partially explained. Only three of the five directors voted for it, and even Barras, who proposed it, was lukewarm, having been persuaded by Germaine de Staël that Talleyrand would be a faithful retainer. For firsthand accounts, see 2 *Memoirs of Barras: Member of the Directorate* 530–573, George Duruy, ed. (New York: Harper and Brothers, 1895); Madame Anne-Louise Germaine de Staël, 1 *Considerations on the Principal Events of the French Revolution* 381–382 (London: Baldwin, Cradock, and Joy, 1819); 2 *Mémoires de Larevellière-Lépeaux* 114–115 (Paris: Plon, 1895); Hippolyte Carnot, 2 *Mémoires sur Carnot* 116 (Paris: Pugnerre, 1863); Charles Maurice de Talleyrand-Périgord, *Mémoires, 1754–1815* 191, Paul Louis Couchoud and Jean Louis Couchoud, eds. (Paris: Plon, 1982). The most useful secondary source attempting to reconcile the conflicting firsthand accounts is Bernard, *Talleyrand*. See especially pp. 179–186.

19. Madelin, *Talleyrand* 56. "*Il faut y faire une fortune immense, une immense fortune, une immense fortune, une immense fortune.*" Michel Poniatowski, *Talleyrand et le Directoire* 161 (Paris: Librarie Académique Perrin, 1982). It would appear that Talleyrand replaced Charles Delacroix not only in the foreign ministry but also in the matrimonial bedroom. Upon assuming office, Talleyrand appointed Delacroix ambassador to Holland. While Delacroix was in The Hague, the new foreign minister took up with Madame Delacroix, and their son, Eugène Delacroix, the famous painter, was born in April 1798. Charles Delacroix assumed paternity, but there was little doubt that Talleyrand was the actual father. Eugène Delacroix looked like Talleyrand, exhibited many of his behavioral traits, and was anonymously supported by the foreign minister during his early years. Bernard, *Talleyrand* 210.

20. Talleyrand to Létombe, August 1, 1797. Subsequently, Talleyrand wrote that the rejection of Pinckney had been "regrettable" and "involved nothing personal against Mr. Pinckney. . . . We shall do everything necessary when the commissioners arrive to exhibit fully our peaceful intentions." To Létombe, September 1, 1797, Archives du Ministère des Affaires Étrangères, 48 *Correspondance Politique: États-Unis* 154–155, 214–215. Hereinafter cited as *CPE-U*.

21. Pitcairn to King, August 3, 1797, 39 Rufus King Papers, cited in Stinchcombe, *XYZ Affair* 47, note 5.

22. Georges Lefebvre, *The Thermidorians and the Directory: Two Phases of the French Revolution* 313, 338, Robert Baldick, trans. (New York: Random House, 1964); William Stinchcombe, "Talleyrand and the American Negotiations of 1797–1798," 62 *Journal of American History* 575, 577 (1975).

23. Stinchcombe, *XYZ Affair* 46, notes 2 and 3 and the sources cited therein.

24. 1 *Preussen und Frankreich von 1795 bis 1807, Diplomatische Correspondenzen* 155 (Oct. 25, 1797), Paul Bailleu, ed. (Leipzig: G. Hirzel, 1880).

25. Sittings of October 17, November 17, and December 24, 1797, Archives Nationales, Paris.

26. Pinckney to Pickering, December 24, 1796, 3 *Marshall Papers* 127, note 8; Stinchcombe, *XYZ Affair* 35.

27. Murray to Marshall, September 2, 1797, 3 *Marshall Papers* 127–128.

28. *Ibid.* Murray's emphasis.

29. Madame Tallien has been described as "tall and lissom, with beautiful shoulders and splendid arms, jet-black hair, tiny feet, and a musical voice. It was she who, in the depths of winter—the hardest winter of the century—started the fashion of wearing Greek robes, with bare arms, transparent tunics, and bare feet shod with sandals." Albert Mathiez, *After Robespierre: The Thermidorian Reaction* 88, Catherine Alison Phillips, trans. (New York: Grosset & Dunlap, 1965). Also see Schama, *Citizens*; Arsène Houssaye, *Notre Dame de Thermidor* (Paris: H. Plon, 1866); Marie-Helene Bourquin, *Monsieur et Madame Tallien* (Paris: Librairie Académique Perrin, 1987); L. Gastine, *Madame Tallien*, J. Lewis May, trans. (New York: Lane, 1913).

30. William Gilmore Simms, "A Memoir of the Pinckney Family of South Carolina," 2 *Historical Magazine* 134–139, 2nd series (1867).

31. Pinckney's mother once marvelled that he had "lived to near twenty-three years of age without once offending me." Marvin R. Zahniser, *Charles Cotesworth Pinckney: Founding Father* 18 (Chapel Hill: University of North Carolina Press, 1967).

32. John Marshall, *An Autobiographical Sketch* 24, John Stokes Adams, ed. (Ann Arbor: University of Michigan Press, 1937).

33. Zahniser, *Pinckney* 98.

34. Marshall to Polly, September 9, 1797, 3 *Marshall Papers* 130–132.

35. *Ibid.*

36. Marshall to Pickering, September 9, 1797, *ibid.* 132–135.

37. For the coup of 18 Fructidor (September 4) 1797, see Georges Lefebvre, 2 *The French Revolution from 1795 to 1799* 197–208, John Hall Stewart, trans. (New York: Columbia University Press, 1964).

38. Marshall to Pickering, September 9, 1797, 3 *Marshall Papers* 132.

39. *Ibid.* 135.

40. Marshall to Pickering, September 15, 1797, *ibid.* 136–138. A State Department notation indicates that this letter was received in Philadelphia on November 22, 1797—three weeks before Marshall's letter of September 9 arrived.

41. *Ibid.* Marshall's pessimism, which is apparent in his letter to Washington, intensified following a visit he and Pinckney received from Colonel John Trumbull, the American artist who had served as Jay's secretary during the negotiations with Britain in 1794. Trumbull, although based in England, had wanted to apprise the envoys of the details of Jay's negotiations, but Talleyrand had refused him a visa to travel to France. He caught up with the envoys in Holland and, in addition to providing details of the treaty, declaimed at length about Talleyrand's capriciousness and the difficulties of dealing with the French. See Carl Ludwig Lokke, "The Trumbull Episode: A Prelude to the 'XYZ' Affair," 7 *New England Quarterly* 100–114 (1934).

42. See 3 *Marshall Papers* 142, note 3.

43. Henry Rutledge to Edward Rutledge, October 2, 1797, *ibid.* 147, note 6.

44. Murray to Marshall, September 24, 1797, *ibid.* 149–150.

45. Edmund S. Morgan, "The Puritan Ethic and the American Revolution," 24 *William and Mary Quarterly* 195–208, 3rd series (1977).

46. See especially S. E. Morison, "Elbridge Gerry, Gentleman-Democrat," 2 *New England Quarterly* 6–33 (1929).

47. Abigail Adams to William Smith, June 9, 1798, Smith-Carter Collection, Massachusetts Historical Society.

48. George Athan Billias, *Elbridge Gerry: Founding Father and Republican Statesman* xiii-xviii

(New York: McGraw-Hill, 1976). When Adams presented Gerry's name to the cabinet, James McHenry of Maryland, the amiable secretary of war, after a long pause observed, "If, Sir, it was a desirable thing to distract the mission, a fitter person could not perhaps be found. It is ten to one against his agreeing with his colleagues." Bernard C. Steiner, *The Life and Correspondence of James McHenry* 224 (Cleveland, Ohio: Burrows Brothers, 1907).

49. James T. Austin, 2 *The Life of Elbridge Gerry* 303 (Boston: Wells, 1829).

50. Mary Pinckney to Margaret Manigault, October 5, 1797. Quoted in Stinchcombe, *XYZ Affair* 54.

51. James Cole Mountflorence was a Frenchman by birth who fought in the American Revolution, became a member of the North Carolina bar, returned to Paris as a land agent in 1791, and became American vice consul shortly thereafter.

52. 48 *CPE-U* 120.

53. "Mémoire sur les Relations entre la France et les États-Unis de 1792 à 1797," September 1797, 36 Désagés, French Foreign Ministry Archives, Paris. See William Stinchcombe, "A Neglected Memoir by Talleyrand on French-American Relations, 1797–1798," 121 American Philosophical Society *Proceedings* 195–205 (1977).

54. Envoys to Pickering, October 22, 1797, 3 *Marshall Papers* 255–268.

55. The report of the envoys' meeting with Talleyrand is from the journal [hereinafter cited as "Paris Journal"] that Marshall kept. Whether it was because he was the youngest of the envoys, or whether it was simply on his own initiative, Marshall began to keep a record of the discussions in Paris, and it was that record that became the basis for the dispatches that were sent to Pickering and subsequently published. When Marshall returned to Philadelphia in June 1798, he gave the journal to Pickering, who assigned State Department clerks to transcribe it. The original has since been lost, but the transcribed copy, which is located among the Pickering Papers at the Massachusetts Historical Society, is reprinted in *ibid.* 153–242. It was considered by the editors of the *Marshall Papers* to be genuine. The quotations appear on pp. 159–160.

56. Stinchcombe, "A Neglected Memoir," 206.

57. *Ibid.* At the conclusion of his memorandum, Talleyrand stressed that the envoys' explanation must be given "beforehand; only then will we reveal our willingness to cooperate in every way with sincerely peaceful intentions in reestablishing between both nations a harmony consistent with the dignity of the Republic, mutual interests, and former treaties."

58. Stinchcombe, "Talleyrand and American Negotiations," 575–590.

59. Marshall to Charles Lee, October 12, 1797, 3 *Marshall Papers* 246–251.

60. Antoine-Eustache, baron d'Osmond (1754–1823), served as Talleyrand's private secretary until 1815.

61. "Paris Journal," October 14, 1797, 3 *Marshall Papers* 161–162.

62. *Ibid.*

63. "Paris Journal," October 15, 1797, *ibid.* 162–163.

64. *Ibid.*

65. Deane may have received a *douceur* as well. In 1780 he received a payment of 24,000 livres as "extraordinary aid," from the King's private funds. "Affaires de l'Amérique, 7 December 1780," *Décisions du roi, 1760–1792.*

66. 1 *Preussen und Frankreich* 168.

67. *Ibid.*

68. "Paris Journal," October 15, 1797, 3 *Marshall Papers* 162–163.

69. "Paris Journal," October 30, 1797, *ibid.* 183; Stinchcombe, *XYZ Affair* 60–63.

70. Baldridge, "Talleyrand's Visit to Pennsylvania," 159; 3 *Marshall Papers* 164, note 17; Stinchcombe, *XYZ Affair* 60–61.

71. John Marshall was also responsible for the loan negotiated by James. See Pieter J. Winter, 2 *Het Aandeel van de Amsterdamsche handel aan den opbouw van het Amerikaansche Gemeenebest* 280 (The Hague: M. Nihouf, 1927); Albert J. Beveridge, 2 *The Life of John Marshall* 259 (Boston: Houghton Mifflin, 1916); Stinchcombe, *XYZ Affair* 60.

72. "Paris Journal," October 30, 1797, 3 *Marshall Papers* 183.

73. "Paris Journal," October 18, 1797, *ibid.* 164.

74. *Ibid.* Also see envoys to Pickering, October 22, 1797, *ibid.* 255–267.

75. "Paris Journal," October 30, 1797, *ibid.* 165.

76. *Ibid.*

77. Statement, October 19, 1797, *ibid.* 252–254.

78. "Paris Journal," October 30, 1797, *ibid.* 166.

79. *"Il sera aussi prélévé sur cet Emprunt certaines sommes pour faire les distributions d'usage en affaires diplomatiques."* Statement, October 19, 1797, *ibid.* 254.

80. "Paris Journal," October 20, 1797, *ibid.* 166.

81. *Ibid.*

82. "Paris Journal," October 20, 1796, *ibid.* 166.

83. *Ibid.* 167.

84. When he had given the marked copy of Adams's speech to the envoys, Bellamy then dictated a statement that was transcribed by Hottinguer setting out the specific French demands. The envoys were told they must disavow in writing Adams's reference to "the speech of citizen President Barras"; they must agree that the Directory's decree of March 2, 1797, authorizing the seizure of American vessels was not "contrary to the treaty of 1778"; and there must be "a formal declaration" that when Adams complained about efforts to divide "the government and people of the United States," he was not speaking of "the government of France, [or] its agents." For text, see the envoys' message to Pickering, October 22, 1797, *ibid.* 260–261.

85. *Ibid.*

86. *Ibid.*

87. "Paris Journal," October 20, 1797, *ibid.* 166–167.

88. *Ibid.*

89. Envoys to Pickering, October 22, 1797, *ibid.* 261–262.

90. *Ibid.* 262. Emphasis added.

91. *Ibid.* 263.

92. "Paris Journal," October 21, 1797, *ibid.* 167–168.

93. Gerry's memorandum has been lost but is summarized in the envoys' letter to Pickering of October 22, 1797, *ibid.* 263.

94. *Ibid.* 264–265.

95. *Ibid.*

96. Envoys to Pickering, November 8, 1797, *ibid.* 276–292.

97. Marshall to Murray, October 21, 1797, *ibid.* 254.

98. Marshall to Washington, October 24, 1797, *ibid.* 267–271.

99. Mary Pinckney to Margaret Manigault, October 22, 1797, Manigault Family Papers, University of South Carolina.

100. Pinckney to Murray, October 30, 1797, quoted in 3 *Marshall Papers* 254, note 1. Emphasis added.

101. Gerry to Murray, October 30, 1797, *ibid.*

102. *Ibid.* 168, note 25 and the sources cited therein.

103. In September 1798, long after the XYZ affair had exploded, Marshall wrote to Pickering more or less exonerating Hauteval, whom he said "is a conciliatory character. There are few Frenchmen who are as well disposed to our country—but yet he is devoted to Mr. Talleyrand." *Ibid.* 508–509. Also see Hauteval to Talleyrand, June 1798, reprinted in 9 *Annals of Congress* 3526–3527.

104. Mary Pinckney to Margaret Manigault, October 22, 1797, Manigault Family Papers, University of South Carolina.

105. Envoys to Pickering, November 8, 1797, 3 *Marshall Papers* 276–292, at 280.

106. Stinchcombe, *XYZ Affair* 57.

107. For Talleyrand's time in Boston, see Richard M. Brace, "Talleyrand in New England: Reality and Legend," 16 *New England Quarterly* 399, 405 (1943).

108. "Paris Journal," October 23, 1797, 3 *Marshall Papers* 169.

109. The Treaty of Campo Formio, October 26, 1797. For a brief description of French gains un-

der the treaty, see R. R. Palmer, 2 *The Age of Democratic Revolution* 302–310 (Princeton, N.J.: Princeton University Press, 1964).

110. "Paris Journal," October 27, 1797, 3 *Marshall Papers* 170–174.
111. *Ibid.*
112. Zahniser, *Pinckney* 169.
113. "Paris Journal," October 27, 1797, 3 *Marshall Papers* 170–174. Marshall's emphasis.
114. *Ibid.* 175.
115. "Paris Journal," October 28, 1797, *ibid.* 174–175; Stinchcombe, "Talleyrand and the American Negotiations," 584–586; "Paris Journal," October 28, 1797, 3 *Marshall Papers* 175, note 50.
116. *Ibid.*
117. *Ibid.* 176.
118. "Paris Journal," October 29, 1797, *ibid.* 176–178.
119. *Ibid.*
120. *Ibid.*
121. Talleyrand's offer of October 30, 1797, transmitted to the envoys by Bellamy, was attached as Exhibit A in the envoys' letter to Pickering, November 8, 1797, *ibid.* 290–291.
122. "Paris Journal," October 29, 1797, *ibid.* 180.
123. *Ibid.* 183.
124. *Ibid.* 180.
125. Envoys to Pickering, November 8, 1797, Exhibit B (Paris, October 30–31, 1797), *ibid.* 291–292.
126. Hottinguer did not permit the envoys to copy Talleyrand's letter, but the editors of the *Marshall Papers* suggest that it may have been the undated document inserted November 11, 1797, in the archives of the French Foreign Ministry, 48 *CPE-U*. See 3 *Marshall Papers* 288, note 7.
127. Talleyrand was personally acquainted with both Madison and Burr, and he actually had earlier indicated his preference for the two in conversations with his Paris neighbor, Joseph Pitcairn. See Pitcairn to John Quincy Adams, October 20, 1796, cited in Stinchcombe, "WXYZ Affair," 594.
128. "Paris Journal," November 3, 1797, 3 *Marshall Papers* 183–185. Also see envoys to Pickering, November 8, 1797, *ibid.* 289–290.
129. Marshall to Lee, November 3, 1797, *ibid.* 273–274.
130. 2 *Ibid.* 124–126. Pierre-Augustin Caron de Beaumarchais was as well known as a musician and playwright as he was as a financier. One of ten children of a Parisian clockmaker, he became watchmaker to Louis XV and the music master for the king's sisters. Two fortuitous marriages brought wealth and title, and by the 1770s, he had become a trusted agent of the crown, handling a variety of complex and delicate transactions including the arming of the American colonies, for which he engaged a fleet of forty vessels. At the same time he wrote a series of popular comedies, the most important being *Le Barbier de Seville* (1775) and *Le Mariage de Figaro* (1784), subsequently set to music by Rossini and Mozart respectively. In 1785 he cofounded the Water Company of Paris. He hailed the Revolution, but like many who had been employed by the old regime, was imprisoned during the Terror. He fled to Holland and then Great Britain, and did not return to Paris until 1796. L. de Loménie, *Beaumarchais et son temps*, H. S. Edwards, trans., 4 vols. (London: Addey, 1856); Paul Phillippe Gudin de la Brenellerie, *Beaumarchais* (Paris: L. Collin, 1809). For a discussion of Beaumarchais's role during the American Revolution, see 1 *Diplomatic Correspondence of the American Revolution* 35–39, Jared Sparks, ed. (Boston: Hale and Gray & Bower, 1829).
131. Beaumarchais to Marshall, November 7, 1797; Marshall to Beaumarchais, November 8, 1797, 3 *Marshall Papers* 275–276.
132. Beaumarchais to Talleyrand, October 17, 1797; Beaumarchais to Bellamy (copy to Talleyrand), December 26, 1797. Cited in Stinchcombe, "WXYZ Affair," 601, note 39.
133. Pinckney to Mountflorence, November 6, 1797, 3 *Marshall Papers* 275.
134. "Paris Journal," November 7, 1797, *ibid.* 185–187.
135. *Ibid.*

136. Envoys to Pickering, November 8, 1797, 3 *Marshall Papers* 276–292. Over 80 percent of the dispatch was taken verbatim from Marshall's journal.

137. Envoys to Pickering, November 27, 1797, *ibid.* 305–307.

138. Marshall to Pickering, November 27, 1797, *ibid.* 301–305.

139. *Ibid.* 305.

140. Létombe to Delacroix, June 7, 1797, *Correspondence of the French Ministers to the United States, 1791–1797*, Frederick Jackson Turner, ed., in 2 *Annual Report of the American Historical Association for the Year 1903* 1043 (Washington, D.C.: Government Printing Office, 1904).

141. Stinchcombe, *XYZ Affair* 55. Joel Barlow (1754–1812) gained early literary fame as the author of a massive epic poem, "The Vision of Columbus" (1787), describing in rhymed couplets the discovery, settlement, and future of America. A dedicated republican, he moved to Paris in 1788 and made a fortune after the Revolution investing in the confiscated property of the French nobility. A close friend of Jefferson's and James Monroe's, he may be best known as the author of "Hasty Pudding" (1796), a witty ballad fusing New England memories and European settings. Barlow returned to the United States in 1805, settled in Washington in a lavish home he called "Kalorama," and began work on a history of the United States. In late 1811 President Madison sent him back to France to intercede with Napoléon (with whom Barlow was acquainted) on behalf of American commerce. Napoléon's Russian campaign was then under way, and Barlow journeyed to Warsaw to meet the emperor, but he never obtained an interview. He became ill while in Poland and died December 24, 1812. His history of the United States was never completed. For fragments, see Christine M. Lizanich, "'The March of this Government': Joel Barlow's Unwritten History of the United States," 33 *William and Mary Quarterly* 315–330, 3rd series (1976).

142. Gerry to Ann Gerry, November 25, 1797, Gerry Papers, Letterbook 1797–1801, New York Public Library.

143. For a biography of Madame de Villette, see Jean Stern, *Belle et Bonne: Une fervente amie de Voltaire* (Paris: Librarie Hachette, 1938).

144. *Ibid.* 14.

145. S.G. Tallentyre, 2 *The Life of Voltaire* 287–288 (London: Smith, Elder, 1903).

146. Stern, *Belle et Bonne* 124; Stinchcombe, *XYZ Affair* 66–68.

147. Stern, *Belle et Bonne* 124. Also see Haydn Mason, *Voltaire: A Biography* 137 (Baltimore: Johns Hopkins Press, 1981); Jean Orieux, *Voltaire* 477, Barbara Bray and Helen Lane, trans. (New York: Doubleday, 1979); C. E. Vulliamy, *Voltaire* 335–336 (Port Washington, N.Y.: Kennikat Press, 1930); L. Gastine, *Madame Tallien* 127, J. Lewis May, trans. (New York: Lane, 1913).

148. Murray to Marshall, September 2, 1797, 3 *Marshall Papers* 127–128.

149. Stinchcombe, *XYZ Affair* 68.

150. See Salvatore Mondello, "John Vanderlyn," 52 *New York Historical Society Quarterly* 161–183 (1968).

151. The miniature is about 2½ by 2 inches in size, is set in a brass frame, and is owned by Mrs. Benjamin Woodruff of Charleston, West Virginia. Andrew Oliver, *The Portraits of John Marshall* 6–7 (Charlottesville: University Press of Virginia, 1976).

152. Gerry to Ann Gerry, November 25, 1797, Gerry Papers, Library of Congress, quoted in 3 *Marshall Papers* 300, note 7.

153. Marshall to Polly, *ibid.* 299–301.

154. Frances Norton Mason, *My Dearest Polly* 113 (Richmond: Garrett & Massie, 1961).

155. As Eliza wrote to her friend Frances Caines, "My much loved sister fell into a deep melancholy from which no one could relieve her . . . only her husband who might have by his usual tenderness (had he been here) dissipated this terrible gloom." Eliza Jaquelin Ambler Papers, Colonial Williamsburg Foundation, Williamsburg, Va.

156. Mary Pinckney to Margaret Manigault, March 8, 1798, Manigault Family Papers, University of South Carolina. Quoted in 3 *Marshall Papers* 300, note 7. Mrs. Pinckney's emphasis.

157. On December 17, 1797, *Mahomet* opened at the Odéon.

158. Marshall to Pinckney, December 17, 1797, 3 *Marshall Papers* 311–312. Also see Zahniser, *Pinckney* 175.

159. Fulwar Skipwith had been the American consul in Paris, but because of his close ties to

Monroe and Jefferson, he resigned following Adams's election in 1797. He speculated in
Parisian real estate and owned numerous houses in the city as well as several country estates.

160. Marshall to Skipwith, April 21, 1798, 3 *Marshall Papers* 464. Once back in America, Marshall
also requested Caron de Beaumarchais to remember him to "rue Vaugirard." Marshall to
Beaumarchais, November 20, 1798, *ibid.* 528–529.

161. Marshall to Pinckney, April 21, 1798, *ibid.* 463–464.

162. The allegation derives from a lengthy message sent by the envoys to Pickering, December
24, 1797, in which Pinckney, among other things, reported that he had been approached by
a lady "who is well acquainted with M. Talleyrand" with another request for a loan to
France. For text, see *ibid.* 318–319. The lady is unidentified in the dispatch. Theodore Lyman, writing in 1826, was the first to claim that it was Madame de Villette, but James T.
Austin, writing two years later, effectively rebutted Lyman's contention. Lyman, 2 *Diplomacy
of the United States* 336 note (Boston: Wills & Lilly, 1826); Austin, 2 *Life of Gerry* 202 note. Several modern writers, such as Alexander DeConde, Albert H. Bowman, and Marvin R. Zahniser, have revived the accusation, and cite a letter from Margaret Pinckney to Margaret
Manigault, March 9, 1798. Mrs. Pinckney mentions Madame de Villette in the letter, but in
no way links her to the December 24 approach to General Pinckney, nor in any way with Talleyrand. She does, however, speak of Madame de la Forest, and from the context, it is clear
that it was the latter who approached Pinckney, not Madame de Villette. The entire matter
was considered at length by William Stinchcombe in his definitive work on the XYZ affair,
and he concludes that the woman in question was Madame de la Forest, not Madame de Villette. That, too, was the judgment of the editors of the *Marshall Papers*. See Alexander De-
Conde, *The Quasi-War* 52 (New York: Charles Scribner's Sons, 1966); Albert Hall Bowman,
The Struggle for Neutrality 317 (Knoxville: University of Tennessee Press, 1974); Zahniser,
Pinckney 176. Compare William Stinchcombe, *XYZ Affair* 65, 68, 75–76; 3 *Marshall Papers*
318, note 7. Mrs. Pinckney's letter can be found among the Manigault Family Papers, which
are preserved at the University of South Carolina.

163. Ministre des Puissances Étrangères, File F 7 6152, Dossier 918, Villette (Marquise de);
Beaumarchais (la Famille de), Document 332, Archives Nationales, Paris.

164. *Ibid.* Document 333.

165. Talleyrand to the Minister of Police, April 25, 1798, 49 *CPE-U* 339.

166. The exact date of the dinner has been the subject of some controversy. Marshall recorded it
in his journal as "*ca.* December 2, 1797," although Gerry, in a letter to his wife, listed it
prospectively on November 26. Compare 3 *Marshall Papers* 189 and Gerry to Ann Gerry, November 25, 1797, *Elbridge Gerry's Letterbook: Paris, 1797–1798* 22–25, Russell W. Knight, ed.
(Salem, Mass.: Essex Institute, 1966).

167. "Paris Journal," ca. December 2, 1797, 3 *Marshall Papers* 189; Billias, *Elbridge Gerry* 273.

168. "Paris Journal," December 14, 1797, *ibid.* 189–190; Pinckney to King, December 14, 1797,
King Papers, Library of Congress. Pinckney told King that "Attempts are made to divide the
envoys and with that view some civilities are shewn to M[r.] G[erry] and none to the two others. I am in hopes such attempts will be without success. The American Jacobins here pay
him great court."

169. "Paris Journal," December 17, 1797, 3 *Marshall Papers* 190–192. The entire journal entry was
transmitted to Pickering on December 24, 1797.

170. *Ibid.*

171. "Paris Journal," December 18, 1797, *ibid.* 192.

172. *Ibid.*

173. Envoys to Pickering, December 24, 1797, Exhibit C, *ibid.* 324.

174. *Ibid.* 323–324.

175. Marshall to King, December 24, 1797, *ibid.* 315–316. Also see envoys to Pickering, December 24, 1797, *ibid.* 317–324.

176. *Ibid.* On December 27 Pinckney wrote to King in virtually identical terms. "I have not now
the least hope that we shall make a treaty with this government, for in order to do so, tribute, under the guise of a loan . . . and a private douceur of fifty thousand pounds sterling
must be stipulated: and these degrading terms must be offered by us even before we can be

received." Pickering Papers, Massachusetts Historical Society. Also see the equally pessimistic letter of Gerry to Vans Murray, December 28, 1797, Gratz Collection, Historical Society of Pennsylvania, quoted, *ibid*. 316–317, note 1.

177. King's letter to Marshall was written December 23, 1797. King had been informed of the situation in Paris by John Trumbull, and had anticipated what Marshall asked. See King to Marshall, *ibid*. 313–315.

178. King was much more explicit in a letter to Pinckney written the same day.

> If I do not mistake its import, we are in danger from a quarter in which I confess I have not felt wholly secure, but where I thought integrity and honest though sometimes mistaken patriotism would overcome any miserable vanity and a few little defects of character that I have [known] for a long time to exist, and which I now fear have been discovered by those who will be assiduous to turn it to mischief. You must not appear to suspect what you may really know. You must appear to act as you would do, did the most perfect harmony exist. You must in short save him [Gerry] and in doing so prevent the division that would grow out of a schism in your commission.

King to Pinckney, December 24, 1797, File F 7 4269, Archives Nationales, Paris.

179. King to Marshall, December 23, 1797, 3 *Marshall Papers* 313–315. Emphasis added.

180. Marshall to Pickering, November 27, 1797, *ibid*. 305.

181. Zahniser, *Pinckney* 173.

182. Gerry to Murray, December 28, 1797.

183. *Ibid*.

184. For text, see 3 *Marshall Papers* 331–381. The memorial is dated January 17, 1798, which is the date Marshall completed the final draft.

185. Beveridge, 2 *Life of Marshall* 297.

186. Murray to J. Q. Adams, February 20, 1798, "Letters of William Vans Murray to John Quincy Adams, 1797–1803," Worthington C. Ford, ed., in 2 *Annual Report of the American Historical Association for the Year 1912* 379, 395 (Washington, D.C.: Government Printing Office, 1914).

187. Envoys to Talleyrand, January 17, 1798, 3 *Marshall Papers* 381.

188. Pierre Samuel du Pont de Nemours (1739–1817), like Hottinguer and Bellamy, was connected politically and financially with Talleyrand. See Mack Thompson, "Causes and Circumstances of the DuPont Family's Emigration," 6 *French Historical Studies* 59–77 (1969), and more generally, Ambrose Saricks, *Pierre Samuel DuPont* (Lawrence: University of Kansas Press, 1965).

189. "Paris Journal," February 1, 1798, 3 *Marshall Papers* 194. du Pont called regularly on the Pinckneys during the next two months, explaining that he intended to emigrate to the United States and wanted information concerning land purchases. His role was to keep Talleyrand informed as to whether Pinckney was going to force a break in the negotiations. Stinchcombe, *XYZ Affair* 107.

190. "Paris Journal," February 2, 1798, 3 *Marshall Papers* 194–195.

191. Aide-mémoire of Talleyrand, February 15, 1798, cited in Morison, "Elbridge Gerry, Gentleman-Democrat," 25. Also see Gerry to Adams, March 24, 1798, Adams Papers, Massachusetts Historical Society.

192. "Paris Journal," February 4, 1798, 3 *Marshall Papers* 195–197.

193. *Ibid*.

194. Pinckney shared Marshall's apprehension about Gerry. As he wrote to his brother, Thomas Pinckney:

> Every art is used by Talleyrand and the French Americans here to divide the envoys, and if possible to detach Mr. Gerry from his colleagues. Confidential communications and proposals are made to him by Mr. Talleyrand, under conjunction to conceal them from us, and he considers himself as pledged to comply with this request. . . . I however still think he will act properly. In every public measure we have yet adopted we have been unanimous; but he is habitually suspicious; and hesitates so much, that it is very unpleasant to do business with him. Charles C. Pinckney to Thomas Pinckney, February 24, 1798, Pickering Papers, Massachusetts Historical Society.

195. "Paris Journal," February 7, 1798, 3 *Marshall Papers* 195–197.
196. *Ibid.*
197. Marshall recorded the name as "Dutrimont." "Paris Journal," February 10, 1798, *ibid.* 198–199.
198. *Ibid.*
199. "Paris Journal," February 14, 1798, *ibid.* 199–200.
200. "Paris Journal," February 19, 1798, *ibid.* 200.
201. "Paris Journal," February 20, 1798, *ibid.* 200–202. Beaumarchais gave Marshall a letter summarizing his views. *Ibid.* 388.
202. "Paris Journal," February 26, 1798, *ibid.* 202–209.
203. See C. C. Pinckney to Thomas Pinckney, March 13, 1798, Pickering Papers, Massachusetts Historical Society.
204. "Paris Journal," February 26, 1798, 3 *Marshall Papers* 202–209. For Gerry's version of the meeting, see Gerry to Adams, July 8, 1799, Adams Papers, Massachusetts Historical Society.
205. "Paris Journal," February 26, 1798, 3 *Marshall Papers* 208.
206. "Paris Journal," March 1, 1798, *ibid.* 214–215.
207. *Ibid.*
208. "Paris Journal," February 27, 1798, *ibid.* 209–213. See Envoys to Talleyrand, February 27, 1798, *ibid.* 394.
209. The report of the interview with Talleyrand is in "Paris Journal," March 2, 1798, *ibid.* 215–219. Also see Envoys to Pickering, March 9, 1798, *ibid.* 402–411.
210. "Paris Journal," March 3, 1798, *ibid.* 219–220.
211. *Ibid.*
212. "Paris Journal," March 5, 1798, *ibid.* 221–223.
213. "Paris Journal," March 6, 1798, *ibid.* 223–228.
214. *Ibid.*
215. Washington to the Secretary of War, March 4, 1798, 36 *The Writings of George Washington* 179, John C. Fitzpatrick, ed. (Washington, D.C.: Government Printing Office, 1931).
216. Jefferson to Madison, February 15, 1798, 8 *The Works of Thomas Jefferson* 368, Paul Leicester Ford, ed. (New York: G. P. Putnam & Sons, 1904).
217. Madison to Jefferson, April 15, 1798, 6 *The Writings of James Madison* 315, Gaillard Hunt, ed. (New York: G. P. Putnam & Sons, 1909).
218. Jefferson to Madison, April 6, 1798, 8 *Works of Jefferson* 403.
219. Washington to Pickering, April 16, 1798, 13 *The Writings of George Washington* 495, Worthington C. Ford, ed. (New York: G. P. Putnam's Sons, 1889).
220. Quoted in Page Smith, 2 *John Adams* 960 (Garden City, N.Y.: Doubleday, 1962). The Federalists, of course, were delighted. House Speaker Theodore Sedgwick wrote to Rufus King that "The effect of the publication [of the dispatches] . . . on the people has been prodigious. . . . The leaders of the opposition were astonished and confounded at the profligacy of the French." May 1, 1798 2 *The Life and Correspondence of Rufus King* 318–319, Charles R. King, ed. (New York: G. P. Putnam's Sons, 1896).
221. Jefferson to Edmund Pendleton, January 29, 1799, 10 *The Writings of Jefferson* 86, Andrew A. Lipscomb ed. (Washington, D.C.: The Thomas Jefferson Memorial Association, 1903).
222. Marshall to Washington, March 8, 1798, 3 *Marshall Papers* 399–402.
223. Marshall to Charles Lee, March 10, 1798, *ibid.* 397.
224. "Paris Journal," March 13 and 14, 1798, *ibid.* 228–231.
225. *Ibid.*
226. *Ibid.*
227. *Ibid.*
228. Talleyrand subsequently stated about Gerry that "The advantages that I prized in him are common to all Americans who have not manifested a predilection for England. Can it be believed that a man who shall profess a hatred or contempt of the French republic, or who should manifest himself the advocate for royalty, can inspire the directory with a favorable opinion of the government of the United States?" Quoted in Austin, 2 *Life of Gerry* 241 note.
229. Talleyrand to Envoys, March 18, 1798, 3 *Marshall Papers* 413–422. For an English translation, see 9 *Annals of Congress* 3432.

230. "Paris Journal," March 22, 1798, 3 *Marshall Papers* 232.
231. Vans Murray to J.Q. Adams, April 3, 1798, quoting Pinckney, "Letters of William Vans Murray," 391.
232. On January 24, 1798, Talleyrand, who should have known better, informed the Directory that the United States "is pushing with all its force for a break between the two Republics. Such a motive is the only possible explanation for the continual abuse levelled against us in the gazettes [of the United States]." 49 *CPE-U* 191–192.
233. "Paris Journal," March 22, 1798, 3 *Marshall Papers* 232.
234. For the final text, April 3, 1798, see *ibid.* 428–459. Albert Beveridge was more partisan in his assessment of Marshall's effort: "History, reason, evidence, march through these pages like infantry, cavalry, and artillery going into battle. Marshall's paper was irresistible. Talleyrand never escaped from it." Beveridge, 2 *Life of Marshall* 329.
235. 3 *Marshall Papers* 447.
236. *Ibid.* 448.
237. "Paris Journal," March 22, 1798, *ibid.* 232.
238. "Paris Journal," March 23, 1798, *ibid.* 232–234.
239. "Paris Journal," March 30, 1798, *ibid.* 235.
240. *Ibid.* 236.
241. "Paris Journal," April 11, 1798, *ibid.* 239–242.
242. *Ibid.*
243. *Ibid.*
244. "Paris Journal," April 10, 1798, *ibid.* 238.
245. "Paris Journal," April 11, 1798, *ibid.* 239–242.
246. *Ibid.* 239.
247. *Ibid.* 241.
248. *Ibid.*
249. *Ibid.*
250. *Ibid.*
251. *Ibid.*
252. Talleyrand to Marshall, April 13, 1798, *ibid.* 461–462; Marshall to Talleyrand (replying), April 13, 1798, *ibid.* 462.
253. "Paris Journal," April 3, 1798, *ibid.* 236–238.
254. Pinckney to Rufus King, April 16, 1798, Pinckney Family Papers, Library of Congress. Pinckney added that contrary to Gerry, "General Marshall is a man of extreme ability, of manly candour, and an honest heart."
255. Mary Pinckney to Margaret Manigault, April 15, 1798, Manigault Family Papers, University of South Carolina.
256. Marshall to Pinckney, April 21, 1798, 3 *Marshall Papers* 463–464.
257. Zahniser, *Pinckney* 190. The Pinckneys arrived in Bordeaux July 8 but were unable to book passage until August. In the interim, General Pinckney visited the prisons in Bordeaux, compiled a list of all American seamen being held, lodged a formal complaint with French authorities about prison conditions, and urged Pickering to take prompt remedial action. He also made arrangements to lend money to needy Americans in Bordeaux and assisted those wishing to return to the United States to book passage. Pinckney to Pickering, July 26, 1798; Pinckney to David Steinmetz, August 3, 1798, Pinckney Family Papers, Library of Congress.
258. On April 4, 1798, Gerry wrote to Talleyrand that he would agree only "to confer informally and unaccredited on any subject respecting our mission and communicate to the government of the United States the result of such conferences, being in any individual capacity unauthorized to give them an official stamp." 50 *CPE-U* 293–294.
259. "Had I left Paris with the other Envoys, war without doubt, would have been the consequence," Gerry wrote Adams, January 21, 1799, *Elbridge Gerry's Letterbook* 71. Also see Gerry to Ann Gerry, March 26, 1798, quoted in Morison, "Elbridge Gerry, Gentleman-Democrat," 26.
260. Billias, *Elbridge Gerry* 280–282.
261. Gerry to Adams, April 26, 1798, Gerry Papers, Library of Congress.

262. For details of American actions, see Samuel Flagg Bemis, *A Diplomatic History of the United States* 118 (New York: Holt, 1950).

263. Jefferson advised Victor du Pont, Létombe's successor in Philadelphia, that the only means of saving the Republican party was for France to conciliate the United States quickly. Samuel Eliot Morison, "Dupont, Talleyrand and the French Spoliations," 49 Massachusetts Historical Society *Proceedings* 72 (1915–1916).

264. 9 *The Works of John Adams* 287, Charles Francis Adams, ed. (Boston: Little, Brown, 1850).

265. The new U.S. mission was headed by Murray and included Chief Justice Oliver Ellsworth of Connecticut and William R. Davie of North Carolina, best remembered today as a former governor and founder of the University of North Carolina.

266. Pichon to Talleyrand, July 18, August 1, 1798, 50 *CPE-U* 81–88, 139–142. Talleyrand acknowledged as much when he replied to Pichon that "It is important to make some impression on the men devoted to the administration of Mr. Adams." Talleyrand thought it might be possible to influence Adams through them. August 15, 1798, *ibid.* 166.

9: To Congress from Richmond

1. John Marshall, *An Autobiographical Sketch* 24–25, John Stokes Adams, ed. (Ann Arbor: University of Michigan Press, 1937).

2. Robert Troup to Rufus King, June 23, 1798, King Papers, New York Historical Society.

3. Jefferson to Madison, June 21, 1798, 8 *The Works of Thomas Jefferson* 439–440, Paul Leicester Ford, ed. (New York: G. P. Putnam's Sons, 1904).

4. Marshall to Pickering, June 18, 1798, 3 *The Papers of John Marshall* 467 (Chapel Hill: University of North Carolina Press, 1979).

5. Jefferson to Madison, June 21, 1798, 8 *Works of Jefferson* 439–440.

6. Page Smith, 2 *John Adams* 965 (Garden City, N.Y.: Doubleday, 1962); Alexander De Conde, *The Quasi-War* 95 (New York: Charles Scribner's Sons, 1966).

7. 3 *Marshall Papers* 471, note 8.

8. 8 *Works of Jefferson* 439–440.

9. *Philadelphia Gazette and Universal Daily Advertiser*, June 19, 1798. For Washington's first inauguration, see James Thomas Flexner, *George Washington and the New Nation, 1783–1793* 185–191 (Boston: Little, Brown, 1970).

10. *Porcupine's Gazette* (Philadelphia), June 19, 1798. Compare the Republican *Aurora* of June 21, 1798: "What an occasion for rejoicing! Mr. Marshall was sent to France for the *ostensible* purpose . . . of effecting an amicable accommodation of differences. He returns without having accomplished that object, and on his return the Tories rejoice. This certainly looks as if they did not want him to succeed. . . ." Aurora's emphasis.

11. Elias Boudinot to Mrs. Boudinot, June 21, 1798, 2 *The Life, Public Services, Addresses and Letters of Elias Boudinot* 141, J. J. Boudinot, ed. (New York: Da Capo Press, 1971). Also see Henry Glen to John Jay, June 22, 1798, Special Collections, Columbia University.

12. Julian Ursyn Niemcewicz, *Under Their Vine and Fig Tree: Travels through America in 1797–1799* 121–124, Metchie J.E. Budka, trans. (Elizabeth, N.J.: The Grassmann Publishing Company, 1965). Also see Jefferson to Madison, June 21, 1798, 8 *Works of Jefferson* 439–440; Jefferson to Thomas M. Randolph, June 21, 1798, Jefferson Papers, Massachusetts Historical Society.

13. *Claypoole's American Daily Advertiser* (Philadelphia), June 22, 1798; Tristram Dalton to Benjamin Bartlett, June 21, 1798, Adams Papers, Massachusetts Historical Society.

14. Responding to a testimonial from the grand jury of Glouster County, New Jersey, Marshall noted his support for the president, who was "so worthy of the public confidence [for] his continuing vigilance and wisdom." June 22, 1798, 3 *Marshall Papers* 470.

15. Marshall to militia officers, June 22, 1798, *ibid.* 471.

16. Jefferson to Marshall, June 23, 1798, *ibid.* 471–472.

17. Marshall to Jefferson, June 23, 1798, *ibid.* 472.

18. All sixteen toasts were reported in *Claypoole's American Daily Advertiser*, June 25, 1798. They

are reprinted in Albert Beveridge, 2 *The Life of John Marshall* 349–350, note 1 (Boston: Houghton Mifflin, 1916).

19. Niemcewicz, *Vine and Fig Tree* 122–124.

20. William F. Worner, "John Marshall in Lancaster," 28 *Papers Read before the Lancaster County Historical Society* 113–117 (1924); *Gazette of the United States* (Philadelphia), June 28, 1797.

21. "When future generations pursue the history of America," said Washington, "they will find the name of Marshall on its sacred page as one of the brightest ornaments of the age in which he lived." *Virginia Gazette and General Advertiser* (Richmond), August 14, 1798. For the Richmond address, see 3 *Marshall Papers* 478–481.

22. *Ibid.* 482–484.

23. Marshall to Pickering, August 11, 1798, *ibid.* 484–486. Marshall's letter was initially mislaid by Pickering, causing Marshall to write again on September 5 to request payment. See Pickering to Marshall, September 4, 1798, and Marshall to Pickering, September 5 and September 15, 1798. *Ibid.* 490–493.

24. Jefferson, March 21, 1800, *The Complete Anas of Thomas Jefferson* 355, reprint ed. (New York: Da Capo Press, 1950). See Chapter 7.

25. For Marshall's envoy account, see 3 *Marshall Papers* 509–510.

26. Beveridge, 2 *Life of Marshall* 372.

27. 2 *United States Statutes at Large* (February 18, 1793); 3 *ibid.* 126 (March 2, 1799). The attorney general, who had no administrative responsibilities, received $3,000. The High Federalists in the Sixth Congress, venting their displeasure at President Adams over the Ellsworth mission to Paris, voted to limit the annual emolument for ministers plenipotentiary henceforth to $9,000. 1 *ibid.* (May 10, 1800).

28. Fisher Ames to Timothy Pickering, June 4, 1798, 1 *Works of Fisher Ames* 228, Seth Ames, ed. (Boston: Little, Brown, 1854).

29. Wilson Cary Nicholas to Marshall, August, 1798, 3 *Marshall Papers* 488–490.

30. "An act to augment the Army of the United States, and for other purposes," approved July 16, 1798, 9 *Annals of Congress*, Appendix, 3788–3787. See also Richard H. Kohn, *Eagle and Sword: The Federalists and the Creation of the Military Establishment in America* 47–48 (New York: Free Press, 1975).

31. On July 14, 1798, Congress passed the Evaluation Act, designed to raise $2 million by placing a direct tax on houses and slaves. 1 *United States Statutes at Large* 597–605; 9 *Annals of Congress* 3758–3763, 3778–3786.

32. *Ibid.* 2114, 2120.

33. The texts of the four acts are in 1 *United States Statutes at Large* 570–572, 577–578, 596–597; 9 *Annals of Congress* 3739–3742, 3744–3746, 3753–3754, 3776–3777; and James Morton Smith, *Freedom's Fetters: The Alien and Sedition Laws and American Civil Liberties* 435–442 (Ithaca, N.Y.: Cornell University Press, 1956). A useful analysis of the alien and sedition laws is found in Walter Berns, "Freedom of the Press and the Alien and Sedition Laws: A Reappraisal," *The Supreme Court Review* 109–159 (1970).

34. De Conde, *Quasi-War* 99. Also see, Harry Ammon, "The Jeffersonian Republicans in Virginia," 71 *Virginia Magazine of History and Biography* 159–160 (1963).

35. Leonard W. Levy, *Legacy of Suppression: Freedom of Speech and Press in Early American History* 221–225 (Cambridge, Mass.: Harvard University Press, 1960).

36. Marshall to Pickering, August 11, 1798, 3 *Marshall Papers* 484–486.

37. Washington had accepted the position of lieutenant general subject to the condition that he not be called to assume active command until or unless war began. John Alexander Carroll and Mary Wells Ashworth, *George Washington: First in Peace* 518–521 (New York: Charles Scribner's Sons, 1957); Bernard C. Steiner, *The Life and Correspondence of James McHenry* 309–315 (Cleveland, Ohio: Burrows Brothers, 1907); Adams to Washington, June 22, 1798, 8 *The Works of John Adams* 573, Charles Francis Adams, ed. (Boston: Little, Brown, 1854).

38. For an interesting insight by a Jefferson partisan, see Claude G. Bowers, *Jefferson and Hamilton* 382–383 (Boston: Houghton Mifflin, 1926).

39. John Marshall, 5 *The Life of George Washington* 759–760, reprint ed. (Fredericksburg, Va.: The Citizens' Guild, 1926). For a list of Virginia incumbents in the Fifth Congress, see the *Bio-*

graphical Directory of the American Congress. 1774–1961 60 (Washington, D.C.: Government Printing Office, 1961). For their voting record, see Manning J. Dauer, *The Adams Federalists* 311–314 (Baltimore: The Johns Hopkins Press, 1968). The boundaries of Virginia's nineteen congressional districts are specified in William Waller Hening, 13 *The Statutes at Large: Being a Collection of All of the Laws of Virginia* 331–332 (Richmond, Va.: Samuel Pleasants, 1809–1823).

40. Editorial note, 3 *Marshall Papers* 494.
41. George Washington to Bushrod Washington, August 27, 1798, 14 *The Writings of George Washington* 75, Worthington C. Ford, ed. (New York: G. P. Putnam's Sons, 1889).
42. 4 *The Diaries of George Washington* 283–284, John C. Fitzpatrick, ed. (Boston: Houghton Mifflin, 1925).
43. Marshall to James K. Paulding, April 4, 1835, 2 *Lippincott's Magazine* 624–625 (1868).
44. Martin Van Buren, *The Autobiography of Martin Van Buren*, John C. Fitzpatrick, ed., in 2 *Annual Report of the American Historical Association for the Year 1918* 178 (Washington, D.C.: Government Printing Office, 1920).
45. Marshall to James K. Paulding, April 4, 1835, Marshall Papers, Williamsburg, Va.
46. 4 *Diaries of Washington* 284; *Columbia Mirror and the Alexandria Gazette*, September 6, 1798.
47. Marshall, *Autobiographical Sketch* 28–29.
48. As Jefferson subsequently wrote to Elbridge Gerry, "The alien and sedition acts have already operated in the South as powerful sedatives to the XYZ inflammation." January 26, 1799, 7 *Works of Jefferson* 333.
49. When Marshall died, John Clopton's eldest son was one of the eight men who carried the chief justice's casket to the grave. Handbill, City of Richmond, July 12, 1835. Virginia State Library.
50. Myron F. Wehtje, "The Congressional Elections of 1799 in Virginia," 29 *West Virginia History* 261 (1968).
51. The editors of the *Marshall Papers* assume that Marshall wrote the questions himself. Editorial note, 3 *Marshall Papers* 497.
52. For text, see *ibid*. 502–503.
53. Marshall's full answer is in *ibid*. 503–506. Emphasis added.
54. Wehtje, "Congressional Elections of 1799," 263.
55. Ames to Christopher Gore, December 18, 1798, 1 *Works of Ames* 245–247.
56. Sedgwick to Pickering, October 23, 1798, Pickering Papers, Massachusetts Historical Society. Also see Richard E. Welch, Jr., *Theodore Sedgwick: Federalist: A Political Portrait* 196–197 (Middletown, Conn.: Wesleyan University Press, 1965).
57. Otis's statement is cited in 1 *Works of Ames* 245. For King, see 3 *The Life and Correspondence of Rufus King* 9, Charles R. King, ed. (New York: G. P. Putnam's Sons, 1896); for Murray, see *Letters of William Vans Murray to John Quincy Adams, 1797–1803*, Worthington C. Ford, ed., in 2 *Annual Report of the American Historical Association for the Year 1912* 530 (Washington, D.C.: Government Printing Office, 1914).
58. Pickering to Sedgwick, November 6, 1798, Pickering Papers, Massachusetts Historical Society.
59. Cabot wrote in the *Columbia Centinel* (Boston), October 24, 1798. Six months later he wrote to Rufus King that "Some allowance should be made for the influence of the Atmosphere of Virginia which doubtless makes every one who breathes it visionary and, upon the subject of Fine Government, incredibly credulous; but it is certain that Marshall [in Congress] at Philadelphia would become a most powerful auxiliary to the cause of order and good government, and *therefore* we ought not to diminish his fame which would ultimately be a loss to ourselves." April 26, 1799, in King, 3 *Life of King* 9. Cabot's emphasis.
60. Adams to Pickering, September 13, 1798, 8 *Works of John Adams* 595. James Wilson was financially destroyed in the panic of 1796. He spent the last year of his life fleeing from creditors and mercifully passed away August 21, 1798, in Edenton, North Carolina, at the home of fellow justice James Iredell, who gave him shelter. It was Iredell who informed Adams of Wilson's death. Page Smith, *James Wilson: Founding Father* 382–388 (Chapel Hill: University of North Carolina Press, 1956).

61. 3 *Marshall Papers* 506, 507.

62. Marshall to Pickering, September 28, 1798, *ibid.* 508. Also see Marshall, *Autobiographical Sketch* 26. Washington, a former student of James Wilson's, was nominated by Adams to succeed him on December 20, 1798, and unanimously confirmed by the Senate two days later. He would serve as an associate justice for thirty-two years and was one of the pillars of the Marshall Court.

63. Adams to Pickering, September 26, 1798, 8 *Works of John Adams* 597.

64. "I wish you could find time to make some *proper animadversion* on the infamous conduct of the French government in relation to the commission of the three envoys extraordinary: and I beg you to consider whether the importance of correct information does not require it. Not that the part acted by you and General Pinckney will need vindication with men of sense, even among the French partisans. . . ." Pickering to Marshall, October 4, 1798, 3 *Marshall Papers* 512. Pickering's emphasis.

65. Marshall to Pickering, October 15, 1798, *ibid.* 516–517.

66. *Virginia Gazette and General Advertiser*, October 9, 1798.

67. *The Letters of Curtius* appeared in the *Aurora* (Philadelphia) between December 15 and 26, 1798. A postscript appeared on January 22, 1799. They were reprinted as a pamphlet in 1798 and again in 1802. See John Thomson [*sic*], *The Letters of Curtius Written by the Late John Thomson of Petersburg* (Richmond, Va.: Samuel Pleasants, 1804).

68. *Virginia Gazette and General Advertiser*, October 16, 1798. In this instance, Marshall dodged a bullet that would have been fatal to his campaign. Timothy Pickering, when he heard of the Buckskin-Clopton exchange, wanted to initiate legal action against Clopton on the charge of seditious libel. He wrote to Edward Carrington for the full details, and Carrington, no doubt after consulting Marshall, told Pickering that the charges were groundless and that the matter should be dropped. A government prosecution of Clopton under the Sedition Act would undoubtedly have scuttled Marshall's chances for election. The incident illustrates how far the High Federalists like Pickering, who thought he was doing Marshall a favor, were removed from political reality in Virginia. See Pickering to Carrington, October 23, 1798; Carrington to Pickering, October 30, 1798, Pickering Papers, Massachusetts Historical Society.

69. For additional commentary on the *Letters of Curtius* see especially Henry Adams, *The Life of Albert Gallatin* 212, 227 (Philadelphia: J. B. Lippincott, 1879).

70. *Virginia Gazette and General Advertiser*, December 11, 1798. For other letters supporting Marshall, see *ibid.*, December 25, 1798, January 1, 18, 25, 1799 [by "Procopius"]; January 1, 1799 [by "Thersites"]; and January 15, 1799 [by "Philo-Curtius"]. Additional letters on Marshall's behalf appeared in March and April written by Henry Lee, Fabius, Trump, and Humble Farmer, *ibid.*, March 22, 29, April 5, 12, 16, and 19, 1799.

71. The Kentucky resolutions, adopted by the legislature November 14, 1798, declared that portions of the alien and sedition acts were "altogether void and of no effect." Written by Jefferson and introduced in the legislature by Marshall's old law clerk, John Breckinridge, the resolutions stated that "where powers are assumed [by the Federal government] which have not been delegated [to it], a nullification of the act is the rightful remedy; and that every state has a natural right in cases not within the compact to nullify of their own authority, all assumptions of power by others within their limits."

   The Virginia resolutions, written primarily by Madison, and introduced by John Taylor of Caroline, backed away from asserting the doctrine of nullification and simply declared the acts to be "unconstitutional." Jefferson, who was less concerned with the constitutional implications than Madison, had Taylor add the words "null, void, and of no effect" after "unconstitutional," but at Madison's urging these words were dropped before passage, November 24, 1798. Harry Ammon and Adrienne Koch, "The Virginia and Kentucky Resolutions," 5 *William and Mary Quarterly* 145–176, 3rd series (1948). For the text of the resolutions, see 4 *The Debates in the Several State Conventions on the Adoption of the Federal Constitution* 528–545, Jonathan Elliot, ed. (Philadelphia: J. B. Lippincott Co., 1907). Also see Ralph Ketcham, *James Madison: A Biography* 396–397 (Charlottesville: University Press of Virginia, 1990).

72. "Opinion on the Constitutionality of a National Bank," 6 *Works of Jefferson* 198.

73. See Chapter 20.

74. Merrill Peterson, *The Jefferson Image in the American Mind* 213 (New York: Oxford University Press, 1960); William W. Freehling, *Prelude to Civil War: The Nullification Controversy in South Carolina, 1816–1836* 207–210 (New York: Harper & Row, 1966).

75. Delaware, New York, Connecticut, Rhode Island, Massachusetts, New Hampshire, and Vermont sent negative replies. Maryland, Pennsylvania, and New Jersey dismissed the resolution after a debate. North and South Carolina, Tennessee, and Georgia took no action at all. Vermont said that "It belongs not to the state legislatures to decide on the constitutionality of laws made by the general government; this power being vested exclusively in the courts of the Union." Frank M. Anderson, "Contemporary Opinion of the Virginia and Kentucky Resolutions," 5 *American Historical Review* 45–63 (1899).

76. The class bias of the Virginia resolutions has frequently been overlooked. Like the secessionist movement of 1861, the resolutions reflected the interests of the state's plantation aristocracy. As one historian has written, to the merchants and small farmers of the Potomac, Shenandoah, and Kanawha Valleys, "the compact theory outlined in the Resolutions was nothing more than an attempt to perpetuate the rule of the planter gentry." Norman K. Risjord, "The Virginia Federalists," 33 *Journal of Southern History* 504–505 (1967). Also see Wehtje, "The Congressional Elections of 1799," 256–257; Philip G. Davidson, "Virginia and the Alien and Sedition Acts," 36 *American Historical Review* 336–342 (1931). General Daniel Morgan, Marshall's former commander, captured the spirit in Virginia when he told voters, "You are now to determine whether you will support your union, your independence and national consequence, or dwindle to a state of tributary vassalage." *Columbian Mirror and Alexandria Gazette*, April 18, 1799.

77. Clopton to John Allen (Richmond), February 22, 1799. Similar letters were sent to John C. Littlepage and Captain Nicholas Syme (Hanover county), December 23, 1798; James Apperson (New Kent county), December 23; Richard Apperson (New Kent county), December 30; William Foushee (Richmond), December 30; Colonel Travis (Williamsburg), January 7, 1799; Philip N. Nicholas (Richmond), January 7, 1799. John Clopton Papers, Duke University.

78. Lee's "Plain Truth" essays appeared in the *Virginia Gazette and General Advertiser*, February 5, 8, 12, 5, 19, 22, 26, March 1 and 5, 1799, and were subsequently republished as a pamphlet.

79. Taking their cue from Albert J. Beveridge, a number of scholars have suggested that Marshall drafted the minority address of the Federalists in the Virginia legislature in support of the alien and sedition acts. There is no evidence to support this suggestion apart from the wishful thinking of a Massachusetts High Federalist who wanted to believe that Marshall had recanted the views he expressed in his letter to "a Freeholder." Not only did Marshall not change his position on the unwisdom of the acts, but on January 8, 1799, shortly after the minority address was delivered, he wrote to George Washington reaffirming his opposition to the measures. The ornamental rhetoric of the Virginia minority address reflects the style of Henry Lee, not the lean prose of Marshall, and it was Lee who submitted the address to the House of Delegates. Most important, Marshall explicitly dissociated himself from the address in a letter to St. George Tucker on November 27, 1800. The issue involved the assertion by the minority report that the Constitution had incorporated the common law of seditious libel, giving it precedence over the First Amendment. "This strange and absurd doctrine . . . appeared in Richmond something more than twelve months past," Marshall told Tucker, "but I never suspected that an attempt would be made to represent this as a serious opinion entertained by respectable men." For the text of the minority address, see the December 1798 issue of the *Journal of the House of Delegates of the Commonwealth of Virginia* 90–95 (Richmond, Va.: Thomas W. White, 1828). Also see, Beveridge, 2 *Life of Marshall* 402; Theodore Sedgwick to Hamilton, February 7, 1799, 22 *The Papers of Alexander Hamilton* 469–472, Harold C. Syrett, ed. (New York: Columbia University Press, 1975); Sedgwick to King, March 20, 1799, in King, 2 *Life of King* 581; Marshall to George Washington, January 8, 1799, 4 *Marshall Papers* 3–4; Marshall to St. George Tucker, November 27, 1800, 6 *ibid.* 23–24.

80. James Thompson Callender, *The Prospect Before Us* 126–127, 135, 140 (Richmond, Va.: Jones, Pleasants, and Lyon, 1800).

81. Marshall to Washington, January 8, 1799, 4 *Marshall Papers* 3–4.

82. Madison to Jefferson, January 25, 1799, *Madison Papers*, Library of Congress. Also see Henry Tazewell to Littleton W. Tazewell, January 22, 1799, Tazewell Family Papers, Virginia State Library.

83. Blair initially wrote to Henry on December 28, 1798. The text of that letter has been lost, but see Blair to Henry, June 19, 1799, in William Wirt Henry, 2 *Patrick Henry: Life Correspondence and Speeches* 594–596 (New York: Charles Scribner's Sons, 1891).

84. Henry to Blair, January 8, 1799, *ibid.* 591–594.

85. *Ibid.*

86. *Ibid.* After the contents of Henry's letter supporting Marshall became known, Washington urged Henry to run for the legislature once more. Henry acquiesced, announced his candidacy in Charlotte county, and was elected. He died June 6, 1799, before the legislature convened, and was buried at Red Hill. Marshall delivered the eulogy. See Washington to Henry, January 15, 1799, 37 *The Writings of George Washington* 87–90, John C. Fitzpatrick, ed. (Washington, D.C.: Government Printing Office, 1931–1944).

87. Jefferson to Pendleton, April 22, 1799, 9 *Works of Jefferson* 64–65.

88. Marshall to James Markham Marshall, April 3, 1799, 4 *Marshall Papers* 9–11.

89. 13 Hening 332. For details of Virginia election practices, see Julius F. Prufer, "The Franchise in Virginia from Jefferson through the Convention of 1829," 8 *William and Mary Quarterly* 17–32, 2nd series (1928); Charles S. Sydnor, *Gentleman Freeholders: Political Practices in Washington's Virginia* 18–26 (Chapel Hill: University of North Carolina Press, 1952). Also see James Schouler's classic, "Evolution of the American Voter," 2 *American Historical Review* 665–674 (1897).

90. George Wythe Munford, *The Two Parsons; Cupid's Sports; The Dream; and The Jewel of Virginia* 208–211 (Richmond, Va.: J.D.K. Sleight, 1884); Joseph Shelter Watson, "Letters from William and Mary College," 29 *Virginia Magazine of History and Biography* 176–177 (1921).

91. Washington to Marshall, May 5, 1799, 4 *Marshall Papers* 13.

92. Pickering to King, May 4, 1799, in King, 3 *Life of King* 13. Subsequently Pickering told Marshall that the success of Federalist candidates in Virginia "gives joy to all the real friends of the U. States." May 16, 1799, 4 *Marshall Papers* 14–15.

93. Sedgwick to King, July 26, 1799, in King, 3 *Life of King* 69.

94. Jefferson to Stuart, May 14, 1799, 9 *Works of Jefferson* 67.

95. *Ibid.* Shortly thereafter, Jefferson wrote to Tench Coxe that the Republican losses were attributed to "accidental combinations of circumstances," meaning Marshall and Henry, "not from an unfavorable change of sentiment." May 21, 1799, *ibid.* 69–70.

96. Thomas Marshall's failing health was a recent development. In 1795 George Washington, with whom the elder Marshall retained close ties, wrote to his friend in Kentucky that "I was glad to hear . . . that you continued to enjoy tolerable good health, perfect health at our time of life is not to be expected." Fitzpatrick, 34 *Writings of Washington* 157–158, 415.

97. Jefferson to Wilson Cary Nicholas, September 5, 1799, 9 *Works of Jefferson* 79–81.

98. 2 Call 319 (1798).

99. 11 Hening 39–40.

100. See Winthrop D. Jordan, *White Over Black: American Attitudes Toward the Negro, 1550–1812* 574–578 (Chapel Hill: University of North Carolina Press, 1968).

101. *Virginia: In the High Court of Chancery, March 16, 1798* (Case #38963) 2–3.

102. 5 *Marshall Papers* 541–544, editorial note.

103. The permissible period is usually defined as a life in being plus twenty-one years. Blackstone explains that the law "abhors" a perpetuity, since "estates are made incapable of answering those ends . . . for which property was first established." Sir William Blackstone, 2 *Commentaries on the Laws of England* 173–174 (Oxford: Clarendon Press, 1766).

104. 2 Call 330.

105. The Fifth Congress was divided 56–50 in favor of the Federalists, the Sixth, 63–43. Noble E. Cunningham, Jr., *The Jeffersonian Republicans: The Formation of Party Organization, 1789–1801* 134 (Chapel Hill: University of North Carolina Press, 1957); Manning J. Dauer, *The Adams Federalists* 316, 326 (Baltimore: The Johns Hopkins Press, 1968).

106. Sedgwick to King, July 26, 1799, in King, 3 *Life of King* 69. Secretary of the Treasury Oliver Wolcott shared Sedgwick's assessment. Later in the session he wrote to Fisher Ames that "A number of distinguished men appear from the southward, who are not pledged . . . to support the system of the last Congress; these men will pay great respect to the opinions of General Marshall; he is doubtless a man of virtue and distinguished talents, but he will think much of the State of Virginia . . . ; he will reach and expound the constitution as if it were a penal statute, and will sometimes be embarrassed with doubts of which his friends will not perceive the importance." Wolcott to Ames, December 29, 1799, in Oliver Wolcott, 2 *Memoirs of the Administrations of Washington and John Adams, edited from the papers of Oliver Wolcott, Secretary of the Treasury* 314, George Gibbs, ed. (New York: William Van Norden, 1846).

107. Marshall to James Markham Marshall, December 16, 1799, 4 *Marshall Papers* 44–46.

108. *Ibid*. Secretary of the Treasury Oliver Wolcott had indicated to Adams in his most recent fiscal report that the revenue shortfall for 1799 would approximate $5 million. 2 *Memoirs of Wolcott* 300.

109. The three previous incumbents as Speaker were Jonathan Trumbull of Connecticut, Frederick Muhlenberg of Pennsylvania, and Jonathan Dayton of New Jersey.

110. Welch, *Sedgwick* 190–191.

111. Patrick J. Furlong, "John Rutledge, Jr., and the Election of a Speaker of the House in 1799," 24 *William and Mary Quarterly* 432–436 3rd series (1967).

112. Marshall, *Autobiographical Sketch* 26.

113. Sedgwick to King, December 29, 1799, in King, 3 *Life of King* 163.

114. *Ibid*.

115. "Speech to Both Houses of Congress," 9 *Works of John Adams* 136–140.

116. U.S. Congress, House, *Report of the Committee Appointed to Prepare an Address to Both Houses of Congress*, December 6, 1799. Reprinted in 4 *Marshall Papers* 39–43.

117. As treasury secretary, Oliver Wolcott wrote to Fisher Ames, "It was necessary and proper that the answer to the speech should be prepared by Mr. Marshall. He has had a hard task to perform, and you have seen how it has been executed. The object was to unite all opinions, at least of the federalists; it was of course necessary to approve the [Ellsworth] mission, and yet to express the approbation in such terms as when critically analysed would amount to no approbation at all. No one individual was really satisfied; all were unwilling to encounter the danger and heat which a debate would produce and the address passed with silent dissent." December 29, 1799, 2 *Memoirs of Wolcott* 314.

118. Smith, 2 *John Adams* 1020.

119. Marshall to Charles W. Hanson, March 29, 1832, reprinted in Beveridge, 2 *Life of Marshall* 444–445.

120. 10 *Annals of Congress* 203.

121. *Ibid*.

122. *Ibid*.

123. In his *Life of Washington*, Marshall explicitly gave credit to Lee, "who happening not to be in his place when the melancholy intelligence was received and first mentioned in the House, placed them in the hands of the member who served them." Years later, in a final effort to ensure that Lee got credit, he explained the circumstances in a lengthy letter to Charles W. Hanson of Baltimore, Maryland, which is reprinted in Beveridge, 2 *Life of Marshall* 444–445. Also see Marshall, 5 *The Life of George Washington* 765 (Philadelphia: C. P. Wayne, 1806).

124. Troup to King, January 1, 1800, in King, 3 *Life of King* 171. Also see Dumas Malone, *Jefferson and the Ordeal of Liberty* 442–443 (Boston: Little, Brown, 1962).

125. Joint Congressional Resolution, December 23, 1799, 10 *Annals of Congress* 207–208, 210. The text of Lee's address is at pp. 1305–1311. For the Washington monument, see *The Architectural Drawings of Henry Latrobe*, Charles E. Brownell, ed. (New Haven, Conn.: Yale University Press, 1985). Also see St. George Tucker to Marshall, January 15, 1800, Tucker-Coleman Papers, College of William and Mary Library. It was Tucker who recommended that the monument to Washington be an obelisk, 100 feet tall, inscribed with events from his life.

126. Washington's papers were delivered to Marshall by Tobias Lear, the general's nephew and

secretary, in December 1800. For an approximate inventory, see Lear to Marshall, December 12, 1800, 6 *Marshall Papers* 34–40. For Marshall as biographer and historian, see Chapter 11.

127. Samuel E. Morison, *The Life and Letters of Harrison Gray Otis* 178 (Boston: Houghton Mifflin, 1913).

128. Wolcott to Fisher Ames, December 29, 1799, 2 *Memoirs of Wolcott* 314.

129. Marshall to Ambler, December 29, 1799, 4 *Marshall Papers* 49–50. Ambler, who was Polly's brother, had married Marshall's sister Lucy in 1786. Lucy died in 1795, and in December 1799, Ambler married Catherine Bush Norton. Marshall was writing to congratulate him.

130. Marshall to Ambler, December 29, 1799, *ibid*. 50.

131. Marshall addressed the House on January 7, 1800. For text, see *ibid*. 53–58. Also see Richard H. Kohn, *Eagle and Sword* 260–263.

132. 2 *United States Statutes at Large* 7; 10 *Annals of Congress* 370, 389–404, 425. Marshall spoke briefly on the compromise bill two days before passage, 4 *Marshall Papers* 76–78. See also Marshall to Charles Dabney, January 20, 1800, *ibid*. 75–76. Dabney had commanded "Dabney's Legion" in the revolution and was a close friend of Marshall's.

133. The proposal was passed by the Congress May 14, 1800. 2 *United States Statutes at Large* 85–86; 10 *Annals of Congress* 691–692, 713–716.

134. *Ibid*. 191. In addition to Bayard and Marshall, the committee included Robert Goodloe Harper, Samuel Sewall, and Chauncey Goodrich.

135. William Graham Sumner, 2 *The Financier and the Finances of the American Revolution* 288–300 (New York: Dodd, Mead, 1891). For imprisonment and bankruptcy in general, see Peter J. Coleman, *Debtors and Creditors in America . . . 1607–1900* (Madison: State Historical Society of Wisconsin, 1974).

136. 10 *Annals of Congress* 247.

137. Stevens Thomson Mason to Madison, March 7, 1800, 17 *The Papers of James Madison* 371, William T. Hutchinson et al., eds. (Chicago: University of Chicago Press, 1991).

138. 10 *Annals of Congress* 519–520, 533–534.

139. Sedgwick to King, May 11, 1800, in King, 3 *Life of King* 236. For the text of the Uniform Bankruptcy Act, see 10 *Annals of Congress* 1452–1471. Believing that the Bankruptcy Act favored speculators at the expense of farmers, the Republican Congress repealed the measure in 1803, and it was not until thirty-eight years later that new bankruptcy legislation was enacted. Coleman, *Debtors and Creditors* 20.

140. "In all of our measures, we must never lose sight, of the next election of President," Sedgwick to King, December 12, 1799, in King, 3 *Life of King* 154–155.

141. The citizenship of Nash, alias Robbins, remains murky. At the time he was apprehended, Nash carried with him a certificate attesting that he was an American citizen by the name of Robbins. Moments before he was executed, however, he admitted that he was Thomas Nash and that the British had the right man. The latter view has been accepted by virtually all authorities, but a strong circumstantial case that he was in fact an American has been made by Larry D. Cress in what may be the best single article on the episode. For Nash's confession, see Sir Hyde Parker to Robert Liston, September 9, 1799, 10 *Annals of Congress* 517. Also see John Basset Moore, *A Treatise on Extradition and Interstate Rendition* 90–92 (Boston: Boston Book Company, 1891); DeConde, *Quasi-War* 265; Cunningham, *Jeffersonian Republicans* 175. Compare Ruth Wedgwood, "The Revolutionary Martyrdom of Jonathan Robbins," 100 *Yale Law Journal* 229–368 (1990); Larry D. Cress, "The Jonathan Robbins Incident: Extradition and Separation of Powers in the Adams Administration," 111 *Essex Institute Historical Collection* 99–121 (1975).

142. For an account of the chilling mutiny on the *Hermione*, see William James, 2 *The Naval History of Great Britain from the Declaration of War in 1793 to the Accession of George IV* 115–117 (New York: Macmillan, 1902).

143. Article 27 of the Jay Treaty provided that "all persons . . . being charged with murder or forgery" in either Britain or the United States would be returned to the nation against which the crime was committed, "providing that . . . such evidence of criminality as according to the laws of the place, where the fugitive or person so charged shall be found, would justify his apprehension and commitment for trial, if the offense had been committed there." The

extradition provision of the Jay Treaty was one of the earliest examples of the interstate return of fugitives from justice. 2 *Treaties and Other International Acts of the United States of America* 236, David Hunter Miller, ed. (Washington, D.C.: Government Printing Office, 1948).

144. Pursuant to Adams's decision, Secretary of State Pickering instructed Judge Thomas Bee of the U.S. District Court to deliver Nash to the British if, in accordance with Article 27 of the Jay Treaty, "such evidence of his criminality be produced as, by the laws of the United States or of South Carolina, would justify his apprehension and commitment for trial, if the offense had been committed within the jurisdiction of the United States." In effect, Adams's decision to extradite was contingent upon a final determination of probable cause by the court. On July 25, 1799, following a formal hearing at which Nash (Robbins) was represented by counsel, Judge Bee ordered that Nash (Robbins) "be delivered to the British Consul or his representatives in order that justice might be served."

145. A useful summary of press reaction is in Cress, "Robbins Incident," 106–110. Also see Donald H. Stewart, *The Opposition Press of the Federalist Period* 442–443 (Albany: State University Press of New York, 1969); Jacob Axelrad, *Philip Freneau: Champion of Democracy*, 315–333 (Austin: University of Texas Press, 1967).

146. On February 4, 1800, Livingston moved to request from the State Department all the documentation pertaining to the Nash/Robbins case. The motion passed, and the documents were duly provided by Secretary Pickering, including affidavits from the town clerk and selectmen of Danbury, Connecticut, swearing that no person by the name of Robbins had ever been born in, or resided in, Danbury. That, combined with the news of Nash's gallows confession, made it difficult to argue that Nash was an American, and forced the Republicans to shift their ground. 10 *Annals of Congress* 511–512. Also see William B. Hatcher, *Edward Livingston: Jeffersonian Republican and Jacksonian Democrat* 42–54 (University: Louisiana State University Press, 1940).

147. 10 *Annals of Congress* 526–533; 541–578.

148. Jefferson to Charles Pinckney, October 29, 1799, 9 *Works of Jefferson* 87.

149. Marshall to James Markham Marshall, February 28, 1800, 4 *Marshall Papers* 80–81.

150. 10 *Annals of Congress* 594–595.

151. Marshall's March 7, 1800, speech on the Robbins affair is one of the few that was recorded verbatim in the official *Annals of Congress* (10 *Annals of Congress* 596–619). It is more readily available in 4 *Marshall Papers* 82–109.

152. *Ibid.* 95. Marshall's emphasis.

153. *Ibid.*

154. *Marbury v. Madison*, 1 Cranch 137 (1803).

155. The most recent, and most useful survey of the doctrine of political questions, is Thomas M. Franck, *Political Questions / Judicial Answers: Does the Rule of Law Apply to Foreign Affairs?* 10 ff. (Princeton, N.J.: Princeton University Press, 1992). For its application to the war in Vietnam, see *Mora v. McNamara* 389 U.S. 934 (1967); *Mitchell v. Laird*, 488 F. 2d 611 (D.C. Cir. 1973); *Atlee v. Laird*, 347 F. Supp. 689 (E.D. Pa. 1972), *aff'd. sub nom. Atlee v. Richardson*, 411 U.S. 911 (1973).

156. 4 *Marshall Papers* 104.

157. Compare Justice Sutherland's opinion in *United States v. Curtiss-Wright Export Corporation*, 299 U.S. 304 (1936). Also see Michael J. Glennon, "Two Views of Presidential Foreign Affairs Power: *Little v. Barreme* [Marshall] or *Curtiss-Wright* [Sutherland]," 13 *Yale Journal of International Law* 5–32 (1991); David M. Levitan, "The Foreign Relations Power: An Analysis of Mr. Justice Sutherland's Theory," 55 *Yale Law Journal* 467–497 (1946); Charles A. Lofgren, "*United States v. Curtiss-Wright Export Corporation*: A Historical Reassessment," 83 *Yale Law Journal* 1–35 (1973).

158. 4 *Marshall Papers* 104.

159. Adams, *Life of Gallatin* 232. In discussion of the episode, Adams said that Marshall's speech "stands without parallel in our Congressional debates, superior to the grandest efforts of Clay, Webster, or Calhoun."

160. Joseph Story, "Eulogy to John Marshall," 3 *John Marshall: Life, Character, and Judicial Services* 357–358, John F. Dillon, ed. (Chicago: Callaghan, 1903).

161. *Ibid.*

162. For the House roll-call votes, see 10 *Annals of Congress* 619, 621.

163. *Ibid.* 419.

164 *Ibid.* 423–424.

165. *Ibid.*; Beveridge, 2 *Life of Marshall* 457.

166. For the text of "Mr. Marshall's Motion," April 16, 1800, see 4 *ibid.* 128–130. Also see 10 *Annals of Congress* 177, 179–180, 519–520, 684–685, 715. The revised bill reported by Marshall's committee, April 25, 1800, is at 4 *Marshall Papers* 138–145.

167. 10 *Annals of Congress* 709–710, 713.

168. Sedgwick to King, May 11, 1800, in King, 3 *Life of King* 237.

169. As one historian has written, "From John Adams's viewpoint, the one bright spot in all of this political in-fighting was the increasingly effective leadership of John Marshall in the House. More and more the Virginian demonstrated courage and resourcefulness in supporting the president's policies, and gave Adams cause to respect both his judgment and his integrity." Ralph Adams Brown, *The Presidency of John Adams* 167 (Lawrence: University of Kansas Press, 1975).

170. See Hamilton to Sedgwick, May 4, 1800, 24 *Hamilton Papers* 452–453.

171. According to McHenry's later recounting, Adams castigated Hamilton as "the greatest intriguer in the World—a man devoid of every principle—a Bastard, and . . . a foreigner. He ruled Washington, and would still rule if he could." *Ibid.* 507–512, 551–556.

172. Adams to Senate, May 7, 1800, Records of the U.S. Senate, RG 46, National Archives.

173. Marshall, *Autobiographical Sketch* 27–28.

174. Marshall to Adams, May 8, 1800, 4 *Marshall Papers* 148–149.

175. "Law Papers," May 1800, *ibid.* 156.

176. By statute, members of the House and Senate were paid $6 for each day of attendance, plus 30¢ per mile for transportation to Philadelphia. Fourth Congress, Statute I, chap. III, sec. 2 (1796).

177. Adams to Pickering, May 10, 1800; Pickering to Adams, May 12, 1800; Adams to Pickering, May 12, 1800, 9 *Works of John Adams* 53–55. Also see Pickering to Hamilton, May 15, 1800, 24 *Hamilton Papers* 490.

178. For the Senate confirmation, see Resolution of Consent, May 13, 1800, Entry 342, Senate Confirmation of Presidential Appointments, RG 59, National Archives. Lee's letter and the commission, both dated May 13, 1800, are at 4 *Marshall Papers* 149–150.

179. Mason, *My Dearest Polly* 142–144.

180. Beveridge, 2 *Life of Marshall* 519; 2 *Memoirs of Wolcott* 396. Also see James Bayard to John Rutledge, June 8, 1800, *Papers of James A. Bayard, 1796–1815*, Elizabeth Donnan, ed., in 2 *Annual Report of the American Historical Association for the Year 1913* 112 (Washington, D.C.: Government Printing Office, 1915).

181. Marshall, *Autobiographical Sketch* 28–29.

10: Secretary of State

1. *Aurora* (Philadelphia), May 27, 1800.

2. *Ibid.* Emphasis in original.

3. *Aurora*, June 4, 1800. Sedgwick wrote to King in a similar vein. Marshall's appointment, he said, "was a fortunate event—I believe there is not a man in the U.S. of better intentions, and he has the confidence of all good men—no man regrets more than he does the disunion that has taken place, and no one would do more to heal the wounds inflicted by it." Sedgwick to King, September 26, 1800, Rufus King, 3 *The Life and Correspondence of Rufus King* 309, Charles R. King, ed. (New York: G. P. Putnam's Sons, 1896).

4. Pinckney to McHenry, June 10, 1800, in Bernard C. Steiner, *The Life and Correspondence of James McHenry* 460 (Cleveland: Burrows Brothers, 1907). Pinckney wrote from Virginia, suggesting that Marshall may have conferred with his old friend from Paris before accepting Adams's offer.

5. Abigail Adams to J. Q. Adams, May 15, 1800, Adams Papers, Massachusetts Historical Society. Cabot to Gore, September 30, 1800, in Henry Cabot Lodge, *Life and Letters of George Cabot* 291 (Boston: Little, Brown, 1878).

6. For publishing his pamphlet, *The Prospect Before Us*, Callender was tried for and convicted of violating the sedition act in the U.S. circuit court. The best account of Callender's trial is in James Morton Smith, *Freedom's Fetters* 334–358 (Ithaca, N.Y.: Cornell University Press, 1956).

7. Wilhelmus Bogart Bryan, "Hotels of Washington Prior to 1814," 7 *Records of the Columbia Historical Society* 84, 91 (1904).

8. John Marshall, *An Autobiographical Sketch* 29, John Stokes Adams, ed. (Ann Arbor: University of Michigan Press, 1937).

9. Marshall to Sedgwick, quoted in Sedgwick to King, September 26, 1800, in King, 3 *Life of King* 309.

10. The Virginia statement is in Noble E. Cunningham, *The Jeffersonian Republicans: The Formation of Party Organization, 1789–1801* 228 (Chapel Hill: University of North Carolina Press, 1957).

11. See especially Letter from Alexander Hamilton, Concerning the Public Conduct and Character of John Adams, Esq., President of the United States, 25 *The Papers of Alexander Hamilton* 186–234, Harold C. Syrett, ed. (New York: Columbia University Press, 1977).

12. In this context, see Fisher Ames to Christopher Gore, December 29, 1800, 1 *Works of Fisher Ames* 287, Seth Ames, ed. (Boston: Little, Brown, 1854).

13. Commissioners of the District of Columbia to Marshall, July 3 and 10, 1800, 4 *The Papers of John Marshall* 175, 181–182 (Chapel Hill: University of North Carolina Press, 1984).

14. Marshall and Benjamin Stoddart to D.C. Commissioners, October 22, 1800, *ibid.* 330.

15. Gaillard Hunt, *Department of State of the United States* 191 (New Haven, Conn.: Yale University Press, 1914).

16. Marshall's balanced judgment steered the United States away from foreign adventure. When John Quincy Adams, the minister to Prussia, relayed a Swedish proposal for a joint naval task force in the Mediterranean to protect shipping from the Barbary marauders, Marshall demurred. "Until the differences between the United States and France should be so far accommodated, as that actual hostilities shall cease between them, to station American frigates in the Mediterranean would be a hazard, to which our infant Navy ought not perhaps to be exposed." Marshall to J. Q. Adams, July 24, 1800, 4 *Marshall Papers* 188–189.

17. For the text of Pickering's proposal, see 2 *American State Papers, Foreign Relations* 395–398, Walter Lowrie and Matthew St. Clair Clarke, eds. (Washington, D.C.: Gales and Seaton, 1832). For background, see Bradford Perkins, *The First Rapprochement: England and the United States, 1795–1805* 116–120 (Berkeley: University of California Press, 1967).

18. King to Secretary of State, April 7, 1800, 4 *Marshall Papers* 124–126.

19. King's letter of April 22, 1800, was addressed to the secretary of state, who at that time was Timothy Pickering. It did not arrive in Washington until late July, at which point Marshall had assumed office. For text (two letters) see *ibid.* 132–137.

20. Marshall to Adams, July 21, 1800, *ibid.* 184–185.

21. Adams to Marshall, August 1, 1800, *ibid.* 198.

22. Marshall to Adams, July 26, 1800, *ibid.* 190–191.

23. Adams to Marshall, August 11 and 22, 1800, *ibid.* 212, 229.

24. Marshall to King, August 23, 1800, *ibid.* 282–283. Also see King to Marshall, October 7, 1800, *ibid.* 321; Marshall to King, December 4, 1800, 6 *ibid.* 32–33; February 26, 1801, *ibid.* 82–83.

25. Adams to Marshall, September 18, 1800, 4 *ibid.* 282–283.

26. For details and commentary, see King to Marshall, January 12, 1802; Marshall to King, May 5, 1802; King to Marshall, August 5, 1802, 6 *ibid.* 102–104, 119–120, 121–122.

27. Andrew J. Montegue, "John Marshall," in 2 *The American Secretaries of State* 265, Samuel Flagg Bemis, ed. (New York: Knopf, 1927).

28. Albert Beveridge, 2 *The Life of John Marshall* 507 (Boston: Houghton Mifflin, 1916).

29. Marshall to King, September 20, 1800, 4 *Marshall Papers* 283–297. Marshall sent the letter on September 24 to Adams for his approval. On October 3 Adams notified Marshall that he had read it "with some care and great pleasure. I think it very proper that such a letter should be

sent and I am so fully satisfied with the Representations and Reasonings in it that I shall give it to Gen. Lincoln, the Collector of Boston, to be sent by the first opportunity to London." *Ibid.* 303–304, 312–313.

30. Just prior to leaving office in 1801, Marshall wrote again to King complaining about the courts of vice admiralty "which appear organized for the purpose of legalizing plunder." February 26, 1801, 6 *Marshall Papers* 81–82.

31. Marshall to King, September 20, 1800, 4 *ibid.* 283–297.

32. Quoted in Fisher Ames to Christopher Gore, December 29, 1800, 1 *Works of Ames* 287.

33. Marshall to Adams, July 21, 1800, 4 *Marshall Papers* 184–185. Also see envoys to Secretary of State, April 18, 1800, *ibid.* 131–132.

34. Marshall to Adams, August 25, 1800, *ibid.* 240–241.

35. Adams to Marshall, September 4, 1800, *ibid.* 256–257.

36. Marshall to Adams, September 17, 1800, *ibid.* 279–280.

37. The American negotiators, who went somewhat beyond their instructions to secure an agreement, were reluctant to call the accord a treaty, believing that that sounded too permanent. The French, who had also moved considerably during the course of the negotiations, held out for calling the document a "treaty of amity and commerce." Napoleon, who had just signed the Treaty of St. Ildefonso with Spain transferring Louisiana to France and who wanted to conclude the business with the United States quickly, agreed to call it a "convention," and that settled the matter. See Alexander DeConde, *The Quasi-War: The Politics and Diplomacy of the Undeclared War with France 1797–1801* 255–257 (New York: Charles Scribner's Sons, 1966).

38. The fête is described in *Le Moniteur Universel* (Paris), October 6, 1800; the *Maryland Gazette* (Annapolis), December 11, 1800; and George F. Hoar, "A Famous Fête," 12 *Proceedings of the American Antiquarian Society* 240–259, New Series (1899).

39. Murray to Marshall, October 1, 1800, 4 *Marshall Papers* 310.

40. Ellsworth to Pickering, October 16, 1800, Pickering Papers, Massachusetts Historical Society; Ellsworth to Wolcott, October 16, 1800, in Oliver Wolcott, 2 *Memoirs of the Administrations of Washington and John Adams, edited from the papers of Oliver Wolcott, Secretary of the Treasury* 434, George Gibbs, ed. (New York: William Van Norden, 1846).

41. *Telegraph and Daily Advertiser* (Baltimore), November 7, 1800. William R. Davie did not arrive in Washington with the official text of the convention until December 12, 1800. Blackwell P. Robinson, *William R. Davie* 356–357 (Chapel Hill: University of North Carolina Press, 1957).

42. Marshall to Tucker, November 18, 1800, 6 *Marshall Papers* 14–15.

43. Gallatin to his wife, January 15, 1801, in Henry Adams, *The Life of Albert Gallatin* 252 (Philadelphia: J. B. Lippincott, 1879).

44. Richard Griswold to Fanny Griswold, December 6, 1800, Griswold Papers, Yale University. Also see Constance McLaughlin Green, *Washington: Village and Capital, 1800–1878* (Princeton, N.J.: Princeton University Press, 1962).

45. 2 *Memoirs of Wolcott* 377.

46. Adams to Marshall, September 27, 1801, 4 *Marshall Papers* 306–307. Compare Marshall's final draft, 6 *ibid.* 11–14, with Adams's delivered speech, 10 *Annals of Congress* 723–725.

47. Charles Cotesworth Pinckney to Marshall, December 2, 1800, 6 *Marshall Papers* 31.

48. The prevailing view is that Adams was bitter about his defeat and resented Jefferson's triumph. See Page Smith, *John Adams* 1056 (Garden City, N.Y.: Doubleday, 1962). Recent studies of the Adams administration dispute this interpretation. For example, on December 17, 1800, shortly after learning the results from South Carolina, Adams wrote to his youngest son, "My little bark has been oversett in a squall of thunder and lightning and hail attended by a strong smell of sulphur. . . . Be not concerned for me. I feel my shoulders relieved from a burthen. The short remainder of my days will be the happiest of my life." John Adams to Thomas Boyleston Adams, Adams Papers, Massachusetts Historical Society. For an extensive argument to this effect, see Ralph Adams Brown, *The Presidency of John Adams* 203–206 (Lawrence: University Press of Kansas, 1975).

49. Marshall to Charles Cotesworth Pinckney, December 18, 1800; Marshall to Edward Carrington, December 28, 1800, 6 *Marshall Papers* 41, 44–45.

50. 2 *American State Papers, Foreign Relations* 295–301; 6 *Marshall Papers* 48, note 4.

51. Problems arising during the consideration of the Convention of Môrtefontaine led the Senate to adopt its first set of rules formally setting forth the procedure to be followed when the president laid a treaty before it. Ralston Hayden, *The Senate and Treaties, 1789–1817* 114 (New York: Macmillan, 1920).

52. Otis to Hamilton, December 17, 1800, 25 *Hamilton Papers* 260. Also see James Gunn to Hamilton, December 18, 1800, *ibid.* 263.

53. Ames to Gore, December 29, 1800, 2 *Works of Ames* 289.

54. Sedgwick to Hamilton, December 17, 1800, 6 *Works of Alexander Hamilton* 491–495, Henry Cabot Lodge, ed. (New York: G. P. Putnam's Sons, 1904).

55. Quoted in Robert E. Welch, Jr., *Theodore Sedgwick, Federalist* 210 (Middleton, Conn.: Wesleyan University Press, 1965).

56. 10 *Annals of Congress* 775–776.

57. As a result of the quasi-war, United States trade with France had dropped from $20.2 million in 1795 to $3.2 million in 1799.

58. Also see Albert Gallatin to his wife, January 29 and February 5, 1801, in Adams, *Life of Gallatin* 258–259; Theophilus Parsons to Harrison Gray Otis, January 23, 1801, in 1 *The Life and Letters of Harrison Gray Otis* 214, Samuel Eliot Morison, ed. (Boston: Houghton Mifflin, 1913).

59. King to Marshall, October 31, 1800, 4 *Marshall Papers* 338–339. This letter arrived in Washington in late January 1801.

60. 1 *Journal of the Executive Proceedings of the Senate of the United States* 365–398 (Washington, D.C.: Government Printing Office, 1828); 2 *American State Papers: Foreign Relations* 345. For text, see 2 *Treaties and Other International Acts of the United States of America* 457–487, David Hunter Miller, ed. (Washington, D.C.: Government Printing Office, 1931).

61. Ellsworth's letter of resignation, dated October 16, 1800, was delivered to Adams by Ellsworth's son, December 15, 1800. See William Garrott Brown, *The Life of Oliver Ellsworth* 304–305 (New York: Macmillan, 1905); also see Kathryn Turner, "The Appointment of Chief Justice Marshall," 17 *William and Mary Quarterly* 143, notes 2 and 3, 3rd series (1960).

62. Adams to Jay, December 19, 1800, 9 *The Works of John Adams* 91–92, Charles Francis Adams, ed. (Boston: Little, Brown, 1850); Jay to Adams, January 2, 1801, 4 *The Correspondence and Public Papers of John Jay* 285–286, Henry P. Johnston, ed. (New York: G. P. Putnam's Sons, 1890).

63. Stockton to Adams, February 2, 1801, Adams Papers, Massachusetts Historical Society.

64. For text, see 6 *Marshall Papers* 61–62.

65. Marshall to Adams, February 4, 1801, *ibid.* 73.

66. Adams to Marshall, February 4, 1801, *ibid.* 73–74.

67. Marshall, Memorandum on Foreign Affairs (undated), *ibid.* 65–67.

68. John Paul Frank, *Marble Palace: the Supreme Court in American Life* 62 (New York: Knopf, 1958).

69. Quoted in Charles Warren, *History of the American Bar* 402 (Boston: Little, Brown, 1911).

70. Quoted in Edward S. Corwin, *John Marshall and the Constitution* 52 (New Haven, Conn.: Yale University Press, 1919).

71. James Bryce, 1 *The American Commonwealth* 375 (London: Macmillan, 1891).

11: Opinion of the Court

The headnote quotation is from an article Marshall wrote for the Philadelphia *Union*, April 28, 1819.

1. Marshall to Charles Cotesworth Pinckney, March 4, 1801, 6 *The Papers of John Marshall* 89 (Chapel Hill: University of North Carolina Press, 1990).

2. Alexander Hamilton, "Federalist 78," In Hamilton, James Madison, and John Jay, *The Federalist; A Collection of Essays, Written in Favour of the New Constitution, As Agreed Upon by the Federal Convention, September 17, 1787* (Philadelphia: John and Archibald McLean, 1788). The

citation is found on p. 394 of the Bantam Classic edition, Garry Wills, ed. (New York: Bantam Books, 1982).

3. The first case decided by the Court was *West v. Barnes* at the August term, 1791. 2 Dallas 401. For an eminently readable introduction to the Marshall Court, see R. Kent Newmyer, *The Supreme Court under Marshall and Taney* (New York: Thomas Y. Crowell, 1968).

4. The decisions of the Court from 1790 to 1800 are reported in volumes 2, 3, and 4 of the Reports of Alexander J. Dallas. For several cases decided but not reported, see Charles Warren, 1 *The Supreme Court in United States History* 158, note 2 (Boston: Little, Brown, 1926). For the most part, the Court's cases involved questions of pleading, contract, insurance, bills and notes, land titles, and admiralty. Cases requiring the Court to interpret congressional legislation were as rare as those raising constitutional issues.

5. In *Hylton v. United States*, 3 Dallas 171 (1796), the Court considered whether a federal tax on carriages was a direct tax within the meaning of the Constitution. The facts in the case were fictitious. The government paid the fees of counsel on both sides, and only three justices (Iredell, Paterson, and Chase) heard the case. They held the tax to be constitutional, thereby avoiding a direct clash with Congress, but whether they should have heard the case is questionable. However, although the Court effectively spoke to the issue of the constitutionality of the tax in upholding it, it strains credulity to think that the Court might have been similarly prepared to rule the tax unconstitutional.

6. For a useful survey of Congress's role as the authoritative interpreter of the Constitution during the early years of the republic, see Donald G. Morgan, *Congress and the Constitution* 45–70 (Cambridge, Mass.: Harvard University Press, 1966).

7. *Chisholm v. Georgia*, 2 Dallas 419 (1793).

8. At the last term of the Supreme Court in Philadelphia, August 1800, only Paterson, Moore, and Washington were present. Chief Justice Ellsworth was in Paris, Justice Cushing was ill, and Justice Chase was away campaigning for the Federalist ticket in Maryland. Consequently, the important case of *Talbot v. Ship Amelia (Talbot v. Seeman)*, 4 Dallas 34, was carried over to the next term. See Warren, 1 *Supreme Court* 156–158.

9. Jay to Washington, June 29, 1795, 4 *The Correspondence and Public Papers of John Jay* 177, Henry P. Johnson, ed. (New York: G. P. Putnam's Sons, 1893).

10. Warren, 1 *Supreme Court* 125.

11. Rutledge was defeated by a vote of 10–14, December 16, 1795. For a detailed description of his defeat (the High Federalists opposed Rutledge because of his outspoken opposition to the Jay Treaty), see *ibid.* 129–139.

12. William Wirt, 2 *Sketches of the Life and Character of Patrick Henry* 563–564 (Ithaca, N.Y.: Mack, 1848).

13. Cushing was confirmed by the Senate, January 27, 1796, and declined the office on February 2 without ever taking his place at the head of the Court. See Arthur P. Rugg, "William Cushing," 30 *Yale Law Journal* 128, 140 (1920).

14. William Garrott Brown, *The Life of Oliver Ellsworth* 304–305 (New York: Macmillan, 1905).

15. *Aurora* (Philadelphia), January 8, 1801.

16. Jay to Adams, January 2, 1801, 4 *Jay Papers* 284.

17. As Jefferson expressed it, the executive branch "has been able to draw into this vortex [of political debate] the Judiciary branch of the Government, and by their expectancy of sharing the other offices in the Executive gift to make them auxiliary to the Executive in all its views, instead of forming a balance between that and the Legislature, as it was originally intended." 8 *The Works of Thomas Jefferson* 205, Paul Leicester Ford, ed. (New York: G. P. Putnam's Sons, 1904). In 1800 Edward Livingston of New York introduced a constitutional amendment in the House of Representatives providing that federal judges should hold no other appointment or office. A similar amendment was introduced in the Senate by Charles Pinckney on March 5, 1800.

18. One of the best summaries of improper judicial behavior by Federalist judges in the 1790s is in Albert J. Beveridge, 3 *The Life of John Marshall* 23–49 (Boston: Houghton Mifflin, 1916). Also see Warren, 1 *Supreme Court* 164–167; George L. Haskins and Herbert A. Johnson,

Foundations of Power: John Marshall, 1801–15 159–161, in *The Oliver Wendell Holmes Devise, 2 History of the Supreme Court of the United States* (New York: Macmillan, 1981).

19. Haskins and Johnson, *Foundations of Power* 161, 217.

20. Warren, 1 *Supreme Court* 159, note 1.

21. Jefferson may have expressed public concern best in a letter to Senator Charles Pinckney of South Carolina in August 1800. "I consider all the encroachments made [on the Constitution] heretofore as nothing, as mere retail stuff compared with the wholesale doctrine, that there is a common law in force in the United States of which [the federal] courts have cognizance. . . . Ellsworth and Iredell have openly recognized it. [Bushrod] Washington has squinted at it, and I have no doubt it has been decided to cram it down our throat." 9 *Works of Jefferson* 346. (*N.B.* Charles Pinckney, known to the conservative Pinckney clan as "Blackguard Charlie," was the second cousin of Charles Cotesworth Pinckney. Three times elected governor of South Carolina, he played a critical role in delivering the state's electors to Jefferson and Burr in 1800.)

22. January 26, 1796, 1 *American State Papers: Miscellaneous* 137, 143, Walter Lowrie and Walter S. Franklin, eds. (Washington, D.C.: Gales and Seaton, 1834).

23. *Memorial to Congress from the Commissioners of the Federal City*, February 23, 1798, Legislative branch, National Archives.

24. Papers of the [District] Commissioners, Interior branch, National Archives.

25. January 13, 1801, *ibid.*

26. 10 *Annals of Congress* 914.

27. *Ibid.* 959.

28. Latrobe to James Madison, September 8, 1809, in 2 *The Correspondence and Miscellaneous Papers of Benjamin Henry Latrobe* 765, John C. Van Horn and Lee W. Formwalt, eds. (New Haven, Conn.: Yale University Press, 1986). Also see Latrobe to Jefferson, September 1, 1807, *ibid.* 475–476. What was the north wing of the capitol in 1801 is today that portion of the building that connects the rotunda with the Senate wing. The old Committee Room 2, having undergone various transformations (at one time it housed the Senate barbershop), is currently a small hearing room for the Senate Appropriations Committee. It has two windows facing west, as it did in Marshall's time, and measures 30 feet × 35 feet, with a ceiling that is 18 feet high. The original fireplace has been restored.

29. Alexander Dallas undertook to report the Supreme Court's decisions as an entrepreneurial venture. He was not paid a salary, but sold his reports commercially and kept whatever profit there was. Apparently, it was a small sum. When Dallas relinquished the post, he wrote, "I have found such miserable encouragement for my Reports that I have determined to call them all in, and devote them to the rats in the State House." Quoted in *The Oxford Companion to the Supreme Court of the United States* 215, Kermit L. Hall, ed. (New York: Oxford University Press, 1992).

30. A British visitor contrasted the dingy quarters of the Court with the more opulent facilities enjoyed by Congress. "It is by no means a large or handsome apartment; . . . and the circumstance of its being under ground, give it a certain cellar-like aspect, which . . . tends to create . . . the impression of justice being done in a corner . . . while the business of legislation is carried on with . . . pride, pomp, and circumstance." Thomas Hamilton, 2 *Men and Manners in America* 127 (Edinburgh: William Blackwood, 1833). Also see Haskins and Johnson, *Foundations of Power* 79–82; Warren, 1 *Supreme Court* 169–171; Glenn Brown, 1 *History of the United States Capitol* 24–31 (Washington, D.C.: Government Printing Office, 1900); George C. Hazelton, *The National Capitol: Its Architecture, Art and History* 186–187 (New York: J. F. Taylor, 1907).

31. Justice Cushing, as the senior associate justice, administered the oath to Marshall promptly at 11 A.M., Wednesday, February 4, 1801. The weather that morning was described by Gouverneur Morris in his diary. 10 "Diary of Gouverneur Morris," Library of Congress.

32. The leading Washington newspaper, the *National Intelligencer*, stated only that the justices had "made a court." February 5, 1801. Congressman James A. Bayard, writing to his wife, noted that he had been prepared to argue a case (*Talbot v. Seeman*) before the Court, but that

it had been carried over. He made no mention of Marshall. Bayard's letter of February 6, 1801, is quoted in Warren, 1 *Supreme Court* 85, note.

33. Charles Warren notes an English traveler to the United States in 1828 who wrote that the judges of the Supreme Court wear "plain black silk gowns. They commenced with wigs and scarlet robes, but soon discarded them as inconvenient." (Warren cites a J. P. Cooper, 2 *Notions of the Americans* 48 [1850].) Professor Warren's point is undoubtedly correct, and the citation is accurately quoted, but he (or his researcher) appears to have been taken in by James Fenimore Cooper, not J. P. Cooper, who wrote *Notions of the Americans* in 1828 as a mythical English visitor to the United States. (Reprint ed., New York: Frederick Unger Publishing Co., 1963). For an entertaining essay lamenting robes of any color, see Jerome Frank, "The Cult of the Robe," in Frank, *Courts on Trial* 254–261 (Princeton, N.J.: Princeton University Press, 1949).

34. In a wry tribute to Marshall, Mason, speaking to the Senate on June 13, 1802, referred to: "A State upon her knees before six venerable Judges decorated in party-colored robes, as ours formerly were, or arrayed in more solemn blacks such as they have lately assumed." His remark to the Senate verifies the change to black robes under Marshall. 10 *Annals of Congress* 261. Also see Warren, 1 *Supreme Court* 48, as well as the contemporary reference to scarlet robes worn by Cushing and others cited in Arthur P. Rugg, "William Cushing," 30 *Yale Law Journal* 128, 131 (1920).

35. Arguments were heard in *Course v. Steed's Exors.* and a *per curiam* judgment was entered reversing the circuit court for the district of Georgia. Reflecting the absence of Mr. Dallas and the lack of a replacement, the case was not reported. *Minutes of the Supreme Court of the United States*, February 9, 1801, hereinafter cited as USSC *Minutes*; Haskins and Johnson, *Foundations of Power* 84.

36. Jefferson to Marshall, March 4, 1801; Marshall to Jefferson, March 4, 1801, 6 *Marshall Papers* 88, 89.

37. Madison was ill and did not arrive in Washington until May 1, 1801. The following day he was administered the oath of office by U.S. District Judge William Cranch, who would shortly assume the position Dallas had vacated as Supreme Court reporter. For Madison, see Ralph Ketcham, *James Madison* 406–407 (Charlottesville: University Press of Virginia, 1990). The date of Lincoln's succession is from the *Biographical Directory of the American Congress* 1462 (Washington, D.C.: Government Printing Office, 1961).

38. See particularly Robert G. Seddig, "John Marshall and the Origins of Supreme Court Leadership," 36 *University of Pittsburgh Law Review* 785 (1975).

39. Story to Samuel P.P. Fay, February 24, 1812, in William W. Story, 1 *Life and Letters of Joseph Story* 215 (Boston: Little, Brown, 1851).

40. *Ibid.* Also see Story to Nathaniel Williams, February 16, 1812, *ibid.* 214.

41. As John R. Schmidhauser has noted, "institutional arrangements governing Supreme Court action during the first decade of its existence were conducive to individuality in decision making to a degree that has probably never been approximated since 1800." John Schmidhauser, *The Supreme Court: Its Politics, Personalities, and Procedures* 105 (New York: Holt, Rinehart and Winston, 1960).

42. Cushing discarded the wig in 1790. Warren, 1 *Supreme Court* 48, note 1; Henry Flanders, 1 *The Lives and Times of the Chief Justices of the Supreme Court of the United States* 37 (Philadelphia: Lippincott, 1858). For Cushing generally, see Rugg, "William Cushing," 120ff.

43. 2 Dallas 419, 466.

44. Josiah Quincy, who saw Cushing often in Court, said his mind was strong, though sometimes slow, and his legal attainments "were of high rank. His judgment sound, his habits laborious, and devoted to the duties of his occupation and station." Quoted in Haskins and Johnson, *Foundations of Power* 88. Compare Senator William Plumer to Jeremiah Smith, February 19, 1796, William Plumer Papers, Library of Congress.

45. The first nine paragraphs of the original Judiciary Act are in Paterson's handwriting, the remainder in Ellsworth's. William S. Carpenter, "William Paterson," 14 *Dictionary of American Biography* 294.

46. The *Aurora*, which rarely said anything favorable about a Federalist, later acknowledged that Justice Paterson had "ever been considered one of the ablest lawyers America has produced." Cited in Warren 1 *Supreme Court* 176, note 1.

47. William Paterson, *Laws of the State of New Jersey* (New Brunswick, N.J.: A. Blauvelt, 1800).

48. See especially *Van Horne's Lessee v. Dorrance*, 2 Dallas 304, 308–309 (1795).

49. In the midst of the Senate furor over Marshall's nomination, Paterson wrote to Senator Dayton gently chiding him and emphasizing that he, Paterson, felt "neither resentment nor disgust" at the appointment of Marshall. He told Dayton that Marshall was "a man of genius" whose "talents have at once the lustre and solidity of gold." Paterson to Dayton, January 25, 1801. Quoted in John E. O'Connor, *William Paterson: Lawyer and Statesman, 1745–1806* 262 (New Brunswick, N.J.: Rutgers University Press, 1979); also see Warren, 1 *Supreme Court* 178, note 1.

50. Paterson's letter to Marshall, January 26, 1801, has been lost but it is referred to in Marshall's reply of February 2, 1801. 6 *Marshall Papers* 65.

51. Paterson to Dayton, January 25, 1801, in O'Connor, *Paterson* 262.

52. Paterson was a devoted alumnus and trustee of Princeton, and, following a disastrous fire in the spring of 1802 that destroyed Nassau Hall, he engaged Marshall to help solicit funds for the college. Marshall responded enthusiastically, adding his name to the fund drive, and on September 29, 1802, he was awarded a doctor of laws degree, *honoris causa*. See Marshall to Paterson, April 6, 1802, 6 *Marshall Papers* 105–106. Also see, Alexander Leitch, *A Princeton Companion* 183–184, 330, 353 (Princeton, N.J.: Princeton University Press, 1978).

53. Edward S. Corwin, "Samuel Chase," 4 *Dictionary of American Biography* 35. Also see Jane Shaffer Elsmere, *Justice Samuel Chase* 1–35 (Muncie, Ind.: Janevar, 1980).

54. Chase is credited with bringing fresh instructions to Maryland's delegates on the eve of the decisive vote in Philadelphia, having ridden 150 miles in two days in order to do so. *Ibid.*

55. 3 Dallas 199, 236–243 (1796).

56. 3 Dallas 171, 173 (1796). Chase's definition survived until *Pollock v. Farmer's Loan and Trust* 158 U.S. 601 (1894), when the Court, speaking through Chief Justice Melville W. Fuller, corrected "a century of error." Fuller was subsequently reversed by the adoption of the Sixteenth Amendment.

57. George Jeffreys, the first Baron Jeffreys, "Bloody Jeffreys," Chief Justice of King's Bench, and Lord Chancellor (1685–1688), was a buttress of the Stuart monarchy. Following Monmouth's Rebellion in 1685, Jeffreys presided over the treason trials of the rebels (the "Bloody Assizes"), sentencing approximately 300 to be hanged and 800 to be deported. After the flight of James II in 1688, he was imprisoned in the Tower of London, where he died four months later. Robert Milne-Tyte, *Bloody Jeffreys: The Hanging Judge* 137–151 (London: Andre Deutsch, 1989).

58. Chase presided over the sedition trials of newspaper editor Thomas Cooper and writer James Callender and the treason trial of tax resister John Fries. Fries, having been found guilty, was sentenced by Chase to be hanged, although he was later pardoned by Adams. Francis Wharton, *State Trials during the Administrations of Washington and Adams* 610–648 (Philadelphia: Casey and Hart, 1849). Also see Beveridge, 3 *Life of Marshall* 33–41, and the sources cited therein.

59. 2 Dallas 384 (1798).

60. *United States v. Hudson and Goodwin*, 7 Cranch 32 (1812).

61. Cited in Haskins and Johnson, *Foundations of Power* 96.

62. 1 *Life and Letters of Story* 167–168.

63. George Washington devised his library to Bushrod, as well as his public and private papers, and further provided that after Martha's death, Bushrod would inherit Mt. Vernon and the surrounding 4,000 acres.

64. 1 *Life and Letters of Story* 167–168.

65. Story said that Washington did not indulge in "the rash desire to fashion the law to his own views; but to follow out its precepts, with a sincere good faith and simplicity. Hence, he pos-

sessed the happy faculty of yielding just the proper weight to authority; neither, on the one hand, surrendering himself to the dictates of other judges, nor, on the other hand, overruling settled doctrines upon his own private notions of policy or justice." 2 *Ibid*. 30–32.

66. *The Merrimack*, 8 Cranch 317, 378 (1814), Washington dissenting; *Ogden v. Sanders*, 12 Wheaton 213, 332 (1827), one of Marshall's rare dissents; and *Mason v. Haile*, 12 Wheaton 370, 379 (1827), Washington dissenting. Justice William Johnson, who joined the Court in 1804, later remarked that the two Virginia judges, Marshall and Washington, were "commonly estimated as one judge." Johnson to Jefferson, December 10, 1822, in Donald G. Morgan, *Justice William Johnson: The First Dissenter* 182 (Columbia: University of South Carolina Press, 1954). Also see Lawrence B. Custer, "Bushrod Washington and John Marshall: A Preliminary Inquiry," 4 *American Journal of Legal History* 34 (1960).

67. Donald M. Roper, "Judicial Unanimity and the Marshall Court," 9 *American Journal of Legal History* 118, 128 (1965).

68. Custer, "Bushrod and Marshall," 44. Bushrod's record was not unblemished. In 1821 he sold and transported to Louisiana fifty-four Mt. Vernon slaves, separating many of them from their families. When criticized, he defended his action on the ground that the slaves were property and that he could dispose of them as he chose. See *Niles Weekly Register*, 70–72, September 29, 1821. (Marshall's reaction is undocumented.)

69. J. Davis, "Alfred Moore and James Iredell, Revolutionary Patriots and Associate Justices of the Supreme Court of the United States," 124 N.C. Reports 877, 887 (1899). The best sketch of Moore is that by Leon Friedman in 1 *The Justices of the United States Supreme Court* 269–279, Friedman and Fred L. Israel, eds. (New York: Chelsea House, 1969).

70. Haskins and Johnson, *Foundations of Power* 101–102.

71. See notes 33 and 34.

72. William Wirt, *The Letters of a British Spy* 95 (Baltimore: Lucas, 1803).

73. Story appeared before the Court first in 1808 in *Fletcher v. Peck*, the great Yazoo land case. 6 Cranch 87 (1810). See Chapter 16.

74. Story to Samuel P.P. Fay, February 25, 1808, 1 *Life and Letters of Story* 166–167.

75. 1 Cranch 1 (1801). *Talbot v. Seeman* was originally argued August 11, 12, and 13, 1800, but because of the absence of Chief Justice Ellsworth and Justices Chase and Cushing, the case was "continued for the purpose of hearing a further argument before a fuller Court." 4 Dallas 34. In February 1801, with Paterson and Moore absent, the case was carried over again.

76. *American Daily Advertiser* (Philadelphia), August 18, 1800. Also see the *Aurora*, August 19, 1800.

77. Perhaps the most famous of American warships, the U.S.S. *Constitution* remains afloat in Boston harbor, a memorial to the nascent United States Navy. Its nickname, "Old Ironsides," derives from an 1812 engagement with the British man-of-war H.M.S. *Guerrière*. At the height of the battle, a young American seaman watched a British cannonball bounce harmlessly off *Constitution*'s side. "Good God, her sides are made of iron," he is reported to have said. The ship's preservation is in some measure attributable to the heroic poem "Old Ironsides," written by Justice Holmes's father to protest its decommissioning. See Thomas C. Gillmer, *Old Ironsides* 91–97 (Camden, Maine: International Marine, 1993).

78. John Thompson Mason (b. 1764), was regarded as the leading Republican lawyer of the early 1800s. Jefferson named him United States Attorney for the District of Columbia, and both Jefferson and Madison, on separate occasions, offered to appoint him attorney general, which he declined. Charles Warren, *A History of the American Bar* 246, note 9, reprint ed. (New York: Howard Fertig, 1966).

79. Justice Bushrod Washington's circuit court decision is reprinted at 1 Cranch 3–4.

80. 1 Cranch 1, 10.

81. *Ibid*.

82. *Ibid*.

83. *Ibid*. 15–24.

84. As a social historian of the nation's capital has written, "the justices were barely members of the Washington community, spending only two months a year, usually, at the capital. The unanimity of the case decisions provides little food for political analysis, beyond the obser-

vation that their single-mindedness on policy questions conformed to the fraternal character of their lifestyle. . . . Moreover, they lived such a reclusive existence that the community record does little more than note their presence in the capital. They rarely received guests and they rarely ventured out of their lodgings after hours except to make obligatory appearances at official functions and to pay an annual courtesy call, *en bloc*, at the executive mansion." James Sterling Young, *The Washington Community* 77 (New York: Columbia University Press, 1966).
85. See Chapter 4. Also see Donald G. Morgan, "The Origin of Supreme Court Dissent," 10 *William and Mary Quarterly* 354–355, 3rd series (1953).
86. Haskins and Johnson, *Foundations of Power* 386.
87. See Donald G. Morgan, "Marshall, the Marshall Court, and the Constitution," in *Chief Justice John Marshall: A Reappraisal* 168–185, W. Melville Jones, ed. (New York: Da Capo Press, 1971). Roper, "Judicial Unanimity," 118–134; Seddig, "Origins of Leadership," 785–832.
88. 1 Cranch 1, 28.
89. *Ibid.* 32.
90. *Ibid.*
91. *Ibid.* 36–37.
92. *Ibid.* 37.
93. *Ibid.* 43.
94. *Ibid.*
95. *Ibid.* 44.
96. *Ibid.* 45. The value of the *Amelia* and her cargo totaled $188,326.34. After costs were deducted, Captain Talbot and his crew were awarded $26,405.77, from which they had to pay their own legal costs. USSC *Minutes*, August 11, 1801.
97. 1 Cranch 1, 46.
98. *Aurora*, August 17, 1801; *National Intelligencer*, August 17, 1801.

12: The Gathering Storm

1. The Senate was divided 18–13 for the Republicans, with one vacancy. (Dwight Foster, a Massachusetts Federalist, had resigned during the Sixth Congress and was not replaced until Timothy Pickering was elected in October 1803.) In the House of Representatives, the Republicans had a lopsided 69–36 advantage, also with one vacancy, again from Massachusetts.
2. *United States v. Schooner Peggy*, 1 Cranch 103 (1801), came before the Court on August 12, 1801, but argument was deferred until the December term. *Minutes of the Supreme Court of the United States*, August 12, 1801. Hereinafter cited as USSC *Minutes*.
3. *Ibid.*, December 8, 1801.
4. 11 *Annals of Congress* 11. For the text of Jefferson's message, see 9 *The Works of Thomas Jefferson* 321–342, Paul Leicester Ford, ed. (New York: G. P. Putnam's Sons, 1904).
5. Jefferson explained his action in a letter to Aaron Burr, president of the Senate: "The circumstances under which we find ourselves . . . rendering inconvenient the mode heretofore practiced, of making by personal address the first communications between the Legislative and Executive branches, I have adopted that by Message, as used on all subsequent occasions through the session. In doing this I have had principal regard to the convenience of the Legislature, to the economy of their time, to their relief from the embarrassment of immediate answers, or subjects not yet fully before them, and to the benefits thence resulting to the public affairs." 11 *Annals of Congress* 11. Also see Jefferson to Benjamin Rush, December 20, 1801, 9 *Works of Jefferson* 343–346.
6. In perhaps the most controversial passage of his message, Jefferson assigned the national government the responsibility for external affairs and relations among the states. Everything else belonged to the states. "[T]he States themselves have principal care of our persons, our property, and our reputation, constituting the great field of human concerns. . . ." *Ibid.* 328.
7. *Ibid.* 340. Emphasis added.

8. At the last moment, Jefferson dropped from the message a long, rambling paragraph dealing with the Sedition Act and the authority of each of the three branches of government to interpret the Constitution for itself when "it acts in the last resort." He further asserted that successor administrations were not bound by the constitutional interpretations of their predecessors. "This whole paragraph was omitted," Jefferson noted, "as capable of being chicaned, and furnishing something to the opposition to make a handle of." The text of the omitted paragraph is in Albert J. Beveridge, 3 *The Life of John Marshall*, 605–606 (Boston: Houghton Mifflin, 1916).

9. Ames may have been one of the few to anticipate Jefferson's intentions. To Rufus King he wrote: "The message announces the downfall of the late revision of the Judiciary. . . . The U.S. Government is to be dismantled like an old ship." December 20, 1801, 4 *The Life and Correspondence of Rufus King* 40, Charles R. King, ed. (New York: G. P. Putnam's Sons, 1896). Also see Theodore Sedgwick to King, December 14, 1801, *ibid.* 36; Joseph Hales to King, December 19, 1801, *ibid.* 39.

10. Alexander Hamilton [under the pseudonym Lucius Crassus], *New York Evening Post*, December 29, 1801, reprinted in 25 *The Papers of Alexander Hamilton* 477, Harold C. Syrett, ed. (New York: Columbia University Press, 1977). Hamilton wrote eighteen essays, signed "Lucius Crassus," criticizing Jefferson's message to Congress. They were published in the *New York Evening Post* between December 1801 and April 1802.

11. 1 *The Memoirs of John Quincy Adams* 186, Charles Francis Adams, ed. (Philadelphia: J. B. Lippincott, 1874).

12. See Chapter 10.

13. Charles Warren, 1 *The Supreme Court in United States History* 198–199 (Boston: Little, Brown, 1926).

14. USSC *Minutes*, December 7–17, 1801.

15. Jefferson transmitted the Convention of Môrtefontaine to the Senate on December 11, 1801. For the text of his message, see 2 *American State Papers: Foreign Relations* 345, Walter Lowrie and Matthew St. Clair Clarke, eds. (Washington, D.C.: Gales and Seaton, 1832).

16. The Senate resolution is reprinted in *ibid.*

17. Jefferson's proclamation ratifying the convention is at 2 *Treaties and Other International Acts of the United States of America* 486–487, David Hunter Miller, ed. (Washington, D.C.: Government Printing Office, 1931).

18. In so doing, Marshall explicitly referred to the fact that Jefferson had promulgated the convention and that it now formed part of the supreme law of the land. 1 Cranch 103, 108; USSC *Minutes*, December 21, 1801.

19. See Chapter 9.

20. 1 Cranch 110. Emphasis added.

21. 1 Cranch 45, 87 (1801). The case enjoys some after-the-fact notoriety because Wilson's appeal was argued by Joseph H. Daveiss, the first lawyer from west of the Appalachians to appear before the Supreme Court. Daveiss was United States attorney for Kentucky, and two years after the trial, he married Marshall's youngest sister, Nancy, who had been raised in Kentucky. There is no evidence that Marshall played any role in the courtship. For a contemporary account of Daveiss's frontier manners and his masterly argument before the Court, see *Harper's Weekly* 266 (April 27, 1867).

22. James Madison was a minor holder of a part of the Mason claim, and several of his biographers assert that he was financially injured by the Court's decision. However, there is no primary evidence that he held Marshall responsible, or that relations between them worsened as a result. See Ralph Ketcham, *James Madison: A Biography* 375 (Charlottesville: University Press of Virginia, 1990).

23. Ordinance of Separation from Virginia, subsequently incorporated into Article VIII, section 6, of the Kentucky constitution. The purpose of the law was to settle land titles as quickly as possible and to avoid extended litigation.

24. Section 22 of the Judiciary Act of 1789 provided that "final judgments and decrees in civil actions in a circuit court . . . may be re-examined and reversed or affirmed by the Supreme

Court." 1 *United States Statutes at Large* 84. In Kentucky in 1800, the district court served as the circuit court.

25. 1 Cranch 45, 91–92.

26. *Ibid.* 92.

27. *Ibid.* 102–103.

28. USSC *Minutes*, December 16, 1801.

29. 1 Cranch 137 (1803). John Hart Ely, *War and Responsibility* 55 (Princeton, N.J.: Princeton University Press, 1993).

30. Act of February 27, 1801, 10 *Annals of Congress* 1554; 2 *United States Statutes at Large* 103, 107. The same legislation also authorized the appointment of three judges for the circuit court of the District of Columbia. To these posts Adams appointed his wife's nephew, William Cranch, who subsequently became the Supreme Court's reporter; Marshall's brother, James Markham Marshall; and former Supreme Court Justice Thomas Johnson of Maryland, whom Adams appointed chief judge. Johnson declined to serve, and Jefferson replaced him with a Republican, William Kilty. It is likely that Jefferson initially resented the appointment of Cranch and Thomas Marshall, but when Kilty resigned as chief judge in 1806 to become chancellor of Maryland, Jefferson nominated Cranch to replace him. Alexander Burton Hagner, "William Cranch," in 3 *Great American Lawyers* 87, 91, William Druper Lewis, ed. (South Hackensack, N.J.: Rothman Reprints, 1971).

31. 1 *Journal of the Executive Proceedings of the Senate of the United States* 388, 390 (Washington, D.C.: United States Government Publication Office, 1828). The Senate of the Sixth Congress adjourned *sine die* March 5, 1801; 10 *Annals of Congress* 769.

32. Warren, 1 *Supreme Court* 200–201, and the sources cited therein.

33. As Marshall wrote to his brother James, "I should . . . have sent out the commissions which had been signed and sealed but for the extreme hurry of the time and the absence of Mr. [Jacob] Wagner [chief clerk of the State Department] who had been called on by the President [Mr. Jefferson] to act as his private secretary." John Marshall to James Marshall, March 18, 1801, 6 *The Papers of John Marshall* 90–91 (Chapel Hill: University of North Carolina Press, 1990).

34. Jefferson acted on the theory that, like a deed or a bond, the commissions were not valid until they were delivered. Years later he explained his position to Justice William Johnson as follows: "Among the midnight appointments of Mr. Adams, were commissions to some Federal justices of the peace. These were signed and sealed by him but not delivered. I found them on a table in the Department of State, on my entrance into office, and I forbade their delivery. . . . [I]f there is any principle of law never yet contradicted, it is that delivery is one of the essentials to the validity of a deed. Although signed and sealed, yet as long as it remains in the hands of the party himself, it is *in fieri* [incomplete], it is not a deed, and can be made so [only] by its delivery." Jefferson to Johnson, June 12, 1823, 4 *Memoirs, Correspondence, and Private Papers of Thomas Jefferson* 377, 381–382, Thomas Jefferson Randolph, ed. (London: Colburn and Beatty, 1829).

35. Several years later Jefferson confided to Abigail Adams that "I can say with truth that one act of Mr. Adams' life, and one only, ever gave me a moment's personal displeasure. I did consider his last appointments to office as personally unkind. . . . It seemed but common justice to leave a successor free to act by instruments of his own choice." Jefferson to Mrs. Adams, June 13, 1804, 1 *The Adams-Jefferson Letters* 270–271, Lester J. Cappon, ed. (Chapel Hill: University of North Carolina Press, 1959).

36. Dumas Malone, *Jefferson the President* 144 (Boston: Little, Brown, 1970).

37. *Ibid.* 73; January 6, 1802, 1 *Journal of the Executive Proceedings of the Senate* 404, 417–418, 423.

38. William Marbury (1762–1835), originally a maritime agent in Annapolis, Maryland, had moved to Georgetown in 1799 to assume duties as a purchasing officer for the United States Navy. He speculated successfully in Washington real estate and became a leading figure in the Potomac Company, a venture that sought to link the Potomac and Ohio rivers. Later he became a banker and was the founder and first president of the Farmers and Mechanics National Bank in Georgetown. Wilhelmus Bogart Bryan, 1 *A History of the National Capital* 331

(New York: Macmillan, 1914); Donald O. Dewey, *Marshall versus Jefferson* 83–84 (New York: Knopf, 1970).

39. Malone, *Jefferson the President* 144.

40. *National Intelligencer* (Washington, D.C.), March 23, 1801.

41. Marbury was joined in his suit by three others not reappointed by Jefferson: Dennis Ramsay, Robert Hooe, and William Harper. Ramsay was the most politically active of the four litigants. A former colonel in the Virginia Line, he was twice mayor of Alexandria (1788–89, 1792–94), delivered the town's farewell address to George Washington when he departed to become President of the United States, and was an honorary pallbearer at Washington's funeral. Robert T. Hooe, former sheriff of Fairfax county, was one of the original boosters of Alexandria-Georgetown as the nation's capital. Like Marbury, he speculated heavily and successfully in Washington real estate, and was by far the wealthiest of the four men. A Quaker, he freed his numerous slaves upon his death in 1809. William Harper, the least involved, was an Alexandria merchant and the father of twenty-nine children through several marriages. Also a Quaker, he was an artillery captain during the Revolutionary War, fought at Princeton, Monmouth, and Brandywine, and wintered at Valley Forge. He had the honor of commanding the artillery battery at Washington's funeral.

    All four men were locally prominent Federalists. If they had genuinely desired their posts, it is curious that they did not file their suit at the August 1801 term of the Court. The office of justice of the peace was piddling. Its civil jurisdiction was limited to actions of less than $20, and there was no salary. Whatever remuneration there was resulted only from fees collected. Indeed, as Charles Lee told the Court, "The emoluments, or the dignity of the office, are no objects with the applicants." 1 Cranch 137.

42. *Aurora* (Philadelphia), December 22, 1801.

43. USSC *Minutes*, December 18, 1801.

44. Conventional wisdom, deriving in large measure from the interpretations of Albert Beveridge and Edward Corwin, suggests that Marshall deliberately structured the confrontation with "perfectly calculated audacity" so that he might establish the Court's authority to rule on the constitutionality of acts of Congress. Beveridge, 3 *Life of Marshall* 132. Corwin calls it "a deliberate partisan coup." *The Doctrine of Judicial Review* 9 (Princeton, N.J.: Princeton University Press, 1914). By contrast, Charles Warren suggests that, if anything, Marshall was aiming at the executive branch, not Congress. See Warren, 1 *Supreme Court* 201–204. Dumas Malone, Jefferson's biographer, perhaps more correctly points out that the case was relatively trivial when it commenced, and that one should not "read back" into its inception a calculation that was not there. *Jefferson the President* 146–147.

45. See Monroe's letters to Jefferson, December 21, 1801; February 13, 1802; and March 14, 1802. It would be incorrect to call the latter months of 1801 an "era of good feeling," but Monroe, one of the most partisan of Republicans, advised Jefferson that there would be no objections among the party faithful if the president wanted to retain the services of a number of meritorious Federalists on the government payroll. Monroe to Jefferson, December 21, 1801, 3 *The Writings of James Monroe* 322–323, Stanislaus Murray Hamilton, ed. (New York: G. P. Putnam's Sons, 1900).

46. On December 20, two days after Marshall's "show cause" request to Madison, Jefferson wrote to Dr. Benjamin Rush in Philadelphia that "Our winter campaign has opened with more good humor than I expected. By sending a message, instead of making a speech at the opening of the session, I have prevented the bloody conflict to which the making an answer would have committed them. They consequently were able to set into real business at once, without losing 10 or 12 days in combating an answer. *Hitherto there has been no disagreeable altercations*." Jefferson did not mention Marbury's suit, but he did say that "the suppression of useless offices" and the "lopping off" of Adams's midnight judges would likely produce some difficulty. 9 *Works of Jefferson* 343–346. Emphasis added.

47. Following the decision in *United States v. Schooner Peggy*, the Court devoted the last three days of the December term to two minor cases, *Resler v. Shehee*, 1 Cranch 110 (1801), and *Turner v. Fendall*, 1 Cranch 117 (1801). These cases involved minor civil transactions in the town of Alexandria and came before the Court only because Alexandria had been incorpo-

rated into the District of Columbia and was thus a federal jurisdiction. There were no distinctive federal issues.

    Of passing interest, former attorney general Charles Lee represented the appellant in *Resler* (and lost), and the defendant in *Turner* (and won). His appearance in these two minor cases puts his argument in *Marbury* into perspective. Far from being exceptional, it would seem to have been another routine appearance.

48. Act of February 13, 1801, 2 *United States Statutes at Large* 89.
49. The general thesis is effectively stated by Beveridge in 3 *Life of Marshall* 50–100. For a contrary view, see Malone, *Jefferson the President* 115–116. Also see William S. Carpenter's classic account, "Repeal of the Judiciary Act of 1801," 9 *American Political Science Review* 519–528 (1915). Written the year before Beveridge's spirited biography of Marshall, Carpenter eschews blaming Jefferson and places primary responsibility for repeal on the shoulders of Breckinridge and Mason.
50. One month after his inauguration, Jefferson wrote to Archibald Stuart in Staunton, Virginia, indicating that Adam's "midnight" judicial appointments would stand "till the law is repealed, which we trust will be at the next Congress." April 8, 1801, 8 *Works of Jefferson* 46. Jefferson, of course, did not indicate when at the next session he thought the law should be repealed, and in his letter to Thomas Randolph, he was far less sanguine. Jefferson told Randolph that "a few removals from office will be indispensable. They will be chiefly for real mal-conduct, and mostly in the offices connected with the administration of justice. I shall do as little in that way as possible." March 12, 1801, quoted in George L. Haskins and Herbert A. Johnson, *Foundations of Power: John Marshall, 1801–15* 151, in The Oliver Wendell Holmes Devise, 2 *History of the Supreme Court of the United States* (New York: Macmillan, 1981).
51. Jefferson's desire to lessen hostility and to win the support of moderate Federalists was effectively stated in an August 26, 1801, letter to Attorney General Levi Lincoln. In particular, Jefferson was concerned not to move too hastily to remove Federalist officeholders. "I had foreseen," he wrote, "that the first republican President who should come into office after all the places in the government had become exclusively occupied by federalists, would have a dreadful operation to perform. . . . On him was to devolve the office of an executioner, that of lopping off. I cannot say that it has worked harder than I expected. You know the moderation of our views in this business, and that . . . we determined to proceed with deliberation. This produced impatience in the republicans, and a belief we meant to do nothing." Jefferson told Lincoln that it was essential to bring the "republican federalists" into the fold. He said that if he should ever be convinced that "a healing of the nation into one is impracticable, [that] would be the last moment of my wishing to remain where I am. . . .

    "I am satisfied that the heaping of abuse on me . . . has been with the design and hope of provoking me to make a general sweep of all federalists out of office. But as I have carried no passion into the execution of this duty, I shall suffer none to be excited. The clamor which has been raised will not provoke me to remove one more, nor deter me from removing one less, than if a word had not been said on the subject."

    At the end of the long letter, Jefferson added, almost as a postscript, "The removal of excrescences from the judiciary is the universal demand." 9 *Works of Jefferson* 289–291.
52. Malone, *Jefferson the President* 115–119.
53. The best analysis of the measure is Kathryn Turner's "Federalist Policy and the Judiciary Act of 1801," 22 *William and Mary Quarterly* 3–32, 3rd series (1965). Also see Max Farrand, "The Judiciary Act of 1801," 5 *American Historical Review* 682–686 (1900); Warren, 1 *Supreme Court* 185ff.
54. The Judiciary Act of 1789 had not done so, providing for federal jurisdiction in most cases to be concurrent with that of the state courts. See Charles Warren, "New Light on the History of the Federal Judiciary Act of 1789," 37 *Harvard Law Review* 49–172, esp. 49–65 (1923).
55. The Act of 1801 widened the privilege to remove litigation from the state courts to the federal courts, and in cases involving the Constitution, federal laws and treaties, no minimum amount was required for jurisdiction. There had previously been a minimum of $500. 2 *United States Statutes at Large*, sections 14, 15.

56. *Ibid.*, sections 3, 7
57. See especially Turner, "Judiciary Act of 1801," 4–16, and the sources cited therein.
58. Malone, *Jefferson the President* 114; Warren, 1 *Supreme Court* 219; Turner, "Judiciary Act of 1801," 23–27. Also see Mary K. Bonsteel Tachau, *Federal Courts in the Early Republic: Kentucky, 1789–1816* 167–199 (Princeton, N.J.: Princeton University Press, 1978).
59. 1 Cranch 45.
60. Todd to Breckinridge, February 17, 1802, quoted in Warren, 1 *Supreme Court* 219–220. Emphasis added. See especially Carpenter, "Repeal of Judiciary Act," 522–523. Also see Haskins and Johnson, *Foundations of Power* 153; Malone, *Jefferson the President* 117. Senator James Jackson of Georgia expressed the frontier concern thus during the debate on the repeal: "We have been asked if we are afraid of having an army of Judges. For myself, I am more afraid of our army of Judges under the patronage of the President than of an army of soldiers. The former can do us more harm. They may deprive us of our liberties, if attached to the Executive, from their decisions, and from the tenure of office . . . for we cannot remove them." 10 *Annals of Congress* 47.
61. For a list of Adams's appointees, see February 18, 1801, 1 *Journal of the Executive Proceedings of the Senate* 381, 383. The best analysis of the men selected is Kathryn Turner's "The Midnight Judges," 109 *University of Pennsylvania Law Review* 494–523 (1961). Professor Turner concludes that "As a whole, the group of midnight judges reflected the relatively moderate political positions of the men who had selected them. They were not facsimiles of the fanaticism which had led the Federalists to prosecute the Whiskey Rebels and John Fries for treason and to enforce the Sedition Act with real vigor." At pp. 521–522.

Professor Crosskey comes to a similar conclusion. In his view, judicial nonpartisanship had not yet been established and criticism of Adams is therefore unwarranted. In Crosskey's opinion, the "midnight" judges were an "extraordinarily able group of men [who] will bear comparison with any equal number of judges ever chosen by any President before or since." William Winslow Crosskey, 2 *Politics and the Constitution in the History of the United States* 761 (Chicago: University of Chicago Press, 1953).

Nepotism, however, was not far from the surface. In addition to his wife's nephew, William Cranch, appointed to the D.C. circuit, Adams's appointments included Marshall's brother James Markham, also for the District of Columbia; his brother-in-law, George Keith Taylor, for the Fourth Circuit; and another brother-in-law, William McClung, for the Sixth Circuit. Taylor, who was married to Marshall's sister Jane, was initially recommended by the Federalists in Virginia's congressional delegation, while McClung, married to Mary Marshall, was recommended by Kentucky Senator Humphrey Marshall, who was Marshall's cousin, and whose wife Elizabeth was another of Marshall's sisters. It would be irresponsible to suggest that John Marshall played no role in these appointments, even if it were merely to add his endorsement. See Henry Lee et al. to Marshall, February 10, 1801; Humphrey Marshall to John Marshall, February 15, 1801, 6 *Marshall Papers* 524, 77–78; Turner, "Midnight Judges," 513, 515, 518.
62. Jefferson to John Dickinson, December 19, 1801, 10 *The Writings of Thomas Jefferson* 302, Andrew A. Lipscomb, ed. (Washington, D.C.: The Thomas Jefferson Memorial Association, 1903).
63. Giles to Jefferson, June 1, 1801, quoted in Malone, *Jefferson the President* 116.
64. *Ibid.*
65. The Marshall archives in Williamsburg are barren of political correspondence during this period.
66. In introducing his motion for repeal, Breckinridge complained explicitly that "In Kentucky, non-resident land claimants have gone into Federal Court from a temporary convenience," instead of to the state courts. 11 *Annals of Congress* 25–46. Breckinridge's speech is also reported verbatim in the *National Intelligencer*, January 11–15, 1802.
67. Only two senators, Stevens Thomson Mason of Virginia and James Jackson of Georgia, referred to Mr. Marbury's case. Jackson, in a florid passage likening the judiciary to the "despots of Turkey," spoke of "their attack on the Secretary of State." Mason mentioned the

case only in relation to the removal of justices of the peace, and did not refer to the order to Madison to show cause. 11 *Annals of Congress* 47–48, 61.

Senator Breckinridge did not mention the Marbury matter on the floor, but he wrote to Monroe, "It is supposed that no further proceedings will be had; but that the intention of the gentleman is to stigmatize the Executive, and give the opposition matter for abuse and vilification. The consequences of invading the Executive in this manner are deemed here a high-handed exertion of Judiciary power. They may think that this will exalt the Judiciary character, but I believe they are mistaken." December 24, 1801, Breckinridge Papers, Library of Congress.

In a lengthy reply, Monroe told Breckinridge that he strongly supported the repeal of "the Judiciary law," but he made no mention of the order to Madison. Monroe to Breckinridge, January 15, 1802, *ibid.*

68. 11 *Annals of Congress* 147–150, 154–160, 183.

69. Speaking of the Supreme Court, Giles said, "They have sent a mandatory process, or process leading to a *mandamus*, into the executive cabinet, to examine its concerns. Does this, in the judges, seem unambitious?" *Ibid.* 579–602. Giles's speech is reprinted in the *Aurora*, March 8, 1802.

70. Bayard was an old friend of Marshall's, and it was his shift on behalf of Delaware in January 1801 that had secured Jefferson's election as president. Bayard also enjoyed the reputation of being one of the finest appellate lawyers in America, and he proceeded to give Giles a lesson on judicial procedure. "I deny, sir, that mandatory process has been issued," said Bayard. "Such process would be imperative and suppose a jurisdiction to exist; the proceeding, which has taken place, is no more than notice of the application made to the court and allows the party [at whom it is directed] to show, either that no wrong has been committed, or that the court has no jurisdiction over the subject. Even, sir, if the rule was made absolute, and the *mandamus* issued, it would not be definitive, but it would be competent for the secretary [of state] in a return of the writ, to justify the act which has been done, or to show that it is not subject to judicial cognizance." 11 *Annals of Congress* 614. Also see the *Aurora*, March 16, 1802.

John Randolph, in his summation of the Republican case for repeal, also referred to the Supreme Court's order to Madison, but the reference was tangential to the argument Randolph was making. 11 *Annals of Congress* 662–663.

71. The vote was along party lines, except for one Republican, William Eustis of Massachusetts, who voted with the Federalists. *Ibid.* 982. The measure was signed into law March 8, 1802, 2 *United States Statutes at Large* 132.

72. Article III, section 1 of the Constitution states that "The judicial Power of the United States shall be vested in one supreme Court, and in such inferior Courts as the Congress may from time to time establish."

73. "The Judges, both of the supreme and inferior courts, shall hold their Offices during good Behavior, and shall . . . receive for their Services, a Compensation which shall not be diminished during their Continuance in Office." *Ibid.*

74. Hamilton to James A. Bayard, April 1802, 10 *Hamilton Papers* 609.

75. "An act to Amend the Judicial System of the United States," April 29, 1802, 2 *United States Statutes at Large* 89–100, 156–167. It was passed by the Senate, 16–10, on April 8, and by the House, 46–30, on April 23.

76. 11 *Annals of Congress* 1229 *et seq.* James Monroe also questioned the political wisdom of canceling the next term of the Court. On April 25, 1802, he wrote to Jefferson that such a postponement "may be considered as an unconstitutional oppression of the Judiciary by the Legislature. . . . Suppose the Judges were to meet according to the former law, notwithstanding the postponement, and make a solemn protestation against the repeal and this postponement, denouncing the whole proceedings as unconstitutional. . . . I am of opinion that this postponement would give new colour to their pretensions, new spirits to their party and a better prospect of success." 3 *Writings of Monroe* 342–343.

77. Marshall to Wolcott, April 5, 1802, 6 *Marshall Papers* 104–105.

78. Marshall to Paterson, April 6, 1802, *ibid.* 105–106.

79. *Ibid.*
80. Marshall to Bayard, April 12, 1802, *ibid.* 106–107.
81. Morton Borden, *The Federalism of James A. Bayard* 100 (New York: Columbia University Press, 1954).
82. *Ibid.* 125. Bayard immediately reported his conversation with Marshall to his father-in-law, Richard Bassett, one of the "midnight" judges appointed by Adams. Bayard to Bassett, April 19, 1802, *Papers of James A. Bayard, 1796–1815*, Elizabeth Donnan, ed., in 2 *Annual Report of the American Historical Association for the Year 1913* 153 (Washington, D.C.: Government Printing Office, 1915).
83. These were the words that Marshall used on circuit later that year in dismissing a suit that challenged the repeal of the Judiciary Act of 1801 (*Stuart v. Laird*) and that Justice Paterson paraphrased for the Supreme Court in affirming Marshall's holding. *Stuart v. Laird*, 1 Cranch 298, 308 (1803). For a general discussion of Marshall's mode of statutory construction, "adhering to the letter of the statute, taking the whole together," see Robert K. Faulkner, *The Jurisprudence of John Marshall* 218 (Princeton, N.J.: Princeton University Press, 1968).
84. Richard E. Ellis, *The Jeffersonian Crisis: Courts and Politics in the Young Republic* 60 (New York: Oxford University Press, 1971).
85. Diary of Gouverneur Morris, April 24, 1802, Library of Congress.
86. Bayard also informed Alexander Hamilton of Marshall's views. According to Bayard, "Upon the subject of the Judiciary, I have had an opportunity of learning the opinions of the Chief Justice. He considers the late repealing Act operative in depriving the Judges of all power derived under the Act repealed." April 25, 1802, 25 *Hamilton Papers* 613–614.
87. Diary of Gouverneur Morris, April 24, 1802, Library of Congress.
88. *Ibid.* Quoted in Borden, *Bayard* 125.
89. Marshall to Paterson, April 19, 1802, 6 *Marshall Papers* 108–109.
90. See Chase to Marshall, April 24, 1802, *ibid.* 109–116; Marshall to Paterson, May 3, 1802, *ibid.* 117–118; Paterson to Marshall, June 11, 1802, *ibid.* 120–121; Paterson to Marshall, June 18, 1802, *ibid.* 121.
91. Marshall to Paterson, April 19, 1802, *ibid.* 108–109.
92. Marshall to Paterson, May 3, 1802, citing Justice Washington's earlier reply, *ibid.* 117–118.
93. Cushing's reply is quoted in Paterson to Marshall, 1802, *ibid.* 120–121.
94. Quoted in Hannah Cushing to Abigail Adams, June 25, 1802. See *ibid.* 118, note 6. No reply from Justice Moore has been found, but Marshall referred to him in a letter to Paterson on May 3, and it is assumed that he agreed with the majority. *Ibid.*
95. Chase to Marshall, April 24, 1802, *ibid.* 109–116. Chase's lengthy reply provided abundant ammunition should Marshall have wanted to resist riding circuit, but it is clear that he did not.
96. *Ibid.* 117.
97. Warren, 1 *Supreme Court* 271.
98. Malone, *Jefferson the President* 133–135.
99. Marshall to King, May 5, 1802, 6 *Marshall Papers* 119–120.
100. Marshall to Pinckney, November 21, 1802, *ibid.* 124–126.

13: *Marbury v. Madison*

The headnote quotation is from Marshall's decision in *Marbury v. Madison*, 1 Cranch 137, 178 (1803).

1. 2 *United States Statutes at Large* 157–158.
2. The United States circuit court for the district of Virginia convened on May 22 and November 22 each year for terms that ran two to three weeks. Over the next thirty-three years, five different district judges served with Marshall: Cyrus Griffin (1802–1810), John Tyler (1811–1812), St. George Tucker (1813–1824), George Hay (1825–1829), and Philip Barbour (1830–1835).

    The circuit court for the North Carolina district also convened twice annually, either before or after the Virginia circuit, usually for a term of two to three days and never for more than six. Sitting with Marshall for his entire thirty-three years on the Raleigh bench was U.S. District Judge Henry Potter, who survived the chief justice by many years.

Most of Marshall's decisions on circuit were given orally and were not reported. A collection of eighty-eight of Marshall's written opinions, involving "cases of real difficulty," was published in 1837 by John W. Brockenbrough based on rough notes made by Marshall. *Reports of Cases Decided by the Honorable John Marshall . . . in the Circuit Court of the United States for the District of Virginia and North Carolina,* 2 vols. (Philadelphia: James Kay, 1837).

3. In this context, see especially Richard E. Ellis, *The Jeffersonian Crisis: Courts and Politics in the Young Republic* 57–68 (New York: Oxford University Press, 1971).

4. The centerpiece of this campaign was a widely reprinted pamphlet by one of the "midnight judges" entitled *The Solemn Protest of the Honorable Judge Bassett.* Richard Bassett of Maryland, who was James Bayard's father-in-law, claimed to be speaking for all of the midnight judges, and insisted on pursuing the issue despite the fact that Bayard had explicitly written to him stating that Marshall believed the repeal to be constitutional. See Chapter 12.

5. George Cabot to Oliver Wolcott, October 21 and December 20, 1802, *Life and Letters of George Cabot* 327–329, Henry Cabot Lodge, ed. (Boston: Little, Brown, 1878); Linda K. Kerber, "Oliver Wolcott: Midnight Judge," 32 *Connecticut Historical Society Bulletin* 25–30 (1967).

6. For Jefferson's views, see Dumas Malone, *Jefferson the President: The First Term* 143 (Boston: Little, Brown, 1970).

7. Ellis, *Jeffersonian Crisis* 62–63; *National Intelligencer* (Washington, D.C.), October 4, November 1, December 17, 1802; *Independent Chronicle* (Boston), October 7, 1802.

8. *Ibid.,* October 11, 21, 28, 1802; Levi Lincoln to Jefferson, October 29, 1802.

9. *Joseph Reed v. Joseph Prudden,* cited in Charles Warren, 1 *The Supreme Court in United States History* 272, note (Boston: Little, Brown, 1926).

10. There is no published record of Marshall's circuit court decision, although the details are reported in the headnotes of the Supreme Court case, *Stuart v. Laird,* 1 Cranch 298, 301–302 (1803). The quotation from Lee appears at p. 306.

11. *Ibid.* 302.

12. Jonathon Mason, "Diary of Mason," 2 *Proceedings of the Massachusetts Historical Society* 21, 2nd series (1885–1886).

13. Sallie Ewing Marshall, "Chief-Justice John Marshall," 12 *Magazine of American History* 69 (1884).

14. Marshall to Polly, January 2, 1803, 6 *The Papers of John Marshall* 145–146 (Chapel Hill: University of North Carolina Press, 1990).

15. In addition to the cases reported by Brockenbrough, eighteen cases from the federal circuit are contained in John Haywood's *Cases Adjudged in the Superior Courts of North Carolina* (Raleigh, N.C.: Turner and Hughes, 1843).

16. 2 Cranch 272 (1804).

17. *Ogden v. Blackledge* was a test case involving claims of British creditors that antedated the Revolutionary War. The issue involved the application of a North Carolina statute of limitations (seven years). The statute conflicted with Article 4 of the Treaty of Paris, which stipulated that creditors should meet with "no lawful impediment" to the recovery of debts contracted before the war. The result of the decision was the upholding of the treaty and its related implementing legislation over the state's statute of limitations. 2 Cranch 272, 279.

18. *Raleigh Register,* January 4, 1803.

19. *Minerva* (Raleigh), January 4, 1803.

20. *Ibid.*

21. 11 *Annals of Congress* 30–31, 427–442. For an insightful discussion of the judges' strategy, see George L. Haskins and Herbert A. Johnson, *Foundations of Power: John Marshall 1801–15* 177–180, in The Oliver Wendell Holmes Devise, 2 *History of the Supreme Court of the United States* (New York: Macmillan, 1981).

22. *Aurora* (Philadelphia), February 2, 1803, printing a dispatch "From Washington," January 27, 1803.

23. 11 *Annals of Congress* 434–436.

24. *Ibid.* 438.

25. *Ibid.*

26. *Ibid.* 440.

27. *Ibid.* 70.

28. *Ibid.* 67.

29. *Ibid.* 74.

30. *Ibid.* 68.

31. *Ibid.* 78. Theodore Foster of Rhode Island, a nominal Federalist elected on a Law and Order ticket, voted with the Republicans, thus avoiding a tie vote.

32. William Harper appears to have dropped out of the proceedings. He did not present the December 1801 court order to Madison to show cause why his commission should not be delivered, nor did he join in the effort to obtain a copy of the Senate's journal.

33. 11 *Annals of Congress* 32–34.

34. In the late eighteenth and early nineteenth centuries, the Senate acted on all appointments in executive session, and the records of those sessions were not published.

35. 11 *Annals of Congress* 35–36.

36. *Ibid.* 40.

37. *Ibid.* 37.

38. *Ibid.* 48.

39. *Ibid.* 50. Once again Theodore Foster voted with the Republicans.

40. *Aurora*, February 4, 1803. Emphasis in original.

41. 1 Cranch 137 (1803).

42. According to the statute, "The Supreme court . . . shall have power to issue . . . writs of *mandamus*, in cases warranted by the principles and usages of law, to any courts appointed, or persons holding office, under the authority of the United States."

43. *Minutes of the Supreme Court of the United States*, February 10, 1803. Hereinafter cited as USSC *Minutes*.

44. On March 18, 1801, Marshall had replied to an inquiry from his brother James that he had "not sent out the commissions because I apprehended such as were for a fixed time [the justice of the peace commissions were for five years] to be completed when signed and sealed, and such as depended on the will of the President which might at any time be revoked. To withhold the commission of the Marshal is equal to displacing him, which the president I presume has the power to do, but to withhold the commissions of the Justices is an act of which I entertained no suspicion." 6 *Marshall Papers* 90.

    Given Marshall's direct involvement in the case, it is reasonable to ask why he did not recuse himself. An answer often suggested is that since Justice Cushing was absent during the February 1803 term, and since Alfred Moore did not arrive in Washington until February 18 and thus missed hearing argument in the case, the Court would not have had quorum (four justices) if Marshall had not taken part. That answer may be correct. On the other hand, the inability to make quorum would have been an excellent excuse if the Court had wanted to avoid the hot potato that *Marbury v. Madison* had become. A more plausible explanation is that Marshall recognized that the Court was in an exceedingly complex and difficult situation, and trusted himself to find a way of resolving it.

45. 1 Cranch 137, 142.

46. *Aurora*, February 15, 1803. The report of the proceedings in the *Aurora* is much fuller than that in Cranch's Report, which appears to have been taken verbatim from the *National Intelligencer*, March 18, 1803.

47. *Ibid.* The commissions were never located, and to this day it is not known what happened to them.

48. *Ibid.*

49. 1 Cranch 137, 144.

50. *Aurora*, February 15, 1803.

51. 1 Cranch 137, 145.

52. *Ibid.*

53. *Ibid.* 146. The Court record indicates that "on a subsequent day, and before the Court had

given an opinion," Lee introduced an affidavit from Hazen Kimball, a former clerk in the office of the secretary of state, attesting the existence of justice of the peace commissions made out to James Marbury and Robert Hooe. *Ibid.* 153.

54. *National Intelligencer*, February 14, 1803; Warren, 1 *Supreme Court* 239.

55. USSC *Minutes*, February 15, 1801.

56. February 14, 16, 25, 1803, 11 *Annals of Congress* 95–96.

57. All of the quotations from Marshall's decision in *Marbury v. Madison* are from 1 Cranch 137, 153–180.

58. Marshall's precedents have not gone unchallenged. See especially Susan Law Bloch and Maeva Marcus, "John Marshall's Selective Use of History in *Marbury v. Madison,*" *Wisconsin Law Review* 301–337 (1986).

59. Pursuant to the act of 1789 "for the safe-keeping of the Acts, Records, and Seal of the United States," the secretary of state was to be paid ten cents a sheet for "making out and authenticating copies of records." 1 *United States Statutes at Large* 68–69.

60. Much of the confusion on these points is attributable to the Supreme Court itself, which, in recent years, has asserted constitutional supremacy, citing Marshall's decision in *Marbury v. Madison* as the authority. For example, in the 1958 case of *Cooper v. Aaron*, a unanimous Court, in a unique opinion signed by all nine justices, quoted Marshall's statement that the Constitution was "the fundamental and paramount law of the nation." It went on to say, speaking of *Marbury v. Madison*, that "This decision declared the basic principle that the federal judiciary is supreme in the exposition of the law of the Constitution, and that principle has ever been respected by the Court and the Country as a permanent and indispensable feature of our constitutional system." 358 U.S. 1, 18 (1958). Marshall certainly said that the Constitution was the fundamental and paramount law, but the latter reference is a carefully worded embellishment.

In *Baker v. Carr*, 369 U.S. 186, 211 (1962), Justice Brennan, speaking for the Court, referred to the Supreme Court "as ultimate interpreter of the Constitution." That allusion was cited by Chief Justice Berger, speaking for another unanimous Court in *United States v. Nixon*, and linked by Berger with Marshall's statement in *Marbury* that "It is emphatically the province and duty of the judicial department to say what the law is," thus invoking Marshall on the side of judicial supremacy. 418 U.S. 683, 703–705 (1974).

Justice Stevens, speaking for the Court in *Thompson v. Oklahoma*, 487 U.S. 815, 833, note 40 (1988), cited Marshall to the same effect. "That the task of interpreting the great, sweeping clauses of the Constitution ultimately falls to us has been for some time an accepted principle of American jurisprudence." See *Marbury v. Madison*, 1 Cranch 137, 177 (1803).

In fact, the valid precedent for judicial supremacy in constitutional matters is not Marshall but Chief Justice Roger Brooke Taney in *Scott v. Sandford*, 19 Howard 393 (1857), but it is understandable that the Court would prefer not to cite the Dred Scott case when conventional wisdom attributes the same holding to Marshall in *Marbury v. Madison*.

61. 1 Cranch 299, 308 (1803). Marshall, having tried the case on circuit, recused himself, and Justice Cushing was absent. That left Paterson as the senior justice on the bench, and it was in that capacity that he delivered the opinion of the Court.

62. *Ibid.* 309.

63. For a comprehensive survey of Republican and Federalist reaction to the holding in *Marbury v. Madison*, see Warren, 1 *Supreme Court* 243–268.

64. Even such adamant defenders of popular sovereignty as Patrick Henry, Samuel Adams, and Elbridge Gerry acknowledged the authority of the Supreme Court to declare acts of Congress unconstitutional. Despite his vigorous opposition to the Constitution, Henry told the Virginia ratification convention, "I take it as the highest encomium on this country that the acts of the Legislature, if unconstitutional, are liable to be opposed by the Judiciary. . . . The Judiciary are the sole protection against a tyrannical execution of the laws." Adams told the Massachusetts ratification convention that any law made by the federal government inconsistent with the Constitution "will be an error and adjudged by Courts of law to be void." Gerry, also addressing the Massachusetts convention, said that the judiciary "will have a sufficient check against encroachments in their own department by their exposition

of the laws, which involve a power of deciding on their constitutionality." *The Debates in the Several State Conventions on the Adoption of the Federal Constitution* II, 131; III, 324, 537; V, 151, Jonathan Elliot, ed. (Philadelphia: J. B. Lippincott Co., 1907).

65. At the time the Constitution was adopted, Jefferson shared the general view that the judiciary provided a valuable safeguard against legislative or executive tyranny. Writing to Madison on March 15, 1789, he said that an important argument for the addition of a Bill of Rights to the Constitution was that it put a "legal check" into the hands of the judiciary. 14 *The Papers of Thomas Jefferson* 659, Julian G. Boyd, ed. (Princeton, N.J.: Princeton University Press, 1958).

Jefferson expressed a similar view in 1798 to Archibald H. Rowan. "The laws of the land, administered by upright Judges, would protect you from any exercise of power unauthorized by the Constitution of the United States." September 25, 1798, 8 *The Works of Thomas Jefferson* 217, Paul Leicester Ford, ed. (New York: G. P. Putnam's Sons, 1907).

In 1804, in a well-known letter to Abigail Adams, Jefferson once again referred to the authority of the Supreme Court to declare acts of Congress unconstitutional in cases before it and asserted the right of the president and Congress to interpret the Constitution within their spheres of action. "The instrument meant that its co-ordinate branches should be checks on each other." September 11, 1804, 10 *ibid.* 88.

The question of whether Jefferson's position on judicial review had changed by the time he became president is argued pro and con by Wallace Mendelson and Samuel Krislov. See Mendelson in 10 *Journal of Public Law* 113–124 (1961) and 29 *University of Chicago Law Review* 327–337 (1962). Edward S. Corwin, after the most exhaustive examination of Jefferson's writing, noted that "I cannot find that Jefferson ever actually denied the right of the Supreme Court to judge the validity of Acts of Congress." "The Supreme Court and Unconstitutional Acts of Congress," 4 *Michigan Law Review* 629 (1906).

Not until 1807 did Jefferson go on record opposing the decision in *Marbury v. Madison*, and then, in a letter to George Hay, the United States Attorney prosecuting Aaron Burr, his concern was with Marshall's comments about Marbury's right to his commission, not with the exercise of judicial review. Jefferson to Hay, June 2, 1807, 10 *Works of Jefferson* 396. Jefferson's sharpest comments were made a year before his death, when he complained to Justice William Johnson about the judiciary in general. But even then his anger was directed at what he considered Marshall's *obiter dictum* pertaining to Marbury's commission. Jefferson to Johnson, June 12, 1823, 4 *Memoirs, Correspondence, and Private Papers of Thomas Jefferson* 377–382, Thomas Jefferson Randolph, ed. (London: Colburn and Beatty, 1829).

66. Inexplicably, Albert J. Beveridge writes that Marshall's opinion "received scant notice at the time of its delivery. The newspapers had little to say about it." 3 *The Life of John Marshall* 153 (Boston: Houghton Mifflin, 1916). Charles Warren, after reprinting an extensive collection of press commentary from 1803, observes that "[Beveridge's] statement as to newspapers does not appear to be supported by the facts." 1 *Supreme Court* 245–256, note 2.

67. *National Intelligencer*, March 18, 21, 24, 1803.

68. *New York Spectator*, March 30, April 2, 1803.

69. *Aurora*, March 23, 26, 1803.

70. *Washington Federalist*, March 17–22, 1803.

71. *Ibid.*, March 11, 1803.

72. *Aurora*, April 26, 1803.

73. 3 *Journal of the Council of State of Virginia* 221–222, Wilmer L. Hall, ed. (Richmond, Va.: Virginia State Library, 1952).

74. Acts of October 1787, *Journal of the House of Delegates of the Commonwealth of Virginia* 141 (January 8, 1788); William Waller Hening, 12 *The Statutes at Large: Being a Collection of All of the Laws of Virginia* 507 (Richmond, Va.: Samuel Pleasants, 1809–1823).

75. "If [Congress] was to make a law not warranted by the powers enumerated," said Marshall, "it would be considered by the judges as an infringement of the Constitution which they are to guard. They would not consider such a law as coming under their jurisdiction. They would declare it void." Elliot, 3 *Debates* 553.

76. *Ogden v. Blackledge*, in Haywood, 2 *Cases Adjudged in the Superior Courts of North Carolina* 227–229. Reprinted in 6 *Marshall Papers* 147–149.

14: The Center Holds

1. The Supreme Court was in session from February 7 to March 2, 1803. During those three weeks, it decided nineteen cases and listened to arguments in four more, which were carried over to the 1804 term. Marshall delivered the opinion in ten cases: *Marbury v. Madison*, 1 Cranch 137; *Clark v. Young*, 1 Cranch 181; *Wilson v. Lenox and Maitland*, 1 Cranch 194; *Hooe & Co. v. Groveman*, 1 Cranch 214; *Wood v. Owings and Smith*, 1 Cranch 239; *Thompson v. Jameson*, 1 Cranch 282; *Mandeville and Jameson v. Joseph Riddle Co.*, 1 Cranch 290; *Hamilton v. Russell*, 1 Cranch 309; *Hepburn and Dundas v. Auld*, 1 Cranch 321; and *Hodgson v. Dexter*, 1 Cranch 345. Justice Paterson delivered the opinion in *Stuart v. Laird* (1 Cranch 299), four cases were decided *per curiam*, and four were dismissed after argument without judgment being rendered. With the exceptions of *Marbury v. Madison* and *Stuart v. Laird*, none of the cases before the Court involved constitutional issues, and over half were minor civil actions in the District of Columbia.

    What is noteworthy is that it was the same group of attorneys who appeared in all of these cases, often in pairs, and in a kaleidoscopic mix, changing partners as their clients changed. Charles Lee appeared in ten cases, Thomas Swann in eight, Edmund J. Lee in seven, John T. Mason in six, Charles Simms in six, Luther Martin and Philip Barton Key in two each, and Levi Lincoln and Robert Goodloe Harper in one each. For brief biographical sketches, see Charles Warren, *A History of the American Bar* 256–263 (Boston: Little, Brown, 1911).

2. Dumas Malone, *Jefferson the President: The First Term* 418–484 (Boston: Little, Brown, 1970). Jefferson's opinion was shared by Madison, Levi Lincoln, and treasury secretary Albert Gallatin. Madison's moderate views made him continuously suspect among the radical Republicans. Levi Lincoln's role in *Marbury v. Madison* has already been described. Gallatin's views are best stated in a letter he wrote to Jefferson. "It is important for the permanent establishment of those Republican principles for which we have successfully contended, that they should rest on the broad basis of the people, and not a fluctuating majority, that it could be better to displease many of our political friends than to give an opportunity to the irreconcilable enemies of a free government of including the mass of the federal citizens to make a common cause with them." August 10, 1801, 1 *The Writings of Albert Gallatin* 33, Henry Adams, ed. (Philadelphia: J. B. Lippincott, 1879). See generally, Richard E. Ellis, *The Jeffersonian Crisis: Courts and Politics in the Young Republic* 69–107, 233–237 (New York: Oxford University Press, 1971).

3. Giles to Jefferson, March 16, June 1, 1801, Jefferson Papers, Library of Congress. Also see 11 *Annals of Congress* 596.

4. John Quincy Adams, then a United States Senator, reports a conversation that took place before the fireplace off the Senate chamber in which Giles "treated with the utmost contempt the idea of an *independent* judiciary [and] said there was not one word about such independence in the Constitution." 1 *The Memories of John Quincy Adams* 322, Charles Francis Adams, ed. (Philadelphia: J. B. Lippincott, 1874). J. Q. Adams's emphasis.

5. 6 *The Papers of John Marshall* 187 (Chapel Hill: University of North Carolina Press, 1990).

6. Chase to John F. Mercer, March 6, 1803, "Letters of Some Members of the Old Congress," J.C. Willie, ed., 29 *Pennsylvania Magazine of History and Biography* 205–206 (1905). Chase's emphasis.

7. Last Will and Testament, July 9, 1799, 37 *The Writings of George Washington* 284 John C. Fitzpatrick, ed. (Washington, D.C.: Government Printing Office, 1904).

8. Bushrod Washington to Lear, June 13, 1800, cited in 6 *Marshall Papers* 226, note 2. Also see Lawrence B. Custer, "Bushrod Washington and John Marshall: A Preliminary Inquiry," 4 *American Journal of Legal History* 48 (1960).

9. Bushrod Washington to Caleb P. Wayne, September 8, 1800, Dreer Collection, Pennsylvania Historical Society.

10. Wayne to Marshall, October 3, 1800, 4 *Marshall Papers* 314.

11. Lear to Marshall, December 12, 1800, 6 *ibid.* 34–40. The bulk of Washington's papers were shipped by Bushrod to Marshall in Richmond some time in July 1801. See Bushrod Washington to Hamilton, November 21, 1801, 25 *The Papers of Alexander Hamilton* 432–433, Harold C. Syrett, ed. (New York: Columbia University Press, 1979).

12. John Marshall, *The Life of George Washington* 5 vols. (Philadelphia: C.P. Wayne, 1805–1807).
13. Compare Marshall's secular tone with David Ramsay, *The History of the American Revolution*, 2 vols. (Dublin: William Jones, 1793), and Mercy Otis Warren, *History of the Rise, Progress and Termination of the American Revolution*, 3 vols. (Boston: Larkin, 1805).
14. Marshall to Monroe, January 3, 1784, 1 *Marshall Papers* 113.
15. Marshall to Wayne, September 3, 1804, 6 *ibid.* 328.
16. The best summary of the commercial arrangements concerning Marshall's *Life of Washington* is contained in the editorial note in 6 *Marshall Papers* 219–230.
17. Bushrod Washington to Wayne, December 22, 1803; Marshall to Wayne, December 23, 1803; Wayne to Marshall, December 31, 1803; Marshall to Wayne, January 10, 1804, *ibid.* 237–240, 239, note 3, 244, 250–252.
18. Wayne to Marshall, February 17, 1803, quoted in Albert J. Beveridge, 3 *The Life of John Marshall* 230 (Boston: Houghton Mifflin, 1916). This letter does not appear in the *Marshall Papers*. It is part of the Dreer Collection of the Pennsylvania Historical Society.
19. Mason Locke Weems, or "Parson Weems," as he is generally known, was an American original. Born in Maryland in 1759 into a family of nineteen children, he studied medicine, entered the Episcopal church, and served briefly as rector at Pohick Church in Mount Vernon Parish, Virginia. The ministry offered little remuneration, and Weems became a traveling book salesman, perhaps the most successful in American history. He went on horseback wherever it seemed possible to sell a book or a Bible, carrying his samples in his saddlebags. He was a natural orator, a born entertainer, and an expert violinist, all of which talents he employed in his book-selling activities.

    Dissatisfied with merely selling books, Weems began to write, and biography proved his *métier*. Weems wrote short, anecdotal books that were full of moral examples, some of which were fictitious. His 200-page *Life of Washington* became an instant best-seller and is the source of such myths as Washington cutting down a cherry tree and throwing a silver dollar across the Rappahanock. Misinformation aside, Weems became as successful at writing as he was at selling. In addition to the biography of Washington, his books include *Life of Francis Marion* (1805); *Life of Benjamin Franklin* (1817); *Life of William Penn* (1819); and *Drunkard's Looking Glass*, a best-selling temperance tract.
20. Marshall to Potter, January 10, 1804, 6 *Marshall Papers* 252–253.
21. Bushrod Washington to Wayne, March 23, November 24, 1803, Dreer Collection. Washington's emphasis.
22. Wayne to Bushrod Washington, November 27, 1803, *ibid.*
23. William Raymond Smith, *History as Argument: Three Patriot Historians of the American Revolution* 39 (The Hague: Mouton & Co., 1967).
24. By way of comparison, David Ramsay's *History of the American Revolution*, the first book to deal in any substantial way with the struggle for independence, sold only 1,600 copies over a period of ten years. Rollo G. Silver, *The American Printer, 1787–1825* 98, 173–174 (Charlottesville: University Press of Virginia, 1967).
25. On October 18, 1806, the Marshall syndicate paid £14,000 sterling to General Philip Martin, the brother and heir of Denny Martin Fairfax. William Murdock, a London merchant, acted as the Marshalls' agent. The funds were raised through the sale of various parcels of South Branch Manor, plus Marshall's royalties. For the South Branch sales, see 6 *Marshall Papers* 543–545. In addition to John and James Marshall, the syndicate included John Ambler and Rawleigh Colston. Articles of Agreement, September 6, 1801, *ibid.* 93–94.
26. In 1831 Marshall completed a slightly condensed two-volume edition of *The Life of George Washington* that commenced with Washington's birth and omitted the material pertaining to the settlement of the colonies. The two-volume format was misleading, since the type used was much smaller and there was little white space. "The work was originally composed under circumstances which might afford some apology for its being finished with less care than its importance demanded," said Marshall in the Preface. "The immense mass of papers which it was necessary to read, many of them interesting when written, but no longer so, occupied a great part of that time which the impatience of the public could not allow for the appearance of the book itself. It was therefore hurried to the press without that previous

careful examination, which would have resulted in the correction of some faults that have been perceived. In the hope of presenting the work to the public in a form more worthy of its acceptance, and more satisfactory to himself, that author has given it a careful revision." John Marshall, 1 *The Life of George Washington* iv (Philadelphia: Crissy, 1832).

27. John Marshall, *The Life of George Washington*, American Statesmen Series, Arthur Schlesinger, Jr., general ed. (New York: Chelsea House, 1983).

28. In the preface to the abridged school text, Horace Binney wrote, "It is quite remarkable that the Chief Justice . . . should have given a portion of his busiest days to the preparation of an abridgement, in which he was not required to exercise, to any considerable extent, the powers of his remarkable understanding. The fact must be explained, I think, by his cordial attachment to the men and principles of the Revolution, by his conscientious approval of the measures of General Washington's administration, both as a system of public policy, and as an exposition of the Constitution,—and by his paternal solicitude for the youth of our country, upon whom he desired to impress his own feelings and convictions on all these subjects." John Marshall, *The Life of George Washington, written for the Use of Schools* (Philadelphia: Crissy, 1832).

29. "Lives of Washington," 13 *Edinburgh Review* 150 (October 1808). Also see 17 *Blackwood's Magazine* 179 (1808).

30. Adams to Jefferson, July 13, 1813, 2 *The Adams-Jefferson Letters* 349, Lester J. Cappon, ed. (Chapel Hill: University of North Carolina Press, 1959). Earlier, upon receiving the first three volumes from Marshall, Adams had replied, "*Exegisti monumentum aere perennius.* [You have erected a monument more durable than bronze.] As it is certainly more rational, I hope and believe it will be a more glorious and desirable Memorial to your Hero, than a Mausoleum would have been, of dimensions Superiour to the proudest pyramid of Egypt." Adams to Marshall, February 4, 1806, 6 *Marshall Papers* 425.

31. Jared Sparks journal entry, April 25, 1827, cited in Herbert Baxter Adams, 2 *The Life and Writings of Jared Sparks* 36–37 (Boston: Houghton Mifflin, 1893).

32. Marshall to John Adams, July 6, 1806, 6 *Marshall Papers* 451–452.

33. Madison thought that "the bias of party feeling" was obvious in volume 5 and that Marshall "would write differently at the present day and with his present impressions." Madison was speaking in 1827. Adams, 2 *Life of Sparks* 37.

34. See, in particular, the introduction by Marcus Cunliffe in the 1983 Chelsea House reissue of the *Life of Washington*; also see William Raymond Smith, "The Necessity of Circumstances: John Marshall's Historical Method," 26 *The Historian* 19–35 (1963). Marshall's casual footnote citations and heavy reliance on secondary sources, particularly in volume 1, would not pass muster today, and that has led to criticism by some academic historians. See, for example, William A. Foran, "John Marshall as a Historian," 43 *American Historical Review* 51–64 (1937).

35. Ulysses S. Grant, *Personal Memoirs of U.S. Grant*, 2 vols. (New York: C. L. Webster, 1885).

36. In an era before the publication of official documentary collections, Marshall's *Life of Washington* provided the first access to Washington's correspondence and speeches. The Farewell Address, for example, is reprinted in its entirety, as is Washington's speech to the Continental Congress resigning his commission. In 1827 Jared Sparks, then editor of the *North American Review*, persuaded Marshall and Bushrod to allow him to publish a multivolume set of Washington's papers. Under their arrangement, Sparks received half the royalties and the other half was split by Marshall and Bushrod. In 1837 Sparks paid the heirs of the two justices $15,384.63, and continued to make payments for the next two decades. Sparks subsequently became McLean Professor of History at Harvard and later, president of Harvard (1849–1853). See Daniel J. Boorstin, *The Americans: The National Experience* 346–347 (New York: Random House, 1965).

37. Jared Sparks, *The Life of George Washington*, preface (London: Henry Colburn, 1839).

38. Washington Irving, *Life of George Washington*, 3 vols. (New York: G. P. Putnam, 1855).

39. 26 *North American Review* 38 (1828). Story was reviewing Marshall's *A History of the Colonies Planted by the English on the Continent of North America, From their Settlement, to the Commencement of That War, Which Terminated in Their Independence*, (Philadelphia: Abraham Small, 1824).

40. Charles A. Beard, *An Economic Interpretation of the Constitution of the United States* 296–299 (New York: Macmillan, 1914).
41. Charles A. Beard, *Economic Origins of Jeffersonian Democracy* 237 (New York: Macmillan, 1915). In contrast to Beard, Albert J. Beveridge, writing one year later, is surprisingly snide about Marshall's abilities as a biographer. Exactly why is unclear, but it is apparent that Beveridge chose not to examine the *Life of Washington* for any insight into Marshall's thought. Beveridge, 3 *Life of Marshall* 223–273.
42. Stanley Elkins and Eric McKitrick, *The Age of Federalism* (New York: Oxford University Press, 1993). In this context, see particularly Elkins and McKittrick, "The Founding Fathers: Young Men of the Revolution," 76 *Political Science Quarterly* 181 (1961).
43. Professor Robert Kenneth Faulkner, the most acute analyst of Marshall's thought, may have been the first to recognize the importance of *The Life of Washington* as a key to Marshall's jurisprudence. "It reveals Marshall's considered judgment on the Constitution's origins, the conditions it was to face, and its practical working during the first crucial decade." *The Jurisprudence of John Marshall* xviii–xix (Princeton, N.J.: Princeton University Press, 1968).
44. 4 Wheaton 316 (1819).
45. 6 Cranch 87 (1810).
46. 9 Wheaton 1 (1824).
47. *Dartmouth College v. Woodward*, 4 Wheaton 518 (1819).
48. I am indebted to Professor Faulkner for calling this passage to my attention. *Jurisprudence of John Marshall* 116–117.
49. Marshall, 5 *Life of Washington* 378 (1807). The quoted paragraph is from Marshall's summation of Washington. It is preceded by the following, which is equally emblematic of Marshall's thought:

> Respecting, as the first magistrate in a free government must ever do, the real and deliberate sentiments of the people, their gusts of passion passed over, without ruffling the smooth surface of his mind. Trusting to the reflecting good sense of the nation for approbation and support, he had the magnanimity to pursue its real interests, in opposition to its temporary prejudices; and, though far from being regardless of popular favour, he could never stoop to retain, by deserving to lose it. In more instances than one, we find him committing his whole popularity to hazard, and pursuing steadily, in opposition to a torrent which would have overwhelmed a man of ordinary firmness, that cause which had been dictated by a sense of duty.

Ibid. 377–378.
50. Jefferson to Barlow, May 3, 1802, 9 *The Works of Thomas Jefferson* 372, Paul Leicester Ford, ed. (New York: G. P. Putnam's Sons, 1904).
51. Napoleon's precipitous decision to dispose of Louisiana was ancillary to his decision to renounce the 1801 Peace of Amiens with Great Britain and resume hostilities. On April 11, 1803, France severed diplomatic relations with Britain, and that same day Talleyrand advised Robert Livingston, the resident American minister, that Napoleon wanted to sell the whole of Louisiana immediately. After some brief haggling over price, the treaty of cession was signed on April 30.
    For Napoleon, it was a matter of concentrating his forces for the coming war with England. He and Talleyrand had initially sought Louisiana from Spain to anchor a new French empire in North America. However, the failure of the French army to defeat Toussaint L'Ouverture's black republic in Santo Domingo (50,000 French troops perished from the combination of war and yellow fever) left the overseas empire stillborn and Louisiana became superfluous. See, in particular, E. Wilson Lyon, *Louisiana in French Diplomacy, 1795–1804* (Norman: University of Oklahoma Press, 1934).
52. Jefferson to Breckinridge, August 12, 1803; Jefferson to Madison, August 25, 1803; and Jefferson to Wilson Cary Nicholas, September 7, 1803, 10 *Works of Jefferson* 407–411, 412–415, 417–420.
53. The October 20, 1803 Senate vote was 24–7, Jonathan Dayton of New Jersey voting with the Republicans. 1 *Journal of Executive Proceedings of the United States Senate* 449–451 (Washing-

ton, D.C.: United States Government Publication Office, 1828). Also see, Senator William Plumer to Jeremiah Smith, February 7, 1805, in Andrew Preston Peabody, *Life of William Plumer* 328 (Boston: Phillips, Samson, 1857).

54. *American Insurance Co. v. Canter*, 1 Peters 511 (1828). The case involved the 1819 treaty with Spain by which the United States acquired Florida, but the issue was the same as that in the Louisiana purchase.

55. *Ibid*. 540.

56. For Jefferson's reasoning, see Malone, *Jefferson the President* 303–310.

57. When pressed about West Florida by Robert Livingston, the U.S. minister in Paris, Talleyrand said, "I can give you no direction. You have made a noble bargain for yourselves, and I suppose you will make the most of it." *Ibid*. 306.

58. *Foster v. Neilson*, 2 Peters 253 (1829). Emphasis added.

59. For Marshall's decisions in *Owen v. Adams* (December 7, 1803) and *Blane v. Drummond* (December 9, 1803), see 6 *Marshall Papers* 206–219.

60. The circuit court's written decisions in five minor cases are reprinted with explanatory notes in *ibid*. 245–249.

61. Marshall to Potter, January 10, 1804, *ibid*. 252–253.

62. "*Resolved*, That a committee be appointed to inquire into the official conduct of Samuel Chase, one of the Associate Justices of the Supreme Court of the United States, and to report their opinion whether the said Samuel Chase hath so acted in his judicial capacity as to require the interposition of the Constitutional power of this House." January 5, 1804, 13 *Annals of Congress* 806.

63. Randolph was especially critical of Jefferson for surrounding himself with men "whose Republicanism has not been the most unequivocal"—a reference to Madison, Gallatin, and Levi Lincoln. Randolph to Joseph H. Nicholson, January 1, 1801, Nicholson Papers, Library of Congress.

64. Representative Samuel Taggart to the Reverend John Taylor, January 13, 1804, "Letters of Samuel Taggart," cited in Richard E. Ellis, *The Jeffersonian Crisis* 304 (New York: Oxford University Press, 1971).

65. Senator William Plumer, who dined with Jefferson that evening, reports that the president was surprised to hear what Randolph had done, inquired what the grounds were for impeaching Chase, and then, speaking in a disgruntled tone, dismissed the subject, saying "This business of removing Judges by impeachment is a bungling way." William Plumber Memorandum, February 3, 1804, William Plumer Papers, Library of Congress. Also see Malone, *Jefferson the President* 468–469; Richard Ellis, "The Impeachment of Samuel Chase," in *American Political Trials* 65, Michael R. Belknap, ed. (Westport, Conn.: Greenwood Press, 1981).

66. January 8, 1804, 13 *Annals of Congress* 875.

67. Chase's letter was dated January 13, 1804. It has been lost, but its contents can be inferred from Marshall's reply of January 23, 1804. 6 *Marshall Papers* 347–348.

68. Marshall to Chase, January 23, 1804, *ibid*.

69. *Ibid*. Marshall concluded with a rare biblical allusion: "the little finger of democracy [crossed out] is heavier than the loss of _____," a paraphrase of Chronicles 10:10, "My little finger shall be thicker than my father's loins." (Also see 1 Kings 12:10.)

70. 2 Cranch 64 (1804).

71. "I hold the right of expatriation to be inherent in every man by the laws of nature," Jefferson wrote to Albert Gallatin. "[It is] incapable of being rightfully taken away from him even by the united will of every other person in the nation." June 26, 1806, 10 *Works of Jefferson* 273. For the basic Republican position, see George Hay, *A Treatise on Expatriation* (Washington, D.C.: A & G Way, 1814). For the Federalist rejoinder, see John Lowell, *Review of "A Treatise on Expatriation" by a Massachusetts Lawyer* (Boston: Russell Cutler, 1814).

72. For the official battle report of the *Constellation*, see 2 *Naval Documents Related to the Quasi-War Between the United States and France* 326–327 (Washington, D.C.: Government Printing Office, 1938). . . . 103–110 (New York: A. S. Barnes & Co., 1968). Like the *Constitution*, the *Constellation* remains afloat as a monument to the early American navy and is anchored in Baltimore's inner harbor.

73. 2 Cranch 64, 118. Note Marshall's words, "as understood in this country." That is the traditional formulation that permits each nation to interpret its own obligations under international law.

74. *Ibid.* 120. Marshall's emphasis.

75. *Ibid.* 120–121. Marshall's emphasis.

76. *Ibid.* 124. According to Marshall, "a public officer entrusted on the high seas to perform a duty deemed necessary by his country, and executing according to the best of his judgment the orders he has received, if he is a victim of any mistake he commits, ought certainly never to be assessed with vindictive or speculative damages."

77. 2 Cranch 170 (1804).

78. *Ibid.* 179.

79. *Youngstown Sheet & Tube v. Sawyer*, 343 US. 579, 660–662 (1952).

80. After failing in the Supreme Court to avoid liability for their actions, Captains Murray and Little sought relief from Congress, which approved special acts by which the United States understood to pay the judgments against them. 14 *Annals of Congress* 985, 994, 1005; 15 *ibid.* 230–231, 260–261. Also see *Report from the Committee of Claims* . . . (December 10, 1804) s. #9599 in *American Bibliography: A Preliminary Checklist for 1805*, Ralph R. Shaw and Richard H. Shoemaker, eds. (New York: The Scarecrow Press, 1958).

81. Plumer to Dr. John Parton, February 14, 1804, Plumer Papers, Massachusetts Historical Society. Justice Moore died in Bladen county, North Carolina, October 15, 1810.

82. From 1796 until 1824, the Republican party nominated its candidates for president and vice president by congressional caucus. On February 25, 1804, 108 of the party's senators and representatives met and unanimously renominated Jefferson. Aaron Burr was dropped as vice president, replaced by Governor George Clinton of New York, who defeated John Breckinridge of Kentucky for the nomination, 67–20. The Federalists, whose organizational structure was looser, informally chose Charles Cotesworth Pinckney for president and Rufus King for vice president.

83. Gallatin to Jefferson, February 15, 1804, 1 *Writings of Gallatin* 178.

84. Johnson was thirty-two years and three months of age when he was named by Jefferson. Joseph Story, who was appointed by Madison in 1811, was thirty-two years and two months old.

85. Plumer to Jeremiah Smith, March 23, 1804, Plumer Papers, Massachusetts Historical Society.

86. *Ibid.*

87. Story to Samuel P.P. Fay, February 25, 1808, 1 *Life and Letters of Joseph Story*, 168, W. W. Story, ed. (Boston: Little, Brown, 1851). On Johnson generally, see Donald G. Morgan, *Justice William Johnson: The First Dissenter* (Columbia: University of South Carolina Press, 1954).

88. Deposition of Jonathan Snowden to the Committee to enquire into the Official Conduct of Samuel Chase, reprinted in the *National Intelligencer* (Washington, D.C.) March 14, 1804. The reference was apparently to Callender's published attacks on Jefferson in the Richmond *Recorder* in 1802. Among other things, Callender accused Jefferson of having an extended affair with the slave "Dusky Sally" [Sally Hemings] and of attempting to seduce the wife of his friend John Walker. Richmond *Recorder*, September 1, 15, 22, 29, 1802 (Hemings); October 13, 27, and November 17, 1802 (Walker).

89. Deposition of John Marshall, March 2, 1804, 6 *Marshall Papers* 269.

90. In addition to *Murray v. Schooner Charming Betsy* and *Little v. Barreme*, Marshall delivered the opinion of the court in *Faw v. Marsteller*, 2 Cranch 10; *Pennington v. Coxe*, 2 Cranch 33; *Head & Amory v. Providence Insurance Co.*, 2 Cranch 127; *Dunlop & Co. v. Ball*, 2 Cranch 180; *Church v. Hubbart*, 2 Cranch 187; and *Mason v. Ship Blaireau*, 2 Cranch 240. Because he had tried the case on circuit, Marshall recused himself in *Ogden v. Blackledge*, and the decision was delivered by Cushing, the senior justice present. 2 Cranch 272.

91. *Head & Amory v. Providence Insurance Co.*, 2 Cranch 127, and *Church v. Hubbart*, 2 Cranch 187.

92. February 17, 1804, 1 *Memoirs of J. Q. Adams* 295.

93. U.S. Congress, Senate 1 *Trial of Samuel Chase, Associate Justice of the Supreme Court of the United States, Impeached by the House of Representatives for Higher Crimes and Misdemeanors* 1–4 (Washington, D.C.: Samuel H. Smith, 1805).

94. On May 2, 1803, Chase was presiding over the circuit court in Baltimore and, with Marshall's restraining influence removed, launched into another tirade against Republican rule, viciously criticizing not only the national government but the state government of Maryland and the Supreme Court itself for the decision in *Stuart v. Laird*. "The bulk of mankind are governed by their passions, and not by reason," said Chase. "The late alteration of the federal judiciary by the abolition of the office of the sixteen circuit judges, and the recent change in our state Constitution by the establishing of universal suffrage . . . will in my judgment take away all security for property and personal liberty. The independence of the national judiciary is already shaken to its foundation. . . . Our Republican Constitution will sink into a mobocracy, the worst of all possible governments . . . the modern doctrines by our late reformers, that all men in a state of society are entitled to enjoy equal liberty and equal rights, have brought this mighty mischief upon us." 14 *Annals of Congress* 675–676.
95. Marshall to James Markham Marshall, April 1, 1804, 6 *Marshall Papers* 277–278.
96. Ordinarily, Congress commenced the first week in December. Because of the pending Chase impeachment trial, the second session of the eighth Congress began a month early, on November 5, 1804.
97. U.S. Circuit Court, Va., 4 Order Book 421, 427–429, 432 (1804).
98. 6 *Marshall Papers* 291, note 3.
99. Sentence, *United States v. Logwood*, (C.C.D. Va. 1804), *ibid*. 290–291. Marshall's emphasis.
100. William C. Bruce, 2 *John Randolph of Roanoke* 218 (New York: G. P. Putnam's Sons, 1922).
101. Paul S. Clarkson and R. Samuel Jett, *Luther Martin of Maryland* 213, 306 (Baltimore: Johns Hopkins Press, 1970). In addition to Martin, Chase's defense team included Robert Goodloe Harper (chief counsel), James A. Bayard, Joseph Hopkinson, Philip Barton Key, Charles Lee, and Philip Wickham. All served without pay.
102. After representing Maryland in the landmark case of *McCulloch v. Maryland*, 4 Wheaton 316 (1819), Martin suffered a paralytic stroke from which he never recovered. The Maryland legislature, recognizing his plight, unanimously enacted a truly extraordinary statute requiring every lawyer in the state to contribute $5 annually for Martin's support. Cited in William H. Rehnquist, *Grand Inquests* 25 (New York: William Morrow and Co., 1992).
103. The House approved eight charges against Chase. The first dealt with his conduct at the Fries trial, the next five pertained to his overbearing behavior and procedural errors during the Callender trial, the seventh dealt with his hectoring of a grand jury in Delaware, and the last with his partisan jury charge in Baltimore. U.S. Congress, Senate, 1 *Trial of Samuel Chase* 85.
104. In addition to Randolph, the House managers included Caesar Rodney, Joseph H. Nicholson, George Washington Campbell, Peter Early, John Boyle, and Christopher Clark. 14 *Annals of Congress* 86–92.
105. *Ibid*. 101–151.
106. Entry of February 9, 1803, *William Plumer's Memorandum of Proceedings in the United States Senate, 1803–1807* 280, Everett S. Brown, ed. (New York: Macmillan, 1923).
107. The argument for a latitudinarian interpretation of "high Crimes and Misdemeanors" was vigorously put by Senator William Branch Giles of Virginia. "The power of impeachment was given without limitation to the House of Representatives; and the power of trying impeachments was given equally without limitation to the Senate. . . . A trial and removal of a judge upon impeachment need not imply any criminality or corruption in him . . . nothing more than a declaration of Congress to this effect [is required]: you hold dangerous opinions, and if you are suffered to carry them into effect you will work the destruction of the nation. We want your offices, for the purpose of giving them to men who will fill them better." 1 *Memoirs of J. Q. Adams* 322.
108. Article II, section 4, of the Constitution states that "The President, Vice President, and all civil Officers of the United States, shall be removed from Office on Impeachment for, and Conviction of, Treason, Bribery, or other high Crimes and Misdemeanors." The meaning of "high Crimes and Misdemeanors" is not defined. For the legal and constitutional precedents, see especially Peter Charles Hoffer and N.E.H. Hall, *Impeachment in America, 1635–1805* (New Haven, Conn.: Yale University Press, 1984); Raoul Berger, *Impeachment: The Constitutional Problems* (Cambridge, Mass.: Harvard University Press, 1973). Also see

Richard B. Lillich, "The Chase Impeachment," 4 *American Journal of Legal History* 49–72 (1960); Richard Ellis, "The Impeachment of Samuel Chase."

109. For Marshall's testimony, see 6 *Marshall Papers* 350–357.

110. *Ibid.* 352–353.

111. Beveridge, 3 *Life of Marshall* 192–196.

112. 14 *Annals of Congress* 664–669.

113. 1 *Memoirs of J. Q. Adams* 364. George Clinton of New York, Jefferson's vice president-elect, explained Chase's acquittal thus:

> I will only observe that several of the members who voted for his acquittal had no doubt that the charges against him were substantial and of course that his conduct was unproper and reprehensible, but considering that many parts of it were sanctioned by the practice of the other judges . . . and that the act with which he was charged was not prohibited by any express and positive law they could not consistently with their ideas of justice find him guilty of high crimes and misdemeanors. It was to such refined reasoning of some honest men that he owes his acquittal.

George Clinton to Pierre Van Cortlandt, March 3, 1805, Van Cortlandt Papers, New York Public Library.

114. Ellis, *Jeffersonian Crisis* 103–104. The six Republicans would vote consistently for acquittal: Bradley, Mitchell, Israel Smith, the two John Smiths, and Gaillard are assumed to have been influenced by Madison. See George L. Haskins and Herbert A. Johnson, *Foundations of Power: John Marshall, 1801–15* 244, in 2 *History of the Supreme Court of the United States* (New York: Macmillan, 1981).

115. Plumer to his son, March 3, 1805, *Plumer Memorandum* 325. Chase was sixty-four years old at the time, not seventy.

116. Ellis, *Jeffersonian Crisis* 102.

117. *Ibid.* 102–104.

118. Jeremiah Smith to William Plumer, February 11, 1804, Plumer Papers, Library of Congress; J. Q. Adams to his father, March 8, 1805, 3 *The Writings of John Quincy Adams*, Worthington C. Ford, ed. (New York: Macmillan, 1913).

119. 14 *Annals of Congress* 662. Also see *ibid.* 160, 651–652.

120. For Chase's later years, see Jane Shafer Elsmere, *Justice Samuel Chase* (Muncie, Ind.: Janevar Publishing Co., 1980). Elsmere's biography of Chase, along with Chief Justice Rehnquist's treatment of the trial, provide the best blow-by-blow description of Chase's trial before the Senate. See Rehnquist, *Grand Inquests*.

121. *National Intelligencer*, May 5, 1805. For the text of Chase's charge, see his notebook of original jury charges, Chase Manuscripts, Maryland Historical Society.

122. See especially the argument of Richard Ellis in *Jeffersonian Crisis* 233–249.

15: Treason Defined

1. Of the twenty-three cases decided in 1805, Marshall delivered the opinion of the Court in eighteen, three were decided *per curiam*, and in two cases, *Lambert's Lessee v. Paine*, 3 Cranch 95, and *Marine Insurance Company of Alexandria v. Wilson*, 3 Cranch 187, Marshall recused himself and the opinions were given *seriatim*.

2. 2 Cranch 358 (1805). A second constitutional case, though minor in impact, was *Hepburn and Dundas v. Ellzey*, 2 Cranch 445 (1805), in which the Court, speaking through Marshall, held that the District of Columbia was not a constituent state of the Union. As a result, residents of the district were not entitled to bring suits in federal court under the diversity of citizenship provisions of Article III of the Constitution. Marshall said it was up to Congress to provide a remedy. "It is extraordinary that the courts of the United States, which are open to aliens, and to citizens of every state of the union, should be closed upon *them*. But this is a subject for legislative not for judicial consideration." 2 Cranch 445, 453. Marshall's emphasis. Congress ignored the disparity until 1940, when it finally passed legislation opening the

federal courts to residents of the district. See *National Mutual Insurance Co. v. Tidewater Transfer Co.*, 337 U.S. 582 (1949).

3. 1 *United States Statutes at Large* 512–516, § 5.

4. See Chapter 9.

5. 2 Cranch 358–385.

6. 4 Wheaton 316 (1819).

7. 2 Cranch 396.

8. Alexander Hamilton, "Opinion on the Constitutionality of an Act to Establish a Bank," February 23, 1791, 8 *The Papers of Alexander Hamilton* 97–134, Harold C. Syrett, ed. (New York: Columbia University Press, 1965).

9. John Marshall, 5 *The Life of George Washington* 3–11, note 3 (Philadelphia: C. P. Wayne, 1807). According to Dumas Malone, Marshall's rendition of the memoranda of Hamilton and Jefferson was the first account of these important documents to appear in print. Malone, *Jefferson the President: Second Term* 358 note 35 (Boston: Little, Brown, 1970).

10. Marshall, 4 *Life of Washington* 497.

11. For a representative survey of Marshall's 1805 cases on circuit in Richmond and Raleigh, see 6 *The Papers of John Marshall* 383–402, 407–424 (Chapel Hill: University of North Carolina Press, 1990).

12. When the Ninth Congress convened, Randolph reintroduced his constitutional amendment for the removal of judges, stating that Chase's acquittal had established the principle that "an officer of the United States may act in as corrupt a manner as he pleases, without there being any constitutional provision to call him to account." 15 *Annals of Congress* 446.

13. "That part of the Constitution which relates to the impeachment is a nullity," said Representative John Smilie of Pennsylvania. "I do religiously believe that we cannot convict any man on an impeachment." *Ibid.* 503.

14. *Marine Insurance Company of Alexandria v. Tucker*, 3 Cranch 357; *United States v. Heth*, 3 Cranch 390; and *Randolph v. Ware*, 3 Cranch 503.

15. *Simms and Wise v. Slacum*, 3 Cranch 300, 309–310 (1806).

16. Johnson to Jefferson, December 10, 1822, in Donald G. Morgan, *Justice William Johnson: The First Dissenter* 181–182 (Columbia: University of South Carolina Press, 1954).

17. Marshall to Caleb P. Wayne, June 27, 1806, 6 *Marshall Papers* 448–449.

18. Justice Paterson and Rufus King were awarded Doctor of Law degrees along with Marshall. Minutes, President and Fellows of Harvard College, July 16, 1806; Minutes, Overseers of Harvard College, August 21, 1806; *Columbia Centinel* (Boston), September 6, 1806.

19. His adversary, an obscure Federalist named Jones, angered by Livingston's published barbs, had "caught him by the nose and struck him" while Livingston was strolling innocently on the Battery. Livingston challenged Jones to a duel, which was fought across the Hudson in Hoboken, New Jersey. Gerald T. Dunne, "Brockholst Livingston," in 1 *The Justices of the United States Supreme Court* 396, Leon Friedman and Fred L. Israel, eds. (New York: Chelsea House, 1969). For Livingston's comments on the Court, see Dunne, "The Story-Livingston Correspondence, 1812–1822," 10 *American Journal of Legal History* 224 (1966).

20. See, for example, *Lenox v. Prout*, 3 Wheaton 520 (1818); *Dugan v. United States*, 3 Wheaton 172 (1818); *The Euphrates*, 8 Cranch 385 (1814); *The Struggle*, 9 Cranch 71 (1815); and *The Estrella*, 4 Wheaton 298 (1819).

21. 1 *Life and Letters of Joseph Story* 167, William W. Story, ed. (Boston: Little, Brown, 1851).

22. Dunne, "Story-Livingston," 225.

23. *Finley v. Lynn*, 6 Cranch 238 (1810).

24. Fred L. Israel, "Thomas Todd," in Friedman and Israel, 1 *Justices of the Supreme Court* 411.

25. *Dougherty's Heirs v. Edmiston*, 1 Cooke (Tenn.) 136 (1812).

26. Quoted in Charles Warren, 1 *The Supreme Court in United States History* 301 (Boston: Little, Brown, 1926).

27. Morgan, *Justice William Johnson* 371.

28. Quoted in Josiah Quincy, *Figures of the Past* 189–190 (Boston: Roberts Brothers, 1883).

29. Walter Flavius McCaleb, *The Aaron Burr Conspiracy* 12 (New York: Wilson, Erickson, 1936).

30. In the early 1790s, Felipe Neri, Baron de Bastrop and a Dutch subject of Spain, received

from the Spanish crown a grant to 1.2 million acres located in the Washita River valley in the Louisiana Territory (now Oklahoma). In 1798 Bastrop sold his claim to Abraham Morehouse, a Kentucky speculator who resold the land in 1804 to Edward Livingston of New Orleans and Charles Lynch of Shelby County, Kentucky. Lynch got 700,000 acres, and in 1806, Burr arranged to purchase half of those. Milton Lomask, *Aaron Burr: The Conspiracy and Years of Exile, 1805–1836* 111 (New York: Farrar, Straus, Giroux, 1982).

31. Charles F. Hobson, 7 *Marshall Papers* 3, editorial note.
32. Literature on the "Burr conspiracy" is extensive. In addition to the trial record cited below, see Lomask, *Burr: Conspiracy*; Malone, *Jefferson: Second Term* 211–370; McCaleb, *Aaron Burr Conspiracy*; Thomas P. Abernathy, *The Burr Conspiracy* (New York: Oxford University Press, 1954); Nathan Schachner, *Aaron Burr: A Biography* (New York: F. A. Stokes, 1937).
33. See Malone, *Jefferson: Second Term* 223–225, 237–238.
34. *Ibid.* 259.
35. "Proclamation Against Burr's Plot," November 27, 1806, 10 *The Works of Thomas Jefferson* 301–302, Paul Leicester Ford, ed. (New York: G. P. Putnam's Sons, 1905).
36. Jefferson to Langdon, December 22, 1806, 19 *The Writings of Thomas Jefferson* 157–158, Andrew A. Lipscomb, ed. (Washington, D.C.: Thomas Jefferson Memorial Association, 1903). Also see Jefferson to Caesar Rodney, December 5, 1806, 10 *Works of Jefferson* 322–323; and Jefferson to the Reverend Charles Clay, January 11, 1807, *ibid.* 338.
37. Cited in Lomask, *Burr: Conspiracy* 182.
38. Entry of December 27, 1806, *William Plumer's Memorandum of Proceedings in the United States Senate, 1803–1807* 544, Everett S. Brown, ed. (New York: Macmillan, 1923).
39. 16 *Annals of Congress* 334–359.
40. *Ibid.* 39–43.
41. Adams to Rush, February 2, 1807, cited in Albert J. Beveridge, 3 *The Life of John Marshall* 338, note 2 (Boston: Houghton Mifflin, 1916).
42. The Sixth Amendment states that "In all criminal prosecutions, the accused shall enjoy the right to a speedy and public trial, by an impartial jury of the State and district wherein the crime shall have been committed. . . ."
43. Reflecting several years later on Wilkinson's actions, Jefferson wrote to J. B. Colvin that "a strict observance of the written laws is doubtless *one* of the highest duties of a good citizen: but it is not the *highest*. The laws of necessity, of self-preservation, of saving our country when in danger, are of higher obligation. To lose our country by a scrupulous adherence to written law, would be to lose the law itself, with life, liberty, property and all those who are enjoying them with us; thus absurdly sacrificing the ends to the means." Jefferson's emphasis. September 20, 1810, 12 *Writings of Jefferson* 418–422. For Jefferson's role generally, see Malone, *Jefferson: The Second Term* 252–288; Leonard W. Levy, *Jefferson and Civil Liberties: The Darker Side* 70–92 (Cambridge, Mass.: Harvard University Press, 1963).
44. Warren, 1 *Supreme Court* 302–303.
45. William Cranch to his father, February 2, 1807, reprinted *ibid.* 304.
46. Rufus King wrote that Giles's effort to suspend *habeas corpus* was "religiously believed to have been made at the instigation of the president." 4 *The Life and Correspondence of Rufus King* 543–549, Charles R. King, ed. (New York: G. P. Putnam's Sons, 1896). Also see George L. Haskins and Herbert A. Johnson, *Foundations of Power: John Marshall, 1801–15* 256, in The Oliver Wendell Holmes Devise, 2 *History of the Supreme Court of the United States* (New York: Macmillan, 1981); Warren, 1 *Supreme Court* 302. Cf. Malone, *Jefferson: Second Term* 271. Also see J. Q. Adams to John Adams, January 27, 1807, 3 *The Writings of John Quincy Adams* 158, Worthington C. Ford, ed. (New York: Macmillan, 1913).
47. 16 *Annals of Congress* 44.
48. King, 4 *Life of King* 543.
49. Remarks of James Elliott of Vermont, 3 *Writings of J. Q. Adams* 402–425.
50. *United States v. Bollman*, 24 F. Cas. 1189 (C.C.D.C. 1807) (No. 14,622). Also see 4 Cranch 75, note (b) (1807).
51. Lee's appearance that day was on behalf of another alleged conspirator, James Alexander,

who, like Bollman and Swartwout, had been seized by Wilkinson in New Orleans and sent by ship to Washington. *Ex Parte Bollman and Ex Parte Swartwout*, 4 Cranch 75 note (a).

52. Marshall was joined by Cushing, Livingston, and Washington. Chase and Johnson dissented.

53. 4 Cranch 93. By insisting that the Court's authority derived exclusively from statute, Marshall was rejecting the argument made by Robert Harper that the power to issue writs of *habeas corpus* was one of the "incidental powers" of all superior courts in England and America.

54. 1 *United States Statutes at Large* 81–82 (1789).

55. 1 Cranch 137 (1803).

56. 4 Cranch 101.

57. Article III, section 3. The Constitution goes on to state that "No Person shall be convicted of Treason unless on the Testimony of two Witnesses to the same overt Act, or on Confession in open Court."

58. The justices divided two to two as to whether General Wilkinson's affidavit was admissible for purposes of committing the prisoners. Marshall said that "under this embarrassment it was deemed necessary to look into the affidavit," and then proceeded to discuss its contents as if it were admissible. 4 Cranch 75 at 129.

59. 1 *The Memoirs of John Quincy Adams* 459, Charles Francis Adams, ed. (Philadelphia: J. B. Lippincott, 1874).

60. Immediately after the Court's decision, Judge Cranch, who was also the Supreme Court reporter, wrote that "It happened, from a singular and unforeseen coincidence of strange circumstances, that I should be the first to resist the hand of arbitrary power. Although I have not for a moment doubted the correctness of my opinion, yet it is a source of great satisfaction to find it confirmed by the highest judicial tribunal in the Nation. I congratulate my country upon the triumph of reason and law over popular passion and injustice—upon the final triumph of civil over military authority, and of the practical principle of substantial personal liberty over the theoretical doctrine of philosophic civil liberty." Warren, 1 *Supreme Court* 308.

61. *Marshall v. Currie*, 4 Cranch 172 (1807). Because of Humphrey Marshall's involvement, the chief justice recused himself.

62. Capt. Daniel Bissell to Gen. Andrew Jackson, January 5, 1807, 16 *Annals of Congress* 1017–1018. This letter was included with the evidence Jefferson presented to Congress on January 22, 1807.

63. McCaleb, *Aaron Burr Conspiracy* 219–220.

64. Cowles Mead to Secretary of War, January 13, 1807, 16 *Annals of Congress* 1018.

65. Return of the Mississippi Grand Jury, February 3, 1807, reported in the *Orleans Gazette*, February 20, 1807. The grand jury went on formally to post "a grievance" against calling out the militia against Burr and the "destruction of personal liberty" by General Wilkinson in New Orleans.

66. Randolph to Joseph H. Nicholson, March 25, 1807, in Henry Adams, *John Randolph* 220 (Boston: Houghton Mifflin, 1882).

67. Malone, *Jefferson: Second Term* 294.

68. 4 Cranch 126.

69. Malone, *Jefferson: Second Term* 297–299.

70. William Waller Hening and William Munford, *The Examination of Colonel Aaron Burr before the Chief Justice of the United States* 26, S.#12528 in *American Bibliography: A Preliminary Checklist for 1807*, Ralph R. Shaw and Richard H. Shoemaker, eds. (New York: The Scarecrow Press, 1961).

71. Rodney told Jefferson he had no doubt that Hay would "conduct the business in the most correct, prudent, and efficient manner." Rodney to Jefferson, May 6, 22, 1807, in Malone, *Jefferson: Second Term* 306.

72. William Blackstone, 4 *Commentaries on the Laws of England* 293 (Oxford: Clarendon Press, 1765–69).

73. Marshall's opinion was printed in the Richmond *Enquirer*, April 13, 1807. 7 *Marshall Papers* 13–21.

74. *United States v. Burr*, (C.C.D. Va 1807). 7 *Marshall Papers* 13–21.

75. *Ibid.* 16–17.

76. Jefferson to James Bowdoin, April 2, 1807, 4 *Memoirs, Correspondence, and Private Papers of Thomas Jefferson* 71–73, Thomas Jefferson Randolph, ed. (London: Colburn and Beatty, 1829).

77. Jefferson to Giles, April 20, 1807, *ibid.* 73–75.

78. Jefferson to Madison, April 14, 1807, 10 *Works for Jefferson* 383. These funds were in addition to the money regularly appropriated for the conduct of criminal prosecutions. Beveridge, 3 *Life of Marshall* 391.

79. Jefferson to Hay, May 20, 1807, 10 *Works of Jefferson* 394–401.

80. *Ibid.* General Andrew Jackson, who had made the journey from Nashville to Richmond to be present at the trial, wrote that "this thing has . . . assumed the shape of a political persecution," and placed the blame on Jefferson. Jackson to W. Patten Anderson, June 16, 1807, in James Parton, 1 *Life of Andrew Jackson* 334 (New York: Mason Brothers, 1861). Winfield Scott, a young Richmond lawyer who would later command American forces in Mexico, also attended the trial, noting that "It was President Jefferson who directed and animated the prosecution. Hence, every Republican clamored for [Burr's] execution. Of course, the Federalists . . . comported themselves on the other side." Winfield Scott, 1 *Memoirs of Lieutenant-General Scott* 13 (New York: Sheldon, 1864).

81. 1 *Reports of the Trials of Colonel Aaron Burr* 79–81, David Robertson, ed. (Philadelphia: Hopkins and Earle, 1808).

82. *Ibid.* 97. Citing the procedural requirements of the Fourth Amendment, Marshall said that "In the cool and temperate moments of reflection, undisturbed by that whirlwind of passion . . . which most generally produces acts or accusations of treason . . . the people of America have believed the power even of commitment to be capable of too much oppression in its execution to be placed, without restriction, even in the hands of the national legislature. Shall a judge disregard those barriers which the nation has deemed proper to erect?" Opinion, U.S. Circuit Court, Virginia, May 28, 1807, *ibid.* 97.

83. *Ibid.* 106.

84. Washington Irving, who was covering the trial for several New York papers, wrote jokingly to a friend that the recess was necessary so that the jurors "might go home, see their wives, get their clothes washed, and flog their negroes." Irving to Mrs. Hoffman, June 4, 1807, 1 *Life and Letters of Washington Irving* 192, Pierre Munroe Irving, ed. (New York: G. P. Putnam, 1863).

85. Years later Burr reciprocated Martin's generosity. After Martin suffered a stroke that left him paralyzed, Burr had the aged lawyer moved into his own home in New York and supervised his case for the remaining three years of Martin's life. Lomask, *Burr: Conspiracy* 376.

86. See Jefferson to Hay, May 26, 1807 ("Go into any expense necessary for this purpose . . ."); May 28, 1807 (instructions for examining witnesses); June 2, 1807 (rejection of *Marbury v. Madison* as precedent); June 5, 1807 (discharge of grand jury). 11 *Writings of Jefferson* 209–210, 210–211, 213–216, 218–219.

87. Jefferson to John Eppes, May 28, 1807, 10 *Works of Jefferson* 412–413.

88. The documents sought included a letter from General Wilkinson to Jefferson describing Burr's activities, Jefferson's reply to Wilkinson, and the president's instructions to the army and navy to apprehend the former vice president. 1 *Burr Trials* 113–114, 119.

89. *Ibid.* 112–119.

90. Hay to Jefferson, June 9, 1807, quoted in Beveridge, 3 *Life of Marshall* 434.

91. 1 *Burr Trials* 127–128. Jefferson to Hay, June 19, 1807, 10 *Works of Jefferson* 402–403.

92. 1 *Burr Trials* 130–133.

93. *Ibid.* 137–145.

94. Jefferson to Hay, June 19, 1807, 10 *Works of Jefferson* 402–403.

95. *United States v. Burr*, Opinion, U.S. Circuit Court, Virginia, June 13, 1807, *ibid.* 177–189. Also see 7 *Marshall Papers* 37–50.

96. 1 *Burr Trials* 178. Before turning to the question of whether a subpoena *duces tecum* could be directed to the president, Marshall disposed of the prosecution's argument that an accused

person had no right to the subpoena power in a grand jury hearing. Citing precedent, the Sixth Amendment and statute, he held that "Upon immemorial usage then, and upon what is deemed a sound construction of the Constitution and law of the land, the court is of the opinion that any person charged with a crime in the courts of the United States has a right, before as well as after indictment, to the process of the court to compel the attendance of his witnesses." *Ibid.* 180.

97. *Ibid.* 182. Marshall went on to say "The court would not lend its aid to motions obviously designed to manifest disrespect to the government, but the court has no right to refuse its aid to motions for papers to which the accused may be entitled and which may be material to his defence." *Ibid.*

98. In reading his opinion, Marshall used the word "wished" instead of "expected." When he concluded, Alexander MacRae, on behalf of the government, queried the word, at which point Marshall assured him that it was not the court's intention "to insinuate that the attorneys for the prosecution, or that the administration, had ever wished the conviction of Colonel Burr, whether he was guilty or innocent." When court adjourned for the day, Marshall announced that he had expunged the offending word from the record. *Ibid.* 189, 197.

99. *Ibid.* 188.

100. Haskins and Johnson, *Foundations of Power* 275.

101. Jefferson to Hay, June 12, 1807, 10 *Works of Jefferson* 398–400. Hay read the president's letter into the record on June 16, 1807. 1 *Burr Trials* 210–211.

102. "All nations" said Jefferson,

> have found it necessary, that for the advantageous conduct of their affairs, some of these proceedings, at least, should remain known to their executive functionary only. He, of course, from the nature of the case, must be the sole judge of which of them the public interests will permit publication. . . . The respect mutually due between the constituted authorities, in their official intercourse, as well as sincere dispositions to do for every one what is just, will always insure from the executive, in exercising the discrimination confided to him, the same candor and integrity to which the nation has in like manner trusted in the disposal of its judiciary authorities. Considering you as the organ for communicating these sentiments to the Court, I address them to you for that purpose. . . .

Jefferson to Hay, June 17, 1807, 10 *Works of Jefferson* 400–402. Jefferson's letter was read into the record by Hay on June 20, 1807. 1 *Burr Trials* 254–255.

103. 10 *Works of Jefferson* 406–407. Jefferson's personal note is undated. Dumas Malone joins it to the president's June 17 letter to Hay, and I have adopted Malone's chronology. Compare Beveridge, 3 *Life of Marshall* 518–520.

104. 10 *Works of Jefferson* 407.

105. *Ibid.* 350.

106. Indictment against Aaron Burr, Document 3, R.G. 21, National Archives. This indictment went on to assert that Burr "in order to fulfil and bring into effect the said traitorous compassings . . . with a great number of persons . . . to wit to the number of thirty persons and upwards, armed and arrayed in a warlike manner . . . with guns, swords, and dirks . . . being them and the traitorously assembled . . . did . . . array and dispose themselves against the said United States." Also see 1 *Burr Trials* 430–432.

107. There is evidence that the grand jury may have indicted Burr on the treason charge because of Marshall's definition of levying war in *Bollman.* On August 7, 1807, Harman Blennerhasset recorded in his journal that "two of the most respectable and influential members of [the grand jury] have declared they mistook the meaning of Chief Justice Marshall's opinion as to what sort of acts amounted to treason [and] that it was under the influence of this mistake they concurred in finding such a bill against A. Burr, which otherwise would have probably been ignored." William H. Safford, *The Blennerhasset Papers* 314 (Cincinnati: Moore, Witstach & Baldwin, 1864). Also see Joseph C. Cabell to Thomas Ritchie, September 10, 1807, Cabell Papers, University of Virginia; 7 *Marshall Papers* 6.

108. Marshall to Cushing, June 27, 1807, *ibid.* 60–62. Marshall wrote to each associate justice, but only the letter to Cushing survives. All of their replies have been lost or destroyed, but it is reasonable to assume that each replied and that Marshall took their views into account in his subsequent rulings.

109. *Ibid.* Justice Chase's biographer confirms Chase's role in fashioning Marshall's ultimate ruling in *United States v. Burr.* See Jane Shaffer Elsmere, *Justice Samuel Chase* 316–317 (Munice, Ind.: Janevar, 1980).

110. 1 *Burr Trials* 415–416.

111. *Ibid.* 425.

112. *Ibid.*

113. The trial jury was composed of foreman Edward Carrington, David Lambert, Richard Parker, Hugh Mercer, Christopher Anthony, James Sheppard, Reuben Blakey, Benjamin Graves, Miles Bott, Henry Coleman, John Sheppard and Richard Curd. *Ibid.* 430.

114. *Ibid.* 448. Hay's emphasis, as reported by Robertson.

115. *Ibid.* 459.

116. *Ibid.* 454.

117. *Ibid.* 469–472. Also see 7 *Marshall Papers* 70–74.

118. 1 *Burr Trials* 473.

119. *Ibid.* 485.

120. *Ibid.* 529.

121. *Ibid.* 530.

122. *Ibid.* Marshall's emphasis.

123. *Ibid.* 531.

124. Quoted in Lomask, *Burr: Conspiracy* 270.

125. 1 *Burr Trials* 549–550.

126. 2 *Ibid.* 3.

127. *Ibid.* 4.

128. The elegance of Wirt's allusions dazzled the courtroom as he compared Blennerhasset's Island to a garden of Eden traduced by the serpent Aaron Burr, who had extended the poisoned apple of ambition to Harman and Margaret Blennerhasset. Throughout the nineteenth century, Wirt's speech appeared regularly in textbooks on rhetoric, and generations of schoolchildren have memorized his glittering passage. *Ibid.* 96–97. Also see John P. Kennedy, 1 *Memoirs of the Life of William Wirt* 179–187 (Philadelphia: Blanchard and Lea, 1856).

129. This was Harman Blennerhasset's expression for the great advocate. Safford, *Blennerhasset Papers* 377.

130. 2 *Burr Trials* 378.

131. Beveridge notes that Marshall invoked more references to precedent in his Burr decision than in all of his great constitutional holdings combined. 3 *Life of Marshall* 504.

132. All of the quotations are from Marshall's August 31, 1807, decision in *United States v. Burr,* most readily available in 7 *Marshall Papers* 74–116. Also see 2 *Burr Trials* 401–445; 4 Cranch 470 (1807).

133. In his decision, Marshall referred to the Eighth Amendment but was speaking of what today is the Sixth Amendment. Originally twelve amendments were proposed in the Bill of Rights, but two were not ratified.

134. The jury verdict, delivered by foreman Edward Carrington, states, "We of the jury say that Aaron Burr is not proved guilty under this indictment by any evidence submitted to us. We therefore find him not guilty." 2 *Burr Trials* 446.

135. *Ibid.* 448.

136. *Ibid.* 451–452.

137. Wirt was more circumspect. As he wrote immediately after Marshall's decision came down: "We [the prosecution] were governed by our construction of the opinion of the Supreme Court [in *Bollman*]. If we were mistaken, it was an error common to those enlightened men who were on the grand jury, and whose minds are as much illuminated as those of any men in this state; and an error I believe most men of intelligence might commit. The court how-

ever has said that the opinion of the Supreme Court has been misconceived; but no blame ought to be attached to us for that, [as] the misconception was general and common to the ablest men in this country." 2 *Burr Trials* 499.

Hay told Jefferson that "The opinion of the C[hief] Justice is too voluminous to be generally read, and on the great question about the overt act of levying war too obscure and perplexed to be understood." Hay to Jefferson, September 1, 1807, in Malone, *Jefferson: Second Term* 337. Hay had become seriously ill during the trial and later said that by cutting off the trial, Marshall had saved his life. *Ibid.* 340.

138. Jefferson to Hay, September 4, 1807, 11 *Writings of Jefferson* 360.

139. Jefferson to Hay, September 7, 1807, *ibid.* 366.

140. Burr was charged with violating a 1794 statute that made it a "high misdemeanor" to "begin or set on foot or provide or prepare the means for any military expedition or enterprise to be carried on . . . against the territory or dominions of any foreign prince or state with whom the United States are at peace." 1 *United States Statutes at Large* 384.

141. T. Carpenter, 3 *The Trials of Colonel Aaron Burr* 107–110. (Washington, D.C.: Westcott, 1808).

142. The testimony of these witnesses is collected in 17 *Annals of Congress* 401–683.

143. *United States v. Burr*, 25 F. Cas. 201 (C.C.D. Va. 1807) (No. 14, 694a).

144. *Virginia Argus* (Richmond), November 10, 1807; *Aurora* (Philadelphia), November 21, 1807. For a sampling of newspaper criticism, see Warren, 1 *Supreme Court* 309–311.

145. Message to Congress, October 27, 1807, 17 *Annals of Congress* 17–18. In his original draft, Jefferson had asked "whether there was a radical defect" in the administration of the law and had gone on at some length to attack the "refractoriness" of the trial court. At the suggestion of Albert Gallatin and Caesar Rodney, those passages were deleted. 10 *Works of Jefferson* 503–510 note.

146. On November 5, 1807, Senator Giles introduced a constitutional amendment calling for the removal of federal judges by a majority vote of both houses of Congress, and on February 11, 1808, he proposed legislation that would ease prosecution for treason. Both measures failed passage. 17 *Annals of Congress* 21, 108–133.

147. Marshall to Peters, November 23, 1807, 7 *Marshall Papers* 164–165.

148. Scholars have divided over Marshall's handling of the Burr trial. Modern writers, concerned with civil liberties, have uniformly applauded his rejection of the common law doctrine of constructive treason. See Bradley Chapin, *The American Law of Treason* 108–113 (Seattle: University of Washington Press, 1964); Robert K. Faulkner, *The Jurisprudence of John Marshall* 272–277 (Princeton, N.J.: Princeton University Press, 1968); James Willard Hurst, *Treason in the United States* (Westport, Conn.: Greenwood Press, 1945); Leonard Levy, *Jefferson and Civil Liberties: The Darker Side* 75–80 (Cambridge, Mass.: Belknap Press, 1963); Richard B. Morris, *Fair Trial* 119–120, 147–150 (New York: Knopf, 1952).

Others, such as Edward S. Corwin, have sharply criticized Marshall for jettisoning the British rule that in treason all are principals. In Corwin's view, Marshall's emphasis on an overt act testified to by two witnesses has made it virtually impossible to convict anyone of treason. *John Marshall and the Constitution* 98–111 (New Haven, Conn.: Yale University Press, 1919).

Professor Corwin, writing immediately after World War I, was imbued with the spirit of American patriotism. He was sharply critical of Holmes's clear and present danger test in *Schenck v. United States*, 249 U.S. 47 (1919) ("biographical detail converted into constitutional history"); disparaged the dissents of Holmes and Brandeis in *Abrams v. United States* 250 U.S. 616, 626–627 (1919); and lamented the Court's expansion of the guarantees of the Fourth and Fifth amendments in *Boyd v. United States*, 116 U.S. 616 (1886) and *Counselman v. Hitchcock*, 142 U.S. 547 (1892). A justifiably renowned constitutional scholar, Professor Corwin was a staunch advocate of executive power and was not sympathetic to a latitudinarian interpretation of the Bill of Rights. See Corwin, "Freedom of Speech and Press Under the First Amendment: A Resume," 48 *Yale Law Journal* 48 (1920); "Constitutional Law in 1919–1920," 14 *American Political Science Review* 656 (1920); "The Supreme Court's Construction of the Self-Incrimination Clause," 29 *Michigan Law Review* 205–206 (1930); *American Constitutional History* 166 (New York: Harper & Row, 1964).

16: Yazoo

1. Frances Norton Mason, *My Dearest Polly* 195–196 (Richmond: Garrett & Massie, 1961).
2. Bishop William Meade, 2 *Old Churches, Ministers and Families of Virginia* 222 (Philadelphia: J. B. Lippincott, 1861).
3. Albert J. Beveridge, 4 *The Life of John Marshall* 67 (Boston: Houghton Mifflin, 1919).
4. Marshall to Rawlings, July 28, 1829, in Mason, *My Dearest Polly* 308–309.
5. Marshall to Louis Marshall, December 23, 1816, Private Collection, copy supplied by Papers of John Marshall, Williamsburg, Va.
6. Maria Newton Marshall, *Recollections and Reflections of Fielding Lewis Marshall* 150 (Orange, Va.: private printing, 1911).
7. Mason, *My Dearest Polly* 202–203; Samuel Mordecai, *Richmond in By-Gone Days* 62 (Richmond, Va.: G. M. West, 1856); Mary Virginia Hawes Terhune (Mary Harland, pseud.), *Some Colonial Homesteads and Their Stories* 91, (New York: G. P. Putnam's Sons, 1912).
8. Quoted in Mason, *My Dearest Polly* 203. Also see Terhune, *Colonial Homesteads*, 93; Henry Howe, *Historical Collections of Virginia* 266 (Charleston, S.C.: Babcock, 1845).
9. Related by Professor J. Franklin Jameson, from personal interviews with old residents of Richmond, and retold to Albert Beveridge. See 4 *Life of Marshall* 67–68.
10. "Lines Written for A Lady's Album," in Marshall's handwriting, is in the Swem Library, College of William and Mary.
11. Story to Fay, February 24, 1812, 1 *Life and Letters of Joseph Story* 215–217, William W. Story, ed. (Boston: Little, Brown, 1851).
12. Marshall to Polly, January 30, 1831, in Mason, *My Dearest Polly* 328.
13. See Marshall to John Randolph, March 4, 1816, 8 *The Papers of John Marshall* 127 (Chapel Hill: University of North Carolina Press, 1995).
14. Details of the judges' conference are sketchy at best. That the judges made a practice of adjourning at eight is inferred from a letter written by artist Chester Harding, describing a sitting by Marshall for a portrait. "When I was ready to draw the figure into his picture," writes Harding, "I asked him, in order to save time, to come to my room in the evening. . . . An evening was appointed; but he could not come until after the 'consultation,' which lasts until about eight o'clock." Quoted in Andrew Oliver, *The Portraits of John Marshall* 73 (Charlottesville: University Press of Virginia, 1976).
15. See R. Kent Newmyer, *Supreme Court Justice Joseph Story* 78 (Chapel Hill: University of North Carolina Press, 1985).
16. 1 *Life and Letters of Story* 215–217.
17. 4 Cranch 358 (1808).
18. The Delaware court acted pursuant to a statute of 1786, 2 *Delaware Laws* 831, and was authorized to do so by the Judiciary Act of 1789, which permitted the states to continue to exercise the maritime jurisdiction theretofore theirs. See George L. Haskins and Herbert S. Johnson, *Foundations of Power: John Marshall, 1801–15* 399, in The Oliver Wendell Holmes Devise, 2 *History of the Supreme Court of the United States* (New York: Macmillan, 1981).
19. The case for the United States was presented by Attorney General Caesar Rodney, *Minutes of the Supreme Court of the United States*, March 1–4, 1808.
20. 4 Cranch 366.
21. 2 Cranch 280 (1804), 4 Cranch 209 (1804).
22. 4 Cranch 320 (1808).
23. Marshall was absent when *McIlvaine* was initially argued and took no formal part in the decision. However, as Herbert Johnson notes, "Cushing as the presiding justice delivered the opinion, a lengthy and erudite statement that seems well beyond his capacities at that time, and perhaps beyond his professional ability even at a younger age." Haskins and Johnson, *Foundations of Power* 384.
24. 4 Cranch 434 (1808).
25. See Madison to Jefferson, June 22, 1810, 8 *The Writings of James Madison* 103–104, Gaillard Hunt, ed. (New York: G. P. Putnam's Sons, 1908).
26. Justice Todd did not participate in the decision.

27. Justice Washington added a concurring opinion in *Croudson v. Leonard*, 4 Cranch 438.
28. In addition to *McIlvaine v. Coxe's Lessee*, in which the decision was delivered by Cushing, Marshall recused himself in *Dawson's Lessee v. Godfrey*, 4 Cranch 320 (decision by Johnson), and *Blaine v. Ship Charles Carter*, 4 Cranch 327 (decision by Chase).
29. In *Hudson v. Guestier*, 4 Cranch 293, Chase and Livingston filed a written dissent, and in *Rose v. Himely*, 4 Cranch 240, Johnson wrote a dissent. Livingston dissented without stating the reasons in *Higginson v. Mein*, 4 Cranch 415, 419. Similarly, in *Croudson v. Leonard*, 4 Cranch 434, Livingston and Chase dissented without filing an opinion.
30. Acts of December 22, 1807, January 9, 1808, March 12, 1808, and April 25, 1808, 18 *Annals of Congress* 2814–2815, 2815–2817, 2839–2842, 2870–2874.
31. As Jefferson wrote Governor Charles ["Blackguard Charlie"] Pinckney of South Carolina, "In order to give this law the effect it intended, we find it necessary to consider any vessel suspicious, which has on board any article of domestic produce in demand at foreign markets, and most especially provisions." Letter, July 18, 1808, quoted in Charles Warren, 1 *The Supreme Court in United States History* 325, note 1 (Boston: Little, Brown, 1926). Compare 8 *The Writings of Thomas Jefferson* 322–324, H. A. Washington, ed. (New York: H. W. Derby, 1861).
32. Jefferson to Gallatin, May 6, 1808, 1 *The Writings of Albert Gallatin* 386, Henry Adams, ed. (Philadelphia: J. B. Lippincott, 1879).
33. Samuel Eliot Morison, *The Oxford History of the American People* 373–375 (New York: Oxford University Press, 1965).
34. *Charleston Courier*, May 26, 28, 30, 31, 1808.
35. *Gilchrist v. Collector of Charleston*, 10 F. Cas. 355 (C.C.D. S.C. 1808) (No. 5, 420).
36. *Ibid*. 356. Johnson family tradition holds that Justice Johnson took his walking stick, put on his hat, boarded the vessels in Charleston harbor, and personally wrote out sailing orders for the captains. Donald G. Morgan, *Justice William Johnson: The First Dissenter* 59 (Columbia: University of South Carolina Press, 1954).
37. For an extensive survey of press response, see Warren, 1 *Supreme Court* 326–329.
38. Morgan, *Justice William Johnson* 73–74; Warren, *Supreme Court* 329.
39. Rodney's opinion is printed in full in the *Aurora* (Philadelphia), August 9, 1808.
40. 10 F. Cas. at 359.
41. *Ibid*. 364.
42. Rodney to Jefferson, October 31, 1808, reproduced in Warren, 1 *Supreme Court* 336–337.
43. *Ibid*.
44. The constitutionality of the embargo was upheld by District Judge John Davis, a Federalist appointee, sitting in Salem, Massachusetts. *United States v. Brig William*, 28 F. Cas. 614 (D. Mass. 1808) (No. 16, 700).
45. 2 Cranch 358 (1804). See Chapter 15.
46. For a discussion on this point, see Warren, 1 *Supreme Court* 343–350.
47. 9 Wheaton 1, 191 (1824). Emphasis added. Justice Johnson, in his concurring opinion in *Gibbons v. Ogden*, claimed even more extensive power for the national government than Marshall had done.
48. As John Quincy Adams reported to Ezekiel Bacon, "The District Court, after sitting seven or eight weeks and trying upwards of 40 cases, has at length adjourned. Not one instance has occurred of a conviction by jury." Letter, December 21, 1808, 3 *The Writings of John Quincy Adams* 277, Worthington C. Ford, ed. (New York: Macmillan, 1913). Also see Adams to Giles, December 20, 1808, and January 16, 1808, *ibid*. 287.
49. Monroe was supported by a dissident group of Republicans who had broken with Jefferson for various reasons. The group included John Randolph, John Taylor of Caroline, Littleton Tazewell, and two of Marshall's Richmond neighbors, George Hay and John Brockenbrough. For Monroe's campaign, see Harry Ammon, *James Monroe: The Quest for National Identity* 270–282 (Charlottesville: University Press of Virginia, 1990).
50. Virginia, the most populous state in the union, was entitled to twenty-two seats in the House of Representatives. The Federalists did better than Marshall had predicted, winning five seats. Daniel P. Jordan, *Political Leadership in Jefferson's Virginia* 150 (Charlottesville: University Press of Virginia, 1983).

51. Marshall to Pinckney, September 21, 1808, 7 *Marshall Papers* 182–183.
52. In the 1808 election, only Virginia and Rhode Island chose their electors at large. All other states selected them either on the basis of congressional districts or by the state legislature, thus allowing the state's electoral vote to be split. Congressional Quarterly, *Guide to U.S. Elections* 204 (Washington, D.C.: Congressional Quarterly, 1975). For the Virginia law, see William Waller Hening, 13 *The Statutes at Large: Being a Collection of All of the Laws of Virginia* 536–540 (Richmond, Va.: Samuel Pleasants, 1809–1823). Also see Tadashisa Kuroda, *The Origins of the Twelfth Amendment: The Electoral College in the Early Republic* 153ff. (Westport, Conn.: Greenwood Press, 1994).
53. Marshall to Pinckney, September 21, 1808, 7 *Marshall Papers* 183.
54. Marshall to Pinckney, October 18, 1808, *ibid.* 184–185.
55. *Ibid.*
56. Madison carried eleven states with 122 electoral votes, to Pinckney's 47. New York gave 6 electoral votes to Clinton.
57. *Virginia Argus* (Richmond), November 1, 1808.
58. 19 *Annals of Congress* 353 *et seq.*
59. At the Virginia ratification convention, Madison had deferred to Marshall for the defense of the judiciary article of the Constitution, acknowledging Marshall's greater familiarity with the subject. See Chapter 5.
60. For a restatement of New England's arguments, see Warren, 1 *Supreme Court* 362–365.
61. In 1793, following the decision of the Supreme Court in *Chisholm v. Georgia*, 2 Dallas 419, Georgia had successfully challenged the Article III authority of federal courts to hear cases against a state brought by citizens of another state. The Eleventh Amendment to the Constitution, adopted in 1798, vindicated Georgia's concerns. In Pennsylvania, the issue of federal jurisdiction first arose in *Huidekoper's Lessee v. Douglass*, 3 Cranch 1 (1805), but the state governor ultimately vetoed a resolution by the legislature rejecting federal authority. See Haskins and Johnson, *Foundations of Power* 317–322.
62. Commonly known as the Olmstead Case, the issue had been in litigation for about twenty-five years. During the Revolution, a sea captain named Olmstead had obtained a judgment in the old Federal Court of Appeals in a prize case, *The Sloop Active*, against the rival claim of the State of Pennsylvania. For a discussion of the case, see Beveridge, 4 *Life of Marshall* 18–22.
63. *Olmstead v. The Active*, 18 F. Cas. 680 (C.C.D. Pa. 1803) (No. 10, 503a).
64. Section 2, Act of April 2, 1803, 17 *Pennsylvania Statutes* 472, 479.
65. Judge Peters, who had presided with Justice Chase in the treason trial of John Fries, was targeted by John Randolph along with Chase for removal from the bench, but the House failed to return an indictment. See Chapter 14.
66. *United States v. Peters*, 5 Cranch 115 (1809).
67. *Ibid.* 133.
68. *Ibid.* 135.
69. 21 *Annals of Congress* 2267.
70. Warren, 1 *Supreme Court* 382–383.
71. 21 *Annals of Congress* 2269.
72. Warren, 1 *Supreme Court* 385–386. The following month, after the disturbance died down, President Madison tempered justice with mercy and granted Bright a pardon.
73. *Aurora*, April 20, 1809.
74. Morris to Marshall, December 2, 1809, 7 *Marshall Papers* 219–220.
75. *Ibid.*
76. Marshall to Morris, December 12, 1809, *ibid.* 220–221.
77. *Ibid.* Emphasis added.
78. Morris to Marshall, December 28, 1809, *ibid.* 222–224.
79. 1 Cranch 137 (1803).
80. 6 Cranch 87 (1810).
81. 4 Wheaton 316 (1819).
82. *Dartmouth College v. Woodward*, 4 Wheaton 518 (1819).

83. 9 Wheaton 1 (1824).

84. 6 Peters 515 (1832). Between 1810 and 1832, the Marshall Court invalidated seventeen pieces of state legislation. In addition to those listed in the text, the Court declared state laws unconstitutional in: *New Jersey v. Wilson*, 7 Cranch 164 (1812); *Terrett v. Taylor*, 9 Cranch 43 (1815); *Sturgis v. Crowninshield*, 4 Wheaton 122 (1819); *McMillan v. McNeil*, 4 Wheaton 209 (1819); *Farmers' and Mechanics' Bank v. Smith*, 6 Wheaton 131 (1821); *Green v. Biddle*, 8 Wheaton (1823); *Society for the Propagation of the Gospel v. New Haven*, 8 Wheaton 464 (1823); *Osborn v. Bank of the United States*, 9 Wheaton 738 (1824); *Ogden v. Saunders*, 12 Wheaton 213 (1827), Marshall dissenting; *Brown v. Maryland*, 12 Wheaton 419 (1827); *Craig v. Missouri*, 4 Peters 410 (1830); and *Boyle v. Zacharie and Turner*, 6 Peter 635 (1832).

85. Oliver Wendell Holmes, Jr., *Collected Legal Papers* 295–296 (New York: Harcourt, Brace and Howe, 1920).

86. See Robert K. Faulkner, *The Jurisprudence of John Marshall* 18–19 (Princeton, N.J.: Princeton University Press, 1968).

87. 6 *The Works of John Adams* 280, Charles Francis Adams, ed. (Boston: Little, Brown, 1850). For Jefferson, "the true foundation of republican government is the equal right of every citizen, in his person and property." John Taylor of Caroline was more outspoken. In a vitriolic attack on the Marshall Court following its decision in *McCulloch v. Maryland*, Taylor wrote that "the rights of man include life, liberty and property. The last right is the chief hinge upon which social happiness depends." 10 *The Works of Thomas Jefferson* 39, Paul Leicester Ford, ed. (New York: G. P. Putnam's Sons, 1905); John Taylor, *Construction Construed and Constitutions Vindicated* 67 (Richmond, Va.: Shepard and Pollard, 1820).

88. C. Peter Magrath, *Yazoo: Law and Politics of the New Republic* 4–15 (Providence, R.I.: Brown University Press, 1966).

89. Georgia's 1790 population numbered 83,000 persons, of whom 30,000 were slaves. The population density was .6 persons per square mile, making Georgia the most sparsely settled state in the Union. U.S. Bureau of the Census, 1 *Historical Statistics of the United States: Colonial Times to 1970* 26 (Washington, D.C.: Government Printing Office, 1975).

90. Henry Adams, 1 *History of the United States of America* 303 (New York: Charles Scribner's Sons, 1889).

91. For text, see 1 *American State Papers: Public Lands* 156–158, Walter Lowrie and Matthew St. Clair Clarke, eds. (Washington, D.C.: Gales and Seaton, 1832).

92. Joel Chandler Harris, *Stories of Georgia* 134–135 (New York: American Book Co., 1896). A useful historical survey of the Yazoo sale is provided by Horace E. Hagan, "Fletcher v. Peck," 16 *Georgetown Law Journal* 1–40 (1927).

93. Editorial note, 7 *Marshall Papers* 226. Also see Chapter 14.

94. For analysis of the factors suggesting an "arranged case," see Haskins and Johnson, *Foundations of Power* 343–345.

95. The decision of the circuit court is unreported. The records of the case are located in Massachusetts Circuit Court Records, RG 21, Federal Records Center, Boston. Also see Magrath, *Yazoo* 53–56.

96. John Quincy Adams, who originally appeared for Peck (and was replaced by Story when Adams was appointed ambassador to Russia), explained the dismissal as follows:

> With respect to the merits of the case, the Chief Justice added verbally, that, circumstanced as the Court are, only five justices attending [Chase and Cushing were absent], there were difficulties which would have prevented them from giving any opinion at this term had the pleadings been correct; and the Court more readily forebore giving it, as from the complexion of the pleadings they could not but see that at the time when the covenants [between Fletcher and Peck] were made the parties had notice of the acts covenanted against; that this was not to be taken as part of the Court's opinion, but as a motive why they had thought proper not to give one this term.

Entry of March 11, 1809, 1 *The Memoirs of John Quincy Adams* 547, Charles Francis Adams, ed. (Philadelphia: J. B. Lippincott, 1874).

97. Henry P. Goddard, *Luther Martin: The "Federal Bull-Dog"* 35 (Baltimore: J. Murphy, 1887).

Some have suggested that Martin's inebriated performance evidenced his collusion with those representing the land companies. Given Martin's habits, that seems unwarranted. Magrath, *Yazoo* 82.

98. The financial interests of Harper and Story in the Yazoo cause are detailed in *ibid*. 64–69.

99. *Fletcher v. Peck*, 6 Cranch 87, 140.

100. *Ibid*. 128.

101. In the words of Charles Warren, "Nothing could more certainly bring the Court into violent conflict with the Legislative branch of the Government than any such judicial attempt to investigate its motives, and to set aside a statute, upon a judicial finding of corruption." Warren, 1 *Supreme Court* 398.

102. As Chief Justice Waite noted while speaking for the Court in *Munn v. Illinois*, 94 U.S. 113, 134 (1877), "For protection against abuses by legislatures, the people must resort to the polls, not to the courts."

103. Marshall's broad definition of contracts to include an obligation of the grantor not to violate the terms of his grant was a restatement of well-understood legal principles, articulated succinctly by Sir William Blackstone, whom Marshall cited. See 2 *Commentaries on the Laws of England* 443 (Oxford: Clarendon Press, 1766–1769). Marshall's definition elicited no criticism at the time, although progressive historians, writing in the late nineteenth and early twentieth centuries, suggested he had erred. See, for example, Benjamin F. Wright, *The Contract Clause of the Constitution* 28–34 (Cambridge, Mass.: Harvard University Press, 1938). Dean Roscoe Pound put the controversy in perspective. Speaking of Marshall's usage, Dean Pound wrote:

> Contract was then used, and was used as late as Parsons on Contracts in 1853, to mean what the French now call *acte juridique*. It might be called "legal transaction." Not merely contract as we now understand it, but trust, will, conveyance, and grant of a franchise are included. . . . The writers on natural law considered that there was a natural legal duty not to derogate from one's grant. . . . This is the explanation of *Fletcher v. Peck* and no doubt is what the [contract clause] meant to those who wrote it into the Constitution. God and the devil and the king were bound to contract and *a fortiori* [all the more] the Commonwealth.

Professor Theophilus Parsons, whom Dean Pound cited, is certainly explicit. He opened his highly regarded 1853 book on contracts with these words:

> The law of contracts in its widest extent may be regarded as including nearly all the law which regulates the relations of human life. Indeed, it may be looked upon as the basis of human society. All social life presumes it, and rests upon it; for out of contracts, expressed or implied, declared or understood, grow all rights, all duties, all obligations, and all law. Almost the whole procedure of human life implies, or, rather is, the continual fulfillment of contracts.

Theophilus Parsons, 1 *The Law of Contracts* 3 (Boston: Little, Brown, 1853); Roscoe Pound, "The Charles River Bridge Case," 27 *Massachusetts Law Quarterly* 19–20 (1942). Also see Wallace Mendelson, "B. F. Wright on the Contract Clause: A Progressive Misreading of the Marshall-Taney Era," 38 *Western Political Quarterly* 262–275 (1985); Nathan Isaacs, "John Marshall on Contracts: A Study in Early American Judicial Theory," 7 *Virginia Law Review* 413–428 (1921).

104. As he always did, Marshall read the text of the Constitution precisely: "Since the Constitution uses the general term contract, without distinguishing between those which are executory and those which are executed, it must be construed to comprehend the latter as well as the former." 6 Cranch 135.

105. Benjamin Wright, whose book on the contract clause is often cited in casebooks on constitutional law, asserted that Marshall had overstepped the intent of the Framers and that the contract clause was not meant to apply to state contracts. Yet Wright offered no documentation for his assertion and ignored substantial evidence to the contrary. For example, the Northwest Ordinance enacted by the Continental Congress in July 1787 stated that "no law

ought to . . . have force in said territory that shall in any manner whatever interfere with or affect *private* contracts . . . previously formed." Emphasis added. At the Constitution Convention six weeks later (August 28, 1787), Rufus King moved to include a similar ban concerning private contracts in the Constitution. The Committee of Style (Gouverneur Morris, Dr. Johnson, King, Hamilton, and Madison), which reported on September 14, deleted the qualifying word "private" and referred simply to "contracts." If the Framers had wanted the clause to apply merely to private contracts, they could easily have said so. See Max Farrand, 2 *Records of the Federal Convention of 1787* 439, 597 (New Haven, Conn.: Yale University Press, 1936).

Hamilton and Madison, explaining the contract clause in *The Federalist*, both refer to it in general, all-inclusive terms. See *The Federalist; A collection of Essays, Written in Favour of the New Constitution, As Agreed Upon by the Federal Convention, September 17, 1787* No. 44 (Madison), No. 81 (Hamilton) (Philadelphia: John and Archibald McLean, 1788). Justice James Wilson, who played an equally prominent role at the Convention, asked rhetorically in *Chisholm v. Georgia*, "What good purpose could this constitutional provision secure if a state might pass a law impairing the obligation of its own contracts, and be amenable, for such a violation of right, to no controlling judiciary power?" 2 Dallas 419, 464 (1793). Justice William Paterson, the author of the "New Jersey plan" at the convention, was even more explicit in *Van Horn's Lessee v. Dorrance*, 4 Dallas 14 (1800), when he held that the state of Pennsylvania could not impair its own contractual obligations.

Aside from the text of the Constitution itself, the fact that Hamilton, Madison, Wilson, and Paterson all spoke of the contract clause in general terms and did not restrict it to private contracts appears conclusive. Compare Wright, *Contract Clause* 15–18.

106. 6 Cranch 137.

107. In volume 5 of his biography of Washington, in his discussion of the internal state of affairs after Washington's inauguration, Marshall had written that the new Constitution "was understood to prohibit all laws impairing the obligation of contracts" and that this "had in a great measure restored what confidence which is essential to the internal prosperity of the nation." John Marshall, 5 *The Life of George Washington* 178 (Philadelphia: C. P. Wayne, 1807).

108. Johnson rested his opinion on natural law, which he called "the reason and the nature of things: a principle which will impose laws even on the deity." 6 Cranch 143. At the conclusion of his opinion, Johnson alluded to the possibility that the case had been arranged between friendly parties. "I have been very unwilling," he said, "to proceed to the decision of this cause at all. It appears to me to bear strong evidence, upon the face of it, of being a mere feigned case. It is our duty to decide on the rights, but not on the speculation of parties. My confidence, however in the respectable gentlemen who have been engaged for the parties, has induced me to abandon my scruples, in the belief that they would never consent to impose a mere feigned case upon this court." *Ibid.* 147–148.

109. In 1805, in the often-overlooked case of *Huidekoper's Lessee v. Douglass*, 3 Cranch 1, the Marshall Court unanimously held that the state of Pennsylvania was bound by the contract clause. The decision did not overturn state legislation, but Marshall, in interpreting the relevant statute, stated, "This is a contract, and although the state is a party, it ought to be construed according to those well regulated principles which regulate contracts generally." *Ibid.* 70. Also see Mendelson, "B. F. Wright," 268; Isaacs, "Marshall on Contracts," 418–426.

110. There is no evidence to suggest that the Court's decision aroused substantial public reaction or was unpopular. Press reaction was subdued. New England papers approved the decision; the *Aurora* remained silent; and two southern newspapers, the Richmond *Enquirer* and the *Savannah Republican*, habitually critical of Marshall, reprinted the decision without editorial comment. For an exhaustive review of press commentary, see Magrath, *Yazoo* 225, note 13. Professor Magrath concludes: "My examination of the *Annals of Congress* for 1810 and 1811, and of some dozen leading eastern newspapers in the period March–May 1811—certainly rough barometers of public concern—uncovered little excitement over the Supreme Court's decision." Cf. Beveridge, 3 *Life of Marshall* 595.

111. See Chapter 14. Madison, along with Albert Gallatin and Levi Lincoln, recommended to Jefferson that 5 million acres be set aside to settle the Yazoo claims "The interest of the United

States, the tranquility of those who thereafter may inhabit that territory, and various equitable considerations . . . render it expedient to enter into a compromise on reasonable terms." 1 *American State Papers, Public Lands* 134–135. For the administration's favorable reaction to *Fletcher v. Peck*, see Irving Brant, 4 *James Madison* 240 (Indianapolis: Bobbs-Merrill, 1956).

112. 3 *United States Statutes at Large* 116–120 (1814). Ultimately, a total of $4,282,151.12 was disbursed, the last claims being dismissed in 1864. 3 *American State Papers, Finance* 281–283; *New England Land Company v. United States*, 1 Court of Claims 135 (1864).

113. On the relation between *United States v. Peters* and *Fletcher v. Peck*, see especially Joseph M. Lynch, "*Fletcher v. Peck*: The Nature of the Contract Clause," 13 *Seton Hall Law Review* 1–20 (1982).

114. The term "vested rights" is most frequently attributed to Edward S. Corwin, "The Basic Doctrine of American Constitutional Law," 12 *Michigan Law Review* 255 (1914).

115. Pennsylvania (1790); Kentucky (1792); Tennessee (1796). Wright, *Contract Clause* 60–61.

116. Eleven of these states were from west of the Appalachians, where ideas of popular sovereignty were presumably strongest. *Ibid.* 86–87.

117. Magrath, *Yazoo* 114.

118. *Hudson and Smith v. Guestier*, 6 Cranch 281, 285 (1810), which upheld the jurisdiction of the French courts. This case had been decided during the 1808 term, *Hudson v. Guestier*, 4 Cranch 293. Marshall wrote the decision, but Chase and Livingston filed a rare written dissent pertaining to the locus of capture. When the case was regarded in 1810, Livingston convinced his colleagues of the correctness of his original position. The Court reversed itself on this minor jurisdictional point. The judgment, however, did not change. Marshall's brief, lighthearted dissent evidences perplexity rather than principle.

17: "A Band of Brothers"

1. W. M. Paxton, *The Marshall Family* 99 (Cincinnati: Robert Clarke & Co., 1885).

2. Frances Norton Mason, *My Dearest Polly* 206–208, 225 (Richmond, Va.: Garrett & Massie, 1961).

3. Marshall's letter to Washington, April 12, 1810, has been lost. Its contents are referred to in Bushrod's reply of May 2, 1810, 7 *The Papers of John Marshall* 244–245 (Chapel Hill: University of North Carolina Press, 1993). Marshall had evidently seen a newspaper advertisement placed by Antoine Cazanove announcing the arrival of a shipment of "London Particular Madeira Wine" from Murdock, Yuille, Wardrop & Co., English wine merchants.

4. *Ibid.*

5. Marshall's reply has not been found, but presumably, the sixty-three gallons of Madeira he ordered made it to Richmond.

6. Latrobe to Marshall, June 5, 1810, 7 *Marshall Papers* 254–256.

7. The courtroom had a vaulted ceiling that supported the floor of the Senate chamber. During construction, the ceiling collapsed, killing the superintendent of work. *Connecticut Courant*, September 28, 1808.

8. For the itemized account, see Message from the President to Congress, January 15, 1811, S#24231, R.R. 233, National Archives.

9. Marshall to Latrobe, June 9, 1810, 7 *Marshall Papers* 261.

10. Charles J. Ingersoll, *Inchiquin: The Jesuit's Letters* 52 (New York: Riley, 1810).

11. *Ibid.*

12. Jefferson to Gallatin, September 27, 1810, 11 *The Works of Thomas Jefferson* 152–155, note, Paul Leicester Ford, ed. (New York: G. P. Putnam's Sons, 1905).

13. Jefferson's view that all three branches of government should be responsible to the popular will is expressed in a letter to Edmund Randolph: "The whole body of the nation is the sovereign legislative, judiciary, and executive power for itself. The inconvenience of meeting to exercise these powers in person, and their inaptitude to exercise them, induce them to appoint special organs to declare their legislative will, to judge and execute it. *It is the will of the nation which makes the law obligatory. . . .*" Jefferson to Randolph, August 18, 1799, 9 *Works of Jefferson* 74. Emphasis added.

14. Jefferson to Giles, November 17, 1810, quoted in Charles Warren, 1 *The Supreme Court in United States History* 402 (Boston: Little, Brown, 1926).

15. Jefferson to Madison, May 25, 1810, 11 *Works of Jefferson* 139–141.

16. Tyler to Jefferson, May 12, 1810, in Lyon G. Tyler, 1 *The Letters and Times of the Tylers* 244–247 (Richmond, Va.: Whittet & Shepperson, 1884). Two weeks later Jefferson replied that

> We have long enough suffered under the base prostitutions of law to party passions in one judge [Marshall], and the imbecility of another [Griffin]. In the hands of one the law is nothing more than an ambiguous text, to be explained by his sophistry into any meaning which may subserve his personal malice. Nor can any milk-and-water associ-ated maintain its own [in?] dependence, and by a firm pursuance of what the law re-ally is, extend its protection to the citizens or the public. I believe you will do it, and where you cannot induce your colleague to do what is right, you will be firm enough to hinder him from doing what is wrong, and by opposing sense to sophistry, leave the ju-ries free to follow their own judgment.

Jefferson to Tyler, May 26, 1810, 11 *Works of Jefferson* 141–143, note. On June 9, 1810, Tyler graciously replied but made no reference to Marshall, Griffin, or the judiciary. Tyler, 1 *Letters and Times of the Tylers* 249.

17. See Marshall to Monroe, January 3, 1784, 1 *Marshall Papers* 113–114.

18. Years later Tyler's son, President John Tyler, reflecting on Richmond at the time when his father was governor (young Tyler was eighteen), described the illustrious members of the city's bar, noting respectfully that Marshall had, years before, "put on the robes of the Chief-Justice. How he wore them is too well known to require me to say." 1858 address of former President John Tyler, "Richmond and its Memories," in Tyler, 1 *Letters and Times of the Tylers* 219–225. For Judge Tyler's basic concurrence with Marshall, see Dumas Malone, *The Sage of Monticello* 64 (Boston: Little, Brown, 1977).

19. Jefferson to Gallatin, September 27, 1810, 11 *Works of Jefferson* 152–155, note.

20. Jefferson to Madison, October 15, 1810, *ibid.* 150–154.

21. *Ibid.* Jefferson's reference to Story as a "pseudo-republican" is in his letter to Henry Dear-born, July 16, 1810, *ibid.* 142–145.

22. *Ibid.*

23. Madison to Jefferson, October 9, 1810, 8 *The Writings of James Madison* 110–111, Gaillard Hunt, ed. (New York: G. P. Putnam's Sons, 1900).

24. Madison to Lincoln, October 20, 1810, quoted in Warren, 1 *Supreme Court* 408.

25. Lincoln to Madison, November 27, 1810, *ibid.* 409.

26. See, for example, Rodney to Lincoln, January 1811, *ibid.* 409–410.

27. Lincoln to Madison, January 20, 1811, *ibid.* 410.

28. It was widely assumed that Jefferson was pulling the strings behind the scene. As John Ran-dolph wrote to Joseph H. Nicholson, "The truth seems to be that [Madison] is President *de jure* only. Who exercises the office *de facto* I know not, but it seems agreed on all hands that 'there is something behind the throne greater than the throne itself.'" February 14, 1811, in Henry Adams, *John Randolph* 238–240 (Boston: Houghton Mifflin, 1882). Madison's biogra-pher disputes Jefferson's role and suggests that Wolcott was recommended by Joel Barlow, Marshall's acquaintance from Paris, who was then living in Washington. Irving Brant, *James Madison: The President, 1809–1812* 170 (Indianapolis: Bobbs-Merrill, 1956).

29. The immediate crisis was perhaps less serious than the one that might have resulted had Wolcott been confirmed, since he subsequently went on record that any judge who declared a law unconstitutional had usurped legislative power and should be impeached. Richard J. Purcell, *Connecticut in Transition* 397 (Washington, D.C.: American Historical Association, 1918).

30. For a summary of press reaction, see Warren, 1 *Supreme Court* 415.

31. Marshall to Pickering, February 28, 1811, 7 *Marshall Papers* 270.

32. J. Q. Adams to Madison, June 3, 1811, 4 *The Writings of John Quincy Adams* 93, Worthington C. Ford, ed. (New York: Macmillan, 1913).

33. Madison to Adams, November 15, 1811, 8 *Writings of Madison* 165.

34. J. Q. Adams to Madison, June 3, 1811, 4 *Writings of J. Q. Adams* 95. Adams was more candid writing to his brother, Thomas Boylston Adams. "I am conscious of too little law even for practice at the bar, still less should I feel myself qualified for the bench of the Supreme Court of the United States. I am also, and always shall be, too much of a political partisan for a judge. . . ." *Ibid*. 47–48. Also see Adams's lengthy explanation to his father, June 7, 1811, *ibid*. 98–102.

35. Chase rode the fourth circuit, which included the states of Maryland and Delaware.

36. See Madison's memorandum of April 11, 1811, quoted in Warren, 1 *Supreme Court* 423, note 1.

37. The adjective is from Joseph Story, who described Duvall as unfailingly "urbane and courteous, with a gentle manner, firm integrity, independence, and sound judgment." 2 Howard xi (1835).

38. For Madison's close friendship with Duvall, see Brant, *Madison: The President* 171. Mrs. Duvall was less well liked, especially by Mrs. Madison and her sisters. Lucy Payne Washington, Dolley's beautiful younger sister who subsequently married Justice Todd, wrote after the wedding that she was "very much provoked at that old hag Mrs. Duvall [whose] disposition to venom" was unparalleled—a view that Dolley Madison apparently shared. Lucy Todd to Dolley Madison, April 18, 1812, cited in Ralph Ketcham, *James Madison: A Biography* 520 (Charlottesville: University Press of Virginia, 1990).

39. Duvall may or may not have lived up to Madison's expectations. During his twenty-three years on the Court, he wrote only seventeen decisions. All were erudite and nicely crafted, but none dealt with major issues. He dissented in the great case of *Dartmouth College v. Woodward*, 4 Wheaton 518, 713 (1819), and, although a slaveowner himself, was the most assiduous of the justices in defending the rights of blacks. See his eloquent dissent in *Mima Queen and Child, Petitioners for Freedom v. Hepburn*, 7 Cranch 290, 298 (1813) as well as his opinion for the Court in *Le Grand v. Darnall*, 2 Peters 664 (1829). Given the collegial style of the Marshall Court, however, a mere compilation of written decisions provides little insight into the role that each justice played in conference. Marshall and Story respected Duvall's judgment, and that surely counts for something. Compare David P. Currie's tongue-in-cheek article, "The Most Insignificant Justice: A Preliminary Inquiry," 50 *University of Chicago Law Review* 466–480 (1983); and Frank H. Easterbrook's rejoinder, "The Most Insignificant Justice: Further Evidence," *ibid*. 481–501. Duvall's decision are catalogued at 500–501.

40. Warren, 1 *Supreme Court* 415. "The facts surrounding this highly unexpected appointment remain a legal historical mystery."

41. 6 Cranch 87 (1810).

42. Joseph Story, *A Selection of Pleadings in Civil Actions* (Salem, Mass.: Bernard Macanulty, 1805).

43. Joseph Chitty, *A Practical Treatise on Bills of Exchange . . .* , Joseph Story, ed. (Boston: Farnand, Mallory & Co., 1804); Charles Abbott *A Treatise on the Law Relative to Merchant Ships and Seamen*, Joseph Story, ed. (Newburyport, Mass.: E. Little, 1810); and Edward H.V. Lawes, *A Practical Treatise on Pleading in Assumpsit*, Joseph Story, ed. (Boston: James W. Burditt, 1811).

44. R. Kent Newmyer, *Supreme Court Justice Joseph Story* 71 (Chapel Hill: University of North Carolina Press, 1985).

45. David P. Currie suggests, not entirely in jest, that the characterization "John Marshall and the Six Dwarfs" provides the best description of the Court during this period. See "The Most Insignificant Justice: A Preliminary Inquiry," 466, 469. Currie, a sometime witness to the common law origins of the infield fly rule (*ibid*. 466, note 2), has fallen victim to Marshallian mythology. The more appropriate appellation, "a band of brothers," is Shakespeare's phrase, used by Henry V to rally his troops at Agincourt ("We few, we happy few, we band of brothers." *Henry V*, Act IV, scene 3.). It was usefully employed by Lord Nelson to describe the symbiotic relationship among his captains at the Battle of the Nile. See 3 *The Dispatches of Vice Admiral Lord Viscount Nelson* iv, 91, Sir Nicholas Harris Nicolas, ed. (London: Henry Colburn, 1840). Just as the British victory over a superior French fleet required an instinctive understanding by each captain of the rules of engagement, so the unanimity of the Marshall Court required fundamental agreement among the justices as to the purpose and

meaning of the Constitution. Nelson's captains fought their ships independently, just as the justices of the Marshall Court arrived at their common conclusions via different routes.

46. Felix Frankfurter, *The Commerce Clause Under Marshall, Taney and White* 5 (Chapel Hill: University of North Carolina Press, 1937).

47. See particularly Julius Goebel, Jr., "The Common Law and the Constitution," in *Chief Justice Marshall: A Reappraisal*, W. Melville Jones, ed. (Ithaca, N.Y.: Cornell University Press, 1956).

48. Newmyer, *Story* 81. I have drawn heavily on Professor Newmyer's insight concerning the Marshall Court, and I take this opportunity to acknowledge my indebtedness to him.

49. Donald G. Morgan, *Justice William Johnson: The First Dissenter* 20, 287 (Columbia: University of South Carolina Press, 1954).

50. Newmyer, *Story* 20–36.

51. *Ibid.* 24.

52. *Ibid.* 81–82.

53. The text of Monroe's letter has been lost, but Madison's November 5, 1811, message to Congress was reprinted in the *National Intelligencer* (Washington, D.C.) the following day. See 7 *Marshall Papers* 272, note 1.

54. Marshall to Monroe, November 8, 1811, *ibid.* 272.

55. 15 F. Cas. 660 (C.C.D. Va. 1811) (No. 8,411).

56. Livingston's declaration contained eight counts, but the issue turned on Jefferson's third plea challenging the jurisdiction of the court. The pleadings are examined in detail from a legal perspective by Ronan E. Degnan in "*Livingston v. Jefferson*—A Freestanding Footnote," 75 *California Law Review* 115–128 (1987).

57. The local action rule, reinforced by Marshall's holding in *Livingston v. Jefferson*, remains the basic principle that determines the venue of land title actions in federal courts. See Charles Alan Wright, Arthur R. Miller, and Edward H. Cooper, *Federal Practice and Procedure* section 3822, 204, 2nd ed. (St. Paul: West Publishing Co., 1986); Jack H. Friedenthal, Mary K. Kane, and Arthur R. Miller, *Civil Procedure* section 2.16, 85–87 (St. Paul, Minn.: West Publishing Co., 1985); John J. Cound, Jack H. Friedenthal, Arthur R. Miller and John E. Sexton, *Civil Procedure: Cases and Materials* 301–303, 307–308, 4th ed. (St. Paul, Minn.: West Publishing Co., 1985).

58. 15 F. Cas. at 663.

59. *Doulson v. Matthews*, 4 T.R. 503, 100 Eng. Rep. 1143 (King's Bench, 1792). "It is now too late," said Justice Buller, "for us to enquire whether it were wise or politic to make a distinction between transitory and local actions: it is sufficient for the Courts that the law has settled the distinction, and that an action *quare clausum fregit* is local."

60. Act of Sept. 24, 1789, section 11, 1 *United States Statutes at Large* 73, 78. For discussion of this point, see Degnan, "*Livingston v. Jefferson*," 122–123; Charles Wright, *Federal Courts* 138, 4th ed. (St. Paul, Minn.: West Publishing Co., 1983).

61. 15 F. Cas. at 663–665.

62. Livingston eventually regained his *batture* land and sold it at a profit. Denied the opportunity to sue Jefferson, he brought suit in New Orleans against the United States marshal who had seized the land. On August 3, 1813, Judge Dominick Augustin Hall of the United States district court entered judgment in favor of Livingston ordering the marshal "to put the plaintiff in the peaceable and quiet possession of the premises." Following the return of his property, Livingston dropped proceedings for damages. United States District Court for the District of Louisiana, Minute Book No. 3 227 (1811–15).

63. John Tyler to Jefferson, May 17, 1812, in Tyler, 1 *Letters and Times of the Tylers* 263–264.

64. Marshall to Story, July 13, 1821, Story Papers, Massachusetts Historical Society. Also see Malone, *Sage of Monticello* 69.

65. Mason, *My Dearest Polly* 209–214.

66. Bishop William Meade, 2 *Old Churches, Ministers and Families of Virginia* 221–222 (Philadelphia: J. B. Lippincott, 1861).

67. 7 Cranch 116 (1812).

68. Letter, John Bassett Moore to Albert J. Beveridge, cited in Beveridge, 4 *The Life of John Marshall* 121, note (Boston: Houghton Mifflin, 1919).

69. Warren, 1 *Supreme Court* 425.

70. Joseph Story, 2 *Commentaries on the Constitution of the United States* 460–461 (Boston: Hilliard, Gray & Co., 1833). Also see Note, "Jurisdictional Immunity for Foreign Sovereigns," 63 *Yale Law Journal* 1148 (1954); Clark C. Stewart, "Reciprocal Influence of British and United States Law: Foreign Sovereign Immunity Law from The Schooner Exchange to the State Immunity Act of 1978," 13 *Vanderbilt Journal of Transnational Law* 761, 762–773 (1980); M. L. Marasinghe, "A Reassessment of Sovereign Immunity," 9 *Ottawa Law Review* 474, 480–482 (1977).

71. The case for *The Exchange* was argued by Alexander Dallas, the United States Attorney for Pennsylvania, and Attorney General William Pinkney. The statement is by Dallas at 7 Cranch 126.

72. Marshall to Josiah Quincy, April 23, 1810, 7 *Marshall Papers* 242.

73. See, for example, the unanimous decision of the Rehnquist Court terminating the financial claims against Iran that were then pending in federal courts. That decision affirmed the arrangements made by the Carter administration for the release of the American hostages in Tehran. *Dames & Moore v. Regan*, 453 U.S. 654 (1981).

74. Five decisions were *per curiam*, and two cases were dismissed.

75. *Schooner Paulina's Cargo v. United States*, 7 Cranch 52, 68 (1812).

76. *Walken v. Williams*, 7 Cranch 278, 279 (1812).

77. The view of many in Washington was that Justice Todd was as interesting as "still champagne," but Lucy, in her honeymoon letters to Dolley, draws the point of an ardent lover determined to get her pregnant. Back in Kentucky, Todd asked his wife to tell the president "that he [Todd] has got the apple in the dumpling" (the best of the Payne sisters), but left "the hows, and whens, for him [Madison] to conjecture." Lucy Todd to Dolley Madison, April 18 and May 29, 1812, quoted in Ketcham, *Madison* 519–520.

78. Marshall to Randolph, June 18, 1812, 7 *Marshall Papers* 332–333.

79. Marshall to Monroe, June 25, 1812, *ibid*. 333–334.

80. Randolph's letter has been lost. Marshall's reply, *infra*, indicates its contents.

81. Marshall to Randolph, June 26, 1812, 7 *Marshall Papers* 334–337.

82. Benjamin Stoddert to James McHenry, July 15, 1812, in Bernard C. Steiner, *The Life and Correspondence of James McHenry* 581–582 (Cleveland: Burrows Brothers, 1907). The episode is discussed in James H. Broussard, *The Southern Federalists, 1800–1816* 139–143 (Baton Rouge: Louisiana State University Press, 1978).

83. Marshall to Smith, July 27, 1812, 7 *Marshall Papers* 337–340.

84. Pinckney to James Milnor et al., August 24, 1812, Pinckney Family Papers, Library of Congress.

85. John Marshall, 5 *The Life of George Washington* 12–18 (Philadelphia: C. P. Wayne 1807).

86. Washington to Governor Benjamin Harrison, January 18, 1784, 9 *The Writings of George Washington* 11–13, Jared Sparks, ed. (Boston: Little, 1855).

87. In his letter to Harrison, Washington pointed out that if the people of the West should have their trade "flow through the Mississippi or the St. Lawrence; if the inhabitants thereof should form commercial connections, which we know lead to intercourses of other kinds, they would in a few years be as unconnected with us, as are those of South America." *Ibid*.

88. Editorial note, *Ibid*. 356.

89. *River Commission Report*, December 26, 1812. The report was originally published in the Richmond *Enquirer*, January 7 and 9, 1813, and is reprinted in 7 *Marshall Papers* 361–378. The original map made by the party has been lost, but a copy is among the records of the Virginia Board of Public Works in Richmond.

90. See especially Douglas R. Egerton, *Charles Fenton Mercer and the Trial of National Conservatism* 100–105 (Jackson: University Press of Mississippi, 1989); Philip Morrison Rice, "The Virginia Board of Public Works, 1816–1842," 45–66, unpublished M.A. thesis, University of North Carolina, 1947.

91. Editorial note, 7 *Marshall Papers* 359; Wayland Fuller Dunaway, *History of the James River and Kanawha Company*, 75, 100–104 (New York: Columbia University Press, 1922).

92. Marshall to Monroe, January 18, 1813, 7 *Marshall Papers* 380–381.

93. St. George Tucker, *Blackstone's Commentaries: With Notes of Reference to the Constitution and Laws of the Federal Government of the United States; and of the Commonwealth of Virginia*, 5 vols. (Philadelphia: Birch and Small, 1803).

94. See Chapter 15.

95. See, for example, *Evans v. Jordan and Morehead* (C.C.D. Va. 1813), in which Marshall and Tucker, unable to agree, certified the case to the Supreme Court. The Court, speaking through Justice Washington, affirmed Marshall's view. 9 Cranch 199 (1815).

96. Marshall to Tucker, February 3, 1813, 7 *Marshall Papers* 381–382.

97. Marshall delivered the opinion of the Court in seventeen cases, Story in seven, Livingston in six, Johnson and Washington in four each, and Duvall in two. Four decisions were *per curiam*, and two case were dismissed. Duvall dissented once, and Johnson three times. The remainder of the decisions were unanimous. Two of Johnson's dissents were from decisions written by Story: *Mills v. Duryee*, 7 Cranch 481, and *Fairfax's Devisee v. Hunter's Lessee*, 7 Cranch 603.

98. For a useful summary of cases, see George L. Haskins and Herbert A. Johnson, *Foundations of Power: John Marshall, 1801–15* 531–545, The Oliver Wendell Holmes Devise, 2 *History of the Supreme Court of the United States* (New York: Macmillan, 1981); Charles J. Ingersoll, 1 *Historical Sketch* Chap. 2 (Philadelphia: Lea & Blanchard, 1845).

99. Vigilance Committee Minute Book, 1–4, 6–7, 11, 16, cited in 7 *Marshall Papers* 413–414, note 1.

100. "Report on Fortifications," June 28, 1813, *ibid.* 412–413.

101. Mason, *My Dearest Polly* 223–225.

18: National Supremacy

1. As Justice Johnson said of the war, speaking for an unanimous Court in *The Rapid*, 8 Cranch 155 (1814), "The whole nation are embarked in one common bottom and must be reconciled to submit to one common fate."

2. Between 1812 and 1816, Story dissented seven times, exclusively on questions related to the war powers of the government. That was more than any other justice, including William Johnson, who is often regarded as the great dissenter, and more than the total number of dissents by all the justices during the first eleven years of the Marshall Court. See R. Kent Newmyer, *Supreme Court Justice Joseph Story* 93 (Chapel Hill: University of North Carolina Press, 1985).

3. 8 Cranch 110 (1814).

4. Marshall's decision in *Brown* reversed Story's holding on circuit. In deferring to the ultimate authority of Congress, the chief justice's opinion was consistent with his earlier decision in *Little v. Barreme*, 2 Cranch 170 (1804).

5. Story was joined by an unnamed colleague, but it very likely was Bushrod Washington. This surmise is based on Washington's decision in *The Venus*, 8 Cranch 253 (1814), with which Story concurred and from which Marshall dissented. Washington's reasoning in *The Venus* conforms to the basic thrust of Story's dissent in *Brown*.

6. 8 Cranch 253 (1814).

7. *Ibid.* 288. Livingston joined Marshall in dissent, and Johnson abstained.

8. Of the forty-five cases on the docket, Marshall delivered the opinion in twelve, Story in ten, Washington in seven, Johnson in six, Livingston in four, Duvall in two, and Todd in one. Two cases were decided *per curiam*, and one was dismissed. Story and Livingston each dissented twice, Johnson once, and Marshall once.

9. *National Intelligencer* (Washington, D.C.), February 24, 1814.

10. Story to Samuel P. Fay, March 6, 1814, 1 *Life and Letters of Joseph Story* 251–253, William W. Story, ed. (Boston: C. Little and James Brown, 1851).

11. Mr. Samuel Harrison Smith to Mrs. Kirkpatrick, March 13, 1814, in Margaret Bayard Smith, *First Forty Years of Washington Society* 96, Gaillard Hunt, ed. (New York: Charles Scribner's Sons, 1906). Pinkney's proclivity to play to the women in the audience was notorious. As William Writ wrote, describing a scene in the Supreme Court several years later, "There were ladies present, and Mr. Pinkney was expected to be eloquent at all events. So, the mode he adopted was to get into his tragical tone in discussing the construction of an act of Congress. Closing his speech in this solemn tone he took his seat, saying to me, with a smile, 'that will do for the ladies.'" Wirt to Francis Gilmer, April 1, 1816, in John Pendleton Kennedy, 1 *Memoirs of the Life of William Wirt* 404 (Philadelphia: Lea and Blanchard, 1856).

12. Latrobe to Congress, November 28, 1816, quoted in Charles Warren, 1 *Supreme Court in United States History* 459 (Boston: Little, Brown, 1926).

13. *Ibid.*

14. Marshall to Washington, December 29, 1814, 8 *The Papers of John Marshall* 63 (Chapel Hill: University of North Carolina Press, 1995).

15. Treaty of Peace between Great Britain and the United States, December 24, 1814, 2 *Treaties and Other International Acts of the United States* 574, David Hunter Miller, ed. (Washington, D.C.: Government Printing Office, 1931).

16. George Ticknor to his father, February 1815 [day omitted], 1 *Life, Letters, and Journals of George Ticknor* 38–40, Anna Ticknor and George S. Hillard, eds. (Boston: J. R. Osgood, 1877). In commenting that the justices "were fully powdered," Ticknor may have been taking poetic license for his father's benefit. Paintings of Marshall's indicate that his hair had become steel gray, but do not suggest the use of powder. That was not Marshall's style.

17. *Ibid.*

18. Justice Livingston dissented from the majority opinion written by Story in *Speake v. United States*, 9 Cranch 37 (1815), and Story dissented from Marshall's opinion in *The Nereide*, 9 Cranch 388 (1815).

19. 9 Cranch 388 (1815).

20. Mr. Pinto was represented by J. Ogden Hoffman and Thomas Emmet of New York; the captors by Alexander Dallas, William Pinkney, and Robert Harper.

21. *New York Evening Post*, March 15, 1815. Also see 1 *Life, Letters, and Journals of Ticknor* 38, 41.

22. Justice Johnson, concurring with Marshall, said, "To the Legislative power alone, it must belong to determine when the violence of other nations is to be met by violence; to the Judiciary, to administer law and justice as it is, not as it is made to be by the folly or caprice of other nations." 9 Cranch 432.

23. For the United States position, see Green Haywood Hackworth, 7 *Digest of International Law* 1–12 (Washington, D.C.: Government Printing Office, 1943); Charles Chaney Hyde 3, *International Law Chiefly as Interpreted and Applied By the United States* 2041–2045, 2nd rev. ed. (Boston: Little, Brown, 1945).

24. 11 Faculty Records, March 20, 1815, Harvard University, in 8 *Marshall Papers* 84, note 2.

25. *Ibid.* 82, note 1.

26. Marshall to Washington, March 16, 1815, *ibid.* 81–82.

27. Washington to Marshall, May 2, 1810, 7 *ibid.* 244–245. See Chapter 17.

28. Marshall to Willing & Francis, May 2, 1815, 8 *ibid.* 89–90.

29. Marshall to Thomas Willing, Jr., November 5, 1817, *ibid.* 158–159.

30. Marshall to Cogswell, April 9, 1815, *ibid.* 83–84.

31. Marshall to Cogswell, April 23, 1815, *ibid.* 398 (Appendix).

32. Marshall to Cogswell, May 29, 1815, *ibid.* 398–399.

33. Marshall to Phillip Slaughter, September 22, 1827; Marshall to James Keith Marshall, April 7, 1828; copies in the Marshall Papers, Williamsburg, Va.

34. Marshall to Washington, April 3, 1815, 8 *Marshall Papers* 82–83. Also see Marshall to Washington, June 26, 1820, 9 *ibid.* (in press).

35. Herbert B. Adams, 1 *The Life and Writings of Jared Sparks* 389–413 (Boston: Houghton Mifflin, 1893).

36. Peters to Marshall, October 4, 1815. Letter not found, but see 8 *Marshall Papers* 100.

37. Marshall to Peters, October 12, 1815, *ibid.*

38. *Ibid*. Marshall's emphasis.

39. The first appeal from a state court judgment was *Olney v. Arnold*, 3 Dallas 308 (1797), involving the construction of a federal statute by the Rhode Island supreme court.

40. *United States v. Peters*, 5 Cranch 115 (1809). See Chapter 16.

41. The Virginia legislature solemnly resolved that in disputes "between the General and State Governments a tribunal is already provided by the Constitution of the United States (to wit, the Supreme Court) more eminently qualified to decide the disputes aforesaid in an enlightened and impartial manner than any other tribunal which could be created." See Warren, 1 *Supreme Court* 443.

42. *New Jersey v. Wilson*, 7 Cranch 164 (1812).

43. 1 Wheaton 304 (1816).

44. This complex litigation has been described by numerous authors, but never with the exactitude displayed by Charles F. Hobson, editor of *The Papers of John Marshall*, in his note, "Marshall and the Fairfax Litigation," 8 *Marshall Papers* 108–126. Compare: John Alfred Treon, "*Martin v. Hunter's Lessee*: A Case History," unpublished Ph.D. dissertation, University of Virginia, 1970; F. Thornton Miller, "John Marshall versus Spencer Roane: A Reevaluation of *Martin v. Hunter's Lessee*," 96 *Virginia Magazine of History and Biography* 297–314 (1988); William Winslow Crosskey, 2 *Politics and the Constitution in the History of the United States* 785–817 (Chicago: University of Chicago Press, 1953).

45. See Chapter 6.

46. In the distribution of Lord Fairfax's personal estate, James Markham Marshall had acquired the parcel in Shenandoah County that David Hunter contested. James Marshall had, in turn, sold the land long before the case came to the Supreme Court, but he was the principal party to the suit. 8 *Marshall Papers* 114ff.

47. Marshall to Charles Lee, May 7, 1810, 7 *Marshall Papers* 246–247.

48. Contrary to the conventional wisdom that enshrouds *Martin v. Hunter's Lessee*, title to the entirety of Lord Fairfax's estate was not at issue. That had been firmly resolved by the compromise enacted by the Virginia legislature in 1797. The question before the Court was where the 739-acre parcel fit. See especially Hobson, "Marshall and the Fairfax Litigation," 114–116.

49. 7 Cranch 603 (1813).

50. Marshall and Todd did not participate in the case, and Justice Johnson dissented. The majority was composed of Story, Duvall, Livingston and Washington.

51. Newmyer, *Story* 107–108.

52. The Supreme Court's mandate was sent out in August 1813. In the spring of 1814, the Virginia court of appeals heard argument on whether it should obey the writ, but did not render its decision until September 1815, a majority of Virginia's judges not wishing to challenge federal authority while the conflict with Britain was still under way. 8 *Marshall Papers* 116–117.

53. 4 Munford 58–59 (1815). Judge Cabell said that the Court "should decline obedience to the mandate": Judge Brooke, that "obedience to the mandate ought to be refused"; Judge Roane, that "this Court is at liberty and is bound to follow its own convictions on the subject"; and Chief Judge Fleming, that "it is inexpedient for this Court to obey the mandate." *Ibid. passim*.

54. Roane, who served on the Virginia court of appeals from 1794 to 1821, is usually referred to as the chief judge or chief justice of the Virginia high court. In fact, William Fleming occupied that position ("president") throughout Roane's tenure.

55. 4 Munford 25–54.

56. Newmyer, *Story* 107–108.

57. *Martin v. Hunter's Lessee*, petition for Writ of Error, December 16, 1815, reproduced in 8 *Marshall Papers* 121–122.

58. Marshall dispatched the petition to Justice Washington, who immediately granted the writ of error and signed a citation to David Hunter summoning him to appear before the Supreme Court during the 1816 term. *Martin v. Hunter's Lessee*, Appellate Case No. 793, R.G. 267, National Archives. For an analysis of the celerity with which the Marshall Court acted, see G. Edward White, *The Marshall Court and Cultural Change, 1815–35* 496–497, in The

Oliver Wendell Holmes Devise, 3–4 *History of the Supreme Court of the United States* (New York: Macmillan, 1988).

59. I am indebted to Dr. Charles Hobson for the thoughts and much of the phraseology of this paragraph. See 8 *Marshall Papers* 117–118.

60. In *Granville's Devisee v. Allen*, (C.C.D. N.C. 1805), a case involving the Treaty of Paris of 1783 that raised points similar to those at issue in the Fairfax litigation, Marshall stepped aside, stating that he "should feel much delicacy in deciding the present question." 6 *Marshall Papers* 400. Similar considerations prevented him from participating in *Smith v. Maryland*, 6 Cranch 286 (1810), and *Orr v. Hodgson*, 4 Wheaton 465 (1819).

61. Marshall to St. George Tucker, May 26, 1823, Tucker-Coleman Papers, College of William and Mary Library.

62. 1 Wheaton 304 (1816).

63. 7 Cranch 603.

64. "Are then the judgments of this Court to be reviewed by every court of the Union? And is every recovery of money, every change of property, that has taken place under our process, to be considered as null, void, and tortious?" asked Johnson. "We are constituted by the voice of the Union, and when decisions take place . . . ours is the superior claim upon the comity of the state tribunals." 1 Wheaton 323–391.

65. 8 *Marshall Papers* 119; U.S. Supreme Court Dockets, App. Cas. No. 793.

66. The term was coined by the *Columbia Centinel* of Boston, July 12, 1817.

67. Monroe received 183 electoral votes; 34 votes were cast for Rufus King. Shaw Livermore, Jr., *The Twilight of Federalism: 1815–1830* 34 (Princeton, N.J.: Princeton University Press, 1962).

68. Harry Ammon, *James Monroe: The Quest for National Identity* 366–395 (Charlottesville: University Press of Virginia, 1990).

69. Monroe intended to take the oath in the chamber of the House of Representatives, as his predecessors had done, but Speaker Henry Clay refused to grant permission. See Monroe to Marshall, and Marshall to Monroe, March 1, 1817, 8 *Marshall Papers* 151.

70. *National Intelligencer* (Washington, D.C.), March 15, 1817.

71. Quoted in John Wentworth, *Congressional Reminiscences* (Chicago: Fergus, 1882).

72. One case, *United States v. Bevan*, 3 Wheaton 386 (1818), deserves comment because Marshall carefully steered the Court away from expanding federal admiralty jurisdiction and an impending confrontation with the state of Massachusetts. William Bevan, a marine sentry on the U.S.S. *Independence*, had allegedly murdered a cook's mate while the ship lay at anchor in Boston harbor. Bevan was tried and convicted in the U.S. circuit court in Massachusetts, but his appeal raised the question of whether his offense was within the jurisdiction of the state of Massachusetts or that of the federal court. By the time the issue reached the Supreme Court, it had acquired considerable notoriety. Daniel Webster argued the appeal for Bevan, and Attorney General Wirt for the United States.

Marshall's decision, in which all of his colleagues concurred, interpreted the relevant acts of Congress narrowly, declined to apply the common law of admiralty, and held that the states, not the federal courts, had jurisdiction over crimes committed in their harbors. It would appear that Marshall had convinced his colleagues that it would be impolitic to hold otherwise. Justice Story said afterward that he had written a dissenting opinion but had declined to deliver it. "The truth is . . . I put the opinion [aside] with a view at some future day perhaps to publish it, and I should have delivered it in Court, if I had not felt a delicacy in request to the Chief Justice. . . . Upon the point as to the exemption of a public ship of war from State jurisdiction, a majority of the Court held the same opinion as myself, although . . . that opinion was suppressed from motives of delicacy." Story to Henry Wheaton, April 10, 1818, 1 *Life and Letters of Story* 305.

73. In the forty-two cases reported during the 1817 term, Marshall delivered the opinion of the Court fifteen times; Johnson, Story and Washington each delivered eight decisions; Duvall delivered one; and two were *per curiam*. In 1818 the Court decided thirty-eight cases. Marshall announced seventeen; Story, Livingston and Johnson each announced four; Washington, three; Todd, two; Duvall, one; and three were *per curiam*.

74. *Shipp v. Miller*, 2 Wheaton 316, 326 (1817).

75. *The Aeolus v. Wood*, 3 Wheaton 392, 407 (1818).

76. *New York Commercial Advertiser*, February 7, 1818.

77. Marshall to Polly, February 14, 1817, 8 *Marshall Papers* 149–150.

78. 5 *The Memoirs of John Quincy Adams* 322–323, Charles F. Adams, ed. (Philadelphia: J. B. Lippincott, 1882).

79. William M. Meigs, *Life of Charles Jared Ingersoll* 123 (Philadelphia: J. B. Lippincott, 1897).

80. Frances Norton Mason, *My Dearest Polly* 241 (Richmond, Va.: Garret & Massie, 1961).

81. In the early nineteenth century, Fauquier White Sulphur Springs was a prosperous rival to the more famous White Sulphur Springs in what is now West Virginia. It is described at length in Perceval Reniers, *The Springs of Virginia* 155–158 (Chapel Hill: University of North Carolina Press, 1941).

82. Marshall to Louis Marshall, December 7, 1817, 8 *Marshall Papers* 159–160. Also see Marshall to Polly, February 16, 1818, in which Marshall notes that their son Jaquelin had written to him concerning her poor health. *Ibid*. 179.

83. Story to Henry Wheaton, December 9, 1818, 1 *Life and Letters of Story* 312.

84. *National Intelligencer*, March 13, 1818.

85. *Dartmouth Collage v. Woodward*, 4 Wheaton 518 (1819).

86. Justice Todd, who might have joined Duvall, remained in Kentucky and did not attend the 1819 session of the Court. His position is therefore unrecorded. For a useful analysis of the thinking of the justices, see White, *Marshall Court* 612–622.

87. For treatments of the origins of the *Dartmouth College* case, see Francis N. Stites, *Private Interest and Public Gain: The Dartmouth College Case, 1819* (Amherst: University of Massachusetts Press, 1972); John M. Shirley, *The Dartmouth College Causes and the Supreme Court* (St. Louis, Mo.: G. I. Jones 1877); John King Lord, *A History of Dartmouth College, 1815 1909* (Concord, N.H.: Rumford, 1913).

88. Warren, 1 *Supreme Court* 484.

89. Quoted in White, *Marshall Court* 613.

90. Jefferson followed the events in New Hampshire closely. On July 21, 1816, shortly after the legislature had acted, he wrote a letter of support to Governor Plumer. "The idea that institutions established for the use of the Nation cannot be touched or modified, even to make them answer their end, because of rights gratuitously supposed in those who manage them in trust for the public may, perhaps, be a satisfactory provision against the abuses of a monarch, but it is most absurd against the nation itself." Jefferson to Plumer, July 21, 1816, 7 *The Writings of Thomas Jefferson* 19, H.A. Washington, ed. (New York: H. W. Derby, 1861).

91. Webster was joined by Jeremiah Smith of New Hampshire, Jeremiah Mason of Maryland, and Joseph Hopkinson of Pennsylvania; William Wirt, joined by Congressman John Holmes of Maine, argued the case for the state of New Hampshire. See Warren, 1 *Supreme Court* 480.

92. 4 Wheaton 558.

93. Quoted in Samuel Gilman Brown, 1 *Works of Rufus Choate* 187–188 (Boston: Little, Brown, 1862).

94. Marshall's decision in *Dartmouth College v. Woodward* begins at 4 Wheaton 624.

95. Marshall's assertion, bold as it may seem, was not very controversial in 1819. It accorded with common law principles that a grant was a contract and with the Court's holding in *Fletcher v. Peck* that a grant by a state was as much a contract as one between individuals. See Charles F. Hobson, Editorial Note, *Dartmouth College v. Woodward*, 8 *Marshall Papers* 220.

96. *Bracken v. College of William and Mary*, Virginia Court of Appeals, 3 Call 577–579, 589–597 (1790), See Chapter 6. Also see Florian Bartosic, "With John Marshall from William and Marry to Dartmouth College," 7 *William and Mary Law Review* 259–266 (1966).

97. See Bruce A. Campbell, "*Dartmouth College* as a Civil Liberties Case," 70 *Kentucky Law Journal* 643–706 (1981–82).

98. 4 Wheaton 650.

99. To have held differently would have put at risk the charters of Harvard, Princeton, Yale, and William and Mary, all of which traced their existence to royal grants, and would have made the colleges easy targets for populist state legislatures eager to establish state university systems.

100. 4 Wheaton 654. Duvall dissented, but did not file an opinion. Todd, who was absent, did not participate in the judgment. The Court's majority was composed of Marshall, Washington, Johnson, Livingston, and Story.

101. See note 96.

102. Webster to Jeremiah Mason, February 4, 1819, quoted in *Memoirs and Correspondence of Jeremiah Mason* 213, George Stillman Hillard, ed. (Cambridge, Mass.: Riverside Press, 1873).

103. Hopkinson to Francis Brown, February 2, 1819, 1 *The Private Correspondence of Daniel Webster* 301, Fletcher Webster, ed. (Boston: Little, Brown, 1857).

104. *Boston Daily Advertiser*, February 8, 1819.

105. *Columbia Centinel*, February 10, 1819.

106. *Stone v. Mississippi*, 11 Otto 816 (1879). Also see *The Binghamton Bridge*, 3 Wallace 73 (1865); *Pearsall v. Great Northern Railway*, 161 U.S. 660 (1895).

107. Webster to Hopkinson, March 14, 1818, quoted in Warren, 1 *Supreme Court* 480.

108. As one historian has written of Marshall's conciliatory role in the *Dartmouth College* case, "[H]e had an ardent social nature, a seductive personal magnetism; he was a delightful companion, fluent and facile in conversation, and . . . the most eloquent listener in the Union. He was full of sly, waggish humor, genial and convivial; his temper was serene and imperturbable, his patience almost inexhaustible, and his judgment cool, wary, and calculating. . . . He was a born diplomatist . . . a natural politician." Shirley, *Dartmouth College Causes* 377.

109. Donald G. Morgan, *Justice William Johnson: The First Dissenter* (Columbia: University of South Carolina Press, 1954).

110. *Ibid*. 149–151.

111. 6 Cranch 87 (1810).

112. In *Fletcher v. Peck*, Johnson had based his concurrence on "general principles" rather than the contract clause. In *Dartmouth College v. Woodward*, he endorsed Marshall's explicit use of the contract clause rather than Story's concurring opinion, which was rooted in general principles. The personal chemistry was not unimportant. Johnson and Marshall were close; Johnson and Story were not.

113. 4 Wheaton 122 (1819).

114. Sturgis sued in the United States circuit court in Boston. After hearing arguments in October 1817, Justice Story and district court judge John Davis divided, certifying the case to the Supreme Court. Story was profoundly interested in bankruptcy legislation, and there is evidence that he and Judge Davis divided intentionally in order to facilitate the Supreme Court's review. See White, *Marshall Court* 633 and the sources cited therein.

115. According to Article I, section 8, of the Constitution, "The Congress shall have Power . . . To establish an uniform Rule of Nationalization, and uniform Laws on the subject of Bankruptcies throughout the United States."

116. Story confronted the issue in Boston in 1812 in *Babcock v. Weston*, 2 F. Cas. 306 (C.C.D. Mass. 1812) (No. 703) and *Van Reimsdyck v. Kane*, 28 F. Cas. 1062 (C.C.D. Mass. 1812) (No. 16,871). Washington dealt with the matter in Philadelphia in *Golden v. Prince*, 10 F. Cas 542 (C.C.D. Pa. 1814) (No. 5,509).

117. *Adams v. Storey*, 1 F. Cas. 141 (C.C.D. N.Y. 1817) (No. 66).

118. *Hannay v. Jacobs*, an unreported case cited by counsel in *Sturgis v. Crowninshield*, 4 Wheaton 135. Daniel Webster, who listened to the arguments in the case, wrote afterward that "the general opinion is that the six judges now here will be equally divided." Webster knew the Court better than most, however, and noted that he personally thought the decision "will be against the state laws." Webster to Jeremiah Mason, February 15, 1819, 16 *Writings and Speeches of Daniel Webster* 49–50, J. McIntyre, ed. (Boston: Little, Brown, 1903).

119. *Odgen v. Saunders*, 12 Wheaton 213, 272–273 (1827).

120. 4 Wheaton 196. The pragmatic nature of the holding, no doubt reflecting the arguments Marshall made in conference, is reflected in his phraseology: "It does not appear to be a violent construction of the Constitution, *and is certainly a convenient one*, to consider the power of the States as existing over such cases as the laws of the Union may not reach." *Ibid*. 195. Emphasis added.

121. Marshall to Washington, April 19, 1814, 8 *Marshall Papers* 34–35.

122. This is consistent with the letter Marshall wrote to Bushrod Washington in 1814, in which he said, "The words of the Constitution are prospective. 'No State shall' etc. . . . It may be doubted whether a bankrupt law applying to contracts after its passage may fairly be termed a law impairing the obligation of contracts. Such a contract is made with a knowledge that it be acted on by the law." April 19, 1814, *ibid.* 34–35.

123. 12 Wheaton 272–273.

124. When that issue came before the Court in 1827, a majority of the justices sustained the state law, with Marshall, Duvall, and Story dissenting. *Ogden v. Saunders*, 12 Wheaton 213, 332. This was Marshall's only dissent in a constitutional case during his thirty-five years as chief justice.

125. 4 Wheaton 316 (1819).

126. Albert J. Beveridge, 4 *The Life of John Marshall* 282 (Boston: Houghton Mifflin, 1919).

127. John Marshall, 4 *The Life of George Washington* 299 (Philadelphia: C. P. Wayne, 1807).

128. The Republican Congress had attempted to charter the bank a year earlier, but Madison had vetoed the measure. The president made clear, however, that he did not dispute its constitutionality. Madison said he waived the question of Congress's power to incorporate the bank "as being precluded in my judgment by repeated recognition under varied circumstances of the validity of such an institution in acts of the legislature, executive, and judicial branches of the Government." His objection was to the details. Veto Message to the Senate of the United States, January 30, 1815, 8 *The Writings of James Madison* 327, Gaillard Hunt, ed. (New York: G. P. Putnam's Sons, 1908). In December 1815 Madison suggested to Congress that they try again. In his State of the Union message, the president said "the probable operation of a national bank will merit consideration." 1 *A Compilation of the Messages and Papers of the Presidents, 1798–1897* 566, James D. Richardson, ed. (Washington, D.C.: Government Printing Office, 1896).

129. The Maryland tax applied to every banknote issued by non–state-chartered banks and ranged from 10¢ to $20, depending on the size of the note. The tax could be avoided by prior payments of an annual fee of $15,000. The methods adopted in other states varied. Illinois and Indiana flatly prohibited banks not chartered by the state. Georgia, Kentucky, North Carolina, Ohio, and Tennessee imposed taxes generally more burdensome than Maryland's. See Warren, 1 *Supreme Court* 505–506.

130. In May 1819 McCulloch was officially charged with embezzlement, having, among other things, misappropriated more than $500,000 of the bank's funds for his personal use. Criminal proceedings continued for several years but he was ultimately acquitted, the state of Maryland having no statute against embezzlement. Bray Hammond, *Banks and Politics in America from the Revolution to the Civil War* 268ff. (Princeton, N.J.: Princeton University Press, 1957).

131. *McCulloch v. Maryland*, 4 Wheaton 316, 426 (1819). The case was argued from February 22 through March 3, 1819.

132. *Ibid.* 363.

133. Story to Stephen White, March 13, 1819, 1 *Life and Letters of Story* 325.

134. 4 Wheaton 316, 400.

135. White, *Marshall Court* 486–487.

136. Charles F. Hobson, Editorial Note, 8 *Marshall Papers* 258.

137. Walter Berns, *Taking the Constitution Seriously* 207–208 (New York: Simon and Schuster, 1987).

19: Steamboats

1. For an extensive survey of press coverage, see Charles Warren, 1 *Supreme Court in United States History* 511–525 (Boston: Little, Brown, 1926).

2. Webster to Story, March (no date) 1819, 16 *Writings and Speeches of Daniel Webster* 56, J. McIntyre, ed. (Boston: Little, Brown, 1903).

3. *Boston Daily Advertiser*, March 13, 1819.

4. *National Intelligencer* (Washington, D.C.), March 13, 1819.

5. *Augusta Chronicle*, March 31, 1819.

6. *Kentucky Gazette*, March 19, 1819.

7. *Natchez Press*, quoted in Warren, 1 *Supreme Court* 519.

8. *Niles Weekly Register* (Baltimore), March 13, 1819.

9. For the Junto's reaction to *Martin v. Hunter's Lessee*, see Marshall to Story, April 28, 1819, 8 *The Papers of John Marshall* 309–310 (Chapel Hill: University of North Carolina Press, 1995).

10. Judge Brockenbrough's son, John W. Brockenbrough, subsequently collected and published Marshall's circuit court opinions, a singular service to history and the law. *Reports of Cases Decided by the Honorable John Marshall . . . in the Circuit Court of the United States for the District of Virginia and North Carolina, from 1802 to 1833*, 2 vols. (Philadelphia: James Kay, 1837).

11. As John Randolph noted, the principle of implied power announced by Marshall was sufficient to allow Congress to "emancipate every slave in the United States." Quoted in Albert J. Beveridge, 4 *The Life of John Marshall* 420 (Boston: Houghton Mifflin, 1916).

12. *Enquirer* (Richmond), March 23, 1819.

13. Marshall to Story, March 24, 1819, 8 *Marshall Papers* 280. Marshall's emphasis.

14. Marshall to Washington, March 27, 1819, *ibid*. 281. Emphasis added.

15. Brockenbrough's *nom de guerre*, "Amphictyon," derives from the term used to describe the league of Greek city-states ("Amphictyony") in the seventh-century B.C. The implication was that Brockenbrough was a citizen in a confederacy of independent states, not a consolidated Union. For more on the Amphictyony, see 1 *Encyclopaedia Britannica* 885–886 and the sources cited therein, 11th edition (Cambridge: Cambridge University Press, 1910).

16. The second essay appeared in the *Enquirer*, April 2, 1819. The text of both essays is reprinted in Gerald Gunther, *John Marshall's Defense of McCulloch v. Maryland* 52–77 (Stanford, Calif.: Stanford University Press, 1969).

17. Brockenbrough wrote "everyone must admit" that Marshall's opinion was very able.

> This was to be expected, proceeding as it does from a man of the most profound legal attainments, and upon a subject which has employed his thoughts, his tongue, and his pen, as a politician, and an historian, for more than thirty years. The subject, too, is one which has . . . heretofore drawn a broad line of distinction between the two great parties in this country, in which line no one has taken a more distinguished and decided rank than the judge who has thus expounded the supreme law of the land. It is not in my power to carry on a contest . . . with a man of his gigantic powers, but I trust it will not be thought rash or presumptuous to endeavor to point out the consequences of some of the doctrines maintained by the supreme court.

Enquirer, March 30, 1819.

18. For Jefferson's view on this issue, see his lengthy letter to Justice Johnson, October 27, 1822, 12 *The Works of Thomas Jefferson* 246–252, Paul Leicester Ford, ed. (New York: G. P. Putnam's Sons, 1905). Also see Jefferson to Thomas Ritchie, December 25, 1820, *ibid*. 175–179.

19. "Amphictyon," April 2, 1819, in Gunther, *Marshall's Defense* 77.

20. For the Agricola (Monroe)—Aristides (Marshall) exchange, see Chapter 7.

21. Marshall's essays appeared in the Philadelphia *Union* on April 24 and April 28, 1819. They are reprinted in Gunther, *Marshall's Defense* 78–105. Also see 8 *Marshall Papers* 287–308.

22. Marshall to Washington, May 6, 1819, *ibid*. 311–312.

23. *Ibid*. The corrected essays were published in the *Gazette and Alexandria Daily Advertizer*, May 15, 17, and 18, 1819. See Gerald Gunther, "Unearthing John Marshall's Major Out-of-Court Constitutional Commentary," 21 *Stanford Law Review* 449 (1969).

24. Marshall to Story, May 27, 1819, 8 *Marshall Papers* 313–314.

25. Marshall, "A Friend to the Union," in Gunther, *Marshall's Defense* 79–81.

26. Quoted in *ibid*. 18.

27. For generations, historians assumed that Roane was the author of the Amphictyon essays. The correct authorship and chronology of the various articles was pieced together and is carefully documented by Professor Gunther in *Marshall's Defense*.

28. Marshall to Washington, May 6, 1819, 8 *Marshall Papers* 311.

29. Like Marshall, Roane was a vigorous defender of judicial independence. See his opinion in *Kamper v. Hawkins*, 1 Va. Cases 20 (1794).

30. The assertion was made originally by Professor William Edward Dodd in "Chief Justice Marshall and Virginia," 12 *American Historical Review* 776 (1907). Dodd cites no evidence to support his contention.

31. See Chapter 11. By 1819 there is no question that Jefferson would have preferred Roane, or virtually anyone other than Marshall, as chief justice, but those were not his feelings when he took office in 1801.

32. Alexander McRae (published anonymously), *Letters on the Richmond Party . . . by a Native Virginian* 27 (Washington, D.C.: Washington Republican, 1823). The sketch on Roane in the *Dictionary of American Biography*, edited by Dumas Malone, agrees with McRae's assessment. 8 *DAB* 642–643 (New York: Charles Scribner's Sons, 1933).

33. Roane's essays appeared in the *Enquirer*, June 11, 15, 18, and 22, 1819. They are reprinted in Gunther, *Marshall's Defense* 106–154. Roane did not oppose the Court's holding that the Bank of the United States was constitutional. In fact, three weeks before Marshall delivered his opinion, Roane purchased fifty shares of stock in the bank at $98 each on behalf of his son, confident that the Supreme Court would sustain the holding. Roane to his son, February 16, 1819, 1 *John P. Branch Historical Papers of Randolph-Macon College* 136, William Edward Dodd, ed. (Ashland Va.: Randolph-Macon College, 1901).

   By contrast, Marshall, who had owned seventeen shares of stock in the bank since its inception, disposed of his holdings as soon as he learned the case was coming forward. Marshall's power of attorney directing the sale was dated January 21, 1819, and was published in 53 *Niles Weekly Register* 51 (1837). See 8 *Marshall Papers* 402 as well as *Correspondence of Nicholas Biddle* 283–289, 291–293, Reginald C. McGrane, ed. (Boston: Houghton Mifflin, 1919).

34. Spencer Roane, "Hampden," June 11, 1819, in Gunther, *Marshall's Defense* 110. In view of Roane's investment in the bank, skepticism is warranted regarding his censure of "the *luxuries* of banking. A money-loving, funding, stock-jobbing spirit has taken foothold among us. We are almost prepared to sell our liberties for 'a mess of pottage.'" *Ibid.* 112.

35. Charles F. Hobson, Editorial Notes, 8 *Marshall Papers* 285.

36. Gunther, *Marshall's Defense* 140–141, 146.

37. *Ibid.* 151.

38. Marshall to Washington, June 17, 1818, 8 *Marshall Papers* 316–317.

39. Marshall to Washington, June 28, 1819, *ibid.* 317–318.

40. Marshall to Washington, June 17, 1819, *ibid.* 316–317.

41. *Ibid.*

42. Gunther, *Marshall's Defense* 18.

43. *Ibid.* 197.

44. *Ibid.* 214.

45. Drew R. McCoy, *The Last of the Fathers: James Madison and the Republican Legacy* 99–101 (Cambridge: Cambridge University Press, 1989). Madison said that the decision "seems to break down the landmarks intended by a specification of the power of Congress, and to substitute for a definite connection between means and ends a Legislative discretion as to the former to which no practical limit can be assigned. . . . It was anticipated, I believe, by few if any of the framers of the Constitution that a rule of construction would be introduced as broad and pliant as what has occurred." Madison to Roane, September 2, 1819, 3 *Letters and Other Writings of James Madison* 143, William C. Rives and Philip R. Ferdall, eds. (Philadelphia: J. B. Lippincott, 1865).

46. Jefferson to Roane, September 6, 1819, 12 *Works of Jefferson* 135–140. For Jefferson on the Bank of the United States in the context of *McCulloch*, see his letter to John Adams, November 7, 1819, *ibid.* 144–146.

47. *Journal of the House of Delegates of the Commonwealth of Virginia* 56–59, 105 (1819–1820) (Richmond, Va.: Thomas W. White, 1828).

48. G. Edward White, *The Marshall Court and Cultural Change, 1815–35* 567, in The Oliver Wendell Holmes Devise, 3–4 *History of the Supreme Court of the United States* (New York: Macmillan, 1988).

49. Roane to Barbour, December 29, 1819, reprinted in 10 *William and Mary Quarterly* 7, 1st series (1901).

50. 35 *Annals of Congress* 107–108.

51. Letter to J. S. King, February 6, 1820, 6 *The Life and Correspondence of Rufus King*, Charles R. King, ed. (New York: G. P. Putnam's Sons, 1900).

52. Harry Ammon, "The Richmond Junto, 1800–1824," 60 *Virginia Magazine of History and Biography* 395, 411–412 (1953).

53. 35 *Annals of Congress* 107–108. Emphasis in original.

54. Story to Stephen White, February 27, 1820, 1 *Life and Letters of Joseph Story* 361–362, William W. Story ed. (Boston: C. Little and James Brown, 1851).

55. Roane to Monroe, February 16, 1820, 10 *Bulletin of the New York Public Library* 175 (1906), quoted in Harry Ammon, *James Monroe: The Quest for National Identity* 455 (Charlottesville: University Press of Virginia, 1990).

56. 36 *Annals of Congress* 1566–1588.

57. *United States v. Smith*, 5 Wheaton 153, 164 (1820).

58. *Blake v. Doherty*, 5 Wheaton 358, 367 (1820).

59. *Enquirer*, March 7, 1820.

60. John Taylor, *Construction Construed and Constitutions Vindicated* (Richmond, Va.: Sheppard & Pollard, 1820).

61. Quoted in Beveridge, 4 *Life of Marshall* 335. For Taylor, see Robert E. Stalhope, *John Taylor of Caroline: Pastoral Republican* (Columbia: University of South Carolina Press, 1980); Henry H. Simms, *Life of John Taylor* 178–179 (Richmond, Va.: William Byrd Press, 1932).

62. *Bracken v. College of William and Mary*, 7 Va. Cases 579–588 (1790). See Chapter 6.

63. Taylor, *Construction Construed* ii.

64. *Ibid*. 84.

65. *Ibid*. 314.

66. In 1822 Taylor published *Tyranny Unmasked*, a slashing attack on the federal judiciary, and in 1823, *New Views of the Constitution*. Those texts, together with *Construction Construed and Constitutions Vindicated*, became standard references for the states rights movement.

67. Jefferson to Holmes, April 22, 1820, 12 *Works of Jefferson* 150–160. Also see Jefferson to Charles Pinckney, September 30, 1820, *ibid*. 164–166.

68. Jefferson to Ritchie, December 25, 1820, *ibid*. 175–179.

69. Jefferson to Gallatin, December 26, 1820, *ibid*. 185–189.

70. Jefferson to Thweat, January 9, 1821, *ibid*. 196–197.

71. Jefferson to Roane, March 9, 1821, *ibid*. 201–202.

72. Jefferson to Ritchie, December 25, 1820, *ibid*. 177–178. Jefferson never surrendered the view that the Court should be required to announce its views *seriatim*. Writing to James Pleasants the following year, he said that "Another most condemnable practice of the Supreme Court to be corrected is that of cooking up a decision in Caucus and delivering it by one of their members as the opinion of the court, without the possibility of our knowing how many, who, and for what reasons each member concurred." December 26, 1821, *ibid*. 213–217. Two years later Jefferson attempted to get Madison to intervene with Dolley's brother-in-law, Justice Todd, and, because of "your antient intimacy," with Justice Duvall. "If [Justice] Johnson could be backed by them in the practice [of *seriatim* decisions], the others would be obliged to follow suit and this dangerous engine of consolidation would feel a proper constraint." Madison, who agreed with Jefferson on this point, replied that to approach the judges "may be a delicate experiment" and let the matter drop. Jefferson to Madison, June 13, 1823, *ibid*. 295–296; Madison to Jefferson, June 27, 1823, 3 *Letters of Madison* 327.

73. Act of May 3, 1802, *United States Statutes at Large*.

74. For the history of lotteries in America and their fund-raising use by government, see John Samuel Ezell, *Fortune's Merry Wheel* 101–136 (Cambridge, Mass.: Harvard University Press, 1960).

75. Pinkney's letter was published by *Niles Weekly Register* on September 2, 1820. It was signed by Thomas Emmet, David B. Ogden, Walter Jones, and John Wells, in addition to Pinkney himself.

76. For a summary of the arguments mounted, see White, *Marshall Court* 505–510.

77. For an account of the debate in the General Assembly, see *Niles Weekly Register*, December 2, 1820 and January 20, 1821.

78. 6 Wheaton 264 (1821).

79. Marshall to Washington, February 8, 1821, 9 *Marshall Papers* (in press).

80. Philip Barbour was the brother of Senator James Barbour. On December 28, 1835, Jackson appointed him to replace Gabriel Duvall. (Roger Brooke Taney was nominated the same day to replace Marshall.) Barbour served on the Court for five years and wrote twelve opinions, the most important of which was his pro-slavery opinion in *New York v. Miln*, 11 Peters 102 (1837), holding that people were not commerce and that the states could restrict their movement.. That decision was explicitly overruled in *Edwards v. California*, 314 U.S. 160, 177 (1941).

81. 6 Wheaton 344.

82. *Ibid.* 401.

83. *National Intelligencer*, March 23, 1821.

84. 6 Wheaton 434–440.

85. Compare the dissent of Justice Thomas, writing for himself, Chief Justice Rehnquist, and Justices O'Connor and Scalia in *U.S. Term Limits v. Thornton*, 93–1456 (1995). Like Spencer Roane, Justice Thomas asserted that "the ultimate source of the Constitution's authority is the consent of the people of each individual state, not the consent of the undifferentiated people of the Nation as a whole." Two pages later Thomas lifted from context Marshall's remark in *McCulloch* that "no political dreamer was ever wild enough to think of breaking down the lines which separate the States, and of compounding the American people into one common mass." What Chief Justice Marshall meant is exactly what he wrote in reply to Roane: "The question discussed by the Court was not whether the Constitution was the act of the people in mass, or in the States, but whether the Constitution was the act of people or the State governments." The context makes that clear. Marshall's meaning cannot in good faith be misunderstood.

86. Marshall to Monroe, February 20, 1821, 9 *Marshall Papers* (in press).

87. Harry Ammon, *James Monroe* 473–475.

88. In the 1821 term, in addition to the twelve decisions delivered by Marshall, Story and Johnson each delivered seven, Livingston six, Todd one, and eight were *per curiam.*

89. Marshall to Story, July 13, 1821, 9 *Marshall Papers* (in press).

90. "We have heard much of the opinion of the Court delivered this morning in the case of Cohen and others. We request that the Court will have the goodness to allow us to Spread it on the column of the *National Intelligencer*." Gales & Seaton to Marshall, March 3, 1821, 9 *Marshall Papers* (in press). Marshall replied that he had made "one or two verbal inaccuracies in reading the opinion" and that he had no objection to its being published. "But it is the property of the Court and I shall ask the other Judges this evening whether they will part with the original, having no copy." Marshall added that if the *Intelligencer* published the opinion as to jurisdiction, they should also publish the one on the merits of the case. Marshall to Gales and Seaton, March 3, 1821, *ibid.*

91. *New York American*, May 8, 1821.

92. *Southern Patriot* (Charleston, S.C.), March 31, 1821. A week later the *Patriot* criticized Virginia's opposition to the Court's holding as "not a little remarkable" and said that the Old Dominion "seemed unnecessarily more sensitive to her rights than the rest of the States." Warren, 1 *Supreme Court* 560.

93. *Enquirer*, March 23, April 6, 1821.

94. Roane to Madison, April 17, 1821, Madison Papers, Library of Congress.

95. Madison to Roane, May 6, 1821, 3 *Letters of Madison* 217–222. Also see Ralph Ketcham, *James Madison: A Biography* 632–633 (Charlottesville: University Press of Virginia, 1990); W. Ray Luce, *Cohens v. Virginia* 165 (New York: Garland Publishing Co., 1990).

96. Madison to Roane, June 29, 1821, 3 *Letters of Madison* 222–224.

97. Algernon Sidney (1622–1683), an inveterate foe of royal prerogative and the author of a celebrated political tract, *Discourses Concerning Government*, was beheaded for treason during the reign of Charles II.

98. Roane's articles appeared in the *Enquirer*, May 25, 29, June 1, 5, 8, 18, and 21, 1821. They are reprinted in 2 *John P. Branch Historical Papers* 78–183.

99. *Ibid.* 123–124. Roane's emphasis.

100. Marshall to Story, June 2, 1821, 9 *Marshall Papers* (in press). Marshall's emphasis.

101. Marshall to Story, June 15, 1821, *ibid.*

102. Marshall to Washington, June 15, 1821, *ibid.*

103. Story to Marshall, June 27, 1821, *ibid.* Story's emphasis.

104. For the text of Jefferson's letter to Jarvis, September 28, 1820, see 12 *Works of Jefferson* 161–164. Jefferson wrote to thank Jarvis for sending him a copy of his book, *The Republican*, in which Jarvis discussed the role of the judiciary at some length. "You seem to consider the judges as the ultimate arbiters of all constitutional questions," wrote Jefferson. "[This is] a very dangerous doctrine indeed, and one which would place us under the despotism of an oligarchy. . . . Their maxim is *boni judicis est ampliare juridictionem* [a common law maxim meaning that it is the duty of a good judge to enlarge or extend justice], and their power the more dangerous as they are in office for life, and not responsible, as the other functionaries are, to the elective control." Also see Dumas Malone, *Sage of Monticello* 353–355 (Boston: Little, Brown, 1977).

105. Story to Marshall, June 27, 1821, 9 *Marshall Papers* (in press). Story's emphasis.

106. Marshall told Story that he appreciated the New Englander's expression of affection. "The harmony of the bench will, I hope and pray, never be disturbed. We have external and political enemies enough to preserve internal peace." Marshall to Story, July 13, 1821, *ibid.*

107. *Ibid.*

108. Marshall to Henry Lee, October 25, 1830, Marshall Papers, Williamsburg, Va.

109. Jefferson to Roane, June 27, 1821, 12 *Works of Jefferson* 202–203; Malone, *Sage of Monticello* 357–358.

110. *Enquirer*, July 17, 1821.

111. Also see Jefferson to Samuel H. Smith, August 2, 1823, in which the former president again referred to the federal government and the states as "two co-ordinate governments, each sovereign and independent in its department. . . . The one may be strictly called the Domestic branch of government which is sectional but sovereign, the other the foreign branch of government [which is] equally sovereign on its own side of the line. . . . On every question of the usurpation of State powers by the Foreign or General government, the same men rally together. . . . The judges are at their head as heretofore, and are their entering wedge." 12 *Works of Jefferson* 300–302.

112. For Calhoun's role mobilizing the press response, see 6 *The Papers of John C. Calhoun* 259–260 (Columbia: University of South Carolina Press, 1959); Luce, *Cohens v. Virginia*.

113. Quoted in White, *Marshall Court* 523.

114. *Ibid.*

115. Marshall to Story, September 18, 1821, 9 *Marshall Papers* (in press).

116. White, *Marshall Court* 523–524. Senator Johnson, an exceptionally flamboyant figure, was elected vice president by the Senate in 1847 after none of the candidates received a majority in the electoral college. In 1840 he ran for reelection on a ticket with Van Buren against William Henry Harrison and John Tyler. To counter Harrison's military appeal ("Tippecanoe and Tyler too"), Johnson's supporters coined the limerick:

> Rumpsey, Dumpsey
> Rumpsey, Dumpsey
> Colonel Johnson killed Tecumseh

—a campaign slogan described by one historian as the most imbecilic in American history.

117. Webster to Story, January 14, 1822, 1 *The Private Correspondence of Daniel Webster* 319, Fletcher Webster, ed. (Boston: Little, Brown, 1857).

118. Jefferson to Hammond, August 18, 1821, Jefferson Papers, Library of Congress. Also see Jefferson to Nathaniel Macon, November 23, 1821, *ibid.* For Jefferson's criticism of the Court, see his August 19 and October 20 letters to Macon, and to James Pleasants, December 26, 1821, all three in 12 *Works of Jefferson*, 207–208, 213–217. Jefferson expressed his resentment

most vividly in a May 3, 1822, letter to Benjamin Ruggles. The former president told Ruggles that he "reads with comfort everything which reprobates the apostasizing heresies of the case of Cohens. According to the doctrines of the Supreme Court in that case, the States are provinces of the Empire, and a late pamphlet gives to that Court the infallibility of the Pope. Caesar has only to send out his Proconsuls and with the *Sanction of our Pope* all is settled, but the battle of Bunkers hill was not fought to set up a Pope." Jefferson Papers, Library of Congress. Jefferson's emphasis.

119. *Enquirer*, March 12, 1822.
120. Luce, *Cohens v. Virginia* 243–244.
121. Once again the decisions were distributed widely. In 1822, Marshall spoke for the Court fifteen times, Story six, Livingston three, Johnson and Todd two each, Washington one, and two decisions were made *per curiam*. In 1823 Story led with ten, followed by Marshall with eight, Johnson with five, Washington with three, Duvall and Livingston with 1 each, and two were *per curiam*. Justice Johnson filed separate concurrences in three cases.
122. In 1822 Duvall, Johnson, and Livingston dissented from an opinion by Story in a case involving common law issues, *Evans v. Eaton*, 7 Wheaton 256, 435. In 1823 Johnson dissented from Story's opinion in an admiralty case, *The Luminary*, 8 Wheaton 407, 413.
123. In *Green v. Biddle*, 8 Wheaton 1 (1823), the Court, speaking through Washington, reaffirmed and expanded an earlier decision by Story that had overturned two Kentucky land statutes under the contract clause. Marshall declined to sit because members of the Marshall family claimed title to over 400,000 acres in Kentucky. For discussions of the significance of *Green v. Biddle*, see White, *Marshall Court* 641–648; Warren, 1 *Supreme Court* 633–642.
124. 6 *The Writings of James Monroe* 216–284, Stanislaus Murray Hamilton, ed. (New York: G. P. Putnam's Sons, 1898).
125. Marshall to Monroe, June 13, 1822, 9 *Marshall Papers* (in press).
126. Story to Monroe, June 24, 1822, Monroe Papers, Library of Congress.
127. William Bennett Bizzell, *Judicial Interpretation of Political Theory* 115 (New York: G. P. Putnam's Sons, 1914).
128. Johnson to Monroe, undated, Monroe Papers, Library of Congress. Johnson suggested that Monroe have the decision in *McCulloch v. Maryland* printed "and dispersed through the Union." Donald G. Morgan, *Justice William Johnson: The First Dissenter* 123–124 note (Columbia: University of South Carolina Press, 1954).
129. In 1793 President Washington requested the Supreme Court's opinion concerning American obligations under treaty and international law in the conflict then under way between Britain and France. Chief Justice John Jay, on behalf of his colleagues, replied on August 8, 1793, that it would be inappropriate for the Supreme Court, as "a court of last resort" and as a separate branch of government, to render an advisory opinion to the president, 3 *The Correspondence and Public Papers of John Jay* 633–635, Henry P. Johnston, ed. (New York: G. P. Putnam's Sons, 1893). That position has been consistently reaffirmed by the Court.
130. The second-longest interval of continuous membership—five years eight months—occurred between the appointment of John Paul Stevens (November 28, 1975) and the resignation of Potter Stewart (July 31, 1981).
131. During the twelve years he was on the Court, Livingston delivered the opinion of the Court twenty-eight times and dissented on six occasions.
132. Marshall to St. George Tucker, December 27, 1817, 8 *Marshall Papers* 177–178.
133. Van Buren, who had his own presidential ambitions, was attempting to resurrect the New York–Virginia electoral alliance of Jefferson's day, and March 1822 he had visited the ailing Spencer Roane in Richmond and had praised Roane's attacks on the Court. That did not endear him to Marshall and his colleagues. See David B. Cole, *Martin Van Buren and the American Political System* 116–117 (Princeton, N.J.: Princeton University Press, 1984).
134. Story to Marshall, June 22, 1823, 9 *Marshall Papers* (in press).
135. Marshall to Story, July 2, 1823, *ibid*.
136. Ammon, *James Monroe* 513–514.
137. Van Buren to Thompson, June 4, 1823, quoted in White, *Marshall Court* 313.
138. Reflecting on the episode years later, Van Buren concluded that it had ended properly. In his

view, Thompson "was as eminently qualified [for the Court] as he was unfit for political life." Martin Van Buren, *Autobiography of Martin Van Buren*, John C. Fitzpatrick, ed., in 2 *Annual Report of the American Historical Association of the Year 1918* 141 (Washington, D.C.: Government Printing Office, 1920).

139. White, *Marshall Court* 307–317. For Smith Thompson generally, see Donald M. Roper, *Mr. Justice Thompson and the Constitution* (New York: Garland Publishing Company, 1987).

140. Ann Polk to Thompson, April 1, 1824, Miscellaneous Papers, New York Public Library.

141. Marshall to Story, June 1, 1823, 9 *Marshall Papers* (in press).

142. *Ibid.*

143. Story to Marshall, June 22, 1823, *ibid.*

144. Detailed excerpts from the letters were first published by Charles Warren in 1941. See "The Story-Marshall Correspondence, 1819–1831," 21 *William and Mary Quarterly* 1–26, 2nd series (1941).

145. The case was *Bank of the United States v. Dandridge*, reported in the *Enquirer*, June 10, 1823. As Marshall anticipated, he was reversed by the full Court in 1827 (12 Wheaton 64). He wrote a lengthy dissent.

146. Marshall to Story, July 2, 1823, 9 *Marshall Papers* (in press).

147. Marshall to Story, November 24, 1823, *ibid.*

148. Marshall to Story, October 12, 1823, *ibid.*

149. Marshall to Story, September 26, 1823, *ibid.*

150. Johnson's decision was published in the *National Intelligencer*, September 8, 1823, and in many other papers shortly thereafter.

151. Marshall to Story, September 26, 1823, 9 *Marshall Papers* (in press).

152. *The Brig Wilson*, 1 Brockenbrough 423 (1820). The issue did not involve a conflict between state law and the Constitution, which freed Marshall of the obligation of overturning the statute. The brig *Wilson* had attempted to land a cargo of Africans at Norfolk in contravention of the Virginia statute, but the issue before the circuit court was whether the vessel was subject to seizure by the federal government for violating the United States law prohibiting the importation of slaves. Marshall upheld the seizure, noting that the commerce clause covered the slave trade and that "Every power that pertains to navigation [is] rightfully exercised by Congress." *Ibid.*

153. *Charleston Mercury*, August 15, 1823. For a survey of press reaction, see Donald G. Morgan, "Justice William Johnson and the Treaty-making Power," 22 *George Washington Law Review* 187–215 (1953).

154. *Niles Weekly Register*, September 6, 1823. Also see the issues of August 23 and September 20, 1823.

155. Johnson to Jefferson, August 11, 1823, Jefferson Papers, Library of Congress. For the previous ten months, the justice and the former president had conducted a brief but ardent correspondence, exchanging no fewer than seven letters. Jefferson applauded Johnson's biography of General Nathanael Greene; encouraged him to write a history of political parties in the United States as a corrective to "the five-volumed libel" written by Marshall; and urged him to break with his colleagues on the Court and restore the practice of *seriatim* opinions. "The very idea of cooking up opinions in conclave begets suspicion that something passes which fears the public ear." As recently as June 12, 1823, two months before the decision in *Elkison v. Deliesseline*, Jefferson had written at great length to Johnson deploring the decision in *Cohens*, praising Roane's articles in the *Enquirer* ("they appeared to me to pulverize every word which had been delivered by Judge Marshall"), and urging that the original intent of the Framers be the basis on which the Constitution was interpreted. Jefferson to Johnson, October 27, 1822, March 4, June 12, 1823, 12 *Works of Jefferson* 246–259, 277–280. On August 11, 1823, Johnson wrote Jefferson that disunion, "the greatest evils," was rampant in Charleston and that he feared for "the destiny of our beloved country." Johnson to Jefferson, August 11, 1823, Jefferson Papers, Library of Congress. Jefferson's failure to respond indicates that he had written off Johnson. The correspondence is treated extensively by Johnson's biographer, who concludes that the effect of the justice's final plea to Jefferson was negligible. Donald G. Morgan, *Justice William Johnson* 147–189.

156. *Ibid.* 198.

157. Jefferson to Robert J. Garnett, February 14, 1824, 12 *Works of Jefferson* 341.

158. Marshall to Story, December 9, 1823, 9 *Marshall Papers* (in press).

159. Marshall had the highest regard for Clay's judgment. Questioned in late December 1823 about his choice for president, Marshall ostensibly declined to take sides. He said that the majority of Virginians supported William Crawford and that Clay was second. "For myself I can say that I consider Mr. Clay as an enlightened Statesman who has ever since his mission to Europe acted on a system which displays enlarged and liberal views; and I think him entitled to particular credit for having brought the Missouri conflict to a pacific conclusion." Marshall might not have wanted to take sides, but his preference for Clay was obvious. Marshall to Charles Hammond, December 28, 1823, *ibid.*

160. Marshall to Clay, December 22, 1823, *ibid.*

161. 9 Wheaton 1 (1824).

162. Charles Warren, *History of the American Bar* 396 (Boston: Little, Brown, 1911).

163. Quoted in Warren, 1 *Supreme Court* 598.

164. The most complete recitation of the early cases is in Maurice Glen Baxter, *The Steamboat Monopoly* 8–36 (New York: Knopf, 1972). Also see Thomas Campbell, "Chancellor Kent, Chief Justice Marshall, and the Steamboat Monopoly," 25 *Syracuse Law Review* 497–534 (1974); Beveridge, 4 *Life of Marshall* 405–412.

165. Act of February 18, 1793, 1 *United States Statutes at Large* 305–318. There was long-standing animosity between Gibbons and Ogden over a variety of issues. Gibbons once challenged Ogden to a duel, and Ogden subsequently won an $8,000 judgment against Gibbons for trespass. *Ogden v. Gibbons*, 5 N.J.L. 987 (1820). See D. Kendall, "Mr. Gibbons and Colonel Ogden," 26 *Michigan State Bar Journal* 22 25 (1947).

166. According to Article I, section 8, of the Constitution, "The Congress shall have Power . . . To regulate Commerce with foreign Nations, and among the several States, and with the Indian Tribes. . . ."

167. Quoted in Warren, 1 *Supreme Court* 599.

168. 9 Wheaton 11–17.

169. *Washington Republican*, February 4, 1824. Also see the *National Intelligencer*, February 6, 1824.

170. Story's remarks are quoted in Everett P. Wheeler, *Daniel Webster: Expounder of the Constitution* 59 (New York: G. P. Putnam's Sons, 1905).

171. Warren, 1 *Supreme Court* 603.

172. *New York Statesman*, February 7, 1824.

173. Bibb to John J. Crittenden, March 8, 1824, quoted in Warren, 1 *Supreme Court* 606.

174. Accounts of Marshall's fall are contained in the *New York Commercial Advertiser* (February 24, 1824) and the *New York American* (February 25, 1824). Also see Frances Norton Mason, *My Dearest Polly* 261–262 (Richmond, Va.: Garrett and Massie, 1961).

175. Marshall to Polly, February 23, 1824, 9 *Marshall Papers* (in press).

176. *New York Statesman*, March 4, 1824. Also see the *New York Commercial Advertiser*, March 3, 1824.

177. *Ibid.*, March 5, 1824.

178. *New York Statesman*, March 5, 1824.

179. *Gibbons v. Ogden*, 9 Wheaton 186ff.

180. Beveridge, 4 *Life of Marshall* 429–430.

181. 9 Wheaton 227.

182. For a survey of press reaction, see Warren, 1 *Supreme Court* 613–616.

183. *Charleston Courier*, March 17, 1824.

184. Randolph to John Brockenbrough, March 3, 1824, in Hugh A. Garland, 2 *The Life of John Randolph of Roanoke* 212 (New York: D. Appleton, 1851).

185. Quoted in Warren, 1 *Supreme Court* 618.

186. See B. H. Meyer and C. E. Macgill, *History of Transportation in the United States*, 107–108 (Washington, D.C.: Carnegie Institution, 1917).

187. Harlan F. Stone, "Fifty Years Work of the United States Supreme Court," 14 *American Bar Association Journal* 128, 130 (1928).

188. The Court decided forty-one cases in 1824, of which thirty-seven were unanimous. Marshall, despite his injury, wrote fifteen. Story wrote eleven, and the remainder were distributed more or less evenly. Johnson dissented four times, but not on constitutional issues.
189. Marshall to Polly, March 23, 1824, 9 *Marshall Papers* (in press).

20: The Chief Justice and Old Hickory

1. See Marshall's letters to Bushrod Washington, May 24, May 31, October 6, and December 11, 1824, 9 *The Papers of John Marshall* (in press).
2. Lafayette's visit lasted from August 15, 1824, to September 25, 1825. The best description is that written by his aide and secretary, Auguste Levasseur, *Lafayette in America in 1824 and 1825*, John D. Goodman, trans. (Philadelphia: Carey and Lea, 1829).
3. *National Intelligencer* (Washington, D.C.), September 14, 1824; Robert D. Ward, *An Account of General Lafayette's Visit to Virginia* 114–117 (Richmond: West Johnson, & Co., 1881).
4. Details of Lafayette's reception in Norfolk and Richmond are provided by the *National Intelligencer*, November 1, 5, 1824, and *Niles Weekly Register* (Baltimore), November 6, 1824.
5. *National Intelligencer*, November 1, 1824.
6. *Niles Weekly Register*, November 6, 1824. Lafayette replied with equal generosity. "Amidst the flattering circumstances of my reception, I much value the honor I have to be addressed in the name of our comrades, by you, my dear sir; and in the Chief Justice of the United States, the eloquent historian of the revolution, and of its matchless military chief, to recognize a brother officer in more arduous times, and a personal friend."
7. *National Intelligencer*, November 5, 1824.
8. The poem, in Marshall's handwriting, is now part of a Maryland family's private collection. A copy of the original is in the Marshall Papers, Williamsburg, Va. It was reprinted in 6 *Tyler's Quarterly Historical and Genealogical Magazine* 1–2 (July 1924).
9. Marshall to Randolph, March 6, 1828, Marshall Papers, Williamsburg, Va. Also see Frances Norton Mason, *My Dearest Polly* 277 (Richmond, Va.: Garrett and Massie, 1961).
10. 6 *Tyler's Quarterly* 1.
11. See Marshall to Clay, April 14, 1825, 9 *Marshall Papers* (in press).
12. Monroe and Marshall had become exceptionally close during Monroe's second term, and in December 1824 they once again exchanged felicitous letters. The president sent Marshall a copy of his final state of the union message with a generous inscription; the chief justice responded in kind. "While I take the liberty to express my personal regrets that your retirement approaches so nearly . . . I may be permitted to congratulate you on the auspicious circumstances which have attended your course as chief Magistrate of the United States, and which crown its termination. You may look back with pleasure to several very interesting events which have taken place during your administration, and have the rare felicity not to find the retrospect darkened by a single spot the review of which ought to yourself or your fellow citizens." Marshall to Monroe, December 13, 1824, *ibid.*
13. Marshall to James Markham Marshall, February 14, 1825. *ibid.*
14. John Marshall, *A History of the Colonies Planted by the English on the Continent of North America, from their Settlement, to the Commencement of that War, which Terminated in their Independence.* (Philadelphia: Abraham Small, 1824).
15. Marshall to Monroe, March 7, 1825, 9 *Marshall Papers* (in press). Monroe replied graciously on March 10. "The favorable opinion which you have expressed . . . affords me the highest gratification. We began our careers together in early youth, and the whole course of my Public conduct has been under your observation. Your approbation therefore of my administration of the affairs of our Country, deserves to be and will be held by me in the highest estimation." *Ibid.*
16. *The Antelope*, 10 Wheaton 66 (1825).
17. Article I, section 9, of the Constitution prevented Congress from prohibiting the slave trade until 1808. On March 2, 1807, in anticipation of the end of that restriction, Congress passed the first act barring the importation of slaves. 2 *United States Statutes at Large* 416 (1807).

18. 3 *ibid.* 450 (1818); *ibid.* 600 (1820).
19. In 1819 Congress had enacted an "Act in Addition to the Acts prohibiting the slave trade," which authorized the president to secure the "safekeeping, support, and removal beyond the United States" of Africans found on ships illegally engaged in the slave trade. *Ibid.* 532 (1819).
20. 10 Wheaton 81.
21. An excellent account of the case is provided by John T. Noonan, Jr., *The Antelope: The Ordeal of the Recaptured Africans in the Administrations of James Monroe and John Quincy Adams* 93–117 (Berkeley: University of California Press, 1977).
22. In addition to the treatment in Noonan, useful analyses of *The Antelope* are contained in G. Edward White, *The Marshall Court and Cultural Change, 1815–1835* 682–703, in The Oliver Wendell Homes Devise, 3–4 *History of the Supreme Court of the United States* (New York: Macmillan, 1988); Donald M. Roper, "The Quest for Judicial Objectivity: The Marshall Court and the Legitimization of Slavery," 21 *Stanford Law Review* 532–539 (1969); and R. Kent Newmyer, "On Assessing the Court in History: Some Comments on the Roper and Burke Articles," *ibid.* 540–547.
23. 10 Wheaton 119–120.
24. The most detailed description of the disposition is in Noonan, *The Antelope* 133–152.
25. 2 Peters 150 (1829).
26. Charles Warren, 1 *Supreme Court in United States History* 710–711 (Boston: Little, Brown, 1926).
27. 2 Peters 156.
28. Marshall to Elliott Cresson, February 22, 1835, in *Niles Weekly Register*, May 9, 1835; also see Robert K. Faulkner, *The Jurisprudence of John Marshall* 50–51 (Princeton, N.J.: Princeton University Press, 1968).
29. Marshall to Pickering, March 20, 1826, 9 *Marshall Papers* (in press).
30. Marshall to Lafayette, August 26, 1825, and May 2, 1827, La Fayette Collection, Cornell University. Cited in Leonard Baker, *John Marshall: A Life in Law* 719 (New York: Macmillan, 1974).
31. Marshall to Edward Carrington Marshall, February 15, 1832, Marshall Papers, Williamsburg, Va.
32. Marshall to Rev. R. R. Gurley, December 14, 1831, *ibid.*
33. Quoted in Faulkner, *Jurisprudence of Marshall* 51.
34. Mason, *My Dearest Polly* 252.
35. P. J. Staudenraus, *The African Colonization Movement: 1816–1865* 18–29. (New York: Columbia University Press, 1961).
36. Mason, *My Dearest Polly* 258.
37. *Ibid.* 259. Compare the American Colonization Society Memorial to the Virginia Assembly, December, 13, 1831, Virginia State Library.
38. Marshall's comments, which were printed under the title "Emancipation," concluded with the hope "of a people at present degraded, and who must . . . remain degraded while they continue on any part of this continent, forming a free, equal society, governed on humane and liberal principles until it should be capable of governing itself, placed in a situation from which the lights and advantages of Christianity and civilization may be spread over an immense continent. I can perceive nothing in any other direction, which promises such advantages to our coloured population." Letter, February 8, 1835, 12 *African Repository and Colonial Journal* 165 (1836). Between its founding in 1816 and the Civil War, the society organized the transportation of 10,572 Africans from the United States to Liberia. Staudenraus, *African Colonization* 251.
39. Sallie E. Marshall Hardy, "John Marshall," 8 *The Green Bag* 488 (December 1896). Marshall's sons shared the chief justice's views. When the issue of emancipation came before the state legislature in 1832, Thomas Marshall, representing Fauquier county, took the lead in pressing its approval. Slavery, he said, was an "evil that admits no remedy." Edward Carrington Marshall, the chief justice's youngest son, freed all of his slaves in 1854 and later gave each of them twenty-five acres of land in Fauquier county, some of which is still owned by their

descendants. *Virginia Slavery Debate* 6 (Richmond, Va.: Richmond Enquirer, 1832). Baker, *John Marshall* 715.

40. Story wrote that the debate on the Court was "somewhat pungent and acrimonious" but otherwise without effect. It was "one of the safety valves by which we let off some of our superabundant steam." 1 *Life and Letters of Joseph Story* 495, William W. Story, ed. (Boston: Little, Brown, 1851).

41. U.S. House of Representatives, 19th Congress, 1st session, December 13, 1825. For the efforts to curtail the Court, see Warren, 1 *Supreme Court* 652–685.

42. U.S. Senate, 19th Congress, 1st session, April 7, 1826.

43. *Ibid.* April 14, 1826.

44. Wirt to Monroe, May 5, 1823, in John Pendleton Kennedy, 2 *Memoirs of the Life of William Wirt* 133 (Philadelphia: Blanchard and Lea, 1849).

45. Quoted in Mason, *My Dearest Polly* 293.

46. Marshall to Washington, April 9, 1825, 9 *Marshall Papers* (in press).

47. Marshall to Washington, June 12, 1825, *ibid.*

48. Marshall to Polly, February 5, 1826, *ibid.*

49. Justice Story reports that Todd's decisions on circuit provided the "prevailing influence on the decisions of the state authorities; and his decisions on the circuit were rarely reversed in the Supreme Court." Story's moving eulogy to Todd appears at 13 Peters iii–viii (1839). Also see Story to C. S. Todd, March 2, 1839, 1 *Life and Letters of Story* 497–499.

50. "I'm glad our brother Trimble has passed the Senate *Malgré* [in spite of] Mr. Rowan," Marshall wrote to Story immediately afterward. Marshall to Story, May 31, 1826, 9 *Marshall Papers* (in press).

51. There is no biography of Trimble, but see the sketch by Fred L. Israel in, 1 *The Justices of the United States Supreme Court* 513–532, Leon Friedman and Fred L. Israel, eds. (New York: Chelsea House, 1969).

52. When the justices were informed on February 20 of Todd's death, they resolved to wear crêpe armbands for the remainder of the term. *Minutes of the Supreme Court of the United States*, February 20, 1826. Story wrote that "the Court has been engaged in its hard and dry duties, with uninterrupted diligence," Story to Samuel Fay, March 8, 1826, 1 *Life and Letters of Story* 492–493.

53. Marshall to Polly, February 12, 1826, 9 *Marshall Papers* (in press). In the thirty-five years of Marshall's tenure as chief justice, Polly never once accompanied him to Washington.

54. Marshall to Polly, March 12, 1826, *ibid.* Marshall told Polly that he had dined with John Randolph. "He is absorbed in the party politics of the day, and seems as much engaged in them as he was twenty-five years past. It is very different with me. I long to leave this busy bustling scene and to return to the tranquility of my family and farm."

55. Marshall's affection for Johnson is apparent in a letter he wrote to Henry Lee. See Marshall to Lee, March 21, 1826, *ibid.* Lee was writing a history of the southern campaign in the Revolution and, in an earlier letter to Marshall, had been critical of General Nathanael Greene's role in the origins of that campaign. Marshall disagreed with Lee's analysis and said that in any further edition of the *Life of Washington*, he would treat the issue very cautiously. Marshall stressed his concern for Justice Johnson's feelings. *Niles Weekly Register*, January 19, 1828.

56. *Ibid.*

57. Marshall to Sparks, March 16, 1826, 9 *Marshall Papers* (in press). Also see Marshall to Sparks, December 10, 1826, *ibid.*; and the 1826 correspondence between Sparks and Bushrod Washington in Herbert B. Adams, 1 *The Life and Writings of Jared B. Sparks* 395–413 (Boston: Houghton Mifflin, 1893).

58. *Ibid.* 421–422.

59. Marshall to Story, May 31, 1826, 9 *Marshall Papers* (in press). The chief justice told his colleague that circuit court in North Carolina proved shorter than he anticipated.

> A cause was for trial between two New England clergymen in which one had charged the other with very serious crimes; and on being sued, had pleaded that the words

written, for it is libel, were true. [*Whitaker v. McPheetors* (C.C.D. N.C. 1826).] They have taken depositions of almost all New England, and I am told by lawyers that the testimony is very contradictory. All was ready; but the combatants seemed to fear each other, and the course was continued. . . . Notwithstanding my knowledge of the persevering firmness with which gentlemen of the sacred profession pursue their objects, I was surprised at this obstinacy till I was informed that it was Presbyterian vs. Unitarian.

60. Monroe's financial predicament is discussed fully in Harry Ammon, *James Monroe* 553–560 (Charlottesville: University Press of Virginia, 1990).

61. Marshall to Monroe, July 13, 1825, 9 *Marshall Papers* (in press). "I can perceive no reason why you should not receive as much as has even been allowed to others for similar services; and I trust this reasonable expectation will not be disappointed." *Ibid.*

62. Mason, *My Dearest Polly* 295.

63. Dumas Malone provides a summary of Jefferson's financial situation in Appendix II of *The Sage of Monticello* 505–512 (Boston: Little, Brown, 1981). By Malone's calculation, the former president owed various creditors $107,273.63, at his death.

64. *Ibid.* 482.

65. Irwin S. Rhodes, 2 *The Papers of John Marshall: A Descriptive Calendar* 267 (Norman: University of Oklahoma Press, 1969). Also see Mason, *My Dearest Polly* 295.

66. For Judge Fay and his immediate family, see Christina Hopkinson Baker, *The Story of Fay House* 53–94 (Cambridge, Mass.: Harvard University Press, 1929); also see O. P. Fay, *Fay Genealogy: John Fay of Marlborough and His Descendants* (Cleveland: J.P. Savage, 1898).

67. Marshall to Judge Fay, September 15, 1826, 9 *Marshall Papers* (in press).

68. Baker, *Fay House*, 55–56.

69. Marshall to Judge Fay, October 15, 1826, 9 *Marshall Papers* (in press). In 1830 Harriet married the noted sculptor William Horatio Greenough, a Harvard classmate of Edward's.

70. Marshall to Story, November 26, 1826, 9 *Marshall Papers* (in press). Story delivered his address in August, 1826. The portion to which Marshall referred is reprinted in 1 *Life and Letters of Story* 503–505.

71. Mason, *My Dearest Polly* 294.

72. Albert J. Beveridge, 4 *The Life of John Marshall* 80 (Boston: Houghton Mifflin, 1919).

73. Marshall to Story, September 30, 1829, 14 *Proceedings of the Massachusetts Historical Society* 341 2nd series (Boston: Massachusetts Historical Society, 1901).

74. I am indebted to Charles F. Hobson, editor of the *Marshall Papers*, for this observation.

75. 12 Wheaton 419 (1827). Justice Thompson dissenting.

76. *Brown v. Maryland* is notable for the first appearance before the Court of future chief justice Roger Brooke Taney, then Maryland's attorney general. Taney lost the case but years later, speaking for the Court in *Almy v. California*, 24 Howard 169 (1861), he acknowledged that Marshall's decision was correct. For a vivid description of Taney in *Brown*, see John E. Semmes, *John H.B. Latrobe and His Times* 202–203 (Baltimore: Norman, Remington, 1917).

77. 12 Wheaton 213 (1827).

78. *Ibid.* 365–367.

79. Aside from the long-standing division over state bankruptcy legislation, Marshall dissented from his colleagues in *Bank of the United States v. Dandridge*, 12 Wheaton 64, and Thompson dissented in *Brown v. Maryland*. Of the forty-seven decisions, Marshall wrote fifteen, Story nine, Trimble eight, Johnson six, Thompson four, Washington two, and two were *per curiam*.

80. Humphrey Marshall to Marshall, January 7, 1827, Marshall Papers, Williamsburg, Va.

81. Marshall to Clay, January 20, 1827, R.G. 59, National Archives. Thomas Marshall was passed over by Adams and in 1831 was elected to Congress. He was subsequently appointed to the Kentucky supreme court, where he served for twenty-three years, the last six as chief justice.

82. The incident is described by Philip Slaughter's descendants. See William B. Slaughter, *Reminiscences of Distinguished Men* 113 (Madison, Wisc.: private printing, 1878).

83. *Ibid.*

84. Marshall to Slaughter, September 22, 1827, Marshall Papers, Williamsburg, Va.

85. Slaughter, *Reminiscences* 113.
86. Marshall spoke for the Court twenty-four times, Story and Trimble each delivered seven decisions, Thompson six, Johnson five, Duvall three, and one decision was *per curiam*. Johnson dissented twice in *Minor v. Mechanics Bank*, 1 Peters 46 (Story), and *Governor of Georgia v. Madrazo*, 1 Peters 110 (Marshall).
87. The one exception, *American Insurance Co. v. Canter*, 1 Peters 511 (1828), in which Marshall, speaking for a unanimous Court, upheld the Louisiana Purchase, was discussed in Chapter 12.
88. Wirt to William Pope, October 14, 1828, Wirt Papers, Maryland Historical Society.
89. Marshall to Story, December 15, 1828, Marshall Papers, Williamsburg, Va.
90. Marshall to Lafayette, May 2, 1827, Lafayette Collection, Cornell University.
91. *Marylander* (Baltimore), March 22, 1828.
92. Marshall to John H. Pleasants, March 29, 1828, reprinted in *Niles Weekly Register*, April 12, 1828.
93. Clay to Marshall, April 8, 1828, Marshall Papers, Williamsburg, Va. Marshall replied on May 1 that "The note you mention was drawn from me very unwillingly, and the opinion it expressed, was the necessary result of evidence on a mind not predisposed to condemn. If it draws upon me a portion of that scurrility, which has been lavished on others, I must console myself with the reflection that I have not voluntarily intruded myself upon a controversy, which has been carried on with such unexampled virulence." *Ibid.*
94. Story to Marshall, April 10, 1828, not found, but referred to by Marshall in his reply to Story. Marshall to Story, May 1, 1828, Marshall Papers, Williamsburg, Va.
95. *Ibid.* The chief justice explained to Story that one of his nephews

> for whom I feel great regard . . . was asked in Baltimore by a gentleman of that place if he knew my opinion respecting the candidates for the Presidency. On his answering that I seldom mentioned the subject, but that he had heard me say that though I had not voted for upwards of twenty years I should probably vote at the ensuing election, the gentleman observed then he supposed I should consider the election of Jackson as a virtual dissolution of the government. This observation was received with a smile and some light expression of its extravagance, and upon the strength of this circumstance a communication was made which produced the publication in the *Marylander*. . . . My nephew stated the affair to me while [I was] in the mountain country, and was too much chagrined for me to add to his mortification by blaming him.

96. Jackson polled 56 percent of the popular vote and carried all of the southern and western states, Pennsylvania, and most of New York, winning 178 electoral votes to Adams's 83.
97. Clay to Marshall, October 23, 1828, not found, but referred to by Marshall in his reply to Clay. Marshall to Clay, November 20, 1828, Marshall Papers, Williamsburg, Va.
98. *Ibid.*
99. Clay to Marshall, December 22, 1828, *ibid.*
100. Marshall to Polly, February 1, 1829, *ibid.*
101. Marshall to Polly, March 5, 1829, *ibid.*
102. Jackson met with McLean before his appointment and secured his commitment not to contest the presidency. Nevertheless, McLean, like Smith Thompson, never completely surrendered his political ambitions. See Frank Otto Gatell, "John McLean," in 1 *Justice of the Supreme Court* 538–540.
103. For a sample of Whig reaction, see Warren, 1 *Supreme Court* 705–706.
104. Marshall to Joseph Hopkinson, March 18, 1829, Marshall Papers, Williamsburg, Va. The chief justice has been instrumental in securing the appointment for Hopkinson. See Marshall to Hopkinson, March 16, 1827, and also (no date) in 1828, *ibid.* On the subject of political removals, see Marshall to his son Thomas, March 20, 1829, *ibid.*
105. Justice Benjamin Curtis, after McLean's dissent in *Cooley v. Board of Wardens*, 12 Howard 299 (1852), called him one of "the most high-toned federalists on the bench." Gatell, "McLean," 542.
106. Justices Johnson and Thompson dissented from Marshall's opinion in *Weston v. City Council of Charleston*, 2 Peters 449 (1829), overturning an attempt by Charleston to tax stock of the

United States. Overall, in addition to the seventeen opinions by Marshall, Story delivered eleven, Washington six, Johnson five, Thompson two, Duvall one, and two were *per curiam*.

107. Marshall to Polly, March 5, 1829 and Marshall to Committee of Richmond Citizens, March 25, 1829, Marshall Papers, Williamsburg, Va.

108. Marshall to Story, September 20, 1829, *ibid*.

109. Marshall to Story, June 11, 1829, *ibid*.

110. Ralph Ketcham, *James Madison: A Biography* 636–637 (Charlottesville: University Press of Virginia, 1990).

111. Mason, *My Dearest Polly* 309–310.

112. *Ibid*. 311–312.

113. Hugh Grisby to Horace Binney, February 23, 1869, John Marshall Miscellaneous Papers, New York Public Library.

114. Julius F. Prufer, "The Franchise in Virginia," 8 *William and Mary Quarterly* 28–29, 2nd series (1928); Faulkner, *Jurisprudence of Marshall* 122–124.

115. Hugh Blair Grigsby, *The Virginia Convention of 1829–30* 919, reprint ed. (New York: Da Capo Press, 1969).

116. Slaughter, *Reminiscences* 120–122.

117. Quoted in Baker, *John Marshall* 712.

118. Notes by Charles Campbell, representing Washington county, reported in 3 *Southern Literary Messenger* 237–238 (1836).

119. Grigsby, *Virginia Convention* 619.

120. Compare Marshall's initial committee report to the convention (*ibid*. 33) with Article V of the 1830 Constitution (*ibid*. 901–902).

121. Marshall to Story, October 15, 1830, Marshall Papers, Williamsburg, Va.

122. Madison to Lafayette, February 1, 1830, 4 *Letters and Other Writings of James Madison* 59–60, William C. Rives and Philip R. Ferdall, eds. (Philadelphia: J. B. Lippincott, 1868).

123. During the twenty-nine years they served together on the Court, Marshall and Washington differed in only three cases. Later Marshall wrote to Joseph Hopkinson that Washington "was indeed one of the worthiest and best, and therefore one of the most beloved of men. In amiableness of manners, in excellence of heart, in professional acquirements and in soundness of intellect he was all that you have represented him. His loss is deplored by no person more than myself." December 17, 1830, Hopkinson Papers, Historical Society of Pennsylvania.

124. Gibson's candidacy was backed vigorously by Vice President John C. Calhoun. But Jackson was in the process of distancing himself from the South Carolinian, and Gibson may have been a casualty of that. At the time, Gibson strongly opposed the right of the judiciary to rule on the constitutionality of legislative acts, and his dissent in *Eakin v. Raub*, 12 Serg. Rawle 320 (S.C. Pa. 1825), presents the classic argument against Marshall's holding in *Marbury v. Madison*. In 1845, in *Norris v. Clymer*, 2 Pa. 277, 281, Gibson recanted his earlier position and acknowledged the necessity of judicial review.

125. Story to his wife (Sarah Waldo Story), January 31, 1830, 1 *Life and Letters of Story* 35.

126. Webster to Jeremiah Mason, January 6, 1830, 16 *Writings and Speeches of Daniel Webster* 191–192, J. McIntyre, ed. (Boston: Little, Brown, 1903).

127. January 17, 1830, 8 *The Memoirs of John Quincy Adams*, Charles Francis Adams, ed. (Philadelphia: J. B. Lippincott, 1876).

128. Marshall to Polly, January 31, 1830, Marshall Papers, Williamsburg, Va.

129. *Ibid*.

130. *Shanks v. Dupont*, 3 Peters 242 (Story); *Finley v. King*, 3 Peters 346 (Marshall); and *Craig v. Missouri*, 4 Peters 410 (Marshall).

131. 4 Peters 410 (1830). Marshall, Story, Duvall and Baldwin in the majority; Johnson, Thompson and McLean dissenting, each for different reasons.

132. 4 Peters 514 (1830).

133. Marshall's decision in *Providence Bank* provided the foundation for Chief Justice Taney's opinion in *Charles River Bridge v. Warren Bridge Co.*, 11 Peters 420 (1837), which, as most

scholars now recognize, was not a reversal of the Marshall's Court's contract jurisprudence but simply an extension of the great chief justice's holding in the *Providence* case.

134. For a survey of reaction, see Warren, 1 *Supreme Court* 714–715.

135. In the *South Carolina Exposition and Protest*, written anonymously in 1828, Calhoun, like the Richmond Junto, argued that the Constitution was a compact among the states whereby the states delegated certain specific and limited powers to the federal government. But Calhoun went beyond Roane and argued that if a state believed the federal government had overstepped its authority, the state could nullify the offending measure. If this did not achieve the desired end, the state was then free to secede.

136. Hayne spoke on January 19 and 25, 1830. U.S. Senate, 21st Congress, 1st Session.

137. *Ibid.* January 26 and 27, 1830.

138. William MacDonald, *Jacksonian Democracy, 1829–1837* 149 (New York: Harper Brothers, 1906).

139. 21 *North American Review* 537–546 (October 1830).

140. Quoted in Samuel Eliot Morison, *The Oxford History of the American People* 432 (New York: Oxford University Press, 1965).

141. Marshall to Story, October 15, 1830, Marshall Papers, Williamsburg, Va.

142. 2 Peters 245 (1829). See Chapter 19.

143. Marshall to Polly, January 30, 1831, Marshall Papers, Williamsburg, Va.

144. Edward Everett to his wife, February 25, 1831, Everett Papers, Massachusetts Historical Society.

145. Richard Peters to Joseph Hopkinson, March 18, 1838, Hopkinson Papers, Historical Society of Pennsylvania.

146. "You may probably have heard of the breaking out of Judge Baldwin's insanity," Daniel Webster wrote to Warren Dutton. "When I was in Philadelphia he was under medical treatment and was somewhat calm." January 4, 1833. Webster Papers, Dartmouth College. Also see P. C. Brooks to Edward Everett, January 3, 1833, Everett Papers, Massachusetts Historical Society.

147. Story was scarcely one to back down. As he wrote to Joseph Hopkinson, who sat with Baldwin on circuit court in Philadelphia, "I have long thought that you would find him uncomfortable, conceited, willful, and wrongheaded—the opinions, which you refer to, are so utterly wrong in principle and authority, that I am sure he cannot be sane. And indeed, the only charitable view which I can take of his conduct is that he is partially deranged at times." Story to Hopkinson, May 9, 1833, Hopkinson Papers, Historical Society of Pennsylvania.

148. Of the forty-two decisions rendered in 1831, Marshall wrote thirteen; Story and McLean each wrote seven; Johnson five; Baldwin and Thompson four each; and two were *per curiam*. In addition to Baldwin's nine dissents, Johnson disagreed with his colleagues in three cases, and Story and Thompson in one each.

149. Marshall to Story, May 3, 1831, Marshall Papers, Williamsburg, Va.

150. Marshall to Story, June 26, 1831, *ibid.*

151. *Ibid.*

152. Story to Marshall, May 29, 1831, *ibid.*

153. Marshall to Story, June 26, 1831, *ibid.*

154. Marshall [from Raleigh] to Polly, May 12, 1831, *ibid.*

155. Marshall to Story, October 12, 1831, *ibid.*

156. Dr. Physick was then Emeritus Professor of Surgery and Anatomy at the University of Pennsylvania. His reputation rested not only on his surgical dexterity but also on his pioneering development of cataract extraction ("Physick's Operation") and his success in removing stones from the bladder, a technique (lithotomy) he devised in 1793. Alexander Randall, M.D., F.A.C.S., "Philip Syng Physick's Last Major Operation," 9 *Annals of Medical History* 133–141 (1937). For Dr. Physick generally, see *Biography of Eminent American Physicians and Surgeons* 384–407, R. French Stone, ed. (Indianapolis: C. E. Hollenbeck, 1898).

157. Marshall to Polly, October 6, 1831, Marshall Papers, Williamsburg, Va.

158. Marshall to James Keith Marshall, October 12, 1831, *ibid.*

159. Randall, "Physick's Last Operation," 139.

160. Marshall to Polly, October 12, 1831, Marshall Papers, Williamsburg, Va.
161. Marshall to James Keith Marshall, October 12, 1831, *ibid.*
162. Marshall to Story, October 12, 1831, *ibid.*
163. Randall, "Physick's Last Operation," 139.
164. *Ibid.*
165. *Ibid.*
166. A detailed description of the surgical procedure is provided by Dr. Randall in "Physick's Last Operation," 137–138. It makes for gruesome reading, and I have decided against quoting it.
167. *Ibid.*
168. Marshall to Polly, November 8, 1831, Marshall Papers, Williamsburg, Va.
169. Marshall to Story, November 10, 1831, *ibid.*
170. Marshall to Richard Peters, November 23, 1831, *ibid.*
171. Marshall to James Markham Marshall, December 19, 1831, *ibid.*
172. Mason, *My Dearest Polly* 342–343.
173. Story to Sarah W. Story, March 4, 1832, 2 *Life and Letters of Story* 86–87.
174. For the complete text, see Mason, *My Dearest Polly* 343–344.
175. *Johnson and Graham's Lessee v. McIntosh*, 8 Wheaton 543 (1823).
176. *Cherokee Nation v. State of Georgia*, 5 Peters 1 (1831).
177. The circumstances of the execution are described in the *Enquirer* (Richmond), December 9, 1830; January 4, 8, 1831.
178. *Niles Weekly Register*, January 8, 1831.
179. 5 Peters at 14. The Court divided 4–2, with Marshall, McLean, Baldwin, and Johnson in the majority; Story and Thompson dissenting.
180. 6 Peters 515 (1832).
181. Quoted in Baker, *John Marshall* 742.
182. Story to George Ticknor, March 8, 1832, 2 *Life and Letters of Story* 83.
183. Horace Greeley, 1 *The American Conflict* 106 (Hartford, Conn.: O. D. Case, 1864). For a more detailed analysis of what Jackson may have said, see Warren, 1 *Supreme Court* 758–760.
184. In early 1837 Worcester and Butler accepted a pardon from Governor Wilson Lumpkin, thus ending the case. In 1992 Georgia granted a second and more generous pardon, calling the incident "a stain on the history of criminal justice in Georgia." *The New York Times*, November 23, 1992. Also see Joseph C. Burke, "The Cherokee Cases: A Study in Law, Politics, and Morality," 21 *Stanford Law Review* 500, 525–530; Newmyer, "On Assessing the Court in History," *ibid.* 540, 544–547; Warren, 1 *Supreme Court* 762–769.
185. *Greenleaf's Lessee v. Birth*, 6 Peters 302 (Story).
186. *United States v. Arredondo*, 6 Peters 691 (Baldwin).
187. Marshall to Story, August 2, 1832, Marshall Papers, Williamsburg, Va.
188. Marshall to Story, September 22, 1832, *ibid.*
189. When the electoral votes were tabulated in 1832, Jackson received 219, Clay 49, Wirt 7, and John Floyd, a state's rights South Carolinian, 11. In popular votes, Jackson's victory was equally overwhelming: 701,780 to Clay's 484,205.
190. For the text of Jackson's proclamation, see 1 *Major Problems in American Constitutional History* 378–386, Kermit L. Hall, ed. (Lexington, Mass.: D. C. Heath & Co., 1992). Also see Warren, 1 *Supreme Court* 779, note citing Jackson's conversation to the same effect with the Georgia congressional delegation.
191. Marshall to Story, December 25, 1832, Marshall Papers, Williamsburg, Va.
192. Story to Sarah W. Story, January 27, 1832, 2 *Life and Letters of Story* 119.
193. Story to Sarah W. Story, January 20, 1833, *ibid.* 116.
194. Justices Johnson and McLean dissented from Story's opinion in *Ex Parte Watkins*, 7 Peters 568. Overall, Marshall wrote fourteen decisions, Story eight, Thompson six, McLean six, Johnson four, and three were *per curiam*.
195. 7 Peters 243 (1833).
196. Joseph Story, *Commentaries on the Constitution of the United States* (Boston: Hilliard, Gray, & Co., 1833).

197. Marshall to Story, April 24, 1833, Marshall Papers, Williamsburg, Va.
198. *Charles River Bridge v. Warren Bridge Co.* 11 Peters 420 (1837); *Briscoe v. Commonwealth Bank of Kentucky*, 11 Peters 257 (1837); and *New York v. Miln*, 11 Peters 102 (1837). The cases were carried over in the 1835 term, as well, and were not decided until after Marshall's death.
199. 8 Peters 122 (1834).
200. Justices Baldwin and Thompson dissented in *Wheaton v. Peters*, 8 Peters 591 (1834).
201. Charles Sumner, March 3, 1834, 1 *Memoirs and Letters of Charles Sumner* 135–136, Edward L. Pierce, ed. (London: Sampson Low, Marston, Searle & Rivington, 1878).
202. *Niles Weekly Register*, January 17, 1835.
203. Warren, 1 *Supreme Court* 795–796.
204. While the nomination was pending, Marshall wrote to his friend Senator Benjamin Watkins Leigh of Virginia in support of Jackson's choice. "If you have not made up your mind on the nomination of Mr. Taney," said Marshall, "I have received some favorable information I wish to communicate." Quoted in Samuel Tyler, 1 *Memoir of Roger Brooke Taney* 63 (Baltimore: Murphy, 1872).
205. Justice Duvall had consistently refused to resign until he was satisfied that the president would name a congenial replacement. Taney, a fellow Marylander, satisfied that requirement. Irving Dillard, "Gabriel Duvall," in 1 *Justices of the Supreme Court* 427.
206. Justice Baldwin dissented twice; McLean and Thompson once.
207. 9 Peters 711 (1835).
208. Marshall to John Marshall, Jr., December 7, 1834, Marshall Papers, Williamsburg, Va.
209. Marshall to James Keith Marshall, February 14, 1833; Thomas Marshall to Marshall, October 29, 1833; and Marshall to James Keith Marshall, April 13 and May 22, 1835, *ibid*.
210. Marshall to James Keith Marshall, April 13, 1835, *ibid*.
211. Marshall to Peters, April 30, 1835, *ibid*.
212. As reported in the *Enquirer*, June 10, 1835.
213. Allan Bowie Magruder, *John Marshall* 282 (Boston: Houghton Mifflin, 1885).
214. *Enquirer*, July 10, 1835.
215. Jackson to Horace Binney, September 18, 1835, Jackson Papers, Library of Congress.

Bibliography

Unpublished Papers and Manuscripts

Adams Papers. Massachusetts Historical Society.

Eliza Jaquelin Ambler Papers, Colonial Williamsburg Foundation. Williamsburg, Virginia.

Breckinridge Papers. Library of Congress.

Cabell Papers. University of Virginia.

Caley, Percy B. "Dunmore: Colonial Governor of New York and Virginia." Unpublished Ph.D. dissertation. University of Pittsburgh, 1939.

Chase Papers. Maryland Historical Society.

John Clopton Papers. Duke University.

Constable-Pierpoint Papers. New York Public Library.

Cowden, Gerald Steffens. "The Randolphs of Turkey Island: A Prosopography of the First Three Generations, 1650–1806." Unpublished Ph.D. dissertation, College of William and Mary, 1977.

Nathan Dane Papers. Library of Congress.

Diary of Justice Joseph P. Bradley. New Jersey Historical Society.

Dreer Collection. Pennsylvania Historical Society.

Everett Papers. Massachusetts Historical Society.

Fairfax of Cameron Manuscripts. Manuscript collection. Gays House, Holyport, Berks, Great Britain.

Gelback, Clyde Christian. "Spencer Roane of Virginia: 1762–1822." Unpublished Ph.D. dissertation, University of Pittsburgh, 1955.

Gerry Papers, Letterbook 1797–1801. New York Public Library.

Gratz Collection. Historical Society of Pennsylvania.

Griswold Papers. Yale University.

Hemphill, Edwin W. "George Wythe: America's First Law Professor and Teacher of Jefferson, Marshall, and Clay." Unpublished M.A. thesis, Emory University, 1933.

Hobson, Charles F. "The Early Career of John Randolph." Unpublished Ph.D. dissertation, Emory University, 1971.

Hoes, Rose Gouveneur. "James Monroe's Childhood and Youth." MS Collection, James Monroe Law Office, Fredricksburg, Virginia.

Hopkinson Papers. Historical Society of Pennsylvania.

Jackson Papers. Library of Congress.

Keith Family Papers. Virginia Historical Society.

King Papers. New York Historical Society.

Lafayette Collection. Cornell University.

Madison Papers. Library of Congress.

Manigault Family Papers. University of South Carolina.

John Marshall Miscellaneous Papers. New York Public Library.

Marshall Papers. Williamsburg, Virginia.

Monroe Papers. Library of Congress.

Diary of Gouverneur Morris. Library of Congress.

Nicholson Papers. Library of Congress.

William Paterson Papers. New Jersey Historical Society.

Timothy Pickering Papers. Massachusetts Historical Society.

Pinckney Family Papers. Library of Congress.

Pitcairn Papers. Cincinnati Historical Society.

William Plumer Papers. Library of Congress.

Rice, Philip Morrison. "The Virginia Board of Public Works, 1816–1842." Unpublished M.A. thesis, University of North Carolina, 1947.

Russell, Triplett T., and John K. Gott. "An Historical Vignette of Oak Hill." Unpublished paper of the Fauquier County Commission on the Bicentennial of the United States Constitution, Marshall, Virginia, September 26, 1987.

Sellers, John R. "The Virginia Continental Line 1775–1780." Unpublished Ph.D. dissertation, Tulane University, 1968.

Shockley, Martin Staples. "John Marshall and the Richmond Theatre." Unpublished paper, Marshall Papers Project, Williamsburg, Virginia.

Smith-Carter Collection. Massachusetts Historical Society.

Story Papers. Massachusetts Historical Society.

Swindler, William. "Marshall's Law Notes." Unpublished manuscript, Swem Library, College of William and Mary.

Tazewell Family Papers. Virginia State Library.

Treon, John Alfred. "*Martin v. Hunter's Lessee*: A Case History." Unpublished Ph.D. dissertation, University of Virginia, 1970.

Tucker-Coleman Papers. College of William and Mary Library.

van Cortlandt Papers. New York Public Library.

George Washington Papers. Library of Congress.

William and Mary College Papers, Bound Volumes, Notes on Professors' Lectures A–M. Swem Library, College of William and Mary.

Wirt Papers. Maryland Historical Society.

Official Publications

Accounts of Military Stores, July 31, 1780, Box 37, War Office Papers, Virginia State Library.

Acts of the Assembly Now in Force in the Colony of Virginia, Williamsburg, Va.: W. Hunter, 1769.

"Affaires de l'Amérique, 7 December 1780," *Decisions du roi, 1760–1792*.

American Archives. 6th series. Peter Force, ed. Washington, D.C.: Matthew St. Clair Clarke and Peter Force, 1833–1846.

American State Papers. Walter Lowrie et al., eds. Washington, D.C.: Gales and Seaton, 1832–1834.

Angelokos, Peter. "Arrangements of the several regiments of the First Virginia Brigade." September 14, 1778. National Archives, Orderly Book No. 28, Record Group 93.

Annals of Congress.

Annual Report of the Monticello Association. 1936.

Archives du Ministère des Affaires Étrangères. *Correspondance Politique: Étas-Unis.*

Bevans, Charles I., ed. *Treaties and the International Agreements of the United States of America, 1776–1949.* Washington, D.C.: Government Printing Office, 1974.

Biographical Directory of the American Congress, 1774–1961. Washington, D.C.: Government Printing Office, 1961.

Davis, J. "Alfred Moore and James Iredell, Revolutionary Patriots and Associate Justices of the Supreme Court of the United States." In North Carolina Reports, vol. 124. Raleigh, N.C.: Turner and Hughes, 1843.

Haywood, John. "Reports of Cases Adjusted in the Superior Courts of Law and Equity, Court of Conference and Federal Court for the State of North Carolina, from the year 1791–1806." In North Carolina Reports, vol. 2. Raleigh, N.C.: Turner and Hughes, 1843.

Hening, William Waller. *The Statutes at Large: Being a Collection of all of the Laws of Virginia.* Richmond, Va.: Samuel Pleasants, 1809–1823.

————.*The Statutes at Large of Virginia, from October Session 1792 to December Session 1806.* Samuel Sheperd, ed. Richmond, Va.: Samuel Sheperd, 1835–1836.

Hening, William Waller, and William Munford. *The Examination of Colonel Aaron Burr before the Chief Justice of the United States.* S.#12528. In *American Bibliography, A Preliminary Checklist for 1807,* Ralph R. Shaw and Richard H. Shoemaker, eds. New York: The Scarecrow Press, 1961.

Journal of Executive Proceedings of the Senate of the United States. Washington, D.C.: Government Publishing Office, 1828.

Journal of the Council of State of Virginia. Wilmer L. Hall, ed. Richmond, Va.: Virginia State Library, 1952.

Journal of the House of Delegates of the Commonwealth of Virginia 1781–1785. Richmond, Va.: Thomas W. White, 1828.

Journal of the Proceedings of the Convention, held at Richmond on the 20th Day of March, 1775. Williamsburg, Va.: Alexander Purdie, 1775.

Journals of the Continental Congress, 1774–1789. Worthington C. Ford, ed., 4 vols. Washington, D.C.: Government Printing Office, 1904–1937.

Marshall, John. Affidavit to support William Payne's pension claim. National Archives, Pension File 8938, Record Group 15.

McRae, Sherwin, ed. *Calendar of Virginia State Papers.* Richmond, Va.: Superintendent of Public Printing, 1886.

"Mémoire sur les Relations entre la France et les États-Unis de 1792 à 1797." Désagés, vol. 36, French Foreign Military Archives, Paris.

Memorial to Congress from the Commissioners of the Federal City, February 23, 1798. Legislative Branch, National Archives.

Miller, David Hunter, ed. *Treaties and Other International Acts of the United States.* 8 vols. Washington, D.C.: Government Printing Office, 1931–1948.

Minute Book, Office of the Clerk, Fauquier County Circuit Court, Warrenton, Virginia.

Minutes of the Supreme Court of the United States.

Naval Documents Related to the Quasi-War Between The United States and France. Washington, D.C.: Government Printing Office, 1938.

Papers of the [District] Commissioners. National Archives.

Potter, J. "Rank Roll of Virginia Line Officers." September 8, 1778. National Archives, Orderly Book No. 28, Record Group 93.

Preussen und Frankreich von 1795 bis 1807, Diplomatische Correspondenzen, Paul Bailleu, ed. Leipzig: G. Hirzel, 1880.

Report of the Committee of Claims . . . (December, 1805) S.#9599. In *American Bibliography: A Preliminary Checklist for 1805,* Ralph R. Shaw and Richard H. Shoemaker, eds, New York: The Scarecrow Press, 1958.

Richardson, James D., ed. *A Compilation of the Messages and Papers of the Presidents, 1789–1897.* 10 vols. Washington, D.C.: Government Printing Office, 1896–1899.

U.S. Bureau of the Census. *Historical Statistics of the United States: Colonial Times to 1970.* Washington, D.C.: Government Printing Office, 1975.

U.S. Bureau of the Census. *Statistical History of the United States: From Colonial Times to the Present.* New York: Basic Books, 1976.

U.S. Congress. *Biographical Directory of the American Congress.* Washington, D.C.: Government Printing Office, 1972.

U.S. Congress, Senate. *Trial of Samuel Chase, Associate Justice of the Supreme Court of the United States, Impeached by the House of Representatives for High Crimes and Misdemeanors.* Washington, D.C.: Samuel H. Smith, 1805.

Virginia Calendar of State Papers. Virginia State Library.

Virginia Constitution: 1776. Williamsburg, Va.: Alexander Purdie, 1776.

Books

Abbott, Charles. *A Treatise on the Law Relative to Merchant Ships and Seamen.* Joseph Story, ed. Newburyport, Mass.: E. Little, 1810.

Abernethy, Thomas P. *The Burr Conspiracy.* New York: Oxford University Press, 1954.

Abrams, M. H. et al. *The Norton Anthology of English Literature.* 4th ed. 2 vols. New York: Norton, 1979.

Adams, Henry. *History of the United States During the Administration of Thomas Jefferson.* Reprint ed. New York: Literary Classics of the United States, 1986.

———. *History of the United States of America.* 9 vols. New York: Charles Scribner's Sons, 1889–1891.

———. *John Randolph.* Boston: Houghton Mifflin, 1882.

———. *The Life of Albert Gallatin.* Philadelphia: J. B. Lippincott, 1879.

Adams, Herbert B. *The Life and Writings of Jared Sparks.* 2 vols. Boston: Houghton Mifflin, 1893.

Adams, John. *Familiar Letters of John Adams and his wife Abigail Adams during the Revolution.* Charles Francis Adams, ed. New York: Houghton Mifflin, 1875.

———. *The Works of John Adams.* 10 vols. Charles Francis Adams, ed. Boston: Little, Brown, 1850–1856.

Adams, John Quincy. *The Memoirs of John Quincy Adams.* 12 vols. Charles Francis Adams, ed. Philadelphia: J. B. Lippincott, 1874–1877.

———. *The Writings of John Quincy Adams.* 7 vols. Worthington C. Ford, ed. New York: Macmillan, 1913–1917.

Ambler, Charles Henry. *Sectionalism in Virginia from 1776 to 1861.* Chicago: University of Chicago Press, 1910. Republished, New York: Russell & Russell, 1964.

Ames, Fisher. *Works of Fisher Ames.* 2 vols. Seth Ames, ed. Boston: Little, Brown, 1854.

Ammon, Harry. *The Genet Mission.* New York: W. W. Norton, 1973.

———. *James Monroe: The Quest for National Identity.* Charlottesville: University Press of Virginia, 1990.

Anburey, Thomas. *Travels through the Interior Parts of America.* 2 vols. London: W. Lane, 1789.

Anderson, D. R., ed. *Richmond College Historical Papers.* Richmond, Va.: Richmond College, 1915.

Anderson, Peter John, ed. *Fasti Academiae Mariscallanae Aberdonensis; Selection from the Records of The Marischal College and University, 1593–1860.* 3 vols. Aberdeen: New Spalding Club, 1889–1898.

Anderson, Troyer S. *The Command of the Howe Brothers During the American Revolution.* New York: Oxford University Press, 1936.

Austin, James T. *The Life of Elbridge Gerry.* 2 vols. Boston: Wells and Lilly, 1828–1829.

Axelrad, Jacob. *Philip Freneau: Champion of Democracy.* Austin: University of Texas Press, 1967.

Bacon, Matthew. *A New Abridgement of the Law.* 6 vols. London: E. and R. Nutt and R. Gosling, 1736.

Baker, Christina Hopkinson. *The Story of Fay House.* Cambridge, Mass.: Harvard University Press, 1929.

Baker, J. H. *An Introduction to English Legal History.* London: Butterworths, 1971.

Baker, Leonard. *John Marshall: A Life in Law.* New York: Macmillan, 1974.

Baldwin, Leland D. *Whiskey Rebels: The Story of a Frontier Uprising.* Pittsburgh: University of Pittsburgh Press, 1939.

Bancroft, George. *History of the United States of America from the Discovery of the Continent*. 6 vols. New York: D. Appleton, 1885.

Barras, Paul. *Memoirs of Barras: Member of the Directorate*. George Duruy, ed., C. E. Roche, trans. 4 vols. New York: Harper and Brothers, 1895–1896.

Bartlett, Ruhl J., ed. *The Record of American Diplomacy*. New York: Knopf, 1964.

Bastide, Louis. *Vie religieuse et politique de Talleyrand-Périgord*. Paris: Faure, 1838.

Baxter, Maurice Glen. *The Steamboat Monopoly*. New York: Knopf, 1972.

Bayard, James A. *Papers of James A. Bayard, 1796–1815*. Elizabeth Donnan, ed. In 2 *Annual Report of the American Historical Association for the year 1913*, 2 vols. Washington, D.C.: Government Printing Office, 1915.

Beard, Charles A. *An Economic Interpretation of the Constitution of the United States*. New York: Macmillan, 1914.

———. *Economic Origins of Jeffersonian Democracy*. New York: Macmillan, 1915.

Beeman, Richard R. *The Old Dominion and the New Nation*. Lexington: University Press of Kentucky, 1972.

———. *Patrick Henry: A Biography*. New York: McGraw-Hill, 1974.

Bemis, Samuel Flagg. *A Diplomatic History of the United States*. New York: Holt, 1950.

———. *Jay's Treaty: A Study in Commerce and Diplomacy*. New York: MacMillan, 1923.

Bemis, Samuel Flagg, ed. *American Secretaries of State and Their Diplomacy*. 10 vols. New York: Knopf, 1927–1929.

Berger, Raoul. *Congress v. the Supreme Court*. Cambridge, Mass.: Harvard University Press, 1969.

———. *Impeachment: The Constitutional Problems*. Cambridge, Mass.: Harvard University Press, 1973.

Bernard, Jack F. *Talleyrand: A Biography*. New York: Putnam, 1973.

Berns, Walter. *Taking the Constitution Seriously*. New York. Simon and Schuster, 1987.

Beveridge, Albert J. *The Life of John Marshall*. 4 vols. Boston: Houghton Mifflin, 1916–1919.

Biddle, Nicholas. *Correspondence of Nicholas Biddle*. Reginald C. McGrane, ed. Boston: Houghton Mifflin, 1919.

Bill, Alfred H. *Valley Forge: The Making of an Army*. New York: Harper, 1952.

Billias, George Athan. *Elbridge Gerry: Founding Father and Republican Statesman*. New York: McGraw-Hill, 1976.

Billings, Warren M., John E. Selby, and Thad W. Tate. *Colonial Virginia: A History*. White Plains, N.Y.: KTO Press, 1986.

Binney, Horace. *An Eulogy on the Life and Character of John Marshall*. Philadelphia: J. Crissy and G. Goodman, 1835.

Bizzell, William Bennett. *Judicial Interpretation of Political Theory*. New York: G. P. Putnam's Sons, 1914.

Blackburn, Joyce. *George Wythe of Williamsburg*. New York: Harper & Row, 1975.

Blackstone, Sir William. *Commentaries on the Laws of England*. 4 vols. Oxford: Clarendon Press, 1766–1769.

Bland, Theodorick. *The Bland Papers*. 2 vols. Charles Campbell, ed. Petersburg, Va: E. and J. C. Ruffin, 1839–1843.

Blumenthal, Walter Hart. *Women Camp Followers of the American Revolution*. New York: Arno Press, 1974.

Boatner, Mark Mayo III. *Encyclopedia of the American Revolution*. New York: David McKay, 1966.

Boorstin, Daniel J. *The Americans: The National Experience*. New York: Random House, 1965.

———. *The Mysterious Science of the Law: An Essay on Blackstone's Commentaries*. Cambridge, Mass.: Harvard University Press, 1941.

Borden, Morton. *The Federalism of James A. Bayard*. New York: Columbia University Press, 1954.

Boudinot, Elias. *The Life, Public Services, Addresses and Letters of Elias Boudinot*. J. J. Boudinot, ed. New York: Da Capo Press, 1971.

Bourquin, Marie-Helene. *Monsieur et Madame Tallien*. Paris: Librairie Académique Perrin, 1987.

Bowden, James. *The History of the Society of Friends in North America*. 2 vols. London: C. Gilpin, 1850–1854.

Bowers, Claude G. *Beveridge and the Progressive Era*. Boston: Houghton Mifflin, 1932.

————. *Jefferson and Hamilton*. Boston: Houghton Mifflin, 1925.

Bowman, Albert Hall. *The Struggle for Neutrality*. Knoxville: University of Tennessee Press, 1974.

Boyd, Thomas A. *Light-Horse Harry Lee*. New York: Charles Scribner's Sons, 1931.

Braeman, John. *Albert J. Beveridge*. Chicago: University of Chicago Press, 1971.

Brant, Irving. *James Madison, The President: 1809–1812*. Indianapolis: Bobbs-Merrill, 1956.

————. *James Madison: Secretary of State, 1800–1809*. Indianapolis: Bobbs-Merrill, 1956.

————. *James Madison: The Virginia Revolutionary*. Indianapolis: Bobbs-Merrill, 1941.

Breen, T. H. *Tobacco Culture: The Mentality of the Great Tidewater Planters on the Eve of the Revolution*. Princeton, N.J.: Princeton University Press, 1985.

Brigham, Clarence Saunders, ed. *British Royal Proclamations Relating to America: 1603–1783*. Worcester, Mass.: American Antiquarian Society, 1911.

Brockenbrough, John W. *Reports of Cases Decided by the Honorable John Marshall . . . in the Circuit Court of the United States for the District of Virginia and North Carolina*. Philadelphia: James Kay, 1837.

Broussard, James H. *The Southern Federalists, 1800–1816*. Baton Rouge: Louisiana State University Press, 1978.

Brown, Glenn. *History of the United States Capitol*. 2 vols. Washington, D.C.: Government Printing Office, 1900–1903.

Brown, Imogene. *American Aristides: A Biography of George Wythe*. Rutherford, N.J.: Fairleigh Dickinson University Press, 1981.

Brown, Ralph Adams. *The Presidency of John Adams*. Lawrence: University Press of Kansas, 1975.

Brown, Robert E., and B. Katherine. *Virginia, 1705–1786: Democracy or Aristocracy?* East Lansing: Michigan State University Press, 1964.

Brown, Stuart E., Jr. *Virginia Baron: The Story of Thomas 6th Lord Fairfax*. Berryville, Va.: Chesapeake Book Co., 1965.

Brown, William Garrott. *The Life of Oliver Ellsworth*. New York: Macmillan, 1905.

Brownell, Charles E., ed. *The Architectural Drawings of Henry Latrobe*. 2 vols. New Haven, Conn.: Yale University Press, 1985.

Bruce, Philip Alexander. *Institutional History of Virginia in the Seventeenth Century*. New York: G. P. Putnam's Sons, 1910.

Bruce, William C. *John Randolph of Roanoke*. 2 vols. New York: G. P. Putnam's Sons, 1922.

Bryan, Wilhelmus Bogart. *A History of the National Capital*. 2 vols. New York: Macmillan, 1914–1916.

Bryce, James. *The American Commonwealth*. London: Macmillan, 1891.

Buchan, Peter. *An Historical and Authentic Account of the Ancient and Noble Family of Keith*. Peterhead: P. Buchan, 1820.

Bulloch, John Malcolm. *A History of the University of Aberdeen, 1495–1895*. London: Hodder & Stoughton, 1895.

Burk, John Daly. *The History of Virginia from its First Settlement to the Present Day*. 4 vols. Petersburg, Va.: Dickson and Pescud, 1804–1816.

Burk, W. Herbert. *Historical and Topographical Guide to Valley Forge*. Philadelphia: Winston, 1910.

Burlamaqui, Jean Jacques. *The Principles of Natural and Politic Law*. Thomas Nugent, trans. London: J. Nourse, 1763.

Burnaby, Andrew. *Travels Through the Middle Settlements of North America in the Years 1759 and 1760*. 3rd ed. London: A. Wessels, 1798.

Burt, A. L. *The United States, Great Britain, and British North America from the Revolution to the Establishment of Peace after the War of 1812*. New Haven, Conn.: Yale University Press, 1940.

Burton, John Hill. *The Scot Abroad*. 2 vols. Edinburgh: William Blackwood & Sons, 1864.

Byrd, William. *The Secret Diary of William Byrd of Westover 1709–1712*. Louis B. Wright and Marion Tinling, eds. Richmond, Va.: The Dietz Press, 1941.

————. *The Writings of Colonel William Byrd of Westover in Virginia*. John Spencer Bassett, ed. New York: Doubleday, Page & Co., 1901.

Cabot, George. *Life and Letters of George Cabot*. Henry Cabot Lodge, ed. Boston: Little, Brown, 1878.

Calhoun, John C. *The Papers of John C. Calhoun*. 13 vols. Columbia: University of South Carolina Press, 1959–1980.

Callahan, North. *Daniel Morgan: Ranger of the Revolution.* New York: Holt, Rinehart, and Winston, 1961.

Callender, John Thomas. *The Prospect Before Us.* Richmond, Va.: Jones, Pleasants, and Lyon, 1800.

Campbell, Charles. *History of the Colony and Ancient Dominion of Virginia.* Philadelphia: J. B. Lippincott, 1860.

Cappon, Lester J., ed. *The Adams-Jefferson Letters.* 2 vols. Chapel Hill: University of North Carolina Press, 1959.

Carnot, Hippolyte. *Memoires sur Carnot.* 2 vols. Paris: Pagnerre, 1861–1869.

Carpenter, Thomas. *The Trials of Colonel Aaron Burr.* Washington, D.C.: Westcott, 1808.

Carroll, John Alexander, and Mary Wells Ashworth. *George Washington: First in Peace.* 7 vols. New York: Charles Scribner's Sons, 1948–1957.

Carson, Jane. *James Innes and His Brothers of the F.H. C.* Williamsburg, Va.: Colonial Williamsburg, 1965.

Cattelain, Fernand. *Étude sur l'influence de Montesquieu dans les constitutions américaines.* Besançon: Millot frères, 1927.

Catterall, Helen Tunnicliff. *Judicial Papers Concerning American Slavery and the Negro.* Washington, D.C.: Carnegie Institution of Washington, 1926–1937.

Chalmers, George. *Collection of Treaties between Great Britain and Other Powers,* vol. 1. London: J. Stockdale, 1790.

Chapin, Bradley. *The American Law of Treason.* Seattle: University of Washington Press, 1964.

Chidsey, Donald B. *Valley Forge.* New York: Crown Publishers, 1959.

Chinard, Gilbert. *Pensees choisies tirees du Commonplace Book de Thomas Jefferson.* Paris: Société d'edition "Les Belles Lettres," 1925.

———. *Thomas Jefferson, The Apostle of Americanism.* Boston: Little, Brown, 1929.

Chitty, Joseph. *A Practical Treatise on Bills of Exchange.* Joseph Story, ed. Boston: Farnand, Mallory & Co., 1804.

Choate, Rufus. *Works of Rufus Choate.* Samuel Gilman Brown, ed. Boston: Little, Brown, 1862.

Choper, Jesse H. *Judicial Review and the National Political Process: A Functional Reconsideration of the Role of the Supreme Court.* Chicago: University of Chicago Press, 1980.

Christian, Ashbury W. *Richmond: Her Past and Present.* Richmond, Va.: L. H. Jenkins, 1912.

Christison, General Sir Philip. *Bannockburn: The Story of the Battle.* Edinburgh: Scottish National Trust, 1962.

Chroust, Anton-Hermann. *The Rise of the Legal Profession in America.* Norman: University of Oklahoma Press, 1965.

Churchill, Charles. *The Prophecy of Famine.* London: private printing, 1763.

Cipolla, Carolo M. *Clocks and Culture.* London: Walker, 1967.

Clarkin, William. *Serene Patriot: A Life of George Wythe.* Albany, N.Y.: Alan Publications, 1970.

Clarkson, Paul S., and R. Samuel Jett. *Luther Martin of Maryland.* Baltimore: Johns Hopkins Press, 1970.

Clinton, Sir Henry, and Earl Charles Cornwallis. *Narrative of the Campaign of 1781.* Philadelphia: J. Campbell, 1865.

Coke, Sir Edward. *The first part of the Institutes of the Laws of England: or A commentary upon Littleton.* 12th ed. London: E. and R. Nutt and R. Gosling, 1738.

Cole, David B. *Martin Van Buren and the American Political System.* Princeton, N.J.: Princeton University Press, 1984.

Coleman, Peter J. *Debtors and Creditors in America, 1607–1900.* Madison: State Historical Society of Wisconsin, 1974.

Colmache, M. *Reminiscences of Prince Talleyrand.* London: H. Colburn, 1850.

Combs, Jerald A. *The Jay Treaty: Political Background of the Founding Fathers.* Berkeley: University of California Press, 1970.

Conway, Moncure Daniel. *Omitted Chapters of History Disclosed in the Life and Papers of Edmund Randolph.* New York: G. P. Putnam's Sons, 1888.

Cooch, Edward W. *The Battle of Cooch's Bridge.* Wilmington, Del.: W. N. Cann, 1940.

Cooke, Jacob E. *Alexander Hamilton.* New York: Charles Scribner's Sons, 1982.

Cooke, Jacob E., ed. *The Federalist.* Middletown, Conn.: Wesleyan University Press, 1961.

Cooper, James Fenimore. *Notions of the Americans.* 2 vols. Reprint ed. New York: Frederick Ungar Publishing Co., 1963.

Correspondence of the French Ministers to the United States, 1791–1797. Frederick Jackson Turner, ed. In 2 *Annual Report of the American Historical Association for the Year 1903*, Washington, D.C.: Government Printing Office, 1904.

Corwin, Edward S. *American Constitutional History.* New York: Harper & Row, 1964.

———. *The Doctrine of Judicial Review.* Princeton, N.J.: Princeton University Press, 1914.

———. *John Marshall and the Constitution.* New Haven, Conn.: Yale University Press, 1919.

———. *The President's Control of Foreign Relations.* Princeton, N.J.: Princeton University Press, 1917.

Cound, John J. et al. *Civil Procedure: Cases and Materials.* St. Paul, Minn.: West Publishing Co., 1985.

Cox, Isaac Joslin. *The West Florida Controversy 1798–1813; A Study in American Diplomacy.* Baltimore: Johns Hopkins Press, 1918.

Crockford's Clerical Directory. London: Oxford University Press, 1960.

Crosskey, William Winslow. *Politics and the Constitution in the History of the United States.* 2 vols. Chicago: University of Chicago Press, 1953.

Cullen, William. *A Treatise of the Materia Medica.* Benjamin Smith Barton, ed. Philadelphia: Edward Parker, 1812.

Cunningham, Noble E., Jr. *The Jeffersonian Republicans: The Formation of Party Organization, 1789–1801.* Chapel Hill: University of North Carolina Press, 1957.

Curti, Merle. *The Growth of American Thought.* 3rd ed. New York: Harper & Row, 1943.

Curtis, George Ticknor. *Life of Daniel Webster.* 2 vols. New York: D. Appleton, 1870.

Dabney, Virginius. *Richmond: The Story of a City.* Garden City, N.Y.: Doubleday, 1976.

———. *Virginia: The New Dominion.* Garden City, N.Y.: Doubleday, 1971.

Daniels, Jonathan. *The Randolphs of Virginia.* Garden City, N.Y.: Doubleday, 1972.

Dargo, George. *Jefferson's Louisiana: Politics and the Clash of Legal Traditions.* Cambridge, Mass.: Harvard University Press, 1975.

Dauer, Manning J. *The Adams Federalists.* Baltimore: The Johns Hopkins Press, 1968.

Daveiss, Joseph Hamilton. *View of the President's Conduct Concerning the Conspiracy of 1806.* Frankfort, Ky.: J. M. Street, 1807.

Davis, Michael, and Frederick A. Elliston. *Ethics and the Legal Profession.* Buffalo, N.Y.: Prometheus Books, 1986.

Davis, Richard Beale. *Intellectual Life in Jefferson's Virginia.* Chapel Hill: University of North Carolina Press, 1964.

DeConde, Alexander. *Entangling Alliance: Politics and Diplomacy under George Washington.* Durham, N.C.: Duke University Press, 1958.

———. *The Quasi War.* New York: Charles Scribner's Sons, 1966.

Dennis, John. *The Age of Pope (1700–1744).* London: George Bell and Sons, 1901.

Dewey, Donald O. *Marshall versus Jefferson.* New York: Knopf, 1970.

Dewey, Frank L. *Thomas Jefferson: Lawyer.* Charlottesville: University Press of Virginia, 1986.

Dickens, Charles. *Bleak House.* Philadelphia: Getz and Buck, 1853.

Dickinson, Josiah L. *The Fairfax Proprietary.* Front Royal, Va.: Warren Press, 1959.

Dickson, William Kirk. *The Jacobite Attempt of 1719.* Edinburgh: Edinburgh University Press, 1895.

Dillon, John F., ed. *John Marshall: Life, Character, and Judicial Services.* Chicago: Callaghan and Company, 1903.

Dodd, William Edward, ed. *The John P. Branch Historical Papers of Randolph-Macon College.* 5 vols. Ashland, Va.: Randolph-Macon College, 1905.

Dood, Merrick. *American Business Corporations Until 1860.* Cambridge, Mass.: Harvard University Press, 1954.

Dowdey, Clifford. *The Virginia Dynasties.* Boston: Little, Brown, 1969.

Draper, Theodore. *A Struggle for Power: The American Revolution.* New York: Times Books/Random House, 1996.

Duke, Maurice, and David P. Jordan, eds. *A Richmond Reader, 1733–1783.* Chapel Hill: University of North Carolina Press, 1983.

Dumbauld, Edward. *Thomas Jefferson and the Law*. Norman: University of Oklahoma Press, 1978.

Dunaway, Wayland Fuller. *History of the James River and Kanawha Company*. New York: Columbia University Press, 1922.

Eckenrode, Hamilton J. *The Randolphs: The Story of a Virginia Family*. Indianapolis: Bobbs-Merrill, 1946.

———. *The Revolution in Virginia*. Boston: Houghton Mifflin, 1916.

Egerton, Douglas R. *Charles Fenton Mercer and the Trial of National Conservatism*. Jackson: University Press of Mississippi, 1989.

Elkins, Stanley, and Eric McKitrick. *The Age of Federalism*. New York: Oxford University Press, 1993.

Eliot, Jonathan, ed. *The Debates in the Several State Conventions on the Adoption of the Federal Constitution*. 5 vols. Philadelphia: J. B. Lippincott Co., 1907.

Ellis, Richard E. *The Jeffersonian Crisis: Courts and Politics in the Young Republic*. New York: Oxford University Press, 1971.

Elsmere, Jane Shaffer. *Justice Samuel Chase*. Muncie, Ind.: Janevar Publishing Company, 1980.

Ely, John Hart. *War and Responsibility*. Princeton, N.J.: Princeton University Press, 1993.

Engeman, Thomas S., Edward J. Erler, and Thomas B. Hofeller, eds. *The Federalist Concordance*. Middletown, Conn.: Wesleyan University Press, 1980.

Ernst, Robert. *Rufus King: American Federalist*. Chapel Hill: University of North Carolina Press, 1968.

Ezell, John Samuel. *Fortune's Merry Wheel*. Cambridge, Mass.: Harvard University Press, 1960.

Faden, William. *North American Atlas*. London: W. Faden, 1777.

Fairchild, Hoxie Neale. *Religious Trends in English Poetry*. 5 vols. New York: Columbia University Press, 1939.

Farrand, Max, ed. *The Records of the Federal Convention of 1787*. 3 vols. New Haven, Conn.: Yale University Press, 1911.

Faulkner, Robert K. *The Jurisprudence of John Marshall*. Princeton, N.J.: Princeton University Press, 1968.

Fay, O. P. *Fay Genealogy: John Jay of Marlborough and his Descendants*. Cleveland: J. P. Savage, 1898.

Ferling, John E. *The First of Men: A Life of George Washington*. Knoxville: University of Tennessee Press, 1988.

Fischer, David Hackett. *The Revolution of American Conservatism: The Federalist Party in the Era of Jeffersonian Democracy*. New York: Harper & Row, 1965.

Flanders, Henry. *The Lives and Times of the Chief Justices of the Supreme Court of the United States*. 2 vols. Philadelphia: Lippincott, Grambo and Company, 1855–1858.

Flexner, James Thomas. *George Washington and the New Nation, 1783–1793*. Boston: Little, Brown, 1970.

Fortescue, Sir John, ed. *The Correspondence of King George the Third*. London: Macmillan, 1927.

Forty, George and Anne. *They Also Served*. Speldhurst, Kent: Midas Books, 1979.

Foster, Francis B. *Old Homes and Families of Fauquier County, Virginia*. Berryville, Va.: Virginia Book Company, no date.

Franck, Thomas M. *Political Questions/Judicial Answers: Does the Rule of Law Apply to Foreign Affairs?* Princeton, N.J.: Princeton University Press, 1992.

Frank, John Paul. *Marble Palace: The Supreme Court in American Life*. New York: Knopf, 1958.

Frankfurter, Felix. *The Commerce Clause Under Marshall, Taney, and White*. Chapel Hill: University of North Carolina Press, 1937.

Fraprie, Frank Roy. *The Castles and Keeps of Scotland*. Boston: L. C. Page & Co., 1907.

Freehling, William W. *Prelude to Civil War: The Nullification Controversy in South Carolina, 1816–1836*. New York: Harper & Row, 1966.

Freeman, Douglas Southall. *George Washington: A Biography*. 7 vols. New York: Charles Scribner's Sons, 1948–1957.

Friedenthal, Jack H., Mary K. Kane, and Arthur R. Miller. *Civil Procedure*. St. Paul, Minn.: West Publishing Co., 1985.

Friedman, Leon, and Fred L. Israel, eds. *The Justices of the United States Supreme Court*. New York: Chelsea House, 1969.

Gallatin, Albert. *The Writings of Albert Gallatin*. 3 vols. Henry Adams, ed. Philadelphia: J. B. Lippincott, 1879.

Garland, Hugh A. *The Life of John Randolph of Roanoke*. New York: D. Appleton, 1851.

Garnett, James M. *Lectures on Female Education*. 4th ed. Richmond, Va.: Thomas W. White, 1825.

Gastine, L. *Madame Tallien*. J. Lewis May, trans. London: Lane, 1913.

The George Washington Atlas. Lawrence Martin, ed. Washington, D.C.: George Washington Bicentennial Commission, 1932.

Gerry, Elbridge. *Elbridge Gerry's Letterbook: Paris, 1797–1798*. Russell W. Knight, ed. Salem, Mass.: Essex Institute, 1966.

Gilbert, Felix. *To the Farewell Address*. Princeton, N.J.: Princeton University Press, 1961.

Gillmer, Thomas C. *Old Ironsides*. Camden, Maine: International Marine, 1993.

Gilman, Daniel. *American Statesman: James Monroe*. Boston: Houghton Mifflin, 1890.

Gilmer, Francis Walker. *Sketches, Essays and Translations*. Baltimore: Lucas, 1828.

Glass, D. V., and Eversley, D.E.C., eds. *Population in History*. London: Edward Arnold, 1965.

Goddard, Henry P. *Luther Martin: The "Federal Bull-dog."* Baltimore: J. Murphy, 1887.

Goebel, Julius, Jr. *Antecedents and Beginnings to 1801*. In The Oliver Wendell Holmes Devise. *History of the Supreme Court of the United States*. vol. 1. New York: Macmillan, 1971.

Goodwin, Edward Lewis. *The Colonial Church in Virginia*. Milwaukee: Morehouse Publishing Co., 1927.

Graham, James. *The Life of General Daniel Morgan*. New York: Derby & Jackson, 1856.

Grant, Ulysses. *The Personal Memoirs of U.S. Grant*. 2 vols. New York: C. L. Webster, 1885.

Gray, Horace. *An Address on the Life, Character and Influence of Chief Justice Marshall*. Washington, D.C.: Pearson, 1901.

Gray, Lewis Cecil. *History of Agriculture in the Southern United States to 1860*. 2 vols. Gloucester, Mass.: Peter Smith, 1958.

Graydon, Alexander. *Memoirs of His Own Time*. Philadelphia: Lindsay and Blakiston, 1846.

Greeley, Horace. *The American Conflict*. 2 vols. Hartford, Conn.: O. D. Case, 1864–1866.

Green, Constance McLaughlin. *Washington: Village and Capital*. Princeton, N.J.: Princeton University Press, 1962.

Green, Raleigh Travers. *Genealogical and Historical Notes on Culpeper County, Virginia*. Culpeper, Va.: R. T. Green, 1900.

Greenbaum, Louis S. *Talleyrand Statesman-Priest: The Agent-General of the Clergy and the Church at the End of the Old Regime*. Washington, D.C.: Catholic University of America Press, 1970.

Greene, Evarts B., and Virginia Harrington. *American Population Before the Federal Census of 1790*. New York: Columbia University Press, 1932.

Greene, Francis Vinton. *General Greene*. New York: D. Appleton, 1913.

Greene, George Washington. *The Life of Nathanael Greene*. 3 vols. New York: Hurd and Houghton, 1871.

Grigsby, Hugh Blair. *The History of the Virginia Federal Convention of 1788*. 2 vols. Richmond, Va.: Virginia Historical Society, 1890–1891.

———. *The Virginia Convention of 1829–1830*. Reprint ed. New York: Da Capo Press, 1969.

Groome, Harry C. *Fauquier During the Proprietorship*. Richmond, Va.: Old Dominion Press, 1927.

Grotius, Hugo. *The Rights of War and Peace*. London: Irvy and Marby, 1738.

Gudin de la Brenellerie, Paul Phillippe. *Historie de Beaumarchais*. Paris: H. Plon, 1888.

Gunther, Gerald. *John Marshall's Defense of McCulloch v. Maryland*. Stanford, Calif.: Stanford University Press, 1969.

Hackworth, Green Haywood. *Digest of International Law*. 8 vols. Washington, D.C.: Government Printing Office, 1943.

Hale, Sir Matthew. *Historia Placitorum Coronae*. 2 vols. London: E. and R. Nutt and R. Gosling, 1736.

Hall, Evelyn Beatrice. *The Life of Voltaire*. Stephen G. Tallentyre, pseud. London: Smith, Elder, 1903.

Hall, Kermit L., ed. *Major Problems in American Constitutional History*. Lexington, Mass.: D.C. Heath and Co., 1992.

————. *The Oxford Companion to the Supreme Court of the United States*. New York: Oxford University Press, 1992.

Hamilton, Alexander, James Madison, and John Jay. *The Federalist; A Collection of Essays, Written in Favour of the New Constitution, As Agreed Upon by the Federal Convention, September 17, 1787*. Philadelphia: John and Archibald McLean, 1788.

————. *The Papers of Alexander Hamilton*. 8 vols. Harold C. Syrett, ed. New York: Columbia University Press, 1961–1987.

————. *Works of Alexander Hamilton*. 12 vols. Henry Cabot Lodge, ed. New York: G. P. Putnam's Sons, 1904.

Hamilton, Charles. *Braddock's Defeat*. Norman: University of Oklahoma Press, 1959.

Hamilton, Thomas. *Men and Manners in America*. 2 vols. London: William Blackwood, 1833.

Hammond, Bray. *Banks and Politics in America: From the Revolution to the Civil War*. Princeton, N.J.: Princeton University Press, 1957.

Harrell, Isaac. *Loyalism in Virginia*. Durham, N.C.: Duke University Press, 1926.

Harris, Joel Chandler. *Stories of Georgia*. New York: American Book Co., 1896.

Hart, James D. *The Popular Book: A History of American Literary Taste*. New York: Oxford University Press, 1950.

Haskins, George L., and Herbert A. Johnson. *Foundation of Power: John Marshall, 1801–15*. In The Oliver Wendell Holmes Devise. *History of the Supreme Court of the United States*. vol. 2 New York: Macmillan, 1981.

Hatcher, William B. *Edward Livingston: Jeffersonian Republican and Jacksonian Democrat*. University: Louisiana State University Press, 1940.

Hawkins, William. *A Treatise of the Pleas of the Crown*. 2 vols. London: E. and R. Nutt and R. Gosling, 1724–1726.

Hay, George. *A Treatise on Expatriation* Washington, D.C.: A & G Way, 1814.

Hayden, Ralston. *The Senate and Treaties, 1789–1817*. New York: Macmillan, 1920.

Hazelton, George C. *The National Capitol: Its Architecture, Art and History*. New York: J. F. Taylor, 1907.

Headley, Joel T. *Washington and His Generals*. 2 vols. New York: Baker and Scribner, 1847.

Heaton, Ronald E. *Valley Forge, Yesterday and Today*. Norristown, Pa.: Heaton, 1956.

Henry, William Wirt. *Patrick Henry: Life, Correspondence and Speeches*. 3 vols. New York: Charles Scribner's Sons, 1891.

Higginbotham, Don. *Daniel Morgan: Revolutionary Rifleman*. Chapel Hill: University of North Carolina Press, 1961.

Hirschman, Albert O. *The Passions and the Interests: Political Arguments for Capitalism Before its Triumph*. Princeton, N.J.: Princeton University Press, 1977.

Hobbes, Thomas. *Leviathan*. C.B. Macpherson, ed. London: Penguin Books, 1968.

Hoffer, Peter Charles, and N.E.H. Hull. *Impeachment in America, 1635–1805*. New Haven, Conn.: Yale University Press, 1984.

Holmes, Oliver Wendell, Jr. *Collected Legal Papers*. New York: Harcourt, Brace, and Howe, 1920.

————. *The Common Law*. Boston: Little, Brown, 1881.

Hornblow, Arthur. *A History of the Theater in America from its Beginnings to the Present Time*. Philadelphia: B. Blom, 1919.

Horsnell, Margaret E. *Spencer Roane: Judicial Advocate of Jeffersonian Principles*. New York: Garland Publishing, 1986.

Houssaye, Arséne. *Notre Dame de Thermidor*. Paris: H. Plon, 1866.

Howe, Henry. *Historical Collections of Virginia*. Charleston, S.C.: Babcock and Co., 1845.

Hughes, Charles Evans. *The Supreme Court of the United States*. New York: Columbia University Press, 1928.

Hughes, Rupert. *George Washington*. 3 vols. New York: W. Morrow, 1926–1930.

Humboldt, Wilhelm Freiherr von. *Neue Briefe an Schiller, 1796–1803*. F. C. Ebrard, ed. Berlin: Paetel, 1911.

Hume, David. *Essays and Treatises on Several Subjects*. 4 vols. London: A. Millar, 1758.

————. *A Treatise of Human Nature*. 2 vols. London: J. Noon, 1739.

Hume, Ivor Noël. *1775: Another Part of the Field*. New York: Knopf, 1966.

Hunt, Gaillard. *The Department of State of the United States*. New Haven, Conn.: Yale University Press, 1914.

Hurst, James Willard. *Treason in the United States*. Westport, Conn.: Greenwood Press, 1945.

Hyde, Charles Chaney. *International Law Chiefly as Interpreted and Applied by the United States*. 2nd rev. ed. Boston: Little, Brown, 1945.

Idzerda, Stanley J., ed. *Lafayette in the Age of the American Revolution: Selected Letters and Papers*. Ithaca, N.Y.: Cornell University Press, 1977–1983.

Ingersoll, Charles J. *Historical Sketch*. 2 vols. Philadelphia: Lea & Blanchard, 1845–1849.

———. *Inchiquin: The Jesuit Letters*. New York: I. Riley, 1810.

Irving, Pierre Munroe, ed. *Life and Letters of Washington Irving*. 3 vols. New York: G. P. Putnam, 1863–1864.

Irving, Washington. *The Life of George Washington*. 5 vols. New York: G. P. Putnam, 1855–1859.

Isaac, Rhys. *The Transformation of Virginia: 1740–1790*. Chapel Hill: University of North Carolina Press, 1982.

James, William. *The Naval History of Great Britain From the Declaration of War in 1793 to the Accession of George IV*. 6 vols. New York: Macmillan, 1902.

Jay, John. *The Correspondence and Public Papers of John Jay*. 4 vols. Henry P. Johnston, ed. New York: G. P. Putnam's Sons, 1890–1893.

Jefferson, Thomas. *The Complete Anas of Thomas Jefferson*. Reprint ed. New York: Da Capo Press, 1950.

———. *The Family Letters of Thomas Jefferson*. Edwin Morris Betts and James Adam Bear, Jr., eds. Columbia: University of Missouri Press, 1966.

———. *The Literary Bible of Thomas Jefferson: His Commonplace Book*. Gilbert Chinard, ed. Baltimore: The Johns Hopkins Press, 1928.

———. *Memoirs, Correspondence, and Private Papers of Thomas Jefferson*. 4 vols. Thomas Jefferson Randolph, ed. Charlottesville, N.C.: F. Carr and Company, 1829.

———. *Notes of the State of Virginia*. William Peden, ed. Chapel Hill: University of North Carolina Press, 1955.

———. *The Papers of Thomas Jefferson*. 25 vols. Julian P. Boyd, ed. Princeton, N.J.: Princeton University Press, 1950–1992.

———. *The Works of Thomas Jefferson*. 12 vols. Paul Leicester Ford, ed. New York: G. P. Putnam's Sons, 1904–1905.

———. *The Writings of Thomas Jefferson*. 20 vols. Andrew A. Lipscomb, ed. Washington, D.C.: The Thomas Jefferson Memorial Association, 1903–1904.

———. *The Writings of Thomas Jefferson*. 9 vols. H. A. Washington, ed. New York: H. W. Derby, 1861.

Jeffreys, Thomas. *American Atlas*. Amsterdam: Theatrum Orbis Terraum, 1974.

———. *A General Topography of North America and the West Indies*. London: Sayer, Jefferys, 1768.

Jensen, Merrill. *The New Nation: A History of the United States During Confederation, 1781–1789*. New York: Knopf, 1950.

Jillson, Willard Rouse. *The Kentucky Land Grants*. Louisville, Ky.: Standard Publishing Co., 1925.

———. *Old Kentucky Entries and Deeds*. Louisville, Ky.: Standard Printing Co., 1926.

Johnston, Henry P. *The Campaign of 1776 Around New York and Brooklyn. Including a New and Circumstantial Account of the Battle of Long Island at the Loss of New York*. Brooklyn, N.Y.: Long Island Historical Society, 1878.

———. *The Storming of Stony Point*. New York: James T. White & Co., 1900.

Jones, W. Melville, ed. *Chief Justice John Marshall: A Reappraisal*. New York: Da Capo Press, 1971.

Jordan, Daniel Pendleton. *Political Leadership in Jefferson's Virginia*. Charlottesville: University Press of Virginia, 1983.

Jordan, Winthrop D. *White Over Black: American Attitudes Toward the Negro, 1550–1812*. Chapel Hill: University of North Carolina Press, 1968.

Kaminski, John P. et al., eds. *Documentary History of the Ratification of the Constitution*. 16 vols. Madison: State Historical Society of Wisconsin, 1976–1993.

Kapp, Friedrich. *The Life of John Kalb*. New York: Henry Holt, 1884.

Keith, Alexander. *A Thousand Years of Aberdeen*. Aberdeen: Aberdeen University Press, 1972.

Kennedy, John P. *Memoirs of the Life of William Wirt*. 2 vols. Philadelphia: Blanchard and Lea, 1856.

Ketcham, Ralph. *James Madison: A Biography*. Charlottesville: University Press of Virginia, 1990.

Kimball, David. *Venerable Relic: The Story of the Liberty Bell*. Philadelphia: Eastern National Park and Monument Association, 1989.

King, Charles R., ed. *The Life and Correspondence of Rufus King*. 6 vols. New York: G. P. Putnam's Sons, 1894–1900.

King, Larry. *Keith Kinfolks: Descendants of James Keith, Sr*. Hendersonville, Tenn.: King, 1979.

Knox, Thomas Wallace. *The Life of Robert Fulton and a History of Steam Navigation*. New York: G. P. Putnam's Sons, 1896.

Kohn, Richard H. *Eagle and Sword: The Federalists and the Creation of the Military Establishment in America, 1783–1802*. New York: Free Press, 1975.

Konkle, Burton Alva. *Joseph Hopkinson, 1770–1842. Jurist, Scholar, Inspirer of the Arts, Author of Hail Columbia*. Philadelphia: University of Pennsylvania Press, 1931.

Kunst, H. *Montesquieu und die Verfassungen der Vereinigten Statten von Amerika*. Munich: Ullstein, 1922.

Kuroda, Tadashisa. *The Origins of the Twelfth Amendment: The Electoral College in the Early Republic*. Westport, Conn.: Greenwood Press, 1994.

La Cour-Gayet, Georges. *Talleyrand: 1754–1838* 3 vols. Paris: Payot, 1928–1934.

Lancaster, R. A. Jr. *Historic Virginia Homes and Churches*. Philadelphia: J. B. Lippincott Co., 1915.

La Revallière de Lepeaux, Louis Marie de. *Mémoires de Larevellière-Lépeaux*. 3 vols. Paris: E. Plon, Nourrit et cie, 1895.

La Rouchefoucauld-Liancourt, Francois Alexandre Frédéric. *Travels Through the United States of North America*. 4 vols. London: R. Phillips, 1799–1800.

Latrobe, Benjamin Henry. *The Correspondence and Miscellaneous Papers of Benjamin Henry Latrobe*. 3 vols. John C. Van Horn and Lee W. Formwalt, eds. New Haven, Conn.: Yale University Press, 1984–1988.

Lawes, Edward H.V. *A Practical Treatise on Pleading in Assumpsit*. Joseph Story, ed. Boston: James W. Burditt, 1811.

Leake, Isaac Q. *Memoirs of the Life and Times of General John Lamb*. Albany, N.Y.: J. Muncell, 1850.

Lebsock, Suzanne. *The Free Women of Petersburg: Status and Culture in a Southern Town, 1784–1860*. New York: W. W. Norton, 1984.

Lee, Charles. *The Lee Papers*. 4 vols. New York: New York Historical Society, 1872–1875.

Lee, Henry. *Memoirs of the War in the Southern Department*. General Robert E. Lee, ed. New York: University Publishing Co., 1869.

Lee, Richard Henry. *The Letters of Richard Henry Lee*. 2 vols. James Curtis Ballagh, ed., New York: Macmillan, 1911–1914.

Lefebvre, Georges. *The French Revolution from 1795 to 1799*. 2 vols. John Hall Stewart et al., trans. New York: Columbia University Press, 1962–1964.

———. *The Thermidorians and the Directory: Two Phases of the French Revolution*. Robert Baldick, trans. New York: Random House, 1964.

Leitch, Alexander. *A Princeton Companion*. Princeton, N.J.: Princeton University Press, 1978.

Lenman, Bruce. *The Jacobite Cause*. Glasgow: Richard Drew Publishing, 1986.

Levasseur, Auguste. *Lafayette in America in 1824 and 1825*. John D. Goodman, trans. Philadelphia: Carey and Lea, 1829.

Levy, Leonard W. *Jefferson and Civil Liberties: The Darker Side*. Cambridge, Mass.: Harvard University Press, 1963.

———. *Legacy of Suppression: Freedom of Speech and Press in Early American History*. Cambridge, Mass.: Harvard University Press, 1960.

Little, Lewis Payton. *Imprisoned Preachers and Religious Liberty in Virginia*. Lynchburg, Va.: J. P. Bell, 1938.

Livermore, Shaw, Jr. *The Twilight of Federalism: 1815–1830*. Princeton, N.J.: Princeton University Press, 1962.

Locke, John. *An Essay Concerning Human Understanding*. London: T. Basset, 1690.

Lockmiller, David A. *Sir William Blackstone*. Chapel Hill: University of North Carolina Press, 1938.

Lomask, Milton. *Aaron Burr.* 2 vols. New York: Farrar, Straus, Giroux, 1979–1982.

Loménie, Louis Leonard de. *Beaumarchais and His Times.* H. S. Edwards, trans. London: Addey, 1856.

Longman, F. W. *Frederick the Great and the Seven Years' War.* New York: Charles Scribner's Sons, 1890.

Lord, John. *A History of Dartmouth College.* Concord, N.H.: Rumford, 1913.

Loss, Richard, ed. *The Letters of Pacificus and Helvidius.* Delmar, N.Y.: Scholars Facsimilies and Reprints, 1976.

Lossing, Benson J. *The Pictorial Field-Book of the Revolution.* 2 vols. New York: Harper and Bros., 1851–1852.

Lowell, John. *Review of "A Treatise on Expatriation" by a Massachusetts Lawyer.* Boston: Russell Cutler, 1814.

Luce, W. Ray. *Cohens v. Virginia.* New York: Garland Publishing Co., 1990.

Lyman, Theodore. *Diplomacy of the United States.* Boston: Wells & Lilly, 1826.

Lyon, E. Wilson. *Louisiana in French Diplomacy, 1795–1804.* Norman: University of Oklahoma Press, 1934.

McCaleb, Walter Flavius. *The Aaron Burr Conspiracy.* New York: Wilson-Erickson Inc., 1936.

McCants, David A. *Patrick Henry, the Orator.* Westport, Conn.: Greenwood Press, 1990.

McCardell, Lee. *Ill-starred General: Braddock of the Coldstream Guards.* Pittsburgh: University of Pittsburgh Press, 1958.

McCoy, Drew R. *The Last of the Fathers: James Madison and the Republican Legacy.* Cambridge: Cambridge University Press, 1989.

McDonald, Forrest. *We the People: The Economic Origins of the Constitution.* Chicago: University of Chicago Press, 1958.

Macdonald, William. *Jacksonian Democracy, 1829–1837.* New York: Harper Brothers, 1906.

Macinnes, Allan L. *Charles I and the Making of the Covenanting Movement.* Edinburgh: John Donald, 1991.

Mack, Maynard. *Alexander Pope: A Life.* New York: W. W. Norton, 1985.

McLaughlin, Andrew C. *The Confederation and the Constitution.* New York: Collier Books, 1962.

McLynn, Frank. *The Jacobites.* London: Routledge & Kegan Paul, 1985.

McMaster, John Bach, and Frederick D. Stone. *Pennsylvania and the Federal Constitution, 1787–1788.* Lancaster, Pa: Inquirer Publishing, 1888.

McRae, Alexander (published anonymously). *Letters on the Richmond Party . . . by a Native Virginia.* Washington, D.C.: Washington Republican, 1823.

McRee, Griffith J. *Life and Correspondence of James Iredell.* 2 vols. New York: Appleton, 1857–1858.

McRoy, Drew R. *The Last of the Fathers: James Madison and the Republican Legacy.* Cambridge: Cambridge University Press, 1989.

Madelin, Louis. *Talleyrand: A Vivid Biography of the Amoral, Unscrupulous, and Fascinating French Statesman.* Rosalie Feltenstein, trans. New York: Roy, 1948.

Madison, James. *Letters and Other Writings of James Madison.* 4 vols. William C. Rives and Philip R. Ferdall, eds. Philadelphia: J. B. Lippincott Co., 1865–1868.

———. *The Papers of James Madison.* 17 vols. William T. Hutchinson et al., eds. Chicago: University of Chicago Press, 1962–1991.

———. *The Writings of James Madison.* 9 vols. Gaillard Hunt, ed. New York: G. P. Putnam's Sons, 1900–1910.

Magrath, C. Peter. *Yazoo: Land and Politics in the New Republic.* Providence, R.I.: Brown University Press, 1966.

Magruder, Allan B. *John Marshall.* Boston: Houghton, Mifflin, 1890.

Mairobert, Mathieu François Pidanzat de. *L'Espion Anglais ou Correspondance Secrète entre Milord All Eye et Milord All Ear.* 10 vols. London: J. Adamson, 1777–1786.

Maitland, Frederick W. *Equity, also the Forms of Action at Common Law.* A. H. Chaytor and W. J. Whittaker, eds. Cambridge, Mass.: Harvard University Press, 1929.

Malone, Dumas, ed. *Dictionary of American Biography.* New York: Charles Scribner's Sons, 1933.

Malone, Dumas. *Jefferson and the Ordeal of Liberty.* Boston: Little, Brown 1962.

———. *Jefferson the President: First Term.* Boston: Little, Brown, 1970.

————. *Jefferson the President: Second Term*. Boston: Little, Brown, 1974.

————. *Jefferson and the Rights of Man*. Boston: Little, Brown, 1951.

————. *Jefferson the Virginian*. Boston: Little, Brown, 1948.

————. *The Sage of Monticello*. Boston: Little, Brown, 1977.

Marsh, Philip. *Monroe's Defense of Jefferson and Freneau against Hamilton*. Oxford, Ohio: privately published, 1948.

Marshall, John. *An Autobiographical Sketch*. John Stokes Adams, ed. Ann Arbor: University of Michigan Press, 1937.

————. *A History of the Colonies Planted by the English on the Continent of North America, from their Settlement, to the Commencement of that War, which Terminated in their Independence*. Philadelphia: Abraham Small, 1824.

————. *The Life of George Washington*. 5 vols. Philadelphia: C. P. Wayne, 1805–1807.

————. *The Life of George Washington*. 2 vols. Philadelphia: Crissy, 1832.

————. *The Life of George Washington*. 5 vols. Reprint ed. Fredericksburg, Va.: The Citizens' Guild, 1926.

————. *The Papers of John Marshall*. 8 vols. Charles R. Hobson, et al., eds. Chapel Hill: University of North Carolina Press, 1974–1995.

————. *The Political and Economic Doctrines of John Marshall*. John Edward Oster, ed. New York: The Neale Publishing Co., 1914.

Marshall, Maria Newton. *Recollections and Reflections of Fielding Lewis Marshall*. Orange, Va.: private printing, 1911.

Marshall, Senator Humphrey. *History of Kentucky*. Frankfort, Ky.: Henry Gore, 1812.

Martineau, Harriet. *Harriet Martineau's Autobiography*. Maria Weston Chapman, ed. London: Smith, Elder & Co., 1877.

————. *Retrospect of Western Travel*. 2 vols. London: Saunders and Otley, 1838.

————. *Society in America*. Seymour Martin Lispet, ed. Garden City, N.Y.: Doubleday, 1962.

Mason, Frances Norton. *My Dearest Polly*. Richmond, Va.: Garret and Massie, 1961.

Mason, George. *The Papers of George Mason*. 3 vols. Robert A. Rutland, ed. Chapel Hill: University of North Carolina Press, 1970.

Mason, Haydn. *Voltaire: A Biography*. Baltimore: Johns Hopkins University Press, 1981.

Mason, Jeremiah. *Memoirs and Correspondence of Jeremiah Mason*. George Stillman Hillard, ed. Cambridge, Mass.: Riverside Press, 1873.

Mathews, Mitford M., ed. *Dictionary of Americanisms on Historical Principles*. Chicago: University of Chicago Press, 1951.

Mathiez, Albert. *After Robespierre: The Thermidorian Reaction*. Catherine Alison Phillips, trans. New York: Grosset & Dunlap, 1965.

Mayer, Henry. *A Son of Thunder: Patrick Henry and the American Republic*. New York: Franklin Watts, 1986.

Mays, David John. *Edmund Pendleton, 1721–1803: A Biography*. Cambridge, Mass.: Harvard University Press, 1952.

Meade, Bishop William. *Old Churches, Ministers and Families of Virginia*. 2 vols. Philadelphia: J. B. Lippincott, 1861.

Meade, Robert Douthat. *Patrick Henry: Practical Revolutionary*. 2 vols. Philadelphia: J. B. Lippincott, 1957–1969.

Meigs, William M. *Life of Charles Ingersoll*. Philadelphia: J. B. Lippincott, 1897.

Metzger, Charles H. *The Quebec Act*. New York: United States Catholic Historical Society, 1936.

Meyer, B. H., and C. E. Macgill. *History of Transportation in the United States Before 1860*. Washington, D.C.: Carnegie Institution, 1917.

Middleton, Arthur Pierce. *Tobacco Coast: A Maritime History of Chesapeake Bay in the Colonial Era*. Newport News, Va.: Mariners' Museum, 1953.

Miller, Helen Hill. *George Mason: Gentleman Revolutionary*. Chapel Hill: University of North Carolina Press, 1975.

Miller, John C. *Alexander Hamilton: Portrait in Paradox*. New York: Harper & Row, 1959.

————. *Triumph of Freedom*. Boston: Little, Brown, 1948.

Milne-Tyte, Robert. *Bloody Jeffreys: The Hanging Judge*. London: Andre Deutsche, 1989.

Minot, George Richards. *History of the Insurrection in Massachusetts in 1786 and of the Rebellion Consequent Thereon.* Reprint ed. New York: Da Capo Press, 1971.

Mitchell, Silas Weir. *The Youth of Washington Told in the Form of an Autobiography.* New York: Century, 1904.

Mitchell, Stewart. *New Letters of Abigail Adams.* Boston: Houghton Mifflin, 1947.

Monroe, James. *The Writings of James Monroe.* 7 vols. Stanislaus Murray Hamilton, ed. New York: G. P. Putnam's Sons, 1898–1903.

Montesquieu, Baron de. *The Spirit of the Laws.* 2 vols. Thomas Nugent, trans. London: J. Nourse and P. Vaillant, 1750.

Moore, John Bassett. *A Treaties on Extradition and Interstate Rendition.* 2 vols. Boston: Boston Book Co., 1891.

Mordecai, Samuel. *Richmond in By-Gone Days.* Richmond, Va.: G. M. West, 1856.

Morgan, Donald G. *Congress and the Constitution.* Cambridge, Mass.: Harvard University Press, 1966.

———. *Justice William Johnson: The First Dissenter.* Columbia: University of South Carolina Press, 1954.

Morgan, Edmund S. *The Stamp Act Crisis.* Chapel Hill: University of North Carolina Press, 1953.

———. *Virginians at Home: Family Life in the Eighteenth Century.* Charlottesville: University Press of Virginia, 1952.

Morgan, George. *The Life of James Monroe.* Boston: Small, Maynard, 1921.

———. *The True Patrick Henry.* Philadelphia: J. B. Lippincott, 1907.

Morison, Samuel Eliot. *The Life and Letters of Harrison Gray Otis.* 2 vols. Boston: Houghton Mifflin, 1913.

———. *The Oxford History of the American People.* New York: Oxford University Press, 1965.

Morris, Anne Cary, ed. *The Diary and Letters of Gouverneur Morris.* London: Kagan, Paul, Trench, 1899.

Morris, John E. *Bannockburn.* Cambridge: Cambridge University Press, 1914.

Morris, Richard B. *Fair Trial.* New York: Knopf, 1952.

———. *The Peacemakers.* New York: Harper & Row, 1965.

Morton, Richard Lee. *Colonial Virginia.* 2 vols. Chapel Hill: University of North Carolina Press, 1960.

Muhlenberg, Henry A. *The Life of Major-General Peter Muhlenberg.* Philadelphia: Carey and Hart, 1849.

Munford, George Wythe. *The Two Parsons; Cupid's Sports; The Dream; and the Jewel of Virginia.* Richmond: J.D.K. Sleight, 1884.

Murray, William Vans. *Letters to William Vans Murry to John Quincy Adams 1797–1803.* Worthington C. Ford, ed. In 2 *Annual Report of the American Historical Association for the Year 1912*, pp. 341–708. Washington, D.C.: Government Printing Office, 1914.

Nash, Howard P. *The Forgotten Wars: The Role of the U.S. Navy in the Quasi-War with France.* New York: A. S. Barnes & Co., 1968.

Nelson, Paul David. *Anthony Wayne.* Bloomington: Indiana University Press, 1985.

Nelson, William H. *The American Tory.* Oxford: Clarendon Press, 1961.

Newmyer, R. Kent. *Supreme Court Justice Joseph Story.* Chapel Hill: University of North Carolina Press, 1985.

———. *The Supreme Court under Marshall and Taney.* New York: Thomas Y. Crowell, 1968.

Nicholas, Sir Nicholas Harris, ed. *The Dispatches and Letters of Vice-Admiral Lord Viscount Nelson.* London: Henry Colburn, 1845–1846.

Niemcewicz, Julian Ursyn. *Under Their Vine and Fig Tree: Travels through America in 1797–1799.* Metchie J.E. Budka, trans. Elizabeth, N.J.: The Grassman Publishing Company, Inc., 1965.

Noonan, John T. Jr. *The Antelope: The Ordeal of the Recaptured Africans in the Administrations of James Monroe and John Quincy Adams.* Berkeley: University of California, 1977.

O'Connor, John E. *William Paterson: Lawyer and Statesman, 1745–1806.* New Brunswick, N.J.: Rutgers University Press, 1979.

Odell, George C.D. *Annals of the New York Stage.* New York: Columbia University Press, 1927.

Oliver, Andrew. *The Portraits of John Marshall*. Charlottesville: University Press of Virginia, 1976.

Orieux, Jean. *Voltaire*. Barbara Bray and Helen Lane, trans. Garden City, N.Y.: Doubleday, 1979.

Orkin, Mark M. *Legal Ethics*. Toronto: Cartwright, 1957.

Oster, John Edward. *Political and Economic Doctrines of John Marshall*. New York: Neale, 1914.

Palmer, John McAuley. *General Von Steuben*. New Haven, Conn.: Yale University Press, 1937.

Palmer, Robert R. *The Age of the Democratic Revolution*. 2 vols. Princeton, N.J.: Princeton University Press, 1959–1964.

Parsons, Theophilus. *The Law of Contracts*. 2 vols. Boston: Little, Brown, 1853–1855.

Parton, James. *Life of Andrew Jackson*. 3 vols. New York: Mason Brothers, 1861.

Paterson, William. *Laws of the State of New Jersey*. New Brunswick, N.J.: A. Blauvelt, 1800.

Paulding, James K. *A Life of Washington*. 2 vols. New York: Harper Brothers, 1835.

Paxton, William M. *The Marshall Family*. Cincinnati: Robert Clarke & Co., 1885.

Peabody, Andrew Preston. *Life of William Plumer*. Boston: Philips, Samson, 1857.

Pecquet du Bellet, Louise. *Some Prominent Virginia Families*. 4 vols. reprint ed. Baltimore: Genealogical Publishing Co., 1976.

Pendleton, Edmund. *The Letters and Papers of Edmund Pendleton, 1734–1803*. 2 vols. David John Mays, ed. Charlottesville: University Press of Virginia, 1967.

Perkins, Bradford. *The First Rapprochement: England and the United States, 1795–1805*. Berkeley: University of California Press, 1967.

Perry, William Stevens. *Historical Collections Relating to the American Colonial Church*. 5 vols. Hartford, Conn.: The Church Press, 1870–1878.

Peterson, Merrill D. *Jefferson and Madison and the Making of Constitutions*. Charlottesville: University Press of Virginia, 1987.

————. *The Jefferson Image in the American Mind*. New York: Oxford University Press, 1960.

————. *Thomas Jefferson and the New Nation*. New York: Oxford University Press, 1970.

Petrie, Sir Charles. *The Jacobite Movement: the Last Phase, 1716–1807*. London: Eyre & Spottiswoode, 1932.

Phillips, Henry. *Historical Sketches of the Paper Currency of the American Colonies*. Roxbury, Mass.: W. Elliot Woodward, 1865.

Pickering, Danby. *The Statutes at Large*. 44 vols. Cambridge: Joseph Bentham, 1762–1807.

Plucknett, Theodore F.T. *A Concise History of the Common Law*. 5th ed. London: Butterworth, 1956.

Plumer, William. *William Plumer's Memorandum of Proceedings in the United States Senate, 1803–1807*. Everett S. Brown, ed. New York: Macmillan, 1923.

Pole, J. R. *Paths to the American Past*. New York: Oxford University Press, 1979.

Poniatowski, Michel. *Talleyrand et le Directoire*. Paris: Librairie Academique Perrin, 1982.

Pope, Alexander. *An Essay on Man*. Maynard Mack, ed. London: Methuen, 1950.

Pufendorf, Samuel, Freiherr von. *On the Law of Nature and Nations*. London: Varnan and Osborne, 1716.

Quaife, Milo M., Melvin J. Weig, and Roy E. Appleman. *The History of the United States Flag from the Revolution to the Present*. New York: Harper & Row, 1961.

Quincy, Josiah. *Figures of the Past*. Boston: Roberts Brothers, 1883.

Quisenberry, Anderson Chenault. *The Life and Times of Hon. Humphrey Marshall*. Winchester, Ky.: Sun Publishing Co., 1892.

Ramsay, David. *The History of the American Revolution*. 2 vols. Dublin: William Jones, 1793.

Randall, Henry S. *The Life of Thomas Jefferson*. 3 vols. New York: Derby & Jackson, 1858.

Randall, Willard Sterne. *Benedict Arnold: Patriot and Traitor*. New York: William Morrow and Co., 1990.

Randolph, John. *Collected Letters of John Randolph of Roanoke to Dr. John Brockenbrough, 1812–1833*. Keith Shorey, ed. New Brunswick, N.J.: Transaction Books, 1988.

Randolph, Robert Isham. *The Randolphs of Virginia*. Chicago: private printing, 1936.

Randolph, Roberta Lee. *The First Randolphs of Virginia*. Washington, D.C.: Public Affairs Press, 1961.

Randolph, Wassell. *William Randolph I of Turkey Island*. Memphis, Tenn.: Seebode Mimeo Service, 1949.

Reardon, John J. *Edmund Randolph: A Biography*. New York: Macmillan, 1975.

Reed, John F. *Campaign to Valley Forge: July 1, 1777–December 19, 1777*. Philadelphia: University of Pennsylvania Press, 1965.

Rehnquist, William H. *Grand Inquests: The Historic Impeachments of Justice Samuel Chase and President Andrew Johnson*. New York: William Morrow and Co., 1992.

Remini, Robert V. *Henry Clay: Statesman for the Union*. New York: W. W. Norton, 1991.

Reniers, Perceval. *The Springs of Virginia*. Chapel Hill: University of North Carolina Press, 1941.

Rhodes, Irwin S. *The Papers of John Marshall: A Descriptive Calendar*. 2 vols. Norman: University of Oklahoma Press, 1969.

Richardson, Edward W. *Standards and Colors of the American Revolution*. Philadelphia: University of Pennsylvania Press, 1982.

Richardson, William H. *Washington and the "Enterprise Against Paulus Hook."* Jersey City, N.J.: New Jersey Trust Co., 1938.

Ritcheson, Charles R. *Aftermath of Revolution: British Policy Toward the United States, 1783–1795*. Dallas: Southern Methodist University Press, 1969.

Rives, William C. *History of the Life and Times of James Madison*. 3 vols. Boston: Little, Brown & Company, 1859–1868.

Robertson, David, ed. *Reports of the Trials of Colonel Aaron Burr*. Philadelphia: Hopkins and Earle, 1808.

Robinson, Blackwell P. *William R. Davie*. Chapel Hill: University of North Carolina Press, 1957.

Rolle, Sir Henry. *Un Abridgement des Plusieurs Cases et Resolutions del Common Ley*. London: A. Crooke, W. Leake, 1668.

Roper, Donald Malcolm. *Mr. Justice Thompson and the Constitution*. New York: Garland Publishing Co., 1987.

Rouse, Parke, Jr. *James Blair of Virginia*. Chapel Hill: University of North Carolina Press, 1971.

Rowland, Kate Mason. *The Life of George Mason*. 2 vols. New York: Russell & Russell, 1964.

Rudko, Frances Howell. *John Marshall and International Law*. Westport, Conn.: Greenwood Press, 1991.

Rush, Benjamin. *The Autobiography of Benjamin Rush*. George W. Corner, ed. Princeton, N.J.: Princeton University Press, 1948.

Russell, T. Triplett, and John K. Gott. *Fauquier County in the Revolution*. Warrenton, Va.: Fauquier County American Bicentennial Commission, 1976.

Sabine, Lorenzo. *Biographical Sketches of Loyalists of the American Revolution*. Boston: Little, Brown, 1864.

Safford, William H. *The Blennerhasset Papers*. Cincinnati: Moore, Wilstach and Baldwin, 1864.

Sale, Edith Tunis. *Interiors of Virginia Houses of Colonial Times*. Richmond, Va.: W. Byrd Press, 1927.

Sanchez-Saavedra, E. M. *A Guide to Virginia Military Organizations in the American Revolution, 1774–1787*. Richmond, Va.: Virginia State Library, 1978.

Sargent, Winthrop. *History of an Expedition against Fort Du Quesne in 1755; under Major-General Edward Braddock*. Philadelphia: Historical Society of Pennsylvania, 1855.

Saricks, Ambrose. *Pierre Samuel DuPont*. Lawrence: University of Kansas Press, 1965.

Schachner, Nathan. *Aaron Burr: A Biography*. New York: F. A. Stokes, 1937.

———. *Alexander Hamilton*. New York: D. Appleton-Century, 1946.

Schama, Simon. *Citizens: A Chronicle of the French Revolution*. New York: Knopf, 1989.

Schmidhauser, John. *The Supreme Court: Its Politics, Personalities, and Procedures*. New York: Holt, Rinehart, and Winston, 1960.

Schoepf, Johann David. *Travels in the Confederation*. 2 vols. Alfred J. Morrison, trans. Philadelphia: W. J. Campbell, 1911.

Scott, Winfield. *Memoirs of Lieutenant-General Scott*. New York: Sheldon, 1864.

Seilhamer, George O. *History of the American Theatre*. 3 vols. Philadelphia: Globe Printing House, 1888–1891.

Selby, John E. *The Revolution in Virginia: 1775–1783*. Williamsburg, Va.: The Colonial Williamsburg Foundation, 1988.

Semmes, John E. *John H.B. Latrobe and His Times*. Baltimore: Norman, Remington, 1917.

Shaw, W. A. *The Knights of England*. 2 vols. London: Sherratt & Hughes, 1906.

Shirley, John M. *The Dartmouth Causes and the Supreme Court.* St. Louis, Mo.: G. I. Jones, 1877.

Sibley, Agnes Marie. *Alexander Pope's Prestige in America, 1725–1835.* New York: King's Crown Press, 1949.

Silver, Rollo G. *The American Printer, 1787–1825.* Charlottesville: University Press of Virginia, 1967.

Simms, Henry H. *Life of John Taylor.* Richmond, Va.: William Byrd Press, 1932.

Sklarsky, I. W. *The Revolution's Boldest Venture.* Port Washington, N.Y.: Kennikat Press, 1965.

Slaughter, Philip. *History of St. Mark's Parish.* Baltimore: Innes and Co., 1877. Reprinted in Raleigh Travers Green, *Genealogical and Historical Notes on Culpeper County, Virginia.* Culpeper, Va.: R. T. Green, 1900.

Slaughter, William B. *Reminiscences of Distinguished Men.* Madison, Wisc.: private printing, 1878.

Smith, James Morton. *Freedom's Fetters: The Alien and Sedition Laws and American Civil Liberties.* Ithaca, N.Y.: Cornell University Press, 1956.

Smith, Margaret Bayard. *First Forty Years of Washington Society.* Gaillard Hunt, ed. New York: Charles Scribner's Sons, 1906.

Smith, Page. *James Wilson: Founding Father, 1742–1798.* Chapel Hill: University of North Carolina Press, 1956.

———. *John Adams.* Garden City, N.Y.: Doubleday, 1962.

Smith, Samuel Stelle. *The Battle of Monmouth.* Monmouth Beach, N.J.: Philip Freneau, 1964.

Smith, William Raymond. *History as Argument: Three Patriot Historians of the American Revolution.* The Hague: Mouton & Co., 1967.

Smyth, John Ferdinand Dalziel. *A Tour in the United States of America.* 2 vols. London: Robinson, 1784.

Sosin, Jack M. *Whitehall and the Wilderness.* Lincoln: University of Nebraska Press, 1961.

Sparks, Jared, ed. *Diplomatic Correspondence of the American Revolution.* 12 vols. Boston: N. Hale and Gray & Bower, 1829–1836.

———. *The Life of George Washington.* 2 vols. London: Henry Colburn, 1839.

———. *Life of Gouverneur Morris.* 3 vols. Boston: Gray & Brown, 1832.

Spruill, Julia Cherry. *Women's Life & Work in the Southern Colonies.* New York: Russell and Russell, 1938.

Spurlin, Paul M. *Montesquieu in America.* Baton Rouge: Louisiana State University Press, 1940.

Staël, Baroness de (Anne-Louise Germaine). *Considerations on the Principal Events of the French Revolution.* 3 vols. London: Baldwin, Cradock, and Joy, 1818.

Stalhope, Robert E. *John Taylor of Caroline: Pastoral Republican.* Columbia: University of South Carolina Press, 1980.

Staudenraus, P. J. *The African Colonization Movement: 1816–1865.* New York: Columbia University Press, 1961.

Steiner, Bernard C. *The Life and Correspondence of James McHenry.* Cleveland: Burrows Brothers, 1907.

Stephen, Sir Leslie, and Sir Sidney Lee, eds. *Dictionary of National Biography.* London: Oxford University Press, 1917.

Stephenson, Richard W. *The Cartography of Northern Virginia: Facsimile Reproductions of Maps Dating From 1608–1915.* Fairfax County, Va.: History & Archaeology Section, 1981.

Stern, Jean. *Belle et Bonne: Une fervent amie de Voltaire.* Paris: Librairie Hachette, 1938.

Stevenson, David. *The Covenanters: The National Covenant and Scotland.* Edinburgh: The Saltire Society, 1988.

Stewart, Donald H. *The Opposition Press of the Federalist Period.* Albany: State University of New York Press, 1969.

Stewart, Dugald. *The Philosophy of the Active and Moral Powers of Man.* 2 vols. Boston: Wells & Lilly, 1828.

Stinchcombe, William. *The XYZ Affair.* Westport, Conn.: Greenwood Press, 1980.

Stites, Francis N. *Private Interest and Public Gain: The Dartmouth College Case, 1819.* Amherst: University of Massachusetts Press, 1972.

Stone, R. French, ed. *Biography of Eminent American Physicians and Surgeons.* Indianapolis: C. E. Hollenbeck, 1898.

Storing, Herbert J., ed. *The Complete Anti-Federalist*. Chicago: University of Chicago Press, 1981.

Story, Joseph. *Commentaries on the Constitution of the United States*. 3 vols. Boston: Hilliard, Gray & Co., 1833.

————. *A Selection of Pleadings in Civil Actions*. Salem, Mass.: Bernard Macanulty, 1805.

Story, William Wetmore, ed. *Life and Letters of Joseph Story*. 2 vols. Boston: Charles C. Little and James Brown, 1851.

Stoudt, John, J. *Ordeal at Valley Forge*. Philadelphia: University of Pennsylvania Press, 1963.

Strachey, William. *The Historie of Travell into Virginia Britannia*. Louis B. Wright and Virginia Freud, eds. London: Hakluyt Society, 1953. (Originally published in 1612.)

Stryker, William S. *The Battle of Monmouth*. Princeton, N.J.: Princeton University Press, 1927.

Sumner, Charles. *Memoirs and Letters of Charles Sumner*. 2 vols. Edward L. Pierce, ed. London: Sampson, Low, Marston, Searle & Rivington, 1878.

Sumner, William Graham. *The Financier and the Finances of the American Revolution*. New York: Dodd, Mead, 1891.

Sutherland, Stella H. *Population Distribution in Colonial America*. New York: Columbia University Press, 1936.

Sydnor, Charles S. *Gentlemen Freeholders: Political Practices in Washington's Virginia*. Chapel Hill: University of North Carolina Press, 1952.

Szatmary, David P. *Shays's Rebellion: The Making of an Agrarian Insurrection*. Amherst: University of Massachusetts Press, 1980.

Tachau, Mary K. Bonsteel. *Federal Courts in the Early Republic: Kentucky, 1789–1816*. Princeton, N.J.: Princeton University Press, 1978.

Talleyrand-Périgord, Charles Maurice de. *Mémoires, 1754–1815*. Paul Lois Couchoud and Jean Louis Couchoud, eds. Paris: E. Plon, 1982.

————. *Memoirs of the Prince de Talleyrand*. 5 vols. Albert, duc de Broglie, ed., R. Ledos de Beaufort, trans. New York: G. P. Putnam's Sons, 1891–1892.

Talleyrand-Périgord, Dino, Charles Maurice Camille de. *Étude sur la République des États-Unis D'Amérique*. New York: Hurd and Houghton, 1876.

Taylor, Frank H. *Valley Forge: A Chronicle of American Heroism*. Philadelphia: J. W. Nagle, 1905.

Taylor, John. *Construction Construed and Constitutions Vindicated*. Richmond, Va.: Sheppard and Pollard, 1820.

Taylor, Robert J. *Western Massachusetts in the Revolution*. Providence, R.I.: Brown University Press, 1954.

Terhune, Mary Virginia Hawes (Mary Harland, pseud.). *Some Colonial Homesteads and Their Stories*. New York: G. P. Putnam's Sons, 1912.

Thayer, James Bradley. *John Marshall*. Boston: Houghton Mifflin, 1904.

Thayer, Theodore. *The Making of a Scapegoat: Washington and Lee at Monmouth*. Port Washington, N.Y.: Kennikat Press, 1976.

Thian, Raphael P. *Legislative History of the General Staff of the Army*. Washington, D.C.: Government Printing Offices, 1901.

Thompson, John. *The Letters of Curtius*. Richmond, Va.: S. Pleasants, 1804.

Ticknor, George. *Life, Letters, and Journals of George Ticknor*. Anna Ticknor and George S. Hillard, eds. 2 vols. Boston: J. R. Osgood, 1877.

Tillotson, Geoffrey. *Pope and Human Nature*. Oxford: Oxford University Press, 1958.

Trevelyan, George. *The American Revolution*. 4 vols. New York: Longmans, Green, 1905–1922.

Trumbull, John. *The Autobiography of John Trumbull*. Theodore Sizu, ed. New Haven, Conn.: Yale University Press, 1953.

Tucker, Nathaniel Beverley. *The Principles of Pleading*. Boston: C. C. Little and J. Brown, 1846.

Tucker, St. George, ed. *Blackstone's Commentaries with Notes of Reference to the Constitution and Laws of the United States and to the Commonwealth of Virginia*. Philadelphia: Birch and Small, 1803.

————. *The Life of Thomas Jefferson*. 2 vols. Philadelphia: C. Knight, 1837–1838.

Tyler, Lyon G. *The Letters and Times of the Tylers*. 3 vols. Richmond, Va.: Whittet and Shepperson, 1884–1896.

Tyler, Samuel. *Memoir of Roger Brooke Taney*. Baltimore: Murphy, 1872.

Uhlendorf, Bernhard A., and Edna Vosper, eds. *Letters from Major Baurmeister to Colonel von Jungkenn*. Philadelphia: Historical Society of Pennsylvania, 1936.

Van Buren, Martin. *The Autobiography of Martin Van Buren*. John C. Fitzpatrick, ed. In 2 *Annual Report of the American Historical Association for the Year 1918*. Washington, D.C.: Government Printing Office, 1920.

Van Bynkershoek, Cornelius. *A Treatise on the Law of War*. Philadelphia: Farrand and Nicholas, 1790.

Vattel, Emmerich. *The Law of Nations*. Dublin: L. White, 1792.

Vulliamy, Colwyn E. *Voltaire*. Port Washington, N.Y.: Kennikat Press, 1970.

Wall, Charles Cecil. *George Washington: Citizen-Soldier*. Charlottesville: University Press of Virginia, 1980.

Wallace, Willard M. *Appeal to Arms: A Military History of the American Revolution*. New York: Harper & Brothers, 1951.

Ward, Christopher. *The War of the Revolution*. New York: Macmillan, 1952.

Ward, Harry M., and Harold E. Greer, Jr. *Richmond During the Revolution: 1775–1783*. Charlottesville: University Press of Virginia, 1977.

Ward, Robert D. *An Account of General Lafayette's Visit to Virginia*. Richmond, Va.: West Johnson & Co., 1881.

Warden, Lewis C. *Life of Blackstone*. Charlottesville, Va.: The Michie Company, 1938.

Warren, Charles. *Bankruptcy in United States History*. Cambridge, Mass.: Harvard University Press, 1935.

———. *History of the American Bar*. Boston: Little, Brown, 1911.

———. *The Supreme Court in United States History*. Boston: Little, Brown, 1926.

Warren, Mercy Otis. *History of the Rise, Progress and Termination of the American Revolution*. Boston: E. Larkin, 1805.

Washington, George. *The Diaries of George Washington*. 4 vols. John C. Fitzpatrick, ed. Boston: Houghton Mifflin, 1925.

———. *The Writings of George Washington*. 39 vols. John C. Fitzpatrick, ed. Washington, D.C.: Government Printing Office, 1931–1944.

———. *The Writings of George Washington*, 14 vols. Worthington C. Ford, ed. New York: G. P. Putnam's Sons, 1889–1893.

———. *The Writings of George Washington*. 12 vols. Jared Sparks, ed. Boston: Little, Brown, 1855.

Waterman, Thomas Tileston. *Mansions of Virginia*. Chapel Hill: University of North Carolina Press, 1946.

Watson, John F. *Annals of Philadelphia and Pennsylvania*. 2 vols. Philadelphia: J. F. Watson, 1844.

Webster, Daniel. *The Private Correspondence of Daniel Webster*. Fletcher Webster, ed. Boston: Little, Brown, 1857.

———. *Writings and Speeches of Daniel Webster*. 18 vols. J. McIntyre, ed. Boston: Little, Brown, 1903–1908.

Weems, Mason Locke. *The Life of George Washington*. Reprint ed. Boston: Harvard University Press, 1962.

Weis, Frederick Lewis. *The Colonial Clergy in Virginia, North Carolina, and South Carolina*. Baltimore: Genealogical Publishing Co., 1976.

Welch, Richard E., Jr. *Theodore Sedgwick, Federalist: A Political Portrait*. Middletown, Conn.: Wesleyan University Press, 1965.

Wentworth, John. *Congressional Reminiscences*. Chicago: Fergus, 1882.

Wertenbaker, Thomas J. *Norfolk: Historic Southern Port*. 2nd ed. Marvin W. Schlegel, ed. Durham, N.C.: Duke University Press, 1931.

Westin, Alan, ed. *An Autobiography of the Supreme Court*. New York: Macmillan, 1963.

Wharton, Francis. *State Trials during the Administrations of Washington and Adams*. Philadelphia: Carey and Hart, 1849.

Wheeler, Everett P. *Daniel Webster: Expounder of the Constitution*. New York: G. P. Putnam's Sons, 1905.

White, Douglas H. *Pope and the Context of Controversy*. Chicago: University of Chicago Press, 1970.

White, G. Edward. *The Marshall Court and Cultural Change: 1815–35.* In the Oliver Wendell Holmes Devise. *History of the Supreme Court of the United States*, vols. 3–4. New York: Macmillan, 1988.

White, Lynn. *Medieval Technology and Social Change.* Oxford: Clarendon Press, 1963.

Wildes, Henry E. *Valley Forge.* New York: Macmillan, 1938.

Wilkinson, L. P. *Horace and His Lyric Poetry.* Cambridge: Cambridge University Press, 1951.

Williams, Charles R. *The Life of Rutherford Birchard Hayes.* Columbus: Ohio State Archaeological and Historical Society, 1928.

Winter, Pieter J. *Het Aandeel van de Amsterdamsche handel aan den opbouw van het Amerikaansche Gemeenebest.* The Hague: M. Nijhoof, 1927.

Wirt, William. *The Letters of a British Spy*, 2nd ed. Richmond, Va.: S. Pleasants, 1803.

———. *Sketches of the Life and Character of Patrick Henry.* Ithaca, N.Y.: Mack, Andrus, 1848.

Wolcott, Oliver. *Memoirs of the Administration of Washington and John Adams, edited from the papers of Oliver Wolcott, Secretary of the Treasury.* 2 vols. George Gibbs, ed. New York: William Van Norden, 1846.

Wolfe, Christopher. *The Rise of Modern Judicial Review: From Constitutional Interpretation to Judge-made Law.* New York: Basic Books, 1986.

Woodman, Henry. *The History of Valley Forge.* Oaks, Pa.: J. Francis, 1922.

Woody, Thomas. *A History of Women's Education in the United States.* New York: Science Press, 1929.

Wright, Benjamin F. *The Contract Clause of the Constitution.* Cambridge, Mass.: Harvard University Press, 1938.

Wright, Charles. *Federal Courts.* St. Paul, Minn.: West Publishing Co., 1983.

Wright, Charles Alan, Arthur R. Miller, and Edward C. Cooper. *Federal Practice and Procedure.* St. Paul, Minn.: West Publishing Co., 1986.

Wright, Chester Whitney. *Economic History of the United States*, 2nd ed. New York: McGraw-Hill, 1949.

Young, James Sterling. *The Washington Community.* New York: Columbia University Press, 1966.

Zahniser, Marvin R. *Charles Cotesworth Pickney: Founding Father.* Chapel Hill: University of North Carolina Press, 1967.

Zweiben, Beverly. *How Blackstone Lost the Colonies: English Law, Colonial Lawyers, and the American Revolution.* New York: Garland, 1990.

Articles

"The Ambler Family." *Richmond Critic* (January 1889).

Ammon, Harry. "Agricola *Versus* Aristides: James Monroe, John Marshall, and the Genet Affair in Virginia." *Virginia Magazine of History and Biography*, vol. 74 (1966), pp. 312–320.

———. "The Jeffersonian Republicans in Virginia." *Virginia Magazine of History and Biography*, vol. 71 (1963), pp. 153–167.

———. "*The Richmond Junto, 1800–1824.*" Virginia Magazine of History and Biography, vol. 60 (1953), pp. 395–418.

Ammon, Henry, and Adrienne Koch. "The Virginia and Kentucky Resolutions." *William and Mary Quarterly*, vol. 5, 3rd series (1948), pp. 145–176.

"The Ancestors and Descendants of John Rolfe with Notes on Some Connected Families." *Virginia Magazine of History and Biography*, vol. 24 (1916) pp. 327–333.

Anderson, Dice Robins. "The Teacher of Jefferson and Marshall." *South Atlantic Quarterly*, vol. 15, no. 4 (October 1916), pp. 327–343.

Anderson, Frank M. "Contemporary Opinion of the Virginia and Kentucky Resolutions." *American Historical Review*, vol. 5 (1899), pp. 45–63.

Anderson, Jefferson Randolph. "Tuckahoe and the Tuckahoe Randolphs." *Virginia Magazine of History and Biography*, vol. 45 (1937), pp. 55–86.

Angelokos, Peter. "The Army at Middlebrook, 1778–1779." *New Jersey Historical Society Proceedings*, vol. 70 (1952), pp. 98, 105–106.

Arkes, Hadley. "On the Moral Standing of the President as an Interpreter of the Constitution." *PS*, vol. 20 (Summer 1987), pp. 637–642.

Baldridge, Edwin R. "Talleyrand's Visit to Pennsylvania, 1794–1796." *Pennsylvania History*, vol. 36 (1969), pp. 145–160.

Baroway, Aaron. "The Cohens of Maryland." *Maryland Historical Magazine*, vol. 18 (1923), pp. 363–373.

Bartosic, Florian. "With John Marshall from William and Mary to Dartmouth College." *William and Mary Law Review*, vol. 7 (1966), pp. 259–266.

Beach, Rex. "Spencer Roane and the Richmond Junto." *William and Mary Quarterly*, vol. 22, 2nd series (1942), pp. 1–17.

Bedini, Silvio A. "Marshall's Meridian Instrument." *Professional Surveyor*, vol. 7 (July/August 1987), pp. 26ff.

Bemis, Samuel Flagg. "Washington's Farewell Address, A Foreign Policy of Independence." *American Historical Review*, vol. 39 (1934), pp. 254–255.

Berns, Walter. "Freedom of the Press and the Alien and Sedition Laws: A Reappraisal." *Supreme Court Review*, (1970), pp. 109–159.

Bessell, Edmund P. "The Storming of Stony Point." *National Historical Magazine*, vol. 72 (1938), p. 47.

Bloch, Susan Low and Maeva Marcus. "John Marshall's Selective Use of History in *Marbury v. Madison*." *Wisconsin Law Review*, (1986), pp. 301–337.

Bond, B. W. "The Quit-Rent System in the American Colonies." *American Historical Review*, vol. 17 (1912), pp. 496–516.

Brace, Richard M. "Talleyrand in New England: Reality and Legend." *New England Quarterly*, vol. 16 (1943), pp. 397–406.

Brant, Irving. "Edmund Randolph, Not Guilty." *William and Mary Quarterly*, vol. 7, 3rd series (1950), pp. 179–198.

Brock, Dr. R. A. "Vestry Book of Henrico Parish, Virginia 1730–1773." In J. Staunton Moore, ed., *History of Henrico Parish, 1611–1904*. Richmond, Va.: Bossieux, 1904.

Brown, John. "Glimpses of Old College Life." *William and Mary Quarterly*, vol. 9, 1st series (October 1900), pp. 18–23 and 75–136.

Bryan, Wilhelmus Bogart. "Hotels of Washington Prior to 1814." *Records of the Columbia Historical Society*, vol. 7 (1904) pp. 84–91.

Brydon, Rev. G. McLaren. "The Virginia Clergy." *Virginia Magazine of History and Biography*, vol. 32 (1924), pp. 333–334.

Burke, Joseph C. "The Cherokee Cases: A Study in Law, Politics and Morality." *Stanford Law Review*, vol. 21 (February 1969), pp. 500–530.

Burton, Rev. Lewis D. "Annals of Henrico Parish." In J. Staunton Moore, ed., *History of Henrico Parish, 1611–1904*. Richmond, Va.: Bossieux, 1904.

Campbell, Bruce A. "Dartmouth College as a Civil Liberties Case." *Kentucky Law Journal*, vol. 70 (1981–1982), pp. 643–706.

Campbell, Thomas. "Chancellor Kent, Chief Justice Marshall, and the Steamboat Controversy." *Syracuse Law Review*, vol. 25 (1974), pp. 497–534.

Carpenter, William S. "William Patterson." *Dictionary of American Biography*, vol. 14, pp. 293–295.

———. "Repeal of the Judiciary Act of 1801." *American Political Science Review*, vol. 9 (1915), pp. 519–528.

Carrington, Elizabeth Ambler. "An Old Virginia Correspondence." *Atlantic Monthly*, vol. 84 (1899), pp. 535–547.

Chase, Edward M. "Valley Forge." *Quartermaster Review*, vol. 32 (1952), pp. 44–46.

Childs, Francis S. "A Secret Agent's Advice on America: 1797." In Edward Meade Earle, ed. *Nationalism and Internationalism*. New York: Columbia University Press, 1950, pp. 18–26.

C.M.C. "The Home Life of Chief Justice Marshall." *William and Mary Quarterly*, vol. 12, 2nd series (1932), pp. 67–69.

Cooke, John Esten. "Early Days of John Marshall." *Historical Magazine and Notes and Queries Concerning the Antiquities, History and Biography of America*, vol. 3. (June 1859), pp. 165–169.

Corwin, Edward S. "The Basic Doctrine of American Constitutional Law." *Michigan Law Review*, vol. 12 (1914), pp. 247–276.
———. "Constitutional Law in 1919–1920." *American Political Science Review*, vol. 14 (1920), p. 656.
———. "Freedom of Speech and Press Under the First Amendment: A Resume." *Yale Law Review*, vol. 48 (1920), p. 48.
———. "Samuel Chase." *Dictionary of American Biography*. New York: Charles Scribner's Sons, 1935, pp. 35–38.
———. "The Supreme Court and Unconstitutional Acts of Congress." *Michigan Law Review*, vol. 4, (1906), pp. 616–630.
———. "The Supreme Court's Construction of the Self-Incrimination Clause." *Michigan Law Review*, vol. 29 (1930), pp. 205–206.
Coues, William P. "Washington's Campaign Against Smallpox in the Continental Army." *New England Journal of Medicine*, vol. 202 (1930), pp. 254–259.
Cress, Larry D. "The Jonathan Robbins Incident: Extradition and Separation of Powers in the Adams Administration." *Essex Institute Historical Collection*, vol. 111 (1975), pp. 99–121.
Cullen, Charles T. "Completing the Revisal of the Laws in Post-Revolutionary Virginia." *Virginia Magazine of History and Biography*, vol. 82 (1974), pp. 84–99.
———. "New Light on John Marshall's Legal Education and Admission to the Bar." *American Journal of Legal History*, vol. 16 (1972), pp. 345–351.
Currie, David P. "The Most Insignificant Justice: A Preliminary Inquiry." *University of Chicago Law Review*, vol. 50 (1983), pp. 466–480.
Custer, Lawrence B. "Bushrod Washington and John Marshall: A Preliminary Inquiry." *American Journal of Legal History*, vol. 4 (1960), p. 34.
Davidson, Philip G. "Virginia and the Alien and Sedition Acts." *American Historical Review*, vol. 36 (1931), pp. 336–342.
Degnan, Ronan E. "*Livingston v. Jefferson*—A Freestanding Footnote." *California Law Review*, vol. 75 (1987), pp. 115–128.
Diamond, Martin. "The Federalist." In Leo Strauss and Joseph Cropsey, eds. *History of Political Philosophy*. Chicago: University of Chicago Press, 1963, pp. 573–593.
Dodd, William E. "Chief Justice Marshall and Virginia." *American Historical Review*, vol. 12 (July 1907), pp. 776–787.
Dunne, Gerald T. "Brockholst Livingston." In Leon Friedman and Fred L. Israel, eds. *The Justices of the United States Supreme Court*. New York: Chelsea House, 1969.
———. "The Story-Livingston Correspondence, 1812–1822." *American Journal of Legal History*, vol. 10 (1966), pp. 224–236.
Easterbrooke, Frank H. "The Most Insignificant Justice: Further Evidence." *University of Chicago Law Review*, vol. 50 (1983), pp. 481–503.
Elkins, Stanley, and Eric McKitrick. "The Founding Fathers: Young Men of the Revolution." *Political Science Quarterly*, vol. 76 (1961), pp. 181–216.
Ellis, Richard. "The Impeachment of Samuel Chase." In Michael R. Belknap, ed., *American Political Trials*. Westport, Conn.: Greenwood Press, 1981, pp. 56–78.
Engdahl, David E. "Immunity and Accountability for Positive Government Wrongs." *University of Colorado Law Review*, vol. 44 (1972), pp. 1–21.
Evans, Emory. "Private Indebtedness and the Revolution of Virginia." *William and Mary Quarterly*, vol. 28, 3rd series (1971), pp. 349–374.
Farrand, Max. "The Judiciary Act of 1801." *American Historical Review*, vol. 5 (1900), pp. 682–686.
Fletcher, William F. "History of the Judge Advocate General's Corps, United States Army." *Military Law Review*, vol. 4 (1959), pp. 89–92, 116–117.
Foran, William A. "John Marshall as a Historian." *American Historical Review*, vol. 43, (1937), pp. 51–64.
Foster, Frances B. "Oak Hill." In *Old Homes and Families of Fauquier County*, Virginia (The W.P.A. Records). Berryville, Va.: Virginia Book Company, no date, pp. 147–150.
Frank, Jerome. "The Cult of the Robe." In Frank, *Courts on Trial*. Princeton, N.J.: Princeton University Press, 1949.
Freund, Paul. "Forward: On Presidential Privilege." *Harvard Law Review*, vol. 88 (1974), pp. 13–31.

Furlong, Patrick J. "John Rutledge, Jr., and the Election of a Speaker of the House in 1799." *William and Mary Quarterly*, vol. 24, 3rd series (1967), pp. 432–436.

Furman, Bess. "Signed, Sealed and Forgotten! The Story of a Premier Promoter of the Revolution." *Daughters of the American Revolution Magazine*, vol. 71 (1937), pp. 1004–1009.

Fyers, Evan W.H. "General Sir William Howe's Operations in Pennsylvania, 1777." *Society of Army Historical Research Journal*, vol. 9 (1930), pp. 173, 187.

"Genealogy of the Fleming Family." *Virginia Magazine of History and Biography*, vol. 23 (1915), pp. 325–326.

"The Genesis of Fauquier." *Bulletin of the Fauquier County Historical Society*, vol. 1 (July 1922), pp. 109–113.

"Germantown, Fauquier's First Settlement." *News and Notes from the Fauquier Historical Society*, vol. 30 (Summer 1981), pp. 1–2.

Gibson, James E. "The Role of Disease in the 70,000 Casualties in the American Revolutionary Army." College of Physicians of Philadelphia Transactions, vol. 17 (1949), pp. 121–127.

Glennon, Michael J. "Two Views of Presidential Foreign Affairs Power: *Little v. Barreme* or *Curtiss-Wright*." *Yale Journal of International Law*, vol. 13 (1991), pp. 5–32.

Goebel, Julius Jr. "The Common Law and the Constitution." In W. Melville Jones, ed., *Chief Justice Marshall: A Reappraisal*. Ithaca, N.Y.: Cornell University Press, 1956.

Goodwin, Rutherford. "The Reverend John Bracken, Rector of Bruton Parish and President of the College of William and Mary in Virginia." *Historical Magazine of the Protestant Episcopal Church*, vol. 10 (1941), pp. 354–389.

Gunther, Gerald. "Unearthing John Marshall's Major Out-of-Court Constitutional Commentary." *Stanford Law Review*, vol. 21 (1969), pp. 449–547.

Hagan, Horace E. "*Fletcher v. Peck*." *Georgetown Law Journal*, vol. 16 (1972), pp. 1–40.

Hagner, Alexander Burton. "William Cranch." In William Druper Lewis, ed., *Great American Lawyers*. South Hackensack, N.J.: Rotham Reprints, 1971.

Hamer, Philip M. "Great Britain, the United States, and the Negro Seamen Acts, 1822–1848." *Journal of Southern History*, vol. 4 (1935), pp. 3–28.

Hamilton, J. G. de Roulhac. "A Society for the Preservation of Liberty." *American Historical Review*, vol. 32 (1927), pp. 550–552.

Hardy, Sallie E. Marshall. "John Marshall as Son, Brother, Husband, Friend." *The Green Bag*, vol. 8 (1896), p. 480.

———. "Some Virginia Lawyers of the Past and Present." *The Green Bag*, vol. 10 (1898), pp. 23–24.

Hardy, Stella Pickett. "Fauquier County Keiths." In *Colonial Families of the Southern States of America*. Baltimore: Genealogical Publishing Co., 1968.

Harrison, Fairfax. "Virginians on the Ohio and Mississippi Rivers in 1742." *Virginia Magazine of History and Biography*, vol. 30 (1922), pp. 203, 205–206.

Harrison, Joseph H.J. "Oligarchs and Democrats: The Richmond Junto." *Virginia Magazine of History and Biography*, vol. 78 (1970), pp. 184–198.

Hoar, George F. "A Famous Fête." *Proceedings of the American Antiquarian Society*, vol. 12, New Series, (1899), pp. 240–259.

Hobson, Charles F. "The Recovery of British Debts in the Federal Circuit Courts of Virginia, 1790 to 1793." *Virginia Magazine of History and Biography*, vol. 92 (1984), pp. 176–200.

Holmes, Oliver Wendell. "Cinders from the Ashes." *Atlantic Monthly*, vol. 23 (January, 1869), pp. 115–123.

Hooker, Richard J. "John Marshall on the Judiciary, the Republicans, and Jefferson, March 4, 1801." *American Historical Review*, vol. 53 (April, 1948), pp. 518–520.

Hughes, Robert M. "William and Mary, The First American Law School." *William and Mary Quarterly*, vol. 2 (2nd series, 1922), pp. 40–48.

Hurley, John. "Aboriginal Rights, the Constitution and the Marshall Court." *Revue Juridique Themis*, vol. 17 (1983), pp. 403–443.

Isaacs, Nathan. "John Marshall on Contracts: A Study in Early American Judicial Theory." *Virginia Law Review*, vol. 7 (1921), pp. 413–428.

Johnston, F. Claiborne Jr. "Federalist, Doubtful, and Antifederalist: A Note on the Virginia Convention of 1788." *Virginia Magazine of History and Biography*, vol. 96 (1988), pp. 333–344.

"Journals of Captain John Montresor." *New York Historical Society Collection, 1881*. New York: New York Historical Society, 1882.

"Judge Spencer Roane of Virginia: A Champion of States Rights—Foe of John Marshall." *Harvard Law Review*, vol. 66 (1953), pp. 1242–1259.

"Jurisdictional Immunity of Foreign Sovereigns." *Yale Law Journal*, vol. 63 (1954), pp. 1148–1172.

Keim, C. Ray. "Primogeniture and Entail in Colonial Virginia." *William and Mary Quarterly*, 3rd series, vol. 25 (1968), pp. 545–586.

Kemper, Charles E. "The Early Westward Movement of Virginia, 1722–1734." *Virginia Magazine of History and Biography*, vol. 13 (1906), pp. 362–370.

———. "The History of Germantown." *Bulletin of the Fauquier County Historical Society*, vol. 2 (July 1922), pp. 125–133.

Kendall, D. "Mr. Gibbons and Colonel Ogden." *Michigan State Bar Journal*, vol. 26 (1947), pp. 22–25.

Kennedy, Duncan. "The Structure of Blackstone's Commentaries." *Buffalo Law Review*, vol. 28 (1978–79), pp. 205–382.

Kerber, Linda K. "Oliver Wolcott: Midnight Judge." *Connecticut Historical Society Bulletin*, vol. 32 (1967), pp. 25–30.

Krislov, Samuel. "Jefferson and Judicial Review: Refereeing Cahn, Commager and Mendelson." *Journal of Public Law*, vol. 9 (1960), pp. 374–381.

Kukla, Jon. "A Spectrum of Sentiments: Virginia's Federalists, Antifederalists, and Federalists Who Are for Amendments." *Virginia Magazine of History and Biography*, vol. 96 (1988), pp. 286–287.

Lambdin, Alfred B. "Battle of Germantown." *Pennsylvania Magazine of History and Biography*, vol. 1 (1877), p. 377.

Lassiter, Francis Rives. "Arnold's Invasion of Virginia." *Swanee Review*, vol. 9 (1901), pp. 78–93.

Lee, Richard Henry. "Letters from the Federal Farmer." In Michael Kammen, ed., *The Origins of the American Constitution: A Documentary History*. New York: Penguin Books, 1986.

Levitan, David M. "The Foreign Relations Power: An Analysis of Mr. Justice Sutherland's Theory." *Yale Law Journal*, vol. 55 (1946), pp. 467–497.

Lillich, Richard B. "The Chase Impeachment." *American Journal of Legal History*, vol. 4 (1960), pp. 49–72.

"Lives of Washington." *Edinburgh Review*, vol. 13, no. 150 (October 1808).

Lizanich, Christine M. "'The March of this Government': Joel Barlow's Unwritten History of the United States." *William and Mary Quarterly*, vol. 33, 3rd series (1976), pp. 315–330.

Lodge, Henry Cabot. "John Marshall, Stateman." *North American Review*, vol. 172 (February 1901), pp. 191–204.

Lofgren, Charles A. *"United States v. Curtiss-Wright Export Corporation*: A Historical Reassessment." *Yale Law Journal*, vol. 83 (1973), pp. 1–35.

Lokke, Carl Ludwig. "The Trumbull Episode: A Prelude to the 'XYZ' Affair." *New England Quarterly*, vol. 7 (1934), pp. 100–114.

Luce, W. Ray. "The Cohen Brothers of Baltimore." *Maryland Historical Magazine*, vol. 68 (1973), pp. 288–308.

Lutz, Donald S. "The Relative Influence of European Writers on Late Eighteenth-Century American Political Thought." *American Political Science Review*, vol. 78 (March 1984), pp. 189–197.

Lynch, Joseph M. *"Fletcher v. Peck*: The Nature of the Contract Clause." *Seton Hall Law Review*, vol. 13 (1982), pp. 1–20.

Lyon, E. W. "The Closing of the Port of New Orleans." *American Historical Review*, vol. 37 (1932), pp. 280–283.

———. "The Directory and the United States." *American Historical Review*, vol. 43 (1938), pp. 514–516.

Macfarlan, Douglas. "Revolutionary War Hospitals in the Pennsylvania Campaign 1777–1778." *Picket Post*, vol. 59 (1958), pp. 23–30.

Marasinghe, M. L. "A Reassessment of Sovereign Immunity." *Ottawa Law Review*, vol. 9 (1977), pp. 480–482.

Marshall, John. Anniversary Eulogy to Mary W. Marshall, December 25, 1832. Virginia State Library, Richmond, Va.

———. "Letter to a Freeholder." *Virginia Herald*, 2 October 1798.

Marshall, Sally Ewing. "Chief-Justice John Marshall." *Magazine of American History*, vol. 12 (1884), p. 69.

Mason, George. "Objections to the Constitution." In Michael Kemmon, ed., *The Origins of the American Constitution: A Documentary History*. New York: Penguin Books, 1986.

Mason, Jonathan. "Diary of Mason." *Proceedings of the Massachusetts Historical Society*, vol. 2, no. 21, 2nd series (1885–1886).

Maxwell, Helen. "My Mother." *Lower Norfolk County Virginia Antiquary*, vol. 2 (1828), p. 137.

McDonald, A. H. "The Style of Livy." *Journal of Roman Studies*, vol. 47 (1957), p. 155.

McKnight, Marshall. "The Marshalls of Kentucky." *Kentucky Progress Magazine*, pp. 29–30.

McMichael, Henry. "Diary of Lieutenant James McMichael of the Pennsylvania Line, 1776–1778." *Pennsylvania Magazine of History and Biography*, vol. 16 (1892), pp. 129–159.

Mendelson, Wallace. "Jefferson on Judicial Review." *Journal of Public Law*, vol. 10 (1961), pp. 113–124.

———. "B. F. Wright on the Contract Clause: A Progressive Misreading of the Marshall-Taney Era." *Western Political Quarterly*, vol. 38 (1985), pp. 262–275.

———. "Was Chief Justice Marshall an Activist?" In Stephen C. Halpern and Charles M. Lamb, eds., *Supreme Court Activism and Restraint*. Lexington, Mass.: Lexington Books, 1982, pp. 57–77.

Miller, F. Thornton. "John Marshall versus Spencer Roane: A Reevaluation of *Martin v. Hunter's Lessee*." *Virginia Magazine of History and Biography*, vol. 96 (1988), pp. 297–314.

Mondello, Salvatore. "John Vanderlyn." *New York Historical Society Quarterly*, vol. 52 (1968), pp. 161–183.

Montague, Andrew J. "John Marshall." In Samuel Flagg Bemis, ed., *The American Secretaries of State*, vol. 2. New York: Knopf, 1927.

Montresor, John. "Journals of Captain John Montresor." *New York Historical Society Collections, 1881*, vol. 445–446. New York: 1882.

Morgan, Donald G. "Justice William Johnson and the Treaty-Making Power." *George Washington Law Review*, vol. 22 (1953), pp. 187–215.

———. "Marshall, the Marshall Court, and the Constitution." In W. Melville Jones, ed. *Chief Justice John Marshall: A Reappraisal*. New York: Da Capo Press, 1971.

———. "The Origin of Supreme Court Dissent." *William and Mary Quarterly*, vol. 10, 3rd series (1953), pp. 354–355.

Morgan, Edmund S. "The Puritan Ethic and the American Revolution." *William and Mary Quarterly*, vol. 24, 3rd series (1977), pp. 195–208.

Morison, Samuel Eliot. "DuPont, Talleyrand and the French Spoilations." Massachusetts Historical Society Proceedings, vol. 49 (1915–1916), pp. 72–84.

———. "Elbridge Gerry, Gentleman-Democrat." *New England Quarterly*, vol. 2 (1929), pp. 6–33.

"Narrative of Bacon's Rebellion." *Virginia Magazine of History and Biography*, vol. 4 (1897), pp. 117–153.

Nelson, William E. "The Eighteenth-Century Background of John Marshall's Constitutional Jurisprudence." *Michigan Law Review*, vol. 76 (1977–1978), pp. 893–904.

Newmyer, R. Kent. "On Assessing the Court in History." *Stanford Law Review*, vol. 21 (1969), pp. 540–547.

O'Fallen, James M. "Marbury." *Stanford Law Review*, vol. 44 (January 1992), pp. 219–260.

"Original Records of the Phi Beta Kappa Society." *William and Mary Quarterly*, vol. 4, 1st series (April 1896), pp. 213–261.

Peak, Mayme Ober. "Oak Hill: The Fauquier Home of Chief Justice Marshall." *House Beautiful*, vol. 49 (April 1921), p. 288.

Phillips, P. L. "Virginia Cartography." In *Smithsonian Miscellaneous Collections*. Washington, D.C.: Government Printing Office, 1896.

Pigón, Jakub. "Helvidius Priscus, Eprius Marcellus, and *Judicum Senatus*: Observations on Tacitus, *Histories* 4.7–8." *Classical Quarterly*, vol. 42 (1992), pp. 235–246.

Plous, Harold J., and Gordon E. Baker. "McCulloch v. Maryland: Right Principle, Wrong Case." *Stanford Law Review*, vol. 9 (1957), pp. 710–730.

Potter, J. "The Growth of Population in America, 1700–1860." In D. V. Glass and D.E.C. Eversley, eds., *Population in History*. London: Edward Arnold, 1965, pp. 631–688.

Pound, Roscoe. "The Charles River Bridge Case." *Massachusetts Law Quarterly*, vol. 27 (1942), pp. 19–20.

Prufer, Julius F. "The Franchise in Virginia from Jefferson through the Convention of 1829." *William and Mary Quarterly*, vol. 8, 2nd series (1928), pp. 17–32.

Randall, Alexander. "Philip Syng Physick's Last Major Operation." *Annals of Medical History*, vol. 9 (1937), pp. 133–141.

Rhodes, Irwin S. "John Marshall and the Western Country, Early Days." *Bulletin of the Historical and Philosophical Society of Ohio*, vol. 18 (April 1960), pp. 116–136.

Risjord, Norman K. "The Virginia Federalists." *Journal of Southern History*, vol. 33 (1967), pp. 486–517.

Robson, Eric. "British Light Infantry in the Eighteenth Century: The Effect of American Conditions." *Army Quarterly*, vol. 62 (1891), pp. 209–222.

Roper, Donald M. " In Quest of Judicial Objectivity: The Marshall Court and the Legitimation of Slavery." *Stanford Law Review*, vol. 21 (1969), pp. 532–539.

———. "Judicial Unanimity and the Marshall Court." *American Journal of Legal History*, vol. 9 (1965) pp. 118–134.

Rugg, Arthur P. "William Cushing." *Yale Law Journal*, vol. 30 (1920), pp. 128–144.

Sanchez-Saavedra, E. M. "All Fine Fellows and Well-Armed." *Virginia Calvacade*, vol. 14 (1974), pp. 4–11.

Schmidt, Gustavus. "Reminiscences of the Late Chief Justice Marshall." *Louisiana Law Journal*, vol. 1 (May 1841), pp. 80–99.

Schouler, James. "Evolution of the American Voter." *American Historical Review*, vol. 2 (1897), pp. 665–674.

Scott, Austin. "*Holmes v. Walton*: The New Jersey Precedent." *American Historical Review*, vol. 4 (1899), pp. 456–460.

Seddig, Robert G. "John Marshall and the Origins of Supreme Court Leadership." *University of Pittsburgh Law Review*, vol. 36 (1975), p. 785.

Seybolt, Robert F. "A Contemporary British Account of General Sir William Howe's Military Operations in 1777." *American Antiquarian Society Proceedings*, vol. 40 (1930), pp. 1–76.

Shepard, E. Lee. "Breaking into the Profession: Establishing a Law Practice in Antebellum Virginia." *Journal of Southern History*, vol. 48 (1982), pp. 393–410.

Sheridan, Richard B. "The British Debt Crisis of 1772 and the American Colonies." *Journal of Economic History*, vol. 20 (1960), pp. 168–181.

Sherry, Suzanna. "The Founders Unwritten Constitution." *University of Chicago Law Review*, vol. 54 (1987), pp. 1127–1177.

———. "The Richmond Theatre." *Virginia Magazine of History and Biography*, vol. 60 (1952), pp. 421–436.

Simms, William Gilmore. "A Memoir of the Pinckney Family of South Carolina." *Historical Magazine*, vol. 2, 2nd series (1867), pp. 134–139.

Smith, William Raymond. "The Necessity of the Circumstances: John Marshall's Historical Method." *The Historian*, vol. 26 (1963), pp. 19–35.

Stanard, W. G. "Major Robert Beverley and his Descendants." *Virginia Magazine of History and Biography*, vol. 3 (1896), pp. 261–271.

Stervey, Tracy E. "Albert J. Beveridge." In William T. Hutchinson, ed., *The Marcus W. Jernegan Essays in American Historiography*. Chicago: University of Chicago Press, 1937.

Stewart, Clark C. "Reciprocal Influence of British and United States Law: Foreign Sovereignty Immunity Law from the Schooner Exchange to the State Immunity Act of 1978." *Vanderbilt Journal of Transnational Law*, vol. 13 (1980), pp. 761–773.

Stinchombe, William. "The Diplomacy of the WXYZ Affair." *William and Mary Quarterly*, vol. 34, 3rd series (1977), pp. 590–617.

———. "A Neglected Memoir by Talleyrand on French-American Relations, 1797–1798." American Philosophical Society *Proceedings*, vol. 121 (1977), pp. 195–205.

———. "Talleyrand and the American Negotiations of 1797–1798." *Journal of American History*, vol. 62 (1975), pp. 575–590.

Stone, Harlan Fiske. "Fifty Years of the United States Supreme Court." *American Bar Association Journal*, vol. 14 (1928), pp. 428–436.

Story, Joseph. "Chief Justice Marshall's Public Life and Services." *North American Review*, vol. 27 (January 1828), pp. 1–40.

———. "Eulogy to John Marshall." In John F. Dillon, ed. *John Marshall: Life, Character and Judicial Services*. Chicago: Callaghan, 1903.

———. "Review of: A History of the Colonies Planted by the English on the Continent of North America, From their Settlement to the Commencement of that War Which Terminated in Their Independence." *North American Review*, vol. 26 (1828), pp. 1–40.

"A Strange Story of the Firing of the Courthouse." *William and Mary Quarterly*, vol. 4, 1st series (1895–1896), pp. 115–116.

Swindler, William F. "John Marshall's Preparation for the Bar." *American Journal of Legal History*, vol. 11 (1967), pp. 207–213.

Talleyrand-Périgord, Charles Maurice de. "Commercial Relations to the United States with England." Boston: Thomas B. Wait, 1809.

———. "An Essay upon the Advantages to be Derived from New Colonies." Boston: Thomas B. Wait, 1809.

Tate, Thad W. "The Social Contract in America, 1774–1787: Revolutionary Theory as a Conservative Instrument." *William and Mary Quarterly*, vol. 22, 3rd series (1965), pp. 371–391.

Tazewell, Littleton Waller. "Sketches of his own family written by Littleton Waller Tazewell for the Use of his children." Norfolk, Va.: 1823. Tazewell Family Papers, Virginia State Library.

"Thomas Marshall." *Bulletin of the Fauquier County Historical Society*, vol. 1 (July 1922), pp. 140–141.

Thompson, Mack. "Causes and Circumstances of the DuPont Family's Emigration." *French Historical Studies*, vol. 6 (1969), pp. 59–77.

Thomson, Robert P. "The Reform of the College of William and Mary, 1763–1780." *Proceedings of the American Philosophical Society*, vol. 115 (1971), pp. 187–213.

Turner, Kathryn. "The Appointment of Chief Justice John Marshall." *William and Mary Quarterly*, vol. 17, 3rd series (April 1960), pp. 143–163.

———. "Federalist Policy and the Judiciary Act of 1801." *William and Mary Quarterly*, vol. 22, 3rd series (1965), pp. 3–33.

———. "The Midnight Judges." *University of Pennsylvania Law Review*, vol. 109 (1961), pp. 494–523.

Tyler, Lyon G. "The Old Virginia Line in the Middle States During the American Revolution." *Tyler's Quarterly Historical and Genealogical Magazine*, vol. 12 (1930), pp. 1–42, 90–141.

Uhlendorf, Bernard A., and Edna Vosper, eds. "Letters of Major Baurmeister during the Philadelphia Campaign." *Pennsylvania Magazine of History and Biography*, vol. 59 (1935), pp. 399–401.

"Virginia Council Journals, 1726–1753." *Virginia Magazine of History and Biography*, vol. 32 (1924), pp. 55–56.

"Virginia Gleanings in England." *Virginia Magazine of History and Biography*, vol. 18 (1910), pp. 80–92.

"Virginia's Soldiers in the Revolution." *Virginia Magazine of History and Biography*, vol. 19 (1911), p. 406.

Waldo, Albigence. "Diary Kept at Valley Forge by Albigence Waldo, Surgeon in the Continental Army, 1777–1778." *Historical Magazine*, vol. 5 (1861), pp. 129–134.

Warren, Charles. "New Light on the History of the Federal Judiciary Act of 1789." *Harvard Law Review*, vol. 37 (1923), pp. 49–172.

———. "The Story-Marshall Correspondence, 1819–1831." *William and Mary Quarterly*, vol. 21, 3rd series (1941), pp. 1–26.

Watson, Joseph Shelter. "Letters from William and Mary College." *Virginia Magazine of History and Biography*, vol. 29 (1921), pp. 176–177.

Wedgwood, Ruth. "The Revolutionary Martyrdom of Jonathan Robbins." *Yale Law Journal*, vol. 100 (1990), pp. 229–368.

Wehtje, Myron F. "The Congressional Elections of 1799 in Virginia." *West Virginia History*, vol. 29 (1968), pp. 261–279.

Whitaker, A. P. "The Retrocession of Louisiana in Spanish Policy." *American Historical Review*, vol. 39 (1934), pp. 454–476.

Wild, Ebenezer. "The Journal of Ebenezer Wild." *Massachusetts Historical Society Proceedings*, vol. 6, 2nd series (1890), pp. 78–160.

Wilkins, Fred J. "Steuben Screamed But Things Happened and an Army was Born at Valley Forge." *Picket Post*, no. 20 (1948) pp. 7–13.

Wilkinson, H. F. "Here Was born a Nation." *Quartermaster Review*, vol. 10 (1930), pp. 9–25.

Willie, J. C. "Letters of Some Members of the Old Congress." *Pennsylvania Magazine of History and Biography*, vol. 29 (1905), pp. 205–206.

Worner, William F. "John Marshall in Lancaster." *Lancaster County Historical Society Papers*, vol. 28 (1924), pp. 113–117.

Wright, John W. "The Rifle in the American Revolution." *American Historical Review*, vol. 29 (1924), pp. 293–299.

———. "Some Notes on the Continental Army." *William and Mary Quarterly*, vol. 11, 2nd series (1931), pp. 81–105, 185–209.

Wyatt, Edward A. IV. "George Keith Taylor, 1769–1815." *William and Mary Quarterly*, vol. 16, 2nd series (1936), pp. 16–17.

Newspapers

Alexandria Gazette.
American Daily Advertiser. Philadelphia.
Augusta Chronicle.
Aurora. Philadelphia.
Boston Daily Advertiser.
Charleston Courier.
Charleston Mercury.
Claypool's American Daily Advertiser. Philadelphia.
Columbia Centinel. Boston.
Columbia Mirror.
Commercial Advertiser. New York.
Connecticut Courant. Hartford.
Enquirer. Richmond.
Gazette and Alexandria Daily Advertizer. Alexandria.
Gazette of the United States. Philadelphia.
Independent Chronicle. Boston.
Kentucky Gazette. Lexington.
Maryland Gazette. Annapolis.
Marylander. Baltimore.
Le Moniteur Universel. Paris.
Minerva. Raleigh.
Natchez Press.
National Intelligencer. Washington, D.C.
New York American.
New York Commercial Advertiser.
New York Evening Post.
New York Spectator.
New York Statesman.
Niles Weekly Register. Baltimore.
Orleans Gazette. New Orleans.

Paris Journal.
Philadelphia Gazette and Universal Daily Advertiser.
Porcupine's Gazette. Philadelphia.
Raleigh Register.
Recorder. Richmond.
Salem Gazette.
Savannah Republican.
Southern Patriot. Charleston, S.C.
Telegraph and Daily Advertiser. Baltimore.
Union. Philadelphia.
Virginia Argus. Richmond.
Virginia Gazette and General Advertiser. Richmond.
Virginia Gazette. Williamsburg.
Virginia Independent Chronicle. Richmond.
Washington Federalist.
Washington Republican.

Acknowledgments

Many people have helped to make this book possible. My greatest debt is to Dr. Charles Hobson and the late Laura Gwilliam of the Marshall Papers Project in Williamsburg, Virginia. Without their help and support this biography could not have been written.

I am also especially indebted to my editorial associate, Gillian Manning, and my illustrations editor, Elisabeth Zaritzky. Gillian did yeoman service pulling the manuscript together; Elisabeth possesses a unique talent for discovering illustrations to complement the narrative.

Because I write in longhand, I am eternally grateful to those who can read my scribbling and convert it to typescript. My special debt is to Hyla Levy of the University of Toronto and to her colleagues Marian Reed and Brenda Samuels.

To those who have read the manuscript, I am indebted beyond measure. Their comments have been invaluable, and I thank them for the time and effort they have generously granted. They include: William Beaney, Walter Berns, Jane Bradley, Karl Kahandaliyanage, Sanford Lakoff, Rebecca Murphy, William Nelson, Thomas Pangle, Beverly Pasian, Louis Pauly, Julie Rosenthal, John Seaman, Jeannie Sears, Bernadette Vano, Helen, Niki, and Vicki Vokas, Melissa Williams, and Joanne Wong. The bibliography was prepared by David Bronskill and Anissa Seguin. The copy editing was done by Debra Manette. Jeanne Tift supervised production; Megan Butler handled publicity.

Another debt I would like to acknowledge is to the staff of the Library of the University of Toronto, especially to those in the interlibrary loan division. Their unflagging support has been an essential ingredient in the timely completion of the book.

Generous financial support was provided by the Social Science and Humanities Research Council of Canada and the Bellagio Study Center of the Rockefeller Foundation.

Once again, my final debt is to Elizabeth Kaplan of the Ellen Levine Agency and to my editor at Henry Holt, Marian Wood. There are none better.

Illustration Credits

Architect of the Capitol: 49.
Albert J. Beveridge, *The Life of John Marshall*, Boston: Houghton Mifflin, 1916: 54.
Boston Athenaeum: Frontispiece.
Circuit Court, City of Baltimore: 40.
Collection, Château de Valençay: 13.
Collection of the Supreme Court of the United States: 22, 23, 24, 27, 28, 29, 30, 31, 32, 35.
Corcoran Art Gallery: 41, 46.
Dartmouth College: 44.
Harvard University Art Museum: 15.
Library of Congress: 4, 16, 18, 21, 37, 39, 45, 51, 52.
Library of Virginia: 1, 2, 5, 11, 12, 25, 42, 43, 47, 53, 55.
B. J. Lossing, *Washington and the American Republic*, New York: Worthington, 1851: 9, 10, 20.
Mariners' Museum: 38.
Francis Norton Mason, *My Dearest Polly*, Richmond, Virginia: Garrett and Massie, 1961: 3.
New York Historical Society: 17, 36.
New York Public Library: 14.
P. W. Norton Gallery: 6.
Trinity College, University of Toronto: 34.
United States Senate: 19, 48.
University of Virginia: 26.
Valentine Museum: 8.
Virginia Historical Society: 50.
William and Mary Library: 7.
William E. Wiltshire III: 33.

Index